Venice
and the
Islamic World
828–1797

Institut du Monde Arabe, Paris
October 2, 2006 – February 18, 2007

The Metropolitan Museum of Art, New York
March 27 – July 8, 2007

Cover:
cat. 144. *Pair of doors* (detail)
Venice, ca. 1575–1600

cat. 35, 38, 36. Anonymous Painter from Verona or Follower
Portraits from a Series of Ottoman Rulers
Orhan, Murad III, Mehmet I
Venice, 1578 or later

cat. 15. Johannes
Marco Polo's Departure from Venice (detail) *from a copy of Il Milione*
England, ca. 1400–10

The Metropolitan Museum of Art: (hc) and (pbk)
Yale University Press: (hc)

ISBN: 978-0-300-12430-9
Library of Congress Number: 2006938864

Printed in Italy by GECA, Milan

Venice and the Islamic World 828–1797

The Metropolitan Museum of Art
New York
Yale University Press
New Haven and London

ORGANIZATION OF THE EXHIBITION

The exhibition was organized by The Metropolitan Museum of Art, New York and the Institut du Monde Arabe, Paris.

The Metropolitan Museum of Art
Philippe de Montebello, Director
Mahrukh Tarapor, Associate Director for Exhibitions / Director for International Affairs, Geneva Office

Institut du Monde Arabe
Yves Guéna, President
Mokhtar Taleb-Bendiab, Chief Executive Director
François Baudet, Associate Director

CURATORS

General Curator
Brahim Alaoui
Director of the Museum and Exhibitions Department – Institut du Monde Arabe

Chief Curator
Stefano Carboni
Curator and Administrator
Department of Islamic Art
The Metropolitan Museum of Art

Assisted by
Trinita Kennedy
Research Associate
Department of Islamic Art
The Metropolitan Museum of Art
Noha Hosni
Curator, Institut du Monde Arabe
Aurélie Clemente-Ruiz
Deputy Curator, Institut du Monde Arabe
Djamila Chakour
Assistant Curator, Institut du Monde Arabe

THE METROPOLITAN MUSEUM OF ART

Press Relations
Harold Holzer
Senior Vice President for External Affairs
Elyse Topalian
Deputy Vice President
and Chief Communications Officer
Mary Flanagan
Senior Press Officer

Exhibition Design
Michael Batista
Senior Exhibition Designer
Sue Koch
Senior Graphic Designer
Clint Coller
Senior Lighting Designer
Rich Lichte
Senior Lighting Designer

CATALOGUE

General Editor
Stefano Carboni

Coordination, Institut du Monde Arabe
Éric Delpont
Djamila Chakour

Coordination, The Metropolitan Museum of Art
Stefano Carboni
Trinita Kennedy
Elizabeth Marwell

ÉDITIONS GALLIMARD

Editor
Jean-Loup Champion

Supervising Editor
Audrey Gregorczyk

Copy Editor English-language Edition
Christine Schultz-Touge

Translation from the French
Deke Dusinberre

Proofreader English-language Edition
Rebecca Brite

Designer
Anne Lagarrigue

Layout
Constance Clavel
Isabelle Flamigni
Assisted by Florence Pierrelée

Typesetting
Dominique Guillaumin

Head of Production
Christian Delval

Production
Amélie Airiau

Heads of Press Communications
Brigitte Benderitter
Béatrice Foti

Press Officer
Françoise Issaurat

Head of International Rights and Coeditions
Hélène Clastres

Catalogue entries written by:
Qamar Adamjee (QA)
Sylvia Auld (SA)
Carmen Bambach (CB)
Andrea Bayer (AB)
Stefano Carboni (SC)
Walter Denny (WD)
Trinita Kennedy (TK)
Wolfram Koeppe (WK)
Francesca Leoni (FL)
Roberta Marin (RM)
Maria Antonietta Marino (MAM)
Pia Palladino (PP)
Stuart Pyhrr (SP)
Francesca Saccardo (FS)
Wendy Thompson (WT)
Nicholas Warner (NW)

In New York, the exhibition is made possible by The Hagop Kevorkian Fund.

Additional support is provided by The Andrew W. Mellon Foundation, the Oceanic Heritage Foundation, and the National Endowment for the Arts.

Contents

Acknowledgments

The Institut du Monde Arabe and The Metropolitan Museum of Art are grateful to all the lenders who have made this exhibition possible:

AUSTRIA / LIECHTENSTEIN

Vaduz, Sammlungen des Fürsten von und zu Liechtenstein
Vienna, Liechtenstein Museum
Dr. Johann Kräftner; Michael Schweller; Beatrice Capaul

FRANCE

Château d'Écouen, Musée National de la Renaissance
Thierry Crépin-Leblond; Alain Erlande-Brandenburg; Chantal Bor
Paris, Bibliothèque Interuniversitaire de Médecine
Guy Cobolet; Bernadette Molitor
Paris, Bibliothèque Nationale de France
Jean-Noël Jeanneney; Monique Cohen; Antoine Coron; Nathalie Leman; Catherine Goeres; Thierry Grillet; Béatrice Coulmeau
Paris, Cité de la Musique – Musée de la Musique
Laurent Bayle; Christine Laloue; Monique Blanc; Martine Depagniat
Paris, Institut du Monde Arabe
Yves Guéna; Denis Bauchard; Mokhtar Taleb-Bendiab; François Baudet; Brahim Alaoui; Noha Hosni; Éric Delpont; Aurelie Clemente-Ruiz; Djamila Chakour
Paris, Musée du Louvre
Henri Loyrette; Vincent Pomarède; Carel van Tuyll; Francis Richard; Sophie Makariou; Marc Bascou; Rachel Beaujean-Deschamps; Danielle Gaborit-Chopin; Catherine Loisel; Marlène Mengant; Cécile Bourdillat-Oudeyer
Sèvres, Musée National de Céramique
Antoinette Hallé; Marie-Chantal de Tricornot; Christine Lahaussois; Lionel Pinon

GERMANY

Berlin, Fioritura Collection, Heinz & Jertha Kuckei
Heinz Kuckei; Beate Kuckei-Funke; Carsten Sternberg
Berlin, Staatliche Museen zu Berlin
Peter-Klaus Schuster; Astrid Holmgren
Berlin, Gemäldegalerie
Bernd Wolfgang Lindemann; Gisela Helmkampf; Roberto Contini
Berlin, Museum für Islamische Kunst
Claus-Peter Haase; Jens Kröger; Almut von Gladiß; Astrid Holmgren
Berlin, Kunstgewerbemuseum
Angela Schönberger; Susanne Netzer
Berlin, Kupferstichkabinett
Heinrich Schulze Altcappenberg; Holm Bevers; Ingrid Rieck
Dresden, Sächsischen Landesbibliothek – Staats und Universitätsbibliothek Dresden
Thomas Bürger; Katrin Nitzsche
Düsseldorf, Gemäldegalerie
Bettina Baumgärtel; Kathrin Bürger
Düsseldorf, Glasmuseum Hentrich
Helmut Ricke; Karl Amendt
Düsseldorf, Stiftung Museum Kunst Palast
Jean-Hubert Martin
Frankfurt, Museum für Angewandte Kunst
Ulrich Schneider; Siegried Rehberg; Andrea Schwarz
Munich, Bayerische Staatsgemäldesammlungen, Staatsgalerie in der Residenz Würzburg
Reinhold Baumstark; Cornelia Syre; Ingrid Huber; Christina Schwill
Stuttgart, Staatsgalerie
Christian Von Holst

ITALY

Bologna, Biblioteca Universitaria
Biancastella Antonino; Laura Miani
Cividale del Friuli, Museo Archeologico Nazionale
Serena Vitri; Valeria Poletto; Fabiana Vio
Cividale del Friuli, Parrocchia di Santa Maria Assunta
Florence, Museo Nazionale del Bargello
Beatrice Paolozzi Strozzi; Marco Spallanzani; Maria Grazia Vaccari
Milan, Pinacoteca di Brera
Luisa Arrigoni; Emanuela Daffra; Mariolina Olivari
Padua, Comunità Ebraica di Padova
Davide Romanin Jacur; Gianni Parenzo
Padua, Museo d'Arte Medievale e Moderna
Davide Banzato; Franca Pellegrini
Pistoia, Museo Diocesano
Don Luciano Tempestini
Rome, Galleria Nazionale d'Arte Antica di Palazzo Barberini
Angela Negro; Maria Grazia Bernardini; Giuliana Forti
Venice, Armeria di Palazzo Ducale
Giandomenico Romanelli; Daniela Andreozzi
Venice, Basilica di Santa Maria Gloriosa dei Frari
Padre Domenico Carminati; Fra Leopoldo Fior
Venice, Biblioteca Nazionale Marciana
Marino Zorzi; Annalisa Bruni; Susy Marcon; Tiziana Plebani; Silvia Pugliese
Venice, Chiesa di San Sebastiano
Don Gastone Barecchia
Venice, Gallerie dell'Accademia
Giovanna Nepi Sciré; Roberto Fontanari
Venice, Istituto di Storia dell'Arte - Fondazione Giorgio Cini
Giuseppe Pavanello; Rossella Patrizio; Fabrizio Speziale
Venice, Museo Civico Correr
Giandomenico Romanelli; Camillo Tonini; Piero Lucchi
Venice, Galleria G. Franchetti alla Ca' d'Oro
Adriana Augusti; Francesca Saccardo; Gloria Tranquilli
Venice, Museo di Palazzo Mocenigo
Chiara Squarcina
Venice, Museo Storico Navale
Rudy Guastadisegni; Alessandro Ronconi; Lorenzo Sferra
Venice (Murano), Museo Vetrario
Giandomenico Romanelli
Venice, Procuratoria di San Marco
Giorgio Orsoni; Mons. Antonio Meneguolo; Paolo Gasparotto
Venice, Provincia Veneta di Sant' Antonio dell'Ordine dei Frati Minori
Frate Rino Sgarbossa; Padre Giannangelo Marchetto
Venice, San Pietro in Castello
Don Luigi Libralon
Venice, Scuola Grande di San Rocco
Franco Posocco; Ermes Farina (†); Silvio Bonavita; Enrico Zane; Marcella Battiston
Verona, Museo di Castelvecchio; Musei Civici
Paola Marini; Francesca Rossi; Rossella Pasqua; Silvia D'Ambrosio
Verona, Soprintendenza per i Beni Archeologici del Veneto; Giuliana Cavalieri Manasse; Maurizia De Min

SINGAPORE

Singapore, Joli Quentin Kansil Collection
Joli Quentin Kansil

SWITZERLAND

Geneva, Aga Khan Trust for Culture
Prince and Princess Sadruddin Aga Khan
Amanda Monney; Benoît Junod

TURKEY

Istanbul, Topkapı Sarayı Müzesi (Museum and Library)
Ilber Ortayli

UNITED KINGDOM

Chatsworth, Trustees of the Chatsworth Settlement
Charles Noble; Diane Naylor
London, Courtauld Institute of Art Gallery
Deborah Swallow; Julia Blanks
London, Rainer Zietz Ltd
Rainer Zietz; Karoline Weser
London, The British Library
Lynne Brindley; Barbara O'Connor; Robert Davies; Greg Buzwell; Bella Nolan
London, The British Museum
Neil MacGregor; Philip Attwood; Sheila Canby; Hugo Chapman; Venetia Porter; Lindsey Belcher; Jill Maggs; Marianne Eve; Maureen Theobald
London, The Nasser D. Khalili Collection of Islamic Art
David Khalili; Michael Rogers; Nahla Nassar
London, The National Gallery
Charles Saumerez Smith; David Jaffé; Carol Plazzotta; Simona Pizzi; Claire Hallinan
London, Victoria and Albert Museum
Mark Jones; Reino Liefkes; Tim Stanley; Mariam Rosser-Owen; Liz Wilkinson; David Packer; Ruth Hibbard
London, Wellcome Library
Harold Cook; Julia Nurse; Lara Artemis; Sue Chapman; William Schupbach
Oxford, Ashmolean Museum
Christopher Brown; Oliver Watson; Chezzy Brownen; Nicholas Mayhew; Catherine Whistler; Polly Holbrook; Helen Hovey
Oxford, The Bodleian Library, University of Oxford
Reginald P. Carr; Richard Ovenden; Bruce C. Barker-Benfield; Colin Wakefield; Dana Josephson
Windsor, The Provost and Fellows of Eton College
Michael Meredith; Nicholas Baker
Windsor Castle, The Royal Collection
Her Most Gracious Majesty Queen Elizabeth the Second; The Honorable Lady Jane Roberts; Theresa-Mary Morton; Martin Clayton

UNITED STATES

Baltimore, The Walters Art Museum
Gary Vikan; Regine Schulz; William Noel; Morten Steen Hansen; Martina Bagnoli; Abigail Quandt; Betsy Dahl; Liz Flood; Barbara Fegley; Terry Drayman-Weisser
Corning, NY, The Corning Museum of Glass
David Whitehouse; Tom Knotts; Warren Bunn
New York, The Metropolitan Museum of Art
Philippe de Montebello; Mahrukh Tarapor; Doralynn Pines; Michael Barry; Larry Becker; George R. Goldner; Laurence B. Kanter; Marco Leona; Stuart Pyhrr; Marjorie Shelley; Kenneth Soehner; Ian Wardropper; Florica Zaharia; Andrea Bayer; Carmen Bambach; Sarah Brooks; Tom Campbell; Keith Christiansen; James Draper; Maryam Ekthiar; Wolfram Koeppe; Jessie McNab; Wendy Thompson; Clare Vincent; Melinda Watts; Martin Bansbach; Mecka Baumeister; Mindell Dubansky; Jean-François De Laperouse; Lisa Pilosi; Janina Poskrobko; Adriana Rizzo; Nobuko Shibayama; Yana van Dyke; Simona Artusi; Warren Bennett; Tim Caster; Alessandra Cereda; Paola Chadwick; Annick Des Roches; Britt Eilhardt; Trish Sclater-Booth; Denise Marie Teece; Kit Basquin; Lisa Beidel; Aileen Chuk; Deanna Cross; Christine Coulson Scornavacca; Martha Deese; Ronald Fein; Elizabeth Hammer; Drue Heinz; Julia E. Kameron; Andrea Kann; Amanda Maloney; Nestor Montilla; Rebecca Noonan Murray; Ren Murrell; Thomas Reynolds; Fredy Rivera; Susie Rubin Schein; Denny Stone; Linda Sylling; Diana Vought; Fran Wallace; Emily Vanderpool
New York, The Pierpont Morgan Library
Charles E. Pierce, Jr.; William M. Voelkle; Lucy R. Eldrige; Patricia Courtney; Inge Dupont; John Bidwell

Princeton, Princeton University Art Museum
Susan Taylor; Laura Giles; Karen Richter; Alexia Hughes; Calvin Brown
Saint Louis, Saint Louis Art Museum
Brent R. Benjamin; Sidney Goldstein; Angela Carter; Jeanette Fausz
Washington D.C., Folger Shakespeare Library
Gail Kern Paster; Heather Wolfe; Bettina Smith

National, Regional, Local, and Ecclesiastical Authorities, Italy

Ministero per i Beni e le Attività Culturali, Dipartimento per i Beni Archivistici e Librari
Luciano Scala
Ministero per i Beni e le Attività Culturali, Divisione VI
Daniela Cecchini
Ufficio Promozione Beni Culturali, Curia Patriarcale di Venezia
Don Gianmatteo Caputo; Irene Galifi
Curia Arcivescovile di Udine, Ufficio per i Beni Culturali
Don Sandro Piussi
Pontificia Commissione per i Beni Culturali
Mons. Mauro Piacenza
Soprintendenza Speciale per il Polo Museale di Firenze, Prato e Pistoia
Antonio Paolucci
Soprintendenza per il Patrimonio Storico Artistico ed Etnoantropologico per le Province di Firenze, Pistoia e Prato
Bruno Santi; Caterina Caneva; Lia Brunori
Soprintendenza per il Patrimonio Storico Artistico ed Etnoantropologico per le Province di Milano, Bergamo, Como, Lecco, Lodi, Pavia, Sondrio, Varese
Maria Teresa Fiorio
Soprintendenza Speciale per il Polo Museale Romano
Claudio Strinati; Silvana Grosso
Soprintendenza per i Beni Architettonici e il Paesaggio, e per il Patrimonio Storico e Demoetnoantropologico del Friuli Venezia Giulia
Giangiacomo Martines
Soprintendenza per il Patrimonio Storico Artistico per le Province di Venezia, Belluno, Padova e Treviso
Fabrizio Magani
Soprintendenza Speciale per il Polo Museale Veneziano
Giovanna Nepi Scirè; Roberto Fontanari
Soprintendenza per i Beni Ambientali ed Architettonici, Storici, Artistici ed Etnoantropologici di Venezia e Laguna
Renata Codello; Giorgio Rossini; Gabriella Delfini; Emanuela Zucchetta; Grazia Fumo; Roberto Noé
Soprintendenza per il Patrimonio Storico Artistico ed Etnoantropologico delle Province di Verona, Vicenza, Rovigo
Anna Maria Spiazzi
Arcidiocesi di Udine, Ufficio Arte Sacra e Beni Culturali
Don Guido Genero; Beatrice Bertone; Antonio Barba

Our sincere thanks also go to all those who provided help during the preparatory stages of this exhibition, notably:

His Excellency Yves Aubin de la Messuzière, French ambassador to Italy (Rome)
Raffaella Anna Pavanello and Emmanuelle Ferrari, French cultural attachés in Italy (Venice)

M. Massimo Cacciari, mayor of Venice
Dante Bartoli, Doctoral candidate, Texas A&M University
Jessica Batty, The Art Institute, Chicago
Daniel Berger, Rome and Venice
Josephine Berger-Nadler, New York
David Alan Brown, National Gallery, Washington, D.C.
Caroline Campbell, The Courtauld Institute, London
Lora Chin, J.-P. Getty Museum, Los Angeles
Franco Colosimo, Cropani
Anne Costa, Université Marc Bloch, Bibliothèques des Arts Photographiques
Padre Francesco Critelli, Collegiata di Santa Maria Assunta, Cropani
James Cuno, The Art Institute, Chicago
Adrienne D'Angelo, New York
Enrico De Pascale, Bergamo
Daniela Degl'Innocenti, Museo del Tessuto, Prato
François-Marie Deyrolle, Musées de Strasbourg
Consuelo W. Dutschke, Rare Book and Manuscript Library, Columbia University
Larry Feinberg, The Art Institute, Chicago
Vincenzo Franco, Archivio di Stato, Venice
Jane Gallagher, The National Trust, Great Britain
Arianna Gambirasi, Venice
John Garton, Cleveland Institute of Art
Roland Gilles, Institut du Monde Arabe
Mons. Pierantonio Gios, Biblioteca Capitolare, Padua
Audrey Mathieu Girard, Musée des Tissus et des Arts Décoratifs, Lyon
Margaret Gray, Powis Castle
Eric Grunberg, Paris
Marie-Hélène Guelton, Musée des Tissus et des Arts Décoratifs, Lyon
Navina Haidar, The Metropolitan Museum of Art
Rachel Hasson, L.A. Mayer Memorial, Jerusalem
Catherine Hess, J.-P. Getty Museum, Los Angeles
Adrienne Jeske, The Art Institute, Chicago
Sue Kaoukji, The Al-Sabah Collection, Dar al-Athar al-Islamiyyah, Kuwait
Vladimir Kovačić, Civic Museum, Poreč
Bozena Anna Kowalczyck, Venice
Karen Lawson, The Picture Library, Royal Collection Enterprises Ltd.
Florence Lhuillier
Rosamond Mack, Washington, D.C.
Louise Mackie, The Cleveland Museum of Art
Stefania Mason, University of Udine
Audrey Moutardier, Institut du Monde Arabe
Federica Olivares, Edizioni Olivares, Milan
Roberto Della Porta, Rome
Jennifer Pruitt, Doctoral candidate, Harvard University
Nassim Rossi, Doctoral candidate, Columbia University
Raffaele Santoro, Archivio di Stato, Venice
Paul Saenger, Newberry Library, Chicago
Michela Scarazzola, Venice
Alessandra Schiavon, Archivio di Stato, Venice
Carlotta Sembenelli, Edizioni Olivares, Milan
Saverio Simi, Accademia di Belle Arti, Venice
Eleanor Sims, London
Milton Sonday, New York
Ellen South, J.-P. Getty Museum, Los Angeles
Katy Spurrell, Rome
Giorgio Vercellin, University of Venice
Mathilde Voinchet
Daniel Walker, The Textile Museum, Washington, D.C.
as well as Mrs. Patti Cadby Birch
And at the Direction of the Musées des France:
Francine Mariani-Ducray, Jean-Paul Mercier-Baudrier, and Sandra Calvados.

The curators extend special thanks to Elizabeth Marwell, Department of Islamic Art, The Metropolitan Museum of Art.

The Institut du Monde Arabe is grateful to the following representatives of the Total Group, which generously supported this exhibition in Paris:
Thierry Desmarest
Jean-Jacques Guilbaud
Yves-Marie Dalibard
Yves Le Goff
Françoise Trobas
Sylvain Gauduchon

Philippe de Montebello
Director
The Metropolitan Museum of Art

In 1494 the Milanese priest Pietro Casola recorded his awestruck reaction to the wealth of merchandise in the Venetian marketplace: "Who could count the many shops so well furnished that they also seem to be warehouses, with so many cloths of every make—tapestry, brocades, and hangings of every design, carpets of every sort, camlets of every color and texture, silks of every kind; and so many warehouses full of spices, groceries, and drugs, and so much beautiful white wax!" Many of the products that caught Casola's eye, including the carpets, brocades, silks, and spices, came from the Eastern Mediterranean and beyond, brought to the lagoon by Venetian merchants active in places like Cairo, Alexandria, Istanbul, Bursa, Acre, Damascus, Aleppo, Trebizond, and Tabriz. No other city in Western Europe cultivated as assiduously and successfully a Levantine trade and diplomatic network as Venice, and, as the Byzantine Empire gradually gave way to Islamic sultanates in the region, Venetians came increasingly into contact with Muslims and their ideas, culture, and way of life. Venice's prosperity depended almost entirely on her role as Europe's gateway to the richer civilizations in the East.

Venice and the Islamic World, 828–1797, co-organized by the Institut du Monde Arabe and The Metropolitan Museum of Art, explores the artistic consequences of Venice's interaction with the Islamic world over nearly a millennium. During this time an impressive number of works of art traveled from East to West, and sometimes vice versa, through diplomatic or commercial exchange or as booty. Among these many objects are rock-crystal vases in the Treasury of the Basilica of San Marco, Persian manuscripts in the Biblioteca Nazionale Marciana, the great carpet in the Scuola Grande di San Rocco, ceramics in the Museo Correr, and inlaid metalwork and brocaded vestments in Santa Maria Assunta in Cividale del Friuli. Many works of Islamic art now in major Western museums passed through Venice and were acquired there in the 18th and 19th centuries.

This ambitious exhibition reunites these works, taking into account the ideas Venice borrowed from her Muslim neighbors, including those in the realms of philosophy and science. It also gathers works of art indicative of Venetian attitudes—whether fascination, ambivalence, or fear—towards Muslims, among them, most importantly, the paintings and drawings of Gentile Bellini, Carpaccio, Mansueti, Tiepolo, and Guardi. Finally, the exhibition demonstrates the degree to which Venetian craftsmen sought to emulate the finest Islamic styles, motifs, and techniques in glassmaking, lacquerware, ceramics, bookbinding, textiles, and arms and armor. The Serenissima seems to have been touched in endless ways by Islamic culture, not only in the visual arts, but also in her structural appearance. Architecture cannot, of course, be a part of this exhibition, but major monuments such as the Basilica of San Marco, the Palazzo Ducale, and the Fondaci dei Tedeschi and dei Turchi, as well as public and private palaces with Islamic-style windows, crenellations, and courtyards, reflect the city's connections to the Islamic Near East.

Assembling an exhibition of nearly 200 works of art in such a broad range of media from all over the world has been a challenging task, but lenders have responded to our requests with remarkable generosity, in many cases agreeing to lend works that seldom travel. By the same token, the Institut du Monde Arabe and the Metropolitan Museum, in our first cooperative venture, have worked together seamlessly, belying the newness of the relationship.

Stefano Carboni, Curator and Administrator of the Department of Islamic Art at the Metropolitan Museum, is ideally suited to bringing this project to fruition. Born near the Rialto Bridge in the heart of Venice, he has studied Islamic art in his native city and abroad and has been a member of the Museum staff for many years. The exhibition and catalogue represent for him a synthesis of nearly 20 years of scholarship. Dr. Carboni assembled a team of international specialists to write the essays and entries for the catalogue. As a result, this project presents the most up-to-date ideas and the newest evidence regarding Venice's role in the cultural interchange of the Mediterranean.

The exhibition is particularly welcome, coming, as it does, when the Islamic galleries at the Metropolitan Museum are closed for redevelopment and only a small selection of the permanent collection remains on view. *Venice and the Islamic World* is intended not just for enthusiasts of Islamic art, however, but also for those interested more generally in European art, especially since many visitors are not familiar with Venice's close rapport with the Eastern Mediterranean. The exhibition encourages us all to view art across cultures and without bias, two notions at the heart of the experience offered by the Institut du Monde Arabe and The Metropolitan Museum of Art.

For the New York presentation, we are most grateful to have the generous support of the Hagop Kevorkian Fund, whose commitment to furthering scholarship in this field is truly inspiring. We are also grateful to the Andrew W. Mellon Foundation, the Oceanic Heritage Foundation, and the National Endowment for the Arts for their additional support.

Yves Guéna
President

Mokhtar Taleb-Bendiab
Chief Executive Director
Institut du Monde Arabe

As celebrations for its 20th anniversary approach, the Institut du Monde Arabe in Paris is proud to host *Venice and the Islamic World, 828–1797.* Daily events continue to remind us that the exhibition's theme of cultural exchange remains crucial to peaceful coexistence among peoples.

The Metropolitan Museum of Art in New York has long shown its support for the Institut's exhibitions by generously loaning works of art. For *Venice and the Islamic World,* the two institutions have forged a veritable partnership. We are sincerely grateful to everyone who has contributed to this effort.

Over the years, the Institut has been eager to explore various historical eras when intercultural dialogue thrived. Earlier exhibitions, for example, studied the realms of science and the Middle Eastern art of living, in which the accomplishments of Islamic civilizations have benefited the world as a whole. Other shows have revealed the Orient's revitalizing effect on European painting during key stages of artistic change—Delacroix captured its light, while Matisse embraced the aesthetics of Eastern art. Finally, the dawn of the new millennium provided an occasion to examine how the spirit of Islamic Andalusia, ten centuries ago, made it possible for various faiths and ethnic groups to live together in a moment of grace.

Close relationships between Venice and the Islamic world extended over a surprisingly long period of time. Between 828,when the relics of St. Mark were translated to the City of the Doges, and 1797, the year the Venetian Republic fell, political and military history was dotted by numerous conflicts ranging from Christian Crusades to Ottoman coups. But these belligerent interludes should not make us overlook the consistently fruitful exchanges—from East to West, and vice versa—in the realms of ideas, arts, and crafts, as well as in the understanding and recognition of the Other, going beyond the ambivalence of people's beliefs. The Venetian and Islamic artworks and artifacts presented in this exhibition speak, each in their own language, to that ongoing dialogue between two highly different cultures. Apart from the varying influences of the East on Venetian painting, the show also reveals the great assimilation of skills and motifs by Venice's master craftsmen—to the point that we sometimes forget that the original model came from the East. And, in turn, it demonstrates the influence of that Venetian creativity on those who first inspired it. How, then, can we view cross-Mediterranean relations as purely antagonistic? *Venice and the Islamic World* proves that these relations also followed more rewarding routes.

Thierry Desmarest
Chief Executive Officer
Total

Venice's unique geographic location between East and West enabled the City of the Doges to maintain a special relationship with the most powerful Islamic dynasties over hundreds of years. The artistic refinement and scientific progress of Islamic society, notably in the areas of medicine, mechanics, astronomy, and mathematics, considerably shaped Venetian attitudes towards Eastern culture. Always eager for new knowledge, Venetian craftsmen and merchants enthusiastically acquired objects and imitated Eastern techniques in the production of glassware, leather, and textiles. Venetian art, culture, and imagination steadily took on an Oriental attitude during centuries of dialogue and exchange with the East.

Every culture draws nourishment from its own roots, yet truly blossoms only on contact with other cultures. The exhibition *Venice and the Islamic World* illustrates this intercultural blossoming, based on an exchange of learning, savoir-faire, and cultural values through the channels of art, trade, and migration. Today, Total seeks to preserve and promote such cultural diversity through its patronage program. Present in 130 countries on five continents, Total employs thousands of men and women of every background, culture, and origin. In extending its oil and gas activities, the corporation favors dialogue and cooperation, seeking to establish harmonious, lasting relationships with all the communities that welcome them.

For over 90 years, Total has cultivated long-term partnerships in the Middle East, based on respect for each host country, on a transfer of technology, and on training local personnel. By supporting the exhibition *Venice and the Islamic World*, Total is once again demonstrating its interest and respect for the Arab world's culture and heritage.

Moments of Vision: Venice and the Islamic World, 828–1797

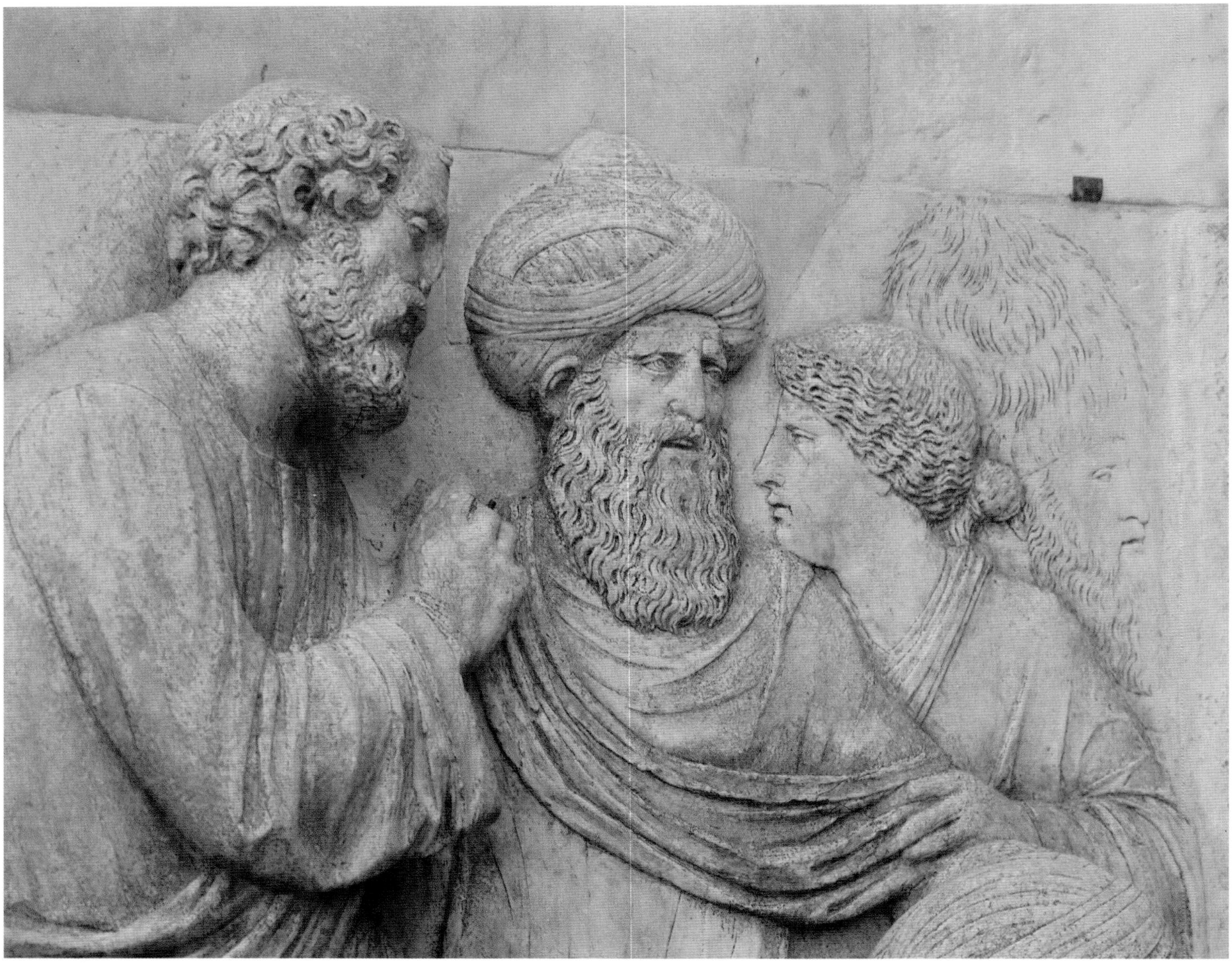

Stefano Carboni

It was the year 828. The Venetian chronicles recount that two merchants[1] from the emergent and ambitious city on the lagoon succeeded in purloining the relics of St. Mark the Evangelist from their resting place in the Coptic church of the same name on the shores of Mazarita in Alexandria (cats. 46b and 47) and delivered them triumphantly to Doge Giustiniano Partecipazio (r. 827–29) in the recently erected Palazzo Ducale.[2] The Egyptian city at the time was under the control of the ʿAbbasid governor of Cairo, ʿAbdallah ibn Tahir ibn al-Husayn, in a particularly confused political period in Egypt.[3] Giustiniano's successor, Giovanni Partecipazio (r. 829–37), immediately began building the Doge's Chapel, better known today as St. Mark's Basilica (see fig. 1, p. 121), as a *cappella palatina* connected directly to one side of the palace. The chapel was meant to contain the body of St. Mark and thus imbue the power of the Serenissima with a compelling and commanding spiritual patron, in a period when such secular and religious marriages were particularly poignant, in order to establish a supremacy over other medieval cities. Venice would not become the seat of the patriarchate until 1451—the patriarch had his seat in the northeastern city of Aquileia establishing an important link between Christian Orthodox Byzantium and the Catholic pope in Rome. Venice's bishop resided in the cathedral of San Pietro (see fig. 6, p. 79),[4] which presided over the entrance of the port (fig. 1) and, according again to Venetian sources, was given in these very years the purported stone seat of the first bishop, St. Peter himself, adorned with verses from the Qur'an

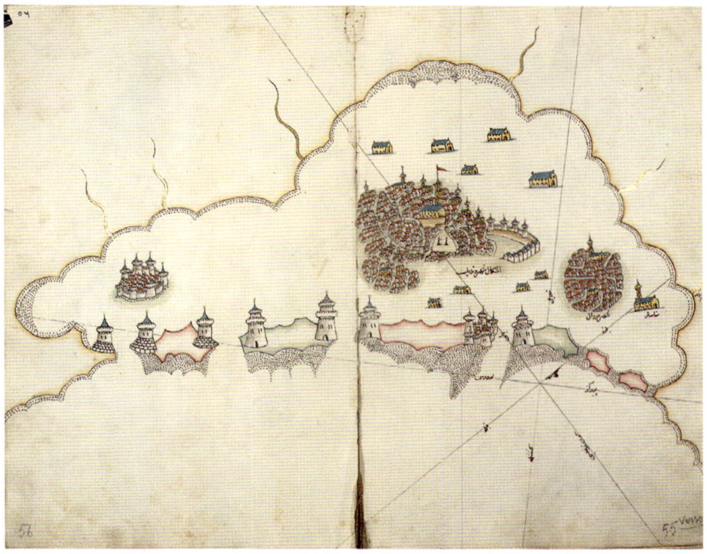

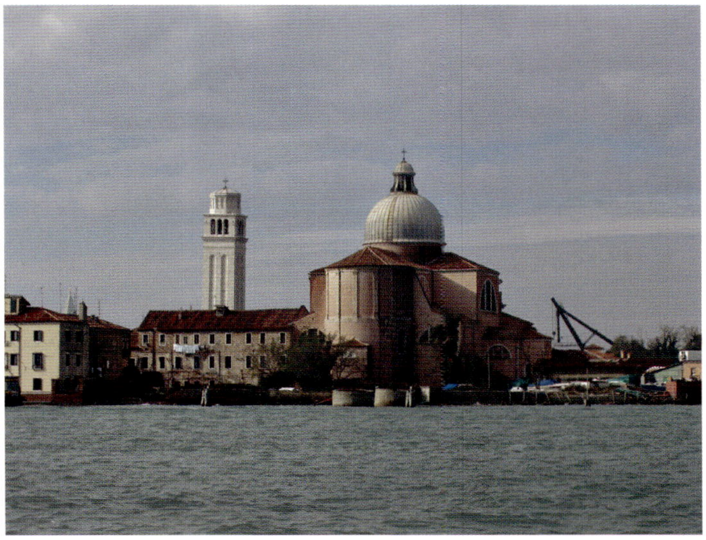

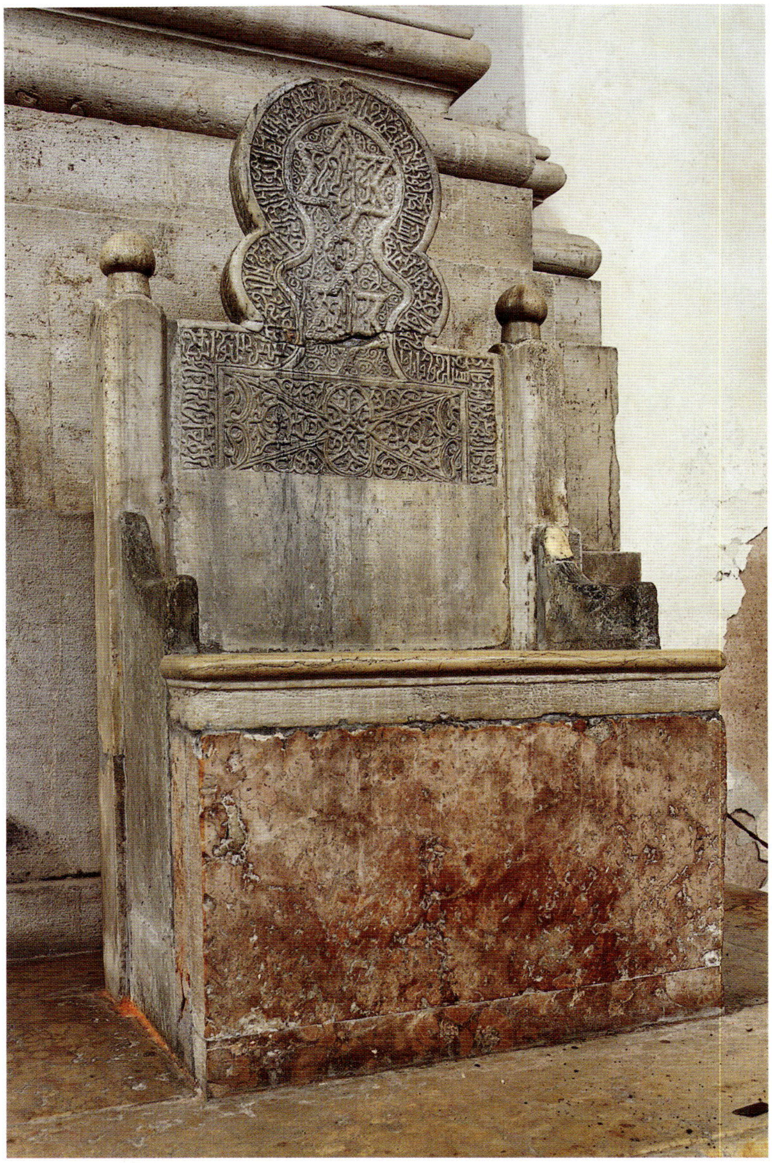

cat. 87. *"Chair of St. Peter"*
Eastern Mediterranean,
backrest ca. 11th–12th century
Basilica con Cattedrale di
San Pietro di Castello, Venice

Preceding pages:
fig. 5. Tullio Lombardo, *St. Mark Healing Anianus* (detail), 1489–90

cat. 47. *Seyyed Nuh*
Kitab al-bahr al-aswad
wa al-abyad ("The Book of the Black and White Sea")
Istanbul, Turkey,
second half of 17th century
Biblioteca Universitaria, Bologna

fig. 1. Church of San Pietro di Castello, Venice, seen from the lagoon

(cat. 87) and donated to the city by the Byzantine emperor in appreciation for Venice's help in trying unsuccessfully to wrest Sicily from the Arabs.[5]

"In the second year of Doge Giustiniano the body of St. Mark was brought to Venice from Alexandria in Egypt. It happened as follows. The caliph of the Saracens had ordered the erection of a magnificent palace in Alexandria, but he lacked the construction materials necessary and decreed therefore that the marble columns be removed from the Christian churches of Egypt so as to be available for the new building. His order caused horror and despair among the Egyptian clergy. Right at that time the tribunes Bono di Malamocco and Rustico di Torcello—two prominent figures involved in large-scale trade—who, despite a ban decreed a few years earlier, set anchor with three ships loaded with everything imaginable in the port of Alexandria, having been swept there by a fierce storm. During their stay in Egypt the crew frequented Mass in the Church of St. Mark where the saint's body was preserved. One day Bono and Rustico went to the church and found two Greek clergymen, the monk Stauracio and the presbyter Teodoro, in great despair. They asked the clergymen what it was that troubled them and thus they learned of the caliph's decree. So the two Venetians said: 'The precious treasury you preserve in your church is in grave danger of being desecrated and ill-treated by the Saracens. Give it to us for we will know how to honor it as it deserves. In recognition our doge shall not fail to bestow upon you great rewards.' Persuaded by the Venetians' reasoning, the two clergymen obliged; but first of all it was necessary to circumvent as much the watchfulness of the Christians of Alexandria as that of the Saracen customs agents. The Christians were swindled by the shrewdness of the Venetians and their two Greek accomplices, who switched the body of the Evangelist with that of another saint, while the customs agents were deceived by the top of the box which, amongst the sacred relics, contained ham and other cuts of pork meat which, as everyone knows, was as offensive to the Saracens as it was to the Jews. When the box was opened at the customs office, the agents began to cry *'khinzir, khinzir!'* a word that certainly expresses repugnance and horror,[6] and of course they authorized the consignment [straight away]. Bono and Rustico joyfully transported their treasury to Venice (fig. 2)."[7]

The legend of St. Mark's relics also extended to unlikely places, such as the small village of Cropani in the Gulf of Squillace in Calabria, the region at the "foot" of the Italian peninsula.

Local history relates that, when the ship containing the saint's relics bound for Venice was caught in a fierce storm, the only way to avoid sure death was the promise to leave St. Mark's kneecap in the village as a relic. For this reason—and here is the practical aspect of the deal—Cropani's merchants enjoyed tax exemptions in Venice and in her dominions. Similarly, another sea story from Cropani claims that the image of the *Dormitio Virginis* that can be found today above the altar of the Duomo—painted by no other than Mark's companion, St. Luke the Evangelist—was left there by a Byzantine ship from Constantinople in order to be able to leave the harbor that had miraculously become deadly calm (fig. 3).[8]

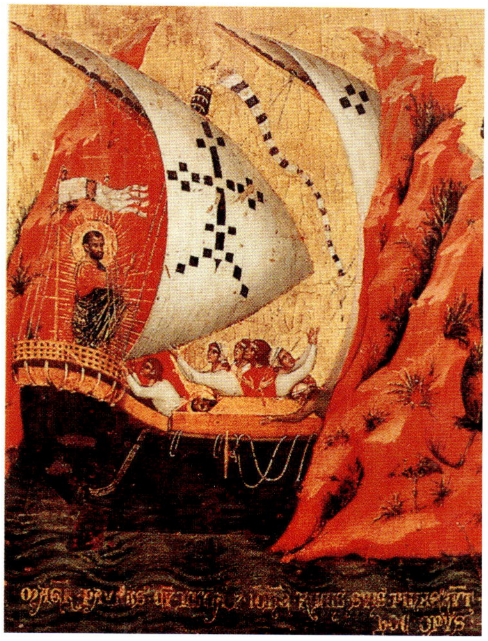

fig. 2 Paolo Veneziano, *A Scene from the Life of St. Mark* (*The Saint Saving the Ship Transporting His Dead Body to Venice*), panel of the Pala Feriale, 1345. St. Mark's Basilica, Venice

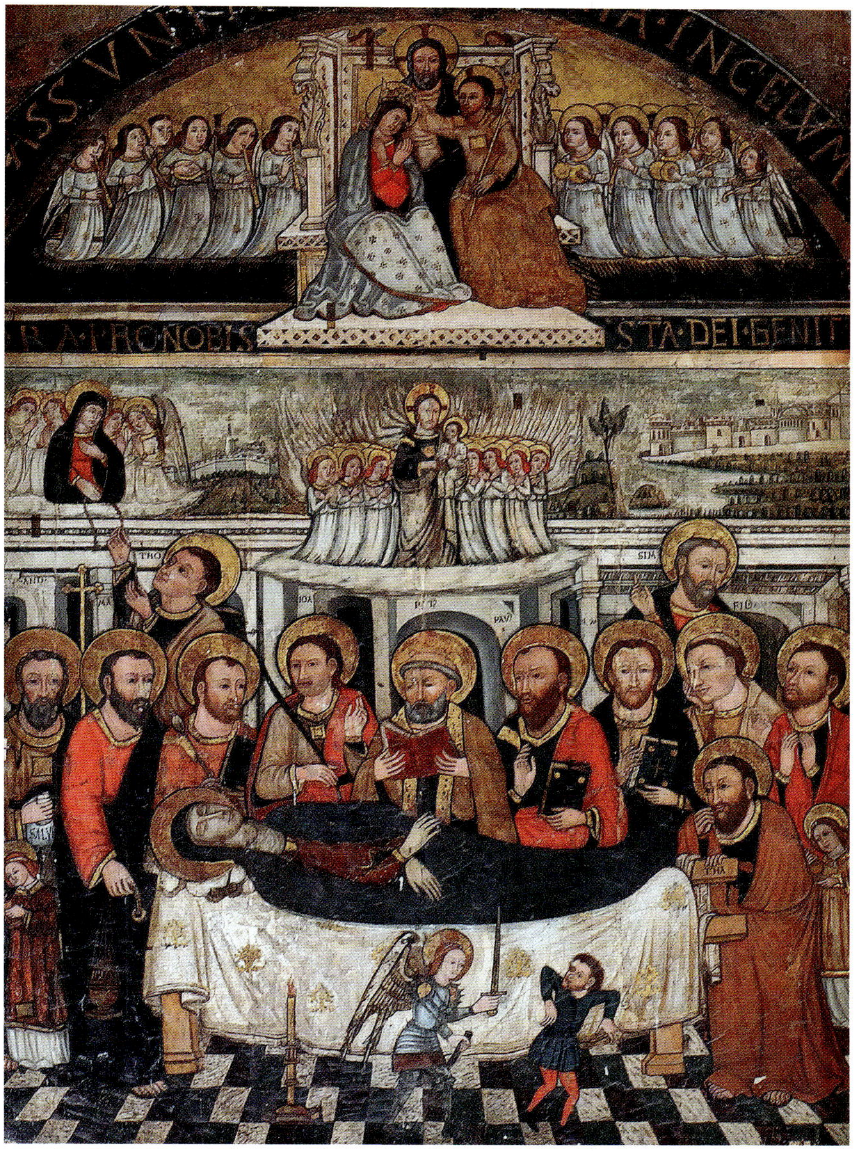

fig. 3 Anonymous Italo-Byzantin, *The Dormition of the Virgin*, probably 14th century, Cathedral, Cropani

The feat of bringing St. Mark to his final resting place—giving origin to both the myth of St. Mark and Venice's identification as the New Alexandria (see fig. 7, p. 129),[9] both so intimately linked with the history of the city—represented a great boost for the city's ability to expand her trade in the eastern and southern Mediterranean, to become an important point of departure for pilgrimage to the Holy Land, and to establish herself as what has been aptly defined as the "hinge" between Europe and the East or as the "liquid frontier" between these two seemingly antithetical worlds.[10] Venice's liminal and pivotal role implies that the definition "antithetical" does not truly apply to her history and the present exhibition and catalogue intend to emphasize this city's different and unique approach to, and understanding of, a world that has too often been described as "the other."

Pragmatism is probably the term that best characterizes Venice's relationship with the Islamic Near East: it underlines at the same time the acumen of her ruling elite in dealing with political matters as well as a remarkable amount

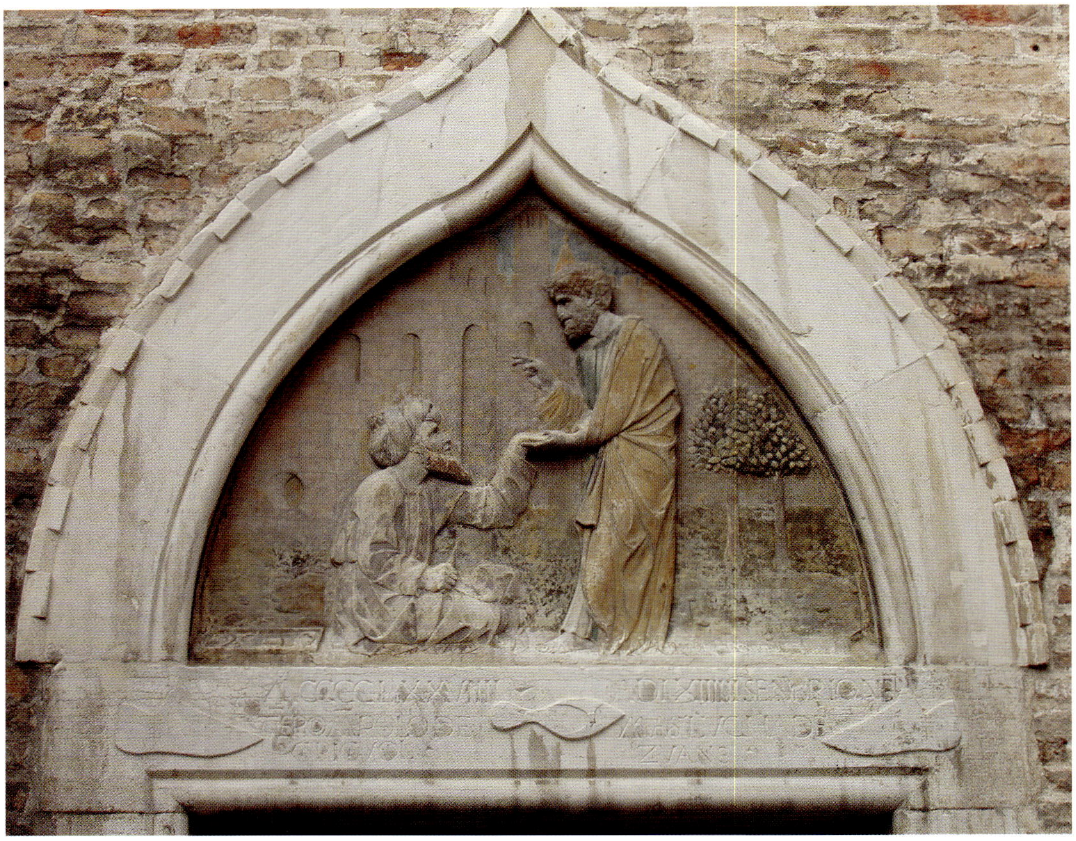

fig. 6. Pietro Lombardo (attr.), *St. Mark Healing Anianus*, late 15th century. Façade (lunette) of the Scuola dei Calegheri, Campo San Tomà, Venice

of cynicism in taking care of her own interests, which allowed a city with little or no *terra firma* possessions until the 15th century to enjoy a thriving economy and play a powerful political role in the world for many centuries, surviving for over a millennium until modern times.

It was this almost perfect balance and interaction of religious esprit, chameleonic diplomacy, and an unsentimentally practical mercantile system that turned Venice into the most respected trading and political partner of the Near East. The city needed to maintain good diplomatic relations especially with the Mamluks and the Ottomans in order to survive and at the same time could not relinquish her role as one of the defenders of Christendom in Europe, which represented the other half of her economic subsistence.[11] Hence, the policy of the carrot and the stick and diplomatic subterfuges were common practice. Too much emphasis has been given thus far to Venice's alignment with the various holy leagues that were established throughout the centuries and on her periods at war with the Grand Turk.[12] As a matter of fact, the times of peace were much longer, capitulations[13] were regularly renewed after the accession of a new ruler, and, even during times of hostility, diplomacy was always hard at work and trade virtually never came to a halt.

It was the continuous presence of Venetian diplomats and the prolonged residence of Venetian merchants in the main cities of the Islamic Near East (fig. 4)[14]—together with the frequent visits of Mamluk and Ottoman emissaries to the Serenissima—that distinguished this city from all other European powers. It resulted in a direct, sometimes intimate, knowledge of the Muslims' customs, religion, philosophy, science, technology, and—the obvious focus of a museum exhibition—their arts. That is why it sounds incorrect or at least misleading to read about an "Orientalist" curiosity towards the Ottomans on the part of the Venetians,[15] at least in the 15th and 16th centuries, or to view the presence of well-observed Mamluk and Ottoman characters in the religious paintings and façade decorations for the Venetian *scuole* and *scuolete* (figs. 5 and 6) as the inescapable representation of the fear-provoking Muslim enemy after the fall of Constantinople.[16]

The first half of the 9th century represents the dawn of Venice's complex relationship with the Islamic Near East, which already contained *in nuce* all the elements of the millenary script: the flag of St. Mark and his lion whenever it was necessary to show religious zeal; the on-and-off confrontation with the Islamic powers along the shores of the Mediterranean (in this period the surging Aghlabids in Tunisia and Sicily at a time when Venice was still under Byzantium's sphere of influence);[17] the first emissaries to the main trading cities in the Near East; and, finally, the already familiar sight of Venetian merchants in Alexandria, which was a determining factor in their odds to flee from the city with the saint's supposed relics.

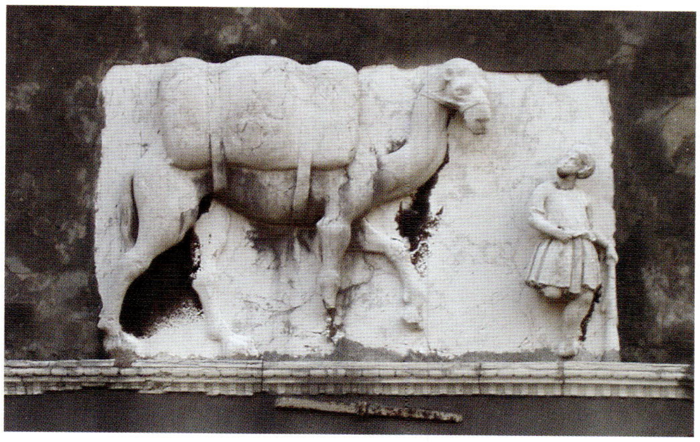

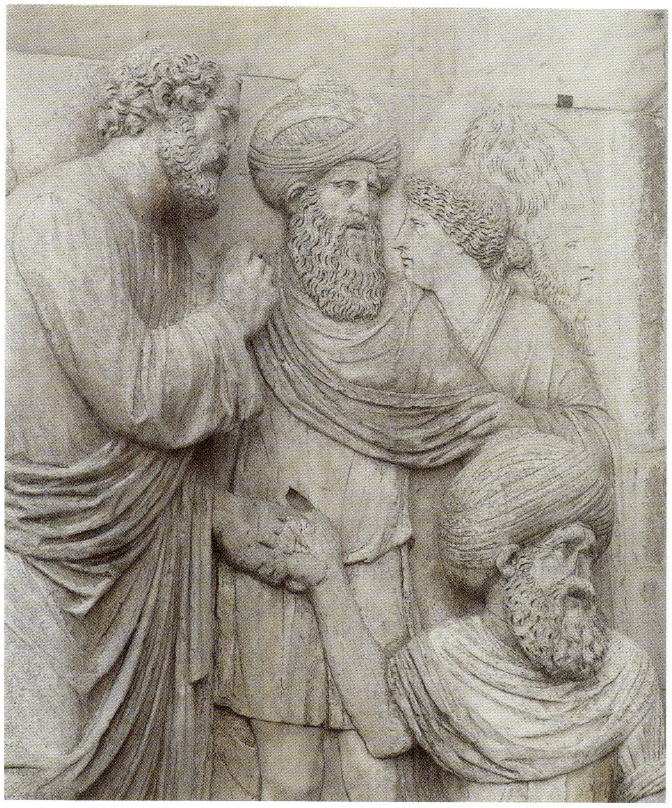

fig. 4. Bas-relief with merchant and camel, probably 14th century. Façade of Palazzo Mastelli, Venice

fig. 5. Tullio Lombardo, *St. Mark Healing Anianus* (detail), 1489–90. Bas-relief on the façade of the Scuola Grande di San Marco, Venice

The recurrence of occasions on which the Venetian oligarchy made an effort to come to terms with the Islamic world, circumventing the religious, philosophical and idealistic disputes that were so predominant in other European cities and focusing on diplomatic, political, and practical issues, prompted me to include in the original title of the exhibition the phrase "Moments of Vision." The title was subsequently shortened to the present "Venice and the Islamic World, 828–1797." The original title was inspired by a series of lectures given by Richard William Southern at Harvard University in 1961, which were subsequently published under the title *Western Views of Islam in the Middle Ages.*[18] The third lecture, or Chapter Three in the book, was entitled "The Moment of Vision" in reference to an aborted attempt in the mid-15th century to do something about Islam, that is, to discuss rationally the thorny issue of the perception of the Islamic world in Europe at a time when Islam had to be treated not only as a moral and intellectual danger but also as a military and political threat to the West soon after the fall of Constantinople in 1453. It was with a mindset of fear and hope that three future cardinals and a future pope exchanged correspondence on the possible solution to the cultural divide. Southern regarded it as a "moment of vision" based on the solid ground of textual criticism that was, in his opinion, a far cry from the imaginative fabrications of the early 12th century and from the bold and hopeful speculations of the 13th.

The four interlocutors were the Spaniard John of Segovia, archbishop of Caesarea in 1453; the German Nicholas of Cusa, made cardinal by Nicholas V in 1448; the French Jean Germain, bishop of Nevers and Chalon-sur-Saône; and the Italian Aeneas Silvius from the Piccolomini family, bishop of Siena, who became Pope Pius II in 1458. One of them, John of Segovia, who was based in Caesarea and thus had firsthand knowledge of some of the Near Eastern complexities, dreamed of organizing a *contraferentia,* a sort of *conferentia* (from the Latin *cum ferre,* or "bring together"), with the fundamental difference being that it was devised as a useful meeting of hostile parties, Christians and Muslims, though the obvious goal was the establishment of the preeminence of the Christian Catholic faith. In order to prepare for the great conference, Nicholas of Cusa proposed "to have merchants summoned from Cairo, Alexandria, Armenia, and Greece (fig. 7)[19] who would describe at first hand the ideas and practices of Islam." And when this information had been collected, he wanted to have intermediaries sent from the West to the Islamic countries, preferably, he says, "temporal princes, whom the Turks prefer to priests."[20]

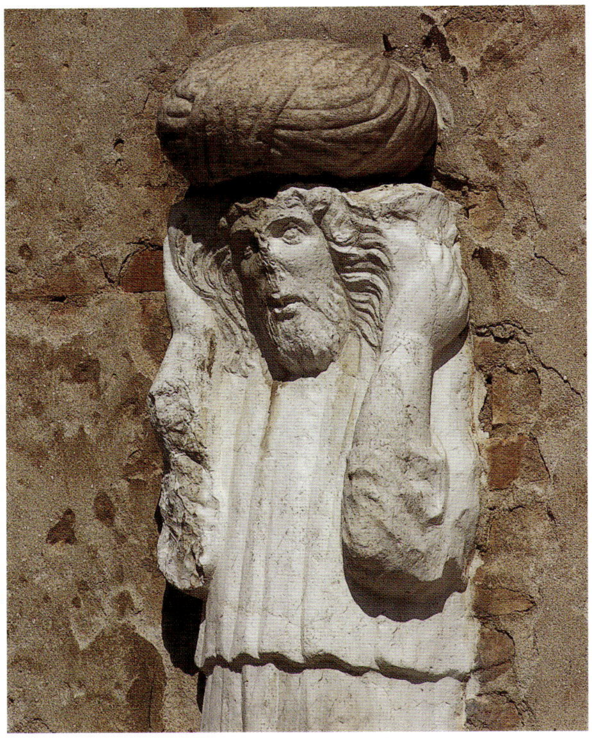

fig. 7. Detail of figure with turban, probably late 13th–early 14th century. Statue in Campo dei Mori, Venice

Pius II (1405–1464), one of the most interesting and complex personalities of the 15th century, organized at the end of his life a rather pathetic attempt to lead a Crusade against the Ottoman sultan with the help of the Venetian fleet leaving from the port of Ancona in central Italy.[21] The *contraferentia* never happened for various reasons, one of them being Piccolomini's accession to the papal seat, and perhaps because the project was too audacious and ambitious for the political climate of the time in Europe, but the vast epistolary exchange among these four men remains the best attempt in pre-Renaissance Europe to address the full complexity of the problem and give Islam a distinct role in world history.

The Oxonian Thomas Gascoigne wrote that a few decades earlier in the Quattrocento there were three main causes for Muslims to abhor conversion to the Christian faith: "Firstly, the diversity and contradiction among Christians in various sects and on various subjects; secondly, the evil lives of the Christians; and thirdly, the ill-faith of the Christians, and especially of the Genoese and the Venetians."[22] This was, of course, Gascoigne's point of view, not that of the Muslims, but it is not surprising that he included Venice, which had already been excommunicated by the pope a couple of times for trading with the infidel, among the "ill-faithed" Christians.[23]

It was indeed Venice's (and Genoa's to a much lesser degree) especially close relationship with the Islamic world in terms of trade and diplomacy that often made her suspicious to Christian Europe. For the Venetians, there was in fact no single moment but instead several "moments of vision" throughout the centuries (hence the plural in the original title of the exhibition) for they always had a rational approach to the Islamic world based on a direct and practical knowledge of it. For this reason, if we exclude the heavily Islamized areas of the Iberian Peninsula and southern Italy, Venice was the first and in many ways the only European city to understand and appreciate Islamic philosophy and science and to open channels of communication that also included artistic, visual, and technological information.

It was the year 1204. The Fourth Crusade was the most successful Venetian-led military campaign in the Near East, but it was far from being a confrontation with Muslim rulers. The Ayyubids (1171–1260), then reigning over Jerusalem and many other cities where Venetian merchants traded actively, were a relatively stable power and favored commerce with Europe. In fact, the Fourth Crusade resulted in a devastating attack on Constantinople, the Byzantine capital of the Eastern Orthodox faith.[24] After the bloody three-day-long sack of the city by Crusaders, with the decisive help of the Venetian fleet, the schism between Catholic Europe and Orthodox Byzantium was complete and no attempt was made to march on Jerusalem to wrest it from the Muslims. Only two years earlier, in 1202, Pope Innocent III (r. 1198–1216) had shown no qualms about inflicting a first excommunication upon the Serenissima after she captured Zara in Dalmatia, noting that the city put her colonial and economic interests over the flag of Christendom. But he had promoted this expedition, convincing the doge to provide the fleet and gather the Crusaders in Venice. In frustration after the sack of Constantinople, the pope complained that the Crusaders had vowed to free the Holy Land but ended up fighting Christians instead of Muslims.[25]

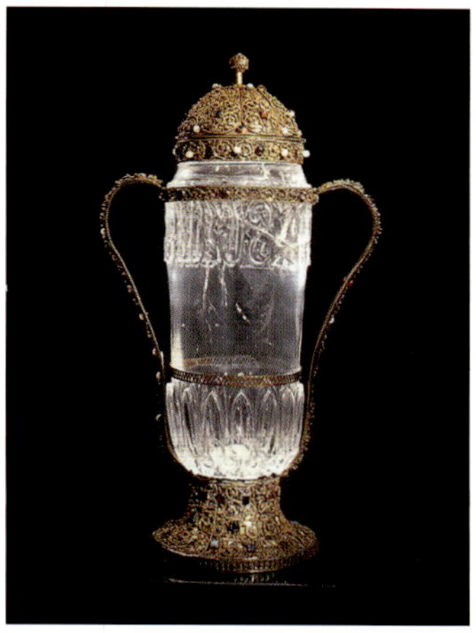

cat. 88. *Rock crystal vase with mount*
Vase: Egypt, late 10th century;
Mount: Venice, mid-13th century
Treasury of St. Mark's, Venice

The booty of Constantinople and many Byzantine possessions in the Eastern Mediterranean—Venice was rewarded a "quarter and a half" or three-eights of the Peloponnesus together with a series of commercial colonies and the island of Crete— represented the most valuable profit ever achieved by the Serenissima Republic in her history.

This was also the moment when the famed four bronze horses were brought to Venice and installed on the façade of St. Mark's Basilica and when the church's treasury became legendary in Europe because it was so greatly enriched with luxury objects looted by the Venetians in Constantinople.[26] In addition to the large number of Byzantine works, there were also several objects that the emperor had evidently obtained through diplomatic or other means from Muslim courts, most notably that of the Fatimids of Egypt and Syria (969–1171). Not surprisingly, this was the symbolic start of the history of collecting Islamic works of art in Venice—or at least the beginning of a constant stream of such works that either arrived and remained in or passed through the city, which culminated in the 16th century.

It may well be that the earliest works of Islamic art that survive in Venice in the Church of San Pietro di Castello (see cat. 87, p. 14) and in St. Mark's Treasury (cats. 88 and 150) can be interpreted more as *spolia*, trophies, or booty rather than expressions of an early appreciation and collection of Islamic artistic culture. The reutilized Kufic stele in San Pietro that became the backrest for the Venetian bishop's seat could be seen as a victory of Christianity over Islam; as for the several rock-crystal and relief-cut glass objects in the treasury, the doge may have been profiting indirectly via Constantinople from the dispersal of the fabled Fatimid treasure in Cairo in the third quarter of the 11th century.[27]

Later, true collecting trends can be established and there is plenty of evidence today in two major Venetian institutions, the Marciana Library and the Correr Museum. The library, created in 1468 after Cardinal Bessarione's gift of his famed collection of Latin and Greek texts to the

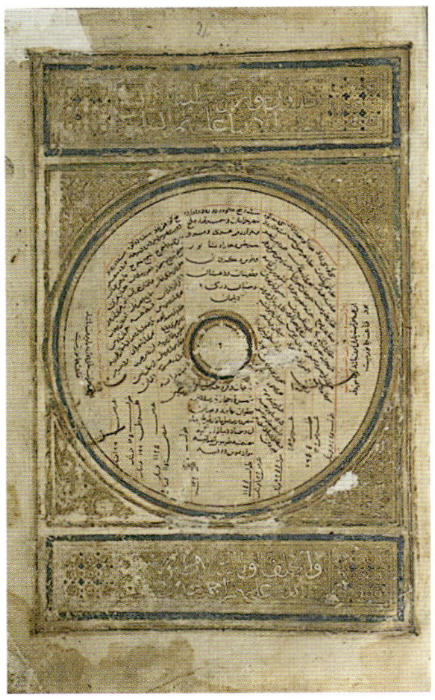

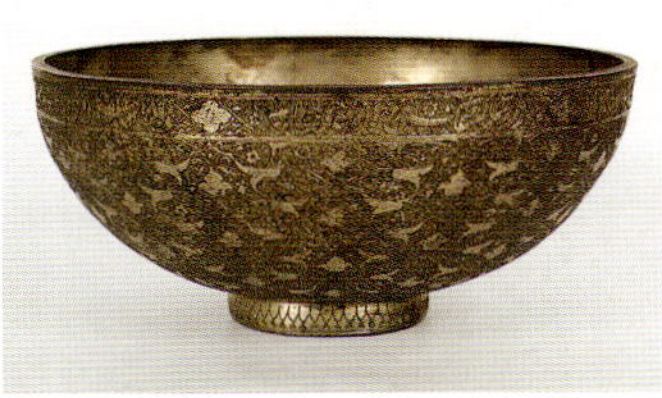

cat. 1. *Tarikh-i tabari*
Iran, ca. 1290–1320
Biblioteca Nazionale Marciana, Venice

cat. 114. *Wine cup*
Iran, late 16th–early 17th century
Museo Civico Correr, Venice

Venetian Republic, was kept for a long time in storage in St. Mark's Basilica; it found a permanent home in the current Sansovino building in the Piazzetta only about a century later.[28] Bessarione continued to add volumes to his collection until his death in 1472 and the possibility that some of the Arabic, Persian, and Turkish manuscripts now in the Marciana Library were acquired by the cardinal himself should not be discounted. The largest and most important gift of "Oriental" manuscripts, however, enriched the library at the end of the 18th century through the collection of Giacomo Nani (see cats. 1 and 3), an important figure in late Venetian political history who endowed the Marciana with his library at his death in 1797, the very year of the demise of the Serenissima Republic.[29]

The Correr Museum was established much later than the Marciana Library. At the end of the 18th century, it was initially a personal collection available to the public in Teodoro Correr's palace at San Zan Degolà (S. Giovanni Decollato), then became a civic museum in 1836. Correr (1750–1830) was one of the most enthusiastic and heterogeneous collectors in the history of Venice. For him, collecting was a real passion, almost an obsession, and he acquired, in particular, existing collections and objects from the Venetian oligarchy as well as from established families, which for the most part had had contacts with the Near East in the past.[30] He is not known to have singled out works of Islamic art or to have been expressly appreciative of its artistic idiom, but his collection of Ottoman weapons and paraphernalia that belonged to Francesco Morosini (see cat. 77, p. 65; cats. 113 and 134, p. 238), along with the many works of Islamic art that are housed today in the Correr Museum (see cat. 48, p. 108; cats. 95–96, p. 65; cat. 114, p. 20; cat. 178, p. 131; cat. 179, p. 283), exemplify at once his admiration for these objects and the presence in Venice of older collections that included Islamic works. Incidentally, from 1880 to 1922 the museum was housed in the newly restored Fondaco dei Turchi on the Grand Canal (see fig. 2, p. 94) before it was moved to the new wing of St. Mark's Square, where it remains today. The works of Islamic art in the museum are perhaps not of great overall quality, reflecting the fact that Correr bought entire collections of eclectic nature, but together they form one the largest single collections of its kind in Italy. The list of collectors of works of Islamic art in Venice, however, does not stop with the end of the Republic but continues into modern times with the distinguished figures of Mariano Fortuny y De Madrazo (1871–1949; moved to Venice in 1889),[31] Baron Giorgio Franchetti (d. 1922; he bought the Ca' D'Oro, or Santa Sofia Palace, in 1894 and willed it to the city of Venice at his death),[32] and Count Vittorio Cini (1885–1977; he established a cultural center, the Giorgio Cini Foundation, on the island of San Giorgio in front of St. Mark's Square; see cat. 12).[33]

It was the year 1291. The painter and craftsman Gregorio from Napoli di Romania (Nauplia in the Peloponnesus, which was under direct Venetian control for two centuries from 1388) moved to Venice at a time when the glass industry on the lagoon had developed into a profitable business. The trade in glass cullet from the Eastern Mediterranean coast had long been established and also recently regulated, and the hazardous glass factories were about to move from the market area of Rialto to the island of Murano in order to create a safe and less congested area

cat. 3. Taj al-Din Ibrahim ibn Khidr Ahmadi
Iskandarnama
("The Book of Alexander")
Turkey, probably Edirne, mid-15th century
Biblioteca Nazionale Marciana, Venice

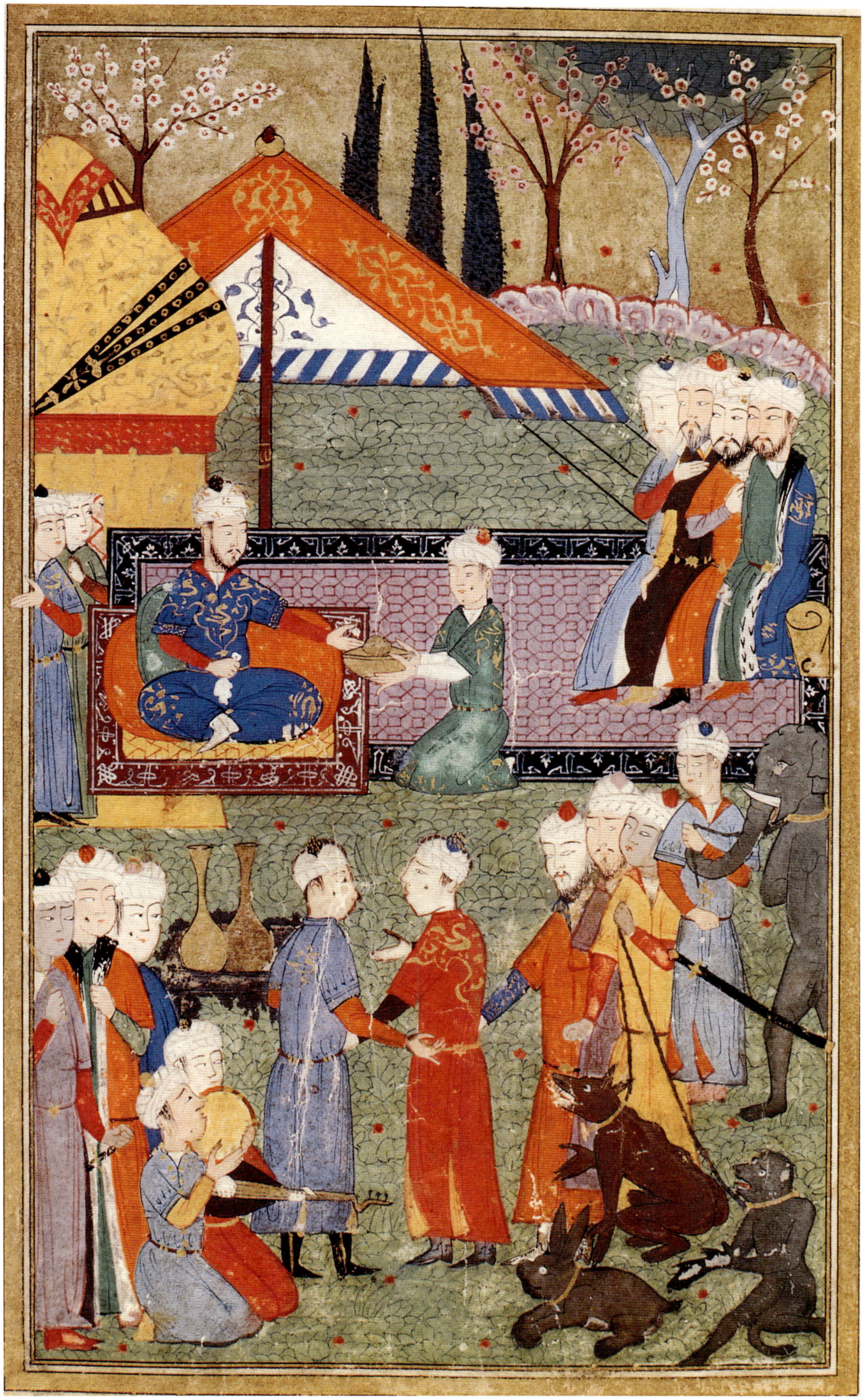

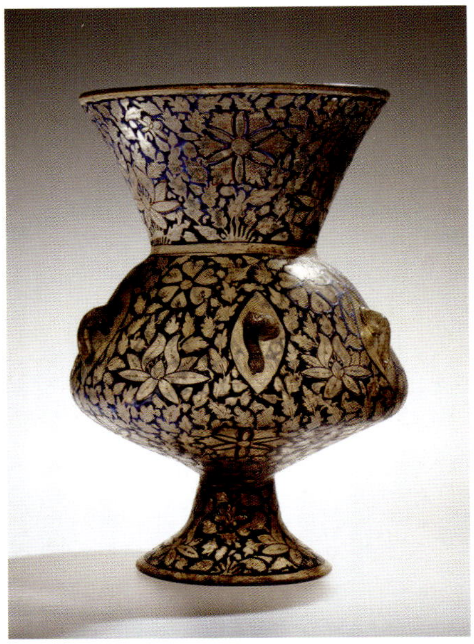

cat. 153. *Mosque lamp*
Cairo, Egypt, ca. 1356–63
The Victoria and Albert Museum, London

where the industry could develop under the government's control and support. Islamic artists and craftsmen had for several centuries been undisputedly in the avant-garde of glass technology, technique, and artistic decoration and Venice had been at the receiving end of this industry, learning and absorbing its mysteries.[34]

In particular, Syrian and Egyptian glass painters had decorated objects with gold and colored enamels for about a century (cat. 153), mastering this difficult firing technique and at the same time creating splendid objects that had caught the attention of sultans as well as European knights and princes.[35] Gregorio and other artists undoubtedly became familiar with the Islamic enameled and gilded works that arrived in Venice, saw the potential of this type of decorated glass, joined forces with the Venetian makers of *moioli* (beakers), and started local production for export to Europe—based on the same technology and materials they had become familiar with from their Islamic counterparts. This became a successful business, which lasted for several decades (cats. 156–59, pp. 257–58),[36] and established the Venetian glass trademark for centuries to come.

Enameled glass production in Venice in the late 13th century can be regarded as the earliest example of Venetian craftsmen's flirtation with artistic creations from the Islamic lands, in this case encouraged by a constant and well-established commercial flow as well as by a novel artistic and technical challenge for the creativity of the surging Venetian industry. As a constant equation in Venice's history, therefore, trade was of paramount importance in the development of her artistic language.

Trade and economy were indeed at the core of everything in Venice and influenced all other aspects of life in the city. While Gregorio and his colleagues were painting hundreds of beakers, the Republic, confident in her economic stability, coined the first gold ducat in 1284, which became known as the *zecchino,* a term derived directly from the Arabic *sikka* ("mint"). In the meantime, Marco Polo (1254–1324) returned from his 25-year-long absence from Venice in 1295, bringing with him valuable information about the Asian trade routes (cat. 15, p. 58).

In the same years, Polo's contemporary Marin Sanudo the Elder (ca. 1260–1338) was thundering against the Muslims and trying to revive the spirit of the Crusades by making use of economic, rather than religious, means of persuasion. We know from his *Liber secretorum fidelum crucis* (later enlarged into a three-part text entitled *Opus terrae sanctae*; cat. 41, p. 62) that he had spent long periods abroad and traveled extensively in the eastern Mediterranean. Although filled with religious zeal, his theory was that the Muslims could be subjugated only if their role of intermediaries along the spice trade route was annihilated and the Christian fleets took control of the coasts of the Indian Ocean. This was a remarkable ideological assessment for his time and almost visionary of what the Portuguese would achieve two centuries later. Sanudo's was a grandiose, if overambitious plan, which occupies an important place today in the understanding of medieval trade routes and especially in the development of cartography (see cats. 42–43, pp. 55 and 63), therefore overriding his original intentions, but it could have been conceived only by a native Venetian who had both the opportunity to travel extensively and a good network at his disposal.

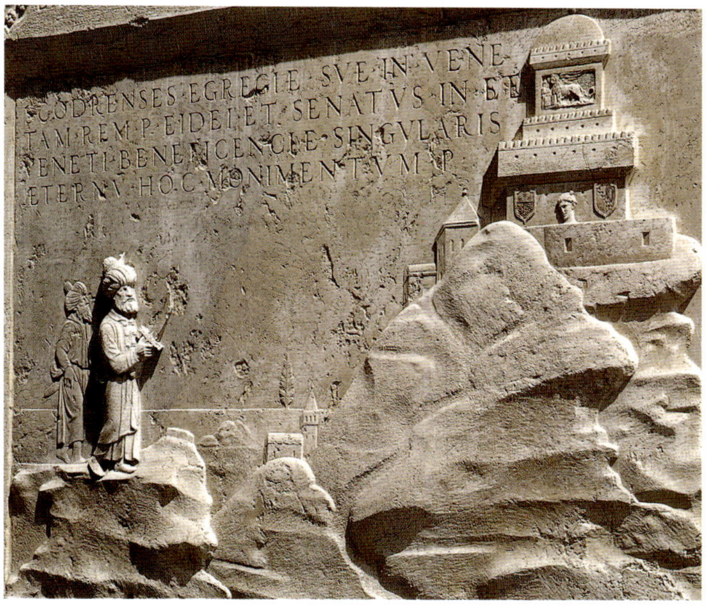

fig. 8. Bas-relief showing Mehmet II before the fortress of Scutari, formerly on the façade of the Scuola degli Albanesi, late 15th century

It was the year 1479. *"Zentil belin optimo pytor,"* "Gentile Bellini the excellent painter," was sent to Istanbul by the Venetian Signoria following the wish of Mehmet II, the Conqueror of Costantinople, to have at his court a good painter, a sculptor, and a bronze founder. Only twenty-five years after the final fall of Byzantium, the Western world was trying to come to terms with the new order established by the Ottomans, sharing uneasy borders in Eastern Europe. For Venice, the moments of vision must have been several in a relatively short time-span that included: the hopeful years of Francesco Foscari's long rule (r. 1423–57; cat. 21, p. 189), during which were built the new Doge's Palace as we admire it today (see fig. 1, p. 76) and the Fondaco dei Tedeschi; the uncertainties following the capture of Constantinople; the immediate renewal of the existing capitulations; a long war to try to salvage a few possessions in the eastern Mediterranean; and an attempted alliance with Uzun Hasan of the White Sheep Turcomans in order to engage the Ottoman's army on their eastern border (see cat. 150). Finally, there was a rather smart peace treaty that left Venice with only a few lost territories (one of these was Scutari, an important and tragic event for Venice's Albanian community, which was recorded in their *scuola* and is still visible to the attentive visitor; fig. 8) and many untouched ones, and which brought, notably, an inspired awareness that Mehmet II had a keen interest in seeking legitimization among the royal European entourage. As Pedani appropriately put it, in these years Venice's "attitude towards the Turks was at the same time of reverential fear and a realistic search for the positive aspects of a peaceful agreement."[37]

The decision to send to Mehmet's court perhaps the most celebrated living Venetian artist and a famous portraitist, who was at that time also engaged by the government to paint canvases for the new Doge's Palace, must be viewed as an intelligent effort to appeal to the narcissistic side of the Ottoman ruler and portray Venice to him as a great Renaissance court, while diplomacy was working incessantly. So much has been brilliantly written on Gentile's two years at the Ottoman court, in the catalogue of a recent exhibition,[38] that it is easy to overestimate the influence of his visit not only on Venetian painting of the late 15th and the early 16th centuries but also on the decorative arts that in those very years began to display an interest in the language of Islamic art through a process of imitation in many different media.

If Gentile Bellini's visit was the most prominent means of transmission and an extraordinary *trait d'union*—also able to influence Ottoman art (see cats. 5–6)—it is principally thanks to the multitude of diplomats and anonymous merchants covering the Muslim areas that Venetian artists and craftsmen appreciated and became familiar with Mamluk and, later, Ottoman and Persian bindings (see cats. 124 and 128), Islamic inlaid metalwork (see cats. 89 and 108), Ottoman textiles (cats. 70–75, pp. 186–87), Iznik pottery (cat. 173; cats. 174–75; cats. 176–77, pp. 288–89; cat. 178), and Chinese blue-and-white porcelain (cat. 172) predominantly in this period.

Page 24:
cat. 6. Haydar Reis Nigari
Portrait of Admiral Haireddin "Barbarossa"
Istanbul ca. 1540–45
Topkapı Sarayi Müzesi Library, Istanbul

Page 25:
cat. 5. *Portrait of Mehmet II the Conqueror*
Istanbul ca. 1479–81
Topkapı Sarayi Müzesi Library, Istanbul

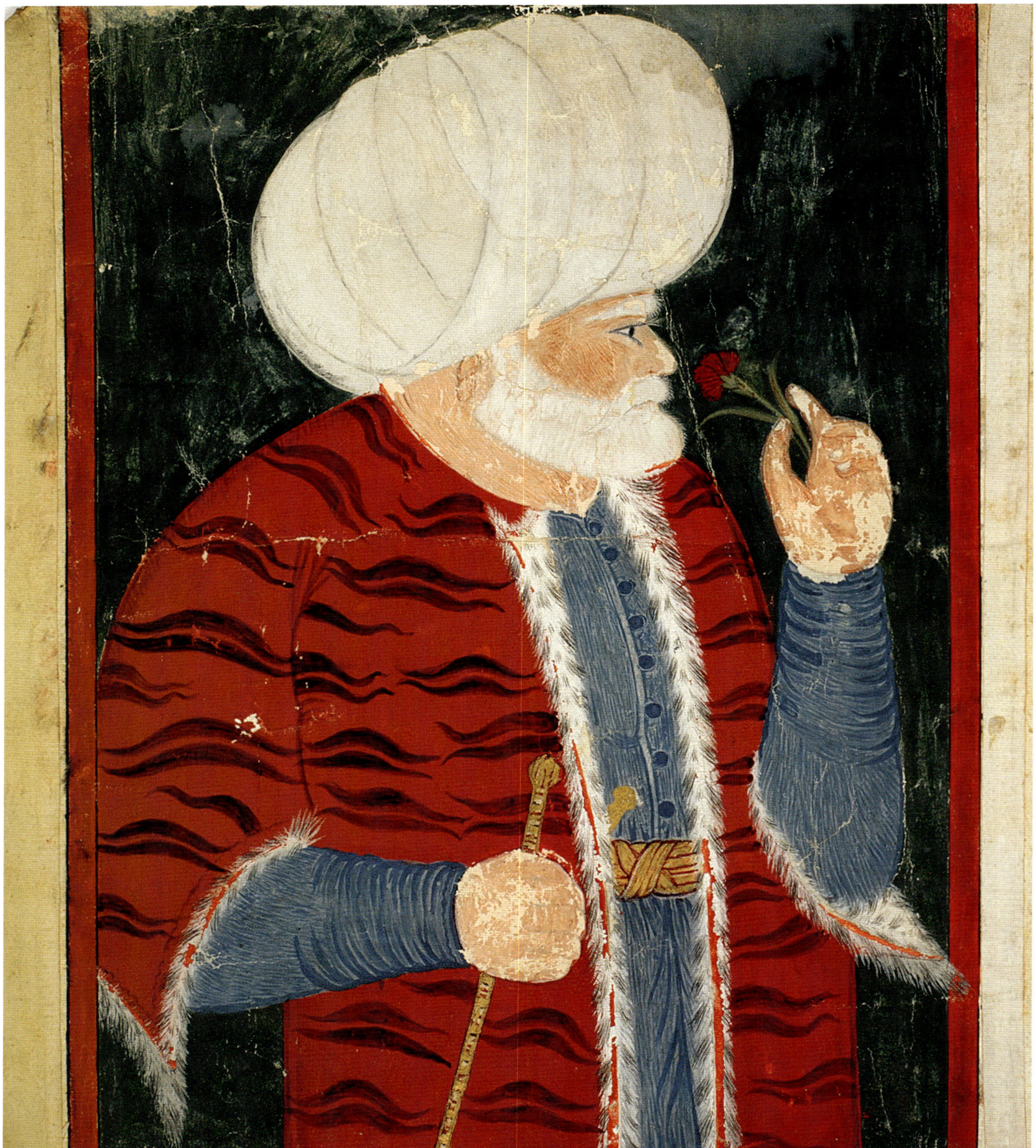

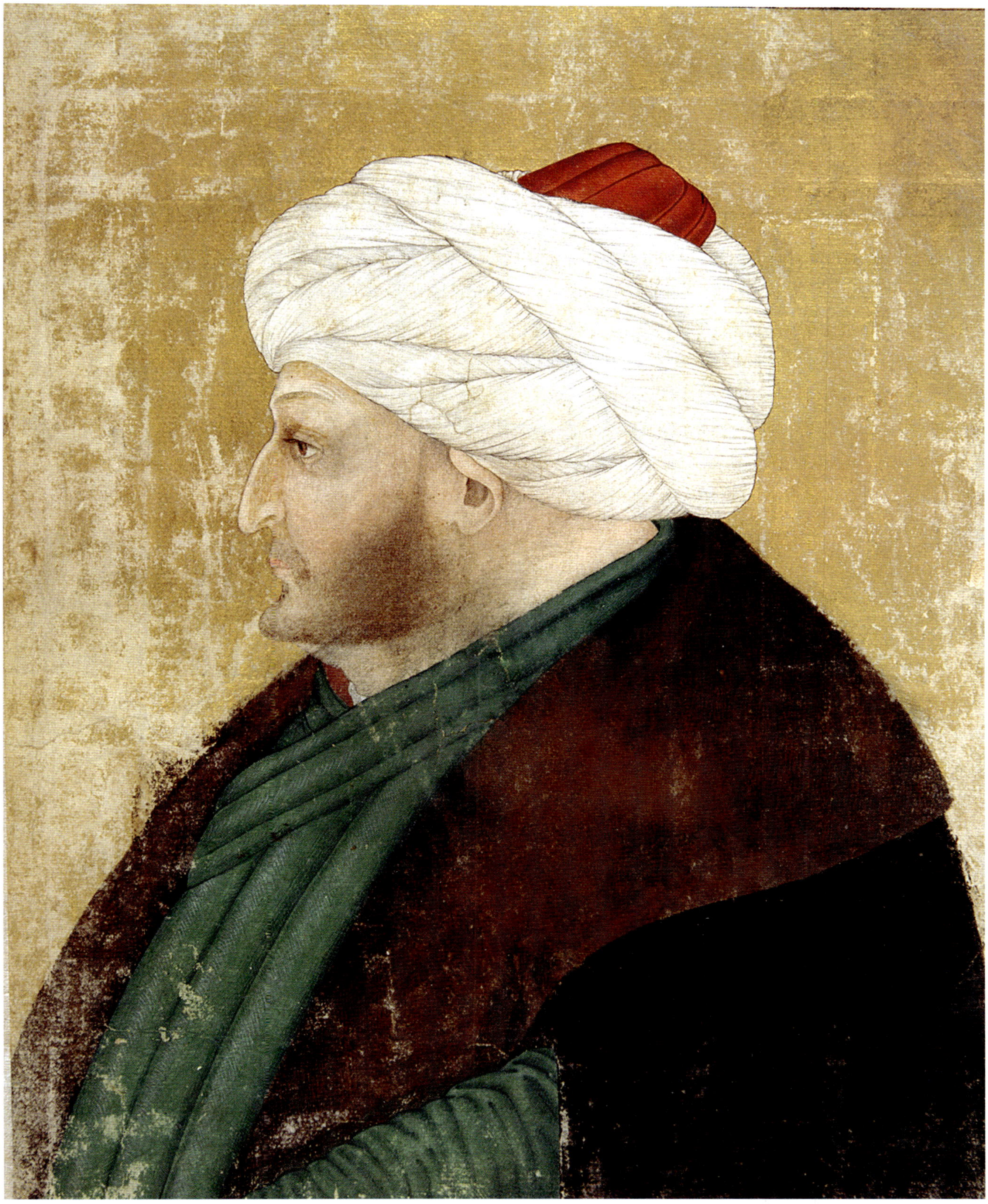

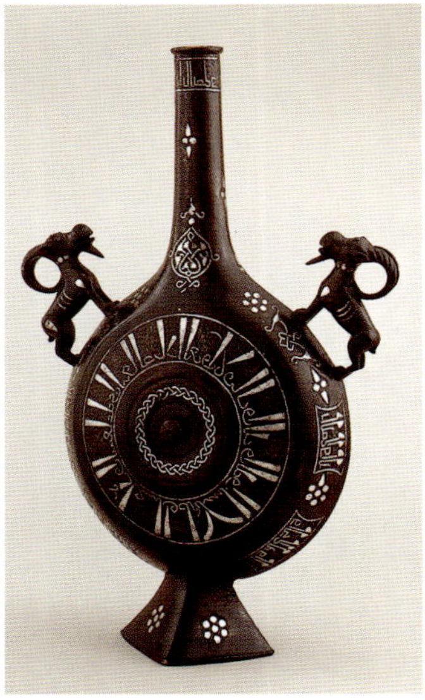

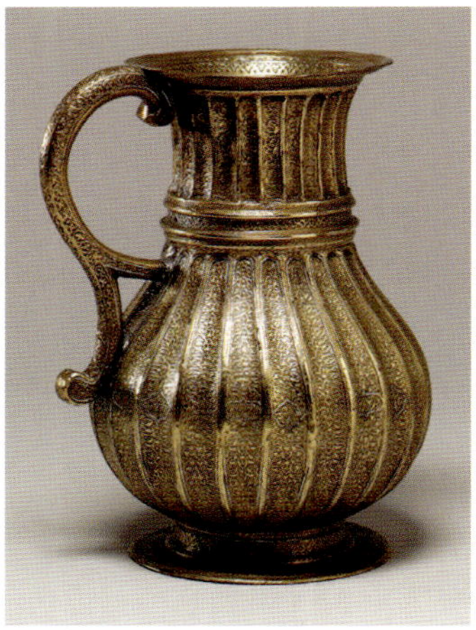

In Venetian painting, the important point is that "Orientalism" in the second half of the 15th century does not have the same connotation and should not be mistaken for the much later, 19th-century European phenomenon that was born out of colonialism. In Bellini and his followers, such as Mansueti (cat. 26), we have indeed the feeling of a neutral attitude, if not a sympathetic one, towards the Mamluks and the Ottomans, as if they were part of an acknowledged historical phenomenon or a sort of natural landscape necessary to illustrate the life of St. Mark in its original setting. A change in the perception and the role of Muslim characters in Venetian painting happened only with Carpaccio's late works in the second decade of the 16th century, a time also marked by the end of the Mamluk sultanate, Venice's most successful trading partner, and by the perception that the Ottomans were becoming all too powerful. Of the extant four canvases from the Scuola di Santo Stefano, the only one populated exclusively with Ottoman figures represents the stoning of St. Stephen, as if Muslims ought to be the only characters responsible for evil acts against Christians (cat. 31).

It was the year 1533. Marin Sanudo the Younger died at the age of 67 leaving, among other things, a detailed chronicle, which the perceptive and analytical insider of the Venetian Senate had compiled from the year 1496 until his death. Sanudo became a member of the Maggior Consiglio at the age of 20 and a senator in 1498, a remarkable career for a young man without powerful political supporters in the Venetian mature oligarchic system. He was a careful observer and an obsessive recorder of every word, look, and gesture exchanged in the Senate and he also had access to the classified state archives. His *Diarii*, published in their entirety only at the beginning of the 20th century in 58 volumes,[39] are without a doubt the most important source for any scholar who hopes to gain a deeper understanding not only of the mere facts but also of the political frame of mind of the Serenissima during one of the most eventful periods in her history. In the context of the present study, Sanudo's reports of the frequent visits of Ottoman envoys, from

cat. 89. *Flask*
Khurasan or the Punjab, ca. 1200
The British Museum, London

cat. 108. Qasim
Ewer
Possibly northwest Iran
or southeast Anatolia,
late 15th–early 16th century
The Walters Art Museum, Baltimore

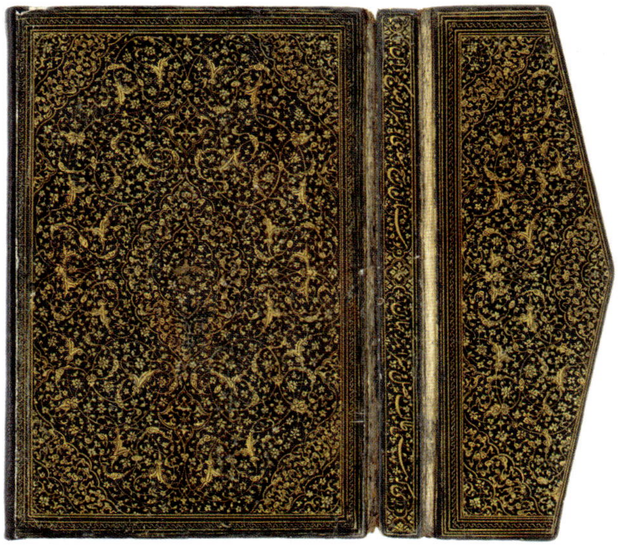

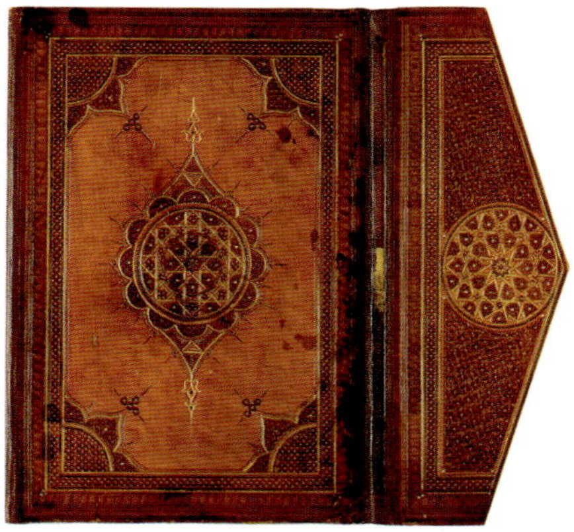

cat. 128. Sa'di
Bustân
Istanbul, after 1530
The Nasser D. Khalili Collection of Islamic Art, London

cat. 124. *Second volume of a 30-part Qur'an manuscript*
Egypt, late 14th century
The Walters Art Museum, Baltimore

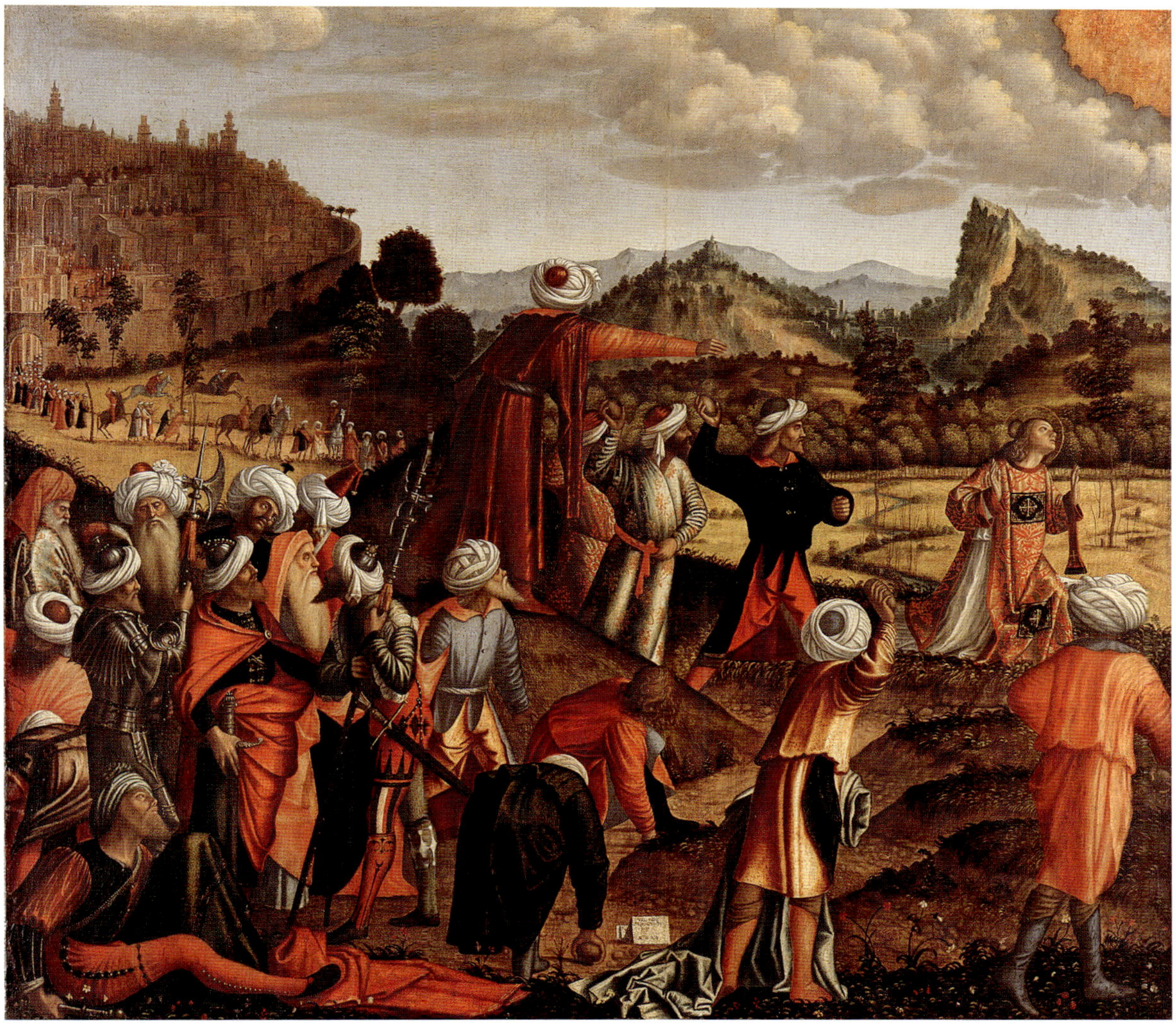

cat. 31. Vittore Carpaccio et atelier
La Lapidation de saint Étienne
Venise, 1520
Stuttgart, Staatsgalerie

the moment they were lodged in the city to the time they left, and the innumerable references to discussions, arguments, and decisions made in the Doge's Palace regarding Near Eastern policies, as well as his anecdotal accounts of the activities and efforts of Venetian merchants to do business in the eastern Mediterranean, represent an invaluable and largely untapped wealth of information. The diaries are still mostly unknown to the international scholarly audience, especially since information must be extrapolated from a verbose text written in a wonderful blend of Renaissance Italian and Venetian dialect.[40]

For example, the art historian is thrilled to learn, from Sanudo's *Diarii*, about the encrusted gold tiara sold for the astronomical sum of 115,000 ducats by the Rialto jewelers Caorlini and Levriero to Süleyman the Magnificent and displayed in the Doge's Palace before it was sent off to Istanbul (cat. 59, p. 112),[41] or about the decorated leather boxes brought to Venice by the envoy Ali Bey in 1514 that may have helped to promote an interest in the production of gilded leather with Islamic patterns later in the century in Venice (cats. 135–42).[42]

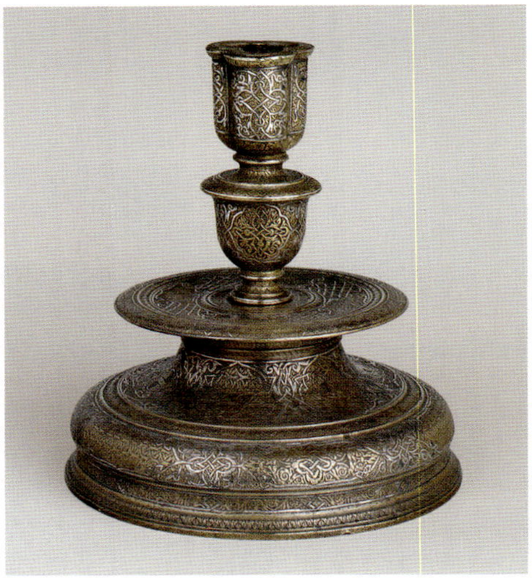

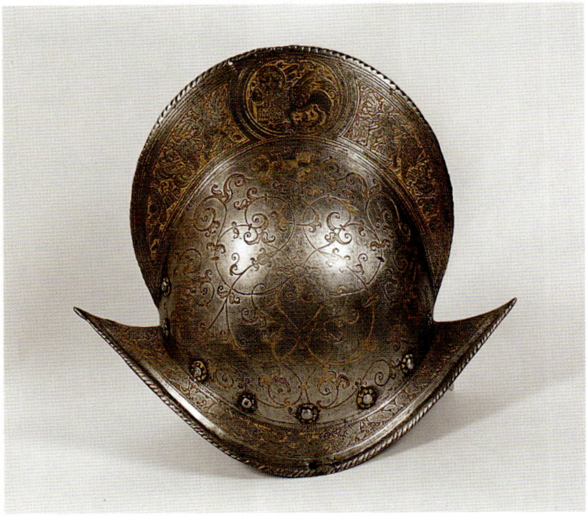

cat. 121. *Candlestick*
Europe, possibly Venice, 16th century
The Metropolitan Museum of Art, New York

cat. 122. *Morion*
Brescia, third quarter of the 16th century
Armory of the Palazzo Ducale, Venice

Sanudo's witty remarks and skeptical attitude are even more fascinating and sometimes amusing. Thus, in the episode on the talismanic, poison-detecting narwhal horns in St. Mark's Treasury—one of which the Venetians reluctantly gifted to the Ottoman sultan through the request of Yunus Bey in 1529–31—we learn that a rumor was deliberately circulated that a horn had been stolen, to avoid admitting that such a priceless amulet had been given to an opponent of the Christians. (See p. 372 of Appendix, extracts from Marin Sanudo's *Diarii,* vol. 53, col. 536; vol. 54, col. 291; vol. 55, col. 178.) Or, in reference to the news of the Ottoman victory over the Safavids in the battle of Çaldiran in 1514, readily conveyed to Venice by Selim I's envoy Mehmet, Sanudo dryly remarks that "we know through the grapevine that the Ottomans got the short end of the stick."[43]

The last years of Sanudo's careful notes correspond to the ascent of Süleyman the Magnificent to the Ottoman throne (r. 1520–66), a period of unusual frequency in diplomatic missions and in exchanges of gifts, of a strong presence of Venetian merchants and noblemen in Istanbul and other Ottoman cities, and of a lasting peace interrupted only by a brief period of conflict in 1537–40.[44] A brief survey of the works that are included in the present catalogue reveals that this is also the period that marks the closest proximity in artistic production between Venice and the Ottomans or, better, that denotes a peculiar vogue in Venice for "Oriental" patterns—clearly those that were most familiar to them—as a sort of chinoiserie *ante litteram.*

Each medium—textiles, inlaid metalwork (see cats. 121–22), tooled and gilded leather, painted and lacquered wood, enameled glass, and maiolica (see cat. 181)—must be analyzed individually[45] in order to understand the different circumstances that brought artists and craftsmen from each guild to work in the Islamic style. It is important, however, to emphasize that this fashion was a pervasive and—until now—scarcely observed phenomenon by modern scholars that was part of the Venetian artistic idiom for a few decades in the 16th century. When one also considers the pattern books with different *rabeschi* that were printed in those years (cat. 58) as well as the bold efforts to publish religious and secular texts in Arabic with movable type (cat. 60) during an exciting pioneering moment for Venice's publishers, the picture becomes clearer as an overall effort to create a different taste, aimed at pleasing local and foreign patrons, which the city on the lagoon was in a unique position to accomplish.

This use of Islamic patterns in the Venetian arts in the 16th century can be read on various levels that range from a mere effort to find a different and appealing marketing tool on the part of the artists, or a conscious patronage on the part of sophisticated sponsors, to intricate symbolic connotations that take into account the complex and unique cultural, philosophical, and political relationship between Venice and the Ottomans in particular. It would be too ambitious to try to offer a satisfactory interpretation at the present time, but the pragmatic attitude that the Serenissima demonstrated in her dealings with the Islamic world should always provide a useful guideline.

It was the year 1603. The envoys of the Persian Safavid ruler Shah ^{c}Abbas I (r. 1571–1629) visited the Serenissima in an effort to discuss the common "Ottoman" problem. For Venice,

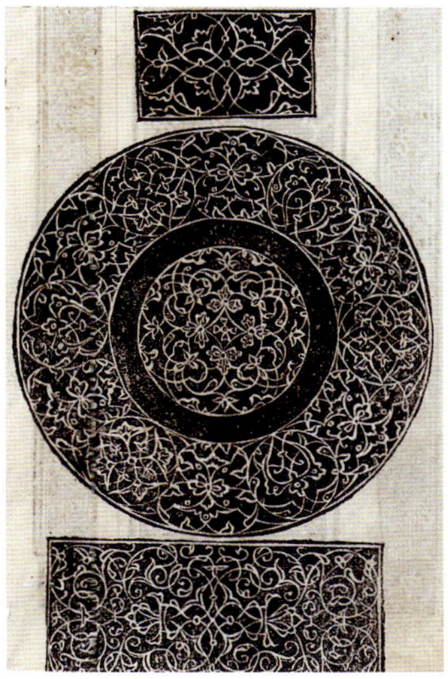

cat. 58. Giovanni Antonio Tagliente
Arabesque Interlace in Circle
Venice, ca. 1465–1527
The Metropolitan Museum of Art, New York

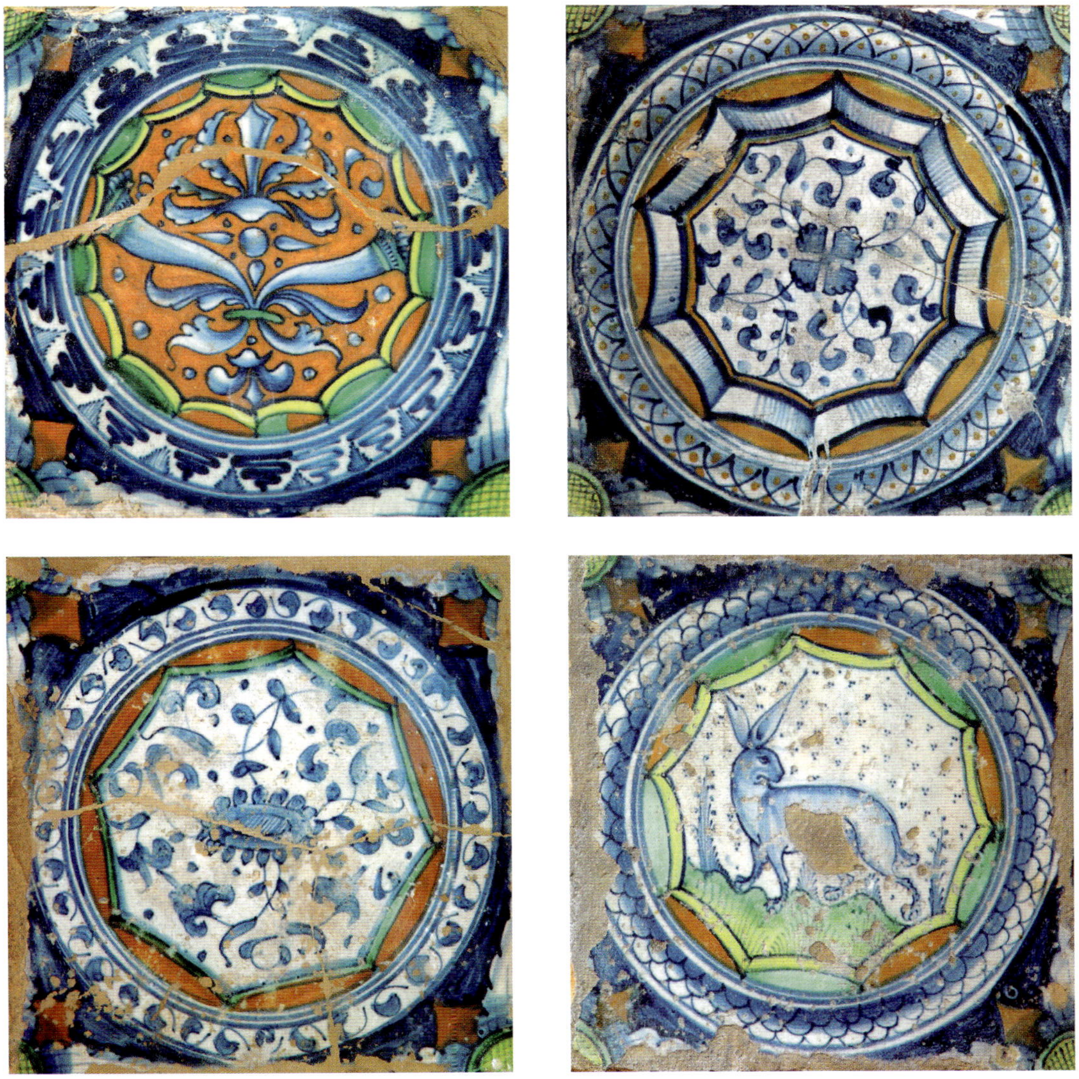

cat. 181. *Four tiles from the floor of the Cappella Lando, Church of San Sebastiano, Venice*
Probably Venice, ca. 1510
Church of San Sebastiano, on loan to the Museo Franchetti alla Ca' d'Oro, Venice

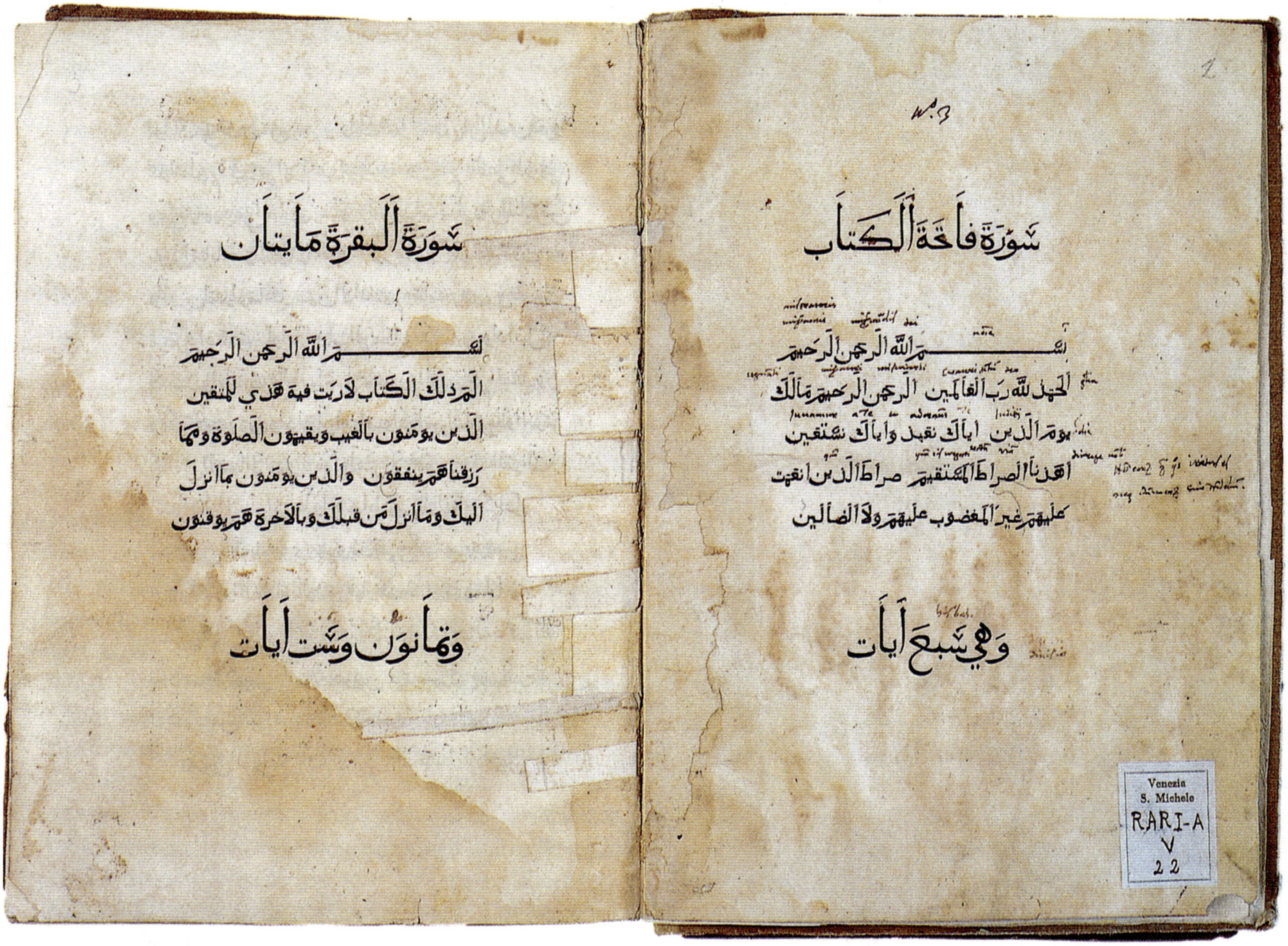

cat. 60. *Printed Qur'an in Arabic*
Venice, 1537–38
Provincia Veneta di S. Antonio dell'Ordine dei Frati Minori, Venice

things had changed dramatically after the death of Süleyman the Magnificent in 1566. While commercial enterprise was as active as ever in the late Cinquecento, diplomatic missions with the Ottomans started to dwindle and the Battle of Lepanto of 1571—in itself not a particularly significant event—marked nonetheless a change of attitude on both sides of the equation. In Venice, rhetoric prevailed over pragmatism in this instance and the minor victory at Lepanto became a cause for huge celebrations and an opportunity for the Venetian oligarchy to align with the rest of Europe, which still bore the scars of the 1529 siege of Vienna, in her role as champion of the Christian faith (see cat. 34, p. 93).[46] On the other hand, following the revolution in the trade routes that had given the Portuguese direct access to the Indian Ocean bypassing the Mediterranean,[47] the Ottomans perceived that Venice's ability to maintain a central role as an economic and political partner was diminishing at a fast pace. From this period, the Ottoman sultans sent fewer and fewer embassies to the Serenissima,[48] becoming snobby about their dealings with her and favoring more powerful European courts, while the role of the *bailo* in Istanbul was no longer essential. The "Venetian Gulf" was turning into the "Ottoman Lake" and Venice inevitably had to reinvent herself as a regional, rather than an international, marketplace, turning her back to that sea that had provided her with wealth and power for so many centuries.

The Safavid envoys gifted the doge with several court-production silk and silver-wrapped-thread luxury carpets made in Isfahan, five of which are still on display today in the St. Mark's Basilica Museum (cat. 83, p. 180). Although official diplomatic missions are scarce in the history of Venetian-Persian relations,[49] especially as compared to those with the Ottomans, these emissaries were certainly aware of the appreciation of carpets and textiles and the role they played both in the economic and the social life of the Serenissima. The doge deposited the Persian carpets in the Basilica Treasury because it was common practice to lay these precious items at the foot of the main altar in a celebratory religious context during specific feasts,[50] to place them on the floor at the church's entrance and exhibit on them gold and silver objects from the treasury once a year, or to use them as a floor spread for the bier of the dead doge as a symbolic bed of flowers.[51]

Religious institutions, such as the Scuola Grande di San Rocco in the 1540s, acquired and perhaps directly commissioned carpets in Cairo and elsewhere to cover the large tables around which the trustees had their meetings (cat. 81, p. 178); churches were often at the receiving end of such gifts from the government, as in the case of the recorded gift to the Church of the Redentore in 1571[52] and, probably, of the splendid dragon carpet acquired by von Bode in Burano (cat. 86, p. 179). Many Venetian paintings exemplify the use of Oriental carpets in a religious setting (see fig. 4, p. 179) but none is more symbolic of the transfer of their significance from a sacred to a secular setting than the "Star Ushak" rug wrapping the steps in front of the doge's seat in the religiously charged illustration of the *Return of the Ring to the Doge* by Paris Bordone in 1534 (see fig. 3, p. 177),[53] which was part of the cycle of paintings begun by Gentile Bellini for the Scuola Grande di San Marco (see cat. 28, p. 83).[54]

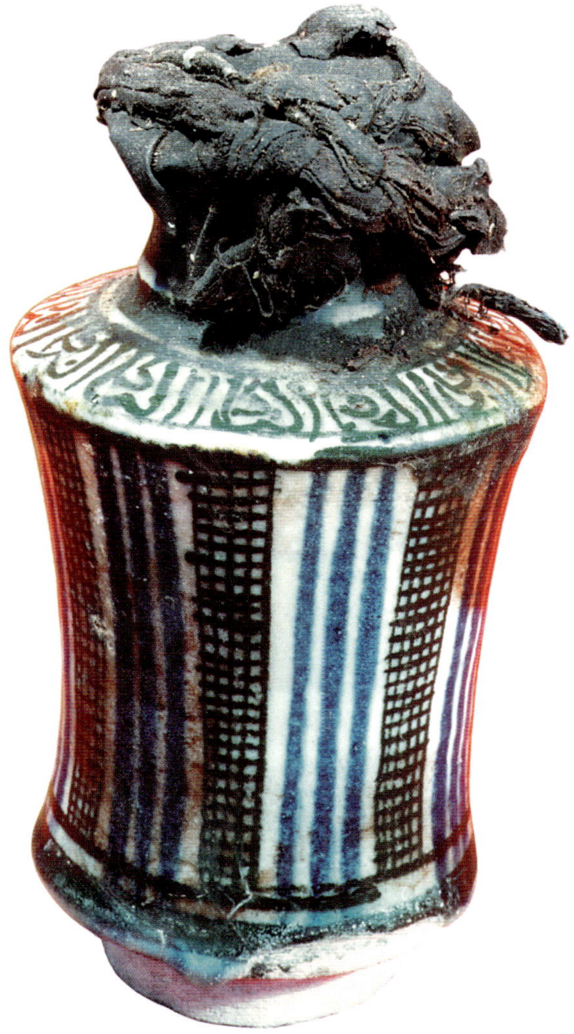

fig. 9. *Albarello*, reused as a reliquary, Syria, 14th century. Tomb of San Nicolò, Church of San Nicolò, Lido, Venice

In Venice there was never an effort to imitate Mamluk, Turkish, or Persian carpets, or at least there was never a successful one, and this is why they were regarded as high-end status-symbol objects also in a domestic context (cat. 33, p. 63). Textiles, instead, were the most successful in-kind currency both on the diplomatic and the commercial level (see cat. 18), representing the artistic production that brought the Venetian and the Ottoman weavers as close as they could ever get. Envoys in Venice and Istanbul expected to receive a munificence of garments and lengths of cloths-of-gold and velvets and would compare them among each other, bitterly complaining if they were not satisfied. For the government, the selection and number of textiles it gave away was a way to make a point of the importance in which it held the mission. On the commercial side textiles single-handedly represented well over 50 percent of the recorded transactions and exemplify the intense exchanges between the two areas.[55] They were so intimately linked with the Islamic world that when an Ottoman envoy was in town with his retinue all the shops in the Mercerie between St. Mark's Square and the Rialto Bridge displayed their best textiles in the hope of a good sale and prices automatically went up at Rialto during his stay in Venice.[56]

The 17th and the 18th centuries are relatively uninteresting in regard to the artistic relationship explored in the present exhibition. It is not a period of fruitful exchanges and reciprocal interest, but one of a general adjustment in Venice to the common European view that the Turk was truly "the other" and had to be described and illustrated in either a confrontational or a derisive way, the latter being one of the aspects of early Orientalism. Thus, Francesco Morosini's galley going to war in the battle of Candia in the 1660s was decorated with the figure of a naked, bareheaded Turk in chains (cat. 149, p. 47), who in his turn was transformed into a circus acrobat in an 18th century print (cat. 66). On a more sophisticated level, the Venetian painters Giambattista Tiepolo and Antonio Guardi had no interest in seeking inspiration in the large early-16th-century canvases full of Mamluk and Ottoman characters in the Scuola di San Marco when they began to work on their series for *Gerusalemme Liberata* and the *quadri turcheschi* (cats. 39–40, pp. 137–38). Rather, they illustrated a world that was stimulated by contemporaneous prose, poetry, and opera librettos, then in vogue in the European capitals.

The demise of the Serenissima Republic, in the end, did not come at the hands of the West's preferred common enemy, the Muslim world, which in good and bad times had been a lifeline for Venice's own existence. It came from Europe, embodied in the figure of Napoleon Bonaparte, which the city had decided to rely upon in order to extend her survival in a dramatically changed environment. **It was the year 1797**.

Facing page:
cat. 18. Stefano Veneziano
Madonna and Child Enthroned
Venice, 1369
Museo Civico Correr, Venice

Following page:
cat. 66. Francesco Basilicata (attr.)
Turk on a Horse
Venice, 1618
Museo Civico Correr, Venice

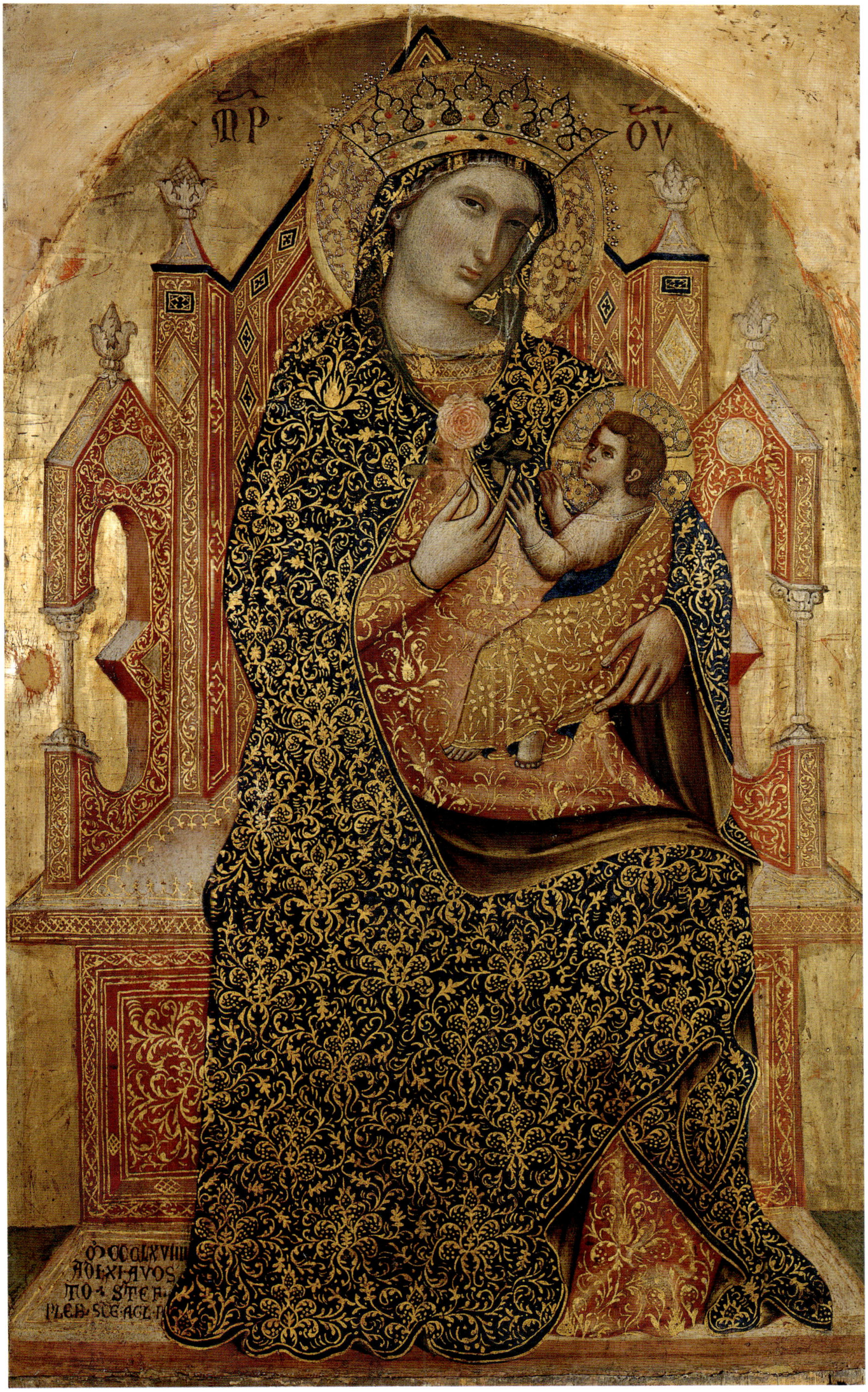
MP ΘV
M CCCLXVIIII
ADI XI AVOS
TO · STEF
PLEB SCE AGL

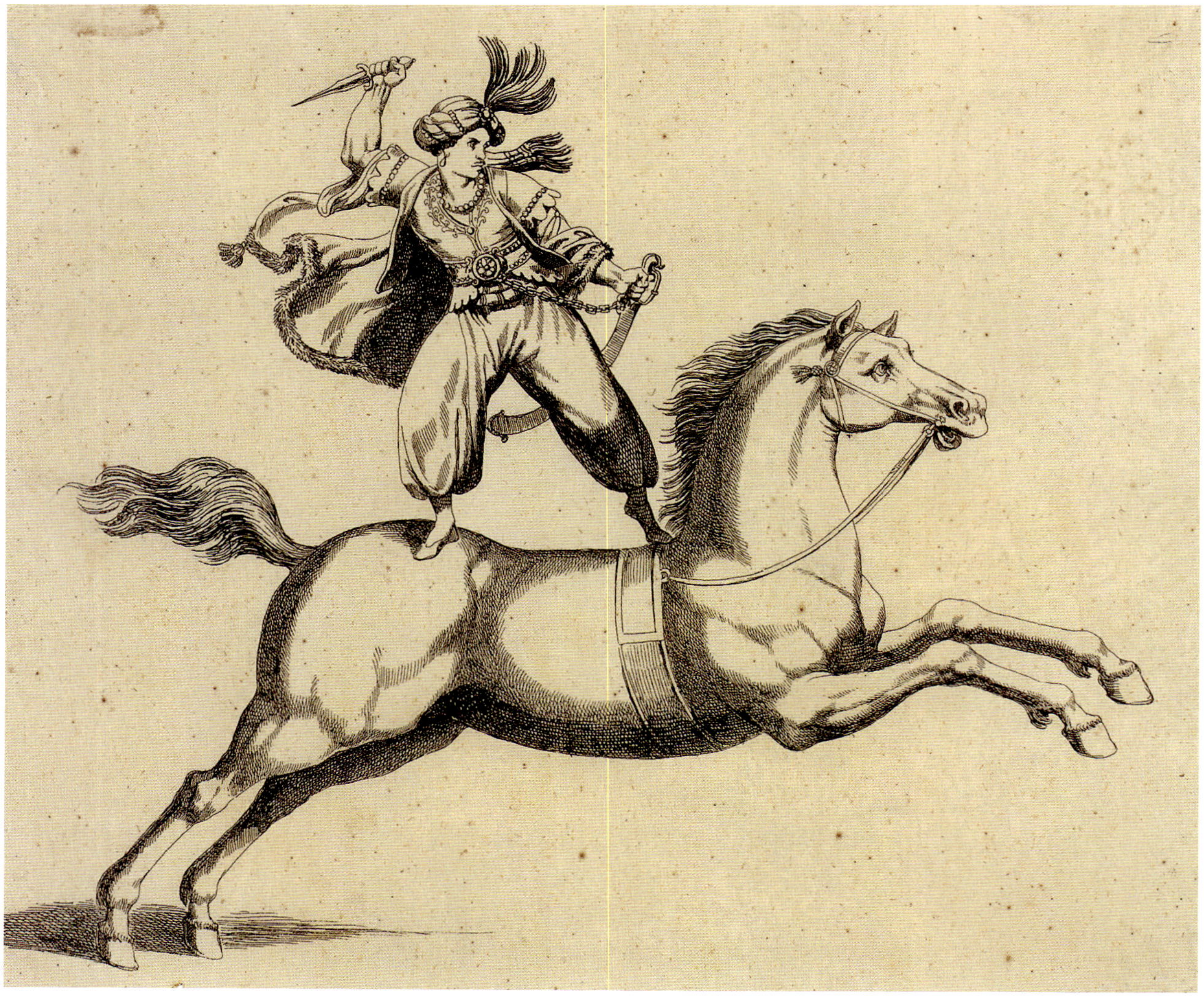

Notes

1 Their names have been recorded as Bono da Malamocco and Rustico da Torcello. The village of Malamocco (Metamauco) lies on the Lido and the island of Torcello was one of the very first settlements on the lagoon where the Church of Santa Maria Assunta was also built. The construction of the Doge's Palace began in 811.

2 The earliest brief mention of the translation of the body from Alexandria to Venice is in Giovanni Diacono's *Cronaca veneziana* from the beginning of the 10th century (Diacono 1890). The legend about the shrewd purloining of the relics (see the citation below and note 8) probably developed in the mid-11th century and was codified in the mid-14th century by the doge/historian Andrea Dandolo in his *Chronica* (Dandolo 1937). For a brief critical survey of the legend, see Lebe 1981, pp. 39–52.

3 For this historical period, see Kennedy 1981; Saliba 1985.

4 Today known as San Pietro di Castello after the name of one of the six Venetian quarters into which the city was later subdivided, in 1171.

5 Strika 1978; see a survey of the purported history of the chair under cat. 87.

6 The Arabic word simply means "pig."

7 Translated from the Latin from Dandolo 1937, pp. 146-47. *"Secundo ducis anno, corpus sanctissimi Marci evangeliste de Alexandria, translactum est Veneciam. . . .*

. . .que quidem translactio taliter facta est. Rex Saracenorum, apud Babilonem palacium sibi construere volens, mandavit ab ecclesis christianorum et aliis vulgaribus locis accipi lapides, ut splendidam sibi faceret domum. Accedentes autem ad ecclesiam beati Marci, more solito, Bonus tribunus methamaucensis et Rusticus torcelensis, qui contra Venetorum eddicta, cum X navibus mercibus honeratis, impelente vento, Alexandriam iverant, videntque Stauracium monachum et Theodorum sacerdotem, ecclesie custodes, admodum tristes; erant autem Greci. Querunt igitur causam tristicie, et audiunt quia impio regis eddicto devastacionem ecclesie metuunt. Rogant illi corpus sanctum sibi dari, ut Veneciam deferrant, promitentes eos apud ducem Venecie magnis extolli honoribus. . . .

Videntes autem custodes ecclesie devastacionem et personis iminere periculum, votis petencium condescendunt, et diem statuunt, quo corpus sanctum accipiant. Iacebat autem in clamide de serico involutum, et clausum in eodem a capite usque ad pedes, multis sigilis. Portant itaque beate Claudie corpus . . . indeque corpore beati Marci extracto, beate Claudie corpus imponunt, sigilis intactis manentibus. Tanta autem civitatem replevit odoris flagrancia subito, ut cuncti stuperent miraculum; nonnulli quoque dubitarent corpus evangeliste fore submotum. Curunt proinde ad ecclesiam, capsam aperiunt, clamidem sigilatam inveniunt; sic, delusi, ad propria redierunt. Ad navem autem portantes, superpositis herbis et carnibus porcinis, querentibus quid portarent ostendunt; at Saraceni horrentes; Ganzir, Ganzir, clamaverunt. . . .

Cum vero Venecia portaretur . . . Dux, clerus et populus occurrunt, et cum laudibus in capela ducis corpus deponent."

8 The stories are found in the texts of the friar Giovanni Fiore da Cropani (1622–83), recently reprinted in Fiore 1999–2001.

9 See in particular Botti 1992 on the identification between Venice and Alexandria in the paintings of the Scuola Grande di San Marco executed by the Bellinis and their followers in the late 15th and early 16th centuries.

10 Respectively, McNeill 1974 and Braudel 1973.

11 Obviously, the goods on which Venice strove to obtain a virtual monopoly in her dealings with the Near East—mostly spices—needed to be redistributed to the various European cities in order to earn profits, especially those of the

Hanseatic League of which Venice was a powerful member.

12 The term "Grand Turk," a common pejorative for the Ottoman sultan, was forbidden in Venice's official speeches and documents as of 1479 in favor of "il Gran Signore." See Pedani 1994, p. 106.

13 Capitulations were agreements extending trading and other economic and diplomatic privileges to Venetian individuals residing in the Near East, especially in Ottoman times.

14 See, for example, Howard 2003. Fig. 5 shows the relief of a man pulling a camel by its harness, set on the façade of Palazzo Mastelli along the Fondamenta Gaspare Contarini in the quarter of Cannaregio, which is said to have belonged to the three merchants whose statues are found in the nearby Campo dei Mori (see fig. 4 and note 20 below).

15 This point of view was offered most recently, for example, by Souren Melikian in his review of the exhibition "Bellini and the East" in the *International Herald Tribune*, June 10–11, 2006, p. 9.

16 Several historians of Venetian painting have offered this interpretation in the past. In the present catalogue, Barry leans toward a similar view through a meticulous line of reasoning.

17 On the Arab conquest of Sicily, see Michele Amari's translation from the 12th-century Arabic historian Ibn al-Athir's *Al-Kamil fi al-tarikh* in Gabrieli and Scerrato 1979, pp. 697-705; see also the brief historical survey by Gabrieli in the same volume, pp. 36-53.

18 Southern 1962.

19 Fig. 7 illustrates one of the marble statues set on one side of Campo dei Mori ("of the Moors"), which Venetian legend says are the effigies of three 12th-century merchants from the region of Morea whose names have been recorded as the brothers Rioba, Sandi, and Alfani and who took the family name of Mastelli (see above, note 14). Although most likely just a story—like the one claiming that Campo dei Mori takes its name from a Fondaco degli Arabi nearby, which never existed—the presence of the three statues and the camel relief are symbolic of the established commercial links between Venetian merchants and the Near Eastern market.

20 Southern 1962, p. 93, citing the *Epistula ad Joannem de Segovia* in R. Klibansky and H. Bascour, *Nicolai de Cusa De Pace Fidei* (*Medieval and Renaissance Studies*, III, suppl.), 1956, p. 97.

21 See fig. 5 in Barry's essay in this volume.

22 Southern 1962, p. 83, citing Gascoigne's *Loci e libro veritatum*, ed. by J. E. Thorold Rogers (Oxford, 1881), pp. 102–3.

23 On papal bans against Venice in her trading with the Levant, see Ortalli 1996.

24 The literature on the history and consequences of the Fourth Crusade is enormous. Among the most recent studies, see Phillips 2004 and Lace 2006.

25 On Pope Innocent III, see recently Moore 1999 and 2003.

26 Gallo 1967; Hahnloser 1971; *Treasury* 1984.

27 On the Fatimid treasury and its dispersal see Shalem 1996 and the text and notes under cat. 88 in this volume.

28 A complete history of the Marciana Library is in Zorzi 1987, esp. chapters 2–6.

29 The number of Arabic and Persian manuscripts available in Venice must have been extremely large. In the 16th century, Hobson (1989, p. 148) reports, Diego Hurtado de Mendoza, Charles V's ambassador to the Serenissima, acquired 268 Arabic manuscripts while residing in Venice.

30 The best source of information for Teodoro Correr and the Museo Correr is Musei Civici 1988, in particular Giandomenico Romanelli's essay on pp. 13–25.

31 On Mariano Fortuny and his life and work in the Palazzo Fortuny in Campo San Beneto, see in particular Osma 1980; Davanzo Poli 1997; Venice 1999; Deschodt and Davanzo Poli 2001.

32 For general surveys on Franchetti and his collection in the Ca' D'Oro Palace on the Grand Canal, see Barilli *et al.* 1999; Augusti and Saccardo 2002.

33 On the figure of Vittorio Cini see Siciliano 1978; Benvenuti and Romano 1998.

34 See Barovier's and Carboni's essay in this volume.

35 Lamm 1929–30, pp. 243–64; Ward 1998; Carboni and Whitehouse 2001, pp. 203–7, cat. 113–35

36 See Carboni 1998; Krueger 1998; Barovier's and Carboni's essay in this volume.

37 Pedani 1994, p. 109.

38 Campbell and Chong 2005.

39 Sanudo 1879–1902.

40 In the Appendix edited by Giovanni Curatola the reader can have a glimpse of Sanudo's style (as well as of the unfeasibility of a proper translation), in a selection from his *Diarii* that is relevant to the subject of this study.

41 Kurz 1969, p. 250, citing Sanudo 1879–1902, vol. 56, col. 7.

42 Pedani pp. 82–83, note 83.

43 "*Se intende per molte vie el Signor Turco haver auto la pezor*" in Sanudo 1879–1902, vol. 19, col. 302.

44 After the peace, Venice lost, among others, Nauplia in the Peloponnesus (the painter Gregorio was from Nauplia; see above, note 37). This is the time, for example, of the dandified figure of Alvise, the out-of-wedlock son of Doge Andrea Gritti, who lived a high-society life in a mansion in the Pera section of Istanbul and was known as the *beyoğlu*, or "son of the Signore," a name that still survives in the homonymous quarter of the modern city.

45 This is the overall intent of the section of essays devoted to the different mediums in Part II of the present volume.

46 For Venice's celebrations after the Battle of Lepanto, see Gombrich 1967 and Fenlon 1988.

47 Alvise Ca' Da Mosto (1432–1488), ironically a Venetian captain hired by the Portuguese prince Henrique "The Seafarer" (1394–1460), spearheaded the discovery of the African route reaching the Cape Verde Islands in 1456. Vasco da Gama (1469–1524) completed Africa's circumnavigation reaching Calicut in India in 1488.

48 In the 17th century Ottoman embassies became rare events and the last recorded mission happened under Ahmet III at the beginning of his reign in 1703. The Ottomans always sent special envoys to foreign countries and never created permanent embassies in Europe until the reign of Selim III (1789–1807), when Venice was also considered as a potential seat in 1795, just two years before the end of the Republic.

49 Berchet 1865; Pedani 1994, p. 69, note 48; Rocca 2002.

50 On Venetian civic and religious festivities, see Michiel 1829; Mazzarotto 1961; Muir 1981.

51 The practice is still in effect in the Vatican, for everyone to see during the televised broadcast of the exposition of John Paul II's bier in 2005.

52 Pedani 1994, p. 77, note 71.

53 The painting illustrates a legend that emphasizes St. Mark's legitimate final resting place in Venice. A fisherman gives the doge the ring that St. Mark had handed him as a proof of the old man's help in sinking a boat full of demons who were getting ready to cause a terrible storm over the lagoon. The fisherman had rowed the saints Mark, George, and Nicholas to the mouth of the port at the Lido, where they were able to sink the demons' boat. Incidentally, inside St. Nicholas's tomb in the homonymous church at the Lido, which was recently exhumed, there is a 15th-century Mamluk albarello containing relics (fig. 9).

54 For the history of the *scuola*, see, among others, Sohm 1982.

55 See in particular Molà 2000.

56 Pedani 1994, p. 172.

Venice and the Turks

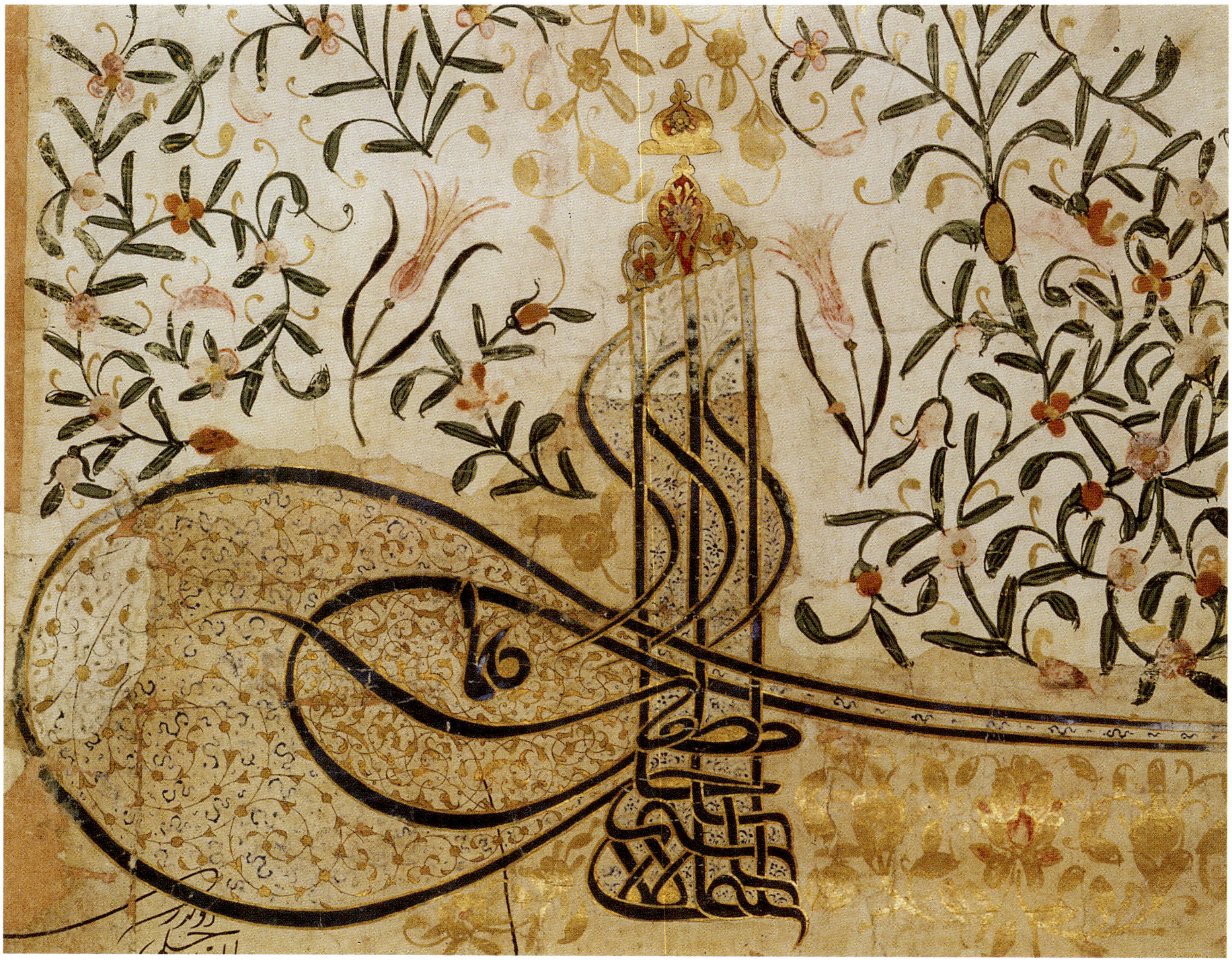

Jean-Claude Hocquet

In 1300 the Islamic world was still multifarious yet was on the verge of handing over its political leadership—and its military and naval fate—to newcomers, the Turks. After having served as a rampart for the Christian West against recent invaders—the Mongols, who also came from east-central Asia but headed back eastward—the Turks inspired dread as soon as they completed their conquest of the last shreds of the Byzantine Empire. By the 15th century the frontier of the continental Turkish Empire reached the Danube to the northwest, while to the west it bordered the Republic of Venice's *stato da mar,* a long ribbon of ports, headlands, and islands dotting the maritime routes stretching between Venice and the ports of the Levant.[1] The Venetians feared a direct confrontation with the Turks. Indeed, the Republic's pantheon-church of SS. John and Paul (Santi Giovanni e Paolo, known in Venetian dialect as San Zanipolo), a vast Gothic temple built for the Dominicans on land given to them in the 13th century by Doge Giacomo Tiepolo, the conqueror of Crete, served as a tomb and monument to fallen heroes. An urn there contained the skin of Marcantonio Bragadin, the noble who commanded the defense of Famagusta on Cyprus when besieged by the Turkish army in 1571. After surrendering, the Venetian military leaders were mutilated and killed—Bragadin was flayed alive—while the Albanian and Greek soldiers taken prisoner were transported on Turkish ships to Candia and freed. Yet this cruel incident, of great political significance (not only the torture of the noble commander but also the liberation of captives from populations subject to the Venetian Empire) was just one part of the long history of relations between Venice and Constantinople (thenceforth called Istanbul). The Venetians had extended their reach as far as Cyprus; and throughout the Levant, wherever they encountered the Turks, their relationship was not solely belligerent but also, and often, peaceful, to mutually beneficial commercial, cultural, and artistic ends. In Venice the Turks maintained a *fondaco* (inn) with *hammam* (Turkish bath) and a mosque while the Venetian Republic appointed a *bailo,* or permanent ambassador, to the sultan.[2]

cat. 49. *Firman including a treaty granted by Süleyman the Magnificent to the Republic of Venice* (detail)

Trade and Venetian Thalassocracy

Venice, a populous island city with little agricultural land, was obliged to import food from the outside and to live from maritime trade and from its role of intermediary between East and West: it systematically exploited the markets that opened onto the Mediterranean.[3] Venetian navigation eastward took place within a triangle bordered by Byzantium, by Levantine ports and calling places along the Syro-Palestinian coast, and by the great Egyptian port of Alexandria to the south. The island port of Candia played the role of pivot in this geography of trade. If the political and religious situation disturbed peaceful trade, notably in Byzantium where the *basileus* or emperor always had some score to settle with the Italians (judged too powerful and hegemonic in his own city and ports), then Venetian merchants could always call at Alexandria (the outlet for trade arriving from the Red Sea), or else could explore new routes in the west, towards the Muslim Maghreb (from Tripoli and Djerba to Tunis and as far as Ceuta at the gates of the Atlantic Ocean).[4] From the end of the 12th century, Venetian ships and merchants traveled along all Mediterranean routes and paths of navigation that shared a common passage, outward and inward, through the channels of the eastern Adriatic islands under Venetian control, from Modone (Modon) and Corfu in the south to Venice in the north. The Romania–Black Sea route sailed around Cape Maléa, called at Negroponte, and then at Constantinople before continuing on to Tana (on the north shore of the Sea of Azov) or Trebizond. An intermediate route called first at Candia then visited the ports of Cyprus and Syria, especially Beirut (the terminus of the silk route arriving from Samarkand and Tabriz).[5] At Candia the convoy for Alexandria took a southern route to reach the great Egyptian port where it loaded spices, foodstuffs from the crop economies, dye-plants, and ingredients for medieval pharmacopoeia that arrived by sea from the shores of the Pacific (Moluccas) and the Indian Ocean (Indonesia, Ceylon, India).[6] Merchant vessels also took on shipments of salt and voluminous products such as Syrian cotton.[7] Venice always had two alternate routes, in case upheavals in the vastness of Asia or its European fringes blocked one of them. In the second third of the 15th century it opened the Barbary route, which brought products from North Africa into the major trans-Mediterranean trade stream—hides, fleeces, grains, and cereals, plus articles, gold, and slaves from sub-Saharan Africa brought by caravan across the long trans-Saharan trails. The Barbary route called at Tunis, Annaba, Bejaia, Algiers, Oran, and Honein before sailing on to Cadiz, Valencia, and Barcelona, returning to Venice via the strait of Sicily, Djerba, and Tripoli. In 1492, by instituting the *trafego* route, Venice established direct relations, via its outpost in Modone, between Alexandria and Djerba, Tunis, and Barbary, in order to supply the Maghreb with Oriental products and to offer a passage to Muslim travelers on their way to Mecca.[8] Distant shorelines also fueled the grand trans-Mediterranean paths towards Venice, notably Ras al-Makhbaz on the Tripoli coast, Larnaca on Cyprus, the Crimean salt marshes to the north, and, to the south, the salt lagoons of Alexandria and Damietta (fig. 1).[9]

Despite trading privileges obtained from Byzantium, which Venice had helped to defend against Saracen and Norman assailants, relations between Venetians and the Greek population of the imperial capital were often tense and tinged with religious hostility. The Fourth Crusade,

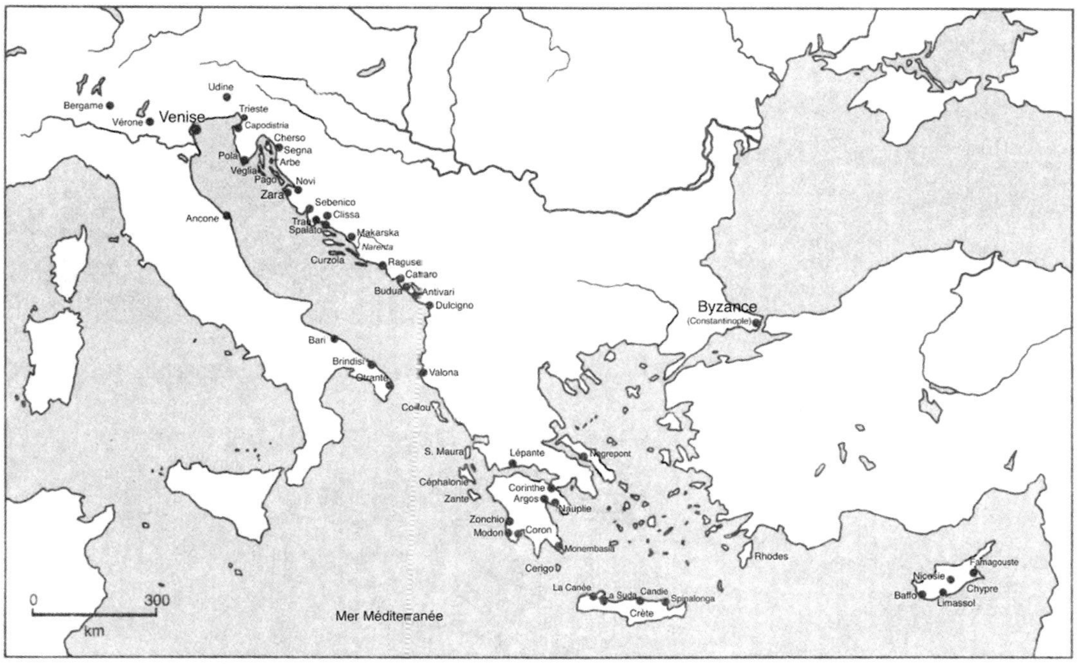

led by Doge Dandolo, had captured Constantinople in 1204. With this victory the Venetians recovered privileges enjoyed in the past, claiming hold to them throughout the empire: in the capital itself, in Thrace, in several ports from Albania to Morea, in the Ionian Islands, in Eubea (Negroponte), and even more so in Crete—in short, in all the coastal and island territories that dotted and controlled trade routes in and out of the Adriatic, and offered ports of call for provisions of water under the protection of garrisons that monitored and guarded these routes from pirates and competitors.[10] The Venetians also seized the archipelagos of the Aegean Sea, the Cyclades and Sporades. Venice successfully defended this maritime empire against competition from Genoa and from the Byzantine emperor once he was reinstalled in his capital (1261).

fig. 1. Venetian thalassocracy and the domination of Levant trade routes

The Eastern Mediterranean Becomes a Turkish Lake

The Diversity of the Turkish Peoples

The Turkic languages belong to the Altaic family,[11] the original cradle of Turkic-, Tungusic-, and Mongolian-speaking peoples. In the 10th to 12th centuries, literate Turks began using the Arabic alphabet to write the words of the Muslim religion. From the 13th century onwards, the Turkic language of Central Asia (common Turkish) evolved in its written form into three new groups, which became consolidated in the 16th century: western Turkic (Seljuq, then Oghuz), northern Turkic (Kipchak), and eastern Turkic (Uzbek-Uighur).[12] Turkophone peoples therefore constituted a veritable conglomeration that stretched between Turkey and what old geography textbooks pertinently labeled Russian and Chinese Turkestan, those vast lands that

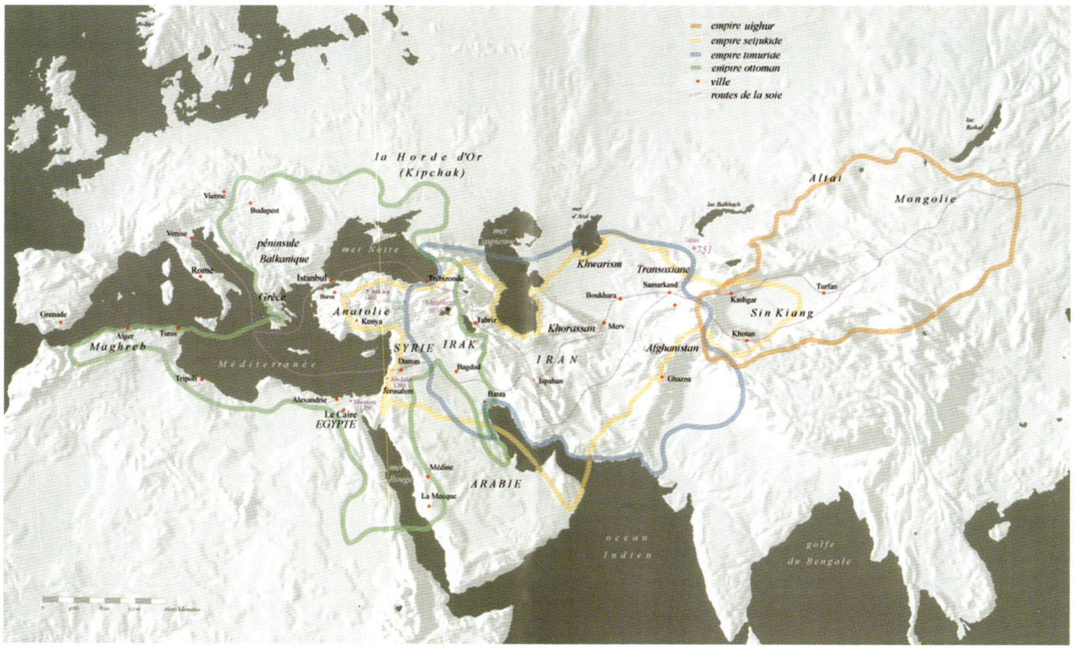

fig. 2. Extension of the Turkish world and the push westward

curve from Central Asia all the way to the Pacific, if we include the non-written Turkic languages of eastern Siberia (fig. 2).[13]

These peoples lived mostly on the steppes stretching across the semi-arid continental regions between the Russo-Siberian taiga to the north and huge mountain chains rising in the center of the Asian continent.[14] In 545, calling themselves "Turks" (*türük*), they came into contact with the two empires then sharing the Middle East, namely the Greek Byzantine Empire and the Iranian Sasanian Empire. As early as 568 they sent an embassy to Constantinople to form an alliance against the Sasanians. The allies defeated the Sasanians in 628, thus paving the way for an Arabo-Muslim victory over a weakened Iran in 651, until the Turks put a halt to Arabic conquests to the north in Transoxania (750); the Turks later allied themselves with the young 'Abbasid caliphate in Baghdad to repulse the Chinese army of the Tang Dynasty at the battle of Talas in 751. From that date onwards, the ancient caravan trail known as the Silk Route, which traversed the continent of Asia from oasis to oasis, was under control of Turkish peoples along almost its entire extent. These Oghuz Turks began to convert to Islam in the first quarter of the 8th century but, living on the Arab world's northern frontier, they remained victims of raids from the south. Turkish prisoners were incorporated in the guards of slaves that 'Abbasid caliphs started recruiting in the 820s. Arab sources referred to the converts as *turcomans* or Turkmen in order to distinguish them from the Oghuz, who were still infidels practicing the Nestorian Christianity, Buddhism, and Mazdaism that were all part of the East's religious syncretism. Among these infidels was an Oghuz warrior chief called Seljuq, who ultimately converted to Islam in the late 10th century.[15]

The Turkish Conquest

The Turkish tribes continued to be jostled by Eastern peoples squeezed by the Chinese Empire, so they in turn headed west and threatened their neighbors. In 1040 Seljuq's grandsons, Tughril Beg and his brother, defeated the army of the Ghaznavid monarch Mas'ud, who governed Afghanistan and northeastern India. This victory gave them control of Iran and Afghanistan. The 'Abbasid caliph considered using them to free himself of control by Iranian shi'ites. In 1055 Tughril Beg entered Baghdad, hailed as the sultan of the Sunnites. From Baghdad in the heart of the caliphate, the Seljuq sultan consolidated his power in Central Asia and extended control over the old Arabo-Muslim lands of Syria and the Mediterranean coast, thus coming into contact with two established states: the Christian empire of Byzantium to the north and the shi'ite Muslim empire of Fatimid Egypt to the south. Tughril's successor, his nephew Alp-Arslan, defeated the Byzantine army at Manzikert (1071), a victory that opened the way to Anatolia, where the Seljuq tribal chiefs formed principalities (*beyliks*) and the sultanate of Rum[16] (1081) with its capital at Konya. It was this Seljuq sultanate with whom the Christian Crusaders clashed in the 12th century. In the 13th century, the great Seljuq leader Malik-Shah, son of Alp-Arslan, who governed Iran, Iraq, Syria, and Turkestan along with western Afghanistan, gave way to a new threat—the Mongols. In 1141, a Seljuq defeat near Samarkand by the Karakhitai confederation provoked a resurgence of autonomous regions that facilitated the later invasion by Mongols supported by Turkish tribes who resented Seljuq hegemony. The sultan of Rum was defeated in turn at Sivas (Anatolia) in 1243. Hulegu, one of the sons of the conqueror Ghengis Khan, sacked Baghdad in 1258 and turned Iraq and Iran into a vassal kingdom of the Mongol Empire, run by the Il-khanids (*il-khan,* a subordinate *khan,* or king).[17]

Mamluk Egypt

The Mongol expansion was soon halted by a powerful group of military slaves (*mamluks*) originally recruited among the Turks of the Kipchak steppes by the Ayyubid sultans of Egypt. Slave dealers shipped the soldiers either via the maritime route from Byzantium and Cyprus westward, or by overland routes passing further east through Tabriz. The Mamluks were commanded by emirs who eliminated Turan Shah, the Ayyubid sultan in Cairo, and then placed the government in the hands of Aybak the Turkmen, who founded the Mamluk Dynasty, a military oligarchy that selected its sultan from among the emirs. These warrior slaves saved Islam from two threats: one was "the Franks" (the Crusaders, halted at the battle of al-Mansura in 1249), the other was the Mongols (repulsed at Ayn Jalut in 1260). "Turk" thus referred to Mamluks of all ethnic origins, the Mamluk sultanate being called *Mulk al-turk.* Profiting from his victory over the Mongols, a Mamluk officer called Baybars seized power; he was legitimized by the installation as caliph in Cairo of al-Mustansir, the 'Abbasid ruler who had fled from Baghdad and delegated all power to Baybars. The Mamluk state dominated Egypt, Syria, and Palestine until 1517; three naval campaigns against Cyprus had led to its conquest in 1426, reducing its Christian king to the status of vassal.[18] The Mamluks' elective system was often disrupted by coups that greatly weakened it, especially in the 15th century, but generally it encouraged the development of trade and the maintenance of friendly relations and commercial treaties with Venice, its best customer in the West.[19]

The Alexandria Cog

On June 22, 1391, the Venetian Senate launched a public call for bids by owners of cogs (square-rigged sailing vessels) of over 400 tons who wished to make the trip to Alexandria. According to the decree, a majority vote of senators would determine which ship would be commissioned to make the voyage. This ship had to be completely outfitted and armed, with a full crew plus six crossbowmen to defend it. In Venice it could take on cargo up to July 22, and had to weigh anchor on July 25. It could carry heavy merchandise—including copper, wrought copper, tin, and lead—as well as articles usually transported by unarmed ships, especially costly goods shipped in chests, but nothing that contravened Church prohibitions. In payment for transport, the owner of the ship would receive a charter fee of three ducats per thousand pounds of metal, plus the going cargo rates for the other goods. Two ducats of the charter fee would go to the ship, while the third was destined for the galleys on the trip—the owner would give this third ducat to the commander of the convoy at Alexandria. The ship was to sail directly to Modone and Corone [Coron], where it would remain two days, taking on merchandise for Alexandria, then at Candia where the ship would stay for four days. At ports of call it was prohibited from loading merchandise outlawed by the Church. To the benefit of this cog and these galleys, no other ship would be authorized to load cargo in Venice destined for Alexandria. On arrival in Alexandria, the ship would wait one week after the arrival of the galleys before leaving port. For its own subsidy, the cog was authorized to load cargoes of cotton and all other goods authorized for import by ship, keeping the charter fees, and to take on Alexandrian salt up to one-half foot from the water line if it were a two-decked vessel, for which it would receive the agreed price. If it took on light goods (spices), the charter fee would be divided in two halves, one for the cog, the other for the *Comune* (municipality). On his return the commander of the galleys would report on whether space remained on board, in which case he would be compensated for his loss by one half of the charter fee received by the municipality. The owner of the cog also had to carry, for free, the Senate's ambassador to the sultan, along with his baggage and retinue.

Hence the real purpose of this voyage was explained only at the end of the document: namely to convey an ambassador to the Mamluk sultan in good, safe, and comfortable conditions not found on galleys. To finance the trip, the cog was allowed to carry cargo that would not compete with the galleys, to whom it would pay one-third of the charter fee. It could not contravene papal decrees by delivering weapons or strategic materials to the Muslims. Finally, the only merchandise that it could freely bring back from Alexandria was Egyptian cotton and salt, on condition that the ship was not overloaded. Given the tricky situation of managing several monopolies at the same time, coordinating the navigation of galleys and the profitability of a vessel mobilized for an official mission, Venice prohibited all other ships from sailing this route to Alexandria, and it meticulously stipulated the merchandise to be loaded, also taking into account the totality of the charter fees to be divided, as fairly as possible, among all the participants on the voyage.[20]

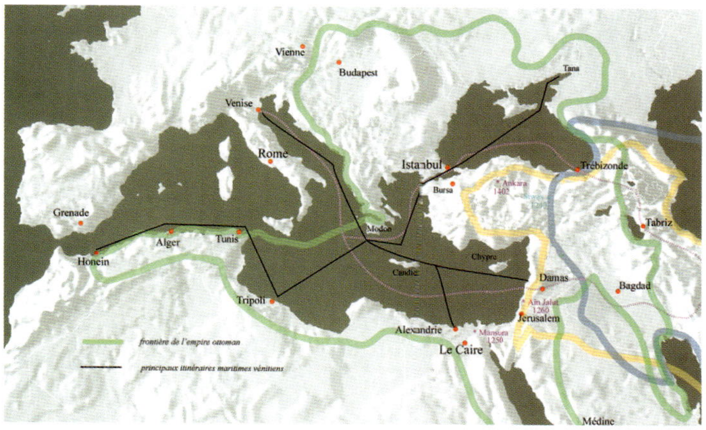

fig. 3 Venetian control of the Mediterranean in the 16th century

The Founding of the Ottoman Empire

Halted in the south, the Mongols pushed northward and in 1322 the Il-khanids from Iran annexed the Seljuq sultanate of Rum, allowing some Seljuq *beyliks* to remain. One of these *beylik* rulers would play a crucial role—Osman (an Oghuz form of the Arab 'Uthman), established in Bithynia in northwestern Anatolia. His successors were called Osmanli (or "men of Osman"), which became Ottomans. After three centuries of Turkish occupation, the primarily Greek Christian population of Anatolia had undergone a slow process of religious and linguistic acculturation and it thenceforth supplied the Ottoman army with ample military personnel. One of Osman's descendants, Bayezid I, ran up against the final incarnation of the Mongol invasion—in the West, at least—in the person of Timur (also known as Tamerlane), who took him prisoner at the battle of Ankara in 1402. The Turks' defeat afforded the Byzantines in Constantinople a certain respite, but in 1453 the young sultan Mehmet II—who became known as Mehmet Fatih, or Mehmet the Conqueror—finally captured the city and destroyed what remained of the Byzantine Empire. He then went on to conquer the last Greek principalities of Trebizond and Morea,[21] whereas his successors conducted a vast war against the Mamluk sultanate (1485–91), and a quarter of a century later annexed Egypt (1517), which became a province of the Ottoman Empire, governed from Syria. The caravan termini and all the main Levantine ports of Venetian maritime routes thus fell under the control of a single master, the Ottoman sultan. It was thenceforth impossible for Venice to exploit local rivalries between hostile states. The Ottoman Turks had created a monopoly situation for themselves (fig. 3).

Venice's Relationship with the Ottomans

Venice did not carry out an aggressive policy against Islamic sovereigns, and had only taken part in the Crusades in order to prevent all the spoils going to its Genoese, Pisan, and Norman rivals; at Acre and Tyre it obtained its share of commercial advantages conceded upon the Latin conquest of the Levant. Venice maintained trading relations with the Nasrid kingdom of Granada, Morocco, Hafsid Egypt, Fatimid (and, later, Ayyubid and Mamluk) Egypt, and even with the Seljuq Dynasty in southeastern Anatolia.[22] She found it hard in the 14th century not to violate the pontifical embargo against Alexandria and Egypt, and in 1415 signed a commercial treaty with the Mamluk sultan. Yet Venice lived in fear of the Ottoman peril. In the 15th century, "the Turk" required the Venetians to be constantly vigilant. The two empires shared a long frontier because the Republic of Venice had built its maritime state (*stato da mar*) upon all its Mediterranean

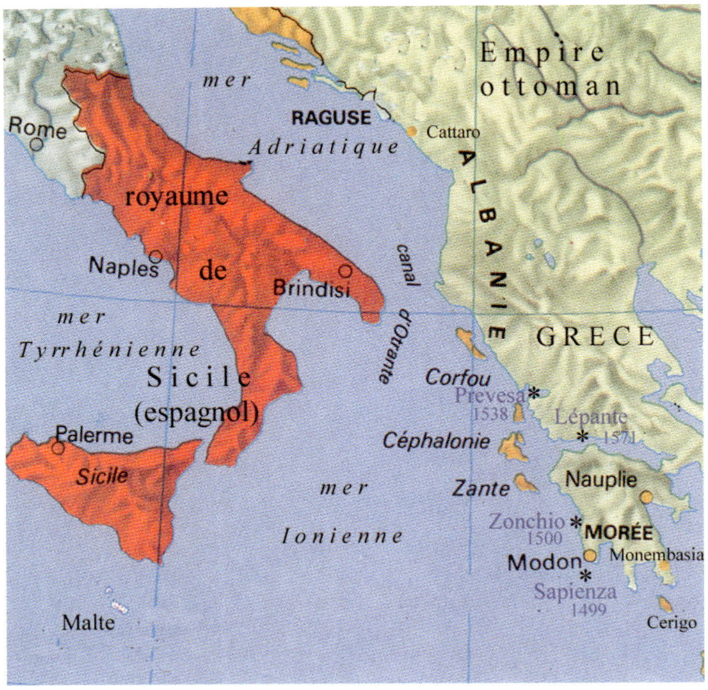

fig. 4. Main naval battles during Venetian-Turkish wars of the 16th century

possessions conquered from the Byzantines—which thenceforth bordered, given Ottoman expansion, Turkish lands subject to the sultan. All the naval resources of Venice went on the alert whenever the Turks put to sea, even with a limited squadron, for the Republic trembled at the thought that its powerful, inconvenient neighbor might cut its extensive navigation routes throughout the Levant. Seeking some breathing room, the Turks obstinately nibbled away at Venetian islands and shores; Venice was ultimately embroiled in six naval and land wars, with varying outcomes that usually resulted in further losses of Venetian territory, despite a favorable balance of forces at sea (fig. 4).

The first clash was deceptive. In 1415 Turkish vessels incautiously molested Venetian galleys returning from the Black Sea ports of Tana and Trebizond, and then threatened to attack Negroponte; hence in May 1416 a small squadron led by Pietro Loredan crushed the Ottoman fleet commanded by officers unfamiliar with naval tactics. The first truly serious war, however, broke out in 1463 when Venice sought to liberate Morea, which the Turks had invaded; it lost Negroponte in 1470, and a treaty signed in Istanbul on January 25, 1479, confirmed the loss of Albanian strongholds (which had nevertheless held out against a long siege) and Morea. Furthermore, Venice agreed to pay damages of 100,000 ducats and an annual tribute of 10,000 ducats for the privilege of continuing to trade in the Levant and maintaining an ambassador (*bailo*) in Istanbul.[23] The Republic thus abandoned the entire Aegean, and crescent-bearing banners even flew over Valona, at the mouth of the Adriatic. Venice filled this gap with compensatory maritime routes: in 1489 it convinced the queen of Cyprus, Caterina Cornaro, originally from Venice, to hand over the island to the Republic; it also occupied ports in Puglia (Otranto, Brindisi, Bari) on the western shore of the Strait of Otranto, opposite Valona.

The second war, despite Venice's total mobilization of its naval resources—placed, alas, under the command of a timorous officer—was characterized by indecisive battles in the Ionian Sea off the coast of Morea (summers of 1499 and 1500). The treaty signed on May 20, 1503, confirmed the Republic's right of free trade, but Venice lost Modone and Corone and only kept the Ionian islands in return for a tribute of 500 ducats—the news met with no signs of joy, no festivities, no ringing of bells in the lagoon. The Venetians, who expected no help from Christian powers, feared they would soon find themselves under the Turkish yoke.[24] They were also aware of the considerable significance of recent Portuguese and Spanish explorations of the Atlantic and Indian Oceans.

Venice's Isolation within the New World Order

The world underwent considerable expansion at the end of the 15th century thanks to two discoveries: a maritime route around the Cape of Good Hope that re-directed the spice trade towards Portugal's Atlantic coast; and a new continent—America—that made the Habsburg monarch of a recently unified Spain a truly powerful sovereign as well as head of the Holy Roman Empire. The Mediterranean began to lose its central role as the crossroads of the three continents of the ancient world. The conflict between the Turks and their neighbors took on new scope: the ongoing expansion of the Ottoman Empire henceforth threatened Austria,[25] ruled by the brother of Holy Roman Emperor Charles V. However, Sultan Selim I (1512–20) also had to keep his eye on Iran, where the new Safavid Dynasty (1501–1722) established shi'ism as the state religion and forged an alliance with the Portuguese in the Indian Ocean.[26] The Ottoman sultan, who united all the Arabic-speaking Islamic nations, also established his domination along the northern coasts of Africa, which enabled him to monitor Spain and maritime traffic in the Western Mediterranean. From the moment of his accession in 1520, Selim's son, Süleyman (whose victories would earn him the title of Süleyman the Magnificent), waged war against the Safavids to the east and captured Belgrade to the west (1521), thereby reaching the doorstep of Hungary and acquiring a good staging post for an assault against Vienna and the Habsburg Empire. He annexed Algiers, which he entrusted to the pirate Khayr al-Din Barbarossa, who also took Tunis in 1535.[27] All the ports on the eastern and southern shores of the Mediterranean (except for Morocco) were now under Ottoman control. Venice felt truly isolated in a world turned upside down.

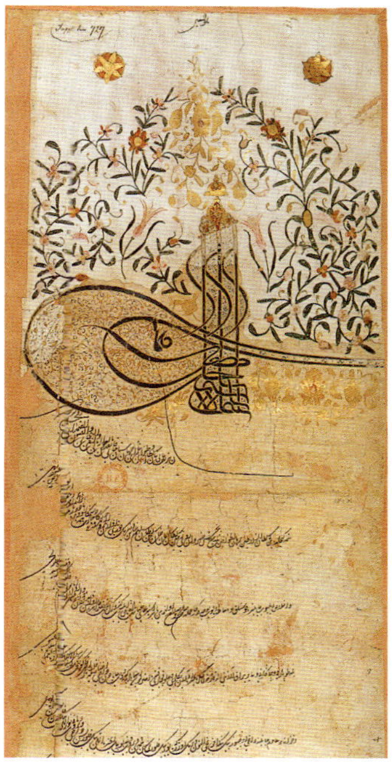

cat. 43. *Firman including a treaty granted by Süleyman the Magnificent to the Republic of Venice*
Istanbul, October 2, 1540
Bibliothèque Nationale de France, Paris

The naval respite had lasted for some 30 years, but in 1537 Süleyman laid siege to the Venetian island of Corfu, which guarded entry to the Adriatic. Pope Paul III managed to createe an anti-Turkish alliance in February 1538, uniting the papacy, the Holy Roman Emperor, the duke of Austria, and the Republic of Venice. Andrea Doria, from Genoa, was named commander of the allied fleet.[28] At the battle of Prevesa (September 1538) the Venetians realized that, reduced to their own forces, they could never overcome the Turks, who benefited from a vast empire and immense human resources. Venice therefore had to find allies with naval forces, but its allies could never manage to overcome their mutual mistrust and fear of fighting the Turks at sea—hence the weight of naval warfare would be borne above all by Venice. The battle of Preveza therefore conferred supremacy of the Mediterranean on the Turks. A treaty signed on October 2, 1540, cost Venice its last bastions in Morea (cat. 49) (Monemvasia, Napoli di Romania). Four European capitals were nevertheless actively concerned with halting Ottoman expansion: Venice, Madrid, Vienna, and Rome. Venice pursued its usual policy of simultaneously seeking diplomatic support from afar, namely the czar of Moscow and the shah of Iran,[29] thereby attempting a backdoor operation on the Ottoman Empire's northern and eastern flanks because it realized that Christian monarchs were too divided and too busy elsewhere: France was occupied with wars of religion and anyway remained loyal to its friendship with the Turks, useful allies against Spain; Spain, meanwhile, was dealing with rebellion in the Low Countries and limited its Mediterranean horizons to a defense of the western basin; the pope was trying to marshal his forces against the Protestants.

Peace held once again for 30 years, but in February 1570 a Turkish envoy demanded that Venice yield Cyprus. The Turks landed on the island during the summer, occupying Nicosia. Plague had greatly weakened the Venetian fleet stationed in Cyprus, and thus from the start

Venice was at a distinct disadvantage in the fourth of its wars with the Ottomans. On May 25, 1571, a Holy League was formed by Pope Pius V, Phillip II of Spain, and Venice. On October 7, the allied fleets carried the battle of Lepanto but were unable to exploit this brilliant success by concluding a decisive victory. After long negotiations, on March 7, 1573, Venice signed a secret treaty in Constantinople: it relinquished Cyprus, paid war damages of 300,000 ducats, and agreed to increase the annual tribute for the island of Zacinto to 1,500 ducats, but won confirmation of the validity of existing commercial treaties—which was the most important issue—and recovered possession of its captured merchant vessels. Making this separate peace, however, was hardly conducive to reinforcing trust among the former allies.

Venetians began to think that maybe the most treacherous enemy was the king of Spain, allied to the pope, both of whom wanted to become masters of the whole of Italy. In addition, the Spanish king's relative—the Habsburg duke in Vienna—had designs on the Adriatic and secretly supported marauding Christian pirates who, operating out of the Gulf of Quarnero, attacked not only Turkish but Venetian vessels (accusing them of being lukewarm in the struggle against the infidels).[30] In the 1590s, Venice's response to the pope's constant desire to form a league of Christian powers, ran as follows: Venice lived constantly under the Turkish threat but did not want to see her trade comprised by a new war; leagues were "were fine and grand in appearance but of little substance."[31] It was absurd to ask Venice to contribute money and soldiers at the very moment it was facing threats on its borders from the king of Spain, with whom it was supposed to ally itself, and from Emperor Rudolf II, who protected the piratical bandits.

Venice: an Armed Pacifism

An English observer staying in Venice, during this contentious time, noted that the Venetians were solely occupied with retaining their lands and seemed to have renounced all desire of annexing the possessions of their neighbors—they hated any kind of war, especially against the Turks.[32]

A lack of resources and manpower imposed this pacifist behavior on Venetians. In his *Discorsi Politici* (Political Discourses, 1559), Paolo Paruta justified Venice's "neutrality" as an active force in diplomatic negotiations, thanks to which the Republic oversaw the maintenance of peace in Italy and, through its ambassadors and diplomatic networks, disposed of unrivaled information in Europe that taught it just how wars drained state treasuries and alienated public opinion in order to produce, at best, fleeting territorial gains.[33] In 1593, the Most Serene Republic built a fortress at Palmanova, expressing its conviction that money was better invested in a fortress, than spent on helping the Habsburg emperor in Vienna, which would have merely triggered Turkish reprisals. Venice clearly displayed its propensity to come to terms with, rather than fight, the Turks. And the emperor rightly realized that Palmanova was directed more against his own ambitions than those of the Turks, his diehard enemies.[34]

Venice nevertheless fought two more trying wars against the Turks in the 17th century. The fifth war lasted 25 years (1645–1669) and, despite a few fine naval victories, Venice was

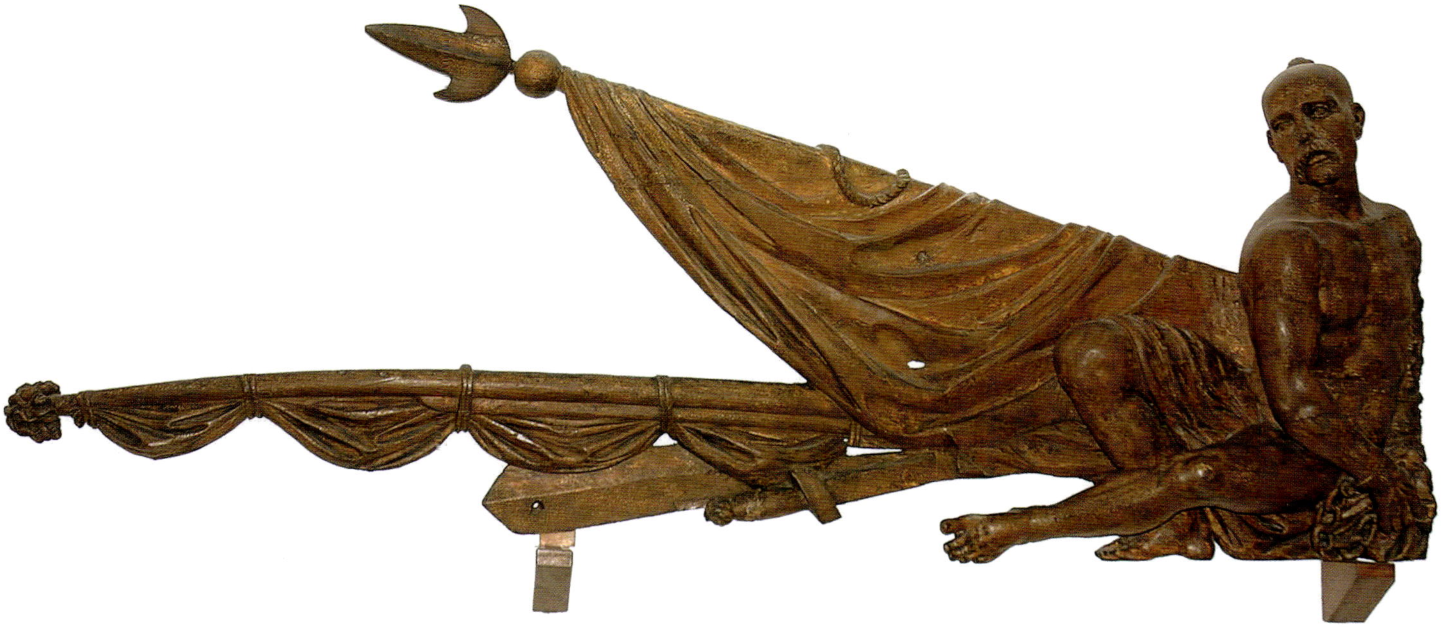

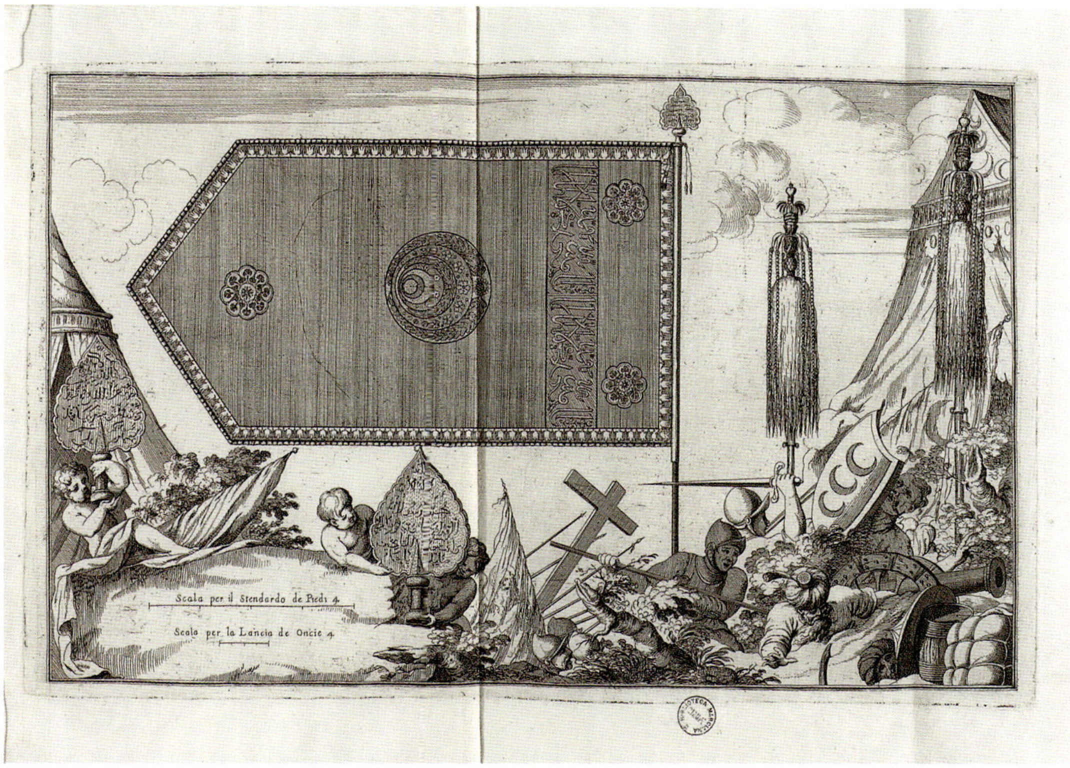

cat. 149. *Stern decoration from the* bastarda *of Commander in Chief Francesco Morosini*
Venice, mid-17th century
Museo Storico Navale, Venice

cat. 67. *Turkish banner*
Venice, 1650–1718
Biblioteca Nazionale Marciana, Venice

obliged to surrender Candia even though it retained the right to keep garrisons in two strongholds on the island in order to keep a port of call and a supply depot on its trade routes in the Levant. The Turks successfully continued their obstinate policy of steadily dismantling the *stato da mar,* begun four centuries earlier. But they were unable to gain a decisive victory over the Habsburgs and they suffered a serious defeat near Graz in 1664. Venice took advantage of the situation to reinforce its presence in Dalmatia and Albania, easing the Turks' grip. Twenty years later, in the summer of 1683, the Turks got as far as the walls of Vienna, which was saved by the king of Poland, Jan Sobieski. Venice thereupon agreed to join an anti-Ottoman coalition (May 1684). As the imperial army took the offensive on the Danube and captured first Buda and then Belgrade,

Francesco Morosini conquered Morea (cat. 149). In 1699, the treaty of Carlowitz awarded Venice its conquests of Morea, Dalmatia, and the island of Santa Maura, and finally Tinos (cat. 67).[35] It was the first Venetian victory in a long time—but a fragile one. In 1716 the Turks went to war again and reconquered Morea. In the treaty of Passarowitz (1718), the Venetians, ever faithful to their policy, managed to retain four strongholds on the Ionian coast in Albania (Butrinto) and Greece (Parga, Preveza, and Vonitsa). Ever since Lepanto—hence throughout the 17th century—the Turks appeared weaker on the sea, while the powerful Venetian fleet remained strong, On land, however, the Ottoman armies regained their offensive superiority, thanks to recruitment across a vast empire. Venice was fully aware of this situation and so its major concern was to maintain its control of the sea, especially the important bases along the coastline.

Venetian Perception of the Turks

Venetians were soon forced to face the facts, even though at the beginning they had displayed a certain contemptuous condescension towards the Turks, those skillful horsemen from the steppes who were versed in equestrian arts but ignorant in naval arts, to the point where Pietro Loredan, victor of the battle of Gallipoli who massacred all the Christian officers and men serving in the Turkish fleet, could write to Venice: "Henceforth we can say that the power of the Turks in this sea [the strait and the Aegean] has been destroyed for a long time to come and that they will never be able to arm a squadron nor recruit crews."[36] But as the Turks steadily conquered Greek and Albanian lands, plus the islands of the Aegean archipelago, they recruited war-hardened sailors and skillful boat-builders, and thus made such progress on the seas that the attitude of the Venetians changed.

In the Senate, two parties sprang up in the debates over peace or the continuation of war following the battle of Preveza, which confirmed Turkish naval superiority in the Mediterranean. In 1551 Francesco Longo reported the arguments of the League's adversaries, who were favorable to peace and who felt that the pope and the Spanish were the Republic's worst enemies. "Our commonwealth has retained its state and wealth intact thanks to friendship with the Turks, who protected you from the damage that Christian princes wanted to inflict upon you. When the mainland state was occupied by the enemy, camped at Marghera and at Ca' Fusina,[37] you felt no fear because the maritime routes remained open, there were plenty of supplies, trade continued, galleys departed on voyages, and the Republic maintained its government—it did not waver. When the Turks headed towards Hungary and Friuli they were protecting you from the threats of Charles V and Ferdinand who, if they had not feared the Turks and your treaty with them . . . might have been tempted once again to plunder you."[38]

And yet Venice was wracked by a Turkish nightmare when it learned that Istanbul was assembling a squadron to continue its expansion westward in order to seize Levantine realms. Venice, wrote historian Paolo Preto, "trembled, armed itself, resisted, fought, lost, and resigned itself to withdrawal throughout a century-long history that ended only at the close of the

17th century. The fear of the Turks was the fear of a distant, powerful, invincible, *barbarian* enemy. The myth of Turkish power was also expressed in the fear of ubiquitous espionage, since the Turks had a good intelligence service in Venetian lands—Cyprus, Candia, Corfu, and even Venice itself. Naturally, people saw the work of Turks behind the fire in the Arsenale in 1569; accomplices were thought to come from the Jewish community, the perfidious Jew being the natural ally of infidels."[39] This opinion was not shared by all. One contemporary, Cardinal Agostino Valier, expressed his reaction to the separate peace concluded by Venice shortly after the Holy League's victory at Lepanto. "The Republic lives and even prospers in the face of most powerful princes, it enjoys its freedom and maintains its own laws. But it suffers from scandalmongering by those who want it to assume unbearable expenses, until its strength is spent. True, the Turk is an infidel; but he has not abandoned the law of peoples (*il jus delle genti*) which means that, unless we give him a good reason, he is not about to violate the peace treaty."[40]

The Venetian-Turkish relationship was not marked solely by bellicose antagonism, for the pair also enjoyed long periods of peace and friendly relations on the commercial and political levels. In fact, the two adversaries could accommodate one another, both being aware of the pressure of foreign competition. Indeed, they needed one another: Venice because it wanted to discourage English, Dutch, and French activities in the Orient,[41] Istanbul because Venice remained its best customer, even if the caravan trade across the Middle East had lost much of its luster. This is what a disillusioned Venetian merchant, who set up business in Aleppo in the mid-16 century, wrote:

> 1556, Jan. 22nd, to Mr. Jeronimo Soranzo, Venice
>
> We must abandon this country, where in truth we are mistreated. They take our goods and want to pay for them in their own way; worse still, they say they never received the money, which is what the pasha did even though he devoured over 500 sequins, but he said he gave them to the Jew who served as our interpreter and who is now dead. Of business very little is done, neither for cash nor barter, there is no silk, and even though spices here cost little there aren't any. You can find walnuts, cloves, mace, and ginger in good quantities and at decent prices, but the sellers stubbornly insist on 15%, may God be their guide! I must also tell you that the caravan from Mecca arrived at Damascus, very poor compared to previous years, when it brought few spices that we could buy; but this year is even worse because the camels died during the outward journey for lack of water and during their return due to cold; furthermore, many pilgrims on their way to Mecca died for the same reasons. Some Damascus merchants remained there, they say that Barbary and Provençal coral sold at very low prices, that raw amber didn't sell well and that they could do nothing with worked amber. [Woolen] cloth of all kinds fetched good prices. At Mecca, pepper, cloves, ginger, and mace were bought for cash, but there was neither cinnamon nor nutmeg. The caravan brought back 800 sommes of which 200 were pepper, 50 to 60 were cloves, 30 to 40 ginger, 10 to 12 mace, and the rest of indigo, lacquer, silk and cotton fabrics. We cannot hope to buy more than 100 *sommes,*

> because all these goods are for local consumption. But they say that in Alexandria this year, by the grace of God, business will be good because the merchants who stayed in Mecca regularly send spices to Cairo via the Tur route. Some of it may get this far, in small quantities, on day-to-day caravans.[42]

The important question still remains: "Who were these Turks?" The answer is not straightforward; in the West we do not draw sufficient distinctions concerning what, in the Orient, involves ethnicity (and language) when it comes to Turks, Arabs, and Iranians (all of whom then used the Arabic alphabet for their written language), or when it comes to the political and dynastic history of various states (Seljuq, Ottoman, Ilkhanid), or to religion (sunnite, shi'ite), to mention only the major differences. And these distinctions must be superimposed on prior ones, notably ethnic and religious (the least stable being dynastic, often overturned following a defeat or palace revolution). Venetians were familiar with the Turks and they used the term "Turkish subjects" for the old Christian populations that the Ottoman conquest had amalgamated in Anatolia, in Greece, along the coasts of the Black Sea, in Albania and Bosnia, in Armenia and, later, in Cyprus and Crete. The Venetians had established close relations with these peoples—some of whom were later Islamized—as a result of trade, cultural connections, and political or military domination. The Turks imposed their administration on these various populations, as well as their garrisons (often composed of Christian mercenaries), but let them practice their religion. The sultan's income consisted above all of *jizya* and *kharaj,* taxes on non-Muslim subjects that yielded ever-greater revenue as conquered lands grew. Turks and Venetians both shared a reputation for tolerance and a fairly liberal welcome for persecuted religious minorities, such as Protestants and Jews driven out of Spain, who brought their capital and their skills to the Ottoman Empire.[43] And both states were also shrewd enough to leave the door open when it came to maintaining, and even extending, trade relations, a role played by Spalato in Venetian Dalmatia and by Ragusa, a free republic on the Adriatic flank of the Ottoman Empire, two ports through which merchants and merchandise passed.[44] Venetian merchants were well received in Constantinople and Smyrna and the empire continued to supply the Republic, as it had in the past, with raw silk, cotton, coral, and especially grains.[45] Finally, as proof that the Mediterranean had not lost all importance, the English and Dutch signed commercial treaties ("capitulations") with Istanbul, and sent growing numbers of ships to Ottoman ports in order to sell the products of their industries. Turkey steadily integrated itself into Europe's trade networks, and a new attitude of Turkophilia began to emerge in the cultivated circles and salons of the Enlightenment era.[46]

Notes

1 Cozzi and Knapton 1986; Cozzi, Knapton, and Scarabello 1992; Hocquet 2006; Tenenti and Tucci 1991.
2 Sagredo and Berchet 1860.
3 Abulafia 2004; Hocquet 1999.
4 Hocquet 2002.
5 Gonzales Clavijo 1990.
6 Ashtor 1976.
7 Lane 1973.
8 Hocquet 2004.
9 Hocquet 1978–79.
10 Tenenti 1999.
11 The Altai Mountains now form the border between Russian Siberia and western Mongolia, source of Siberia's Ob and Yenisey Rivers.
12 Oghuz languages are still spoken today in Anatolia, Cyprus, the Balkans, Azerbaijan, Khorassan (northeastern Iran), and by the Turkmen of Iraq and Turkmenistan. It corresponds to the Turkish (or Turkish-influenced) peoples of the former Ottoman Empire in its European and Asian components, the remainder of the empire being populated above all by Arab speakers (Middle East and North Africa). The northern group (Kipchak) forms the Tatar language of the former Gold Horde centered on the Volga, the Crimea, and the Caucasus, as well as Kyrgyz and Kazakh. The eastern group corresponds to the Uighur of China's Xinjiang. See Roxburgh 2005 and Golden 2005.
13 Golden 2005.
14 The favored lifestyle of Turkish peoples was nomadic raising of livestock (horses and goats); their socio-political organization was based on the tribe. Tribes came together in confederations that obeyed the *khan,* and they contested lands for the passage and pasturage of herds. Starting in the second half of the 5th century they began a slow migration towards the west that carried the Oghuz to the steppes of the Volga and the Black Sea.
15 Golden 2005.
16 Rum designated the land of the Romans, or Romania. The Byzantine emperor, successor to Roman emperors, was officially "emperor of the Romans" even though most of the people in his empire spoke Greek.
17 *EF,* see "Iran."
18 *EF,* see "Mamluk"; Petry 1998; Ayalon 1979; Darrag 1961 Garcin 1995–2000.
19 Ashtor 1976; Ashtor 1978; Cahen 1977; Jacoby 1979; Labib 1965; Müller-Wiener 1992; Vallet 1999.
20 Senato, Misti, reg. 42, fol. 4, Archivio di Stato, Venice.
21 Babinger 1956; Inalcik 1978; Mantran 1989; Hitzel 2001; Karpov 1986.
22 Zachariadou 1983.
23 Valensi 1987.
24 Gullino 1996; Mallett and Hale 1984; Pertusi 1973; Pryor 1988.
25 Braudel 1966.
26 Inalcik 1977, discussion of V. Magalhães Godinho, p. 91; Rota 2002.
27 Braudel 1966.
28 Cozzi 1994.
29 Ibid.
30 Benzoni 1974; Beck, Manoussacas and Pertusi 1977; Setton 1991.
31 Cozzi 1994, p. 66.
32 Fynes Moryson, *Shakespeare's Europe* (London: 1903), pp. 138–39, quoted in Hale 1994, p. 239.
33 Candeloro Giorgio (ed.), *Paolo Paruta: Discorsi politici* (Bologna, 1963), p. 330, cited by Hale 1994, p. 241.
34 Eickhoff 1991.
35 Cozzi 1997.
36 Romanin 1973, vol. 4, pp. 54–56, published Loredan's entire letter to the Venetian doge and Signoria, based on the text of Sanudo's *Diarii;* Gullino 1996.
37 That is to say, in the days of the League of Cambrai, a vast anti-Venetian coalition formed by the pope and almost all European nations in 1509.
38 Cozzi 1994, p. 32.
39 Preto 1994, p. 221.
40 Cozzi 1994, p. 54. Agostino Valier, bishop of Verona in 1565, was made a cardinal in 1583 and was a member of the *Savi agli Ordini* (one of the committees of the *Collegio,* or "cabinet," the Republic's executive arm), then went on to teach philosophy to numerous young noblemen, including Alvise Contarini, who became Venice's "official historian"(Cozzi 1963–64), authoring a history of Venice and a treatise on educating young patricians (Valier 1787, p. 485).
41 Eldem 1999.
42 Tucci 1957.
43 Arbel 1995; Ashtor 1983; Setton 1976–84; Levy 1994.
44 Krekić 1997; Paci 1971.
45 Inalcik 1978.
46 Grube 1989; Preto 1975; Schwoebel 1967.

Venice and the Islamic World in Light of Archival Documents

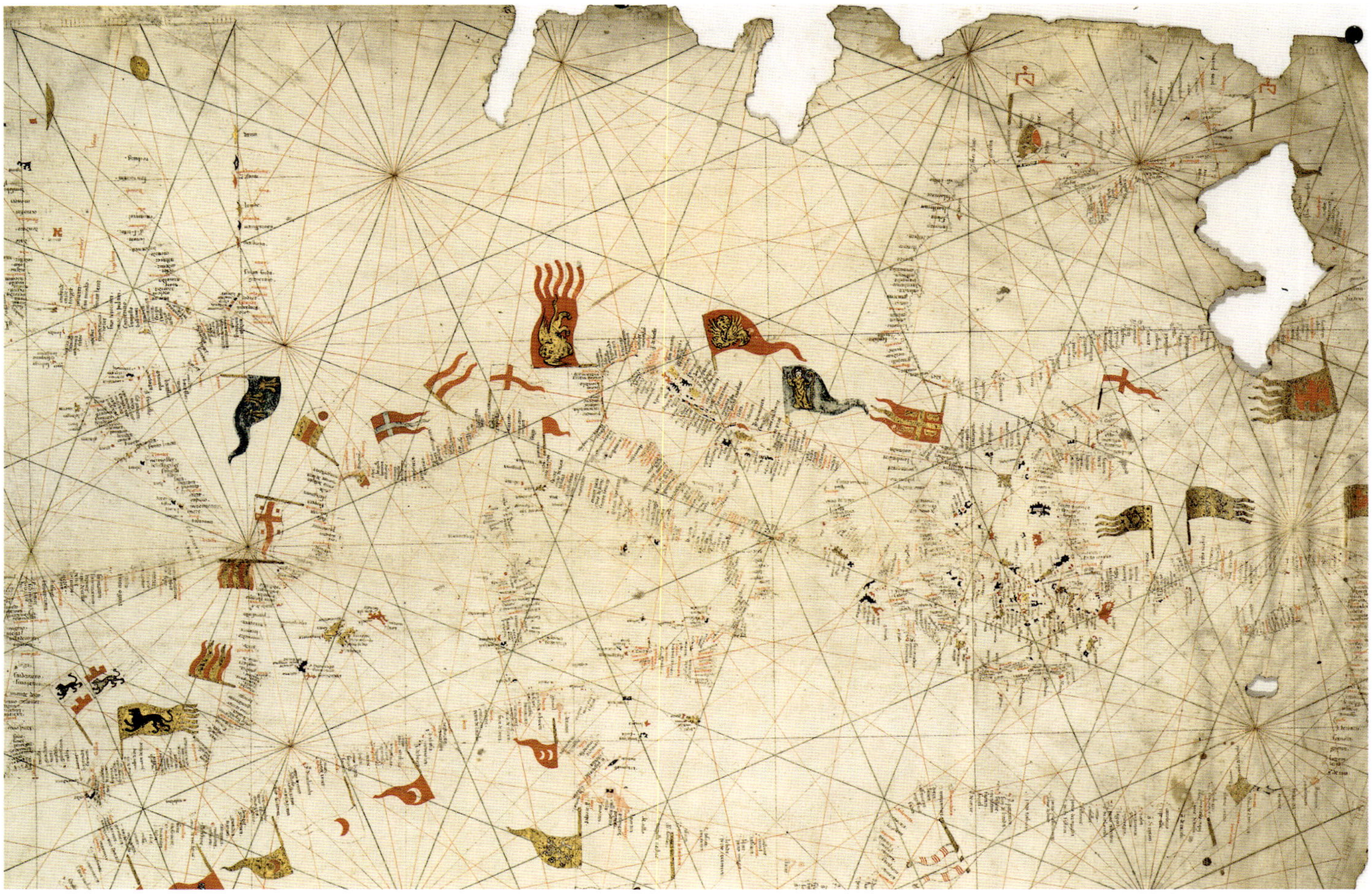

Giovanni Curatola

Using the vast quantity of surviving archival documents to define the centuries-long relationship between Venice and the Islamic world requires a certain number of preliminary comments. For centuries, Venice struggled for commercial and political hegemony in the Mediterranean against the Mamluk, Ottoman, and Persian Empires and competed with them for strategic and often disputed trading posts at places exemplified by Cyprus. Venice was a city-state endowed with an eminently special structure, highly active on international markets yet practically devoid of major mainland territory able to contribute to production; hence local production was limited to a few specific sectors such as textiles (cat. 78), which, along with silk manufacturing, was the most advanced, while glassmaking also enjoyed a special status (cat. 167). Venetian business therefore rested primarily on trade and intermediary activities: the purchase of European merchandise destined for sale in the Orient and, above all, the importation of widely consumed Oriental goods (largely, but not exclusively, spices) in order to distribute them throughout Europe, which yielded large profit margins thanks to attempts to ensure and maintain a monopoly in this sphere. This is a well-known story. What has not been sufficiently stressed is the fact that while Venice's wealth and the maintenance of its status as a regional power actually depended on the Orient, the same was not true for Islamic potentates. Trade with the West did not play a crucial role for the Mamluk[1] and Ottoman[2] Empires. This was particularly true for the Ottomans, and we know that the Mamluk sultans' attempts to monopolize the pepper trade for their sole use—and exclusive profit—thereby provoked discontent among Venetian merchants, who boycotted the port of Alexandria even though the value of the product sold by the sultan represented just a modest part of their overall business.[3] Finally, we are dealing with a classic case in which the balance of payments was heavily tipped in favor of one of the parties. This was a factor of extreme importance in the stability and survival of the Venetian Republic, as well as its credibility on the main markets—to such an extent that it was no coincidence that its collapse had two concomitant causes, namely the new Portuguese maritime routes around Africa and the Spanish gold and silver arriving from the New World at a time when the flow of German capital into the Rialto slowed as the they increasingly used the port of Ragusa. It is important to stress—and to keep in mind—the

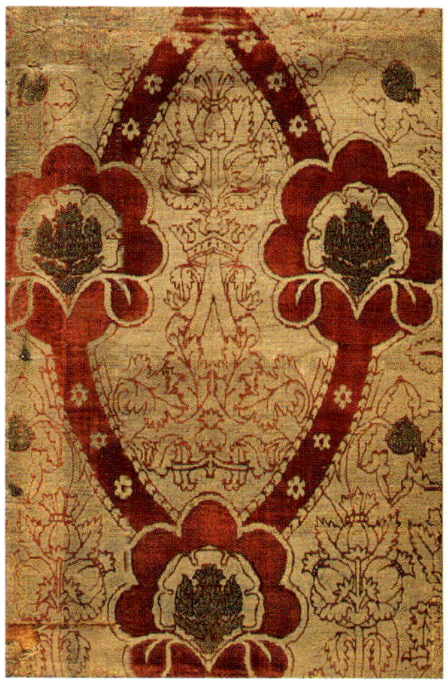

cat. 78. *Fragment of velvet fabric*
Venice, 15th century
Museo di Palazzo Mocenigo, Venice

cat. 42. Francesco de Cesanis
Portolan (detail)

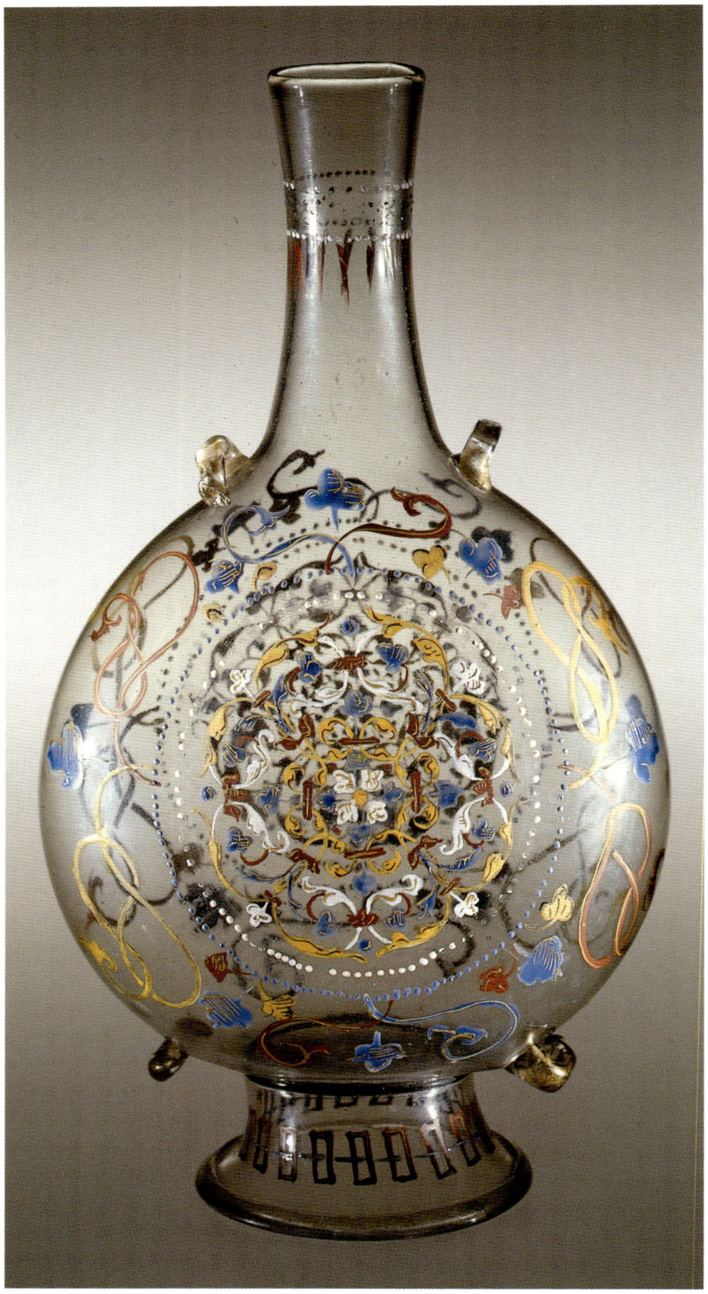

cat. 167. *Pilgrim flask*
Venice, ca. 1500–25
The Metropolitan Museum of Art, New York

fact that there was no reciprocity in relations between Venice and the Islamic world, and that the struggle—not only diplomatic and military, but also political—inevitably reflected this context, which basically remained unchanged through the centuries. Venice's leading representatives were certainly aware of this factor, and the very organization of the city reflected the great attention paid to ensuring and maintaining this "privilege" as long as possible. The highest state offices in Venice were held by an oligarchy for which successful trading activities with the Orient represented a mandatory stage in attaining the highest posts. Of course, the private and public sectors remained strictly separate in theory, but in reality—as was also the case with relations with the Jewish community—great attention was brought to bear on the Orient. Profits from trade enriched not only merchants but the whole city, which was therefore organizationally focused on that activity. For example, we need merely think of the highly structured fleet of galleys—built in the gigantic state-owned Arsenal—as well as the way in which the Venetian Senate decreed, in precise detail, the length and itineraries of voyages, not to mention the shipping taxes to be paid by merchants. In fact, defense and protection of the Arsenal (against greatly dreaded fires—whether criminal or accidental—and against Turkish espionage, the two threats most often cited in documents[4]) was a crucial task entrusted to this extraordinary Republic (which was, in reality, an oligarchy above all else).[5] Venice's relations with the Islamic Orient were not only constant and special, they also influenced every aspect of its existence and defined its basic framework. The period of the *mude*, when convoys of ships prepared to sail for other Mediterranean ports, was one of intense activity in the Rialto, where people readied merchandise destined for trade and attempted to anticipate the way the market would develop in the future. During the 14th century, Venetian merchants personally sailed on adventurous maritime journeys backed by their own capital, but in the 15th century families started banding together through marriage to form *de facto* companies (cat. 42). In this kind of organization, one partner, usually the main supplier of capital, resided in Venice while the other partner acted as the agent at the ports of call and became well integrated in the commercial and political system, forming a close relationship with the Republic's *bailos* (official representatives).[6] The agent in the Orient, who often acted for several Venetian merchants at the same time and would also conduct financial operations on his own behalf, was considered a worthy man whose dispatches would not only be read in the city with great attention but would be meticulously preserved. Along with account

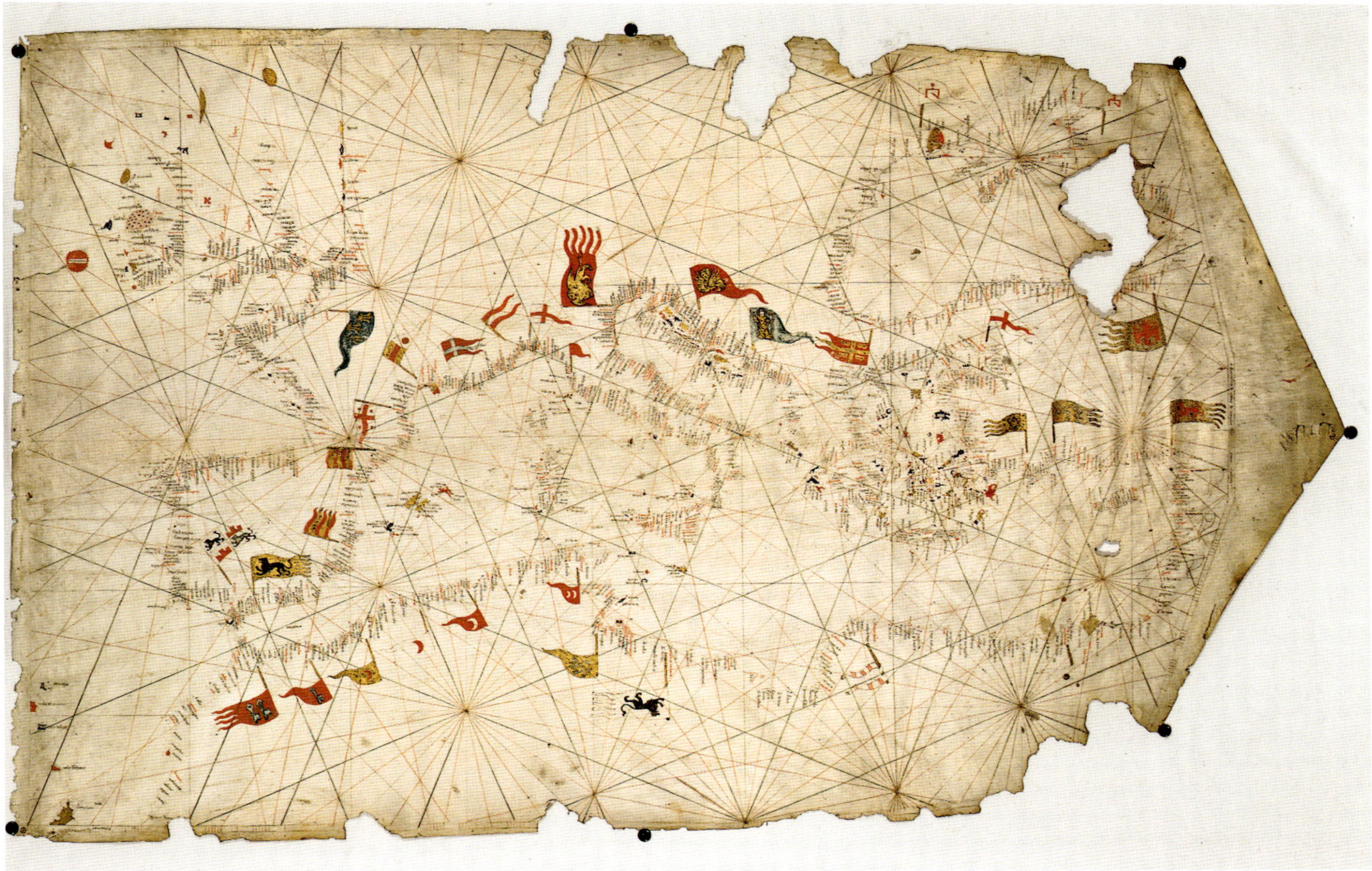

books, they served as documentation and evidence in the case of lawsuits, which were far from rare, in courts where complicated commercial disputes were tried. This meant that in Venice, knowledge of the Islamic world, whether it came from Pera (a neighborhood of Istanbul), Aleppo, Damascus, Acre, Alexandria, or Cairo, was not a secondary or fortuitous thing, but something that ran very deep. The attention paid to Levantine issues can be seen clearly, for example, in the highly strict and detailed health laws involving quarantines of imported merchandise.[7] In short, the Islamic world with its laws, habits, and customs held no mystery for Venetians. They succumbed to the appeal of exoticism far less so than today. Abundant written and material traces of it survive, such as the famous *Diarii* kept by historian Marin Sanudo,[8] which are known to constitute a mine of information and an indispensable firsthand source for anyone keen to know and understand the history of Venice in the late 15th and early 16th centuries. The Archivio di Stato, or state archives, housed in the former Monastero dei Frari, boasts documents covering over 60 kilometers of shelves that record every aspect of the Most Serene Republic, providing an inexhaustible resource for historians. In the end, the extensive scale of documentation—a veritable sea of paper—combined with the complexity of the structure of the Venetian state (each magistracy issued its own edicts and rulings, and no aspect of life escaped from some form of control or another) can make research highly difficult, indeed frustrating. It can also yield satisfaction on an equal scale. One particularly interesting series of documents, relating to Turkish affairs, was analyzed by Alessio Bombaci, an eminent specialist.[9] These documents were recently inventoried and filed anew in a highly rigorous manner by an archivist at the Archivio di Stato.[10] They provide a crucial point of departure even though, unfortunately, they cannot yet be compared with Venice-

cat. 42. Francesco de Cesanis
Portolan
Venice, 1421
Museo Civico Correr, Venice

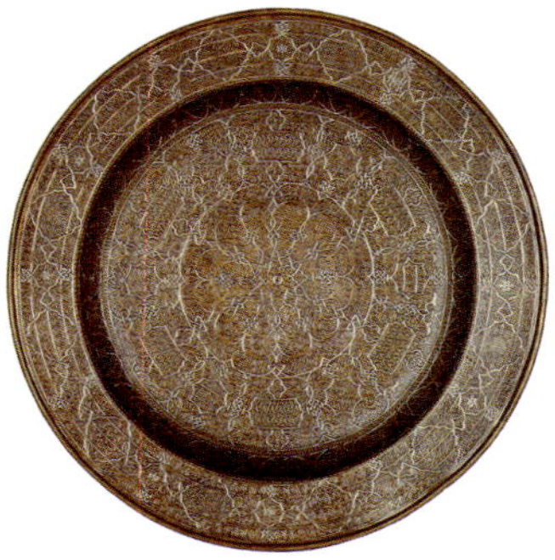

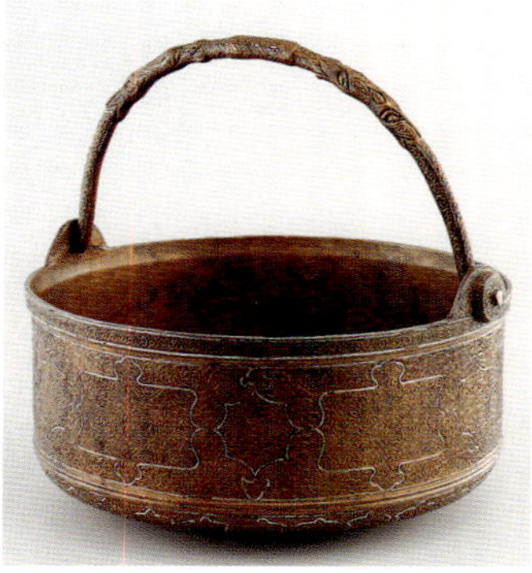

cat. 109. *Salver*
Possibly northwest Iran or southeast Anatolia, late 15th century
Museum für Islamische Kunst, Berlin

cat. 112. *Bucket*
Islamic Near East or possibly Venice, 16th century
Parrochia Santa Maria Assunta, Cividale del Friuli

related documents in Ottoman archives, which are hard to access, leading to reconstitutions that are not only partial but, in certain cases, completely one-sided.

Commercial exchange with the Muslim world continued uninterrupted even during the most trying periods, that is to say at the height of the struggle for control of the Mediterranean as well as during other more minor clashes. The enormous mass of archive documents relates above all to the spice trade and shipments of merchandise. The quantities are so well documented that F. C. Lane was able to draw up a chart of the Venetian economy between 1363 and 1510.[11] In contrast, it is much more difficult to know which of those items that might generically be defined as artistic products—those featured in this catalogue—actually reached Venice not as a steady stream of imports, but as rare curiosities. Three categories can nevertheless be established: textiles, carpets, and metalwork (notably the pieces formerly known as Veneto-Saracenic [cats. 109 and 112]). This last is of distinct interest despite the absence—for the time being, at least—of detailed documentation. This metalwork is amply discussed in other essays in this catalogue, but I would like to draw attention to a study published a few years ago by Bertrand Jestaz, who shed new light on the "Veneto-Saracenic" issue.[12] By studying the inventory of property belonging to a certain Bernardin di Redaldi, drawn up in 1527, we can deduce that he had assembled, in addition to a collection of Chinese porcelain comprising no fewer than 72 pieces (from a total list of roughly 200 items),[13] damascened metalwork that Jestaz judges to be of Islamic origin, based on thoroughly argued reasoning. Most of them are allegedly Syrian pieces, probably old, notably from the Mamluk period. Indeed, a certain number of documents seem to confirm the existence in Venice of works of Islamic origin, including *uno candelabro magno damaschino* (a large damascened candelabrum), valued at two ducats.[14]

Letters from Lorenzo da Pavia to Isabella d'Este (1508–11) leave no doubt about the presence in Venice of Islamic metalwork brought back from the east by galleys (cat. 112), valued at the remarkable sum of eight ducats.[15] In the late 15th century, the Senate seemed concerned by the spread of luxury items and prohibited their manufacture. *"È sta principiato a fare chavedoni d'arçento de man de orese cum grandissima fortuna, et come uno principia a fare simel spexe, tuti seguiscono… L'anderà parte che dicti chavedoni che fossero lavoradi d'oro et d'arçento o ala damaschina et similiter cassete che intervenisse or et Arçento siano bandide."* [January 14, 1495, m.v.][16] This decision must undoubtedly be related to the issue of the circulation of coinage and the fear of tying up an excessive amount of gold at the entire community's expense. The stress was placed on gold and silver. While Bernardin de Redaldi was indisputably a 16th century collector of exotic works of great interest, the terminology used in the inventory of his goods leaves a few gray areas that will probably never be cleared up, such as the distinction between "damascened" and "damascene-like"—the former might be interpreted as indicating an Islamic origin, while the latter would be applied to an imitation. The same goes for the expression *a la azzemina* (from the Arabic word *'ajam,* meaning "Persian" or, more generally, "foreign"), and above all for the recurring descriptive term, *lavorado d'arzento e d'oro* (silver and gold work). I understand it to mean the widespread Islamic metalworking technique, but we cannot rule out the possibility that the term simply refers to the use of these precious metals as raw materials (which would prove the Senate correct, legitimizing its decision to outlaw their manufacture). The inventory also includes enamel,[17] little employed overseas; thus item 55 is listed as *"uno vaso de rame dorà tien circa un secchio, item uno homo a cavallo"* ("a vase of gilded copper"—which might designate an Ottoman piece—"roughly as large as a *secchio* [unit of measure], with a rider depicted on it"). It is hard to find a good comparison for this object in surviving works of Islamic art.

We can take consolation in the fact that Venetian archives nevertheless constitute a mine that may one day provide the answer to this enigma—indeed, may also deliver other valuable information concerning Islamic artifacts and merchandise (glass, ivory, leather, books, ceramics) that passed through San Marco and the Rialto before winding their way into the labyrinthine alleys of Venice.

Notes

1 Gaudefroy-Demombynes 1923; Little 1970.
2 Inalcik 1994; Simon 1984.
3 Lane 1982, pp. 191–93.
4 Preto 1994, pp. 95–109, 247–60, 306–13.
5 Valensi 1989.
6 Coco and Manzonetto 1985.
7 Vanzan Marchini 2004.
8 Sanudo 1879–1902. The 58 printed volumes of the *Diarii* obviously contain various types of information on different subjects.
9 Bombaci 1949 and Bombaci 1965.
10 Pedani Fabris 1994.
11 Lane 1982, pp. 188–89.
12 Jestaz 1990, pp. 23–60.
13 ASV, Notarile, Cancelleria Inferiore, Miscellanea Notai diversi, b. 34.
14 ASV, Procuratori di San Marco, Misti, b. 145.
15 Jestaz 1990, p. 44.
16 ASV, Senato Terra, reg. 12, f. 120. "Goldsmiths have begun to make silver *chavedoni* [chests or coffers] with great success, and once people begin to make such expenditures everyone follows. . . . Such *chavedoni* of gold, of silver, or damascened, and other coffers of similar type in gold and silver, are prohibited."
17 Jestaz 1990, p. 45.

Venice as an "Eastern City"

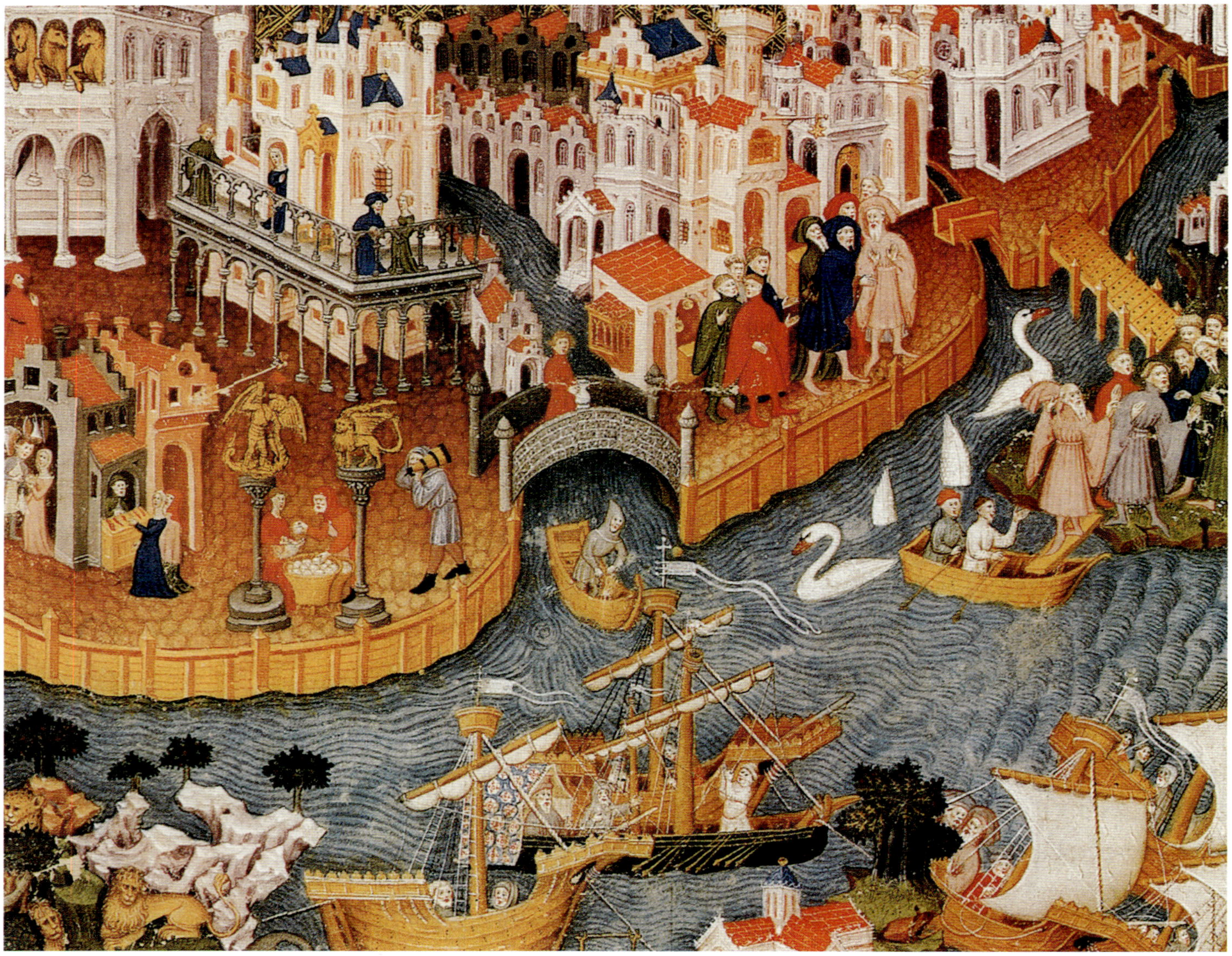

Deborah Howard

For medieval Europe, the lands to the east embodied a range of material and spiritual associations, as the source of exotic and precious commodities and the perceived location of Paradise. From at least the 9th century, Venice's political and economic viability depended on commercial links with the East, and over the centuries the city came to acquire a hybrid identity infused with Eastern characteristics. As John Ruskin wrote in *The Stones of Venice,* "the Venetians deserve especial note as the only European people who appear to have sympathized to the full with the great instinct of the Eastern races."

In contrast with most other European powers of the Middle Ages, the members of the Venetian ruling elite were not great feudal landowners but international merchants. Inhabiting a group of marshy islands in a shallow lagoon, they had no natural resources except for fish and salt, and only gradually acquired a hinterland. Thus the city's livelihood depended on long-distance travel and daring trading ventures. The theft of St. Mark's body from Alexandria in 828 was only possible because the appearance of Venetian merchants in the Egyptian port caused no surprise. In the same year the testament of Doge Giustiniano Partecipazio revealed that he himself had huge investments in overseas trading voyages.[1] Over the centuries, Venice struggled to achieve supremacy over her rivals in Levantine trade, especially Pisa and Genoa. By the 15th century, however, it had achieved undeniable dominance in the import of Eastern merchandise into Europe. Overseas commercial voyages, threatened by piracy, shipwreck, and warfare, always involved a degree of risk. Yet the enticement of lucrative profits was irresistible. As the Venetian diarist Marin Sanudo, remarked, "it is worthy of note that, just as they have been merchants from the beginning, so the Venetians continue to be from year to year."[2]

When traveling abroad, merchants such as Marco Polo could pay no higher compliment to any foreign city than the term *mercadantesca* (cat. 15).[3] Literally translated as "mercantile," the word implied a dazzling array of goods in the bazaars and bustling cosmopolitan crowds. Visitors to Venice, in their turn, were fascinated by the profusion of Oriental goods. In 1494 the markets of the Rialto stunned the Milanese priest Pietro Casola: "Who could count the many shops so well furnished that they also seem warehouses, with so many cloths of every make—tapestry,

cat. 15. Johannes, *Marco Polo's Departure from Venice* (detail)
The Bodleian Library, Oxford

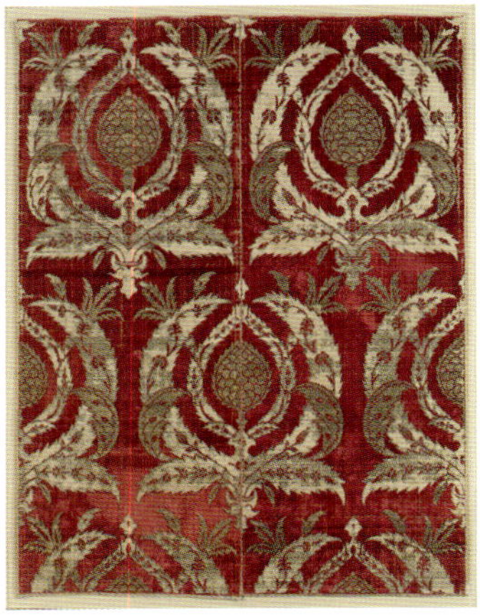

brocades, and hangings of every design, carpets of every sort, camlets of every color and texture, silks of every kind; and so many warehouses full of aromatics, spices, and drugs, and so much beautiful white wax!" (cat. 71).[4]

In the streets, marketplaces, and family homes, the adventures of overseas traders were a constant topic of conversation. The infiltration of Arabic and Greek words into Venetian dialect mirrored the whole spectrum of colonial experience.[5] At the foot of the Rialto Bridge stood a loggia of marble and wood, where the merchant nobility could meet to plan their voyages, using a world map painted on the wall (fig. 1).[6]

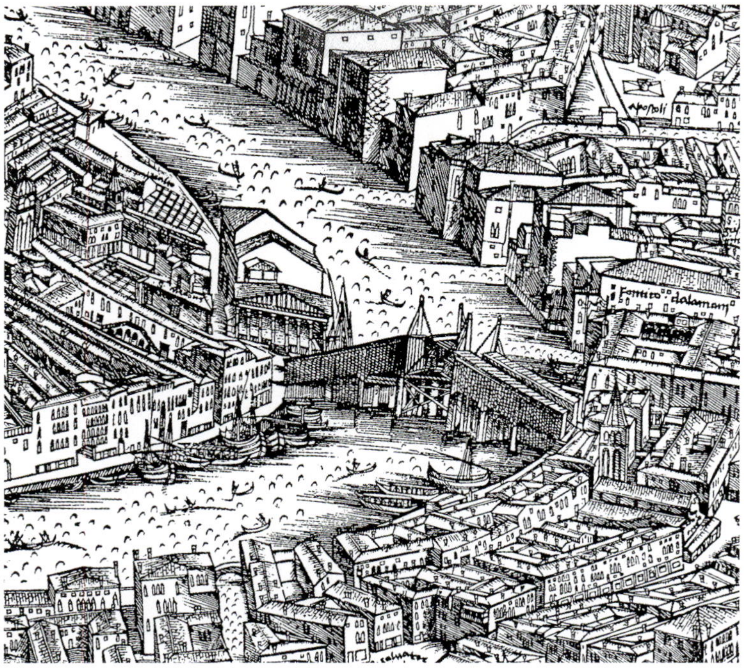

Unlike Spain and Sicily, Venice was never ruled by any Islamic caliphate. Originally an outlying colony of the Byzantine Empire, the Republic gradually established its cultural and political independence. After the First Crusade in 1099, the Venetians lost no time in establishing trading bases in the Kingdom of Jerusalem, based on the model of their trading privileges in Constantinople since 1082.[7] Thus, from the era of the Crusades onwards, Venice enjoyed a network of trading posts, known as "colonies," in the Levant and Central Asia.[8] Some of these were in Mediterranean seaports such as Acre and Alexandria, or on the Black Sea, including Tana and Trebizond, while others were in inland cities, ranging from Damascus to Tabriz. Venetian commerce depended on the maintenance of smooth relations with Muslim trading partners.

cat. 71. *Pieced panel of brocaded silk*
Probably Bursa, second half of 16th century
The Metropolitan Museum of Art, New York

fig. 1. Rialto market, with the loggia at the foot of the bridge. Detail from a bird's-eye view of Venice, engraved by Jacopo de' Barbari in 1500

"Colonial" life was not the privilege of the elite alone. Traveling merchants came from a wide range of backgrounds. At the lowest end of the scale were the oarsmen, who were allowed to collect indulgences at a local pilgrim site and to peddle their modest possessions when moored in a foreign port.[9] A consul represented the interests of the Venetian community, and the priest served as notary as well as chaplain. Most "colonies" had a *fondaco* for storage and lodgings, a church, a bakery, and a public bathhouse. In some cities, such as Damascus, Venetians lived outside the *fondaco* in rented property in the town alongside the local population. Skilled artisans from home served the daily needs of the visiting or resident merchants: these included barbers and tailors, bakers and cooks, goldsmiths and pharmacists.[10] Barbers could serve as surgeons, and we also have documentary evidence of physicians accompanying consuls and ambassadors to the East.[11] (cat. 191)

The Crusader colonies in the Kingdom of Jerusalem had provided the only context in which family life could be recreated in the ports of the Eastern Mediterranean.[12] After the fall of Acre, the last bastion of the Kingdom of Jerusalem, to the Mamluks in 1291, the chance for whole families to settle permanently in the East became restricted to Venice's true colonies in Crete,

cat. 191. *Barber's dish*
Veneto, 17th century
Museo Civico Correr, Venice

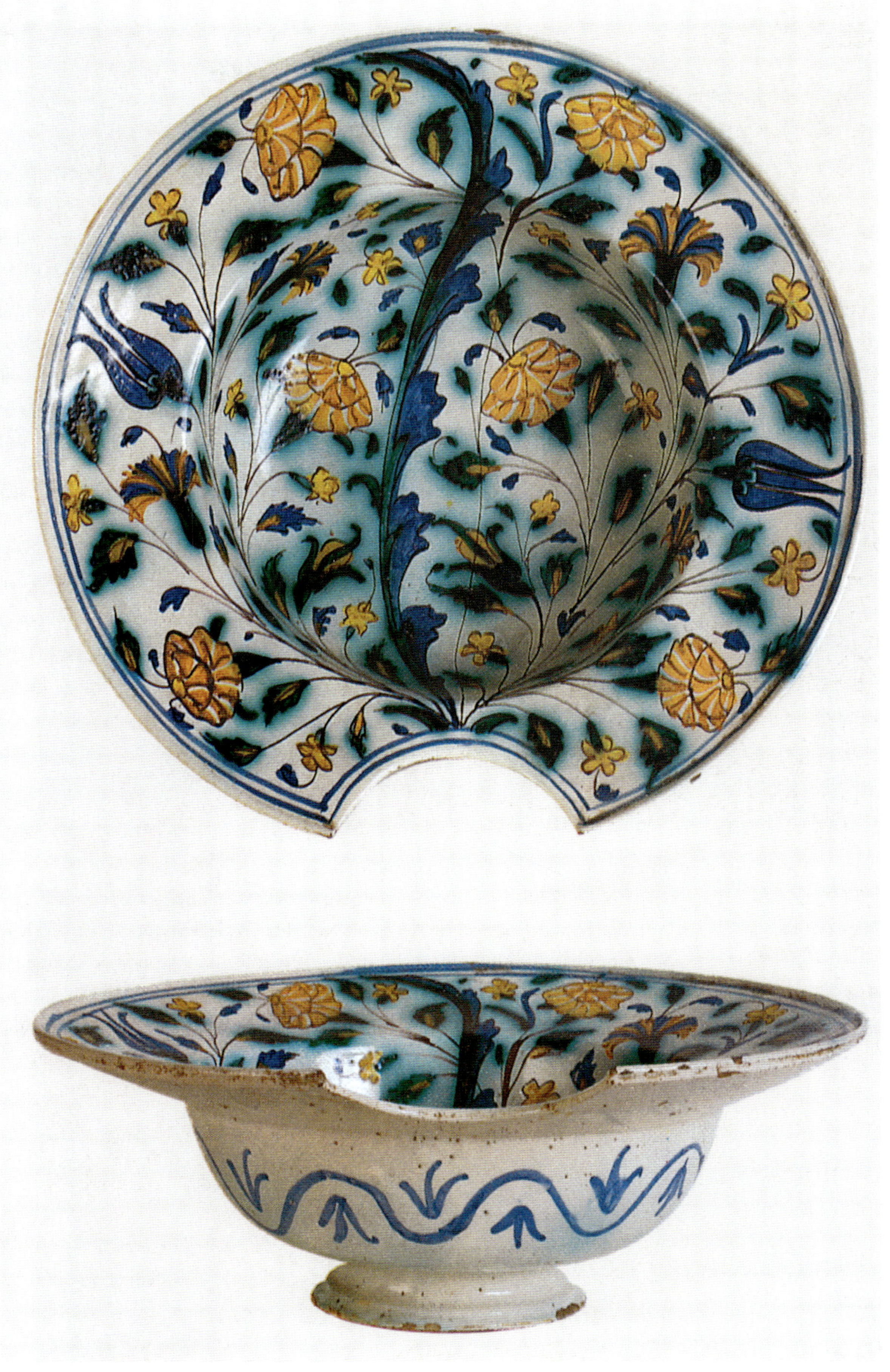

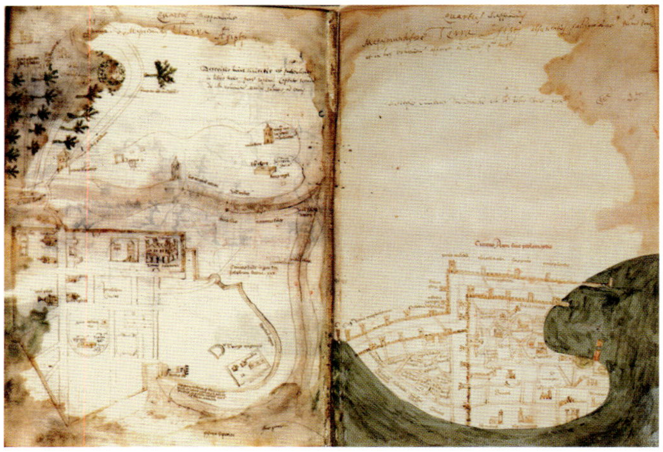

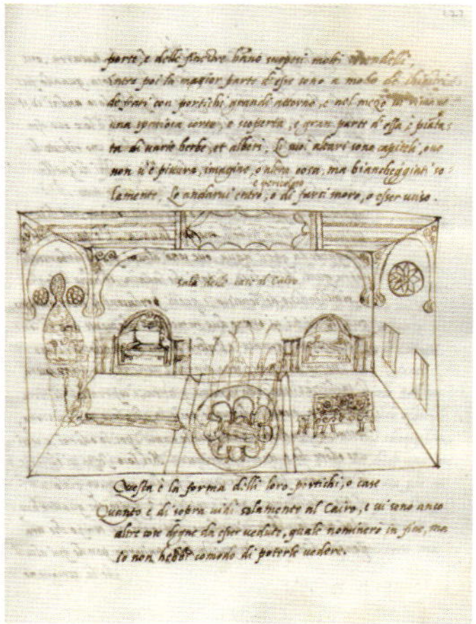

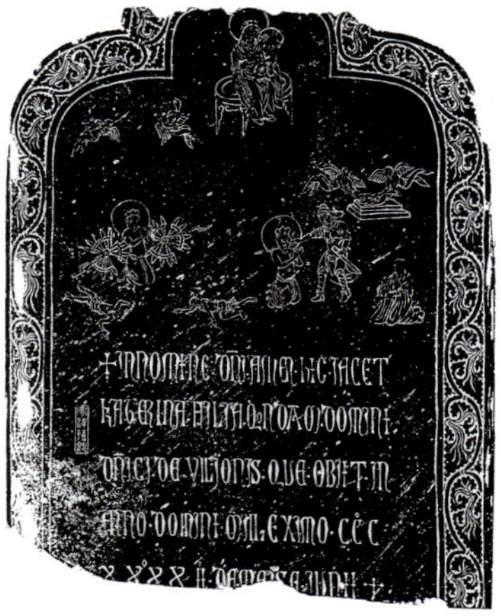

cat. 41. Workshop of Pietro Vesconte
City views of Jerusalem and Acre from *Liber secetorum fidelum crucis*
Venice, ca. 1330
The British Library, Manuscript Collections, London

cat. 54. "Interior of a house in Cairo" from the *Travel Diary of Alessandro Magno*
Venice, southeastern Mediterranean, Brescia, and London, ca. 1557–65
Folger Shakespeare Library, Washington, D.C.

fig. 2. *Tomb of Caterina Vilion* (d. 1342), Yangchow, China. Print taken from F. Rouleau, "The Yangchow Tombstone," *Harvard Journal of Asiatic Studies* 17 (1954), pl. 1

Cyprus, and the Aegean (cat. 41). Elsewhere, from the 14th century onwards, Venetian residents overseas were exclusively male. In the colonies in Mamluk Egypt and Syria, as well as those on the Black Sea and in Central Asia, there is little evidence of any Venetian female presence.[13]

Within this masculine domain a remarkable exception is the Italian woman Caterina Vilion, who died in 1342 in Yangchow, China, where her tombstone still survives today (fig. 2). She was presumably descended from the Venetian Pietro Vilion who made his will in Tabriz in 1264.[14] Much later, in the 1430s, Nicolò de' Conti's wife and family accompanied him to Cairo, where she and two of the children died of the plague.[15] Otherwise the Venetian merchant abroad had to make do with slaves and concubines. During his youth as a merchant in Constantinople, the future Doge Andrea Gritti (r. 1523–1538) fathered three illegitimate children, one of whom, Alvise, was to become a close friend of Sultan Süleyman's Grand Vizier Ibrahim Pasha.[16]

The all-male character of Venetian colonial life exerted a decisive influence on the East-West transmission of culture. Venetian overseas merchants remained in close contact with their native city, encouraging the maintenance of an efficient East-West system of communication.[17] The return of a husband, father, or brother after a long period of absence colored the domestic scene with traveler's tales and treasures to be unpacked and admired. In 1592, for example, the historian Antonio Paruta arranged to bring home the "furnishings, most beautiful things" that he had acquired in Constantinople.[18]

This mosaic of individual world-views transmitted back to Venice contributed to a shared culture of great complexity and richness. The ambassador to Persia, Giosafat Barbaro, for instance, did not see any need to describe Aleppo in his account of a journey made in 1478 "being a place with which we are familiar, and a very famous one."[19] Even a single individual rapidly gained a broad spectrum of geographical knowledge. By the age of 25, Francesco Suriano, for instance, had already made at least 16 voyages to various Oriental destinations.[20] The tradition of sending Venetian merchants abroad as teenagers—to learn Arabic, bookkeeping, and trading acumen—allowed the ports of the Eastern Mediterranean to color their formative years. (cat. 54)

Trade penetrated deeply into Venetian family life. Though rarely present in the overseas colonies, women at home were deeply implicated in commercial deals. Many mercantile documents involve females, acting either independently or on behalf of their husbands (whether living abroad or dead) or young sons.[21] Letters exchanged between merchants passed on affectionate messages to their families.[22] Meanwhile, the wives left behind in Venice bore sole responsibility for

cat. 33. Cesare Vecellio
Family Portrait
Venice, ca. 1555–70
Museo Civico Correr, Venice

cat. 43. *Atlas with Three Portolans (Atlante di tre carte nautiche)*
Venice, first half of the 15th century
Biblioteca Nazionale Marciana, Venice

cat. 174. *Fragment of a large plate*
Iznik, Turkey, ca. 1570
Museo Franchetti alla Ca'd'Oro, Venice

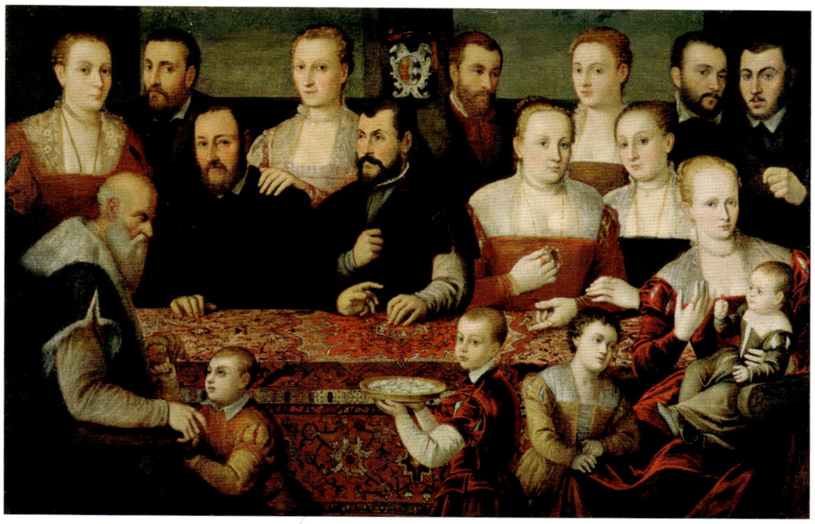

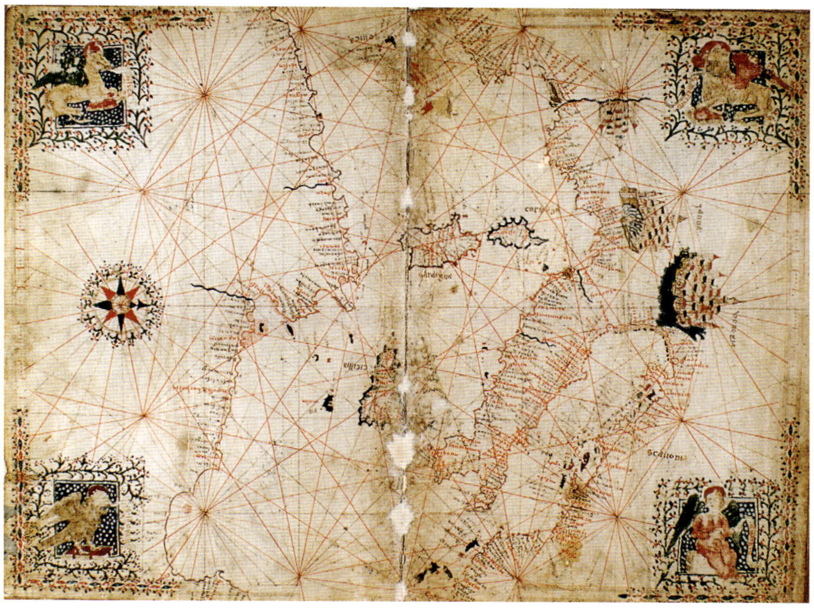

raising the children in the absence of their husbands.[23] Men making their wills abroad included poignant references to their wives in Venice, often wondering whether they might be pregnant or leaving them specially treasured valuables.[24] In Acre in 1227 Giovanni Natale even left a string of pearls to his mother-in-law.[25] Similarly, on his death in Damascus in 1455, Stefano Ravagnino left two coral rosary beads, or paternosters, to his beloved sister in Venice.[26]

From the point of view of the rapid infusion of Oriental elements into Venetian culture, the split families proved a deeply involving line of communication. The family home in Venice became the repository, not only of possessions to keep, goods to sell, and capital to invest, but also of memories, travel narratives—both oral and written—and maps for planning and discussing past and future voyages (cat. 43).[27]

Within its walls, as Francesco Sansovino observed, "the noble families, who have flourished for centuries in public life and trade, have always added to their possessions with the greatest delight. However much their ancestors dedicated themselves to parsimony, their houses were also splendidly furnished."[28] We know that Islamic furnishings such as textiles, inlaid woodwork, carpets (cat. 33), glass, ceramics (cat. 174), and metalwork (cats. 95–96, p. 65) were imported by returning travelers.[29] The inventory of Marco Polo's possessions after his death in 1324 included a number of Oriental items, probably from Central Asia, including a white outfit *alla tartaresca*, pieces of white and yellow silk from Cathay, silk cloth decorated with "strange animals," and bed covers with Tartar embroidery (cat. 68, p. 64).[30] As the most public space, the *portego* (or long central hall) exhibited coats of arms and the trophies of war such as banners and weapons, asserting the family's lineage and honor (cat. 77, p. 65). Sea-chests and trunks are often mentioned in inventories, as well as maps and shipping charts.[31]

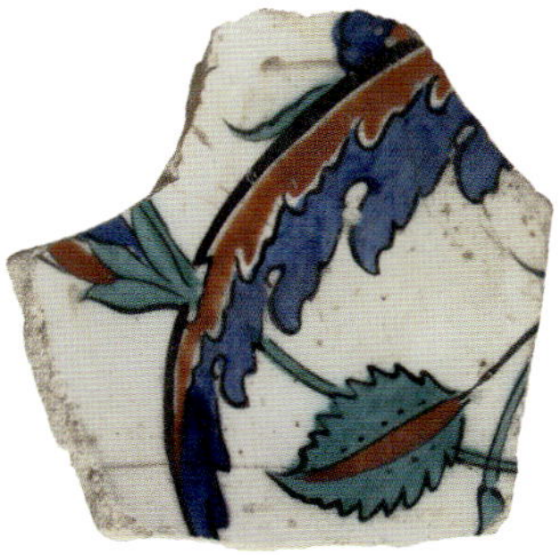

We can gain some impression of the acquisitiveness of Venetian overseas travelers through inventories drawn up in the colonies. Some itemize the possessions of travelers who had died on the outward voyage, such as Nicolo de Ruzino, who died on the Beirut galley in 1457.[32] His possessions were limited to various clothes, money, books, three bunches of garlic, a sugar loaf, two pillows, a bundle of candles, and several rosaries. Apart from the clothes and some gold on his person and two books to read on board, all was packed away in one chest and one small cloth bag. Another seafarer had a parrot and a supply of birdseed on board ship.[33] The contrast with the

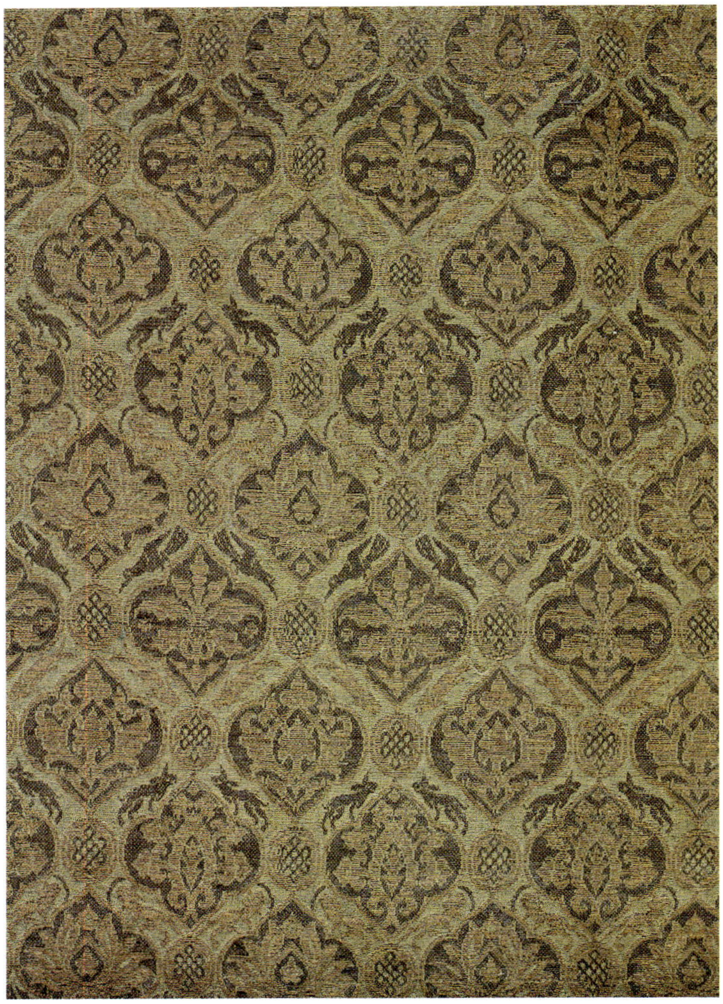

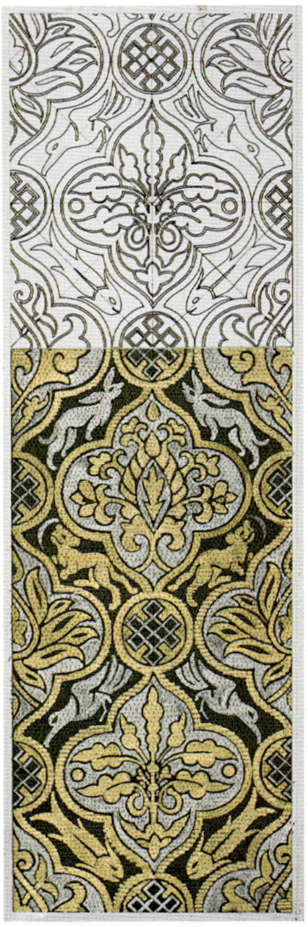

inventories of resident Venetians who died in Damascus in the same years is dramatic. For instance, the wealthy merchant Stefano Ravagnino, who died in 1455, left large amounts of money and jewelry, papers recording dealings with Arab merchants, inlaid boxes and furniture, embroidered clothes and handkerchiefs, cushions, carpets, and bedding, as well as textiles in a separate warehouse and books from the local bazaar.[34] Many other possessions were clearly acquired in Damascus, such as the writing stand with its silver scales, silver stylus with a copper nib, and cover *"alla moresca."* His handkerchiefs were embroidered *"alla damaschina,"* he had knives *"all'arabesca"* with bone handles, and even his prayer book "in good paper" had a damascene cover.

cat. 68. *Fragment of cloth from the tomb of Cangrande I della Scala (d. 1329)*
Possibly northwest Persia, early 14th century
Musei Civici, Verona

Of course, the backbone of Venetian trade was not simply the acquisition of personal wealth and luxury objects to fill the palaces on the Grand Canal. The Republic's commercial supremacy depended first and foremost on the city's role as an entrepôt. The imports included spices, dyes, aromatics, silks, carpets, and gems (imported by convoys of small, maneuverable galleys), as well as bulk cargoes such as cotton and sugar (transported by huge cogs or roundships) (fig. 3, p. 76). While the Venetians themselves specialized in overseas trade, their principal clients were merchants from mainland Europe, especially Germany. Traders from north of the Alps had their own headquarters in Venice, known as the Fondaco dei Tedeschi, where they could lodge while transacting their business at the Rialto market. In exchange for the purchase of Eastern commodities, they brought to Venice large quantities of metals (especially copper, tin, and silver), wool, and timber to fill the Venetian ships on their outgoing voyage.

Venice's position at the node linking two great trading arteries—the land route over the Brenner Pass into Germany and the Adriatic Sea leading to the Mediterranean—had profound implications for the city's artistic development in the later Middle Ages. Affinities between Gothic and Islamic visual culture included a love of vegetal ornament, pointed arches, delicate traceries and exquisite low-relief carving. Within the city of Venice itself these two strands were interwoven into the fabric of the medieval city, to create an exceptionally rich architectural tradition. Just as Arabic words infused Venetian dialect, so too the city's housing stock imported elements from the

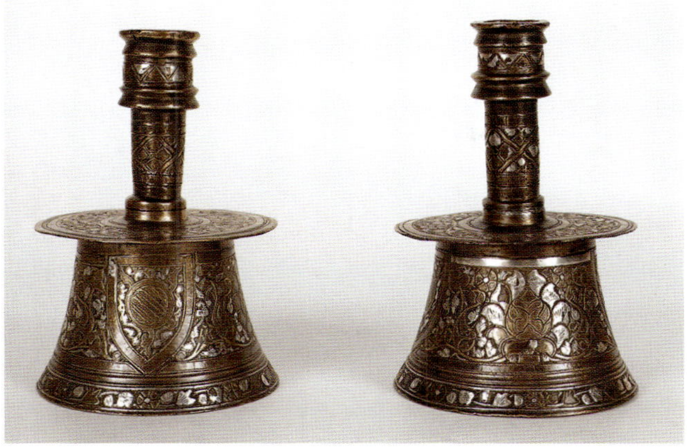

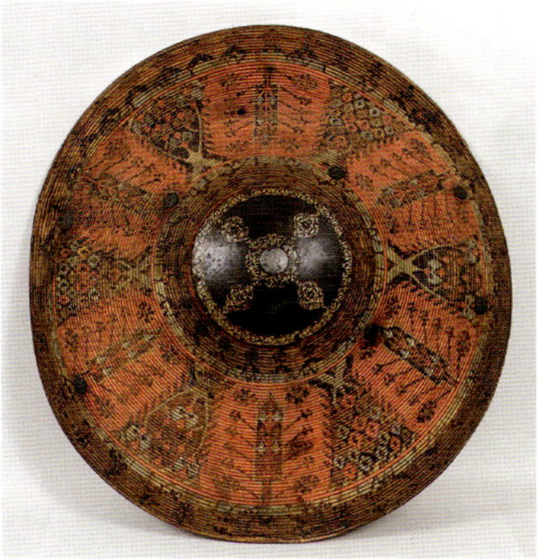

cats. 95–96. *Two candlesticks with the arms of Venetian families*
Probably Damascus, Syria, early 15th century
Museo Civico Correr, Venice

cat. 77. *Shield*
Turkey, 17th century
Museo Civico Correr, Venice

East—whether trophies such as Oriental marbles or sculptural panels, or a more generalized love of colorful and elaborate ornament. Shared features of domestic space, such as labyrinthine street networks, secluded courtyards, rooftop platforms, and covered balconies, established a continuum between home and the overseas colonies.

Some of the imported Eastern motifs were deliberately intended to be recognized, assuming a degree of familiarity (whether direct or secondhand) among the Venetian public. The motivations behind such "borrowings" may be divided into four different categories. First of all, the establishment of the Venetian oligarchy as a cohesive ruling class, united by generations of overseas trading, encouraged architectural self-definition. On the one hand, the ruling nobility began to specify its membership more precisely, beginning with the famous *serrata* (or closure) of the Great Council in 1297. Meanwhile, following the invention of the nautical compass, which allowed winter voyages and hence doubled the number of potential sailings, the state began to provide armed escorts for galley convoys from 1303 onwards. Thus the nobility sought to protect its own interests in trade while, in parallel, defining its identity visually, both in the Doge's Palace and in private domestic buildings. Elements that recalled Eastern models helped to advertise the specialization of Venetian traders as importers of merchandise from the markets of the Levant.

Secondly, Venice began to emulate aspects of the identity of Alexandria in order to create a more authentic setting for the relics of St. Mark. As a great antique metropolis, Alexandria was familiar to Venetian scholars through classical authors such as Strabo and Diodorus of Sicily. After the Fourth Crusade of 1204, Venice acquired the confidence to assert greater independence over her Byzantine heritage, and proudly displayed the spoils of victory on St. Mark's Square, including quantities of priceless marbles and, of course, the four bronze horses from the Hippodrome in Constantinople. Significant modifications were made to the decoration of the church, placing increasing emphasis on Egyptian subject matter, especially in the mosaics. Meanwhile, the low Byzantine domes were crowned by soaring outer structures, in emulation of the bulbous domes of Egyptian funerary structures (figs. 3-4). The adoption of an Islamic model seems to have been accepted in the interests of allusion to an authentic biblical and classical location, familiar to generations of Venetian merchants. Similarly, new doorways in St. Mark's, crowned by attenuated ogee arches, hinted at memories of exotic Eastern destinations (fig. 5).

A third motivation for specific recourse to the Eastern visual repertoire was an aspiration to emulate the biblical figure of Solomon. The Venetian Republic aimed to exemplify the virtues of Justice and Wisdom, for which Solomon was the outstanding scriptural paradigm.[35] Analogies may be drawn between biblical accounts of the Palace of Solomon and the Doge's Palace, as it was

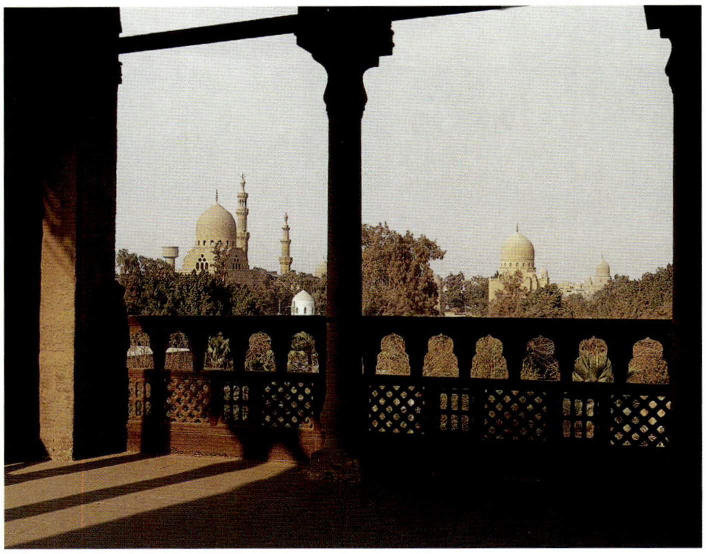

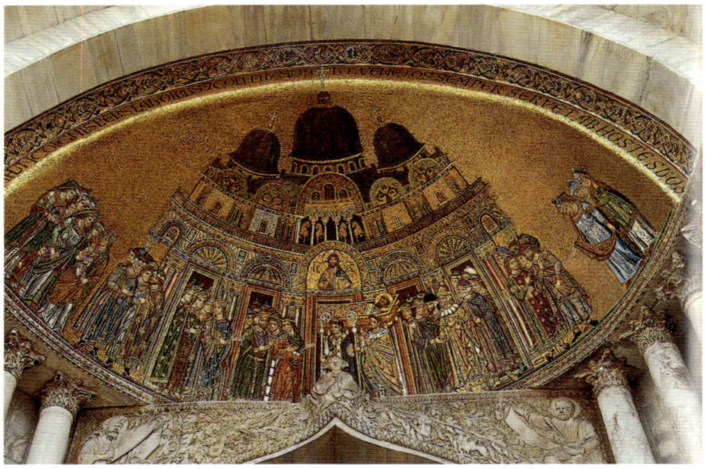

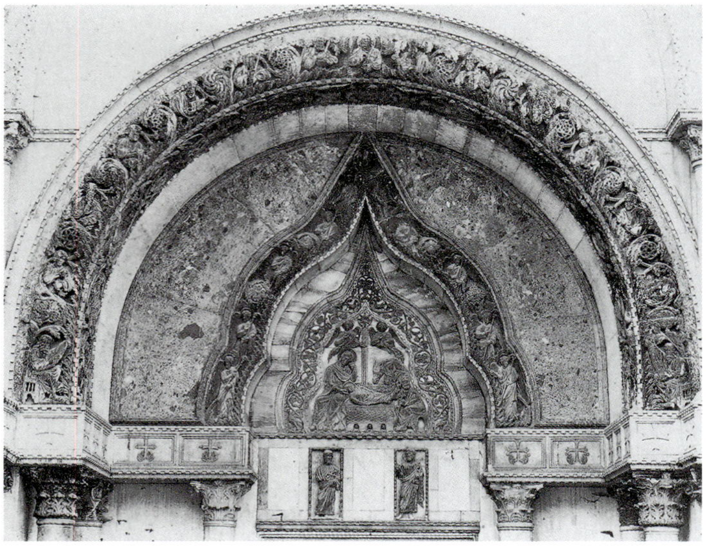

rebuilt from 1341 onwards. According to the description in the First Book of Kings 7:7–12, for example, Solomon's Hall of Judgment had big hewn stone blocks at the base, with walls of fine dressed stone above; the ruler's own residence was set at the back of a colonnaded courtyard; the main hall was paneled with cedar wood; and two giant columns stood outside, all features recognizable at the Doge's Palace (fig. 6). The desire to emulate both Alexandria and Jerusalem, although mainly connected with Christian beliefs, led Venetians to look very closely at these cities as they then were, and to refer to their present-day appearance, thereby adopting Islamic characteristics almost unwittingly.

Finally, Venice dominated the transport of pilgrims to the Holy Land. Venetian entrepreneurs offered a package tour of the sacred sites, complete with overland guides, regulated by the state. Pilgrim galleys moored alongside the merchant fleet in front of the Doge's Palace, where pilgrims could select their berths. Lying at the point of embarkation on the sacred journey to Jerusalem, Venice sought to acquire the identity of a holy city in its own right.[36] Pilgrims passed the weeks before their departure from Venice visiting relics, sightseeing, and shopping for their journey.

Official documents tend to skew the interpretation of history because of their concentration on mishaps and conflicts. The Venetian archives document in exhaustive detail the impact on overseas trade of war, piracy, and extortion. Yet lurking in private notarial records and collections of merchant letters lies copious evidence of sustained, often friendly, and highly profitable commercial exchange with Islamic trading partners. In the late Middle Ages Arabic culture seemed eminently worthy of emulation, being sophisticated and scientifically advanced, especially in medicine (cat. 64, p. 70), technology, astronomy (cat. 90, p. 70), and the use of Arabic numerals.

Venetians in the Islamic world eagerly picked up new skills, from bookkeeping to remedies and recipes (cats. 14 and 57, p. 69). Travelers to the Levant from other European countries were advised to consult Venetian expatriates about local customs, ranging from self-defense to the wearing of local dress and the hire of animals.[37]

The cultural impact of Venice's Eastern commerce over the period of this exhibition falls into several distinct phases. During the period 1300-1500 numerous Islamic elements were incorporated into the fabric of the city, especially St. Mark's and the Doge's Palace, as well as commercial and domestic buildings. These imported features blended easily with the rich northern Gothic transmitted by the other principal axis of Venetian trade. In parallel, Venetian craftsmen began to emulate the manufacturing skills of the East, especially in glass and textiles (cat. 163, p. 69).

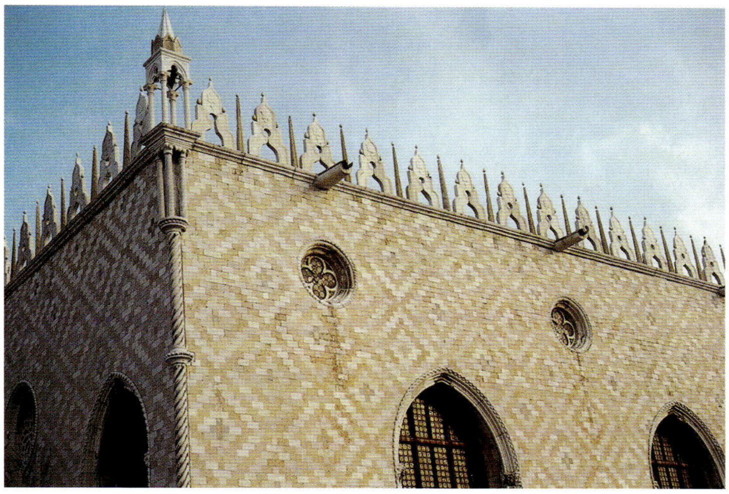

fig. 6. Façade of diamond-patterned brick topped by decorative merlons of Islamic inspiration, Doge's Palace, Venice

It is an intriguing feature of cultural exchange that the rate of transmission tends to accelerate during periods of conflict. At times of tension, diplomatic initiatives intensified, and information gathering increased. Meanwhile, gift exchange heightened the significance of material goods acquired from overseas. This effect may be observed in the aftermath of the fall of Constantinople to the Ottomans in 1453, when an exponential increase in depictions of the East in Venetian painting occurred, intensified by the visit of Gentile Bellini to the court of Mehmet II in 1479–81 (cat. 23, p. 68). At the same time, Mehmet himself began to show ever-growing interest in the achievements and culture of the West.

After 1500, we begin to detect a gradual shift in Venetian attitudes to Eastern culture. On the one hand, the collecting of Eastern artifacts and their display within the home had never been greater; similarly, the emulation of Eastern manufactures in metalwork, ceramics, glass, and leather intensified dramatically (cat. 138, p. 70).[38] Meanwhile, however, on the exterior, the city began to seek a more Roman identity, asserting the virtues of the Republic's Roman constitution and its legendary foundation by refugees at the end of Roman Empire. The Republic's position within the world economy was beginning to change. With the discovery of America and the Cape Route to the Indies, the center of gravity of international commerce began to shift. Although trade with the Ottoman Empire, especially Turkey and Syria, continued almost uninterrupted, the number of nobles in the overseas colonies declined as more and more of the trade was carried out by agents. Still, however, Venetian adventurers continued to travel overseas and even to settle far afield. At Elefante in India around 1580, the Venetian jeweler Gasparo Balbi came upon a flourishingship shipbuilding industry producing both large and small galleys, thanks to the expertise of "a good master from Venice called Domenico da Castello, who makes them rather well."[39]

The identity of Venice as a world emporium was crucial to the city's self-definition. In 1500, Jacopo de' Barbari's huge woodcut bird's-eye view map of Venice celebrated the universality of Venice, surrounded by eight cherubic winds like a world map (fig. 7, p. 70). At the top Mercury, the god of trade, looks down on the city from a nest of fluffy clouds ringed by a Latin inscription reading "I Mercury shine favorably upon this above all other emporia."[40] Significantly, this

fig. 3. Mamluk cemetery, known as the City of the Dead, Cairo

fig. 4. The translation of St. Mark's remains to St. Mark's Basilica. Mosaic on the Saint' Alipio portal, late 13th century

fig. 5. Friori doorway (north side of cloister), St. Mark's Basilica, Venice, probably 13th century

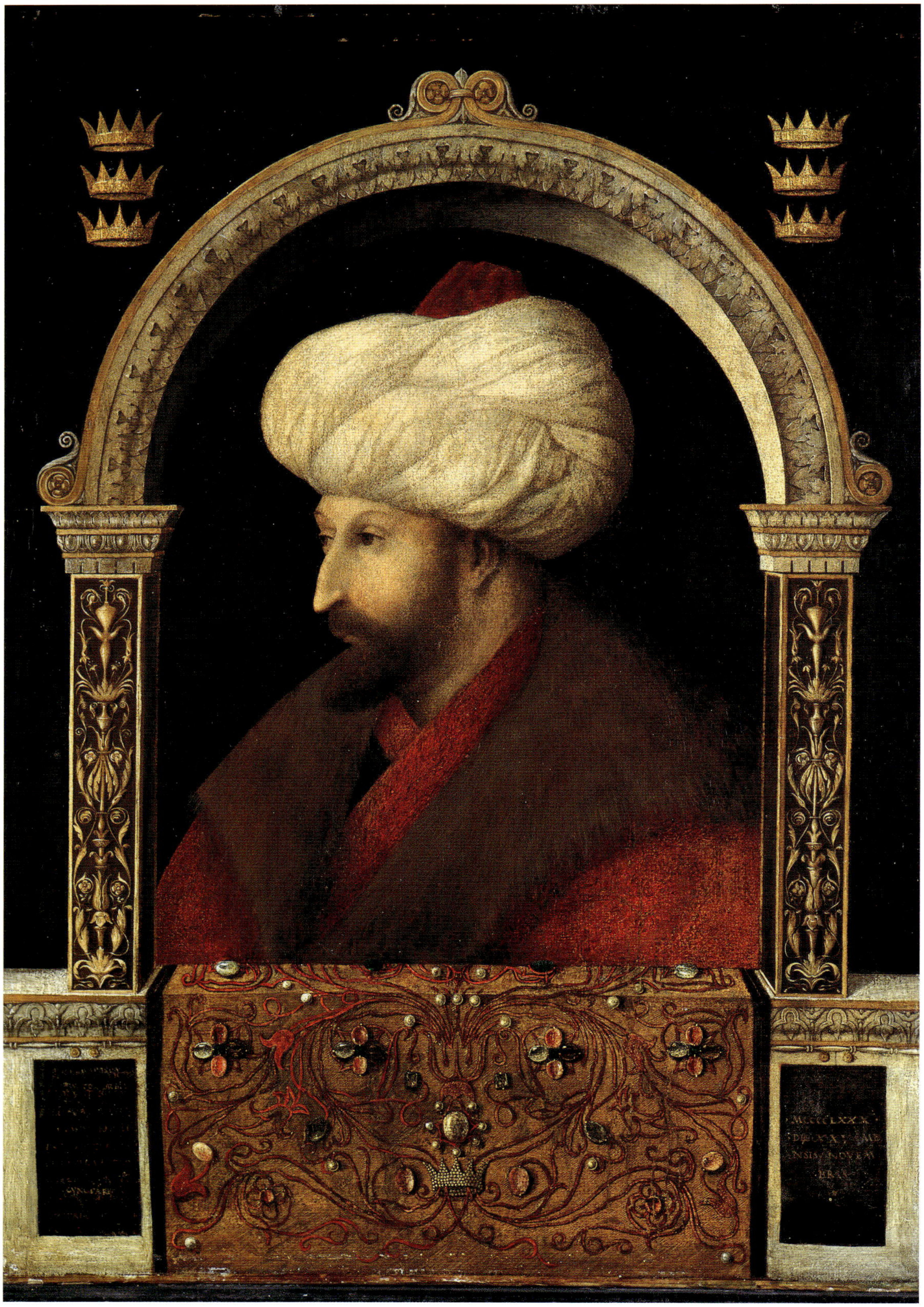

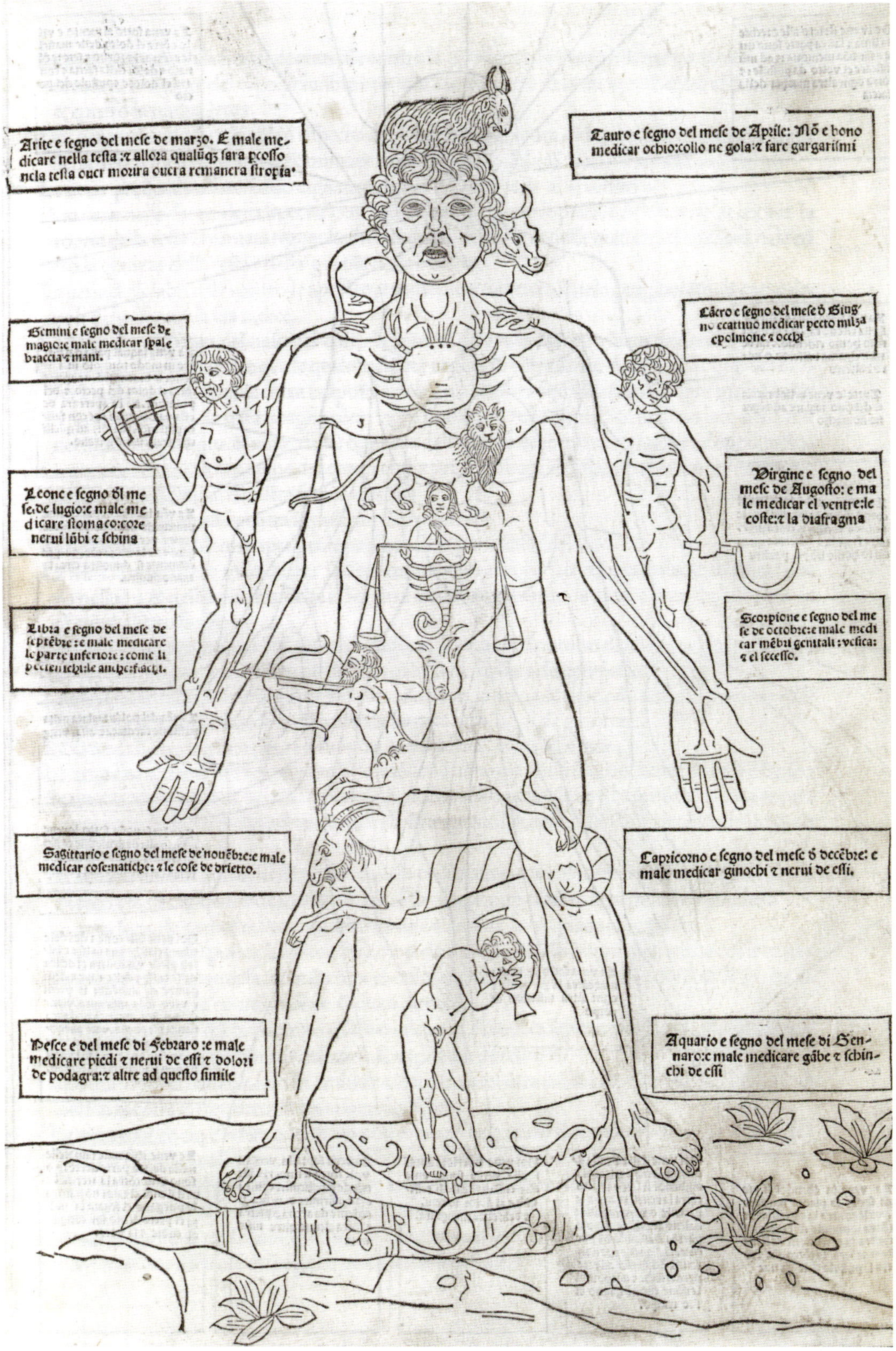

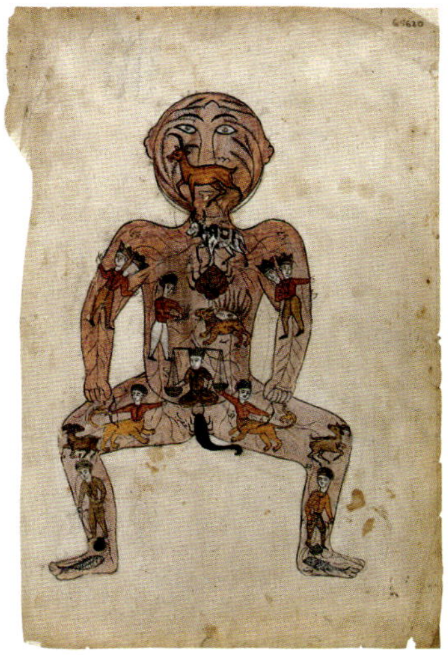

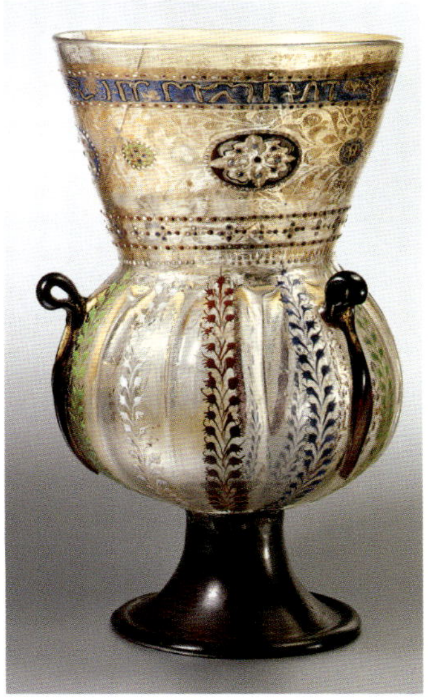

cat. 57. Johannes de Ketham (Johannes von Kirckheim?)
"The Zodiac Man"
Venice, dated February 5, 1493
The Metropolitan Museum of Art, New York

cat. 14. *Zodiac Man*
Iran, 18th–19th century
The Wellcome Library, London

cat. 163. *Mosque lamp*
Possibly Venice, ca. 1500
Glasmuseum Heutrich, Düsseldorf,

cat. 23. Gentile Bellini
Portrait of Sultan Mehmet II
Istanbul, dated November 25, 1480
The National Gallery, London

date marks the climax of Venice's trading supremacy. From this time onwards, the ideals of the great Eastern emporium were absorbed into a fictive construct, promoted in print and displayed in the private interiors of Venetian collectors, while the true supremacy passed into the hands of the Portuguese and later the Dutch.

Still, today, we think of "orientation" as positive, and "disorientation" as negative. For Venetians in the period of this exhibition, symbiosis with the East was the *raison d'être* of the city's existence. Whereas historical memory was infused with myth, Venetian communal culture embraced extensive and detailed geographical knowledge, whether acquired through direct experience or at secondhand. Every traveler's tale contributed to the city's shared experience of the East, creating a mosaic of evocative memories of distant lands. Constantly updated by merchant handbooks and diplomatic reports, this vivid picture of life in the Islamic world colored the production and interpretation of art and architecture at home in Venice.

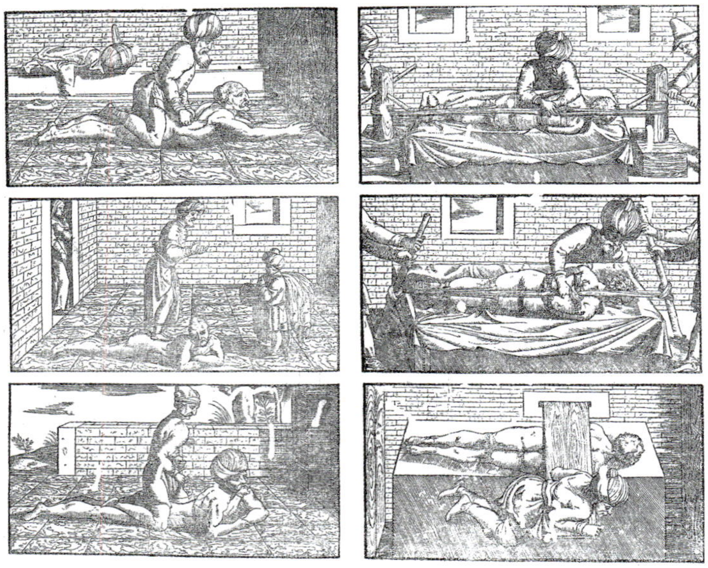

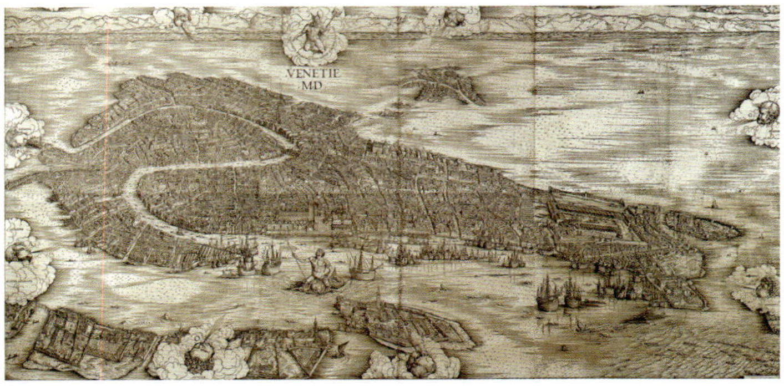

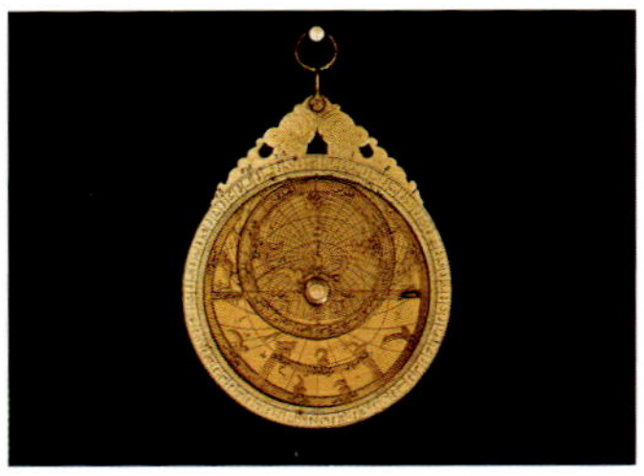

cat. 64. Avicenna (Ibn Sina)
Canon
Venice, 1595
Bibliothèque interuniversitaire
de médecine, Paris

fig. 7. Bird's-eye view of Venice, engraved by Jacopo de' Barbari, 1500

cat. 90. *Astrolabe*
Iraq (1306–7) and Turkey (1685–86)
Musée de l'Institut du Monde Arabe, Paris

cat. 138. *Shield*
Venice, late 16th century
Armeria di Palazzo Ducale, Venice

Notes

1 Lopez and Raymond 1955, pp. 38–41.
2 Sanudo 1980, p. 28: *"Et è da saper che Venetiani, cussì come sono stato nel principio mercadanti, cussì ogni anno seguono."*
3 Howard 2000, pp. 47–48, with references.
4 Newett 1907, p. 129.
5 Words derived from Arabic tend to refer to trade (such as *doana* or *tariffa*) or luxury living (for example, *sofa* and *divan),* whereas those of Greek derivation are often connected with religion (such as *patriarca* and *nicopeia*). See Howard 2000, p. 22, with further references in the notes.
6 Howard 2000, pp. 117–18. The loggia, opened in 1284 and rebuilt in 1424, was destroyed in the great fire of 1514.
7 The first colony in Constantinople, authorized by the Byzantine emperor in 1082, formed the model for future overseas bases. See Brown 1920 and Nicol 1988, pp. 60–64, 88–90.
8 Howard 2000, pp. 29–36.
9 Howard 2000, pp. 33, 190
10 Ashtor 1983, pp. 408–9.
11 Howard 2000, p. 35.
12 Prawer 1973, p. 638.
13 Ashtor 1983, pp. 407–8.
14 Rouleau 1954. Pietro Vilion's testament is published in Cecchetti 1883, pp. 161–65. Less plausibly, Zorzi (1988a, p. 38) wondered whether Caterina might be related to Marco Polo (who was known as Milion). Lopez claimed her for the Genoese (Lopez 1988, p. 290). Nothing is known about her at all, except her name and that of her father, the fact that she was a Christian, and the date of her death, known from her tomb in Yangchow, which is very similar to an Islamic stele, still existing there today. See Howard 2000, p. 34.
15 De' Conti 1929, introduction by Mario Longhena, p. 23.
16 On Andrea Gritti's connections with Constantinople, see Viallon 1995, pp. 186–92. See also Finlay 1984; Cacciavillani 1995, p. 55. As Sanudo remarked disapprovingly, *"Uno che ha tre bastardi in Turchia non dovrebbe essere fatto doge."* (Sanudo 1879–1902, 34, col. 158).
17 See Braudel 1972, vol. 1, pp. 358–69, mainly based on 16th-century sources.
18 Tucci 1973, p. 369.
19 Lockhart *et al* 1973, p. 164: *"per esser luogo assai domestico e molto noto."*
20 Suriano 1949, p. 1. Suriano became a Franciscan friar and was later the Guardian of Mount Sion, but he began his career as a merchant.
21 See Morozzo della Rocca and Lombardo 1940, vol. 1, pp. 176–79. Women took delivery of goods sent from the East, accepted repayments of loans, raised capital, and handled transactions regarding property in the colonies. Examples may be found in Morozzo della Rocca and Lombardo 1940, vol. 1, pp. 38–39, 53, 162, 181–82; vol. 2, pp. 42–43, 77–78, 370–71.
22 See the letter of Vanino in Alexandria to Pignol Zucchello in Venice, 1347 (Morozzo della Rocca 1957, p. 109); letter of Andrea Berengo from Aleppo, 1556 (Tucci 1957, p. 321).
23 See for instance, Renouard 1955, p. 94.
24 Morozzo della Rocca and Lombardo 1954, vol. 2, p. 177.
25 Morozzo della Rocca and Lombardo 1954, vol. 2, p. 176.
26 Bianchi and Howard 2003, testament cited in Appendix 3, Doc. no. 2, pp. 259–60.
27 Most surviving references to the display of maps in Venetian private houses date from the 16th century onwards. Sanudo, for instance, proudly displayed his *mappamondo* to a group of scholarly visitors in 1511 (Thornton 1990, p. 88, citing Sanudo 1879–1902, vol. 12, col. 293, December 5, 1511). See also Ambrosini 1981.
28 Sansovino 1663, p. 384: *"A ciò s'aggiunge, che le case nobili, per centinaia d'anni, stando tuttavia in fiore per i magistrati, & per le facende del mare: hanno sempre ampliato le cose loro à colmo di grande felicità. Et quantunque i passati si dessero alla parsimonia, erano però ne gli addobbamenti di casa splendidi grandemente."*
29 See Mack 2002; Tucci 1973, pp. 357, 363; and Thornton 1997, pp. 78, 206. The Damascus inventories published in Bianchi and Howard 2003 list quantities of such material that was to be returned to Venice on the deaths of the owners.
30 Inventory published in Cecchetti 1886, pp. 123–29.
31 Crouzet-Pavan 1992, vol. 1, pp. 402–6.
32 Bianchi and Howard 2003, Appendix 4, Doc. no. 5, pp. 284–86.
33 Molmenti 1905, vol. 1, pp. 446–47, Doc. no. 8.
34 This passage is based on text in Howard 2000, p. 60. The inventory is published in Bianchi and Howard 2003, Appendix 4, Doc. no. 2, pp. 270–75. See also Howard 2003.
35 Howard 2000, pp. 180–83; Rosand 2001, pp. 96–116.
36 Howard 2000, pp. 189–216.
37 Howard 2000, p. 38.
38 See Howard's forthcoming article "Cultural transfer between Venice and the Ottomans in the 15th and 16th centuries," in *The Fashioning of Self: Forging a European Identity c. 1400–c. 1700,* ed. Herman Roodenburg and Bernd Roeck (Cambridge University Press, forthcoming).
39 *"Buon maestro da Venetia, chiamato Maestro Domenico da Castello, il qual le fà assai belle."* (Balbi 1590, p. 63)
40 *"MERCVRIVS PRECETERIS HVIC FAUSTE EMPORIIS ILLVSTRO.*

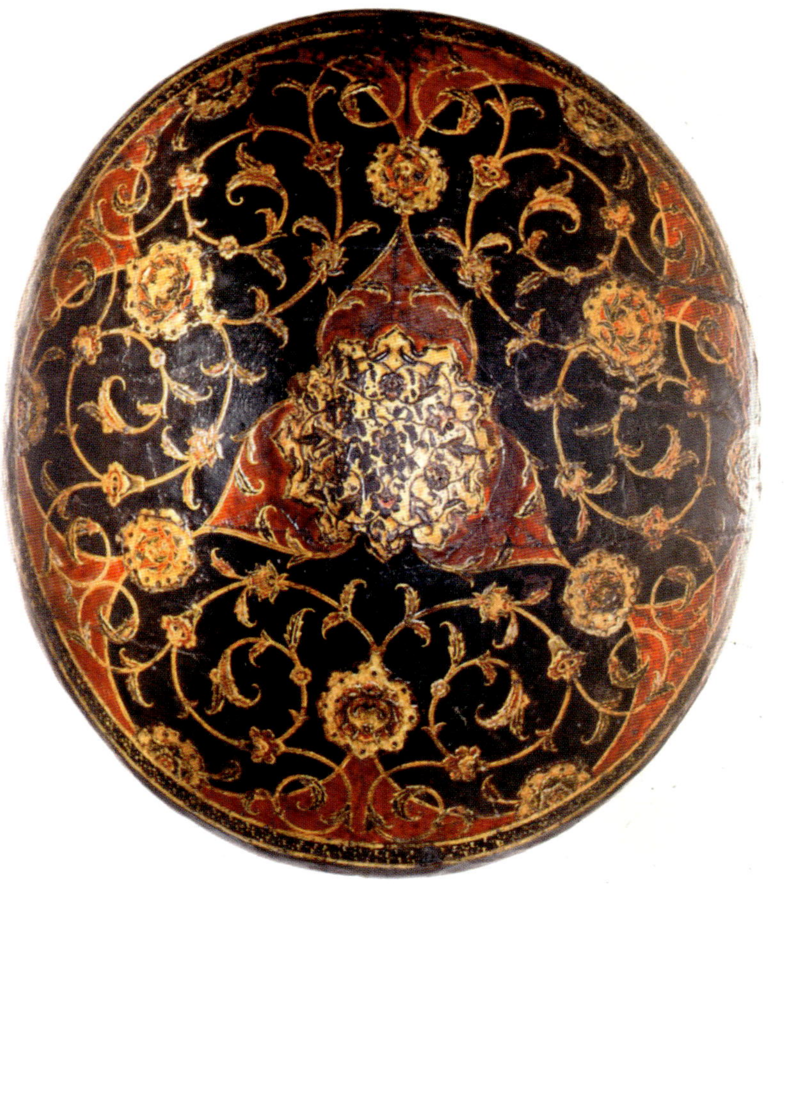

Venice and the Mamluks

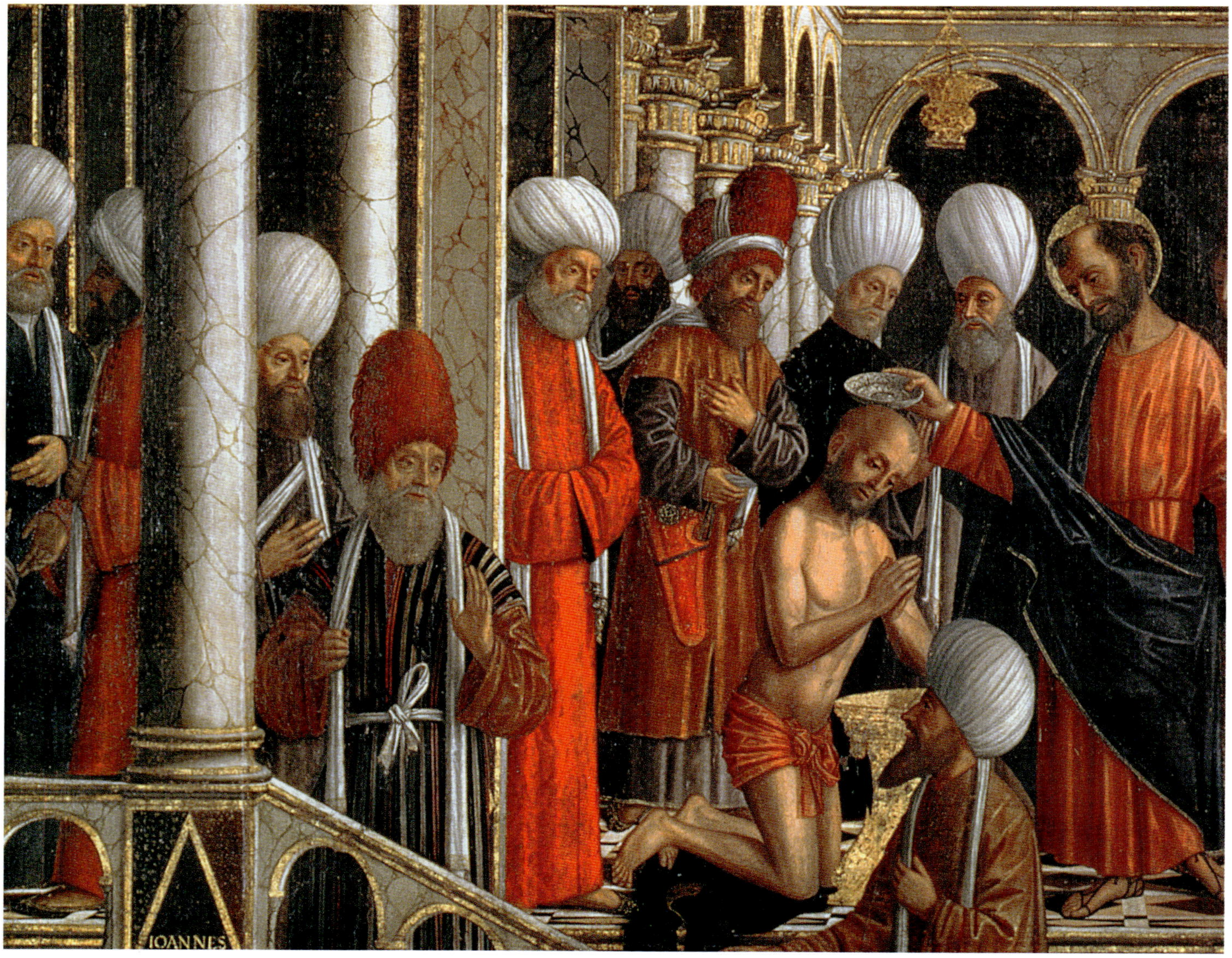

Deborah Howard

The Mamluks

The Mamluks were the rulers of a vast area of the Eastern Mediterranean stretching from Egypt to Syria from 1250 until 1517. As such they were the principal trading partners of the Venetian Republic during its rise to commercial supremacy in the Eastern Mediterranean.[1] This fragile but remarkably durable cooperation exploited the particular assets of each, transferring huge quantities of valuable merchandise between Asia and Western Europe. Whereas the Venetians traded almost exclusively at sea, the Mamluks were landlubbers. Their principal cities lay inland, and they hardly even troubled to fortify their coastal ports. Thus, in effect, the Mamluks depended on Venetian naval strength and goodwill to protect their Mediterranean littoral.

The word *mamluk* literally means "owned," but its meaning was extended to comprise not only slaves but also freed slaves in the military. The Mamluk lands were ruled by an elite militia of emancipated slaves, captured from outside their own territory, mainly from the Steppes of Central Asia.[2] The sultan himself was drawn from this self-perpetuating military oligarchy, racially distinct from the inhabitants who were mainly Arabs. During the period of the Bahri Mamluks who reigned from 1250 until 1390, succession passed, in theory at least, through the blood line, although there were many discontinuities. In 1382, control began to pass to the Burji or Circassian Mamluks, whose succession operated, instead, through patronage. Both periods were characterized by recurrent instability, interspersed by the long steady reigns of individual, powerful sultans. The two most successful sultanates, those of al-Nasir Muhammad (1293–1341, with two breaks at the start) and Qa'itbey (1468–96), span the two centuries of Venice's greatest commercial success.

As successors to the Ayyubids, the Mamluks were Sunni Muslims, in contrast to the earlier Shi'ite rulers of Egypt, the Fatimids (969–1171). It was the Mamluks who drove the Frankish Crusaders out of their last stronghold in Acre in 1291, branding themselves as the true successors of Saladin (Salah al-Din, d. 1193), while on their eastern frontier they resisted Mongol and

cat. 28. Giovanni Mansueti
St. Mark Baptizing Anianus (detail)

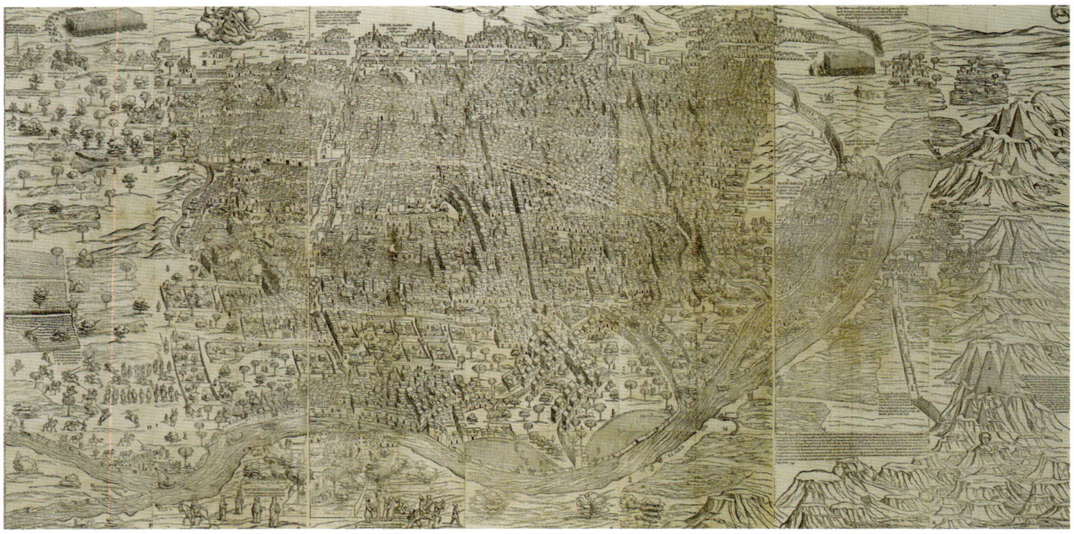

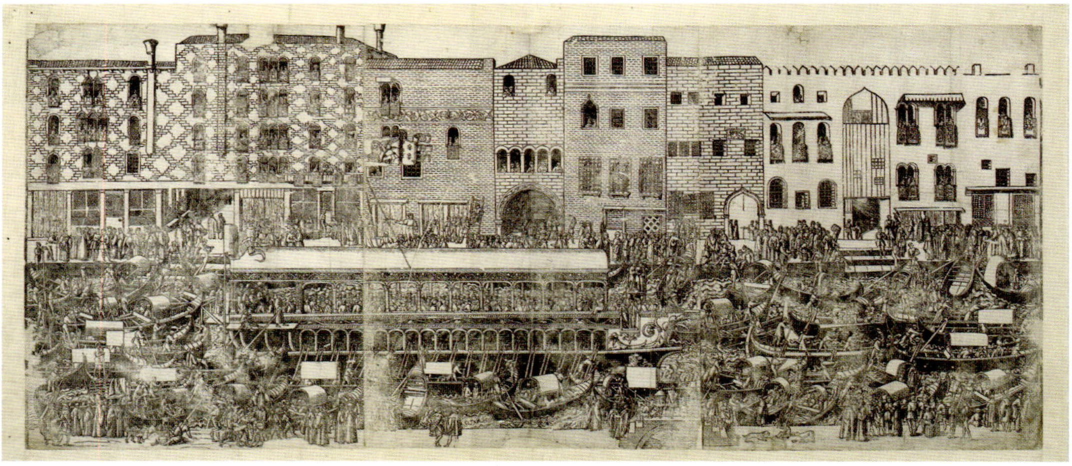

Persian advances. Yet once their territory was defined they traded avidly on both frontiers. The incursions of Timur (Tamerlaine) in 1400–1401 devastated both Aleppo and Damascus, but control was quickly reestablished. Mamluk rule finally came to an end when first Syria and then Egypt fell to the Ottomans in 1516–17.

Drawn from non-Arab bloodstock, the Mamluk sultans lived isolated from their citizens within a highly ritualized, disciplined military elite.[3] The rulers asserted their presence in the cities by building impressive mosque complexes and funerary structures, usually associated with charitable endowments.[4] Their blazons and inscriptions identified the individuality of each reign, while their emirs (high officials) emulated them by erecting urban palaces and smaller mosque complexes (cat. 69).[5] A remarkable consistency in architecture, arts, and crafts over the whole period helped to counteract the recurrent instability of the regime.[6]

cat. 44. Matteo Pagano
La Vera Descritione de la Gran Cita del Caiero
Venice 1549 (?)
Staatliche Museen zu Berlin, Kupferstichkabinett, Berlin

cat. 56. Anonymous Venetian
The Doge in the Bucintoro *being rowed to the Marriage of the Sea*
Venice, ca. 1501–21
The British Museum, London

cat. 46b. *View of Alexandria*
Turkey, ca. 1670
The Nasser D. Khalili Collection of Islamic Art, London

cat. 69. *Textile fragment with Mamluk emblem*
Egypt, ca. 1468–96
The Metropolitan Museum of Art, New York

The Mamluk capital, Cairo, a city of around 200,000 inhabitants, was the greatest metropolis of the age (cat. 44).[7] In 1326, the North African traveler Ibn Battuta visited the city during the sultanate of al-Nasir Muhammad: "From Dimyat [Damietta] I traveled up the Nile until at length I arrived at the city of Misr [Cairo]. Mother of cities and seat of pharaoh the tyrant, mistress of broad provinces and fruitful lands, boundless in multitude of buildings, peerless in beauty and splendor . . . she surges as the waves of the sea with her throngs of folk and can scarce contain them for the capacity of her situation and sustaining power."[8]

Mamluk-Venetian Relations

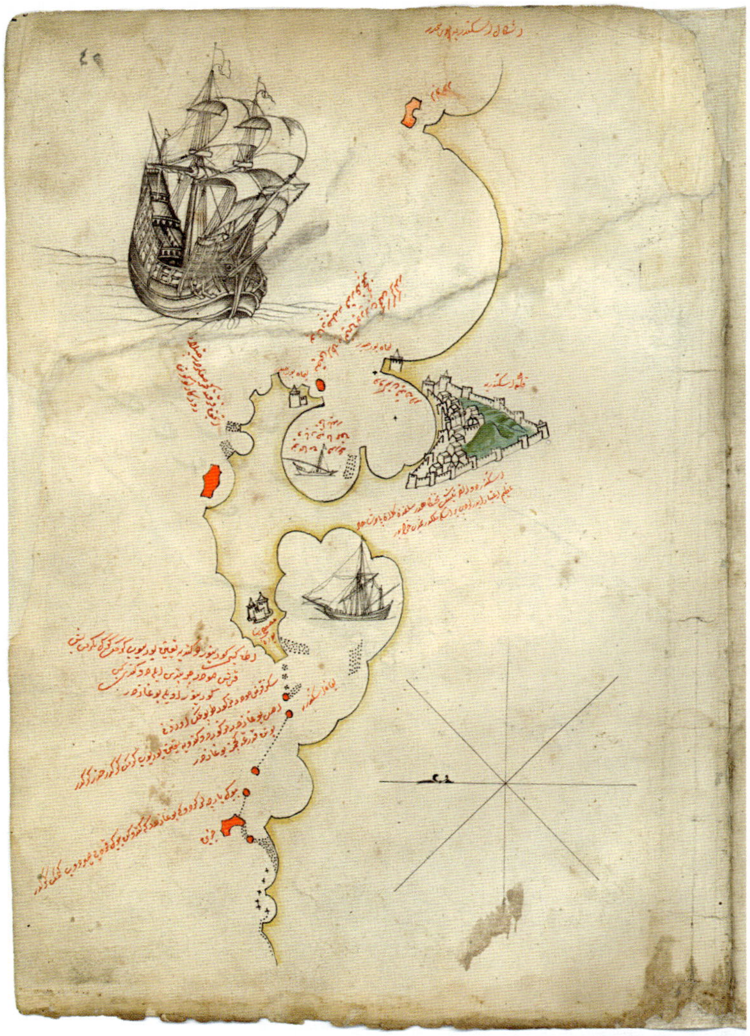

Although it was the Mamluks who finally drove the Crusaders out of the Levant and took control over the holy places, in Venice the fall of Acre in 1291 was perceived as a tragedy for trade, rather than a calamity for Christianity. From the start of the Mamluk sultanate, Venetians had been trading intensively in Alexandria, and after the expulsion of the Franks from Acre they lost no time in renegotiating commercial privileges to allow their continued use of the port.[9] By the early 14th century intense trading activity with both Egypt and Syria had resumed, despite energetic opposition from the papacy.[10] From 1308 onwards the Venetian Republic's official armed galley convoys set sail from the Riva degli Schiavoni and the Molo di San Marco in front of the Doge's Palace, laden with European linen and wool; olive oil, nuts, dried fruit, and honey were acquired from southern Italy, Crete, and Cyprus during the voyage (cat. 56). In the Mamluk ports, these were exchanged for spices, dyestuffs, silks and alkali, as well as quantities of Syrian cotton (cat. 46b). The most valuable Venetian exports, copper, tin, and silver, were discouraged in these early years by the papal embargo, which forbade the export of wood and metals to Muslim states.

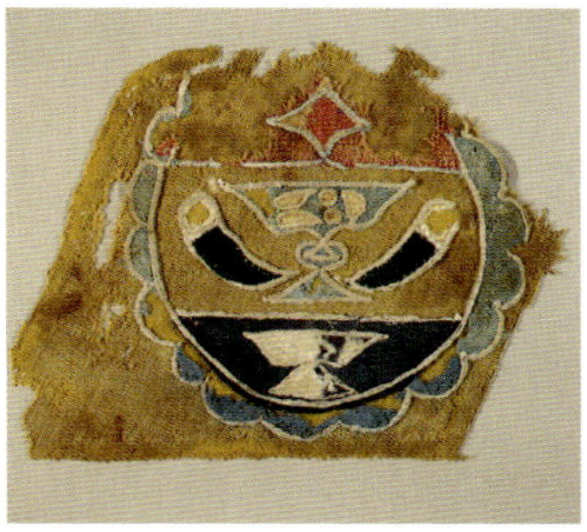

Papal interference eventually deteriorated into an outright ban on all trade with Muslims in 1320, and in 1326 a bull of Pope John XXII imposed excommunication on anyone who violated the prohibition.[11] The protests from Doge Giovanni Soranzo that Venice had no other livelihood than trade "in the total absence of vineyards and fields" fell on deaf ears.[12] The Venetian state was forced to accept the ban.

Nonetheless, there is considerable evidence that some individuals could not resist the temptation of seductive profits. In their wills Venetian merchants described in poignant dialect the pain of excommunication, and pleaded to be forgiven for carrying on their business activities in defiance of papal opposition.[13] Some merchants found a compromise solution by trading through Crete and Cyprus. Eventually Pope John XXII agreed to allow shipping to resume by means of the purchase of special licenses, and he finally lifted the ban in 1344.[14] Although the new treaty between Venice and the Mamluk sultan in 1345 claimed that no Venetian ship had docked in Alexandria for 23 years, this probably referred only to official convoys.[15]

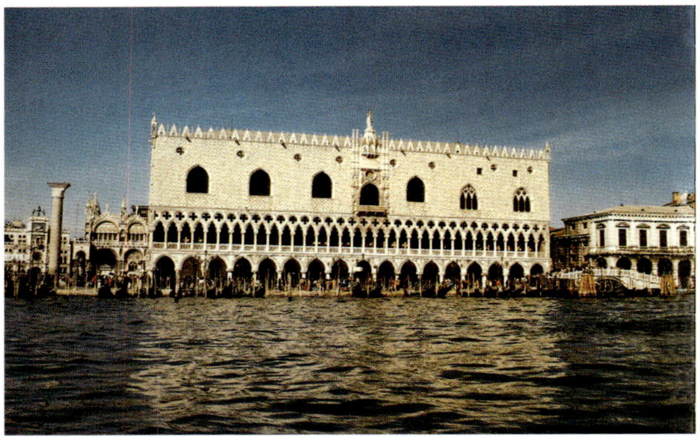

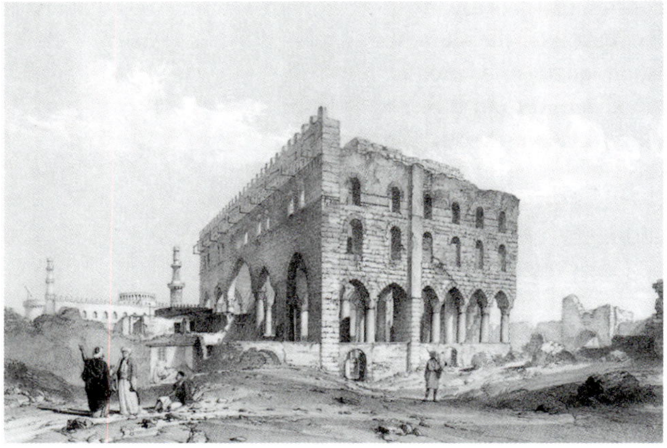

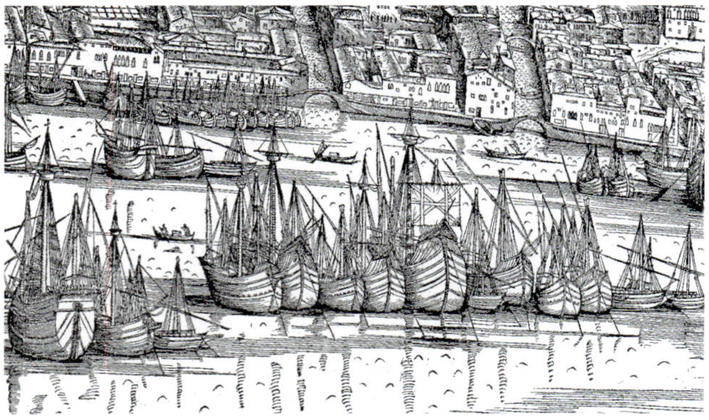

fig. 1. Doge's Palace, Venice

fig. 2. Sultan al-Nasir Muhammad's audience hall (Iwan al-Kabir) in Cairo, 1333–34

fig. 3. Detail of the bird's-eye view of Venice engraved by Jacopo de' Barbari in 1500, showing the large hulls of the cogs

This phase of papal interference in Venetian trade coincided with the long third reign of Sultan al-Nasir Muhammad (1310–41). Those merchants who continued to visit Egypt during the ban must have been astonished by the ambitious architectural patronage of the Mamluk ruler.[16] The early part of his reign, when he was still very young, had been twice interrupted by rivals, but already in the first two phases (1293–94 and 1299–1310) he had founded a splendid madrasa-mosque complex in Cairo, re-erecting a Crusader Gothic portal from a church in Acre to form the entrance.[17] Similarly, in a bold assertion of rulership, spoils from earlier Ptolemaic, Roman, and Christian buildings were incorporated into the stately mosque that he founded in the citadel of Cairo.[18] Local decorative tradition was enriched by the import of craftsmen from Persia. We can only guess at the splendour of al-Nasir Muhammad's magnificent domed palace in the citadel, destroyed in the 19th century.[19]

It was in the very year of the death of Sultan al-Nasir Muhammad that the Venetians began the rebuilding of the Doge's Palace, the center of Republican administration, overlooking the quay where the Levantine galleys moored. As the symbol of the Venetian mercantile nobility, the new Doge's Palace unashamedly vaunted the Oriental interests of the ruling class (fig. 1).[20] Its rooftop crenellations had no military use, but instead adopted a form of decorative cresting reminiscent of Mamluk mosques, madrasas, khans, and funerary complexes. With its spacious arcade at the base, topped by more solid, crenellated walls above, the new Doge's Palace evoked the typology of the imposing audience hall of Sultan al-Nasir Muhammad in Cairo, the Iwan al-Kabir, built in 1333–34 (fig. 2). Meanwhile the diaper pattern on the upper walls recalled Seljuq lozenge-design brickwork decoration, perpetuated in the delicate tilework of the Il-khanid rulers of Iraq and Iran, where Venetians had continued to trade avidly during the period of the papal ban.[21]

The Black Death of 1348 had a devastating impact on both Venice and the ports of the Levant. Alexandria had been shrinking ever since the late Antique period, and the shift of Mamluk power and investment inland had only exacerbated this process. Whereas Venice revived relatively quickly after the great plague, Alexandria's *dar-al-tiraz,* the state-run textile industry along the Nile Delta, collapsed and the city never recovered its former size.[22] The port continued to function, but the compelling dominance of Cairo left Alexandria as a marginal outpost. The coastal ports of Syria, too, suffered from underinvestment, but for different reasons. After the final expulsion of the Crusaders, the Mamluks had deliberately damaged their harbors to forestall future Christian invasions, and cities such as Tyre and Ascalon never recovered, although both Acre and Beirut continued to remain active in international trade.[23]

The unsuccessful "Crusade" by King Peter of Cyprus, who invaded Egypt in 1365, had a knock-on effect on all European traders, but as usual the diplomatic efforts of the Venetians allowed the rapid resumption of their privileges in Mamluk ports.[24] The Alexandria galley convoys resumed in 1370, and five years later a galley route to Beirut was established. From then on, regular convoys to both Alexandria and Beirut allowed the establishment of sustained and almost uninterrupted trade between Venice and the Mamluks, a link that was highly valued by both parties. As well as the consulate in Alexandria, with its two *fondaci,* reopened in 1302, the consulate in Damascus was established in 1375, and subsidiary consulates existed on and off in all the major market-towns of Syria (including Beirut, Acre, Tripoli, Hama, and Ramla).

It was during the last quarter of the 14th century, after the War of Chioggia in 1378–81, that the Venetians finally achieved supremacy in Mediterranean trade over their main rivals, the Genoese. As well as the regular armed galley convoys, the Venetians began to make increasing use of cogs or roundships, the huge round-bellied sailing ships that figure so prominently in Jacopo de' Barbari's bird's-eye view map of Venice (fig. 3). Cogs were ideal for transporting bulk cargoes of lesser value, such as cotton, grain and sugar. Meanwhile, the gradual decline in industrial investment in Mamluk lands allowed European manufactured goods to find a ready market in Egypt and Syria. Technological advances in the West, especially in the use of waterpower, made products such as paper and textiles highly competitive in the Mamluk market.[25] As well as exporting huge quantities of cloth from other parts of Europe, the Venetians themselves acquired expertise in soap and sugar production and, even more profitably, in the manufacture of luxury textiles and glassware (cat. 151, p. 78).

Nevertheless, the period of the Burji or Circassian Mamluks from 1382 onwards was not always easy for Venetian traders. The incursions of Timur (Tamerlaine) into Syria in 1400 and 1401 left a trail of destruction in both Aleppo and Damascus, two of their most important mercantile destinations. The reign of Sultan Barsbay (1422–38), in particular, vexed the merchants of Venice, for he imposed a monopoly on the sale of pepper, supplanting the Karimi middlemen.[26] This measure dramatically raised the price of pepper, one of the staple commodities of Venetian trade. Official documents complain of extortion and ill-treatment by Mamluk officials. To make matters worse, Sultan Barsbay expelled the Franciscans from their guardianship of the sacred sites of Jerusalem and closed the holy places to Christian pilgrims. Meanwhile in Venice, however, under Doge Francesco Foscari (1423–57) expansion on to the mainland continued to underpin Venetian strength. The rebuilding of the Doge's Palace was extended along the Piazzetta frontage, confidently retaining the exotic, Orientalizing decoration and openness of the original Bacino wing. In 1438 a new ceremonial entrance known as the Porta della Carta was begun in a flamboyant Gothic

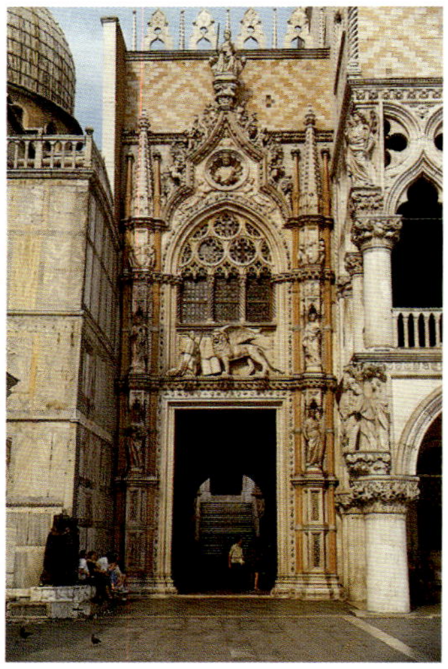

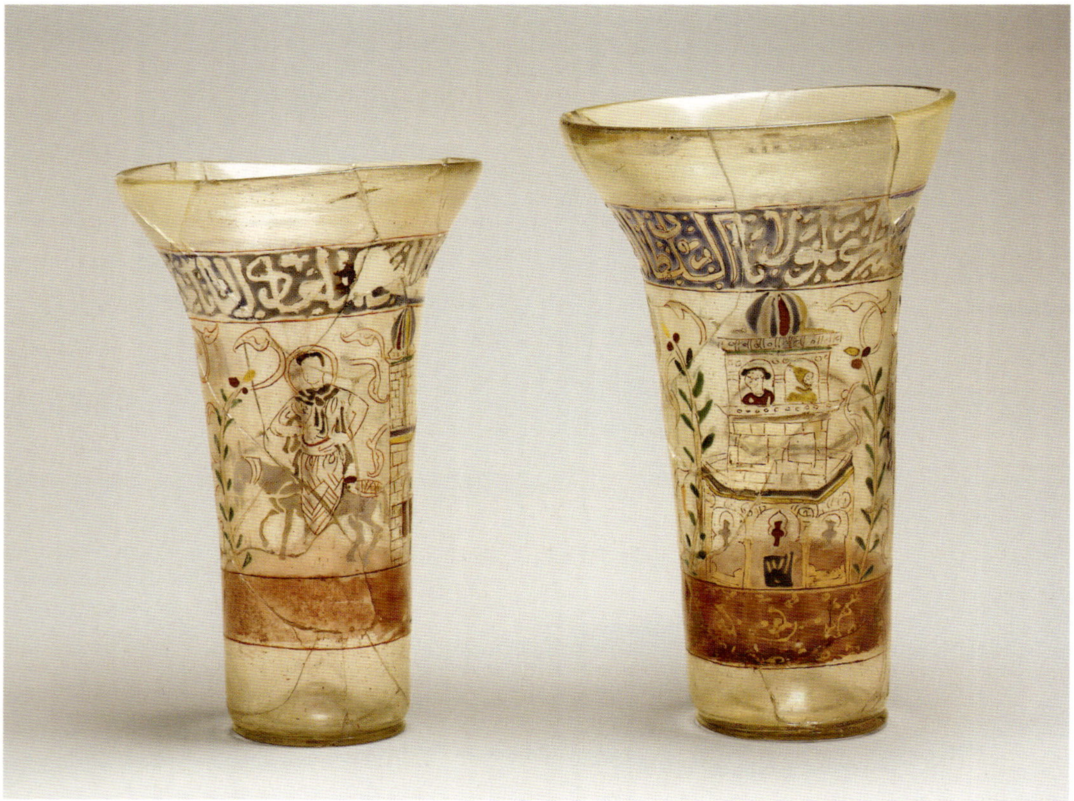

fig. 4. Porta della Carta, Doge's Palace, Venice

cat. 151. *Two beakers*
Syria, ca. 1260
The Walters Art Museum, Baltimore

style, set within a tall narrow cleft like the ornate portals of great Mamluk mosque complexes (fig. 4). The insertion of the main entrance in a recess suggests that Venetians, who knew the eastern Mediterranean, would have recognized the affinity.

After the death of Barsbay in 1438, intensive diplomatic activity resulted in a new set of trading privileges between Venice and the Mamluks. The treaty, signed in 1442, makes clear the special position of Venetian traders in Egypt and Syria.[27] They were allowed to wear local dress and to ride on horseback rather than on mules or camels when traveling overland; and in both Damascus and Amman they were free to live anywhere in the city, rather than being confined to the *fondaco.* Competition from the Genoese was by now mainly confined to the Black Sea trade. By this time, the papacy had ceased to interfere, although the export of arms to the Islamic world was still prohibited. The Mamluks and Venetians were united not only by their common trading interests, but also by the rise of Ottoman power, which threatened the territories of both parties. During the long sultanate of Qa'itbey (1468–96) both Venice and the Mamluks were involved in wars with the Ottomans, the Venetians at sea (1463–79) and the Mamluks on land (1485–91). In 1489 the Venetians took over Cyprus when Queen Caterina Cornaro, Venetian widow of the last king of the island, agreed to hand over the territory to her home country. Nevertheless, a duty to the Mamluk overlords was still payable, much of it delivered in the form of luxury cloth.[28] Like Crete and Corfu, Cyprus played a major role in securing the safety of the maritime trade routes.

It was during the sultanate of Qa'itbey that one of the most remarkable landmarks of Egypt, the great Pharos of Alexandria, was finally obliterated in order to build a fortress on the site (fig. 5). Earlier Mamluk rulers had shown little interest in fortifying the coastline—the damage resulting from the "scorched earth" policy at the end of the Crusades had never been reversed. The old lighthouse, one of the Seven Wonders of the Ancient World, had been deteriorating through neglect and periodic mutilation under Islamic rule, but portolan (mariners') guides indicate that it was still a crucial point of orientation for Venetian sailors entering the port of Alexandria.[29] In the erection of Qa'itbey's new fortress from 1477 to 1480, much of the gleaming white stone from the old Pharos was reused. Venetian visitors continued to refer to this as the "Farion" (or great lighthouse), because of the familiarity of the site and the imposing dimensions of the fort. The Venetian response to the destruction of a celebrated monument of Antiquity was to recreate the Pharos of Alexandria on Venetian soil between 1482 and 1488, when the campanile of the cathedral of Venice, San Pietro di Castello, was re-clad in snow-white masonry, emulating the form of the famous Hellenistic lighthouse.[30] In 1482, the architect Mauro Codussi traveled in person to the quarries in Istria to select the best quality stone for this project. Although this belltower lost its domed top storey in the late 17th century, it still forms a prominent beacon for ships entering the lagoon (fig. 6).

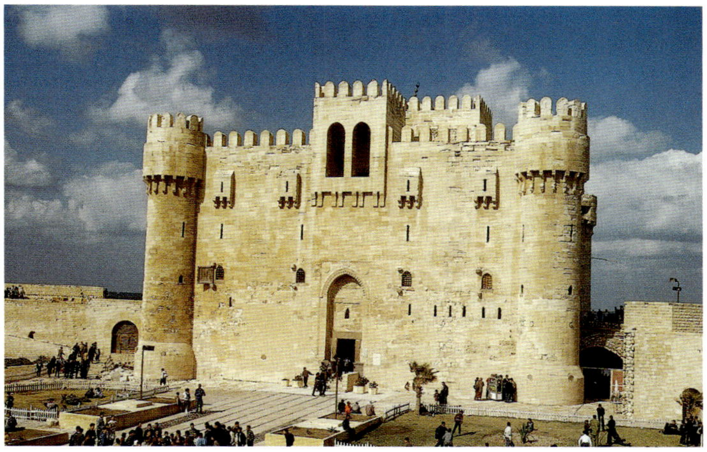

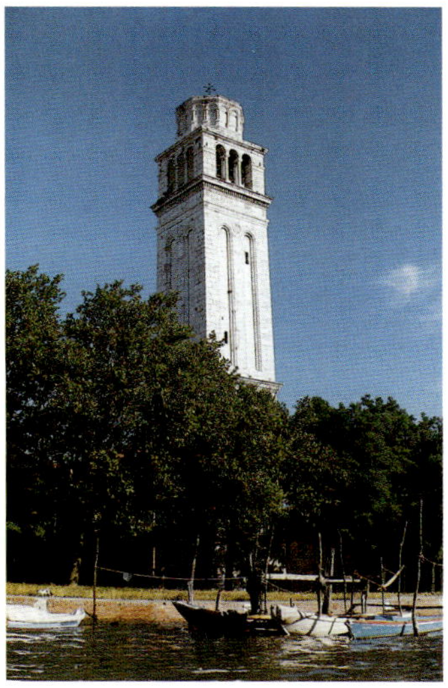

By the end of the 15th century, trade with the Mamluks amounted to 45% of all Venetian investment in overseas commerce.[31] The main sailings of the official galley convoys to Alexandria and Beirut in late summer were regulated by the Venetian state, to allow an official trade fair or *mudda* to take place on the return of the laden ships in October.[32] A second, less important trade fair in July followed the spring sailings. During the 15th century a dazzling array of goods was transported in both directions.[33] Venetians were crucial providers of metals, especially gold, silver, copper, tin, lead, and mercury, which were in short supply in Egypt and Syria.[34] Some of the gold and silver was reexported from Mamluk territories further east to India and the Far East. Other valuable exports included textiles (woolens and linens from elsewhere in Europe and luxury silks and velvets made in Venice) (cat. 79, p. 80) a variety of furs from northern and Eastern Europe, Baltic amber, and coral acquired from the shores of Italy and North Africa. Among the manufactured goods, hats play a surprisingly important role, in addition to glass, soap, and paper.[35] Venetian hat manufacture seems to have boomed towards the end of the 15th century, and it is tempting to suppose that the Mamluk passion for flamboyant headgear may have stimulated export production in the millinery workshops of Venice. In return the Alexandria and Beirut galleys imported a huge range of spices (dominated by pepper), pigments, medicinal drugs, pearls, precious stones, and damasks.

fig. 5. Qa'itbey's fortress in Alexandria, 1477–80

fig. 6. Campanile of San Pietro di Castello, re-clad in stone by Mario Codussi, 1482–88

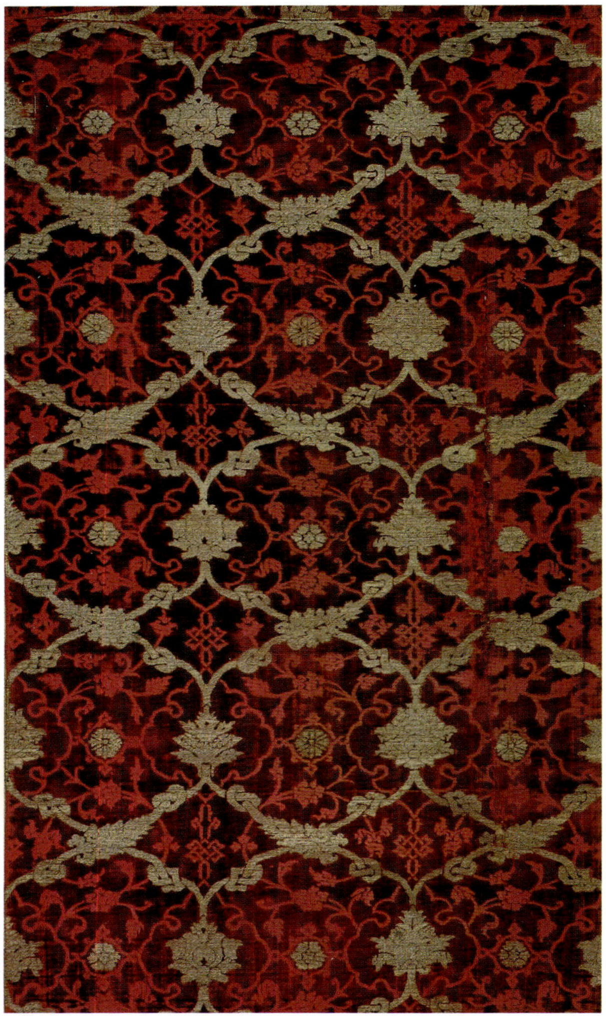

cat. 79. *Loom-width piece of velvet*
Probably Bursa, Turkey, possibly Venice, late 15th century
The Metropolitan Museum of Art, New York

It was during the reign of Sultan Qansuh al-Ghuri (1501–16) that the Fontego dei Tedeschi, headquarters of the German merchant colony in Venice, was destroyed by fire in 1505. Recognizing the crucial role of the Germans as purchasers of Venice's Oriental merchandise, the state decided to rebuild the *fondaco* immediately on the same site. In a rationalization of the earlier building on the site—a piecemeal agglomeration of three courtyards—the new *fondaco,* erected from 1505 through 1508, seems to reflect the scale and layout of some of the recent *khan*s and *wikala*s of Cairo. These were trading posts consisting of warehousing and lodgings for traveling merchants—the urban equivalent of the *caravanserai.*[36] In particular, the newly completed *wikala* of al-Ghuri in Cairo (1504–5), with its spacious cistern court surrounded by corridors and its lodgings opening outwards on to the street, offered a fitting prototype (fig. 7).

The rule of Sultan Qansuh al-Ghuri was a trying time for Mamluks and Venetians alike, for both were threatened on their land frontiers. In 1509 the forces of the League of Cambrai, a formidable alliance of European powers eager to stop Venice's territorial expansion, invaded the Veneto and very nearly obliterated Venetian hegemony. In the long and expensive war that ensued, Venice managed to recover most of the *terra firma,* but the economic and political stress was considerable. Meanwhile the Mamluks were under pressure from the Safavids on the east and the Ottomans in the north. Venetian diplomacy was tested to its limits. In 1511 the Venetian consul in Damascus, Pietro Zen, was accused by the Mamluks of having contacts with the Persian rulers.[37] This accusation was justified, for the Venetians recognized the Safavids as potential allies in the face of relentless Ottoman expansion (cat. 65). Only a few years later, the Ottomans overran Syria in 1516 and Egypt in 1517, ending two and a half centuries of Mamluk rule.

Trade, Diplomacy, and Pilgrimage

Three main activities drew Venetian travelers to Mamluk lands: trade, diplomacy, and pilgrimage. Each of these occupations proved a highly effective channel of cultural transfer, for all were associated with the transport of both material goods and information. The motivation of the journey added value and significance to each object or letter carried, while the place and circumstances of the acquisition attached an individual narrative to every article or consignment. Thus, to a greater or lesser extent, each acquisition transmitted a range of information and experience about life in the Eastern Mediterranean back to Venice.

Overseas merchants spoke the language of trade: that of supply and demand, prices, quality, weights and measures, and barter. The shared mercantile mentality easily crossed boundaries of religious belief, language, and race. Merchants had to be tough in their negotiations, but they understood each other's points of view. Although interpreters were available, many Venetian merchants learned Arabic and bookkeeping during periods spent in the East in their youth, to avoid the risk of misunderstanding and, even worse, deception. Venetian commercial documents reveal many instances of direct contact with Muslim traders, and even of deals drawn up in the houses of local inhabitants.[38] Indeed, at times local merchants were almost as aggravated by the interference of Mamluk officials as were the visiting Venetians.

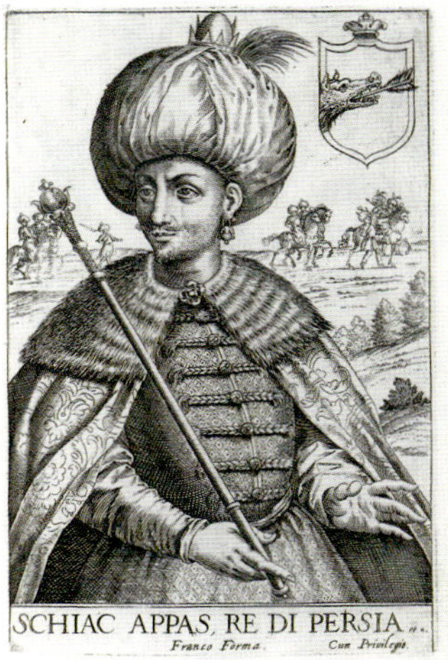

The inventories of Venetians who died overseas reveal, on the one hand, a desire to replicate the values and entertainments of life at home, and on the other a chameleon-like ability to adapt to local customs and culture. In 1436 one merchant in Damascus left several musical instruments, including a harpsichord, a viola da gamba in a painted case, and a lute, while among his books was a songbook with all the sonnets of Petrarch on parchment.[39] The list of his pieces of furniture mentioned a wardrobe from Padua painted in chiaroscuro for storing cloth. Another Venetian who died in Damascus in 1455 had a roasting spit from Germany operated by counterweights, symbolic of his broad international horizons.[40] Most inventories included Christian altarpieces and religious books. At the same time, Venetian residents acquired locally made metalwork, especially items for use in their offices or studies, such as inkwells, pen boxes, candlesticks, pomanders, and bells, not to mention useful tools such as scales, rulers, scissors, and padlocks (cat. 97, p. 82).[41] Mamluk carpets, characterized by their rich red, green, and blue coloring, were a favorite acquisition, usually to be placed on tables or sideboards.[42] As the trading treaty renegotiated with the Mamluks in 1442 allowed Venetians to dress in Arab-style dress, several of the overseas residents owned items of local clothing including long underdrawers, an example of which has survived in Brussels (fig. 8, p. 82).

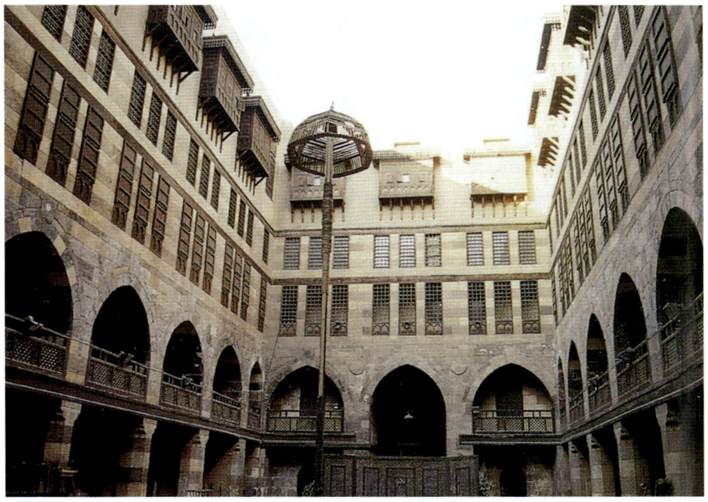

cat. 65. Giacomo Franco
"Schiac Appas, Re di Persia"
("Shah 'Abbas, King of Persia")
Venice, 1550–1620
The Metropolitan Museum of Art, New York

fig. 7. *Wikala* of al-Ghuri, Cairo

The idea that numerous Muslim merchants themselves frequented the markets of the Rialto, and that Muslim craftsmen practiced their trade in Venice, is a 19th-century myth, fostered by the conspicuous appearance of Orientals in narrative paintings of around 1500.[43] In reality, Venetian traders had a virtual monopoly in the sale of Oriental products at the Rialto. The so-called Fondaco dei Persiani, demolished in 1908, had probably been an inn for German merchants and pilgrims, while the Casa dei Mori in Cannaregio was not a Muslim trading base but the house of a Venetian spice merchant.[44] The Fondaco dei Turchi was not finally established until 1621.[45] No documentary evidence has yet been found of any Muslim craftsmen active in Venice in the Mamluk period—even the Dalmatian and Albanian residents were

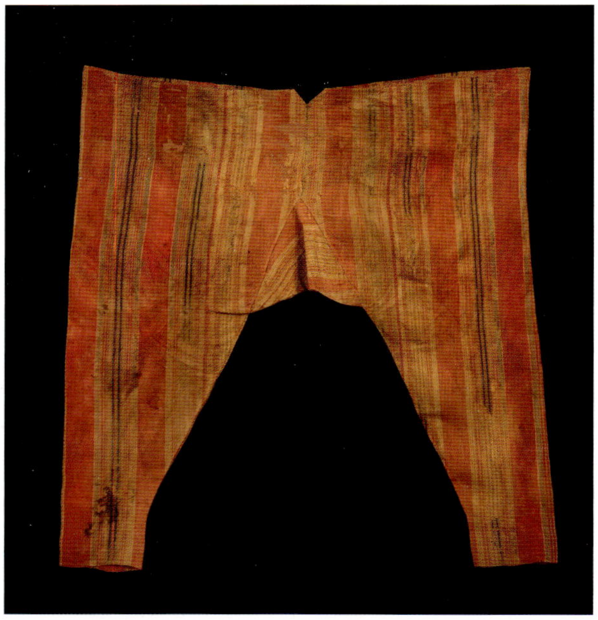

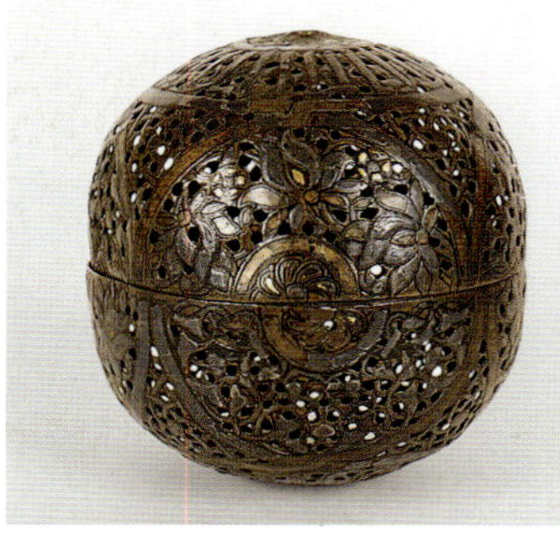

fig. 8. Mamluk underdrawers, 15th century. Musées Royaux d'Art et d'Histoire, Brussels

cat. 97. *Incense burner*
Probably Egypt, first half of the 14th century
Museo Civico Correr, Venice

fig. 9. Vittore Carpaccio, *The Miracle of the True Cross on the Rialto Bridge*, 1494. Gallerie dell'Accademia, Venice

cat. 28. Giovanni Mansueti
St. Mark Baptizing Anianus
Venice, ca. 1518
Pinacoteca di Brera, Milan

Christians. The few Muslim visitors to Venice in the Mamluk period were official envoys, such as the Turkish Ambassador Lufti Bey and the Mamluk dragoman Taghribirdi, who traveled on Venetian ships and whose visits aroused intense curiosity, as we know from Sanudo's diaries.[46] The appearance of Orientals in the paintings of Gentile Bellini, Carpaccio, and Mansueti either indicated an Oriental locality or, in the case of Venetian scenes, recalled the exotic dress and demeanor of the official envoys (fig. 9; cat. 28). Some of the darker-skinned figures were slaves, brought back by merchants from their Eastern travels, but these were usually manumitted and given Christian names.[47]

Because of the need to lubricate the wheels of trade, the Venetian Republic's sophisticated diplomatic service enabled relations with the Mamluks to survive many a crisis. Consuls were appointed to serve in the principal "colonies" in Mamluk lands, while smaller trading bases had to make do with vice-consuls; consular presence overseas was essential to deal with urgent problems because of the time-lag imposed by the slow pace of seaborne communications. If, for example, one or more Venetians were detained by Mamluk officials in Alexandria, a letter could take three months to reach Venice. The consul's residence, usually in the Venetian *fondaco* in the overseas "colony," played an important part in the social life of visiting merchants—the well-appointed kitchen of Marino da Molin, consul in Damascus in 1453–57, suggests generous hospitality.[48] In contrast to the merchants, the consuls wore Venetian ceremonial robes to express the dignity of office.[49] In addition to the frequent dispatches, they had to write a full report or *relazione* on their return giving all details of the history, geography, and customs of the locality.

Whenever a particular crisis arose, a special envoy or "orator" would be appointed to go east to negotiate directly with the sultan. One of the most celebrated Venetian diplomats, Giovanni Dario, whose various embassies took him to Constantinople, Egypt, and Persia, was not even a noble, but a *cittadino* or citizen, originally from Crete, who began his career in public service as a notary in the ducal chancery in Venice.[50] Yet as late as 1484 he still described himself in a letter to the doge as a *mercadante*, for like most diplomats he had gained his youthful experience of the *oltremare* through trade.[51] Dario's own palace in Venice, datable to the 1480s, was adorned with precious colored marbles, which he presumably acquired on a diplomatic mission or a trading voyage (fig. 10, p. 84).[52] Although these marbles were applied to the façade by Venetian masons in the manner of cosmatesque floor-paving, Dario may have tried to evoke the rich palaces of the East, such the palace of the amir Bashtaq in Cairo, where a similar design of small discs arranged in a circle appears.[53] It seems that Dario's palace on the Grand Canal was recognized by the Republic as having Oriental qualities, for on three occasions in 1515 and 1516, envoys of the Ottoman sultan were housed there while on diplomatic missions to Venice.[54]

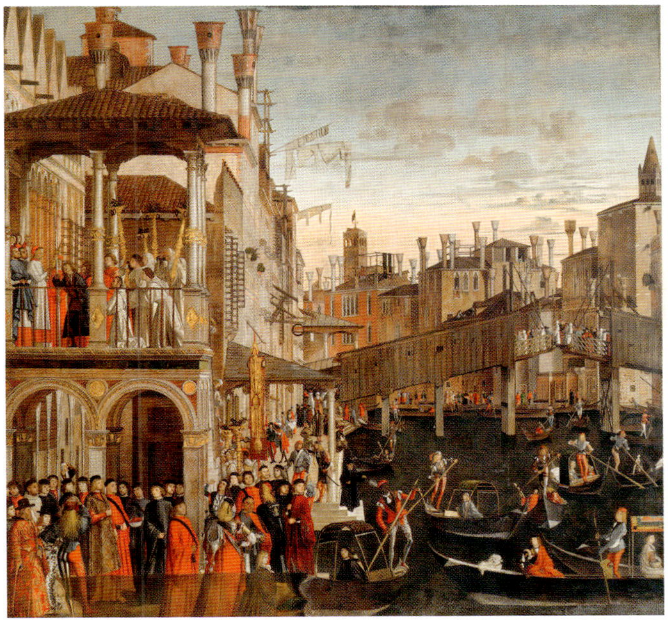

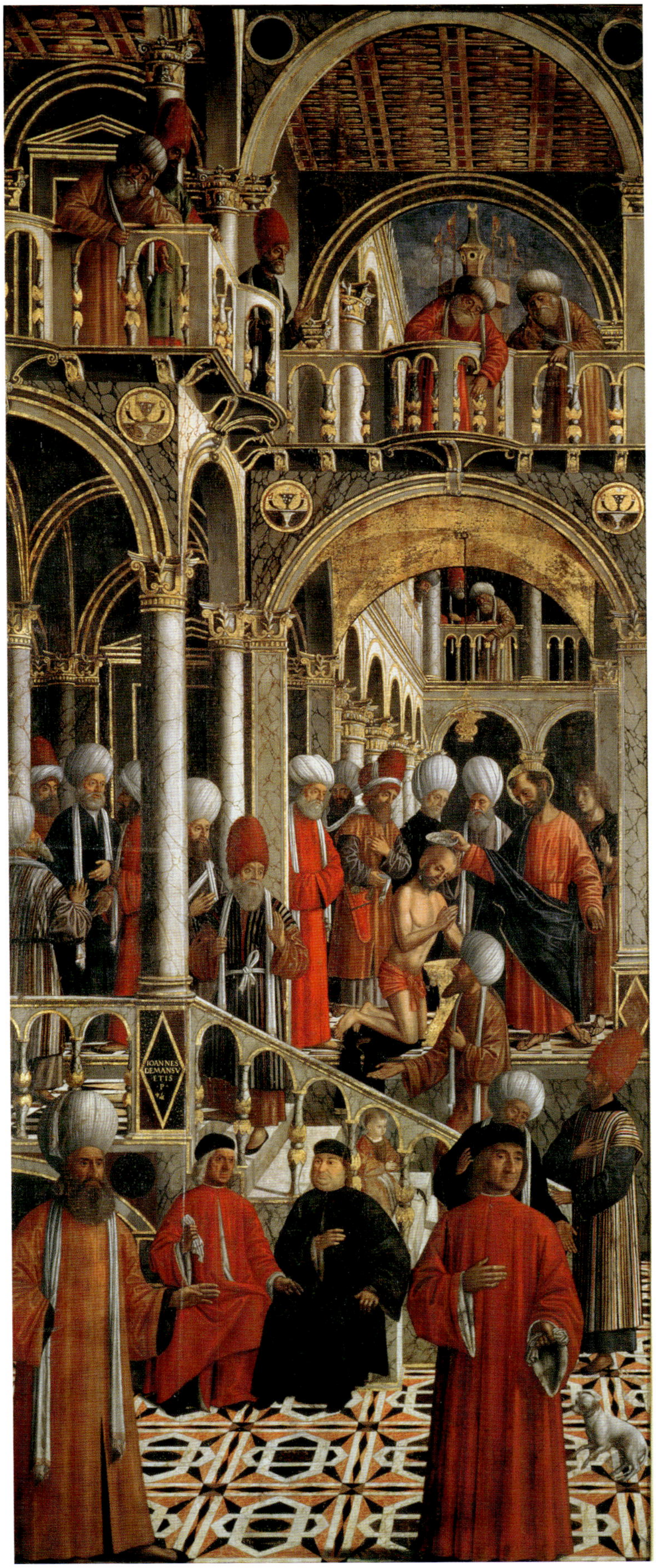
IOANNES
DEMANSV
ETIS
·P·

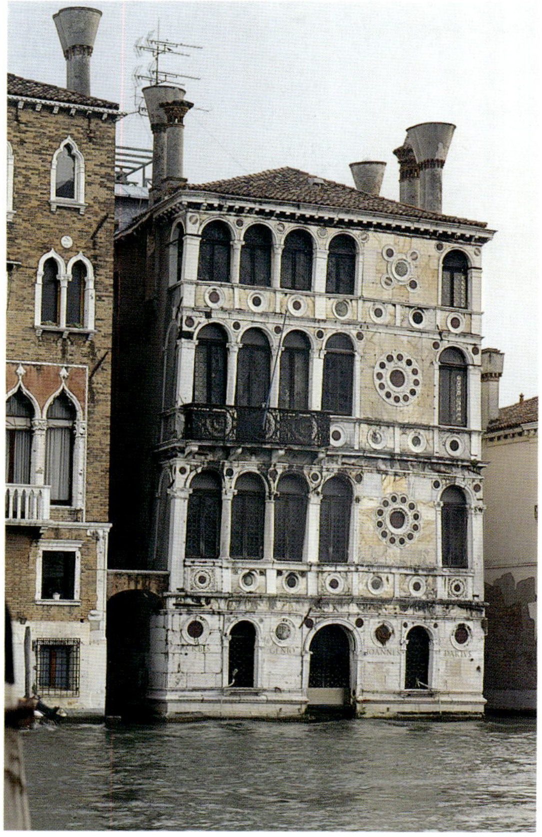

fig. 10. Giovanni Dario's palace, Venice

Reports of diplomatic visits highlight the importance of display, ritual, and gift exchange. For example, in 1502 the Venetian envoy Benedetto Sanudo ceremonially presented the amir in Alexandria with various sorts of fine cloth and some cheese, Parmesan-style cheeses being among the most valued diplomatic gifts.[55] In Cairo, Sanudo's official gifts to the sultan included luxury textiles, furs, and yet more cheese, and in return he received chickens, sweetmeats, and watermelon.[56] At the climax of his visit he was ceremonially robed in a gown of silk woven with gold thread and lined with ermine, "and with this we returned home in triumph."[57] The gifts from the sultan for the doge included twenty pieces of porcelain of various sizes.

The most spectacular record of the arrival of a Venetian diplomat in Mamluk lands is the anonymous painting *The Reception of the Venetian Ambassadors in Damascus,* now in the Louvre (cat. 29). Recent restoration of this painting has revealed a date of 1511.[58] If this date refers to the event depicted, it may represent the ceremonial welcome of Consul Nicolò Malipiero, who succeeded the unlucky Pietro Zen, detained by the sultan in Cairo because of his suspected contacts with the Safavids, as already mentioned. The diarist Marin Sanudo records that Malipiero had already reached Cyprus by August 1511, but his party was delayed by an epidemic on board ship, which caused the death of the chaplain, the barber, and several others. [59] Malipiero's letter (undated) describing the details of his entry into Damascus was eventually received in Venice on February 15, 1512 (still 1511 in the Venetian calendar).[60] Alternatively, it has been suggested that the ambassador shown arriving in Damascus is none other than Pietro Zen himself, and that the picture responds to the events of 1511, although Zen himself was in Cairo throughout that year.[61]

In 1512, Domenico Trevisan was sent on a special mission to Sultan Qansuh al-Ghuri in Cairo, to settle the "Zen affair" as well as disputes over the price of pepper and access to the pilgrim sites. Accounts of his visit to Egypt highlight the ways in which each nation tried to impress the other. In Alexandria Trevisan was ceremonially welcomed by the Mamluk amir, accompanied by the Mamluk cavalry in splendid livery, and taken to the amir's palace for an exchange of letters and civilities, before going to his own lodgings (cat. 51, p. 87).[62] During the voyage up the Nile from Rosetta to Cairo, the Venetians themselves played fanfares of trumpets and drums as they passed each village, employing "instruments new to the moors and much appreciated by them," as Trevisan's letter to his brother proudly reported.[63] The musicians and liveried bowmen were provided by the Venetian colony in Alexandria to add luster to their distinguished representative. In Cairo, Domenico Trevisan was flattered to be housed in a magnificent palace, which had belonged to one of the former sultan's wives. He described his quarters as "extremely costly, all paved from corner to corner with marbles, porphyry, and serpentine, like the Church of San Marco, and much better carved than ours, with gilded ceilings and rich ornament *a la damaschina.*"[64] Some of the sultan's own tapestries had been hung

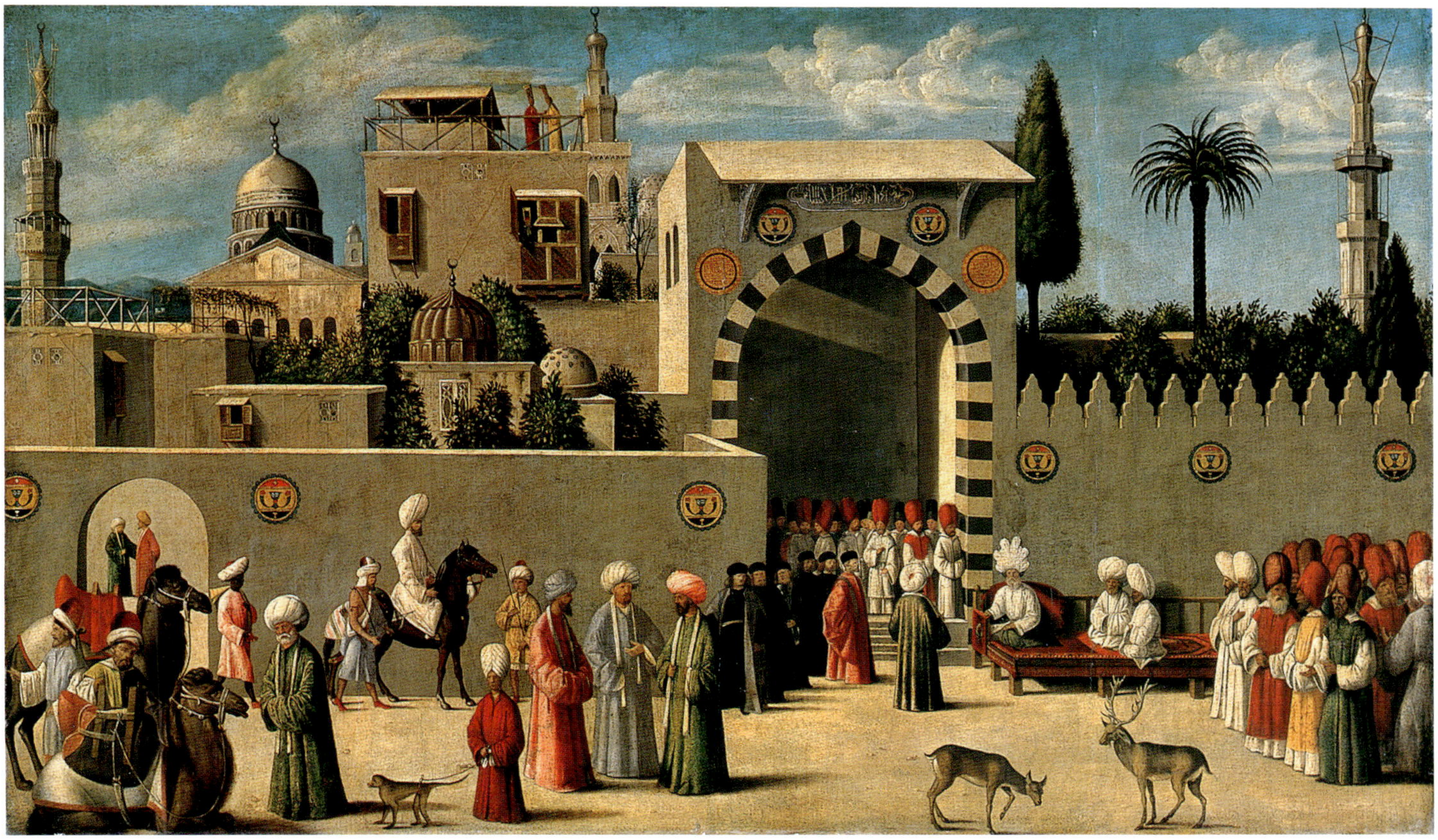

cat. 29. Anonymous Venetian
The Reception of the Venetian Ambassadors in Damascus
Venice, 1511
Musée du Louvre, Paris

on the walls: "a novelty in these lands and much appreciated by the moors."[65] The account of his official reception by the sultan in the citadel in Cairo described in detail the robes, carpets, rituals, and musical fanfares. A letter from an observer, Marc'Antonio Marcello, to his brother in Venice reported that the sultan had shown the envoy the unprecedented privilege of escorting him in person on horseback around his gardens, and eating and drinking with him.[66] Trevisan himself described the garden as *"un paradiso terrestre,"* but he was realistic about the toughness of the negotiations.[67]

Just as the Venetian fanfares aroused curiosity along the banks of the Nile, so, too, the Mamluk envoy, Taghribirdi, fascinated the local public during his ten-month stay in Venice in 1506–7.[68] After a Venetian ambassador, Alvise Sagundini, had unexpectedly died in Cairo in 1506, the Mamluk sultan sent his experienced dragoman on a mission to Venice to complete the interrupted negotations. Together with his retinue of 20, Taghribirdi was welcomed in Venice by scarlet robed senators and lodged in Ca' Pasqualigo on the Giudecca. While in Venice, he went about the city escorted by his pages and mace-bearers in military formation "with the usual pomp," as the Venetian diarist Marin Sanudo recorded.[69]

Just as diplomacy and trade were inextricably linked, so, too, pilgrimage was implicated in both. The Mamluk possession of the Christian pilgrimage sites in the Holy Land provided the sultans with additional bargaining power. In 1512 Ambassador Trevisan, for example, had to address the issue of the expulsion of the Franciscans from Jerusalem. Thanks to their usually amicable relations with the Mamluks, the Venetians were well placed to provide galleys for the transport of pilgrims from elsewhere in Europe to the Holy Land. Pilgrims could select their berth on one of the galleys moored in front of the Doge's Palace, and in the weeks before embarkation, the state provided official guides to show them the most sacred relics and churches of Venice, and to take them shopping.[70] By the late 15th century, departing pilgrims were personally embraced by the doge in a ceremony in the Doge's Palace. On arrival in Jaffa the pilgrims were provided with a guide to escort them to the sacred sites.

While in the East, Venetian merchants often took advantage of the proximity of the holy places to undertake personal devotional visits. Stefano di Bossina, who died in Damascus in 1455, had a wooden chest filled with items of pilgrim's luggage. He also owned pilgrim souvenirs in such quantity that he himself may have dealt in holy objects: these included six "ropes from Jerusalem for measuring the Holy Sepulchre"; sixteen "small crosses of mother-of-pearl of various sorts"; and eight "wooden rosaries from Jerusalem."[71] Nicolò de Ruzino, who died aboard the Beirut galley in 1457, had pilgrim girdles and *paternostri* from Jerusalem in his sea chest, as well as religious (and secular) reading matter, both in his deck luggage and in the hold.[72]

The relatively short overland journey from Damascus to Jerusalem encouraged Venetian merchants to make devotional visits and, of course, to earn indulgences. In 1514, Barbon Morosini stayed on longer in the Holy Land than the other merchants in his party, who returned to Damascus after two weeks.[73] Disguised as a Muslim, Morosini even succeeded in visiting the interior of al-Aqsa Mosque, which he believed to be the Temple of the Virgin. The sharing of holy sites impressed him greatly—at the Church of the Nativity in Bethlehem he found more Muslims than Christians, and remarked that they showed greater devotion (with tears and moans in abundance). Morosini's friendly contacts with Muslims allowed him to roam freely among the holy sites in search of spiritual consolation. His travel diary frequently includes detailed architectural descriptions, pointing out features such as rare marbles, mosaics, and leaded domes that would be meaningful to his compatriots at home: the *mihrab* (prayer niche) of the al-Aqsa Mosque, for instance, was surrounded by marbles, and inlays of serpentine and porphyry, and even perhaps jasper, although in the dark it was difficult to be sure—mosques could only be visited with "difficulty and great expense." Because the inclusion of architectural description in a pilgrim narrative heightened its significance, such personal accounts proved a highly effective channel of transmission of architectural information, just as diplomatic gifts and pilgrim souvenirs sent home to Venice carried specific associations of place, as well as political or religious nuances.

By the end of the Mamluk era, Venice was recognized as Europe's principal source of Oriental spices and luxury goods. For example, prominent wealthy Florentines, such as Filippo Strozzi in 1475–76, procured Chinese porcelain and Syrian blue-and-white ceramics in Venice (cat. 172, p. 88).[74] The Venetian Republic's long symbiosis with the Mamluk sultanates not only reflected the mercantile acumen and maritime adventurousness of its traders. The long-lasting partnership also demonstrated the value of constant diplomatic effort to smooth over difficulties—whether overt hostilities or misunderstandings. While Venetian merchants

cat. 51. Giovanni Mansueti (attr.)
Three Standing Mamluk Dignitaries
Venice, early 16th century
The Royal Collection, Windsor Castle

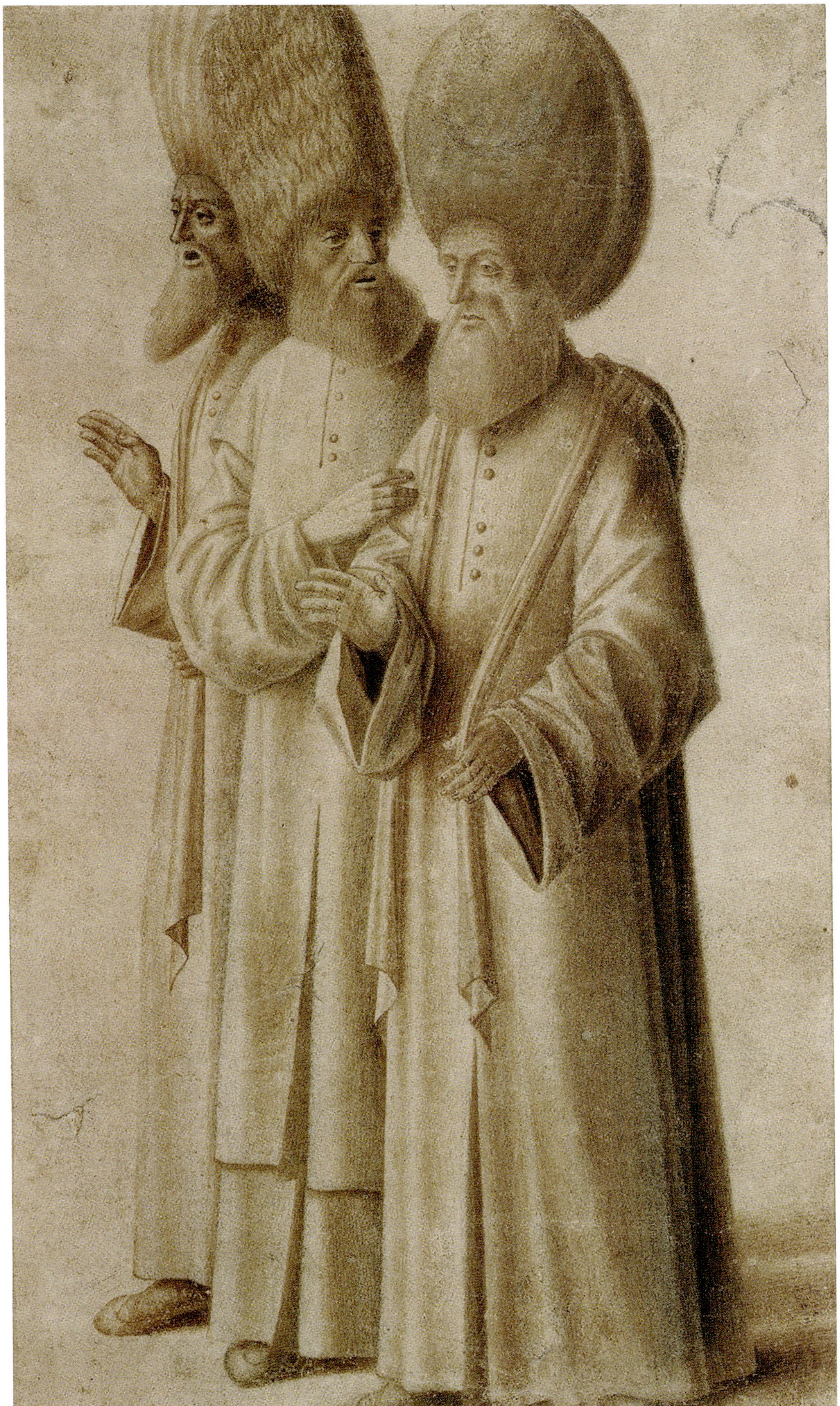

themselves, especially in Syria, interacted relatively informally with Muslim traders, diplomacy was highly ritualized. The detailed documentation that accompanied every diplomatic exchange, and the prominence of the official gifts that oiled the wheels of the trading treaties, assured the transmission of both written and visual information from East to West. Venetian diplomats could even exploit the Rialto's profusion of top-quality luxury goods for embassies elsewhere in Europe: in 1518 the Venetian ambassador in London, Sebastiano Giustiniani, suggested a gift of 12 to 15 Damascus carpets to Cardinal Wolsey, but evidently the gesture was considered inadequate, and two years later no fewer than 60 fine Oriental carpets were shipped to London.[75] Finally, we must remember that the cooperation of the Mamluks was essential to the success of the Venetian "package-tour" service to the biblical sites. Through pilgrimage, the distinctive character of Mamluk architecture, craftsmanship, and clothing gradually came to be associated in the Western mind not only with the marketplace, but also with the Holy Land, its treasures, and the dress of its inhabitants.

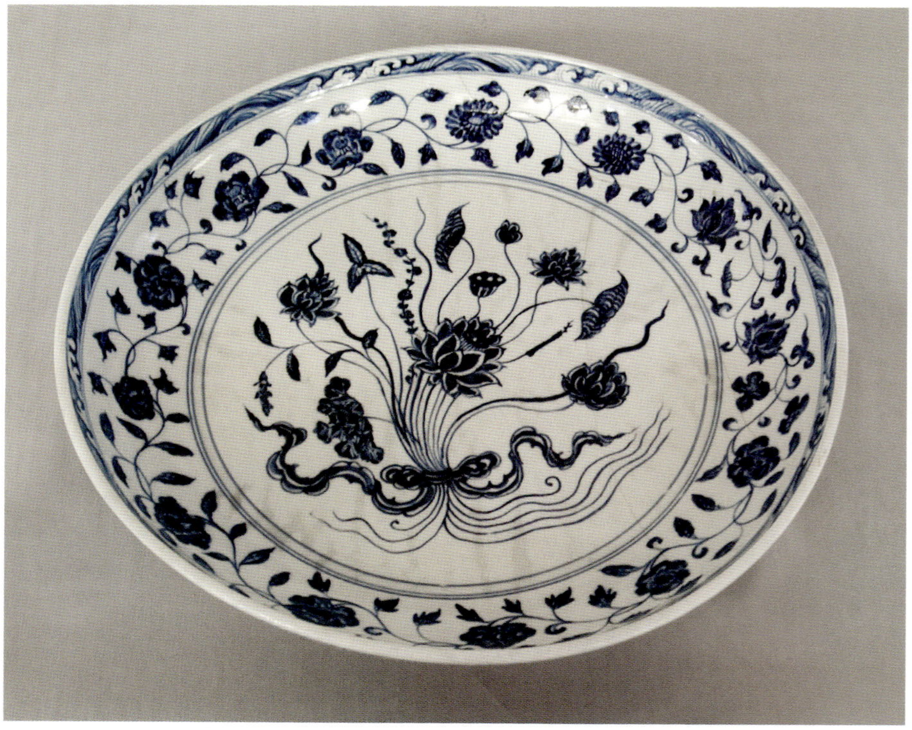

cat. 172. *Bowl*
China, early 15th century
Topkapı Sarayi Müzesi, Istanbul

Notes

1 For a general survey of this theme, see Gabrieli 1966.
2 Irwin 1986, pp. 1–23.
3 Stowasser 1984.
4 See, for example, Williams 1984; Blair and Bloom 1994; O'Kane 1996, pp. 70–96.
5 Ibrahim 1984.
6 For surveys of the state of research in Mamluk art and architecture, see Grabar 1984; Bloom 1999.
7 Raymond 1984; Williams 1984.
8 Ibn Battuta 1958, vol. 1, p. 41.
9 Irwin 1986, p. 73; Ashtor 1983, p. 26.
10 Ashtor 1983, pp. 12–29.
11 Ibid., pp. 44–53.
12 Thomas 1880, vol. 1, pp. 208–9, Doc. no. 105: *"civitas nostra . . . in mare constitua caret totaliter vineis atque campis."*
13 See Stussi 1965, pp. 87–88, 152.
14 Ashtor 1983, pp. 64–67.
15 Ashtor 1983, p. 45.
16 Williams 1984, pp. 35–38; Irwin 1986, p. 117.
17 Blair and Bloom 1994, p. 77.
18 Blair and Bloom 1994, p. 80.
19 Rabbat 1995, pp. 199–213 on the Qasr al-Ablaq erected in 1313–14, and pp. 244–63 on the Iwan al-Kabir built in 1333–34.
20 Howard 2000, pp. 175-80.
21 Howard 2000, p. 178.
22 Irwin 1986, p. 147; Mackie 1984, p. 127; Walker 2000, p. 169.
23 Fuess 2001.
24 Ashtor 1983, pp. 88–102; Irwin 1986, pp. 146–47.
25 Ashtor 1977, p. 319.
26 The Karimis were private merchant families who dominated imports from Asia through the Persian Gulf and the Red Sea.
27 Wansbrough 1965a.
28 Arbel 2004, p. 67.
29 Howard 2000, p. 98.
30 Ibid., p. 94.
31 Ashtor 1983, pp. 478–79.
32 Lane 1957b.
33 Arbel 2004.
34 Allan 1984, pp. 91–92; Rogers 1990, pp. 63–67.
35 Arbel 2004, p. 55.
36 Hillenbrand 1994, pp. 331–76, especially pp. 356–58; Constable 2001; Constable 2003, pp. 234–65.
37 Lucchetta 1968.
38 Howard 2000, pp. 36–42.
39 ASV, Cancelleria Inferiore, busta 122, Atti Tebaldo Manfredi, registro dated 1420–65, July 3, 1436, among goods belonging to Ruberto Morosini in the house of Piero da Molin, f. 16 sin., 24 sin. Dr. Susan Connell Wallington kindly drew these documents to my attention.
40 Bianchi and Howard 2003, p. 243.
41 Howard 2003, p. 147; Bianchi and Howard 2003, pp. 252–53.
42 ASV, Cancelleria Inferiore, busta 122, Atti Tebaldo Manfredi, registro dated 1420–65, July 3, 1436, f. 15 sin. mentions two *"Tappedi . . . da tavola"* and 16 *"da case"* including one for a credenza (sideboard). See also Walker 2000, 183–85; Howard 2003, pp. 148–50; Bianchi and Howard 2003, pp. 251–52.
43 For a survey of scholarship on this issue, see Auld 2004, pp. 36–43. See also Huth 1970; Auld 1989.
44 Concina 1997, pp. 118, 140, 240–44; Howard 2000, pp. 8–9, 126, 150–51, 223, n. 54, p. 238, n. 145.
45 Preto 1975, pp. 132–33; Tucci 1985, pp. 51–55; Concina 1997, pp. 219–40.
46 Zele 1989; Wansbrough 1963.
47 Howard 2000, pp. 34, 64.
48 Bianchi and Howard 2003, p. 244.
49 Howard 2000, p. 33.
50 Babinger 1961; Tiepolo 2002.
51 Babinger 1978, p. 78.
52 McAndrew 1980, pp. 215–21; Sgarbi 1984.
53 Howard 2000, pp. 153–54.
54 Sanudo 1879–1902, vol. 20, col. 543, August 21, 1515; vol. 22, col. 454–55, August 23, 1516; vol. 23, col. 361, December 23, 1516.
55 Biblioteca Marciana, Venice, cod. Marc. Its. XI, 66 (=6730), f. 268 v.
56 Biblioteca Marciana, Venice, cod. Marc. Its. XI, 66 (=6730), f. 269.
57 Biblioteca Marciana, Venice, cod. Marc. Its. XI, 66 (=6730), f. 269 v.: *"et con quella tornassemo a casa con triompho."*
58 Personal e-mail communication from Professor Jaynie Anderson, May 20, 2005.
59 Sanudo 1879–1902, vol. 12, col. 503, September 13, 1511, mentioning a letter from Cyprus dated August 10; vol. 13, col. 126, October 19, 1511, reporting letter of August 18.
60 Sanudo 1879–1902, vol. 13, col. 480, February 15, 1511 *more veneto* (=1512), reporting the receipt of Malipiero's letter: *"come è intrato consolo, et scrive di quelle particularità, ut in litteris."*
61 Campbell and Chong 2005, 22–23.
62 Thénaud 1884, pp. 171–73; Sanudo 1879–1902, vol. 14, cols. 500–501, July 21, 1512, quoting letter from Alexandria of April 16; cols. 551–52, August 4, 1512, quoting letter sent from Corfu on July 14, 1512.
63 Sanudo 1879–1902, vol. 15, cols. 194–99, October 12, 1512, quoting letter of July 1512: *"sono instrumenti novi a' mori e molto apreziati dal loro, sichè jubilavano per tuto."*
64 Sanudo 1879–1902, vol. 15, col. 194: *"La qual fabricha è de una spexa extrema, e tuta salizada in ogni canto di marmori, porfidi e serpentini, come è la chiexia de San Marcho, e molto meglio lavorati che è nostri, soffità tuta d'oro con lavori alla damaschina con intagli."* See also Thénaud 1884, p. 181.
65 Sanudo 1879–1902, vol. 15, col. 194: *"Fu adornata per l'orator con le sue tapezarie, che sono cosse nove in quelli paexi e molto apreziate da mori."*
66 Sanudo 1879–1902, vol. 15, col. 24, September 5, 1512, quoting letter of August 12, from Setia.
67 Sanudo 1879–1902, vol. 15, col. 197.
68 Wansbrough 1963.
69 Wansbrough 1963, pp. 515–16, quoting Sanudo 1879–1902, vol. 7, col. 24.
70 Howard 2000, pp. 192–95.
71 Bianchi and Howard 2003, pp. 248–49; Howard 2003, p. 151.
72 Bianchi and Howard 2003, pp. 244–45, 248–9; Howard 2003, pp. 147, 151.
73 Biblioteca Marciana, Venice, cod. Marc. It, Cl. VI, 6 (=5887), ff. 1–6 v., *Viaggio di Barbon Morosini nei luoghi di Terra Santa fatto l'anno 1514 e da lui stesso descritto.*
74 Spallanzani 1978, pp. 50–52; Mack 2002, pp. 104–105. On Syrian underglazed blue- and white-ware, see Jenkins 1984.
75 Erdmann 1966, pp. 529–32.

The Serenissima and the Sublime Porte: Art in the Art of Diplomacy 1453–1600

. . . e chi vol aver ben in queli paesi, bisogna donar
(Marin Sanudo, December 1516)[1]

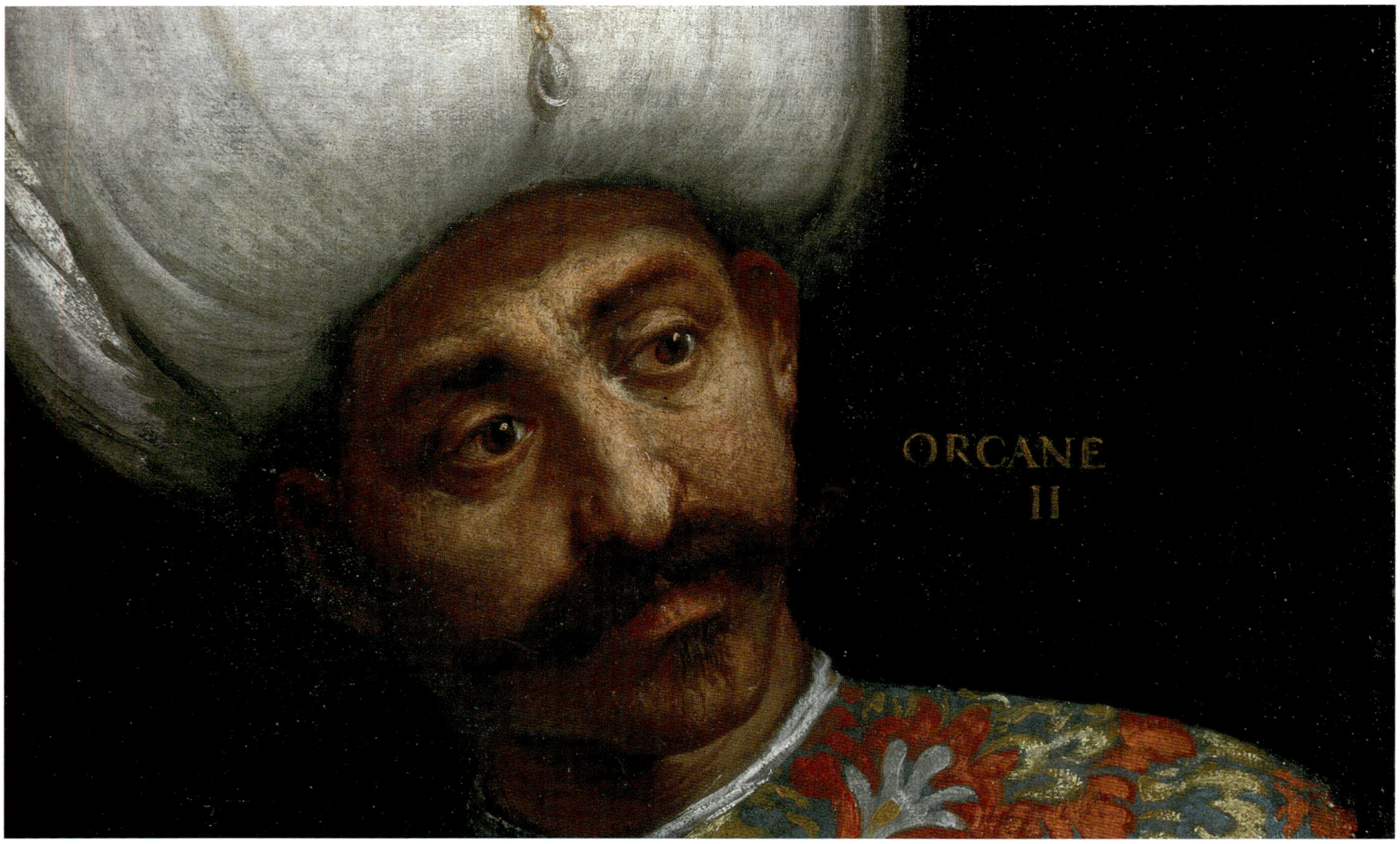

Julian Raby

In Pietro Aretino's comedy *La Cortigiana*, Flaminio, the servant of the lovelorn Parabolano, talks excitedly about Venice, its *vertuosi* and *galanti uomini* and relates how he passed by a band of painters and sculptors, and the artists who had gone to Istanbul with the exceptional Luigi Caorlini.[2] The revised version of the play was produced—with a strong pro-Venetian slant—in Venice in 1534. The reference would have been plain to Aretino's audience, for here were artists who two years earlier had gained celebrity for taking a treasure of bejeweled objects to the court of Venice's most feared enemy, the Grand Turk. Their risks were personal and financial, and, while this particular venture was a huge success, a similar one a few years later was a personal catastrophe for Luigi Caorlini.[3] The incidents reveal the dual nature of the Venetian image of the Grand Turk—danger and opportunity, threat and temptation.[4] That image was succinctly conveyed in 1571 in a woodcut by Nicolò Nelli that portrays an Ottoman as man of substance and—turned 180 degrees—as diabolic beast (fig. 1).[5]

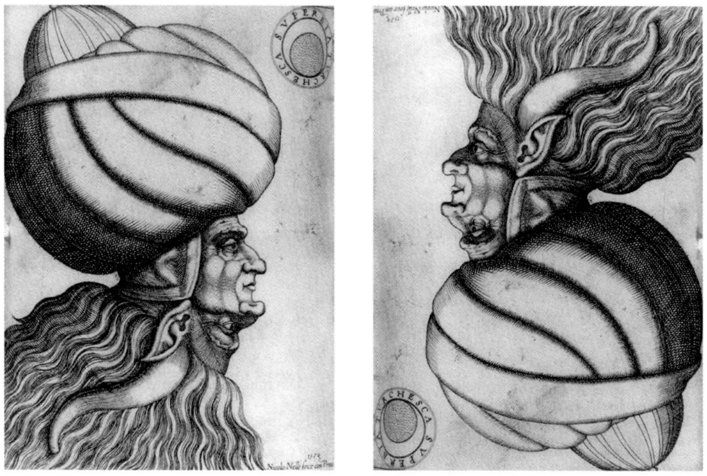

fig. 1. Nicolò Nelli, *Turkish Pride,* 1571. Biblioteca Comunale, Mantua

The Serenissima's relations with the Ottomans are often depicted as a ceaseless struggle, the Venetian Republic as the standard bearer of Christendom. Following the fall of Constantinople in 1453, the next 250 years were punctuated by major wars and periodic skirmishes between these rivals, but there were long periods of peaceful, if fraught, interaction. For some 70 years, from the battle of Zonchio in 1499 to the battle of Lepanto in 1571, the Venetians were obliged to accept Ottoman naval hegemony in the Mediterranean, a fact underlined by their defeat at the battle of Prevesa in 1538.[6] They even invited Ottoman forces into Italy after the battle of Agnadello in 1509, when the Venetians faced an alliance of all the major European powers, including the Holy Roman Empire. This was one invitation the Venetian nobility preferred to gloss over,[7] but Habsburg observers writing to Charles V accused the Venetians in 1526 of encouraging the Ottomans to invade Italy, so bitter had

cat. 35. Anonymous Painter from Verona or Follower of Veronese
Portraits from a Series of Ottoman Rulers
Venice, 1578 or later
Orhan (detail)

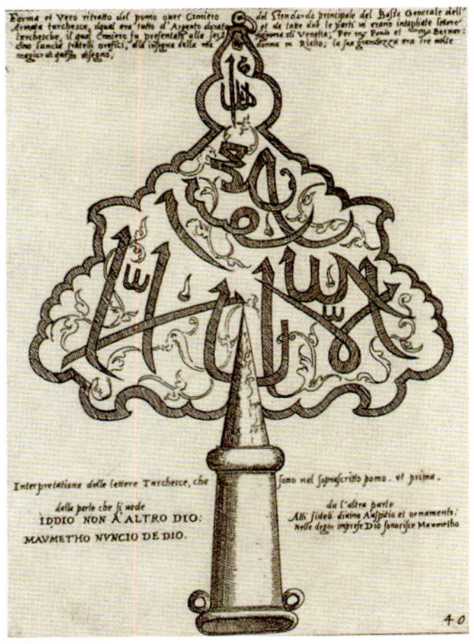

cat. 62. Giovanni Francesco Camocio
Finial of Turkish Standard Given to the Venetian Senate after Victory at Lepanto, 1571
Venice, after August 1574
Biblioteca Nazionale Marciana, Venice

their feud with the Holy Roman Empire become.[8] The following year, in the wake of the sack of Rome, the Habsburg ambassador in Venice urged that now was the time to strike a blow against a people that was a "constant accomplice of the Turks."[9]

In other instances the Venetians chose to congratulate—discreetly at least—the sultan on his victories, and withstood pressure to join an anti-Turkish league.[10] In 1571 they did join the Holy League, and the victory at Lepanto was interpreted as a major reversal of fortune, unleashing an unprecedented array of triumphalist imagery in Venice (cats. 34, 62).[11] But with the loss of Cyprus reality soon set in, and in 1573 the Venetians negotiated a humiliating accord with the Ottomans that initiated another stretch of 70 years of largely peaceful, if often discordant, accommodation.[12] For the rulers of Venice it may have been more advantageous, both at home and abroad, to project a picture of opposition, but both *realpolitik* and commercial necessity demanded a modus operandi of regular trade and established diplomacy.[13] And among both populace and patricians there was a grudging sense of awe at the Ottoman achievement.[14]

Venice lay at the threshold of Europe and the Ottoman Empire, and the Venetians were quick to reconfirm their "capitulations" with the Ottomans after the fall of Constantinople in 1453.[15] Capitulations gave the recipient the status of "favored trading nation," and the Venetians cemented their position in Istanbul by establishing a permanent diplomatic presence through their *bailo,* a presence reinforced by the periodic dispatch of ambassadors. The bailo combined the roles of consul and ambassador, and oversaw the Venetian merchants in Istanbul. So important was the Ottoman Empire to the Venetians that this was regarded as the most senior foreign posting in the Venetian diplomatic service, and was the highest paid.[16]

The system of capitulations, the difficulty of gaining access to Ottoman officials, and the problems of language all contributed to giving considerable scope to intermediaries—Greeks, Armenians, Jews, and Gasmoules (mixed Latins and Greeks).[17] Here Venice enjoyed advantage over most of its European rivals in that the city had large communities of each. Venice further benefited from its close connections with Ragusa.[18] Even in times of conflict, Venetians succeeded in maintaining a level of trade with the Ottomans by using Jewish or Ragusan front men.[19]

Venice further enjoyed the advantage that some of those who rose to the highest power at the Ottoman court were born in Venetian territories in Greece and the Aegean, and avowed, at least when it suited them, vestigial fondness for Venice. A case in point is the most powerful Grand Vizier of the first part of Süleyman the Magnificent's reign, Ibrahim Pasha, who was born in Parga on the coast of Epirus, opposite Corfu, and who claimed "he greatly loved the Signory of Venice as he had been born under its dominion."[20] The most famous case, as we shall see, was that of the "Venetian" wife of Selim II, and mother of Sultan Murad III, Nur Banu.[21]

cat. 34. Paolo Veronese
Allegory of the Battle of Lepanto
Venice, ca. 1571–72
Gallerie dell'Accademia, Venice

In addition, Venice was the only city in Europe that for several centuries received a regular stream of Ottoman dignitaries and visitors,[22] and Venice was the only city, with

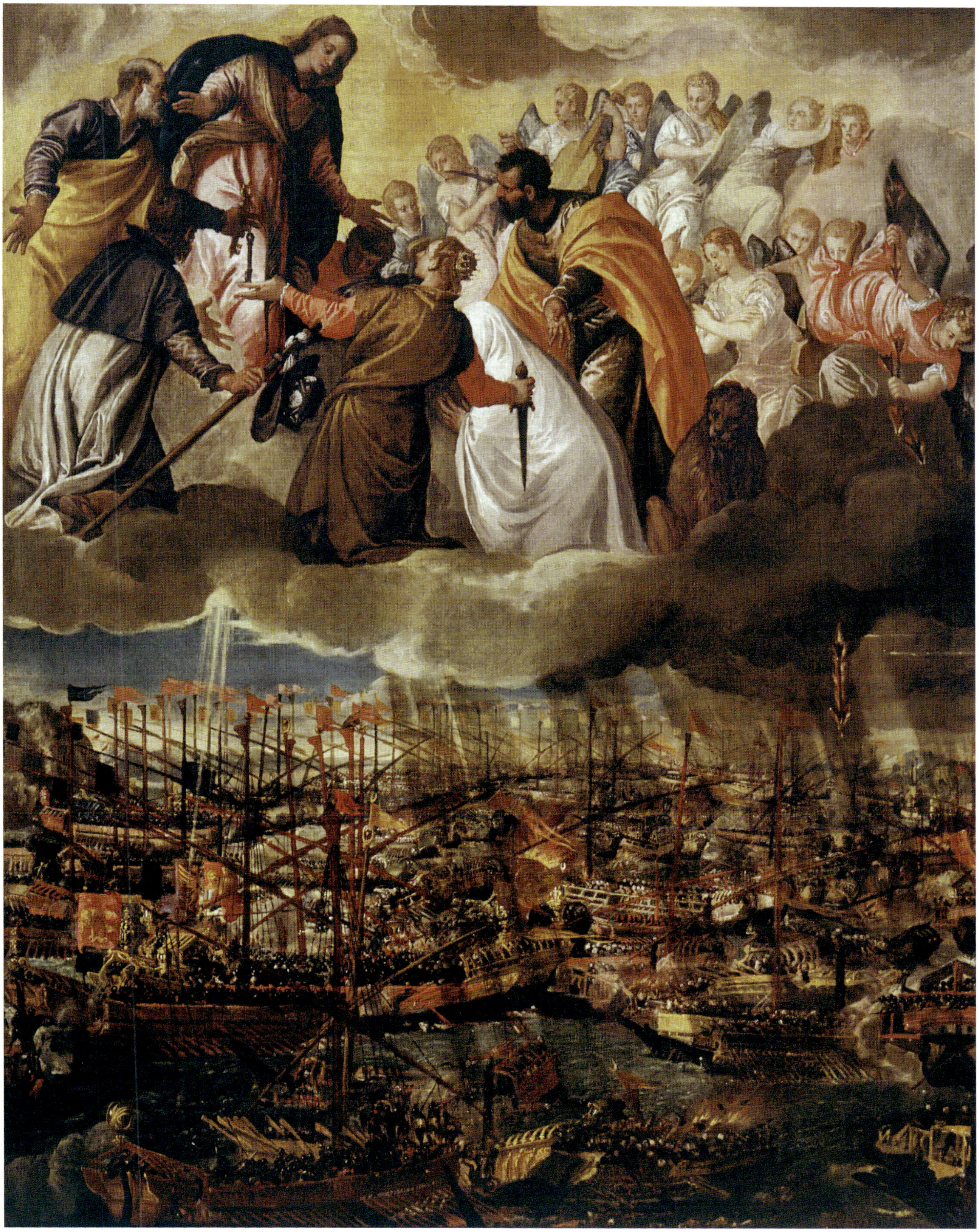

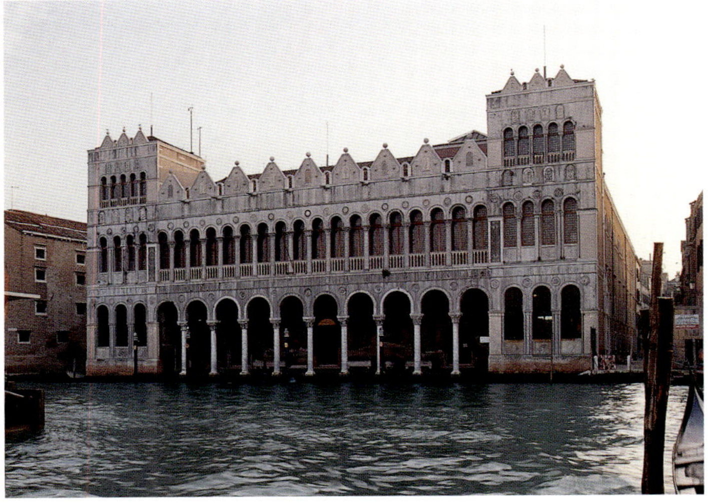

fig. 2. Fondaco dei Turchi, Venice

the exception of Ancona, where there was an established presence of Turkish merchants and Ottoman subjects from domains such as the Balkans.[23] There were a good number of Ottoman Muslim merchants in Venice at the outbreak of the war in 1571, and after the declaration of peace in 1573, their numbers rose, until it was finally decided in 1612, following increasing popular complaints, that it was disruptive for them to continue to occupy different residences, including houses of ill repute, as they had for most of the 16th century, and that the state should provide safe lodging for them, a decision which led to the purchase of the palace of the Dukes of Ferrara as the Fondaco dei Turchi in 1621 (fig. 2).[24]

Venice relied on the Ottomans for a supply of wheat,[25] as well as other primary commodities such as spices, raw silk, cotton, and leather and, from the Ottoman provinces of Syria and Egypt, calcined ashes for the Murano glass industry.[26] In return, it mostly exported finished goods, notably textiles, glass, soap, and paper. As Tommaso Garzoni wrote in 1585: "Venetian cloths, Flemish kerseys, tin, bronze, glass, paper, chests, mirrors and numberless other Venetian wares have an excellent sale in the various parts of the Levant."[27]

It was in the realm of luxury goods that Venice excelled, usurping production of what had been previously the province of Near Eastern workshops—fine silks, glass, and rock crystal. The development of Venetian luxury crafts reflected a broader shift that took place, over the course of several centuries, in the balance of trade between Europe and the Muslim world.[28] In Venice this shift received some acknowledgement in the adoption of Eastern forms and motifs, and to some extent technology.[29] The Venetians were also adept in the fields of cartography and horology, and here too they catered to Ottoman demand, even if in clocks and watches it was the Germans who were the principal suppliers.

Much of the demand was met through the normal channels of trade, through Venetian merchants resident in Pera, Ottoman merchants resident in Venice, and visiting Ottoman imperial merchants (*hassa tuccar*).[30] Much, however, was supplied through diplomatic channels, and in a variety of ways. This essay looks at the role of gift exchange in cementing Ottoman-Venetian relations, and the role of European and in particular Venetian luxury goods in feeding a cosmopolitan demand among the Ottoman elite.

*

On occasion, the Ottomans dispatched buying agents to Venice, and used diplomatic channels to assure the success of their missions. In 1546 the Beylerbeyi of Rumelia, Semiz Ali Pasha, wrote to Doge Francesco Donato about the agent he was sending to Venice to buy silk (*ibrishim*) for Sultan Süleyman's wife, Hürrem Sultan.[31] In 1569 Grand Vizier Sokollu Mehmet Pasha asked the *bailo* to write to the Venetian authorities about an agent whom the Beylerbeyi of Buda (his nephew) wished to send to Venice to buy cloth.[32] In 1589 a palace treasurer, Mustafa, was dispatched to secure an order of 2,000 *braccia* of cloth-of-gold, more than 1,100 meters, for the royal treasury. The accompanying Turkish letter noted that it was the old custom of the Sublime Porte to have *panni d'oro* made in Venice, and that in this instance the order was to be paid for with tribute money from Ragusa, and the Ragusan authorities had been notified accordingly.[33]

Formal diplomatic gifts were, of course, regularly given: the Venetian doge mirrored the Muslim practice of granting robes (*hil'at*) to Ottoman emissaries,[34] and textiles formed the principal category of gift taken by Venetian ambassadors to the Sublime Porte.[35] Although Venice had in the 15th century paid the Ottomans an annual tribute for some of the territories it held in the Balkans and the Ionian and Aegean seas—tribute that mostly took the form of specie and worked silver—during most of the 16th century there was no tribute and no annual public presentation of gifts,[36] and certainly nothing to compare to the *Türkenverehrung*, the euphemistic name for the annual tribute of 30,000 ducats and clocks and automata which the Ottomans exacted from the Habsburgs from 1548 until 1606. The Habsburg "presents" comprised gold and silver vessels, which were usually goblets to hold the specie, and clocks and automata, which had always to be to a new design.[37]

In the absence of regular tribute, the Venetians had to make sporadic, but frequent, gifts to members of the Ottoman court. They could demonstrate a disarming sense of cultural sensitivity. In 1586 when the bailo Lorenzo Bernardo gave Grand Vizier Siyavush Pasha two clepsydras for the mosque he was constructing, Siyavush was so taken aback that a Christian would make a gift to a mosque that he asked for the text to be translated—twice.[38]

Cultivating good relations was the most common motive. As the Venetian Senate wrote to the *bailo* in 1552, *"et vi si manderà più presto si potrà per il desiderio che tenimo di far cosa grata a sua Signoria."*[39] In some instances, though, the gifts were intended less to win favor than to assuage anger. This was the case in 1584 when an unusually large circle of courtiers was given gifts in the wake of a major diplomatic incident. A Venetian squadron under the command of Gabriele Emo had massacred those on board the galley of the young regent of Tripoli, Mehmet Bey of Jerba. Both Mehmet Bey and his mother died in the incident, and the Ottomans were universally incensed that women were among those killed.[40] The Senate immediately granted permission for the *bailo* to spend money on gifts: robes and money for the sultan's tutor, Hoca Sa'deddin, and for two sisters of the sultan, one of whom was the wife of Grand Vizier Osman Pasha, the other the widow of Piyale Pasha;[41] and urgent efforts were made to acquire two large chairs that the Grand Vizier had previously ordered. The sultan received gyrfalcons, including a white one of great value. The *nishançı* Mehmet was sent a velvet robe, glass lamps, and windowpanes. A velvet robe was also given to Cafer Agha, a Venetian who had been captured in his youth and had risen to become the Chief White Eunuch (*has odabashı*), while it was agreed that his mother, Franceschina Zorzi Michiel, should be given the first office available in Venice that yielded an income of 10 ducats a month.[42] Gifts were also made to Esther Kira, the Jewish confidante of Murad III's wife, Safiye Sultan. Perhaps the most irate member of the court was the Grand Admiral Uluç (Kılıç) Ali, who had been a close friend and ally of Mehmet Bey's father, and who had helped the young Mehmet Bey succeed his father. It was known that the Grand Admiral wanted a rock-crystal and silver casket worth several thousand ducats, and this was ordered immediately. The *bailo,* Giovanni Francesco Morosini, also acted by giving gifts—more velvet robes to other officials, and a purse of 2,000 gold ducats to Mesih Pasha, who was serving as Grand Vizier in Osman Pasha's absence; and sugar loaves and cheese to Hoca Sa'deddin.[43]

As often as not, the Venetians received overt requests for items. The principal demand was for textiles, but requests ranged from cheese to an organ, lapdogs, and *mappamundi.*[44] A particularly personal request—and one guaranteed to win favor—was for reading glasses. In 1532 the Defterdar asked the vice-*bailo* Pietro Zen for a pair of glasses (*ochiali*), and was given one with silver frames.[45] In February 1576 the bailo asked for glasses and a magnifying glass for the sultan's tutor, and in 1577 for two sets of reading glasses for Siyavush Pasha.[46]

In many instances, the correspondence from the *bailo* fails to specify who was expected to pay for the order. One should not, however, assume that in every case the items were expected gratis. In March 1553 a letter from the Senate to the *bailo* stated that an invoice was being sent for the glass, textiles, and clocks that had been loaded on a ship bound for Istanbul.[47] Specific reference to payment also occurs in Nur Banu's request to Niccolò Barbarigo in April 1578.

Even when an offer was made to pay, the Venetian Senate might choose, as in the last instance, to make a present of the items. The bailos sometimes pressed the Senate to make a gift. Marc'Antonio Barbaro made it clear how pleased Sokollu Mehmet Pasha would be if the Venetian government paid for the glass mosque lamps which, as we shall see, he requested in 1569: ". . .so that if you lay out the money, at least the person for whom the expense is incurred will be pleased. . ."[48] In other instances, no concession was made, as is clear from three documents in the Ragusan archives, from 1571 and 1572, which also relate to requests for glass from Sokollu Mehmet and his wife, Princess Ismihan Sultan; the 1572 document specifies the costs and notes that freight will be an additional charge.[49] Thus, requests made through the bailo were not necessarily made to avoid payment, but to expedite the order.

Given that these gifts lay outside a regulated gift-giving structure, the boundaries between gift, bribe, and purchase are often difficult to judge. On a few occasions the gifts were clandestine: in an attempt to pacify Grand Vizier Ibrahim Pasha in 1530, the Venetian Council of Ten sent him a *rubino* worth 4,000 ducats, and pressed him to keep the gift secret.[50] In other cases, the gift was part of long-term cultivation of goodwill, which required patience and generosity, as we can see by looking at the *bailo*'s dealings with two of his contemporaries whose influence was critical to Venetian interests. One was Sokollu Mehmet Pasha, who was Grand Vizier between 1565 and 1579, the other Nur Banu.

Two Demanding People: Sokollu Mehmet Pasha and Nur Banu

Even a partial list of the requests Sokollu made to Venice, especially alongside those he made to the Habsburg ambassador, conveys a sense of how demanding and particular he was, often providing drawings as well as written instructions. In 1567 he requested a clock from the Habsburgs as well as a silver goblet filled with some 1,000 ducats,[51] and the next year he asked the Venetians for *cesendelli,* long and thin cylindrical hanging lamps, for his mosque in Lüleburgaz.[52] In 1569, apart from asking for the *bailo*'s help with the agent of the Beylerbeyi of Buda, he asked the bailo for more lanterns and no fewer than 900 glass lamps (cat. 170, p. 98).[53] The *bailo*'s dispatch included outline drawings of the two different shapes of lamp (see figs. 11-12, p. 170). He also wanted a lantern of the type used in grand rooms, referred to in a later dispatch as *"un fernal grande, over fanò di quelli che si adoperano nelle sale."* In September that year he was also looking for eight or ten lanterns for his mosque.[54]

In 1573 he asked the Habsburgs for a watch,[55] and in 1576 he requested multiple examples of a spherical clock in two differing styles, for which he provided instructions and drawings.[56] In 1578 he asked for some 2,000 round glass window panes;[57] the same year he gave the Venetian bailo samples of the type of textiles he wanted, and in March of that year the Venetian authorities sent a box filled with cloth-of-gold.[58] In June Barbarigo delivered the textiles to the Grand Vizier, who was evidently delighted as he said he had not seen such fine cloth from Venice for several years. Later in 1578 Sokollu asked the Venetians to supply portraits of past Ottoman sultans, a request we shall come back to later. In addition he wanted six saddlecloths, four quivers, and four bow cases in the colors and styles indicated on his drawings (cats. 141, 142, p. 99). The saddlecloths were evidently unusual as the Senate wrote back to say that they could not be sent promptly ("*per essere di lavoro inusitato in queste parti*").[59] In 1579 he had a French ambassador, Jacques de Germigny, send a drawing of a spherical clock to Henri III.[60]

Given the seclusion of Muslim women, it is easy to assume that the majority of requests came from male members of the Ottoman elite such as Grand Vizier Sokollu Mehmet Pasha. This is to reckon, however, without such formidable female bastions of the Ottoman court as Nur Banu, the mother of Sultan Murad III, or Murad's wife Safiye Sultan, key figures in what is often called the "Sultanate of Women."[61] They found ways to send their demands to the Venetian *bailo* through letters and through intermediaries, the most notable of whom were Jewish, including several women, in particular Esther Kira whom we have already met in connection with the scandal of the slaying of Mehmet Bey of Jerba. It was no wonder, then, that Esther herself put in requests to the *bailo.*[62] Like their male counterparts, these Ottoman ladies most frequently demanded textiles.

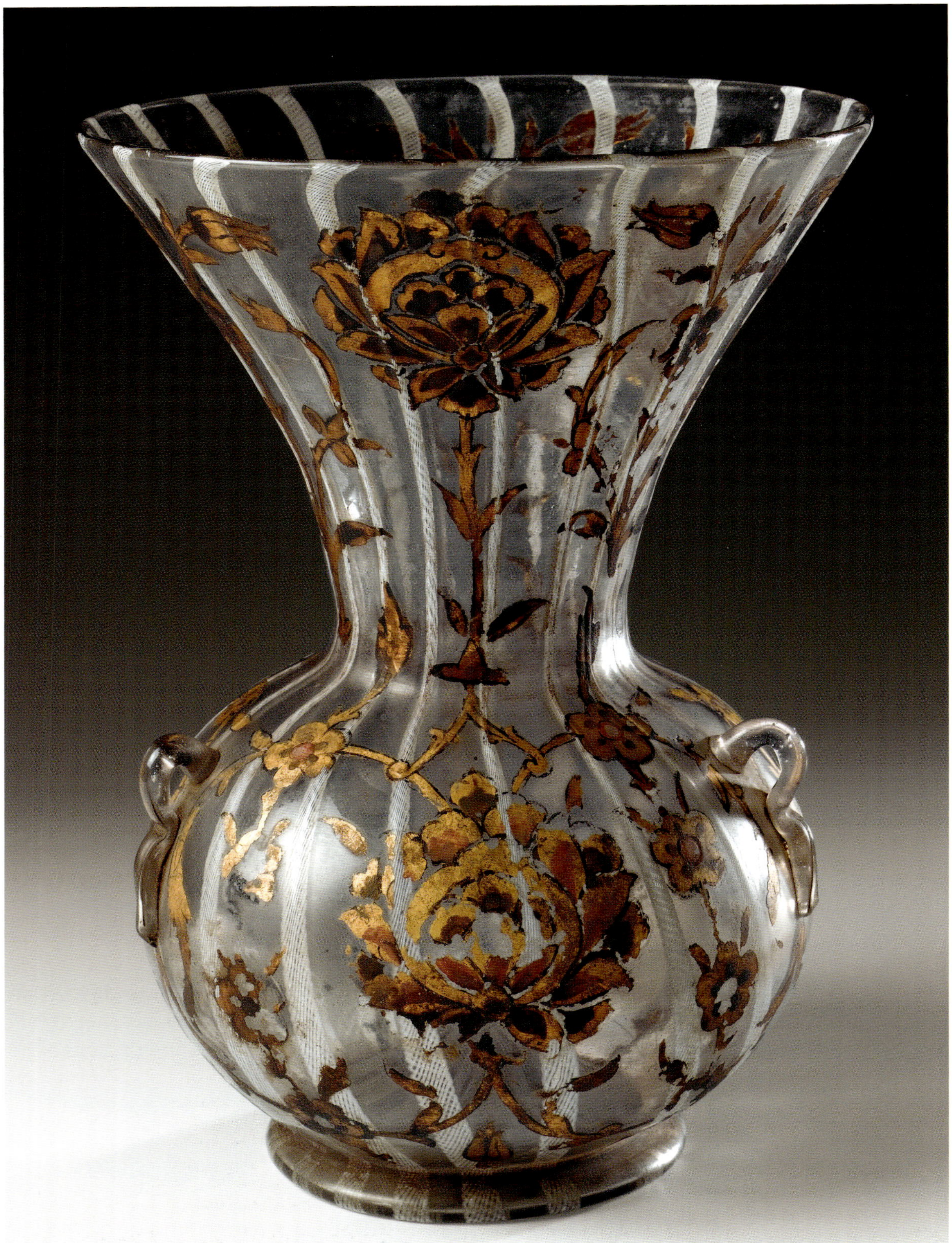

Safiye's best-known requests were addressed to Queen Elizabeth I of England, as it were sister to sister, queen to queen.[63] Nur Banu (d. 1583) was, from the Venetian viewpoint, a more intriguing case, because it was alleged she was of Venetian origin, a member of the patrician family of Venier on the Aegean island of Paros.[64] This lineage had obvious appeal to the Venetians, especially as her putative second cousin, Sebastiano Venier, was one of the heroes of Lepanto, and became doge in 1577. In the long run, however, the Senate was uncertain about her origins.[65] Nur Banu played on Venetian ambiguity to personal advantage: in her later years she still claimed that she came from a family that owned a house on the Grand Canal, though without specifying the family's name.[66]

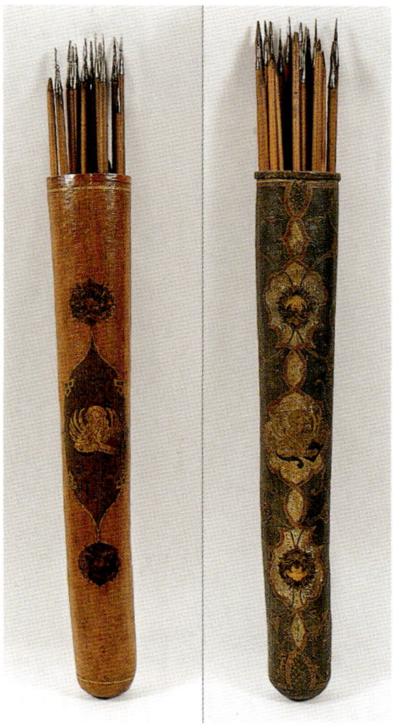

cats. 141–42. *Two Quivers*
Venice, second half of the 16th century
Armeria di Palazzo Ducale, Venice

At the beginning of April 1578 the Senate wrote to the *bailo,* Niccolò Barbarigo, that it had dispatched 50 *brazze* of white satin for the Queen Mother, following a request she had made for only 36 *brazze*.[67] That same month, the *bailo* received a request from Nur Banu delivered by Esther Kira and Salamon Eschinasi for textiles in a dazzling array of different colors and types, all to be delivered as soon as possible, and to be made as exquisitely as possible, as they were for the sultan and his mother, whose custom it was both to wear robes of the same quality and color on the same day! Salamon, who was originally from Udine, successfully urged Barbarigo to write immediately, as the Queen Mother "*ha l'assoluto imperio della volontà del Signor.*" [68]

Esther presented written instructions about the textiles, and insisted that the Signoria should inform Barbarigo of the cost, because her mistress only wanted the items at her own expense. Esther must also have brought samples of at least three types of cloth with her, because Barbarigo responded that *panno* of such a light type was not made in Venice, and he had never seen that sort of *damasco* in Venice. As for the cloth-of-gold, the sultana knew that it was not made in Venice, but advised the Venetians to get it from Bologna or Milan.

Writing on June 2 that year Barbarigo emphasized how fastidious both the sultan and the sultana were, though he evidently thought the demand extraordinary as he later in the year refers to the cloths as *"suoi pazzi di seta et di oro."*[69] Meanwhile, the Senate was discovering how difficult a request this was. On September 12, 1578, it wrote to Barbarigo that the silk costumes (*panno di seta*; *veste*) had come out "quite well" (*assai bene*), but that any attempt to replicate the cloth-of-gold had met with no success, and that efforts were under way to have them made elsewhere in Italy, though no one had been found who would undertake to make them according to the samples. The costumes that had been made in Venice would be sent at the earliest opportunity.[70]

It must have been evident that this would be a troublesome request, which raises the issue that to the recipient "value" or merit could lie in both the process and the present itself. Gratification, in other words, was to be had not just at Venetian success but at their overt expenditure of effort. Whether the sultana's insistence on paying for the textiles was a genuine offer or a veiled disguise to ensure that the textiles were sent as gifts, is difficult to decide. As the objects were of high quality and not all from Venice, it is possible that the Queen Mother

cat. 170. *Mosque lamp*
Venice, 16th century
Topkapı Sarayi Müzesi, Istanbul

cared more about Venetian assistance than she did about the cost. In any event, it suggests that customarily the Serenissima made a present of such items to Nur Banu, and in this case the doge stressed in his letter to Barbarigo that the robes should be presented "in our name" (*in nome nostro*).[71]

If the Venetians' aim was to keep Nur Banu happy, the right presents had the desired effect. In December 1578 she received cloth-of-gold and other items. In the letter Esther Kira subsequently wrote to the Doge she referred to them as "such pretty things," and said they brought her mistress "great pleasure and joy."[72] But the Queen Mother was not always pleased, and in June 1583 she wrote a peevish note to the bailo Gianfrancesco Morosini, complaining about the two lapdogs he had sent: they were too big and long-haired. . . . "Let them be white and let them be little."[73]

In the late 1560s Marino Cavalli summarized how vital it was to keep her content, and how crucial presents were in the process: "*. . . mi pareria che non fusse se non bene di tenerla presentata, perchè con tal mezzo guadagnandosi l'animo suo, et in detto modo obligandosela, potria esser instrumento di rimover dall'animo del Signore qualche sinistro pensiere che d'altra parte le fusse messo inanzi a maleficio dell cose di V.ra Ser.ta.*"[74] The Venetians duly continued to court her favor for almost the next 20 years. In the last year of her life, she had Esther write to the doge and the Senate to say that the sultana wished to assure them that she "is very attached to that Seignory and that she retains so many remembrances of her homeland, and that every kind of favor may be expected from her Highness."[75] As if true to her word, that same year she was credited by the *bailo* Morosini with preventing an Ottoman attack on Crete.[76]

Structures of Gift Exchange

This list of examples, even though partial, begins to read like a litany intended to confirm an Orientalist stereotype of official greed and an untamed appetite for trivia. Even some seasoned Venetian diplomats, such as Jacopo Soranzo, the ambassador to Murad III in 1582, wrote despairingly of the need to give lavishly: *"Non donando, e largamente, non si ottiene cosa alcuna a quella Porta."*[77] And sometimes the demands seem to verge on the redundant or the ridiculous. In 1558 the French ambassador requested help from a colleague in Venice after Sultan Süleyman had two or three times asked him to get some small chiming watches—he wanted to wear 10 or 12 when he went hunting.[78] *Bailo* Agostino Nani's exasperation was understandable when he was asked in 1601 to provide dolls—of the type made by nuns—for the sultan's children and dwarf; as he wrote back to Venice, "they believe the *bailo* of Venice has an open shop for every type of ware."[79] However, to put such requests in some perspective, it is said that Catherine de' Medici asked the Ottomans in 1584 to provide her with 12 Abyssinian slaves, an elephant, a giraffe, and other exotic animals.[80] And to reduce the gifts and requests to the level of greed and trivia is to ignore the fact that in many instances the Ottomans were using the *bailo*'s good offices not to obtain a gift, but to expedite orders that they were quite willing to pay for, and more importantly, to ignore the structure and symbolism of gift exchange in Ottoman society.

In the medieval and early modern Muslim world, munificence was not so much a personal predilection, as a fundamental expression of magnificence. To give and to receive were the very essence of privilege. They were more than manifestations of power and success—they were duties.[81]

This applied not only to the sultan but to all members of the Ottoman elite. Thus, in 1563 the Grand Vizier explained that a gift was more an issue of honor than value, and complained that the French were constantly making demands without bringing the smallest present, be it a watch or a basket of fruit.[82] The French seemed slow to learn, though Jacques de Germigny emphasized in 1583 how much the Venetians helped their cause by being generous with their presents to the Ottomans, Nur Banu in particular.[83] Marc'Antonio Barbaro countered the view among officials in Venice that gifts were a costly and unproductive means to an end by stressing how important gifts were in ensuring that there were members of the sultan's court who were favorable to the Venetians.[84] The gift was such a vital part of Venetian diplomacy at the Ottoman court that in 1616 Cristoforo Valier added a small treatise at the end of the *relazione* he presented on his return from the Ottoman capital.[85]

The extrinsic value of the gift lay in its recognition or conferral of status, and offense could be caused if the gift did not meet the standard expected or was not accompanied by the appropriate marks of respect. A *çavush*, for example, refused to leave Venice if he was not given a gift as good as that given to his predecessor.[86] Instead of reading this as an act of petulant pride, we should appreciate that he might have had understandable concern that a lesser present would reflect badly on his mission.

For Nur Banu, as Contarini explained in 1583, what mattered was not so much the quality of the present as the display of respect she expected from all princes, the doge most of all, given that "she had been born in Venice."[87] This is borne out by the letter she wrote on February 20, 1579, thanking the *bailo* for the gift of 40 robes. She was sending two imperial robes (*due veste di Sig.ria*) for the doge, and one for the *bailo,* and expressly used the phrase "and let it be with pardon" (*et sia con perdono*), which, the *bailo* comments, meant "please excuse me if the present is not appropriate and what is deserved." But this politesse was immediately followed by a rebuke at the Venetians' lapse in protocol: she had not included a letter of thanks to the doge because he had not sent a letter to her.[88]

Gifts often elicited return gifts. Here too protocol was to be observed. Acts of reciprocity are often mentioned in the Venetian documents,[89] but they fail to mention the redistributive dynamic of Ottoman gift exchange.[90] Gifts given to a patron were often passed out to "clients." It was this centrifugal process that ensured that foreign textiles became, quite literally, part of the fabric of Ottoman elite society and its myriad dependents. It also assured the spread of Italian velvets to rival Muslim powers. In 1503, for example, Sultan Bayezid presented, among other gifts, Italian *alto basso* velvets to the Mamluk sultan, Qansuh al-

Ghuri;[91] and in 1560 Sultan Süleyman's envoy brought Shah Tahmasp several types of European textiles, including crimson velvets.[92]

In other instances, such as Sokollu Mehmet Pasha's request in 1576 for four spherical clocks of the same type, it seems clear that he was ordering the clocks as presents, not for his own use. The same was true, as we shall see, of the organ that Piyale Pasha ordered as a present for Sultan Murad.

A monotonous listing of presents and requests tends to give the impression that dealings between the *bailo* and members of the Ottoman court never rose above the impersonal and the acquisitive. But there were instances of a more personal exchange of gifts, the best known being the portrait of Marc'Antonio Barbaro, variously attributed to Paolo Veronese or Lambert Sustris, which depicts him holding a document inscribed to *"IMO domino Mahomet Musulmano[rum] Visiario amico optimo."* That Barbaro referred to Sokollu Mehmet Pasha as his "dearest friend," when the Grand Vizier had kept him under house arrest for much of his stay in Istanbul, is impressive, and illustrates that, for all the posturing on both sides, there was still room for mutual understanding and courtesy.[93]

Marino Cavalli, who expressed reservations about the utility of gifts and bribes, and urged the Venetians to put greater emphasis on the reputation of the state, supported by strong military force, presented Sultan Süleyman in 1559 with a manuscript containing a discourse on old age that his ancestor Andrea Foscolo had heard Murad II deliver to Mehmet II.[94] This was the most thoughtful of presents, for it combined the philosophical and the personal. The present was a reminder of a link between their families that went back more than a century, and it touched on a topic very much on the aged Süleyman's mind.

Classes and Singularities: the Categories of Venetian Gifts

Many of the items that the Ottomans acquired through the Venetian *bailo* fall into three categories, each of which was a standard appurtenance of Muslim sovereignty in the medieval and early modern periods: silk textiles, jewels, and mechanical marvels.

The Venetians never enjoyed a monopoly in supplying the Ottoman market with European textiles, even though they attempted to negotiate one in 1509.[95] The requests from Nur Banu in 1578 underline how well informed the Ottomans could be about the latest European products, and how difficult it could be for the Venetians to satisfy their demands. Not all the textiles ordered from Venice were necessarily in a European style. The occasional reference to drawings accompanying orders suggests that some may have been made to Ottoman designs,[96] and indeed there are examples of velvets in the Topkapı Palace that have long been regarded as prime examples of Turkish weaving, but which are in fact of Italian manufacture.[97] On the other hand, both Murad III and his wife Safiye Sultan evinced a taste for the latest European fashions. In the wake of the Mehmet Bey affair, the *bailo* advised the Senate that

Safiye Sultan was especially fond of "new" textiles.[98] Murad's passion is borne out by an incident that took place the following year, when three times during an audience he pressed the French ambassador Monsieur de Germigny to write to Henri III to send Paris cloth in scarlet, green, violet, and a delicate white. The request was followed up by Rabbi Salamon and then by the Grand Vizier, who gave proof of the sultan's eagerness by offering to send a small galley (*fusta*) from Algiers to Marseilles to pick up the cloth.[99]

Jewels feature more prominently in Ottoman-Venetian exchanges in the first half of the 16th century than in the second half. In the first half of his reign Sultan Süleyman was regarded as having a greater fondness for jewels than any of his Ottoman predecessors.[100] By contrast, his grandson Murad III's passion was said to be for artistic clocks.[101] These were European perceptions that helped guide the choice of gifts. Certainly, by the second half of the 16th century the presents that seemed to have elicited the most enthusiastic response were clocks, automata, and organs. Before the *Türkenverehrung*, the most notable items were those made in 1532 for Francesco Zen, son of the vice-*bailo* Pietro Zen, to take to Istanbul for sale to the sultan: they included a watch so small it fitted into a ring, and yet still chimed on the hour. Other items sent at this time were a mechanical *nef* for the table and a dancing female doll that Marin Sanudo dismissed as a *"puta di legno qual con certa arte camina."*[102] Pietro Aretino was no more flattering when he referred to the items as "being only good for making little girls smile."[103] Mechanical marvels enjoyed, however, a long pedigree at Middle Eastern courts,[104] and the Ottomans' fascination with such objects differed little from that of the Habsburgs or, in later times, the Ching emperors.[105]

The Germans came to dominate the field of horology in the 16th century, and there must have been little incentive for the Venetians to compete with the Habsburgs' *Türkenverehrung*.[106] Nonetheless, even as late as 1589 the Venetians sent a large counter-weighted clock by Maestro Gherardo to the sultan,[107] and in 1594 they gave the Grand Admiral three clocks, one of which was almond-shaped.[108] On at least one occasion clocks were sent from Istanbul to Venice for repair.[109]

The Habsburgs' rivals had better fortune with mechanical organs. In 1568 the Venetians were asked to supply Piyale Pasha with an organ that he and his wife, the princess Gevherhan Sultan, daughter of Selim II, wanted as a gift for the sultan.[110] When the organ arrived in June 1569, Barbaro sent one of his sons to demonstrate how to use and maintain it. Piyale Pasha's enthusiasm was evident, but what most surprised Barbaro was that his wife came to hear it, along with all her ladies and the household, and that she stayed a long time, in utter disregard of the fact that Barbaro's men were present. Small wonder, then, that Barbaro wrote, "nothing here has ever been given that has given greater satisfaction."[111]

The Venetians were not so well placed to provide the Ottomans with another standard item of imperial gift exchange, live animals, though they did present gyrfalcons to the sultan on one occasion, and were asked to supply hunting dogs on another.[112] Hunting animals were emblematic of imperial prestige, whereas Nur Banu's lapdogs fall into what in the Muslim context was the surprising category of dog as pet, more of a fashion accessory in the Venetian manner.

The gyrfalcons remind us that Venice served as a conduit for objects from other parts of the world, not just from Venice and the Veneto. Another reminder is the "unicorn" horn that Ibrahim Pasha was so insistent on receiving and that Pietro Zen took to Istanbul in 1531. From the description it was clearly a narwhal horn.[113] Yet understandably it was Venetian specialties that were most often in demand.

The most requested type of object, other than textiles, was architectural glass, particularly roundel panes (*rui*).[114] The spate of construction in Istanbul and the provinces during the 16th century placed a severe strain on the local glassworking industry.[115] It was a gap the Venetians were prompt to fill, and many notables, especially in the second half of the 16th century, sought the Venetian *bailo*'s help to secure their needs. In 1578 the *bailo,* in addition to ordering *rui* for Sokollu Mehmet Pasha, expedited an order for thousands of *rui* for the mosque of the Grand Admiral;[116] in 1586 the *bailo* Lorenzo Bernardo gave Siyavush Pasha window glass for his mosque,[117] and in 1592 glass was requested for an imperial kiosk, to list a few examples.[118] One might have expected that *rui* would have been available in quantity on the open market, and the cargo of the *Gagiana*, which sank off the Dalmatian coast in 1583, confirms a sizable export.[119] The requests from members of the Ottoman court must sometimes, then, have been a means of acquiring the items gratis. This was certainly the case in June 1569 when the Agha of the Janissaries was so insistent about getting window glass that Barbaro bought what he wanted in Istanbul, even though there was an order of *rui* due from Venice. Barbaro said that if the latter arrived, he would try to get money back on them, but if they had not yet been sent, there was need to do so.[120] Little, then, would have prevented the Agha of the Janissaries from acquiring these items in Istanbul himself.

There was also much demand for luxury glass, especially *cristallo*, glass of such clarity that it resembled rock crystal. The Venetians also exported quantities of glass beads and mirrors, and even mirrored hanging balls.[121] An order for the Topkapı Palace in 1555–56 included, for example, lamps and glass panes, *cristallo,* and mirrors.[122] The Murano craftsmen were ceaselessly inventive, and it comes as no surprise to hear of an order from the sultan in 1590 for 75 vases made out of "chalcedony glass," one of Murano's more remarkable achievements (see cat. 168, p. 261).[123]

True rock crystal was used in Venice in the late 16th and early 17th centuries for a majestic style of gilt metal casket that incorporated large panes of crystal, and lacquered decoration in an Ottomanizing style.[124] These caskets (cat. 145) were popular with European royalty and, to judge from the descriptions, with the Ottoman court: one was given to Grand Admiral Uluç Ali in 1584 to appease his anger over the Mehmet Bey affair; and another, ordered by the sultan in 1590, took a full three years to produce.[125]

Papal bans prevented the Venetians from supplying the Ottomans with military technology or raw materials that could be used for military purposes. It did not, however, stop the Ottomans from asking. In 1559 a man claiming to be an envoy from Prince Selim arrived in Venice asking the doge to supply the prince with 500 German harquebuses, a request that was duly refused, as were requests on other occasions for anchors.[126] One of the more unusual demands came from Sultan Süleyman's daughter Mihrimah, who asked for steel for hewing tools which the Ottomans needed to cut a conduit to bring water from Mount ʿArafat to the Kaʿba, a massive project that took nine years to complete, from 1562/63 to 1572. Again, the request was refused on the grounds of the papal ban, though the *bailo* was told in 1569 that the tools were for the benefit of poor pilgrims, not for martial purposes.[127]

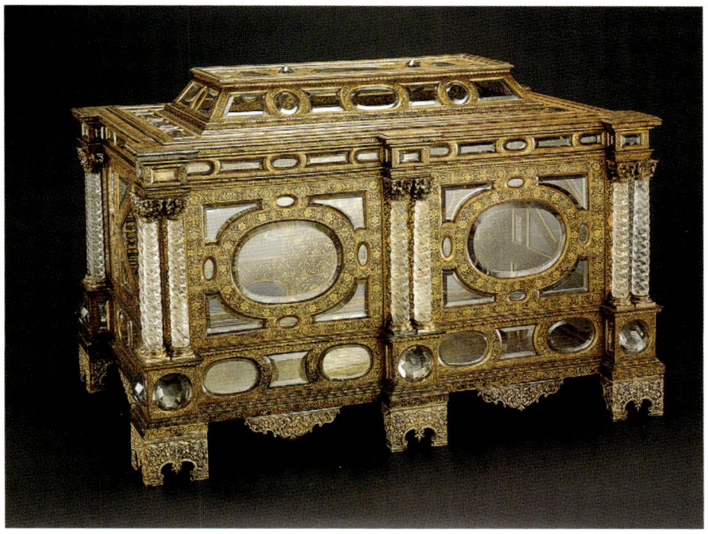

cat. 145. *Casket*
Venice, late 16th century
St. Louis Art Museum, St. Louis

An area where the Venetians were willing to oblige was cartography, for in the mid-16th century the city was a leading center of geographical knowledge. The most intriguing exchange occurred in the early 1550s, when Venice was asked to provide world maps for two, possibly all three, of the Ottoman princes then battling each other for the right to succeed their father, Sultan Süleyman. A request from Prince Bayezid came via a special envoy in December 1552, and, as no suitable map could be found, the Senate commissioned a new map that was presented to Bayezid in Edirne two years later. Unless there is a serious confusion in the Senate records over the names of the princes, Bayezid's ultimately successful rival, Prince Selim, also received a wall map; and Andrea Morosini (1557–1618), the Republic's official historian, records that Prince Mustafa asked for a terrestrial globe, which was sent, though it was not delivered due to his death on October 5, 1553.[128] If indeed the three main rivals to Süleyman's throne all asked the Venetians for a world map within the space of a year, it suggests that the maps were seen more as aids in their deadly struggle for power than as "a prestigious and symbolic product of Venetian cartography."[129] The explanation may lie in the fact that Venice was home at this time to a remarkable network of scholars with an interest in world geography and in the East in particular. They included Giovanni Battista Ramusio, the cosmographer and compiler of the most important collection of travel accounts of the new discoveries; Giacomo Gastaldi Piemontese, who painted the maps in the Sala dello Scudo in the Doge's Palace between 1550 and 1553, and who also drew all the maps for Ramusio's *Navigazioni e viaggi;*[130] and Michele Membré, the Serenissima's senior dragoman, who collaborated with Gastaldi in producing a map of Asia in the 1550s.[131]

The Senate's undisguised willingness to provide items of potential strategic importance to the three contenders to the Ottoman throne contrasts with its ambivalence 15 years later when the *provedditore* of Cefalonia, Marc'Antonio Giustiniani, had 150 copies printed of a cordiform world map with a long inscription and place-names in Arabic (cat. 45ab).[132]

The princely request for world maps was not the only such request from the Ottomans, but it was unusual enough to throw into relief how, typologically at least, the overwhelming

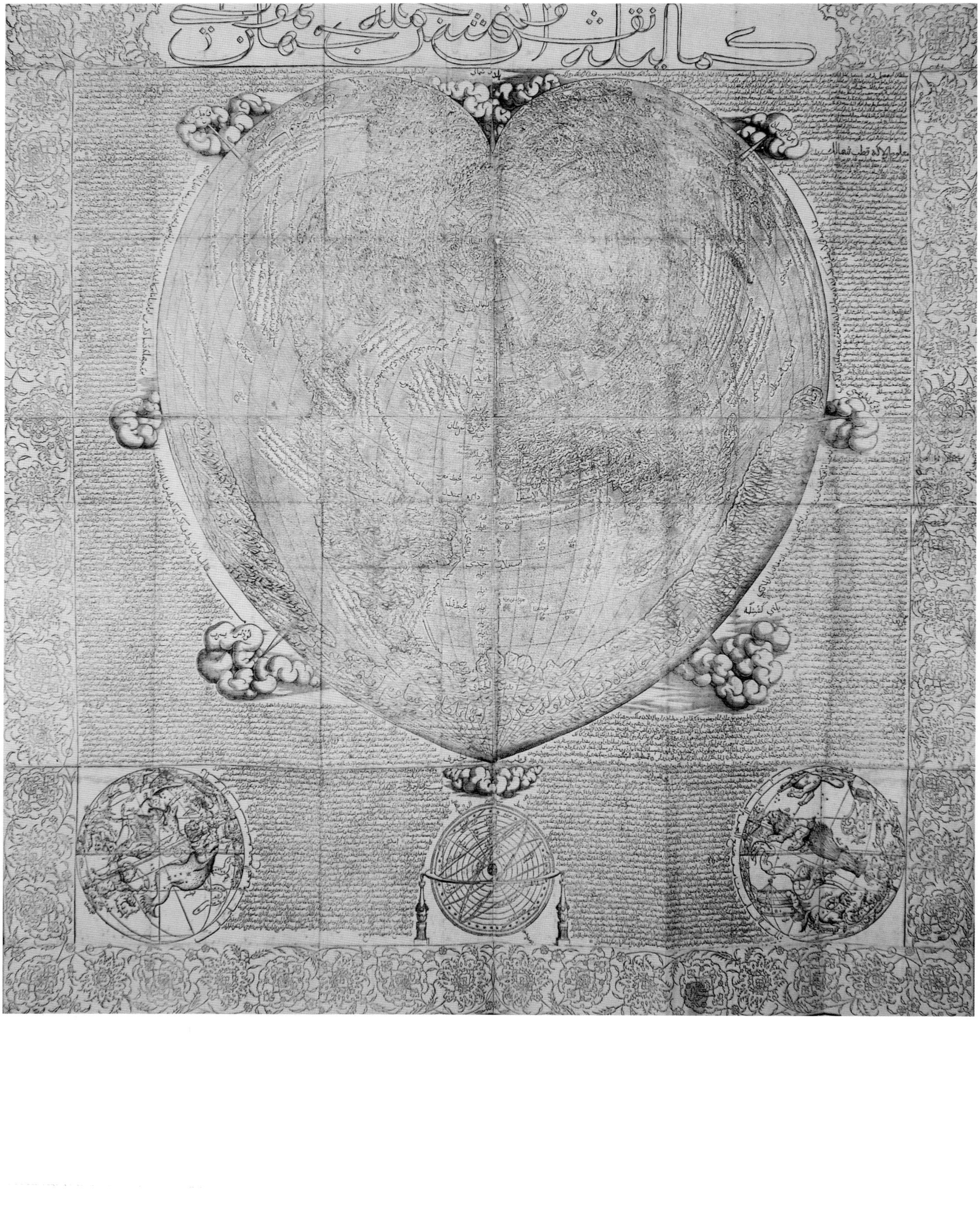

majority of gifts and requests were highly repetitive (cat. 48, p. 108). In the case of robes-of-honor, this can be explained by their official, ritual nature. The personal requests focused on commodities and luxuries. In the 16th century there was almost no demand for painting and sculpture, and almost no demand for services.[133] The exceptions are intriguing. The one sultan who showed a consistent interest in European artists was Mehmet the Conqueror (r. 1451–81) (cat. 24, p. 109; see also cats. 116–17, p. 134). The visit of Gentile Bellini to his court in 1479 has become the stuff of legend, but the emphasis on Bellini has tended to obscure the broader trends of Mehmet's Western patronage. First, Bellini's visit was the culmination of several attempts, some successful, some not, over the course of more than 20 years to get portrait painters and medallic sculptors to Istanbul from Rimini, Naples, Ragusa, and Venice. The Venetians were not officially involved in these exchanges until the last two years of Mehmet's life, because from 1463 until 1479 they were waging a bitter war with the Ottomans. Second, the request to Venice did not specify Bellini by name, but was part of a request for a painter, a sculptor, and a builder, and perhaps also glassmakers. This request for a range of skilled artists and craftsmen suggests the sultan was interested in more than the graphic and glyptic portraits for which his patronage is celebrated—perhaps an architectural project in his new palace.[134]

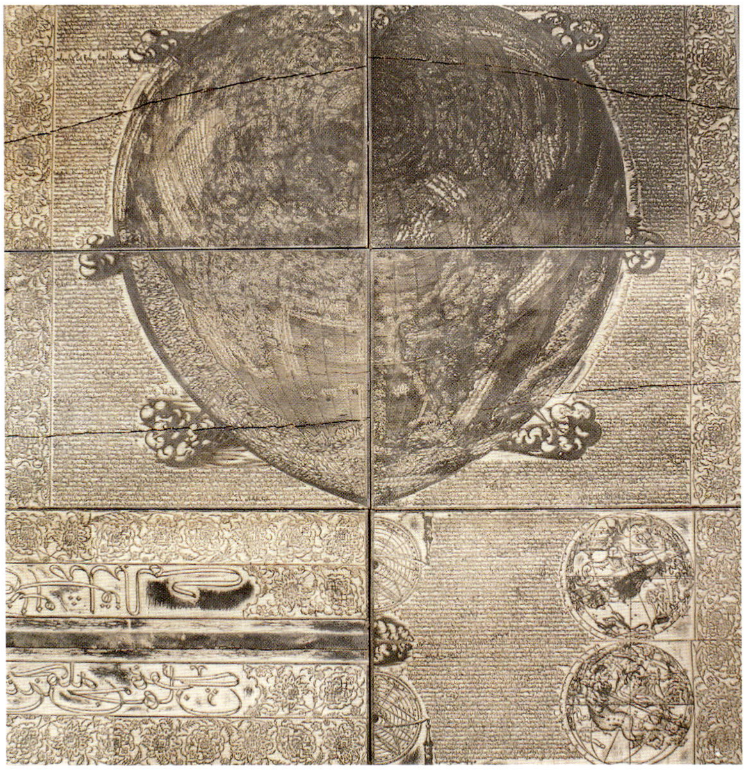

cat. 45ab. Hajji Ahmed
Six woodblocks and print of the *Perfect and complete engraving and description of the entire world*
Venice, 1795
Biblioteca Nazionale Marciana, Venice

Mehmet's successor, Bayezid II, was as averse to figural painting as his father had been fond. However, it was Bayezid who extended invitations to Leonardo and to Michelangelo, in 1502 and 1506, respectively. His interest, though, was in engineering ventures, in particular a bridge over the Golden Horn that would have linked the Muslim and European quarters of the Ottoman capital. His son Selim I, in contrast, invited Michelangelo specifically for his abilities as a figural painter and sculptor, but this invitation too came to naught.[135]

Throughout the remainder of the 16th century there were no known invitations to figural artists, and no opportunity for the Venetians to influence the Ottomans in the use of painting as an expression of imperial symbolism, allegory, and magnificence. In 1578, almost exactly one century after Bellini's visit, Sokollu Mehmet Pasha asked the bailo for his help in acquiring European portraits of past sultans. Barbarigo replied that he knew of no such series except printed ones whose quality he did not regard as worthy. In the end the Senate commissioned portraits from a Veronese painter (cats. 35-38, p. 110), but these arrived too late to be of major influence on the Ottoman project to create an album of imperial portraits, the *Kitafetü'l-insaniye* (cat. 10, p. 111). In fact, it was a printed work, the *Promptuarium*

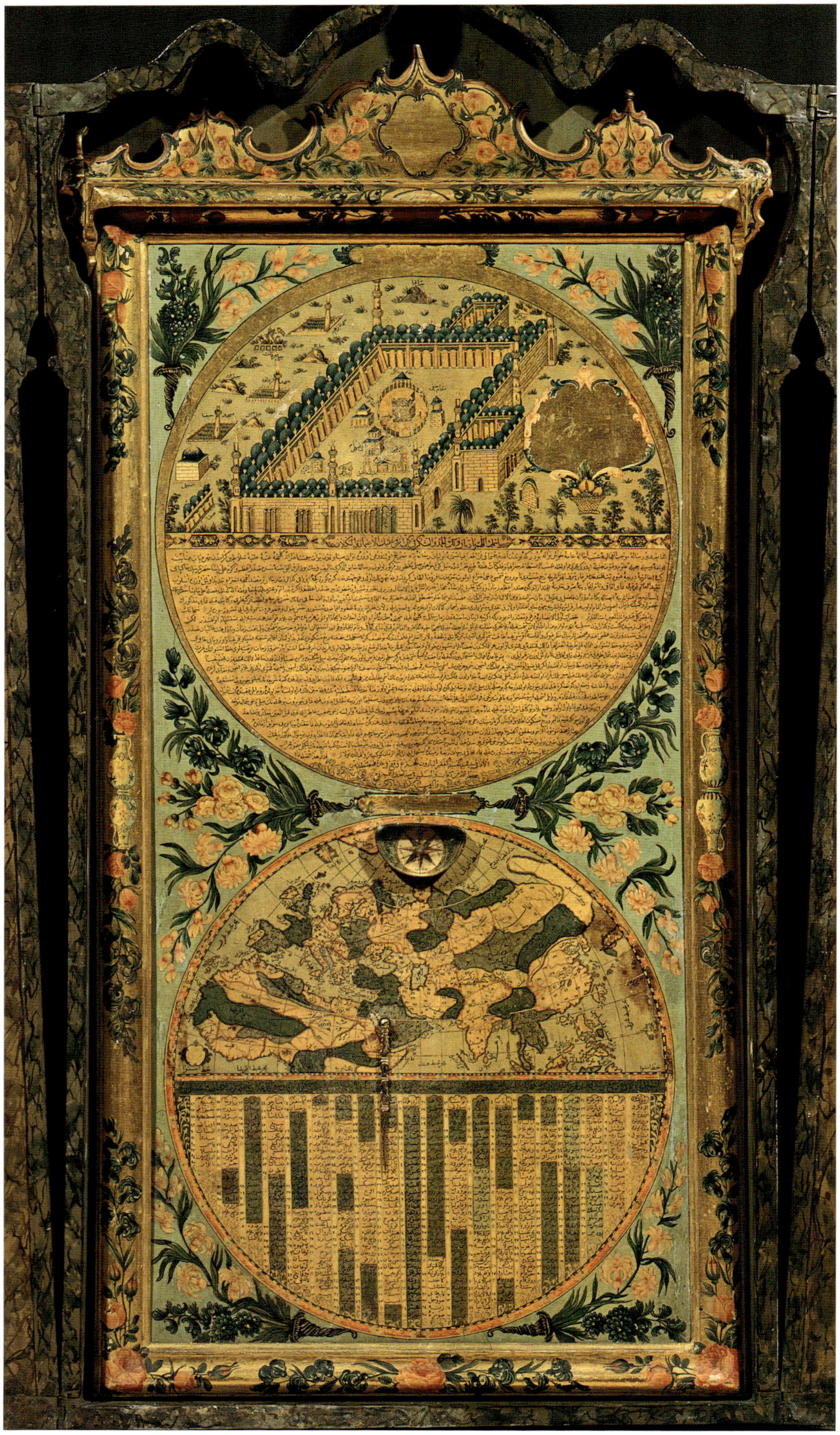

Iconum published by Guillaume Rouillé (Rovillius) in Lyon in 1553, that proved the most influential European source for the individual portraits, the very type of work Barbarigo sought to dissuade Sokollu from consulting.[136] The concept of the series may have been stimulated by the publication of Rouillé's compendium and other European printed portrait books with images of the Ottoman sultans, notably two works by Paolo Giovio published in 1575 and 1577.[137] However, the portraits themselves had a more complex genesis, part Timurid imagery, part European. European influence was perhaps seminal, but it was not sufficient.[138]

The lack of figurative influence from Venice in the 16th century meant that the items sent from Venice fell mostly into the realm of the minor and decorative arts, including jewelry. One example, however, shows how these could be developed to create a highly symbolic program. This was the helmet and other imperial insignia, including a scepter, that were produced by the craftsmen referred to by Flaminio in *La Cortigiana.*

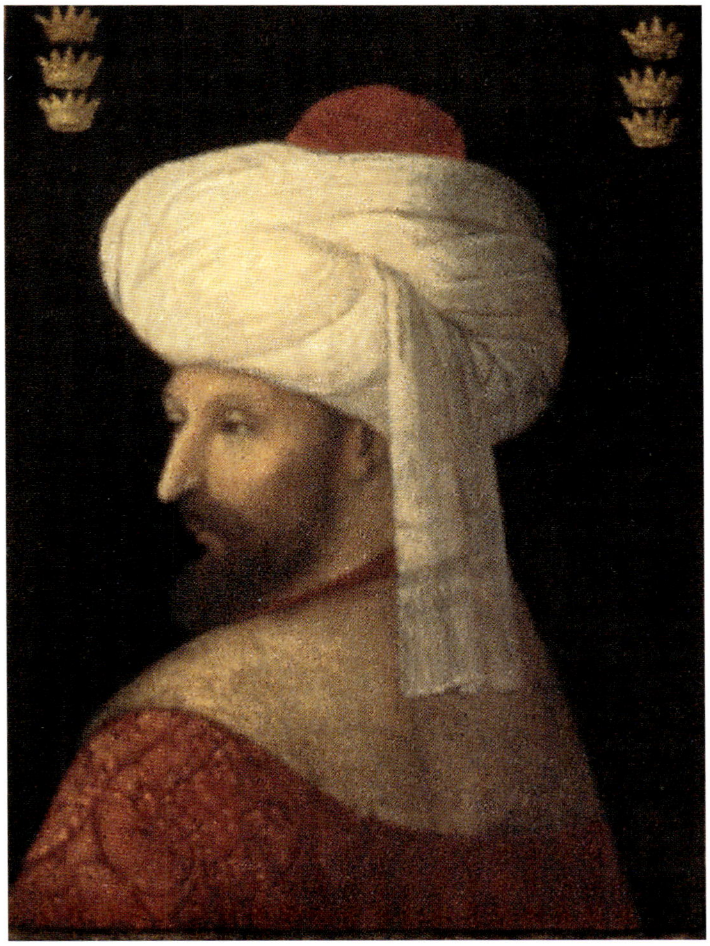

cat. 24. Anonymous Venetian (associated with Gentile Bellini)
Portrait of Mehmet II
Venice, ca. 1510
Joli Quentin Kansil Collection, Singapore

In 1532 Venetian and German entrepreneurs produced a panoply of jeweled objects for sale to the sultan, including a scepter and a jewel-studded saddle and saddlecloth.[139] The central item was a four-tiered crown, modeled on the three-tiered tiara that Cristoforo Foppa, Il Caradosso (c. 1452-d. 1526/67), had begun producing for Pope Julius II in 1510.[140] These imperial insignia were key elements of an elaborately orchestrated theater of magnificence that turned Süleyman's march on Vienna in 1532 into a parade that projected his right to universal rule.[141]

The helmet and other regalia were not items that the sultan officially ordered through the *bailo.* Prime movers in this venture were Alvise Gritti, who was credited with designing the helmet, the scepter, and a crystal mirror, and Alvise's patron and protector, Grand Vizier Ibrahim Pasha.[142] As Alvise was the bastard son of the reigning doge, Andrea Gritti, and the business sponsors comprised leading members of several Venetian patrician families, including the ambassador and vice-*bailo,* Pietro Zen, the enterprise nonetheless enjoyed quasi-official status; and almost all the Senatorial Pregadi came to see the helmet the day it was brought for viewing in the Doge's Palace.[143]

Four years later, in 1536, the same jewelers attempted to sell more regalia to the sultan, including an imperial parasol designed by Jacopo Sansovino, but the attempt failed. Not only did Ibrahim Pasha die on March 15, 1536, but corsairs captured the ship taking the jewels to Istanbul.[144] This ended the most elaborate attempt by Venetians to assist

cat. 48. *Map with qibla indicator*
Istanbul, Turkey, 1738
Museo Civico Correr, Venice

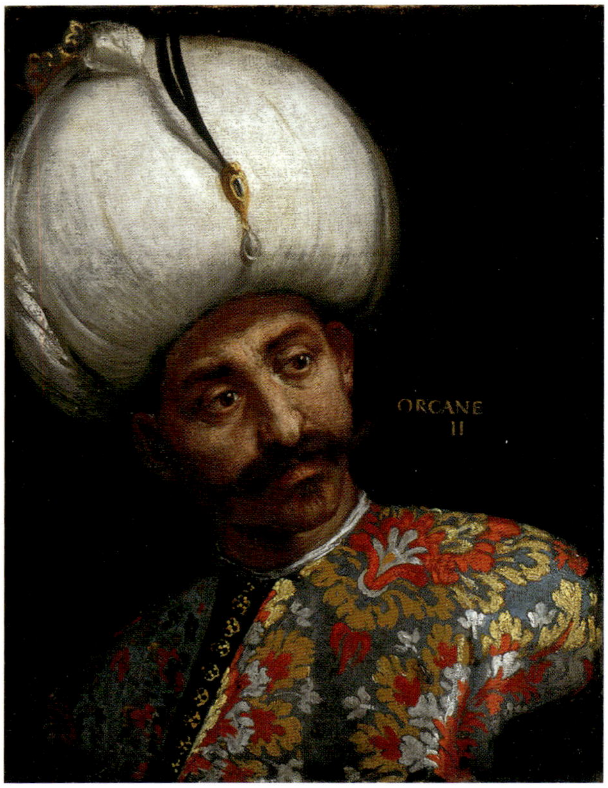
ORCANE
II

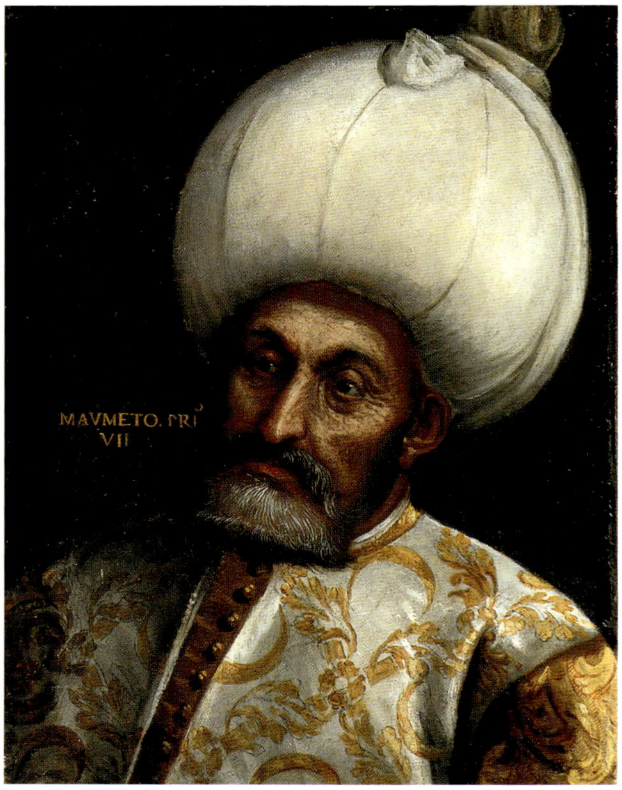
MAVMETO. PRI
VII

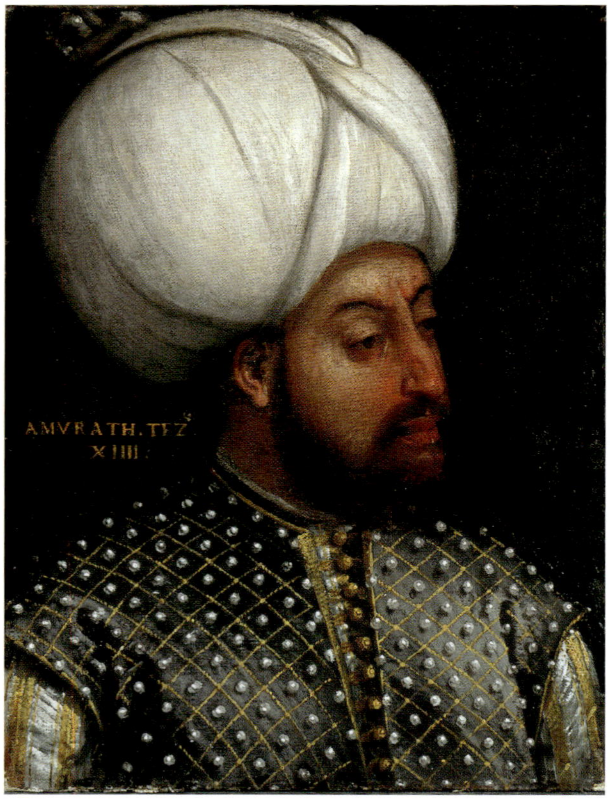
AMVRATH. TEZ
XIIII

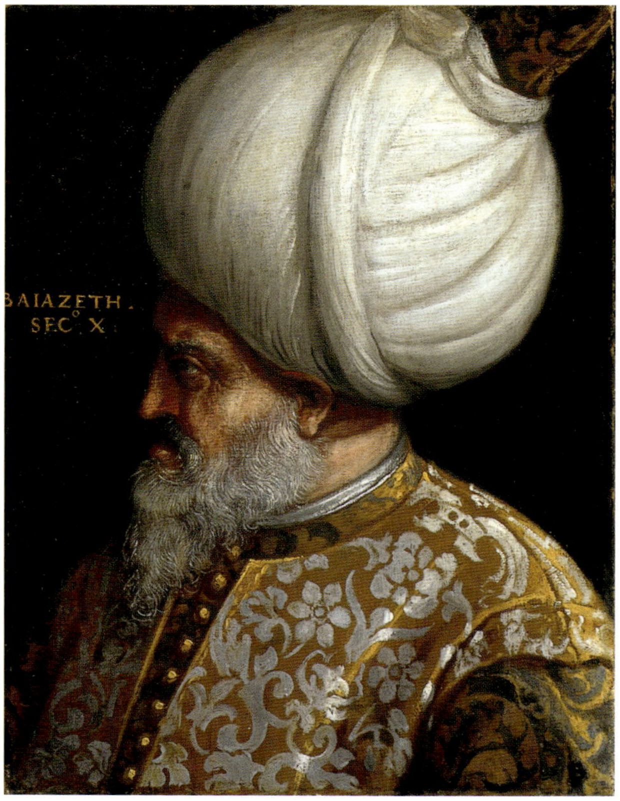
BAIAZETH.
SEC.° X

in fashioning the Ottoman imperial image. Although there are several European woodcut depictions of Süleyman wearing the crown (cat. 59, p. 112), including one of him seated on a horse with a bejeweled caparison, the regalia had no long-term role in Ottoman imperial propaganda.

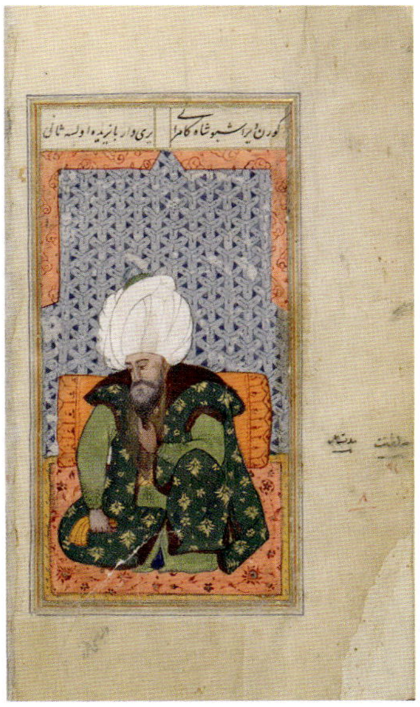

cat. 10. Seyyid Lokman
Kitafetü'l-insaniye fi şema'ilü'l-osmaniye
Probably Baghdad, Iraq, ca. 1595
The Nasser D. Khalili Collection of Islamic Art, London

No other objects supplied by the Venetians to the Ottomans could compare in cost, sumptuousness, or iconographic intent. Nevertheless, we should not underestimate the cumulative influence of the commodities and luxuries mentioned earlier. That influence might exert itself through repetition over time or through an aggregate effect at any one moment. An example of iterative influence is the way in which the Venetians' gifts of crimson velvet robes must have confirmed the Ottoman predilection for a fabric type that in Venice was a prerogative of the nobility. This was clearly an Italian, not an Eastern taste, and so embedded was it at the Ottoman court, at least until the reforms of Rüstem Pasha in the mid-16th century, that the sultan is known to have presented ceremonial robes made of Italian velvet to European dignitaries such as the Imperial ambassador Sigmund von Herberstein in 1541.[145] Another example is that of clocks and watches, the demand for which became so great that a colony of watchmakers established itself in Galata in the last quarter of the 16th century, providing an item for the open market whose influence went far beyond display, inculcating a concept of time supplementary to that imposed by the Muslim calls to prayer.[146]

It is more difficult to gauge the effect created by an aggregate of European goods. So little 16th-century palatial architecture has survived, other than the Topkapı Palace, that we cannot tell if there were attempts to create quasi-European interiors. And we cannot extrapolate from the surviving religious architecture, as this was governed by a self-conscious and carefully coded Ottoman aesthetic.[147] Public decorum was no obstacle, however, to private license, and it is possible that some palaces were more eclectic in taste that we might suppose.[148] In the last three decades of the 16th century there were requests for Venetian furniture, including a room-lantern and chairs,[149] as well as lengths of gilded and varnished leather (*cuoridoro*).[150] A pair of doors inlaid with plaques of semi-precious stones (cat. 144, p. 237) might have been intended for a cupboard recess in an Ottoman interior: their size and proportions recall the mother-of-pearl inlaid cupboard doors in Murad III's quarters in the harem of the Topkapı Palace; their system of hinging is related; and the keyhole cover is in the form of a crescent moon, a motif inextricably linked in the European mind with the Ottomans.[151] These doors may, then, be the only known surviving item of European furniture produced for the Ottomans. European furniture and furnishings might, in the end, have been too few and too dispersed to affect interior decoration in Ottoman palaces, but one element of European furniture had a long-term influence on royal imagery. This was the armchair, which influenced the form of the royal throne in the early 17th century, largely displacing the bench-style throne of the 16th century. The Serenissima presented chairs to the sultan and sultana on the occasion of their wedding in 1584, and of other royal weddings, thus perhaps encouraging a new appreciation of the chair as a symbol of status.[152]

cats. 35–38. Anonymous Painter from Verona or Follower of Veronese
Portraits from a series of Ottoman rulers: Orhan, Mehmet I, Bayezid II, Murad III
Venice, 1578 or later
Bayerische Staatsgemäldesammlungen, Munich

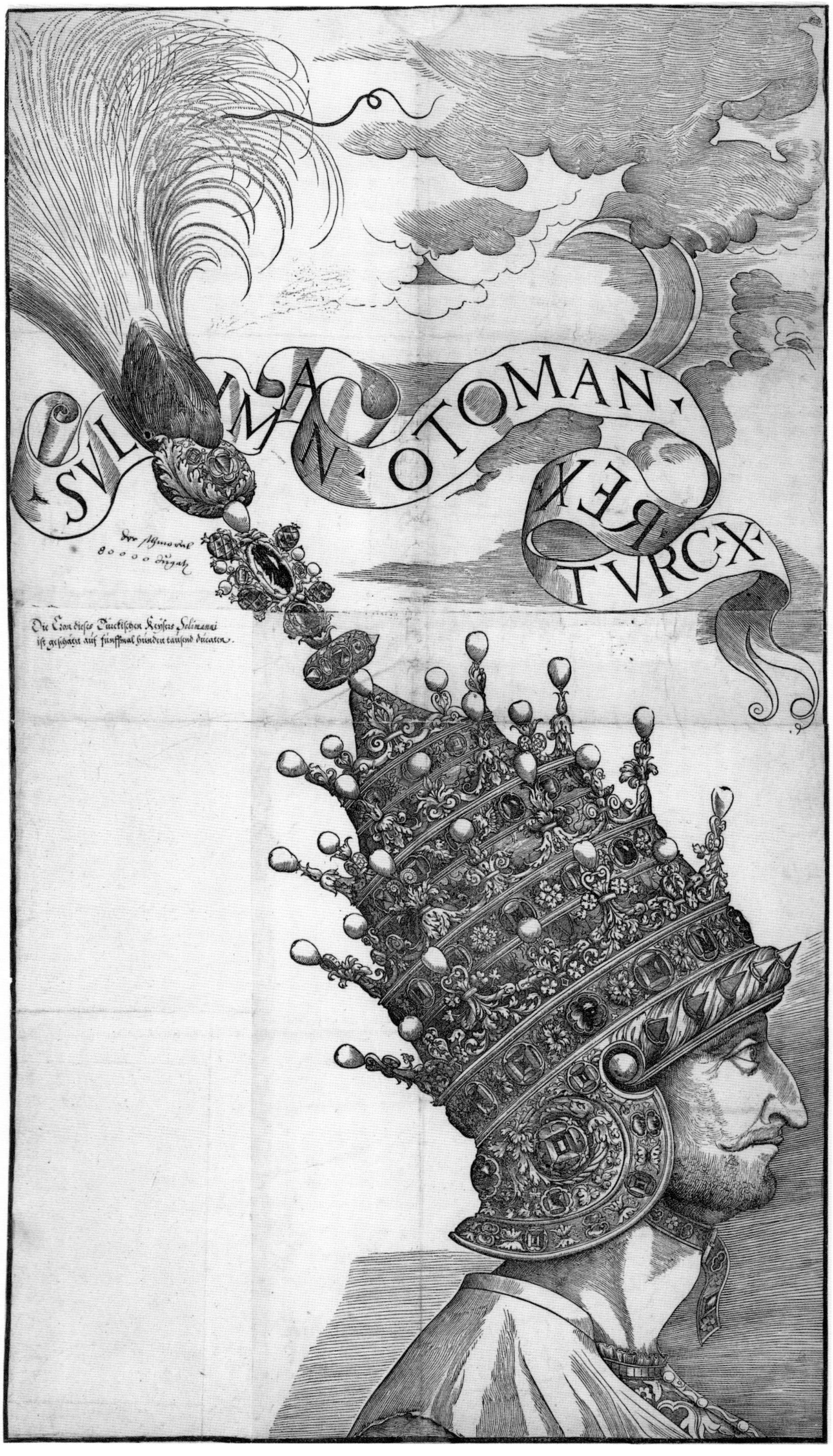
SVL
MAN · OTOMAN ·
REX
TVRCX
Die Cron dieses Türckischen Keysers Solimanni
ist geschätzt auf fünffmal hundert tausend ducaten.

This emphasis on durable objects distracts from the possibility of a performative influence from one of the great vehicles of Venetian self-representation in the 16th century—the pageant. Venetian pageants became increasingly elaborate in the course of the 16th century, with allegorical and symbolic floats and *tableaux vivants.* Exultant pageants such as those that followed the battle of Lepanto, and those surrounding the visit of Henri III in 1574, were theatrical displays of state propaganda. They embraced patricians and populace, and foreign visitors and residents were prime members of the audience.[153] The Venetian pageants may have helped inspire the extraordinary festivities for the circumcision of Murad III's sons in 1582, in which the guilds of Istanbul and subjects of the Ottoman Empire paraded their wares and their talents in processions and on floats, in full sight of the foreign powers whom the sultan took care to invite.[154]

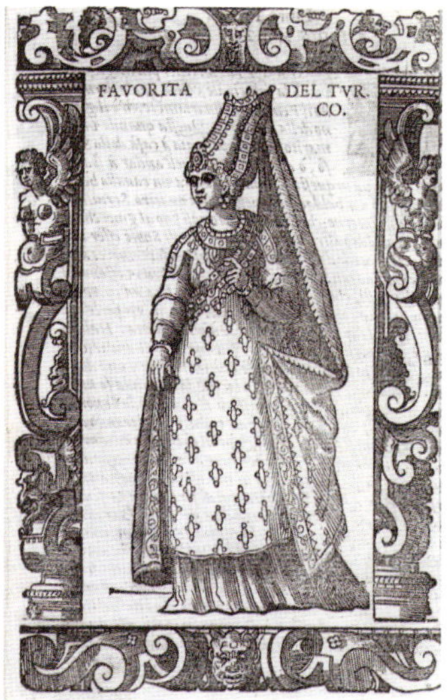

cat. 63. Cesare Vecellio
La Favorita del Turco
Venice, 1590
The Metropolitan Museum of Art, New York

A Cosmopolitan City

A pictorial analog of the pageant of 1582, in which the Ottoman capital paraded itself before the world, was the Ottoman costume book, a visual record of the plurality of Ottoman society. The last quarter of the 16th century saw the beginnings of a tradition of Ottoman costume albums that lasted into the 19th century (cat. 13, pp. 114–15). Initiated by Europeans for Europeans, with captions in at least one European language, these albums came to be produced by Ottoman artists, and they served as a practical vade mecum to, and a memento of, the hierarchies of the court, the military and the religious establishments, the trades and guilds of the city, and the diverse mix of races and nations in Istanbul and Pera.[155] The last quarter of the 16th century also saw the publication in Venice of Cesare Vecellio's celebrated costume book, *Habiti antichi et moderni di tutto il mondo* (1590; cat. 63).[156]

Whereas Ottomans figured prominently in Vecellios's compendium (Book VII was devoted to the *Habiti dei Turchi*), the Frankish component in the Ottoman costume books was comparatively small. This difference is telling. For the Venetians, the Ottomans were the defining "other," the foreigners whose looming presence spurred reflection on Venetian identity. For the Ottomans, their empire stretched in all the cardinal directions, across the "seven climes," and though Venice was a critical point in their Western frame, their political, religious, and cultural horizons lay predominantly to the East. Europeans were far from a dominant element in the Ottomans' image of their empire.

The Ottoman elite was not closed to the rest of the world, as many might imagine. On the contrary, in the mid-16th century the Imperial ambassador de Busbecq asserted: "No nation in the world has shown greater readiness than the Turks to avail themselves of the useful inventions of foreigners, as is proved by their employment of cannons and mortars, and many other things invented by the Christians."[157] Openness existed not only in the realm of technology, but also on the cultural side.[158]

For the Ottomans, European goods were only one component of their global self-image. The European items came, though, without the religious and cultural underpinning of

cat. 59. Anonymous Venetian
Sultan Süleyman the Magnificent Wearing the Jewel-Studded Helmet
Venice, ca. 1532
The Metropolitan Museum of Art, New York

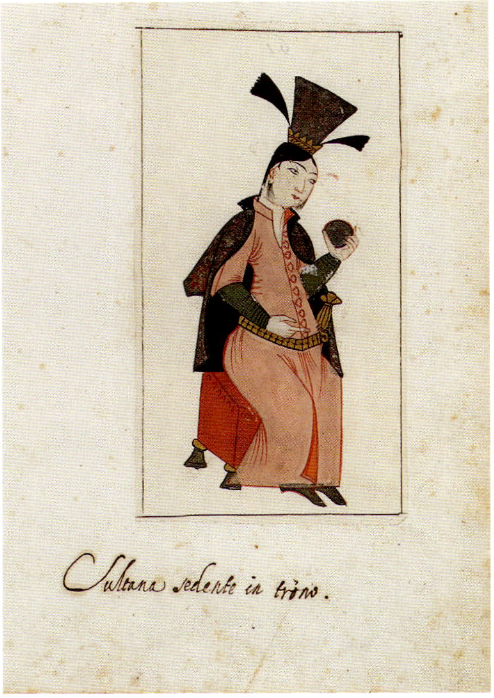

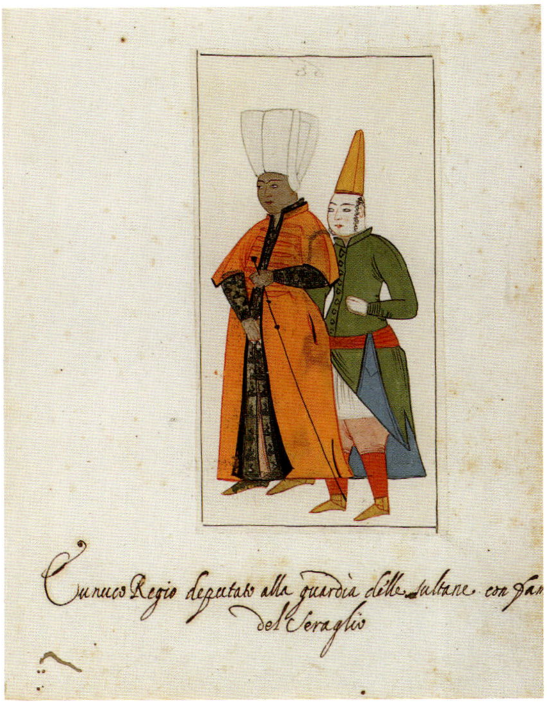

so many Arab and Persian cultural imports. They tended to be in the realm of luxuries and the decorative arts, not of complex symbolism and iconography. There were exceptions: Mehmet the Conqueror's interest in the concept and meaning of European portraiture owed much to his contacts with Italian humanists, while half a century later Alvise Gritti, whose household included Italian scholars and literati, and who nearly succeeded in persuading Pietro Aretino to come to the Ottoman capital, played a vital role as cultural bridge-maker. But just as the death of Mehmet was followed by a reaction against European-style portraiture, so too the death of Alvise and his patron Ibrahim Pasha ushered in a period of sobriety and more restrained ostentation at Süleyman's court. By the 1550s Ottoman imperial art and architecture had achieved a distinctly Ottoman voice.[159] Under Grand Vizier Rüstem Pasha, there was an eschewal of imports from either Iran or Europe, and a corresponding promotion of Ottoman artistic products and style. This change of policy had both an ethical and an economic dimension, for if consumption was a sultanic duty, it should be to the benefit of the sultan's own subjects. The focus on an Ottoman cultural expression in the mid 16th century reflected a new sense of Ottoman self-identity, and a growing shift from the more syncretic tendencies under Mehmet II or early in Süleyman's reign.

By contrast, in the last three decades of the 16th century the taste for European luxuries and goods grew stronger, both on a diplomatic level and through the open market. The market began to open up with the arrival of the northern Europeans, such as the English who were granted capitulations in 1580.[160] At the courtly level, the taste remained largely behind closed walls. In public there was a conservative insistence on custom, on the imitation of ancestral mores; in private there was greater room for fashion, for the imitation of strangers and adoption of the exotic. This dichotomy obtained until the later 18th century when there was renewed interest in European modes of imperial representation.

Venice was both supplier and broker in the Ottomans' cultural exchanges with Europe. For the Ottomans, the "gifts" from Venice were proof of state power and of per-

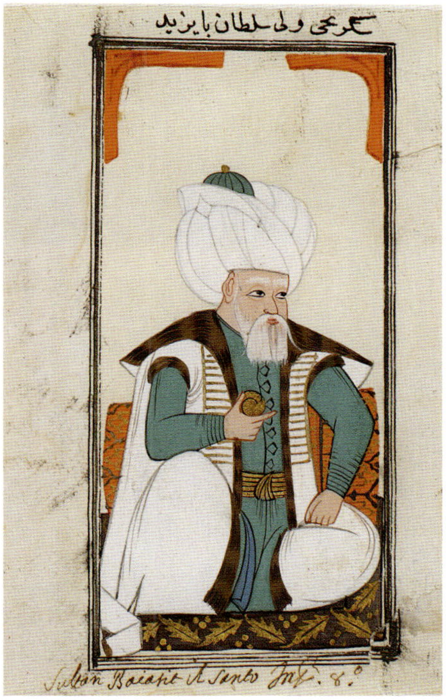

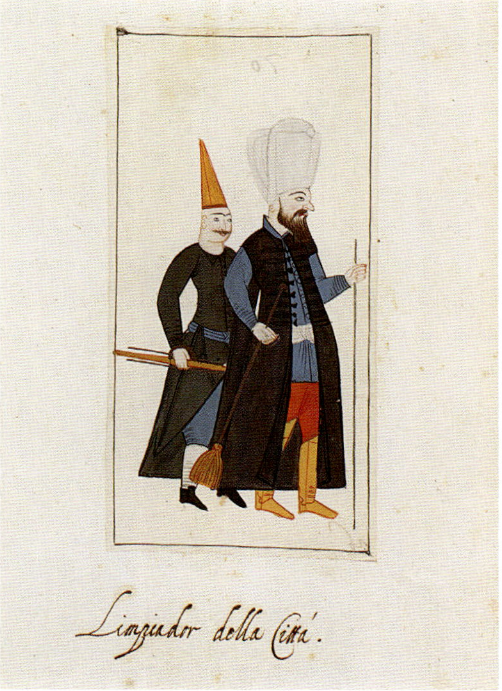

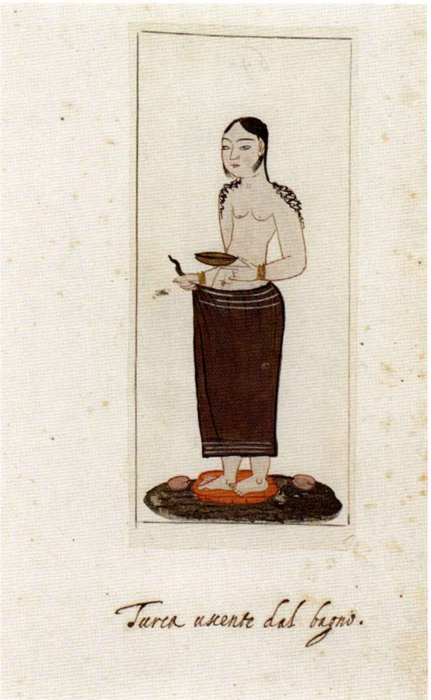

cat. 13. *Fogge diverse di vestire de' Turchi* ("Diverse dressing habits of the Turks")
Turkey, probably Istanbul, 17th century
Biblioteca Nazionale Marciana, Venice

sonal contacts—metonyms of collective or individual status. For the Venetians, the gifts were an indispensable means of achieving their prevailing diplomatic goal—a military stasis that would allow trade to flourish. The arts of Venice were not, then, just items of trade, but an indispensable apparatus of political business.

As Marc'Antonio Barbaro vividly declared, diplomacy was like juggling with a glass ball: *"Si può dire che'l negotiare sia a similitudine del giocar con una balla di vetro che è necessario sostentarla con destrezza sempre in aere non la lasciando nè dar in terra nè ribattendola con furia di posta, perchè la romperebbe, ma prendendola destramente et poi con opportunità rimandandola vivamente."*[161] In this diplomatic juggling act a well-occasioned gift could not guarantee success, but it might assure attention.

Notes

1 "If one wants to have possessions in those countries, one must first bring gifts." Sanudo 1879-1902, vol. 23, col. 286. I owe thanks to Trinita Kennedy and, above all, to Kelly Swain for their considerable help in tracking down copies of many of the bibliographical items cited here.
2 Aretino 1971, Act III, scene VII, p. 157, and esp. p. 160; see also p. 163 on Flaminio saying he wants to go Venice, but, if not to Venice, then to Constantinople to serve Alvise Gritti, on whom see below, notes 25, 141, 143.
3 See below, notes 138–43.
4 Istanbul was a city of opportunity: in the 1580s Reinhold Lubenau noted that there were European, including Italian, clockmakers and gem-engravers in Galata, "for the most part young people who return to Europe as soon as they have made some money"; cited by Kurz 1975, p. 49.
5 Wilson 2003, pp. 52-53, fig. 19.
6 On the peace treaty, see Bombaci 1943; Wittek 1952.
7 Preto 1975, pp. 36-53; Preto 1993, p. 201.
8 Finlay 1984, p. 82.
9 Ibid., p. 84.
10 See, for example, Preto 1993, p. 202; cf. Finlay 1984, p. 95, on the Venetian ambassador being the sole ambassador who failed to attend a meeting called by Pope Clement, for fear of offending the Turks. In 1548 Sultan Süleyman sent Ferhad Çavush to Venice to tell the doge to celebrate the Ottomans' victory over the Safavids, as in other parts of the Ottoman Empire (Gökbilgin 1979, p. 289). On the other hand, the *bailo* Pietro Zen made no disguise of Venetian delight at the Ottoman victory over the Imperial forces at Mohacs in 1526: he draped the Venetian residence with cloth-of-gold and had a fountain spouting wine: Bertelè 1932, p. 42; Finlay 1984, p. 83.
11 Sinding-Larsen 1956; Gombrich 1967. On poetic output in praise of the victory, see Preto 1975, pp. 260-268. On the battle, and some of its subsequent imagery, see Morin 1985. See also Perkins 1868, p. 211.
12 In general, see Preto 1975, pp. 55ff., esp. pp. 58-59. Muraro (1977, p. 165) has suggested that the Signoria avoided the possibility of offence by avoiding depictions in the Doge's Palace of battles against the Turks; after the battle of Lepanto this and other images were commissioned that showed Venice as defender of Christianity.
13 Preto 1975, pp. 25ff.; Preto 1993, p. 201. On Andrea Gritti and the Zen family, fine exemplars of the Venetian patrician-cum-merchant, as proponents of accommodation with the Ottomans, see Concina 1984. On a shift from trading to land-holding among the Venetian nobility in the second half of the 17th century, see Muir 1979, esp. p. 72; Fabris 1991, p. 56.
14 Preto 1975, pp. 22-23; Olivieri 1979.
15 April 18, 1454: Bertelè 1932, pp. 35ff.
16 Simon 1985; Dursteler 2001.
17 Mantran 1982. Reliance on intermediaries applied not only in Istanbul, but also in Venice, where Ottoman merchants might encounter language problems: see Vercellin 1980, p. 55. On the role of Jews in the trade with Ragusa, with a more comprehensive recent bibliography, see Orfali 2002. Jews were often intermediaries between tax-farmers and traders (Mantran 1982, p. 130). For the role, for example, of Jews in the glass trade by the second half of the 16th century, see Han 1973.
18 To take a single example, in 1483 the Ragusan authorities served to expedite an order from the *sancakbey* of Herzegovina for Venetian window glass of the type previously received by the *sancakbey* of Bosnia, Davud Pasha. In both cases the orders were to go through a Ragusan merchant known as Johannes de Florio, also known as Turchinovich. The incident exemplifies the importance of the Balkans in both the consumption of, and transit trade in, Venetian products. See Han 1973, pp. 165-66. For other examples, also relating to glass, see below, note 49.
19 Preto 1993, p. 201. This device could not, of course, provide a substitute for all the former level of trade, and it is understandable that Ragusan custom revenues rose during periods of conflict between Venice and the Ottomans (on which see Kafadar 1986, p. 195).
20 Sanudo 1879-1902, vol. 35, col. 259: *"...amava grandemente la Signoria di Venezia in quanto egli era nato sotto il suo dominio"*; quoted by Finlay (1984, p. 81). He told the Venetian ambassador he was a "*suddito*" of Venice, and another vizier referred to Ibrahim Pasha as *"veneziano vostro"* (Finlay 1984, p. 81). Cf. Concina 1994, p. 145.
21 Another person who claimed special recognition on the grounds that he had born on Venetian territory was Süleyman's dragoman Yunus. For the letter to the doge presented on December 4, 1539, see Gökbilgin 1964, p. 168, doc. 39; Gökbilgin 1979, p. 289; Pedani Fabris 1994, p 109, doc. 412. He was from Modone, with relatives in Zante (Necipoğlu 2005, pp.485–6). For several other cases of Venetian converts who gained high positions at the Ottoman court, see Pedani 2000, pp. 19-23, 25. For a Venetian noble who was captured at the battle of Prevesa and rose to be the *alfiere* of Prince Mustafa, and who wished to send news to his parents in Venice in 1553, see Fabris 1989, p. 11, note 26. Others, of course, were Italian renegades. On renegades, see Kissling 1961; Preto 1975, pp. 169-252; Benzoni 1985a.
22 Preto 1975, pp. 121-25; Pedani Fabris 1994; Pedani Fabris 1996. On a few recorded unofficial visitors, see Fabris 1991, p. 54.
23 Vercellin 1979; Vercellin 1980; Kafadar 1986, pp. 195-98.
24 Bertelè 1932; Turan 1968, esp. p. 261; Preto 1975, pp. 126-43. On the building, see Turan 1968, and Schulz 1995. On the institution of the *fondaco*, see Concina 1997; Constable 2001; Constable 2003.
25 In general, see Aymard 1966; also Braudel 1949, pp. 447-71, and Preto 1975, p. 27. It is probable that both Andrea and Alvise Gritti dealt in wheat, a commodity Andrea Gritti was still dealing in when he was elected doge in 1523. During the famine of 1527, the doge had to defend himself against accusations relating to the import of grain to Venice by two of his illegitimate sons, Zorzi and Alvise: Finlay 1984, p. 103, note 10, p. 107, note 51, p. 110, note 78. On the boom in the wheat trade in the 1550s, see also Berindei 1989, p. 209. On Alvise Gritti and the trade in wheat, see Gökbilgin 1979, p. 282.
26 In general, Preto 1975, p. 60. On the soda ash, see Rogers 1990-92, p. 68, note 16; see, in particular, Jacoby 1993. On an incident in 1589 when one of the imperial merchants, Çavush Cafer, sent two men, Hasan and Mehmet, to Venice carrying with them 14.5 *yük* of raw silk to buy merchandise for the sultan, see Turan 1968, p. 253, with reference to ASV *Documenti Turchi*, b. 4, no. 64; Pedani Fabris 1994, p. 252, doc. 992. Pedani Fabris gives the çavush's name as Halil, Turan as Cafer. As the silk *yük* (*harir yükü*) was equivalent to about 61.5 kg, they brought just under 900 kg of raw silk.
27 Quoted in Charleston 1966, p. 23. In general, see Turan 1968, p. 254; Preto 1993, p. 201. On the import of paper, see Babinger 1931. Venice also served as a source of Mediterranean coral and Baltic amber: Rogers 1983, p. 241. Garzoni's comments are borne out by the cargo of a ship wrecked off the Dalmatian coast, most probably the *Gagiana* which was lost in November 1583 en route to Turkey; see Gasparetto 1973; Petricioli 1973; Gasparetto 1976; Rogers 1983, pp. 253-54.
28 Abulafia 1987.
29 For example, early enameled glass from Venice is often linked to the enameled glass of the Ayyubids and early Mamluks, but there were significant differences in technology: see Carboni 1989; Tait 1999.
30 On the career of one such merchant-envoy-spy, see Skilliter 1976. On Pasqualino Lioni, who traded for 20 years in the Levant, and had begun selling silk and cloth-of-gold textiles to the Sublime Porte in the late 1580s, see Villain-Gandossi 1969, pp. 30-31.
31 Gökbilgin 1964, p. 172; Turan 1968, p. 253; Pedani Fabris 1994, p. 155, docs. 603, 604. On Semiz see Necipoğlu 2005, p. 385.
32 ASV *Senato. Dispacci da Costantinopoli*, Filza 4: April 16, 1569. At the same, the Agha of the Janissaries asked for glass *rui*, and Ahmed Pasha, the former Grand Vizier, wanted a glass *cesendello.*
33 For the Ottoman text of Murad III's letter to Doge Pasquale Cicogna, see Turan 1968, p. 252 and esp. pp. 278-79, Appendix, doc. iv (ASV, *Documenti Turchi*, b. 4, no. 72). For a synopsis of the Italian translation, see ASV, *Documenti Turchi* b. 8, no. 991: Pedani Fabris 1994, p. 252. In more detail, see Curatola 1999, p. 109: *"secondo l'antico costume della Porta di far confezionare a Venezia drappi d'oro per conto del tesoro imperiale, ora viene commissionata la 'presente' confezione di 2000 braccia di detto drappo che il tesoriere Mustafa, inviato a questo scopo a Venezia e incaricato di ritirare: il prezzo sara pagato col tributo di Ragusa e a tale scopo gia stati inviati ordini ai signori di quella citta."* According to Curatola there was a similar sale of *panni d'oro* in 1593, though it does not appear to be recorded in Pedani Fabris 1994.
34 For example, in 1480 Mehmet II's envoy to Venice was noted wearing a red velvet robe; on the feast of Pentecost he was given a gold robe and each member of his mission a scarlet robe: Fedalto 1980, p. 525. On the Ottoman tradition of *hil'at* (Ar. *Khil'at*), see M. F. Köprülü *Islâm Ansiklopedisi*, Istanbul, 1940-86, vol. 5, s.v. "Hil'at"; and Baker 1991.
35 The Venetian ambassadors sent in 1517 to congratulate Selim I on his recent victories took a long list of robes and textiles, carefully graded according to the recipient: Sanudo 1879-1902, vol. 25, cols. 626-32.
36 Spremi 1971.
37 Kurz 1975, p. 28. These "presents" were valuable both intrinsically and rhetorically, as when Sultan Süleyman in 1559 asked the Habsburg ambassador Ogier Ghiselin de Busbecq to present the gifts "in the camp, in the sight of the army, as fresh proof to his subjects that he and the Emperor were firm friends."

38 Fabris 1991, p. 53; Curatola 1999, p. 105. The Venetians tended to be more nuanced in their dealings with lesser officials than the approach recommended by the Imperial ambassador Joachim von Sinzendorff in 1578, who believed that special attention should be paid to wishes of the sultan and Grand Vizier, whereas others would take what they were given (Mraz 1980, p. 52).

39 "We shall send [the presents] as soon as possible because we eagerly want to please the Sultan." Fabris 1989, p. 8; cf. Fabris 1989, p. 10: *"et si è usata diligentia tal che speramo che quel signor che ho la richiesto potrà restar ben satisfatto."*

40 Mehmet Bey was the son of the recently deceased Beylerbeyi of Tripoli, Ramazan Pasha, a Sardinian renegade. His entourage included several Italians, including a lutenist, a carpenter, and a tailor. On the incident, see Fabris 1990, and, in brief, Fabris 1991, p. 53. See also Pedani Fabris 1994, p. 235, doc. 934, p. 240, docs. 941 and 943.

41 Piyale Pasha was married to Gevherhan Sultan, one of Selim's daughters, Necipoğlu 2005, p. 422.

42 On Franceschina Michiel, mother of both Cafer Agha and Gazanfer Agha, see Pedani 2000, p. 14.

43 Fabris 1990, esp. p. 104.

44 On *"formaggi piacentini,"* along with a writing case with elaborate mechanism, given to Ibrahim Pasha in 1533, see Bertelè 1932, p. 74, note 54.

45 Sanuto 1879-1902, vol. 56, col. 402: Bertelè 1932, p. 75; Kurz 1975, p. 21, note 1.

46 Pedani 2000, p. 12, note 10.

47 Fabris 1989, p. 9; Arbel 2002, p. 22.

48 See below, note 53.

49 On April 20, 1571, the Ragusan authorities instructed the emissaries they were sending to Istanbul to inquire whether the Grand Vizier wished the glass he had ordered to be ferried by land or, when opportunity arose, by sea. Transport by cart (*vettura*) would cost more than the goods themselves. On September 30 of the same year, another Ragusan envoy was to relay the information that they could not transport the lamps by land, as there was too great a risk of breakage, and the items were to be held in Ragusa until they could be shipped. On March 10, 1572, the Ragusans instructed their envoy that 1,030 items of window glass ordered by the sultana, presumably Sokollu Mehmet's wife, the Princess Ismihan Sultan, had been sent to Istanbul in 12 barrels. Here it was specifically stated that the cost of the window glass amounted to 83.26.15 [*sic*] gold ducats, and that freight from Dubrovnik to Istanbul would be additional. Han (1983, pp. 173-76) suggests (p. 175) that these orders were in fact for glass produced in Dubrovnik rather than for glass just trans-shipped from Venice. See also Rogers 1983, p. 252, note 47, who gives a somewhat different account of these documents. On the construction activities of Sokollu Mehmet Pasha and Ismihan Sultan, see Necipoğlu 2005, pp. 331ff.

50 This occurred in February 1530; see Finlay 1984, p. 109, note 66.

51 Mraz 1980, p. 46.

52 Necipoğlu 2005, p. 348, and p. 544, note 386: see ASV, *Dispacci* filza 3, dispatch 4, March 23, 1568, June 5, 1568, June 14, 1568, September 3, 1568. On *cesendelli* in general, see Zecchin 1970, with reference to a document of 1569 that refers to *cesendelli "alla turchesca, alla romana, alla ceciliana."* See also Carboni 1989, p. 153.

53 ASV Senato, *Secreta* III, Costantinopoli filza 4, fols. 104-9: Rückert 1963; Charleston 1966; Gasparetto 1973, p. 84; Zecchin 1970, p. 26; Rogers 1983, pp. 252-53; Carboni 1989. The glass arrived late in the year, as Barbaro wrote on January 4, 1570 (m.v. 1569), that he had given the order to Sokollu, along with a lantern, on which see the following note, and that he had expressed profuse thanks to the doge *("ne ringratiò con molte grate parole la Serenità Vostra, mostrando che le cose presente le fussero state carissime")*: Marciana MS VII.390 (8872), fol. 265r.

54 Quoted from copies of Barbaro's letters: Marciana MS VII.390 (8872), fol. 116v, see also fols. 227r, 265r. The original order refers to *fanò da salla grande*: Rogers 1983, p. 253; Carboni 1989, p. 151. See also note 119 below.

55 Mraz 1980, pp. 47–48. In fact he was mistakenly given two clocks that had been ordered—to designs sent from Turkey—by his colleague Ahmed Pasha.

56 One of the drawings was signed by his resident clockmaker, Oswald Kayser. On Oswald, see Kurz 1975, p. 48.

57 ASV *Senato. Deliberazioni Costantinopoli (Secreta)*, Reg. 5 (1575-79) fol. 98b. I am grateful to Gülru Necipoğlu for this reference.

58 ASV *Senato. Deliberazioni Costantinopoli (Secreta)*, Reg. 5 (1575–79), fol. 90v, dated March 25, 1578.

59 ASV *Senato. Deliberazioni Costantinopoli (Secreta)*, Reg. 5 (1575–79), fols. 119r–v, dated January 16, 1579 (m.v. 1578).

60 Charrière 1848–60, vol. 3, p. 822.

61 Pierce 1988 and Pierce 1992; Pedani 2000; Necipoğlu 2005, p. 281.

62 She was the widow of Elijah Handali, and originally from Jerez de la Frontera in Spain. She was in Nur Banu's service by September 1569 and joined Safiye's service from Nur Banu's death in 1583 until her own death in 1588 (Skilliter 1982a, p. 518). See also Wittek 1952; Pedani 2000, p. 12. On another powerful Jewish woman in Istanbul, see Orfali 2002. See also Galante 1941-42.

63 Skilliter 1982b.

64 Spagni 1900; Rossi 1953; and, most importantly, Arbel 1992.

65 The conflicting reports about Nur Banu began in 1559 with the arrival of a supposed envoy from Prince Selim: Arbel 1992.

66 Skilliter 1982a, p. 516, with a reference to the Albèri *Relazioni* III, 3, Florence 1855, p. 235: Arbel 1992.

67 ASV Senato *Deliberazioni Costantinopoli (Secreta)*, Reg. 5 (1575-79) fol. 92r, dated April 5, 1578. In July (?) of that year she thanked the bailo for a bale of satin: Skilliter (1982a, p. 520) translates the passage as "a bale of silk," but the Turkish letter and its contemporary Italian translation are clear that it was of satin (p. 527: *"bir top atlas,"* p. 528: *"la pezza di raso"*).

68 "She has complete control of the Sultan's will." The visit occurred on April 12, 1578, and Barbarigo's letter was dated April 15: ASV *Dispacci da Costantinopoli*, Filza 12, April 15, 1578, partially summarized by Spagni (1900, pp. 312-13). On Barbarigo, see F. Babinger, "Barbarigo, Niccolò," *Dizionario Biografico Italiano,* Rome, 1964, vol. 6, pp. 76-78.

69 ASV *Dispacci da Costantinopoli*, Filza 12, fol. 275r (in cipher, transliterated fol. 271r), dated October 10, 1578.

70 ASV *Senato Deliberazioni Costantinopoli (Secreta)*, Reg. 5 (1575-79), fol. 107r. They were dispatched by land; see ASV *Senato. Deliberazioni Costantinopoli* Reg. 5 (1575-79), fol. 119r-v on their dispatch by land; cf. ASV *Dispacci da Costantinopoli*, Filza 12, fol. 275r, Barbarigo writing to the doge on October 10, 1578. Forty robes, 21 bi-color and 19 of cloth-of-gold, arrived on February 19, 1579 (m.v.1578): ASV *Dispacci da Costantinopoli*, February 20, 1578 (m.v.), quoted by Spagni 1900, p. 313. In return, Nur Banu sent two cloth-of-gold robes for the doge, and one for the bailo, and the son of the Kira affirmed that the Queen Mother offered the Venetians help in dealings with her son, the sultan: Spagni 1900, p. 313. And see below, notes 75 and 76.

71 November 12, 1578: ASV *Senato. Deliberazioni Costantinopoli.* Reg. 5 (1575-79), fol. 111v.

72 Spagni 1900, p. 341, doc. II; Skilliter 1982a, p. 522, p. 530 *"de cosas tan lindas que fue de mucha satisfacion y contiento de Su alteza."*

73 Skilliter 1982a, p. 525; the contemporary Italian translation politely omits the optative demand of the original Turkish (p. 533). On another well-known complainant, the dragoman Yunus Bey, see Necipoğlu 2005, p. 486. Nur Banu was still making requests little more than a month before she died, asking for 12 cushions of cloth-of-gold in two sizes: Skilliter 1982a, pp. 527 and 536.

74 "In my opinion it is highly desirable to give her presents because we can both ingratiate her and make her feel she owes us something; in this way, she could remove from the mind of the Sultan some ominous ideas that could be extremely detrimental to your Highness' affairs." Bertelè 1932, p. 132, note 53.

75 Skilliter 1982a, pp. 522 and 530.

76 Spagni 1900, pp. 342-45; Skilliter 1982a, p. 527. See also Necipoğlu 2005, p. 281.

77 The passage is worth quoting more fully: *"Non donando, e largamente, non si ottiene cosa alcuna a quella Porta, e andandosi a parlare la prima volta a qualche grande uomo, la seconda volta non si è ammesso se non si porta."* ("It is impossible to obtain anything from the Ottoman court without presenting generous gifts, and if you are admitted to the presence of an important individual for the first time, the second time you will not be allowed if you do not bear gifts.") Preto 1975, p. 239.

78 Kurz 1975, p. 25. Given Süleyman's generally severe demeanor in his latter years, one can appreciate his wish for a little levity.

79 Pedani 2000, p. 12.

80 The Ottoman response was to send her balsam and *terra sigillata*: Pedani 2000, p. 16.

81 F. Rosenthal in EI^2, pp. 342-44, s.v. "Hiba" on the gift in Muslim society; and B. Spuler, s.v. "Hiba" in EI^2, vol. 3, pp. 349-50, on diplomatic gifts in the Ottoman Empire.

82 Charrière 1848-60, vol. 2, pp. 717-18, note; Kurz 1975, p. 25.

83 Spagni 1900, p. 309: Jacques de Germigny (December 13, 1583) wrote *"Les seig.rs Venitiens en tiroient beaucoup de bons offices pour se dire de leur nation qu'à cause des grands et frequents présens que ilz lui faisoient,"* i.e. from Nur Banu. That same year—1583—the sultan was contemptuous of getting only a watch from the French king (Kurz 1975, p. 26, with reference to *Calendar of State Papers Venice* VIII, 1894, p. 85). One of Germigny's predecessors, François de Noailles, Bishop of Acqs, proudly told Charles IX how little he had paid for a clock he gave the sultan (May 8, 1572):

Kurz 1975, p. 26; Charrière 1848-60, vol. 3, p. 266. In the 17th century, the French ambassador encountered problems with the vizier Ahmed Köprülü, as he was five years late in presenting a gift to Ahmed (see Spuler, s.v. "Hiba" in *EI*², vol. 3).

84 Spagni 1900, p. 310, quoting Marciana cl. VII, cod. 404, fol. 46v: *"Ma quello che si deve considerare per ritrarne ogni maggior beneficio è che sarebbe necessario havere persone nel Serraglio che con amore servissero la Ser.tà V.ra et che con buona occasione et giuditio sapesse accompagnare il dono con ufficii grati et amorevoli et in tal caso crederei che fosse molto utile alla Ser.tà V.ra."*

85 Preto 1975, p. 240.

86 Preto 1975, p. 123, note 16, with a reference to Sanudo 1879-1902, vol. 19, cols. 309, 366.

87 *"perchè in vero non si può mancar di questo complimento desiderandolo lei non per la qualità del presente ma per poter di simile recognitione certificarsi della stima che ambisce sia fatto della sua persona da tutti i Principi e specialmente dalla Ser.tà V.ra per essere nata in questa città."* Cited in Spagni 1900, p. 310.

88 *"Et perchè non mi è stata mandata una lettera ne anco io non ho mandato de li."* Spagni 1900, p. 313; Skilliter 1982a, pp. 521, 528 and, on the phrase *"con perdono,"* Skilliter 1982b, p. 139, note 63.

89 For example, in 1503 Hersekoğlu Ahmed wrote to Andrea Gritti asking for *panni di raso*; Andrea in return sent carpets, furs, and camlets: Curatola 1999, with reference to ASV *Documenti Turchi*, b. 1, docs. 93 and 94; see Pedani Fabris 1994. On the close friendship between Andrea Gritti and Hersekoğlu Ahmed Pasha, see Concina 1994, p. 126. In general, see Heller 1961. It was not, of course, just a custom of returning gift with gift, but sometimes of expressing more extended thanks. For example, when Paolo Contarini left for Venice in November 1582, Nur Banu gave him not only a customary robe of honor, but three of the Ottomans' most prized medicaments, all items of great value and prestige: *terra sigillata*, theriac, and balsam (Spagni 1900, pp. 323-24). On the Ottomans and *terra sigillata*, see Raby 1995. On balsam, see Millwright 2001.

90 On the redistributive process in general: Curtin 1984, esp. pp. 13-14.

91 Barkan 1979, pp. 321–22, item 181; J.M. Rogers in Tezcan 1980, p. 16.

92 Uzunçarılı 1960, esp. p. 107.

93 A seal follows the legend. There are two versions of this portrait, one in the Kunsthistorisches Museum in Vienna, the other in the collection of the Gallerie dell'Accademia in Venice, dated 1572: Yriarte 1885; Bertelè 1932, p. 138; Howard 2003b, p. 310; Necipoğlu 2005, p. 98, fig. 91. On Barbaro's life and career, see Yriarte 1885. Barbaro's description of Sokollu Mehmet Pasha in his *relazioni* is *"assez conventionelle"*: Lesure 1972, p. 136, see also pp. 137–38 on relations between the two men (see also Lesure 1976 p. 127), and Lesure 1972, p. 141-43, 153-54 on the changing nature of the house arrest. During the time he was under house arrest, Ottoman merchants took refuge on his property in Venice: Kafadar 1986, p. 201.

94 On the book see Rossi 1937; Rossi 1938; Preto 1975, p. 240.

95 Heyd 1923, vol. 2, p. 351.

96 In 1554 the Beylerbeyi of Egypt, Dukakinzade Mehmet, wrote to a friend in Venice, a former bailo in Aleppo, about some textiles he wanted woven in Venice: he had sent designs through the Venetian bailo in Cairo, and wondered if his friend could speed up delivery. For the letter, dated Shawwal 961/September 1554, see ASV *Documenti Turchi*. Busta XVII, serie VI, no. 17; Gökbilgin 1964, pp. 219, doc. 99; Turan 1968, p. 252; Gökbilgin 1979, p. 283; Rogers 1990-92, p. 68, note 18; Pedani Fabris 1994, p. 180, doc. 714.

97 Mackie 2001, pp. 188-90, and esp. fig. 38.

98 Morosini wrote that Safiye loved *"gli ormesini da Fiorenza et li tabini [scialli] da Venezia, di colori di tutte le sorti, ma specialmente di quelli più vaghi et novi"*: Fabris 1990, esp. p. 104.

99 Charrière 1848-60, vol. 3, p. 822. De Germigny said that Murad seemed to be "dying" to have them at the earliest opportunity. And the sultan's verbal request was then followed up by the Grand Vizier sending word to Germigny through Rabbi Salomon that the merchant who brought the textiles would be paid, if the king did not see fit to send them as a present.

100 Sanudo 1878–1902, vol. 55, col. 635: *"Questo Signor Turco ha piacer di zoie, che mai più la caxa othomana non havea piacer nè le stimavano."* In 1524, for example, he paid 24,000 ducats for a large diamond that Venetian merchants had bought for 16,000 ducats: Bertelè 1932, p. 78; cf. p. 74 on Marco Minio taking Ibrahim Pasha jewels as a present in 1527. On the decline in the demand for jewels, see Necipoğlu 1989.

101 According to the Habsburg ambassador, David von Ungnad, cited by Mraz 1980, p. 49.

102 Sanudo 1879–1902, vol. 55, cols. 14, 636.

103 Aretino 1913, p. 369, letter cccii; Aretino 1997, pp. 407–09, letter 297, esp. p. 407: December 17, 1537. See also Kurz 1975, p. 22.

104 Kurz 1975.

105 See Born 1937. On the gifts of European clocks to the Chinese court in the 18th century, see Pagani 2001.

106 In general, see Kurz 1975; more specifically on the Imperial gift of clocks, see Mraz 1980. The Austrian court ordered most of the clocks for the annual Ottoman tribute from Augsburg. The French ambassador admitted in 1584 that the clock Catherine de' Medici had intended as gift for Nur Banu could not compete with the esteem in which German clocks were held: Charrière 1848-60, vol. 4, p. 275, note; Kurz 1975, p. 30, note 1. . .

107 Fabris 1991, p. 52, with no reference, where he also mentions that in 1545 the Sancakbeyi of Herzogovina was given an iron clock to send on to Istanbul

108 Fabris 1991, p. 52. Fabris (1991, p. 53) also mentions the gift of 11 clocks sent at the conclusion of the war of Candia in 1670.

109 Arbel 2002, p. 22.

110 ASV *Dispacci da Costantinopoli*, Filza 3, fasc. 35, fol. 251r; cf. loc. cit. fol. 277v, where Barbaro emphasizes the importance of keeping Piyale Pasha happy as he is a favorite of the sultan; loc. cit. fol. 344r, where the princess's insistence is stressed. The texts are also given in Marciana MS VII.390 (8872) fols. 3r, 12v, 46r, respectively. In 1533 a German organ was sent, along with a German organist, to Istanbul. It was played in a church in Venice before it was sent: Concina 1994, p. 138.

111 *". . .et prometto à Vostra Serenità, che quà non é stata donata mai cosa, che habbia dato maggior satisfattione,"* and he had heard that the organ was going to be sent to the sultan immediately. Barbaro's dispatch dated June 24, 1569, is quoted here from Marciana MS VII.390 (8872) fols. 122v-123r. See Fabris 1991, p. 53, with references to ASV *Senato. Deliberazioni Costantinopoli* Reg. 4, fols. 109v, 118, 124, 131. The Venetians' success was repeated 25 years later by the English: Mayes 1956; Kurz 1975, pp. 42-44.

112 Respectively, anno 1579 (Charrière 1848-1860, vol. 3, pp. 796) and anno 1519 (Bertelè 1932, pp. 75, note 54).

113 Bertelè 1932, p. 74, note 54; Necipoğlu 1989. On the image of the unicorn in Muslim culture, see Ettinghausen 1950.

114 Fabris 1991, pp. 52; Rogers 1990–92.

115 On glassmaking in Istanbul, see Eyice 1967; Rogers 1982, p. 292–94; Rogers 1983 is perhaps unduly negative.

116 On this complex, see Necipoğlu 2005, pp. 428–38.

117 Fabris 1991, p. 52.

118 Ibid. Nishancı Mehmet Pasha requested Murano oil lamps and glass panes from the Venetian Senate on October 12, 1584, for his mosque in Istanbul; they were shipped out at the end of that year.

119 See above, note 27.

120 June 24, 1569: Marciana MS VII.390 (8872), fol. 122v. Likewise, on January 4, 1570 (m.v. 1569), Barbaro wrote that the Kapudan pasha had asked the doge to send glass for his lantern *(fanò)*, but that he had been able to find some in Pera which he had sent on, much to the Kapudan pasha's delight: Marciana MS VII.390 (8872), fol. 265r.

121 On the *paternostrami* beads, see Han 1973, p. 173; Charleston 1966, p. 23; Curatola 1999, p. 105. On mirrors, see Charleston 1966, p. 19, and Curatola 1999, p. 105. On the mirrored balls, see Rogers 1983, p. 244, esp. note 19; Necipoğlu 2005, p. 107. The Ottomans seem to have had a fondness for glass balls with small galleons inside them: Charleston 1966, p. 23; cf. Necipoğlu 2005, p. 175 on a glass ball with a wood model of a mosque inside of it.

122 Rogers 1983, pp. 244-45. The invention of *cristallo* is traditionally attributed to Andrea Barovier in the mid-15th century, but it now appears that the technological breakthrough occurred earlier: Jacoby 1993. Mehmet the Conqueror asked the Venetians in 1479 for craftsmen to make *christallini*. Otto Kurz (1975, p. 21) suggested that this referred to rock-crystal reading glasses.

123 Fabris 1991, p. 52. On chalcedony glass, see McCray et al. 1995. One of the more unusual requests was for "feathers" made out of Murano glass; Safiye Sultan bought large quantities but asked the bailo to stop the import from Venice, which was only resumed after they had gone out of fashion (Pedani 2000, p. 12).

124 Huth 1968; Huth 1971; Grube 1989.

125 On the Mehmet Bey affair, see above, note 40. See also Fabris 1991, p. 53 for the sultan's casket; he also mentions that this or another (?) casket for Uluch Ali took the goldsmith Giovanni Battista Rizzoletti and the illuminator Francesco Moro a year and a half to make. Incidentally, the largest surviving such casket, now in the Museo de Arte Antiga in Lisbon, was reportedly sold by Venetian merchants to the ruler of Hormuz, and subsequently given by a "Moor" to the Portuguese Primate of the Church of the Indies: Huth 1971, p. 16, note 13. On the European princely connections, see Huth 1971, esp. pp. 7-8; see also Auerpserg-Trautson 1998, p. 4.

126 On the 1559 incident, see Arbel 1992. On the requests for anchors in 1546 and 1593, see Fabris 1991, p. 54.
127 See Barbaro's letters in Marciana MS VII.390 (8872), fols. 116v, 227r, and 265r. On the project, with further references, Necipoğlu 2005, pp. 300–1. See also Costantino di Garzoni, *Relazione di Costantinopoli del 1574*, Museo Correr, MS Dandolo PD.c.975/57 (unpaginated, but fol.14v). On the papal bans, Ortalli 1996.
128 Fabris (1989) believed there was only one request, that from Prince Bayezid. Arbel (2002) argues that requests were received from all three princes.
129 *Pace* Arbel 2002, p. 23. It is worth noting that Bayezid asked for the best and most detailed map available.
130 Gastaldi was entrusted with drawing the *mappamundi* for Prince Selim. Ramusio's *Navigazioni* was ready for publication in 1553, but it was delayed by a fire and not issued until 1559: Ménage 1958, p. 305, note 3.
131 Ménage 1958; Fabris 1989, p. 14; Arbel 2002, p. 23.
132 Ménage 1958; Almagia 1959-60; Bellinger & Vercellin 1985; Fabris 1989; Arbel 2002. On the sensitive issue of supplying maps to the Ottomans, it is worth recalling the protracted consequences of Matteo de Pasti's aborted visit to Mehmet II, taking, among other things, maps from Sigismondo Malatesta of Rimini (see Raby 1987). The Venetians put on trial the patrician Valerio Marcello for daring to give Dragoman Yunus a detailed map of Dalmatia and Istria (Fabris 1991, p. 56).
133 Military engineers and technicians were in demand but the Ottomans knew all too well that the Venetians could and would not supply them, so instead they relied on renegades and prisoners-of-war. On renegades, see above, note 21.
134 Raby 1980; Raby 1982a; Raby 1987. For the most recent publication, see Campbell and Chong 2005.
135 Babinger 1952; reprinted with some modifications in Babinger 1963a; Raby 2000a. On Michelangelo's connections with Bayezid, see Condivi 1746, p. 21 § www and p. 47 §<U5àé Condivi–Wohl 1999, pp. 35, 94; with Selim, Michelangelo-Poggi 1967, vol. 2|é pp. 176-77, Letter)+WW5W; Frey 1899, p. 139; Sarre 1909.
136 Raby 2000b.
137 Notably Paolo Giovio's *Elogia Virorum Bellica Virtute Illustrium* published in Basle in 1575 and, most importantly, his *De rebus et vitis imperatorum Turcarum usque ad Solymanum II*, part of his *Vitae illustrium virorum tomis duobus*, published posthumously by Pietro Perna in Basle in 1577 and 1578. See also Francesco Sansovino's *Sommario et Alboro delli Principi Othomani*. On the relationship between these European sources and Ottoman imperial portraits, see Raby 2000b.
138 See the contributions by Gülru Necipoğlu and Filiz Çağman in Istanbul 2000.
139 On some of those involved in the consortium, see Concina 1984, p. 277.
140 Julius II's tiara was recorded in drawings (c. 1726) by Francesco Barboli; for a reproduction, see Hope 1983, p. 31
141 Kurz 1969 (reprinted in Kurz 1977); and, most importantly, Necipoğlu 1989. On Süleyman's expressed desire to take Rome, see Finlay 1984, pp. 82, 84–85.
142 Alvise was one of three sons born to a Greek woman when Andrea Gritti was pursuing his merchant business in Istanbul in the late 15th century. According to Paolo Giovio, Alvise personally designed the helmet, scepter, and crystal mirror (Giovio *Elogia* vol. 3 of *Opera Omnia* Basle 1596, pp. 197-99).
143 Sanudo 1879–1902, vol. 55, col. 636.
144 Aretino 1997, vol. 1, letter 74. To compound matters, Alvise Gritti had died in the meantime, in 1534. Sanudo 1879-1902, vol. 56, col. 7.
145 Wearden (1985), who identifies the textiles depicted in a woodcut showing von Herberstein robed *alla turca* with surviving pile-on-pile and voided Italian velvets; Atasoy et al. 2001, pp. 32–33. The overwhelming majority of imperial velvet kaftans surviving in the Topkapı Palace are of European velvet, though whether they are Venetian remains to be established: Mackie 2001, pp. 182–90. On the use of Italian velvets on bookbindings made for the library of Mehmet II, see Raby and Tanındı 1993.
146 Kurz 1975.
147 Necipoğlu 2005.
148 The architectural glass supplied by Venice, much of it for use in mosques, was so integral to the vocabulary of Ottoman architecture that its European origin was irrelevant and unremarkable.
149 On the chairs, see Fabris 1991, p. 51.
150 Contadini 1989, p. 233; Contadini 1999, p. 15: regarding orders for Ibrahim Bey in 1569. He was so taken by the beauty of this leatherwork that he ordered a second batch. In 1578 Sokollu Mehmet Pasha complained to the bailo that a slave of his—a "good painter"—had failed to return after he had been manumitted, and that he needed him badly now, so Barbarigo believed, for a room he was building in his palace. It is not certain that he was Italian, but Barbarigo offered the Grand Vizier the services of a young painter from Verona whom he had in his service. The dispatch is dated August 3, 1578: ASV *Dispacci da Costantinopoli*, Filza 12, fol. 167r.
151 Some of the plaques are of lapis, agate, and jasper.
152 Pedani 2000, p. 18. On the earlier style of throne, see Preyger 1973.
153 On Venetian pageantry, Muir 1979, pp. 36ff. On the Lepanto pageants, see Gombrich 1967; Fenlon 1988. The woodcut by Matteo Pagan showing a ducal procession in the mid-1550s has Turkish onlookers prominently featured (Necipoğlu 2005, p. 100, fig. 104). Similarly, a painting by Il Vicentino (Andrea Michieli) depicting the "Coronation of Dogaress Morosina Grimani" in 1597 has a disproportionate number of Turkish observers (Muir 1979, fig. 10, and pp. 47-48). This was not a contemporary record, and the Ottomans were, one assumes, portrayed prominently as synecdochic of Venice's Eastern connections.
154 For the pictorial record of these festivities, see Atasoy 1997. Doris Behrens-Abouseif (2004) has recently suggested that the *Bucintoro* may have inspired the golden barge used for the Khalij Festival in Cairo in the later Mamluk period.
155 S. Yerasimos in Paris 1990, cat. nos. 317 and 319. See also Ünver 1958; Taeschner 1925; Kurz & Kurz 1972; Skilliter 1977a; and 1985.
156 Lozzi 1900; Guârin-Dalle Mese 1998; Wilson 2004; Wilson 2005.
157 Busbecq-Forster-Daniell 1881, vol. 1, p. 255; Kurz 1975, p. 28.
158 Cf. Kafadar 1986, p. 211, especially on the contribution of traveling merchants to changing tastes and fashions in Turkey.
159 Necipoğlu 1989, esp. pp. 417–26.
160 Skilliter 1977b.
161 "It can be said that negotiating can be compared to juggling with a glass ball: it is necessary to keep it always in the air skillfully—never letting it drop nor handling it too harshly otherwise it would break—catching it with dexterity and throwing it again spiritedly at the most opportune moment." Spagni 1900, p. 305: quoting from ASV *Senato, Dispacci da Costantinopoli*, Filza 5, June 24, 1569.

"Orientalist" Painting in Venice, 15th–17th Centuries

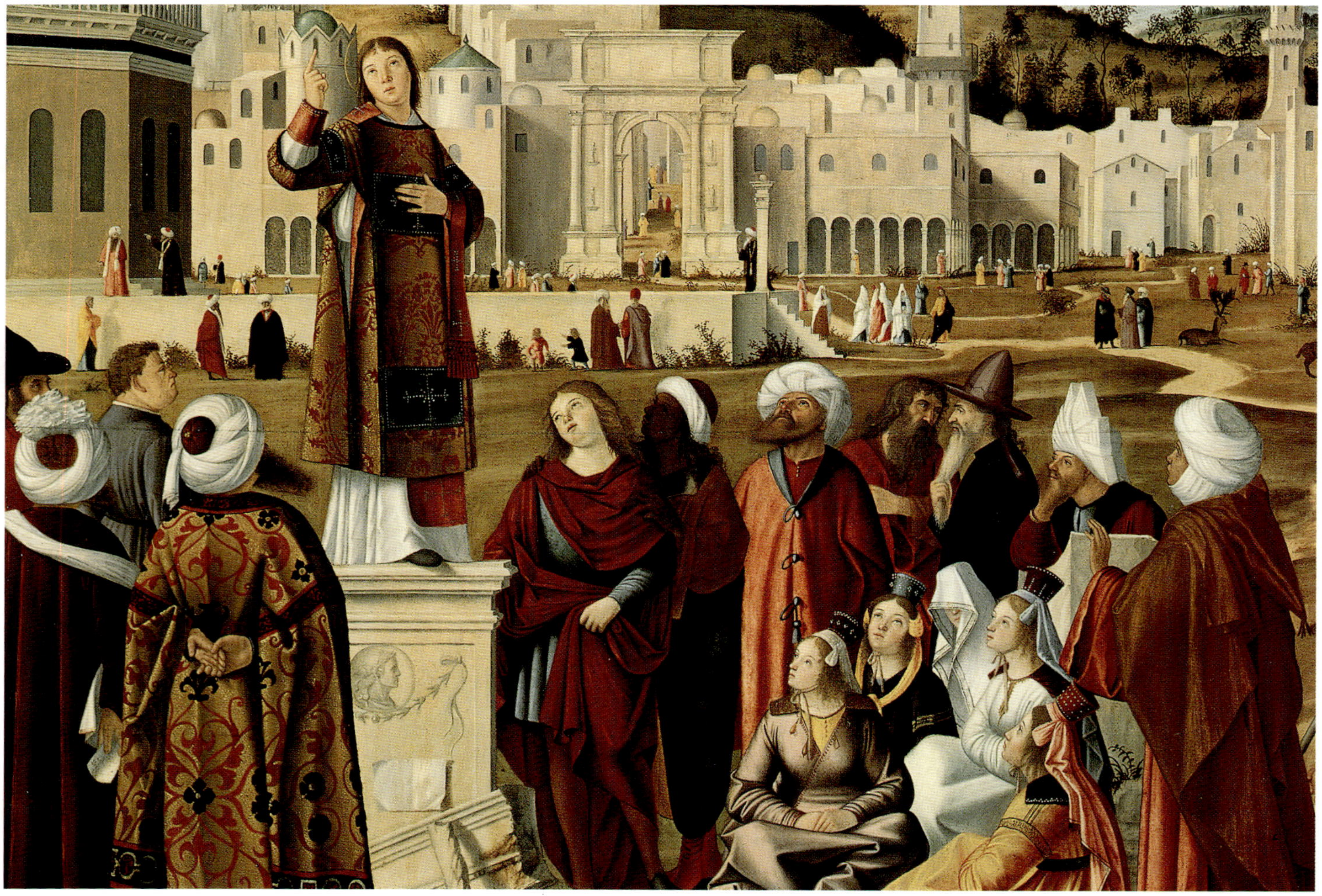

Catarina Schmidt
Arcangeli

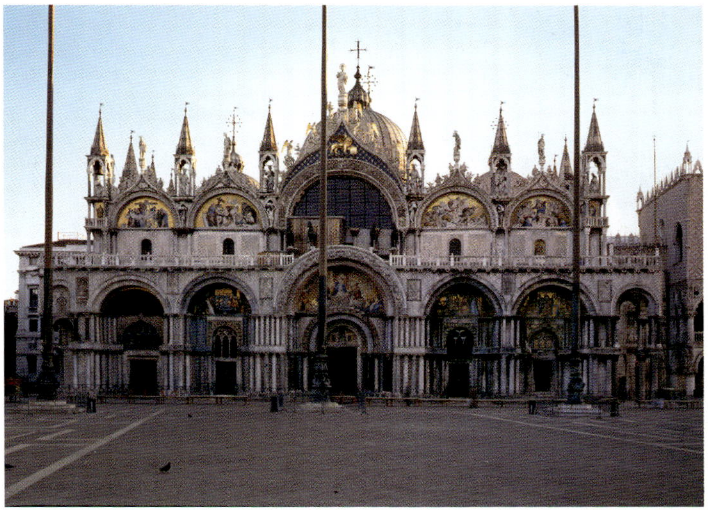

fig. 1. St. Mark's Basilica, Venice

Nearly a quarter century ago Julian Raby first coined the term "Oriental mode" to describe the sudden appearance of Islamic settings, costumes, exotic animals, and luxury objects in late 15th-century Venetian painting.[1] Between the 1490s and the 1520s, the representation of Muslim people and places reached its height in Venice in the large-scale narrative canvases created to adorn the walls of the city's religious confraternities.[2] In the mid- to late 16th century, an interest in portrait cycles and collections flourished in both Italy and the Ottoman Empire, and Venetian painters were increasingly called upon to portray the great rulers and military captains of the Islamic world. By the 17th century, the Near East appears ever more exotic and fantastic in Venetian painting, although arguably the Orientalism of Venice remains distinctive from that of other areas in Europe thanks to the city's close and long rapport with the region. The present exhibition affords an excellent opportunity to trace the different stages in Venetian portrayals of the Islamic world through the centuries.

Even before the dawn of the Oriental mode in the 15th century, aspects of the Near East had already appeared in Venetian art in scenes from the life of St. Mark the Evangelist, the city's powerful patron saint. Mark founded the church in Alexandria, the ancient North African city where he was martyred and first buried. In 828, after Alexandria had come under Muslim control, two Venetian merchants stole the saint's miracle-working body and brought it back to their home city, where they presented it to the doge and a new shrine was erected in his honor, the Doge's Chapel or St. Mark's Basilica (fig. 1). As the final home of St. Mark's relics, Venice became the new Alexandria, and the saint's legend united Orient and Occident. In the centuries that followed, St. Mark's Basilica, modelled on the Byzantine Church of the Holy Apostles in Constantinople, became encrusted with mosaics and was adorned with altarpieces

cat. 28. Vittore Carpaccio
and collaborators
The Sermon of St. Stephen (detail)
Venice, ca. 1514
Musée du Louvre, Paris

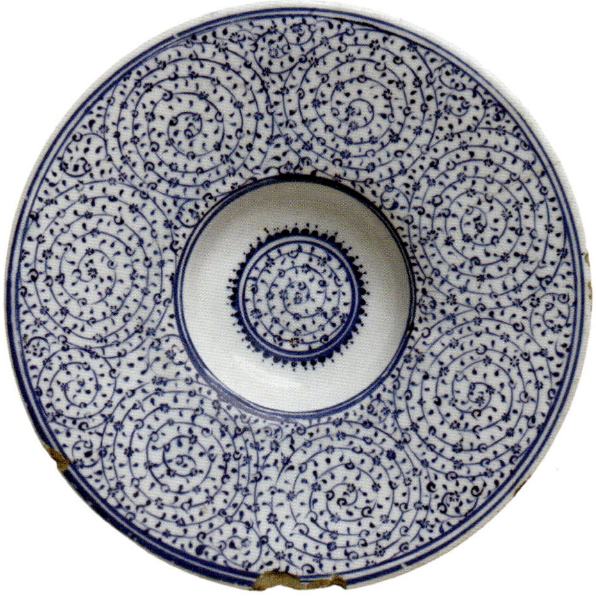

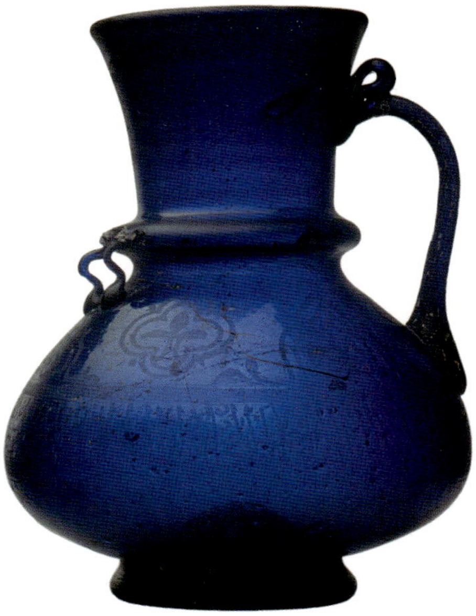

cat. 173. *Plate*
Turkey, Iznik, ca. 1535–45
Ashmolean Museum, Oxford

cat. 154. *Jug*
Syria or Egypt, ca. 1361–63
Ashmolean Museum, Oxford

representing St. Mark's legend.[3] In scenes of his prayer, missionary activities, martyrdom, and the theft of his body, exotic details, such as costumes or architectural motifs, naturally often play a prominent role.[4] The Near East was very much part of the "invented past" created by the Venetians to compensate for their lack of an ancient Roman past.[5] Medieval representations of Alexandria in St. Mark's Basilica therefore were initially linked to Antiquity and not, as in the Oriental mode of the Renaissance, to the contemporary Islamic world.

It is the unique geographical position of Venice between East and West, along with her strong mercantile character, which came to define her special relationship with the Islamic world. Male scions of Venice's most important families, including the Contarini, the Loredan, and the Zorzi, went to work as merchants and diplomats in the eastern Mediterranean. Among these patrician families we also find many of the patrons of the Orientalist painters.

In contrast to the city's merchants, few Venetian artists, with the important exception of the painter Gentile Bellini and the sculptor Bartolomeo Bellano, who were sent to the court of Sultan Mehmet II (r. 1444–46 and 1451–81) (cat. 116, p. 134) in Istanbul as cultural ambassadors of the Venetian Republic between 1479 and 1481, had the opportunity to travel in the Levant. In their depictions of Near Eastern people and places, Venetian painters relied heavily on oral and literary accounts produced by others, and were particularly drawn to illustrated texts, such as Marin Sanudo's *Liber secretum fidelium cruces* ("Book of the Secrets of the Faithful of the Cross"), dated 1316–21 (cat. 41, p. 62). In the late 15th century, Venetian painters frequently drew inspiration from Bernhard Breydenbach´s *Peregrinatio in terram sanctam* ("Pilgrimage to the Holy Land"). Published in Mainz in 1486 and readily available in Venice by the 1490s, the German pilgrimage account is illustrated with woodcuts by the Northern artist Erhard Reuwich, who had accompanied Breydenbach on his journey.[6] In addition to graphic sources, ambassadors visiting Venice from Muslim lands, such as the Ottoman Hasan Bey, who came to negotiate frontiers with Venice in 1480, and the Mamluk Taghribirdi, who came to discuss Venetian commercial treaties in 1507, gave Venetian artists vital insight into the appearance and dress of their Muslim neighbours.[7] A wide variety of Islamic luxury objects, too, were readily visible in Venice in the city's households.[8] Glazed ceramics (cat. 173), patterned

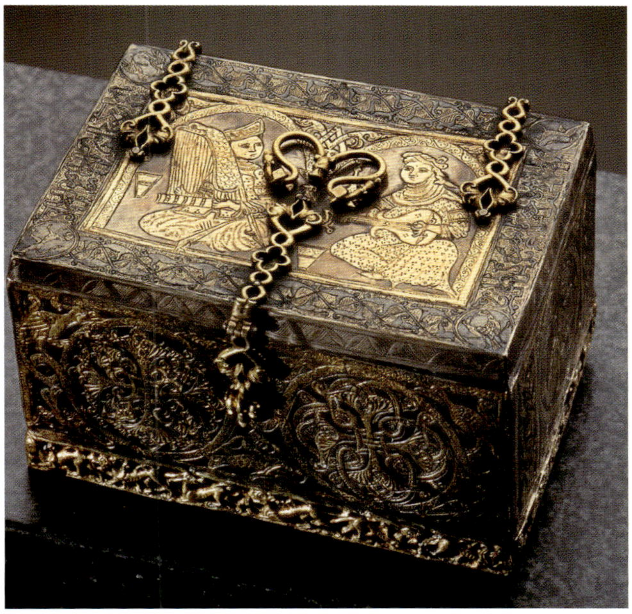

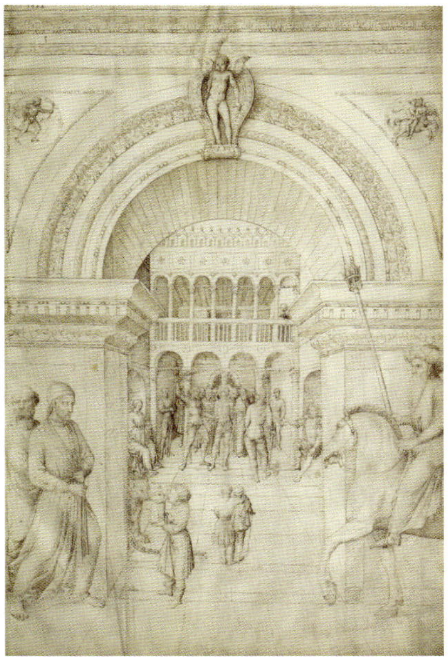

silks, gilded glass (cat. 154), and inlaid metalwork (cat. 93) from the Islamic world appealed to artists for their great beauty and magnificent color as well as the preciousness of their materials, and such objects made a frequent appearance in Venetian painting from the Renaissance.[9]

cat. 93. *Casket*
Southern Italy or Spain, probably late 13th–early 14th century
Procuratoria di San Marco, Venice

fig. 2. Jacopo Bellini, *The Flagellation of Christ in a Palatial Building,* 15th century. Musée du Louvre, Paris

The Bellini Family and the Development of the Oriental Mode

Because of his famous journey to Istanbul, which brought him into direct contact with Ottoman life and culture, Gentile Bellini is widely recognized as one of the chief protagonists of the Oriental mode in Venetian painting. His trip has been the focus of many studies, and the 2005–6 Boston and London exhibition *Bellini and the East* has enhanced our knowledge even further.[10] Far less attention, on the other hand, has been paid to the role of his Venetian contemporaries in the development of the Oriental mode, including most importantly other members of the Bellini family and their workshop.

Jacopo Bellini, Gentile's renowned father, took the first real step in creating settings for modern narratives in the Venetian Renaissance painting, and is best known for his two surviving sketchbooks now in Paris (Louvre) and London (British Museum).[11] In these *libri studiorum,* Jacopo constructed sophisticated pictorial narratives, and his interest in Antiquity and linear perspective served as the basis for religious scenes. He never represented an Islamic setting but did include, as in folio 8 of the Paris sketchbook, turbaned bystanders (fig. 2). The crowded compositions and exotic animals that fill the albums served as a visual dictionary for Venetian painters of the next generation, many of whom trained in the Bellini workshop. In addition, the way Jacopo depicts biblical events as a synthesis of the ancient past and the Venice of his day was extraordinarily influential.[12] His drawings became one of the principal sources of inspiration for the Oriental mode, and it is Jacopo rather than Gentile Bellini who could be called the Father of Venetian Orientalism.

The increased importation of Islamic objects in the latter half of the 15th century inspired their depiction in Venetian painting, even by non-Orientalist painters such as

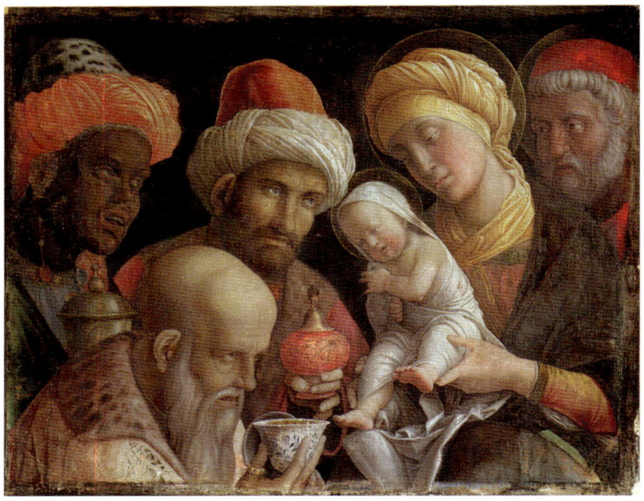

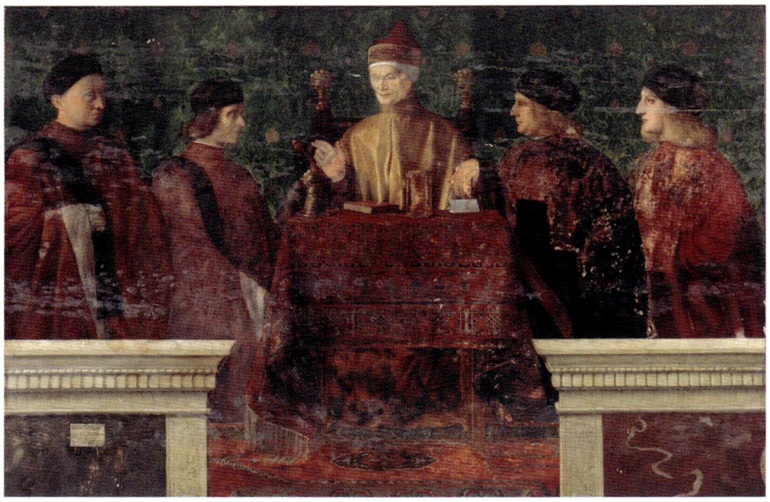

fig. 3. Andrea Mantegna, *Adoration of the Magi,* 1487–1500. J. Paul Getty Museum, Los Angeles

fig. 4. Giovanni Bellini, *Portrait of Doge Loredan and Four Advisers,* 1507. Gemäldegalerie, Berlin

Andrea Mantegna, Jacopo Bellini's son-in-law. Already in the late 1450s, Mantegna draped a small-pattern Holbein carpet from Turkey at the foot of the Virgin's throne in the *San Zeno Altarpiece* (Verona, in situ).[13] Even after he left Padua for Mantua in 1456–57 to work at the Gonzaga court, Mantegna continued to include Islamic objects in his paintings on occasion. In his *Adoration of the Magi* from 1487–1500 (J. Paul Getty Museum, Los Angeles) (fig. 3); , he depicts several Oriental objects, including a small blue-and-white cup with floral scrolls imitating Chinese porcelain, a censer that may be a Turkish *tombak,* and an agate bowl that is perhaps pre-Islamic Persian.[14] Mantua followed Venice's lead in forging diplomatic relations with Muslim potentates,[15] and the Gonzaga collections included Islamic art. Francesco II Gonzaga's own Mamluk tent likely served as the model for the one represented in the *objet de luxe* painting of *Judith with the Head of Holofernes* from ca. 1490 (National Gallery of Art, Washington, D.C.), attributed to Mantegna or his close follower Giulio Campagnola.[16]

Jacopo's son Giovanni Bellini, is more closely associated with Venice's late 15th-century Byzantine revival rather than the Oriental mode, but like his brother-in-law Mantegna he often depicted Islamic objects in his paintings. For example, in his *Coronation of the Virgin* of ca. 1475 (Museo Civico, Pesaro), Giovanni placed a beaker in the hands of Nicodemus, one of the figures represented in the *cimasa*, the painting added to the top of the altarpiece, and this Islamic vessel transmits the exoticism of the Holy Land. [17] In the numerous devotional images of the Presentation in the Temple and the Circumcision made in the Bellini workshop, precious and elaborate Oriental or Orientalizing clothing served as models for the dress of the high priests and bystanders in the Jewish ceremonies.[18] Giovanni's and his patrons' interest in Islamic material culture is further testified by the painter's famous *Portrait of Doge Loredan and Four Advisers*, which features both a Para-Mamluk carpet and an "Ushak" re-entrant prayer rug (fig. 4).[19] These carpets, likely diplomatic gifts from Near Eastern rulers, signify the doge's rank. Objects from both the Near and Far East, including Chinese bowls, an Iznik bowl, and a large vase of Mamluk or Iranian lusterware, also play an important role in Giovanni's *Feast of the Gods* (National Gallery, Washington D.C.), dated 1514.[20]

Giovanni Bellini's pupils and followers showed a similar interest in enriching their compositions with Islamic luxury objects. In *The Dream of St. Ursula* of 1490–95 (Gallerie dell'Accademia, Venice), Vittore Carpaccio represented a Mamluk inlaid metal bucket, converted into a container for holy water, below the tabernacle next to the saint's bed (cat. 110).[21]

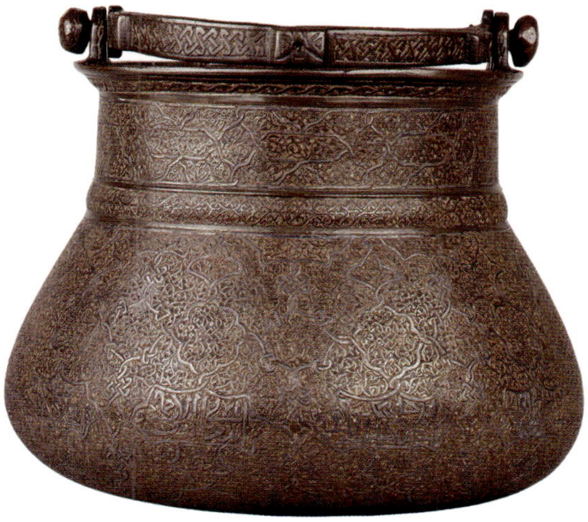

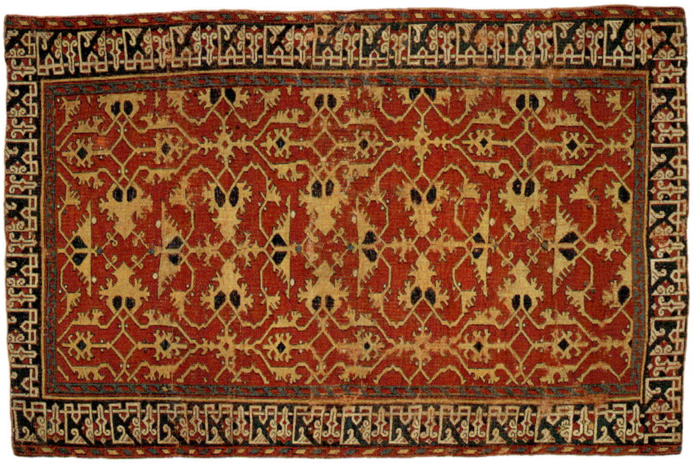

cat. 110. *Bucket*
Probably Egypt or Syria,
late 14th-early 15th century
Museum für Islamische Kunst, Berlin

cat. 84. *Carpet with "Lotto" pattern*
Western Anatolia, early 16th century
The Saint Louis Art Museum, St. Louis

Another painting by Carpaccio, *St. Augustine in his Study* (Scuola di San Giorgio degli Schiavoni, Venice), shows Mamluk rose-water sprinklers on the shelf beside the saint (cat. 98).[22] In his *Madonna with Saints* of 1495 (Kunstmuseum, Düsseldorf), Cima da Conegliano gives the Virgin a nielloed silver bracelet decorated with an Arabic inscription inspired by the *tiraz* bands commonly found on Islamic garments.[23] Later in the 16th century, Lorenzo Lotto became famous for his depictions of Oriental carpets, which he included in religious scenes as well as portraits, such as in *Giovanni della Volta and his Family* in the National Gallery in London (cat. 32, p. 126).[24] In an even more impressive display, Paris Bordone layered a series of large Ottoman carpets (cat. 84) at the feet of the Venetian doge and senators in *The Return of the Ring to the Doge* of 1534 (see fig. 3, p. 177).[25] The variety of Islamic objects that can be identified in Venetian Renaissance paintings demonstrates precisely how plentiful, even commonplace, they were in Venice in this period.

The *Scuole* of Venice and the Oriental Mode

During the late 15th and early 16th centuries, Venetian devotional confraternities, known as *scuole*, decorated their chapels and meeting halls with large narrative canvases representing the pious legends of their patron saints. Since many of those saints had lived in the Eastern Mediterranean or North Africa, Islamic architecture and figures often appear in the scenes as contemporary reflections of these regions. It is in the great *scuole* paintings that Venetian representations of the Islamic world can be seen on a grand scale, and in this essay three of the most exemplary cycles will be discussed.

The first of many Venetian painted narratives in the Oriental mode was made around 1495 for the apsidal chapel in the church of Santa Maria dei Crocifieri by a trio of artists: Cima da Conegliano, Giovanni Mansueti, and Lattanzio da Rimini. Patronized by the small but wealthy guild of silk merchants and weavers known as the Arte dei setaiuoli, the chapel was dedicated to both the Virgin and St. Mark.[26] Its walls were decorated with four scenes from the life of St. Mark on canvas, only two of which survive today.[27] The decision to include so many references to the Islamic world in these paintings seems significant in light of the fact that many members of the Arte dei setaiuoli had business interests in the Eastern Mediterranean.

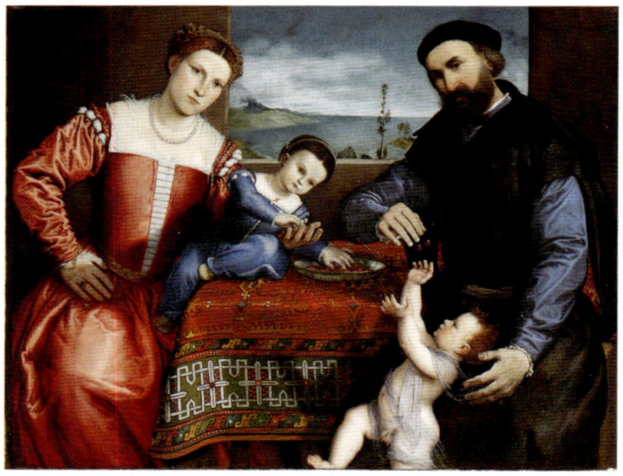

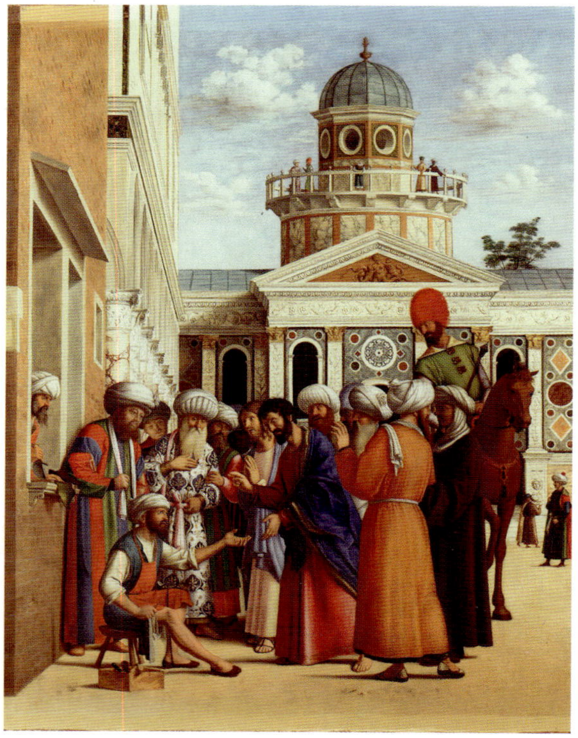

cat. 32. Lorenzo Lotto
Giovanni della Volta with his Wife and Children
Venice, 1547
The National Gallery, London

fig. 5. Cima da Conegliano, *St. Mark Healing the Cobbler Anianus in Alexandria*, 1497–99. Gemäldegalerie, Berlin

cat. 27. Giovanni Mansueti
The Arrest and Trial of St. Mark
Venice, 1499
Sammlungen des Fürsten von und zu Liechtenstein, Vienna

Among them were importers of *seta da mar* (raw silk) from Syria, Egypt, or Persia, while others produced silk thread known as *seta elaborata* that Venice exported to the Islamic world.[28]

In his contribution to the Crocifieri cycle, *St. Mark Healing Anianus* (fig. 5; Gemäldegalerie, Berlin), Cima refashions Alexandria, the city where the event took place, in an image of Venice.[29] The large Renaissance building in the background with a dome, tambour, balustrade, and precious marble inlay closely resembles the Venetian church of Santa Maria dei Miracoli, erected in the heart of the city just a few years earlier. Neither this "temple" nor the porticoed edifice that flanks it evokes Alexandria; instead the setting mirrors contemporary Venice.[30] The reference to Venice as the new Alexandria is not an accident, but rather an explicit reference to the Italian city's long-held claim to be the rightful owner of St. Mark's body.[31] The figures in Cima's scene, however, are Egyptians, dressed in the costume of the contemporary Mamluk Empire. With the exception of St. Mark and his companion, who are dressed in apostolic tunics and wear no head covering, all the figures wear precious Oriental garments and their heads are crowned with either a large bulbous turban or the famous *zamt*, a red bonnet worn by Mamluk military officers.[32]

The second of the two surviving scenes from the Crocifieri cycle is Mansueti's *The Arrest and Trial of St. Mark* (cat. 27). Like Cima before him, Mansueti evokes an urban space similar to that of Renaissance Venice, with buildings characterized by arches, balustrades, and colored marble inlay.[33] But his method differs from Cima's: instead of a cityscape closely connected to actual Venetian buildings, Mansueti derives many of his motifs from Jacopo Bellini's sketchbooks. Notably he was trained in the Bellini family workshop. A detail such as the panther in the foreground can be understood as both homage to Jacopo and as a reminder of how the fierce animal was tamed in the saint's presence.[34] Mansueti clearly took liberties when depicting the setting in all its *venezianità*, but in his representation of contemporary Syro-Egyptian costume he was even more precise than Cima (and most of his other contemporaries). For example, Mansueti crowns the seated dignitary, probably a judge, with an accurate rendering of the kind of Mamluk turban worn by high-ranking officials, characterized by large "horns."[35] This painting shows Mansueti's excellent knowledge of both the decorum and details of Mamluk dress.

Far more important for the development of the Oriental mode was the St. Mark cycle for the *albergo* of the Scuola di San Marco, one of the city's *scuole grandi* (fig. 6, p. 128). As the newly constructed building for the confraternity neared completion at the end of the

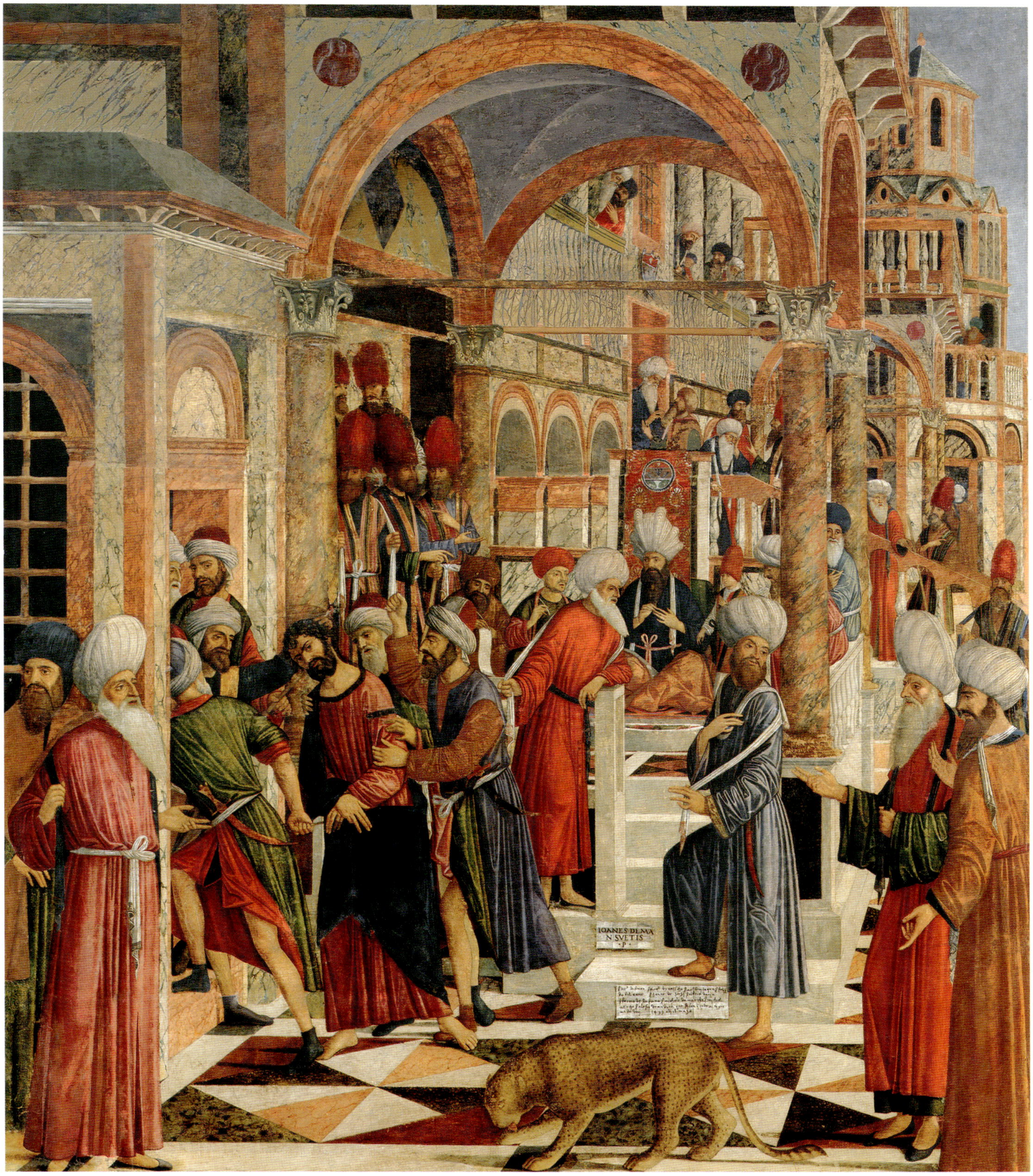
IOANES DE MA
N SVETIS
·P·

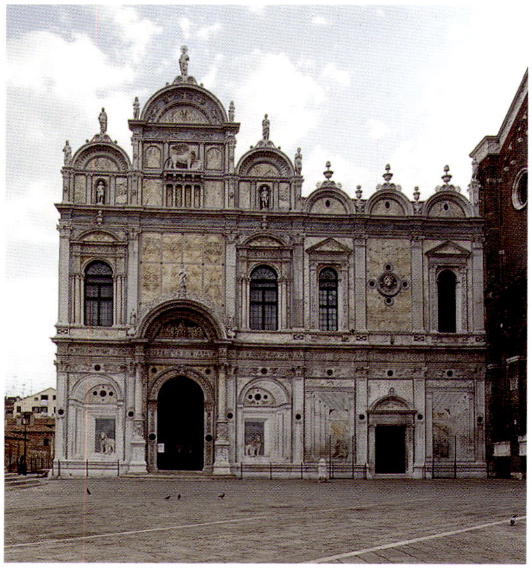

fig. 6. Façade of the Scuola di San Marco, Campo SS. Giovanni e Paolo, Venice

15th century, plans for the decoration of its interior began. In this period the membership roster of the Scuola di San Marco swelled with the names of merchants who shipped merchandise between the Ottoman and Mamluk Empires and Venice. Some members were travelling diplomats, such as the famous Ambrogio Contarini or Giosafat Barbaro, who wrote descriptions of their visits to Tana (on the Black Sea coast) and Persia.[36] Artists, including Gentile and Giovanni Bellini, also belonged to the *scuola*.[37] While serving the *scuola* as the *Guardian da Matin* in 1492, Gentile first extended his offer to decorate the confraternity's *albergo*, although it was more than a decade before the project got under way.

As an artist of notable reputation who had seen the Islamic world first hand, Gentile Bellini was the ideal painter for the Scuola di San Marco cycle. While in Istanbul in 1479–81, he had likely made a number of studies of Ottoman costumes,[38] monuments, luxury goods, and exotic animals, and these drawings became a point of reference for his canvas of *St. Mark Preaching in Alexandria* for the *scuola*. Yet Gentile likely did not visit any other major Near Eastern city, including Alexandria, and therefore, like many other Venetian painters, he turned to Breydenbach's *Peregrinationes* as a guide for depicting Mamluk minarets and costume.[39] But even when quoting a secondary source, Gentile created compositions striking for their originality and unique vision.

St. Mark preaching to the people of Alexandria is recounted in Jacopo da Varagine's *Golden Legend* (written ca. 1269), perhaps the most important source for the lives of the saints in the Middle Ages and Renaissance. The event is one of the most crucial in his apostolic mission to the pagan world, for it resulted in a large number of conversions to the Christian faith, but surprisingly the subject only rarely appears in Venetian art. The city's artists generally focused instead on events with an explicit religious-political significance, such as the translation of his relics from Alexandria to Venice.[40] By selecting a less commonly depicted scene, Gentile Bellini had greater liberty to project the scene onto a space with which he was very familiar: Venice's own Piazza San Marco. As has often been noted, the composition of Gentile's *St. Mark Preaching in Alexandria* (fig. 7) is similar to his earlier *Procession in the Piazza San Marco* (Venice, Gallerie dell'Accademia), but in this case Gentile gave the famous Venetian square an Oriental aura by populating it with exotic animals and figures in Mamluk and Ottoman garments, behind which can be seen monuments of Istanbul, such as the obelisk with pseudo-hieroglyphs and the Column of Diocletian, also known as the Pillar of Pompey.[41] The church in the painting's background displays the characteristics of several different buildings including St. Mark's Basilica in Venice and the Church of the Holy Apostles in Constantinople, while also alluding to the Boucolis church in Alexandria, founded by St. Mark himself and considered to be another important forerunner to St. Mark's.[42] Gentile also made reference to Islamic architecture such as the minaret of the Ibn Tulun Mosque in Cairo with an exterior stair-

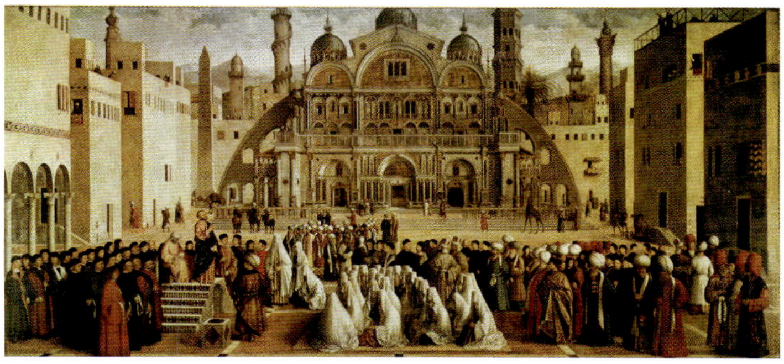

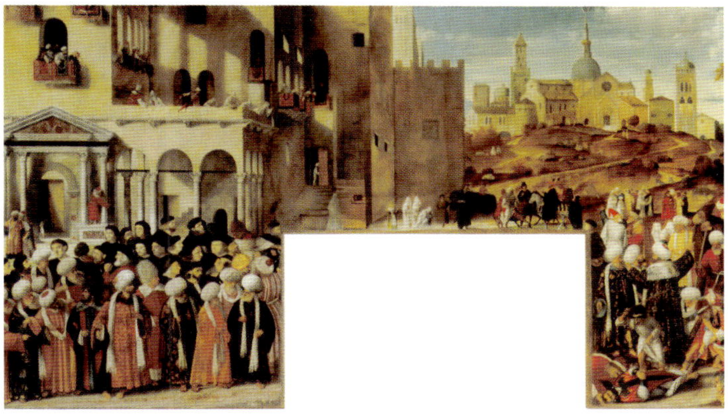

case and the tower of Bab Zuwayla.[43] There are also other minarets and houses with small windows and roof terraces typical of Syro-Egyptian buildings. Finally the painter incorporates the symbol of Alexandria, the Pharos lighthouse.[44] In Gentile's amalgamation of antique and contemporary elements, every time a motif was copied it was also transformed.

fig. 7. Gentile Bellini, *St. Mark Preaching in Alexandria,* 1504–7. Pinacoteca di Brera, Milan

fig. 8. Vittore Belliniano, *The Martyrdom of St. Mark,* 1515–26. Gallerie dell'Accademia, Venice

After Gentile's death in 1507, his brother Giovanni completed *St. Mark Preaching in Alexandria,*[45] and in 1515 the Scuola di San Marco's governors voted to continue the cycle with a second monumental canvas, *The Martyrdom of St. Mark* (Venice, Gallerie dell'Accademia; fig. 8).[46] Although Giovanni conceived and executed much of this painting, his pupil Vittore Belliniano finished it after Giovanni himself died in 1516. The Islamic setting is suggested only through the numerous costumes of Mamluks and Ottomans (cat. 52, p. 130) who, together with the Venetian *confratelli,* witness the saint's death.

In 1518, another painter, Giovanni Mansueti, became involved with the Scuola di San Marco cycle, and before his own death in 1526 or 1527, he contributed three paintings to it: *St. Mark Healing Anianus* (see cat. 50, p. 131 on the subject), *St. Mark Baptizing Anianus* (cat. 28, pp. 74 and 83), and *Scenes from the Life of St. Mark* (Gallerie dell'Accademia, Venice). Mansueti's vocabulary in these canvases is that established earlier in the artist's *Arrest and Trial of St. Mark* for the Crocifieri cycle. In *St. Mark Healing Anianus* the architecture is Venetian, but decorated with the blazon of the Mamluk sultan Qa'itbey (r. 1468–96), while the figures are almost all Mamluks. The crowded stage and the recurrence of stock figures such as the Mamluk officer are the main features of Mansueti's work. Despite the Venetian character of the interior and exterior spaces there is one accurately depicted Islamic object, the Ottoman Iznik bowl (cat. 178, p. 131) placed on the staircase in the *Healing of Anianus.* The painter clearly took liberties when depicting the Islamic world, but in doing so he was not different from most of his Venetian contemporaries also working in the Oriental mode.

Vittore Carpaccio (see cat. 30, p. 133; cat. 31, p. 27), who like Mansueti was close to the Bellini family of painters, has been recognized as the greatest practitioner of the Oriental mode in Venetian Renaissance painting,[47] and perhaps his most exemplary narrative cycle comes from the meetinghouse of the Scuola di San Giorgio degli Schiavoni. Begun in 1502, the series is composed of nine large paintings: two scenes from the life of Christ, three from

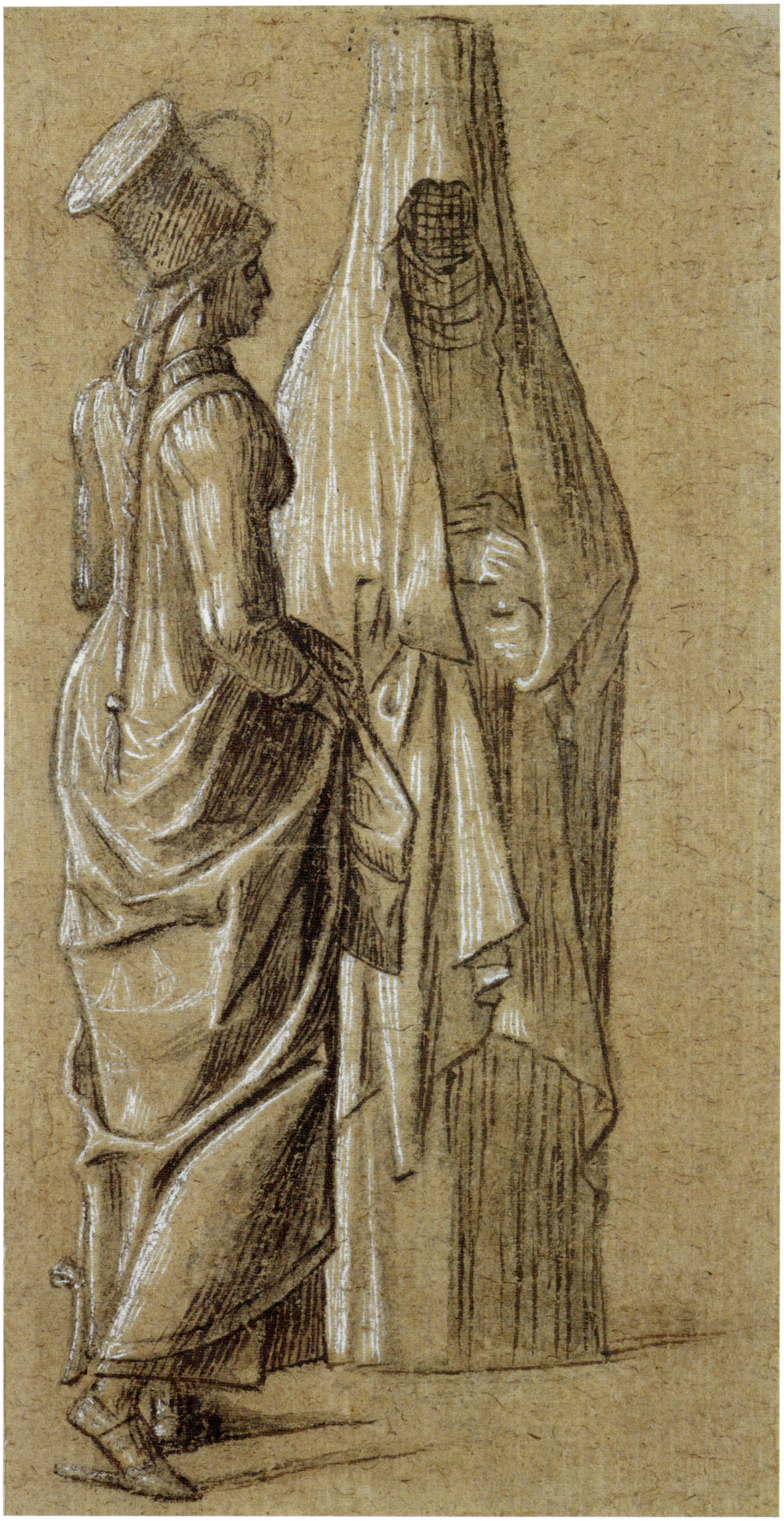

the life of St. Jerome, three from the life of St. George, and one from the life of St. Tyron. With much assistance from his workshop, Carpaccio was able to finish it in just five years. Since 1586, the paintings have been installed on the ground floor of the *scuola*, where they remain to this day.[48]

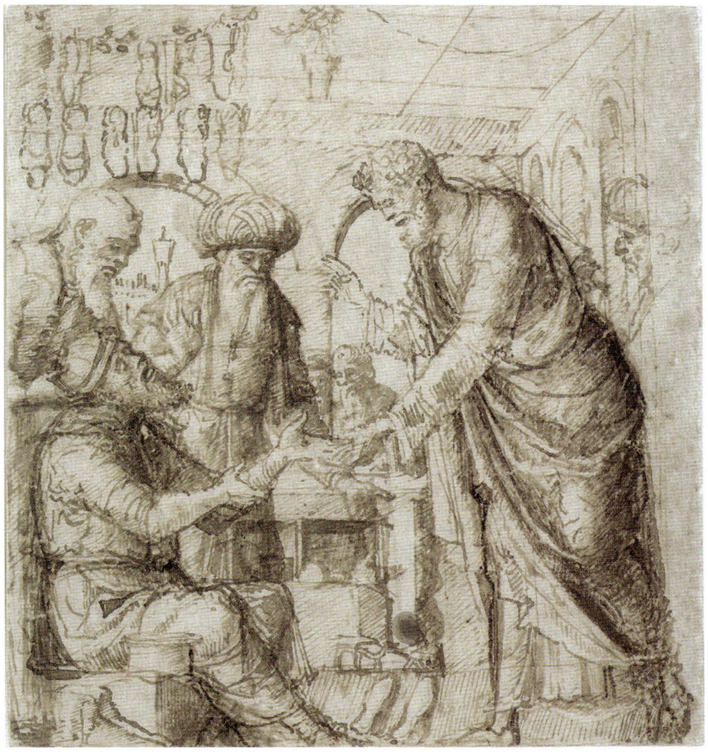

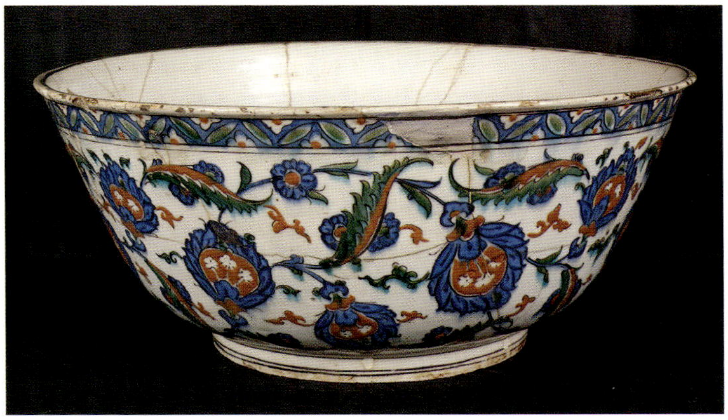

Founded in 1451 for Venice's Dalmatian colony and dedicated to SS. George, Jerome, and Tyron, the Scuola di San Giorgio degli Schiavoni often met to pray for their brethren working on Venetian ships traveling in the Eastern Mediterranean.[49] Dalmatians also financed many of the Venetian galleys in their numerous military battles with the Turks, and their help in defending Rhodes was even honoured by an indulgence of Pope Sixtus IV.[50] More directly confronted with the constant danger of the Ottoman Empire, the members of the Scuola di San Giorgio degli Schiavoni had a more problematic view of the Islamic Levant than those of the Arte dei setaiuoli and the Scuola di San Marco, whose interests focused on peaceful travel to the emporia of the Near East to exchange goods for commercial gain.

The three scenes from the life of St. George in Carpaccio's Scuola degli Schiavoni cycle are *St. George and the Dragon* (fig. 9, p. 132), *The Triumph of St. George*, and *The Baptism of the Selenites* (fig. 10, p. 132). The painter referred to Varagine's *Golden Legend* for the narrative; his visual source of inspiration included Reuwich's illustrations, although Carpaccio likely borrowed Oriental motifs from other places too.[51] The final composition of each scene must have been the result of a long preparatory process, as a number of drawings testify.[52]

In *The Triumph of St. George*, the figures appear in rich Oriental costumes in the foreground, while in the background there is an open square with the Temple of Solomon flanked by other minarets, like the one in the city of Rama, in the background, and by towers similar to those in Reuwich's view of Alexandria. A drawing in the Uffizi, with a lattice-covered window typical of contemporary Cairo as well as a Mamluk minaret and cup, reveals the artist's precision when preparing complex compositions (fig. 11, p. 133). It is worth noting that the minaret in this drawing is given a more precise shape than in Reuwich's illustration, revealing that Carpaccio used other sources as well.[53]

In *The Baptism of the Selenites*, the frieze-like composition shows figures in Ottoman and Mamluk dress, along with two women in Dalmatian costumes.[54] Islamic luxury objects,

cat. 50. Giovanni Bellini
Miracle of St. Mark: The Healing of the Cobbler Anianus
Venice, mid-1480s
Staatliche Museen, Kupferstichkabinett, Berlin

cat. 178. *Bowl*
Iznik, Turkey, 17th century
Museo Civico Correr, Venice

cat. 52. Vittore Carpaccio
Two Standing Women, One in Mamluk Dress (recto)
Venice, ca. 1500
Princeton University Art Museum

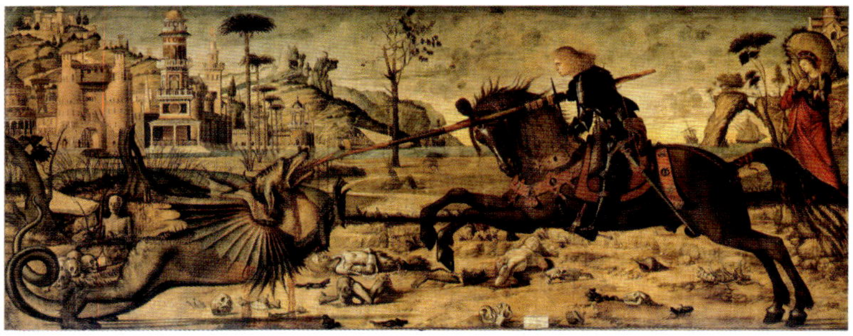

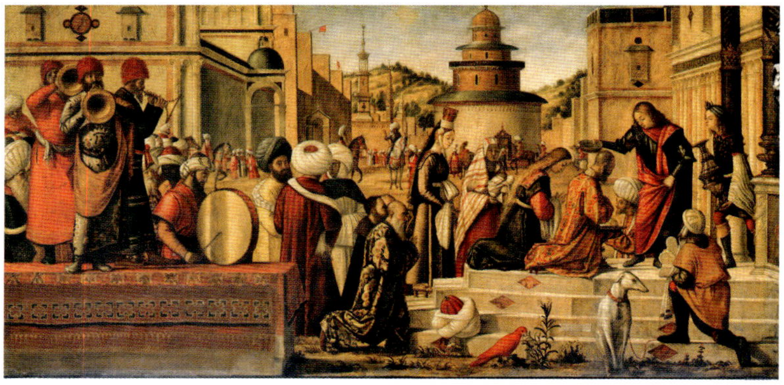

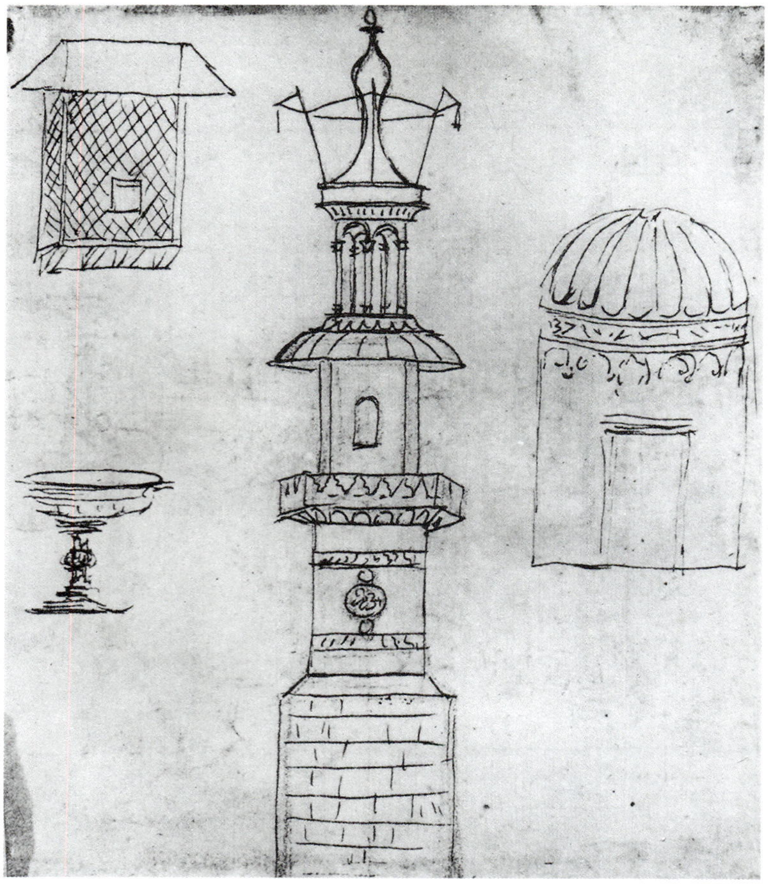

like the Turkish carpet beneath the musicians and the Islamic water bottle held by one of St. George's servants, also have a notable presence in the scene.

The confrontation between Christians and non-believers is the main subject of the St. George legend. Born in Cappadocia (Turkey), he was well known to Crusaders to the Holy Land because of his prominent role in the Byzantine Church. The most captivating aspect of his legend is his fierce nature, demonstrated in his victory over the dragon, but St. George's role as a missionary is relevant too. The importance of this soldier-saint in battles against non-believers is testified by a number of sources.[55] This *militia Christi* had a mission identical to that of all medieval European Crusaders.

Whether this and the other scenes from the life of St. George can be interpreted as a commentary on contemporary politics, as has been suggested by some scholars, must be considered carefully and cautiously.[56] The Scuola degli Schiavoni's Dalmatian *confratelli* were certainly aware of Ottoman military might and keenly felt the loss of important Venetian fortresses such as Modone and Corone, which fell to the Turks in 1499.[57] With the help of Pope Alexander VI, peace was finally reached between the Venetians and Ottomans in 1502. Thus, between 1502 and 1507, the period when the Scuola degli Schiavoni cycle was being painted, there was no military victory over the Turks that would justify an interpretation of the saint's fight with the dragon as emblematic of a Venetian defeat over the Ottomans. Carpaccio's paintings from the life of St. George have to be seen in relation to the legend of a saint who personified the Crusader defeating the non-believer and to the conflicting relationship between two monotheistic religions.[58] Despite the fact that the Turks and other Islamic dynasties had conquered Christian holy sites, Carpaccio's paintings do not transmit danger, fear, or aversion towards them, but instead reflect a peaceful community of Christians, Mamluks, and Ottomans. As if he wanted to accentuate this harmony, in the

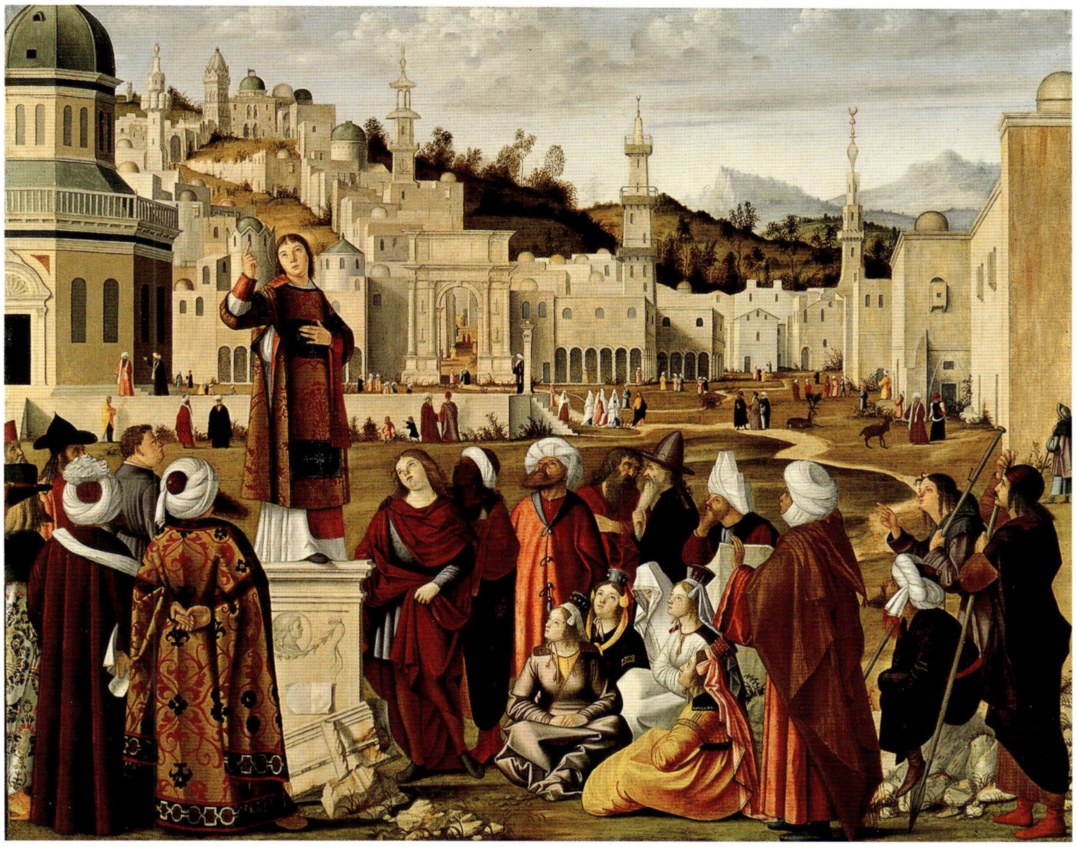

foreground of *The Baptism of the Selenites*, the painter placed a large Ottoman turban on the staircase as a symbol of conversion, while the nearby parrot symbolizes eloquence and redemption.[59]

cat. 30. Vittore Carpaccio and collaborators
The Sermon of St. Stephen
Venice, ca. 1514
Musée du Louvre, Paris

The Reception of the Venetian Ambassadors in Damascus

Among the large-scale narrative paintings with Near Eastern subject matter produced in Venice at the end of the 15th and beginning of the 16th centuries, the anonymous *Reception of the Venetian Ambassadors in Damascus* is in many ways unique (see cat. 29, p. 85).[60] Notably, it does not appear to have formed part of a confraternity cycle, but instead was likely made for an individual, possibly a Venetian *bailo* who had lived and worked in Mamluk Damascus and wanted a visual record of his time abroad. In earlier Venetian paintings, examples of Islamic architecture were incorporated into a stage set to evoke, rather than fully describe, the Islamic world, but here an entire Near Eastern setting is created. This artist saw the Islamic world through an "Oriental filter," depicting the Venetian delegation and the Mamluk dignitaries before a portrait of the city of Damascus. A pointed *iwan* arch with a bi-colored *ablaq* stone flanked by long walls and decorated with Sultan Qa'itbey's blazon provides the backdrop.[61] The Great Umayyad Mosque, with its large dome set atop a double drum and the minarets on

fig. 9. Vittore Carpaccio, *St. George and the Dragon,* 1502–7. Scuola di San Giorgio degli Schiavoni, Venice

fig. 10. Vittore Carpaccio, *The Baptism of the Selenites,* 1507. Scuola di San Giorgio degli Schiavoni, Venice

fig. 11. Vittore Carpaccio, preparatory drawing for *The Triumph of St. George,* ca. 1502. Galleria degli Uffizi, Florence

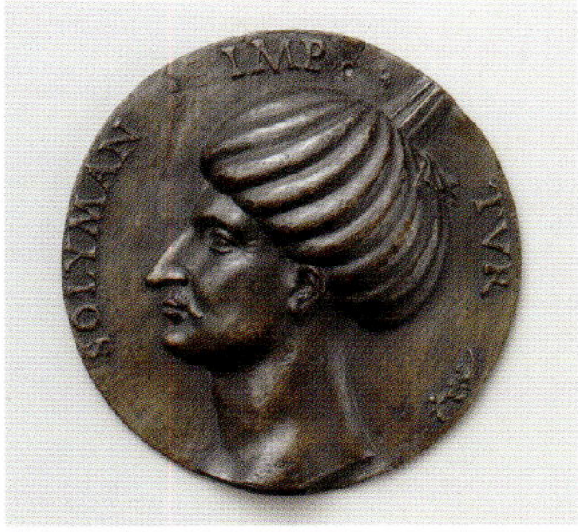

cat. 119. *Portrait Medallion of Süleyman the Magnificent*
Probably Venice, after 1521
The Metropolitan Museum of Art, New York

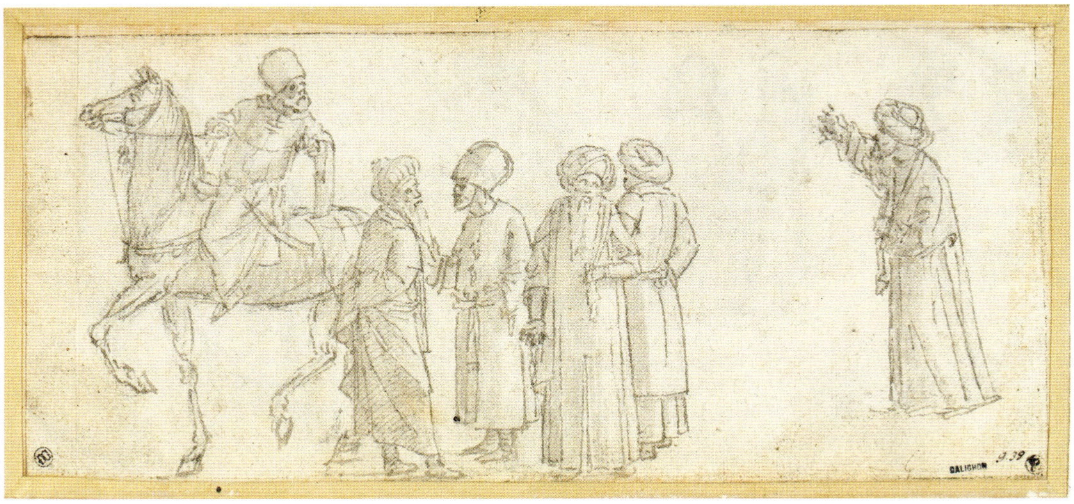

cat. 53. Vittore Carpaccio (attr.)
Six Turkish Figures, One on Horseback
Venice, ca. 1500–10
Musée du Louvre, Paris

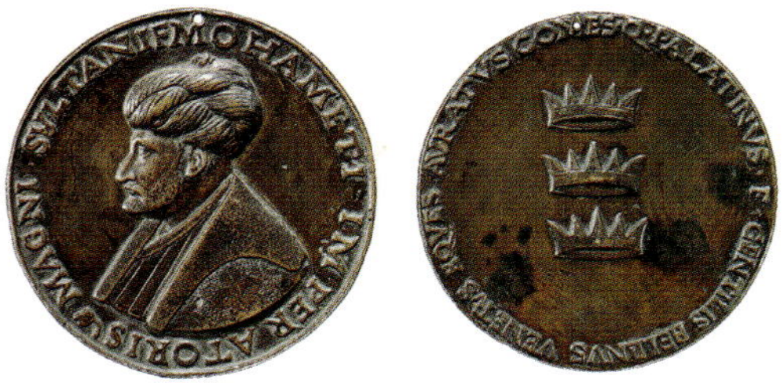

cat. 116. *Medal of Sultan Mehmet II designed by Gentile Bellini*
Istanbul, late 1479–early 1480
The British Museum, London

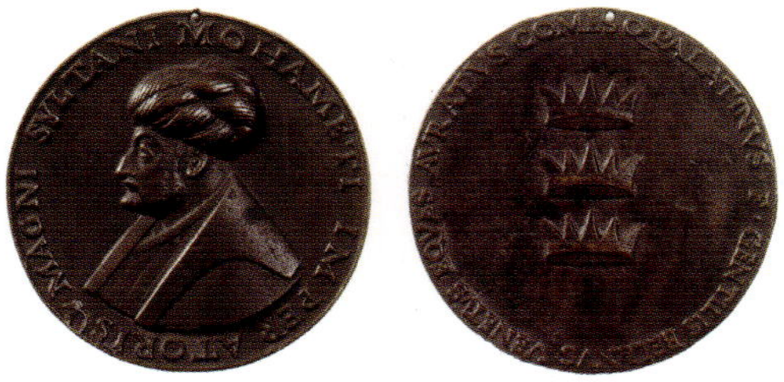

cat. 117. *Medal of Sultan Mehmet II designed by Gentile Bellini*
Istanbul, late 1479-early 1480
Museo Franchetti alla Ca' d'Oro, Venice

either side, identifies the city as Damascus. Moreover, two small domes are depicted, one of them fluted and the other set with "bubble-glass" windows that hint at its function as a hammam.[62] The group of houses with terraces (known as miradors) reflects the painter's knowledge of traditional Syro-Egyptian habitations, and on the right is an accurate depiction of a Mamluk minaret.[63] The western minaret was finished in 1488, and for a long time it provided the only indication of a date for this painting. During the recent restoration, however, an inscription on the painting with the year 1511 was uncovered.[64] This date allows suggestions to be made about the identity of the Venetian ambassador wearing a scarlet toga with open sleeves (*maniche dogali*) in the scene. Caroline Campbell has proposed that the ambassador might be either Pietro Zen or Niccolò Malipiero, both present in Damascus between 1511 and 1513.[65]

The cityscape of the *Reception* is striking, but did not find followers among Venetian painters, although it must have been well known, as the many copies of it reveal.[66] Mansueti and Carpaccio, for example, employed different methods, creating fantastic views of the Islamic world. It is not accidental that Carpaccio signed some of his canvases with the word *"finxit."*[67] The painter thereby confessed that his works, although seemingly realistic, are in fact products of his imagination (cat. 53).

Portraits and Prints

By 1525, the last canvas painted in the Oriental mode for a Venetian *scuola* was in place, many of the city's most important Orientalist painters had died, and the Ottomans had conquered the Mamluk Empire. The Venetian tradition of setting large narrative scenes in the Islamic world had no followers in the late 16th century, when portraits of Muslim, most often

cat. 4. *Mehmet II Smelling a Rose*
Istanbul, ca. 1480
Topkapı Sarayı Müzesi Library, Istanbul

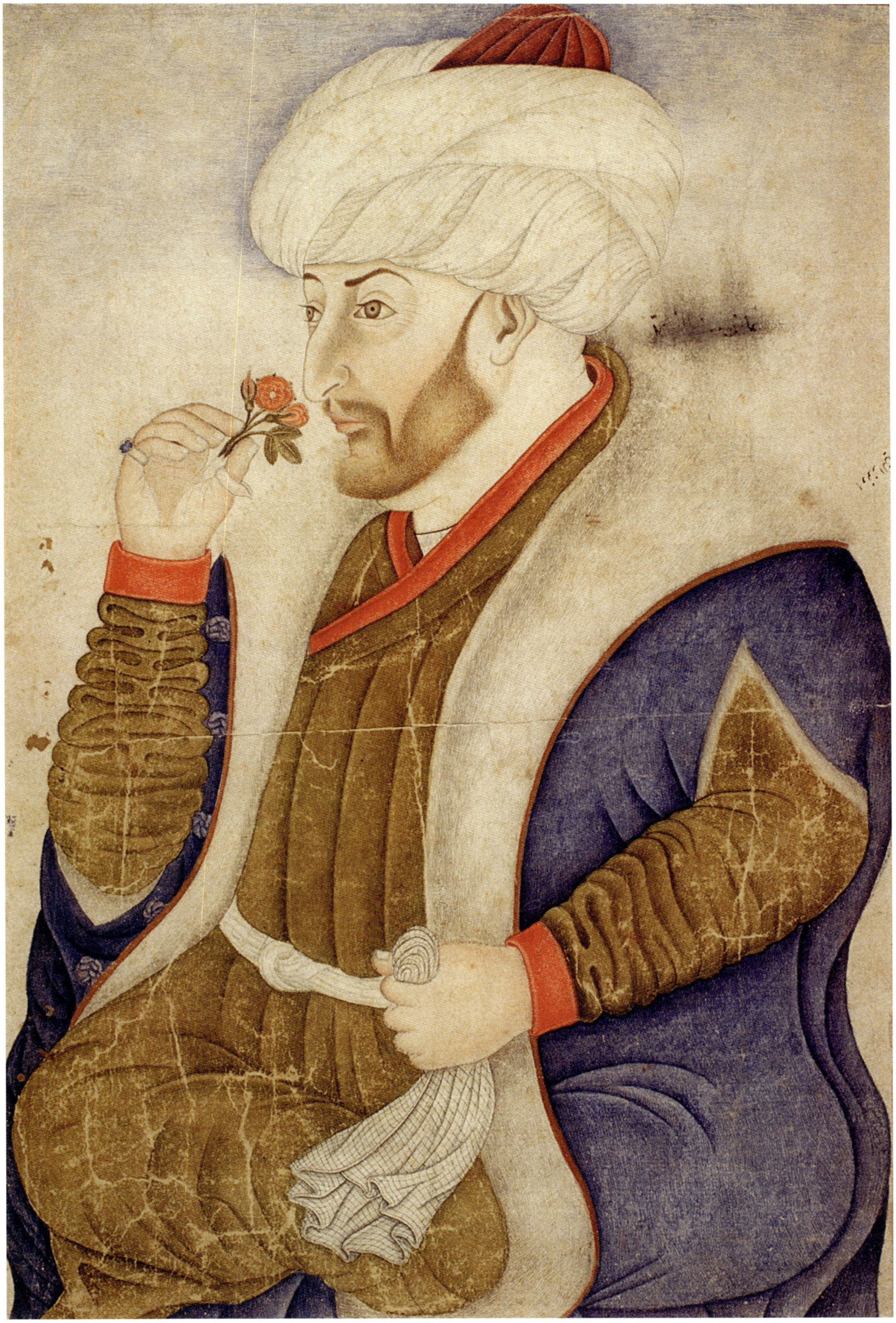

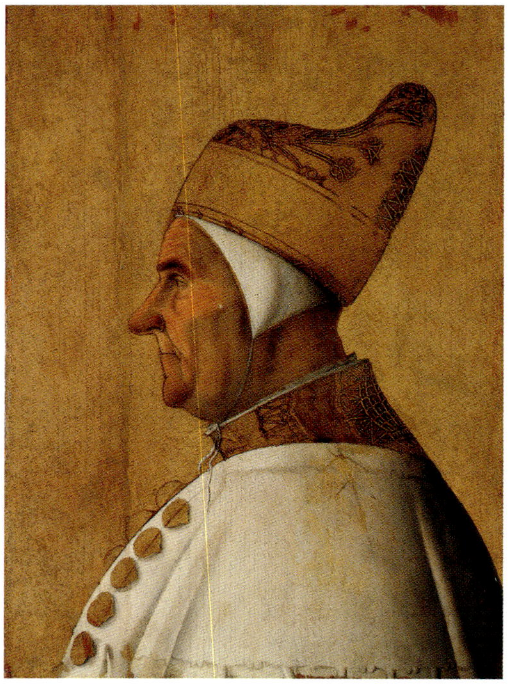

cat. 22. Gentile Bellini
Portrait of Doge Giovanni Mocenigo
1478–79 or 1481–85
Museo Civico Correr, Venice

Ottoman sultans, or the inclusion of a single Muslim figure in a religious scene, were more characteristic.

In this period, an ethnographic/historiographic[68] approach to the Islamic world came to the fore, as costume books and the first world atlas were produced. Cesare Vecellio's famous costume book of 1590 pretended to be historiographically precise, despite the author's many inventions (see cat. 63, p. 113). Studies of "*il costume*," which went beyond costume to include lifestyles and manners of a variety of different cultures, were numerous, but did not represent Islamic architecture and settings.[69] In the 16th century, the portrait became the dominant genre of Orientalist painters, who were very much influenced by the contemporary ethnographic movement. Not a group of wealthy patrons in the *scuole*, but individual patrons—Turks as well as Venetians and other Europeans—were now responsible for the commissions. Instead of *fantasia*, realistic depiction was required: images of sultans were a form of Ottoman state propaganda, and were given as diplomatic gifts as well as collected.

The tradition of Venetian sultan portraiture has its roots in Gentile Bellini's famous painting in the National Gallery, London (see cat. 23, p. 68).[70] As the later copy now in a private collection in Singapore suggests (see cat. 24, p. 109), Gentile and his followers produced a great number of replicas of the portrait, thereby spreading an awareness of the sultan's likeness in Italy.[71] Mehmet must have been more than pleased to have his image painted by a renowned Venetian artist. In addition to paintings, the sultan also commissioned portrait medals by the Italian artists he invited to his court, who included not only Gentile Bellini (cat. 116, p. 134) but also Costanzo da Ferrara (or Costanzo di Moysis), sent from Naples in 1478 (cat. 117, p. 134). At the same time, Mehmet also commissioned portraits of himself from Islamic artists, as exemplified by *Mehmet Smelling a Rose*, a miniature attributed to the Ottoman court painter Ahmed Siblizade (cat. 4, p. 135).

In Venice, Gentile Bellini had frequently produced portraits of doges and other men of power (see, for example, cats. 21 and 22), but in all likelihood he had never confronted a Muslim sitter prior to his trip to Constantinople. For Mehmet II's image, Gentile created a new iconography for sultans. The London portrait makes reference to Mehmet's military prowess with the inscription, "Conqueror of the World" (Victor Orbis),[72] and the seven crowns, three on either side of the arch and one embroidered into the drapery hanging over the parapet, likely symbolize the Ottoman Dynasty, Mehmet II being the 7th sultan in the imperial line.[73]

Especially after the Ottoman Sultan Süleyman the Magnificent (r. 1520–66) conquered Hungary in 1526, European princes became eager to have a portrait of this formidable figure in their galleries of famous men and women (cat. 119, p. 134). Titian painted an image of Süleyman for the Gonzaga of Mantua, several copies of which survive,[74] and he is believed to have represented Roxelana, the sultan's favorite consort, as well.[75] Yet Titian was far from being

cat. 55. Giandomenico Tiepolo
Turkish Lancer and Onlookers Approaching a Town
Venice, ca. 1760–70
The Metropolitan Museum of Art, New York

cat. 40. Giambattista Tiepolo
Two Orientals under a Tree
Venice, ca. 1742–45
The National Gallery, London

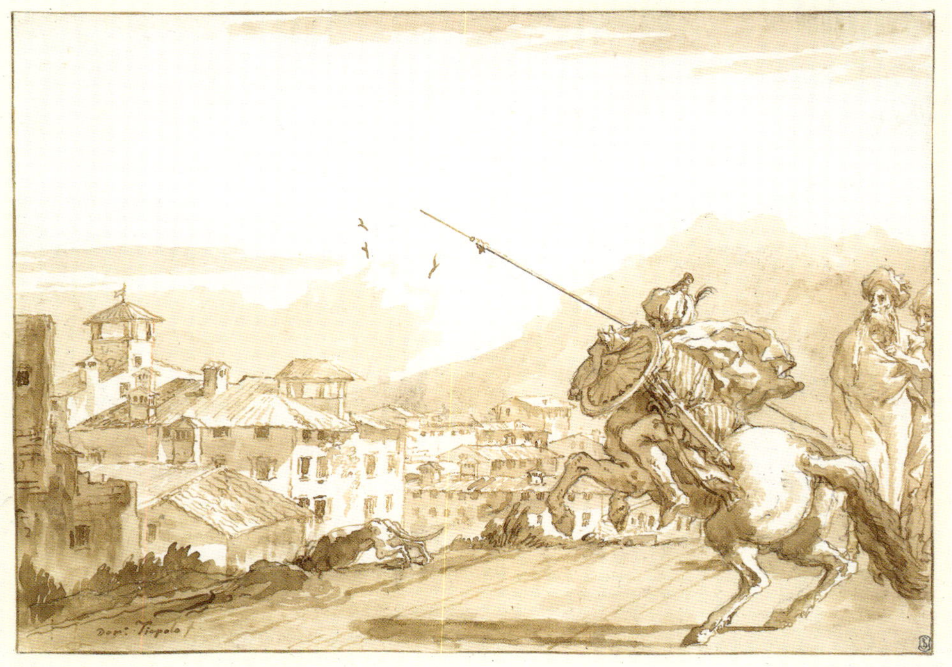

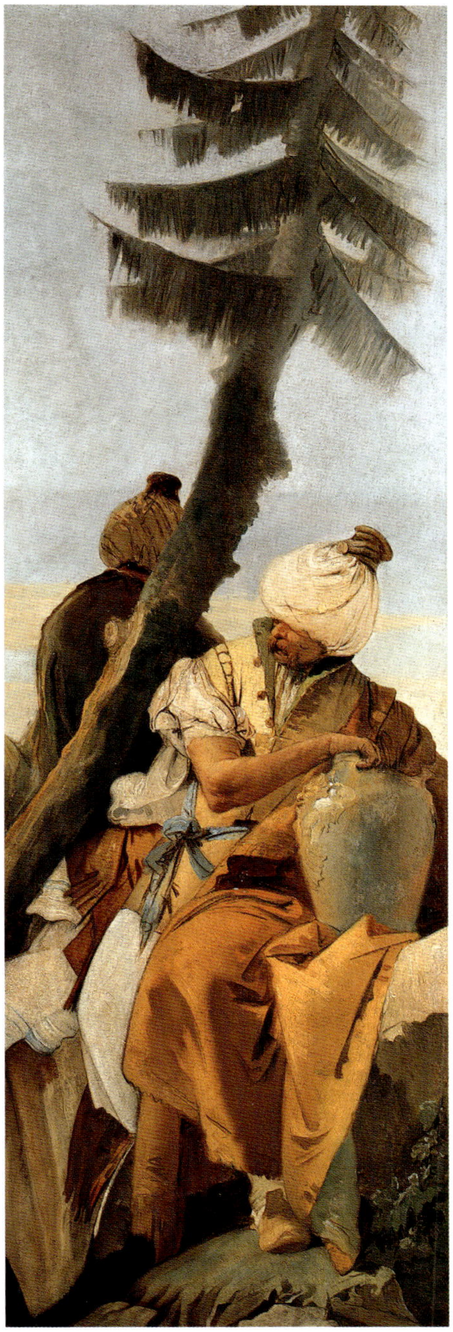

an Orientalist painter. He never depicted an Islamic setting and rarely represented Turkish costume,[76] although there is a Turkish bystander in his *Pesaro Altarpiece* of circa 1519–26 (Santa Maria Gloriosa dei Frari, Venice), and a turbaned sultan on horseback in his *Ecce Homo* of 1543 (Kunsthistorisches Museum, Vienna). Titian's younger contemporary, Jacopo Tintoretto, was even less interested in depicting the Near East, and his Islamic figures are not portraits at all but rather faceless Turks, as in the *Miracle of St. Mark* of 1548 (Gallerie dell'Accademia, Venice). In the *oeuvre* of Paolo Veronese, Muslims have a kind of decorative significance, appearing as background figures in the pageantry of his large feasts for monastic refectories.[77] They can also be found as bystanders in religious scenes such as the *Martyrdom of St. Giustina* (Florence, Gallerie degli Uffizi). In the art of the three greatest painters of the late Venetian Renaissance—Titian, Tintoretto, and Veronese—Islamic people and places thus played no great part, likely because Venetian culture in general turned its attention towards a Roman *renovatio* in the 16th century.[78] Given that this is so, it is not surprising to find that a much lesser local painter assisted the Ottoman royal house in obtaining a portrait series of sultans in 1578 (see cats. 35–38, p. 110).

Representing the Turk in Baroque Venice

In the 17th century, the Islamic Levant as a *topos* in Venetian art survived as an expression of artistic invention or as the result of special commissions like the *turquerie* of Antonio Guardi and his workshop. In 1742–43, Guardi received the commission to paint 43 *quadri turchi* (Turkish pictures) from Marshall Matthias von der Schulenburg.[79] In these works, Guardi focuses on Muslim costume and hardly ever refers to a larger Eastern setting (cat. 39, p. 138). The imaginative basis of the paintings is a marked case of *venezianità*: Venetians in Oriental dress are depicted in *sale di turchi* or in sumptuous fetes on artificial stages.

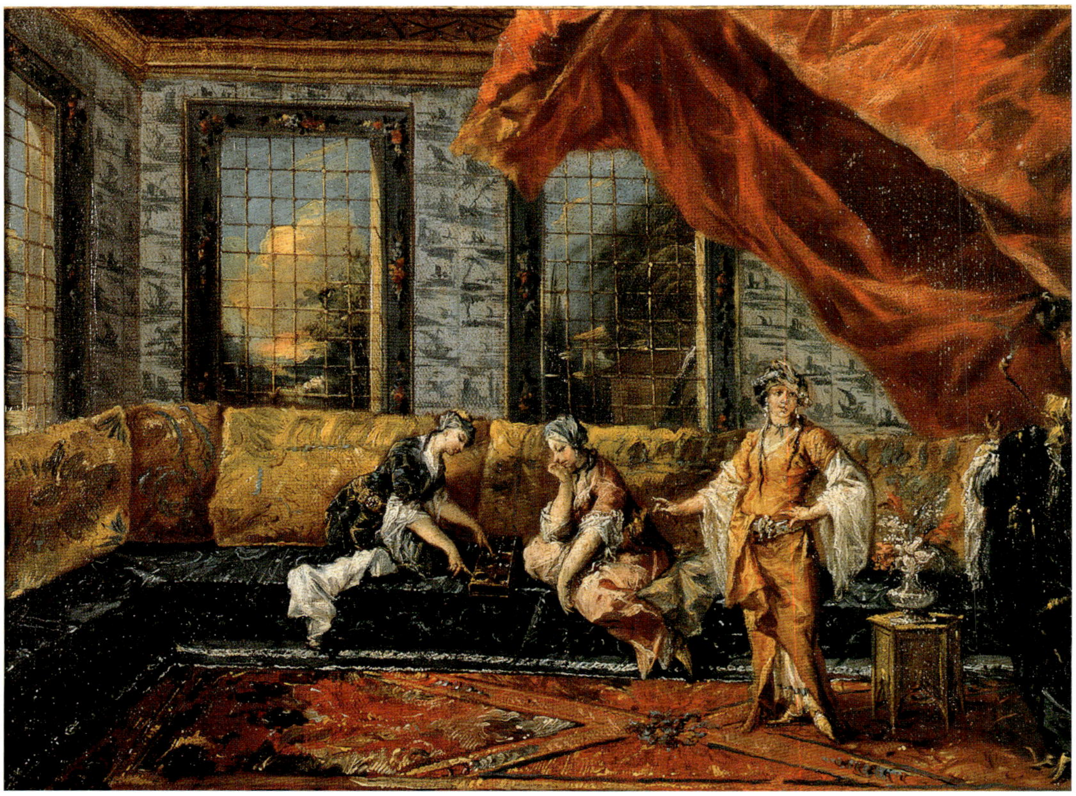

cat. 39. Giovanni Antonio Guardi or Francesco Guardi
Odalisques Playing a Mancala Game in the Harem
Venice, 1742–43
Gemäldegalerie, Düsseldorf,

Giambattista Tiepolo´s landscapes with tall, flowing trees and Muslim figures differ from Guardi's *turquerie*, for it was dreaming "as an activity of the visual mind" that provided the basis for his compositions[80] (cat. 40, p. 137) and Giovanni Domenico's drawing (cat. 55, p. 137). The appearance of Oriental costumes in religious scenes traditionally linked to the East can be seen in Tiepolo's *Adoration of the Magi* of 1753 (Alte Pinakothek, Munich). Islamic figures are inserted by the painter when depicting historical settings, as in *The Meeting of Anthony and Cleopatra* of about 1745–50 (Palazzo Labia, Venice), or to create an ethnographic aspect, as in the *Treppenhaus* at the Residence in Würzburg with frescoes of Africa and Asia.[81]

The paintings of Guardi and Tiepolo are far from the Oriental mode of their Venetian forebears, the Bellini, Carpaccio, and Mansueti. If the painters of the 15th century tried to copy or transform the Islamic world into a Venetian vocabulary, the artists in the 17th century were mostly guided by their own invention and imagination, with few references to actual examples of Islamic architecture or objects. What all these painters had in common, however, was their familiarity with and attraction to the Orient seen through a Venetian filter. Their city was the mirror for any foreign culture, whether they represented Venice as a portrait or as an honorific landscape.

Notes

1 Raby 1982.
2 Fortini Brown 1988.
3 Demus 1960.
4 Howard 2000, pp. 65–94.
5 Fortini Brown 1996.
6 Landau and Parshall 1994, p. 43.
7 Rava 1916, p. 70; Sanudo 1879–1902, vol. 39, cols. 23, 29; Wansbrough 1963; Fortini Brown 1988, p. 168.
8 Spallanzani 1989, pp. 83–100.
9 Shalem 1998; Hoffman 2001; Scarazzolo 2003.
10 Campbell and Chong 2005.
11 Eisler 1989; Degenhart and Schmitt 1990.
12 For an analysis of this concept see Fortini Brown 1996, pp. 189–206.
13 Mills 1983, pp. 14; see also Denny's essay in the present volume.
14 Lightbown 1986, p. 446; Spriggs 1965, p. 73; Spallanzani 1978a, p. 52; Carr 1997.
15 Bourne 1999, p. 62.
16 Mack 2002, pp. 62–63; Boskovits and Brown 2003, pp. 435–43. A comparable fragment from an Ottoman tent is in the Museo Civico Correr, Venice (illustrated in Curatola 1985, p. 187).
17 Auld 1990–91, pp. 84-102 who defines it as either Mamluk or Persian.
18 Heinemann 1962, n. 145a-k; Howard 2005, p. 30.
19 Schmidt Arcangeli 2005, pp. 283–93.
20 Carswell 1993, pp. 180–85; Simon 1997, pp. 305–12, Mack 2002, pp. 105–6; Shalem 2002, p. 507; Hess 2004, p. 20.
21 A similar metal bucket is in Treviso, Museo Diocesano (illustrated in Curatola 1993, p. 313).
22 Shalem 2002, p. 511.
23 Ibid.
24 See Mack 1997, p. 59 on the painter's use of re-entrant prayer, Para-Mamluk, and Lotto rugs.
25 Mack 2002, pp. 92-93.
26 Fortini Brown 1988, p. 197; the panel by Lattanzio can be probably identified with the drawing formerly in Chatsworth, Devonshire Collection.
27 Fortini Brown 1988, pp. 286–87.
28 Molà 2000, p. 241.
29 Humfrey 1983, pp. 82–84.
30 Another picture by Cima of ca. 1495–97 with a similar ambient is *The Presentation of the Virgin* (Gemäldegalerie, Dresden); Humfrey 1983, p. 99.
31 For this belief, known as the *predestinatio*, see Fortini Brown 1997, p. 81.
32 Only one figure in the background is dressed in the Ottoman manner.
33 Together with his signature he adds ten names of the patrons of this cycle, see Miller 1978, p. 91.
34 On the panther as a symbol of the Mamluk sultan see Degenhart and Schmitt 1980, p. 3.
35 Raby 1982, p. 35.
36 On the relation of the *scuola* with Alexandria, see Botti 1992, pp. 47–57; on the members who had relations with the Orient, see ibid, p. 56.
37 Sohm 1982, pp. 240–42.
38 On Gentile's drawings of Turkish costumes, see Meyer zur Capellen, 1983, pp. 168–70; Campbell and Chong 2005, p. 98–105.
39 Raby 1982, p. 41.
40 Scenes of the state propaganda were shown in the mosaics of San Marco. On the hagiographic sources see Daniele, Schmidt Arcangeli, and Vio 1998, pp. 84–89.
41 Meyer zur Capellen 1985, pp. 89–94; Lehmann 1977, p. 8. On the interpretation of the letters VL as reference to the dogate of Leonardo Loredan see Howard 2003, pp. 67–78.
42 Niero 1992, pp. 15–35; idem, 1993, pp. 11–15; Schmidt Arcangeli 1998, pp. 84–91.
43 Botti 1992, p. 43; the painter had already made a cityscape of Cairo for Francesco Gonzaga in 1493.
44 Meyer zur Capellen 1985, p. 91.
45 For Giovanni Bellini´s final touches see Bertelli 2003, pp. 105–7.
46 Fortini Brown 1988, p. 293.
47 Ibid., p. 69.
48 Ibid., p. 288.
49 Pallucchini and Perocco 1961, p. 72; Gentili 1996, pp. 69–74 .
50 Pallucchini and Perocco 1961, p. 72.
51 Raby 1982, pp. 76; Shalem 2002, pp. 509–10.
52 Brooke 2004, pp. 303–14.
53 Raby 1982, p. 72.
54 See a preparatory drawing for two ladies, in Princeton (cat. 52).
55 Blass-Simmen 1991, p. 36. The dragon as an attribute of St. George can be traced only since the 12th century.
56 Gentili 1996, pp. 78–82.
57 Paolo Valaresso himself was the commander of these fortresses.
58 On the Islamic view of the Crusades, see Hillenbrand 1999.
59 Gentili 1996, pp. 55–56 for the discussion of these symbols.
60 Howard 2005, pp. 21–23.
61 Raby 1982, pp. 41–46, 55–65; Contadini 1999, p. 8.
62 Raby 1982, p. 55, suggests that this is the *hammam* of the Suq al Buzuriyya.
63 Meyer zur Capellen 1985, pp. 143–44.
64 The date has been discovered underneath the horse's legs on the left side of the *iwan*.
65Campbell and Chong 2005, p. 22
66 Exceptions are the two copies with little differences in composition and motifs, which were in the collections Stern and Langlade in Paris, reproduced in Meyer zur Capellen 1985, p. 144. The tapestry in Powis Castle, Welchpool is dated 1545; for it, see also Clayton and Wace 1938.
67 For the signature *"finxit"* or *"fingebat"* in Carpaccio´s paintings see Damisch 1984, pp. 137; Matthew 1998, pp. 630, 638–39.
68 For this term, see Ilg 2004, pp. 29-46.
69 Wilson 2005, Chapter 2.
70 Meyer zur Capellen 1985, pp. 17–21, pp. 129–30; Pedani-Fabris 1996–97 and 1999; Raby 2000, p. 80; Campbell and Chong 2005, pp. 78–79; Chong 2005, p. 109.
71 Campbell and Cong 2005, p. 109.
72 The inscriptions originally painted on purple panels on the parapet are very damaged and distorted by later repairs. See a similar composition of the parapet in Giovanni Bellini's *Doge Loredan and Four Advisers* in the Gemäldegalerie in Berlin.
73 The technique of the drapery with attached pearls, rubies, and other precious gems cannot be traced in Islamic textiles and was used only rarely in Venetian garments. The motif of the hanging carpet appears in other paintings by Gentile Bellini such as the *Procession in Piazza San Marco*, see also the miniature of Doge Andrea Vendramin, his secretary and the papal legate, appearing in a window with a hanging carpet (Boijmans Van Beuningen Museum, Rotterdam).
74 Majer 2000, pp. 39, 65; Raby 2000, p. 115.
75 Gronau 1903; Wethey 1971, vol. 2, p. 205.
76 Gould, 1976, p. 234.
77 Cocke 2001, pp. 167–78.
78 Tafuri 1985.
79 For the history of these *scene turchesche* see Bettagno 1993, p. 18.
80 Alpers and Baxandall 1994, p. 46
81 Alpers and Baxandall 1994, p. 27 and pp. 30–33 on questions of Tiepolo´s repertory and his *scherzi* technique.

Pigments in Venetian and Islamic Painting

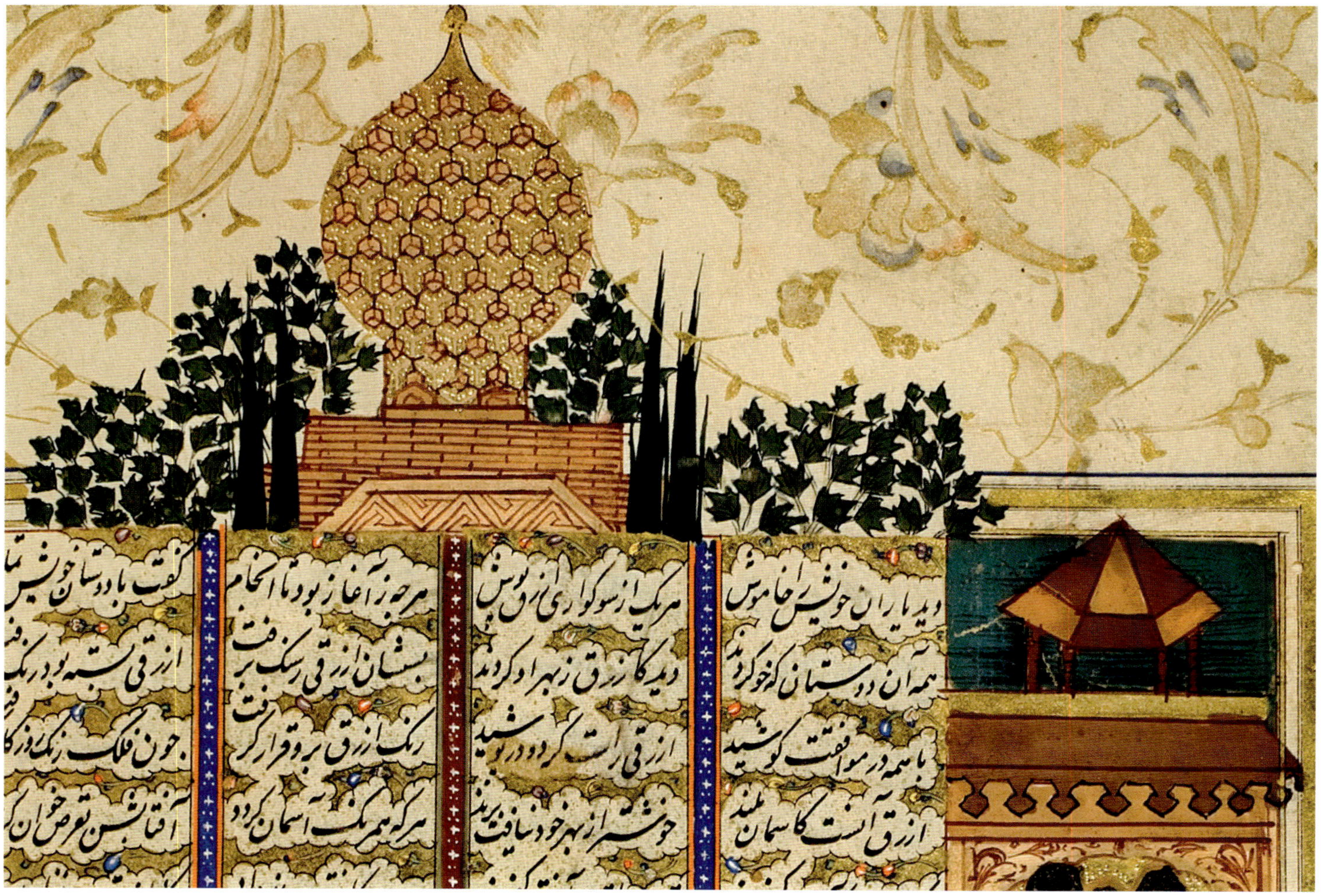

Barbara H. Berrie

Cultural influences moved across Europe and the Islamic world in the early modern era via assimilation by travelers as well as trade in commodities and manufactured goods. Papermaking, textile weaving and dyeing, and glassmaking all contributed to the transfer of technology—their products carrying both intellectual and stylistic content—and stimulated exchange between the two regions. The influence of Islamic ceramics on the development of the Italian maiolica industry is a prominent example of such an exchange. The transmission of the technology and aesthetics of glassmaking has been firmly established. The convergence of pattern and color of many types of textiles from Italian and Ottoman sources is also notable.[1]

The mutual impact of Italian and Islamic painters on each other's materials and techniques has not been studied extensively and, at first sight, it seems perhaps even non-existent, particularly in comparison to the extent of commonality in the mediums mentioned above. Overall, there is also little published comparative research on the materials and methods of the Islamic artists.[2] On the other hand, the colorants used by Venetian artists have been well studied although fugitive organic pigments are often overlooked by technical analysis. The impression that Islamic painting had little or no influence on Italian artists must arise from the subtlety of such influence and the difficulty in isolating it. The painted works of Islamic artists are small in scale, produced on burnished paper, and usually bound into books; Islamic artists did not adopt the easel. The links between Islamic and Venetian painting may well lie in the materials and techniques—rather than in the style and taste of the painters—used by both Western and Eastern artists and in the appearance and color of the paint, but these links can be postulated only through limited factual information and are raised here as hypotheses for further study.

The impact of the aesthetics of the decorative arts on the painters active in Venice has been described.[3] Chromatic effects and dramatic changes in color, emphasized also by the perpetual movement of the reflecting water surface, certainly affected its citizens' sensitivity to nuances in color, pervading many levels of artistic output as well as architecture and

cat. 12. Nizami
Khamsa (Quintet)

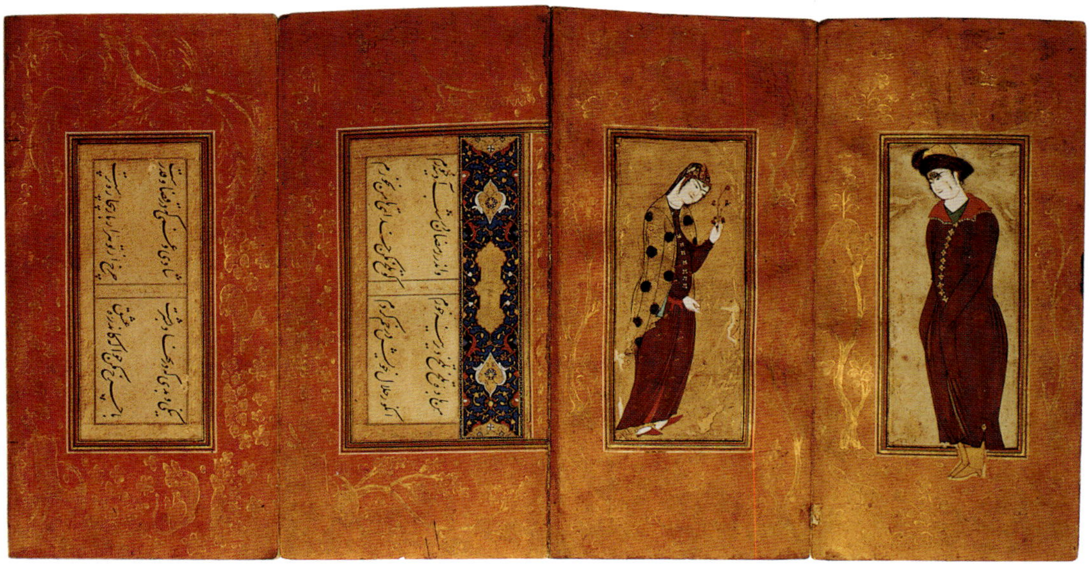

cat. 11. *Album (muraqqa')*
Copied by Mir 'Ali Katib
Iran, second half of 16th century
Biblioteca Nazionale Marciana, Venice

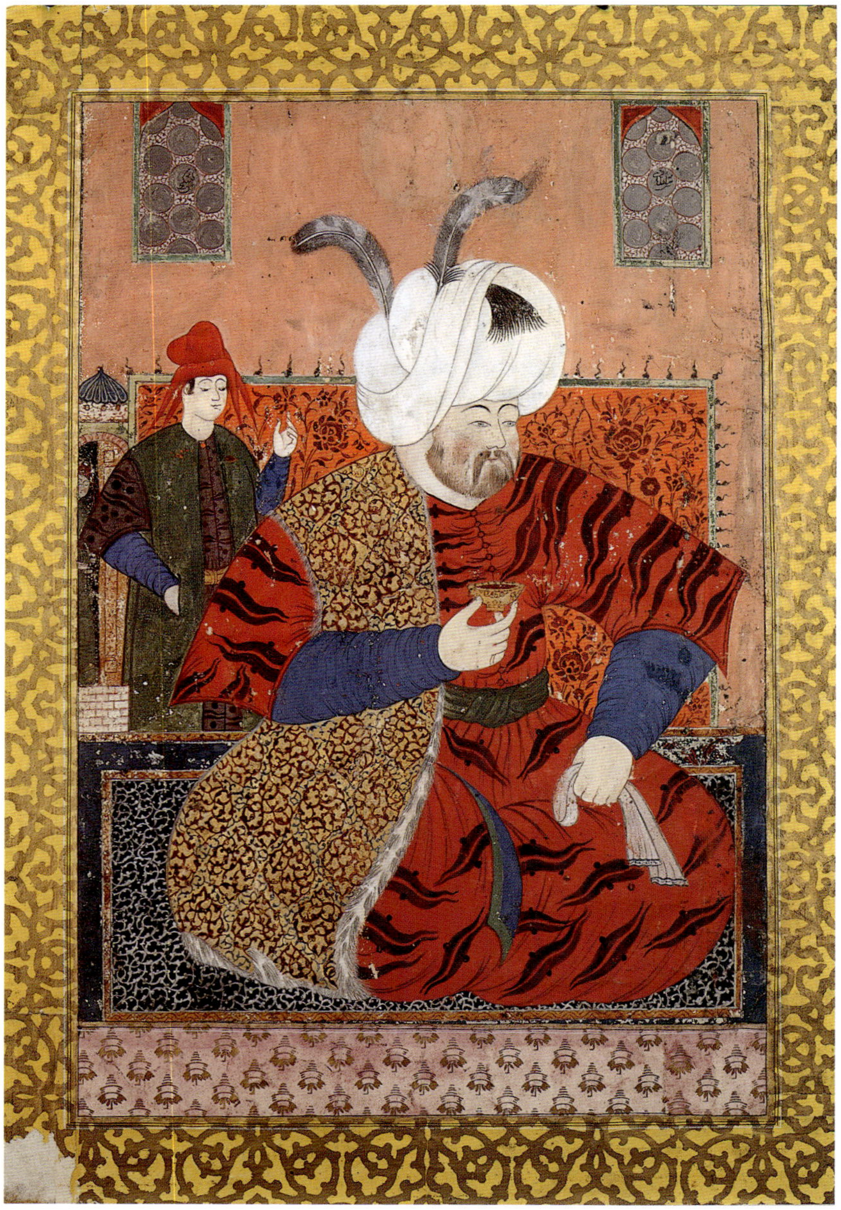

cat. 7. Haydar Reis Nigari
Portrait of Sultan Selim II
Istanbul, Turkey, ca. 1570
Aga Khan Trust for Culture, Geneva

fashion. One may surmise that Venetian patrons were accustomed to and appreciative of a rainbow of hues and of the riot of colors that suffuses many Persian and Turkish paintings (cats. 7 and 12); these same qualities would have excited a Venetian painter's eye as well. The limited analysis performed on the pigments in Persian paintings shows that the palette contained for blues, indigo, azurite, and preeminently ultramarine; for greens, verdigris or orpiment mixed with indigo; for reds, mostly cinnabar (or its synthetic equivalent) and vermilion although artists used hematite and probably also lake pigments such as kermes and lac; for orange, realgar and minium; for blacks, lampblack whereas charcoal was reserved mainly for drawing rather than painting; for white, predominantly white lead; powdered gold and silver complete the palette.[4] Some treatises, of which Qadi Ahmad's is one of the best known,[5] suggest that Islamic artists used some pigments other than those that have been found through analysis, including tin white, turmeric, safflower, malachite, brass and copper fillings, mica, and talc (cat. 11).[6] The difficulty of analyzing the plant dyes makes it problematic to confirm their presence in either Islamic or Italian works; nevertheless, the possibility of their use indicates that artists were striving to obtain and use the widest possible range of colors.

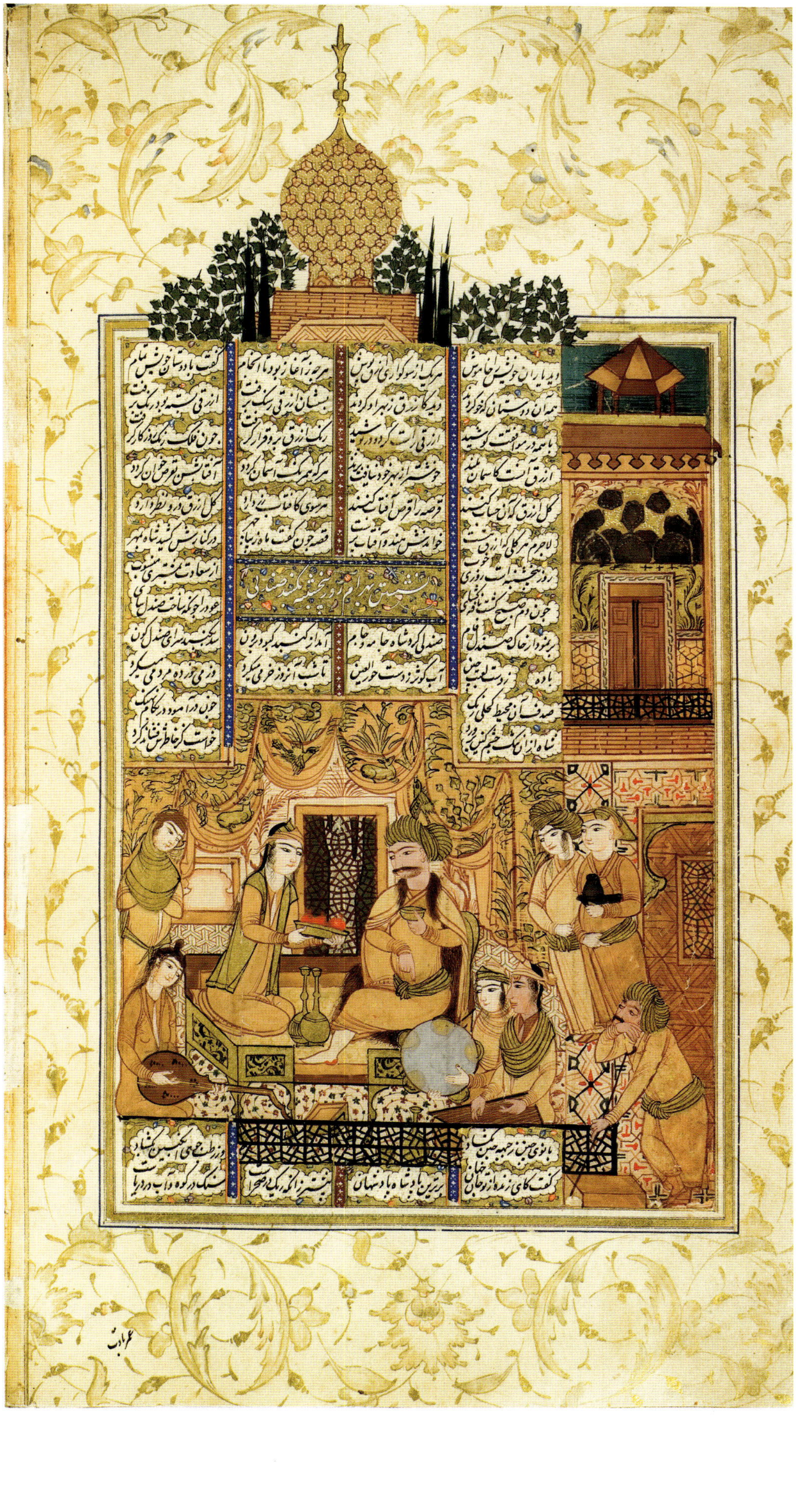

cat. 12. Nizami
Khamsa (Quintet)
Iran, 1624–25
Fondazione Giorgio Cini, Venice

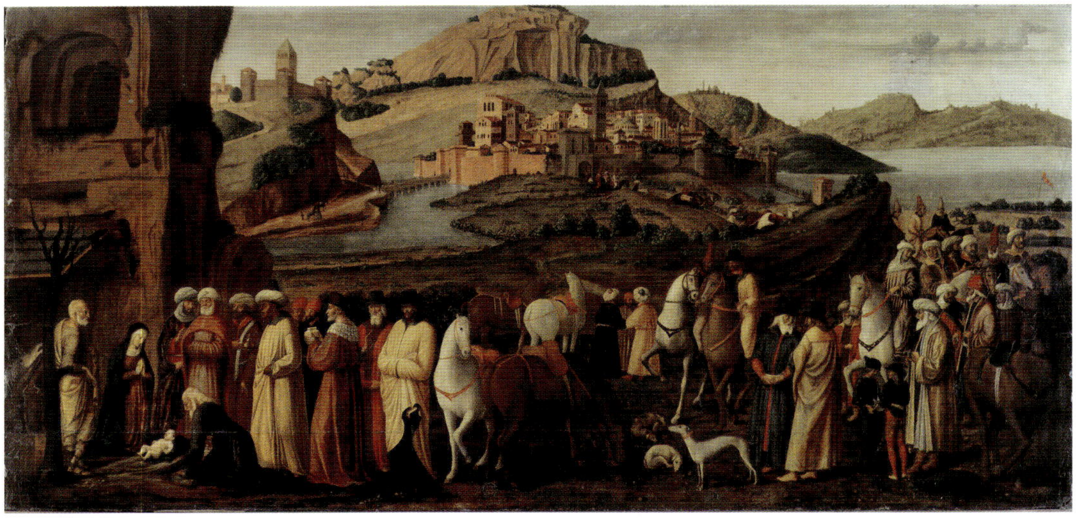

cat. 25. Painter from Verona
The Adoration of the Magi
Venice, early 16th century
Museo d'Arte Medievale e Moderna, Padua

The aqueous medium of Persian paintings ensured a strong, saturated palette; colors obtained using white lead created unusual contrasts of pastel tones of lilac, pink, and pale green. Islamic artists did not shy away from juxtaposing the intense hues of vermilion and verdigris, orpiment, saffron and mixed purples, or minium and ultramarine. The stimulating color schemes of their work may have been the source of inspiration for Venetian artists such as Gentile Bellini and Titian who were beginning to arrange vibrant passages of colors, sometimes pairing clear tones of the complementary pairs orange and blue, yellow and violet, and red and green in their works.

Unfortunately, there are no records of Venetian travelers who acquired Persian miniatures in the East before and during the Renaissance. The only small paintings usually recorded were Christian devotional objects in addition to copper pots, bolts of cloth, and other objects and trinkets.[7] Thus, although trade between Venice and the Levant provided access to a novel style of depiction, it seems that its greatest importance lay in improving access to certain pigments, presumably at affordable prices. From the third quarter of the 15th century the Venetian easel painter's palette was augmented by the addition of several colorants: orpiment and smalt are particularly obvious (cat. 25). Ultramarine, realgar, indigo, and other pigments such as mosaic gold[8] and verdigris became important in their palette. Manuscript illuminators, whose connections to Byzantine art are more readily perceived, had already been using these pigments, but artists painting on wood panels or canvases had restricted the use of these colorants mainly to small touches until some time around the last quarter of the 15th century when they began to employ them in quantity.[9] Giovanni Bellini was among the first to use orpiment in a large painting, in the drapery of his Pesaro *Coronation of the Virgin* dated 1475.

The color names themselves indicate their perceived association with the material sources. Among these we may note lazuli, from the Persian *lajavard* (Arabic *lazuward*) and *narancio* from the Arabic name for the fruit, *naranj* (Persian *narang*), which was used in Italy for the color's name from ca. 1499.[10] Even more direct than the adoption of foreign words for colors are the descriptive names, for example the *colore arabico detto turchino* for a type of turquoise glass colored like the semi-precious stone, which was named for its apparent origin from Turkey.[11] Blue paper, much used by Venetian artists for drawing, was known not only as *carta azzurra* but also as *carta turchina.* Names for pigments that indicate their origin, for example, *endego de baghedad* (Baghdad indigo)[12] and *azzurro damasceno* (damascene blue or smalt), link materials of certain hues and compositions with the East.

The demand in Venice for color-making supplies must have been great indeed, for it was large enough to support the development of a group of shopkeepers known as *vendecolori* who dealt only in pigments and materials related to the manufacture of colorants and paints by the end of the 15th century.[13] The 1534 inventory of one of these shop lists includes, among other artists' materials, fenugreek, brazilwood, indigo, and orpiment, all pigments imported by Venice from the Levant. A 16th-century treatise[14] describes the use of saffron to paint on paper, both unmixed and then mixed with blue to provide green, just as it was used for many Islamic paintings, as well as the use of orpiment mixed in water with indigo for coloring paper green,[15] a combination seen often in both medieval European painting and in Islamic works.

In conclusion, the transformations in Venetian painting from the last quarter of the 15th century are due not so much to the stylistic influence of Islamic artists but to the growing cosmopolitan attitude of its citizens as their access to goods and materials from foreign cultures increased. The availability of large amounts of costly pigments, imported from the eastern coasts of the Adriatic, Damascus, and Constantinople—previously limited to the miniaturists' brush—freed artists to experiment with these colorants, enriching their palettes and surely contributing to the development of Venetian *colore*.

Notes

1 For the mediums above, see the essays by Fontana, Carboni and Barovier, Denny, and Curatola in this volume.

2 A bibliography of publications that describe materials and methods of Islamic painters is available at http://www.sandyaajain.com/art.html.

3 Hills 1999.

4 FitzHugh 1988; Purinton and Watters 1991.

5 Qadi Ahmad 1959.

6 Barkeshli, Zain, and Zekrgoo 2000. Malachite was identified in an early study of pigments in Persian paintings; the wide use of Tyrian purple in early paintings was later replaced by a mixture of ultramarine and red lake. See Laurie 1935.

7 For example, no Islamic paintings were noted in the effects of four Venetians who died in, or en route from, Damascus (Bianchi and Howard 2003).

8 Mosaic gold is an imitation gold composed of tin sulfide. European and Chinese recipes for mosaic gold are known. Although the pigment produced is the same, the chemical paths used to obtain it are completely different on the two continents. See Butler *et al.* 1983.

9 Many of the earliest occurrences of these pigments in tempera and oil paintings, which at that time were generally confined to the miniaturists' palette, occur in the second half of the century in works from Venice and Ferrara.

10 The use of the name orange to describe a color only arose in Italy in the late fifteenth century. See Hills 2002.

11 See Neri 1612, ch. 25 (Neri 2003, p. 42); Zecchin 1987, p. 253. The term *arabico* was used to describe a turquoise color in 1536 in a glassmaker's recipe book created in L'Ecole de Médecine de Montpellier (Zecchin 1987, pp. 253–54).

12 Schweppe 1997, pp. 81–84.

13 Matthew 2002; Matthew and Berrie 2005.

14 Cited in Zecchin 1987, p. 245.

15 Borghini also suggests that these pigments were tempered in glue for painting wooden objects, giving lances and shields as examples; he does not mention, however, their use for oil painting.

Renaissance Venice and Her "Moors"

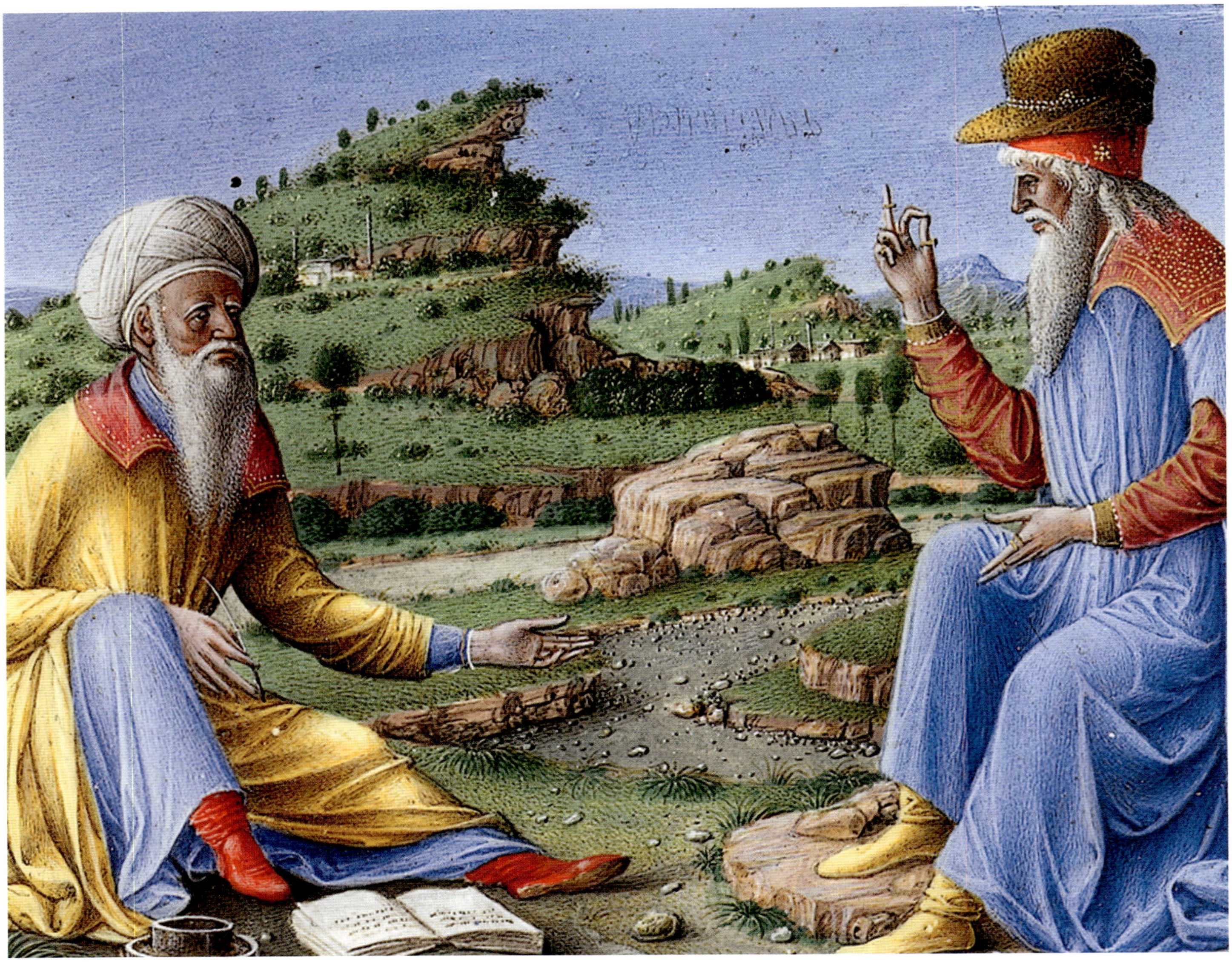

Michael Barry[1]

cat. 17. Girolamo da Cremona and Assistants *Aristotle lecturing Averroës* (detail)

Carved or painted turbaned Muslims—Moors, *Mori*—lurk in wall-niches and canvases of late medieval and Renaissance Venice, just as their real-life counterparts mingled in the throngs of merchants on the quaysides. But in art, most of these grave bearded figures impassively ponder the triumphs and agonies of Venetian Christendom's most venerated martyrs—or point in awe, at St. Stephen preaching; at St. George slaying the dragon; and of course at St. Mark scourged and dragged by his feet to the pyre.

To be sure, Venice's artists—beginning with Gentile Bellini dispatched by the Signoria to paint the Ottoman sultan's portrait in Istanbul (cat. 23, p. 68)—intended to convince their own viewers of the utter realism of their depicted "Moors." Far too many Venetian merchants and diplomatic envoys sailed yearly to the Levant to settle for less than total verisimilitude—and these were the painters' main sponsors.

Gentile Bellini thus sketched dozens of vivid Ottoman types during his stay in Istanbul in 1479–81, such as a crouching janissary with quiver, sword, and taut feline energy as if ready to bound and kill; a pensive hooded Turkish girl perched on towering clogs; or a standing turbaned merchant with bristling mustache and arrogant thumb hooked into his sash (fig. 1). Bellini's visual impressions like these were copied in the best workshops of Venice and also elsewhere in Italy—the better to accompany and illustrate the lives of Christ's saints, and highlight the victory of the Church Militant.

fig. 1. Gentile Bellini, *Standing Turk,* late 15th century, Venice. Musée du Louvre, Paris

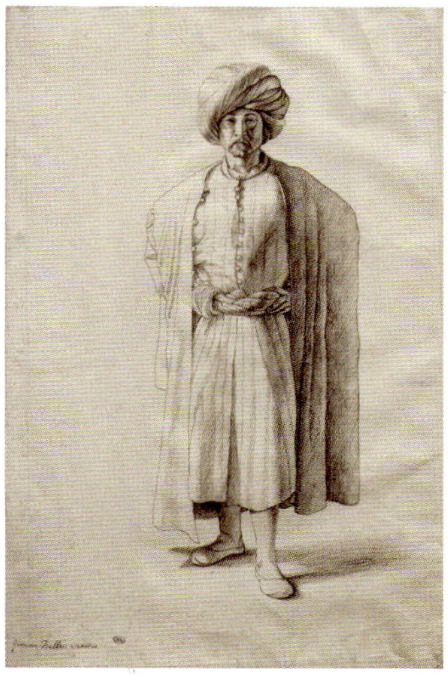

But why this Venetian concern with an Orientalist kind of realism that no other European artists cared to match before the colonial 19th century—and then for completely different reasons? No doubt painters and engravers of the northern Renaissance, Dürer and others, also framed their passions of Christ and his saints with dour and more or less Mamluk- or Ottoman-looking tormentors.

But 15th- and 16th-century Venetian painters remain unique in European art of the time in so determinedly stressing the most accurately possible rendered Moors. Nor might even exacting modern specialists seriously fault the scrupulously reproduced attires of, say, Vittore Carpaccio's Muslim-looking horsemen and dignitaries in his panels for the chapel of

San Giorgio degli Schavioni (St. George of the Slavs), painted between 1502 and 1508 (figs. 9 and 10, p. 132).

Without a doubt, Renaissance Venice's painted Moors do reflect Venetian mercantile dealings with the Near Eastern spice ports. Yet the allegorical meaning of these same "Moorish" figures reaches far beyond the surface of commercial anecdotes—and should be sounded. Aside from preparatory sketches, the Moors of Venetian Renaissance art adorn religious compositions saturated with the Catholic symbolism and Crusader spirit of their own age—like the immense and somber Mannerist-style canvases of Lepanto hung afresh in the Ducal Palace after the fire of 1577.

Messianic prophecies throughout the later 15th and 16th centuries circulated in the lagoon, affirming Venice's miraculous, long-awaited resurrection in the face of so many rivals both Christian and Muslim—indeed, thanks to the Great Turk himself. According to a fervent sermon preached by the tireless 90-year-old monk, Piero Nani, quoted by the chronicler Marin Sanudo under the date of April 30, 1509, the Great Turk, already master of holy Constantinople since 1453, would extend his conquering sway over the entire world and even over Rome itself, and feed his horse in the pope's own christening fount, but then, suddenly, would be struck by grace, convert to Christ, restore universal peace, return unto Venice all it holdings upon the Italian mainland, and finally entrust to the Patriarchate of St. Mark the safekeeping of Palestine, the Holy Land itself, in fief.[2]

St. Mark's Triumph over Islam

Venice's patron saint, as is well known, is Mark. Venetians believed that the Apostle once preached on the shores of the lagoon, where, in a vision, he saw Christ prophesy that he, Mark, would one day find his final resting-place thereabouts. Mark was martyred in Alexandria in about AD 62 or 63. According to medieval Christian legend, the pagan Egyptians were prevented from burning Mark's body by a providential storm that scattered them into flight, and so allowed the faithful to recover and reverentially bury the saint. But, the legend goes on, in 828—some two centuries after the Muslims' conquest of Alexandria in 642—two shrewd Venetian merchants in Egypt, named Rusticus and Tribunus, stole the miraculously preserved body and carried it to Venice, thereby fulfilling Christ's prophecy, and turning the city of the lagoon into an Apostolic See inferior in religious and political prestige only to Rome.

Scholars now believe that the monumental canvas of *St. Mark Preaching in Alexandria* was begun by Gentile Bellini in 1504, and finished after his death by his brother Giovanni in 1507 (fig. 7, p. 129).[3] Gentile Bellini's Apostle in classical drapery preaches from a platform to a lively mixed crowd including both turbaned Muslim men and veiled Muslim women, and long-robed and velvet-capped Venetian senators and merchants of the highest rank (amongst which is Gentile himself). A huge building dominates the "Alexandrian" square, with Byzantine-style rounded arches topped by three majestic domes. The Bellini brothers may have meant this edifice to depict the pagan temple of Serapis, or the future Alexandrian tomb of the saint himself—but also, here, deliberately evoked St. Mark's own basilica in Venice.

Regarding style, Gentile Bellini's painting juxtaposes the legend's successive episodes under a clear sky with bright sharp details and rigorous perspective. Venetian tastes in art would soon shift from such Late Gothic crystalline depictions of a world ablaze under gilded light, in preference for the damper mists and shadowy *sfumato* of Titian's manner: a new foggy aesthetic mood believed first introduced into the schools of the lagoon by the painter Giorgione, inspired by Leonardo da Vinci. But in terms of content, later Venetian artists certainly did not eschew the *allegorical* import of the Bellini school of art, which is limpid here. The Alexandria depicted by the Bellini brothers prefigures Venice. The city where Mark once preached to the Egyptian unbelievers—whether pagans before or Muslims now—was indeed long ago a holy city, an Apostolic See incarnate in its own domed basilica. But ever since Alexandria had submitted to Islam, and so renounced the Apostle by reverting to its ancient unbelief, Mark had transferred his holy presence unto the worthier city upon the lagoon—as Christ had predicted. Venice thus became the new Alexandria, Mark's new and true Apostolic See.

Giovanni Mansueti resorts to similar allegory in his own rendition of *St. Mark Preaching in Alexandria* painted in about 1518, a jumble of scenes again juxtaposed as if in a Mystery play, in an "Alexandrian" setting that is simply the Venetian architecture of St. Mark's Basilica itself, reproduced with multiplied arcades, balconies, and domes, all topped by a cross. Mansueti's impossible Alexandria is ruled by an enthroned emir with a Mamluk horned turban, surrounded by mingled crowds of Egyptian Muslims and Venetian Christians while opaquely draped Egyptian women, as in the Bellini painting, sit upon the ground, in veneration, at the feet of the Apostle.

For such allegory to impress Venetian audiences, the "Egyptians" had to look convincingly real. Whipped turbans and gold-embroidered kaftans are already as richly rendered in Cima da Conegliano's *St. Mark Healing the Cobbler Anianus in Alexandria,* painted in 1497–99 for the Venetian Church of the Crociferi (fig. 5, p. 126), as any by Carpaccio.

Carpaccio's own "Moors," in the painter's twin cycles of Stephen and George, symbolize their own defeat and the triumph of the depicted saint. Carpaccio's Stephen (cat. 30, p. 133; cat. 31, p. 27), Christendom's first martyr, preaches (like Mark) unto a crowd of turbaned infidels cloaked in Ottoman-type kaftans. Carpaccio's George, in the Scuola di San Giorgio, is a fair-haired solar knight on horseback who symbolizes Christ himself as he pierces the dragon of satanic darkness with the sun-like ray of his lance, thereby saving the princess of Trebizond who symbolizes the human soul. George's triumph, in turn, signifies Christ's ultimate victory over Islam, allegorized as the king of Trebizond depicted by Carpaccio as a sultan who doffs his turban in order to receive baptism from the saint. Carpaccio's visual conceit, painted in 1507, of a clearly Muslim-looking ruler kneeling before the dragon-slaying saint, closely coincides with the messianic predictions that had thrilled the Republic for more than a half-century, and were so soon to be revived with fresh zeal in 1509 by the monk Piero Nani, regarding the imminent conversion of Islam's sultan: to the greater benefit and glory of Venice. Venetian mythology at the turn of the 16th century thus nicely reconciled the Republic's urgent Catholic faith with the Republic's no less urgent need to trade with Egypt's and Turkey's spice-lords: if only these would conveniently convert.

Such predictions not only aroused hopes in Venice. The Umbrian artist Pinturicchio, one of Raphael's teachers, borrowed from contemporary Venetian pictorial models to allegorize his own vision of Christ's victory over Islam, in frescoes for the library of Siena Cathedral painted between 1505 and 1507. Pinturicchio shows the ailing Pope Pius II (a scion of the Sienese Piccolomini family) carried on his dais before the harbor of Ancona on July 19, 1464, from where this pontiff had hoped—in vain—to launch a Crusade with Venetian help to recover Constantinople from the Turks (fig. 2). Pope Pius II died soon after, and his Crusade never sailed, but Pinturicchio nevertheless transforms this historical fiasco into a victorious-looking pageant. Before the pope's throne jostle a bearded Byzantine nobleman, as a symbol of Greek Christendom finally submitting to Rome; Doge Cristoforo Moro of allied Venice properly on his knees; and kneeling also—but in gorgeous and realistically rendered Ottoman robes—the Turkish prince Bayezid Osman, half-brother to Sultan Mehmet. This unhappy Turkish prince fled to Rome in 1456 after losing his bid for the Ottoman throne, and convinced a decidedly credulous Pope Calixtus III that his own restoral to the sultanate with papal military help might result in subjecting the entire Ottoman Empire unto Latin Christendom. Most especially, the prince himself submitted to Christian baptism—whence his new name in Christian circles: *Calixtus Ottomanus.*

In this fresco, the Ottoman prince's kneeling posture signifies Pinturicchio's variation on the well-known prophetic theme. The Turkish prince symbolizes universal Islam humbled and converted at last. Moreover, behind this kneeling prince stands his turbaned Turkish squire, squarely facing viewers as if to implicate them in the depicted holy scene—with his thumb proudly hooked in his sash. This seemingly minor detail actually betrays that Pinturicchio directly lifted this figure of a "Standing Turk" from the Gentile Bellini drawing now in the Louvre (or some very close copy thereof). More important, the basic allegorical thrust of Pinturicchio's fresco in Siena stands revealed as exactly the same as that of the Carpaccio painting of George's triumph in Venice, finished in the identical year 1507: the sultan's conversion prefigures that of all Islam.

Giorgione's Arab Philosopher

While most Venetian painted Moors are really stock characters in a religious drama, infidels to be vanquished, one single Moor does emerge in the city's art as the dignified protagonist of a higher order of thought. This figure is Giorgione's "Arab" philosopher. Giorgione's Moor arises only to be cast down and vanquished in turn—but after a bracing spiritual struggle richly symbolized in Giorgione's art. The logic, which humbles the Moors in other Venetian paintings, applies to Giorgione's Moor as well—but on more subtle a level.

Giorgione's famously enigmatic *Three Philosophers* (fig. 4, p. 162), painted between 1504 and 1506, yields us a glimpse of another and no less important aspect of Islam, in Renaissance Venetian minds, than the contemporary Mamluk or Ottoman sultanates: this is the Spanish-Islamic aspect, or rather the Averroan—for the central, noble-looking robed and turbaned figure in the picture, with the brown beard of a man in his 30s, is undoubtedly Averroës, as we shall see.

Averroës in Venice

With the exception of Aristotle himself, no philosopher was more heatedly debated in Venice and the neighboring University of Padua, between the 14th and 17th centuries, than Aristotle's most famous and influential commentator, the Spanish-Arab thinker Ibn Rushd: born in Cordova in 1126, died in Marrakesh in 1198, and whose name was Latinized as Averroës by his medieval European translators. The bulk of Ibn Rushd's Aristotelian commentaries were rendered from Arabic into Latin by Michael Scot, a learned Scots cleric who studied Arabic in Toledo, then worked under the enlightened sponsorship of Emperor Frederick II in Palermo in the 1220s. Scot's Latin renditions of Averroës were considered so important by Frederick II that the enthusiastic monarch sent them on to the University of Bologna, whence they rapidly spread to the University of Paris. The Averroan commentaries deeply impressed Christian clerics, sparked intellectual controversy, but very much worried the leaders of the Church, which ultimately, however, authorized their study by learned clergy and laymen alike.

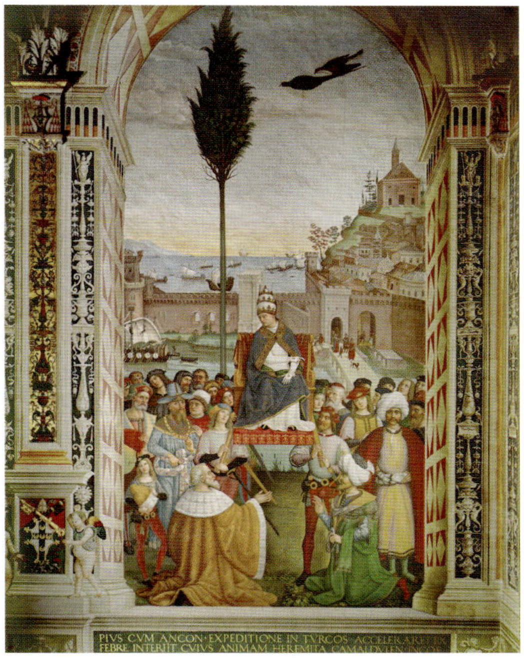

fig. 2. Bernardino Pinturicchio, *Pope Pius II (Aeneas Silvius Piccolomini) in the Port of Ancona*, 1505–7. Piccolomini Library, Cathedral, Siena

After printing presses were established in Venice in 1469, the Republic's publishing shops, then the most prolific in Europe, multiplied copies of Averroës's works from 1472 to 1560, in their medieval Latin translations to be sure, but often revised, on the basis of extant Spanish-Hebrew versions, by learned Venetian Jews such as Elia del Medigo, Calonymos ben David, and Jacob Mantino. Indeed, since most of Averroës's writings have been lost to us in the original Arabic, the philosopher's major works remain mainly known to us today from these Latin editions published in Renaissance Venice. After French ecclesiastical tribunals condemned many theses associated with the name of Averroës at the University of Paris in 1270 and 1277, Latin Christian scholars of the Spanish-Arab philosopher's Aristotelian commentaries found a new and welcoming home, and major center of European-wide influence, in northern Italy and especially in Padua and Venice—rather than at the University of Bologna then mainly specializing in law.

One can even choose to see Averroës's enduring prestige in Venetian civilization in the light of something like a stubbornly vigorous, even astonishing cultural survival, in one rich corner of Europe, of the heritage of Spanish Islam. The domain of the Muslims in southern Spain shrank after their fatal defeat by Castile's knighthood in 1212, and disappeared with the fall of their last stronghold in Granada in 1492. But Averroës's teachings persisted and even flourished in Catholic Padua and Venice. In the eyes of the Muslim Ibn Rushd or Averroës, as for the Catholic Dante after him, the pagan Greek philosopher Aristotle represented the "master of those who know," *il maestro di color che sanno:* that is, the summit of human knowledge attainable by pure speculative reason alone, without the Grace of Divine Revelation.

But again, for Dante and the other Latin Christian scholars of his age, plumbing the extraordinarily difficult writings of the pagan Aristotle in turn required necessary resort to the Muslim Averroës' detailed, lucid, indeed matchless commentary, in depth, of the ancient Greek philosopher. Not that Ibn Rushd had not offered his own original vision of the world, and of the soul, within the context of his own Aristotelian commentaries. Following in the steps of his own great intellectual predecessor, the erudite Spanish-Muslim writer and vizier Ibn Tufayl, Averroës himself had stressed the underlying harmony between the teachings of the Qur'an and those of Aristotle, but also insisted that such harmony might only be perceived by an elite of sages capable of following abstract discourse. In Ibn Rushd's view, however, the common crowd of unlearned believers might only be governed by the clear, simple, even brutal dictates of Divine Law and by the vivid imagery of Holy Writ. Indeed the common people were not capable of Philosophy, and should not be dangerously taught Philosophy, the preserve of the elite. Yet according to Ibn Rushd, Philosophy and Holy Writ do teach the same truths beneath their surface differences. For wherever Philosophy and Holy Writ might appear to contradict one another in the letter, it behooved authentic sages to detect their profound accord in the spirit through ever more logically rigorous reading of the texts. For example, Aristotle taught that the world is eternal. The Qur'an, however, teaches that it was created. But the true sage perceives that Divine Creation occurs outside the bounds of time. Creation's priority pertains, therefore, not to the temporal order, but to the purely logical order of the Necessary First Cause. Hence no real contradiction subsists between the eternity of this world according to Aristotle, and its creation according to the Qur'an.

Latin translations of Averroës, as these became increasingly available to Western clerics by the second third of the 13th century, through the clarity of their argumentation, and the implacable critical rigor of their commentaries on Aristotle, overwhelmingly impressed some of the best minds in the University of Paris: now seduced away from Avicenna's poetic mysticism by what looked to them like the Cordovan master's flawless resort to pure rational logic, raised to the heights of utter intellectual ecstasy without any apparent help from any one particular religious Faith. Bishop Étienne Tempier, in 1270 and again in 1277, hurled accusations of heresy against the Averroist masters in Paris, among whom the brilliant Flemish scholastic, Siger de Brabant, later so much praised by Dante. According to Bishop Tempier, the blinded admirers of Aristotle and of his impious Muslim commentator defied the Church by daring to teach the uncreated eternity of the world; the single identity of all human souls; and worst of all, the pernicious Averroan notion of a Double Truth (never actually professed by the historical Ibn Rushd), whereby a thing might be logically true, and its exact opposite equally true even if logically absurd, if so taught by Holy Writ. Such a notion of a Double Truth, in Bishop Tempier's eyes, sapped the foundations of Faith, if Reason and Faith were perceived not logically to conform.

The friars of the Dominican Order at the University of Paris, who also taught Aristotle and therefore felt stung, defended their orthodoxy and sprang to the offensive by attacking the Averroists in turn. Their greatest master, the Italian monk and professor in Paris Thomas Aquinas (1224–74), wrestled in his writings at every turn with the thought of Averroës, whom he branded as "not so much an Aristotelian as the corrupter of Aristotelian philosophy."[4] Thomas had to absorb, in order to refute, whole sections of the great Averroan glosses to Aristotle, which he nevertheless exploited as indispensable intellectual underpinnings to his own massive writings—from the *Summa contra Gentiles* (Sum against the Gentiles) to the *De unitate intellectus contra Averroistas* (Regarding the Unity of the Intellect, against the Averroists)—in order to affirm the fundamental agreement between Faith and Reason.

As it happens, the real Ibn Rushd himself had argued that apparent contradiction between Reason and Faith could always be resolved by the deeper probings of Reason. Thomas, in his strenuous polemics against the Latin Averroists of his day, actually pursued much the same logical path as the Spanish-Muslim thinker whom he targeted, when insisting, in turn, on the necessary concord between Faith and Reason.

In fact, wherever he struggles to refute Averroës, Thomas often explicitly borrows neo-Platonizing arguments from the other great Muslim philosopher known to him, Avicenna, thereby integrating these two supremely important thinkers, from the twin, opposite horizons of medieval Islamic civilization, the Spanish-Arab and the Persian, into the heart of his Catholic theology. Indeed, ever since Thomas Aquinas's canonization in 1323 as the greatest intellectual champion of his Church since Augustine, mastering the Thomistic system of thought has required all truly serious Catholic theologians and students of Western Christianity to grapple not only with Aristotle, but with the thought of Aristotle's two most eminent Muslim interpreters, as well.[5]

When the later medieval Church enshrined St. Thomas as its guiding philosopher, it was thereby constrained, whatever its initial misgivings, to include the study of Averroës himself in pride of place in its scholastic curriculum: while cautiously defining such a reading of Averroës as a necessary form of intellectual gymnastics in pure philosophy, the better to elucidate the thought of Aristotle and so to affirm, through resort to reason itself, the primacy of faith. The Spanish-Muslim master thereby became, in the great Catholic schools, a philosophical opponent at once respected, reviled, but necessary. According to the well-known medieval cultural habit of psychologically "dissociating aspects" (so perceptively identified by J. Huizinga in his now classic *Waning of the Middle Ages* in 1919), the Church, in Averroës, now admired the philosopher, while condemning the heretic. For all self-respecting clerics, intellectual dueling with the brilliant but heretical thought of Averroës turned into a mandatory scholarly exercise: because it forced Catholic schoolmen to sharpen their wits by constantly targeting Averroës as their most seductive and dangerous mental adversary—to be repeatedly overcome in argument.

In the course of the 14th century, European primacy in Averroan studies passed from the University of Paris—now shaken by the Hundred Years' War between France and England—to the great Italian schools: Bologna and especially Padua. Set in the immediate neighborhood of Venice, the University of Padua consecrated the triumph of Averroism in the sense of enjoining systematic scholastic resort to the Averroan commentaries in order to elucidate Aristotle and so refine the scholars' own critical sense. From Padua, Averroism rapidly spread to the intellectual elite of nearby Venice—especially after Venice annexed Padua itself in 1405 and so turned the town, then one of Italy's most respected scholarly centers, into the official university of the Republic, as it were the Oxford of the Venetian nobility. In Padua, young Venetians studied their Aristotle through Averroës's glosses.

With the advent of printing, Venice further gave the world its very first editions—in Latin versions of course—of the leading classical Muslim philosophers. And this was not limited to the Averroan commentaries on Aristotle. The Paduan scholastic Agostino Nifo, or "Niphus," spread Averroës's original contributions to thought by publishing in Venice, in 1497, the available medieval Latin version of the Spanish-Arab master's *Destructio destructionis (Tahafut al-Tahafut):* Averroës's polemical blast against the anti-philosophical mysticism of the Persian thinker Algazel. Editions of Avicenna and Alpharabius, again in Latin, followed soon after: the world's *editio princeps* of their respective treatises on the soul, combined into a single handy volume, thus saw the light in Venice in 1508.

Ibn Rushd of Cordova's strange posthumous philosophical fate is an almost exclusively European cultural phenomenon, and might give here pause. The Spanish-Arab *Commentator*, as he was so often referred to in Latin, although exploited by Christian Europeans for his cold study of Aristotelian logic, yet also served to convey to Christian Europe something of the fervor of Islamic mysticism, or Sufism, a way of thought almost akin to Hinduism in its yearning for the appeased soul's extinction of individuality within the undifferentiated One. With Averroës, moreover, we see the odd case of a Muslim philosopher born in southern Europe, largely ignored in other Islamic lands but translated, read, discussed, and finally published exclusively in Europe, by and for European Christians and indeed also by and for European Jews. Now, the medieval definition of "Europe" was outlined by Pope Urban II in his momentous sermon at Clermont in central France, in 1095, when he preached the First Crusade: "Of the three parts of the world once known to the Ancients, Asia and Africa now obey the Law of Mahomet, only Europe still observes the Law of Christ." The historical Ibn Rushd himself remained unaware of any such notion of "Europe." The Graeco-Roman purely arbitrary abstract geographical projection of mythologically named "continents" was ignored by medieval Muslim cosmographers, who preferred to divide the terrestrial map into equal bands of seven climatic zones. But "Europe" as defined by Urban II did come to engulf, through war, the Andalusian city where Ibn Rushd was born, when Cordoa was captured (a generation after Averroës's death) by the Castilians in 1236. But since that date, it has become difficult to deny that, at least through Averroës himself, one particular "European" Islamic thinker did come to play a central rôle in European civilization, in fact in European civilization alone—until the final expulsion of Averroan studies from mainstream European culture in the course of the 17th century.

It has sometimes been argued that late medieval and early Renaissance Averroism essentially offered a kind of intellectual breach of freedom for thinkers impatient of Churchly restrictions and keen to discourse on the natural order of things in the light of pure reason alone. Yet Averroës seems more often than not to have served as a sort of convenient intellectual whipping-post for medieval and Renaissance Catholic scholastics, proud to "vanquish" the Moorish philosopher by dint of their own argumentation. Still, as Lucchetta has accurately noted, Venice was concerned enough to insure European-wide influence for the University of Padua to protect, at least to some extent, the university's freedom of expression and thought, hence the flourishing of Averroan and Aristotelian debate.[6] As modern visitors to Venice, we become almost so sentimentally trapped by the sheer visual beauty of the city upon its lagoon that we tend to forget what the Republic of St. Mark also very much represented for Christian Europe between the 14th and 17th centuries: an island of relative intellectual freedom; a haven for a broad measure of religious tolerance, at least by the grim standards of those years; and then the final stronghold of Italian political independence against the repeated and sometimes combined assaults of the papacy, France, and the Austrian and Spanish Habsburgs.

Against Averroës in Venice: the Reaction of the Petrarchists

When Averroism as a dominant intellectual current—that is, an Aristotelianism colored by the comments of the Spanish-Arab philosopher—triumphed in 14th-century Venice and nearby Padua, the trend also provoked angry reactions not only from those partial to the more Platonizing and Augustinian strains in Christianity, but further from defenders of what might be called "good writing", that is, *belles lettres.* In echo, the great 19th-century French Arabist and Hebraist, Ernest Renan, deplored what he called the arid pedanticism of 14th- to 17th-century Venetian Averroism, as a scientific approach perverted by a sterile, endless sparring of logical arguments and counter arguments based upon Aristotle and his Commentator alone—while diverting minds away from a direct and renewed observation of nature.[7] Now, without a doubt, fresh scientific breakthroughs in the 17th century did ultimately shatter the traditional cosmology not only of Aristotle and Averroës, but also of the medieval Catholic Church, which based its scholastic perceptions of the universe on precisely the same scientific data as the ancient Greek philosophers and their medieval Muslim interpreters, however much it might dispute this or that theological conclusion drawn from Aristotle by Avicenna or Averroës. But in the eyes of the humanists of the dawning Italian Renaissance, traditional Aristotelianism with its attendant Averroist glosses, as taught in the Universities of Paris or Padua, sinned on aesthetic grounds as well: by imposing use of an impoverished, desiccated Latin for supposedly practical reasons as a kind of frozen technical style devoid of any literary flavor, emotional resonance, or cultural depth—as it were, a direct prefiguration of the worst kind of modern academic jargon or the sort of deadened, ugly English currently favored in international bureaucracies. As Petrarch (1304–74) put it: "they have rendered Aristotle hideous."[8]

If any one single individual could possibly be credited with inventing the "Renaissance"—that is, the culture of a Christian humanism grounded almost exclusively in the reading of ancient Roman and Greek authors, or in other words a historical fashion in thought which sprouted in Italy in the 14th century, held sway over all cultured Europe from the late 15th to the 17th and even beyond, and whose last traces only just died out in Western schools yesterday in the mid-20th—then this individual would have to be Petrarch. The illustrious Tuscan poet and scholar, as is well known, drew for his inspiration on Cicero for his prose style, on Virgil for his verse, and on Augustine's Platonism for his understanding of Christianity, while heartily recommending all three Latin writers—the pagan and the Christian—as his peerless literary models. But Petrarch also resided for many years in Venice, where he writes how repelled he was by the insipid Latin and arrogant Scholasticism of the city's numerous Averroists—including members of the highest nobility. The Venetian patricians Leonardo Dandolo, Tommaso, Talanto, and Zaccaria Contarini, accompanied by the professional Scholastic Guido da Bagnolo, paid Petrarch a solemn visit in his own house on the Riva degli Schiavoni to argue, deplore, and smugly to mock the poet's ignorance of both Aristotelian science and Averroan logic. Petrarch chose to refute these Venetian Averroists in a long Latin epistle clogged with Classical quotations, composed in 1367: "Regarding my own ignorance and that of many others," *De sui ipsius et multorum ignorantia.* The *editio princeps* of this seminal pamphlet for Renaissance humanism was published in Venice very early in the age of print, in 1501, as a cultural manifesto which landed in the lagoon, dare one say, with a splash: for Petrarch challenged no less than the received text of Aristotle and the sheer pertinence of Averroës' commentaries. Now, this little episode in Renaissance Venetian cultural history is no mere scholarly detail. The lasting intellectual consequences of Petrarch's attitude, down to our own day, have been very grave, and even tragic: because Petrarch explicitly demanded expulsion of all Arabic contributions to the culture of Christian humanism as so much dross—stressing its Greek and Latin sources alone.

Petrarch's assault against Averroës, Avicenna, and other "Arabs" triumphed among Western Europe's literary-minded humanists by the early 16th century and predominated in all the universities, even among physicians and astronomers, by about the second generation of the 17th. To clarify: Western Christian civilization between the 12th and 17th centuries certainly rejected Islam as a religion, but nevertheless consciously integrated those precious Arabic influences considered indispensable to the development of dialectics, medicine, astronomy, and mathematics. By the mid-17th century, however, the study of classical Islamic authors in the "West"—that is, in Catholic and Protestant Europe and its later American extensions—rapidly dwindled to its current abysmal levels: as an exotic, basically superfluous intellectual specialization indulged in by rare scholars (many of them at first Church-trained), when not dismissed out of hand in today's Western universities (mainly on account of modern Islamic fundamentalist hysterics, despite the usual "politically correct" disclaimers on this), as a tedious academic nuisance, drained of any scholarly matter really pertinent and vital for contemporary Western thought. Both Avicenna and Averroës in the course of the 17th century simply dropped from the recognized core curriculum of required readings for Western literary elites. Certainly algebra and other major breakthroughs of medieval Islamic culture left a permanent mark on world science, but world scientific research since the 17th century followed largely fresh paths whence obvious Islamic contributions disappeared. But as it happens, the crucial intellectual debate for or against the place of "Arabism," in Western culture, first mainly raged in Italy, and notably in the Veneto. Even as late as 1560, Venetian printers yet thought it worth their while, both intellectually and commercially, to issue fresh volumes of Averroës in Latin, while Padua's faculty in the early 17th century still taught the art of healing from the old Latin version of Avicenna's medical *Canon,* whose first edition in the original Arabic was actually brought out by the papal press, in Rome, in 1587. Yet Petrarch's 14th-century pamphlet, once put into wide circulation in its 1501 Venetian edition, urged rejection of all these "Arabic" studies. "I hate the whole Arab race," Petrarch further and scathingly scribbled in a letter to Giovanni Dondi (*Contra medicum quemquam invectiva*), in his rage against the enduring influence of Arab medical texts upon the practice of Venetian physicians in his day (fig. 3).[9]

Medieval Christendom had justified its borrowings from Islamic civilization as so much intellectual plunder, booty for thought legitimately seized from the enemy. Jacques Le Goff pointedly quotes the 12th-century English cleric Daniel de Morley, who traveled as far as Toledo to study Arabic and reproduced a familiar argument from St. Augustine's *De doctrina christiana,* to the effect that it was proper to loot the wisdom of infidels in the service of the Church, in the manner in which the Hebrews led by Moses once carried off Egyptian treasures in order to adorn the Tabernacle of their Lord: "We too who have been mystically freed from Egypt, the Lord hath bade us despoil the Egyptians of their treasures by which to enrich the Hebrews. Let us therefore according to the Lord's command and by His help despoil these infidel philosophers of their learning and eloquence, let us despoil these unbelievers that we may become enriched, with their spoils, in our belief."[10]

Rich spoils indeed; Le Goff quotes another English cleric in 12th-century Castile, Adelard of Bath, who also learned enough Arabic to translate philosophical texts: "I have learned from my Arab masters to take reason for my guide."[11]

The intellectual debate in Renaissance Venice really concerned the practical advantage, or not, of yet retaining such philosophical spoils from the Muslim foe. The late 15th- and 16th-century humanists who now shared Petrarch's way of thinking wanted to jettison the "Arabs" altogether, especially since Greek studies henceforth flourished in Venice with the arrival of Byzantine refugee scholars along with scores of original Greek texts. Why any longer read Averroës and other "barbarian" commentators, the humanists wanted to know, when authentic Greek texts of Aristotle and his ancient commentators Themistius and Alexander of Aphrodisias were now made readily available, and in good copies, by the Venetian press? The Scholastic opponents of the Classical-minded humanists at the University of Padua tried to argue, but with shrinking success as the 16th century progressed, that the Arabic contributions remained indispensable at least in terms of actual science—if not for their literary merits.[12]

Yet what might have at least partly justified the stridency of the humanist opponents of Arabism was that 15th- and 16th-century Islamic civilization seemed truly to become almost mentally petrified before Italian eyes—at least in the Mediterranean basin. Those Muslim philosophers whom Renaissance Venetians were actually in a position to read, in two- or three-hundred-year-old Latin versions, included only those writers once known and appreciated in 12th-century Spanish-Islamic civilization (including authors from the Islamic East like Avicenna), that is, shortly before the military collapse of most of Islamic Spain itself under Castilian assault in 1212. Renaissance Venetian readers, regarding Islamic civilization, remained caught in a time lag. They never even suspected the existence and thought of Islamic Spain's last great mystic, Ibn 'Arabi (1165–1240), who, like most of his learned fellow-countrymen, fled the fall of his Iberian homeland in order to live and teach in the East: in Ibn 'Arabi's case, in Ayyubid Syria and in Seljuq Turkish Anatolia. Even more than Avicenna, and certainly far more than Averroës whose very name remained unknown in the East, it was Ibn 'Arabi, fondly referred to by his disciples as the Shaykh Akbar (the supreme sheikh) and as Ibn Aflatun (the son of Plato), who had become consecrated as the guiding spiritual light of all mystically inclined Egyptian, West Asian, and Indian Muslims by the turn of the 16th century.

But of such spiritual trends in contemporary Eastern Islam, the Renaissance Venetians knew nothing. The Ottoman Empire encircled and threatened them, and ever since the Ottoman sultan Selim's crushing victory over the Shi'ite Savafids at the battle of Chaldiran in 1514, walled them off from further contact with lands like Iran and India where Islam's true creativity endured far into the 16th and even 17th centuries and splendid achievements continued to flower in poetry, painting, philosophy, and mysticism. The Ottoman court, however, unlike its own Seljuq predecessors, hardly encouraged serious vocations in philosophy. Like its rival Mamluk sultanate, the Ottoman Empire channeled all its main mental energies into the team arts of war and drill; and admittedly, wherever sternly disciplined, military-like repetition held some aesthetic appeal, did score undeniable visual success in architecture, calligraphy, and such decorative crafts as glass, ceramics, and textiles—but certainly not in original speculative thought, which demands the most acute individual sensitivity. The Ottomans, again like their Mamluk rivals, further committed what can only be branded a cultural suicide: both early 16th-century Near Eastern powers spurned the art of printing, leaving the world's first publications of Islam's earlier philosophical classics to the Renaissance Venetians.

Yet until the very twilight of the 16th century, the Petrarchists in Venice failed to hound the "Arabs" entirely out of the Venetian programs of study, since so many members of the Venetian intelligentsia continued stubbornly to read their Latin Averroës in order to make sense of Aristotle. The Andalusian "Moorish" philosopher therefore remained an imposing intellectual opponent, one constantly to be read, and repeatedly to be contested—hence still a living, commanding cultural presence in Venice in the Renaissance.

Giorgione's Averroës

"The Three Philosophers"

While the Moors in so many Renaissance Venetian paintings are villains in a religious pageant, infidels to be laid low, one Moor at least stands out in early 16th-century Venetian art as the dignified protagonist of a higher order of thought. This is Giorgione's Arab philosopher. Giorgione's Moor stands so tall, to be sure, only to be cast down in turn—but at the outcome of a spiritual struggle pondered by the painter in depth. The logic which fells so many scores of Moors in other Venetian paintings most certainly also applies to Giorgione's great turbaned figure—but at far more subtle a level.

The painting generally called *The Three Philosophers* was finished by Giorgione sometime between 1504 and 1508. It may have been touched up or even partially modified after his death in 1510 by Sebastiano del Piombo, also known as Sebastiano Veneziano. Giorgione's painting shows, against the backdrop of a forest, which clears to the left and there reveals a dawning sun upon the horizon: a venerable white-bearded Elder to the right, draped in the classical manner, who looks in the general direction of the rising sun and also grips a parchment inscribed with the (Arabic) numerals 1504 (= the painting's date?), further adorned with the diagram of a sort of toothed sun or wheel, itself marked with the numerals 1 to 7;[13] to the left, a beardless Youth, also draped in classical style, sits and measures with a compass the celestial revolutions, also looks in the general direction of the sun, but moreover turns his face towards the dark opening of a cave which closes the painting on the left border;[14] this Youth, in addition, turns his back upon the Elder, but nevertheless broadly directs his gaze in the same direction as this Elder; finally, standing in the center between the Youth and the Elder, while directing his gaze *away* from the dawn and instead *towards* the Elder, appears a brown-bearded character aged some 30 years, that is, a Middle-Aged Man by 16th-century standards, wearing the turban and long tunic of a Moor.

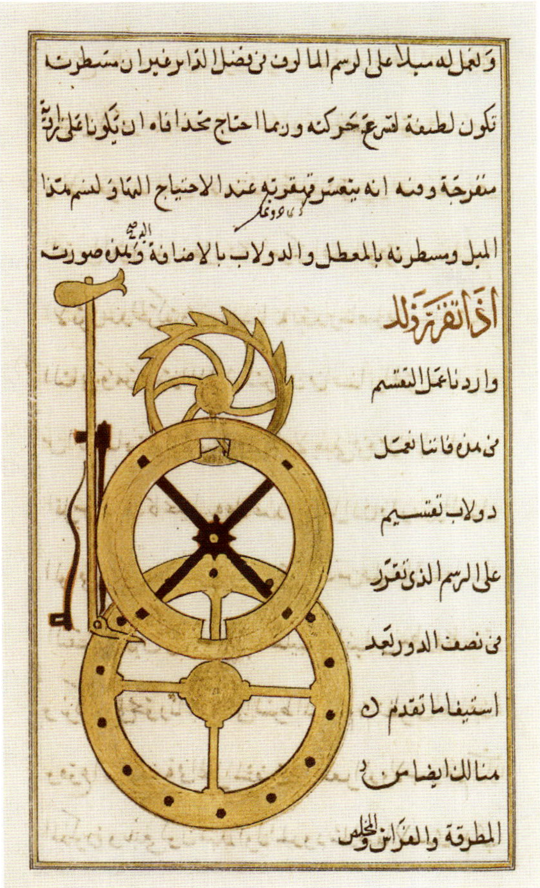

fig. 3. Taqî ad-Dîn Muhammad ibn Ma'rûf, *Al-Kawâkib ad-durriyya* (Brilliant Heavenly Bodies), 1559, Cairo. Bibliothèque Nationale de France, Paris

One aspect of Giorgione's painting hitherto overlooked in the critical literature, at least to my knowledge, is an arresting detail in the Moor's proud stance: he hooks his thumb in his sash. This is a discreet but absolutely unmistakable visual quotation from the sketch of the *Standing Turk* (now in the Louvre, fig. 1, p. 147) by Giorgione's own teacher, Gentile Bellini. We have seen above how Pinturicchio, in Siena in 1507, visually quoted exactly this same figure by Gentile Bellini to make his own allegorical point about the final submission of Islam.

Giorgione's painting has been interpreted in many ways through the centuries. The Venetian Michiel, in 1525, is the first known writer to mention the work and calls it "three philosophers in a landscape" (*3 phylosophy nel paese*); a bill of sale to an English lord in 1638 reads *"3 Astronomers and Geometricians in a Landskip who contemplat and measure";* the painting, after being sold in Brussels in 1649 to the Habsburg archduke Leopold Wilhelm, was described in the Vienna catalogue of 1659 as "a landscape . . . wherein three mathematicians take the measure of the dimensions of the sky's height" (*ein Landschaft . . . warin drey Mathematici, welche di Masz der Höchen des Himmelsz nehmen*); finally, in 1783, with the work now housed permanently in Vienna, it was reinterpreted by Christian Mechel as a representation of the Three Magi: "By Giorgione. The Three Wise Men of the East in a pleasant landscape" (*Von Giorgione. Die Drey Weisen aus Morgenland in einer angenehmen Landschaft*).

In the 20th century, interpretations multiplied beyond measure and even beyond all reason, especially after J. Wilde's examination of the painting under X-ray in 1932 revealed the painter's striking hidden *pentimento:* Giorgione had first sketched beams of light emanating from the fold of cloth draping the Elder's head. Such rays would certainly have evoked the figure of Moses to 16th-century Venetian viewers. But the fact remains that Giorgione deliberately overpainted and so erased these rays. Wilde himself chose to retain Mechel's late 18th-century reading of the work as a depiction of the Three Magi.

Critics since Mechel and Wilde have either agreed with this interpetration of the painting as the Three Magi, or demurred; 20th-century suggested readings have included: the cave over which first appeared the comet announcing Christ's birth;[15] the cave of the Nativity itself;[16] Plato's cave;[17] an allegory of Judaism, Christianity, and Islam.[18] The Elder has been seen as Melchior the Magus;[19]Moses;[20] Ptolemy;[21] Aristotle;[22] Pythagoras;[23] even Solomon.[24] The middle-aged turbaned figure, or Moor, has been successively identified as the Magus Balthazar;[25] Ptolemy also;[26] or as the Arab astronomer al-Battani;[27] even as the Prophet Muhammad himself;[28] or more generally as an allegory of Islam[29] or simply Averroism;[30] not to mention as Hiram king of Tyre who furnished the Temple's building-materials to Solomon.[31] The Youth, in turn, has been thought to represent the Magus Gaspar;[32] the young anti-Averroan late 15th-century Venetian Hellenist Ermolao Barbaro;[33] the early 16th-century German astronomer Regiomontanus;[34] his contemporary the Polish astronomer Copernicus;[35] Hiram the artisan of the Temple;[36] an allegory of humanism in the painter's day;[37] a symbol of Christianity;[38] and even the Antichrist![39]

Some critics[40] have further suggested that Sebastiano del Piombo's intervention after Giorgione's death may have been very heavy-handed indeed, in order intentionally to disguise the painter's true intentions skirting outright heresy.[41]

Giorgione's Riddles

Giorgione da Castelfranco was born in 1477 and died young, of the plague, in 1510. As repeated in every general history of art, he was the first Venetian painter to introduce to the city the *sfumato* technique of Leonardo da Vinci, by softly veiling in damp mists what had been the bright, dry, primary palette of the brothers Bellini. The great Renaissance critic, Giorgio Vasari, praised Giorgione's art as the turning point in Venetian stylistics, in the first edition of his famous *Lives* dated 1550.[42]

But while Giorgione's manner was always admired, his subject matter has repeatedly baffled critics.[43] Even Vasari, by the middle of the 16th century, already admitted puzzlement at Giorgione's frescoes then adorning the façade of Venice's Fondaco dei Tedeschi fronting the Grand Canal; not only were their colors fast eroding in the sharp saline air, but so already was cultural memory of their traditional allegorical code. In the second edition of his *Lives,* dated 1568, Vasari confessed that one could hardly "find there stories which might have any order at all" (*non si ritrovino storie che abbino ordine*).

But the earliest descriptions, by Michiel in 1525, of the three Giorgione paintings which the Venetian writer then saw hanging in the palace of the refined and highly erudite Contarini family—Taddeo and his son Girolamo both read Greek—do already yield some fundamental clues regarding the artist's preferred subjects (notably including the Trojan cycle—as J. Rapp so well grasped); although, of the three paintings in the Contarini palace, only the *Three Philosophers* survives today: "The canvas in oils of the three philosophers in a landscape, two standing and one seated who contemplates the sun's rays, with the rock so marvelously rendered (literally: 'feigned'), was begun by Giorgio da Castelfranco, and finished by Sebastiano Veneziano. The great canvas in oil of Hell with Aeneas and Anchises was by the hand of Giorgio da Castelfranco. The canvas of the landscape with the birth of Paris, with the two standing shepherds, was by the hand of Giorgio da Castelfranco and was one of his first works."[44]

We might begin by taking seriously what Michiel states in 1525: the surviving painting was then indeed regarded as representing "three philosophers." It follows, therefore, that the depicted Moor, at any rate for our earliest-known Venetian witness, was certainly a "philosopher," too. Such an observation appears blatant. Yet it seems worth repeating, given the tortured conceptual mazes into which some of the more far-fetched modern criticism has been stumbling. True, before the 18th century, the term "philosopher" never contradicted that of "astronomer." Like the ancient Greek sages, philosophers of the medieval, Renaissance, or Baroque periods were also supposed to master the entire cosmological system of their own age. The writers of the 17th century descriptions of the painting believed that the three figures were "astronomers," but such a title would not have precluded, for observers writing in 1638, 1649, and 1658, that Giorgione's characters could be philosophers too. Still, the very first term, selected by the Venetian Michiel in 1525, as close as we can come to Giorgione in time and space, specifies: "three *philosophers*." Michiel's early 16th-century choice of words seems worth retaining.

A Moorish "astronomer," if Giorgione had truly wanted to paint such a figure, might normally, in the eyes of an early 16th-century Venetian viewer, have corresponded to Ptolemy: the Greek-writing cosmographer active in Roman Egypt in the 2nd century AD, copies of whose maps and sky charts enjoyed immense popularity in Venice when first brought from Byzantium in 1410 and at once translated into Latin. Now Ptolemy, though Egyptian, had certainly not been a Muslim. But in reference to his Egyptian birthplace, Renaissance and Baroque Italian painters and engravers sometimes—though by no means always—depicted Ptolemy as a contemporary Egyptian: that is, with beard and turban; but if so, then they would always show his turban surmounted by a crown. Ptolemy, in Renaissance and Baroque Italian art, was invariably depicted crowned on account of a willful confusion, on the part of the artists, of this character with Ptolemy the Lagid, Alexander's general who did become king of Egypt in the 4th century BC. Thus the magnificent "portrait" of Ptolemy which adorns the luxurious bilingual (Greek and Latin) Venetian manuscript of his *Geography*, dated 1453 and preserved in the Marciana in Venice, shows the Egyptian cosmographer as a bearded king with crown and ermine-lined robe—but European in appearance, and with no turban.

Another famous Moor in medieval and Renaissance Italian art, Avicenna, often also curiously appears, not as a Muslim-looking philosopher at all, but as an Italian doctor in robe and hood, or then, like Ptolemy, as a Christian-looking king: that is, with no turban—but instead

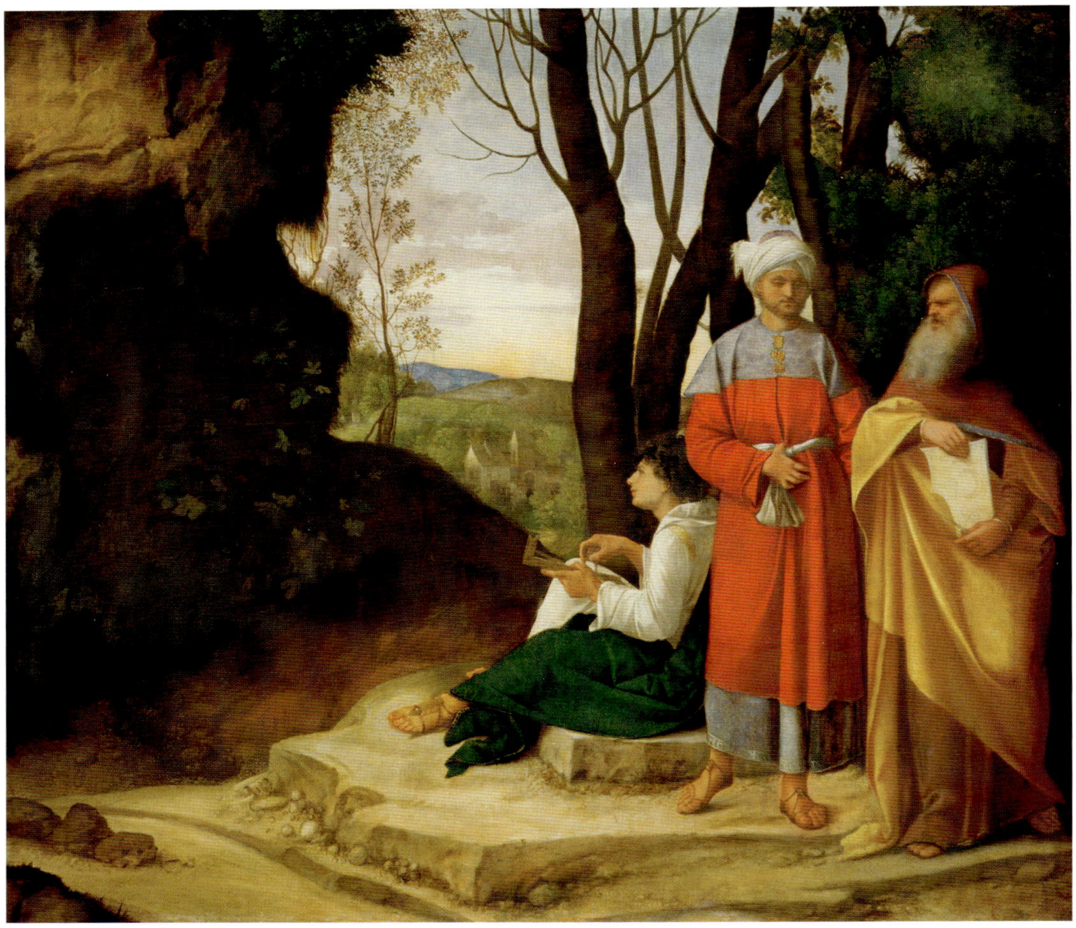

fig. 4. Giorgione, *The Three Philosophers,* 1504–8. Kunsthistorisches Museum, Vienna

with a crown. Some 15th- and 16th-century Italian depictions of Avicenna do bedeck him with an Islamic turban, but in such cases, Avicenna's turban is always shown wound about a crown. The reason again, as Hasse points out,[45] derives from an error of a Latin translator of the 12th-century Toledan school, Giraldus Cremonensis, who rendered the Arabic title of the illustrious Persian Muslim philosopher, *ash-shaykh ar-ra'is* (the leading sheikh), by the words *senex rex* (elder king), thereby spreading belief throughout medieval Western Christendom that Avicenna had not only been an outstanding sage, but also a monarch.

It is thus an Avicenna both crowned and turbaned who appears standing behind "Averroës" wearing a simple turban, in the sumptuous illumination representing the *Turba philosophorum* or "crowd of philosophers," added by hand by the artist Girolamo da Cremona in order to illustrate and personalize, for a rich private patron, a copy of the monumental Venetian printed edition of the complete works of Aristotle with the full Averroan commentaries, published in 1483 (cat. 17). Giorlamo da Cremona's Avicenna, holding his book, is a dignified bearded and turbaned figure—hence identifiable here as a Muslim—but he nevertheless wears the robe of an Italian scholar-physician, unlike his companion "Averroës" cloaked in a simple Arab tunic, and from the folds of "Avicenna's" turban clearly rises a royal crown.

Nardi, in 1955, supposed that in Giorgione's painting, the elder, non-Muslim-looking figure on the right might be the ancient Ptolemy, whereas the turbaned Moor in the center would have been his medieval Arab commentator, al-Battani (869–929), an Iraqi astronomer also translated into Latin in 12th-century Spain under the name Albategnius—a figure hardly represented, however, in medieval or Renaissance Italian art. But Guidoni's 1995–96 article added fuel to

Nardi's "astronomical" argument with interesting reproductions of frontispiece engravings for Galileo's *Dialogue on the System of the World,* published in Florence in 1632 and Trier in 1636; the Florentine picture of 1632 thus shows an aged Aristotle on the left; a bearded middle-aged Ptolemy with turban-crown in the center, contemplating Aristotle with respect; and an equally middle-aged bearded Copernicus on the right, also gazing with reverence upon the Greek sage.[46]

One salient characteristic of these 17th-century representations adduced by Guidoni of contemplative astronomer-sages does lie in their groupings into Triads, a most traditional iconographic motif admittedly going back to depictions of the Three Magi.

The Three Ages of Man, and the Three Wise Men

Giorgione's own Triad, however, sharply differentiates the ages of his three figures, a trait which inspired the last of the traditional interpretations offered by the Austrian Christian Mechel in 1783: the Three Magi.[47] Mechel's understanding had the advantage of invoking one of the most recognizable subjects in Christian mythology, the legend of the Three Wise Men ultimately derived from the Gospel according to Matthew: where they were originally not Three Kings, however, but a group of Zoroastrian Persian priests and astronomers symbolizing the Gentiles in search of salvation, and wise enough to recognize and follow Christ's star. Later Christian tradition reduced their number to three, to symbolize the Three Ages of Man with gifts of gold (in honor of Christ's royalty), frankincense (for Christ's divinity) and bitter myrrh (His suffering humanity); by the late 15th century, in wake of the Portuguese explorations of Africa's coast, the Three Magi were also made to represent the three continents: Asia (the elder king), Europe (the middle-aged king), and Africa (the young black king).

In early 16th-century Venice, Mansueti's variation on *The Adoration of the Magi* (cat. 26) duly shows his Young King as black, but more important, his three royal horsemen are realistically turbaned in the Mamluk style, according to the precise hierarchy of the contemporary Muslim Egyptian court. Mansueti's Elder King thus wears the multiple-horned turban of a Mamluk sultan; his Middle-Aged King, the simpler but still towering turban of a Mamluk provincial governor; and his Young King, the stark clean turban of an officer of the Mamluk realm. Mansueti conflated these various motifs in order to convey, to his Venetian audience, that the homage of the Magi to Christ prefigured the well-known prophecy of the conversion of Islam's sultan.

In connection with the Magi and the image of the cave in Giorgione's painting, Gabriele[48] pertinently draws attention to the *Opus imperfectum in Matthaeum* or "Gloss on Matthew," attributed to the 4th-century Greek father, St. John Chrysostom, in the medieval Latin rendition published in Cologne in 1487 and Venice in 1503:

> The Magi lived near the Mount of Victory (*Mons Victorialis*) and chose twelve in their number amongst the most learned and versed in the celestial mysteries (*studiosores et amatores mysteriorum caelestium*) to observe the coming of the star. For this reason, every

year, they climbed the Mons Victorialis in which opened a cave within a rock (*habens in se quondam speluncam in saxo*), and there, in a spot most pleasant with springs and choice trees (*fontibus, et electis arboribus amoenissimus*), they awaited the coming of the star as they ceaselessly prayed and praised God in silence for three days (*orabant et laudabant Deum in silentio tribus diebus*), until there appeared above the mountain a star formed like unto child, which guided them as far as Judaea.

E. H. Gombrich, likewise convinced that Giorgione intended to represent the Three Magi, pertinently adds Aristotle's interesting observation that "people in deep ditches and dry wells may sometimes see the stars even in full daylight."[49]

Yet Giorgione, besides these *Three Philosophers,* whom both Gabriele and Gombrich, after Mechel, choose to identify as the Three Magi, did paint an explicitly labeled—and absolutely recognizable—*Adoration of the Magi,* now in the National Gallery in London. But this second painting differs in marked respects from his *Three Philosophers.*

In Giorgione's *Adoration,* three, European-type, clearly crowned Kings, an Elder, a Middle-Aged Man, and a Youth, kneel in worship. Unlike the characters in the *Three Philosophers,* here the gazes of all three Kings, and also of Joseph, converge upon the Christ-child presented by his mother. Giorgione adds this noteworthy variation on the theme: behind his first Three Kings, a European knight points towards the Child for the benefit of a second Triad of Kings, who symbolize flawed humanity as a sort of darkened, murky reflection of the first, and more perfect, Triad of Magi. This second, shadow-Triad includes a princely Black Youth; a Middle-Aged Tatar in a furred cap (15th-century Venetian merchants saw Tatars in the Black Sea ports); and finally a Moorish Elder wearing an Ottoman- or Mamluk-type turban. Giorgione's black Youth indeed looks towards Christ, but the Middle-Aged Muslim Tatar, and the equally Muslim Ottoman or Mamluk Elder, both avert their gaze. This detail is important. The only recognizable turbaned Moor in Giorgione's *Adoration of the Magi* is distinctly an unbeliever, not a Magus: he belongs to a Triad, but to a spiritually faulty one.

Giorgione painted still another canvas closely associated with the Magi motif, but which does not, as such, represent the Magi: this is the *Adoration of the Shepherds* now in the National Gallery in Washington. In this painting, all the characters' gazes converge upon the Child, held by the Mother within the cave of the Nativity beneath the star shining in gloom in the form of a cherubi. Giorgione's two shepherds compose, with Joseph, yet another Triad: including one Youthful and one Middle-Aged shepherd, with Joseph as the white-bearded Elder. But a most interesting aspect of this *Adoration* lies in its clear allusions to the Magi motif—a Triad of worshippers who correspond to the Three Ages, before a cave—without namely representing the Three Magi. Obviously Giorgione transfers and applies Magi-linked themes to other subjects: related to, but not identical with, the Three Wise Men.

Before his early death, Giorgione further elaborated the motif of the Three Ages—as distinct from that of the Three Magi—in his so-called *Singing Lesson* now in the Pitti Palace in

cat. 17. Girolamo da Cremona and Assistants
Page from Aristotle, *Works* (with *Commentary* of Averroës and *Isagoge* of Porphyry), fol. 1, 1483
The Pierpont Morgan Library, New York

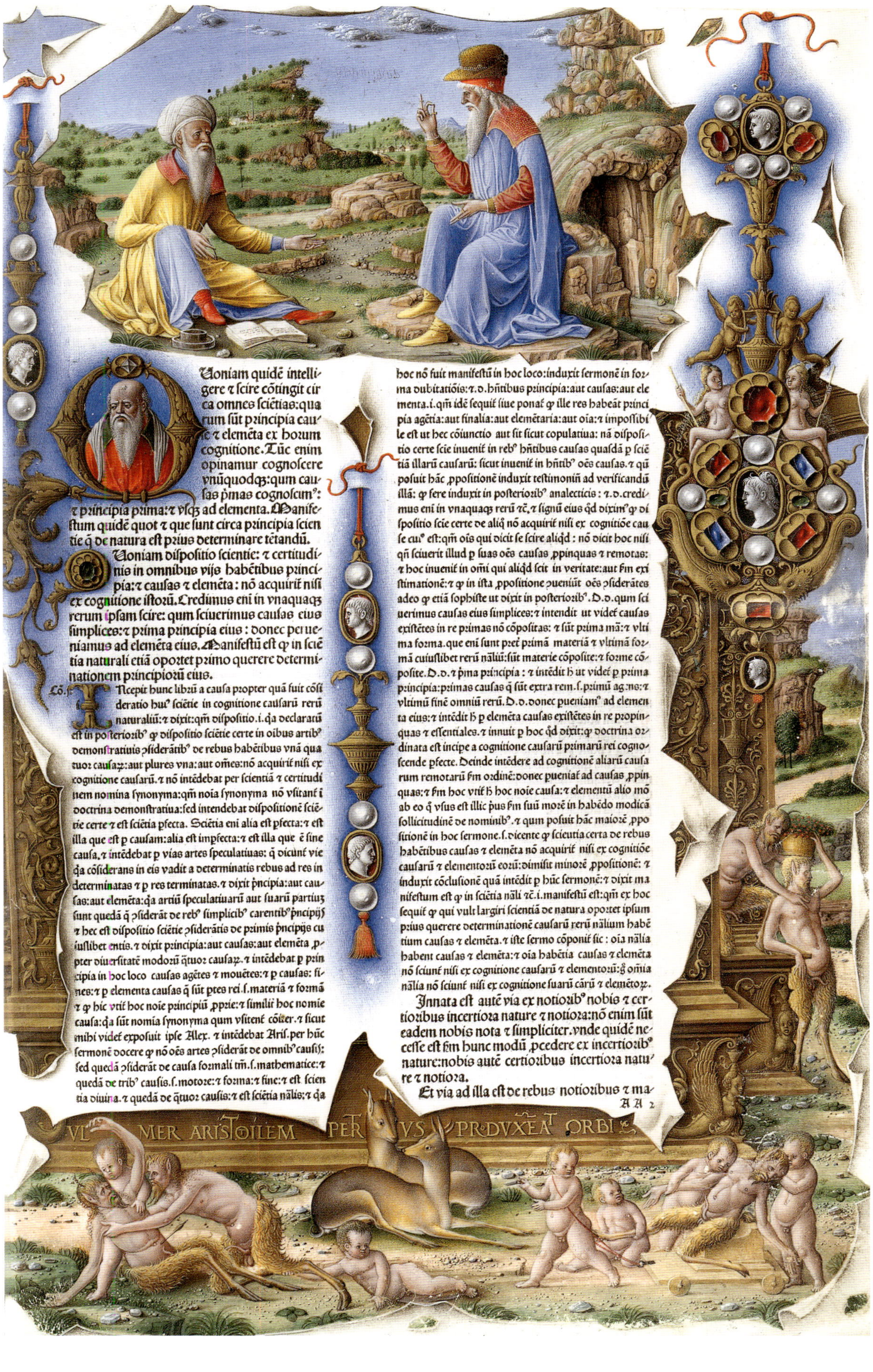

Uoniam quidē intelligere ⁊ scire cōtingit circa omnes sciētias: quarum sūt principia causē ⁊ elemēta ex horum cognitione. Tūc enim opinamur cognoscere vnūquodqꝫ: qum causas ṗmas cognoscim⁹: ⁊ principia prima: ⁊ vsqꝫ ad elementa. Manifestum quidē quot ⁊ que sunt circa principia sciencie q̄ de natura est prius determinare tētandū.

Uoniam dispositio scientie: ⁊ certitudinis in omnibus vijs habētibus principia: ⁊ causas ⁊ elemēta: nō acquirit nisi ex cognitione istorū. Credimus eni in vnaquaqꝫ rerum ipsam scire: qum sciuerimus causas eius simplices: ⁊ prima principia eius: donec perueniamus ad elemēta eius. Manifestū est ꝙ in sciētia naturali etiā oportet primo querere determinationem principiorū eius.

Cō. 1. Incepit hunc librū a causa propter quā fuit cōsideratio hui⁹ sciētie in cognitione causarū rerū naturaliū: ⁊ dixit: qm̄ dispositio. i. q̄a declaratū est in posteriorib⁹ ꝙ dispositio sciētie certe in oibus artib⁹ demonstratiuis ꝯsiderātib⁹ de rebus habētibus vnā quatuor causaꝝ: aut plures vna: aut oēs: nō acquirit nisi ex cognitione causarū. ⁊ nō intēdebat per scientiā ⁊ certitudinem nomina synonyma: qm̄ noia synonyma nō vsitant i doctrina demonstratiua: sed intendebat dispositionē sciētie certe ⁊ est sciētia pfecta. Sciētia eni alia est pfecta: ⁊ est illa que est p causam: alia est impfecta: ⁊ est illa que ē sine causa. ⁊ intēdebat p vias artes speculatiuas: q̄ dicunt vie q̄a cōsiderans in eis vadit a determinatis rebus ad res indeterminatas ⁊ p res terminatas. ⁊ dixit ṗncipia: aut causas: aut elemēta: q̄a artiū speculatiuarū aut suarū partiū sunt quedā q̄ ꝯsiderāt de reb⁹ simplicib⁹ carentib⁹ ṗncipijs ⁊ hec est dispositio sciētie ꝯsiderātis de primis ṗncipijs cuiuslibet entis. ⁊ dixit principia: aut causas: aut elemēta ꝓpter diuersitatē modorū q̄tuor causaꝝ. ⁊ intēdebat p principia in hoc loco causas agētes ⁊ mouētes: ⁊ p causas: fines: ⁊ p elementa causas q̄ sūt ptes rei. s. materiā ⁊ formā ⁊ ꝙ hic vtit hoc noie principiū ꝓprie: ⁊ similit hoc nomie causa: q̄a sūt nomia synonyma qum vsitent cōiter. ⁊ sicut mihi videt exposuit ipse Alex. ⁊ intēdebat Aris. per hūc sermonē docere ꝙ nō oēs artes ꝯsiderāt de omnib⁹ causis: sed quedā ꝯsiderāt de causa formali tm̄. s. mathematice: ⁊ quedā de trib⁹ causis. s. motore: ⁊ forma: ⁊ fine: ⁊ est sciencia diuina. ⁊ quedā de q̄tuor causis: ⁊ est sciētia nālis: ⁊ q̄a hoc nō fuit manifestū in hoc loco: induxit sermonē in forma dubitatiōis: ⁊. d. hn̄tibus principia: aut causas: aut elementa. i. qm̄ idē sequit siue ponat ꝙ ille res habeāt principia agētia: aut finalia: aut elemētaria: aut oia: ⁊ impossibile est ut hec cōiunctio aut sit sicut copulatiua: nā dispositio certe scie inuenit in reb⁹ hn̄tibus causas quasdā p sciētiā illarū causarū: sicut inuenit in hn̄tib⁹ oēs causas. ⁊ qū posuit hāc ꝓpositionē induxit testimoniū ad verificandū illā: ꝙ fere induxit in posteriorib⁹ analecticis: ⁊. d. credimus eni in vnaquaqꝫ rerū ⁊c. ⁊ signū eius q̄d dixim⁹ ꝙ dispositio scie certe de aliq̄ nō acquirit nisi ex cognitiōe cause cui⁹ est: qm̄ ois qui dicit se scire aliq̄d: nō dicit hoc nisi qn̄ sciuerit illud p suas oēs causas ꝓpinquas ⁊ remotas: ⁊ hoc inuenit in omi qui aliq̄d scit in veritate: aut ſm existimationē: ⁊ ꝙ in ista ꝓpositione ꝯueniūt oēs ꝯsiderātes adeo ꝙ etiā sophiste ut dixit in posteriorib⁹. D. d. qum sciuerimus causas eius simplices: ⁊ intendit ut videt causas existētes in re primas nō cōpositas: ⁊ sūt prima mā: ⁊ vltima forma. que eni sunt pret primā materiā ⁊ vltimā formā cuiuslibet rerū nāliū: sūt materie cōposite: ⁊ forme cōposite. D. d. ⁊ ṗma principia: ⁊ intēdit h ut videt p prima principia: primas causas q̄ sūt extra rem. s. primū agens: ⁊ vltimū finē omniū rerū. D. d. donec pueniam⁹ ad elementa eius: ⁊ intēdit h p elemēta causas existētes in re propinquas ⁊ essentiales. ⁊ innuit p hoc q̄d dixit: ꝙ doctrina ordinata est incipe a cognitione causarū primarū rei cognoscende pfecte. Deinde intēdere ad cognitionē aliarū causarum remotarū ſm ordinē: donec pueniat ad causas ꝓpinquas: ⁊ ſm hoc vtit h hoc noie causa: ⁊ elementū alio mō ab eo q̄ vsus est illic ṗus ſm suū morē in habēdo modicā sollicitudinē de nominib⁹. ⁊ qum posuit hāc maiorē ꝓpositionē in hoc sermone. s. dicente ꝙ scientia certa de rebus habētibus causas ⁊ elemēta nō acquirit nisi ex cognitiōe causarū ⁊ elementorū eorū: dimisit minorē ꝓpositionē: ⁊ induxit cōclusionē quā intēdit p hūc sermonē: ⁊ dixit manifestum est ꝙ in sciētia nāli ⁊c. i. manifestū est: qm̄ ex hoc sequit ꝙ qui vult largiri scientiā de natura oportet ipsum prius querere determinationē causarū rerū nālium habētium causas ⁊ elemēta. ⁊ iste sermo cōponit sic: oia nālia habent causas ⁊ elemēta: ⁊ oia habētia causas ⁊ elemēta nō sciunt nisi ex cognitione causarū ⁊ elementorū: g̊ oīa nālia nō sciunt nisi ex cognitione suarū cārū ⁊ elemētoꝝ.

Innata est autē via ex notiorib⁹ nobis ⁊ certioribus incertiora nature ⁊ notiora: nō enim sūt eadem nobis nota ⁊ simpliciter. vnde quidē necesse est ſm hunc modū ꝓcedere ex incertiorib⁹ nature: nobis autē certioribus incertiora nature ⁊ notiora.

Et via ad illa est de rebus notioribus ⁊ ma-

AA 2

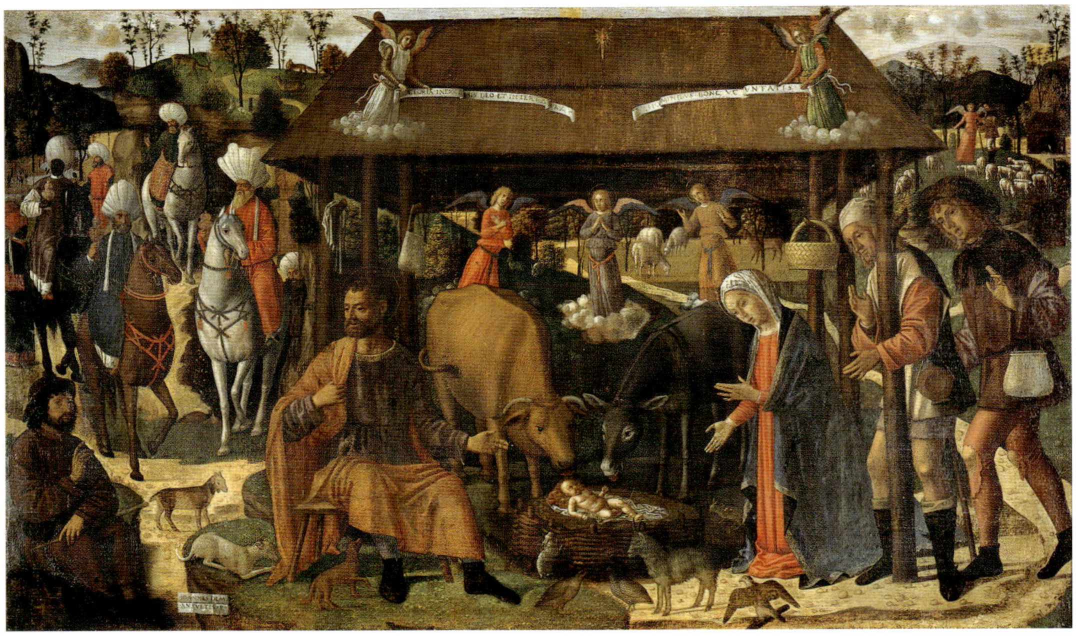

cat. 26. Giovanni Mansueti
Nativity
Venice, early 16th century
Museo di Castelvecchio, Verona

Florence. While the exact identity of Giorgione's three figures here remains, again, in dispute, its allegorical intent to illustrate the Three Ages of Man is clear enough. But no observer has ever considered interpreting the *Singing Lesson* as a representation of the Three Magi.[50] The *Singing Lesson*'s broad theme does run parallel to that of the Magi—it depicts the Three Ages—but it does not depict the Magi.

What truly distinguishes Giorgione's *Three Philosophers* from his other paintings explicitly related to the Nativity lies not only in, say, its three figures' conspicuous lack of royal crowns as befitting the Three Kings. It also resides in the diverging directions of the Three Philosophers' respective gazes. In Giorgione's *Adoration of the Magi,* and also in the *Adoration of the Shepherds,* the three converging gazes of the worshipping Elder, Middle-Aged Man, and Youth focus alike upon the Child, whom they recognize and honor together. In the *Three Philosophers,* by contrast, only the Youth and the Elder fix their gaze upon the rising sun. The Middle-Aged Moor, instead, turns his back upon the rising sun. Why? Only Gombrich seems to have noted, although in passing, that the three figures here do not look in the same direction: or so he implies when he simply remarks that two of the Wise Men appear merely to be awaiting the results of the calculations of their seated companion.[51]

Averroës and the Moor's Last Gaze

Ferriguto in 1933 first briefly suggested that Giorgione's painting, *The Three Philosophers,* might be an allegory of the history of philosophy: representing ancient Aristotelianism, medieval Averroism, and the new humanism breaking with intermediate Averroan tradition to go back directly to ancient sources.[52] I agree. The first known title of the painting given by Michiel in 1525 points in just this direction, to which Anderson in 1996 sensibly invites critics to return, even if for her part she rules out any precise identification of the figures: "Giorgione may have intended to represent particular philosophers, but we may never be able to identify who they are."[53]

In fact, enough clues, I think, do allow us to identify two of them. The Elder is most probably Aristotle, and the Middle-Aged Man, evidently Averroës. The visual motif of a turbaned Averroës, thus identified as a Muslim, depicted on the left as he contemplates an ancient Greek philosopher on the right, recurs in Italian art from about the 14th century. A northern Italian drawing, reproduced in Le Goff, thus confronts two great "pagan" philosophers with their names clearly labeled: on the left is the Arab Averroës as the Aristotelian philosopher, disputing on the right with the Greek neo-Platonic philosopher, Porphyry.[54] Porphyry is clean-shaven and dressed in the fashion of any contemporary cleric in Paris, Bologna, or Padua. But even at so early a date, the Italian draftsman has struggled to make his "Arab" as recognizable as he could, bearded, and with long hair falling from under the folds of a turban, so that the viewer might make no mistake: this philosopher is Muslim, and he is Averroës. In medieval and Renaissance Italian art, Averroës, not Avicenna, stands for the emblematic, all-purpose Muslim.

In his late 15th-century illuminations for the Venetian printed text of Aristotle commented by Averroës, Girolamo da Cremona again resorts to the convention of showing "Averroës" on the left, facing an ancient Greek philosopher—in this case "Aristotle" with a venerable long white beard—on the right (fig. 5; see also cat. 17, p. 165). Then Girolamo carefully depicts upon a sort of balcony, above the twin columns of printed text serving as frontispiece to volume II of Aristotle's works, a group of philosophers meditating on either side of a column. This is Girolamo's representation of the *Turba philosophorum*, the "crowd of philosophers" corresponding to the authors of the curriculum then prescribed at the University of Padua. On the right, Girolamo represents the ancient Greeks conventionally rendered as 15th-century Italians then usually saw them, as contemporary bearded Byzantines in long robes and curious little round brimmed hats. To the immediate right of the column, Girolamo's Aristotle lifts his finger to designate the heavens, and turns his head behind to contemplate his own master, "Plato," while the two great ancient Aristotelian commentators, "Themistius" and "Alexander of Aphrodisias," stand even farther behind, observing reverently. Then, to the immediate left of the column, "Averroës," with a long white beard and the turban and robe of a Muslim, contemplates "Aristotle" from the other side of the central pillar: for of all Aristotelian commentators, Averroës is seen here by Girolamo to have adhered closest to Aristotle. Then, behind "Averroës" on the left, and each holding a volume of his writings, now come "Avicenna," bearded and turbaned as a Muslim to be sure, but also draped in the robe of an Italian physician and wearing his Muslim turban wrapped around a royal crown; and finally, a tonsured and clean-shaven St. Thomas Aquinas in his Dominican habit. To the far right of the balcony squats a monkey adorned with the hood of a buffoon, turning its back upon all these sages, probably to

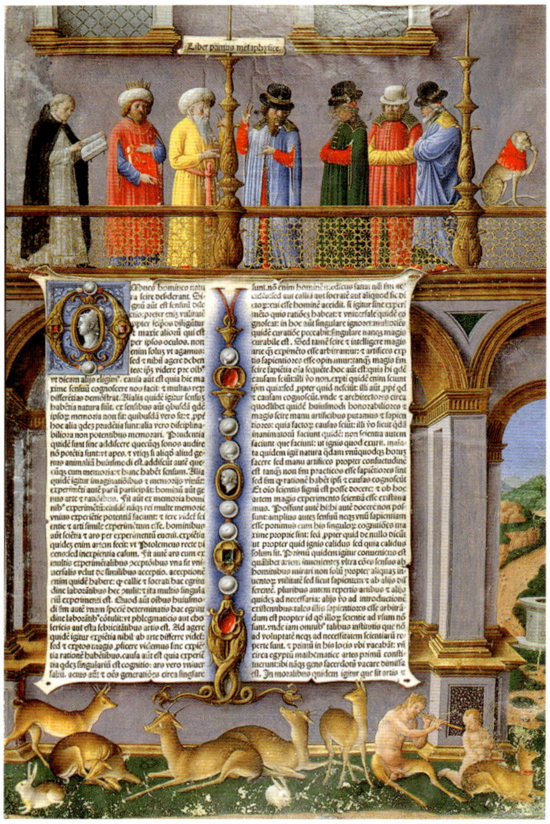

fig. 5. Girolamo da Cremona, *Turba philosophorum.* Aristotle, *Works,* fol. 2, Venice, 1483. The Pierpont Morgan Library, New York

symbolize the grotesque, apelike nature of those human beings who remain ignorant of philosophy.

Dominican art of the 14th-century, however, strove rather to humiliate "Averroës," depicted as a turbaned Muslim with hand pressed in despair against his bearded cheek between the two earlier heretics Sabellius and Arius in a shadow-Triad of the Damned (like Dante's accursed Triad of Brutus, Cassius, and Judas), crushed beneath the feet of a *St. Thomas Enthroned* in the great fresco painted between 1366 and 1368 in Florence's Santa Maria Novella. "Averroës" holds pride of place as the single damned arch-heretic in the *Triumph of St. Thomas* which hangs in the Church of St. Catherine in Pisa, a mid-14th-century work attributed by Vasari to the Pisan master Francesco Traini (fig. 6, p. 172), though now believed by scholars to belong to the Sienese painter Lippo Memmi or his school.[55] Our concern here is with the painting's symbolism, which represents a complete cosmology of the philosophical hierarchies as perceived by late medieval Dominicans.

Enthroned high above the laity, on the right, and the clerical orders, on the left, St. Thomas sits in frontal majesty bathed in a halo of light, surmounted not only by Christ and the Archangels, but also by the prophets of the Old Testament, and the Evangelists of the New, who uphold their writings whence luminous golden rays of inspiration fall upon the open pages of the book propped upon the saint's knees. To the left and right of the saint, but set somewhat lower down because they were ancient pagans though retaining their dignified, long-bearded appearance, Aristotle and Plato in turn brandish their writings whose rays likewise converge upon St. Thomas's open book. This open book is the saint's own *Summa contra Gentiles,* the Sum against the Gentiles, whose initial words, clearly inscribed in the painting, are a biblical quotation.[56] These same words, through emanating rays, overcome a long-haired, long-bearded, turbaned Averroës, lying prostrate beneath the saint's feet and clearly averting his gaze from him, while the Muslim philosopher's own book falls overturned and clamped face downwards. The wisdom of the ancient Greeks, conjoined with the Scriptures, thus illuminates St. Thomas and overcomes Islam. But at least Averroës in this painting remains vanquished in solitary Satanic dignity, as Christian thought's leading intellectual rival and most eminent, seductive, dangerous philosophical foe.

Averroës would however fall much lower still, as Renaissance humanist cultural values increasingly gripped Italian minds. In *The School of Athens* painted in fresco in the Vatican for Pope Julius II in 1508, which is Raphael's own renewed version of the old motif of the *Turba philosophorum,* a Plato standing high in the center among the ancient sages points to the heavens with uplifted finger, while Aristotle by his side, as his full equal, spreads his palm to designate the sublunary world. But Averroës, lost below in the crowd of all these noble Greeks and

Romans as an "exotic" intruder, and so caricatured as a mustachioed and turbaned Ottoman, peers and almost leers over the shoulder of Pythagoras.

Raphael's frozen classicism speaks volumes regarding the coming and final expulsion of Averroës—the Spanish Muslim who, in point of geographical and historical fact, was historically no less European than Raphael's depicted Anatolian, Syrian, and Egyptian Greeks—from the curriculum of European intellectual civilization: as indeed Petrarch had wished.

Between all these extremes—Averroës crushed, degraded, expelled—Giorgione in his way offers a somewhat more refined solution that recognizes, while limiting, the philosophical influence of the Moor. Now, Giorgione and Raphael belong to the same generation, indeed *The Three Philosophers* and *The Schools of Athens* stand as almost exactly contemporary works. Moreover, Petrarch's intellectual influence, in cultivated Italian circles, reached its zenith in just these same opening years of the 16th century. It would of course prove a little contrived to want rigidly to demonstrate how every detail in Giorgione's *Three Philosophers* corresponds to this or that line in Petrarch's *De sui ipsius et multorum ignorantia.* Still, the tone and general imagery of Petrarch's pamphlet, as published in Venice in 1501, coincide so closely with the perceptions of philosophy that Giorgione allows us to glimpse in his own enigmatic painting, that Petrarch's words indeed help throw light on Giorgione's picture—and dissipate much lingering conceptual fog.

Giorgione's pairing of the Elder, on the right, and of the Middle-Aged Moor, to the left of the Elder, reproduces such classically arranged pairings of Aristotle and Averroës as seen in the frontispieces painted by Girolamo da Cremona: even though Giorgione's own specific figure of Averroës is an adaptation of Gentile Bellini's *Standing Turk.* Giorgione's Averroës, as Commentator on the left, looks towards Aristotle on the right: again, a traditional arrangement, as seen in Girolamo da Cremona. But Giorgione here completely transforms the significance of the Moor's gaze upon Aristotle, by adding the figure of the Youth who turns his back upon both of them.

Giorgione's three figures make up a Triad of the Three Ages: Old Age, Middle Age, and Youth clearly differentiated. This motif alludes to the Three Magi, but this Triad does not exactly represent them. Instead, the three figures correspond to the Three Ages of Philosophy as conceived in Giorgione's day by cultured Venetians: the Ancients; the Averroists; the Moderns. Giorgione's "Aristotle," and the Youth, both look in the same direction: towards the rising sun. Averroës, however, averts his gaze from the sun. Instead, Averroës looks back towards Aristotle, meditates the writings of Aristotle and comments upon them, but remains incapable of perceiving the true light even as far as Aristotle once could. For Averroës may only see the sun's light as refracted in Aristotle's writings. The sun, now, symbolizes God's truth. It is a sun, which the pre-Christian "Aristotle" could foresee and divine from the shadowy depths of his pagan forest. But Averroës, as a Muslim, willfully turns his back upon this same sun. Yet Giorgione's Youth, as the Christian, turns his own back upon the mistaken path of Averroës and dares gaze directly at the sun. In so doing, the Youth really looks in the very same direction as Aristotle: but sees farther than Aristotle—and of course far more clearly than Averroës—because his own sight is illuminated by grace.[57]

The Italian humanist Favio Biondo of Forlì (1392–1463), in allusion to the well-known allegory of the Three Ages of Man, in turn invented the concept of the Three Ages of History—Antiquity, the Middle Ages, Modern Times—which still conventionally segments our own perceptions of humanity's career. It is even amusing to note that Giorgione's Middle-Aged "Averroës" ends up rather closely coinciding with the Middle Ages not only as defined by Biondo, but as still perceived by us in our usual Western manuals of the history of philosophy: as a millennium at first dominated by Christian neo-Platonizing patristics, then by a Christian Aristotelianized scholasticism powerfully influenced by Muslim commentators. From this sort of medieval intellectual culture, whether Christianized, Islamicized, or indeed Judaized, we have since all largely turned away—much like Giorgione's own Youth: whatever our current professed religious denominations—or lack thereof.

The natural setting of Giorgione's *Three Philosophers*—if we do recognize two of these to be Aristotle and Averroës—at once becomes meaningful in turn. Aristotle and Averroës dwell in the dark forest, a common medieval and Renaissance allegory for the state of the soul when not illuminated by divine Grace, as absolutely every 16th-century literate Italian (even every literate Italian today) simply learned from the first three utterly familiar verses in Dante's *Inferno:* "In midst of our life's journey, / I found myself within a wood so dark / that the straight path was lost."[58] According to Dante, Averroës, along with Aristotle, Plato, and other eminent non-Christian sages, languishes forever in the twilight of Limbo. The Old Testament Prophets like Moses, whose doctrines were supposed to have even prefigured Plato's,[59] once also dwelt in Limbo, but were redeemed thence by Christ after the Crucifixion in his harrowing of Hell. Dante's pagan philosophers, however, are forever doomed to stay in Limbo: unlike Moses saved by Christ, neither Dante's Aristotle, nor yet his Averroës, may ever emerge from the dark wood of the soul. Yet as told in the very first canto of the *Divine Comedy,* Dante himself, illuminated by grace and spiritually rejuvenated, emerges from the forest and sees the sunlight shine upon the great mountain that leads men's souls up to the heavens.

Giorgione's Youth contemplates these same heavens illuminated by the sun, but also looks upon a cave. Now, this cave does correspond, in part, to that described in Book VII of Plato's *Republic*, a classic image if there ever was one for cultured Renaissance Italians. Plato's dark cave symbolized our lower world upon which flicker projected shadows recognized only by sages as insubstantial illusions. Plato's image was later harmonized with Christian interpretation in a form of allegorical thought which still held full sway in Giorgione's generation, one that sought constantly to reconcile and wed the twin wisdoms taught by the Ancients, and by Scripture. Plato's cave, in Christian understanding, mirrored that other cave in which Christ was born: wherein the Divine Light became humbly incarnate so as to illuminate this dark lower world. Distinct motifs in medieval and Renaissance theology, philosophy, literature, and art need not contradict or cancel one another, but may rather reinforce and significantly point to one another, as mirroring *vestigia* of God's all-encompassing order.

Those cultured Renaissance Italians unfamiliar with Greek, but of course literate in Latin, conveniently found the image of Plato's cave in a prestigiously classical Latinized form, encased in Cicero's *De naturâ deorum,* "On the Nature of the Gods." Moreover, this same Ciceronian version of Plato's cave was precisely that quoted by Petrarch, *in extenso,* in his attack against the Venetian Averroists. In his fundamental study on Averroism in Venice, Renan first identified and quoted part of this key comment from Petrarch's *De ignorantiâ,* which evokes a mental picture so close to what Giorgione paints that it becomes difficult to believe that the artist, or his patron, did not read this pamphlet too:

> If they [the Averroists] did not fear punishment from men far more than from God, they would even dare attack the theory of the world's creation not only according to [Plato's] *Timaeus,* but even according to the Genesis of Moses, to the Catholic Faith, and to the sacred teachings of Christ. But when such apprehension no longer holds them back, and when they feel free to speak without constraint, then they directly wage war against the truth; in their own private meetings, they laugh Christ to scorn, and worship Aristotle—whom they do not even understand. When they argue in public, they protest that they speak of things lying outside the order of Faith: and thus, they seek the truth while rejecting the truth, and the light while turning their backs upon the sun.

Renan did not, however, cite the end of Petrarch's charge, which caricatures the Averroists as thinkers "who wish to plunge into the opaque darkness of the deepest fissures of the earth in order to seek the light there"—a direct allusion to Plato's myth of the cave as read by Petrarch in Cicero.[60]

Against the Averroists, Petrarch further invoked the authority of Aristotle himself, notably in paragraph 86 of the *De ignorantia.* This is because Cicero, Petrarch's own literary and even moral model, himself read Aristotle in a Platonizing light, thus allowing Petrarch to reproduce this whole passage transcribed from Aristotle by Cicero in the *De natura deorum.* In the eyes of Petrarch, of course, the pagan "gods" in the ancient text prefigure the True God (and we might further note, in light of this same text, the stellar signs so eloquently drawn upon the parchment held up by Giorgione's own Ancient Philosopher):

> If there existed men who should have always dwelt beneath the earth in well-appointed and luxurious houses adorned with statues and paintings, in a word, furnished with everything needed to be regarded happy, and should they have never emerged from under the earth but still should have heard of the sway and power of the gods; and then if, all of a sudden, the gates of the earth should have opened, so

that they might emerge from their subterranean dwellings in order to climb up to where we ourselves do dwell, and should have seen, all at once, the land and the seas and the sky, and should have known the beauty and grandeur of the clouds, and should have discovered the grandeur and splendor of the sun, and should have realized its power to produce the day by diffusion of its light throughout the firmament, and then, as soon as night had fallen, should have beheld the heavenly vault adorned with distinct stars, and the changes in the moon's light even as the moon waxes and wanes, and the ascent and descent of the stars in their course as defined and fixed for all time: then, having seen all this, might they indeed believe in the gods.

This is the astral contemplation which Giorgione in turn, in 16th-century Venice, fixed upon his canvas, without thence excluding the Moor: an Averroës philosophically vanquished but still great in his defeat, turning his back upon the light of the sun but yet standing high and proud in the very heart of the Middle Age—the *medium aevum*—of human thought and destiny.

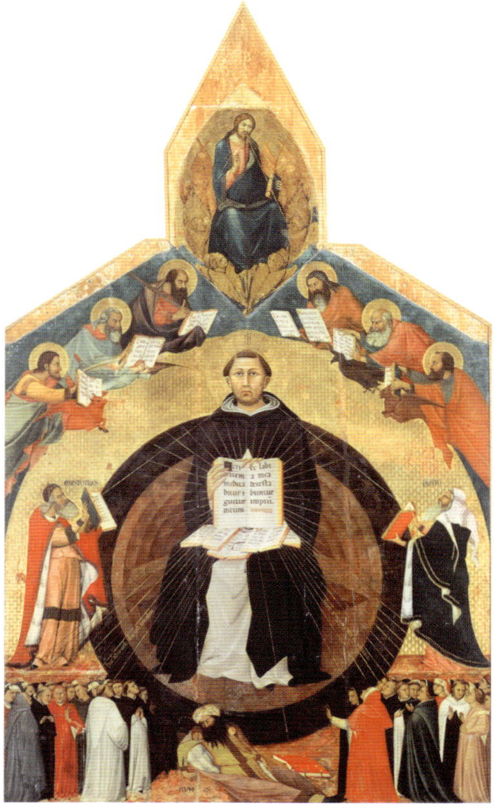

fig. 6. Attributed to Lippo Memmi or his school, *The Triumph of St. Thomas,* ca. 1344. Church of Saint Catherine, Pisa

Notes

1 The author wishes especially to thank Trinita Kennedy, Research Associate at the Metropolitan Museum of Art for the exhibition *Venice and the Islamic World*, and the keepers of the Rare Books collection in Princeton University's Firestone Library, for their precious bibliographical assistance. Unless otherwise noted, all translations are the author's.

2 Tognetti 1985, pp. 86–90.

3 Fortini Brown 1988, pp. 207–209; Campbell and Chong 2005, p. 26.

4 *"Qui non tam fuit Peripateticus quam philosophiae peripateticae depravator."* Thomas Aquinas 1998, vol. 2, par. 59.

5 This is one of the reasons why, in modern times, many of the more profoundly versed Western specialists in Islamic thought have been either Catholic priests or highly educated Catholic laymen, although such scholars as Father Miguel Asín Palacios and Louis Massignon have, as an unfortunate consequence, tended to bend the Islamic philosophical or mystical materials they chose to study to make them agree with far too Catholic an interpretation.

6 Lucchetta 1979, p. 105.

7 Renan 1852.

8 *"Ab his scaber factus Aristotiles."* Francesco Petrarca ("Petrarch") 1906, par. 15.

9 See Renan 1852, pp. 328–29: "I conjure you, so far as my affairs are concerned, to take no note whatsoever of these Arabs, as if they did not even exist; I hate their whole race [*unum, antequam desinam, te obsecro, ut ab omni consilio mearum rerum tui isti Arabes arceantur atque exulent: odi genus universalem*]. I know that Greece has produced learned and eloquent men: philosophers, poets, orators, mathematicians, all come from Greece; in Greece too were born the fathers of medicine. But these Arab physicians! . . . you should know them for what they are worth!"

10 Le Goff 1957, pp. 23–24.

11 Le Goff 1957, p. 59.

12 Schmitt's fundamental study (1979, p. 133) quotes (but does not translate from the original Latin left decently obscure) the vigorous arguments used by the Venetian scholar Tommaso Giunta in defense of his magnificent printed edition of Aristotle in Latin, accompanied throughout with the commentaries of Averroës, in 1550–52: "In truth our own age, as it despises and as it were treads underfoot the teachings of the Arabs, receives nothing, admires nothing, unless it be sure that it be some matter translated from the treasures of the Greeks. Our age cultivates only the Greeks. . . . Some people even proclaim the writings of the Arabs to be nothing but shit, and useless slime." (*Aetas vero nostra, contempta et quasi iam conculcata Arabum doctrina, nihil recipit, nihil miratur, nisi quod a Graecorum thesauris huc norit esse translatum. Graecos solos [aetas nostra] colit...ut Arabum scripta nihil aliud quam faecem et inutile lutum praedicent.*) Schmitt further draws attention to the humanist Pico della Mirandola's own barb against the obsessively anti-"Arab" prejudices of the learned and haughty young Venetian Hellenist Ermolao Barbaro (1454–93) who published a Latin translation of the Greek Aristotelian commentator Themistius: "They prefer to err with the Greeks, than to understand correctly with the Barbarians." (*Malunt cum illis errare, quam cum barbaris recta sentire.*)

13 Probably to show the calculation of an eclipse, according to Ferino-Pagden and Nepi Scirè (2004, p. 180); similar astronomical designs appear in Giorgione's frescoes for the Casa Marta-Pellizzari in his hometown of Castelfranco.

14 The left side of the painting was however truncated in the 18th century; initially, the cave took up far more space on the left, thereby throwing the three characters to the right of the composition.

15 Wilde 1932; Klauner 1955; Gombrich 1986.

16 Gabriele 2004.

17 Meller 1981.

18 Scarpa 1995; Cohen 1995; Borchhardt-Birbaumer 2004.

19 Wilde 1932; Klauner 1955; Gabriele 2004.

20 Cohen 1995; Borchhardt-Birbaumer 2004; Gentili 2004.

21 Nardi 1955.

22 Ferriguto 1933; Witschnitzer-Bernstein 1945.

23 Guidoni 1995–96.

24 MacLennan and Kirkpatrick 2001.

25 Wilde 1932; Klauner 1955; Gabriele 2004.

26 Witschnitzer-Bernstein 1945; Guidoni 1995–96.

27 Nardi 1955.

28 Gentili 2004.

29 Cohen 1995; Borchhardt-Birbaumer 2004.

30 Ferriguto 1933.

31 MacLennan and Kirkpatrick 2001

32 Wilde 1932; Klauner 1955; Gabriele 2004.

33 Branca 1963; but Barbaro had already been dead for more than ten years when Giorgione painted this canvas.

34 Witschnitzer-Bernstein 1945.

35 Nardi 1955; Guidoni 1995–96.

36 MacLennan and Kirkpatrick 2001.

37 Ferriguto 1933.

38 Cohen 1995; Borhhardt-Birbaumer 2004.

39 Gentili 2004.

40 Notably Gentili 2004.

41 The learned and sumptuous catalogue for the Vienna exhibition on Giorgione in 2004 (Ferino-Pagden and Nepi Scirè 2004) lists but does not try to reconcile all these contradictory theses.

42 "Not only did he acquire renown for surpassing Gentile and Giovanni Bellini, but for rivaling those who [then] worked in Tuscany as authors of the modern manner. Nature bestowed upon him such a felicitous spirit in his coloring in oil and in his frescoes, and he rendered some things so vividly and others in a manner so muted, blended, and shadowy [*sfumate*] in their darkness, that this was the reason why many of those who then excelled [in the arts] recognized him [Giorgione] as someone born to breathe the spirit into figures, and especially to counterfeit the freshness of living flesh—and this, more than anyone then painting in Venice or anywhere else."

43 Jürgen Rapp's model essay has recently broken new critical ground in elucidating Giorgione's *Tempest*—which he was the first to recognize as representing Paris abandoning the nymph Oenone (who bore his child) in order to seek out Helen, while the storm clouds of divine wrath threaten Troy in the background—by focusing on those legends and cultural motifs of demonstrated importance to Renaissance Venetians (who revered the Trojans as putative ancestors not only of the Romans, but of the Veneti); Rapp's 1998 essay was re-included in Ferino-Pagden and Nepi Scirè's 2004 catalogue; see Ferino-Pagden's admiring introduction, p. 18.

44 *"La tela a oglio delli 3 phylosophi nel paese, dui ritti e uno sentado che contempla li raggi, con quel sasso finto così mirabilmente fu incominciata da Zorzi da Castelfranco, e finita da Sebastiano Veneziano. La tela grande a oglio dell'Inferno con Enea e Anchise fu de mano de Zorzi da Castelfranco. La tela del paese con el nascimento de Paris, con li due pastori ritti in piede, fu de mano de Zorzo da Castelfranco, e fu una delle suie prime opera."* Torrini 2004, p. 22.

45 Hasse 1997.

46 Nardi 1955; Guidoni 1995. Both Nardi and Guidoni have suggested that Giorgione's Youth might be Copernicus (!), who did study in Padua in 1501–3; but the treaty which made Copernicus famous was only published in 1543, more than three decades after Giorgione's death.

47 This understanding of the painting was accepted by Wilde in 1932 and by many critics since.

48 Gabriele 2004, p. 79.

49 *De generatione animalium,* V, 780, b 21; Gombrich 1986.

50 The Venetian catalogue of 1666, which attributed the painting to Palma il Vecchio, labeled it *"Marcantonio che studia tra due filosofi!"*

51 Gombrich 1986.

52 Ferriguto 1933, pp. 64–65.

53 Anderson 1996, p. 299.

54 Reproduced in Le Goff 1957, p. 122.

55 Meiss 1933; Mallory 1975; Polzer 1995.

56 *"Veritatem meditabitur guttur meum et labia mea detestabantur impium."* (My throat shall meditate the truth, and my lips detest the impious one.)" (Proverbs 8:9)

57 The confessed reliance of Christian Scholastics on the great earlier, non-Christian philosophers was summarized in a famous formula by the 12th-century neo-Platonist Bernard of Chartres: "We are dwarfs perched upon the shoulders of giants, this is why we see better and farther than they."

58 *"Nel mezzo del cammin di nostra vita / mi ritrovai per una selva oscura, / che la diritta via era smarrita."*

59 The parallel traced between Moses and the Greek philosophers, an accepted notion in Church patristics going back to Philo of Alexandria, may well explain the Moses-like rays on the Elder's brow in Giorgione's earlier version of his painting, before he chose to erase them in a *pentimento.*

60 *"Quod quid, oro, est aliud, quam reiecta veritate verum quaerere, et quasi, sole derelicto, in profundissimos et opacos terrae hiatus introire, ut illic in tenebris lumen inveniant."* See Renan 1852, p. 355.

Oriental Carpets and Textiles in Venice

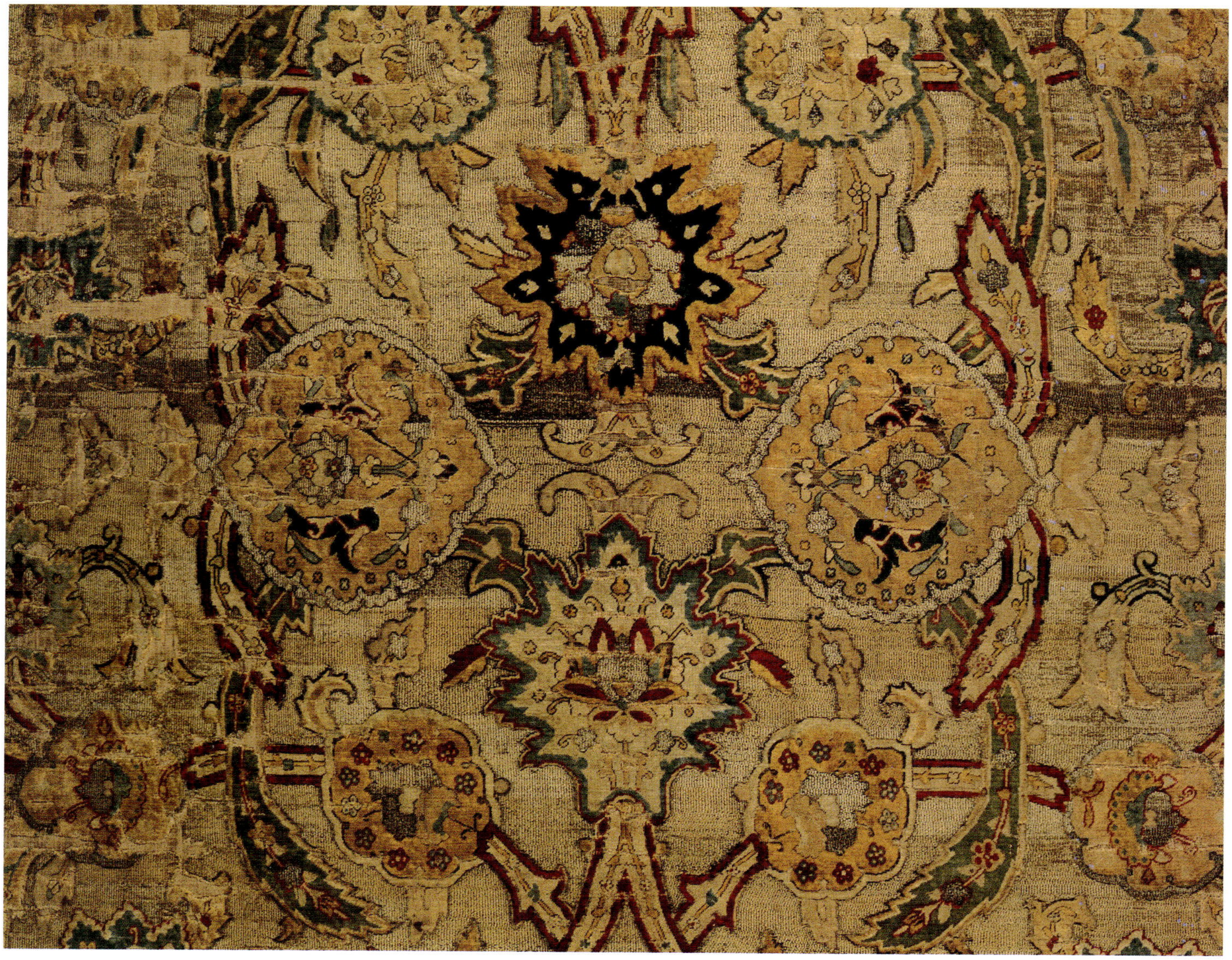

Walter B. Denny

For centuries, Venice served as Europe's primary *porta Orientalis*—its principal Eastern gateway. Venice's three greatest assets—its merchant seafaring tradition, its almost impregnable strategic position behind the Adriatic lagoons, and its location close to the heart of Europe—gave the Most Serene Republic a central role as entrepôt for the importation into Europe of profitable luxury goods such as carpets and textiles, and opened a European door to the Islamic cultures that created those goods.[1] Despite the expenses and depredations of periodic wars with the expanding Ottoman Empire, the Republic derived great income from its trade with the East, and the Orientalism of Venice itself as a city—from the strange and exotic form of St. Mark's, patterned after Byzantine churches in Constantinople and Asia Minor, to its role as a conduit through which Near Eastern luxury goods poured into Europe—meant that aspects of the material culture of the Islamic world were incorporated into Venetian private and civic life and imagery to a degree unprecedented elsewhere in early modern Europe.

Abroad, Venetian diplomats and merchants traveled throughout the Islamic world from the Nile delta to Syria to Constantinople to Azerbaijan, and their *relazioni* or reports to the Venetian authorities still serve as important documentation of Islamic politics, history, economics, and art of those days.[2] For example, in 1474 Giosafat Barbaro served as a Venetian emissary to the court of the White Sheep Turkoman ruler Uzun Hasan in Tabriz. Barbaro recorded his visit to a festivity held outdoors in elaborately decorated tents, where carpets were spread on the ground, and commented that the carpets of local manufacture that he saw there were far more beautiful than the carpets found in the markets of Cairo or Bursa.[3] By the 15th century, Venetians were not only at the forefront of the luxury goods production for both European and Middle Eastern markets, but they were also the foremost in Catholic Europe in their sophistication about the Islamic world, and few surpassed them in their knowledge, admiration, and cultural appropriation of the material products of Islamic culture. Nowhere is this combining of cultures better seen than in the area of textiles and carpets.

cat. 83. *"Presentation" carpet* (detail)

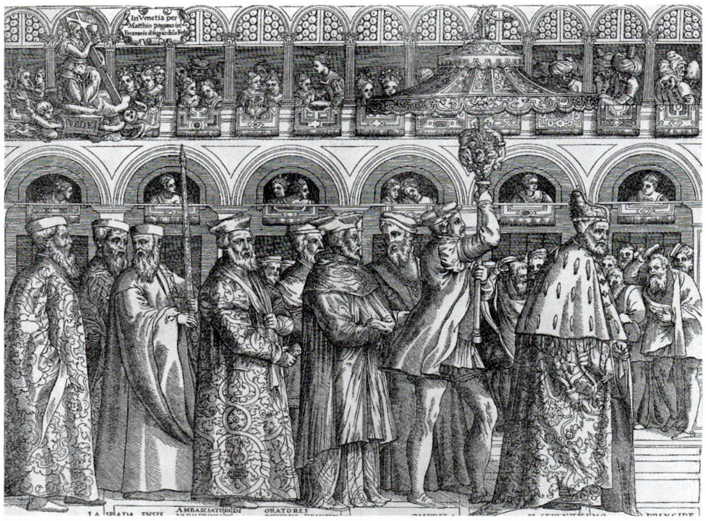

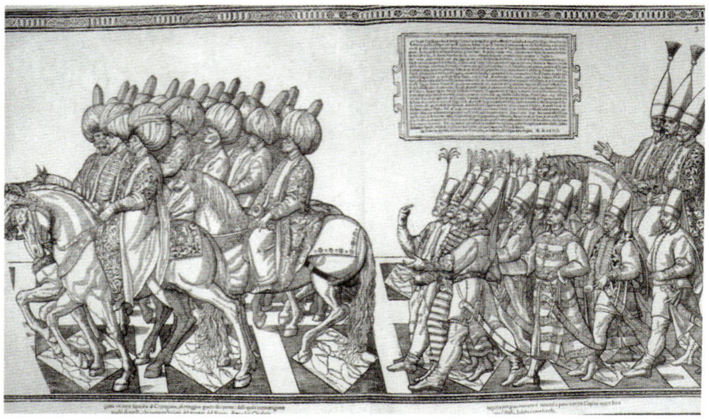

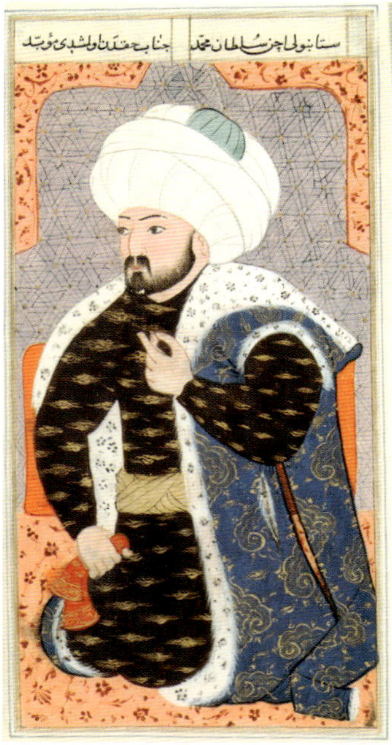

Carpets, Silk, and Venetian Civic Ritual

Around the year 1558, the Venetian artist Matteo Pagan created a suite of copper-engraved prints to be placed end to end in a long frieze that depicted a procession of the doge and the Senate through St. Mark's Square (fig. 1). At almost the very same time, another Venetian artist, Domenico de' Franceschi, created another suite of prints, this time in the technique of wood engraving, showing a procession of the Ottoman sultan Süleyman "the Magnificent" preceded by a procession of gorgeously costumed court officials and military cohorts, going to the Friday noonday prayer in Istanbul (fig. 2). These two emblematic works by Venetian artists provide a convenient starting point from which to embark on a survey of the role of Islamic carpets and textiles in the commerce, culture, and civic rituals of the Republic.

Domenico de' Franceschi's wood engraving displays a distinctly Venetian sensibility in its focus on the details of costumes, caparisons, and fabrics of the sultan, his bodyguards, retainers, and bureaucratic and military servants—a panoply of the entire Ottoman bureaucracy and ruling institution. In the Ottoman Empire, silk textiles and costumes were a primary mode for the projection of power and authority, and details of costumes and headgear, as well as the type of fabrics used, served the knowledgeable observer as signifiers of rank and bureaucratic function (cat. 9). This skillful use of parades and processions to project political power clearly resonated with the Venetian artist.

Matteo Pagan's graphic depiction of the doge and Senate is also remarkable in its attention to documentary detail. Music historians employ it as a primary source for the various kinds of musical instruments in use in Venice in the 16th century;[4] it also records with great realism the contemporary costumes of the oligarchy, in the same sort of detail employed by Domenico de' Franceschi. Silk textile patterns are carefully indicated and the costumes and ceremonial objects are rendered in meticulous detail. For our purposes, a further focus of interest is the Procuratorie, the building on the south side of the square behind the parade, from whose windows well-dressed spectators—all of them female—watch the world unfolding below. Over the balustrade of every window and balcony the artist has depicted a small carpet with geometric designs. Despite a somewhat abbreviated mode of representation employed by Pagan, the types of carpets are easily recognizable as small Turkish ones. We know that such carpets were often employed on ceremonial occasions, sometimes loaned by enterprising carpet dealers as a means of showcasing their wares.[5]

Far from being the sole documentation of the importance of carpets and patterned silk textiles in Venetian civic ritual, Matteo Pagan's engraving in fact stands at the late end of a tradition of representations of such rituals in the art of Venice. Quattrocento painters, in particular Gentile Bellini, Vittore Carpaccio, and Giovanni Mansueti, also depicted Venetian civic rituals,[6] and their paintings abound in depictions of small, mostly Turkish, carpets that show designs today recognizable from surviving early examples. In a similar vein, Paris Bordone's famous 1534 painting of the *The Return of the Doge's Ring,* today in the Accademia, shows the doge enthroned upon a "Star Ushak" carpet from west Anatolia (fig. 3). By 1500 knotted-pile wool carpets and brocaded silk textiles from Egypt, Syria, Anatolia, and Azerbaijan were not only an integral part of Venetian material culture, but through Italian, and in particular Venetian, commerce they were regarded throughout Europe as symbols of sanctity, wealth, power, and taste; as a result, the names of European painters such as Memling, Ghirlandaio, Foschi, Holbein, Lotto, Crivelli, and Bellini have become convenient art-historical labels for standard design types in early Turkish carpets.[7]

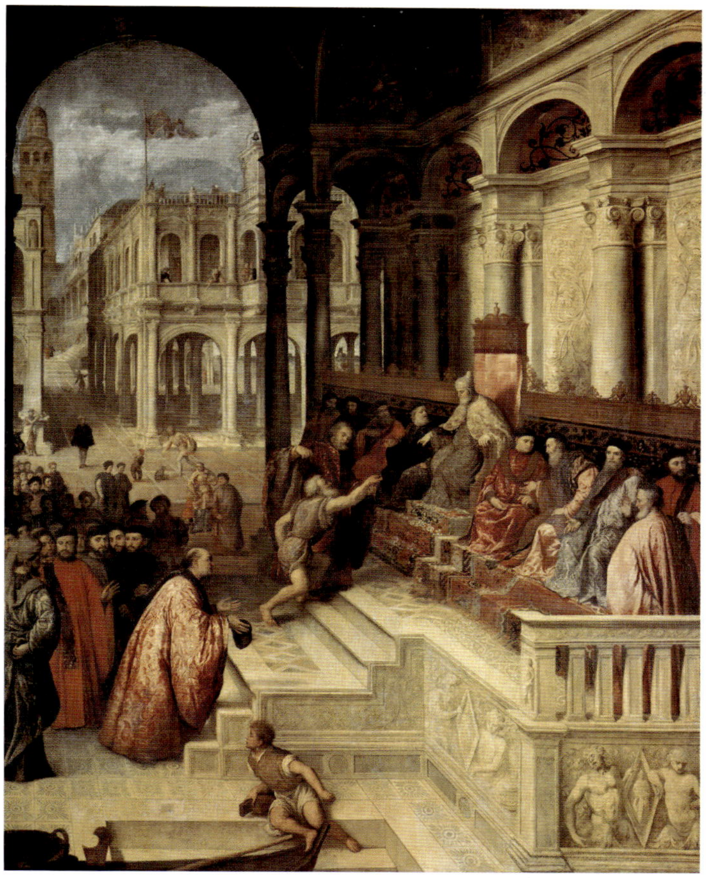

fig. 3. Paris Bordone, *The Return of the Doge's Ring*, Venice, 1534. Gallerie dell'Accademia, Venice

Venice and the Oriental Carpet

In early modern times, there were two general routes by which Oriental carpets woven in Anatolia made their way into Europe: by land and by sea. The land route appears to have crossed the frontier between the Abode of Peace and the Abode of War in the northern Balkans. A celebrated document listing the taxable goods passing overland through the small-town frontier post of Brasov (Brassó, Kronstadt) in Transylvania in the year 1503 mentions an astonishing number of over 500 Turkish carpets in a single eight-month period.[8] Numerous documents from central Europe, Venice, and the Ottoman Empire attest to a veritable flood of early carpets coming in from Turkey in the 15th through the 17th centuries.[9] If this was the case in the war-torn and politically divided lands of central Europe, where overland commerce was fraught with dangers and difficulties, we can imagine that the inherently lower risk and higher volume of maritime shipping from Alexandria and Constantinople to Venice must have included a far greater number of such carpets, a surmise amply supported by the evidence of Venice's primary role as carpet merchant to Western Europe. Moreover, while the smaller carpets of Anatolia could be easily carried on pack animals, larger carpets from the Ushak manufactories in Anatolia or the Damascus and Cairene ateliers in Syria and Egypt were far more safely and conveniently carried by ship. The written documentation from Venetian sources indicates the importance of such carpets in the overall picture of Venetian commerce, and

fig. 1. Matteo Pagan, *Procession of the Doge and Patriarch of Venice* (detail), Venice, 1560. The Metropolitan Museum of Art, New York

fig. 2. Domenico de' Franceschi, *Procession of Süleyman the Magnificent* (detail), Venice, 16th century

cat. 9. Seyyid Lokman *Kitafetü'l-insaniye fi şemâ'ilü'l-osmaniye* *Portrait of Mehmet II* Istanbul, ca. 1585–95 Sächsischen Landesbibliothek-Staats und Universitätsbibliothek, Dresden

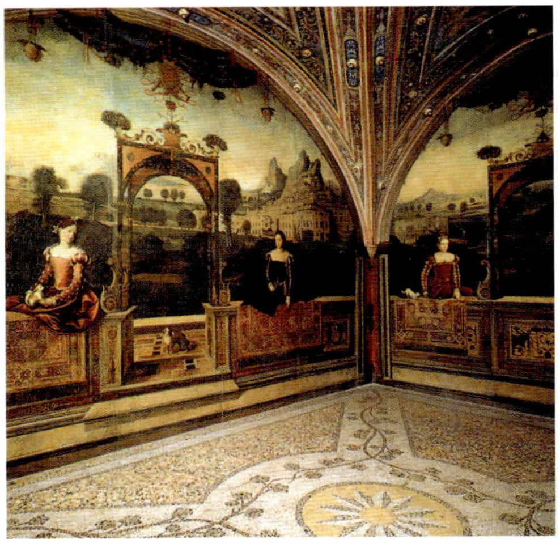

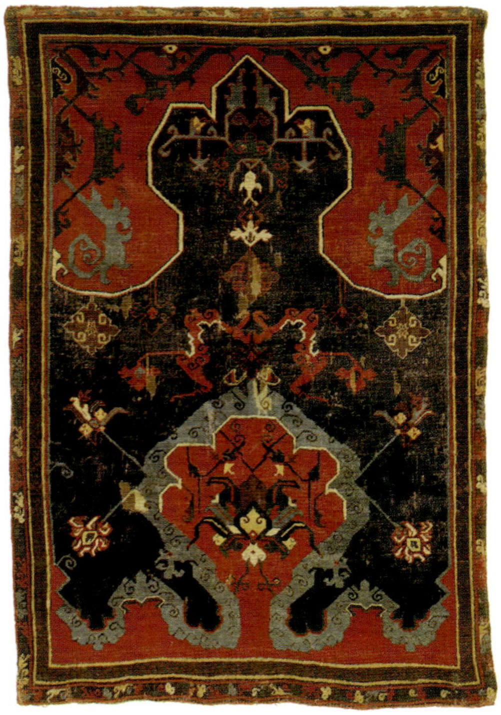

records from Renaissance Italy also attest to the high prices paid for such carpets relative to those prices paid for locally made sculptures and paintings by reputed artists.[10] Other documents indicate that Venetians also served during this period as carpet dealers to the wider European market. A careful look at the geographical distribution of depictions of carpets in Italian painting from the mid-15th century onwards also points towards the northeast of Italy, and thus Venice, as a primary point of diffusion of Islamic carpets from Syria, Egypt, and above all from Anatolia, into the heart of Europe. Finally, a few documents suggest that there may have been attempts to produce carpets in the Venetian territories themselves.[11]

Carpets in Venice

The small carpets that bedecked the balconies of the Piazza San Marco on special feast days consisted almost certainly of Anatolian products. Made in a small size known as a *sajjada* ("for prostration," i.e., a prayer rug) or later as *çeyrek* (literally, "quarter-size"), these small carpets were a standard part of Anatolian manufacture for centuries, and are often depicted in Italian paintings by Carpaccio, Mansueti, Crivelli, Antonello da Messina (who, although from Sicily, encountered Turkish carpets in Venice), Foppa, and others. The wide variety of *sajjada* types available in the marketplace is documented in various Ottoman records from 1545 to as late as 1659.[12] Carpets imported from Egypt tended to be of larger sizes; two huge examples in remarkably good condition recently surfaced in the *Guardaroba* of the Pitti Palace in Florence,[13] and the largest old carpet remaining in Venice is the enormous Mamluk example in the Scuola di San Rocco (cat. 81).[14] Documents suggest that the decision to purchase such a large carpet rather than two smaller ones probably was in part influenced by the sensation its large size would create in Venice, as well as the need to use it to cover an especially large table. Egyptian carpets rarely appear in Italian painting; the notable exception is the depiction of Mamluk rugs in various sizes in Moretto's frescoes in the Palazzo Salvadego in Brescia; these almost certainly arrived in Europe in Venetian shipping (fig. 4).[15]

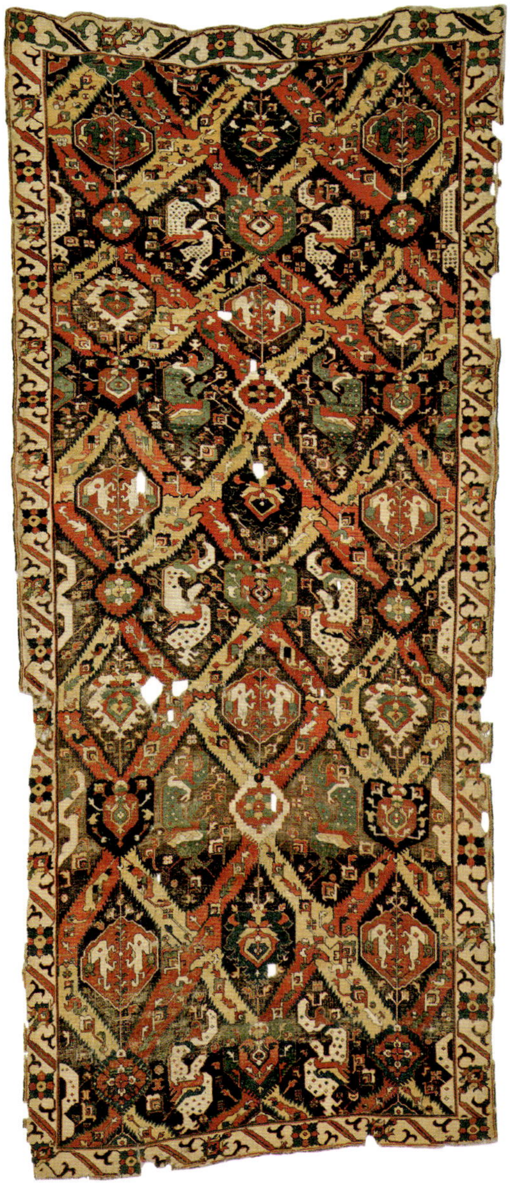

cat. 86. *Dragon carpet*
Eastern Transcaucasia, ca. 1700
Museum für Islamische Kunst, Berlin

Judging from documents of various sorts, which have survived in considerable number, the Venetian consumption of carpets was enormous, but the damp climate of Venice has also meant that over the centuries relatively few old carpets have survived. Giovanni Curatola, the major authority on carpets in Venice, contrasts this situation with that of Florence, where today larger numbers of carpets are found, but few early documents exist.[16] Those preserved in the churches and religious foundations of Venice give some idea of the local taste for carpets, which encompassed a variety of styles and provenances; a wide spectrum of dates suggests that although we have long assumed that the fashion for Islamic carpets faded after around 1600 in Italy, carpets continued to be given or purchased in Venice well into the 18th century and perhaps even beyond.[17]

It is worth noting that Wilhelm von Bode (1845–1929), founding director of the Museum of Painting in Berlin, Germany's greatest scholar of Italian Renaissance art of his time and the author of the first scholarly history of Oriental carpets, acquired a significant number of important carpets for the Berlin collections in Italy, especially in the area around Venice (cats. 85, 86).[18]

An even more interesting insight into Venetian taste and the association of Oriental carpets with decorations for festive occasions was the practice in some ecclesiastical venues of renting out carpets to private individuals for special occasions. This led to legal difficulties when carpets given to the Scuola Grande di San Rocco in Venice, with specific conditions forbidding their being loaned or rented out for any purpose, were then rented by Scuola officials; fines of 50 and 25 ducats were levied on the Guardian Grande and the Sindaci for violating the terms of the original carpet gift. Curatola suggests that the main reason for these stiff fines was concern that the renting practice would result in undue wear or damage to the precious carpets.[19]

Despite Barbaro's own marked preference for the "carpets of Tabriz" expressed in the late 15th century, the vast majority of Islamic carpets arriving in Venice in the 15th and 16th centuries came from the Ottoman Empire—either from Anatolia or from Ottoman Egypt. Iranian carpets became more important in Venice at the beginning of the 17th century, first when Shah 'Abbas I of Iran, pursuing an anti-Ottoman economic policy, sent a gift of "presentation carpets"—Iranian carpets with silk pile and metal brocading created in a royal Iranian workshop for purposes of royal gift-giving—to the Serenissima (cat. 83, p. 180). The new vogue for such carpets prompted the later gift of a similar carpet to the Scuola di San Rocco by one of the Guardian Grande, Silvestro Polognol, listed in the 1709 inventory: "*Un tapedo fondi doro con fiori e Richami d'Argento e seda.*"[20]

cat. 81. *"Mamluk" carpet*
Probably Cairo, Egypt, before 1541
Scuola Grande di San Rocco, Venice

fig. 4. Alessandro Bonvicino, called Moretto, *Frescoes in Palazzo Salvadego showing Mamluk carpets*, Brescia, first half of 16th century

cat. 85. *Prayer carpet (sajjada)*
Western Anatolia (probably Ushak district), ca. 1500–1550
Museum für Islamische Kunst, Berlin

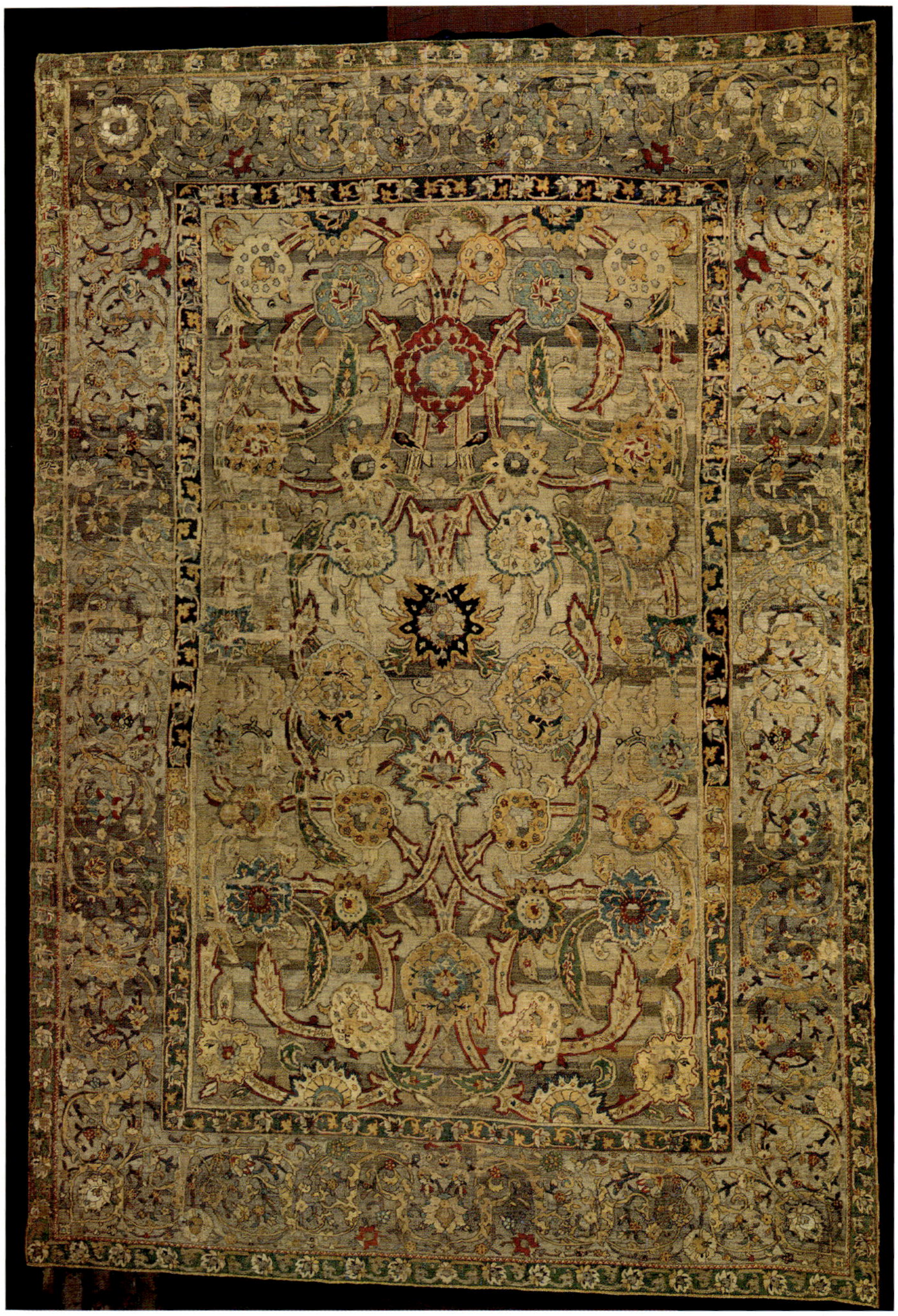

cat. 83. *"Presentation" carpet*
Probably Kashan, Iran, later 16th century
Procuratoria di San Marco, Venice

The Venetians as Carpet Dealers to Europe

In the early 16th century Cardinal Wolsey, first minister to King Henry VIII of England, appears to have been one of the first identifiable examples of a pathological carpet collector in European history; many more have followed in his footsteps in succeeding centuries. According to surviving documents, Wolsey's source for carpets was Venice; Wolsey's correspondence with the Venetian authorities regarding Venetian commercial privileges in England includes references to "gifts" of carpets he was to receive as part of the deal being struck.[21] Wolsey was a true pioneer: from his time onwards, "Oriental rugs" appear repeatedly in connection with the rich and colorful Western tradition of political bribery. As mentioned above, carpets for decorating the palaces fronting the Piazza San Marco during feast days in the 15th and 16th centuries appear largely to have been furnished by Venetian carpet dealers. While a small number of surviving carpets, mainly large ones (including the two recently found in Florence), can be traced to Genoa, Venice's primary competition in the carpet arena in Renaissance Italy, some of the most important surviving examples are far more likely to have passed through Venice, with its diverse population and multiple trading connections in Western Europe, the Balkans, and the Middle East. Curatola has commented that the involvement of the Venetian Jewish community in the carpet industry (see his essay on the subject in this volume), and the importance of carpets in its religious material, is attested to in the survival of a number of early Egyptian carpets with Hebrew inscriptions that were intended for Jewish religious use, a tradition that dates back at least as early as the 14th century in Spain (see cat. 82, p. 182).[22]

The Record of European Paintings

A perusal of the numerous examples of Italian paintings representing carpets suggests from the outset that northern Italian painters have been the primary depicters of carpets in European art. In addition to paintings by the Venetians Carpaccio and Mansueti, the works of near-Venetians such as Giovanni da Udine (1453–1535) and other painters in Italy, such as Crivelli, and adopted Venetians such as Lotto[23] (see cat. 32, p. 126) and Antonello da Messina are especially rich in depictions of carpets. In the landmark article "Carpets in Italian Paintings" by John Mills, one is struck by the number of carpet depictions in paintings either made in or commissioned by entities from northeastern Italian towns in the Venetian cultural orbit.[24] For example, the earliest carpet in the "small-pattern Holbein" design depicted in European painting (as opposed to the earliest depiction) is seen in Mantegna's San Zeno Altarpiece in Verona (fig. 5). The best depiction of an early so-called "Para-Mamluk" carpet (a type likely to have been woven in northern Syria or Azerbaijan, which was already quite old by the time of its depiction in the first half of the 16th century) is by Giovanni da Udine. It depicts the patron saint of Venice, St. Mark, enthroned with saints, and is found in the Cathedral of Udine, a city that like Verona was a part of the Venetian *terra ferma* (fig. 6). Carlo Crivelli, who was born and trained in Venice, painted several types of Anatolian carpets, all of small sizes, and included depictions of a carpet whose design bears his name today in at least two of his works. Although he spent most of his career in the Marches, an area politically subject to Rome, the carpets Crivelli painted probably arrived in Italy through nearby Venice. The geographical nature of the creation and distribution of these and other important paintings points to Venice as the center of European origin for the carpets in the paintings. The varieties of carpets depicted run the full gamut, from the distinctive Cairene or Mamluk production and the so-called "Chessboard" rugs of Syria, to the "Para-Mamluk" rugs from either northern Syria or Azerbaijan, and of course the truly enormous variety of familiar rug types from Anatolia. European documents have even cast light on previously unknown possible places of carpet manufacture in the Middle East, such as Çhemishgezek in Turkey.[25]

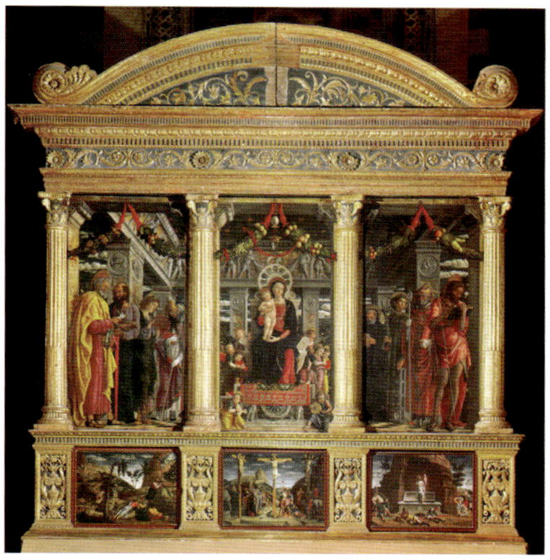

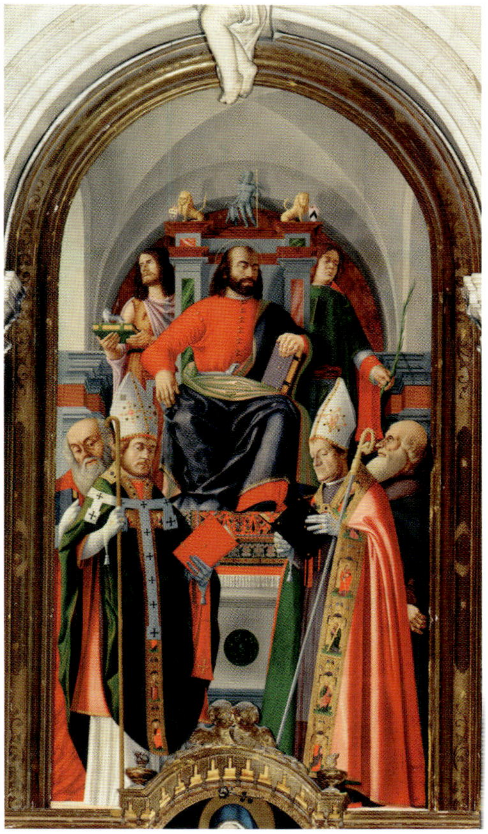

fig. 5. Andrea Mantegna, *San Zeno Altarpiece*, ca. 1457–59. Church of San Zeno, Verona

fig. 6. Giovanni da Udine, *St. Mark Enthroned with Saints*, mid-16th century. Cathedral, Udine

Venetian Copies of Islamic Carpets

A question arises from some documents as to the possibility of carpets having been produced in Venice.[26] Without question, the high prices and prestige of Islamic carpets in Europe led to imitations of Islamic examples being woven there, at first in a robust production in 14th- and 15th-century Spain, and later in smaller numbers in England and France.

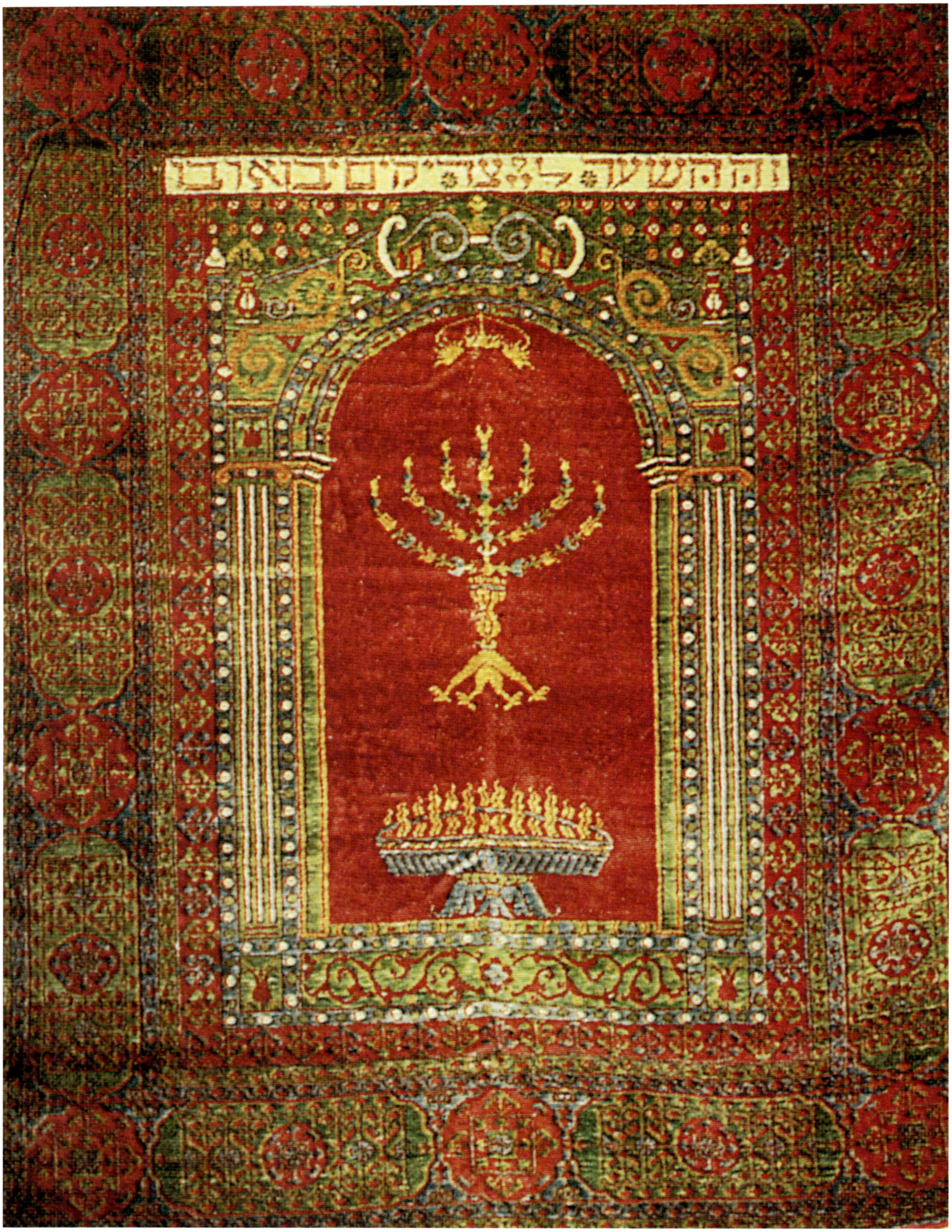
זה השער ל׳׳ צדיקים יבאו בו

However, there are no surviving carpets attributable to Venetian manufacture, nor have any documents about a Venetian manufactory come to light. Since the investment in looms, raw materials, and personnel to weave carpets was substantial, it seems likely that if a production of any significance had existed in Venice, there would have been some surviving local record. There is evidence that an Egyptian weaver—himself possibly of Jewish origin—may have been brought to Italy to weave carpets in the Mamluk style, and one surviving carpet, the famous Padua rug, possibly a Torah curtain (cat. 82), may indeed be associated with this Italian production, although the materials out of which it is made are beyond any doubt Egyptian, as are many details of its design.[27] In all probability, the so-called "Venetian carpets" mentioned in English archives in the 16th century were purchased from or through Venetian dealers, but were unlikely to have been woven in Venice.

cat. 82. *"Mamluk" synagogue carpet*
Probably Cairo, Egypt, mid-16th century
Communità Ebraica di Padova, Padua

Venice and Islamic Silk Textiles

Unlike carpet trade, which appears to have been almost exclusively in an east-to-west direction, textile commerce between Venice and the Islamic Middle East was distinguished by the flow of textile goods in both directions. Venice in the 16th century was a major producer of silk luxury textiles;[28] the raw silk itself was produced in Gilan and Mazandaran on the Caspian shore of northern Persia, and was purchased in the Middle East by Venetian merchants after being transshipped overland through Bursa in Turkey—then the capital of the Ottoman Empire—and later through northern Syria, from whence it was taken by ship to Venice. Venetian luxury silks achieved a high reputation in Europe, and even, as we shall see, enjoyed a flourishing demand in the Ottoman Empire in the early 16th century.

The balance between textile imports and exports in the Venetian economy was in fact an indication of growing European dominance in textile production, which encompassed a wide range of qualities. European technical innovations in weaving in the medieval period, including the water-powered loom, the pedal-operated loom, and the spinning wheel, led to a large-scale export to the Middle East of low-quality cloth, described by a leading economic historian as *"un véritable dumping."*[29] Venetians, in particular, exported to Syria large quantities of Reims linen, and the 15th-century Egyptian historian al-Maqrizi complains of Egyptians dressing themselves in cheap European cloth instead of using higher-quality local products.[30] Venetian textile exports to the Middle East were not confined to lower-quality goods, however. When Barbaro visited Uzun Hasan in Tabriz in 1474, he brought along as gifts fine Venetian silk velvet and brocaded cloth valued at 2,500 ducats.[31] Venetian silk sold in Syria at this time was costly: two ducats per *braccio,* or around 70 ducats for a bolt.[32] The technique of velvet weaving practiced in the Near East from the 14th century onwards may well have originated in Italy.[33] Certain European velvets were so popular in the Middle East in the 15th century that Anatolian rug-weavers actually produced carpets echoing their designs and colors.[34] We

Page 184 :
cat. 72. *Loom-width piece of brocaded silk fabric*
Probably Istanbul, mid-16th century,
Topkapı Sarayi Müzesi, Istanbul

Page 185 :
cat. 74. *Chasuble embroidered with the arms of the Barbaro family*
Probably Istanbul, ca. 1570–80,
embroidered in Venice, late 16th century
Parrocchia di Santa Maria Assunta,
Cividale del Friuli

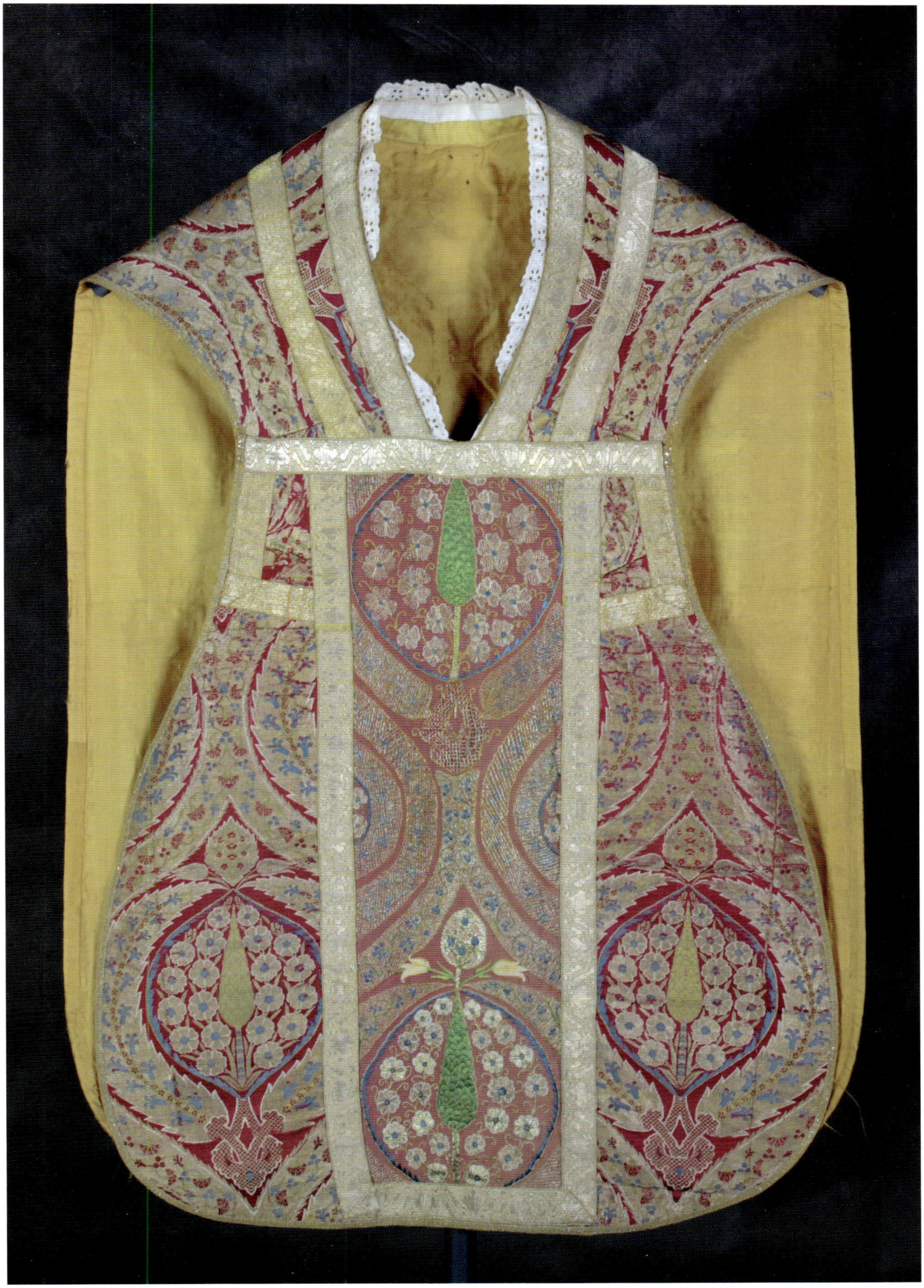

must remember, however, that the silk itself from which Venetians and Florentines wove these luxurious fabrics originated in Iran.[35]

The Use of Middle Eastern Silk Textiles in Venice

Eliyahu Ashtor, one of the great historians of medieval Mediterranean commerce, repeatedly observes that by the 15th century Muslim industry in the Eastern Mediterranean was in decline. Earlier in the Middle Ages, Muslims imported timber and iron from Europe; by the later Middle Ages textiles and manufactured goods had become far more important.[36] During this period of commercial ascendancy and decline of their trading partners, Venetians were highly protective of their own products against competition from foreign goods, whether European (Barbaro, a patriotic Venetian, speaks disdainfully of Florentine fabrics) or Islamic.[37] There is no question that Islamic woven silk and raw silk were both sold in Venice and marketed in Europe by Venetian entrepreneurs, and the evidence alone from 14th-, 15th-, and 16th-century painters would appear to indicate that this importation continued after the mid-15th century despite the European commercial dominance and Islamic decline of the time (cat. 72, p. 184). A 14th- or 15th-century fragment of brocaded silk from Nasrid Granada in Muslim Spain, preserved in the Scuola Grande di San Rocco in Venice (fig. 7), suggests at least a token Venetian interest in luxury goods from the Islamic west, an interest also demonstrated in the development of tin-glazed pottery in Italy (see Fontana's essay in this volume). The available evidence, again largely from paintings, suggests, however, that such textiles from the Mamluk and Nasrid kingdoms and the Ottoman and Safavid Empires were only rarely, if ever, used for Italian secular costume. They found more acceptance as furnishing fabrics, in particular as clerical vestments (cat. 70; cat. 74, p. 185), altar furnishings, and other ecclesiastical applications.[38]

There is evidence from Genoa of Ottoman silk being made into shipboard awnings for a Genoese admiral, and used in other furnishing applications,[39] but a fabric so closely identified with a commercial rival and political and religious adversary is less likely to have been used in public display in Venice. The luxurious brocaded fabrics worn by the Venetian doges in official portraits are almost certainly Venetian products, emblematic of Venetian wealth and power, despite some vague similarities with definable Ottoman motifs or color schemes (cat. 21, p. 189). This is in marked contrast to eastern and central Europe, and in particular Russia, where especially after the middle of the 16th century Ottoman silk fabrics were highly popular, and were used for both clerical and secular costume as well as for a variety of other uses.[40]

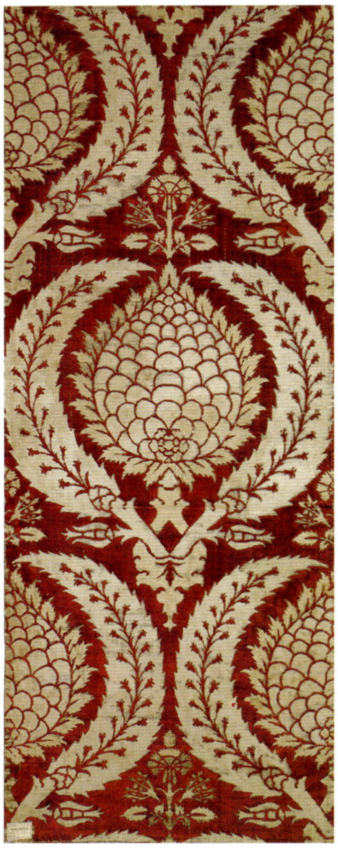

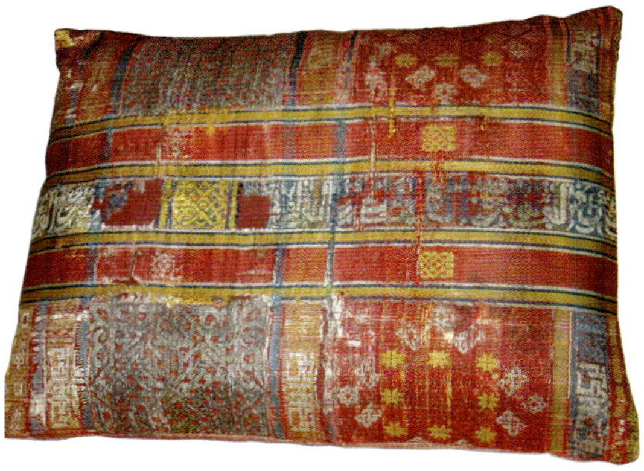

cat. 75. *Loom-width piece of velvet fabric*
Bursa, Turkey, late 16th century
Kunstgewerbemuseum, Berlin

fig. 7. Fragment of brocaded silk. Granada, 14th or 15th century, Scuola Grande di San Rocco, Venice

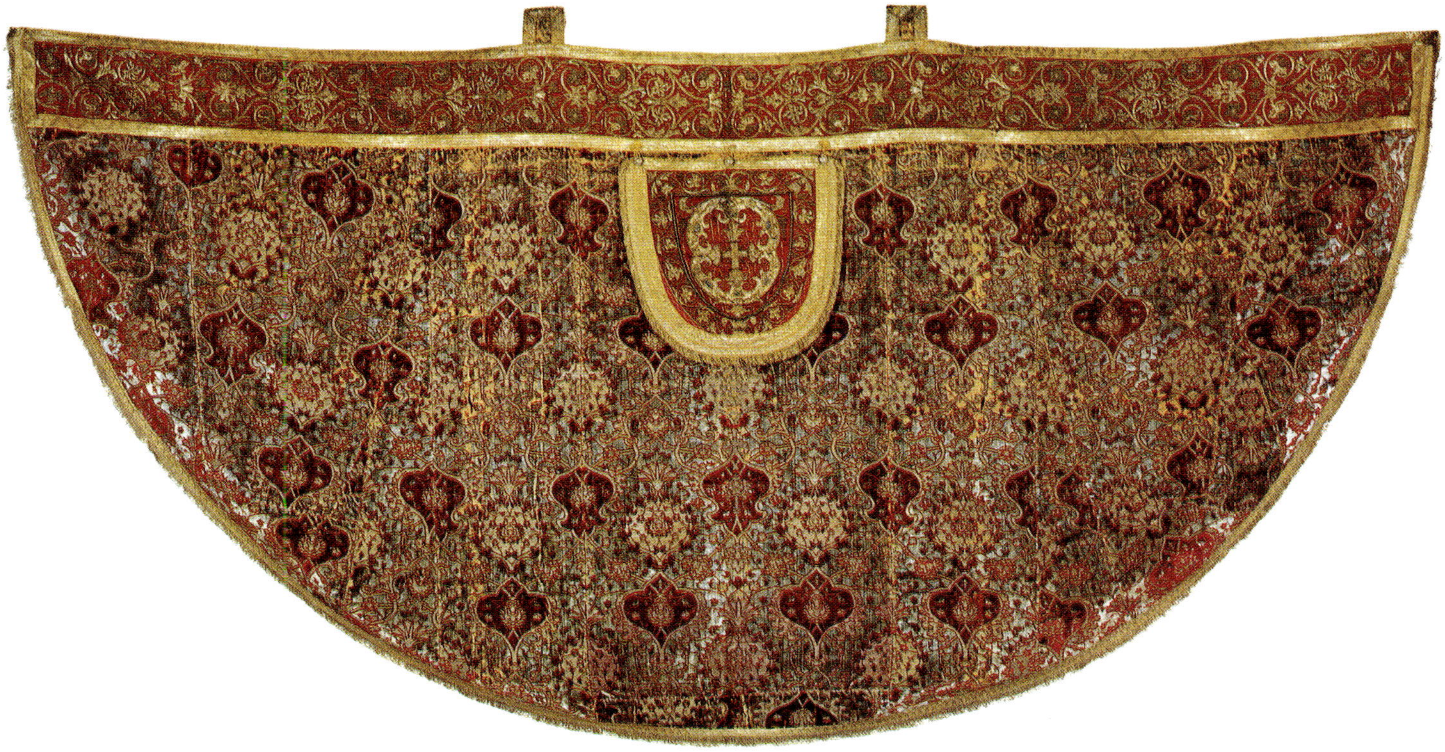

cat. 70. *Ecclesiastical cope (piviale)*
Probably Bursa, Turkey, cut, assembled, and embroidered in Venice, mid-15th century
Basilica di Santa Maria Gloriosa del Frari, Venice

Venetian Textile Manufacture in the Turkish Mode

The large collections of Ottoman dynastic costumes preserved in what is now the Topkapı Palace Museum in Istanbul include over 30 kaftans or ceremonial outer robes executed in silk velvet (cat. 80, p. 188). Some of these are manifestly foreign products, tailored from French or Italian velvet. Others appeared to be of Ottoman manufacture according to their designs, which used the characteristic Ottoman tulip as a primary element of decoration. A closer technical examination, however, proved that many of the latter were in fact also Italian—probably Venetian—velvets, several incorporating the distinctive Italian *alto basso* technique of using both cut and looped velvet pile (fig. 8, p. 189), that apparently had been woven in Turkish designs for the specific purpose of appealing to Ottoman taste, whether to serve as official diplomatic gifts to the sultan or as items of commerce.[41] The Ottoman city of Bursa was in the 15th and 16th centuries one of the most important producers of velvets in the world (cat. 73, p. 189); how do we account for the fact that only three of the velvet kaftans today in the Topkapı Palace collections are without a doubt made from Turkish velvet?

The answer probably lies in a combination of snobbery and rarity. From the later 15th century onwards, the production of velvet in Bursa resulted in its great popularity as furnishing fabric in the Ottoman Empire as well as a significant Ottoman export to the north and west, and the sultan would have been unlikely to wear a ceremonial kaftan fashioned from a fabric that could be seen in every luxury shop in the bazaar and in every wealthy household in

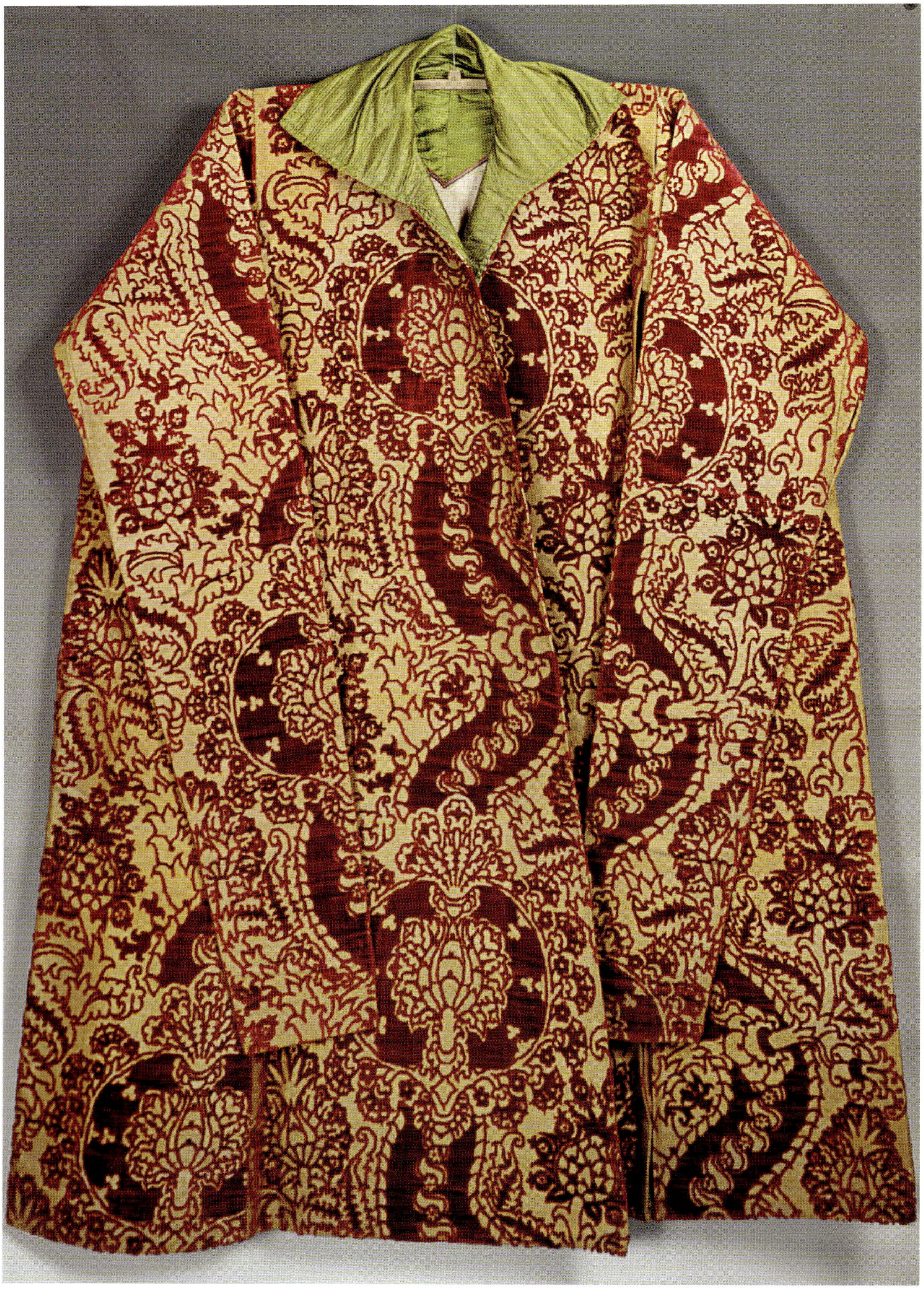

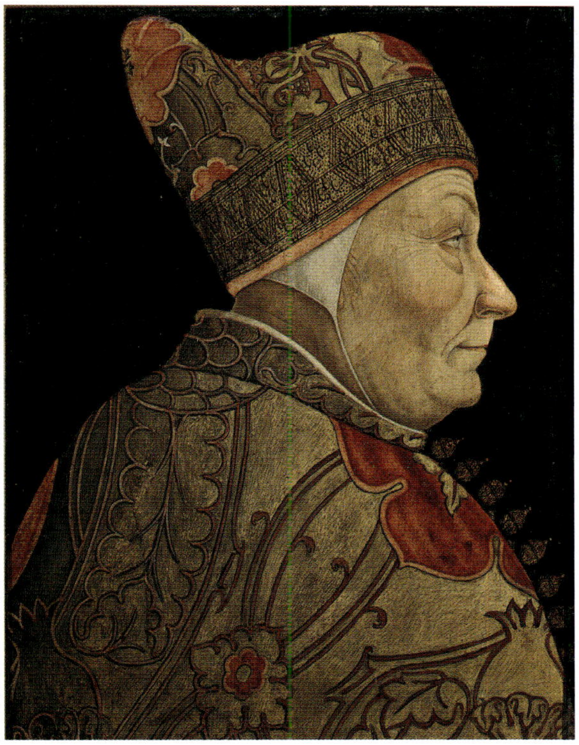

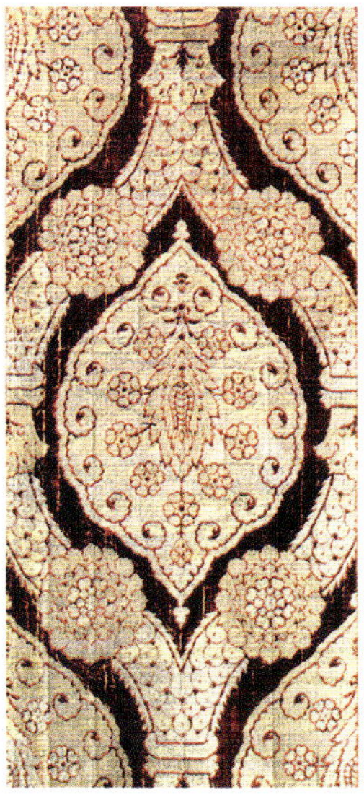

Istanbul. Julian Raby has used the same argument in his memorable explanation for the preference in the Ottoman imperial court for Iranian and Ottoman court-manufactured carpets in place of the famous and popular rugs of Ushak: "If you had been Mehmet II, the Conqueror of Constantinople, would you have been content to rest your felicitous derrière on the type of rugs exported to the *donne mobili* of Venice?"[42]

In a perverse way, the popularity in the first half of the 16th century of Venetian luxury fabrics in the Ottoman Empire may be surmised to have had a significant role in the emergence by the middle third of the century of the spectacular Ottoman fabrics executed in the *kemha* (lampas) and *seraser* (taqueté) techniques that are today recognized as among the supreme artistic achievements of Ottoman art. There is considerable evidence that the Ottoman *sadrazam* or Grand Vizier Rüstem Pasha in the mid-16th century encouraged the development of the Ottoman silk industry for a series of reasons: to produce distinctively Ottoman luxury fabrics for court ceremonial use to replace the reliance on expensive foreign—that is, Venetian—silks; to compete with the Venetians for the lucrative luxury markets in central and eastern Europe and particularly in Russia; and to shift Ottoman tax revenues from the precarious reliance on the tax on raw silk (subject to disruption in the periodic wars between the Ottomans and their eastern neighbors the Safavids, whose domains were the major source of raw silk) to a more dependable and lucrative tax on finished goods, which also brought a higher profit when sold abroad.[43]

These highly effective Ottoman policies notwithstanding, there was apparently a continuing production of Venetian silks in the Ottoman taste, especially in the area of furnishing fabrics. One example that has recently come to light is a handsome velvet *yastık* or pillow cover in the Ottoman style that, because of the unusual density of its pile and its distinctive selvedges, is now thought to be of Italian, almost certainly late 16th-century Venetian, manufacture (fig. 9, p. 190).

cat. 21. Attributed to Lorenzo Bastiani
Portrait of Doge Francesco Foscari
Venice, ca. 1457–60 or mid- to late 1470s
Museo Civico Correr, Venice

fig. 8. Detail of cut and looped velvet pile

cat. 73. *Loom-width piece of velvet fabric*
Probably Bursa, Turkey, late 16th century
Florence, Museo Nazionale del Bargello

cat. 80. *Silk velvet ceremonial robe (kaftan)*
Italian, lined in Istanbul, 16th century
Topkapı Sarayi Müzei, Istanbul

Carpets and Textiles in Venice in the 18th Century

In the age of European *grand goût* promoted by the French in Europe after 1680, the taste for Middle Eastern fabrics declined in France and in places within the French cultural orbit. Their depiction in oil paintings, the major index of popularity of Islamic goods, continued in the prosperous Dutch society, and the 18th century was a period of intense import of Ottoman carpets into central Europe. In Venice, the tradition of using—and renting out—Islamic carpets continued, and whether painters depicted them or not, the commercial flow of Turkish carpets into Venice continued, and many stayed there. The growth of the English and Dutch East India companies, the decline of silk-weaving (but not carpet-weaving) in the 18th-century Ottoman realms, and the commercial decline of Venice itself, altered but did not erase centuries of Venetian traditions regarding the material culture of the Islamic world. Although Venice was no longer Europe's primary *porta Orientalis*, the 18th-century Venetian nostalgia about its own past still incorporated a fascination with the Islamic Orient.

fig. 9. Ottoman-style *yastik* (pillow cover). Late 16th century. Private collection, United States

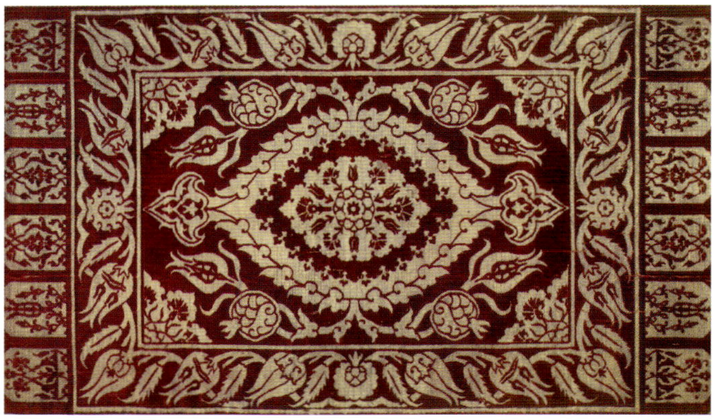

Notes

1 For the most recent general study of Islamic goods in Italy, see Mack 2002. For a general view of Islamic carpets in Europe, see Erdmann 1962; King and Sylvester 1983; and Pinner 1986.
2 Among the many Venetian sources, perhaps the most important is the *Diarii* of Marin Sanudo (1466–1535); see Sanudo 1879–1902.
3 Barbaro and Contarini 1873, pp. 60ff; see also Denny 2002, pp. 24–25.
4 Kurtzman and Koldau 2002 contains numerous illustrations from Matteo Pagan's print of the Procuratorie Vecchie decked out with carpets.
5 Mack (2002, pp. 77–78) gives an account of various ceremonial occasions when carpets were set out in St. Mark's Square, drawing especially on Sanudo's accounts.
6 Among the most important paintings depicting carpets are Bellini's *Procession in the Piazza San Marco*, Mansueti's *Miracle at the Bridge of San Lio*, Carpaccio's *Healing of the Possessed Man*, Bastiani's *Donation of the Relic* (all in Venice's Gallerie dell'Accademia), and a painting cited by Erdmann in a private Viennese collection (Erdmann 1962, p. 26).
7 For the nomenclature and its derivations, see Bode and Kühnel 1984. The use of painters' names for various design groups found in early Turkish carpets is now quite commonplace.
8 See Batari 1994, p. 29; see also Kertesz 2005.
9 Batari 1994, pp. 28–30; see also Raby 1986; Rogers 1986.
10 For prices again see Mack 2002, chapter 4 ("Carpets"), for the widest discussion.
11 The nomenclature "Venetian Carpets" in documents may denote carpets made in Venice, or simply carpets obtained in Venice. There is no surviving Venetian documentation that would suggest carpets were actually woven there; documents do suggest that carpets may have been woven for brief periods in Naples and Mantua in the 15th century (Mack 2002, pp. 92–93).
12 See Inalcik 1986, especially the table dealing with prayer rug production pp. 58–59.
13 See Boralevi 1986.
14 Curatola 1986 discusses the San Rocco Mamluk carpet, which was ordered specifically to be placed on the huge table in the Sala del Guardian Grando, around which the Consiglio di San Rocco held its meetings. It is perhaps significant that while a table of this unusual size could easily have been covered with two or three smaller carpets, a special effort was made to obtain a single carpet large enough to cover the entire table.
15 See Erdmann 1962, p. 18. The Palazzo Salvadego frescoes are unusual; Mack (2002, p. 90) suggests that the scarcity of images of Mamluk carpets in Italian painting is due to the fact that their subtle coloration and complex designs were difficult to portray. The 1534 painting *The Return of the Doge's Ring* in the Accademia by Paris Bordone mentioned above, usually cited because it contains an image of the doge enthroned on a "Star Ushak" carpet, also contains to the left of the Ushak carpet a representation of what was probably a fragment of a large and early Mamluk carpet of an unusual type, represented by a fragmentary example (T. 8348) in the Museum of Applied Arts, Vienna.
16 See Curatola 1986, p. 123.
17 Curatola's (1986) collection of documents spans the years from 1533 to 1790, and he notes that there are thousands of unedited documents remaining to be surveyed, leaving open the possibility of significant future discoveries.
18 Erdmann (1970) discusses a number of Bode's acquisitions, among them a large dragon carpet from the Caucasus acquired in 1905 for 120 lire from a church in Burano near Venice (p. 148; cat. 86), and the famous early Anatolian dragon and phoenix carpet acquired from a church in central Italy (p. 17). Among the non-Bode acquisitions in Berlin, one of the most interesting is the 14th-century fragment of a Spanish carpet "acquired in 1880 from a church in the Tyrol" north of the Veneto (p. 143). Bode gave the Islamisches Museum a donation of several carpets in 1905, most probably acquired in his Italian peregrinations.
19 Curatola 1986, p. 127.
20 Curatola 1986, p. 128.
21 See Hamilton Beattie 1964 for a discussion of the carpets associated with Wolsey and Henry VIII.
22 Boralevi (1984 and 1986) has dealt with the question of carpets made for Jewish religious purposes; see also Denny 2002, pp. 46–54. In addition to the early prayer rug or *sajjada*-sized examples in Padua (woven in Egypt or possibly in Italy of Egyptian wool in Mamluk technique), Washington D.C., and Jerusalem (both using Ottoman court designs and woven in Egypt around the last quarter of the 16th century), there are other later examples, many of them listed in Felton 1997.
23 See Mack 1988.
24 Mills 1986, 1978, 1981, 1991.
25 Rogers 1986, p. 7.
26 See King 1982, p. 300, in which are cited English inventories of 1547 listing over 40 "Venetian" carpets in the English Royal Collections, including "a venyce Carpett of sylke" in the Tower of London of quite a large size, over seven yards long; "Seven Carpettes of venyce making" at Greenwich, all quite small; "vij course carpettes of veanice making with peescoddes fringed at thendes with white cruell" at Westminster, of medium (2 1/2 yards in length) or small size; "fouer Carpettes of Venice making" at Windsor, all of *sajjada* or prayer rug size; and "six carpettes of Venice making" at Hampton Court, also of *sajjada* size. In addition to the possibility that these carpets may simply have been purchased through Venice, some could have been made of Venetian silk velvet.
27 See above, notes 11 and 20; Boralevi 1984. A craftsman named Sabadino Moro from Cairo (suggested to have been Jewish) was evidently in charge of a carpet workshop in Ferrara between 1493 and 1530.
28 See the very useful study Mola 2000. On the sources of the raw silk used in Italy, see also Atasoy, Denny, and Raby 2001, esp. pp. 155–75. The popularity of first foreign and then domestic silk in Italy is demonstrated in its depictions in painting; see Klesse 1967.
29 See Ashtor 1977, esp. p. 319.
30 See Ashtor 1976b, esp. pp. 580–81.
31 See Barbaro's listing of goods and their prices.
32 Ashtor (1978a, esp. pp. 362–67) gives an extensive list of prices for Venetian luxury silk goods in the Middle East.
33 Simple velvets were woven in Italy as early as the 13th century; complex patterned velvets in three colors and two levels of pile (*alto basso*) produced in Lucca in the later 14th century long antedate known velvet production in the Ottoman Empire, suggesting that the technique moved from west to east at the time of the expansion of velvet weaving in Bursa in the 15th century. See Levey 1966, p. 753.
34 See Denny 1999.
35 See Inalcik 1966.
35 Eliyahu Ashtor (1976b, pp. 574–75) calls this phenomenon "the great change on the Levantine trade."
36 See a discussion of Barbaro's comments in Denny 2002, pp. 24–25.
37 See for example a set of ecclesiastical vestments in the possession of the Barberini family discussed by Louise Mackie in Atasoy, Denny, and Raby 2001, pp. 186, 247.
38 See Sims 1990.
39 For an overview of the extensive Russian material, see the discussion in Atasoy, Denny, and Raby 2001, pp. 176–81 and numerous illustrations of material from Russian collections.
40 See Mackie in Atasoy, Denny, and Raby 2001, pp. 182–90.
41 See Raby 1986a, p. 185.
42 For the question of Ottoman independence from a taste for Italian luxury fabrics, sought by the Grand Vizier Rüstem Pasha, see Atasoy, Denny, and Raby 2001, pp. 171-72.

Ottoman or Italian Velvets? A Technical Investigation

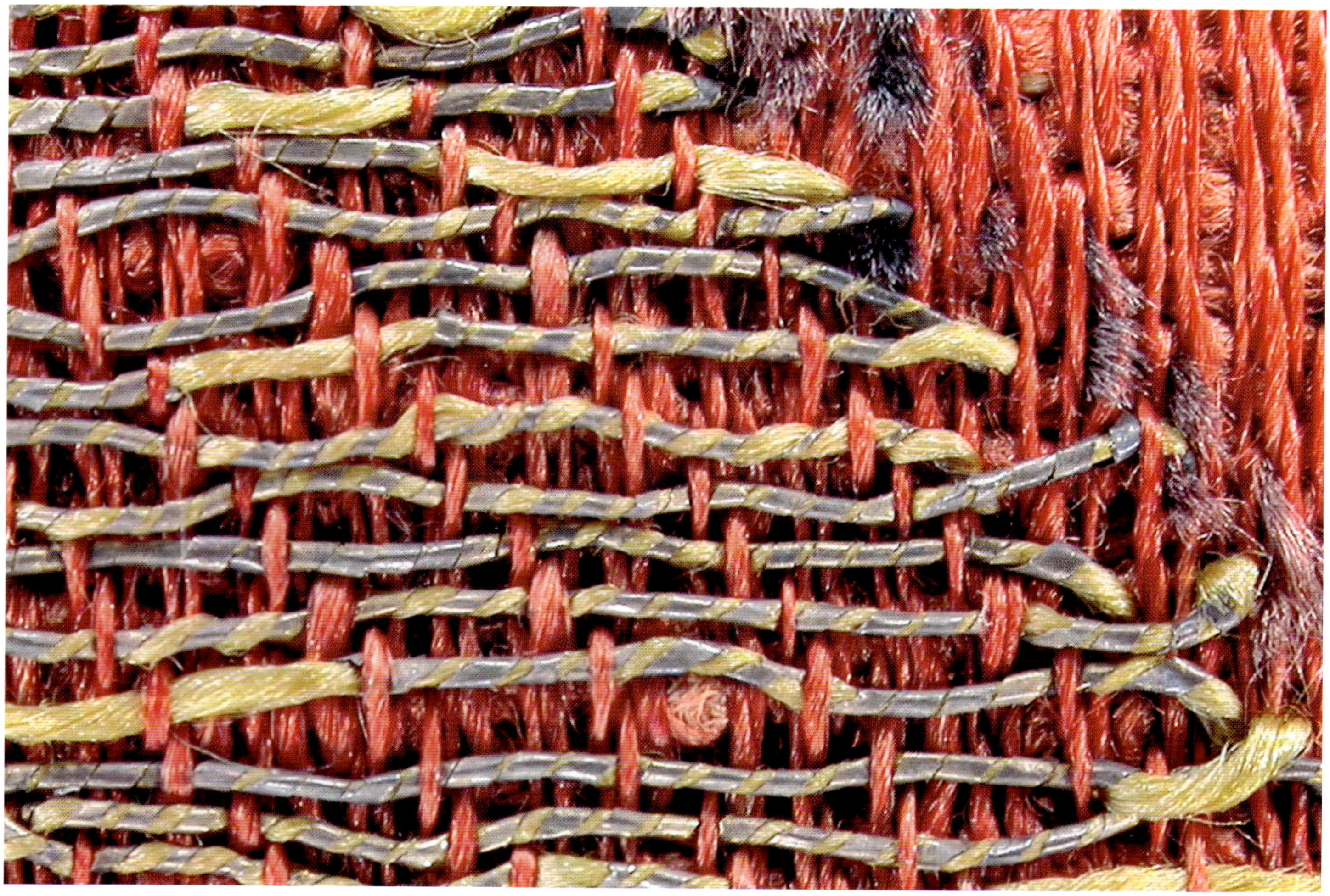

Sandra Sardjono

The rise of commercial trade between the Ottoman Empire and Italy during the 15th and 16th centuries resulted in a mutual exchange of artistic vocabularies, seldom better expressed than in the case of velvet production.[1] During this period, an interesting group of brocaded silk velvets were made whose provenance cannot be determined with certainty on the basis of their patterns alone.[2] The present exhibition and catalogue provide an excellent opportunity to explore the questions of attribution of this problematic group with a scientific method. This was accomplished through an in-depth study of the weaving structure and the materials of a small sample of three related 16th century velvets (figs. 1–3), two in the collection of the Metropolitan Museum of Art (MMA 12.49.5 and MMA 1970.65.9), and one in the Cooper-Hewitt National Design Museum, Smithsonian Institution (CHM 1951-151-1).[3]

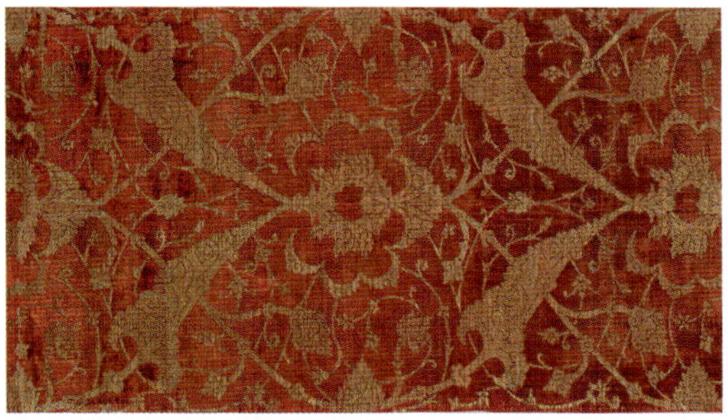

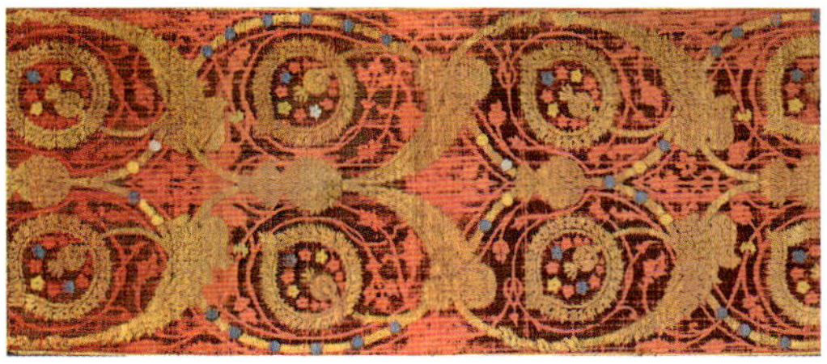

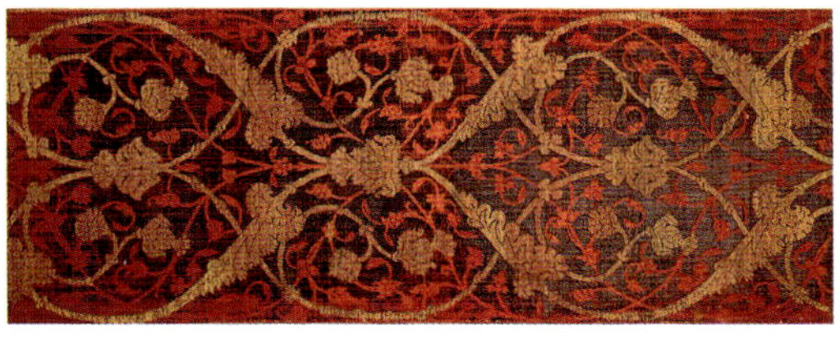

The sumptuous quality of these silk velvets indicates that they were luxury items. They present cut pile loops and areas voided of pile, embellished with brocaded gilded metal wefts. In addition to the use of precious silk and "gold" threads, the prestigious status of these textiles is apparent in the intricacy of their pattern, displaying a complex of three or four superimposed layers of design network. These consist of two overlapping ogival medallions of half serrated sharp-edged leaves together with a central lotus palmette, and one or two linear patterns of scrolling vines. In all three velvets, the voided area serves as the positive image whereas the area with pile forms the background. The selected samples represent three variants of the treatment of the voided areas in relation to the brocaded wefts: in MMA 12.49.5 (fig. 1), the voided area is completely covered with brocaded "gold" wefts; in CHM 1951-151-1 (fig. 3), "gold" wefts fill the two ogival networks and leave the two linear vine patterns exposed; in MMA 1970.65.9 (fig. 2), a similar treatment of selective coverage of the voided area occurs, but, in addition to "gold" wefts, there are also brocaded wefts in colored silks.

Page 192:
fig. 5. Detail of brocaded silk velvet, probably Ottoman Turkey, 16th century

Page 193:
fig. 1. Brocaded silk velvet, probably Ottoman Turkey, 16th century. The Metropolitan Museum of Art, New York (inv. 12.49.5)

fig. 2. Brocaded silk velvet, probably Ottoman Turkey, 16th century. The Metropolitan Museum of Art, New York (inv. 1970.65.9),

fig. 3. Brocaded silk velvet, probably Ottoman Turkey, 16th century. Cooper-Hewitt National Design Museum, New York (inv. 1951-151-1)

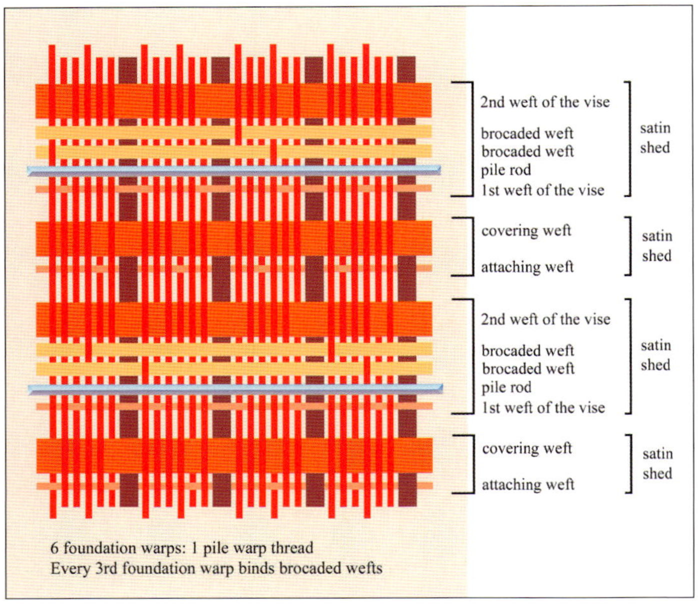

Right:
fig. 4. Warp and weft orders of the three samples under discussion

Weaving Analysis

The three velvets have identical technical features. The foundation structure of each is a 4-and-1 satin weave with an interruption of one. The warp order is six foundation warp threads to every pile warp thread or pile-warp channel (fig. 4).[4] The foundation warps are single thread with firm Z-twist and the warps of the side finishes, which are also a satin weave, are paired threads with Z-twist.

The foundation warps interlace with a pair of wefts in every shed of the satin. The function of this pair of wefts alternates from shed to shed. In one shed, loops of pile warp-threads were pulled up between two wefts that thereby act as a vise. In the next shed the two wefts have two different functions: one weft engages and attaches all pile warp threads to the back of the fabric—otherwise loose when not pulled up between the vise wefts for patterning;[5] the other weft of the pair hides the engaged pile warp threads (fig. 4).[6]

In MMA 12.49.5, the pair of wefts in each shed of the satin are composed of silks of similar weight, whereas in MMA 1970.65.9 and CHM 1951-151-1, the two wefts differ in thickness and character (table 1).[7] The thickness of the wefts generally changes along the same thread, which creates an uneven surface on the back of the velvet. In velvets with two different wefts, two shuttles were clearly used for the weaving of the foundation satin weave. In MMA 12.49.5, where the two wefts are of the same type, however, two shuttles were also used. It is evident from the image (fig. 4) that the attaching weft and the first weft of the vise, shown as a thin line, are the same weft that is carried by one shuttle; likewise, the covering weft and the second weft of the vise, shown as a thicker line, is another weft carried by a different shuttle. Analysis of the selvedges shows that both shuttles were thrown one after the other in the same direction for each opening of the satin shed.

In between two rows of pile lie two brocaded wefts, "gold" or colored silk, which

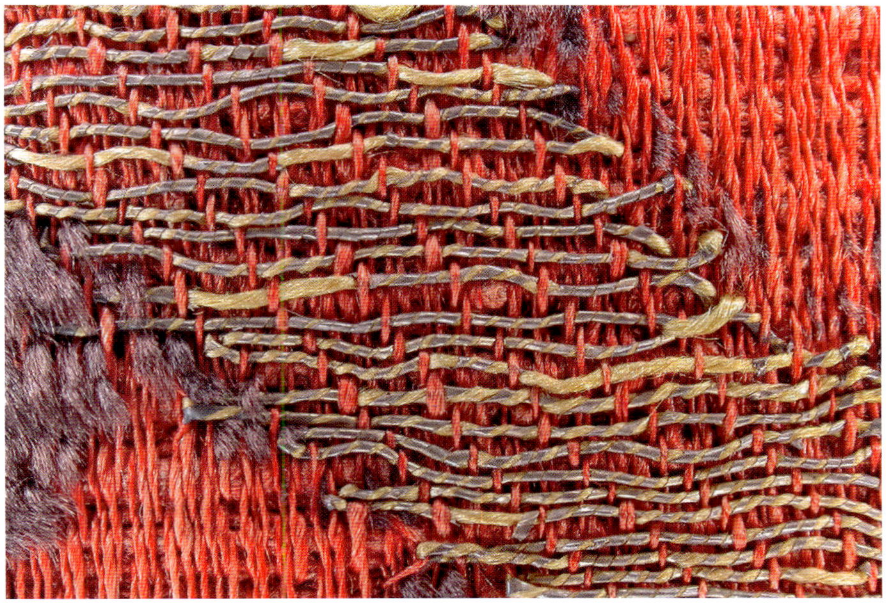

fig. 5. Detail of brocaded silk velvet, probably Ottoman Turkey, 16th century. Cooper-Hewitt Design Museum, New York (inv. 1951-151-1)

are bound on the front of MMA 12.49.5 in a 1-and-4 twill, in the S-direction, by every third foundation warp thread (fig. 5). The "gold" weft is a metal foil wrapped in S-direction around an S-twist yellow silk core thread. It is apparent that the yellow color of the silk core is intended to further enhance the gold-like effect of the metal foil. Many individual bobbins or small shuttles carried the brocaded wefts. Passes of the brocaded wefts turn around on the surface on one end, then on the reverse side of the fabric on the other end (fig. 5).[8] Following a vertical axis of symmetry at the center of the fabric, the turn-around on the surface takes place, for both the left and right half of the fabric, on the edge of the motif that is closer to the axis. On the edge that is closer to the selvedges, the brocaded wefts were taken from the back of the fabric and then returned to the back on the same shed. Brocaded wefts that fall precisely on the axis of symmetry are rendered in the same manner as that on the right.

When the velvets are analyzed with the pattern in their upright orientation and cut pile slanted down (fig. 4), the weft order, from bottom to top, reads as follows: the first shed of the satin is composed of two passes of an attaching weft (shuttle 1) followed by a covering weft (shuttle 2); the next shed has five passes that are made up of a first weft of the vise (shuttle 1), a pile rod,[9] two passes of brocaded wefts (individual bobbins), and a second weft of the vise (shuttle 2). Significantly, this is the same weft order as also observed in the oldest known Turkish velvet dated to the second half of the 15th century.[10]

The overall technical analysis of these velvets is also consistent with the analysis of Ottoman velvets at the Royal Museums of Art and History in Brussels[11] and others in this group that I have had the opportunity to study previously. Such consistency in structure can be seen also in Turkish examples from the 17th century. The three velvets here under discussion, therefore, seem to present a typical Ottoman velvet weave structure from the 15th to the 17th century.

Dye and Metal Analysis

All colored threads were analyzed for their dye content using HPLC.[12] Table 2 shows that insect dyes were found in both MMA textiles. In MMA 12.49.5, lac—a very expensive dye that was imported from India—was used in both the pile and the foundation warp threads. The use of lac in this fabric suggests an Eastern origin since this dye is not commonly found in European fabrics until the end of the 18th century.[13] In MMA 1970.65.9, cochineal dye (either the Mexican or the Armenian type) was used in the foundation warp. Both types have been found in Turkish velvets,[14] the presence of Mexican cochineal indicating a date after the second half of the 16th century, when this dye source first became available in Turkey.[15] The violet color of pile warp threads in MMA 1970.65.9 and CHM 1951-151-1 is composed of a similar mixture of madder, indigo, and another unidentified red dye source. It is interesting to observe that CHM 1951-151-1, presenting arguably the most elegant pattern of the three textiles, does so using madder, a plant dye that is considered a cheaper substitute for insect dyes. The choice of madder, however, may not be related to its cost but rather to the hue or shade of the color sought that may be best achieved with that particular combination of dyestuffs. Intriguingly, an official document issued in Bursa in 1502 mentions the illegal practice of mixing diluted lac (combined with another red dye source) with indigo, which produces an undesirable purple color.[16] Further study is needed to address the interesting subject of the relationship between design, quality, and the expense of dyes and other materials as a measure of the prestige of a textile.

Metal analysis using SEM-EDS was performed on the metal foil of the threads used in all three velvets.[17] The foils were found to be silver, gilded on both sides. The analysis (table 3) indicates the metal composition to be almost-pure silver with a trace amount of copper, one percent or less by weight. Assuming a Turkish origin, this result conforms to a previous study that made a distinction between the composition of metal foil of European threads, consisting of silver alloyed with a large quantity of copper, and that of Turkish (and Persian) threads, consisting of silver that is almost entirely free of copper.[18]

Ottoman versus Italian Velvet

The technical characteristics of Ottoman and Italian velvets discussed in this section are by no means exhaustive. To be able to better understand the differences in the weaving of Ottoman and Italian velvets, further comparative technical studies of securely identified Ottoman and Italian velvets are needed. Certain stylistic features, however, are believed to distinguish Ottoman from Italian velvets. There is a variety of set features associated with different types of Italian velvets of the 15th and 16th centuries.[19] Some velvets—known to have an Italian provenance—have pile warp loops that are cut as well as uncut; others display cut pile in a multitude of heights; many have metal wefts that are fashioned into loops. In regard to side finishes, those of Turkish velvets are not as flat as their Italian counterparts, and do not have cords to reinforce the selvedges.

The absence of covering wefts is another woven feature that may indicate that a velvet is Ottoman.[20] Covering wefts seem to be necessary for velvets with plain weave foundation such as those woven in Italy in the 15th century.[21] Velvets with a satin weave foundation may or may not have covering wefts because of the coverage potential of the long warp floats of the satin. In monochrome velvets with a fine linear pattern, covering wefts are absent due to the satin foundation and because the pile and the foundation warp threads are the same color. Covering wefts are also not found in Italian velvets whose voided areas are completely covered by brocaded metal wefts. On the contrary, in the case of Turkish velvets, covering wefts are always employed even when pile and foundation warp thread color are the same and voided areas are completely covered by brocaded wefts. Accordingly, the use of covering wefts in the presence of one color pile and foundation warp along with a full coverage of the voided areas with "gold" wefts are observed in MMA 12.49.5.

Many 15th- and 16th-century Italian velvets also appear to have a different weft order than the one described above in regard to the entering of the brocaded metal thread. In Italian examples where covering wefts are absent, the weft order is as follows: attaching weft, first weft of the vise, pile rod, second weft of the vise, and two passes of the brocaded metal threads. In these instances, the entering of the brocaded metal threads takes place between sheds whereas in Ottoman velvets it always occurs in a shed between the two wefts of the vise and after the pile rod (fig. 4).

Many Italian brocaded velvets also show a different sequence in pattern lifting of the pile compared to that of Ottoman velvets. In those Italian velvets, the pile warps activated for patterning are lifted again for both passes of the brocaded metal threads. Therefore, pile warps are seen to bind both passes of the metal wefts that traverse pile areas.[22] In Ottoman velvets, on the other hand, pile warps are never lifted over brocaded wefts.

Conclusion

This study demonstrates that an analytical approach to weaving materials and technique may offer substantial clues as to the origin of textiles. The results of weave, dye, and metal analyses, in fact, strongly suggest an Ottoman attribution for all three of these velvets. Firstly, their weave structure is consistent with features considered typical of Ottoman velvets. Secondly, the detection of lac dye in MMA 12.49.5 would be an unexpected occurrence in a textile of European origin of this period, but it is common in the Islamic world. In addition, the high purity of silver in the metal threads found in all three textiles supports a Turkish origin. Naturally, the limits of the small number of samples analyzed in this and other studies must be taken into consideration; all the evidence gathered thus far, however, points to this conclusion. Another attribution that cannot be dismissed is that of an entirely different weaving place outside Turkey and Italy, as suggested by Mackie.[23] Issues surrounding the problem of textile provenance are always complicated by the fact that objects were traded to far-away places and weavers and artisans often relocated, bringing their craft traditions with them.

The earliest surviving examples of Turkish velvet weaving are the *cintamanis* from Bursa, dated to the second half of the 15th century.[24] Their superior quality suggests that—by then—Ottoman weavers had mastered this technique. Records show that Bursa was a great center for the development of textile weaving in the 15th century, thus in all likelihood the city was responsible for a now lost production of velvets prior to that of the *cintamanis.* Because of the lack of surviving examples of these early Turkish velvets there is no way to define common patterns and technical characteristics and there are important questions that cannot be answered at present regarding where and when velvet-weaving technology was introduced to Turkey. One may also question whether features regarded as typical in Turkish velvets are not actually the product of outside influences and the subsequent adoption of foreign practices in the late 15th century, possibly introduced from Spain or elsewhere during the diasporas of Islamic and Jewish weavers brought about by the Inquisition.[25]

To answer these questions, early velvets from regions including Spain, India, and Iran need to be studied further. The analysis of the materials and techniques of the three textiles studied here is a small contribution to a much needed survey of velvets that encompasses all periods and cultures.

Notes

1 A basic description of velvet is the following: A warp-pile weave in which the pile is produced by supplementary warp that is raised in loops through the introduction of rods during the weaving. The loops may be left as loops or cut to form tufts. See Burnham 1980, p. 163.

2 See discussion in Atasoy et al. 2001, pp. 300, 333–34, pls. 67–71. More examples are in De Jonghe *et al.* 2004, cat. V1.1, V.1.6D; Suriano, Carboni, and Peri 1999, cat. 24, pp. 80–82; Erber 1993, cat. G/31, G/32, pp. 107–9.

3 I would like to acknowledge the contribution of Nobuko Shibayama for performing the dye analysis; Mark Wypyski for conducting the metal analysis; Milton Sonday for uncountable advices and challenges; the staff of the Antonio Ratti Center and the Textile Conservation at the Metropolitan Museum of Art for their assistance; Nobuko Kajitani, Thomas Murray, Christine Giuntini, Wayne Barton, Susan Miller, Melinda Watt, Weihua Yan, and Marc Feldman for their support and encouragement.

4 In velvets of this group, each color pile warp is in its own separate channel and is always found within groups of six foundation warps. The issue of warp order with multicolor pile in relation to pile-warp channels is an important one although it cannot be sufficiently addressed in this brief essay. A typical warp order for a two-color pile Ottoman velvet is 4 foundation warps, 1 pile "A" warp, 2 foundation warps, 1 pile "B" warp. Meanwhile, a three-color pile velvet would have a warp sequence of 2 foundation warps, 1 pile "A" warp, 2 foundation warps, 1 pile "B" warp, 2 foundation warps, 1 pile "C" warp.

5 Attaching wefts can easily be seen from looking at the back of the velvets. See Milton Sonday's velvet diagram in Atasoy et al. 2001, p. 221.

6 The terminology used here for the wefts is different from that used by De Jonghe (De Jonghe *et al.* 2004) and Mackie (Atasoy et al. 2001).

7 When the thickness of the two wefts is different, the covering weft and the first weft of the vise are thinner than the covering weft and the second weft of the vise.

8 Also see De Jonghe et al. 2004, pp. 29–30, figs. 9–12.

9 Velvet weaving is done with the front of the cloth face-up. Two people, a weaver and a draw-boy, are required to weave these figured velvets. As the draw-boy lifts pile warp threads in sections according to the pattern, the weaver places pile rods between the surface of the fabric and underneath the lifted pile warp threads. Figure 4 shows the weft order, taking into account the sequence in which the pile rods are placed without showing any pile warp threads lifted over the pile rods. In weaving, pile rods would not be used in the areas voided of pile.

10 See the *cintamani* velvet analysis in De Jonghe et al. 2004, pp. 93–94, cat. V.3.23. For examples of other *cintamani* velvets, see Atasoy et al. 2001, pls. 65–66, fig. 286.

11 De Jonghe et al. 2004, pp. 13–17.

12 The dye analysis with High Performance Liquid Chromatography was performed by Nobuko Shibayama, Associate Research Scientist, Department of Scientific Research, The Metropolitan Museum of Art.

13 See Hofenk de Graaff 2004, p. 86.

14 See Berghe, Maquoi, and Wouters 2004.

15 See Böhmer and Karadag 1993, pp. 69–78.

16 Öz 1950, p. 48.

17 The metal analysis with Scanning Electron Microscopy-Energy Dispersive X-ray Spectroscopy was performed by Mark Wypsyki, Research Scientist, Department of Scientific Research, The Metropolitan Museum of Art.

18 Reath 1927, p. 298. See also description of metal thread in De Jonghe et al. 2004, p. 17.

19 See Monnas 1988.

20 See structural analysis of Italian velvets in Buss, Butazzi, and Pertegato 1983. Some of these analyses, however, were amended in more recent publications.

21 In this type of velvets, covering wefts also function to bind supplementary warps.

22 See Reath 1927, p. 298.

23 See discussion in Atasoy et al. 2001, pp. 224, 334, pl. 67.

24 De Jonghe et al. 2004, pp. 93–94, cat. V.3.23 and Atasoy et al. 2001, fig. 286.

25 I am grateful to Louise Mackie who first brought up this idea in a personal communication.

Table 1. *Weaving Analysis*

Sandra Sardjono, Assistant Conservator, Costume and Textile Department, Los Angeles County Museum of Art

MMA 12.49.5
Overall dimension: 260.5 cm length X 66.2 cm loom width
Width of side finish: 8-9 mm

Technique: cut and voided velvet with brocaded metal weft
Weave of foundation: 4+1 (1) satin
Weave of surface binding for brocaded weft: 1+4 (S) twill
Weave of side finish: 4+1 satin

	Function	Color	Material and make up	Order	Count/cm
WARPS	foundation	crimson	silk, firm Z-twist	6 foundation : 1 pile	12-13 pile tufts
	pile	crimson	silk, no twist		
	side finish	yellow	silk, firm Z-twist, paired or triple		
WEFTS	covering weft and 2nd weft of the vise	red	silk, no twist	covering weft, attaching weft, 1st weft of vise, pile rod, "gold", "gold", 2nd weft of vise	13 pile tufts or 26 "gold" brocaded wefts
	attaching weft and 1st weft of the vise	red	silk, no twist		
	brocaded "gold" weft	gilded foil, wrapped S around a light yellow silk core with S-twist			

MMA 1970.65.9
Overall dimension: 152 cm length X 64.5 cm loom width
Width of side finish: 7-8 mm

Technique: cut and voided velvet with brocaded metal and silk wefts
Weave of foundation: 4+1 (1) satin
Weave of surface binding for brocaded weft: 1+4 (S) twill
Weave of side finish: 4+1 satin

	Function	Color	Material and make up	Order	Count/cm
WARPS	foundation	crimson	silk, firm Z-twist	6 foundation : 1 pile	12 pile tufts
	pile	violet	silk, no twist		
	side finish	yellow	silk, Z-twist, paired or triple		
WEFTS	covering weft and 2nd weft of the vise	orange	silk, Z-twist, in thick bundles	covering weft, attaching weft, 1st weft of vise, pile rod, brocaded weft, brocaded weft, 2nd weft of vise	8 pile tufts or 15-16 brocaded wefts
	attaching weft and 1st weft of the vise	ivory	silk, no twist, thin		
	brocaded silk weft	yellow, blue, light blue	silk, no twist		
	brocaded "gold" weft	gilded foil, wrapped S around yellow silk core with S-twist			

CHM 1951-151-1
Overall dimension: 171.5 cm length X 65.5 cm loom width
Width of side finish: 6 mm

Technique: cut and voided velvet with brocaded metal weft
Weave of foundation: 4+1 (1) satin
Weave of surface binding for brocaded weft: 1+4 (S) twill
Weave of side finish: 4+1 satin

	Function	Color	Material and make up	Order	Count/cm
WARPS	foundation	orange	silk, firm Z-twist	6 foundation : 1 pile	12 pile tufts
	pile	violet	silk, slight S-twist		
	side finish	yellow	silk, firm Z-twist, paired or triple		
WEFTS	covering weft and 2nd weft of the vise	reddish orange	silk, S-twist, in thick bundles	covering weft, attaching weft, 1st weft of vise, pile rod, "gold", "gold", 2nd weft of vise	8 pile tufts/cm or 16 "gold" brocaded wefts
	attaching weft and 1st weft of the vise	reddish orange	silk, slight Z-twist, thin		
	brocaded "gold" weft	gilded foil, wrapped S around yellow silk core with S-twist.			

Table 2. *Dye Analysis*

Nobuko Shibayama, Associate Research Scientist, Department of Scientific Research, The Metropolitan Museum of Art, New York

Object	Description of the samples	Color	Dyes likely used	Color components detected
MMA 12.49.5	foundation warp	red	lac (*Kerria lacca* Kerr) , madder (*Rubia tinctorum* L.?)	laccaic acid, alizarin
	pile warp	red	lac (*Kerria lacca* Kerr) , madder (*Rubia tinctorum* L.?)	laccaic acid, alizarin, purpurin, other anthraquinone type coloring matters contained in madder
	side finish warp	yellow	young fustic (*Cotinus coggygria* Scop.)	3',4' 6 – trihydroxyaurone, fisetin
	covering weft and 2nd weft of the vise	red	madder (*Rubia tinctorum* L.?), gallotannin dyestuff	alizarin, purpurin, other anthraquinone type coloring matters contained in madder, ellagic acid
	attaching weft and 1st weft of the vise	red	madder (*Rubia tinctorum* L.?), gallotannin dyestuff	alizarin, purpurin, other anthraquinone type coloring matters contained in madder, ellagic acid
	silk core of brocaded "gold" weft	yellow	bastard hemp (*Datisca cannabina*, L.)?	flavonoids?, ellagic acid
MMA 1970.65.9	foundation warp	red	cochineal (Mexican or Armenian?), gallotannin dyestuff	carminic acid, ellagic acid
	pile warp	violet	madder (*Rubia tinctorum* L.?), indigo type dye, unknown red dye A'?	alizarin, purpurin, unknown color components, indigo
	side finish warp	yellow	weld (*Reseda luteola*, L.)	luteolin, apigenin, and other flavonoids contained in weld
	covering weft and 2nd weft of the vise	red	madder (*Rubia tinctorum* L.?), gallotannin dyestuff	alizarin, purpurin, other anthraquinone type coloring matters contained in madder, ellagic acid
	attaching weft and 1st weft of the vise	red	madder (*Rubia tinctorum* L.), gallotannin dyestuff	alizarin, purpurin, other anthraquinone type coloring matters contained in madder, ellagic acid
	silk core of brocaded "gold" weft	yellow	weld (*Reseda luteola* L.) and young fustic (*Cotinus coggygria* Scop.)	luteolin, apigenin, and other flavonoids contained in weld, 3',4' 6 – trihydroxyaurone
	brocaded silk weft	yellow	weld (*Reseda luteola* L.)	luteolin, apigenin, and other flavonoids contained in weld
	brocaded silk weft	blue	indigo type dye	Indigo
	brocaded silk weft	light blue	indigo type dye?	indigo? (the sample amount was too small)

CHM 1951-151-1	foundation warp	red	madder (*Rubia tinctorum* L.?) , gallotannin dyestuff	alizarin, purpurin, other anthraquinone type contained in madder, a small mount of ellagic acid
	pile warp	violet	madder (*Rubia tinctorum* L.?), indigo type dye, unknown red dye A?	alizarin, purpurin, unknown color components, indigo
	side finish warp	yellow	weld (*Reseda luteola* L.)	luteolin, apigenin, and other flavonoids
	covering weft and 2nd weft of the vise	red	madder (*Rubia tinctorum* L.?) , gallotannin dyestuff	alizarin, purpurin, some other anthraquinones contained in madder, a small amount of ellagic acid
	attaching weft and 1st weft of the vise	red	young fustic (*Cotinus coggygria* Scop.), Caesalpinia species such as sappanwood, a small amount of madder	brazilein, 3',4' 6 – trihydroxyaurone, fisetin, a small amount of alizarin
	silk core of brocaded "gold" weft	yellow	weld (*Reseda luteola* L.) and young fustic (*Cotinus coggygria* Scop.)	luteolin, apigenin, and other flavonoids contained in weld, 3',4' 6 – trihydroxyaurone

Table 3. *SEM-EDS Elemental Analysis*

By Mark Wypyski, Research Scientist, Department of Scientific Research, The Metropolitan Museum of Art, New York

MMA 12.49.5
The metal strip was found to be gilded silver, with an average width of approximately 0.25 mm. Gilding was found on both sides of the metal strip. EDS analysis performed on a cleaned area of the silver found it to be relatively pure, with a composition of 99.5 % silver and 0.5 % copper.

MMA 1970.65.9
The metal strip was found to be gilded silver, with an average width of approximately 0.12 mm. Gilding was found on both sides of the metal strip. EDS analysis performed on a cleaned area of the silver found it to contain a small amount of copper as well, with a composition of 99.0 % silver and 1.0 % copper.

CHM 1951-151-1
The metal strip was found to be gilded silver, with an average width of approximately 0.27 mm. Gilding was found on both sides of the metal strip. EDS analysis performed on a cleaned area of the silver strip found it to be relatively pure, with a composition of 99.6 % silver and 0.4 % copper.

Venice's Textile and Carpet Trade: The Role of Jewish Merchants

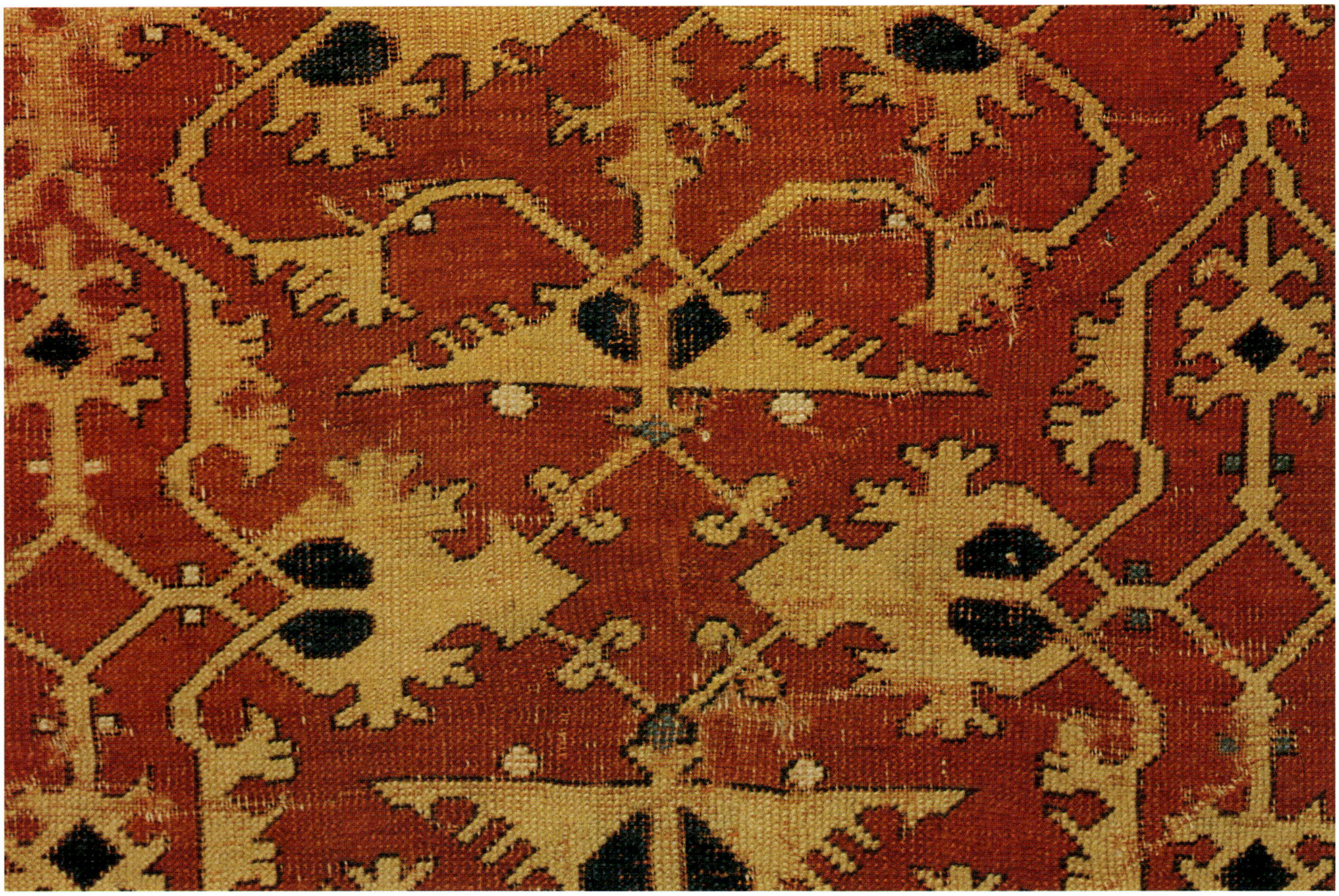

Giovanni Curatola

In addition to spices, the core of East-West trade revolved around textiles. Venice played a double role in this major commerce, as a center of production and a center of exchange. Indeed, even during its periods of greatest inland expansion the Republic never developed an infrastructure for providing raw materials that could compare with the infrastructures of its powerful competitors, so it was therefore in the realm of the transformation of raw materials—in particular wool and silk—that Venice managed to acquire a predominant role.

Despite a distinctly protectionist policy based on a great many laws and regulations issued down through the centuries in order to guarantee its own citizens' privileges (application for Venetian citizenship could be made after 20 years of continuous business activity in the city), the Republic was always careful to cultivate the services of those who, in one way or another, were likely to increase its wealth. Such was the case with silk workshops, whose local development began in 1314 when 32 families from Lucca—members of the Guelph faction—immigrated with their looms to the lagoon.[1] These artisans embodied the heritage of a highly important tradition in Italy, one marked by Oriental influences thanks to the stylistic similarity of their textiles with those from the workshops in Palermo. In 1336 a specialized magistracy was instituted to control the production of silk fabrics,[2] and by 1380 regulations sought to prevent the emigration of weavers specialized in the production of silk and gold-brocade textiles.

Many documents pertaining to textiles have survived in Venice, a city that exported woolen fabrics and imported raw silk and cotton from Flanders. From London and the rest of England it also imported the famous *carisee,* that is to say kersey fabric, whose zones of production progressively extended to include other countries, to the point where some cloth has even been identified as coming from Romania. Venice probably imported various types of kersey, including those woven with silk wastes. In addition to quantities and prices, these documents supply a good deal of information, such as the repeated exhortation—almost like a litany—to buy only the finest quality materials. Terminology in the sphere of textiles is particularly complex, as witnessed by the inventory of a Venetian draper's shop drawn up in the mid-

cat. 84. *Carpet with "Lotto" pattern* (detail)

17th century, recently published by Doretta Davanzo Poli.[3] It provides an idea of the incredible variety of merchandise offered by Bortolo Cargoni in his shop at the sign *Allo Struzzo d'Oro.*[4] Oriental textiles were widespread in Venice by that time. When Marco Polo—who can hardly go unmentioned—died in 1324, he bequeathed to his daughter not only *zendadi* (or *zenale, cendale, cendato, cendà*)[5] which were *blanchi catai,* but also others that were yellow, red (with a rose pattern), and black, as well as a piece of *chamoca blava a bele ovre,*[6] some white silk, and a *chocholario, drapo de seda a straniii animali, nasizo.* The highly interesting term *nasizo*—similar to *nassiccio*—derives from the Arabic *nasîj,*[7] close to *nacco* (*nachetto*), itself derived from *nakhkh,* that is to say, "mat, rug, carpet."

Doge Francesco Dandolo, meanwhile, on his death in 1339 left magnificent garments, including one described—perhaps for the first time—as made of *veluto, vermeio e viride* (red and green velvet). There were also mentions of *samito, cendato, catasamito, camochchac,* and *cambloto.* The last word occurs in various forms (*cammellotto, cambellotto, zambellotto, giamellotto*) and refers to a cloth woven of camel hair, angora, or perhaps even a silk-wool blend.[8]

Ostentatious luxury was discouraged by sumptuary laws,[9] notably by a 1334 *parte* (decree having the force of law) that outlawed *"vestes vel varnimenta aliqua de panno ad aurum laborato ad acu, nec de nassiccio"* (jackets or other garments of fabrics brocaded with gold, including *nassiccio*). An exception was allowed, however, for up to two wedding outfits of velvet. In the 15th century, among the fabrics recurring most often in gift exchanges, we might cite various names whose etymology clearly indicates an Oriental origin—*scarlato, ormesino, fustaneo, mocagiari, panno, caixea, veluto videlicet zetani, damaschino, mussola.* The same is true of *baldacchini* (or *baldechini*) made in Baudac (or Bagad, or Baldac—that is to say, Baghdad), which Marco Polo described as *"lavori di seta e d'oro in drappi a bestie e uccelli"* (cloths of silk and gold patterned with animals and birds).[10] Their typology is similar to the motifs of medallions with fighting animals, typical of the workshops in Lucca, which weavers from that city had brought to Venice.[11]

Italian terminology for clothing is rich in lexical vestiges that recall the Near East, such as *giubba* (jacket), *caffettano* (caftan), and *tabarro* (cloak), just a few of the words attesting to contact with the Orient. Colors also had considerable importance, and among the most frequently cited we find *paonazzo* (a shade of violet-blue, perhaps inspired by peacock feathers), *beretino* (a shade of blue also used in ceramics),[12] *viride* (green), *albo* (white), *nigrum* (black), *grana* (cochineal, the name of a red dye),[13] *turchino, blavo* (blue), *morelo* (purple), and *cremexino* (a blood red, highly appreciated along with *carminio* [crimson][14] and *rubeo* [ruby]). Evidence of this fashion is easy to detect in artworks, as seen in paintings by the Bellini and Carpaccio, where Islamic influence is particularly noticeable (to mention only the pseudo-inscriptions on garments).[15]

The 15th-century records of the Governatori delle Pubbliche Entrate, or tax department, offer a good insight into the problems that Venetian authorities had to solve when it to came to commercial trade in such large volumes.[16]

The magistracy charged with monitoring trade was the Cinque Savi alla Mercanzia,[17] whose records are of great interest. Also worth mentioning is the fact that its jurisdiction extended to Jewish citizens originally from the Mediterranean basin (Levantines), whereas Jews of German origin came within the purview of the Ufficiali al Cattaver.[18] The issue of Jews will be discussed below. Obviously, the Cinque Savi alla Mercanzia had to deal with many questions, some of them concerning merchandise imported from the Orient,[19] notably *"robbe che vengono condotte in questa città dalla Romania Alta e Bassa dai mercadanti levantini"* (merchandise imported from Upper and Lower Romania by Levantine merchants). The magistracy extended for a period of two years the rules and restrictions pertaining to *"sede Belgrado, Vallona, zambellotti, mocaiari, cordovani, montanine, cuori d'ogni sorte desconzi, schiavaine, vallonie, carisee di ponente."*[20] Similarly, a great number of rulings concern customs duties; indeed, one of the main forms of tax evasion involved simply transporting merchandise through the port of Venice (where it returned after having been temporarily warehoused somewhere else), or having it shipped without paying taxes to the *cottimo* (of which there were three—Alexandria, Damascus, and London) by registering it in the name of foreigners. The actual sale of such merchandise could give rise to difficulties, and could not be performed directly if one of the merchants was a foreigner: it then required an authorized intermediary (*sensale*), specialized in certain products.[21] We know that merchandise subsequently passed through a lazaretto, where it was quarantined for a period dictated by Venice's strict health regulations, designed to shield the city from frequent epidemics. A document dated January 23, 1589,[22] contains a passage relating to this health issue, involving a request from *sanseri* (merchants) who sought authorization to enter lazarettos and ships at anchor, accompanied by guards, as had been done in the past (with the obvious intent of getting a jump on the competition). Such permission had been granted to those merchants *"che fanno senseria con Turchi, Armeni et altra simel gente"* (who trade with Turks, Armenians, and other people of that kind); these merchants had been accompanied by guards who, despite everything, were unable to intervene: *"però che parlando il più detti sanseri in turchescho et altre lingue che dalli fanti dell'officio non sono intese, possono facilmente così per questa come per altra causa succeder diversi scandali"* (insofar as said *sanseri* speak above all Turkish and other languages that the guards do not understand, problems may easily arise for that reason, as well as for others). Obviously, this new request was denied and severe penalties were set for violators.

One of the most interesting and most surprising aspects of the relations between Venice and the Orient was linked to the importation of carpets, a subject I have addressed elsewhere.[23] Not only was the carpet trade important, but it also involved the Jewish community, and not only the one in Venice. Studying the way this trade worked is like opening a window onto Venetian society, particularly from the late 15th century onwards. Carpets are mentioned fairly frequently in archive documents, in a consistent way, particularly in inventories of goods belonging to leading families—and only to those families. Carpets clearly constituted a key feature of their estates. In contrast, descriptive detail is very brief, and when size is mentioned it is given in general terms ("large" or "small"); the same is true of function, whether for the floor, to cover a chest, a *scagno* (stool), or table. Their typology was linked to provenance: *caiarino, caierino, cagierino, cagarin* (meaning from Cairo, probably from the term used for the Mamluks), or *cimischasa, cimicasa, cimiscasa* (from Chemishgezek, a village in central-western Anatolia, according to Michael Rogers),[24] or indeed *moschetti* (for the pseudo-Mamluks from Damascus); or typology might be based on the size of "rosettes" (in which case they might refer to Holbein carpets, with patterns of variable sizes). An admittedly late document, dated June 13, 1763,[25] mentions customs duties applicable in Smyrna—expressed in *aspri,* at an exchange rate of 110 *aspri* to one *leone,* or Venetian ducat)—in which, among roughly one hundred categories, we find *tappeti con pelo* (3 1/2 or 2 1/2 or 6 *aspri* apiece), followed by *tappeti della prima qualità, della seconda, della terza* (respectively, 54 *aspri* each for prime quality, 36 for second best, and 18 for third best). As to the *tappeti rigati detti chiliri* mentioned in this same document, I think they must refer to kilims. In these inventories, which merit careful examination, we come across a certain number of terms including *celone* and, more frequently, *stratto* (or *strato*), which Niccolò Tommaseo's famous Italian dictionary defined as *"tappeto o panno che si distende in terra, o altrove, in segno d'onoranza"* (carpet or piece of cloth spread on the ground, or elsewhere, as a mark of honor), which explains the custom of using a *stratto* at Mass (*"habbiano alla Messa l'uso d'un stratto"*).

Camillo Nalin, a popular 19th-century poetaster, described the Festa dei Pugni, celebrated each year in the Dorsoduro district, on the bridge of the same name between Campo San Barnaba and Campo Santa Margherita, as follows: *"Se scomenza abonora / da pergoli e balconi a metter fora / dove che sta i signori / tapei, damaschi, strati / e rossi e verdi e a fiori / de mille e più segnati."*[26] Poetry by such rhymesters includes verses as evocative as they are entertaining: *"Tira su la rebalta ogni botega / e con tapei de Spagna e cagiarini / fa bella mostra e onor"*;[27] and *"O quante de custie co i drappi indosso / tiolte dal strazziarol, o dal zudio / se fa più mamaluchi correr drio / che no fa cani el rosegar d'un osso."*[28]

Here, then, we have a reference to *strazzaria* and Jews, who are central to the issue. Much has been written on Venice and the Jews,[29] and the Most Serene Republic's ambivalent policies towards them are well known. If Jews were confined to the ghetto, and if tolerated rather than protected (and, for that matter, never sure of the future), it was because with their *banchi di imprestito* they facilitated the circulation of money, a crucial activity in a city dedicated to trade. People preferred to borrow from Jews (who could be exploited in various ways) rather than the charitable pawn establishments known as Montes Pietatis (which would have given the Church—and therefore the pope—some control over sources of credit). Jews had to live and work in the ghetto, and the trades they could practice outside it were limited to pawnbroking, medicine, and *strazzaria,* that is to say selling secondhand goods.[30] The *mariegola,* or statutes, governing this latter activity—which was important, if limited—expressly mentioned that it could be performed by Jews; the statutes also list carpets among the goods permitted for resale. Describing this trade, Tommaso Garzoni wrote: *"Hà commercio sopra tutto con gli Hebrei d'ogni sorte, tanto del paese, quanto Levantini,*[31] *perché tutti i stracci fanno recapito in ghetto, come le ciauatte à Novara: e tutti i bazari, ò scauezzacolli, ò baratterie si trovano presso à loro, come i giuochi, e le furberie nelle baccane."*[32] Shakespeare's Shylock inevitably comes to mind when reading the following opinion on secondhand dealers who obviously practiced a trade similar, and sometimes identical, to moneylending: *"Non hanno i stracciaruoli altra cosa di buono in loro, se non che aiutano in un bisogno uno che stia per annegarsi: ma l'aiuto è tanto sinistro, che dall'appendersi ai spini, e à loro c'è poca differenza affatto."*[33] Although the object of menacing contempt, the Jewish merchants who indulged in this trade (pretentiously defined as "the finest profession in the world") organized and defended themselves so well that some of them managed to acquire reputations as *mercanti di gran negozio* entitled to do business with *"diversi nobeli e delli principali di questa eccelsa repubblica"*—such merchants included Isaac Luzzatto, Iseppo della Baldosa, Orso della Man, and Isacco dalla Vida. The latter was highly active in the late 16th century as a furniture dealer (notably during festive celebrations, which was moreover an obligation imposed on the Jewish community, mentioned several times in the *Condotta,* that is to say the collection of laws and duties imposed on Jews by the Venetian Senate).[34] He made repeated requests for authorization to open a shop on the quay overlooking the Rio di Cannaregio (near today's Ponte delle Guglie), hence accessible from both the ghetto and the quay, so that Christians would not be obliged to cross the Jewish quarter to reach his place of business. Moreover, the exercise of this profession gave rise to constant litigation, perhaps epitomized by the admittedly somewhat bold assertion by a used-goods dealer brought to justice—and convicted—in 1568: *"Che noi altri strazzarioli podemo tegnir ogni sorte de robbe, cha sian stà vendute una volta"* (We secondhand dealers can trade in all kinds of merchandise having already been sold one time). This would imply that they had the right to trade in every sphere. Such a claim might justify the 1577 decree specifically prohibiting Jews from buying or selling gold, silver, and jewelry.[35]

Documents concerning legal proceedings in the mid-16th century over carpets have recently been published,[36]certain aspects of which are distinctly interesting, notably the fact that in Cairo there existed, as Tommaso Garzoni reported, workshops placed under the direct control of Venice, which stipulated that *"i tappeti vogliono esser belli di disegno, e haver vaghi colori, e bassi di pelo"* (the carpets must be of handsome design, fine colors, and of shaven wool). Although sources of supply were diverse, Jews exercised control over a luxury item—one of the first to be pawned during straitened times. It is thus natural that Lorenzo Lotto depicted such carpets in his Saint Antonius altarpiece (1542, Church of Santi Giovanni e Paolo, Venice).[37] The well-known story of the purchase of carpets in Venice in 1518 by Cardinal Wolsey, Henry VIII's highly powerful chancellor, who was only able to obtain them after exhausting diplomatic negotiations that lasted several years, attests to the unique role of trade center played by the Republic at that time.[38]

Despite the loss of many documents on the role of Jews in Venetian trade, certain surviving evidence nevertheless indicates its importance. For example, there is an assertion that

Jews in Egypt were dealing in spices on a wholesale basis before the spices reached Alexandria, which obliged the Venetians to open a consulate in Cairo in 1555.[39] And yet the Jews did not always act alone. Thus a memorandum dated 1560 described mixed companies trading between Syria and Cyprus, composed of Jews and Christians.[40] These companies notably enjoyed the advantage—thanks to varying statuses (Jews being designated as *cittadini del sig. Turcho*)—of dodging taxes. "They need only do *consolazo,* and are not obliged to send [merchandise] to Venice, but may do so to Fiume, Ancona, Ferrara, and they pay neither duty nor *cottimo,* in such manner that they impoverish the Republic and enrich Ancona and Ferrara." And, "what is more important, they can conduct their business at the *fontego.*"

It is worth mentioning the vast emigration of Jews from the Iberian peninsula after 1492, in realtion to the carpets painted by Vittore Carpaccio in his famous *St. Ursula* cycle now hanging in the Accademia. The years when the artist was painting this series were precisely those when a great number of Jews arrived, and although it is impossible to document the claim, it is nonetheless tempting to assert that the carpets he depicted came not from Anatolia, as was long believed, but from Spain, inspired by Turkish models. In the same cycle—specifically, in the canvas titled *The Meeting with the Pope*—Carpaccio painted a Jew who is recognizable by his wide-brimmed black hat, worn over a red skullcap. This is just one of many Oriental references by a singular artist whose oeuvre teems with visual allusions to an Orient that was truly at home in Venice.

Relations with Persia, on the other hand, were sporadic, and that country never played an important role in the Republic's commercial dealings, as confirmed in the realm of carpets. Indeed, although Giosafat Barbaro mentioned them during his visit to Tabriz and referred to "Moorish carpets" (1473–78),[41]no document attests to their arrival in Venice prior to the early 17th century when, in 1603, Shah 'Abbas sent one as a gift to the Signoria, accompanied by the recommendation that "each time the Treasury [of Saint Mark's] is displayed outside, it may be placed on this carpet, to its greater beauty."[42] It was, moreover, on the same occasion that Venice received a silk brocade with decoration inspired by a Christian theme (Madonna and Child), now in the Museo Civico Correr.[43] This carpet—also in silk and silver thread—is interesting for its floral motif, whose less than strict symmetry suggests that it was executed from a drawing rather than from a squared-up cartoon.

Thus, Persian carpets benefited from an exotic aura compared to the hundreds, indeed thousands, of rugs that arrived from Anatolia and passed through the hands of travelers and merchants, including Jews.

Notes

1 Bini 1854.
2 Cecchetti 1866.
3 Davanzo Poli 2001.
4 The inventory lists 50 types of fabrics, whose names are still highly difficult to translate: *truffaldà, drapo d'oro richo, samis brocado d'oro, richamo latesin ariento, lastre d'oro ariento, raseti senza cordon, raso cremese, raso latado, raso nero, detto colorado, raso brochado nerro, rigadin nero, satiglioni e rasi brochadi neri, damaschin nero, ochieto, e seghadin, canevazeto nero, raso in opera nero, raso in opera e ochieto, cameloto e raso in opera nero, schachiglia, schacho seda e stame, raso brochado nero, raseto, bavelin nero, terzanela dopia, detta ordenaria, cendà alto, cendal rasado sguardo, detto nero e colorado, spumiglia, ormesin colorado alto a raso, tabini di parangon, detti color di cremese, detto bastardo, detto basso, ormesin tabinadi, ormesin tabin verde, tabin verde basso, ferandine, amuer con ariento, detto cremese oro, amuer in opera neri, detto schieto, cameloto di seda, satiglioni in opera, drogheto seda e lana, detti alla moda, felpa machada, cendeline.*
5 A silk fabric perhaps originating from Sind, similar to taffeta (whose name comes from Persia, more precisely from Taft, a village near Yazd, renowned for its silk industry).
6 Finely worked blue silk.
7 Literally, woven fabric, cloth, material.
8 Marin Sanudo mentioned a great many exchanges of gifts between Ottoman and Venetian ambassadors. See, for example, in the appendix of this volume, pp. 370–72, texts cited in vol. 5, cols. 50 and 993; vol. 15, col. 195; vol. 17. cols. 521 and 545–546; and vol. 47, col. 135.
9 Bistort 1912.
10 Brunello 1986, p. 111.
11 Gabrieli and Scerrato 1979, p. 225. According to Gabrieli, the word *baldracca* (woman of easy virtue, prostitute) strangely shares the same etymology.
12 See the essay by Maria Vittoria Fontana in this catalogue.
13 Cochineal was highly sought after, and its purity had to be monitored, as witnessed by a document dated October 17, 1557: "The cochineals from that city of the Levant in our possession are almost all brought by Jews and, as already mentioned, carry with them various filth, including leaves and bird droppings." Archivio di Stato di Venezia, Cinque Savi, b. 62, f. 165, I. This long text continues by proposing fines of 50 ducats and calling for strict monitoring by the customs officers at the *dogana da mar.*
14 In this case, the term also has an Oriental—more specifically, Persian—etymology, in reference to the small worm ("vermilion") used to make another shade of red dye.
15 Curatola 2003.
16 Archivio di Stato di Venezia, Governatori delle Pubbliche Entrate—466 (38): smuggled silk; 467 (76): duties on white *gottoni* from Turkey; (81/82): velvet smuggling; (94): *mocagiari* (fine fabrics, usually black, with warp of silk and weft of wool); (103): velvet; (117): *gottoni*; (122): smuggled silk (Turkish merchandise); (218): silk. Other files describe lawsuits and disputes with Jews—466 (37): ruling on a dispute concerning a measure of *grana;* 467 (78): Jewish merchants; 469 (183): sale of crimson to Jews. Other documents are also of interest—467 (101): smuggled *zaffare* (ceramics); (147): gold rings brought into Venice; 470 (207): prohibition of maiolica ware from Ravenna; 471 (239): smuggled glass. In 1559 (b. 467, f. 108), a suit was even brought against Domenego Mantoan—known as "the Red"—for smuggling cheese made in Piacenza!
17 Borgherini Scarabellin, 1925.
18 The difficult relations between the two magistracies can be clearly detected in Archivio di Stato di Venezia, Cinque Savi alla Mercanzia, b. 62, f. 165.
19 Archivio di Stato di Venezia, Cinque Savi; folders 639–42: Cairo (years 1745–75); folders 555–56: letters from the *bailo* in Constantinople 1679–97); folders 947–48: Capitular from the *cottimo* in Damascus 1490–1684); folder 965: Venetian merchants established in Aleppo; folder 958: account books of Giacomo Badoer, established in Constantinople, 1436–39 (see Dorini and Bertelé, 1956); folder 966: legal and administrative decisions concerning Armenians, Germans, Turks; folder 968: convoys of commercial galleys 1586–1698.
20 Archivio di Stato di Venezia, Cinque Savi, b. 62, f. 165/1, July 16, 1545.
21 Vercellin 1980.
22 Archivio di Stato di Venezia, Cinque Savi, b. 62, f. 114.
23 Curatola 1986, 1991, 1999, 2004a, 2004b.
24 Rogers 1986, p. 18, n. 19. Giosafat Barbaro passed through this region, but without mentioning carpets; Lockhart, Morozzo della Rocca and Tiepolo 1973, p. 163.
25 Archivio di Stato di Venezia, Cinque Savi, I, b. 369, 4 c.
26 At dawn people commence / draping windows and balconies / of stately dwellings / with carpets, damasks, and *strati* / all red, green, and flowery / and so much more.
27 Every shop draws its curtain / with carpets from Spain and from Cairo / thus bedecking itself with honor.
28 "Many of the [ladies] who wear such garments / bought from the *strazzariol* or the Jew / are followed by *mammaluchi* [young people] / who [worry them] like a dog worries a bone." My emphasis. Quoted in Livingston 1912, pp. 163–188.
29 An excellent overview of the question can be found in *Atti del Convegno internazionale di S. Giorgio maggiore*, Venice (June 5–10, 1983); see also Cozzi 1987. Also worth citing is Arbel 1995.
30 Pullan 1982, pp. 605–6.
31 The question of these Levantines has been the subject of much study. They were usually Jews who had fled Spain and Portugal in the late 15th century, and who passed through Venice—where they were known and often had family ties—before heading on to Salonica or Constantinople, thereby becoming subjects of the Ottoman sultan and hence earning a right of safe-conduct, which Venice was more or less obliged to respect. See Rozen 1993.
32 Garzoni 1587, discourse CLIII: "This trade was above all performed by Jews of all kinds, both local people and Levantines, because all the rags wound up in the ghetto, the way old shoes wind up in Novara. And all the business, trade, and barter is done with them like some game of chance."
33 "The *stracciaroli* are good-for-nothings, at best they might come to the aid of a drowning man, but even then with such clumsiness that it would be not unlike grasping thorns."
34 Curatola 1986, p. 127.
35 Archivio di Stato di Venezia, Archivio alle Arti, Arte dei calegheri, 7.
36 Curatola 2004a.
37 Zampetti 1969, p. 74.
38 Beattie 1964, pp. 4–15.
39 Lane 1978, p. 347.
40 Biblioteca del Museo Correr, Ms PD 397, c. 45.
41 Lockhart, Morozzo della Rocca, and Tiepolo 1973.
42 Gallo 1967, pp. 264–265.
43 Curatola 1993.

Master Mahmud and Inlaid Metalwork in the 15th Century

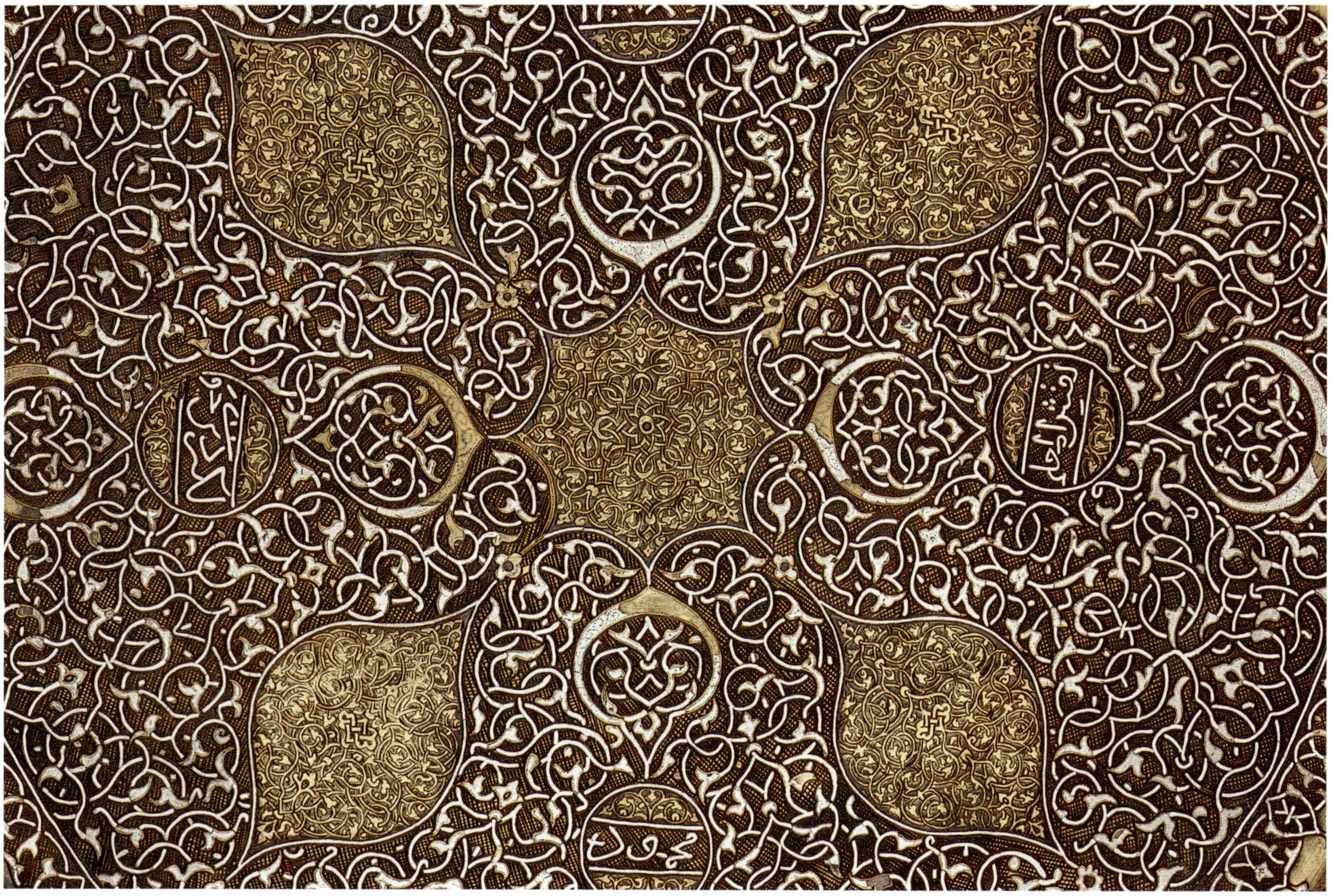

Sylvia Auld

Inlaid metalwork from the Levant became popular in Italy during the 15th century. In the following period its popularity spread north, until a fashion for a design of scrolling vegetal stems and knots pervaded almost every type of European artifact—from textiles to ceramics, from architectural ornamentation to glassware. It is possible to make this bald statement not merely because of the evidence of contemporary paintings, for example by Giovanni and Gentile Bellini, Leonardo da Vinci, and Lorenzo Lotto,[1] but also because of the sheer number of objects including domestic inlaid metal that still exist in museums and other collections (see cats. 92 and 111, p. 214). So widespread are they in Europe that, for reasons explained below, the inlaid metalwares came to be known as "Veneto-Saracenic."[2] By contrast, there are remarkably few such objects in Levantine collections. In order to understand their appeal, it is necessary to take a mental step back in time and in perspective. We are used now to thinking of the countries east of the Mediterranean as being somehow "less" sophisticated, "less" rich, and "less" powerful. This was not so from the 12th to the 17th centuries. In that period, for the rulers of Europe, Muslim forces seemed intent on moving into their territory: the Ayyubids and then the Mamluks were in firm control of Egypt, that indispensable source of cotton, spices, and grain, and of the holy places of Syria and Palestine; and there were successive new threats from the east, by the Mongols, the Timurids, and then the Ottomans. The drive westwards culminated in the final defeat of the Byzantine Empire with the conquest of Constantinople in 1453 by Mehmet II; by 1529 Ottoman forces were at the very gates of Vienna—and in the 1530s even Rome appeared under threat.[3] It was not merely at a political, and thus by extension a religious level (for the one implied the other), that Islam seemed more successful. European visitors to the Turkoman, Ottoman, and Mamluk courts reported back in awe of the riches, the beauty of the buildings, the high level of civilization (street lighting, medical care, diet, cleanliness, learning), and the discipline of the armed forces. The West, in addition, needed the East; among other essentials and luxuries, imported spices were required not merely to make a dish palatable but also for medicine. These had to be transported across the sea in watertight containers.

cat. 101. Mahmud al-Kurdi
Salver (detail)

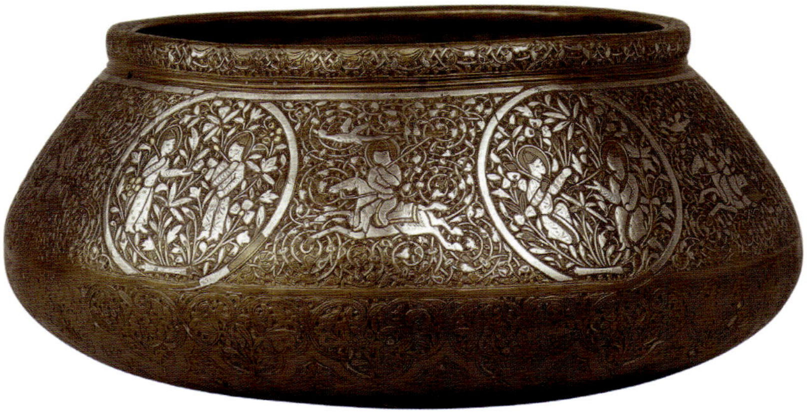

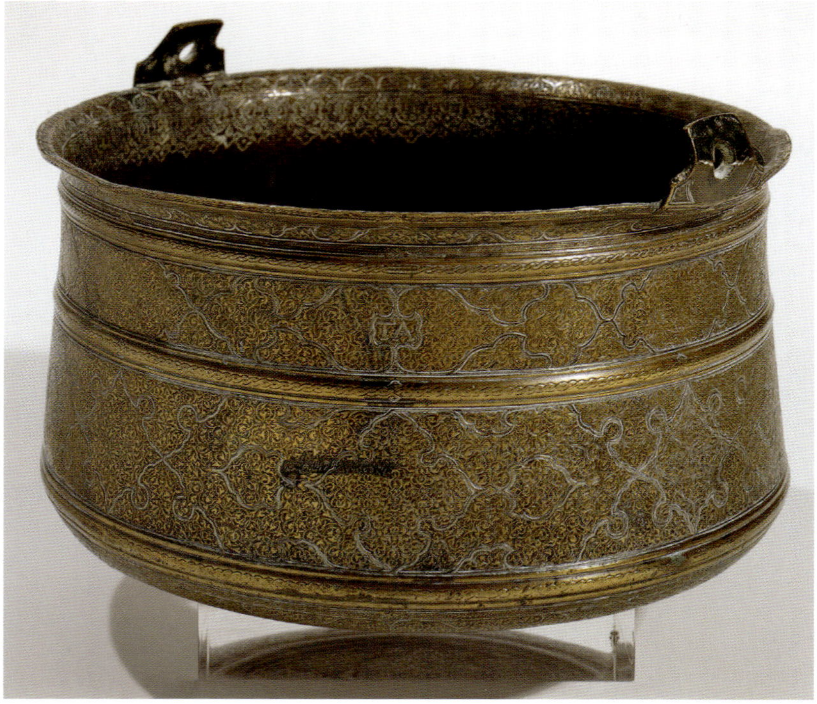

cat. 92. *Bowl*
Iran, probably Shiraz, mid-14th century
Museum für Islamische Kunst, Berlin

cat. 111. *Bucket*
Islamic Near East or possibly Venice, 16th century
Brass inlaid with silver
Museo Nazionale del Bargello, Florence

Politics on the whole did not interfere with trade, and the precious substances were avidly imported into the West through Venice and other seaports on the Mediterranean coast.[4] Like other Italian city-states such as Pisa and Genoa, the Venetian Republic signed successive trading treaties with Mamluk Egypt despite repeated papal injunctions, and their lead was followed by Florence.[5] The Egyptian sultan provided these trading partners with centers (*fondachi*) in Alexandria and Damietta, and later in Cairo, as well as in Aleppo and Damascus. Young men from the leading Venetian families were sent to the Levantine cities not just to learn their trade,[6] but also as a final stage in preparation for life, much like the Grand Tour of the 18th and 19th centuries.[7] In this way, despite a supposedly strict segregation from the local inhabitants, Europeans came to appreciate—and to buy—Muslim artifacts. This probably accounts for some of the number of Mamluk boxes, spherical incense burners, candlesticks, salvers, and ewers that came into European collections. Trade treaties also necessitated an exchange of diplomatic missions to negotiate them. It was so much the custom of the period to present gifts at these times that the negotiations for a new treaty between Egypt and Venice in 1506–7 which did not include them provoked a deal of contemporary comment.[8] This custom may be an explanation for the presence of some of the objects in European collections.[9] It is possible, for example, that a small spherical incense burner in the Museo Correr in Venice may be connected with the Egyptian envoy to Venice at this time, a man called Taghribirdi, one of whose titles was *al-sayfi,* "Sword-Bearer." The incense burner has a Mamluk composite blazon, one element of which is a sword.[10] An embassy to Lorenzo the Magnificent in 1487 included among its gifts *"una grande ampolio di balsami . . . vaso grandi di confectione, mirabolani e giengituo."*[11]

Unfortunately there is no account of how the balsam, sweetmeats, and spices were presented. Presumably the ampoule of balsam was made of glass, but the sweetmeats, myrabolan, and ginger were probably carried in airtight metal containers to preserve their freshness. The association of an exceptional exoticism with these gifts may well have added value to the containers themselves and this may help to explain why the technique of inlaying a base metal with a precious one with arabesques came to be so widely copied by European craftsmen.

Although documents on Islamic manufacturing techniques are tantalizingly rare in both East and West, the comments that have been preserved are of the highest praise for the skill of the Muslim craftsmen. Simone Sigoli, a visitor to Damascus in the mid-1380s, was so enthused by the local crafts—"some of the most beautiful things in the world"—that he added "if you had money in the bones of your leg, without fail you would break it to buy these things."[12] In particular his comments on inlaid metalwares show an appreciation of the way they were made. "Here also are made a great many brass basins and pitchers, and really they appear of gold, and then on the said basins and pitchers are made figures and foliage and other fine work in silver, so that it is a very beautiful thing to see."[13] A French diplomat visiting Cairo in 1511–12 in the company of Louis XII's ambassador commented that "the work always took precedence over the material."[14] Even the notoriously self-congratulatory Benvenuto Cellini was impressed by the skill shown in the manufacture of a number of small metal daggers, which he described as *"turcheschi";* they were, he wrote, "engraved . . . with patterns of beautiful foliage in the Turkish style, which were nicely filled with gold."[15] Giorgio Vasari too commented that inlaid metalwork from Damascus was "excellent."[16]

It is clear that these inlaid objects were equally highly regarded in the Levant. Al-Maqrizi reported that "people [in Egypt in the first half of the 14th century] were very eager to buy inlaid bronzes and I have seen so many of them that their sheer quantity beggars description. There was hardly a house in Cairo and in Egypt which did not possess several inlaid bronzes."[17] Although by the early years of the 1400s fewer of these wares were being made (probably because of a local silver shortage), their manufacture had picked up again by the latter years of the century. One example is a magnificent basin made for the Egyptian sultan Qa'itbey, embellished with gold and silver inlays.[18]

It was not just the manufacturing skills that appealed to both East and West. Complexity of design and an ability to create a sense of wonder in the viewer were also considered essential ingredients. In 1544, a Persian commentator wrote in a preface to an album of paintings that "if a form is not worthy of astonishment, it is not worth a touch of the brush."[19] An underlying geometric constraint combined with an ambiguity in design produced a mental puzzle of the sort that delighted equally the *cognoscenti* of the courts of both East and West. In late Timurid and Turkoman Persia, the traditional belief was that geometry "enlightened the intellect and set one's mind right."[20] In Italy, 16th-century intellectuals and painters were still basing their ideas on Fibonacci, whose *Liber Quadratorum* encouraged men like Leonardo da Vinci and Piero da Francesca to write their own treatises on mathematics and perspective. It is also possible that in Europe there came to be an aura of a talismanic, or at least of apotropaic, value in the Islamic objects. The lid of one round-bottomed box was pierced at some point after manufacture, and illegible "islamizing" inscriptions added in four roundels.[21]

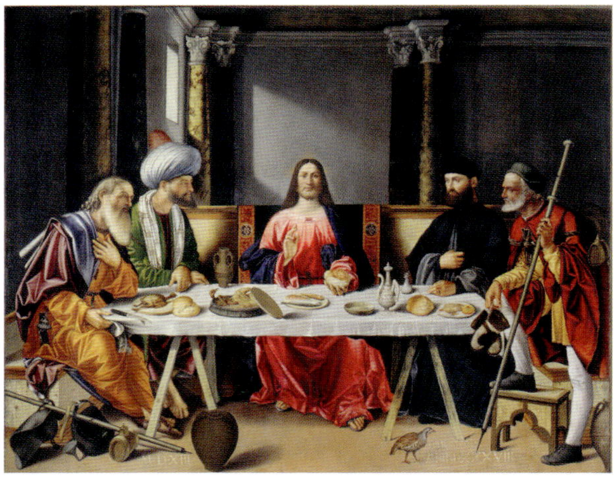

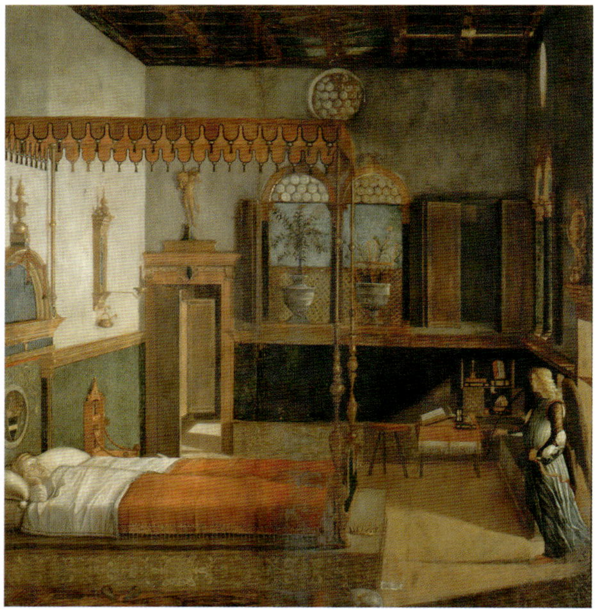

fig. 1. Vittore Carpaccio (attr.), *The Supper at Emmaus,* 1513. Church of San Salvador, Venice

fig. 2. Vittore Carpaccio, *The Dream of St. Ursula,* 1490. Gallerie dell'Accademia, Venice

This is not as extraordinary as it might seem at first, because in the Islamic world knots were believed to have a protective function, and there is some evidence that the scrolling arabesque stems were seen as having planetary associations. Some of the patterns were referred to as "conjunctions" or "knots" (Arabic *ʿuqda*, Persian *girih*); this term has a similar connotation as the Latin word *nodus* (English "node"), which can denote not only a knot but also the orbit of a planet, the place where a leaf is attached to a stem, the point at which a curve intersects itself, or the place where lines and circles meet. It is also probable that there was some underlying meaning to a circle of six fish, their heads pointed towards a central point, an example of which is found on a small box and cover in the Correr Museum (inv. CE XII, 36). This device, known in the West as "fish-pond," is reasonably common in Mamluk metalwork, particularly bowls and boxes. It was believed that waters lay above and below the earth and that the fish thus refer to the heavens; there are contemporary inscriptions in which the sky is called "the fount of the sun."[22]

It is interesting to note here the essential dissimilarity between European and Islamic modes of seeing: whereas the Islamic name for arabesques is never related to specific varieties of plant, the Italian Benvenuto Cellini was analyzing different leaf designs and their origins on the scrolling stems. In Lombardy, he says, they use bryony and ivy (*ellera, vitalba*); in Tuscany and Rome, acanthus (*acanto*), while the Turks use only arum and sunflowers (*gichero, fiorellini di clizia*).[23]

Pilgrims were probably the first collectors of *objets d'art* from the Levant. In addition to textiles, which took on the sanctity of the relics they wrapped, caskets, incense burners, salvers, goblets, and ewers in ivory, metal, enamels, and rock crystal were brought back to Europe and deposited in cathedral treasuries. The majority of these—as might be expected—are from Mamluk Syria and Egypt before ca. 1500. Some of the metalwork pieces appear in paintings as props, presumably to add authenticity to a biblical setting. A Mamluk metal beaker, for example, is shown in the attic section of Giovanni Bellini's *Lamentation over the Dead Christ;*[24] a low Mamluk bowl is depicted on the table in *The Supper at Emmaus,* attributed to Carpaccio, which has now been restored and reinstalled in the Church of San Salvador in Venice (fig. 1). Carpaccio depicts a bucket, similar to one in this exhibition (see cat. 111, p. 214), beside the bed in *The Dream of St. Ursula*[25] (fig. 2). This Venetian painter's cycle of St. George in the Scuola degli Schiavoni includes an image of St. Jerome (or St. Augustine) in his library. Either authentic Levantine or Western copies of rosewater sprinklers (*qumqum*) (see cat. 98) stand on a shelf to the right of the figure, as do candlesticks and a small bucket.[26] It was not just in

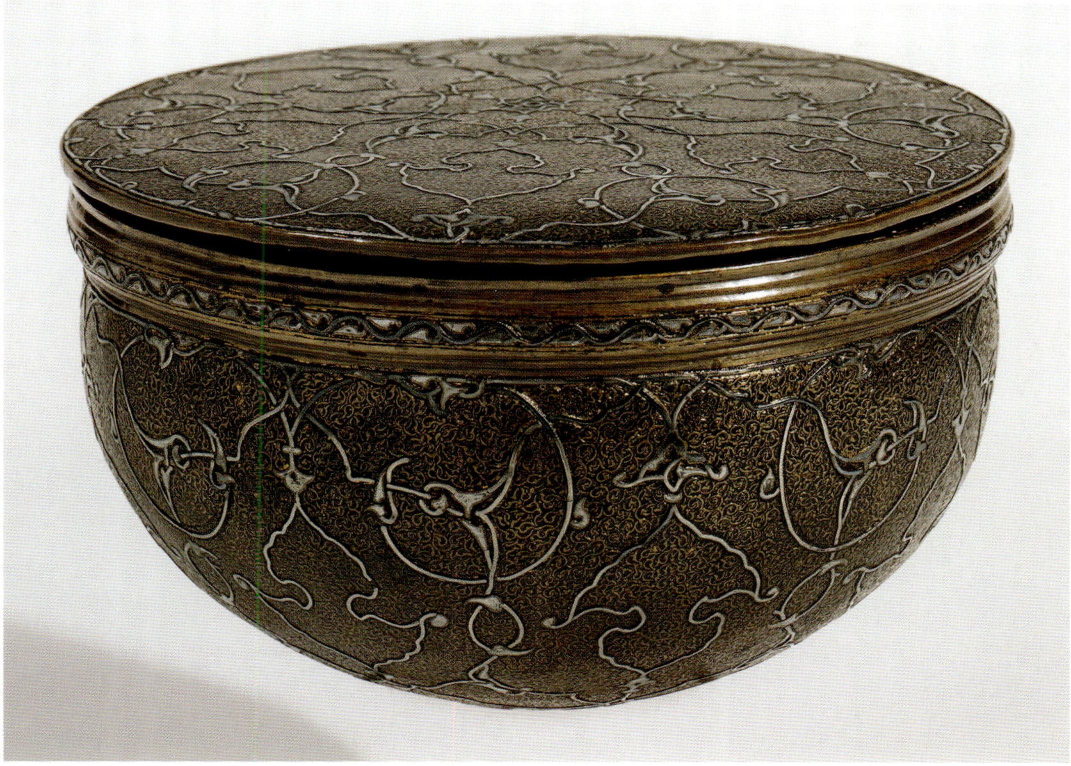

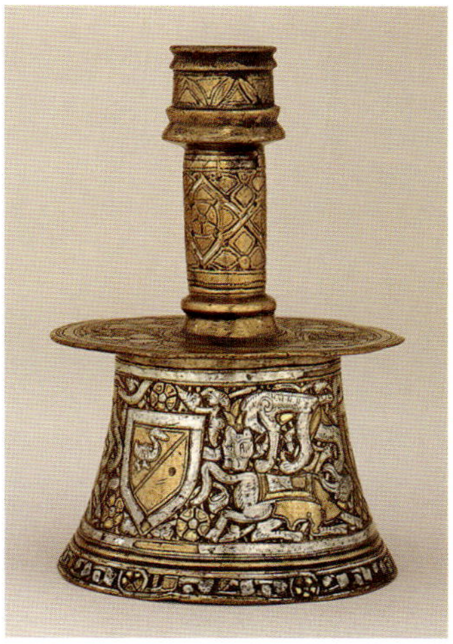

cat. 107. Zain al-Din 'Umar
Box with lid
Possibly northwest Iran or southeast Anatolia, late 15th–early 16th century
Museo Nazionale del Bargello, Florence

cat. 94. *Candlestick with the arms of a Venetian family*
Probably Damascus, Syria, ca. 1400
The British Museum, London

cathedral treasuries that such objects were preserved. European merchant princes and rulers amassed them for their cabinets of curiosities, the original museums.[27] The Museo Nazionale del Bargello in Florence still has a number of objects which were acquired by the Medici family (cat. 107).[28] Many in the Correr Museum in Venice doubtless originated from similar sources. In particular, a number of small candlesticks frequently bear the coats of arms of Italian—specifically Venetian—families (cat. 94; see also cats. 95–96, p. 65). Unfortunately, lack of color and inadequacy in detailing usually prevent attribution to a specific lineage. There is still some debate whether the arms were added at source as part of a commission, or were added later, once the objects had arrived in Italy. Some escutcheons were never completed. No document of importation or commission of the metalwares has yet emerged from Italian archives, although last wills make it clear that the artifacts were treasured.[29] One piece, a salver with an embossed central umbo, breaks this pattern of obscurity. It bears the joint arms of the Venier and Molin families and is thought to mark the mid-15th century marriage between members of the families, although it is still not certain if the salver was made to order rather than adapted later (fig. 3, p. 219).[30]

Although the majority of the "Veneto-Saracenic" pieces are in reality from Mamluk Egypt or Syria, there is another group of domestic metalwork objects—small round-bottomed boxes, salvers, ewers, and incense burners—which were made in a similar way, raised or cast in brass and inlaid with silver, but in a very different style. It is to this group that the objects associated with Mahmud the Kurd belong.[31]

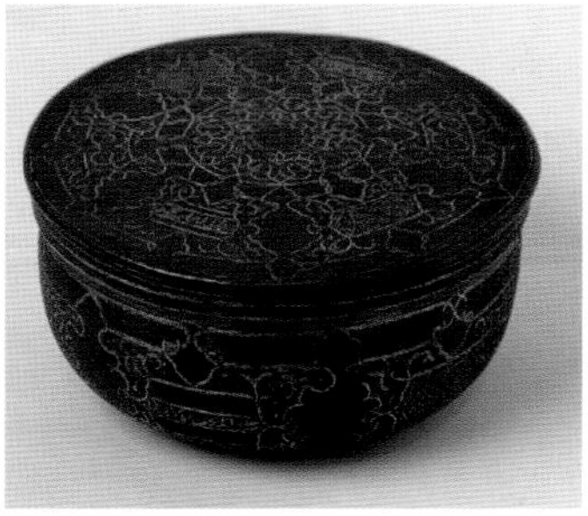

cat. 104. Mahmud al-Kurdi
Box with lid
Possibly northwest Iran or southeast Anatolia, late 15th century
Museo Archeologico Nazionale, Cividale del Friuli

A mystery surrounds the identity of Mahmud al-Kurdi. Nothing is known of his personal details; even the location of his workshop is disputed. Unusually, 12 objects, all of which carry his full name, and a thirteenth without his *nisba* (the Kurd), still exist. None of them bears a coat-of-arms. Five of them are in the current exhibition (cat. 100, p. 219; cat. 101, p. 220; cat. 102, p. 229; cat. 103, p. 221; cat. 104, p. 218). Although the rarity of this number of surviving pieces signed by a single master would ensure interest in his work, it is Mahmud's skill in design and execution that marks him out. His style becomes immediately recognizable. Although the most interesting piece with its double signature (cat. 103, p. 221) was not known at the time, Western attitudes in the 19th century gave rise to the idea that he must have been working in Venice.[32] This led to the metalwork being called "Veneto-Saracenic." Not only was Mahmud exceptionally skilled, but it was also thought the presence of his workshop in the Serenissima would explain the spread of the fashion in Europe for decorating textiles and objects with scrolling stems and knots.

The thesis of Muslims working in Venice, which in point of fact had no real historical basis, was held almost universally for some hundred years until seriously questioned in 1970;[33] even then it was not recognized that the metalwork objects were not from one but from three distinct groups. The Mamluk pieces are decorated in distinct bands of knots, roundels, and scrolling stems, which are clearly demarcated from each other by narrow fillets. A number of other pieces in the second group—to which Mahmud belongs—were in all probability made in northwestern Iran or in eastern Anatolia; and the third group, copying the first two, was fashioned in the West, particularly in Germany and northern Italy. The decoration of Western "copies" is recognizable because the inlay technique is different and the designs are not based on a circular or geometric grid, and sometimes include small human or animal busts among the stems (see, for example, cat. 120, p. 221). That the manufacture of such copies occurred in Germany as well as northern Italy was not coincidental. Germany imported goods from the Levant through Venice and there was a German mercantile depot in the city (Fondaco dei Tedeschi); perhaps Dürer had first encountered the style during one of his visits.[34] It is equally possible that Leonardo da Vinci, who not only designed knots but also sketched a gimbal suspension system for a maritime compass, had seen the device in a spherical incense burner while he was visiting the city.[35]

The extant pieces signed by Mahmud comprise seven round-bottomed boxes, three salvers, one cylindrical box, one bucket, and one spherical incense burner. All are made of brass and are inlaid in silver wire over delicate, intricate arabesque grounds. There is none of the strict confinement to bands of pattern that are a feature of work made in Syria or Egypt. Mahmud delighted in large-scale geometric outlines—shield shapes, circles, squares, trefoils—which stand out from, and act as islands within, the scrolling stems. Each geometric shape is filled with its own design of tiny, engraved arabesque, frequently emerging from a central knot or star-daisy. One has the impression that the geometric figures float over the silver-inlaid background of stems. One of the reasons for placing Mahmud's workshop in Turkoman Iran

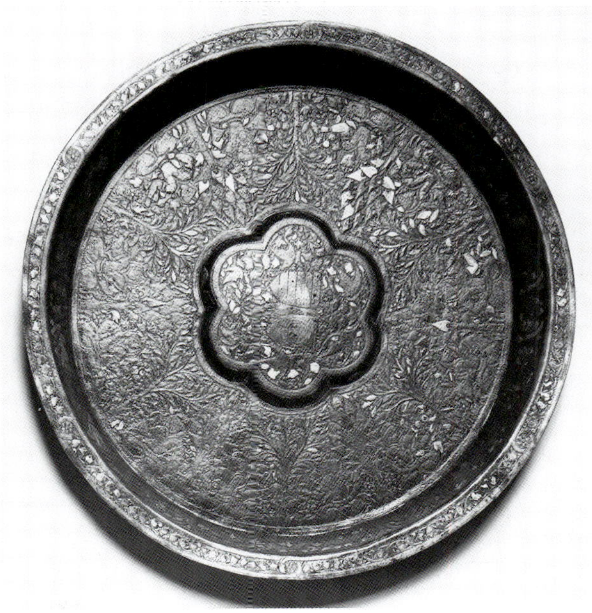

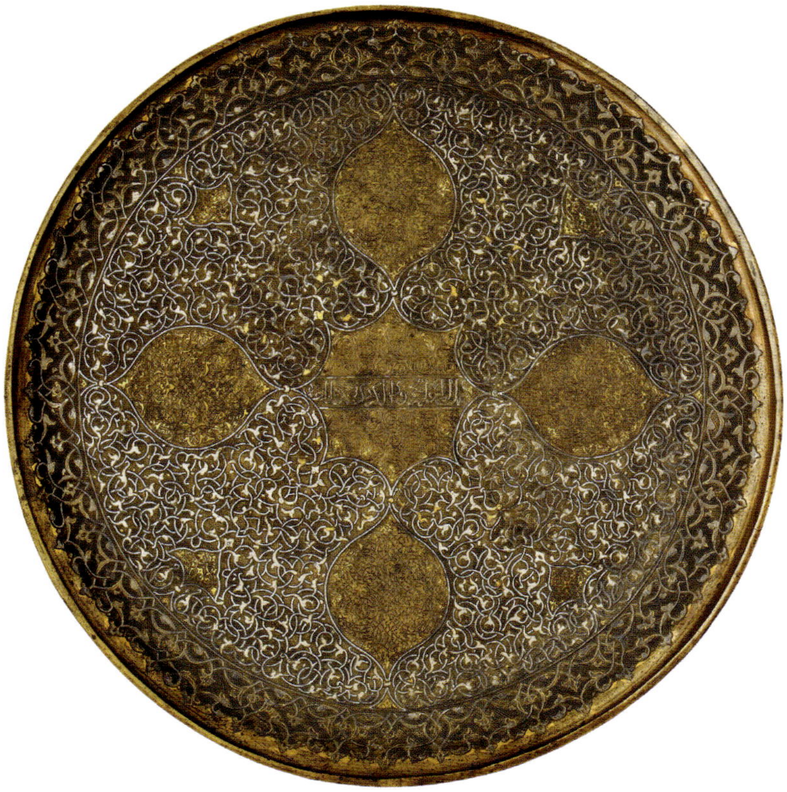

fig. 3. *Salver bearing the arms of the Venier and Molin families.* Museo Nazionale del Bargello, Florence

cat. 100. Mahmud al-Kurdi
Salver
Possibly northwest Iran or southeast Anatolia, late 15th century
Musée du Louvre, Paris

is that similar "floating" geometric shapes, which connect salient points in the underlying geometric grid but stand proud of it, are found in 15th-century Mashhad and Isfahan.[36]

The fineness of Mahmud's work is extraordinary. A magnifying glass is necessary to appreciate fully the precision of the engraved decoration. How was it achieved? Each section must have been worked out in advance. The engraved details within the geometric shapes and the larger-scale areas of scrolling stems that surround them never waver from the underlying circular constraint. Each tiny split-palmette leaf is drawn exactly to correspond to the sweep of a circumference; each spiraling scroll conforms to one. Moreover, from the design of the lid of his round-bottomed boxes it is possible to anticipate the pattern on the base. The two parts of the pattern are proportional to each other, the smaller scale of the lid expanded to fill the walls. It seems likely that the designs were transferred to the metal surface from a preparatory drawing, perhaps using some kind of pounce or indentation with a metal point.[37] Mahmud's technique would have been extraordinarily time-consuming, but labor costs in the 15th century were minimal. The brass of the ground was first cut away, sometimes leaving crosshatching to provide additional texture: the aim was to provide a narrow ridge of base metal standing proud of the surface which would provide the outline of the main design. The hollowed-out ground was then sometimes colored by a black organic substance that has defied modern analysis.[38] Next, the reserved lines were pocked or roughened with an engraving tool, either down the center or, in the case of the split-palmette leaves, around the outline. Soft, almost pure silver, was then rubbed into the grooves to give the impression of a silver wire (fig. 4, p. 222). Sometimes the master's signature forms an integral part of the design; this can be seen on the salvers in the Louvre and in the British Museum (cat. 100; cat. 101, p. 220). On a third tray in the Hermitage Museum, like the example from the Louvre, the name appears across the

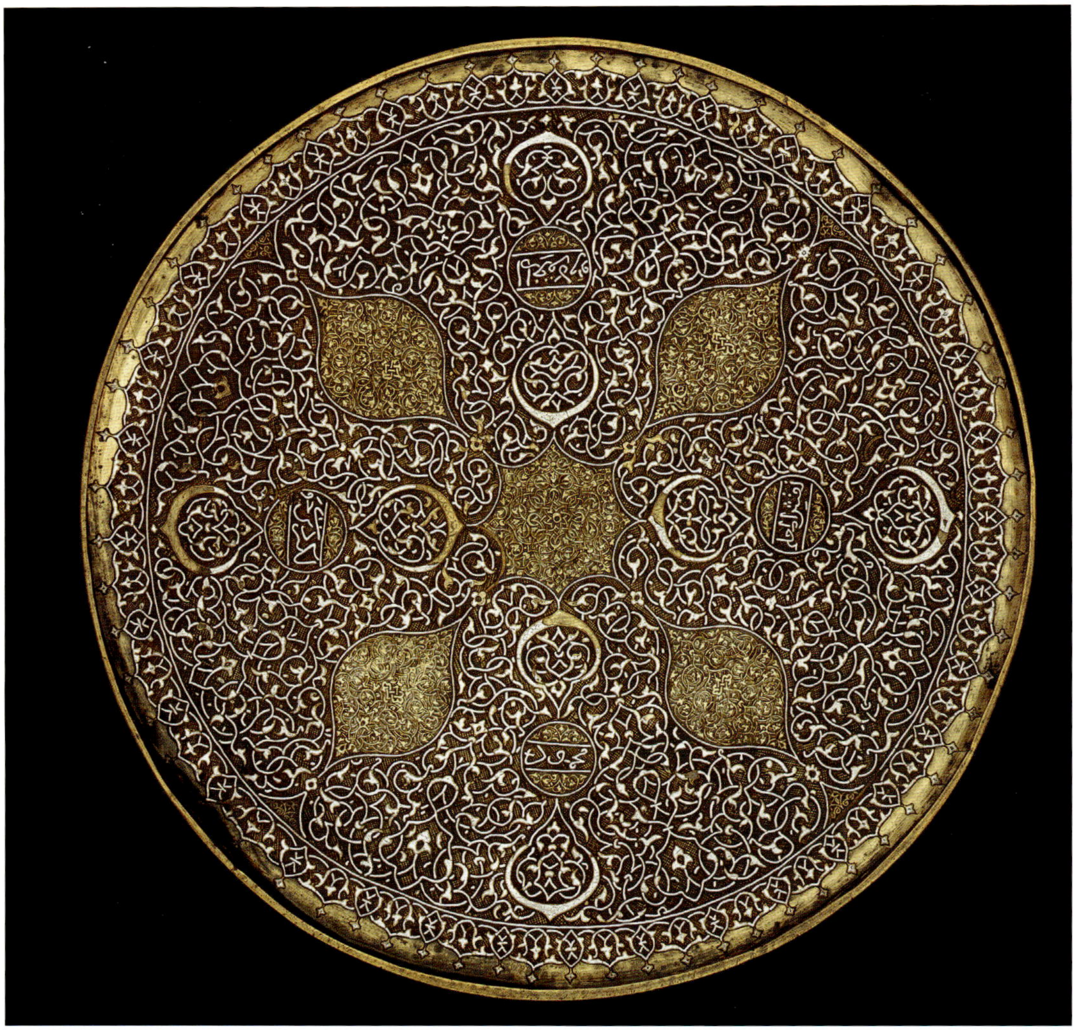

cat. 101. Mahmud al-Kurdi
Salver
Possibly northwest Iran or southeast Anatolia, late 15th century
The British Museum, London

central element of the design (fig. 5, p. 222). Four roundels on the London salver contain sections of his signature (fig. 6, p. 223).[39] On these salvers, this arrangement appears to be a reference to Mamluk emblems that frequently contained the name of the sultan in the later 15th century. Although it is uncommon to find a craftsman's signature in this prominent position, it is also present on the walls of a cylindrical box now in the Museo Stibbert, Florence.[40] On the round-bottomed boxes, Mahmud's name is usually more discreet, hidden under the lid on the narrow lip of the bowl.

It is on one of these boxes (cat. 103) that his most intriguing signature is found. It does not include the final part of Mahmud's name—*al-Kurdi*, "the Kurd"—but in every other way, including the formula "who hopes for forgiveness," it corresponds to the other signed examples. What makes it so interesting is that the signature appears twice—once in Arabic script (although probably in a Persian form) and once in Roman script (*AMELIEMALENMAMUD*: "the work of the master Mahmud").[41]

There is a continuing debate about where Mahmud was working. Opinions differ between Mamluk Egypt or Syria, and Turkoman eastern Anatolia or northwestern Iran. Partly on the basis of the double signature, but, as already explained, also because details of his designs and his metalworking technique correspond closely to late Timurid-Turkoman work, I believe he was working in Iran, at the time of—and perhaps even for—Uzun Hasan, the leader of the

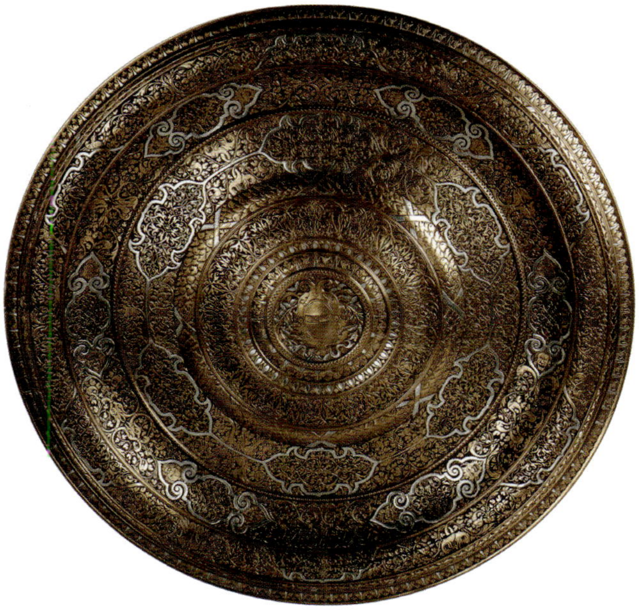

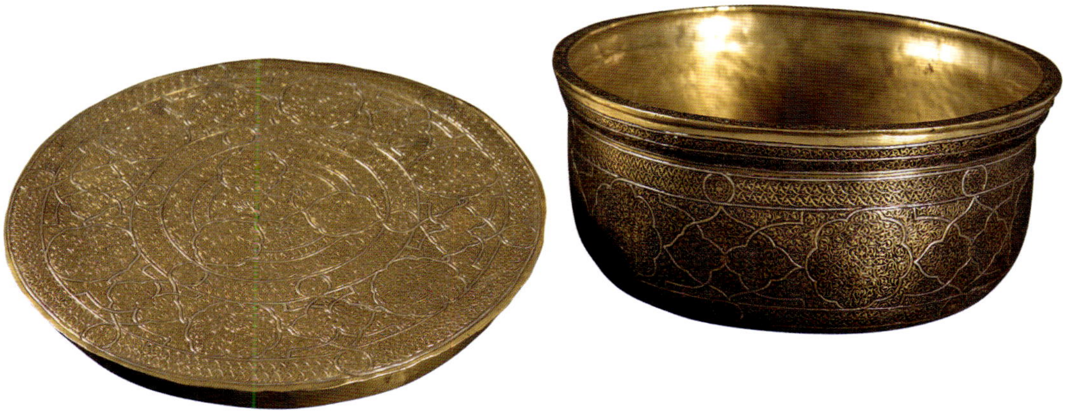

cat. 120. *Salver*
Venice, 16th century
Courtauld Institute of Art Gallery, London

cat. 103. Mahmud al-Kurdi
Box with lid
Possibly northwest Iran or southeast Anatolia, late 15th century
Courtauld Institute of Art Gallery, London

White Sheep (Aq-qoyunlu) Turkomans. Uzun Hasan's capital was Tabriz, a city which earned high praise for its beauty and sophistication.[42] The palace of the Eight Paradises (*Hasht Bihisht*) was described in about 1507 by a Venetian merchant.[43] The city's strategic position on the silk route meant it acted as a gateway for trade between the West and the Far East. Under Uzun Hasan it expanded to become the largest city in the world outside China, but as early as 1325, when it was ruled by the Il-khanids, or Mongols of Iran, a cleric called Odorico da Pordenone described it as *"una città più nobile e migliore di qalsiasi altra che esista oggi al mondo per il commercio . . . e così opulenta che si stenta a credere tutte le cose che vi si possono trovare."*[44] These glories have all but disappeared, but in a *Diwan* of Hafiz, copied in Tabriz in about 1526 and glittering with gold and lapis lazuli (the two most expensive pigments), an illustration allows a glimpse of what it must have been like (fig. 7, p. 223).[45] The floor and walls of the building are depicted covered by tile-work with intricate scrolling arabesques and geometric stars. Similarly, the minute tile-work that still survives from the Blue Mosque (built in 1465) resembles the patterns used by Mahmud. Moreover, there is a direct Venetian connection between Tabriz and Venice because it was to this splendid court of the Aq-qoyunlu leader that successive Venetian embassies were sent in the 15th century, seeking an alliance against the advance of the Ottomans.

The earliest approach by the Serenissima to the Turkoman confederation was in 1463 when overtures were made to two leaders in Anatolia, Ibrahim Qaramani (who subsequently

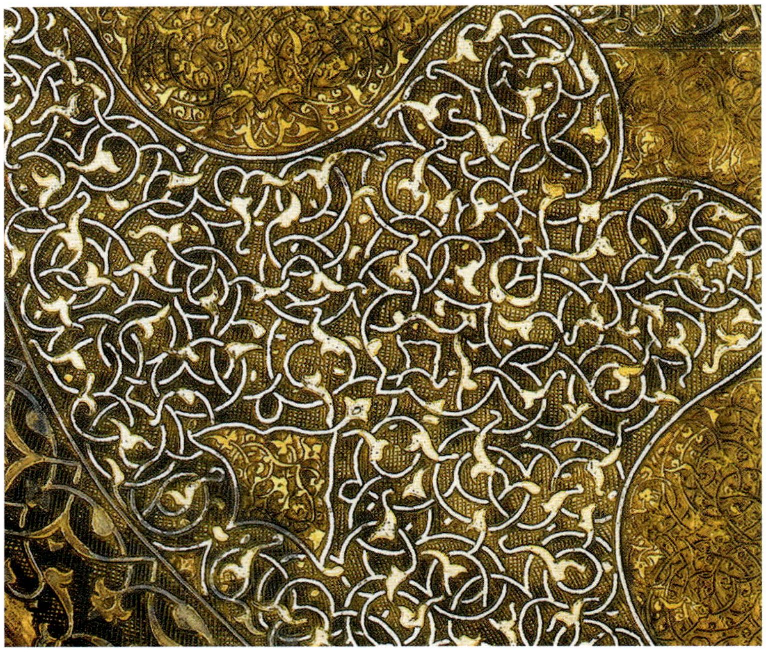

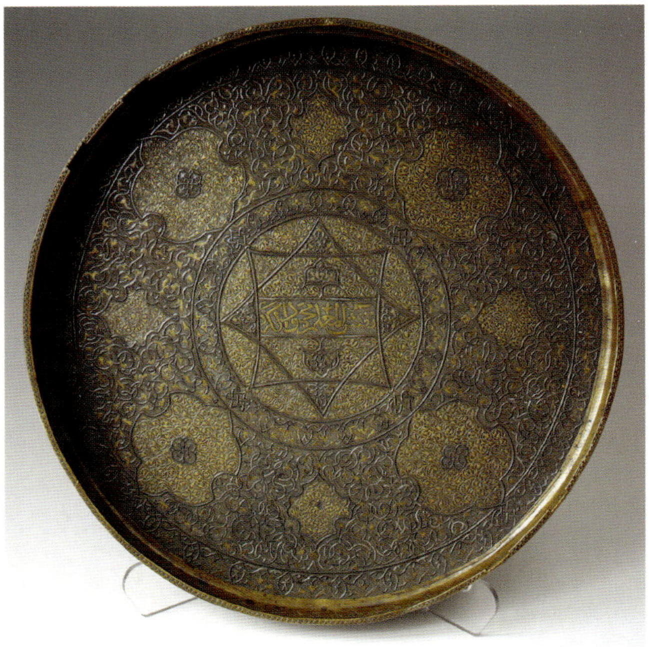

fig. 4. Mamhud al-Kurdi, *Salver,* (detail of cat. 100). Musée du Louvre, Paris

fig. 5. Mamhud al-Kurdi, *Salver.* The Hermitage, St. Petersburg

died) and Uzun Hasan.[46] In response, a Turkoman White Sheep envoy arrived in Venice on March 13 of the following year, crossing the path of a Venetian diplomat, Lazaro Quirini, who was already on his way to Persia.[47] There were further exchanges in 1465 and 1466, but the proposed alliance fell into abeyance until 1470 when Uzun Hasan sent yet another envoy to Venice, who arrived in February 1471. There were further contacts in 1472, 1473, and 1474, and these embassies were accompanied by the customary exchange of diplomatic gifts—a silver vase, cloth of gold, scarlet woolen cloth, and so on, from the Venetians.[48] What the Venetian diplomats received in return is less clear, although detailed records of their visits were kept. One account in particular is of interest as regards the box with the dual signature now in the Courtauld Institute (cat. 103). The Roman script is a transliteration of the Persian/Arabic script rather than a translation; to someone who did not understand the language, the Roman script signature would have been unintelligible.[49] But if the box and cover had been a diplomatic gift, a translator would have been on hand. The Venetian ambassador, Giosafat Barbaro, specifically notes that he had an interpreter when he presented his credentials to Uzun Hasan in 1474.[50] Moreover, as a mark of special favor at an open-air festival arranged for the circumcision of two of Uzun Hasan's sons, Barbaro appears to have been presented with one of a set of bowls or boxes (*tazete*) filled with sweetmeats.[51] Could the box now in the Courtauld be the very one? It is unlikely, but its existence may cast light on both the function of the round-bottomed boxes and how they were used. A question hangs over their curious instability, as mentioned elsewhere. One solution might be that they were intended to be supported on a lacquered or wooden stand, held in place by their projecting rim.

In the West, such was the reputation of Mahmud that his forged "signature" appears to have been added to some objects, presumably to raise their value. This would seem to be the case of the salver now in Baltimore (fig. 8, p. 224), and another in the British Museum.[52] Mahmud was not the only master working in inlaid metalwork at this time. Other contemporary masters worked in a related but not identical style. The most famous are Zayn al-Din (cat. 105, p. 224) and Zayn al-Din ᶜUmar (who may have been his son), who signed seven extant pieces. Zayn

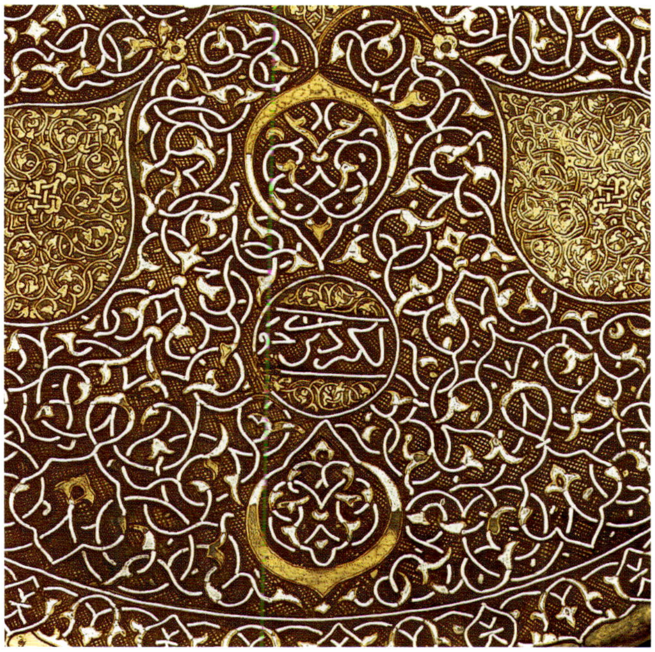

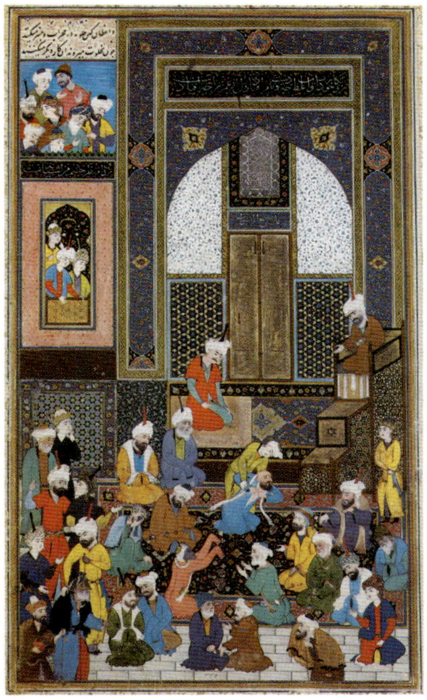

fig. 6. Mamhud al-Kurdi, *Salver* (detail of cat. 101). The British Museum, London

fig. 7. Hafiz, "Scene in a Mosque," *Diwan*, Tabriz, ca. 1526. Private collection

al-Din's spherical incense burner (cat. 106, p. 224) is a particularly fine example. The pieces associated with him have a characteristically "softer" style than al-Kurdi's, with a tendency towards large-scale arabesques and more flowing lines, although they do not have the geometric clarity displayed by works signed by Mahmud. In particular, details of the work of this group point towards a link with styles current in 15th- and 16th-century Ottoman Turkey; these include subdivided split palmettes, linked chain-like roundels, and a tendency towards an infinite, instead of a finite, design. It might be that members of the group were working in the period after Mahmud, possibly training with or under him. Perhaps they were employed in Istanbul, after capture during one of the Ottoman raids on Tabriz in 1474 or 1516. Skilled artisans as well as precious objects were transported to the Ottoman capital as booty. There is no proof of this hypothesis, however, because the name of Zayn al-Din does not appear in the list of the men taken from Tabriz in the published Topkapı registers.[53]

Although some commentators have seen a reference to a planetary or deeper symbolism in the knots, geometric grids, and scrolling stems,[54] Mahmud the Kurd and Zayn al-Din were probably illiterate. Elements of Mahmud's signature are unusual, specifically in the way he divided his words, and point to a blind copying from a prepared script. If so, it seems unreasonable to suppose that the craftsmen would have been aware of any philosophical, literary, or religious basis to the patterns. This does not detract from the value of their work. Indeed, the absence of biographical detail forces the viewer to focus on the objects themselves. The experience is that much the richer and closer to a Renaissance appreciation of skilled craftsmanship for its own sake.

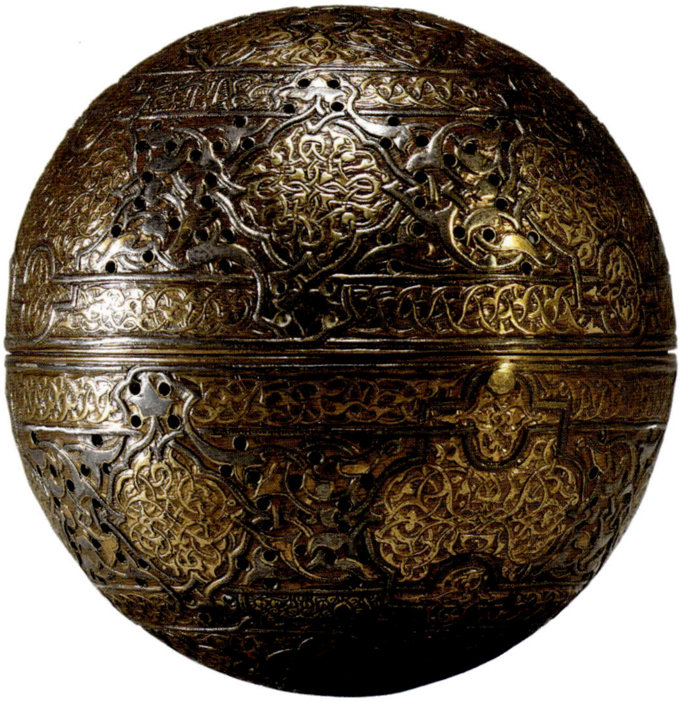

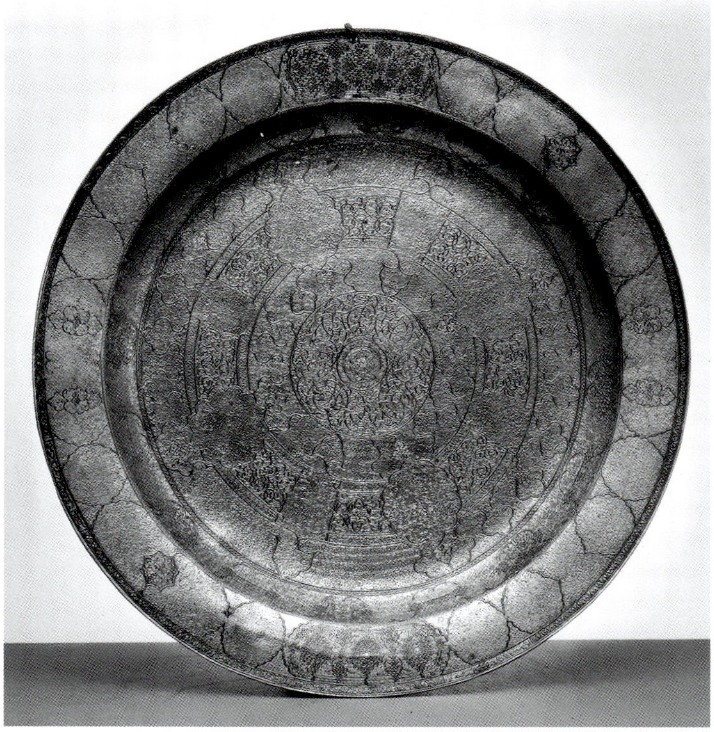

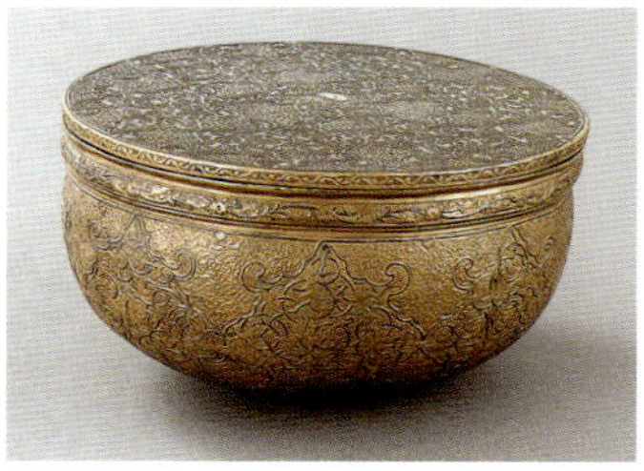

cat. 106. Zain al-Din
Incense burner
Possibly northwest Iran or southeast Anatolia, late 15th–early 16th century
The Walters Art Museum, Baltimore

fig. 8. Salver with forged signature of Mahmud al-Kurdi. The Walters Art Museum, Baltimore

cat. 105. Zain al-Din
Box with lid
Possibly northwest Iran or southeast Anatolia, late 15th–early 16thcentury
Musée du Louvre, Paris

Notes

1 Holbein, *Portrait of Henry VIII at Age 49*, for example (the English king perhaps wore this outfit for his marriage to Anne of Cleves, where knots would be of particular significance), or the carpet in his *The Ambassadors*. Giovanni and Gentile Bellini's interest in, and use of, Islamic textiles in their paintings are widely evident; Gentile Bellini's sojourn in the court of the Ottoman sultan in Constantinople has been investigated by a number of scholars. Mack (2002, pp. 149-70) offers an overview of the connection between the East and the pictorial arts. Lorenzo Lotto, like Holbein, used carpets from Turkey and Egypt in his paintings, meaning that certain designs came to be known as "Lotto" or "Holbein." Leonardo da Vinci's knot patterns were precisely imitated by Albrecht Dürer for embroidery designs, and similar arrangements were used in contemporary pattern books; see Bambach 1991 and Bambach and Whitaker 1991. For an overview, see Mack 2002; on design in general see Evans 1975; Gombrich 1984; Grabar 1992; for a more detailed discussion on the fascination in the West for Muslim artifacts, see Auld 1989.
2 The term seems to have been coined by Stanley Lane-Poole (1886) who followed 19th-century Italian and French scholars in a conviction that the objects were made by Muslim craftsmen working in Venice, known as *azzimini*. This is discussed below. For a brief overview of the art historical views see Auld 2004, pp. 36–43.
3 In 1531, Pietro Zen, the Venetian ambassador to the court of Süleyman the Magnificent, dared to hope that the Ottoman ruler might visit Venice. Certainly, replied the sultan, but he would take Rome first. Letter from Constantinople, 1531 in Sanudo 1879–1902, vol. 55, col. 231.
4 Heyd 1936.
5 Heyd 1936; Wansbrough 1961; Wansbrough 1963; Wansbrough 1965a. For a general overview see Auld 2004, pp. 44–48.
6 On conditions in Syria, see Vallet 1999; Howard 2003. A particularly vivid account of mercantile life away from home is given in Origo 1986.
7 On this aspect, see Deborah Howard's fascinating book *Venice and the East* (Howard 2000).
8 For details of the negotiations, see Wansbrough 1963.
9 See for example Wansbrough 1965a; Wansbrough 1965b.
10 Discussed further in Auld 2004, pp. 49-50; the inventory, number of the object in the Museo Correr is XII 9 (cat. 97).
11 Described in a letter from Pietro da Bibbiena to Clarice de' Medici in Rome. See Fabronius 1784, vol. 2, p. 337: "a large amount of balsam . . . big containers of sweetmeats, myrabolan [Phyllanthus, a member of the genus of the spurge family used for medicinal purposes among others] and ginger."
12 Simone Sigoli, in Sigoli 1944, p. 226.
13 Frescobaldi, Gucci, and Sigoli 1948, p. 182.
14 He was commenting on wooden doors inlaid with what he described as ebony and ivory. See Thénaud, 1530, chap. 2.
15 Cellini 1891, chap. 31, p. 64; Cellini 1956, p. 62.
16 Vasari 1550, chap. 20 (24), pp. 279–80; *"per lavorarsi di ciò [tausia, or alla damascina] in Damasco e per tutto il Levant eccellentemente."*
17 As translated in Rice 1955, pp. 228–29.
18 Now in the Türk ve Islam Eserleri Müsezi, Istanbul.
19 Dost Muhammad in his preface to the album of Bahram Mirza, quoted by Necipoğlu 1995, p. 226, n. 110.
20 Ibn Khaldun 1967, vol. 2, pp. 130–31. He continues "'our teachers used to say that one's application to geometry does to the mind what soap does to a garment.'" The importance of geometry in Islamic design is discussed extensively, if provocatively, throughout Necipoğlu 1995.
21 Naples, Museo di Capodimonte, inv. no. 112121; see Auld 1989, p. 191 for a discussion of this possibility.
22 See Melikian-Chirvani 1982, p. 211; and Baer 1968.
23 Cellini 1891; for a discussion see Auld 1989, pp. 188–89.
24 In the hands of Nicodemus in the attic panel of the Pesaro Altarpiece of 1471–74; now in the Pinacoteca of the Vatican, Rome.
25 Part of the Cycle of St. Ursula of 1490–ca. 1498, now in the Gallerie dell'Accademia; outside Venetian painting, in northern Europe a similar bucket hangs behind the Virgin in the *Mérode Altarpiece* by the Master of Flémalle, and in the *Annunciation* panel of the Ghent Altarpiece by Hubert and Jan van Eyck, which was completed in 1432. For illustrations see Panofsky 1947–1948, vol. 2, pls. 91, 144.
26 The cycle dates from 1502 when the Patriarch of Jerusalem presented the *scuola* with a relic of St. George. Candlesticks and salvers also appear frequently in the paintings of Netherlandish artists such as Dirk Bouts and Jan van Eyck: see, for example, a tall candlestick in

van Eyck's *Lucca Madonna* or the salver in the central panel of Bouts' *Last Supper*, Panofsky 1947–1948 pls. 123 and 217.

27 See Raby 1985, pp. 251–58.

28 Curatola and Spallanzani 1981, pp. 7–9, 10–11, nos. 1, 2.

29 Howard 2003, pp. 143–57.

30 Either in 1449 or 1460; now in Florence at the Museo Nazionale del Bargello; see Spallanzani 1985, pp. 465–78. One Marino da Molin was consul to the Venetian colony in Damascus and an inventory of his possessions was drawn up on May 4, 1457. Although there is no suggestion that the salver belonged to this man, like many other Venetian families, the da Molin were actively engaged in trade with the Mamluks in the eastern Mediterranean.

31 For a full discussion, see Auld 2004.

32 The idea was propagated in particular by Lavoix 1862.

33 See Huth 1970. See also Melikian-Chirvani 1974; Allan 1986; Allan 1989; Auld 1989.

34 Dürer visited Venice twice, once in 1494, and again in 1505–7 when, among others, he encountered Giovanni Bellini.

35 *Codex Atlanticus*, fol. 288 recto; *Codex Madrid*, 1; see Gibbs-Smith and Rees 1978, p. 66, no. 57. The drawing is annotated by Leonardo with the words "method of making rings that can turn in every direction such as a mariner's compass."

36 Masjid-i Jami^c, Mashhad, 1416–18; Masjid-i Jami^c, Isfahan, restored 1475–76; Darb-i Kushk, Isfahan, 1496–97.

37 Designs on paper with small holes to allow a pattern to be transferred have been preserved; for example, although much larger in scale, see Lentz and Lowry 1989, cat. no. 118; for a full discussion, see Auld (forthcoming).

38 For details see Ward and La Niece et al. 1995; Auld 2004, pp. 54–70; and La Niece's essay in this volume.

39 Paris, Louvre, inv. no. 7526; St. Petersburg, Hermitage, inv. no. VC 235; London, the British Museum, inv. no. 187812-30 705.

40 Florence, Museo Stibbert, inv. no. 6121.

41 London, Courtauld Institute of Art Gallery, inv. no. O.1966.GP.204 (cat. 103).

42 The Ottoman artist Matrakçı Nasuh drew the cityscape this year. Later in the 16th century an Ottoman historian, Ta^{c}likizade, still ranked the city as one of the leading conurbations of the world together with Istanbul, Cairo, Delhi, Beijing, and Rome, thus ranking it higher than Samarqand and Herat. Ta^{c}likizade Mehmed Subhi Çelebi ibn Muhammad al-Fenari, *Tebriziye*, ms. R.1299, fol. 38, Topkapı Sarayı Müzesi Kütüphanesi, Istanbul. In 1523–24, another historian, Khwandamir, wrote that Tabriz was the most flourishing city in the inhabited world; see Ghiyath al-Din Khwandamir, *Tarikh habib al-siyar*, ed. by Jalal Huma', 4 vols., Tehran, 1954.

43 A description of the palace and the reference are quoted by Blair and Bloom 1994, p. 52 from Lisa Golombek, "From Tamerlane to the Taj Mahal," in A. Daneshvari (ed.), *Essays in Islamic Art and Architecture in Honor of Katharina Otto-Dorn* (ed.) No further details regarding the original source are given.

44 "... a city more noble and better for commerce than any other that exists in the world today ... so opulent that it is hard to credit all the things that can be found there"; my translation from Barbaro and Contarini 1973, p. 279, n. 247.

45 *"Episode in a Mosque,"* private collection, illustrated in black and white in Lentz and Lowry 1989, fig. 104.

46 Berchet 1865, vol. 3, n. 1; documents vol. 2, pp. 102–4 and vol. 3, p. 104.

47 Berchet 1965, vol. 3, n. 4, quoting the manuscript of Marin Sanudo's *Cronaca*.

48 It was once thought that a turquoise relief-cut glass bowl now in the Tesoro di San Marco in Venice (inv. no. 62), which was first catalogued in the inventory of 1571, was the result of one of these exchanges. For details on these visits and exchanges see Berchet 1865, discussed in Auld 2004, pp. 48–53.

49 However, merchants and diplomats were expected to have some knowledge of Arabic, and Giosafat Barbaro appears to have claimed to have known Persian; see Howard 2000, p. 22 and relevant notes.

50 Lockhart and Morozzo della Rocca 1973, vol. 7, p. 120.

51 Lockhart and Morozzo della Rocca, 1973, vol. 7, pp. 127–28; for a translation see Auld 2004, p. 106, n. 22.

52 Inv. no. 1878 12-30 711.

53 These are not necessarily complete; see Rogers and Köseoğlu 1987, pp. 37–47.

54 For a recent view and bibliography see Necipoğlu 1995.

Master Mahmud and Inlaid Metalwork: A Scientific Perspective

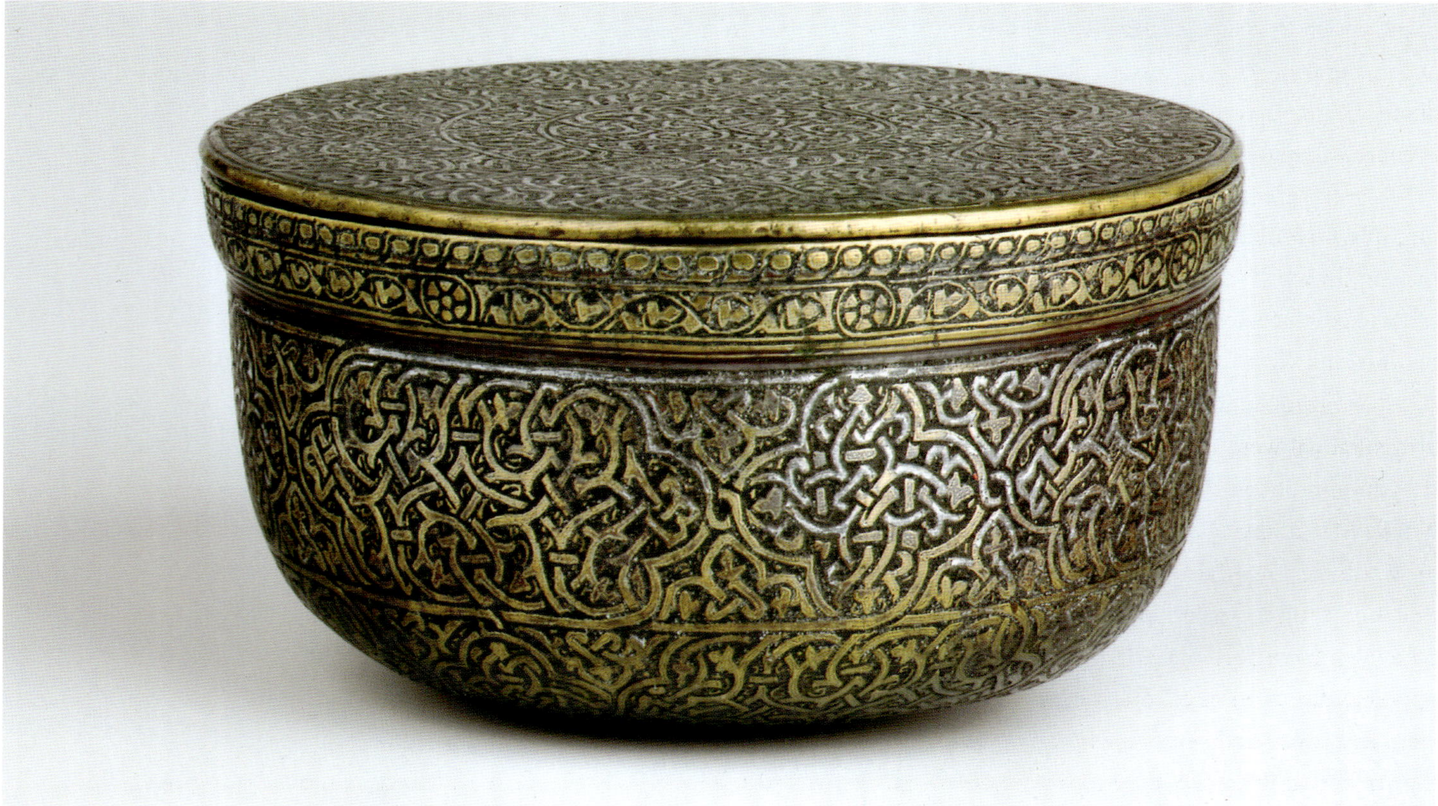

Susan La Niece

Scientific examination provides an additional resource in the study of metalwork and can be used to test the hypotheses of the curator. A case in point is a study of Mahmud al-Kurdi's extant works. Science is able to provide factual information; for example, about what an object is made of and how it was manufactured. By building up a large scientific database we can determine what is standard for each culture, period, or workshop; incidentally this database aids in the identification of modern fakes, whose scientific imprints have different characteristics than those of authentic works.

There are three main tools for the scientific study of metalwork. The first is microscopy, which uses magnification to study the fine detail in tool marks from the manufacture and decoration of the vessels; the second is radiography, which uses X-rays to view hidden details of manufacturing technique, seams, and repairs, both ancient and modern; and the last is chemical analysis, which determines the metal composition.

In principle there are two basic methods of manufacturing metal objects. One is casting, in which molten metal is poured into a mold of the required shape, and the other is hammering, in which a craftsman beats and works a cast lump of metal with a variety of different tools to reach the required shape. In practice, a combination of casting a basic shape, followed by finishing with hand tools, is often most efficient.

From indications left on the metal, it is thought that the round-bottomed boxes or bowls (cat. 99) were made by this combination of casting the basic shape and hammering to deepen and shape the rounded bottom. This technique can still be seen in the markets of North Africa and the Levant: the craftsman rotates the metal, hammering from the center outwards in a regular fashion, thinning and shaping the sides. Intriguingly, it was discovered that one round-bottomed box[1] of what was formerly referred to as the "Veneto-Saracenic" type must have been made by a left-handed craftsman because the hammer marks spiral in the opposite direction of all the others. Using a rotating lathe, probably powered by a workshop assistant, the round box was accurately shaped by holding a sharp tool against the metal, giving particular attention to the rim, where a tight fit with the lid was essential. The lids were

cat. 99. *Box with lid*
Probably Egypt, 15th century

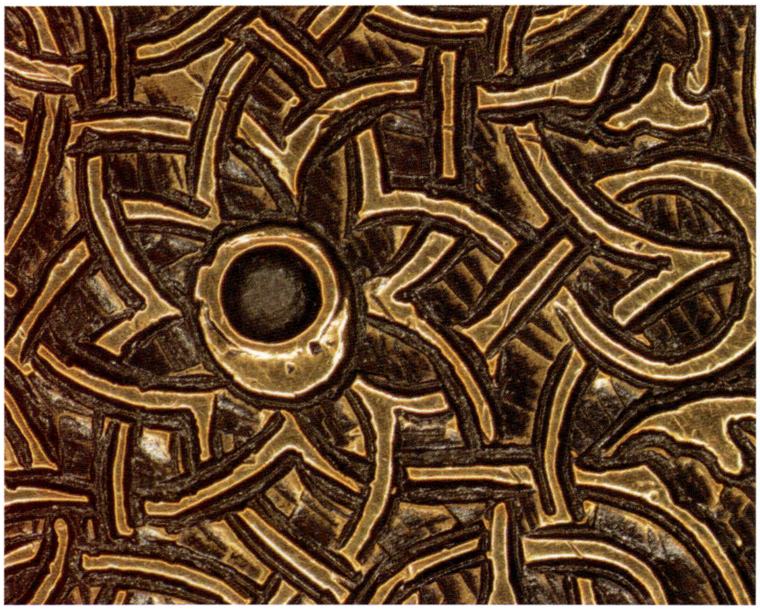

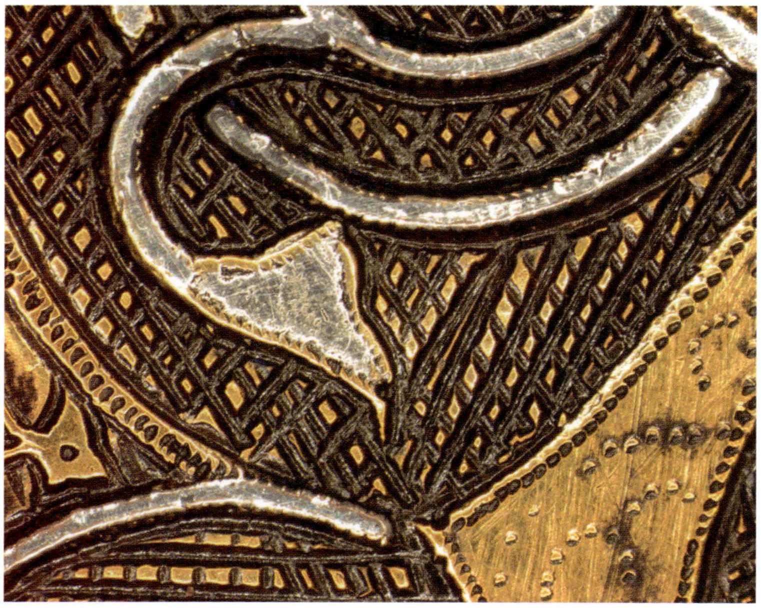

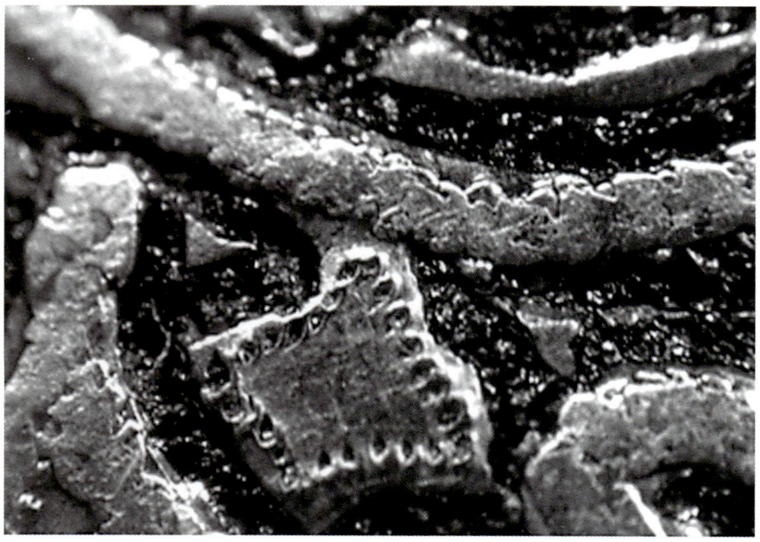

each made from a single piece of metal, in the form of a flattened beret. The centering mark for the lathe and the concentric cut marks in the metal can be seen on many of the objects (fig. 1).[2] The small candlesticks (see cat. 94, p. 217; cats. 95–96, p. 65) were cast in two parts, base and stem, then finished by hand while rotating on a lathe to ensure they were truly circular. The decorative design was accurately marked out, using a pair of compasses, before cutting away and texturing the brass around the decorative motifs.

A characteristic of Mahmud al-Kurdi's work (see cats. 100–104, pp. 218–221 and 229) is fine silver inlay, usually in the form of wire, with small motifs in sheet silver. The silver is of high purity, with only about 2 percent copper; this ensures that the inlay is malleable. Al-Kurdi's wire inlays are characteristically keyed onto narrow ridges with a row of small pits, punched with a sharp tool (cat. 102, p. 229). The silver is lightly hammered into these keying pits, which hold it in place. The ridges serve to accentuate the inlay, highlighting the precious appearance and appeal of the silver. Small sheet silver inlays are applied separately to the wider areas of decoration and are keyed into a neat border of tiny punched pits. In the few examples that have larger inlays, there is additional keying in the center (fig. 2).[3] Mahmud does not appear to have used gold as an inlay material, but the visual effect of smooth areas of polished brass is a very good substitute (fig. 2). These inlay methods can be seen on brass wares throughout the Levant from the 12th century, but this style of keying precious metal inlays with punched pits was not typical of European metalworking.

Many of al-Kurdi's vessels have a black inlay material in the recesses of the design, providing an attractive contrast to the polished brass and silver inlays; this black material is common on much Islamic metalwork from the Levant. Significantly, although black materials such as enamel, niello, and waxes are found on European brasses, the black inlay found on Islamic metalwork is of a different composition. It is often described as bitumen or pine pitch, but its chemical identification is hampered by contamination from many years of use, polishing, and lacquering of the metalwork. It can be generally described as a black organic material, which must have been applied as a hot liquid because it contains tiny bubbles. It fills channels and recessed areas of the decorative design that have a roughened surface to provide keying. On the pieces attributed to Mahmud al-Kurdi the keying for the black inlay is comparatively delicate, with neat steps cut with a straight edged tool around the relief patterns of polished brass (fig. 1). Today, there is usually little of the black inlay remaining on his work in contrast to pieces such as the rosewater bottle (see cat. 98 and fig. 3).[4]

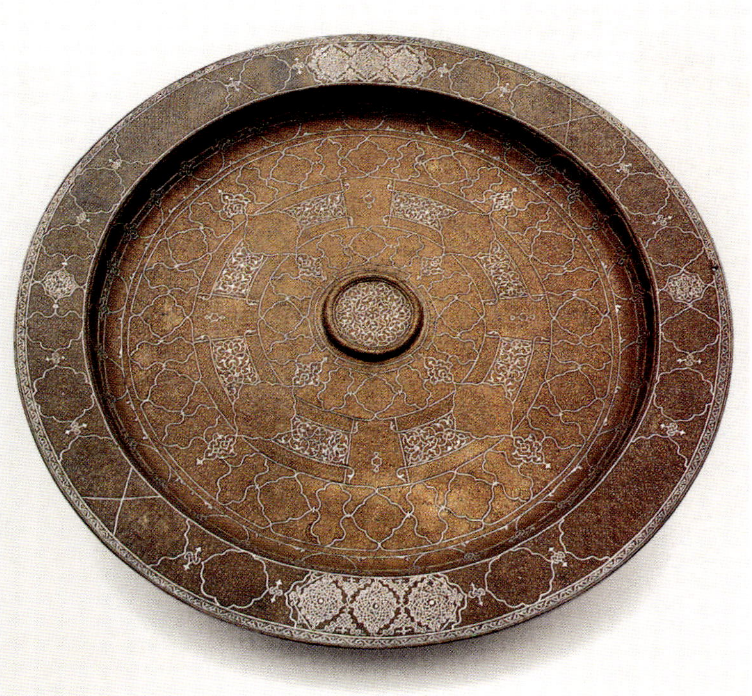

cat. 102. Mahmud al-Kurdi
Salver
Parrochia Santa Maria Assunta, Cividale del Friuli

Chemical analysis of four pieces signed with the name Mahmud al-Kurdi has identified the metal he used as relatively high purity brass (an alloy of copper and zinc), with very low levels of the minor impurities that were always carried over into the metal from the copper and zinc ores.[5] The pieces have very little nickel, an impurity of some copper ores. European metalwork dated to the late 15th century onwards, along with the majority of "Veneto-Saracenic" metalwork pieces, have significantly higher levels of nickel, which has been attributed to copper arriving on the market from central and eastern Europe.[6] From the scientific study it would seem that the workshop of Mahmud al-Kurdi was not using European copper, and the decorative techniques seen on pieces attributed to this workshop are typical of Islamic metalwork, confirming the view that it was situated within the Islamic world, though exactly where is still open to debate.

fig. 1. Detail of salver (cat. 102). The centering mark for lathe and concentric cut marks can be seen on the polished brass surface

fig. 2. Detail of metal inlay and crosshatched decoration (cat. 102). Rows of small pits can be seen where the silver has vanished—the additional keying in the center is unusual

fig. 3. Detail of inlay of silver and an organic black material (cat. 98). The punched pits for silver inlay can be seen on the edge of the central square

Notes

1 The British Museum, inv. no. 1878-12-30-693.
2 The figure shows a detail of the center of the salver (cat. 102) with the deep, round lathe-centering mark. The golden-colored polished brass surface has been cut in steps within the engraved outlines. The background probably once was filled with black organic inlay.
3 The figure shows a detail of the silver inlay-work and cross-hatched decoration on the salver (cat. 102). Rows of dark keying pits can be seen punched into the brass, where the silver is now missing. The additional keying in the center of the large area to the left is unusual in being decorative in its own right.
4 The figure shows a detail of the silver and shiny black organic inlays on the *qumqum* (cat. 98). The punched keying for the silver inlay can be seen around the edge of the square at the center.
5 A salver (1878 12-30 705; cat. 101) and two lidded boxes in the British Museum (1895 5-21, 22, and 23); and a lidded box in the Courtauld Institute (cat. 103). See Craddock, La Niece, and Hook 1998, table 2.
6 Ward et al. 1995.

Venetian Lacquer and Bookbindings of the 16th Century

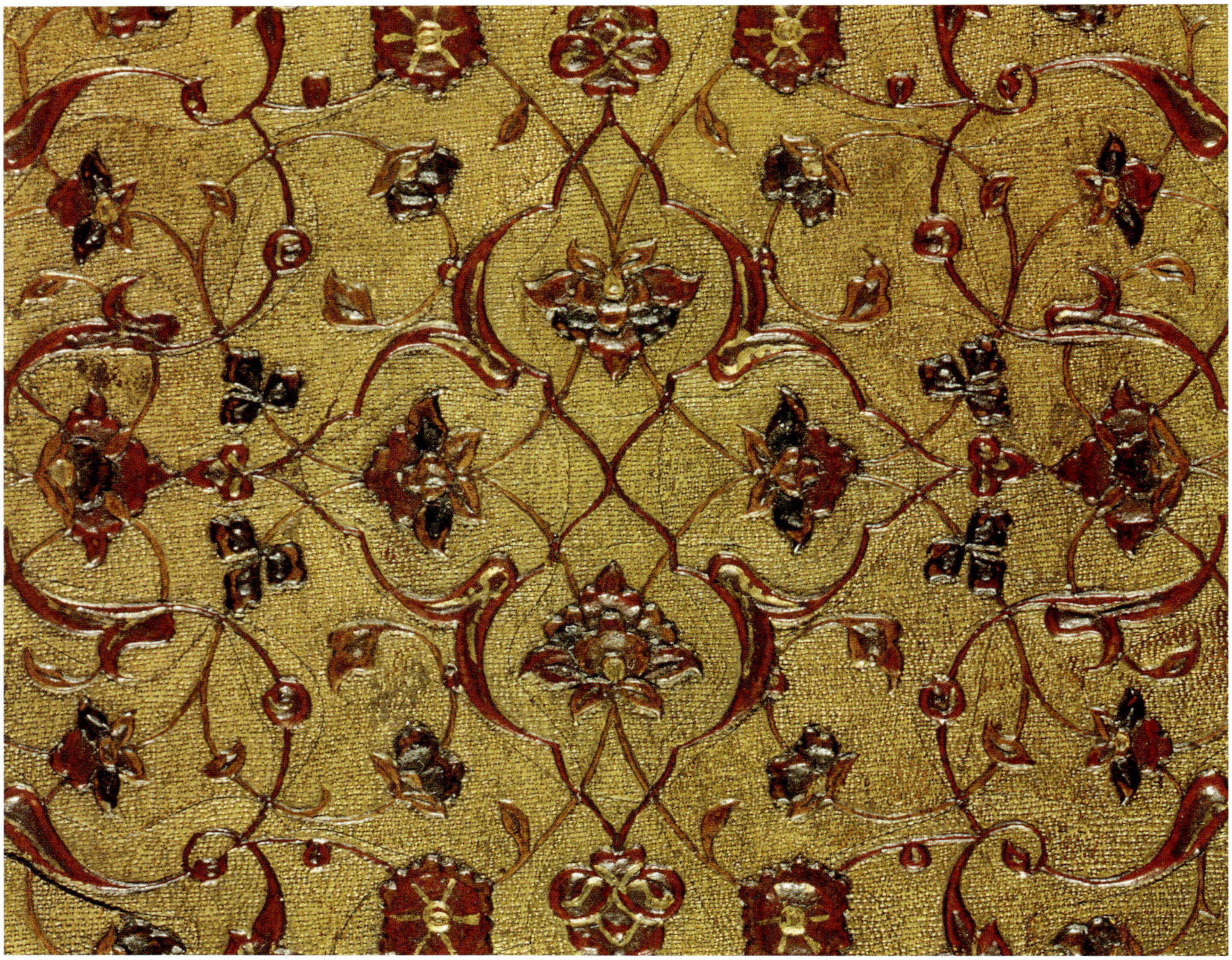

Ernst J. Grube

Among the many manifestations of contact between the art of the Muslim world and the decorative arts of Venice, the most unexpected are undoubtedly the quantity and quality of "lacquer-painted" objects. Authentic lacquered wares are produced from the resinous sap obtained from *Rhus vernicifera* (see Rizzo's essay in this volume). The technique was first used in China and Japan, consequently, the appearance of a seemingly closely related technique in 17th-century Europe—first in England and Holland, shortly after in Germany and France[1]—was generally accounted for by contacts with the Far East. This seemed all the more convincing, as the proliferation of European lacquer-painted decoration occurs primarily on objects decorated with chinoiserie patterns of a certain ingenuity and variety. Only recently has a form of this so-called gilded-lacquer decoration, which first appeared in 16th-century Venice, been connected with earlier, Islamic models. A primary feature of Venetian lacquer-painted objects must be noted immediately: they are not produced using true lacquer but instead are decorated with highly varnished painting on leather or over a chalk or gypsum base on wood, just as are the so-called lacquer-painting objects of the Muslim world.[2]

This technical similarity is not without suggestive significance. In 16th-century Venice, leatherworkers belonged to a special guild. In the early 20th century, the historian Pompeo Molmenti described their manner of working as follows: "The leather . . . was blind-tooled and gilded, stamped with figures, arabesques, flowers, and leaves. . . . Gilded leather was used not only as wall covering but also to wrap chests and caskets and was bent to shape helmets, shields, and quivers on which . . . the Lion of St. Mark stood out. They were sumptuous, delicate works, yet they served regular foot-soldiers."[3] Evidence of this production can be appreciated from the large quantity of extant varnished and gilded fragments of wall coverings[4] and the great variety of objects, including shields,[5] quivers,[6] flatware cases,[7] toilet boxes,[8] bookbindings,[9] cabinets[10] and caskets,[11] picture frames,[12] and musical instruments.[13] Among these, the most spectacular are the often sizable caskets inlaid with semi-precious stones and embellished in large areas with surface veneers of mother-of-pearl, rock-crystal medallions, and columns (cat. 146, p. 232). In his history of Venice, published in 1581, Francesco Sansovino

cat. 132. Fra Giovanni Giocondo da Verona
Syllogue (detail)

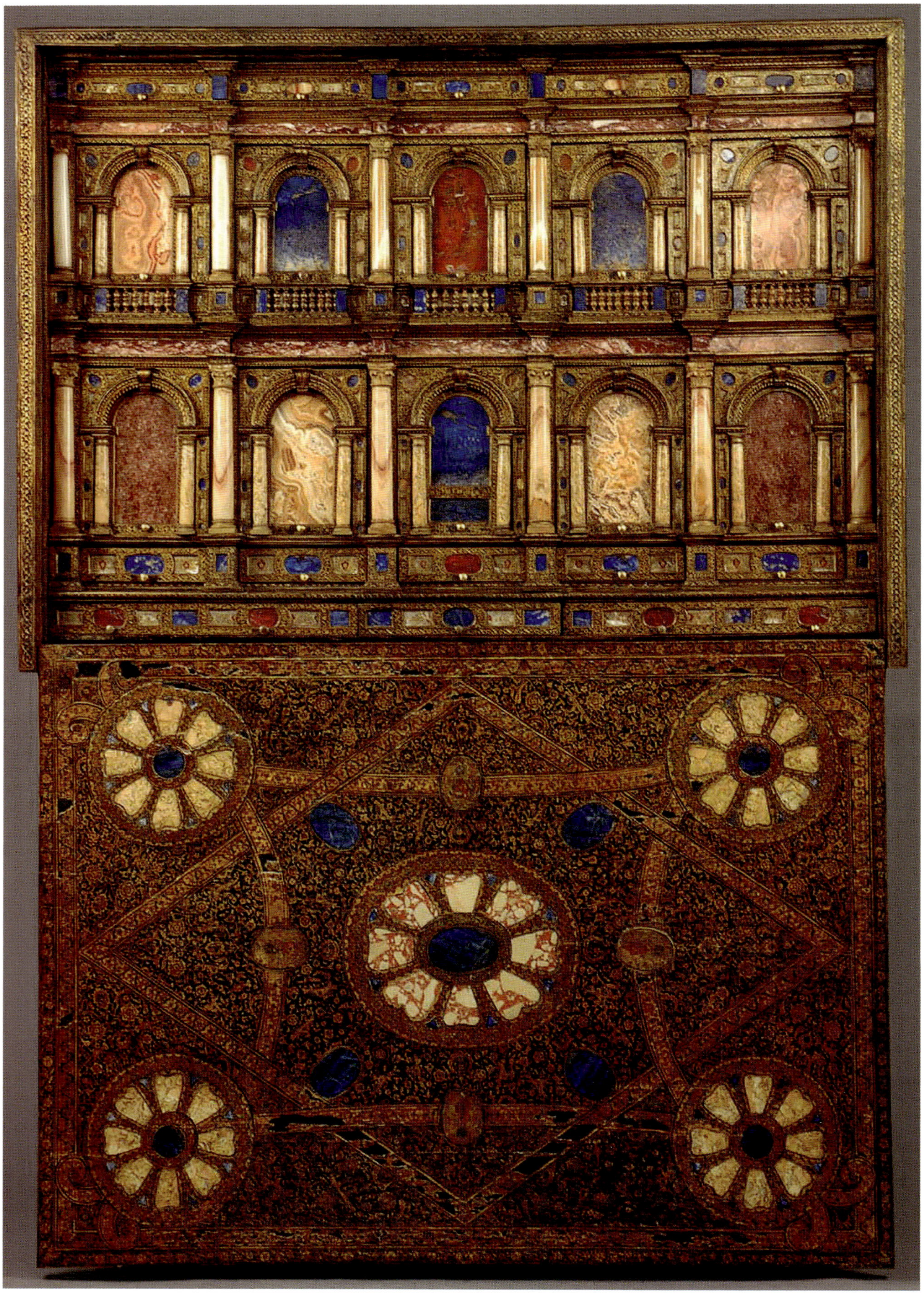

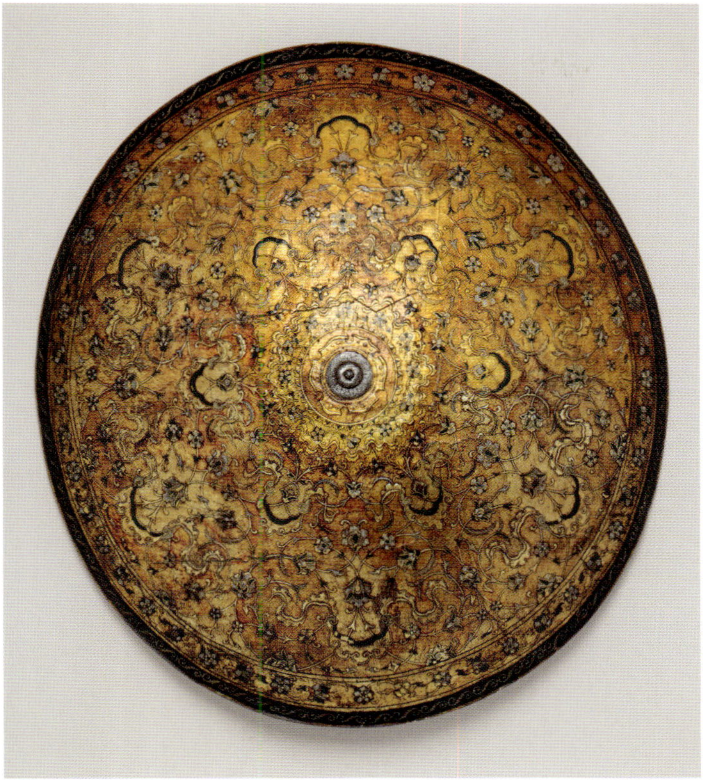

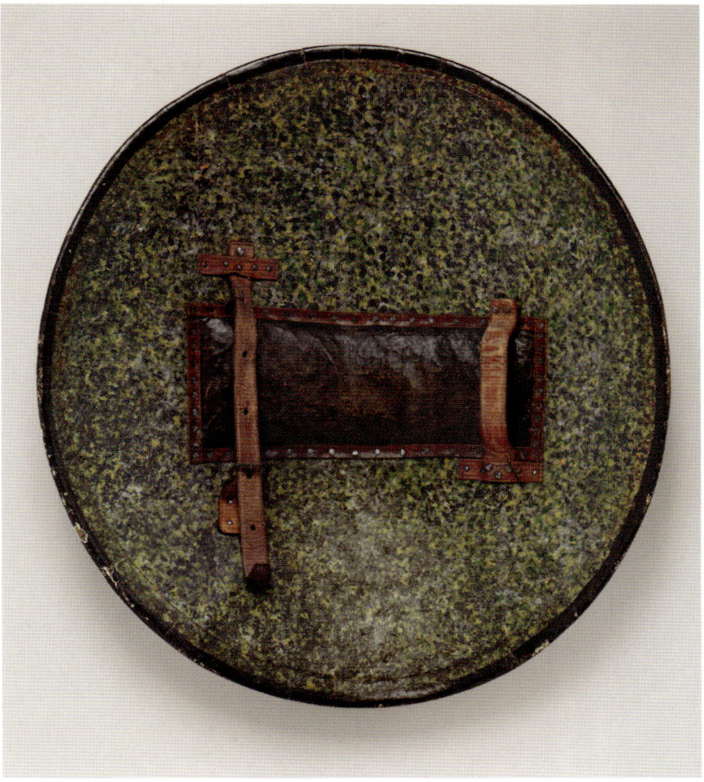

cat. 140. *Parade Shield*
(front and back)
Venice, late 16th century
The Metropolitan Museum of Art, New York

reports having seen in the shop of the jeweler Antonio Maria Fontana in Venice's Ruga dei Oresi "a very large chest of crystal glass that is conceived so that the objects that are placed inside it appear as if they are sculpted outside."[14] A uniquely surviving pair of doors decorated in the manner of these caskets has only recently come to light and is shown in the exhibition (cat. 144, p. 237).[15]

The sheer number of these Venetian lacquer-painted works, and the sometimes astonishing similarity of their decoration to Ottoman Turkish decorative patterns, pose questions that are still not easily answered. While the attribution to Venice has been convincingly resolved by Huth in his study of one of these remarkable caskets (cat. 145, p. 105)[16] the reasons why this fashion of gilded "lacquer decoration"—in the end a rather short-lived fashion—occurred in this period and what, exactly, were the models used by Venetian craftsmen, have not yet been completely explained, although some suggestions are offered below.

Most puzzling are the shields and quivers decorated in the Ottoman style: they were clearly made for use in Venice, as indicated by the application of medallions with the lion of St. Mark in their center, and sometimes by the initials and the coats of arms of renowned Venetian families.[17]

But what was their function? The above-quoted claim in Molmenti—that they were made for "simple foot-soldiers"—does not today seem plausible even though, to my knowledge, this passage remains the only known reference to the specific occasions for which shields were created and used.[18] The answer probably lies in the curious European conceit of the 16th century, in which classical heroes were identified as Turks—or more precisely, in which figures of classical Antiquity were dressed in Turkish clothing. A good example is provided by the figure of Aristotle wearing Turkish garb, in an illuminated Venetian copy of his works (cat. 17, p. 165).[19] Another aspect of this conceit is the extraordinary practice of equipping

cat. 146. *Collector's Cabinet*
Venice, 1565–1680
Kunstgewerbemuseum, Berlin

cat. 135. *Shield*
Venice, late 16th century
Armeria di Palazzo Ducale, Venice

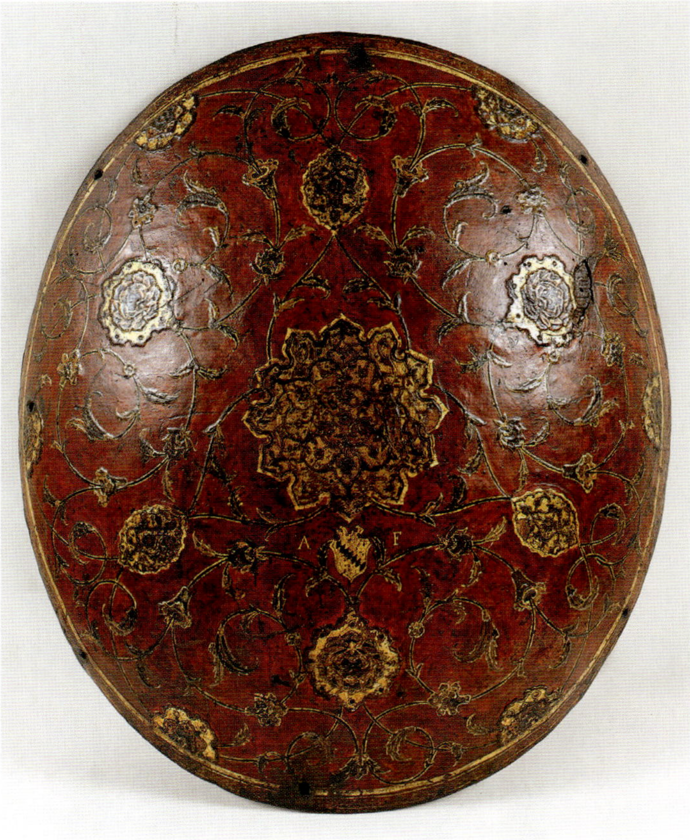

contemporary figures of celebrity with a "Turkish" bodyguard. The most famous of these incidents is recorded, in some detail, in the surviving costume book of the tailor who created garments for the entourage of the future king of Spain, Phillip II, for his entry into the city of Milan in 1548.[20] A similar adoption of Turkish costumes and weaponry is recorded for the cavalry of the archbishop of Salzburg, Prince Wolf Dietrich von Raitenau (1587–1611).[21] Many of these lacquer-painted shields decorated in the Ottoman Turkish style have survived: in Salzburg, where they have been generally regarded as Venetian works made to order for the archbishop (cat. 140, p. 233), in Venice (cats. 135, 136, 137, 139, pp. 234–36),[22] and elsewhere.[23]

The patterns on the Venetian pieces are clearly inspired by Ottoman designs on objects that had come to Venice by many different routes, no doubt partly as booty obtained in the constant battles with the Turks (see cat. 77, p. 65; cats. 113 and 134, p. 238), but equally through commercial contacts with the Ottoman world.[24] One must, of course, take into consideration the much earlier direct contact between Venetian craftsmen and the Turkish capital (cat. 175), of which the story of the famous ceremonial helmet made in Venice for Sultan Sulëyman is the most striking example (cat. 59, p. 112).[25]

It is curious that among the shields of undisputed Turkish manufacture, which can be traced back to the Turkish wars of Archduke Ferdinand II of Tyrol (1529–1596)[26]—yielding a considerable "Türkenbeute" now almost entirely in the Weltliche Schatzkammer in Vienna—none can be considered as a direct model for the European "lacquer-painted" shields. Instead, the majority are made of metal,[27] or are of the more common *kalkan* type (a light, round, convex ceremonial shield made of coiled wicker formed by a spiral coil of reed cable wrapped in silk threads (see cat. 76, p. 238; cat. 77, p. 65), and all are generally decorated with abstract floral, geometric, or cloud-band designs.[28] One exception is represented by a shield in Vienna,[29] which is decorated in the same lacquer-painting technique as the Venetian and Salzburg shields.[30]

cat. 136. *Shield*
Venice, late 16th century
Armeria di Palazzo Ducale, Venice

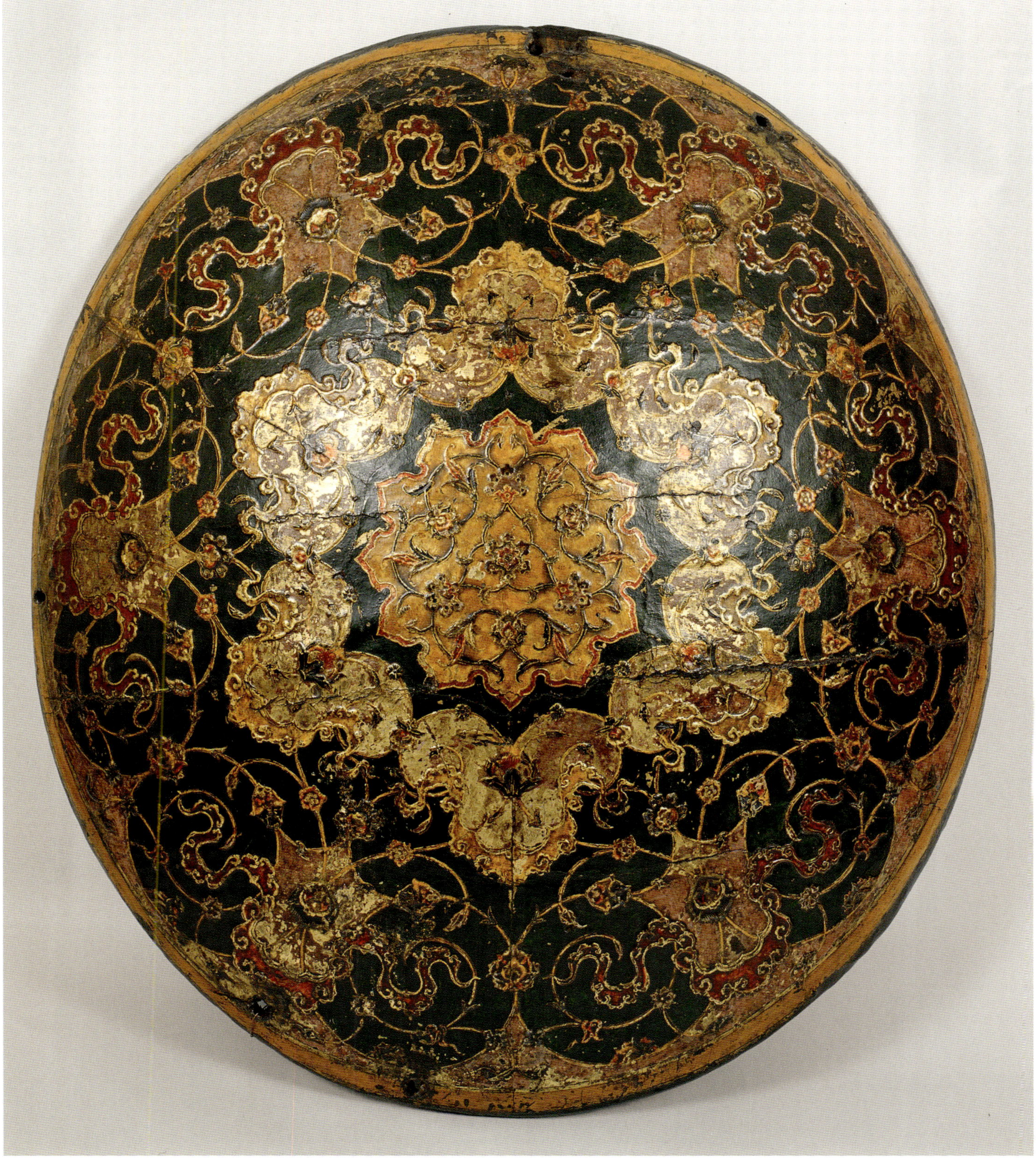

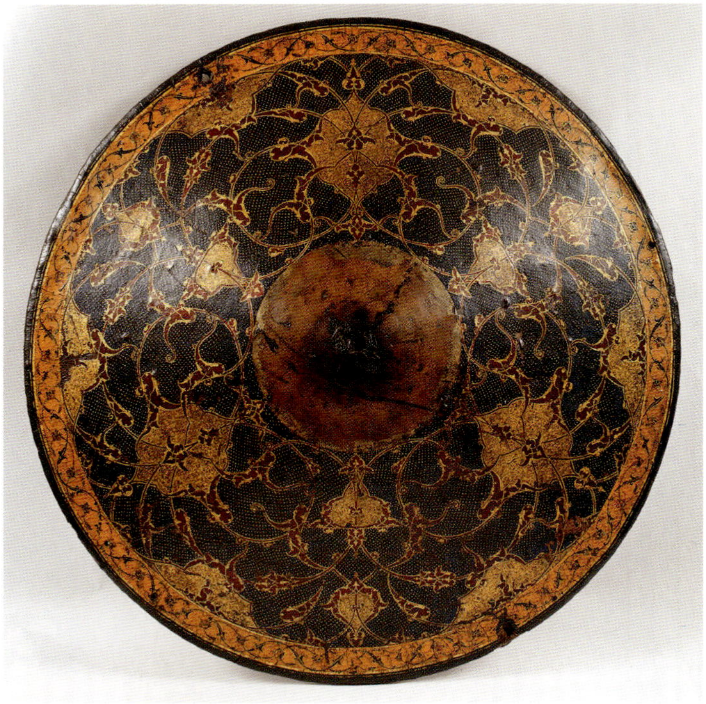

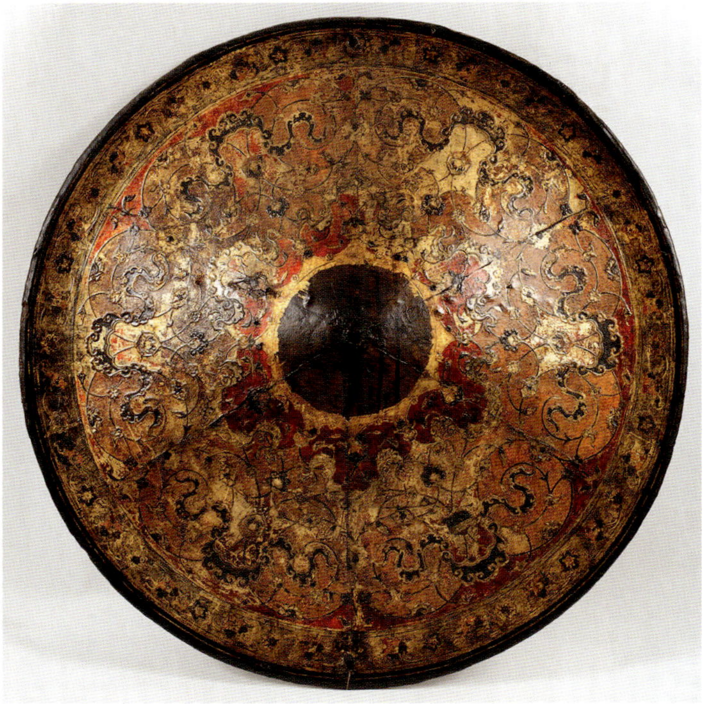

cat. 137. *Shield*
Venice, late 16th century
Armeria di Palazzo Ducale, Venice

cat. 139. *Shield*
Venice, late 16th century
Armeria di Palazzo Ducale, Venice

There is, however, a very fine leather case for a bow and arrows, decorated with elaborate arabesque patterns in gold and colors, that can be dated to the middle of the 16th century coming as it does from the Turkish booty of Ferdinand II during his wars with the Turks in 1566.[31]

By far the largest number of Venetian objects decorated in a decidedly Near Eastern manner consists of bookbindings, which underscores the close involvement of the Venetian humanist scholars in the promotion of this art form.[32] Here the question of models, and of function, is more easily answered. Muslim lacquered—or molded and tooled—bookbindings can be found in many European collections, including the Marciana and Cini libraries and the Correr Museum in Venice. The sheer sumptuousness and splendor of Islamic manuscripts easily explain the impact they must have had on European bookbinders of the period.[33] Turkish and Persian bookbindings of various types (see cats. 126, 127, 129, pp. 239–240) as well as the elaborate tooled bindings of Mamluk Egypt (cat. 125, p. 240)[34] were imitated by European craftsmen (see cats. 130–33, pp. 239–241); their use in various urban centers throughout Europe is well documented and often precisely datable on the basis of the manuscripts or documents they contain. It may seem somewhat strange that the Venetians, of all people, would use unmistakably Ottoman models for the bindings of presentation copies of official documents, yet there seems to have been little hesitation in doing just that, as is made abundantly clear by one of the most splendid examples of the type, the Newberry Library binding containing the document of appointment by Doge Alvise Mocenigo of Girolamo da Mula as *procuratore* of San Marco in 1572 (fig. 1, p. 242).[35]

cat. 144. *Pair of doors*
Venice, ca. 1575–1600
Rainer Zietz, Ltd., London

These bookbindings, not so much by virtue of their large number but rather in their great variety of techniques and patterns, seem to have been the primary medium that provided models for European, especially Venetian, craftsmen. On the bindings may be seen many of the technical qualities, the use of materials, and the specific motifs that are encountered in the decoration of the lacquer-painted Venetian shields. There is an especially intimate connection between the specific forms of arabesque designs painted in gold that appear on some of these

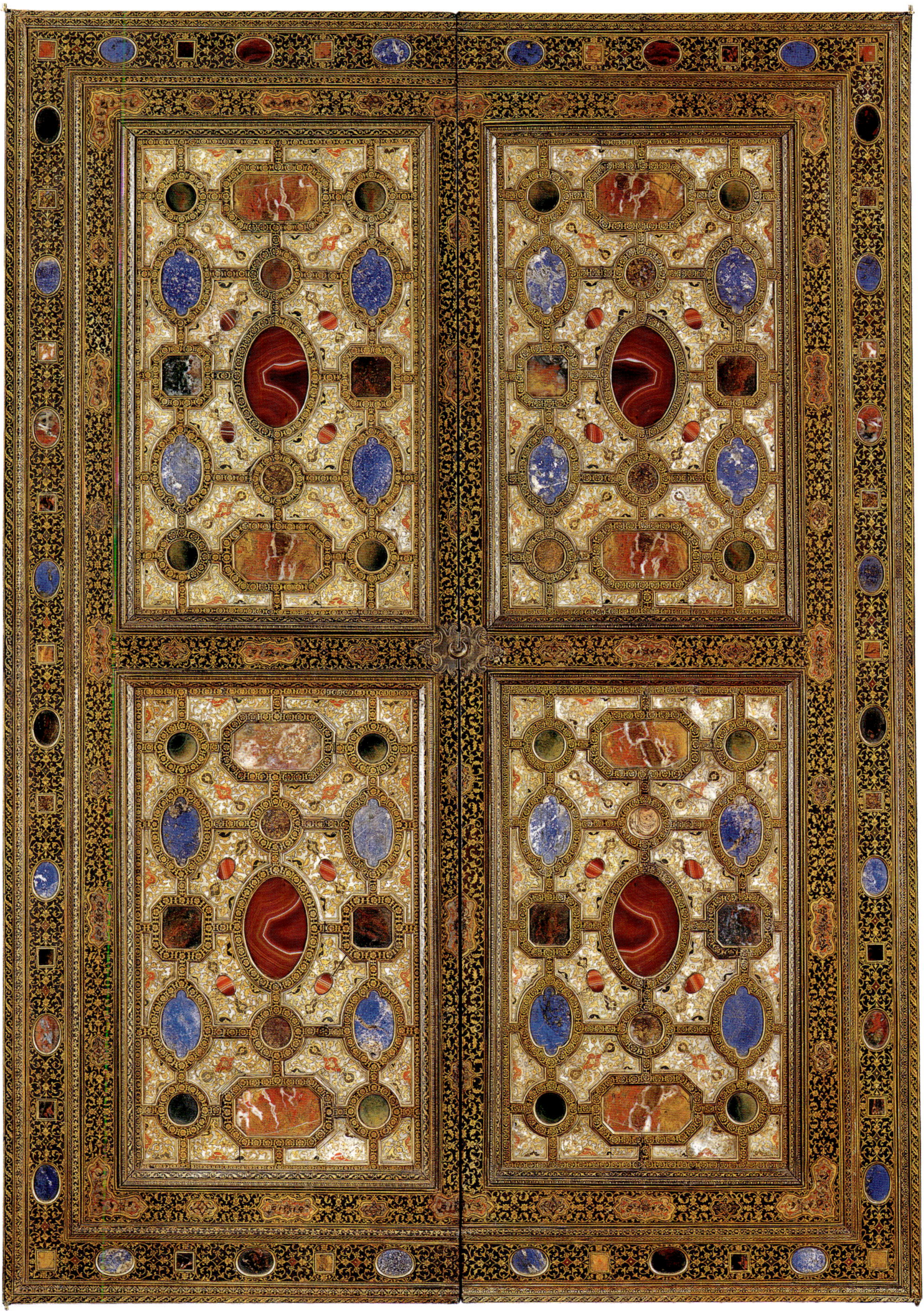

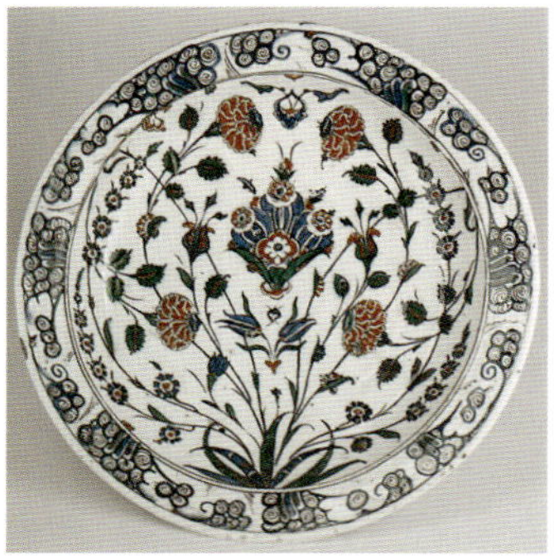

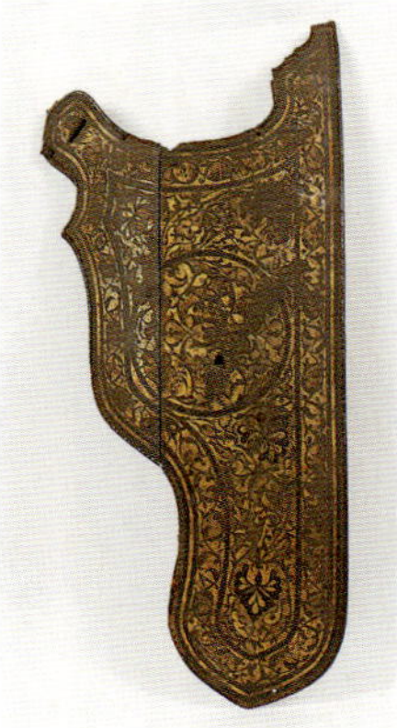

bindings[36] and those on a variety of boxes, both small[37] and large, the latter at times taking the shape of miniature *cassoni*[38] (smaller versions of the famous 15th- and 16th-century Italian dowry chests that are often very richly decorated).[39] The connection between bookbindings and other lacquered objects of this type becomes nowhere clearer than in the decoration of some of the larger cabinets whose doors are frequently painted with designs that resemble open bookbindings.[40]

Equally striking is the reference to Islamic and Islamicizing book-cover designs in the decoration of some Venetian musical instruments of the later 16th century, especially the front case of a set of virginals, such as the one signed by Benedetto Floriani and dated 1571 (cat. 143, p. 242).[41] There are also a number of such 16th-century instruments decorated with patterns that recall bindings made for important and official documents, with the typical overlay in high relief and the sunken sections of irregular shapes, both decorated with a typical short-stemmed arabesque pattern.[42] Finally, others are decorated with patterns that are perhaps not so closely linked to Near Eastern bookbindings but are clearly indebted to similar models, for instance the famous virginal of Queeen Elizabeth I, in the Victoria and Albert Museum in London.[43]

The same scheme of surface decoration can be seen on the extraordinary doors in the collection of Rainer Zietz in London (cat. 144, p. 237).[44] Probably made for an unusually large cabinet or a closet, they combine all the decorative elements that appear on the other lacquer-painted objects here under discussion. Set into a wide frame are four large rectangular panels,

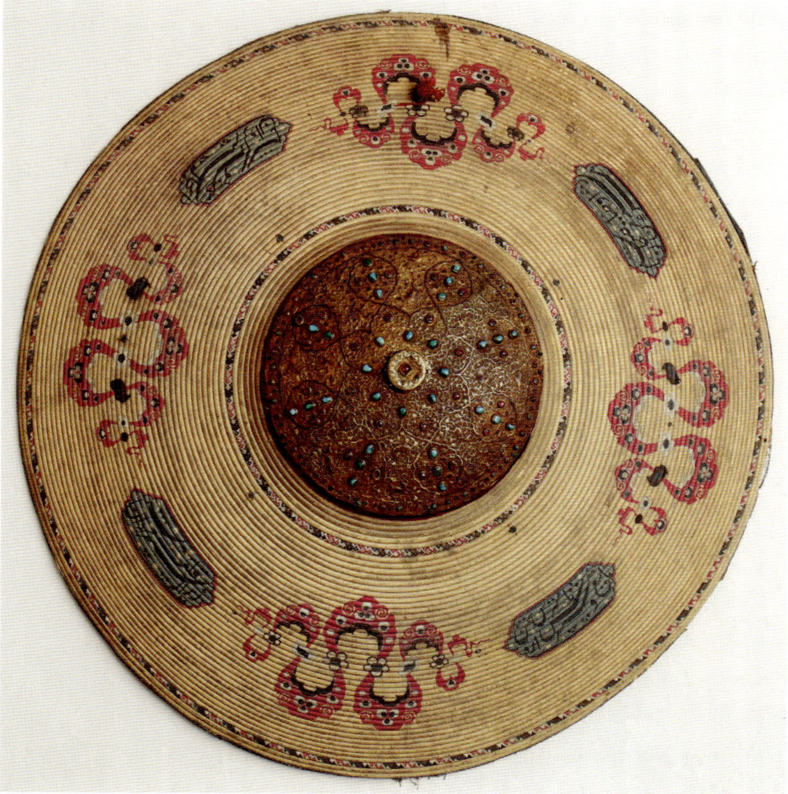

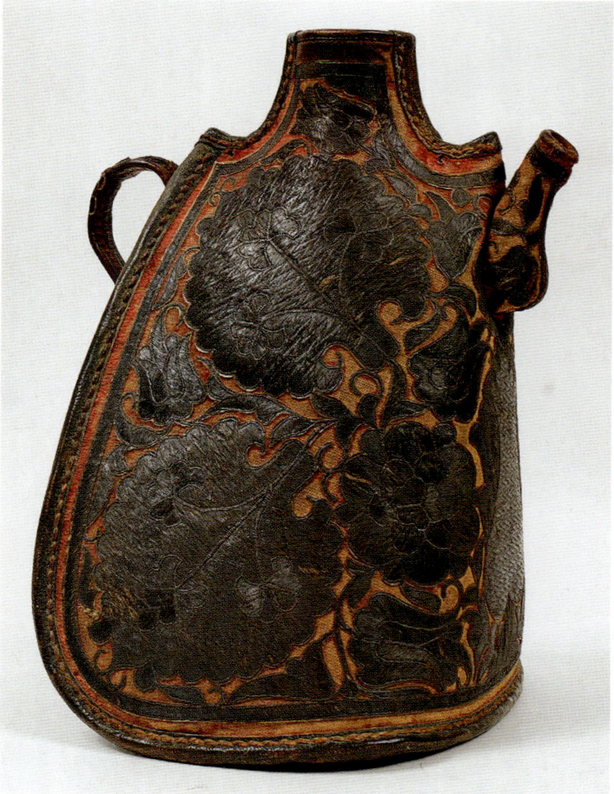

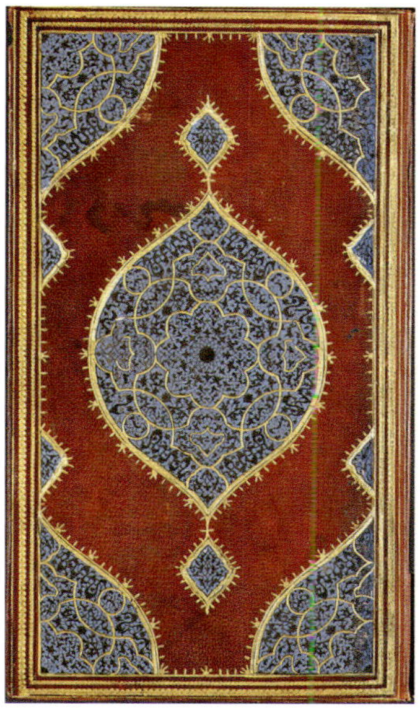

cat. 126. Nizami
Khamsa
Shiraz, Iran, 1510
The Metropolitan Museum of Art, New York

cat. 132. Fra Giovanni Giocondo da Verona
Syllogue
Bound in Venice ca. 1520–30
Trustees of the Chatsworth Settlement, Chatsworth

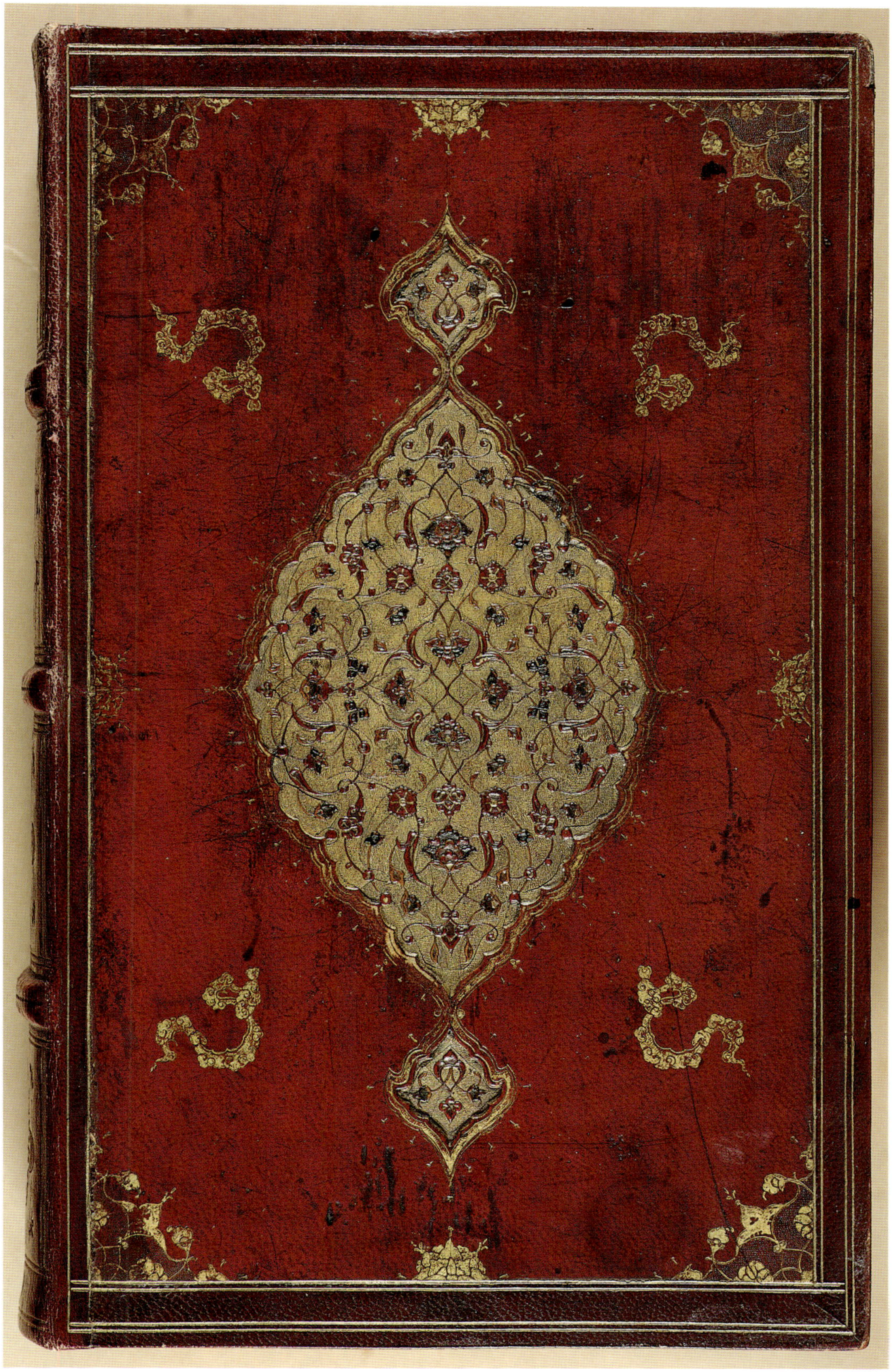

cat. 175. *Plate*
Iznik, Turkey, ca. 1575
Scuola Grande di San Rocco, Venice

cat. 113. *Quiver*
Ottoman Empire, probably the Balkans
17th century
Museo Civico Correr, Venice

cat. 76. *Shield*
Turkey, mid-16th century
Topkapı Sarayi Müsezi, Istanbul

cat. 134. *Flask* (matara)
Turkey 17th century.
Museo Civico Correr, Venice

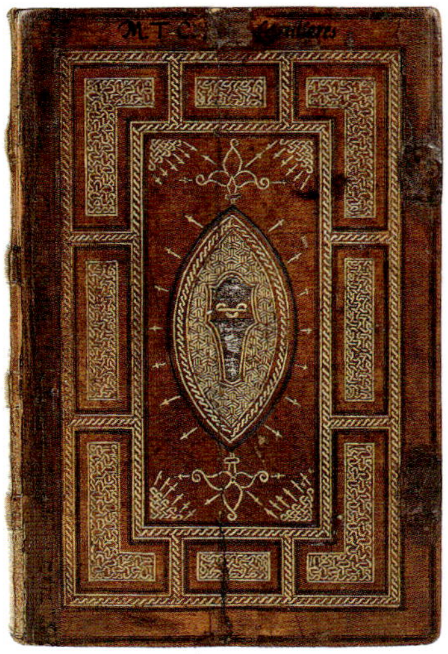
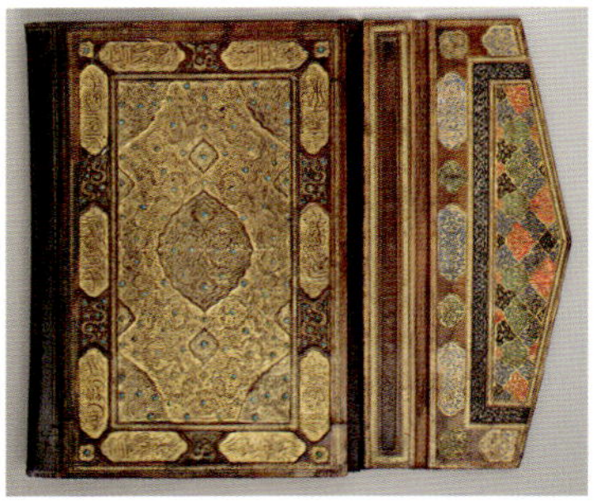
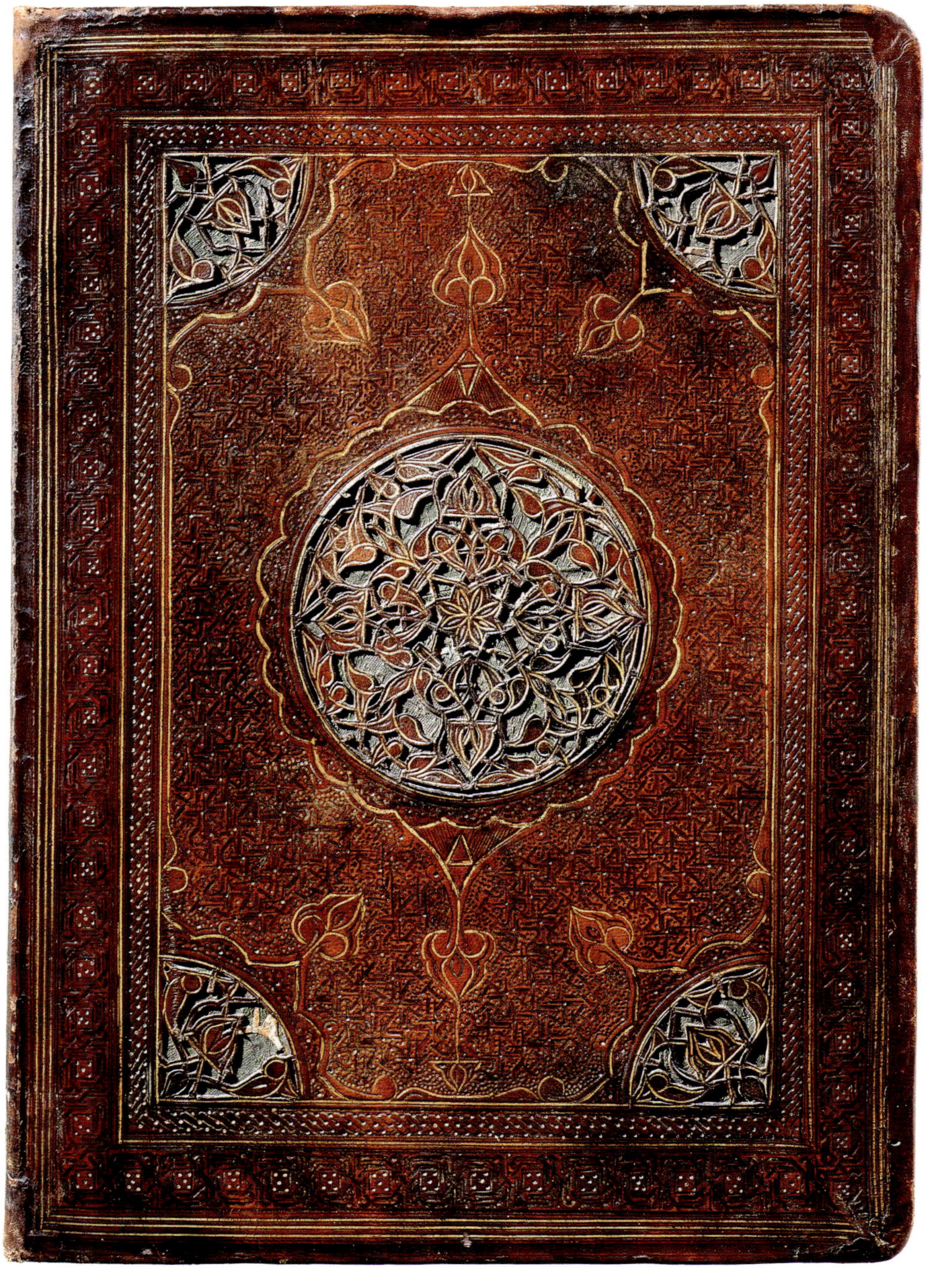

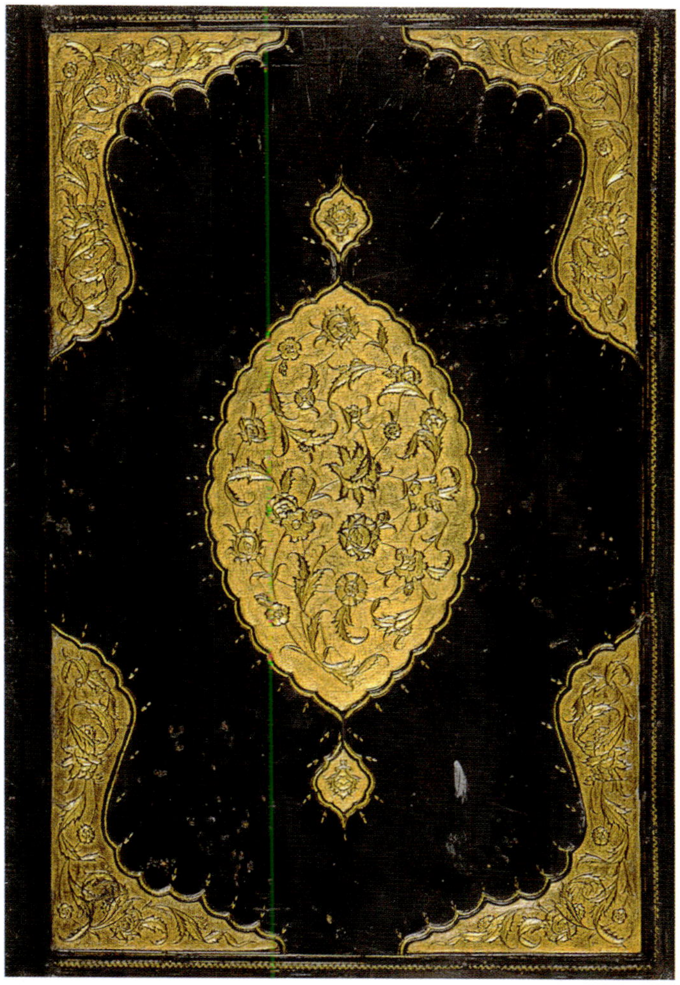

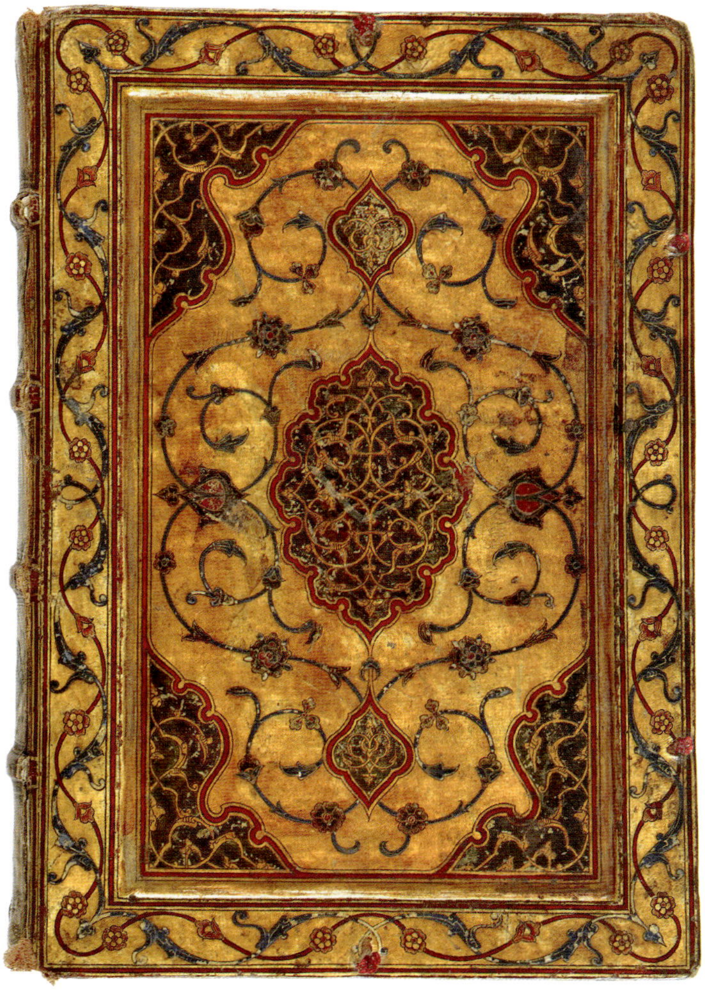

each surrounded by a narrow molded frame and each, again, set into a narrower continuous flat frame consisting of an elaborate interconnected network of raised relief medallions of different sizes and shapes—oval, round, and octagonal—filled with semi-precious stones. The entire pattern is set against a background of mother-of-pearl, sometimes painted with gold, red, and black arabesques, very similar to some of the Venetian bindings and caskets mentioned above. All the frames on the doors are decorated in gold on a black background with a variety of motifs, of which the arabesque patterns in the wider ones are, again, very close to those on Venetian bookbindings as well as the lacquer-painted frames of the later 16th century.[45] Consequently, there can be little question that these doors were produced in Venice towards the end of the 16th century. The unusual use of large semi-precious stones to embellish the four inset rectangular sections of the doors finds close parallels in a number of other Venetian cabinets and boxes. The largest example is in the Palazzo Doria Pamphili in Rome, attributed by Huth to about 1580.[46] Others are very similar in form, size, and decoration to a fine example in the Kunstgewerbemuseum in Berlin (cat. 146, p. 232).[47] It has recently been restored and published in an elaborate report by Bert-Uwe Hellbing, in which 11 recorded pieces are illustrated, so that it can be seen how similar most of them are to the Berlin cabinet.[48]

A small box entirely decorated with lapidary work, reducing to a minimum the framework of the casket holding the stones together, is in the Weltliche Schatzkammer in Vienna.[49] Such a box leads directly to the large and magnificent caskets that are so richly embellished

cat. 127. Al-Bukhar
Sahīh
Turkey, 1529
The Nasser D. Khalili Collection, London

cat. 133. Ludovico Dolce
Le Trasformazioni
Venice, 1553
Fondazione Giorgio Cini, Venice

cat. 129. *Binding for a Qur'an*
Iran, late 16th century
The Metropolitan Museum of Art, New York

cat. 125. *Vol. 22 of a 30-part Qu'ran manuscript*
Egypt, ca. 1388-99
Bibliothèque Nationale de France, Paris

cat. 130. Virgil
Opera
Venice, 1460s
The British Library, London

cat. 131. Cicero
Epistolae ad familiares
Venice or Padua, 1475
Bibliothèque Nationale de France, Paris

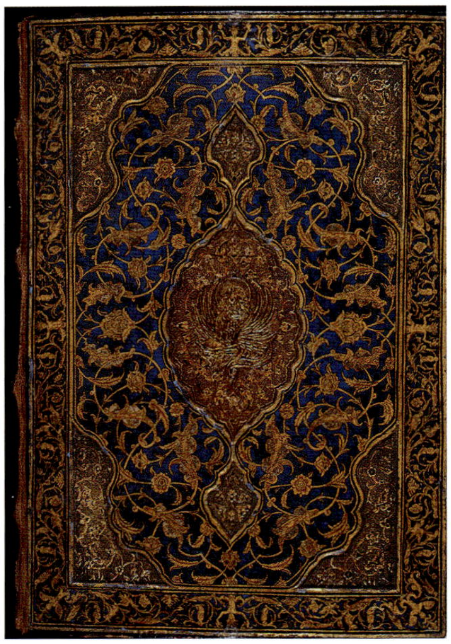

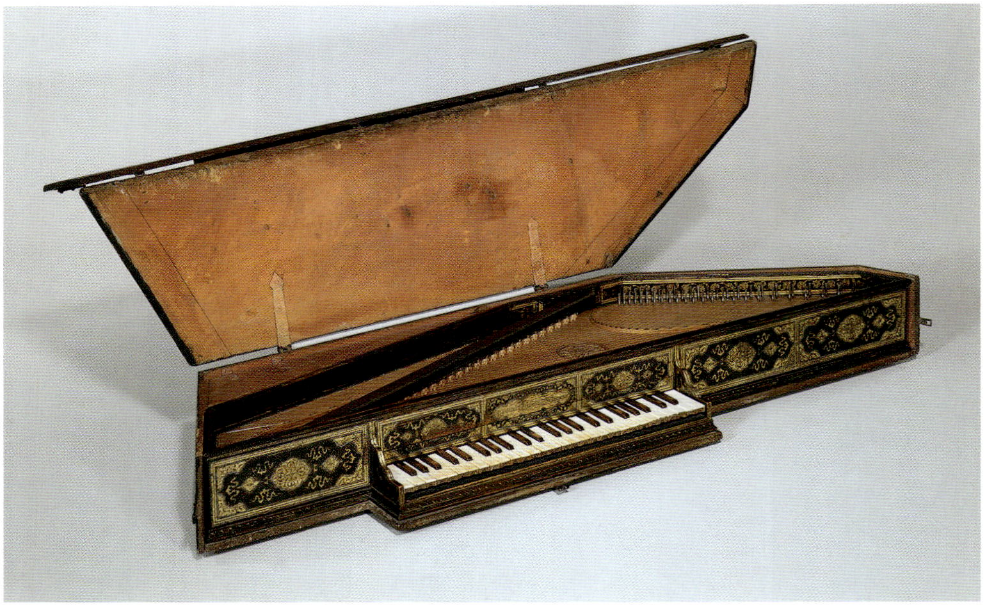

fig. 1. *Commissione* of Girolamo da Mula, 1572. The Newberry Library, Chicago

cat. 143. Benedetto Floriani
Polygonal Virginal (Spinetta)
Venice, 1572
Musée de la Musique /
Cité de la Musique, Paris

with crystal and elaborate gold painting on black "lacquered" wood. Huth has identified these caskets, of which only a few survive (see cat. 145, p. 105),[50] as objects commissioned by the pope to serve as gifts on specific occasions: these rich containers were intended to hold the fine baby linens for the first-born heirs of the Catholic rulers of Europe.[51] The gold decoration of these magnificent caskets is extraordinarily close to contemporary Ottoman designs surviving in a variety of decorative mediums, including "lacquer" bindings.[52]

It can thus be seen that the production of Venetian lacquer in the Ottoman style, although it may have lasted only half a century, is unquestionably one of the more remarkable phenomena in the colorful story of the cultural exchanges between Venice and the Orient. The adherence of the Venetian lacquer-makers to models of Near Eastern design, at times astonishingly close; the application of these to objects of thoroughly European function (with the notable exception of bookbindings); and their apparent creation of that curious genre, the lacquered and densely patterned leather-covered shield, all point to a particularly fascinating moment in the complex history of the relationship between the Turks and the Venetians—if not the Western world—that needs much further study. This important exhibition will undoubtedly contribute greatly to resolving some of these unanswered questions.[53]

Notes

1 See, respectively, Huth 1971, figs. 38–44, 45–47, 49–51, and 52.
2 Huth 1971, pp. 2ff. For a discussion of this technique, see Grube 1974, especially p. 376, note 1. The painted panel, here attributed to the early 17th century, has since been recognized as belonging to a 19th-century Persian atelier, as are a number of other objects published as comparative material in this article (figs. 10 and 15); see Grube 1982, p. 292, group 3, no. 6. For lacquer in the Muslim world, see also the introduction in Khalili, Robinson, and Stanley 1996, p. 11, where the use of the term "lacquer painting" for lacquered and varnished objects in the Muslim world is defended: ". . . as the word lacquer is derived from an Indian term referring to a quite different substance (the lakh mentioned by Kiani) [in Grube 1982, pp. 211–24] and is freely applied in English to a wide range of varnishes and varnished wares, it seems churlish to forbid its use in an Islamic context."
3 For the technique of varnishing and gilding leather in Venice, see especially Fioravanti 1562, captions 57 and 70, pp. 265, 273; Garzoni 1589, pp. 828–29, discorso 127: *"De' Pelliciari, et Cuoiai."* The quote translated in the text is from Molmenti 1910–12, vol. 2, p. 205: *"Le pelli conce, particolarmente di montone o di capra, erano stampate e dorate, impresse a figure, a arabeschi, a fiori, a fogliami, ricoperte di stemmi e d'imprese, modellate a ferro caldo a bassorilievo. Il cuoio dorato non serviva solo a paramenti di stanze, ma anche a coprir casse e cofanetti, e si piegava a formar caschi, scudi e turcassi, sui quali, fra eleganti fregi, spiccava il leone di San Marco: opere di lusso delicato, e che pur servivano ad uso di semplici soldati."*
4 Contadini 1989.
5 Huth 1971, pl. 3, and color pl. 2; Ledermuseum 1974, pl. 7; Boccia 1975, pls. 169–70; Poldi Pezzoli 1985, pl. 372; Grube 1989a, fig. 1; Contadini 1989, figs. 3–10, 12–14; Franzoi 1990, pp. 81–84, cat. 102–31; p.169, figs. 34–37; p. 43, pl. 25; p. 57, pl. 39.
6 Huth 1971, pls. 5–6; Franzoi 1990, pp. 120–21, cat. 378–84; pp. 201–02, figs. 125–26; p. 59, pl. 42.
7 Ledermuseum 1974, cat. no. 1.40.01.
8 Huth 1971, pls. 7–8, 12.
9 Huth 1971, pl. 1; Grube 1989a, figs. 3a, 3b.
10 Huth 1971, pls. 17–20a, 27–28, 37.
11 Huth 1971, pls. 9, 21–26, and color pl. III.
12 Huth 1971, pls. 13–16.
13 Huth 1971, pls. 31–36.
14 Huth 1971, p. 8, cited from Sansovino 1581. The passage reads in Italian: *"una cassa di cristallo molto grande fatta di modo che le cose che si ripongono dentro appariscano tutte scolpite di fuori."* Molmenti 1910–12, vol. 2, p. 174, quotes the same text from an edition of Sansovino of 1563, p. 364. For a list and images of nine such caskets, see Huth 1971, p. 16, note 13. The caskets are in [1] Lisbon, Museu Nacional de Arte Antiga (Huth 1971, pl. 24); [2] St. Louis, City Art Museum (Huth 1971, color pl. I, pl. 26; [3] formerly Hever Castle Collection (Kent), sold Sotheby's London, May 6, 1983, lot 287 and later Christie's, London, December 12, 2000; [4] present whereabouts unknown, formerly Paris, duc de Mouchy (Huth 1971, pl. 23); [5] San Simeon, California, Hearst Castle (Third Heibronner Sale, Paris, 1922, no. 75); [6] present whereabouts unknown, Sale Alfred de Rothschild, London, 1884, no. 189; [7] Present whereabouts unknown, formerly Paris, Baron Alexis de Rede, sold Sotheby's Monaco, May 26, 1975, lot 157, then the Duke of Westminster Collection, Eaton Hall, sold Sotheby's London, June 12, 1995, lot 254; [8] Present whereabouts unknown, sale Robiony, Nice, February 15, 1965, no. 157, pl. 24; [9] Paris, Baron and Baroness Elie de Rothschild. Five more objects must now be added to Huth's list: [10] Mantua, Basilica di Santa Barbara (Chambers and Martineau 1981, pp. 207–8, cat. no. 21; [11] Present whereabouts unknown, Christie's Sale, October 20, 1971, lot 157 (Peter Harris); [12] Lady Rossmore, Christie's Sale, December 8, 1992, lot 15, then Rainer Zietz, London (Auerspach–Trautson 1998, pl. 1, fig. 2; [13] Present whereabouts unknown, formerly Antiquaria Ltd, London (*Apollo*, 127, no. 312, February 1988, advertisement with color illustration on back of front cover); [14] Present whereabouts unknown (Kopplin 1998, p. 24). I am grateful to Rainer Zietz for having provided me with information on several caskets that have changed hands since the list was compiled.
15 Christie's, New York, January 10, 1995, lot 63, now Rainer Zietz Ltd., London. See also Auersperg–Trautson 1989.
16 Saint Louis Art Museum, inv. no. 1958.346; see Huth 1968; Huth 1971, color pl. I, fig. 26; Grube 1989a, p. 221, figs. 4a, 4b.
17 Huth 1971, color pl. II; Franzoi, 1990, p. 169, fig. 36.
18 Molmenti 1911, vol. 2, p. 205.
19 New York, Pierpont Morgan Library, inv. nos. 21194 and 21195; see Fortini Brown 1996, pp. 202–03, pls. 221–22, pp. 270–71.
20 Saxl 1937. The album in which the costumes designed for this reception procession are collected (61 pages, 48 figures) has since been published in a facsimile edition (Saxl *et al.* 1987).
21 Salzburg 1987, p. 370, cat. no. 163 for the illustration of a shield from a surviving inventory of 1664, listing 398 such pieces in the armory of Salzburg castle. See also Tietze 1919, p. 301, note 1; p. 302, fig. 394, where these works are attributed to Venice, ca. 1550; Ledermuseum 1974, color pl. 7, cat. no. 1.40.05; Grube 1989a, p. 220, fig. 1.
22 Franzoi 1990, pp. 80–85, nos. 102–31.
23 For example, in Prague, Museum of Decorative Arts; see Letosnikova 1968, p. 32.
24 Mack 2002, chapter 7: "Bookbinding and Lacquer".
25 Kurz 1969; see also St. Clair 1973, cat. no. 2 for an illustration of Agostino Veneziano's engraving of 1535, which shows the sultan wearing this helmet (cat. 59). For Marin Sanudo's report that he had seen *"il 2 ottobre 1533, a Rialto"* jewelry made in Venice to be offered for sale in Istanbul, see also Molmenti 1910–12, vol. 2, p. 175.
26 See Kupelwieser 1899.
27 Hummelberger 1969; see also Petrasch, Sanger, and Zimmermann 1991, p. 171, no. 117; Istanbul 1999, p. 72, fig. 2; Istanbul 2003, p. 109, cat. no. 22.
28 Zygulski 1999, p. 71: "*Kalkan* is a light, round, convex shield used in many historical countries of the East, especially in Persia and Turkey. . . . The structure of the *kalkan*, like . . . the structure of a basket, is formed by a spiral coil of reed cable called *rotang*, a withe of dogwood, fig, or osier, and woolen, cotton, or silk thread, as well as metal thread, around the central wooden disk, covered on the outside by a metal boss or umbo." For examples see Zygulski 1999, pp. 70, 74–77, figs. 1, 3–6; Washington 1966, cat. no. 234, color illustration on cover; Ingolstadt 1979, cat. no. 45, fig. 7; Istanbul 1983, cat. nos. E.104 and 105; Vienna 1983, pp. 196–97, cat. nos. 16/83, 84, 86; Tenenti 1985, pp. 81–82, figs. 93–94; Recklinghausen 1985, vol. 2, p. 363, cat. nos. 11/21, 22; Falk 1985, p. 307, cat. no. 317; Petrasch 1991, pp. 172–74, nos. 118–21; Atasoy 1992, pp. 50–51, color pl. 110, where they are correctly identified as ceremonial shields, and dated to the mid-16th century; Franzoi 1999, p. 54, pl. 38, pp. 23–124, cat. no. 395, wrongly identified as Persian and connected with the Persian embassy to Venice in 1602; Istanbul 2003, p. 110, cat. no. 23. There are a considerable number of such shields in the Correr Museum in Venice that do not appear to have been published (see cat. 77).
29 Wiener Zeughaus 1977, p. 184, cat. no. 925, pl. 7; Vienna 1983, p. 197, cat. no. 16/87, color illustration before p. 87.
30 Hummelberger 1969, p. 63, no. 94: the shield in question is inv. no. 126.2 29 and is attributed to the second half of the 17th century; Hummelberg 1969 also lists two *kalkan* types, nos. 91 and 92, one of which is illustrated on pp. 22–23 (inv. no. I.N.126.401); see also Contadini 1989, p. 241, note 40, where the attribution of the lacquer–painted shield to Turkey is questioned.
31 Huth 1971, pl. 5, p. 4, where he points out the close relationship of some of the small-scale patterns on this case to the border patterns of some of the boxes discussed below.
32 For a general overview, see Baltimore 1957 as well as Ettinghausen's (1959) comments based on that exhibition. See also Hobson 1989; Grube 1989a, figs. 2–3, 6–7, 17, 22; Hobson 1992; Mack 2002, pp. 125–37, for other examples; Granzotto 1995. Further important information concerning Venetian bookbindings in the Near Eastern manner can be found in De Marinis 1955, 1960, and 1966.
33 Michael Rogers has interpreted the fashion for Near Eastern-type bookbindings in the larger context of "Ornament Prints, Patterns, and Designs" in a penetrating and well-documented study (Rogers 1999). For 15th-century Turkish bindings, which could have served as models for pre-16th-century European designs, see Raby and Tanindi 1993. For the fashion of arabesque designs that developed in Europe, see Berliner 1926.
34 Hobson 1989 for an excellent overview; for Mamluk bindings see especially Bosch, Carswell, and Petherbridge 1981.
35 Huth 1971, pl. I; Grube 1989, color cover; Mack 2002, p. 134, fig. 143.
36 See, for example, the Venetian binding datable to 1550 in the Victoria and Albert Museum, London, inv. no. A.M.25-1881, published in Harthan 1961, p. 27, no. 25; there is another very similar binding in the same collection, inv. no. Ital.VII.1869 (=18134).
37 Huth 1971, pls. 7–8. They are respectively in Vienna (Kunsthistorisches Museum, inv. no. 4103 122, from the Collection of Archduke Ferdinand of Tyrol) and in London (Victoria and Albert Museum, inv. no. 217-1966), both small but tall toilet boxes.
38 Huth 1971, pl. 9.
39 Fleming and Honour 1989, pp. 159–60.
40 Huth 1971, pls. 17–18.
41 One is in Leipzig, Universitätsmuseum, inv. no. 33. See Huth 1971, pl. 32; Grube 1986, p. 226, fig. 18; Fontana and Heise 1998, pl. 14.
42 Huth 1971, pl. 33.
43 Inv. no. 19-1857. See Huth 1971, pl. 31; Patey 1978, pp. 4–5.
44 See above, note 15.
45 Huth 1971, pls. 13–16.
46 Huth 1971, pl. 19.
47 Berlin, Kunstgewerbemuseum, inv. no. 1933.26, see Hellbing 2005.
48 The cabinets are listed and illustrated in Appendix 3 of Hellbing's study: [1] Scloss Bebenhausen, Staatliche Sclösser und Gärten Baden Württemberg, published in Colle 1998, pp. 20–23; [2] Private Collection, sold at Christies, London, March 25, 1999, p. 63, illustrated; [3] Milan, Musei e Gallerie, published in Colle 1996, fig. 256; [4] Private Collection Mr. and Mrs. William J. Robertson, published in Huth 1971, color pl. III; [5] Vienna, Österreichisches Museum für Angewandte Kunst, published in Huth 1971, pls. 17–18, Windisch–Graetz 1983, p. 244; [6] Rome, Palazzo del Quirinale, published in Gonzàlez-Palacios 1996, pp. 42–43; [7] Rome, Palazzo Doria-Pamphili, published in Huth 1971, pl. 19, Riccardi–Cubitt 1992, p. 75; [8] Private Collection (recorded in Photo Archive of the Stefano Bardini Collection, Florence, no. 4400); [9] Ecouen, Musée national de la Renaissance, inv. no. ECL 9928; [10] Scloss Bebenhausen, Staatliche Sclösser und Gärten Baden Württemberg; [11] Hearst Collection, San Simeon, inv. no. 1562, published in Huth 1971, pl. 20a.
49 Huth 1971, pl. 22. The object is illustrated in color in Bauer et al. 1987, p. 256, no. 49.
50 Huth 1971, pls. 23–26; see the list in note 14, above.
51 Huth 1971, pp. 8ff.
52 For early Persian and Turkish bindings with elaborate arabesque decoration in gold on black, see Haldane 1983, pp. 82, cat. no. 3 no. 83; Khalili, Robinson, and Stanley 1996, pp. 22–25, cat. nos. 1–4; Rogers 1995, cat. no. 152.
53 See for this topic see a contribution Grube and Sims (forthcoming).

Venetian "Lacquer": A Scientific Approach

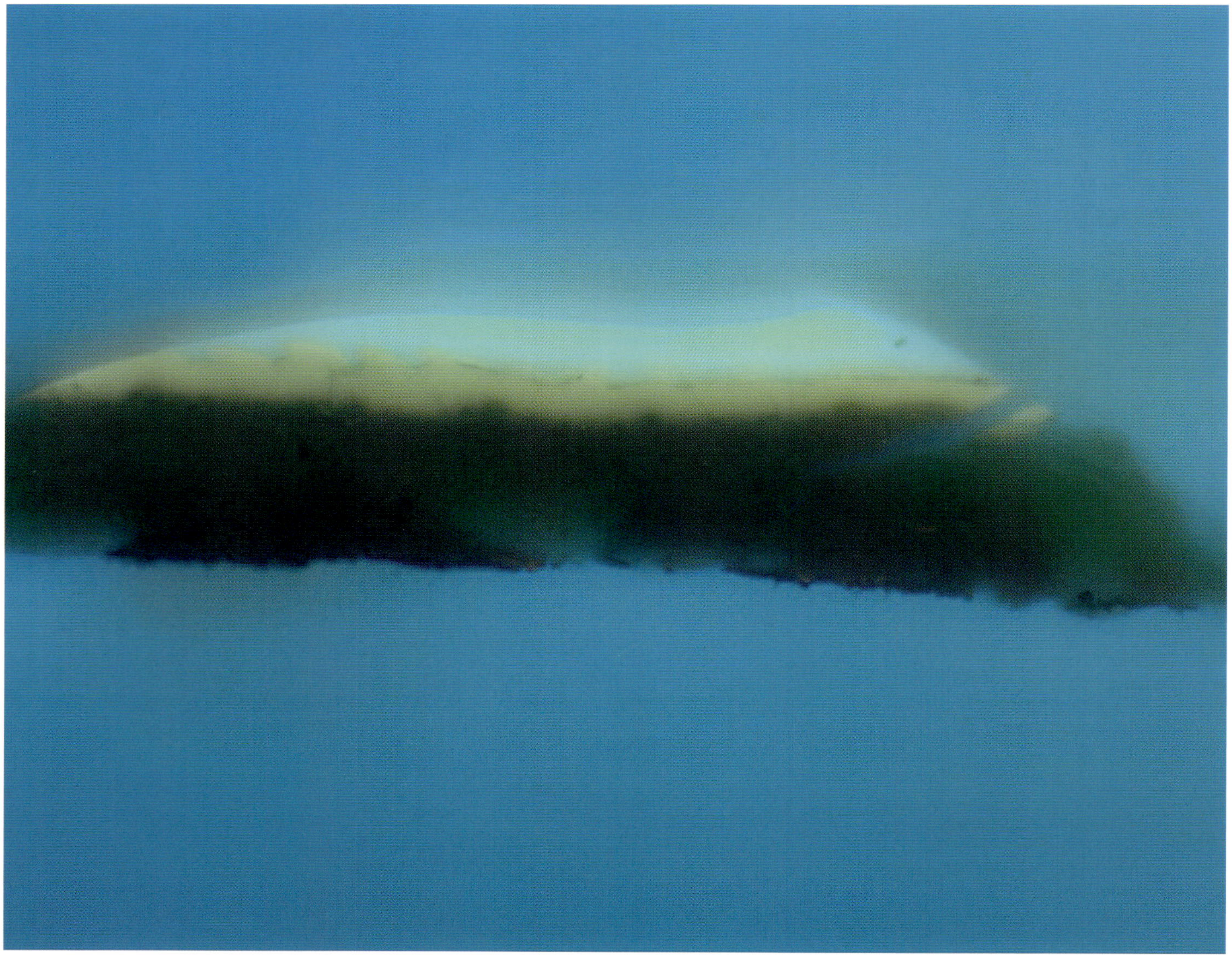

Adriana Rizzo

The word "lacquer" is now commonly used in association with the general glossy appearance of varnished objects rather than with the materials and techniques it originally was used to describe.[1] "True" lacquer, associated with the original lacquerware of China and Japan, can be described scientifically as the sap from the lacquer tree (*Rhus vernicifera*), which grows in China and Southeast Asia. The chemical composition and quality of the raw material, its cumbersome treatments, and application technique produce the unique gloss, hardness, and chemical resistance for which Far Eastern lacquerware is justly famous. On the one hand, its popularity in the regions where it was traded, such as the Near and Middle East and India, led to local imitations. On the other hand, the unavailability outside China and Japan of the original materials and lack of information on techniques for "true" lacquer required the development of new lacquer formulations and methods for achieving similar surface effects and durability. The application of new designs in the Islamic world—inspired by local traditions and other artistic influences while maintaining high-gloss surfaces—made them in turn objects of admiration and imitation in Europe, especially Venice.

The strategic position of Venice and its political and cultural role in trade with the Islamic Levant accounted for its constant exposure to commodities and luxury goods—including lacquerware—from the East.[2] Indian, Persian, and Ottoman lacquerware became increasingly fashionable in Europe—by way of Venice—in the second half of the 16th century. Venetian imitations of Islamic lacquer,[3] especially Ottoman and Persian, were first produced in the city between the end of the 15th and the second half of the 16th century.[4] Perhaps because of the greater availability of Far Eastern lacquerware in museum collections and the necessity to discriminate authentic lacquer from its numerous imitations,[5] thus far scientific research has mainly focused on the analysis of "true" lacquer. As a result, research on both Islamic and Venetian lacquerware has lagged behind.

For centuries Venice relied on trade with Turkey and Iran for the purchase of art materials, such as resins, gums,[6] pigments, and dyestuff.[7] At the same time, knowledge of their properties and applications arrived in Venice and thus local imitations of Persian and Ottoman

fig. 1. Close-up of cross-section of two layers of varnish on a casket (cat. 147)

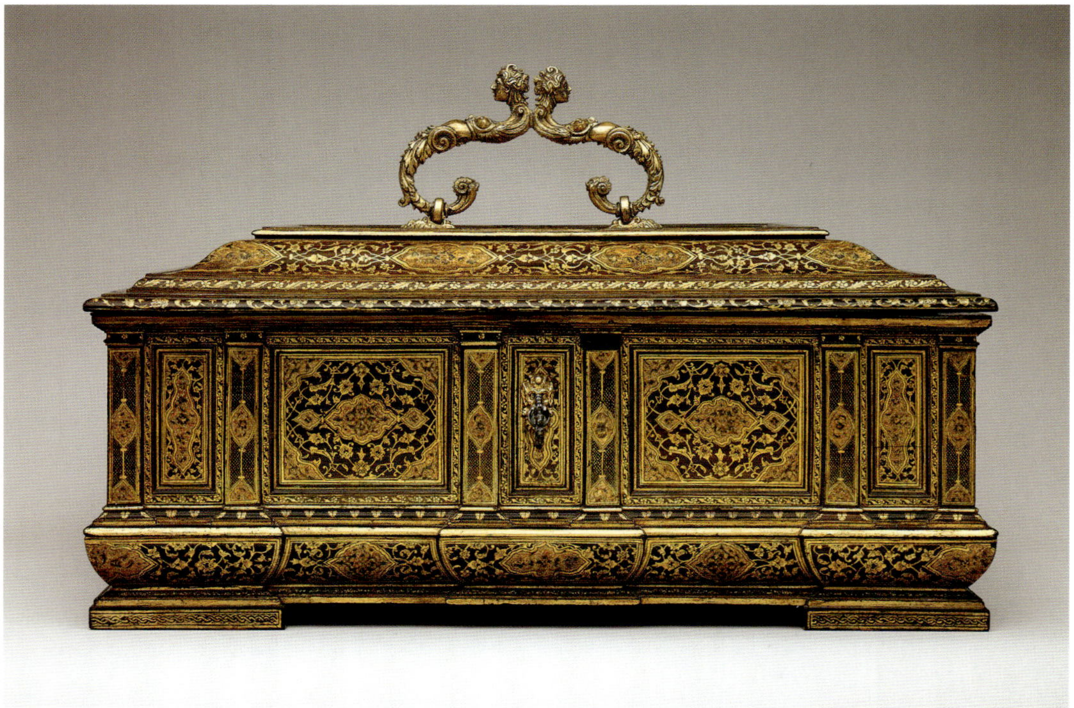

cat. 147. *Casket (Cofanetto* or *Scrigno)*
Venice, ca. 1570–90
The Metropolitan Museum of Art, New York

lacquered objects appeared. Members of the painters (*depentori*),[8] guild who were permitted to decorate a wide variety of objects, including paintings, boxes, and shields, were required to varnish their work prior to delivery to clients.[9] Therefore, the *depentori* must have been the craftsmen in charge of producing varnished objects.

In Iran in the late 15th century, one formulation of lacquer was sometimes adapted for use on leather, papier-mâché, and wood surfaces. The technique was apparently practiced both to protect decorated surfaces and to enhance their brightness.[10] A varnish called "bow gloss"[11] seems to have been applied over leather bookbindings, wooden bows, boxes, and other wares characterized by gold motifs against dark surfaces in order to make them lustrous. Both Islamic and Western 16th- and 17th-century sources[12] agree that this varnish was a formulation of linseed oil, sandarac,[13] and colophony,[14] although they propose different proportions and preparation procedures.[15] In 16th-century Venice, however, other recipes were also available.[16] One in particular was described as applied over silver-coated leather in order to achieve the effect of gold.[17] Objects made in this fashion were called *cuoridoro*.[18]

While written sources on Persian practices were available to Venetians, and sharing of knowledge and expertise must have occurred through trade, there is no evidence during this period of collaboration between craftsmen involved in the making of lacquerware from the Islamic and Western worlds.[19] Scientific analysis of the materials used in Islamic lacquerware and in its Venetian imitations in the 16th century would certainly elucidate whether Venetian imitation of designs was accompanied by the use of original materials described in secret recipes of the period. Studies of Islamic lacquerware exist,[20] but scientific analyses are rare, especially in

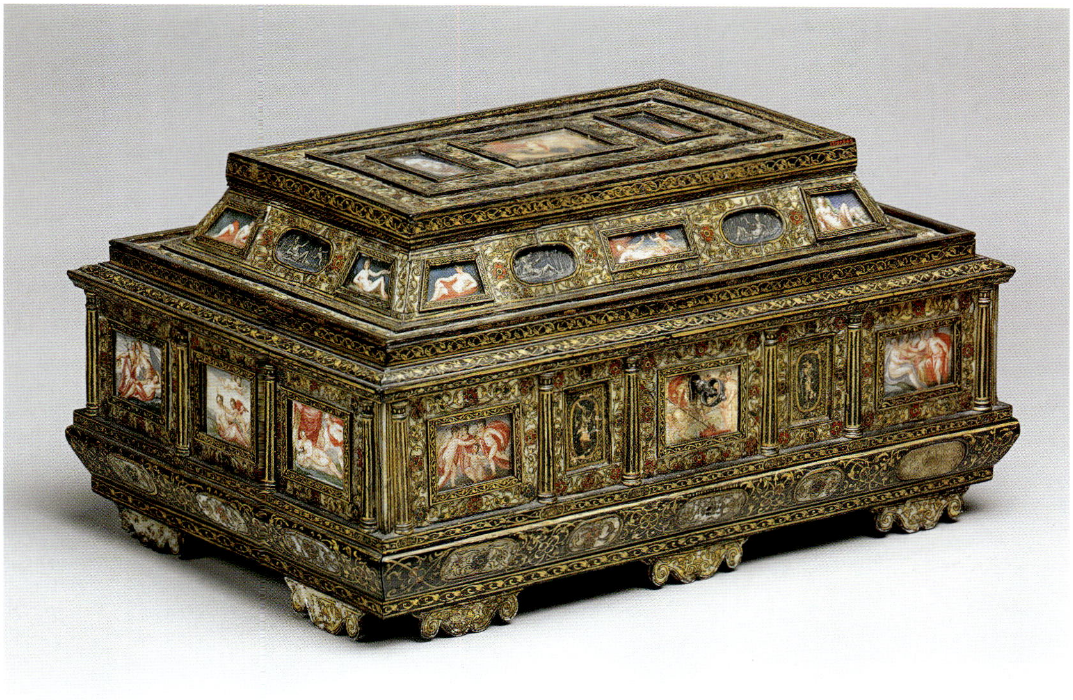

cat. 148. *Casket (Cofanetto* or *Scrigno)*
Venice, ca. 1575–1600
The Metropolitan Museum of Art, New York

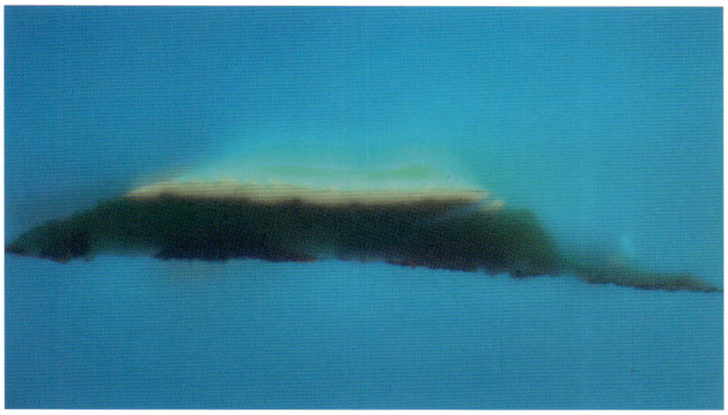

fig. 1. Cross-section of two layers of varnish on a casket (cat. 147)

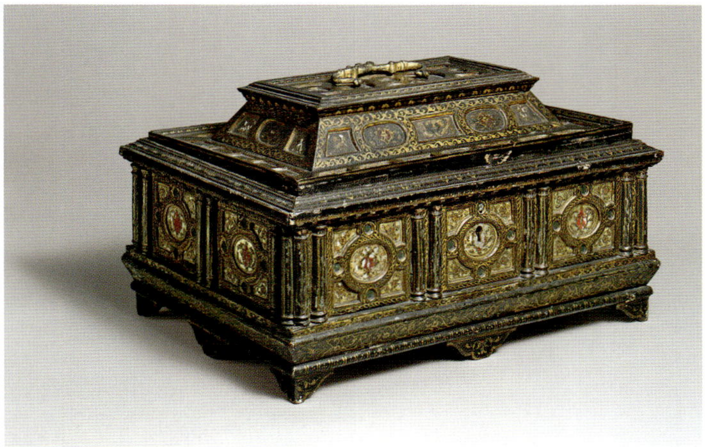

fig. 2. Casket, Venice, 16th century. The Metropolitan Museum of Art, New York

relation to Venetian objects of the mid- and late 16th century. A recent doctoral dissertation,[21] focused on a Venetian cabinet of the second half of the 16th century (cats. 146, p. 232) shows a varnish formulation composed of mastic, linseed oil, Venetian turpentine, and possibly sandarac and colophony as well.[22] It must be noted, however, that varnishes applied at later dates may have contaminated the layer analyzed in that study.

To shed some light on the materials of Venetian lacquer, three 16th-century caskets in the collection of the Metropolitan Museum of Art were examined (cats. 147, 148, and fig. 2). The first casket (cat. 147) displays a technique of decoration that closely relates it to Islamic bookbindings. Gold powder was applied in wiry patterns and floral motifs over the dark wooden background and gold leaf was used as a base for the cartouches and the interior decoration of the lid, where red, blue, and green glazes enhance patterns and floral designs. One of the most distinctive aspects of the casket is the application of an orange varnish with silver flecks over the golden cartouches on the exterior of the object and underneath its lid.[23] In the exterior decoration a similar varnish with silver flecks was also applied over the beveled wooden band at the bottom and on the narrower one below the lid. Two layers of varnish are clearly distinguishable by their fluorescence under ultraviolet light.[24] The original layer displays an orange fluorescence and appears thicker over some gilded areas. The layer can be distinguished in a cross-section over a green glaze applied on the gilded band of the lid (fig. 1) under a more recent layer of varnish.

Microscopic samples of varnish were taken for analysis from four different areas: the varnish engrained in the outer gilded decoration, the varnish embedding silver flecks applied over wood, the orange varnish applied with silver flecks over gold inside the lid, and the uppermost restoration varnish.[25] In particular, the orange varnish was analyzed by FT-IR,[26] GC/MS,[27] and in cross section by SEM/EDS for the presence of pigment. The other samples were characterized simply by GC/MS, which revealed the presence of pine resin and drying oil. Drying oil is suggested by the simultaneous presence of palmitic acid, stearic acid,[28] azelaic acid,[29] and traces of oleic acid.[30] Additionally, a relatively high concentration of suberic acid versus azelaic acid and the presence of low molecular weight dicarboxylic acids indicate that the oil was treated with heat.[31] Linseed oil can be identified with confidence as a component of the varnishes containing silver flecks. The presence of wax[32] and perhaps other contamination from handling prevented a reliable identification of the oil used in the varnish above the gold decoration on the outside. In fact, the measured palmitic to stearic acid ratio would suggest the use of a slow drying oil, which would be highly undesirable in a varnish.[33] For analogy of composition with the other samples it may be speculated that linseed oil was used also in this varnish. The pine resin consistently found in all the samples of original varnish is probably colophony.[34] The several oxidation products of abietic acid (a main component of raw colophony) that were detected confirm its high degree of oxidation. All samples of original varnish display a homogeneous yellow-orange tint, with no clear evidence of inorganic pigments, which may suggest the addition of a dye. Markers for sandarac were not detected in these samples, as would be expected if traditional Persian formulations had been used.

Members of the Venetian painters' guild were familiar with the making of glossy varnishes and their knowledge would have originated from experience in addition to the consultation of "books of secrets" where recipes were revealed for the preparation of pigments, paint, and varnishes. The leading role of Venice in the printing industry would have contributed to the local diffusion of recipe books. Leonardo Fioravanti (1517–1588) was one of the most prominent scientists from the University of Bologna and many of his books were published in Venice. An expert in medicine, alchemy, physics, and natural science, he consolidated his reputation by sharing and broadening his knowledge through his travels across Italy. In one of his writings, Fioravanti describes a varnish formulation, used by *circassi* (Circassians) and Ottomans for coating their bows, based on a heated mixture of colophony and linseed oil.[35] This varnish would have been easier and cheaper to prepare than the Persian sandarac-based "bow gloss" mentioned above, which was used to achieve similar finishes. Fioravanti gives another, similar recipe for the preparation of a varnish for *cuoridori*.[36] The similarity between the application on silver-coated leather and the varnish with silver flecks is striking. The technique of applying golden varnishes to silver backgrounds had been known since the 12th century from the Byzantine world. In the application over the gold cartouches, the use of silver flecks rather than gold may have been dictated by a deliberate aesthetic choice. The light-scattering effect produced by the silver flecks over gold and underneath the varnish would not have been achieved in the same effective manner by gold alone. The use of colophony and linseed oil for the making of a good multipurpose varnish was also mentioned in another 16th-century treatise published in Venice.[38]

Interpreting the results from the finishes in the other two caskets under study is more arduous, as their surfaces were greatly affected by later cleaning and restoration varnishes; thus the results presented here are only preliminary. The two caskets (cat. 148 and fig. 2) are closely related to one another in terms of their decoration, painted cartouches, and gilded and glazed floral motifs over mother-of-pearl inlays. Furthermore, the architectural framework and especially the painted figurines of cat. 148 distinguish it from cat. 147. Cross-section and ultraviolet light examination of these two caskets suggest an inconsistent presence of two varnish applications. Microscopic samples of finishes over mother-of-pearl inlays were taken from the two caskets. GC/MS analysis suggests that the varnish in the casket cat. 148 is a spirit[39] varnish formulated with larch turpentine. This is confirmed by its typical markers, larixyl acetate and larixol. The craquelure and fluorescence over the decoration suggest that the varnish is original. The fact that oil is not present in the formulation is reflected in the poor elastic properties of the film, whose craquelure and discoloration are aggravated by the choice of larch turpentine as a resin. The results for the finish on the other casket (fig. 2) also reveal a formulation based on larch turpentine with the presence of a drying oil, the exact nature of which was not identified because of the use of wax as a contaminant. The surfaces' complexities in these two caskets mean that further analysis is needed to clarify if the varnishes are in fact representative of the original finishes.

This preliminary study of the varnishes of these late 16th century Venetian caskets, in particular of cat. 147, has provided useful information on the choice of materials and the use of the techniques of lacquering on these Islamic-influenced objects. The materials of the original finishes were found to be in agreement with those available in Venice at the time, which are mentioned in contemporary recipes for achieving the desired aesthetic effects. Even though it is not possible to identify the exact lacquering technique on the basis of the lacquer composition, there is an obvious agreement between the "Ottoman" style of the casket (cat. 147) and the "Ottoman lacquer" formulations reported by Fioravanti.

Sandarac resin is mentioned in formulation of Persian-style lacquer and varnishes of the period, but its higher cost, lesser availability, and complex preparation may further account for its absence in Venetian lacquerware. Although oil-sandarac based "lacquer" imparted a more resistant surface compared to the oil-colophony formulations, the function of luxury goods such as caskets would not have required its use. Nevertheless, the strong Islamic influence in the Venetian artistic production and the mention in treatises of sandarac in "lacquer" formulations of the 16th century suggest its potential application in Venice, parallel to that of oil-colophony formulations.

This short study represents a first step in investigating how "lacquer" formulations in Venice may have been chosen according to the style and function of an object. Future systematic scientific analyses of both Islamic and Venetian lacquerware would certainly reveal the extent to which Turkish and Persian artistic influences contributed to the choice of materials used in the Venetian lacquerware that they so clearly inspired.

Notes

1 The etymology of the word is from the material called *lak* in India, corresponding to the resin and dyestuff extracted from *Tachardia lacca*, better known as shellac and red lake, from which Indian imitations of Chinese and Japanese lacquerware, made with *c'hi* or *urushi*, were produced.
2 Since the end of the 14th century the limitation of trade with China saw an increase in luxury goods from India and South Asia. See Pinto 1966, p. 394.
3 For a discussion of the current schools of thought on the definitions of "Islamic lacquer" see Khalili 1997, vol. 1, pp. 10–19.
4 Some extremely refined Persian bookbindings were among the first items to have been imitated and documented in Venice in the late 15th century. See de Marinis 1966, p. 550.
5 In addition to the earlier Eastern imitations of Far Eastern lacquerware, the increased importation of and taste for chinoiserie in the West in the 18th century led to European imitations.
6 The majority of gums and resins featured in an inventory of *vendecolori* (suppliers of art materials in Venice) were imported from the East. Matthew 2002, p. 682; see also Berrie's essay in the present volume.
7 See Balducci Pegolotti 1936 and Berchet 1864 for a description of the materials of the trade, dealers, and suppliers.
8 The guild represented a category of artists and craftsmen whose activities were regulated but not always clearly defined. After the first known documentation in 1271 some classifications were made in the category to better define tasks and responsibilities. In particular, as mentioned in Santini 2003 (p. 44, n. 38), from 1436 a diversification appeared among *depentori, desegnatori, miniatori, cuoridoro, targheri, maschereri, cartoleri,* and *doratori.* (painters; draftsmen; illuminators; craftsmen making gilded leather *targhe* or various types of shields; mask playing cards, and gilders).
9 From 1271 the rule was applied to shields, roundels, and other objects used as weapons. Three to four days were imposed to allow drying to take place, according to the season and the substrate to which the varnish was applied. See Monticolo 1905, pp. 373, 381, 383.
10 Khalili 1997, vol. 1, p. 12.
11 From the Persian *rawghan-i kaman.*
12 For the mention of Islamic sources see Khalili 1997, vol. 1, p. 16. For Western sources see Fioravanti 1675, bk. 4, chap. 68, car. 272. He describes the process of the making the *vernice di sandaracca* or *vernice in grana* as being so troublesome that few craftsmen were able to practice it successfully. However, he reveals its secret ingredients and process, which involves boiling eight parts of linseed oil in a copper vessel, checking the exact point of heating with a feather, then ??? it cool. Then, equal parts of ground sandarac and *pegola di Spagna* (colophony) were added and all was cooked together until the sandarac was completely incorporated.
13 A resin extracted from the North African tree *Callitris quadrivalvis* of the family *Cupressaceae* (sandarac tree or thuya). It was exported from the town of Berenix in North Africa, from which the name *vernice* (varnish) seems to be derived.
14 Solid residue after distillation of oil of turpentine from pine resin. It features among the commodities as *pece greca* and *ragia di pino* in Balducci Pegolotti 1936, pp. 296, 426, 428. The product may have been available in different degree of processing, thus the different names. Colophony is identified as *pegola spagna* in Merrifield 1849, vol. 1.
15 Khalili 1997, vol. 1, pp. 15–16.
16 Other recipes are given in Fioravanti 1675 (bk. 4, chap. 68, car. 273) for a very fine spirit varnish made of *bengioi* (balsamic resin from the *Styracaceae* or storax) and mastic. Other recipes published in the 16th century were available in books of secrets by Alessio Piemontese (Piemontese 1557) and in the so-called Marciana Manuscript (Merrifield 1849, vol. 2). Traditional recipes were available from earlier published sources.
17 Fioravanti 1572, bk. 1, chap. 41, car. 104–104b. A secret recipe from a Neapolitan master is given for the making of such varnish, based on a mixture of four parts of linseed oil (*olio di lino*), two parts colophony (*ragia di pino*), and one part *aloe cavalino,* all boiled until a golden color is achieved.
18 The making of these leather luxury items was particularly profitable for Venice in the 16th century for their trading value in Istanbul wich, in turn supplied Venice with the best leather. See Contadini 1989, p. 233.
19 A reduction in the import of foreign goods was also reflected in the 16th century in confining access to local arts and crafts to artists who were members of the association, thus excluding foreign craftsmen.
20 Khalili 1997, vol. 1, p. 12, where no reference is found for the types of analyses, except for the evidence that similarities existed between objects made of wood and of papier-mâché..
21 Hellbing 2005.
22 The analytical results are given without narrative explanation in Hellbing 2005, p. 51.
23 The metal leaf was identified by SEM/EDS (Scanning Electron Microscopy/Energy-Dispersive X-ray Spectroscopy) by Mark Wypyski as consisting of silver of 99.58% purity.
24 UV fluorescence is the emission of visible radiation by a substance when ultraviolet (UV) radiation is applied by means of a lamp. This non-invasive technique is used as a preliminary diagnostic tool that assists in distinguishing surface coatings by their color. In this case, the uppermost coating was applied later over areas of varnish including silver flecks, with the intention of preserving them from tarnishing. Tarnishing of the flecks is seen where varnish has undergone abrasion.
25 This sample was analyzed to isolate the contribution of the later varnish to the results for the original varnish from inside the lid. GC/MS analysis suggests a mixture of larch turpentine, some drying oil, and probably sandarac, suggested by the presence of totarol and communic acid. This formulation is very different from that found in the original varnish below.
26 Fourier Transform-InfraRed Microspectroscopy.
27 Gas-chromatography/mass spectrometry. Samples were derivatized with a 1:1 solution of the methylating reagent Meth Prep II in benzene, injected in the GC after heating the sample for 1 hour at 60°C. GC/MS analyses were performed in the Scientific Research and Analysis Laboratory of the Philadelphia Museum of Art My sincere thanks to Ken Sutherland, Beth A. Price, and Andrew Lins.
28 The palmitic and stearic acid ratio remains constant through the drying and aging of oil and it is characteristic for the type of oil used.
29 Azelaic acid is a dicarboxylic acid formed upon drying and derives from the oxidation of unsaturated fatty acids.
30 Oleic acid is the monounsaturated fatty acid in the oil that survives longer than the polyunsaturated linoleic and linolenic.
31 Suberic acid and other low molecular weight fatty acids are produced from oxidation of polyunsaturated acids produced by isomerization of linoleic and linolenic acid with the temperature.
32 Natural wax also contributes to the sample with palmitic and acid methylesters, which are indistinguishable from those present in the oil.
33 Walnut oil is rarely mentioned in varnish formulations and it does not feature in inventories of 16th century *vendecolori* in Venice, although it was used as a painting medium. Matthew 2002, p. 684.
34 Mills and White 1994, p. 100.
35 Fioravanti 1675, bk. 3, cited in Rispoli Fabris 1974, p. 22. The recipe is composed of one part linseed oil and three parts *pece greca* (colophony) slowly heated together to homogeneity. The mixture was used as a binder for colors and was reputed good for its covering power. See also Huth 1971, p. 5 and above, n. 16.
36 Fioravanti 1572, bk. 1, chap. 41, car. 104-104b. See also above, n.-17.
37 Marciana Manuscript, p. 405, cited in Merrifield 1849, vol. 2, p. 637. Two parts of linseed oil (*olio di lino*) were boiled, one part of ground colophony (*pece grecha*) and a pinch of burnt and pounded rock alum were combined and the mixture was boiled to the right consistency. The strained varnish was diluted with more linseed oil if needed.
38 Spirit varnishes consist of formulations of resins dissolved in solvents, mainly alcohols, rather than drying oil. The varnish film is then formed on evaporation of the solvent.

Enameled Glass between the Eastern Mediterranean and Venice

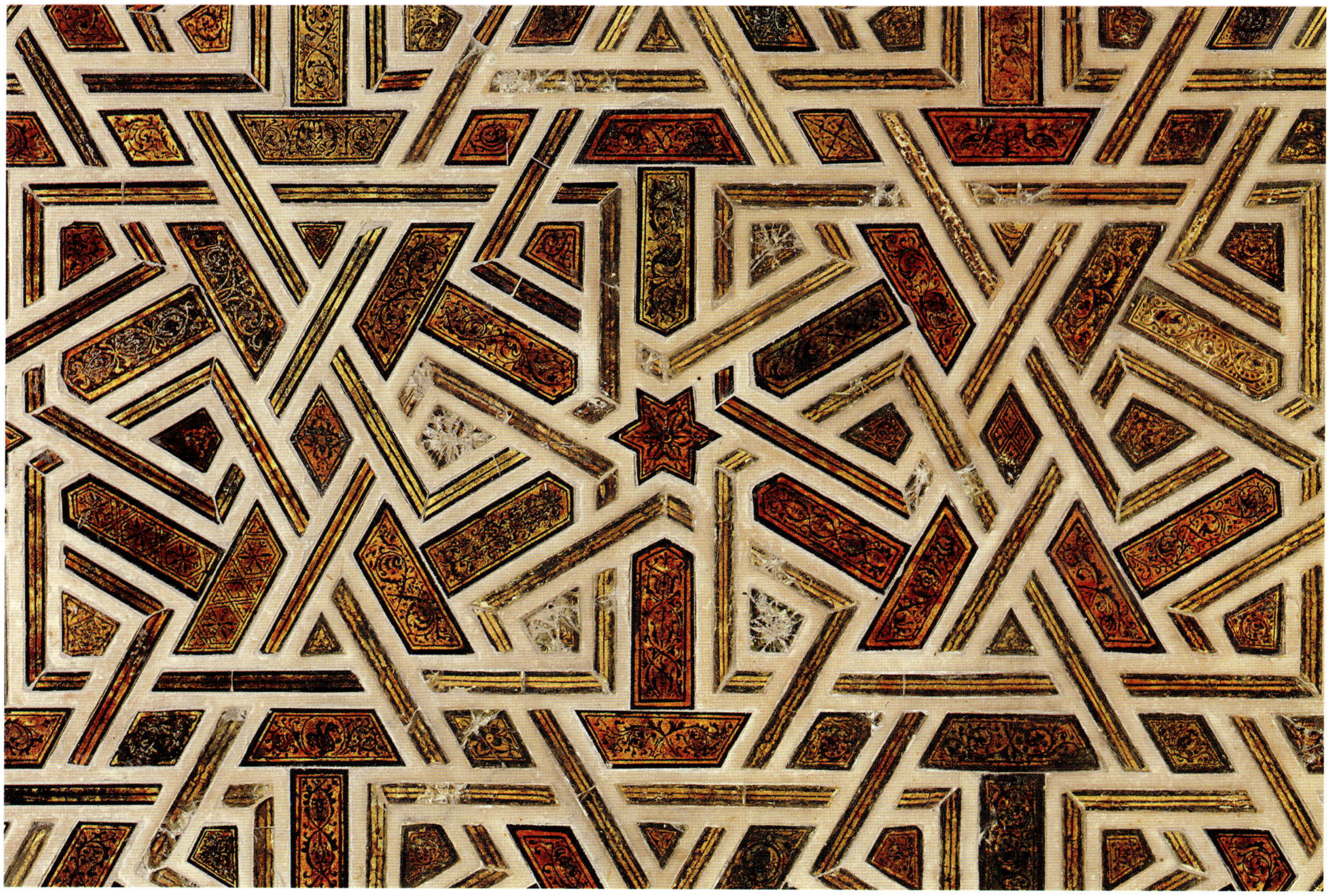

Rosa Barovier Mentasti
and Stefano Carboni[1]

Venice and its factories on the island of Murano are today synonymous with high quality artistic blown glass as well as run-of-the-mill tourist-oriented production. Every visitor to the city on the lagoon inevitably spends a few hours in Murano and is fascinated by the skills of the Venetian craftsmen who create impromptu small blown or lamp-worked objects to his or her amazement (fig. 1). Visitors are well aware that glass in Venice is a big business. Indeed, glassmaking and glass marketing have been one of the most important businesses in Venice at least since its factories were moved from the city center in the vicinity of the Rialto Bridge to the safer, more remote, yet easily accessible island of Murano in the late 13th century.[2] The main reason for relocating was that fires repeatedly broke out in the workshops, threatening surrounding patrician and civilian abodes and other businesses; but their move, perhaps initially spontaneous and later imposed by the authorities, was also an acknowledgment that the industry had become economically viable and that the right moment had arrived for Venice to encourage, support, and market its glass production aggressively.

Glassmaking in the Venetian lagoon has a long history. Archaeological material found on the island of Torcello and neighboring areas suggests that blown and tooled utilitarian vessels were produced there as early as the 9th century.[3] A proper artistic production, however, can be established with certainty only from the 13th century and one of the reasons—if not the principal one—for its development must be Venice's enduring relationship with the Muslim states of the Eastern Mediterranean. Islamic glassmakers or, better, glassmakers who were active in Islamic lands since the 7th century, had inherited the skills of the late Roman and early Byzantine craftsmen. In the early Islamic period, they learned and perpetuated the traditional shapes, technology, decoration, and techniques while at the same time experimenting with new ones.[4] The astounding results included transparent and seemingly weightless masterfully relief-cut vessels; whimsical bi- or tri-colored objects with applied and sometimes marvered trails; the technological innovation of luster painting on colorless works; and splendid and rightly celebrated achievements in enameled and gilded glass (cat. 152, p. 254). Artistic glassmaking in the Islamic world had no serious rival—not by a long stretch—anywhere in Europe.[5]

cat. 155. *Fragment from the pulpit of the Church of San Giovanni Fuorcivitas in Pistoia* (detail)

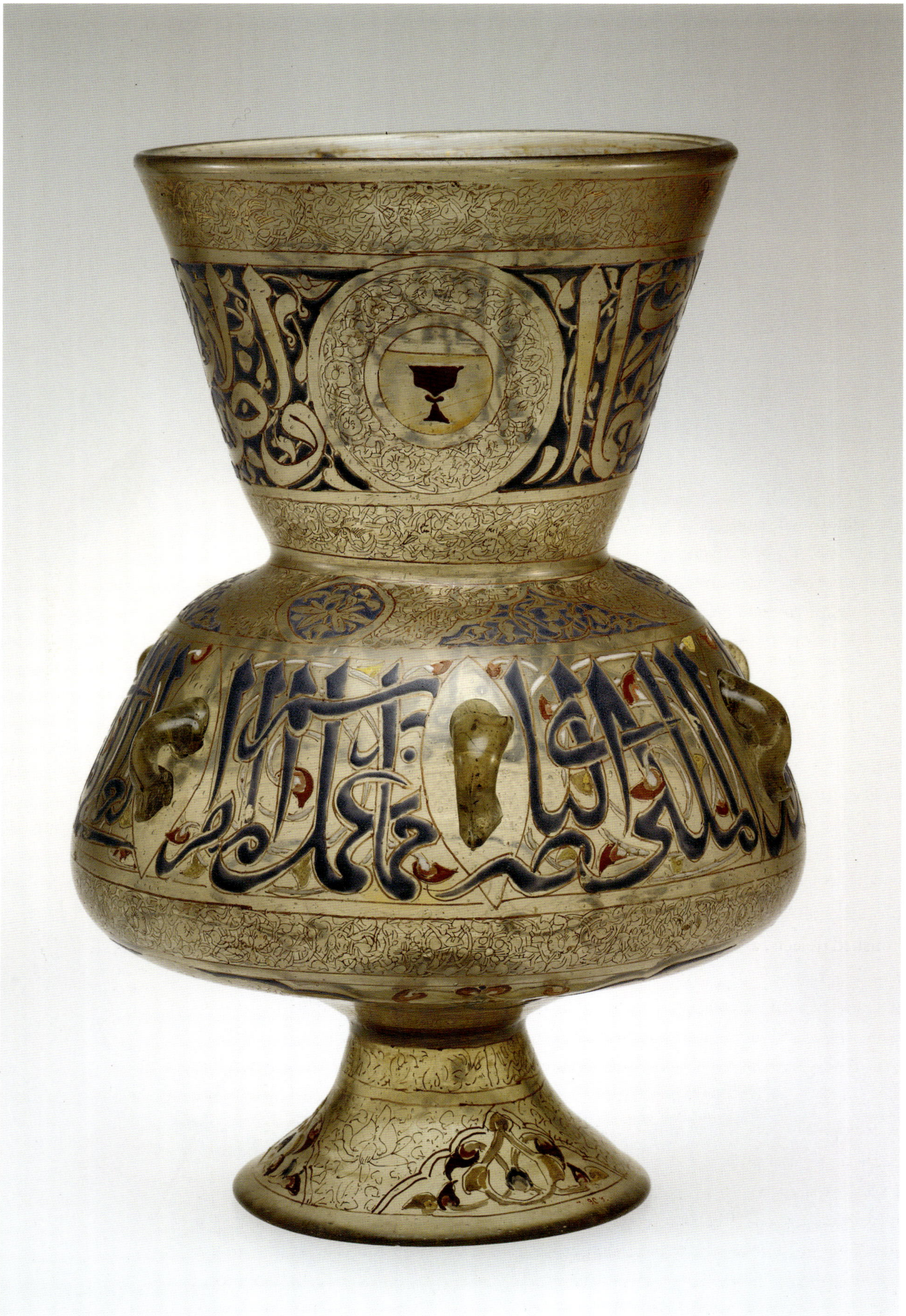

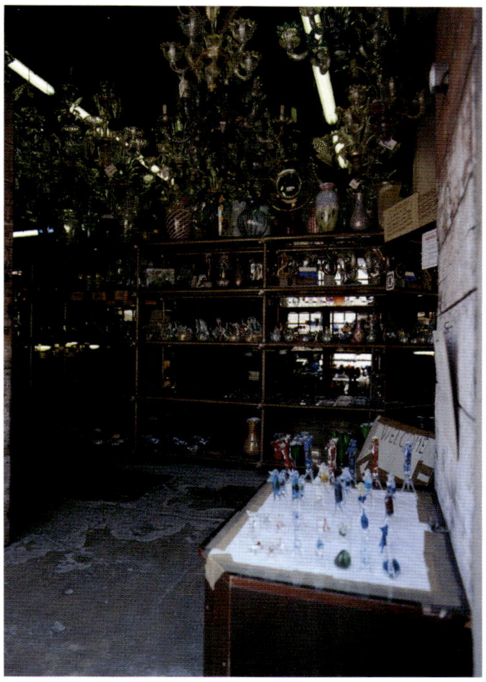

fig. 1. Glasshouse on Murano

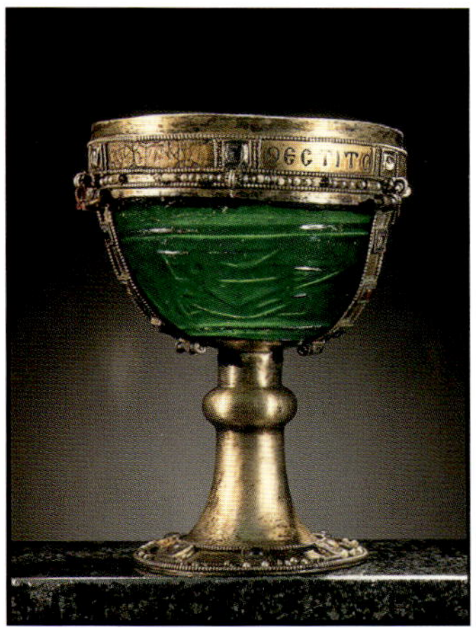

cat. 150. *Cup with mount*
Cup: Probably Iran, 9th–10th century or Egypt, 10th–11th century
Mount: Byzantine, 10th–11th century
Treasury of St. Mark's, Venice

It is not surprising, therefore, that an enterprising trading city like Venice, with a promising glass industry, began to import raw materials as well as cullet to make glass of the same good quality as that produced along the eastern and southeastern Mediterranean coasts. Most importantly, through this trade the Venetians also imported technical and technological information and no doubt they acquired a familiarity with the shapes and the decorative patterns of Near Eastern glass vessels. This progress is documented in the 13th and 14th centuries in the *Atti dei Podestà di Murano* from about 1280,[6] but it can be postulated that the transmission of glass-related information on the routes from Alexandria, Tyre, Antioch, and Acre (to name a few) to Venice had started much earlier. For example, through a well-known treaty signed between the Venetian government of Doge Jacopo Contarini and the prince of Antioch, Bohemond VII, on June 1, 1277, it was established, among other things, that those Venetian merchants who intended to trade cullet (*verre brizé*, or broken glass) in that Eastern Mediterranean city had to pay a tax on it.[7] Such precise reference can only suggest that the Venetians had gotten away with tax-free cullet for quite some time before the Frankish-ruled Antiochians realized that the business was worthy of taxation and ratified such transactions. Glass cullet was important because it could be melted at a lower temperature, thus saving on fuel costs; in addition, it already included the basic soda-lime glass ingredients that the Venetians so admired in high quality Islamic glass. The single most valuable import of raw material, both for glass- and soapmaking, was the *lume catino* or high-grade soda (alkali) that was exported in calcined chunks from the eastern shores of the Mediterranean burning in particular the plant *Salsola kali* (Russian thistle), which was especially suitable for the composition of Venetian glass.[8] The high regard for these materials on the lagoon is proven both by their mandatory use in glassmaking in order to ensure the superior quality of the finished product and by the ban on exporting them from Venice to other European cities.[9]

Finished objects, and not just raw materials, from the Islamic world must have arrived in Venice well before the 13th century through trade and diplomatic gifts, as well as through a personal interest among merchants and ambassadors in acquiring and shipping them home. Several celebrated glass vessels now in the Treasury of St. Mark's, some of which may have arrived in Venice as part of the booty from Constantinople in 1204, provide an isolated but meaningful example of the admiration for this particular artistic medium in an important period of development for the glass industry in Venice (cat. 150).[10]

Perhaps the earliest extant example of the influence of decorative patterns as well as some technical aspects of Islamic art on Venetian glass can be found in the decoration of a marble pulpit datable around 1270, a fragment of which is in the Diocesan Museum in Pistoia (cat. 155, p. 256). This early instance of glass tiles decorated in *verre eglomisé* (i.e., painted on the reverse and set against a flat surface) is reminiscent of the technique of the so-called sandwich glass with gilded decoration that was in vogue in the Syrian area in the 9th or 10th century.[11] In

cat. 152. *Mosque lamp*
Cairo, Egypt, ca. 1329–35
The Metropolitan Museum of Art, New York

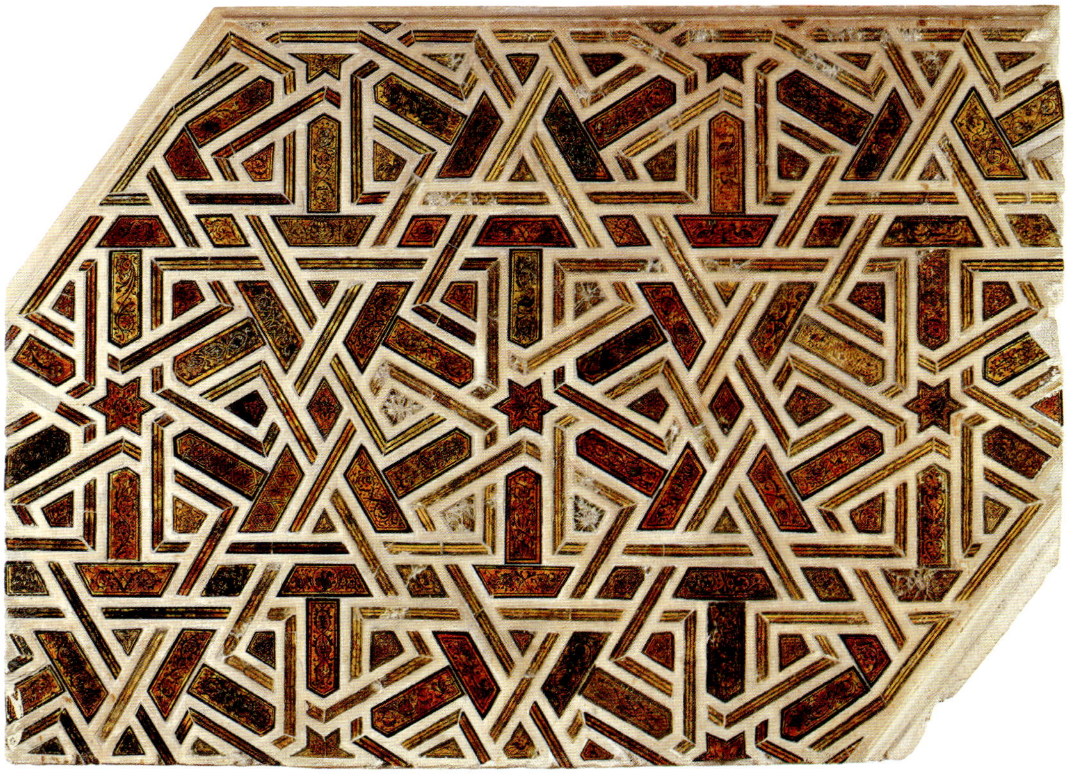

cat. 155. *Fragment de la chaire de l'église San Giovanni Fuorcivitas de Pistoia*
Pistoia, 1270
Pistoia, Museo Diocesano

fig. 2. Mur *qiblî*, mausolée de Sulaymân al-Rifâ'î, 1291, Le Caire

cat. 156. *Beaker*
Venice, late 13th–early 14th century
The British Museum, London

cat. 158. *Beaker*
Venice, late 13th–early 14th century
Glasmuseum Hentrich, Düsseldorf

cat. 159. *Fragmentary beaker*
Venice, late 13th–early 14th century
Soprintendenza Archeologica per il Veneto, Verona

fig. 3. Beaker. Enameled glass, Venice, late 13th–early 14th century. Domschatz, Chur, Switzerland

addition, the individual tiles are arranged following purely Islamic geometric patterns and both their shape and the technique of reverse painting find a close and almost contemporaneous parallel in the decoration of the *qibla* wall in a small mausoleum in medieval Cairo (fig. 2).[12]

Thanks to the so-called Aldrevandin beakers (cats. 156–159) the links between Islamic and Venetian glass can be firmly established. The group was initially identified by the great scholar of Islamic glass Carl Johan Lamm as "Syro-Frankish" in the belief that these enameled and sometimes gilded beakers were made along the Syrian coast to satisfy a European demand for objects inspired by the splendid works then being produced in Syria and perhaps Egypt for a rich clientele.[13] In the past four decades, Luigi Zecchin's discovery of a large number of documents mentioning "painters of beakers" in Venice from around 1280 to the mid-14th century[14] and unmistakable archeological evidence surfacing from innumerable sites in Europe[15] (Lamm based his evidence on a handful of works known in the early part of the 20th century, some of them with a reputed Near Eastern provenance) have firmly established that these beakers, as well as a few other vessels with a similar decoration, have a Venetian origin.[16]

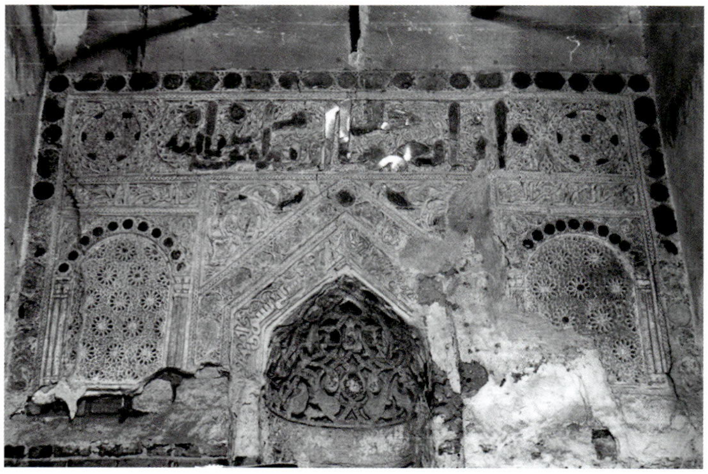

In terms of shape, distinctions among the Aldevandrin beakers can be made. One group is very close to Islamic prototypes, with a small diameter and a slender profile culminating in a wide flared opening (cat. 151, p. 78; cat. 157, p. 258; cat. 159) while another has straighter walls, larger overall diameter, and a generally stocky appearance (cats. 156, 158). Revealing their direct derivation from Islamic models, the first, less numerous group of slender beakers have enamels applied only on their exteriors and, in most cases, gold paint was also used.[17] In the larger group of stockier objects, the enamels are often applied both inside and out and the use of gold is rare. Consequently, it may be suggested that the first group is earlier and has the strongest link between Islamic and Venetian glassmaking, and that the second group corresponds to a local development of the typology after two or three decades of production on the lagoon.

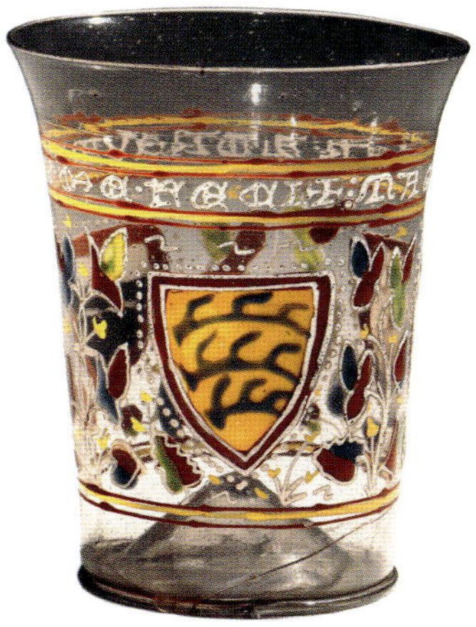

The subjects depicted on these Venetian beakers vary widely, some of them clearly relating and paying homage to their Islamic prototypes, such as the object illustrating camels (cat. 158). In general, however, the same subjects are found on both profiles (slender and stocky as defined above) and can be divided broadly into four main categories, albeit with a number of variants: real or fantastic animals encircling the walls (cat. 157, p. 258); half-size figures of religious significance set within arches supported by columns and flanked by oversize leafy stems (fig. 3); heraldic coats of arms separated by the same vegetal motifs (cats. 156, 159);[18] and courtly subjects, such as lute players and a female figure in the act of placing a garland on the head of a kneeling knight.[19] All these themes are recurrent in, although not limited to, Venetian art of the late medieval period and early Renaissance. Once the glass painters—who decorated these beakers for a European clientele—distanced themselves from the Islamic models, they sought inspiration directly from the buildings of the Venetian city itself: the colorful wall and floor mosaics and the bas-reliefs that adorned the churches of St. Mark in the city center and of the saints Maria and Donato in Murano (figs. 4–5, p. 259); the complex figurative and vegetal patterns of the capitals of the Palazzo Ducale, including the conventional scene of a woman crowning a man with a garland (fig. 6, p. 273);[20] and the inhabited scrolls present in the innumerable *patere* (marble disks carved in relief) that decorated religious and secular buildings throughout Venice.[21] Figures of saints within arches are present, for example, in the 13th-century ciborium of the main altar in St. Mark's as well as in 14th-century marble niches once set in churches in Murano, including the former church of St. Stephen that housed the meeting hall of the Guild of the Glassmakers.[22]

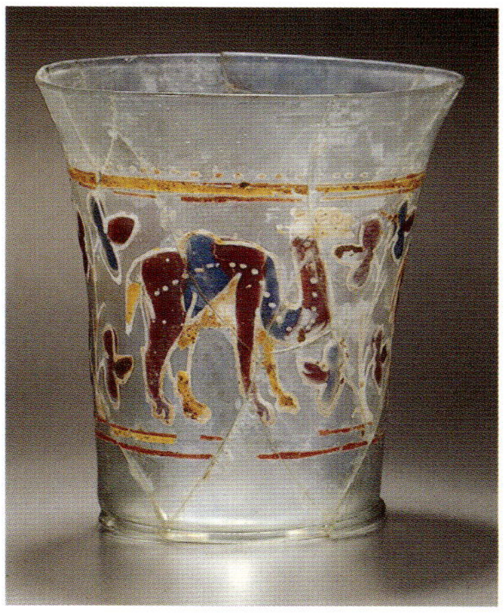

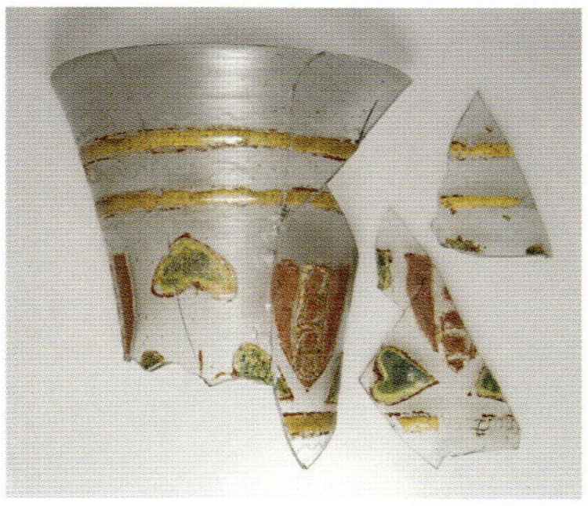

The main reason for a secure attribution of the Aldrevandin beakers to Venice is that some of the names of the glass painters cited in the archival documents, mostly *foresti* or "foreigners"—such as Gregorio, Bartolomeo, Pietro, Zanni, and Donino in addition to a certain Aldrevandinus mentioned as a maker of beakers (*moioli*)—coincide with those signed in a narrow inscriptional band in Latin below the rim of extant objects and fragments found throughout Europe, ranging from London in England to Tartu in Estonia.[23]

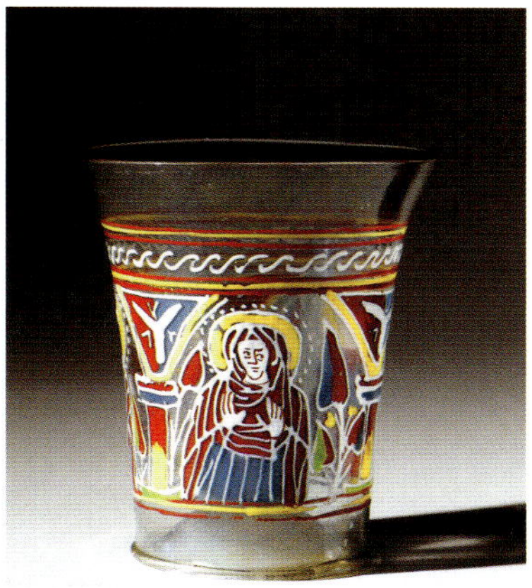

The wide distribution of the Aldrevandin beakers in England, France, Germany, Switzerland, the Netherlands, and further north and east also helps to suggest who may have been instrumental in their initial patronage. Venice was a member of the Hanseatic League, a trading alliance of many cities that favored active commerce throughout Europe.[24] As part of the general market, these cities were among the most obvious recipients of such, perhaps not too expensive but fancy, enameled objects, as proven by many recent archaeological finds.[25] During the early part of the 14th century, the majority of these cities in the

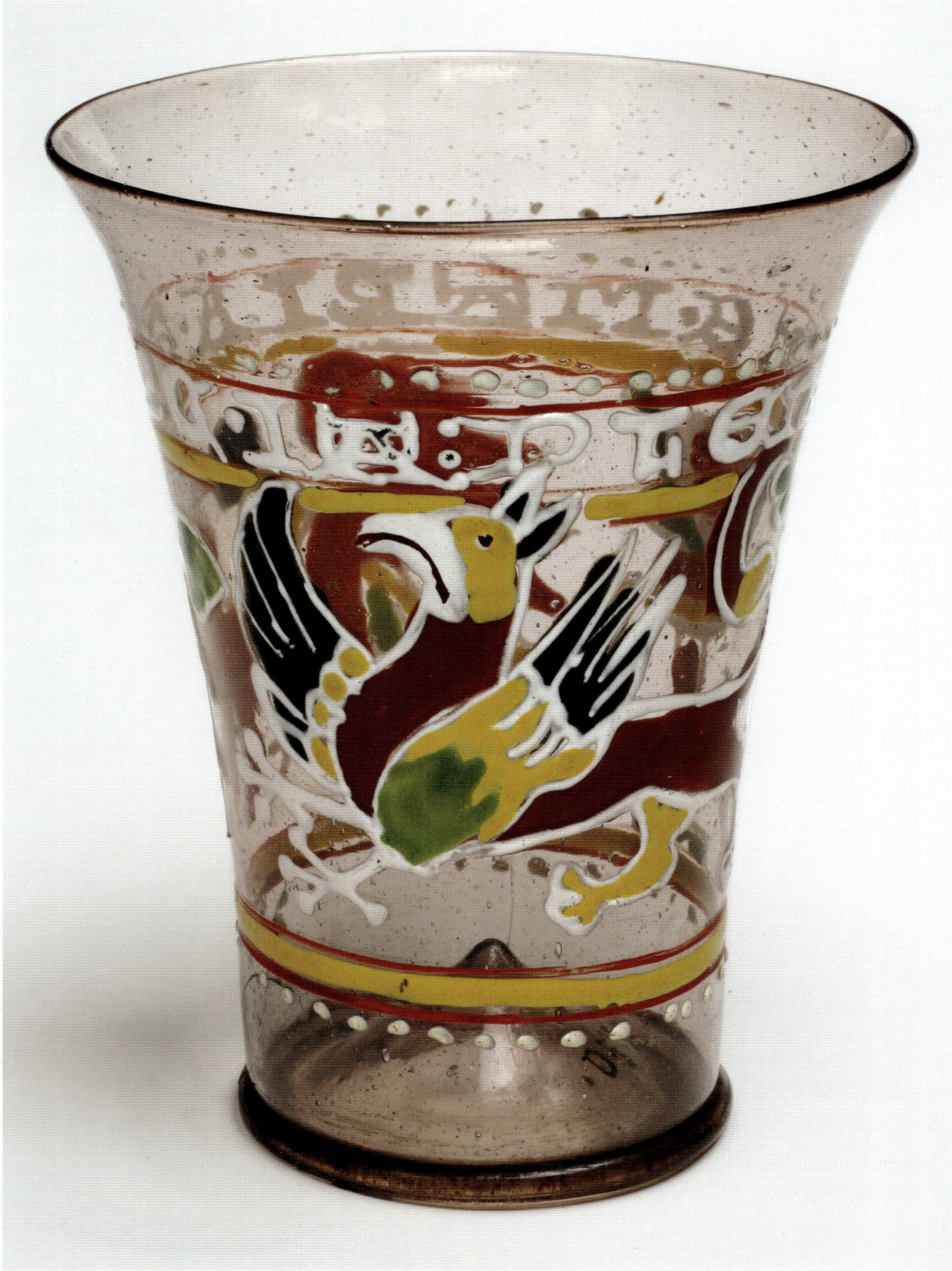

Germanic and northeastern European areas were also subject to the political expansion of the Teutonic Knights, who had significantly held their headquarters in Acre and had also had a considerable presence in Venice until the last Crusaders were expelled from the Holy Land in 1291.[26] Their headquarters were subsequently fully reestablished on the lagoon for the following 20-odd years before they went on to conquer the Germanic world and set up their capital in Marienburg. The knights' strong links to Venice and the Eastern Mediterranean during the early period of production of these beakers, together with their distribution in areas dominated by them later in the 14th century, effectively suggests their involvement in such patronage.

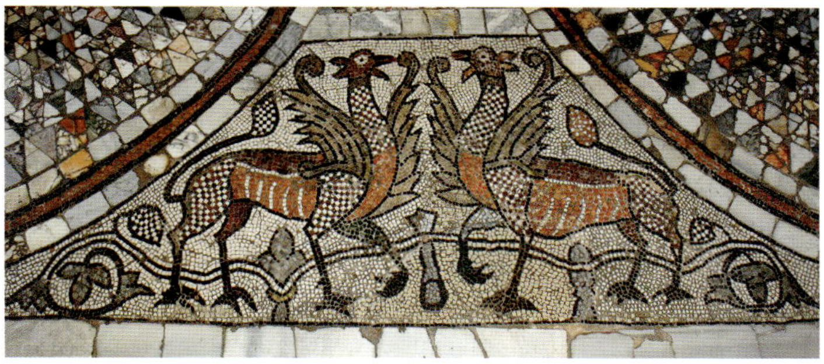

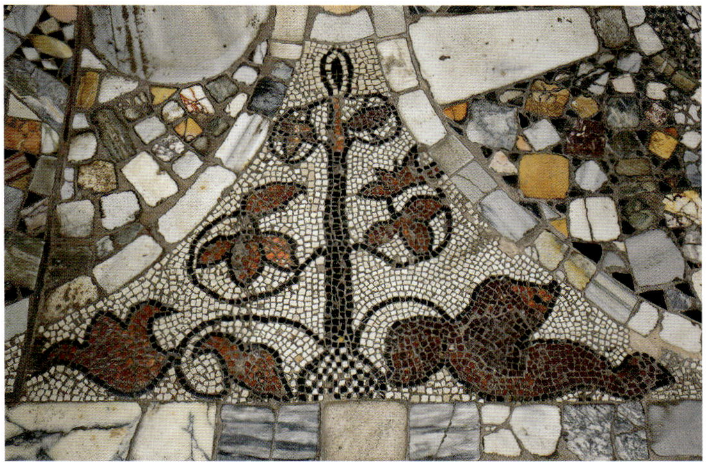

These enameled Venetian beakers seem to have gone out of fashion some time after the middle of the 14th century, during which we can witness the beginning of a decline in patronage—and consequently in technology and creativity—in the glass factories of Cairo under the Mamluks. Such decline becomes painfully evident during the course of the 15th century, since only four mosque lamps of less-than-average quality probably produced in the Egyptian capital survive, as opposed to the more than 200 splendid extant objects from the previous century.[27]

fig. 4. Griffin on floor mosaic (detail), Church of San Maria e Donato, Murano

fig. 5. Floral motifs on floor mosaic (detail), Church of San Maria e Donato, Murano

In Venice, the last reference in the archival documents of the 14th century to a glass painter, a certain Donino, is in 1351. After that, and for almost a century, there is no mention of enameling on glass and the only sporadic indication of enamels is related to jewelry production. The plagues of 1348, 1357, and 1359–61 certainly hurt the glassmaking business, and perhaps some of the masters died without having the opportunity to train enough pupils, leaving a generational gap. In addition, the documents pertaining to the Podestà di Murano for the years 1351–63, which would have likely provided a great deal of information, have unfortunately been lost.

The 15th century, however, corresponds to the establishment of the Murano factories as the leading glass industry in Europe, especially after the "invention" of *cristallo* glass by Angelo Barovier around the middle of the century.[28] It is not surprising, therefore, that the once very active trade in both raw materials and finished objects from the Islamic areas to Venice began to be incontrovertibly and crucially reversed in this period. The many embassies sent by the doge to Alexandria and Cairo in the last years of the Mamluk dynasty in the late 15th and the early 16th centuries (the Ottomans formally ended it in 1517) were loaded with gifts, while trade and exchange were as active as ever.[29] Although there is no specific reference to glass objects sent as presents or commissioned by the Mamluk sultans from the archival

cat. 157. *Beaker*
Venice, late 13th–early 14th century
Museum für Angewandte Kunst, Frankfurt

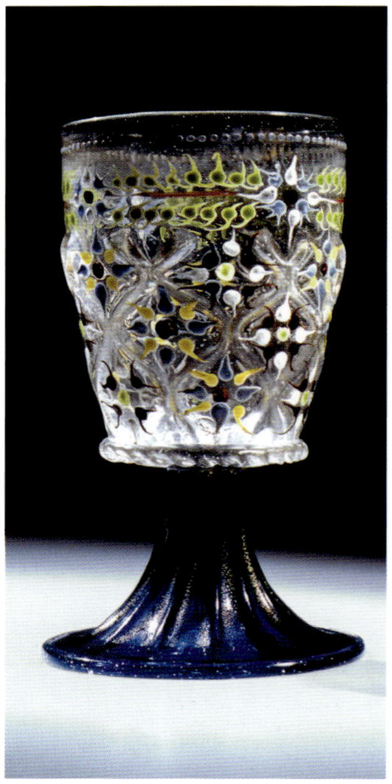

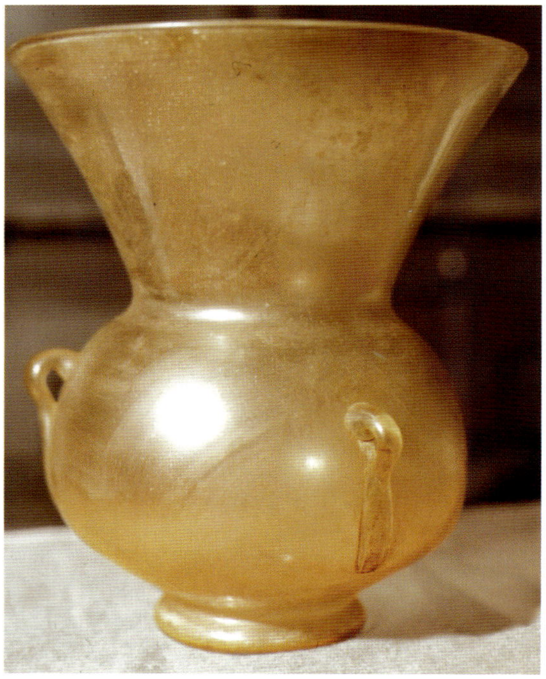

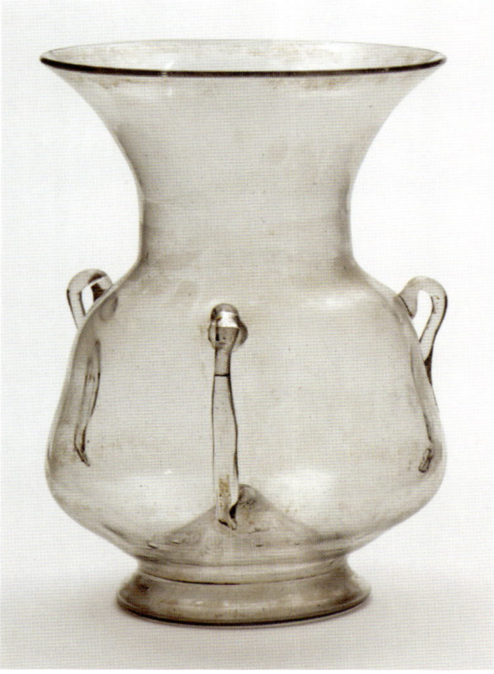

cat. 160. *Goblet*
Venice, late 15th century
Victoria and Albert Museum, London

fig. 7. Mosque lamp. Musem of Islamic Art, Cairo

cat. 162. *Mosque lamp*
Probably Venice, late 15th–early 16th century
Victoria and Albert Museum, London

documents, a number of mosque lamps today in the Museum of Islamic Art in Cairo (fig. 7) as well as a few others in European collections were likely part of shipments of such objects to Egypt in the first years of the 16th century (cat. 162). Also, a small number of clear glass beakers with sparse enameled decoration and a "nipt-diamond-waies" surface pattern are associated with Venetian exports to Mamluk Syria in this same period (cat. 160).

The earliest indication of a revival in enameled decoration seems to be linked to the name of Elena Lando and her work on glass between 1443 and 1445 (*laboreria facta per ipsam super vitris*). Pieces were first delivered to her and then returned to the workshop of Salvatore Barovier, brother of the famous Angelo.[30] This would indeed seem to be the most plausible interpretation of "work on glass" that could be done in her home, that is to say that did not require the bulky equipment and resources of a workshop yet was commissioned by a master glassmaker belonging to the Barovier dynasty—unless, of course, she was simply encasing wine flasks in straw.[31]

The first serious records of the revival of enameling, attested by Venetian documents from 1461 onwards, are related to several members of the Barovier family who headed various workshops.[32] They were all related to Angelo (ca. 1400–60), the inventor of *cristallo* (a highly transparent glass first cited in a document written in Ragusa in 1453) and later of *lattimo* (an opaque milk glass) and chalcedony glass (cat. 168). In the second half of the 15th century the Baroviers constituted the most glamorous dynasty of master glassmakers in Murano. In 1469, at the request of Angelo's son, Marino Barovier, who was a steward of the Arte dei Vetrai (glassmakers' guild), a ducal decree imposed major changes on the guild's *mariegola* (charter), some of them relating to enamel decoration.[33] Masters were notably prohibited from refiring enameled and gilded glass that was not decorated in their own workshops, as well as from selling *schieti*—that is to say, unornamented glass—for the purpose of subsequent decoration. These regulations thus meant, above all, the end of independent production by decorators—which seems to have been a crucial factor during the period of the Aldrevandin beakers (cats. 156–159, pp. 257 and 258)—who could no longer buy raw glass items to be decorated and sold. Contrary to previous assertions, Angelo Barovier and his family never did their own enamel decoration—any more than did other master glassmakers—because, like Marino and Marietta Barovier, for example, they were "too busy to sit at a table and paint glassware."[34] Inventories of items stockpiled in their workshops listed a great quantity of enameled and gilded glass, attesting to the fact that this work was apparently done at their request by other craftsmen.

As had been the case in the previous century, the family names of glass painters that have come down to us suggest that they came from other cities or other states, or belonged to families involved in other businesses. Furthermore, once they obtained the right to start a furnace, they tended to drop their glass-painting business. Such was the case with a painter called Pietro Cortiner in 1471 and probably, in 1517, with Filippo and Bernardo Catani, who developed spiral-effect filigree glass (*filigrana a retortoli*).

cat. 168. *Ewer*
Venice, early 16th century
The Corning Museum of Glass, Corning, New York

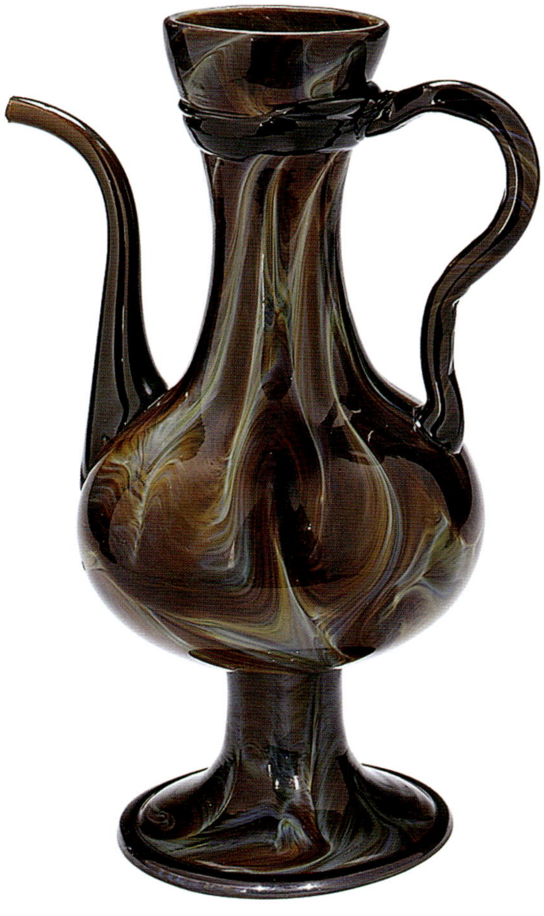

Most concretely, the pressure exerted by the glassmakers' guild to obtain the exclusive right to market enameled glass was justified from a technical standpoint, their effort being much greater than that of decorators. Glass to be painted was first fired then delivered to a decorator, who painted it with a frit or powder of colored glass—itself provided by glassmakers—mixed in an oily medium. After having been painted cold, the item was returned to the glassmaker for reheating in an annealing oven, called an *ara*, set above the furnace. The piece was held by a pontil (a metal rod used by the craftsman to hold the glass) in order to keep the enamel in contact with the flames—thus enamels of the Renaissance and Baroque periods could not have been smelted at low temperatures in a muffle kiln.[35] Study of surviving glassware with handles shows that they were also attached during this final phase, an operation that often led to accidents, as was the case with a goblet of blue glass in Bologna, a veritable masterpiece of enamel painting whose foot is misshapen. Gudenrath's experiments have moreover provided proof that half-molded dishes and plates were also decorated with non-figurative enamel motifs during this phase of refiring.[36]

Up till the 18th century, the two operations during which the glass was attached to the pontil—the shaping of the glass and the firing of enamels—each left a mark in the middle of the base of the object,

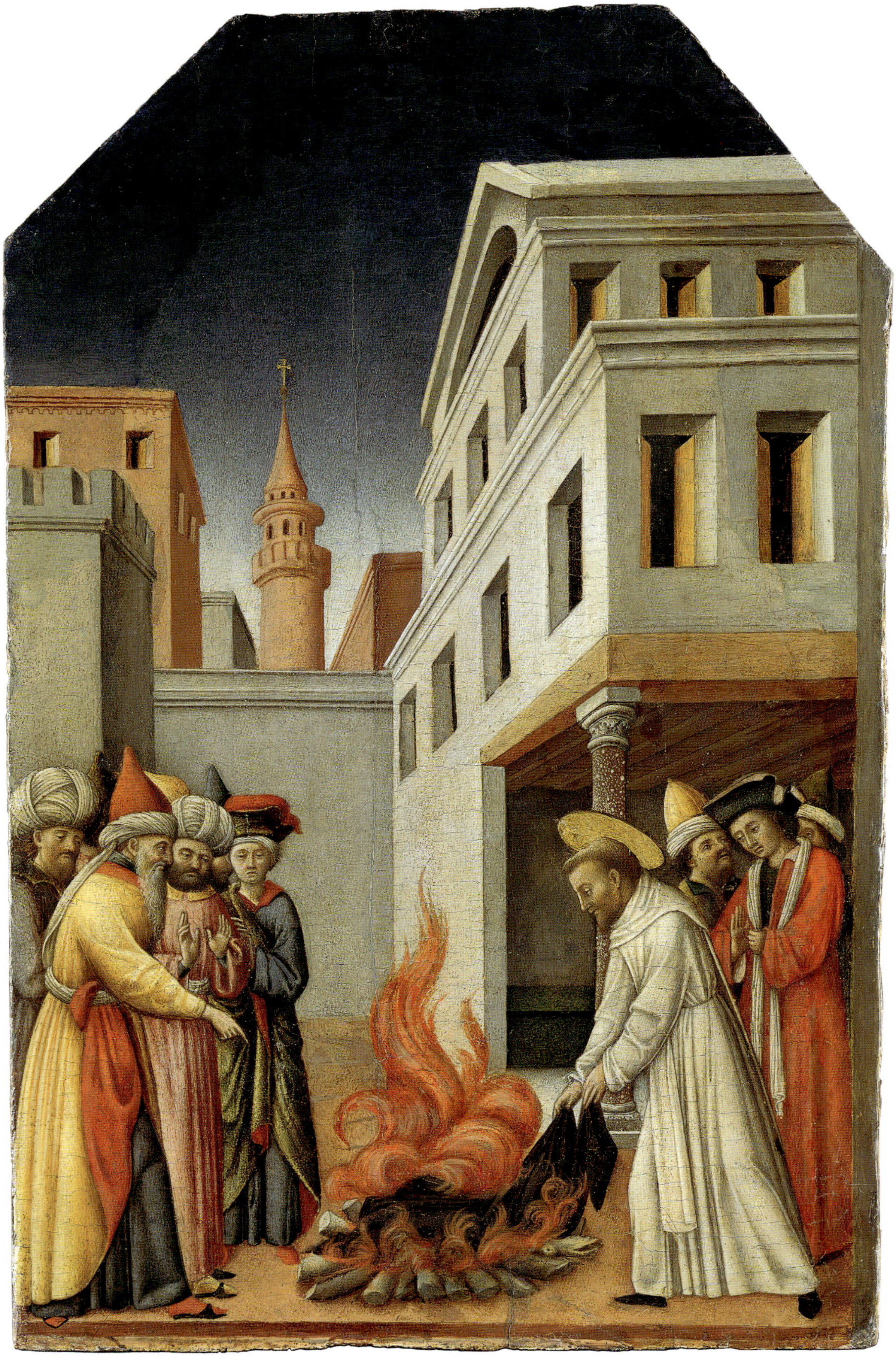

so that today this double pontil mark, which also characterizes enameled glass of the Mamluk period, is taken as proof of an object's age.

Examination of a fairly homogenous group of Venetian enameled glass from the second half of the 18th century, now in the Museo Vetrario on Murano, attests to the variety of techniques used by master glassmakers. Some of them display only a single pontil mark, some have two, while others have one mark in the middle of the base and a second whose shape is similar to a crown; finally, still others bear only the crown-shaped mark. It is therefore difficult to deduce a certain, definitive date of enameled glass based on pontil marks.

The fact that no exhaustive study has been done of Venetian enameled glass during the Renaissance may seem surprising insofar as it was one of the Republic's most brilliant periods of glassmaking, and would constitute a particularly interesting subject in this context.

The oldest enamel-decorated glass to be dated from that period is a blue piece now in the Museo Civico in Bologna, which is moreover one of the rare examples to be decorated with scenes of religious inspiration, perhaps attributable to a painter named Giovanni (fig. 8).[37] This stemmed goblet may serve as a point of departure for establishing whether a date of the early 1460s is the most plausible, or if this date could be pushed back some 10 years, closer to the period when Elena Lando was working (see note 30). The profile of this goblet seems somewhat archaic—a cup with 12 large ribs made by a technique called *a meza stampaura,* that is to say partly molded (see cat. 163, p. 69), plus a rectilinear stem with a knop in the middle and a squat conic foot. The two scenes depicted (the Adoration of the Magi and the Flight into Egypt) alternate with two tondi featuring the busts of two prophets—one with a long beard, the other wearing a beret—who hold an escutcheon. The detail of the garments of some of the figures makes it possible to date this work circa 1440 (the *giornea,* or pleated coat with low waist) or 1450 (puffed upper sleeves, fitted forearms), even though the headgear is typical of the 14th century.[38] These styles of garment remained fashionable until the late 1470s. The wrathful, heavily stylized faces of the two prophets directly evoke the saints on altarpieces by Antonio and Bartolomeo Vivarini (cat. 20), dating from the mid-15th century, before conventional expressive caricature evolved toward a more sober realism. The Flight into Egypt seems to respect a fairly simple scheme with a profile view of Mary on the donkey, based on a model common to paintings of the day. The same is true for the Adoration of the Magi, both in terms of its horizontal composition and its courtly atmosphere.[39] The model directly employed by the glass painter was nevertheless not Gentile da Fabriano's altarpiece, too remote in time and space,[40] but a painting or drawing by his Venetian assistant, Jacopo Bellini—father of Gentile and Giovanni Bellini (cat. 22, p. 136; cat. 23, p. 68; cat. 50, p. 131); in Ferrara there is a predella with the same imagery (ca. 1450) and comparable drawings in the Louvre and the British Museum are dated ca. 1435–40 and 1455–65, respectively.[41] The enameled decoration of this piece furthermore seems closer to a drawing in the Louvre (fol. 31), notably the taste for precious detail and the magical atmosphere typical of the International Gothic style, which suggests an earlier dating of the glass, that is to say ca. 1450–60.

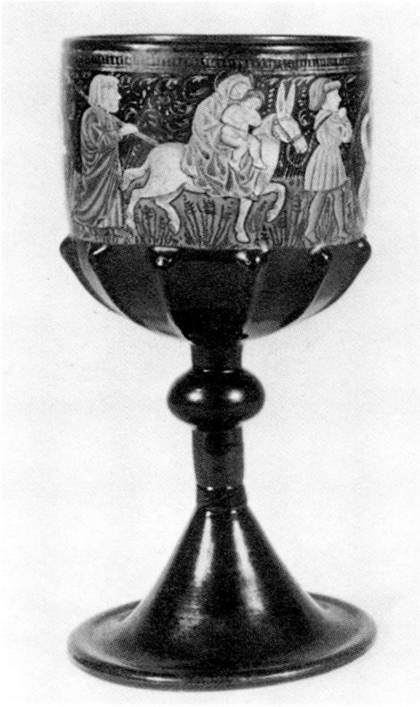

fig. 8. Goblet of blue glass. Museo Civico d'Arte Medievale, Bologna

cat. 20. Antonio Vivarini
St. Peter Martyr Attempting to Burn His Cloak
Venice, ca. 1440–50
Gemäldegalerie, Berlin

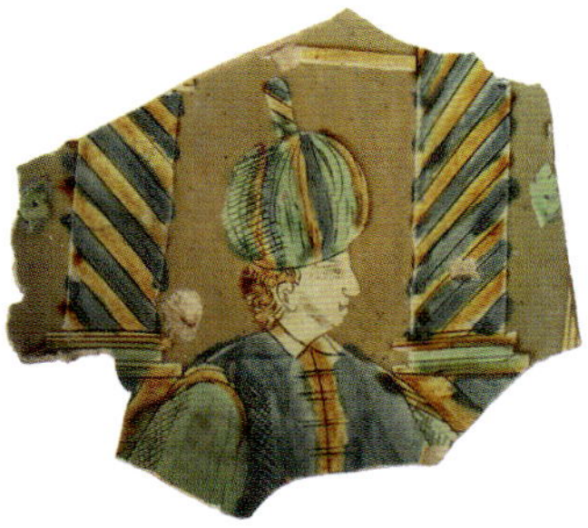

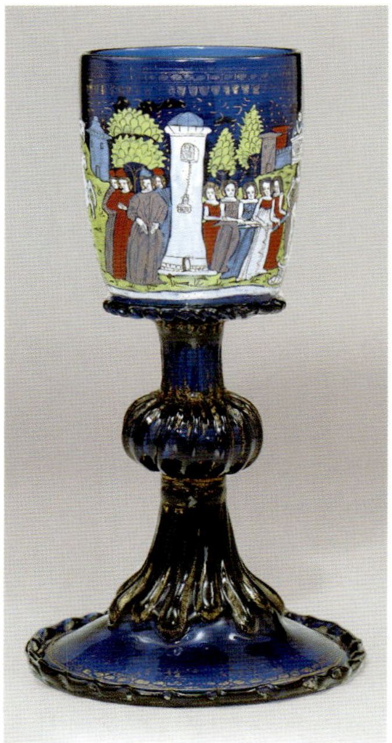

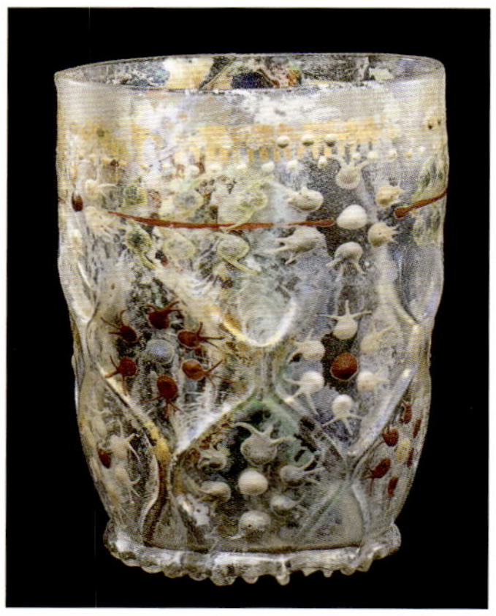

The famous "Barovier cup," now in the Museo Vetrario in Murano, is another of the oldest surviving pieces of Renaissance enameled glass.[42] The first known painted depiction of an identical cup appeared in the Odoni Altarpiece (the British Museum, London), painted by Carlo Crivelli in 1490, a date that serves as *terminus ante quem* for this model. The decoration on this wedding cup is composed of two tondi—one featuring a woman's bust, the other a man's bust—and two scenes of young women (first on horseback, then bathing in the Fountain of Youth). The groom is wearing the traditional beret that appeared in the 14th century, while the bride wears her hair pulled back under a long pointed hat that, in Italy, seems to have been totally out of fashion by the 1470s. Bathing in the Fountain of Youth was a recurring theme in painting and engraving throughout the 15th century. In both the riding scene and the bathing scene certain details seem so similar to the stemmed goblet in Bologna—the tufts of grass, the way the background is patterned with gilded scrollwork, the decorative band of gold beneath the rim—that the two pieces seem to have come from the same workshop. The dating of this cup, usually given as the 1470s or 1480s, should therefore be situated somewhat earlier.

A third item, a purple dish now in the Museo Provinciale d'Arte in Trento, would also seem to merit an early date.[43] The enamel-painted bottom shows the head and shoulders of a woman in profile, similar to late Gothic and pre-Renaissance imagery influenced by medals (see cats. 116, 117, 119, p. 134), which survived in enameled glassware and Venetian ceramics through incised, painted decoration up to the early 16th century (cat. 186).[44] The way in which the painter of this dish drew the features on the woman's face recalls those of the bride on the Barovier cup, which seems to be by the same hand. The rich decoration along the edge of Trento dish is characterized by vine shoots as well as by two peacocks and two birds shown in flight, motifs that are stylistically very similar to Venetian painting of the late Gothic period, in particular that of Pisanello (1395–1455). If we assume that glass decorators painted in a somewhat outmoded style, it was not out of date by many years; indeed, the island of Murano was not only close to Venice but had a direct link to it, and in those days was the site of many summer residences of the Republic's aristocracy, whose members were not only promoters of modernity but also demanding clients thoroughly familiar with prevailing taste.

The blue Bologna goblet, the Barovier cup, and the Trento dish thereby provide a frame of reference for dating similar objects such as the Virgil glass (The Metropolitan Museum of Art, New York) (fig. 9), which displays obvious parallels with the Bologna piece both in terms of shape and in the decoration along the edge. The allegorical scene on this glass, like the one on the Barovier cup, inaugurated a long decorative series on the theme of Triumphs, characterized by processions of male and female figures following a chariot on which ride figures symbolizing various idealized virtues such as Love, Fame, Modesty, and Eternity.[45]

Figurative motifs were used on stemmed cups like the Barovier cup, on cylindrical beakers, and above all on stemmed goblets of an eminently Gothic form. The wide, thick, cone-shaped foot was linked to the bowl by a wavy baluster, including a knop of varying shape.[46] The stem and foot were always ribbed, employing the technique called *a meza stampaura* (half-molded).

In the final 20 years of the 15th century, the rim was often underscored by rosettes produced by a series of tiny, multicolored enamel dots (cat. 161).[47] No explicit reference to this decorative pattern of rosettes has been found in the Murano archives, but it may correspond to an *a la damaschina* style mentioned in a lengthy inventory, drawn up in 1508, of decorated glassware in the workshop of Alvise Dragan.[48] Because it referred to glassware, *damaschina* did not mean the technique of metal inlay, imported from the Near East (see cats. 93–98, pp. 123, 217, 65, 82) but rather a decorative pattern typical of Islamic or Venetian vessels imitating that technique. Indeed, we should not overlook a late allusion, perhaps from the late 15th century, included in a collection of drawings by Jacopo Bellini, now in the Louvre, to a dish edged with this rosette pattern as a being a *vaxo damaschin.*[49]

Another recurring motif was called *a embrici* (overlapping, round-edged scales), mentioned in 1508 in the Dragan inventory by the name of *schiame*. It was obtained by adorning the gold leaf applied to the parison with little dots of enamel (cat. 164, p. 267).

Zigli or *zii,* that is to say lilies of the valley (cat. 166, p. 266; cat. 163, p. 69), were also mentioned in a 1496 inventory of a glasshouse headed by the brothers Giovanni and Marietta Barovier, as well as in the Dragan inventory drawn up 12 years later. Unspecified vegetal motifs, probably foliate scrollwork of Islamic inspiration, were described as *ad foiamina* decoration (with foliage) in an archive document from Murano written in 1474, while enameled pieces *a foiami, non figure* (foliated, not with figures) were requested in a letter sent to Venice by a Venetian merchant living in Istanbul.[50]

Foliate ornamentation would assume a more precise nature when, around 1500, it was used to decorate the opaque white glass known as *lattimo* (fig. 10, p. 267). *Lattimo* was suited for blowing and was developed by Angelo Barovier probably around 1450 or shortly thereafter; it is mentioned in the Murano archives of 1457, in a document concerning a patent granted to Jacopo d'Angelo for a glass called *porcellano,* that is to say resembling Chinese porcelain, the only porcelain available in Europe prior to the 18th century. Chinese porcelain reached Venice via Mamluk Egypt, notably through the port of Alexandria (see cat. 172, p. 88).[51] The earliest evidence of Chinese porcelain belonging to Venetians is found in the estate inventory of the painter Jacobello del Fiore, who died in Venice in 1439, which lists a *bochal de polzenagya,* later corrected to the term *bochal de porzelane* (bowl of porcelain). A few years later, in 1442, the sultan of Egypt gave Doge Francesco Foscari 30 pieces of Ming china.[52] The lively interest in blue-decorated porcelain was reflected in Venetian painting around 1500 and afterwards, as witnessed, for example, by Giovanni Agostino da Lodi's *Christ Washing the Disciples' Feet,* which dates from precisely 1500 and which features in the foreground a large blue and white basin (Gallerie dell'Accademia, Venice). Then there is Giovanni Bellini's *Feast of the Gods,* painted in 1514, which includes three porcelain bowls (National Gallery of Art, Washington). Both Ming china and its Ottoman imitators served as models, at least from 1515 onwards, for the maiolica ware produced in Venice with a *berettino* glaze that included a so-called "porcelain blue" decoration characterized by patterns of leaves and peonies (cat. 185).[53]

cat. 186. *Fragment of a plate depicting a man with a turban*
Venice, second half of the 16th century
Museo Franchetti alla Ca'd'Oro, Venice

fig. 9. "Virgil" goblet. The Metropolitan Museum of Art, New York

cat. 161. *Beaker*
Venice, late 15th century
The Corning Museum of Glass, Corning, New York

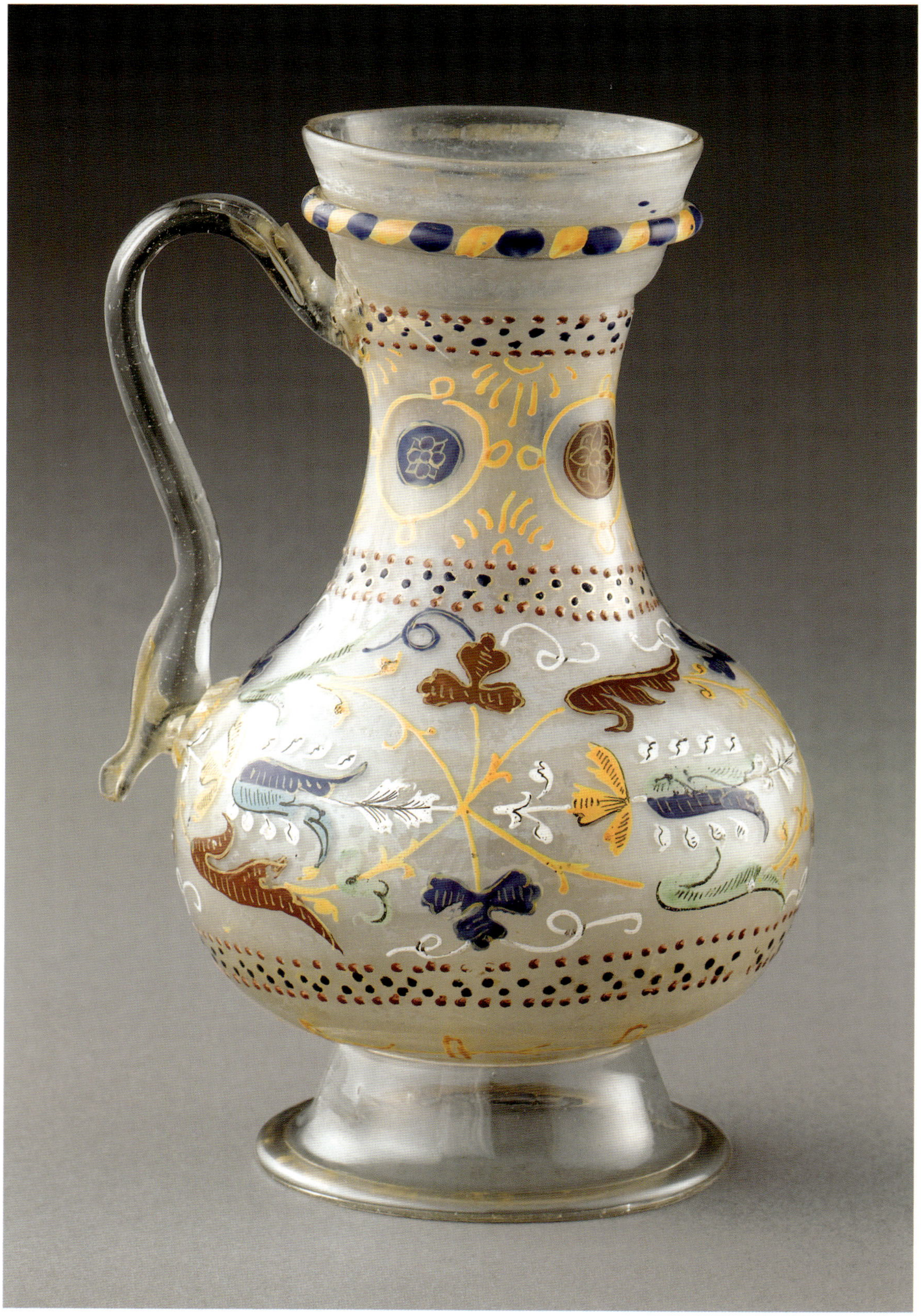

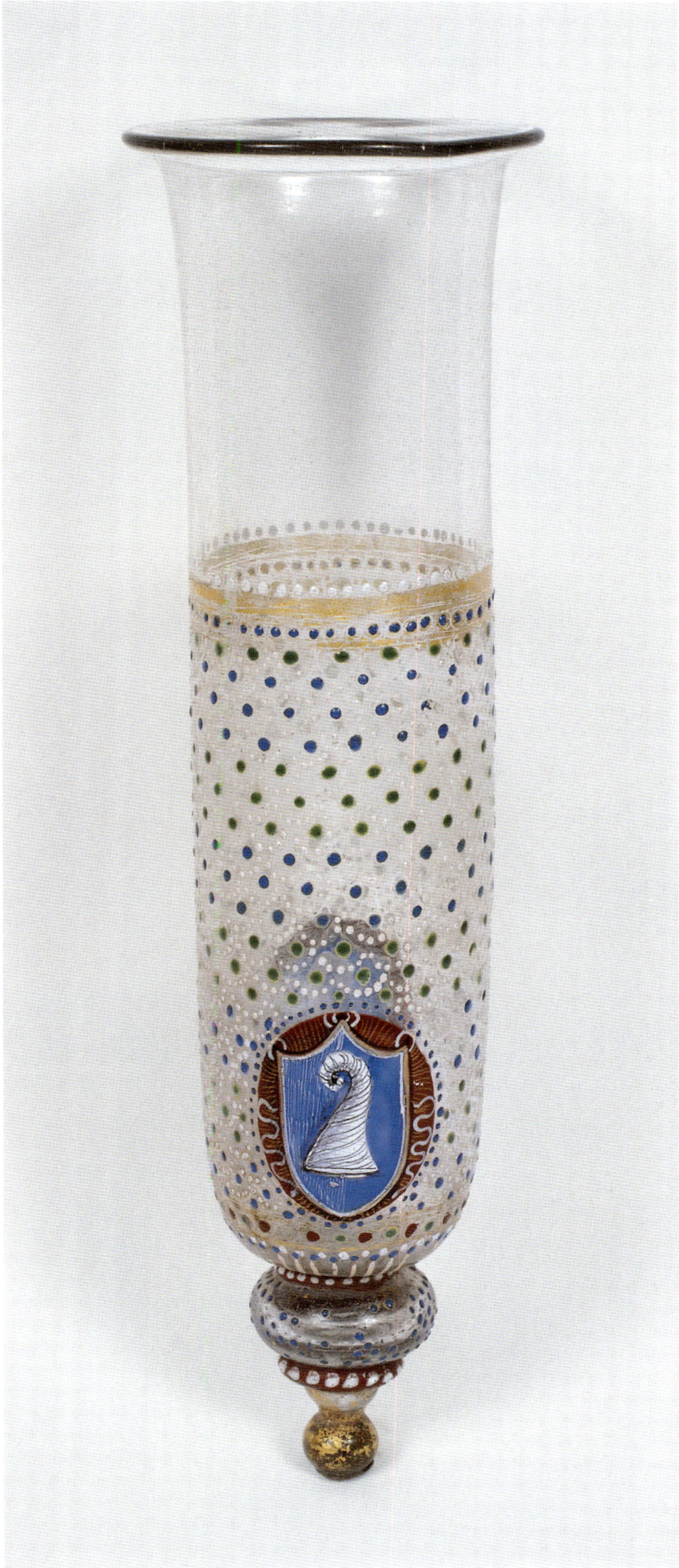

cat. 166. *Jug*
Venice, early 16th century
Musée du Louvre, Paris

cat. 164. *Hanging lamp* (*cesendello*)
Venice, late 15th–early 16th century
Museo Vetrario, Murano, Venice

fig. 10. Pot in *lattimo* glass, Venice, 16th century. The Hermitage, St. Petersburg

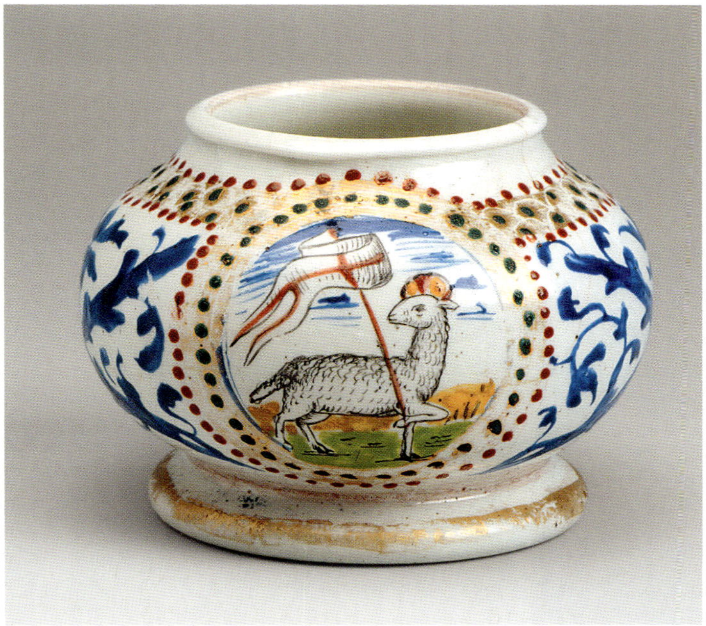

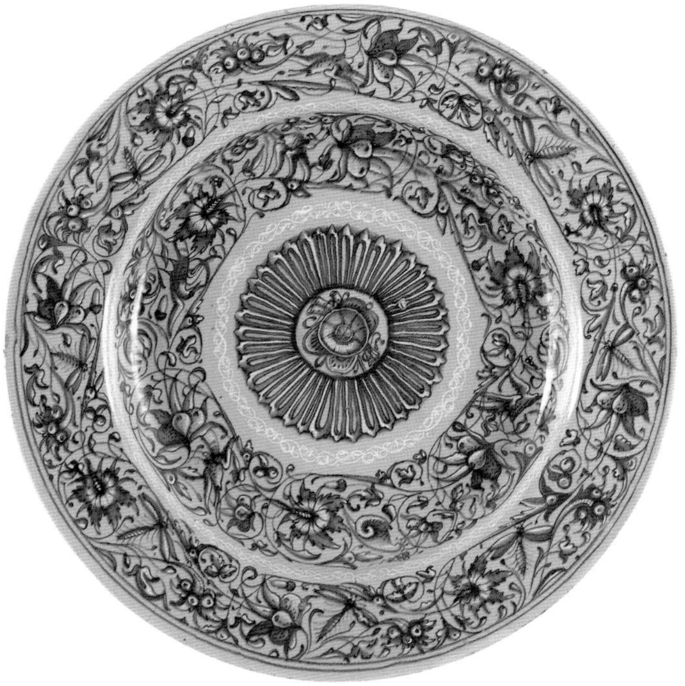

cat. 185. Maestro Lodovico (attr.)
Plate
Venice, ca. 1540–50
Musée National de la Renaissance, Ecouen, France

Even prior to ceramicists, Murano's master glassmakers exploited the fashion for porcelain with their production of *lattimo* from the mid-15th century onwards, while glass decorators developed painted blue enamel decoration on *lattimo* between 1510 and 1520.[54] Timothy Clarke studied a group of 14 pieces of Venetian *lattimo* made during the first two decades of the 16th century, demonstrating the Western and Eastern models behind their decoration, which represented the zenith of Venetian enamel painting on glass. When examined closely, the painting turns out to be of outstanding quality, notably compared to the work done on glass made during the second half of the 15th century, the period of the stemmed goblet in Bologna (fig. 8, p. 263). The quality and colors of the enamel, as well as the artists' technical refinement, make them veritable masterpieces even as the figurative and vegetal motifs link them closely to the Venetian artistic atmosphere of the day. Five of them take as their main motif busts of men and women painted in the style of Carpaccio (see cat. 30, p. 133; cat. 31, p. 27; cat. 52, p. 130; cat. 53, p. 134), who perhaps inspired them. Other pieces of *lattimo* from this group feature various mythological or religious subjects based on contemporary engravings: woodcuts from the *Hypnerotomachia Poliphili* and etchings by Bartolomeo Montagna, Girolamo Mocetto, and others. A few of these pieces have scrolling foliage along the edges with lotus flowers painted in *alla porcellana* blue enamel copied from the Chinese porcelain then fashionable in Venice. While this series seems to have been produced some time after 1520, the scrollwork, combined with other decorative motifs, would reappear on blown glass produced after 1549, this time engraved with a diamond point. However, some pieces of Venetian *cristallo* from the late 15th and first half of the 16th century feature Islamic decorative patterns combined with other, originally Byzantine motifs reworked in Venice through the centuries, along with purely European details (animal or vegetal motifs, knotwork, rosettes, heraldic crests), all in a harmonious fusion that typified not only Venetian art but the entire Venetian lifestyle.

The above-cited letter by an Istanbul-based Venetian merchant—Antonio di Coradi, who placed an order for goods with his brother-in-law in Venice in 1473—contains the first detailed mention of Renaissance blown glass being exported to the Orient by a Venetian dealer. The goods, to be shipped via Candia on Crete, included white, green, and red glass, *cristallo* ware, and chalcedony glass (cat. 168, p. 261). Coradi also ordered *schieti,* that is to say undecorated glassware, yet asked that some be enameled, although *non tanto sontuosamente* (not too lavishly) and *a foiami, non figure* (foliated, not with figures). It is not known whether decoration also featured on the *cristallo* objects given in 1480 to the *diodaro* in Damascus, in an effort to win his favors, by the leader of a group of pilgrims heading for Jerusalem on a ship originating from Venice, which called into the port of Jaffa.[55] In 1512 Martino Merlini, another Venetian merchant, asked his brother, who was traveling to the Near East on business, to find out if it would be feasible to ship enameled glassware made in Vettore di Angelo's workshop on Murano, although we do not know whether this plan was ever pursued. Finally, highly interesting information can be found in another document, dated 1590, namely a list of glassware ready for shipment to Istanbul by Pietro Ballarin, a master glassmaker on Murano. This was a major consignment, to say the least, for it comprised 440 panes of glass and roughly 450 items of blown glass, many of them gilded or silvered, though not enameled. The list includes descriptive terms difficult to interpret (*bembi, soltanie, tapsi, mastrapà, acanini, ocche de fili, catelai, zame*) as well as perfectly comprehensible ones referring to lanterns, basins, vases, bowls, glasses, and hanging lamps called *cesendelli* (cat. 165, p. 270). The most expensive items were "large *cesendelli* with six handles and six roses," valued at two ducats each. It is impossible to know whether these were mosque lamps in the traditional Islamic form or were of the cylindrical type with rounded bottom; in contrast, it is certain that both models were exported to Istanbul, as attested by an order placed by Marcantonio Barbaro for 900 lamps destined for the Grand Vizier Sokollu Mehmet Pasha (figs. 11–12, p. 270; cats. 169 and 171, p. 271; cat. 164, p. 267; cat. 165, p. 270). A lamp now in the Düsseldorf museum (cat. 163, p. 69) must have been made in Venice, or at least in Europe; it features enamel decoration similar to that on a set of glass items found in Damascus and now held in various collections (cat. 160, p. 260; cat. 161, p. 264). These objects testify not only to the volume of exports and made-to-order work by Venetian glasshouses, but also the ability of master glassmakers to adapt to the stylistic requirements of foreign markets.

Meanwhile, grotesques—a combination of human, animal, and foliate motifs devoid of any narrative intent—constituted a style of indigenous decoration typical of the Italian Renaissance.[56] Grotesque motifs were disseminated by engravers such as Agostino Veneziano, active between 1514 and 1536 (cat. 59, p. 112). Dating enameled glassware with grotesque decoration to the period around 1500 therefore seems too early, and it is more likely that this fashion spread to the Murano glasshouses starting in the 1520s.[57]

The period during which enamel painting was done on glass was much more extensive than generally thought, even if it was overtaken by other techniques, such as filigree (*a retortoli,* a spiral effect, or *a reticello,* a lattice effect) and diamond-point engraving. For example, the Sienese copperware merchant Vannuccio Biringuccio spoke of *"pitture d'altri finissimi smalti"* (other extremely fine enamel paintings) in reference to Murano output, in his anthology on *Pirotechnia,* written ca. 1530–35 and published in Venice in 1540. Similarly, it is significant that a 1570 inventory of items in the Ai Tre Mori workshop, belonging to Bortolo d'Alvise, who illegally emigrated to Florence the previous year, lists glassware of all kinds made in various techniques, including gilded glass and notably a *"piatelo dorado con una arma recota"* (small gilded dish with an annealed coat of arms) and *"goti francesi recoti con arme"* (French glass annealed with coats of arms) as well as *"cestelle quatro depente"* (four

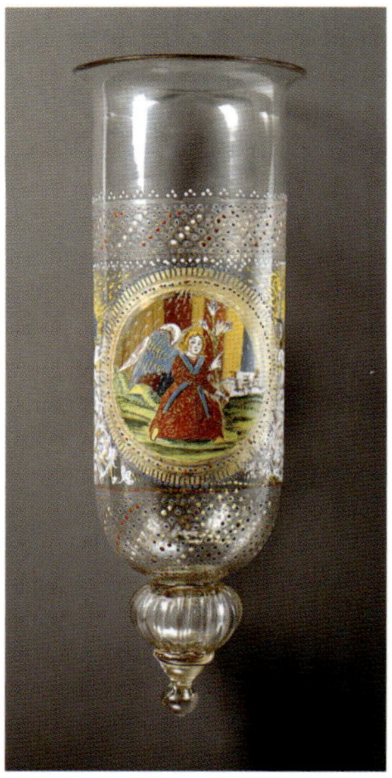

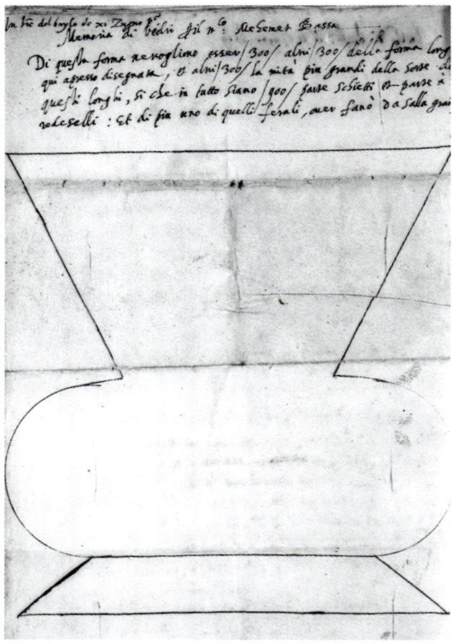

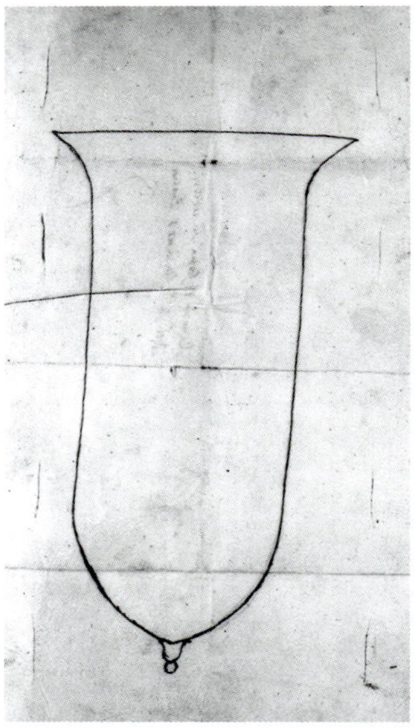

cat. 165. *Hanging lamp* (cesendello)
Venice, late 15th–early 16th century
The Metropolitan Museum of Art, New York

fig. 11. Design for a mosque lamp, probably by Sokollu Mehmet Pasha, 1569. Archivio di Stato, Venice

fig. 12. Design for a *cesendello* (hanging lamp), probably by Sokollu Mehmet Pasha, 1569. Archivio di Stato, Venice

painted baskets). The stress placed on the second firing confirms that we are dealing with smelted enamels here.[58]

In order to confirm the persistence of enameled decoration on Murano up until the middle of the century, it would be useful to make a close study of the coats of arms reproduced on Venetian glass of the 16th century, with the aim of establishing precise dates. Further problems will be posed, however, by Venetian-style glassware bearing German arms, now generally attributed to foreign glasshouses using *façon de Venise* techniques.[59] Up until the second half of the 16th century noble families in Augsburg and Nuremberg ordered ceramics from Venice that were also adorned with coats of arms (cat. 182, p. 272), which were exported along the major trade routes linking the lagoon to Germany.[60] It is highly likely that glassware produced and ordered at Murano also followed these same paths, despite the fact that the major part of these Venetian-style products of the 16th and 17th centuries were done in *façon de Venise.* Reexamination of this issue should be based on glass decorated with typically Venetian figures, in particular Commedia dell'Arte masks and women dressed in Venetian fashion.[61]

Murano's 17th-century archives, such as an inventory of Giacomo Darduin's workshop, drawn up in 1689, make no mention of enameled glass—this type of decoration seems to have died out at least 100 years earlier.[62] In the 18th century, no enameled glass is listed among the gifts offered by Venice to King Frederick IV of Denmark during his stay in the Most Serene Republic in 1709.[63] In 1722, the register of gifts given to the princess of Piedmont and to the prince of Modena, Giovanni Federico, contains no trace of enameled glass among the long list of itemized glassware.[64] *Lattimo,* the milky white glass that imitated porcelain, returned to fashion around 1730, which corresponded to the 18th-century fashion for porcelain and chinoiserie. After the 1708 invention of hard-paste porcelain by Johann Friedrich Böttiger and the founding of Meissen as the first European porcelain manufactory, Venice could pride itself on obtaining Italy's first factory—only the third in Europe—thanks to Giovanni Vezzi, whose firm was active in 1720–27. Vezzi initially benefited from the assistance of Cristoph Konrad Hunger, who had worked at Meissen and Vienna.[65] Later, porcelain was again made in Venice by Geminiano Cozzi, first in partnership with the Helwelckes from Meissen between 1761

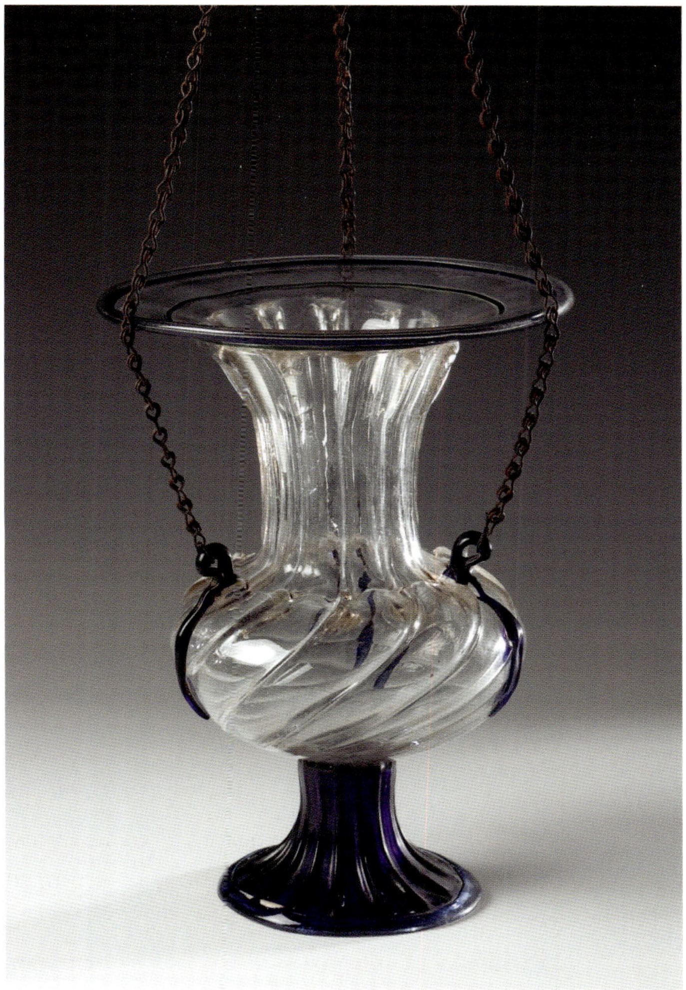

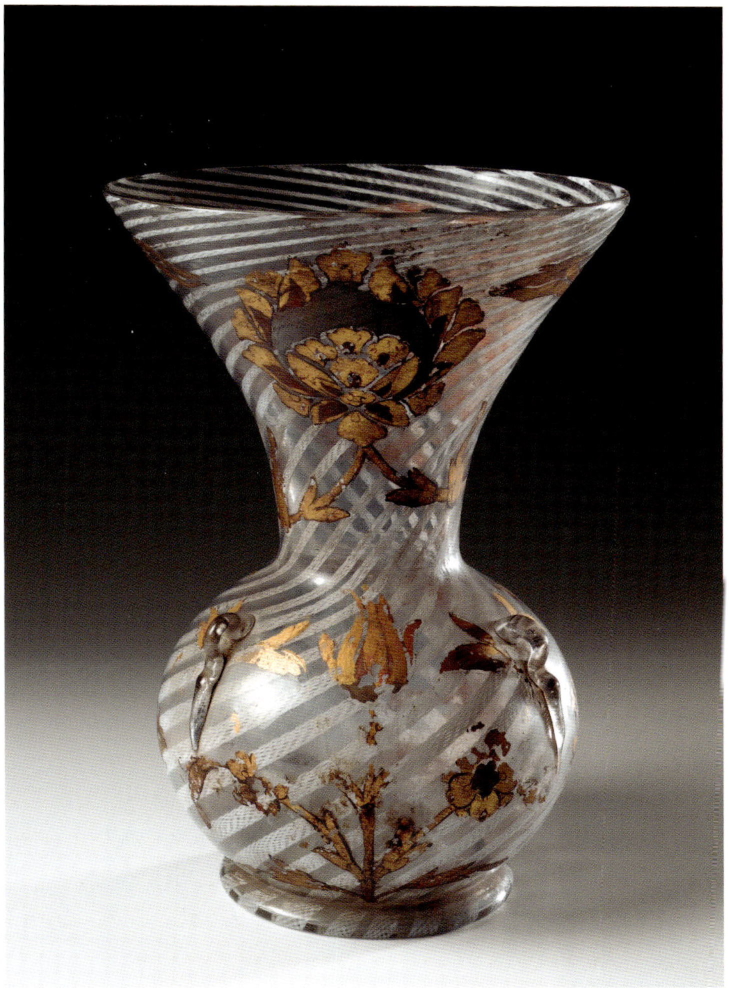

cat. 169. *Mosque lamp*
Venice, 16th century
Topkapı Sarayi Müzesi, Istanbul

cat. 171. *Mosque lamp*
Venice, 16th century
Topkapı Sarayi Müzesi, Istanbul

and 1763, then subsequently as an independent entrepreneur.[66] The period between the closing of Vezzi's factory in 1727 and the launch of Cozzi's in 1761 witnessed the finest Venetian enameled glass of the day, notably those in *lattimo,* which were in fact imitations of porcelain. Thus it can reasonably be asserted that *lattimi* with enameled decoration were designed to fill the void left by the halting of porcelain manufacture in Venice. In this respect, it is significant that the first Venetian enameled glass of this period—dated and inscribed—was made in 1727: namely, a bottle decorated with multicolored flowers framing two figurative scenes, marked on the bottom *AL GESU' MURANO 1727.* This mark belonged to the glasshouse of Vincenzo Miotti (1644–1729) and his son Daniele (1678–1763), which specialized in opaque colored glass and *lattimi.* The Miotti family, known from the mid-16th century, had specialized in the production of enamels, notably once Vincenzo's father, also called Daniele, married into the Darduin family and thus inherited valuable skills. It was the first time that Murano glass—in imitation of porcelain—bore a mark on the bottom.[67] Glass bearing the Miotti workshop mark—or attributed to it—was made between 1727 and 1746. The polychrome floral decoration, often enlivened with a bird perched on a branch or standing on one leg, is similar to—and inspired by—that found on porcelain from the Vezzi manufactory in the years 1724–27.[68] These *lattimi* stand out for the unmistakable finesse of their decoration and it is not impossible that the Miottis hired porcelain decorators. Indeed, we know that the Vezzi warehouse held some 30,000 unglazed pieces that were used, when the firm closed, to pay off employees, who were

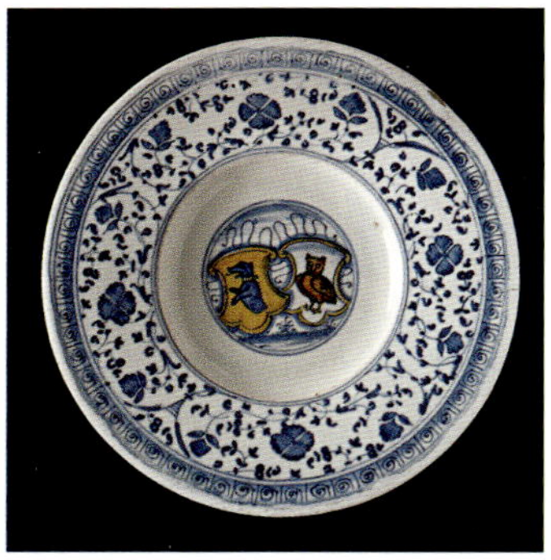

cat. 182. *Plate decorated* alla porcellana *with the arms of the Augsburg families Meuting and Hörwarth*
Venice, ca. 1516
The British Museum, London

entitled to decorate them as they saw fit.[69] Insofar as it was easier and cheaper to refire them, once decorated, in the furnaces of master glassmakers in Murano, this incident may have provided the opportunity for an initial contact, as early as 1727, between porcelain painters and the Miotti firm.[70]

The Miottis' enameled glassware was emulated by Osvaldo Brussa;[71] other known enamel painters include Giovanni Andrea Bertolini and Pietro Bertolini.[72] Closely related to porcelain decoration, figurative motifs based on Chinese, mythological, or pastoral themes were probably derived from drawings. An anonymous artist produced three services of *lattimo* plates at that time—now dispersed in various collections—finely decorated with views of Venice inspired by engravings by Luca Carlevarijs (1703) as well as others by Antonio Visentini (1742) drawn from paintings by Canaletto, which were bought by Horace Walpole and his traveling companions during their stay in Venice as part of their Grand Tour of 1741.[73] This testifies not only to decorators' use of prints as models but also to foreign buyers' penchant for *lattimi* and other opaque colored glass, as distinct from Venetian crystal, which was being supplanted by higher quality products from Bohemia and England.

Venetian enameled glass of the late 18th and early 19th centuries was of mediocre quality, as was its decoration. All sectors of the Venetian glass industry, apart from beads, underwent a deep crisis during the period extending from the fall of the Republic in 1797 to the 1960s. The technique of enameled glass did enjoy a renaissance in 1867 thanks to Salviati & Co., master glassmakers who benefited from the skills of Giuseppe Devers, a ceramics decorator from Turin who had worked at Sèvres and whom Antonio Salviati had met at the Universal Exhibition held in Paris that year.[74] During the two years he spent with the Salviatis, Devers and the firm's technicians managed to achieve high standards of quality in enamel work and decoration, all the while training students. Profiting from the revival movement, masterpieces of the past were copied, from the purple Byzantine bowl in the Treasury of St. Mark's to the Barovier cup via various glass objects belonging to the Slade Collection. Antonio Salviati, who launched a new company in 1877, exhibited at the Paris Universal Exhibition of 1878, as did his first company, which had changed its name in the meantime to the Venice and Murano Glass and Mosaic Company. Their exhibition stands were virtual museums of the art of glassmaking—including enameled glass—from Antiquity up to the Baroque period.[75]

Already in 1867 the new output of Venetian glass attracted the interest of Isma'il Pasha, the khedive of Egypt, who ordered from Salviati 50 mosque lamps based on the model of 14th-century Syrian originals (fig. 13). First submitted to the khedive for approval, they were then shipped to Cairo and perhaps also to Alexandria.[76] This order, and the quality of work it inspired, generated enthusiasm on Murano and in Venice, not only because it indicated a rebirth of enameled glass, but also because it fueled the aspiration of the Murano glasshouses to export their products on a large scale, thus reviving the island's prosperity.[77]

fig. 6. Attributed to Filippo Candelario, "Capital of Love"(detail) featuring a young woman crowning a knight with a wreath, mid-14th century. Doge's Palace, Venice

In 1869, with the khedive's agreement, Napoleon III purchased two of these lamps

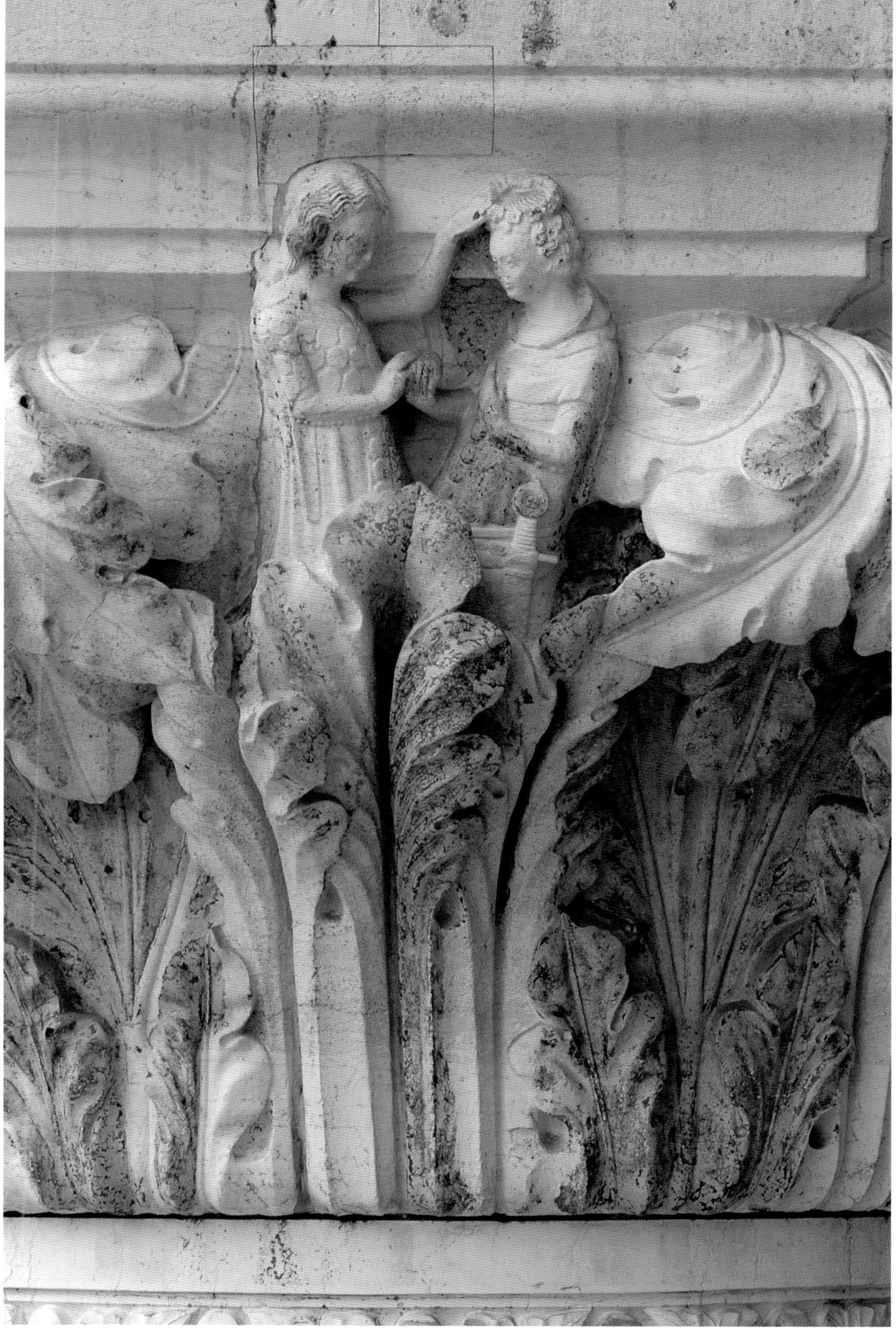

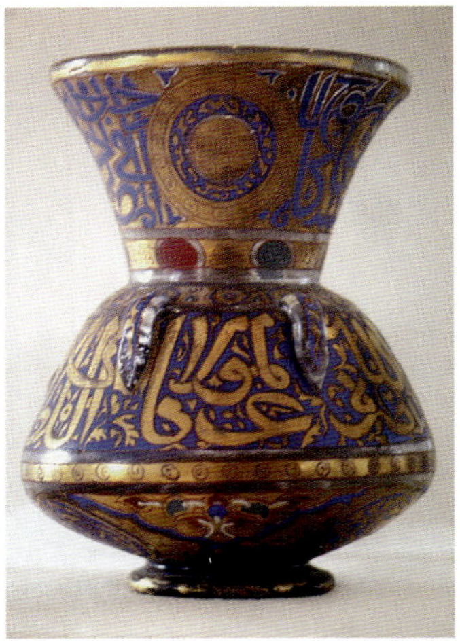

fig. 13. Antonion Salvati, mosque lamp commissioned by the khedive of Egypt, Venice, 1867

for his collection. Thus, during the final third of the 19th century and the early years of the 20th, Islamic lamps with enameled decoration made on Murano were bought as decorative objects or collector's items—in addition to those destined for their original use—as were the lamps and other enameled glass of Islamic inspiration made by Frenchman Philippe-Joseph Brocard for the Universal Exhibition of 1867. Venetian craftsmen then went on to reproduce other Islamic objects—notably a long-necked bottle from the 14th century[78]—characterized by enamel-work similar to the originals (whereas the enamel decoration on French glass was glossier and applied meticulously, sometimes in a light relief that immediately distinguished them from 14th-century originals).

Venetian imitations of Islamic enameled glass such as those in the 19th century have continued almost into the present; therefore, "beyond their intrinsic artistic value and the contribution they made to the revival of Venetian glass, they seem to represent one of the most recent examples of the age-old relationship linking Venice to the main economic and political centers of Asia and Mediterranean Africa. This relationship has undergone alternating phases of reciprocal dependence, yet has often occurred at the level of equal, profitable exchanges that are not only commercial but also cultural."[79]

Notes

1 The initial draft of the first part of this essay was by Stefano Carboni, the second by Rosa Barovier Mentasti. The final text is the result of a close collaboration between the two authors.
2 See, for example, Tait 1991, pp. 148-49.
3 Verità and Toninato 1990; Verità, Zecchin and Renier 2002.
4 Carboni 2001, pp. 15–17; Carboni and Whitehouse 2001, pp. 3–7.
5 The most comprehensive surveys are Lamm 1929–30; Carboni 2001; Carboni and Whitehouse 2001.
6 In particular, see the year-by-year glass chronology, inferred from archival documents until the end of the 14th century, in Zecchin 1973 and 1974.
7 Gerspach (1885, p. 140) is the first author to mention the treaty. See also Lamm 1929–30, p. 491, no. 47; Rückert 1963, p. 228; Carboni 1998, pp. 101-02, n. 12.
8 Jacoby 1993, pp. 67–68; see also Verità 1985, pp. 19–21.
9 Jacoby 1993, p. 70.
10 The Treasury of St. Mark's includes the largest single group of artistic Islamic glass anywhere in Italy. The works that can certainly be attributed to Islamic glassmakers are four (one is cat. 150), although a few others might be from the early Islamic period.
11 Wenzel 1988; Carboni and Whitehouse 2001, pp. 202–3, 221–25, cats. 110–12.
12 Carboni 2003a.
13 Lamm 1929–30, pp. 278–79, pl. 99; Lamm 1941, pp. 77–99.
14 Zecchin 1969, 1970, 1973.
15 The best survey of these European finds is in Baumgartner and Krueger 1988, pp. 126–60, nos. 72–119.
16 Carboni 1998; Verità 1998.
17 Carboni and Whitehouse 2001, p. 303.
18 Baumgartner and Krueger 1988, pp. 126–60.
19 Baumgartner and Krueger 1988, pp. 133–39, cats. 80–89; Krueger 1998.
20 It is one of the most accomplished carved capitals (the so-called Capital of Love) around the Doge's Palace, showing eight scenes from different stages of the life of a couple and probably the work of Filippo Candelario in around the mid-14th century. Wolters (1976, vol. 1, pp. 44, 173–74, 178, vol. 2, fig. 200, cat. 48) notes that some of the scenes are inspired by illustrations of the *Roman de Troyes* and other French texts that were well known in Venice. The French model of the "crowning" scene is also evident from a comparison with an ivory diptych in the Musée de Cluny, Paris, of ca. 1330. See Tigler 1999, p. 23, f. 14.
21 Swiechowski-Rizzi 1982; Barral I Altet 1985, figs. 39, 44, 78, 93; Rizzi 1987; Weigel 1997; Krueger 1998, pp. 107–9, figs. 24.1-.5; Zuliani 2000, pp. 30–34; Dorigo 2003, vol. 2, pp. 451–87.
22 Weigel 1997.
23 Carboni 1998, p. 103, n. 27.
24 Carboni 1998, p. 103, n. 42.
25 See, for example, Baumgartner and Krueger 1988, pp. 129–58, cats. 73, 75-76, 82-83, 86-88, 95, 97–98, 100–101, 104–5, 109–11, 114, 116–17; Krueger 1998; Mäesalu 1999.
26 Carboni 1998, p. 103, n. 35-40.
27 Carboni 2004.
28 Zecchin 1967; Verità 1985.
29 The earliest extant record mentions a request for window glass from Venice by Sultan Zahir Khoshkadam (r. 1461–67); see Zecchin 1980, year 1466, and the entry for cat. 162.
30 Levi was the first to transcribe documents relating to Elena Lando, whom he mistakenly called Elena de Laudo; see Levi 1895, p. 32. Zecchin accepted the interpretation of Lando's work as involving enameled decoration, but

expressed doubts in his later writings. See Zecchin 1987–90, vol. 1, p. 31; vol. 2, pp. 208, 219, 231; vol. 3, pp. 34, 118.
31 Flasks encased in straw were also made on Murano and called *inghistere*, from a term designationg spherical-shaped bottles. A man carrying a flask that hangs from a stick is shown on the blue glass goblet in Bologna.
32 The enamels were worked on a flat, round plate then iron-branded with the name or enseign of the glass manufactory. This practice became mandatory starting in 1469; Zecchin 1987–90, vol. 2, p. 350; vol. 3, p. 40.
33 The original *mariegola* is now in the Museo Civico Correr in Venice, Ms. IV, 26 ; Zecchin 1976.
34 Zecchin 1987–1990, vol. 3, p. 120.
35 *Il libro dei colori: Segreti del secolo XV*, Bologna: Biblioteca Universitaria, Ms. 2861, edited by O. Guerrini and C. Ricci, Bologna, 1887. See Charleston, Archer and Marcheix 1977, pp. 18–19; Zecchin 1987–90, vol. 3, pp. 42–43 and 123.
36 Tait 1991, pp. 235–237; Lanmon and Whitehouse 1993, pp. 3–7.
37 The glass (inv. 1363) was first published in 1814; see Venice 1982, cat. 63. In 1474 a certain Giovanni, painter, decorated a beaker with "a nuntiata," which Zecchin rightly interpreted as an allusion to the Annuciation scene; Zecchin 1979, pp. 64–65.
38 My thanks to Doretta Davanzo Poli for this information.
39 A similar scene figures on the predella of an *Adoration of the Magi* by Gentile da Fabriano, who spent much time in Venice.
40 Gentile's altarpiece (now in the Uffizi, Florence) was painted in 1423 for the sacristy of the Church of Santissima Trinità in Florence, where Jacopo Bellini followed him.
41 Degenhart and Schmitt 1990, vol. 5, p. 148, figs. 126–28; vol. 7, pl. 47; 8, pl. 275.
42 This cup (Museo Vetrario, inv. Cl.VI, n° 1), donated by Teodoro Correr in 1840, was mistakenly attributed to Angelo Barovier by Vincenzo Lazari; Lazari 1859, p. 96, cat. 336.
43 Museo provinciale d'Arte, Castello del Buonconsiglio (inv. mun. n° 4071). This dish was published in the very first systematic study of enameled Venetian glass of the Renaissance period (Schmidt 1911).
44 The most famous painting that includes a double-winged headdress—also called a *sella alla francese*—identical to the one worn by the woman on the Trento dish is Piero della Francesca's *Meeting of Solomon and the Queen of Sheba*, part of his fresco cycle for the Church of San Francesco in Arezzo, executed between 1452 and 1466.
45 The source of these allegorical depictions, highly fashionable in the mid-15th century, was the never-completed poem *Trionfi*, begun by Petrarch in 1352. Although not one of his best works, this poem was nonetheless a source of great inspiration for Italian artists, draftsmen, and decorators, notably painters on glass. The theme of the Triumphs found its most brilliant expression in the *Hypnerotomachia Poliphili*, a book written by Francesco Colonna from 1467 onwards, published by Aldus Manutius in Venice in 1499 with a set of woodcuts often linked to enameled decoration, given the cultural context of the second half of the 15th century; see Colonna, 1499.
46 A glass with ribbed stem and knop is depicted in the *Madonna del Latte*, a late work by Giovanni Boccati, a painter active from 1440 to 1486 (Galleria Nazionale, Perugia); this shape would survive up to the end of the 15th century.
47 This technique is documented in the 16th century—and even in the following century—as seen, for example, in the *Annunciation* in the Church of San Giorgio Maggiore in Venice (ca. 1525–50), as well as in the *The Origin of Love*, a work attributed to Jacopo Tintoretto, executed in 1562. The former painting includes a cylindrical glass with vertical sides, while the latter features a dish with radial sides; see Ivanoff 1976, pp. 42–43; Moore Valeri 1997; and Barovier Mentasti 2001.
48 Zecchin 1987–90, vol. 3, pp. 59–60.
49 Dagenhart and Schmitt 1990, vol. 7, pl. 75, fol. 59.
50 Zecchin 1987–90, vol. 2, pp. 211–12; vol. 3, pp. 58–60, 126.
51 See Deborah Howard's essay in this volume.
52 Zecchin 1987–90, vol. 2, pp. 348–49, nos. 9–10.
53 Alverà Bortolotto 1981, pp. 63–66, pls. 44–47.
54 Clarke 1974.
55 See the account of Santo Brasca's voyage, cited here in the entry for cats. 160–61.
56 The term *grottesca* [grotesque] was derived from grotto when, in the late 15th century, Roman artists discovered the interior decoration of the Domus Aurea, which had been buried. Difficulty of access made it appear to be a natural grotto. The artists drew on what they saw for their own fresco decorations. The first frescoes with "grotesque" motifs appeared at the end of the 15th century and in following years, notably in works by Pinturicchio, Filippino Lippi, and Luca Signorelli. This decorative style enjoyed a great vogue thanks to Raphael's frescoes in the Stanze of the Vatican (1508–17), executed with the help of various assistants, in particular Giovanni da Udine, active in Rome between 1514 and 1527 (that is to say, after Raphael's death).
57 Glassware with grotesque motifs can be seen in 16th-century paintings, including one of *Lot and his Daughters* by Albrecht Altdorfer, from 1537; the glass has a curved bowl and an unribbed conical foot.
58 The same could probably not be said of *vedri christalini indoradi, depenti, intagiadi e lavoradi a mordente* (gilded crystalline glass, painted, cut, and acid-etched), quoted in a 1583 declaration by the master glassmaker Giovanni Luna, who in 1580 had commissioned gilding and painting work from Donato Briati, a glass painter. According to Zecchin (1987–90, vol. 2, p. 174; vol. 3, pp. 72–73), they might have belonged to the category of Venetian crystal that was engraved with a diamond point and gilded and painted cold, not enameled in a furnace.
59 Corning 2004, pp. 20–83.
60 Sauerlandt 1929, pp. 72–73; Alverà Bortolotto 1981, pp. 64–65.
61 Tait 1979, pp. 42–44, cats. 38–41.
62 *Beliconi*—a local corruption of the German word *Willkommen*, used for mugs destined for the German market—are mentioned in the inventory but we do not know whether they were decorated or not; Zecchin 1987–90, vol. 2, p. 168.
63 The gifts numbered at least 200 items, plus many other objects personally acquired by the king; Boesen 1960; Hein 1984, pp. 9–43, nos. 1–97; Hein 1992, pp. 63–78.
64 Boesen 1960, pp. 29–30, 49–50, and 67–68, no. 36. These inventories, as well as those of the Rosenborg collection, refer to *girasoli* glass. This was a translucent white glass made opaque by a treatment with lead arsenate, which mimicked the stone called girasol and possessed opaline qualities. The formula was first given in *Ricettario Darduin*; the original document, dated 1644 and titled *Copia di tutti li secretti de smalti*, figures in *Miscellanea di atti diversi: Manoscritti*, ASV, fol. 41, carta 82v; see Zecchin 1986, pp. 23, 63, and 218. *Girasoli* glass was fashionable up to around 1740, when *lattimo* returned to favor, henceforth called *smalto* (it only recovered its original name in the late 19th century; both terms are used today). During the 17th century, antimony progressively replaced lead and tin as an opacifier.
65 The Venetian factory, which produced high quality porcelain, nevertheless went out of business in 1727 due to the inability of sales to recoup the heavy investment (up to 50,000 ducats).
66 Cozzi's firm closed down in 1812. Stazzi 1967; Mottola Molfino 1976, pp. 26–28; Alverà Bortolotto 1981, pp. 108–131; Melegati 1998.
67 This master glassmaker's mark, which also appeared on his enamels, was Christ's monogram, *I H S* (also found on enameled glass produced in the 18th century. Alternately, one finds *AL GESU* (or *AL GIESU*) or IESUS along with the inscription MIOTTI. See Mariacher 1958, pp. 5–12; Hetteš 1960, no. 197, fol. 51–52; Charleston 1980, no. 72; Barovier Mentasti 1982, pp. 157–70; Zecchin 1987–1990, vol. 1, pp. 195–99; vol. 2, pp. 189–193; and Theuerkauff-Liederwald 1994, p. 129, no. 31.
68 Stazzi 1967, p. 53, pls. 19, 24; Melegati 1998, p. 17, fol. 8, pls. 11, 20, 28, 35.
69 This system made it possible to resolve the problem of the high temperatures required by a second firing, which meant that these items could be sent to Germany, where they were refired. Stazzi 1967, pp. 59 and 422.
70 These hypotheses are shared by Luca Melegati (see Melegati 1998), whom I would like to thank for his comments.
71 Glass made by Brussa is recognizable thanks to the goblet he is seen painting in his portrait now in the Museo Vetrario on Murano. Zecchin 1987–90, vol. 2, p. 192; Barovier Mentasti 1982, fol. 163–64.
72 The Bertolinis, who did not sign their *lattimi*, also attempted to produce porcelain, as witnessed by a 1748 decree by the Council of Ten, but they abandoned it in favor of maiolica ware made on Murano, which by 1753 they could sell, untaxed, in Venice and on the mainland.
73 The prints, never published, were made available by the consul, Joseph Smith. Charleston attributes the plates to the Miottis, while Zecchin ascribes them to the Bertolinis; Charleston 1959, pp. 62–82.
74 Carboni 1989a, pp. 944–45.
75 Paris 1878, pp. 210, 340, f. 560; De Liesville 1878, pp. 695–701; Barovier Mentasti 1982, pp. 217–21.
76 Carboni 1989a, pp. 947–48.
77 Zanetti 1869, p. 14; Colleoni and Errera 1969, pp. 42, 49, and 55; Carboni 1989a, pl. 104–106.
78 Cisotto Nalon and Barovier Mentasti, 2002, pp. 88–91.
79 Quoted from Carboni 1989a, p. 948.

Influence of the Islamic Tradition on the Chemistry and Technology of Venetian Glass

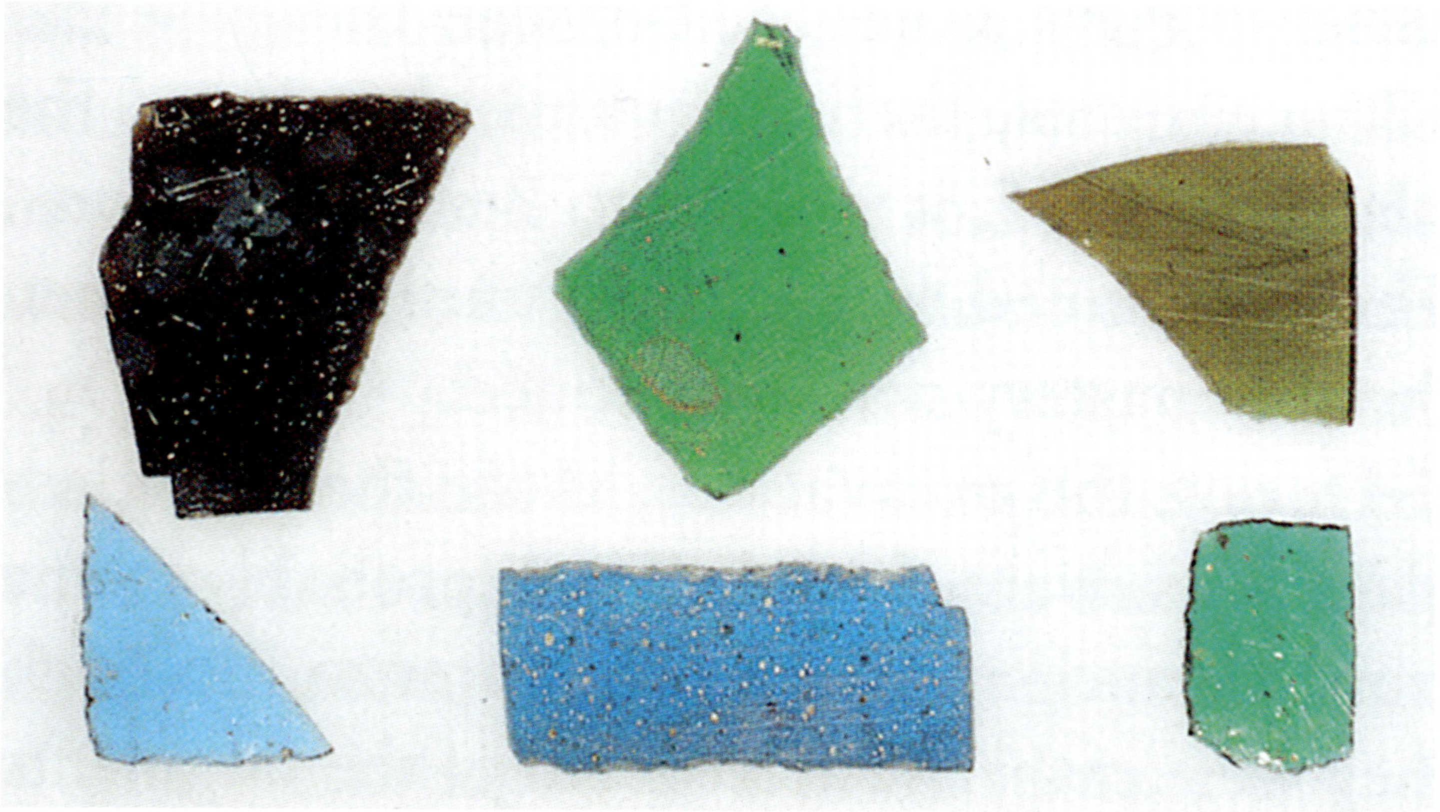

Marco Verità

Several similarities in the chemical composition of both glass and enamels in Islamic and Venetian glassware suggest a close relationship between these two areas. The gathering of data into a workable database with specific information about the chemistry and technology of both productions, however, is not yet complete or comprehensive.

Analytical evidence demonstrates that as early as the Roman period, around the beginning of the Common Era, the basic components of glass in the entire Mediterranean region were soda, lime, and silica. These three components were introduced into glass in the form of two main batch ingredients: natron (a natural form of soda from Egypt) mixed with sand containing silica and lime in a correct ratio (the most famous source is the Belus River in modern Israel), as well as ash obtained by burning certain varieties of littoral or desert plants mixed with silica sand or crushed quartzite pebbles.[1] The respective levels of potassium, magnesium, and phosphorus oxides allow us to distinguish between the two types, the natron glass containing lower levels.[2]

Recent archaeological discoveries and new research in glass analysis have confirmed that, in the Roman period, glassmakers transformed the batch into a molten mass of glass only in a few primary manufacturing centers.[3] From there, chunks of raw, unshaped glass were shipped to secondary workshops where they were softened in small furnaces and subsequently shaped into objects by the glassworkers. Abundant evidence exists for long-distance transport of cullet (broken glass vessels) in ancient times. Shipwrecks containing chunks of raw glass as well as cullet for recycling were also discovered near Venice.[4]

Recent analytical data demonstrates that a transition in composition from natron-glass to plant ash-glass occurred in the Islamic as well as the Byzantine world in the course of the 8th century.[5] Due to a shortage of natron from Egypt, the Levantine glassmakers were probably forced to use the raw materials adopted earlier by glassmakers in Iraq and Iran, which have the characteristic composition of plant ash-glass.[6] In the same period, glassmakers in northern Europe began to use wood ash, which led to the production of potash-lime-silica glass.[7] No presence of wood ash-glass has been found in the Venetian area; however, the

fig. 1. Tesserae from the baptistery of St. Mark's Basilica (detail), Venice, 14th century transition to a type of glass made with soda plant ash similar to the Islamic glass starting in the 8th or 9th century is corroborated by scientific analysis. The transition from natron-glass to plant ash-glass was slow and lasted until the 12th or 13th century, after which natron glass disappeared altogether.[8]

From the same period, it is possible to discern from archaeological finds in the Venetian area the appearance of an almost entirely decolorized glass that replaced the former greenish glass, which was made with pure raw materials and contained low levels of iron and other coloring contaminants.[9] It is likely that the complete process—from batch-melting to glassworking—was not carried out in Venice until the 12th century, for only the resoftening of raw glass and cullet has been ascertained thus far for earlier times.[10]

Slight compositional variations exist between Venetian and Islamic glass, revealing that a similar soda ash and the same ratio between the ash and the silica source were used for glass melting. Only when more analytical results are available for Venetian and Islamic glass, showing the differences in minor and trace components (such as aluminum, iron, and titanium), will scientists be able to distinguish between the two traditions. Clear compositional similarities, of course, are not surprising because for centuries the Levant supplied Venice with both cullet and plant ash.[11] A Venetian document of 1233 mentions the import of *vitreum* (raw glass or glass cullet) from the Levant.[12] A document of 1255 refers again to *vitreum in massa* (in bulk) but also to *alumen album* (white plant ash) from Alexandria.[13] By the late 13th century, Syrian plant ash was preferred and by the early 14th its use was mandatory. The success of the glass industry in Venice was due in part to the import from the Eastern Mediterranean of a high-quality type of soda ash obtained from halophilic plants from saline environments (coastal or desert), such as *Salsola kali*. For the empirical glassmakers of the medieval period it was necessary to get hold of raw ingredients with an appropriate and even ratio of sodium and calcium in order to obtain glass of high quality.

In Venice the import from the Levant of a cobalt-rich mineral is also proved by analytical results. The same mineral rich in cobalt, zinc, and iron that was used for Islamic blue glass was also found in the blue tesserae of the 14th-century mosaics in the baptistery of St. Mark's in Venice (fig. 1).[14] The analyses demonstrated that the cobalt mineral was imported into Venice until the 15th century, after which it was replaced with a mineral imported from southern Germany that contained nickel and arsenic as secondary components.[15]

Important similarities were also found in the analyses of opaque white glass. Tin oxide crystals in a soda-lime glass, containing varying amounts of lead, account for the opacity and color of both the so-called *lattimo* ("milk-like"), the white glass used by Venetian glassmakers, and most of the opaque white Islamic glasses. The origin of this composition, unfortunately, is still unclear and needs further research and analysis. The use of lead and tin scum has been detected in manufactured glass items from northern Europe since the 5th century.[16]

Luster decoration (also called stained decoration) of glass, which was developed by Coptic craftsmen who settled in Egypt before the advent of Islam, is also worthy of mention. Silver and copper were used to create decorative stains on glass vessels as well as lustrous decorative patterns on glazed earthenware. Silver staining appeared later in Western Europe, in particular on 14th-century stained-glass windows. The relation between Venice and the Islamic Levant is confirmed by the recent finding, on a small island in the Venetian lagoon, of the earliest European example of stain-decorated glass thus far recovered, which is attributable to the 9th or 10th century.[17]

Concerning the use and composition of enamels, Venetian documents contain several records of *pictores muzolorum* ("painters of beakers") between 1280 and 1351.[18] Recent research demonstrated that the same enameling technique was used to decorate the so-called Aldrevandin beakers in Venice as well as in the Mamluk Islamic areas for the most precious vessels (cats. 156–59, p. 257).[19] Because the individual colors have different chemical compositions, different temperatures are also required to melt the enamels; therefore, sophisticated knowledge and great experience were necessary to fix them permanently onto the glass surface without softening and distorting the object. It seems likely that Islamic glassmakers in the Levantine area mastered a procedure that solved this problem, and that this technology was exported to Venice.[20] Some differences in the composition of Venetian and Islamic enamels, however, suggest that the trade from the Mediterranean did not include ready-to-use enamels that were simply softened and applied in Venice;[21] on the other hand, the general compositional similarity between them indicates that the knowledge of enameling on glass arrived in Venice by the same route as the glassmakers' raw materials.

As a consequence of the progress of glass technology in Venice, a remarkable reversal of roles began to take place between Venetian glassmakers and their colleagues in the Islamic world. Around the middle of the 15th century Venetian glassmakers perfected a procedure of purification of plant ashes imported from Syria to produce the so-called *cristallo* glass. Some 30 years later, the earliest evidence of this reversed trend is found in the use of soda plant ash, purified in the very same way as the *cristallo* glass, in the production of Iznik glazes in Ottoman Turkey.[22] This development, of course, is mirrored in the trade in glass, which had proceeded exclusively east to west in the medieval period and now reversed its direction as Venetian, Bohemian, and English products were made for export to the Near East.

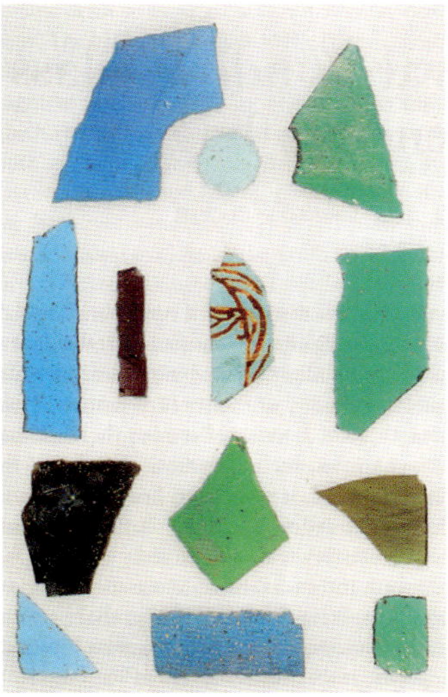

fig. 1. Tesserae from the baptistery of St. Mark's Basilica, Venice, 14th century

Notes

1 The necessary lime was introduced as an impurity of the silica sand in the case of natron-based glass and as a second component of the soda plant ash in the case of plant ash-based glass. The silica introduced as quartzite pebbles is a relatively pure form of SiO_2 (silica oxide); silica sand is less pure.

2 Glasses made with natron generally have K_2O (potassium oxide) and MgO (magnesium oxide) levels of less than 1.5 percent and P_2O_5 (phosphorus oxide) less than 0.2%. Glasses made with soda plant ash contain approximately 2.5 percent K_2O, from 2.5% to 6-7% MgO, and over 0.3% P_2O_5.

3 Brill 1967; Freestone, Gorin-Rosen, and Hughes 2000.

4 Namely, off the coasts of the Lido and of Grado. The former is positioned two miles north of the *bocca di porto* of Malamocco (medieval Metamauco) on the Lido island, the main access to Venice until the 14th century. Its dating is uncertain. The cargo included several hundred kilograms of raw chunks of natron-type glass (Molino et al. 1986). The second shipwreck is that of a Roman ship six miles off the coast of Grado in the northernmost section of the Adriatic Sea and it is datable to the second half of the 2nd century AD. The cargo included a wooden barrel filled with natron glass cullet (Auriemma 1999).

6 Freestone 2002; Freestone, Greenwood, and Gorin-Rosen 2002; Henderson, McLoughlin, and McPhail 2004.

7 Brill 1999, vol. 1, pp. 82–101, vol. 2, pp. 151–205; Whitehouse 2002.

8 Wedepohl 1997.

9 Verità, Zecchin, and Renier 2002.

10 Islamic and Venetian clear glasses usually contain manganese oxide (about 0.5-1.5% MnO). This amount indicates a deliberate addition, either as a decolorizer to offset the green-yellow tints produced by iron impurities or as a colorizer (in larger amount) to give the glass a purple color.

11 Verità, Zecchin, and Renier 2002.

12 Zecchin 1987, 1989 and 1990; Jacoby 1993.

13 Zecchin 1990, p.173.

14 Zecchin 1987, p. 5.

15 Verità 1999.

16 Author's unpublished data; Gratuze et al. 1996.

17 Heck and Hoffmann 2000.

18 Vaghi, Verità, and Zecchin 2004.

19 Zecchin 1990, pp. 114–18; see also Barovier's and Carboni's essay in this volume.

20 Some enamels (yellow, green) are high-lead glasses, others consist of deeply colored opaque glass (white, blue). Red enamels contain iron oxide pigments suspended in a glassy matrix. The composition and manufacturing techniques of the "Aldrevandin" enamels can be related to Venetian glass recipe books of the 15th century.

21 Zecchin 1990, p. 109.

22 Verità 1998; Freestone and Stapleton 1998; Brill 1999.

23 Verità 1985; Paynter et al. 2004.

Islamic Influence on the Production of Ceramics in Venice and Padua

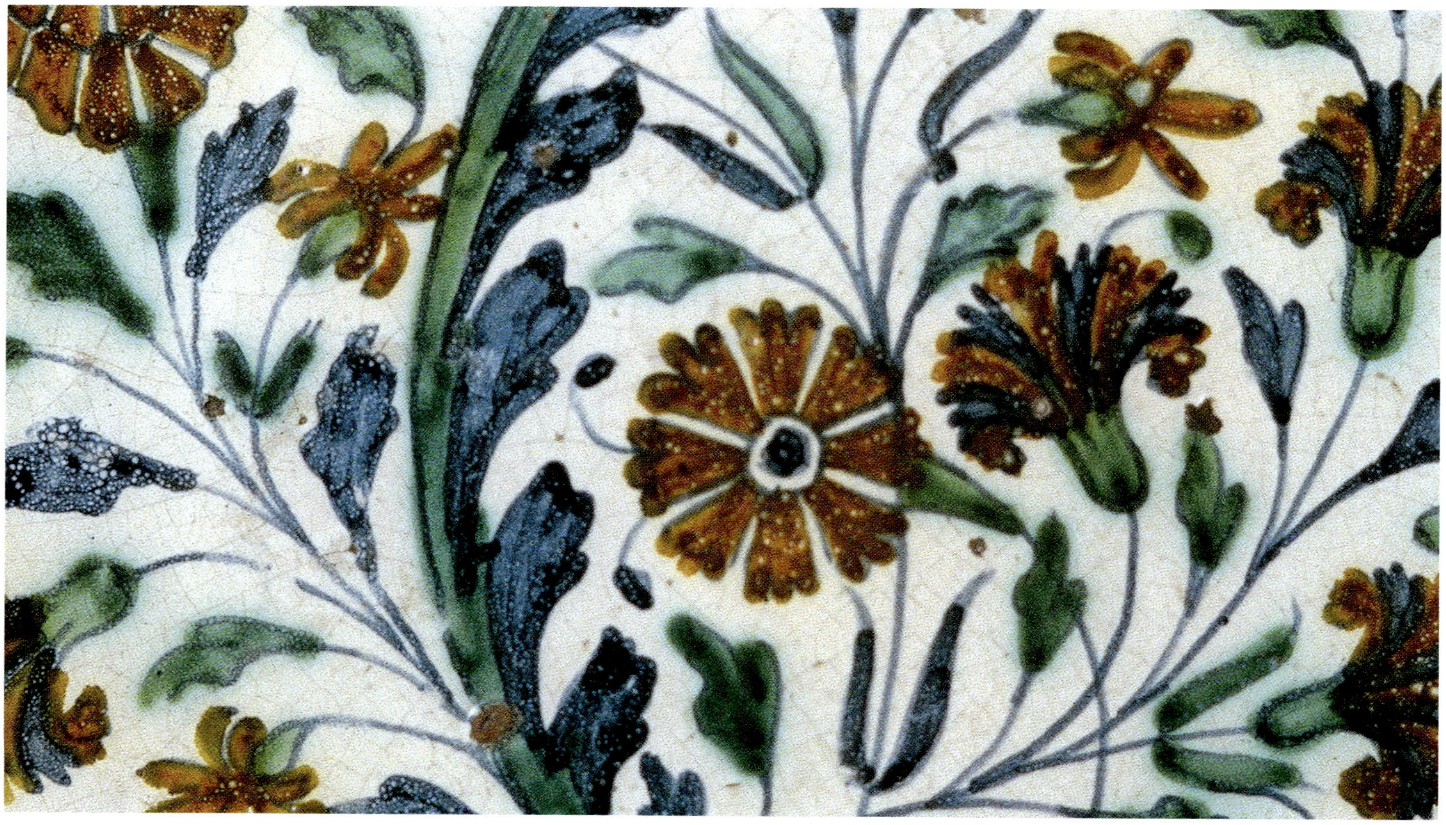

Maria Vittoria Fontana

Islamic Imports

In Italy, knowledge of Islamic ceramics was closely tied to their importation.[1] They constituted one of the most important items of merchandise from the Middle Ages onwards, circulating mainly via maritime routes[2] and providing crucial evidence of trade relations with Crusader states.[3] It was also via the sea that Venice and the Veneto maintained relations with lands of the Eastern and Western Mediterranean,[4] through intense trade with Islamic territories.[5] In the Venetians' expansion abroad, the Fourth Crusade marked a divide: during the preceding period (as early as—even prior to—the 10th century), the Venetians set up "trading posts"[6] rather than colonies, except for Constantinople, while after the Fourth Crusade and the establishment of a Latin Empire in the East in 1204, the situation changed radically—even for the Venetian colony in Constantinople,[7] whose regulations also applied to those in Damascus and Alexandria, outside the empire.[8]

Bacini represent a special case among imports of Islamic ceramics. Imported from the second half of the 11th century to the 13th, an overview of their spread across northern Italy was published by Hugo Blake in 1980.[9] The most recent description of archaeological finds of Islamic ceramics in Venice and the Veneto is found in an essay by three specialists[10] who identified the following seven categories: Siculo-Maghrebi ceramics with green, brown, and yellow decoration beneath a lead glaze; glazed Maghrebi ceramics painted with "cobalt and manganese"; glazed Hispano-Moresque ceramics with blue- or luster-painted decoration; Syro-Egyptian ceramics of the Fatimid period; examples of "Raqqa ware"; Syro-Egyptian fritware of the Mamluk period; and Persian fritware of the Il-khanid period.[11] Some azulejos from the Valencia region (dated ca. 1470) were used to tile two chapels in the church of Sant' Elena in Venice, owned by local aristocratic families, the Giustinians and Borromeos.[12] Moreover, it is highly probable that azulejo tiling from the first half of the 15th century once decorated the Palazzo Da Mula on Murano, as suggested by a fragment found during restoration of that residence.[13] The walls of the oratory in the Villa Nani Mocenigo (16th–17th century) at Monselice in the province of Padua, meanwhile, were lined with polychrome Ottoman tiles.[14]

cat. 188. *Plate with decoration imitating Ottoman Iznik pottery* (detail)

Starting in the 13th century, a certain number of documents provide information on the importation of Islamic ceramics into the Veneto. Thus in 1277 Doge Jacopo Contarini and Bohemond VII, prince of Antioch and count of Tripoli, concluded a treaty bearing on trade in ceramic vessels.[15]

For importation from Spain, the only surviving sources come from Venice. A letter sent from Venice to Florence addressed to the merchant Francesco di Marco Datini—who operated from Prato and who had contacts with Valencia—mentioned the arrival on July 22, 1398, of four chests of *opere di terra* (earthenware objects),[16] originally from Spain, or more precisely from "Maiolica," that is to say Majorca, a commercial outpost of Valencia. In 1401–2, the purchase and shipment to Venice of a batch of maiolica ware from Manises was recorded in the ledgers of Francesco di Marco Datini's trading and banking company.[17] From 1426 to 1665, the Venetian Senate issued a series of decrees outlawing the importation of foreign ceramics (that is to say, produced beyond the borders of Venetian territory), which were invading the local markets at that point. An important exception to this prohibition was granted to Spanish lusterware from Valencia and Majorca.[18] When it comes to Anatolia, evidence of importation can be found in both Venice and Padua.

In Venice itself, it is interesting to note that the exception to the Senate's prohibition excluded not just Spanish ceramics but also porcelain.[19] Dated 1475, an excerpt from account ledgers sent from Venice to Florence, concerning purchases made in the lagoon by Filippo Strozzi, includes the entry: *"duc. 11, sono per 10 schodelle di porciellana: 8 bianche picchole e 2 co' fogliami azzurri"* (ducats: 11, for ten porcelain plates, eight small white and two decorated with blue leaves).[20] It is highly likely that this was Chinese porcelain, both plain white and blue-and-white (see cat. 172, p. 88).[21] We can nevertheless not exclude the possibility, even though it was not necessarily the case here, that in the late 15th century—and especially in the 16th century—no real distinction was made between authentic Chinese blue-and-white porcelain and its Islamic imitations (cat. 179). That is what Marco Spallanzani assumes when it comes to the "porcelain" in Florence, of which enormous quantities figure in Medici inventories.[22] Even if it remains to be demonstrated whether fritware[23] from Syria,[24] Persia, and Ottoman lands[25] should be classed with "porcelain,"[26] various analyses performed on Ottoman pieces and on soft-paste porcelain made in the Medici manufactory have revealed many shared ingredients.[27] Indeed, Islamic fritware, particularly Anatolian, could not always be distinguished from porcelain, and it might be surmised that Ottoman pottery, also described as "porcelain," was imported into Venice in large quantities. Stephan Gerlach, a priest in the retinue of David Ungnad, ambassador in Istanbul for Maximilian II and Rudolf II from 1573 to 1578, mentioned in his diary in September 1577 that Ungnad had sent to Venice a present of ceramic [tiles] from Nicaea (that is to say, Iznik) that cost over 100 ducats.[28] An inventory drawn up in Venice in 1587 listed 30 maiolica objects "coming from Constantinople."[29] Given the current state of knowledge, it seems rather difficult to ascribe to a Venetian family—as Arthur Lane

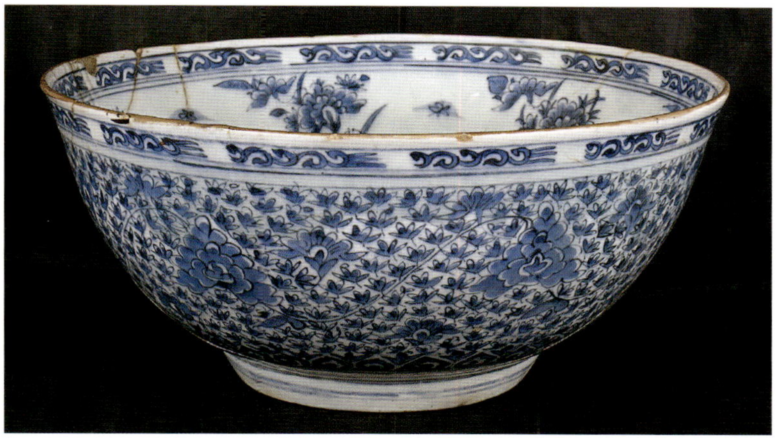

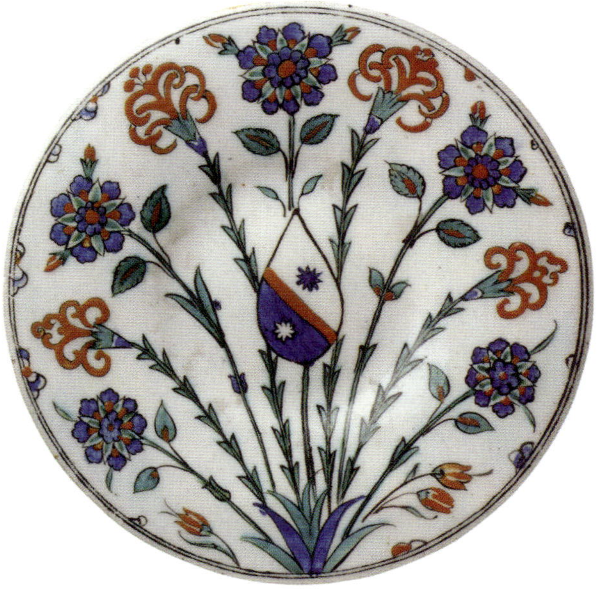

suggested some 50 years ago[30]—the coat of arms on a table service commissioned from an Iznik workshop, probably dated around 1570 (fig. 1).[31] Finally, in Padua, a late transcription of the statutes of the Arte dei Merciai Cittadini (the city's merchants' guild) lists numerous manufactured items as well as *"kinkalie de terra cotta de Armenia e de ogni altra simile sorte"* ("crocks" of terracotta from Armenia and other objects of the same kind)—although this it probably refers to Kütahya pottery.[32]

cat. 179. *Bowl*
Iran, 17th century
Museo Civico Correr, Venice

fig. 1. Plate, Iznik, ca.1570. The Ashmolean Museum of Art and Archæology, Oxford

Venetian Imitations of Islamic Ceramics[33]

Graziella Berti and Sauro Gelichi are correct to assert that, today, we no longer think that . . . the reproduction of ceramics was subject to an entire set of technical skills and knowledge . . . that it is difficult to envisage it without the direct assistance of foreign craftsmen. The convergence of various events must have functioned contextually to lead to the migration of specialized craftsmen. . . . Until now, the mistake was to interpret these phenomena as part of their evolved phase rather than a formative period, but the latter view is now possible thanks to the existence of abundant documentation dating back to the late 13th and 14th centuries, which decisively helps to fill the gaps in information on its origins. . . . Some of the initial types vanished virtually without a trace; . . . in northern Italy the *graffita arcaica padana* [archaic sgraffito, or ceramics with incised decoration, from the Po valley] (derived from the *tirrenica* type) thus replaced the prized *graffite venete.*[34]

Incised Slipware (*Sgraffito*)

Following discoveries of ceramics in the lagoon, a publication by Lorenzo Lazzarini and Ernesto Canal raised the question of the origins of *graffita veneta,*[35] followed three years later by an article by Sauro Gelichi that became a fundamental document on the subject.[36] Gelichi asserted that the presence of kiln wasters and the results of compositional analyses made it possible to date production of sgraffito (incised slipware) in the Veneto to the middle of the 13th century.[37] It is Venice (or various places in the Veneto) that should be credited with the *graffita* (derived from Byzantine Zeuxippus ware, Class I B/C), described as *spirale-cerchio* (fig. 2), which can be dated to the middle of the 13th century on the basis of the *bacini* decorating the walls of the Ferrara church of Sant'Antonio in Polesine.[38] Another type of sgraffito, dubbed *tipo San Bartolo* due to the presence of similarly decorated *bacini* set into the façade of the Church of San Bartolo in Ferrara (late 13th century), is "characterized by coarse incisions, basically geometric, highlighted with spots of color—green or rust yellow—which attest to a derivation from later Byzantine models imported into Venice (Zeuxippus ware [Class II]), and is entirely distince from the type known up till then as *graffita arcaica padana.*"[39] A small group of *graffita* vessels made in Venice was recently identified by Francesca Saccardo as "Sant'Ariano type" dating from the second or third quarter of the 13th century; Saccardo suggests that it served as a kind of prototype for "San Bartolo type" sgraffito (fig. 3).[40]

Graffita veneta, also a sgraffito slipware, was therefore produced no later than the mid-13th century and exported to the Near East, probably by Venetian merchants. Indeed, in the lands conquered by the Crusaders, examples of *graffita veneta* (the sole type produced in central-northern Italy, together with monochrome ceramics also of Venetian origin) were discovered in the same context as the so-called "proto-maiolica"[41] ceramics produced in Apuglia.[42] Gelichi asserts, "it is obvious that in parts of Italy, at least, Zeuxippus ware (along with proto-maiolica) represents the key to a better understanding, thanks to ceramics, of the ramification of the activities of Italian traders in the Levant."[43]

It should thus be kept in mind that, in all likelihood, even though the sgraffito technique—characterized by incisions made on a slip applied to the surface of the vessel, which is then covered with a lead glaze—was certainly of Islamic origin (from the early examples produced in Mesopotamia, probably dating to the 10th century),[44] *graffita veneta,* like the early

fig. 2. Fragment of a dish with *spirale-cerchio* sgraffito, 13th century. Galleria G. Franchetti alla Ca' d'Oro, Venice

fig. 3. Fragment of San Bartolo sgraffito, 13th century. Galleria G. Franchetti alla Ca' d'Oro, Venice

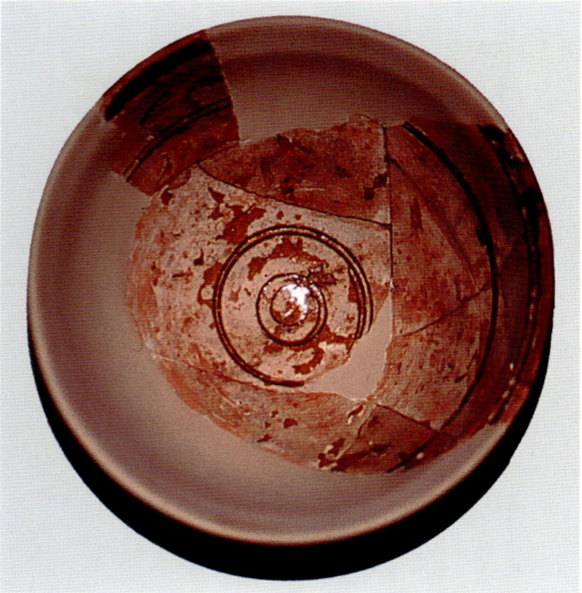

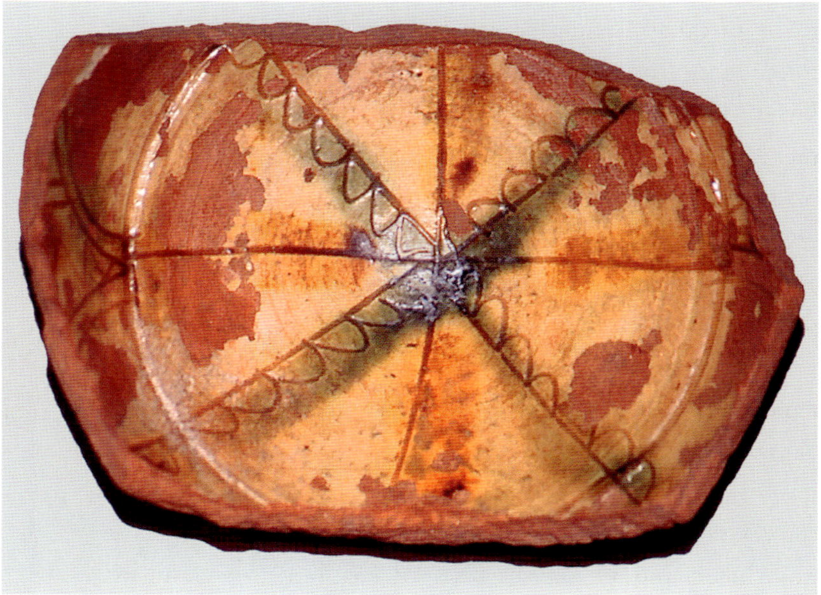

graffita arcaica tirrenica (dating from the last quarter of the 12th century)[45] and the ceramics found above all in Crusader lands (produced by various eastern Mediterranean workshops in the 13th century),[46] all belong to an almost contemporaneous Mediterranean production.[47] It was not until the last quarter of the 14th century that a new type of sgraffito ware appeared in the Veneto, *graffita arcaica padana,* also produced during the 15th century; this was characterized by jasper-colored glazes or by coarse incisions with geometric, or vegetal, or sometimes zoomorphic motifs. Gelichi asserts that "*graffita veneta* is certainly not at the origin of *graffita arcaica padana* . . . a continental type that developed autonomously . . . in two western regions of northern Italy [Lombardy and the Piedmont] and which spread from there to Emilia-Romagna and the Veneto. It is likely that the introduction of this technique occurred via Liguria (that is to say, through *graffita arcaica tirrenica*)."[48] In contrast, Ernst J. Grube posits Islamic models for this type of *graffita,* which was slip-incised with polychrome decoration under a lead glaze.[49] Michelangelo Munarini describes as *graffita rinascimentale canonica*[50] a type of *graffita veneta*—which he dates between the late 15th and early 16th centuries[51]—that includes a large number of cylindrical vessels with four little feet and one or two zoomorphic spouts (the vessel would be divided into two halves inside, separated by a partition), and sometimes having an upper handle. These vessels adopt the shape of *refredadores* (coolers) of the same period produced in Manises and Paterna (fig. 4),[52] whose production is also attested at Padua,[53] Venice, Treviso,[54] and probably Verona.[55] Similar vessels display other types of decoration, such as an example covered with slip and a spotted blue glaze, roughly datable to the mid-16th century,[56] or another in *berettino*[57] decorated with blue scrollwork and belonging, according to Andrea Moschetti, to the Candiana type that imitated Ottoman polychrome ceramics from Iznik (see below).[58]

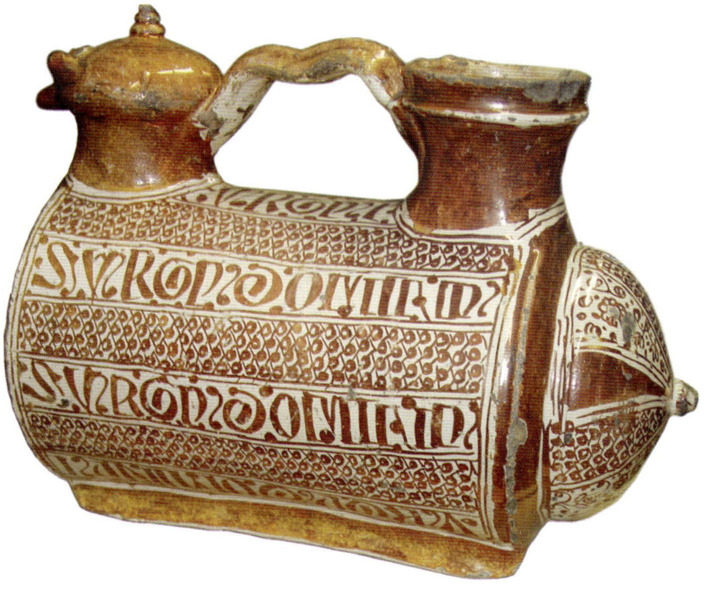

fig. 4. *Refredador,* Manises (Spain), late 15th century. Victoria and Albert Museum, London

Painted Ceramics

An interesting type of ceramic produced in the Veneto is the so-called "Santa Crocetype" (datable to the second or third quarter of the 13th century, named after the church in Ravenna where archaeological excavations took place). It also includes examples covered with a slip and painted in two colors (green and brown) or polychrome (green, brown, yellow, or green, brown, red).[59] The geometric, vegetal (or pseudo-vegetal), and zoomorphic decoration can be found in many Italian products of the 13th century (basically in southern Italy),[60] whereas the use of slip was far less common.[61] On the other hand, the slip, the colors, the lead glaze, and the decoration of Santa Croce-type ceramics all display obvious similarities with Islamic slip-painted decoration. A highly interesting comparison can be made—even if, in the current state of knowledge, the exact link cannot be traced—between a basin uncovered during excavations at the old Sala Borse in Bologna, featuring a bird painted in green and brown plus patterns and ornamental motifs on the bottom and along the edge, and the polychrome slip-paint decoration typical of "Sari" pieces made in the Iranian province of Mazandaran in the 11th and 12th centuries.[62]

Starting in the late 14th or early 15th century[63] there emerged in central Italy a particular type of ceramic dubbed, in the late 19th century, "Italo-Moresque,"[64] a label that has recently led to heated debate among specialists.[65] This style was influenced by models from Islamic Spain, datable to the late 13th or early 14th century, which circulated in great numbers thanks to close trade relations. Spanish pieces were painted in blue and metallic luster, with scrolling vegetal patterns that adopted a spiral form on the oldest ceramics (from Andalusia) or leaves of ivy and byrony[66] on those made in the mid-15th century (Valencia). Carmen Ravanelli Guidotti has drawn up a "map" of the spread of these Italo-Moresque ceramics,[67] and Michelangelo Munarini argues that in both the Veneto and Emilia-Romagna they appeared prior to the middle of the 15th century, probably during the second quarter.[68] A few examples were found in excavations at Concordia Sagittaria in the region of Venice.[69] Giuliana Ericani has noted a small 16th-century bowl found near Belluno, the inside of which is decorated with bryony leaves and small open circles.[70]

There is no doubt that the ornamentation called *a rabesche* was based on an Islamic prototype. Giovan Battista Passeri stated that "*Rabesche* is a type of painting that featured monograms, interlacing, and very fine knotwork adorned with tiny flowers."[71] This *a rabesche*[72] decoration was widely used on maiolica ware in the 16th century, notably in central and northern Italy. Cipriano Piccolpasso di Casteldurante mentioned in his 16th-century treatise, "*rabesches* are used more often in Venice and Genoa than in any other place" (fig. 5).[73] Prototypes for this maiolica ware, which in Venice was painted in various shades of blue under the glaze called *berettino*, probably came from Ottoman ceramics of the Baba Nakkas type, produced around 1480,[74] as well as from other crafts—bookbinding and metalwork—that also served a models.[75] All the most famous workshops, notably those of Jacopo da Pesaro and Maestro Lodovico, were producing Venetian maiolica with *a rabesche* decoration in the middle of the 16th century (cat. 184).[76]

fig. 5. *Trofei/Rabeschi* (Trophies/Arabesques), plate from Cipriano Piccolpasso's book, *Tre Libri dell' Art del Vasaio,* 1556–59. Victoria and Albert Museum, London

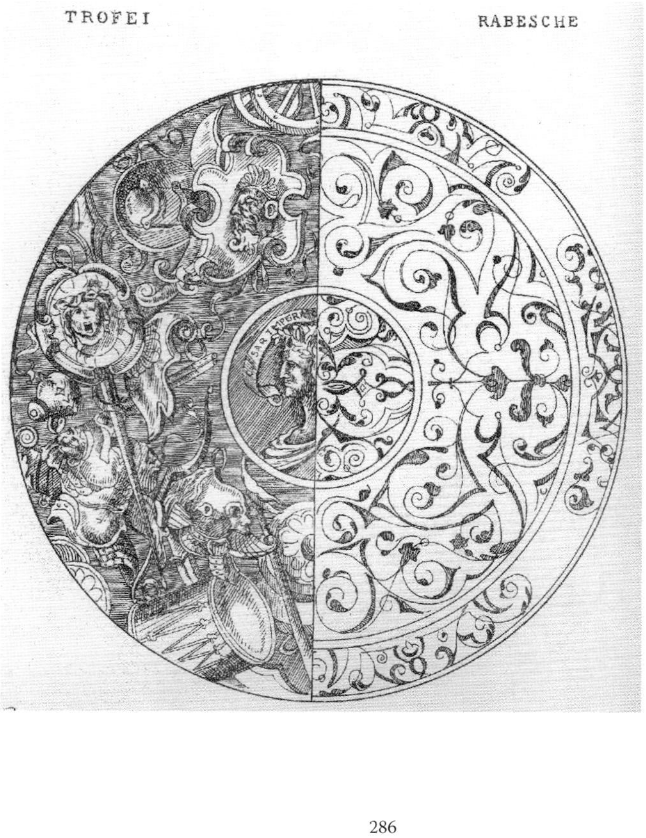

Another decorative style widely used in central and northern Italy starting in the 16th century is called *alla porcellana.* It was defined by Giovanni Battista Passeri as "a kind of painting that involves small, very fine bluish-gray flowers, with tiny leaves and small buds against a white ground."[77] In fact, Venetian *alla porcellana* maiolica often used the bluish *berettino* glaze. The scrolling foliage would be enlivened with peonies, small roses, and other flower buds, ornament typical of the banded rims of blue and white Chinese porcelain of the early 15th century (Ming),[78] or of Ottoman fritware from the 1480s onwards.[79] Piccolpasso used the term *porcelana tirata* for this type of decoration, and when it came to areas of production he asserted that "this type of painting is most widespread,"[80] making it difficult to identify specific centers of manufacture, although Venice was certainly one of them.[81] Maestro Lodovico's workshop in Venice adopted *alla porcellana* ornamentation (against a *berettino* ground) no later than 1515, date of the famous marriage uniting the Lamparten von Greifenstein and Meuting families. On that occasion a service was commissioned, of which one plate survives, in the center of which figure the coats of arms of the two German families (cat. 183, p. 288).[82] *Alla porcellana* pieces were also produced in other parts of the Veneto, for example in Padua[83] and Verona.[84]

The reverse of Maestro Lodovico's plates feature an ornamental band also often labeled *alla porcellana,* yet simpler in style. The scrolling foliage is devoid of flowers, and the leaves are of an attenuated, five-lobed type typical of stylized bryony.[85] In general, such motifs are painted on the back of certain plates, whereas the front displays *alla porcellana* decoration or other—often narrative—subjects.[86] When it comes to the latter, I would suggest that they were influenced by wares from Valencia[87] or by "Italo-Moresque" ceramics.

It is fairly safe to assume that, in Venice, Chinese porcelain and—perhaps above all—Ottoman fritware[88] made in Iznik[89] served as prototypes for attempts to imitate this type of paste from the 16th century onwards (cat. 176, p. 288).[90]

Arthur Lane mentions a letter, published by Urbani de Ghelthof, who said it was written in 1470 by a certain Guglielmo da Bologna and sent from Venice to a friend in Padua, to accompany a bowl and vase from the workshop of Maestro Antonio, located in the parish of San Simeone. The bowl and vase were allegedly *"facti dal maestro con grandissima perfetione perché lui à ridoto le porcelane transparenti et vaghissime con certa bona terra"* (done by the master with great perfection because he has managed to make the most beautiful transparent vessels with a certain good clay). The fact that no trace of this letter has ever been found led Lane to suppose that Urbani de Ghelthof had invented it.[91] Meanwhile, documents attest to attempts to make real porcelain in Venice. Thus on June 4, 1518, Leonardo Peringer sought the privilege *"in questa inclita cità de Venetia de far bone et optime lavori di ogni sorte de porzelane chome sono quele de Levante transparenti."*[92] Other documents refer to *schudelle sette de porcellana contrafacta* (seven small bowls of counterfeit porcelain) bought in Venice by Duke Ercole I d'Este in 1504 as well as *un piatelletto et una scudella de porcellana ficta* (a small plate and bowl of false porcelain), also bought in Venice, by Alfonso I d'Este in 1519.[93]

cat. 184. Maestro Lodovico (attr.)
Plate with tendrils alla porcellana
Venice, ca. 1540–50
Fioritura Collection, Berlin

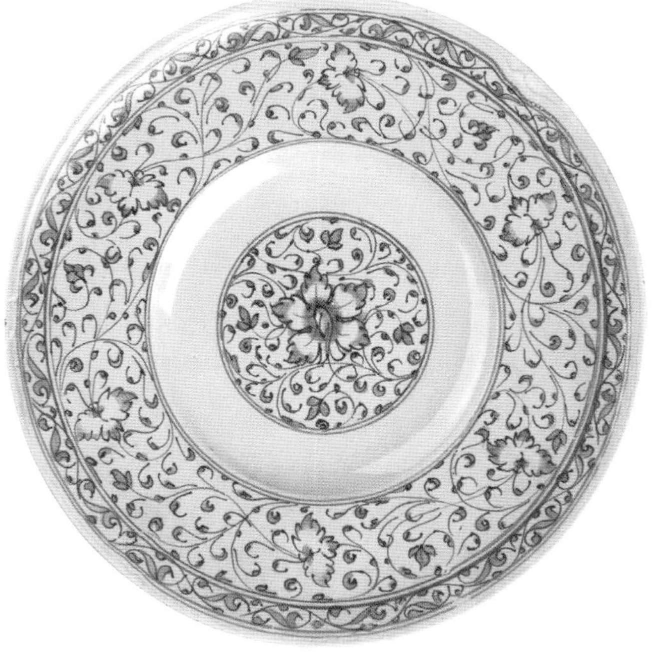

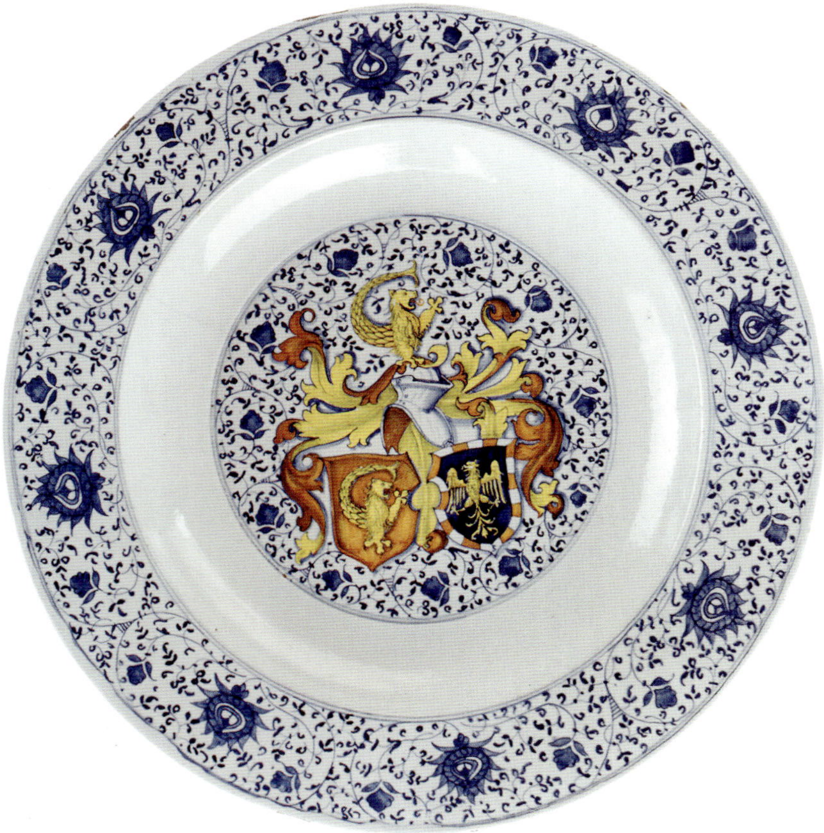

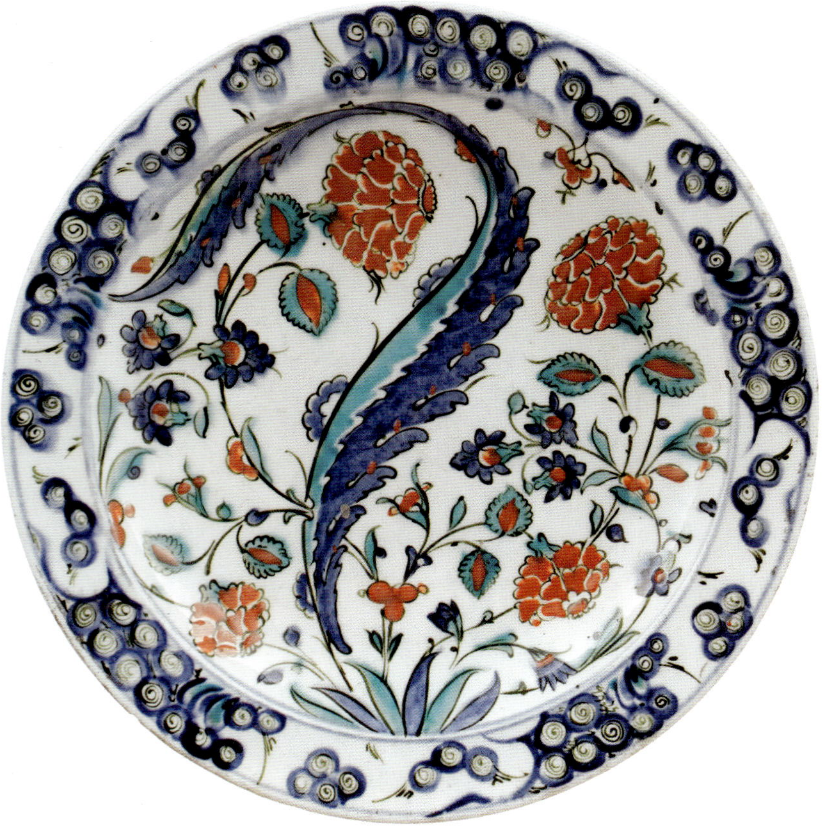

Lane argued that "the Venetian experiments were conducted with opaque white glass painted in enamel colors, and not with clay materials."[94] On the other hand, Angelica Alverà Bortolotto is convinced of the opposite, based on a passage in a letter by Peringer, which reads, *"Uno novo artificio o deficio non più facto né usitato in questa inclita città de Venetia . . . porzelane . . . stano salde da tute viande caldissime et diboto fuogo."* (A new artifice never previously executed or used in this glorious city of Venice . . . porcelains . . . that are not damaged by very hot foodstuffs or fire).[95] Alverà Bortolotto also points out that a kind of soft-paste porcelain, similar to that made at the Medici manufactory, was also produced in Venice. This hypothesis seems to be confirmed by the mention of *fornimenti de terra* (earthen supplies) in two letters sent from Venice to Florence in 1550–51 when Cosimo I de' Medici and his wife, Duchess Eleonore of Toledo, wanted to purchase a service made in Venice, which, "desiring them to be like porcelain, will perhaps have to be expressly made to that end."[96]

On the basis of this Venetian production of soft-paste porcelain, Alverà Bortolotto attributes to Venice two dishes now at the Victoria and Albert Museum in London.[97] The first, painted in monochrome blue, dates from 1638, while the second, in blue, orange, and green, dates from 1627.[98]

What is known as Candiana ware played an important role in Veneto ceramic production in the 17th and 18th centuries (cats. 188–190, 192, pp. 290–91). This was a type of maiolica that imitated Ottoman ceramics, notably the polychrome floral decoration employed during the reigns of Selim II (1566–74) and Murad III (1574–95).[99] Candiana notably copied the use of *saz* leaves,[100] carnations, tulips, hyacinths, roses, and other flowers, painted in blue, green, yellow, and brown, the latter color replacing the brilliant red used at Iznik (cat. 177). Dated examples cover a period ranging from 1613 (fig. 6)[101] to 1705.[102]

It was long thought that Candiana ware was made exclusively in Padua and its environs. For that reason, Bernard Rackham attributed to Padua the two dishes in the Victoria and Albert Museum mentioned above, notably comparing the one dated 1638—whose cavetto is adorned with a landscape and whose outer edges have a vegetal motif similar to Candiana—with a Candiana plate dated 1629, now in the Österreiches Museum für Angewandte Kunst in Vienna.[103] Both pieces display the same combination of decorative motifs, although the landscape on the Vienna plate is painted in the middle of the cavetto and the vegetal ornament typical of Candiana frames the landscape and adorns the edge.[104] As mentioned above, Alverà Bortolotto argues that the two dishes now in London were made in Venice, and hence considers the Venetian or Paduan origin of the one now in Vienna to be uncertain.[105] Furthermore, she also argues that some fragments of Candiana found in the lagoon, now in a private collection,[106] came from a Venetian workshop, which would mean adopting the hypothesis proposed earlier by Luigi Conton concerning a Candiana manufactory in Venice, a theory supported by the great number of shards found in the lagoon.[107]

The production of Candiana is also attested by shards uncovered during kiln excavations at Bassano in the Vicenza region—notably at the Manardi manufactory—probably influenced by the painter Giovan Battista (formerly Ottavio) Salmazzi,[108] who moved to Bassano from Padua in 1669.[109]

cat. 183. *Plate decorated* alla porcellana *with arms of Andreas Imhoff and Ursula Schlaudersbach of Nuremburg*
Venice, ca. 1518–25. Fioritura Collection, Berlin

cat. 176. *Plate*
Iznik, Turkey, ca. 1580
Musée National de la Renaissance, Écouen

cat. 177. *Bowl*
Iznik, Turkey, last quarter of the 16th century. Kunstgewerbemuseum, Berlin

fig. 6. Candiana dish (front and back), marked (back): *M a Suor Isabeta Carrara 1613.* Musei Civici, Padua

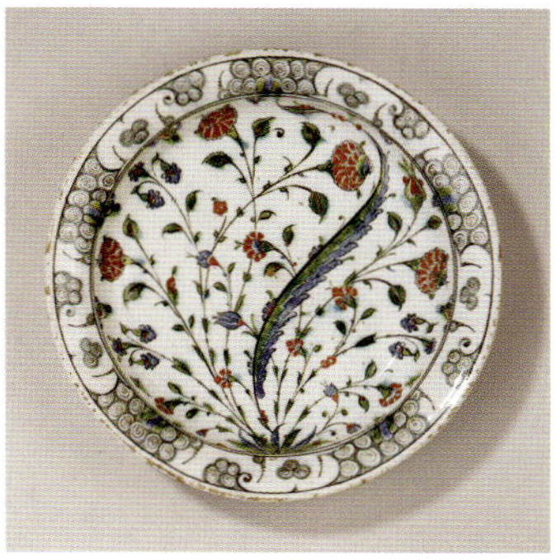

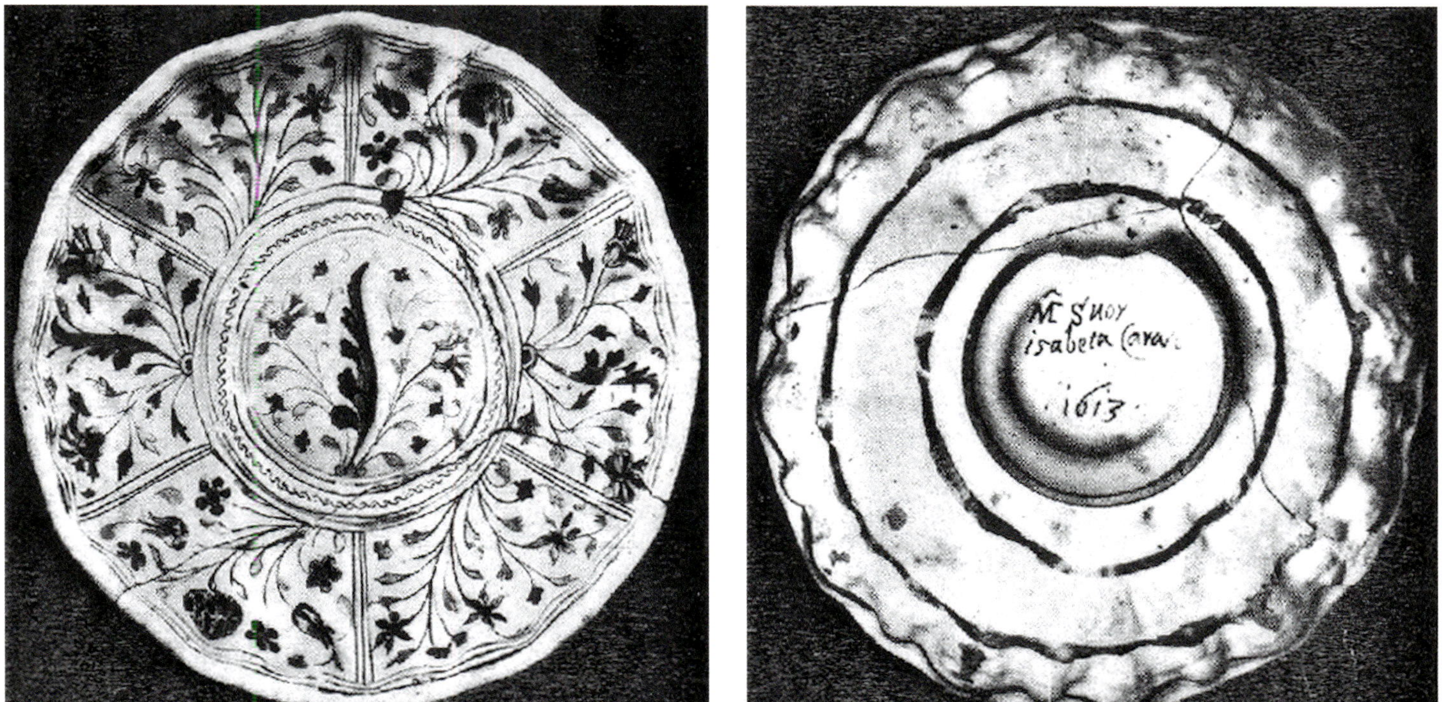

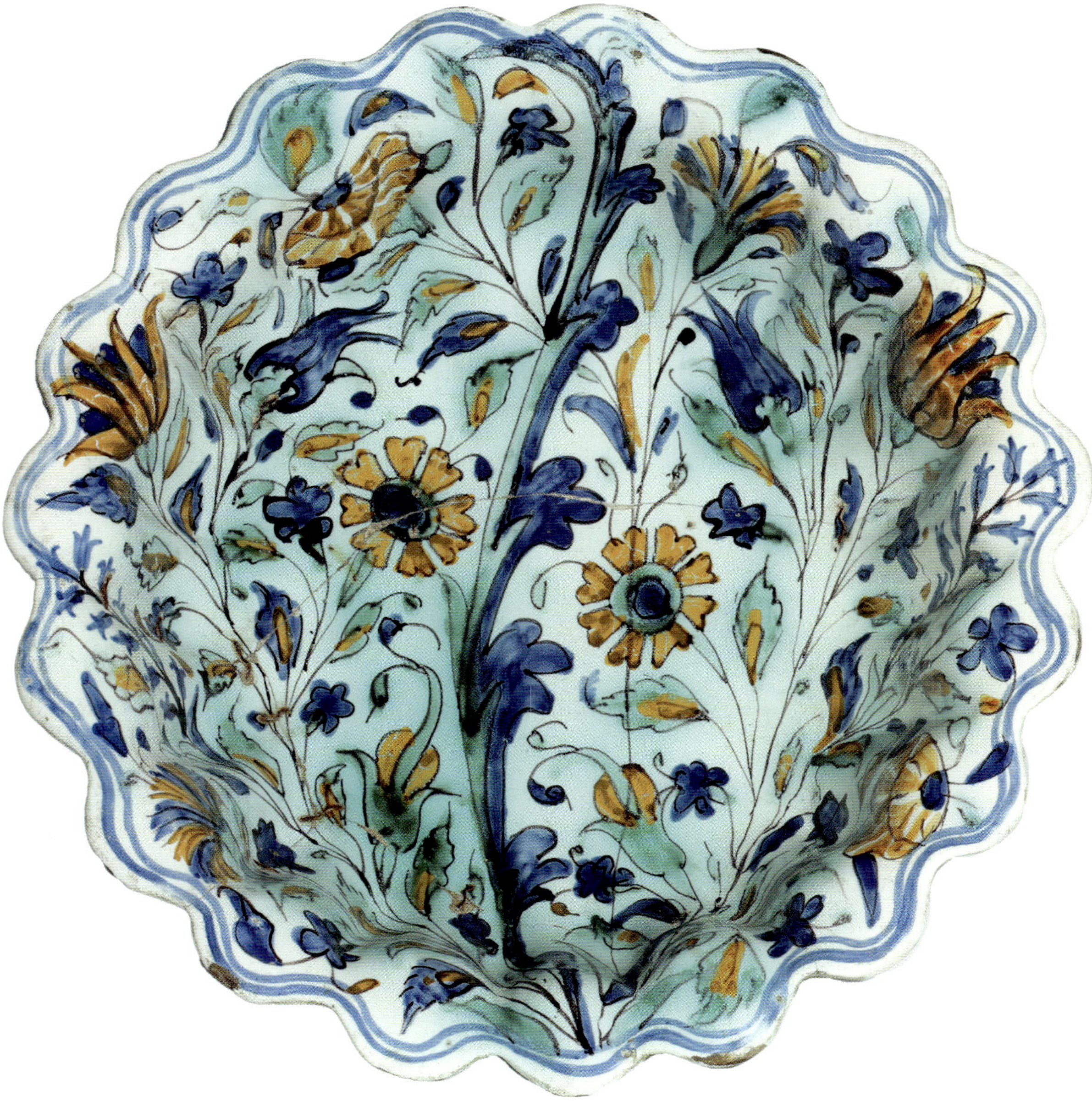

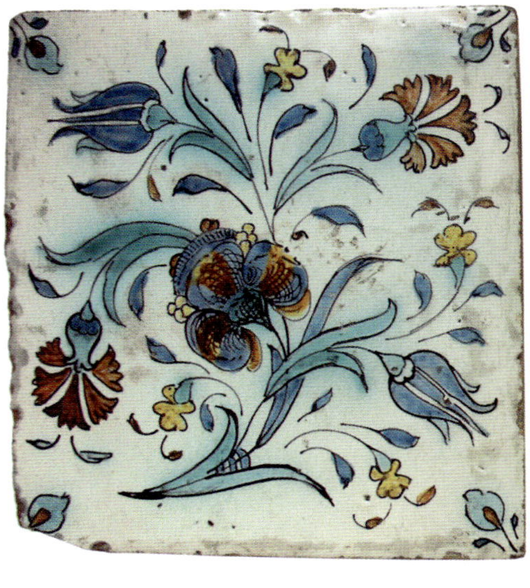

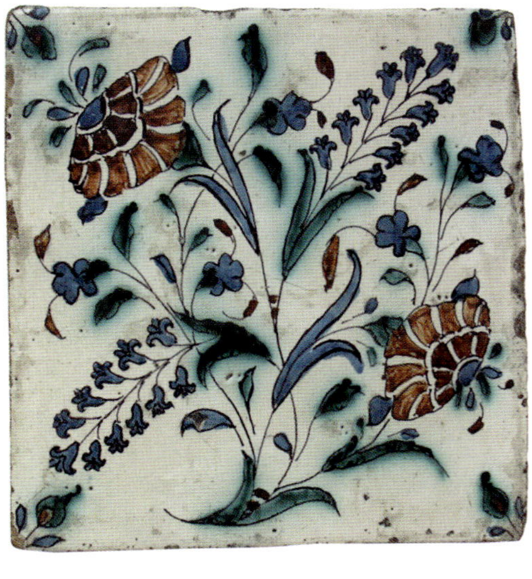

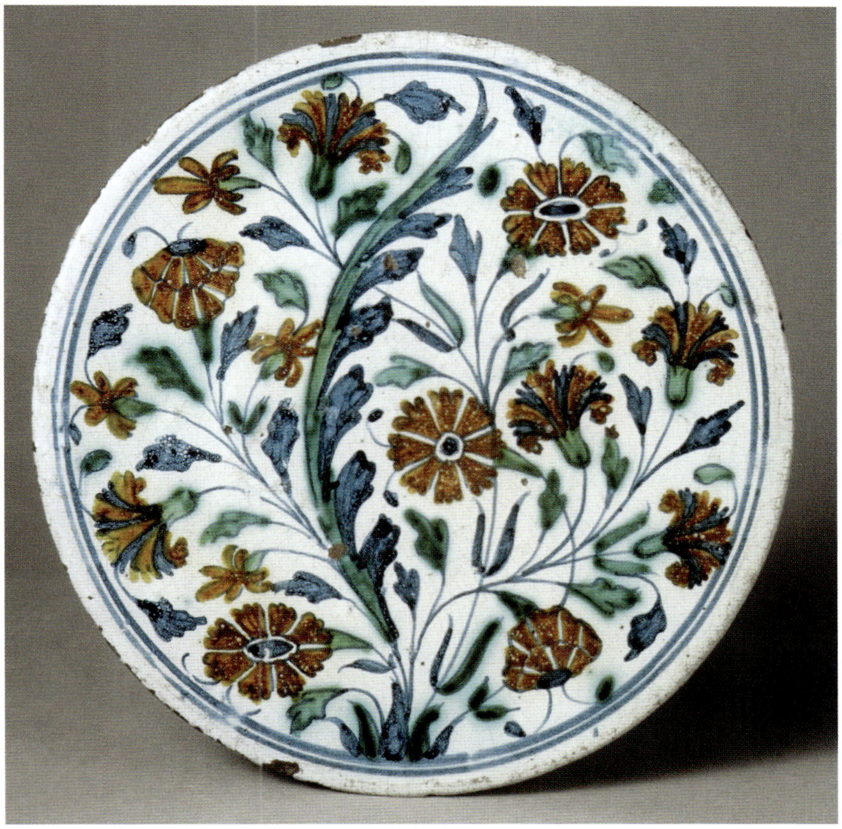

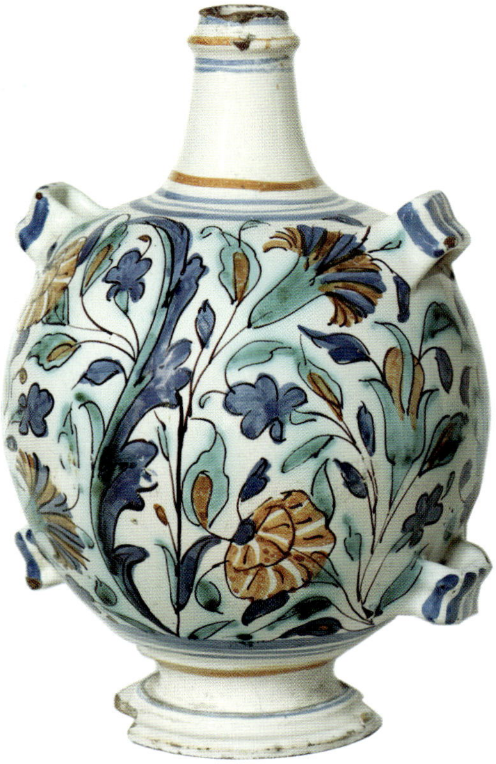

cat. 188. *Plate*
Veneto, 1633
Musée National de Céramique, Sèvres

cat. 192. *Pilgrim flask*
Veneto, 17th century
Museo d'Arte Medievale e Moderna, Padua

Notes

1 The first in-depth analysis of the importation of Islamic ceramics into Italy, especially Venice, was in an essay by Friedrich Sarre (1933) in which he mentioned Syrian fragments from the 12th and 14th centuries and Hispano-Moresque lusterware from the 15th and 16th centuries, as well as the discovery of Ottoman pieces from the 16th and 17th centuries, a subject to which he later returned (Sarre 1939). As to the influence of Oriental ceramics on Italian ceramics of the Renaissance, one of the earliest studies was done by Wallis (1900).
2 See Lewis 1978; Ashtor 1986.
3 See Pringle 1986; Boas 1994.
4 On Venetian navigation in the 13th and 14th centuries, see Tucci 1973, p. 828.
5 See Abulafia 1994, pp. 5–6, 8–9, 11, 13, 16–17.
6 Luzzato, 1995, pp. 52–52: "Trading posts were used above all to facilitate loading and unloading operations, as well as exchanges of merchandise transported on the ships that periodically called at ports, once or twice per year, in convoys or singly. . . . It was usually a question of brief periods of intense activity carried out by a shifting population that nevertheless included a certain number of people who settled, after the First Crusade, on the coasts of Asia Minor, Syria, Palestine, and, somewhat later, Egypt." For a description of Venetian colonies in the Latin kingdom of Jerusalem, notably in the 13th century, see Prawer 1973.
7 Luzzatto 1995, p. 53: "The Venetian quarter underwent notable development and its population grew considerably. In the absence of statistical data . . . the increase in the Venetian population of Constantinople is attested… by the expansion of the quarter, by the increase in the number of port calls, by the augmentation of the number of *fondaci* and warehouses, by the opening of a shipyard for the repair or construction of ships, and finally by the existence—attested shortly afterwards—of banking establishments run by Venetians." See also Cessi 1985, p. 25.
8 Luzzatto 1995, pp. 53–54. See also Heyd 1866–68. On Venetian colonies in the Black Sea, see Nystazopoulou Pélékidis 1973, pp. 551, 553, and 569. On certain treaties between Venice and two emirates in Asia Minor, see Zachariadou 1976.
9 Blake 1980.
10 Saccardo, Lazzarini, and Munarini 2003, pp. 398–404. Among pertinent overviews published previously, it is worth citing: Nepoti 1986, pp. 354–57 and 360–61; Saccardo 1993b, 1995, 1998. On the more specific subject of Fatimid ceramics, see Tonghini 1999, p. 292. On Spanish ceramics, see Conton 1940, pp. 105–17; Nepoti 1986, pp. 360–61; Ravanelli Guidotti 1992, pp. 68–76 and 82–84; Gobbo 1998; and Munarini 1992, pp. 61–68 and 1998.
11 On archaeology's contribution to an assessment of the impact of Islamic culture in southern Europe, see Blake, Tonghini, and Vannini 1998. On fritware, see note 23.
12 See Conton 1940, pp. 105–6; González Martí 1948; Morazzoni 1955, pp. 19–20, and bibliography cited; Concina 1975; Ravanelli Guidotti 1992, pp. 82 and 84.
13 Morazzoni 1955, fig. 10; see Ravanelli Guidotti 1992, p. 84.
14 Now in the Museo Nazionale Atestino (inv. no. 18039) in Este, Padua province. Other examples, probably part of the same decoration and apparently coming from the same building, are preserved at the Musei Civici in Padua (inv. nos. 259, 1142, 1141, plus others with no inventory number); Munarini 1983, pp. 159–64, 168–71, figs. 3–7, 11.
15 See Gelichi 1993a, p. 27, n. 86 (and bibliography cited) and Riavez 2001, n. 89.
16 Spallanzani 1978b, p. 541 and n. 35.
17 Spallanzani 1978b.
18 The edicts are reproduced in the appendices to Drake 1868. See also Sarre 1933, p. 424; Conton 1940, pp. 106–7; Morazzoni 1955, pp. 18–20; Alverà Bortolotto 1981, pp. 17–20; Nepoti 1986, p. 362; Ravanelli Guidotti 1992, pp. 70 and 72.
19 Ravanelli Guidotti (1992, p. 76) refers to an archive note relating to an expedition, which set out from Seville, by the Venetian Andrea Corner between 1412 and 1415; it mentions *veri da specchi e porcellette.* Many Mamluk sultans of the Burji period (1382–1517) sent porcelain to the doge of Venice, starting with the reign of al-Zahir Sayf ad-Dîn Jaqmaq (r. 1438–53), who in 1442 sent porcelain to Doge Francesco Foscari (Heyd 1885–86, vol. 2, p. 697, n. 7; see Mack 2002, p. 178, n. 72). Lane (1963, p. 20 and n. 2 [Lane 1954, p. 1, fn. 2]) and Alverà Bortolotto (1981, p. 94, n. 37) mention Marin Sanudo's assertion that 20 pieces of porcelain were sent in 1461 as a gift to Pasquale Malipiero by Sultan "Abulfet Hamet" [al-Malik al-Mu'ayyad Abu al-Fath Ahmad III, who reigned for only one year in 1461]. In 1473, Sultan Qa'itbey (r. 1468–1496) sent 20 pieces of porcelain to Doge Nicolò Tron (according to a letter given to the doge by Ambassador Giovanni Emo; see Gabrieli 1966, p. 431; see also Mack 2002, p. 23, n. 70, p. 188). Heyd (1885–1886, vol. 2, p. 697, n. 7) mentions shipments to Doge Agostino Barbarigo in 1490 and to the Venetian Signoria in 1498 and 1508 (see also Mack 2002, p. 188, n. 72). Jestaz (1990) reported that the Venetian Bernardin Redaldi acquired prior to 1527, for his own collection, 28 items of blue-and-white porcelain, eight white monochrome pieces, and five blue monochrome pieces (see Spallanzani 1994, p. 43).
20 Spallanzani 1978a, pp. 51–52, 87 and 165.
21 This assumes that we do not consider Venetian production (see below), as brought to light by Spallanzani (1978a, p. 51). Jestaz (1990) convincingly argued that the items described as "porcelain" (white, blue and white, etc.) in Bernardin Redaldi's collection (as listed in his estate

cat. 190. *Bowl*
Veneto, 17th century
Museo d'Arte Medievale e Moderna, Padua

cat. 189. *Two tiles*
Veneto, first half of the 17th century
Museo Franchetti alla Ca' d'Oro, Venice

inventory of 1527, see note 19) are undoubtedly Chinese porcelain.
22 Spallanzani 1994, p. 55.
23 Ceramics with a body of frit were probably being produced in Islamic workshops by the 10th century; for an updated overview of the origins of fritware, see Rugiadi 2005.
24 Spallanzani (1978a, p. 52 and 1989, p. 85) mentions a 1476 document in which Filippo Strozzi in Florence asked Gerolamo Strozzi in Venice to buy for him, among other things, four bowls and a cooler of *porcellana domaschina*. This most likely referred to Syrian ceramics of the Mamluk period, made from frit with blue-on-white painted decoration beneath an alkaline glaze (for such ware, see Marino 2005–6).
25 See Golombek, Mason, and Bailey 1996; Medley 1975.
26 Lane 1954, p. 1 claimed that in the late 15th century the fame of Chinese porcelain in Italy certainly outstripped knowledge of the material itself, even though it was fairly common in Egypt, Syria, and Turkey, countries with which Italian traders had long done vigorous trade. Jestaz (1990, p. 23) argues that by this time there probably existed connoisseurs able to appreciate true Chinese porcelain.
27 See Atasoy and Raby 1989, p. 268 and nn. 26–28.
28 Gerlach (1674, p. 380) explained that the substance was white as chalk, painted with stems and flowers, and went in Latin languages by the name of maiolica (the same material from which they made tiles used by the pasha to decorate his halls, his plates and his drinking goblets). See Ballardini 1925, p. 18; Sarre 1939, pp. 343–44; Atasoy and Raby 1989, p. 264.
29 Thornton 1991, p. 110; Mack 2002, p. 109 and p. 207, n. 76.
30 Lane (1957, p. 279) identified the coat of arms as belonging to the Mocenigo family of Venice, and hypothesized a gift of Iznik ceramics to Doge Alvise Mocenigo.
31 Nine plates survive intact, of three different sizes (currently held by various museums), as well as a fragment uncovered during excavations at Iznik. For a detailed analysis, see Atasoy and Raby 1989, pp. 264–68; see also Mack 2002, pp. 109 and p. 207, n. 76.
32 Munarini 1983, p. 155 and n. 2 (G.F., *Copia del statuto dei merzeri tratta d'altra simile, l'anno 1758 e si può dir raccolta di cose diverse procurate da me*, ms. n° 79, Biblioteca Civica, Padua, p. 15). See also Munarini 1983, pp. 164–67, 171–73 and figs. 8–10.
33 The international conference held in Venice on April 13–15, 2004, *I vasai del Leone: Ceramiche del Veneto e nel Veneto dal VI al XVI secolo*, made a major contribution to the study of ceramics produced in the Veneto.
34 Berti and Gelichi 1995, p. 439. See also Gelichi 1993b, p. 290, and Berti and Gelichi 1999.
35 Lazzarini and Canal 1983.
36 Gelichi 1986.
37 Concerning this date, see Gelichi (1993a, pp. 31–32); Berti, Gelichi and Mannoni 1997, § IV. 3. On likely Venetian production of an older, "original" type of *graffita*, similar to Byzantine Aegean ware and not always employing slip, roughly datable to the first half of the 13th century (although its provenance has not yet be convincingly documented), see Saccardo 1993a, pp. 211–12; Saccardo, Lazzarini, and Munarini 2003, p. 409. See also Berti and Gelichi 1995, p. 428.
38 On the origins and development of these ceramics, following the discovery of a few examples of kiln wasters see Lazzarini 1989. See also Gelichi 1993a, pp. 28–31, especially 32, as well as Berti and Gelichi 1997, pp. 86–89 and figs. 3–7; Saccardo 1993a and 1998.
39 Gelichi 1986, p. 353; see Gelichi 1983–84. On the various decorative motifs used in this type of sgraffito, see Saccardo 1993a. For the results of analyses carried out on two kinds of sgraffito, see Mignucci 2002.
40 Named after a monastery on one of the islands to the north of the lagoon (Saccardo 1997, pp. 409–14). See also Saccardo, Lazzarini, and Munarini 2003, p. 409.
41 What is called proto-maiolica ware—that is to say, maiolica discovered in Corinth and a few sites conquered by the Crusaders in Syro-Palestinian lands (for an overview, see Gelichi 1991b, pp. 200–1, and Gelichi 1993a, n. 83), identified as prototypes for the "later" enameled ceramics produced in Italy—is in fact an Italian product, as Ballardini first realized (1938, p. 37) and Whitehouse (1967, 1980) and Blake (1971) later codified; see also the hypothesis proposed—first in agreement, then in disagreement, with this thesis—by Waagé (1934, p. 132) and Liverani (1937, pp. 4–5, 7). The term proto-maiolica is still used today to refer to the oldest Italian tin-glazed ceramics, produced in southern Italy (for an overview of publications, see Patitucci Uggeri 1997). A map of the dissemination of proto-maiolica in the Latin Kingdom of Jerusalem and neighboring regions was drawn up by Pringle (1986). None has apparently been found either in Istanbul or in the Black Sea trading posts that nevertheless maintained close ties to Italian merchants, especially after the Fourth Crusade.
42 Gelichi 1986, 1991a, 1993a; Riavez 2001. On the exportation of Western ceramics during the subsequent Mamluk period, see Gayraud 1986.
43 Gelichi 1993a, p. 35.
44 On the dating of Islamic sgraffito ware, see Morgan 1994; Northedge 1996; Rugiadi 2001–2, pp. 17–20. It probably began to circulate more widely only in the late 10th or early 11th century.
45 See Lavagna and Varaldo 1986, and Varaldo 1997.
46 Lane 1937–38. Notably at al-Mina and Atlit. For a description of the places that produced this type of sgraffito, known as Port Saint Symeon ware (that is to say al-Mina, formerly Port Saint-Siméon, at Antioch), see Riavez 2001, pp. 505–06; on the spread of sgraffito throughout the Mediterranean basin from the 13th century onwards, see Rugiadi 2001–2, pp. 71–83.
47 See Whitehouse 1971, pp. 275; Berti and Gelichi 1999, p. 33 and n. 34; Riavez 2001, pp. 529–30. For a summary concerning the chronology of incised slipware decoration, see also Berti and Gelichi 2000, pp. 252–53.
48 Gelichi 1991a, p. 345.
49 Grube 1989b, pp. 151–52: "It would appear that it was mainly in Venice and the Veneto that Byzantine pottery was known well enough to have had such an effect on the style and manner of ceramic decoration to allow for a suggested tradition that leads from Chinese T'ang wares through Islamic 'imitations' to Byzantine pottery types that, in turn, inspired the Italian sgraffito wares of the 14th and 15th centuries. . . . It would seem quite possible, especially given the extraordinary closeness of some bichromatic slipcarved wares in Italy to Islamic models of the 10th to 12th centuries, that there was indeed a much closer contact between Italian and early Islamic pottery of this type than has hitherto been recognized." See examples supplied by Grube 1989b, figs. 7 and 6.
50 Munarini 1990a.
51 Munarini (1990a, n. 24) notes that Gelichi (1986, p. 397) attributed it to *graffita arcaica padana* of the first half of the 15th century.
52 The Manises example, late 15th–early 16th century, is now at the Victoria and Albert Museum in London (see González Martí 1944, fig. 366, p. 283; Frothingham 1951, fig. 161); on the use of the term *refredador* for this cylindrical bottle, see Frothingham 1951, p. 193. See also Fontana 1986, p. 128 and figs. 13–14; 1993, p. 468; 1995, p. 313. In the list that the Datini company received from Asmet Zuleima's workshop in Manises in December 1401, concerning the wares sent to Venice (see above and note 17), there also appeared two "coolers" that turn out to be the most costly items (Spallanzani 1978b, pp. 530 and 537), and that perhaps represent the same type of vessel.
53 See the examples dated late 15th–early 16th century now at the Musei Civici in Padua (inv. n° 473 and 480), in Munarini 1990a, ill. p. 81, top, and Munarini and Banzato 1993, cat. 116 and 215.
54 See a late 15th–early 16th century example bearing the inscriptions *OIO* (oil) and *ASE* (vinegar), held by the Victoria and Albert Museum in London (inv. n° C 35–1923); Munarini 1990a, ill. p. 81, lower right; Rackham 1940, ill. 1407; Wilson 1987, fig. 251. An example found in the bed of the Sile River, second half of 15th century, is now in the Museo Civico in Treviso (Bellieni 1990, ill. p. 139, top).
55 See an example for the first half of the 16th century found at Sorgà (province of Verona) and preserved at the Musei Civici in Verona (inv. n° 9202); Ericani 1990a, ill. p. 160, top.
56 Now in the Museo Civico de Bassano del Grappa; see Munarini 1990a, p. 82 and n. 95.
57 Or *berettino,* a gray-blue colored glaze on the body of the ceramic: *"Tal colore nulla ha di quello che mostra, hora ti par bianco, hor scuro, e non è scuro, et così pare d'altri colori, et non è . . . La Etimologia volgare lo dimostra, che è detto barettino da barrar per barcare verbo, cioè ingannare, et Bertino quasi baratino."* (F. Pellegrino, *Del Significato de' Colori e de' mazzolli: Operetta di Fuluio Pellegrino Morato mantouano*, Venice 1551, quoted by Giovanni Conti in Piccolpasso 1976, pp. 221–222, see "bertino."). Piccolpasso supplied the composition, which, in Venice, comprised *marzacotto, stagnio,* and *zaffara* (Piccolpasso 1976, p. 156, corresponding to fol. 46*v* of the manuscript).
58 Moschetti 1931, p. 39, fig. 32, at the Musei Civici in Padua (inv. 134, labeled *borraccia*). See Moschetti 1938, fig. 26, and Munarini 1990d, ill. p. 215, lower left. On Candiana, see below.
59 Gelichi 1993b; see also Berti, Gelichi, and Mannoni 1997.
60 This is true of both glazed ceramics and maiolica ware; for an overview, see Gelichi 1993b, p. 277 and notes.
61 The presence of slip is an exception when it comes to the polychrome decoration in brown, green, and red in ceramics from Ugento, Scribla, and Tarento (see Dufournier, Flambard, and Noyé 1986, p. 261).
62 On the Santa Croce-type polychrome slip-painted basin, see Gelichi 1993b, pp. 291–93, no. and fig. 37. Sari-type slip-painted decoration

has been studied extensively; for an astrological interpretation of this kind of decoration, see Zick-Nissen 1972, cats. 140–41.

63 On the question of this date, already proposed by Sauro Gelichi 1988, see Ravanelli Guidotti 2000.

64 Ballardini 1938, pp. 25 ff.; Ravanelli Guidotti 2000, pp. 370 ff.

65 Ravanelli Guidotti (2000) has drawn up an exhaustive "history" of publications on the "Moresque" origins of Italian maiolica.

66 Bryony (*Bryonia alba* or *Byronia dioica*) is a perennial, twisting climber with five-lobed leaves and little round berries .

67 Ravanelli Guidotti 2000.

68 Munarini 1992, pp. 66 and 68.

69 Croce Da Villa 1989, pp. 67–74; see Munarini 1992, pp. 66–67, and cat. no. 128. MI–001 (probably produced in the Veneto during the second quarter of the 15th century).

70 Museo Civico, Belluno (inv. I.G. 19729); see Ericani 1990a, p. 170, illus. On bryony leaves, see note 66.

71 Passeri 1758, p. 95.

72 The Italian term *rabesche* (or *rabesca*), used during the Renaissance, was the origin of the term arabesque, and it referred to an Islamic type of stylized vegetal decoration, sometimes employing geometric motifs and medallions (see Kühnel 1949). This type of decoration inspired many Italian and European artists from the last quarter of the 15th century onwards (see *Arabesques* 1995).

73 Piccolpasso 1976, p. 203.

74 See Atasoy and Raby 1989, pp. 76–81. In contrast, the later "Tuğrakes spiral type" (from the second quarter of the 16th century onwards) was the prototype for type A, the oldest calligraphic style with Ligurian scrollwork, datable to 1540 from the excavations of the Priamar fortress in Savona (Lavagna 1992).

75 See the articles by Sylvia Auld and Ernst J. Grube in this volume, as well as Fontana 1989, p. 128 and figs. 9–12; 1993, p. 468; 1995, p. 313.

76 Two of the most interesting pieces from each of these two workshops are now in the Victoria and Albert Museum in London (inv. 8389–1863 and 959); see Rackham 1952, pl. 78 and 81a. On the latter, see Alverà Bortolotto 1981, where the entry for plate LVII ascribes it to Maestro Lodovico.

77 Passeri 1758, p. 96.

78 See, for example, Pope 1956, pl. 35.

79 It appeared for the first time on the back of Baba Nakkas ware (Atasoy and Raby 1989, pp. 76–81). On the influence of Chinese porcelain on Ottoman ceramics, see Atasoy and Raby 1989, pp. 121–128.

80 Piccolpasso 1976, p. 210.

81 Alverà Bortolotto 1981, pp. 63–66; Alverà Bortolotto 1983.

82 Museum für Kunsthandwerk, Frankfurt (inv. 6875). Alverà Bortolotto (1981, p. 64, pl. 46) states that there were many German orders for Venetian maiolica and that many examples of *alla porcellana* decoration, dated between 1515 and 1530, have survived. For other *alla porcellana* plates produced by this workshop, see Alverà Bortolotto 1981, pl. XLVIIa–c.

83 A plate dating from 1540, bearing the arms of the Venetian family Da Mula, now in the Victoria and Albert Museum in London (inv. no. 1750–1855), allegedly comes from Venice (Alverà Bortolotto 1981, pl. XLVIId) or Padua (Munarini 1990b, ill. p. 192).

84 Mid-16th century; see Morazzoni 1955, p. 113; Alverà Bortolotto 1981, p. 83, n. 66.

85 Alverà Bortolotto 1981, pl. XLVIIIa–d. On bryony leaves, see note 66.

86 See the large number of examples published in Alverà Bortolotto 1981 (pl. LI–LII, LXII–LXIII, LVII–LXVIII, LXXI–LXXII, LXXVII), which includes items from the Venetian workshop of Maestro Lodovico (up to the mid-16th century) and the Venetian workshop of Maestro Jacopo da Pesaro (ca. 1530–45), as well as other Venetian workshops of the same period. The backs of several Venetian plates are also interesting (one plate is attributed to Maestro Jacopo da Pesaro, ca. 1530–45, now in the Victoria and Albert Museum, London (inv. 968), see Alverà Bortolotto 1981, pl. LXII and 1988, ill. p. 49; a second plate, from another shop working in the same style, is dated 25 April 1550, also in the Victoria and Albert Museum (inv. 965), see Alverà Bortolotto 1988, ill. p. 51, top; finally, a third plate, dated 18 May 1548, is now in the Slezske Museum in Opava (inv. 1118 K, 03.230), see Alverà Bortolotto 1988, ill. p. 69, top) and also features a floral decoration similar to the one on the front of *alla porcellana* plates. For other, later examples made in various areas of the Veneto (mid-16th century), see Alverà Bortolotto 1981, p. 83, n. 66 (Padua and Verona); Munarini 1990c, ill. p. 197 and 202, top (Verona and Padua).

87 Cf. the decoration on the back of several mid-15th-century plates now in the Hispanic Society of America, New York (inv. n° E 634, E 555 and E 589), see Frothingham 1951, figs. 63, 71, and 104).

88 See note 23.

89 On the influence of blue-and-white Chinese porcelain on Ottoman ceramics, see Pope 1972, Raby and Yücel 1983, and Raby in Atasoy and Raby 1989, pp. 121–28; see also Crowe 1976, and Carswell 1985, especially pp. 32–34.

90 See note 26.

91 Urbani de Ghelthof 1877; mentioned in Lane 1963, p. 21, and also Spallanzani 1978a, who published the letter (p. 51 and n. 61).

92 "in this glorious city of Venice to make good and excellent works of porcelain of every kind, like that called Levantine, which is transparent." Lane 1963, p. 21; Alverà Bortolotto 1981, p. 95 and n. 41

93 Lane 1963, p. 21; Alverà Bortolotto 1981, p. 95 and n. 42 and 43; Mack 2002, pp. 104–105 and n. 56, p. 206.

94 Lane 1963, p. 21.

95 Lane, Ibid., offers the hypothesis that this craftsman might have been the same who made the *porcellane* for Alfonso I d'Este, who unsuccessfully sought to employ him for his service. See also Mack 2002, p. 105 and n. 56, p. 206.

96 See Spallanzani 1994, pp. 45–46, 148, who cites a letter of January 8, 1550, sent by Pietro Camaiani in Venice to Pier Francesco del Riccio in Florence. On the reference to a *berettino* bowl decorated with large, three-lobed leaves, now in the Museo Nazionale del Bargello in Florence, see Spallanzani 1994, pl. n. 8.

97 Rackham 1910 and 1936.

98 Alverà Bortolotto 1981, p. 96.

99 See Atasoy and Raby 1989, p. 268.

100 On the *saz* leaf and its origins, see Atasoy and Raby 1989, p. 133

101 Musei Civici, Padua (see Moschetti 1932, pl. XXIV).

102 Museo Correr, Venice (see Ballardini 1940, pl. XIIa). For an overview of studies on the origin of the term Candiana, see Fontana 1989, pp. 129–130, fig. 18 [erroneous caption]–26, and 1993, pp. 483–84, cat. 301; Ericani 1990b, p. 233; see also Atasoy and Raby 1989, p. 268. According to the current state of research, the hypothesis proposed by Azeglio (in Fortnum 1896, p. 312) and Conton (1940), later taken up by Alverà Bortolotto (1981, p. 97) and Mack (2002, p. 109), which links the term to Candia—the former name of Heraklion, the port city on the northern coast of Crete, where much of the merchandise destined for Venice was loaded, along with Ottoman ceramics later copied in the Veneto—no longer seems so incongruous.

103 Inv. Ke. 989; Rackham 1936, fig. E. On this comparison, see also Atasoy and Raby 1989, p. 268 and fig. 591. As far as attributing it to Padua, see also Lane 1963, pp. 26–27, figs. 10–11.

104 It is interesting to note that the outside is painted with a simplifed *alla porcellana* decoration in monochrome blue. Note 86, above, mentions a Venetian maiolica plate dated 1550 (now in the Victoria and Albert Museum, inv. 965) which, like the Viennese example, features a landscape in the cavetto and *alla porcellana* decoration on the back rim; these two ceramics differ in having a three-lobed, fleshy "leaf" motif on the side and edge instead of the typical Candiana foliate motif seen on the Vienna plate. The distinct three-lobed leaves (similar to the ones on the Venetian bowl now in the Bargello, cited in note 96) are a decoration typical of a few plates featuring a central cartouche with a dedication to nuns, which Moschetti categorizes as Candiana (see, for instance, examples in the Museo Civico, Padua; Moschetti 1931, figs. 25–26, 30). For the "monastic" plates with dedications to nuns, see also Bellieni 1990b, p. 232, ill., although they differ in their absence of Ottoman-type decoration. However, many pieces of Candiana bear dedications to nuns (Ballardini 1940, pl. VIIIa).

105 Alverà Bortolotto 1981, p. 96.

106 Ibid., pls. CVIIIb and CIXa.

107 Ibid, p. 97, with a reproduction of fragments of Candiana found in the lagoon by Conton, now in the Galleria Franchetti alla Ca' d'Oro, Venice, pls. CCXXII and CCXXIII; Conton 1940, p. 95.

108 Marini 1990, pp. 247–248. Furthermore, a probable imitation of Candiana can be seen in water jugs attributed to the Grosso workshop in Albisola (Savona province, Liguria), made in 1616 of white maiolica painted with blue floral decoration, a hypothesis formulated by Marzinot 1978 and 1979, p. 352; see Fontana 1989, n. 78, fig. 27.

109 Ericani 1990b, p. 234.

Catalogue of Exhibited Works

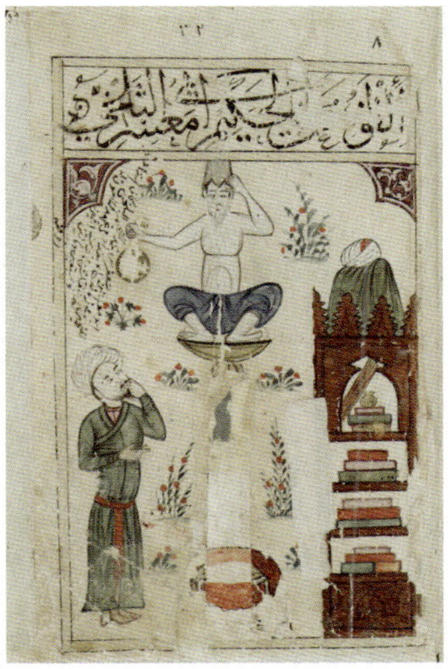

cat. 2

• Works exhibited only in Paris
° Works exhibited only in New York

WORKS ON PAPER

1. *Ta'rikh-i tabari*

"al-Tabari's History" by Balʿami
Iran, ca. 1290–1320
Ink, colors, and gold on paper; tooled leather binding
35 x 25 cm (13 3/4 x 9 7/8 in.)
Biblioteca Nazionale Marciana, Fondo G. Nani 78, Venice
Inv. Cod. Marc. Or. 128 (=171) (ill. p. 21)

The Persian text of this manuscript was written in AD 963 by the Samanid vizier Abu ʿAli Muhammad al-Balʿami (d. 974) as an adaptation of the famous Arabic *History* (*Mukhtasar tarikh al-rusul wa al-mulk wa al-khulafa*, "A Brief History of Prophets, Kings, and Caliphs") by Abu Jaʿfar Muhammad ibn Jarir al-Tabari (839–923). The *Ta'rikh* represents an attempt to write a universal history dealing with Creation, Old Testament patriarchs and prophets, the rulers of ancient Israel and Persia, the prophets before Muhammad, Jesus, and the Persian Sasanians. This account is followed by that on the Prophet Muhammad, which includes detailed sections on the period of conquests, the Umayyad and ʿAbbasid dynasties, and ends in the year AH 302 (AD 915).[1] Al-Balʿami's Persian translation was largely based on the original but is much shorter than al-Tabari's text, being a sort of abridged version. Although he added new sections, he made no attempt to bring the history up to his own time, about 50 years after the chronological end of al-Tabari's text. The importance of Balʿami's *Ta'rikh-i tabari* lies not only in his original additions, but also for being one of the earliest prose works in modern Persian, and the first of Persian historical writings.

This manuscript has 365 folios with some pages missing at the end, and no colophon. Each page of text has 29 lines of neat, small naskh script, with captions and titles in red ink. Though it is not illustrated, the manuscript does have artistically illuminated borders and chapter headings, as well as full-page illuminations (including a *shamsa* or rosette, fol. 3v). It also includes a cosmographic map, a table of geographic sites, and a whimsical genealogical table of the early caliphs and Companions of the Prophet (fol. 68v).

This manuscript formerly belonged to the family library of the Nani, an old and powerful Venetian noble family. Giacomo Nani (1725–1797), a philosopher-patrician and admiral in the Venetian army, bequeathed the collection of nearly 1,000 manuscripts (mostly Greek and Coptic but with a substantial number of Islamic examples) to the Biblioteca Nazionale Marciana (established 1468). He and his family most likely acquired their rare books in Venice or in the Eastern Mediterranean (see cat. 3).

QA

1 A translation of Tabari's *History* volumes in a 15-volume edition was published by M. J. Goeje, Leiden, 1879–1901; recently, some 40 volumes of a complete translated and annotated English version were published in the series "Bibliotheca Persica" of the State University of New York Press.

2. *"The wise Abu Maʿshar al-Balkhi" from the Kitab al-bulhan ("The Book of Wonderment")*

Baghdad, Iraq, late 14th century
Ink, gold, and colors on paper; leather binding
25 x 18 cm (9 7/8 x 7 in.)
The Bodleian Library, University of Oxford
Inv. MS Bodley Or. 133

The *Kitab al-bulhan* is a miscellaneous manuscript including chapters with dates ranging from 1334 to 1435, probably bound together during the reign of the Jalayirid Sultan Ahmad (r. 1382–1410) in the capital Baghdad, with slightly later additions to the text.[1] Its 176 folios include chapters on astronomy, astrology, and divination. There is also a unique section of full-page illustrations captioned by a title on top that begins with "The discourse on . . . ", followed by the subject of the discourse, which can refer to a folktale, a sign of the zodiac, a climate, a *jinn*,[2] or a prophet. The storytelling, however, is left to the painter since no explanatory text was added. For example, some of the most accomplished miniature paintings are "The discourse on the tree of Waq-waq," "Sindibad and the old man of the sea," and "The valley of Sirindib (Sri Lanka) and the gems."[3]

In the introduction to this miscellany, the famous astronomer and mathematician Abu Maʿshar (787–886) from Balkh in northern Afghanistan is indicated as the main author of the astronomical and astrological texts. Jaʿfar ibn Muhammad Abu Maʿshar al-Balkhi was known in Europe as Albumasar and is considered the main original source of Aristotle's theories of nature starting before the middle of the 12th century.[4] In homage to the author, the astronomer also figures prominently in one of the full-page illustrations (fol. 34r), entitled "The discourse on the *hakim* (sage) Abu Maʿshar al-Balkhi."[5] The original numbering of this illustration is also the lowest in the sequence, suggesting that the image of Abu Maʿshar logically represented a sort of frontispiece for the section.

In the painting, Abu Maʿshar seems to be in the middle of an astronomical experiment. He sits in the center under an arch—bare-chested and wearing a hat—inside a large metal bowl placed on the top of a column (now damaged). The vertical composition is balanced by the tools of his knowledge (books, an inkwell, his turban and cloak) on his proper left and by his assistant, his finger raised to his lips in wonderment, on his right. The only element that puts the composition off-balance, and thus becomes the focus of attention, is Abu Maʿshar's outstretched right arm holding a planispheric astrolabe (also damaged) or similar astronomical instrument (see cats. 90–91). A gloss added later to the upper left corner near the instrument provides a brief biography of the astronomer.

Whatever experiment is represented here, Abu Maʿshar, or Albumasar, epitomized Arab astronomers in medieval Europe and images similar to the present one probably appeared inside the manuscripts that were used for the Latin translations of his texts. As a scientist and therefore a philosopher and a *hakim*, his ideal image survives in Venetian illustrations, for example, in the frontispiece of Ptolemy's *Cosmographia* in Eton College (cat. 16).

SC

1 The main study is Carboni 1988, corresponding to a shortened published version of my final dissertation at the University of Venice, completed in 1983, with its bibliography.
2 In Islamic folklore, a *jinn* belongs to a class of spirits that can take human or animal form and can influence humankind in either a positive or a negative manner.
3 Respectively, 43r, 46v, 41v; Carboni 1988, pls. 43, 47, 51.
4 See, for example, Lemay 1962; Pingree 1968; see also Barry's essay in this volume.
5 Carboni 1988, pp. 73–74, pl. 28.

°3. Taj al-Din Ibrahim ibn Khidr Ahmadi (d. 1413) *Iskandarnama ("The Book of Alexander")*

Turkey, probably Edirne, mid-15th century
Ink, gold, and colors on paper; leather binding
24.6 x 17.5 cm (9 5/8 x 6 7/8 in.)
Biblioteca Nazionale Marciana, Venice
Inv. Cod. Marc. Or. 90 (=57) (ill. p. 21)

This exceptional manuscript of the *Book of Alexander* is perhaps the most important Islamic work of art in a Venetian collection today. A narrative in Ottoman Turkish about the life and exploits of Alexander the Great (Iskandar) in his Islamic legendary semblance, the manuscript also includes a section devoted to Ottoman history up to the time of its author's death in the early 15th century. This manuscript and several other "Oriental" codices (see also cat. 1) entered the Biblioteca Marciana in 1797 as part of the bequest of Giacomo Nani (1725–1797), the single largest donation of Islamic manuscripts to the library. Although it is not known how Nani acquired these works, he was a bibliophile and a discerning book collector who likely considered this copy of the *Iskandarnama* a prized possession. Nani, a distinguished patrician, served the Republic as *Provveditore Generale da Mar* (Superintendent in Chief of Maritime Affairs) and often journeyed among the islands of the Eastern and Southern Mediterranean,[1] where he presumably acquired the more than 300 Greek codices as well as the Oriental manuscripts that he left to the Marciana. One of the foremost political figures in a decadent period of the Serenissima Republic,[2] Nani held the title of *Provveditore alle Lagune (Superintendent of the Lagoons)* when the French put an end to the Republic in 1797, which was also the year of his death.

This *Iskandarnama* manuscript contains 277 folios with 66 illustrations and a large number of miniature paintings depicting various episodes of Alexander's life as well as different subjects interspersed throughout: the Ascension of the Prophet Muhammad and his journey to Heaven (fols. 12r, 193r), the poet-author Ahmadi in conversation with a friend (fol. 131v), the Zodiac and the planets (fols. 58r, 132v, 133r), a few episodes derived from the Iranian epic Shahnama ("Book of Kings"), and several illustrations of the history of Islam, the most recent of which is a reception scene at the court of the Ottoman Sultan Bayezid I (r. 1389–1403; fols. 240v–241r). Apart from its many artistically accomplished paintings, the manuscript represents one of a handful of Ottoman codices that can be attributed to the period of the conquest of Constantinople in 1453 and probably to the royal atelier in Edirne, the de facto Ottoman capital on the European continent in the first half of the 15th century. Grube has convincingly argued that the *Iskandarnama*, together with two other related manuscripts, may have been copied under the patronage of Mehmet the Conqueror (r. 1444–46, 1451–81)–Gentile Bellini's future patron (see cat. 23)–just before or after he moved with his court from Edirne to Istanbul.[3]

Grube has identified four hands in the codex, who drew inspiration from earlier 15th-century Timurid painting, especially from the southern Iranian atelier of Shiraz.[4]

SC

1 For example, he was in Tripoli, Libya, in 1764 to ratify a commercial treatise with the local bey. On the career of Giacomo Nani, see Viggiano 1996; Nani 1997.
2 His is the statement "*Bisogna agire con quel che si ha*" (One must act according to what he has in his hands); see the dissertation by Marco Michelon, "*'Bisogna agire con quel che si ha.' La figura del Provveditore da Mar nel '700 e le 'osservazioni' di Giacomo Nani,*" (University of Venice, Studi Storici), 1996–97.
3 Grube 1987, p. 187; see also Venice 1993, pp. 407–9, cat. 261.
4 Grube 1987, p. 189.

4. *Mehmet II Smelling a Rose*

Istanbul, Turkey, ca. 1480
Watercolor on paper
39 x 27 cm (15 3/8 x 10 5/8 in.)
Topkapı Sarayi Müsezi Library, Istanbul
Inv. H. 2153, fol. 10r (ill. p. 135)

Most likely painted in the Ottoman court atelier in the wake of Gentile Bellini's *Portrait of Mehmet II* of 1480 (cat. 23), this miniature testifies to the canonical status that the Venetian painting assumed in the emerging tradition of Turkish sultan portraiture. A comparison of the two works suggests that Mehmet II either implicitly or explicitly challenged other artists at his court to surpass Gentile's masterful likeness of him. Because of the sultan's profound interest in the genre, and seemingly insatiable need for images of himself of all kinds, few Renaissance rulers created such exceptionally fertile ground for new developments in portraiture.[1] His reign is rightfully associated with the advent of the Ottoman portraiture tradition, which drew from Islamic and Italian examples and practices in equal measure.[2]

The present painting has been attributed to Sinan Beg or his pupil Şiblizade Ahmed, but, truth be told, not enough is known about the painters employed in the imperial atelier during Mehmet II's reign to be able to distinguish different personalities and their oeuvres. Nonetheless, the assumption that the author of this painting is from the Near East appears sound on the basis of the artistic choices he made.

To a remarkable extent, the anonymous painter copied the head, turban, and facial features from Bellini's portrait of the sultan, suggesting that these were the aspects of the Venetian painting that most impressed Mehmet II and others at his court. Bellini, however, lavished greater attention on the subtleties of the sitter's appearance, articulating, for example, the shadow cast on the turban by his *taj*, the stubble under his chin, and the crow's feet and bags round his eyes, the latter reminiscent of Lorenzo Bastiani's *Portrait of Doge Francesco Foscari* (cat. 21). Given the frequent diplomatic exchanges between Venice and Istanbul in the late 1470s, it is likely that Mehmet II received Venetian dogal portraits as gifts, and those works could have served as models for this painting as well.[3] In addition, three pen and ink drawings recently reattributed to Gentile—the *Young Greek Woman*, *Seated Janissary*, and *Seated Woman*, all dated to the artist's period in Istanbul (1479–81)—feature a distinctive way of representing the folds of the sleeves that was carefully copied by the unknown artist of the present work.[4]

As in Gentile's *Portrait of Mehmet II*, here the sitter is presented in three-quarter view, but his entire figure, not just his head and shoulders, is depicted. Further distinguishing the two works, a different imperial iconography, one based on late Timurid conventions of royal portraiture, is used in this instance. Thus, instead of Gentile's triumphal arch, crowns, and embroidered cloth, this artist represented the sultan sitting cross-legged, tightly gripping a checkered handkerchief in one hand and holding a trio of red roses in the other. This depiction of the sultan, actively smelling the flowers, is both livelier and more revealing of the sitter's personality than Gentile's. The roses may refer to the sultan's intellectual and spiritual refinement as well as his interest in gardens (or perhaps replace the three crowns of Asia, Greece, and Trebizond used in Gentile's portrait), while the archer's ring round his thumb alludes to his military achievements and skill as a hunter.[5] This portrait, together with cat. 5, is emblematic of the exciting mixture of visual cultures promoted by Mehmet II, especially during the final years of his reign.

TK

1 Atıl 1973; Raby 1980, 1982a, 1987, 2000a; Campbell and Chong 2005.
2 Necipoğlu 2000a, pp. 22–31.
3 Ibid., pp. 29–30.
4 Atıl 1973, pp. 111–13; Campbell and Chong 2005, pp. 98–103. See also the sleeves of the *Seated Scribe* in the Kuwait National Museum (LNS 57 MS) (illustrated in Campbell and Chong 2005, p. 124).
5 Atasoy 2002, p. 126.

5. *Portrait of Mehmet II the Conqueror*

Istanbul, Turkey, ca. 1479–81
Watercolor and gold on paper
26 x 21 cm (10 1/4 x 8 1/4 in.)
Topkapı Sarayi Müsezi Library, Istanbul
Inv. H. 2153, fol. 145v (ill. p. 25)

Like *Mehmet II Smelling a Rose* (cat. 4), this miniature portrait of the sultan has been pasted onto a folio in the so-called Fatih Album (H. 2153), a compilation of works of art owned by Mehmet II that was probably assembled after his death by his son Bayezid II or grandson Selim I.[1] The contents of the volume are eclectic, ranging from Turkoman Aq-qoyunlu watercolors to Florentine prints, though the portraits of Mehmet II are the most famous and often studied.

Powerful despite its small size, this painting is now most often attributed to an unknown Turkish artist, although it is sometimes given to the Italian artist known as Costanzo di Moysis or, alternatively, Costanzo da Ferrara.[2] As early as 1467, Costanzo visited the court of Mehmet II and produced the justly famous bronze portrait medal that characterizes the sultan as an aggressive warrior with a hawk-like stare and imposing physical bulk (see also cats. 116–17).[3] Costanzo's bust-length profile portrait in bronze clearly served as the principal point of departure for this painting, but the draftsmanship and technique confirm that a Turkish miniaturist executed it.[4]

It is possible that this painting dates to the late 1460s or early 1470s,[5] as Raby has argued elsewhere. Another possibility is that Gentile Bellini's arrival at the Ottoman court in fall 1479 marks the beginning of a more serious and sustained dialogue between Turkish and Italian artists, and the work, instead, dates from the period of his sojourn. In support of this theory, the painting recalls some of Gentile Bellini's artistic ideas in addition to Costanzo's, including most importantly, a more somber and sympathetic portrayal of Mehmet II. Furthermore, the sleeves of the sitter in this painting are rendered in the same highly distinctive manner used by Gentile in his drawings of Turkish figures.[6]

As in the two other 15th-century painted likenesses of Mehmet II in this exhibition (cats. 4, 23), the sultan is here crowned with a white turban wrapped around a red *taj* and a fur mantle. The color of his kaftan varies, but it is consistently bold in hue. Perhaps because it reveals so little of the sitter's character and status, the bust portrait is a format rarely employed by Ottoman painters, who generally favored the Timurid-style seated pose showing the entire figure instead (cats. 4, 7–10).

TK

1 Raby 1981; Rogers 2005, pp. 84–93.
2 For the attribution to Costanzo, see, for example, Barry 2004, pp. 41–42.
3 See, for example, Istanbul 2000, p. 90, cat. 7.
4 Ibid.
5 Ibid.
6 On these drawings, and their recent reattribution to Gentile, see Campbell and Chong 2005, pp. 98–105.

6. Haydar Reis Nigari (ca. 1492–1572) *Portrait of Admiral Haireddin "Barbarossa"*

Istanbul, Turkey, ca. 1540–45
Ink and colors on paper
27 x 20 cm (10 5/8 x 7 7/8 in.)
Topkapı Sarayi Müzesi Library, Istanbul
Inv. H. 2134, fol. 9v (ill. p. 24)

This is one of a small number of extant portraits attributed to Haydar Reis, the Ottoman naval commander, poet, and painter better known by the pseudonym Nigari, meaning "the portraitist." Working in a colorful, highly engaging style, Nigari captured the likenesses of Süleyman the Magnificent, his son Selim II (cat. 7), Charles V of Spain, Francis I of France, and, in this instance, Haireddin "Barbarossa" (1466?–1546), the famous Turkish corsair and Grand Admiral of the Ottoman fleet.[1] Operating outside the royal workshop, Nigari successfully revived Turkish portrait painting after it had suffered a decline under Mehmet II's immediate successors.

Combining his skill as both painter and poet, Nigari placed a couplet with his signature on the edge of the portrait, which is likely one of his earliest works.[2] Portraits of mariners are unusual in the Ottoman tradition, and thus this painting is evocative of Haireddin Barbarossa's military achievements and status at the court in addition to his close personal relationship with his fellow seaman Nigari.[3] Never a sultan, Barbarossa is nonetheless depicted in a manner recalling earlier Ottoman portraits of Mehmet II. The half-length profile, for example, is reminiscent of *Mehmet the Conqueror* (cat. 5), while the motif of holding a flower before the nose recalls *Mehmet II Smelling a Rose* (cat. 4), though here the flower is a carnation rather than a rose. Like its important predecessors, this portrait was painted on a single sheet and later pasted into an album.

Both Barbarossa's (lit. "Red Beard") heavy beard and bushy eyebrows are snow white, indicating that this portrait was painted during the later years of the sitter's life. This distinctive aspect of the admiral's appearance is echoed in the white fur trim of his outer coat and rotund turban, while the tiger-striped outer coat is in the same bold red as the carnation. The only other colors in the composition are the blue of the sitter's inner coat and the gold of his belt and baton.

Admiral Barbarossa himself played an instrumental role in the exchange of ruler portraits between the Ottoman Empire and Italy. In 1543, when the French and Ottoman fleets met in Marseille, Barbarossa presented an ebony and ivory box filled with 11 miniature portraits of Ottoman sultans to Virginio Orsini, the Roman commander of several French warships.[4] Once in Italy, these portraits, which Hans Georg Majer posits could have been painted by Nigari,[5] served as the source for the sultan portraits that once decorated the walls of the "Sala de' Turchi" in Paolo Giovio's villa-museum overlooking Lake Como in northern Italy.[6]

Giovio and Barbarossa later corresponded with one another,[7] and the Ottoman corsair may have enclosed a likeness of himself in one of his letters. An Ottoman portrait similar to this one in the Topkapı Sarayi Museum appears to have served as the model for an intriguing painting of Barbarossa (with Captain Sinan the Jew) formerly in Giovio's villa. Now in the Art Institute of Chicago, this northern Italian (possibly Venetian) portrait of the formidable Ottoman mariner was once one of the collector-historian's most prized possessions.[8] Giovio proudly described it as a "*vero ritratto*" in his *Elogia virorum bellica virtute illustrium* of 1575.

TK

1 The most recent assessment of Nigari's oeuvre is Majer 1995 (with earlier bibliography).
2 Çağman and Tanındı 1979, p. 61, cat. 137; Majer 1995, p. 445.
3 Raby 2000b, p. 145. The bond between the two mariners is evoked in the couplet written by Nigari to accompany his portrait of Barbarossa.
4 Raby 2000a, p. 145.
5 Majer 1995; seconded by Raby 2000b, p. 146.
6 On Paolo Giovio, see generally Klinger 1991.
7 Raby 2000a, p. 141.
8 Klinger and Raby 1989, p. 48; Lloyd 1993, pp. 174–78; Raby 2000b, p. 145.

•7. Haydar Reis Nigari (ca. 1492–1572) *Portrait of Sultan Selim II*

Istanbul, Turkey, ca. 1570
44.4 x 31.2 cm (17 1/2 x 12 1/4 in.)
Aga Khan Trust for Culture, Geneva, formerly in the Collection of Prince Sadruddin Aga Khan
Inv. TM5 (ill. p. 142)

The son of Süleyman the Magnificent and his favorite wife, Roxelana, Selim II (r. 1566–74) ascended the throne of the Ottoman Empire at the height of its power and wealth. As sultan, he left military and administrative matters to the grand vizier, devoting himself to leisure and earning the nickname "Selim the Sot" for his excessive drinking. Selim II had already developed a taste for wine, feasting, falconry, poetry, music, and witty conversation as a young prince at the court of Kütahya in western Turkey, where the painter-poet Nigari became one of his fun-loving boon companions.[1] Nigari must have painted this portrait of Selim II after he had become sultan, and its vivid colors and wild patterns successfully capture the festive atmosphere of the court in Istanbul in this period.[2]

In a royal kiosk, Selim I sits cross-legged upon a carpet with a handkerchief in one hand, a pose and attribute symbolic of his sovereignty. A heavy-set man with a short beard, long mustache, and rosy cheeks, the sultan holds a cup of red wine in his other hand rather than the more conventional flower included in other Ottoman portraits (see cats. 4, 6, 8). Known for his extravagant, multi-layered costumes, Selim II wears a scarlet short-sleeved kaftan with an imperial *çintamani* motif in black, a green belt, blue sleeves, and a fur-lined coat with a gold-lobed medallion pattern draped over one shoulder. Two feathers spring from his large, loosely wrapped white turban.

As in an earlier portrait by Nigari of Selim II in the Topkapı Sarayi Müzesi Library,[3] a falconer with a distinctive cap stands behind the sultan. Selim II sits slightly to the right of center and looks and turns toward the right as well. A painted folio with ten figures facing left, now in the Los Angeles County Museum of Art, depicts the rest of the attendees to the sultan's merry gathering, including a pasha, three musicians, and a jester who may be Nigari himself.[4]

TK

1 Majer 1995, p. 445; Necipoğlu 2000, pp. 202-03.
2 Welch and Welch 1982, p. 32
3 Topkapı Sarayi Müzesi Library, H 2134, fol. 3 (illustrated and discussed in Istanbul 2000, pp. 222–25).
4 Los Angeles County Museum of Art, inv. M.85.237.20 (illustrated and discussed in Istanbul 2000, p. 227); see also Binney 1979, pp. 22–23, cat. 11.

8. Seyyid Lokman (d. 1601), *Kitafetü'l insaniye fi şema'ilü'l-osmaniye* Illustrated by Nakkas Osman (active c. 1560–c. 1581) *Portrait of Mehmet II*

Istanbul, Turkey, 1579
Watercolor on paper
23 x 12 cm (9 1/8 x 4 3/4 in.)
Topkapı Sarayi Müzesi Library, Istanbul
Inv. H. 1563

•9. Seyyid Lokman (d. 1601) *Kitafetü'l-insaniye fi şemâ'ilü'l-osmaniye* Illustrated by an anonymous follower of Nakkas Osman active in the Ottoman court atelier *Portrait of Mehmet II*

Istanbul, Turkey, ca. 1585–95
Watercolor on paper
19.3 x 10.3 cm (7 5/8 x 4 in.)
Sächsische Landesbibliothek – Staats und Universitätsbibliothek Dresden
Inv. Ms. Dresd. Eb 373 (ill. p. 176)

Under the aegis of the bibliophile Sultan Murad III (r. 1574–95), illustrated histories, an important genre of Islamic manuscripts, reached new heights at the Ottoman court. In the late 1570s, two luminaries of the imperial scriptorium, the official eulogist and poet Seyyid Lokman and the master painter Nakkas Osman, collaborated on the *Kitafetü'l insaniye fi şema'ilü'l-osmaniye* (*Human Physiognomy Concerning the Personal Dispositions of the Ottomans*). In an ornate literary style, Lokman described the physical, moral, and intellectual characteristics of the 13 sultans from the House of Osman, beginning with the late 12th- early 13th-century founder of the dynasty, Osman I, and ending in the late 16th century with Murad III himself. In an equally graceful visual idiom, Osman completed the text with a colorful likeness of each monarch. Text and image dovetail perfectly, demonstrating the extraordinary degree of cooperation between historian and illustrator.

Made for Murad III and beautifully bound, the celebrated original volume of the *Kitafetü'l-insaniye* (cat. 8) is preserved in the palace treasury; it features portraits by Osman himself along with magnificent calligraphy. Less well known is another volume (cat. 9), one of the numerous high-quality copies made in the scriptorium by Osman's assistants sometime before the end of Murad III's reign. Still bearing the sophisticated imprint of the imperial atelier, its illuminations and calligraphy are nonetheless of a distinctly lesser quality than the original manuscript. A comparison of the portrait of Mehmet II in these two manuscripts shows that even though pose and setting are similar, different color schemes and patterns are employed. Evidently certain distinctions among the various copies were tolerated and perhaps even encouraged. Most surprising is that while Osman depicted Mehmet II smelling a pink rose in one hand, following long-standing tradition (see cat. 4), the anonymous court painter represented him without a flower. The Dresden manuscript is likely one of the copies presented by Lokman to the grand viziers at the court.

The Islamic world inherited the study of physiognomy from Antiquity and invested it with special significance, finding validation for it in the Qu'ran.[1] Research into the character and physical appearance of past sultans played an important role in the preparation of the *Kitafetü'l-insaniye*. To complement the written and visual resources available at the Ottoman court, Grand Vizier Sokollu Mehmet Pasha made an appeal to the Venetian *bailo* Niccolò Barbarigo for sultan portraits from Italy. Because an entire series of painted portraits could not be found on the lagoon, Barbarigo commissioned a new one from his Veronese household painter (see cats. 35–38). Following their arrival in Istanbul in the fall of 1579, the Venetian portraits served as an important point of reference as the new illustrated history was being composed, although Osman remained true to his Ottoman aesthetic sensibilities and did not adopt any foreign conventions in his portraits the way the late 15th century painters did (see cats. 4 and 5).[2]

In this, and several other important instances, most notably during the reign of Mehmet II (see cats. 23, 116–17), the Ottoman court used its diplomatic ties with Venice to help fulfill a desire for sultan portraits. Equally important, Ottoman portraits did not fail to intrigue Western Europeans, as the Dresden example (cat. 9) illustrates so well. Shortly after its production, the

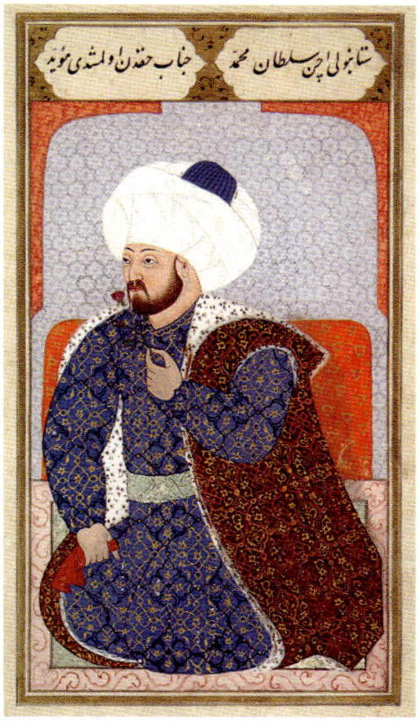

cat. 8

manuscript made its way to Eastern Europe, either through diplomacy or as war booty, and an anonymous European copied it in a manuscript preserved in the Österreichische National Bibliothek in Vienna (A. F. 59).[3] Now in Dresden, this manuscript is one of only five copies of the *Kitafetü'l-insaniye* known outside Istanbul (but see also cat. 10).[4] The original volume (cat. 8) and copies that remained in the Ottoman capital continued to inspire similar illustrated dynastic histories until the empire's end.

TK

1 Çağman 2000, pp. 165–70; Necipoğlu 2000a, pp.33–34.
2 Necipoğlu 2000a, pp. 38–39.
3 Illustrated in Istanbul 2000, p. 268, cat. 46.
4 For a complete list of known manuscripts, see Lokman 1987, pp. 13–14.

10. Seyyid Lokman, *Kitafetü'l-insaniye fi şema'ilü'l-osmaniye*

Probably Baghdad, Iraq, ca. 1595
Watercolor and gold on paper
23.3 x 14 cm (9 1/8 x 5 1/2 in.)
The Nasser D. Khalili Collection of Islamic Art, London
Inv. MSS 870 (ill. p. 111)

Like the two previous catalogue entries, this is an illustrated manuscript of the Ottoman dynastic history known as the *Kitafetü'l-insaniye*. Slightly later than the other two examples, this work dates to after Murad III's reign since it records the sultan as deceased and includes prayers for his successor, Mehmet III.[1] Another distinguishing characteristic of this manuscript is that it appears to have been produced not in the imperial atelier in Istanbul, but rather in a provincial center such as Baghdad (then part of the Ottoman Empire).[2] A grand vizier or other Ottoman statesman likely received this manuscript as a gift; for its original owner, such a glorious illustrated history would have been an important status symbol.[3]

Illustrated here (fol. 42v) is the manuscript's portrait of Mehmet II's son and successor, Bayezid II (r. 1481–1512), the eighth Ottoman sultan. As in many other *Kitafetü'l-insaniye* manuscripts, the sitter is dressed in green (complete with a green *taj*) and sits with one knee up.[4] Ottoman portraitists also consistently emphasized Bayezid II's long beard,[5] and in this instance the painter calls further attention to it by having the sitter tug at it with one hand. All of these features are indicative of Bayezid's extreme piety, reinforcing the accompaning text in Ottoman Turkish that describes him in that way.[6]

In striking contrast to his father, Bayezid II never developed an interest in portraiture, and may have been responsible for selling Gentile Bellini's *Portrait of Mehmet II* in the bazaar of Istanbul ca. 1500 (see cat. 23). Because of the dearth of portraits of him, after his death there was little record of Bayezid II's physical appearance. Extant portraits of him from the late 16th century therefore are usually generalized and emphasize outward signs of his spirituality instead.[7]

A useful comparison can be made between this likeness of Bayezid II and the earlier one in the Venetian portrait series now in Munich (cat. 37). The unknown artist from Verona represented the sultan in a yellow garment, in contrast to the Ottoman tradition, yet clearly knew of Bayezid II's style of facial hair. The painter most likely acquired that knowledge from Paolo Giovio, a man famous for his collection of sultan portraits at his house in Como, who characterized Bayezid II as wearing a long beard in the fashion of "the old Greeks."[8]

MAM / TK

1 Rogers 1995, p. 160, cat. 105.
2 Ibid.
3 Ibid.; Çağman 2000, pp. 178–80.
4 See, for example, Istanbul 2000, p. 166, 37h and p. 169.
5 Raby 2000a, p. 74.
6 Necipoğlu 2000a, p. 35.
7 Raby 2000a, pp. 73–74.
8 Ibid., p. 73.

11. *Album (muraqqa^c)*

Copied by Mir ^cAli Katib
Iran, second half of 16th century
Ink, gold and colors on paper glued on cardboard mounted in accordion format; cardboard binding
22.8 x 11.5 cm (9 x 4 1/2 in.)
Biblioteca Nazionale Marciana, Venice
Fondo G. Nani
Inv. Cod. Marc. Or. 94 (=64) (ill. p. 142)

This album composed of 17 folios, a collection of calligraphy and illustrations, is an example of a *muraqqa^c*. The term, which literally means "patched robe" in Arabic, has been applied to poetic anthologies since the 15th century, and refers to the cloaks worn by Sufi mystics or dervishes. Like these cloaks passed down as spiritual heirlooms, *muraqqa^c*s were treasured for generations. The metaphor also extends to the "patchwork" quality of these courtly books, whose contents were added at different moments in time.[1] This album combines the Persian verses known as the *Rub^cayyat* of Umar Khayyam, copied in *nasta'liq* script in the mid-16th century by the renowned calligrapher Mir ^cAli Katib, together with anonymous paintings executed about a century later.[2] Presented on marbleized paper with decorated margins and connected by an edge-to-edge accordion-style binding, the entire album can be unfolded and viewed in a continuous line.

Among the illustrations are four pages with two colored pictures (fols. 1, 2) and two pencil drawings (fols. 16, 17) executed in the distinctive style of late 16th- and early 17th-century Persia. Common to the style is the representation of figures in three-quarter views, their heads tilting slightly, and their bodies sinuous with bended knees. The first two figures are presented facing one another across the pages; their languid, curved bodies are enhanced with undulating and subtle lines. These do not represent specific persons, but rather are meant to complement the accompanying poetry; as mystical love is the main theme of the *Rub^cayyat*, the amorous young people are well suited to the verses. The great attention to the figures' luxurious clothing reveals a marked interest in contemporary fashion. Both wear maroon robes studded with gold buttons; the woman wears a gold and brown cape, while the man's robe is framed with a red collar that reveals a green undershirt.

Also contained within this album is the figure of a woman dressed in European clothes (fol. 16), revealing the continuous contacts between Europe and the Islamic Safavid court. The finest illustration (fol. 17) represents a drinking scene with two men sitting in a sparsely indicated landscape amidst gold Chinese clouds. This pictorial style developed in the second half of the 16th century with well-known artists such as Sadiqi and Mirza ^cAli, but the undisputed master of this kind of portrait was Riza-i ^cAbbasi, the famous court artist of Shah ^cAbbas I in Isfahan, active from the end of the 16th century through the first half of the 17th century.[3]

MAM

1 Roxburgh 2005a, p. 188.
2 Venice 1993, pp. 443–44, cat. 291.
3 Welch 1976.

12. Nizami *Khamsa* (Quintet)

Shiraz, Iran, AH 1034 / AD 1624–25
Ink, colors and gold on paper; tooled leather binding
27 x 15.5 cm (10 1/2 x 6 1/8 in.)
Fondazione Giorgio Cini, Venice
Inv. Stanza del Tesoro, 23 (ill. p. 143)

This manuscript is an illustrated copy of the popular *Khamsa* of Nizami al-Ganjavi (1141–1204).[1] The colophon states that the manuscript was copied by Muhammad Husayn Dar al-Marzi, a *qadi* (jurist) from Gilan (in northern Iran), in the scriptorium of Lutfallah Mudhahhib Nadir al-Asri in Shiraz.[2] The date on the colophon, AH 1039 / AD 1624–25, suggests that it was produced at the end of the long reign of the Safavid Shah ^cAbbas I (1588–1629), one of the high points in Persian art.

The manuscript, clearly a luxury production, includes all five books of Nizami's text with over 300 folios, 22 full-page paintings, and illuminated borders; the leather binding is probably not original. The text is arranged in four columns and is written in small *nasta^cliq* script. Each of the five books opens with lavish double-page illuminations and headings against a gold background. The double-page frontispiece shows a festive open-air court scene with a seated ruler surrounded by attendants, musicians, food-carriers, two Europeans, a rifle-bearer, and a falconer. The double-page finispiece shows a hunting scene on one side with cheetahs, antelopes, and rabbits, and on the other, a presentation of the game to a seated ruler. Within the manuscript, the paintings are unevenly distributed so that the sections on Khusrau and Shirin, Layli and Majnun, Bahram Gur and the seven princesses (*Haft Paykar*), and Alexander (*Iskandarnama*) have three, two, eight, and five illustrations, respectively. The manuscript also includes a painting of the Night Journey of the Prophet Muhammad (*mi^craj*).

It is unclear how this copy of the *Khamsa* came into the collection of Vittorio Cini (1885–1977), a Ferrara-born entrepreneur and politician, but is one of the finest examples of Persian art in Venetian collections.

QA

1 Speziale 2005.
2 Ibid,, p. 10.

13. *Fogge diverse di vestire de' Turchi (Diverse dressing habits of the Turks)*

Turkey, probably Istanbul, 17th century
Ink, gold, and colors on paper; cardboard binding
24 x 18 cm (9 1/2 x 7 in.)
Biblioteca Nazionale Marciana, Venice
Inv. Cod. It. IV, 491 (5578) (ill. pp. 114–15)

During the second half of the 16th century in Europe, costume books emerged as a popular new genre, reflecting a greater curiosity about foreign cultures derived from travels and new discoveries. Venice and the Veneto, where at least nine examples were published between 1540 and 1610, played a leading role in the costume book's early development.[1] The most famous and important Venetian work is Cesare Vecellio's *Degli abiti antichi et moderni di diverse parti del mondo* of 1590, which became a model of the genre with its over 500 illustrations and special attention to Venetian and Ottoman dress (cat. 63).

Costume books also started to be produced in Ottoman Turkey in the late 15th century, probably after the earliest European models and perhaps even initially illustrated by Western foreigners living in Istanbul.[2] In the 17th century, these codices can be best defined as "bazaar books" because they were not illustrated in the imperial atelier and were popularly sold in the markets of the Ottoman capital. They share with their European counterparts the general format of the illustration, that is, a full-size figure against a plain or nominal background. Unlike them, however, the interest is not anthropologic in order to distinguish different peoples and their habits—specifically focusing on what they wear—since Ottoman "fashion" books rarely depict foreigners. Flipping through their pages, one can enjoy a varied landscape of different social strata of the Ottoman world and their activities, from the sultan all the way down to the barber, the butcher, and the water-seller through the various individuals in the service of the court, such as the chief eunuch, the ceremonies attendant, and soldiers of diverse ranks. It is unclear whether these illustrated books were mostly made for export, providing an instant panorama and categorization of the Ottoman society for a foreign eye,[3] but it may be inferred that they also served a more local purpose within the Turkish upper class, offering a better understanding of their role in society.

The present book (which found its way to the Marciana Library in 1843 through the gift of the 19th-century patrician Girolamo Contarini), is a good example of Ottoman "fashion" books, and with its captions in Italian is most likely representative of the export production of these works. Its 62 miniatures pasted on support pages, one on the recto of each page following the Western format, illustrate six sultans and one sultana, about 20 employees associated with the court, 20 different ranks of officers or soldiers, more than 10 city employees, and the genre scene of a Turkish woman leaving the *hammam* (public bath), thus providing important testimony of daily life in the Ottoman Empire during the 17th century.[4] The "*Attendente all'incanto*" (literally "He who is charge of the auction," better described as a peddler), selling clothes and a pillow and carrying a candlestick on his head, is a particularly endearing illustration of the variegated population of Istanbul's streets.

MAM / SC

1 Wilson 2005, p. 70.
2 Fenerci 1986, pp. 13, 15–30.
3 The Venetian merchant Carlo Helman, for example, owned a manuscript defined in his inventory as *Libro alla Turchesca con Effigie de Turchi*; see Thornton 1997, p. 78.
4 The complete list of the illustrations in is Venice 1993, pp. 412–14, cat. 266.

•14. *Zodiac Man*

Iran, 18th–19th century
Ink and watercolor on paper
31.3 x 21.2 cm (12 3/8 x 8 3/8 in.)
Wellcome Library, London
Inv. IC 582971i (ill. p. 69)

The Islamic image of the zodiac man derives from the ancient Greek tradition that assigns an astrological sign to a specific part of the human body. Aries (the Ram) protects the head; Taurus (the Bull) the neck, shoulders, and throat; Gemini (the Twins) the arms and hands; Cancer (the Crab) the stomach; Virgo (the Virgin) the intestine and diaphragm; Leo (the Lion) the heart; Libra (the Scale) the spine and urogenital system; Scorpio (the Scorpion) the genitals; Sagittarius (the Archer) the thighs; Capricorn (the Kid) the knees; Aquarius (the Water Pourer) the calves; and Pisces (the Two Fish) the feet.[1] In Islamic art, the 12 zodiacal signs sometimes vary from the canonical Greek representations and are usually represented with their planetary lords. Virgo is not a winged woman but a young male farmer (the planet Mercury) holding an ear of corn, following the meaning of the Arabic name of the sign, *sunbula*. Gemini is transformed into Siamese twins with one body and two heads. Leo is painted with the Sun, represented with a circular human face, rising from behind its body, while Sagittarius's tail has an open-mouth dragonhead at its tip.[2]

This colored drawing is a late example of the Islamic zodiac man, whose image first developed in the medieval period. Its iconography, which influenced representations of the zodiac man in Renaissance Venetian printed books such as the *Fascicolo di Medicina* (cat. 57, where a more detailed description of the medical use of the zodiac man can be found), follows texts by celebrated Muslim astrologers such as Abu Maʿshar al Balkhi (9th century, see cat. 2) and al-Biruni (973–1048) although no works survive from these early times.

RM

1 Gyselen 1999, p. 20.
2 Carboni 1997.

°15. Johannes
"Marco Polo's Departure from Venice"

Marco Polo, *Li Livres du Graunt Caam*
England, ca. 1400–10
Tempera and gold on parchment
41.5 x 30 cm (16 x 12 in.)
The Bodleian Library, University of Oxford
Inv. MS Bodley 264 (ill. p. 58)

This well-known and often reproduced miniature introduces one the finest manuscript versions of Marco Polo's *Travels*, written in French prose and described as "*li livre du graunt Caam,*" "The Book of the Great Khan."[1] The illumination, which takes up half the length of the page, shows a bird's-eye view of Venice with three consecutive stages of Marco Polo's departure for China, the land of the Great Khan, in the company of his father Niccolò and uncle Maffeo. Along the way, Marco Polo passed through many Islamic lands, most notably Persia and one of the most fascinating passages in his travel narrative describes his role as escort of a Mongol princess bride to her groom, the great Ilkhanid ruler Ghazan, in Persia.[2]

On the left of this image are the artist's versions of some of the principal monuments of the city: Piazza San Marco with St. Mark's Basilica and the four bronze horses; the nearby Doge's Palace; and the famous pillars with St. Teodoro and the winged lion of St. Mark. To the right of the middle ground, Marco Polo, dressed in pale pink merchant attire, is shown leading his two companions and a group of dignitaries towards the docks, along the Riva degli Schiavoni; further below, they board a small boat that will take them to the galley anchored in the Venetian lagoon. Marco Polo is depicted again in the lower right, sailing away in his ship. Genre scenes enliven the illumination, such as the women buying meat from the butcher's shop in the piazzetta of San Marco and a vendor selling eggs between the two pillars. These picturesque details of everyday life are complemented by the insertion, in the lower left, of an imaginative assortment of wildlife—a leopard, a bear, two lions, ducks, and geese—which are perhaps meant to indicate the exotic, unexplored regions towards which the Polos were headed.[3]

Known in Italian as *Il Milione* (A Million, meaning a "thousand-thousand marvels") Marco Polo's legendary account of his remarkable journey across the Middle East and Asia to the Mongol court in China—where he was to remain for 17 years, from 1275 to 1292—is known today in about 150 medieval manuscript versions, datable from the early 14th to the 15th centuries.[4] These are presumed to be based on a lost original, composed sometime after Marco's return to Venice in 1295; he purportedly dictated his account to fellow convict and author of chivalric poetry, Rustichello da Pisa, while in a Genoese prison. Rustichello's text, written in French or Franco-Italian, enjoyed immediate success and within the first 20 years of its existence it appeared in Tuscan, Venetian, German, and Latin translations, as well as in French prose. The range of descriptions or titles given to the various adaptations, such as *Il Milione, Livre de marveilles* (Book of Wonders), *Livre du Graunt Caam* (Book of the Great Khan), and *Description of the World*, reflects the various perceptions of this work as both a book of marvels and a geographic and ethnographic guide to the East. In the words of one noted scholar, it "told bewildered rather than incredulous contemporaries about the immensely varied life of man and nature in those vast Eastern regions of which he offered the first empirical description to a West long desirous of knowing its secrets and wonders."[5]

The Bodley Marco Polo (fols. 218–71v) is one of two texts that were appended, at an unknown date in the early 15th century, to a 14th-century Flemish manuscript of various Alexander romances (fols. 3–208) and to a Middle-English version of the romance *Alexander and Dindimus* (fols. 209–15v). The manuscript is first recorded, without the additions, in the library of Edward III's youngest son, Thomas, Duke of Gloucester (d. 1397). In 1466, according to an inscription on fol. 274, it was purchased in its present state by Richard Wydevill, Lord Rivers, father-in-law of Edward IV. On this basis Consuelo Dutchke has argued persuasively that the luxuriously produced codex must have belonged to an immediate member of the court circle, who probably commissioned the insertion of the Marco Polo text sometime in the first decade of the 15th century—a dating suggested by the style of the accompanying illuminations.[6]

The decoration of the *Travels* has been attributed to a team of English illuminators, headed by the artist who executed the Venice frontispiece and who signed himself "Johannes" (*Johannes me fecit*), on the Khan's robe in the miniature on fol. 220.[7] While capturing the essential character of the city, with its waterways, bridges, and canals, his view of Venice presents a fanciful reconstruction of its principal sites and monuments in terms of a distinctly English, late-Gothic architectural vocabulary, combined with an imaginative interpretation of their Byzantine-derived elements. Although St. Mark's Basilica is instantly recognizable by the inclusion of the four bronze horses, its structure has little to do with the actual building, whose famous domes have been replaced with the Oriental-looking towers typical of medieval depictions of the East. Similarly the nearby Doge's Palace—with its multiple turrets and hanging balconies—has been reinvented, in accordance with the artist's own experience, as the residence of a feudal lord or prince.

We may presume that Johannes never actually visited Venice but rather drew inspiration from pilgrims' and other travelers' written or verbal descriptions of the city, accounts that perhaps recalled its wonders in the same terms as the marvels of Marco Polo's *Travels*.

PP

1 The full text of the rubric located directly below the miniature reads: "Here begins the Book of the Great Khan which speaks of Great Armenia, of Persia, and of the Tartars, and of India, and of the great Marvels which are in the world."
2 Rossabi 2002, p. 33.
3 In what remains the most comprehensive discussion of this illumination to date, Leonardo Olschki (Olschki 1937, p. 226) points out that the lions might allude to the motto *"hic sunt leones"* ("here are the lions") that appears on medieval maps and nautical charts to indicate the limits of the known or inhabited world.
4 Larner 1999, p. 106.
5 Olschki 1960, p. 2. See also Larner 1999, pp. 106–7.
6 Dutschke 1998, pp. 278–300. Based on textual comparisons, Dutschke is able to establish that the Bodley text of the *Travels* was copied from a 14th-century French manuscript, illuminated in Paris, now in the British Library (Royal 19 D.I), which may have reached England through royal connections.
7 For a full discussion of the division of hands see Scott 1996, pp. 68–73.

16. Leonardo Bellini
"Ptolemy presents his text to a ruler"

Ptolemy, *Cosmographia* (Latin translation by Jacopo d'Angelo), fol. 1
Venice, ca. 1470–75
Tempera and gold on parchment
28.9 x 22.2 (11 3/8 x 8 3/4 in.)
The Provost and Fellows of Eton College, Windsor
Inv. Eton MS 140

Undoubtedly one of the most important events of the early Renaissance was the translation into Latin of Ptolemy's *Geography*. In this text, the famous Greek astronomer and mathematician, active in Alexandria in the 2nd century BC, had laid down the foundations for modern cartography by providing a guide for mapping the then known world based on solid mathematical principles that incorporated, for the first time, the notions of longitude and latitude. Although the *Geography* was translated into Arabic in the 9th century, the Greek text seemed to have disappeared, until a single manuscript was discovered around 1300 in Constantinople. In 1397 a copy of it was brought to Florence by the noted Greek scholar Manuel Chrysoloras (d. 1415), who had been called there to teach and where one of his former students, the apostolic secretary Jacopo d'Angelo da Scarperia (ca. 1360–1410/11), completed his Latin translation around 1409. In the introduction to his Latin text, Jacopo noted that Chrysoloras had translated the Greek title as *Geographia*, but that he would translate it as *Cosmographia*, the name by which the work would be commonly known for the next century.[1]

Jacopo's *Cosmographia* immediately enjoyed a wide diffusion in humanist circles across Italy, often accompanied by luxuriously produced maps and tables. The Eton manuscript, which has no maps, contains only a large introductory miniature and decorative initials at the beginning of each of the eight books, or chapters. The miniature, extending across the page, depicts the fictitious episode of Ptolemy's presentation of his text to an unidentified Muslim ruler, presumably meant to represent the king of Egypt. The king, seated on an elaborately carved, golden throne, is shown leaning forward to accept the volume from the hands of Ptolemy, who kneels before him and holds an astrolabe in his

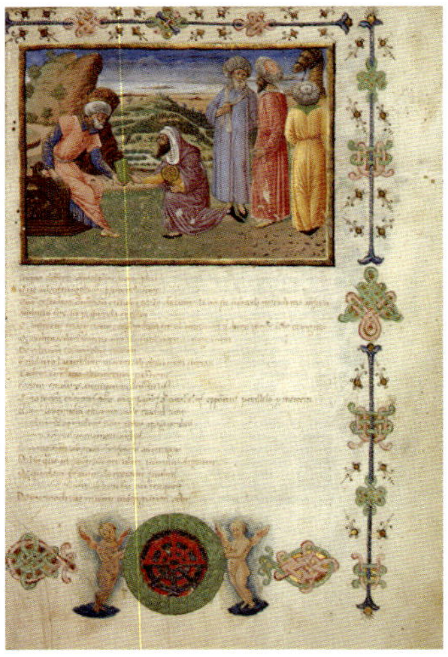

cat. 16

left hand. The exotic setting of this imaginary event is emphasized by the three turbaned figures in attendance behind Ptolemy, one of whom, viewed from the back, appears to be minding a camel. A coat of arms held by two standing putti, at the bottom of the page, identifies the owners of the manuscript as a branch of the prominent Molin family of Venice, with ties to the Venetian colonies in the Levant.[2]

The illuminator of the Eton codex was convincingly identified by Jonathan Alexander as Leonardo Bellini (ca. 1423/25–1490), cousin of the better-known painters Giovanni and Gentile Bellini, and the dominant miniaturist in Venice between 1460 and 1480.[3] The volume's decoration, dated by Alexander to the 1470s, may be compared, more specifically, to the miniatures contributed by the artist, at the beginning of this decade, to prestigious official documents for the city's ruling elite, such as the 1473 *Promissione* of Niccolò Marcello[4] or the *Giuramento* of Andrea Lion, procurator of San Marco, from the same year.[5]

Trained in the workshop of his uncle, Jacopo Bellini, Leonardo developed a personal style that combines figural and compositional elements derived from the Bellini workshop with the decorative idiom of contemporary Ferrarese illumination. In the present case, the scene of Ptolemy's donation appears loosely modeled on the frontispiece in the famous copy of Strabo's *Geography* that was sent by the Venetian condottiere Jacopo Antonio Marcello as a gift to King René of Anjou[6] in 1459—a work most recently attributed to the young Giovanni Bellini.[7] Similarly, the hooded dress and bearded profile of Ptolemy in the Eton miniature—which departs from other contemporary images of the scholar as king—are, coincidentally, strongly reminiscent of the various portraits painted by Gentile Bellini of the erudite Greek Cardinal Bessarion as a monk of St. Basil.[8]

PP

1 For an excellent summary of the text and its versions see Swerdlow 1993.
2 Citing Rietstap's work as a reference (Rietstap 1903–26) the arms were identified by Ker (Ker 1977, p. 759) as those of the Molin of Rovigo. However, according to Di Crollalanza (1888) the same arms belonged to a branch of the Molin, originally from Acre in Syria, who had settled in Venice in the 13th century. The two branches residing in Venice are also discussed by Spallanzani (1985).
3 Alexander 1969, pp. 9–20. On Leonardo Bellini, see most recently Marcon 2004.
4 Venice, Biblioteca del Museo Civico Correr, cod. CL.III, 322.
5 Venice, Biblioteca Nazionale Marciana, ms.Lat. X, 358 [= 3571].
6 Albi, Bibliothèque Rochegude, MS 4.
7 For the debates surrounding the attribution of the Albi Strabo, see most recently: Armstrong 1994, pp. 87–90, which lists the illuminations as "Circle of Jacopo Bellini (Giovanni Bellini?)." The attribution to the young Giovanni Bellini has been tentatively reiterated by Giordana Mariani Canova (Canova 2003a, p. 259).
8 For the iconography of Ptolemy as King of Egypt see Derenzini 1996.

17. Girolamo da Cremona and Assistants
"Aristotle lecturing Averroës"

Aristotle, *Works* (with *Commentary* of Averroës and *Isagoge* of Porphyry), fol. 1
Venice, 1483
Tempera and gold on parchment
40.9 x 27.2 cm (16 1/8 x 10 3/4 in.)
The Pierpont Morgan Library, New York
Purchased by J. P. Morgan Jr., 1919
Inv. PML 21194 (ill. p. 165)

This splendidly illuminated book, opening with the text of the *Physics,* is the first part of a two-volume, printed Latin edition of Aristotle's *Works,* with the commentary of Averroës (ca. 1126–98), that was published in Venice in 1483 by Andreas Torresanus and Bartholomeus de Blavis. The second volume, beginning with the *Metaphysics,* is also in the Pierpont Morgan Library (PML 21195). The two volumes introduced a new Latin edition of the complete works of Aristotle, compiled by the renowned scholar and leading Averroist at the University of Padua, Nicoletto Vernia (1420–99). As stated by the inscription in the lower border of the *Physics* frontispiece—*VLMER ARISTOTILEM PETRVS PRODVXE[R]AT ORBI* ("Peter Ugelheimer has brought [this] Aristotle forth to the world")—the publication was commissioned, and probably financed, by Peter Ugelheimer of Frankfurt, a wealthy German banker and book collector, residing in Venice. Ugelheimer owned some shares in the famous printing workshop run by Nicola Jenson, which after the latter's death, in 1480, had passed on to Torresanus.[1] The Morgan Library Aristotle belongs to a series of lavishly produced, deluxe editions of philosophical and juridical texts printed in Venice between 1477 and 1483, which were decorated for Ugelheimer by some of the greatest illuminators then active in the city.[2]

The remarkable frontispieces at the beginning of each of the Morgan Library volumes constitute the last known masterpieces of Girolamo da Cremona (active 1460–83), the most exquisite and sought-after Italian miniature painter of the second half of the 15th century.[3] Though probably trained by Mantegna in Padua, Girolamo is first documented at the Este court in Ferrara, then at the Gonzaga court in Mantua, and later as being entrusted with major commissions in Padua, Siena, and Florence. In 1474/75 he returned north, to Venice, where the newly introduced art of printing and the growing demand for luxurious, hand-decorated editions offered a great many opportunities. Girolamo's Mantegnesque, classically inspired vocabulary, rendered precious by the addition of realistically painted jewelry, gems, and pearls, was eminently suited to the antiquarian tastes of the wealthy, erudite patrons for whom these ancient Greek texts were being translated and edited.[4]

In the frontispiece to the present volume, Girolamo created his own brilliant version of the so-called "architectural frontispiece," a type first developed in the Veneto, in which classical architectural elements are combined with the illusionistic device of the torn parchment leaf.[5] In this case, the actual page is made to appear torn around the edges to reveal the two worlds behind the ancient text. Visible through an opening at the top is the more tangible realm of the author, Aristotle, who is shown seated in a landscape, dressed in "modern" Greek dress, in the act of lecturing his Arab commentator, Averroës, identified by a turban. In the border below is the other, mythical world of Antiquity, populated by satyrs and putti engaged in various interactions before a golden bronze monument. Several of the motifs, such as the satyr with the basket on his head, are loosely modeled on famous examples of classical sculpture. Hanging from red strings tied through holes in the parchment, on each side and between the two columns of text, are clusters of precious jewels, with cameos encased amid translucent stones and pearls.

PP

1 Ugelheimer's coat of arms appears in one of the painted initials near the end of the second volume (fol. 55). See Armstrong 1994, pp. 204-05.
2 Three of these incunabula are now at the Koninglijke Bibliothek in The Hague (inc. 169 D 1-3), and four are in the Landesbibliothek in Gotha (MSS Mon. Typ. 1477, 2 [12–13]; Mon. Typ. 1479, 2 [4]; Mon. Typ. 1481, 2 [10]). See Toniolo 2003, pp. 264–65.
3 The attribution to Girolamo, now unanimously accepted by scholars, was first advanced by Mirella Levi d'Ancona (Levi d'Ancona 1964), followed by Giordana Mariani Canova in her fundamental study of Venetian Renaissance illumination (Canova 1969, pp. 58–62). For a complete biography and summary of the vast literature on the artist, see Toniolo 2004.
4 Canova 2003a, pp. 258–60.
5 For the development of this motif, first reflected in the work of the so-called Master of the Putti, see Armstrong 1994a, p. 42.

PAINTINGS

18. Stefano Veneziano (active 1369–85)
Madonna and Child Enthroned

Venice, 1369
Tempera and gold on panel
82 x 52 cm (32 1/4 x 20 1/2 in.)
Museo Civico Correr, Venice
Inv. Cl. I n. 2 (ill. p. 33)

The earliest of several works signed and dated by the mid-14th-century Venetian painter Stefano "Plebanus" di Sant'Agnese, or Stefano Veneziano, this *Madonna and Child Enthroned* most likely constituted the central panel of a much larger altarpiece.[1] As is typical of his oeuvre, the artist imbues the figures with majesty and grace while also emphasizing their humanity. The Virgin offers a pink rose in full bloom, a sign of the Passion, to her young son, who opens his hands to receive it.

Stefano Veneziano worked in the tradition established earlier in the Trecento by Paolo Veneziano (active 1324 to 1358), whose triptych with the Madonna and Child in the Louvre and *Madonna and Child with Four Angels* in Carpineta have been identified as archetypes for this panel.[2] Stefano Veneziano, however, introduced a more elaborately ornamented throne and figures with greater solidity and weight.

Religious paintings in which the holy figures are dressed in luxurious costumes offer some of the best evidence for the kinds of Near and Far Eastern fabrics known in Venice during the 14th century, even if painters often freely interpreted textile designs rather than copying them precisely.[3] In Stefano Veneziano's painting, the Virgin and Child wear silks lavishly ornamented with gold threads like those that were making their way to Italy from central Asia via Persia and Syria during the *Pax Mongolica.*[4] Known as *panni tartarici,* these sumptuous foreign fabrics have been discovered in the 14th-century tomb of Cangrande della Scala in Verona (see cat. 68), but could be found in other areas of Italy in this period as well.[5] Trecento Tuscan painters in particular often represented Islamic textiles, but only in Venice,[6] which had especially strong political and commercial ties to the Near East, did this evolve in subsequent centuries into a more profound interest in depicting Islamic figures, costumes, and settings.

The decoration of the wooden throne is also of great interest. Stefano Veneziano painted it to look as if it had been lacquered with red varnish and ornamented with gilded arabesques and ivory inserts, which suggests that Islamic-inspired lacquered furniture may have already been present in Venice in the mid-14th century.[7]

TK

1 Mariacher 1957, p. 216; Romanelli 1985, pp. 49–50; d'Arcais 1992, pp. 71–72.

2 D'Arcais 1992.
3 Hoeniger 1992; Mack 2002, pp. 34–38.
4 Mack 2002, pp. 35–38.
5 Magagnato 1983; Wardwell 1989; Verona 2004.
6 Kleese 1967.
7 On the throne, see also Thornton 1991, p. 98, no. 97. For more on Venetian lacquer, see the essays by Grube and Rizzo in this volume.

19. Michele Giambono (1400–1462) *Madonna and Child*

Venice, ca. 1450
Tempera and gold on panel
57 x 39 cm (23 1/4 x 15 3/8 in)
Inscription: MICHAEL IOHANNIS BONO VENETUS PINXIT
Galleria Nazionale d'Arte Antica di Palazzo Barberini, Rome
Inv. 1660

Iconic images of the half-length Madonna enjoyed enormous popularity in Venice during the Quattrocento,[1] and those painted by Michele Giambono in the first half of the century epitomize the courtly elegance and grace of the International Gothic Style.[2] Inscribed in Latin with the artist's name on the stone parapet, this example now in the Palazzo Barberini in Rome is among the finest and best preserved of Giambono's surviving works.[3]

Unlike the Trecento painter Stefano Veneziano, who clothed the Madonna and Child in intricately patterned garments (see cat. 18), Giambono dressed the holy figures in solid colors, saving the bold pattern for the cloth of honor behind them. Sharply silhouetted against the brocaded textile, Giambono's Virgin and Child assume a three-dimensional presence reminiscent of northern European *Schönen Madonnen* statues of the same period. The extension of the Virgin's garment beyond the parapet, into the viewer's space, further emphasizes the physicality of the figures.

The sorrowful expression and angular features of the Virgin contrast with the round-faced Christ Child who reacts joyfully to the goldfinch, whose presence serves as a premonition of the Passion. Amplifying the theme of Christ's future sacrifice is the sumptuous velvet in the background with large lobate palmettes containing pomegranates, a fruit closely associated with his blood, death, and resurrection.[4] In the 15th century costly imported textiles from the Ottoman Empire and elsewhere in the Islamic world introduced this kind of pomegranate design to Italy, where it immediately became widespread in ecclesiastical and courtly settings.[5] Giambono is among the earliest Italian painters to exploit the iconographic meaning of these textiles in the Christian context. With incredible veracity, he simulates the appearance of dark orange velvet pile set against a luxurious gold satin ground.

Shortly after the arrival in Venice of textiles with pomegranate designs from the Near East, local weavers began producing imitations and thus it is unclear whether the fabric Giambono depicted is Islamic or Venetian.[6] As part of the back and forth of Mediterranean trade, the Venetian versions eventually became sought after in the Near East, as the 16th-century kaftan in this exhibition demonstrates (cat. 80).

TK

1 On the half-length Madonna in Venice, see Goffen 1975; Pächt 2003, pp. 26–37, 157–70.
2 Romanelli 1985, pp. 52–54.
3 For the most recent assessments of Giambono's career, see Land 1974; Pesaro 1992; Franco 1998. On the condition of this painting, see Bernini 1988, pp. 92–97.
4 Bonito Fanelli 1994, pp. 53–54.
5 Bonito Fanelli 1981; Mack 2002, p. 47.
6 On the production of patterned velvets in 15th-century Venice, see Bonito Fanelli 1981, p. 49.

20. Antonio Vivarini (ca. 1419–ca. 1480) *St. Peter Martyr Attempting to Burn His Cloak*

Venice, ca. 1440–50
Oil and tempera on panel
52 x 34 cm (21 1/4 x 13 3/8 in.)
Staatliche Museen zu Berlin-Preussischer Kulturbesitz, Gemäldegalerie, Berlin
Inv. 66 (ill. p. 262)

Antonio Vivarini, the son of a glassmaker from Murano, operated a workshop of painters second in importance in early Renaissance Venice only to that of Jacopo Bellini. Both in collaboration with his partners and independently, Vivarini created narrative altarpieces depicting the lives and miracles of saints in an engaging, colorful style.[1] This small panel belongs to one such altarpiece by Vivarini dedicated to Peter Martyr. Six other fragments from the same polyptych survive and are now dispersed in American and European collections.[2] The original location of the work remains unknown, but it most likely comes from a Dominican foundation in or around Venice.[3] Born in Verona, Peter Martyr (1205–1252; canonized 1253) traveled throughout Italy preaching and performing many miracles, including a trial by fire. The saint demonstrated that his Dominican cloak would not burn, even when placed directly upon the flames, to a heretical young man from the northern Italian city of Como, thereby converting him.[4]

Vivarini offers a distinctive interpretation of the story in this panel, for which he may have relied on a local apocryphal account. The Italian youth, depicted in a red coat and a blue and yellow hat, plays a surprisingly marginal role in the composition, standing behind the haloed saint in the white tunic on the right. The composition is balanced by the group of witnesses to the left of the fire wearing Muslim costumes. Acknowledging the saint's miracle with animated gestures, they represent the non-believers converted by Peter Martyr.

Vivarini took great pains to depict Muslim dress, and in particular the headgear, that plays such a crucial role in his visual narrative. Two of the men are crowned with round, white turbans with both vertical and horizontal folds, the veracity of which can be confirmed through comparisons of Mamluk works of art, such as illustrations of the famous 14th-century *Maqamat* of al-Hariri in the Nationalbibliothek, Vienna (MS A.F. 9). The most prominent Muslim figure in Vivarini's painting, the elderly man with a white beard in the immediate foreground on the left, wears a conical helmet atop his turban. Two other figures standing behind Peter Martyr have similar headgear. Examples of Mamluk helmets with this elegant peaked shape from the 14th and 15th centuries survive in modern museum collections.[5]

Vivarini's painting comes on the heels of Pisanello's famous depictions of Byzantine Greeks, which first fueled an interest in Italy in exotic Eastern dress.[6] The specific sources of Vivarini's knowledge of Mamluk costume remain unknown, but he seems to be one of the earliest Venetian artists to depict it. Indeed, this painting dates several decades earlier than the period when Gentile Bellini and his followers began portraying Muslim figures in their work.

TK

1 The standard study of this family of painters remains Pallucchini 1961.
2 On the other surviving panels, see Pallucchini 1961, pp. 97–98; Zeri 1973, pp. 88–90.
3 For a review of the theories of the provenance of this altarpiece, see Salinger 1938 and more recently Lloyd 1993.
4 Kaftal 1978, pp. 84–85.
5 Mayer 1952, pp. 41–43, pls. VII and VIII; Atıl 1981, pp. 112–13, cat. 41. The Ottomans later adopted this type of helmet as well.
6 Raby 1982, p. 18.

21. Attributed to Lazzaro Bastiani (b. Venice; fl. 1449; d. 1512) *Portrait of Doge Francesco Foscari*

Venice, ca. 1457–60 or mid- to late 1470s
Tempera on panel
52 x 41 cm (20 1/2 x 16 1/8 in.)
Museo Civico Correr, Venice
Inv. Cl. I n. 14 (ill. p. 189)

The distinctive costume of the sitter—comprising a cape with oversized gold buttons and a horned cap known as the *corno* set on top of a white linen coif—renders him immediately recognizable as the doge of Venice, the elected leader of the city's republican oligarchy.[1] This corpulent man with a bullish neck and pronounced bags and crows' feet around his eyes has been identified as Francesco Foscari (1373–1457), whose reign from 1423 to 1457 was the longest of any doge in Venetian history.[2] Controversial from the moment of his election, Foscari was eventually forced to abdicate, and he died just eight days later. During his dogate, he focused Venice's military resources on protecting the city from Genoa and Milan, and the fall of Byzantium to the Turks in 1453 has often been blamed on his preoccupation with the West and indifference towards the East.[3]

Set against a plain, dark background, Foscari's portrait hints at nothing of his contentious personality or the momentous events of his reign, for its function was to depict the doge with timeless dignity and authority. His bust-length profile fills the field like an ancient Roman emperor on a coin. This painting is one of a handful of Venetian dogal portraits of this small format and medium to survive from the 15th century (see also cat. 22).[4] All have been attributed at one time or another to Gentile Bellini, whose role as official painter to the Republic required him to paint portraits of the doges for display in the council chambers of the Palazzo Ducale.[5] Like the great historical narratives that he also made for the palace, Gentile's portraits were destroyed in the great fire of 1577. Extant likenesses of doges like this one of Francesco Foscari may be copies of the Palazzo Ducale portraits made for the homes of the ducal families.[6] Venetian painters other than Gentile could have reproduced the likenesses, and in this case Foscari's portrait is now most satisfactorily attributed to Bellini's contemporary Lazzaro Bastiani.[7] The date of this picture, however, is still a matter of debate, with scholars assigning it either to the late 1450s (during or immediately following Foscari's reign) or the mid-to late 1470s (after Gentile Bellini's appointment as Official Painter to the Republic).

Befitting their status, the doges of Venice always wore conspicuously luxurious fabrics in crimson, scarlet, white, or gold.[8] In this portrait, Foscari's cape and *corno* are cut from the same deep red voided velvet on a silk ground with gold thread. The bold, oversized floral pattern, also seen on actual 15th-century Venetian velvets (see cat. 78), is reminiscent of Ottoman velvets imported to the lagoon in the same period (see Denny's essay in this volume). In the painting's original state, when its surface glazes were still intact, the weave, texture, dye, pattern, and weight of the doge's costume would have been more readily visible for the viewer to admire.[9]

TK

1 Newton 1988, pp. 26–27.
2 For other representations of Foscari, with which this portrait compares favorably, see Meyer zur Capellen 1985, figs. 147–53.
3 Trevor-Roper 1961; Gullino 1997, pp. 306–14.
4 For this group of 15th-century dogal portraits, see Pignatti 1953; Meyer zur Capellen 1981 and 1985, pp. 55–69, 125, 130–34, 139, 176–87.
5 On Gentile as official painter of the Republic, a post he assumed in 1474, see Collins 1970, pp. 8–12.
6 Huse and Wolters 1990, pp. 204–5. For the

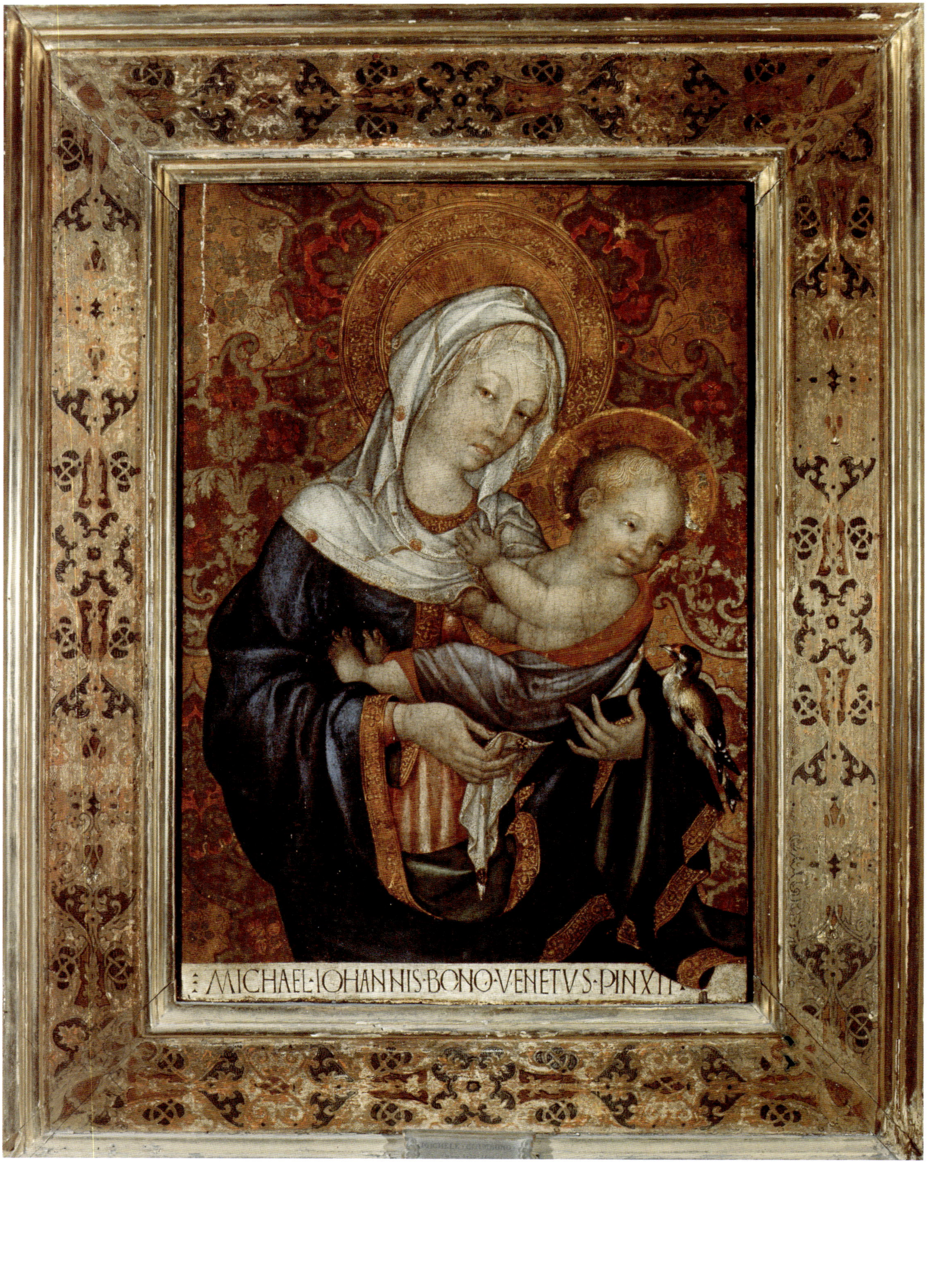

cat. 19

esteem in which Renaissance patrons held copies of important portraits, see Brandt 2003, p. 376. In general, Giorgio Vasari reports that in his day noble Venetian homes were "chockfull" of these portraits.
7 For a history of attributions, see Meyer zur Capellen 1985, p. 176.
8 Newton 1988, pp. 18, 26; Hills 1999, p. 176. Scarlet, a more somber red than crimson, was reserved for mourning.
9 For an excellent discussion of Venetian appreciation for the qualities of luxury fabrics, see Hills 1999, pp. 173–99.

22. Gentile Bellini (1429–1507) *Portrait of Doge Giovanni Mocenigo*

1478/79 or 1481–85
Tempera on panel
62 x 45 cm (24 3/8 x 17 3/4 in.)
Museo Civico Correr, Venice
Inv. Cl. I. n. 16 (ill. p. 136)

The powerful and wealthy Mocenigo family spawned no fewer than six Venetian doges in the Renaissance. This head and shoulders profile portrait depicts Doge Giovanni Mocenigo (1408–1485), who reigned from 1478 to 1485. Two other contemporary painted likenesses of him are known: a votive portrait in the *Madonna and Child Enthroned with Sts. John the Baptist and Christopher* in the National Gallery, London,[1] and another profile portrait in the Frick Collection, New York.[2] In all three cases, the doge wears a luxurious ermine mantle, further embellishing his already sumptuous official dress.[3] In the Correr portrait, the dogal cape and *corno* are made from a cloth of gold, the most rarified and costly fabric, with a raised pomegranate pattern.[4] The gilded background of the picture adds even greater luster to the image.

Like Francesco Foscari's portrait (cat. 21), this work was likely a copy, made for the doge's family, of his now lost Palazzo Ducale portrait. While the former is now attributed to Lazzaro Bastiani, Mocenigo's work has retained its status as an autograph portrait of the renowned 15th-century Venetian painter Gentile Bellini.[5] It remains unclear whether Gentile painted it before or after his visit to the court of Mehmet II in Istanbul between 1479 and 1481.

This exhibition offers the rare opportunity to juxtapose Gentile's portraits of the Venetian Doge Giovanni Mocenigo and the Ottoman Sultan Mehmet II (cat. 23), who were contemporaries. Operating within the long-standing tradition of official dogal portraiture, Gentile depicted Giovanni Mocenigo in the relatively impersonal profile view against a neutral background, his state costume serving as his lone attribute. Only after the turn of the 16th century would Gentile's brother Giovanni break this venerable convention with his frontal portrait of Doge Leonardo Loredan (National Gallery, London).[6] When representing Mehmet II, Gentile had the freedom to experiment with a more revealing three-quarter view and to surround the sitter with symbols of his status and military accomplishments. An important feature that both Gentile's dogal and sultan portraits share, however, is the emphasis on luxury fabrics, esteemed by regal rulers both East and West.

TK

1 Inv. no. 750; attributed to Venetian School. Davies 1961, pp. 419–21.
2 Inv. no. 26.1.2; Gentile Bellini. Frick Collection 1968, pp. 198–202.
3 Ermine became an integral part of dogal attire in the Renaissance; see Newton 1988, p. 26.
4 On cloth of gold in Venice, see Newton 1988, pp. 16–17; Hills 1999, p. 182.
5 Collins 1970, pp. 148–49; Meyer zur Capellen 1985, p. 139.
6 Goffen 1989, pp. 205–12. Notably Carpaccio and other Venetian painters depicted Doge Loredan in profile.

23. Gentile Bellini (1429–1507) *Portrait of Sultan Mehmet II*

Constantinople, November 25, 1480
Oil on canvas
65 x 52 cm (25 5/8 x 20 1/2 in.)
The National Gallery, London
Layard Bequest, 1916
Inv. NG3099 (ill. p. 68)

In a well-known letter written to Mehmet II in 1461, Roberto Valturio, a humanist at the Malatesta court in Rimini, declared the virtue of the portrait as a means of bestowing immortality on its subject.[1] In full agreement, the image-conscious sultan commissioned many Italian and Near Eastern artists to capture his likeness, especially during the last two decades of his life.[2] Just as Valturio promised, these portraits have ensured Mehmet II enduring fame: the physical appearance of no other Ottoman sultan—not even that of Süleyman the Magnificent—is as well known today.

Many Quattrocento Italian artists, including the Venetian master Gentile Bellini (cats. 116–17), produced bronze portrait medals of the sultan, but the most significant Italian portrait of Mehmet II to survive is this painting, most likely made by Gentile during his "state-sponsored" visit to Constantinople. Despite its relatively poor condition and extensive retouching, the painting, which is more iconographically complex than any of the medals, remains essential to our understanding of the sultan's self-image.[3] At the same time, it confirms Gentile Bellini's status as *"un bon depentor che sepia retrazer"* (an excellent painter who knows how to make a portrait).[4]

Set before a dark background, Mehmet II appears in three-quarter view beneath a marble arch and behind a parapet draped with a jewel-encrusted embroidered textile. The sitter is dressed in a red kaftan, a dark brown fur mantle, and a voluminous white turban carefully wrapped around a red *taj*, his signature headdress and a mark of his status as a Muslim.[5] The soft, voluminous contours of the turban contrast with the sultan's thin, angular features, including his sharply pointed nose and neatly trimmed beard. Three golden crowns like those found on Bellini's medal of the sultan (cats. 116–17) and in a later anonymous Venetian portrait of him (cat. 24) adorn the upper left and right corners of this painting. The inscriptions in the porphyry slabs on the left and right sides of the parapet are now only partially legible, but it is still possible to read the date, November 25, 1480, and the phrase identifying Mehmet II as *Victor Orbis*, Conqueror of the World.[6]

The fictive framework within the picture showcases Gentile's ability to create the illusion of three-dimensional space, which, while not a major concern of Ottoman court artists of the period (see, for example, cats. 4–5), was one of the primary virtues of Italian Renaissance painting. Using a parapet to create distance between the viewer and the sitter and as a site for Latin inscriptions are lessons Gentile learned from ancient Roman stelae and tombstones and early Netherlandish portraits.[7] The presence of the arch, though a universal symbol of triumph appropriate for the sultan who conquered Constantinople in 1453, is in a way more curious. Virtually identical marble arches decorated with volutes and candelabra can be found in Venetian ecclesiastical architecture, including the decoration around the portal of the Church of San Zaccaria of ca. 1480, and on paintings of the Madonna Enthroned, such as Bartolomeo Vivarini's *Virgin and Child* of 1465 in the Museo di Capodimonte, Naples.[8] Given the consistently religious context of this motif in Venetian art, it is worth questioning whether the lost Madonna and Child painted by Gentile for Mehmet II also represented this kind of marble arch.[9] If so, the sultan may have requested the elegant form in his portrait as well.

There seems to be a tacit assumption in much of the literature that Gentile painted this portrait before he designed his medal of the sultan; however, the opposite may be true. In the process of making the medal, Gentile designed a distinctive *impresa* for Mehmet II—a trio of vertically stacked crowns, which most likely represent the three lands ruled by the Ottoman sultan: Asia, Greece, and Trebizond. Such emblems are more commonly found on medallic than on painted portraits, and appear incongruous here, floating as they do in thin air. In no other painted portrait by Gentile is the personal device of the sitter depicted in this way.

The provenance of this portrait is far from complete. While it has sometimes been proposed that Gentile painted it after he returned to Venice as a record of his extraordinary mission, the painting is far more likely to have been created in Istanbul for the portrait-loving sultan himself. Just six months after Bellini signed the work, Mehmet II died, and it is believed to have been among the sultan's possessions sold in Istanbul's bazaar by his son and successor, Bayezid II (r. 1481–1521), to help finance his large mosque complex established ca. 1500.[10] Purchased by Venetian merchants trading in the Levant, the portrait may already have been brought to Venice by the early 16th century, for it appears to have served as the prototype for an anonymous portrait of Mehmet II from that period (cat. 24). Nothing certain, however, is known of the painting's whereabouts until ca. 1865, when the distinguished British archaeologist and diplomat Sir Austen Henry Layard acquired it in Venice. In 1916, it entered the National Gallery in London as one of the gems of the Layard bequest.[11] The portrait therefore appears to have been in Istanbul for but a very brief period. Nonetheless, it helped spawn a native portraiture tradition at the Ottoman court that endured for many centuries (see cats. 4–10).

TK

1 The letter is fully transcribed and translated in Spinale 2003, Appendixes B and B1, pp. 310–18.
2 Raby 1982a; Raby 1987.
3 For the most recent estimate of what remains of the original painting, see Campbell and Chong 2005, p. 78.
4 Marin Sanudo described Gentile in these terms (quoted in Chong 2005, p. 107).
5 Raby 1982, p. 21. See also cats. 4 and 5, where Mehmet II similarly has a white turban and red *taj*.
6 Campbell and Chong (2005), p. 78.
7 On the adoption and use of the parapet in Venetian painting, see Goffen 1975, pp. 499–505; Rosand 1983.
8 Longo 1995.
9 For the most recent discussion of the literary sources describing the sultan's Madonna, see Chong 2005, pp. 111–13.
10 Angiolello 1909, p. 121; Blair and Bloom 1995, pp. 217, 234.
11 Meyer zur Capellen 1985, p. 128; Baker and Henry 2001, p. 28; Campbell and Chong 2005, p. 78.

24. Anonymous Venetian (associated with Gentile Bellini) *Portrait of Mehmet II*

Venice, ca. 1510
Oil on wood
21 x 16 cm (8 1/4 x 6 1/4 in.)
Joli Quentin Kansil Collection, Singapore
(ill. p. 109)

This small portrait of Mehmet II painted by an unknown Venetian artist in the opening decades of the Cinquecento appears to shed some light on the early peregrinations of Gentile Bellini's more famous portrait of the sultan now in the National Gallery, London (cat. 23). The latter's whereabouts for the nearly four centuries between 1481, when the Ottoman sultan died, and 1865, when the Englishman Sir Layard acquired it in Venice, have long been shrouded in mystery. If Gentile's portrait served as the prototype for this anonymous work, as the affinities between them strongly suggest, then Bellini's picture must already have made its way from Istanbul, where it was most likely painted, to Venice by the early 16th century.

Among the distinctive features the two paintings share are the position and shape of the sultan's head; his facial features, coloring, expression, and averted gaze; the warm red, gold, brown, and off-white tonalities; the dark background; and the placement of three vertically stacked crowns—Mehmet II's *impresa* devised by Gentile—at the top of the picture on either side of the sitter (see also cats. 116–17).

The anonymous work is much smaller than Gentile's original; it is painted on a miniature scale more common of Ottoman portraits of the sultan (see cats. 4–5, 8–9). The two Venetian paintings diverge in other ways as well. The unknown artist omitted the marble arch (and the parapet underneath) that by the early 16th century had become outmoded. Without the fictive architecture, the sultan's figure is brought closer to the picture plane, significantly altering both the physical and psychological relationship between the sitter and the viewer. The pose and dress of the sultan also vary in the two depictions. Whereas Gentile represented Mehmet II in a three-quarter view, his anonymous follower chose a turning pose fashionable around 1510, first in Venice and then elsewhere on the Italian peninsula.[1] By showing the sitter from the back, looking over his shoulder, the artist both animated the figure and displayed the sultan's sumptuous attire to full effect. Absent in Bellini's picture, the fringed tail of Mehmet II's turban, which brushes his upper back, here plays a prominent role. The sultan is vested in a brocaded silk kaftan with an oversized pomegranate design. Though the mantle wrapped around his shoulders is plain white, the overall effect of the sitter's costume is one of greater magnificence than in Gentile's picture, which, however, includes a luxurious cloth-of-honor missing here. Because of all these changes, some critics consider the present painting superior to the National Gallery portrait.[2]

In several of Vittore Carpaccio's paintings, including the *Sermon of St. Stefano* of ca. 1514 (cat. 30), some of the male figures wear turbans with fringed tails like the one seen here. While Gentile portrayed Mehmet II's turban as neatly wrapped (as he is actually said to have worn it),[3] Muslim men often let the end of the turban cloth, known as the ᶜ*adhaba*, hang between their shoulders or off to one side.[4] Particularly after the turn of the 16th century, the Venetian "Orientalist" painters seem to have grown more attuned to a greater variety of Muslim headdresses.[5] For this reason, and the employment of the turning pose, it seems most appropriate to date the present portrait of Mehmet II to ca. 1510.[6] A contemporary of Carpaccio, the unknown artist was most likely one of the many lesser-known Venetian painters who had trained in Gentile Bellini's large workshop and continued to pay homage to his great master in later, independent works.

TK

1 For more on this kind of portrait, known as *ritratti di spalla*, see Aikema and Martin 1999, p. 335; Cranston 2004; Brandt 2004; Campbell and Chong 2005, p. 23.
2 For this view, see Hare 1935; Collins 1970, pp. 79–80.
3 Necipoğlu 2000, p. 29; in Ottoman portraits of Mehmet II he wears his turban neatly wrapped as well (see, for example, cats. 4, 5, 8, and 9).
4 Björkman 2000, p. 611.
5 See generally Raby 1982.
6 Meyer zur Capellen 1985, p. 130 similarly dates the painting to the beginning of the 16th century; Campbell and Chong 2005 propose a date of 1510–20.

25. Painter from Verona (Francesco dai Libri?, ca. 1450–ca. 1506) *The Adoration of the Magi*

Venice, early 16th century
Oil on panel
103 x 220 cm (40 1/2 x 86 1/2 in.)
Museo d'Arte Medievale e Moderna, Padua
Inv. 425 (ill. p. 144)

For more than a century, scholars have debated the authorship of this *Adoration of the Magi* dominated by figures crowned with Ottoman turbans. Earlier attributions to Gentile Bellini and Giovanni Mansueti have recently been discounted and lesser-known painters from Verona, including Michele da Verona and Francesco dai Libri, have been considered, although there is still no consensus.[1] In addition to Gentile's and Mansueti's work, the painter clearly knew Andrea Mantegna's and Vittore Carpaccio's paintings, as well as the illuminations of Girolamo da Cremona. He therefore probably trained in Padua and Venice, perhaps even in the Bellini workshop, and later in his career, with altarpieces like this one, helped diffuse the "Oriental mode" to the mainland while working for provincial patrons.

Paintings such as this demonstrate just how extensively *simili* drawings were used in the late 15th and early 16th centuries in and around Venice.[2] The painter evidently had access to stock drawings from several different major workshops in the region in addition to firsthand knowledge of many paintings by the leading artists. Thus, for example, the pose and placement of the Virgin and Child reproduces that of Mantegna's Uffizi *Adoration* of ca. 1460, while the horses strongly resemble those in several of Carpaccio's and Mansueti's confraternity cycles from the late 1490s to ca. 1520 and altarpieces, including the latter's *Nativity* in this exhibition (cat. 26). From Girolamo da Cremona, the painter borrowed the black Greek hats together with the unusual stance of several figures with their hands hidden within their sleeves. Carpaccio's and Gentile's paintings and drawings most likely served as the source for the Ottoman costumes. Given its clear dependence on earlier works, the *Adoration* must date to the first decades of the 16th century, rather than to the late 15th century, as has sometimes been proposed.[3]

In terms of both its conception and composition, this painting recalls another anonymous *Adoration* often attributed to Gentile Bellini now in the National Gallery, London, although the two works do not appear to be by the same hand.[4] Particularly in this instance, the painter focused on evoking the Eastern origins of the Magi with an entourage of exotic figures and animals to the point that the protagonists of the story, the Holy Family and the Three Kings, are largely overshadowed. Yet the profusion of personages and details underscores the painter's desire to impress the viewer with pomp, grandeur, and, most of all, spectacular Near Eastern costume.

TK

1 For the attribution history of this painting, see Padua 1991, pp. 86–87.
2 For more on *simili* drawings, see Tietze and Tietze-Conrat 1944 and cats. 51–53 in this volume.
3 Raby attributed this painting to the late 15th century, identifying it as one of the earliest examples of the "Ottoman mode" in Venice (Raby 1982, pp. 21–22).
4 Davies 1961, pp. 135–37, cat. 3098.

26. Giovanni Mansueti (active 1484–1526) *Nativity*

Venice, early 16th century
Oil on Canvas
79.5 x 136.7 cm (31 1/4 x 53 3/4 in.)
Signed "JOHANNES DE MANSVUETIS P"
Museo di Castelvecchio, Verona
Inv. 974-1B276 (ill. p. 166)

This painting of Christ's Nativity, an altarpiece that has been cut down at the top, combines the Adoration of the Shepherds with the Adoration of the Magi. To the right of the manger sheltering the Holy Family two humble shepherds with tattered clothes worship the newborn Child, while on the left the Three Kings in magnificent dress approach on horseback with their small retinue. The male figure seated on the left in the foreground announces their impending arrival to Joseph. The star that guided the Magi throughout their journey appears directly above the Infant's makeshift crib.

The Magi, three astrologers from the East who brought gifts to the Christ Child 12 days after his birth, were often depicted in fanciful Oriental attire in International Gothic and later art. Venetian painters of the late 15th and early 16th centuries were among the very first to represent the wise men in authentic Eastern dress. The anonymous painter of the late 15th-century *Adoration* in this exhibition (cat. 25) portrayed them in Ottoman costume. By contrast, Mansueti dressed the Magi in distinctive Mamluk styles typical of Muslims inhabiting the Holy Land in the early 16th century.[1]

Mansueti casts the Magi's cavalcade in the guise of a Mamluk royal procession, replete with beautifully caparisoned horses. The Magi can be distinguished from their attendants by the gifts that they bear—gold, frankincense, and myrrh—in lidded metal vessels. Melchior, the oldest magus, who has a long, white beard and a red robe, wears the elaborate turban of Mamluk sultans, which is known by a variety of different Arabic names, including *takhfifa kabira*.[2] Balthasar, the middle-aged magus, dressed in blue, has a similarly shaped turban without the "horns." Caspar, the youngest of the three kings, depicted as an African in a purple garment, is crowned with a tall ribbed turban. There are four other turbaned figures in the retinue. The man nearest the African magus, who serves as his guard, wears a *zamt*, the distinctive red bonnet of the Mamluk military corps. Each of these Mamluk court headdresses can also be seen in other late 15th- and early-16th century Venetian paintings, including the anonymous *Reception of the Venetian Ambassadors in Damascus* (cat. 29) and Mansueti's large narrative canvases made for the Scuola Grande di San Marco (see cat. 28) and the Crocifieri cycles (see cat. 27). In every instance, the Venetian painters demonstrated their familiarity with the variety of shapes and sizes of Mamluk ceremonial headgear. Their awareness of the specific rank and profession associated with each style allowed them to create a hierarchy among figures with Islamic costume.[3] It is likely, given Venice's close trading relations with the Mamluks, that the patrons and other contemporary viewers of Mansueti's *Nativity* were familiar with contemporary Syro-Egyptian dress as well.

TK

1 For a related composition by Mansueti in a smaller format, see the *Nativity* in the church of San Martino, Burano, discussed in Merkel 2001, pp. 143–47.
2 Mayer 1952, pp. 16–17; Raby 1982, p. 35.
3 Raby 1982, p. 35.

27. Giovanni Mansueti (active 1484–1526) *The Arrest and Trial of St. Mark*

Venice, 1499
Oil on wood

163.5 x 145.8 cm (64 3/8 x 57 3/8 in.)
Vienna, Sammlungen des Fürsten von und zu Liechtenstein
Inv. GE 857 (ill. p. 127)

In 1495, the prosperous silk-weavers' guild, the *Arte dei Setaiuoli,* in Venice began decorating its new chapel near the high altar of the Church of the Crociferi in the area of Cannaregio. After first commissioning an altarpiece with the Annunciation from Cima da Conegliano (now in the Hermitage in St. Petersburg), the guild ordered a narrative cycle with scenes from the life of St. Mark. Of the four original panels in the series only two survive: Cima's *St. Mark Healing Anianus* (fig. 5, p. 126) and this painting by Giovanni Mansueti, *The Arrest and Trial of St. Mark.*[1] In his work, Mansueti included two *cartellini* (labels), one with his own name in bold majuscule letters, the other with the names of the ten guild members who directly oversaw the commission and the date, which are rendered in a cursive script typical of documents from this period.[2]

Like Cima, Mansueti composed a scene notable for its deep spatial recession and monumental, marble-encrusted architecture. Both painters dressed all the figures, except St. Mark, in contemporary Mamluk costume, although Mansueti gives it much greater prominence and emphasis, incorporating more than twice as many turbaned men in his painting as Cima. Mansueti is often criticized for overpopulating his compositions in precisely this way, yet his approach reveals his extraordinarily extensive knowledge of Mamluk fashion and decorum (see also cat. 28). Only the highest-ranking Mamluks wore the "waterwheel" style turbans with spokes, and thus, appropriately, he depicted the judge condemning St. Mark to prison in one. With equal insight on the part of the Venetian painter, the soldiers each wear a furry red bonnet known as a *zamt,* while the guards, such as those brutally pushing St. Mark through the prison gate, don the *tāqiyya,* the two-toned, flat-topped hat with a white kerchief wrapped around the base.[3] Others, including those in the foreground gesticulating to one another, are crowned with the more common, but no less distinctive high-rising turban worn only in Mamluk Egypt and Syria.[4] In addition to all the finely observed costumes, the presence of scribes recording the official's pronouncements on scrolls lends credence to the theory that Mansueti had learned something about Mamluk court life from Venetian diplomats and merchants with first hand experience in Egypt and Syria.[5]

One thing now certain is that Mansueti did not depend on the anonymous *Reception of the Venetian Ambassadors in Damascus* (cat. 29) for the Mamluk elements in this panel, as scholars previously believed. Indeed, in light of the discovery of the date of 1511 on the Louvre picture, the paintings of the Crocifieri cycle assume new significance as early exponents of the Mamluk mode. However, too many other paintings from this period have been lost to be able to say definitely that these are the first.

New light has also been shed on Mansueti's panel thanks to its recent cleaning in preparation for this exhibition. The removal of centuries of grime has revealed a surprisingly broader range of colors. Like his Venetian contemporaries Gentile Bellini and Vittore Carpaccio, Mansueti typically allowed cinnamon, crimson, indigo, ochre, golden yellow, and various shades of brown to dominate his compositions (see, for example, cats. 30–31), but the newly restored *Arrest and Trial of St. Mark* demonstrates that Mansueti employed paler blues and pinks as well. In this way, Mansueti helped lay the groundwork for the more luminous palette of the anonymous painter of the Louvre *Reception,* who now appears to have been one of his pupils or close followers.

TK

1 The most plausible theory about the original arrangement of the panels is in Fortini Brown 1988, p. 287.
2 Fully transcribed in Fortini Brown 1988, p. 287; for more on the Crocifieri cycle and its patron, see Schmidt Arcangeli's essay in this volume.
3 Raby 1982, pp. 35–41.
4 Ibid., p. 62.
5 Fortini Brown 1988, p. 200.

28. Giovanni Mansueti (active 1484–1526) *St. Mark Baptizing Anianus*

Venice, ca. 1518
Oil on canvas
325 x 135 cm (128 x 53 1/8 in.)
Pinacoteca di Brera, Milan
Inv. 153 (ill. p. 83)

In 1492, Gentile Bellini proposed that he and his brother Giovanni decorate the four walls of the *albergo,* or meeting hall, of the Scuola Grande di San Marco, one of Venice's oldest, largest, and most prestigious confraternities, with scenes from the life of St. Mark, on the condition that no other painters be involved in the commission.[1] Because of their busy schedules and then their deaths in 1507 and 1516 respectively, Gentile and Giovanni finished just one canvas and started another, so that in the end Vittore Belliniano, Giovanni Mansueti, Paris Bordone, and possibly Palma il Vecchio contributed to the program as well.[2] The seven paintings from this series, all of which survive, were dispersed after the suppression of the *scuola* in the early 19th century, and today are divided between the Gallerie dell'Accademia in Venice and the Pinacoteca di Brera in Milan. The confraternity building itself is now a hospital in which the former *albergo* functions as a medical library.

The earliest of the seven scenes, *St. Mark Preaching in Alexandria* (fig. 7, p. 129), established the tone for the rest of the cycle. Largely painted by Gentile and given its final touches by Giovanni Bellini, the monumental canvas presents a fantastic vision of an expansive square in Alexandria populated with men and women in contemporary Mamluk attire. Venetian officers of the Scuola di San Marco, dressed in black or scarlet robes and black berets, also appear. Described even in documents related to the commission as a *fantasia,* the painting nonetheless has an air of historical veracity because of its profusion of Eastern costumes and setting. The architectural backdrop features characteristically Egyptian edifices, such as the obelisk carved with (pseudo) hieroglyphs, minarets, and flat-roofed houses with Islamic tile and lattice-covered windows (*mashrabiyya*).[3] The central and largest structure represented, however, closely resembles Venice's own St. Mark's Basilica (fig. 1, p. 121).

After he became involved in the project ca. 1518, Gentile's protégé Giovanni Mansueti continued working in the same vein, combining Alexandrian and Venetian elements as a way of conflating the history of the two cities united by St. Mark.[4] In total, Mansueti contributed three canvases to the series, including this one, *St. Mark Baptizing Anianus.* Custom-made to fit a tight space between a corner and a window in the *albergo, St. Mark Baptizing Anianus* is the narrowest canvas in the entire cycle, yet the scene is one of the most significant in St. Mark's apostolic activities in Alexandria. Mansueti drew attention to his smaller painting through the extensive use of gold. In the center, Mark, dressed in a red garment with a blue mantle and crowned with a gilded halo, baptizes Anianus, the Alexandrian shoemaker healed by the saint who thereafter converted to the Christian faith. According to the *Golden Legend,* local men began plotting to kill St. Mark immediately thereafter. Imbuing this scene with ominous overtones, Mansueti dressed many of the surrounding figures in the official costumes of the Mamluk military. They wear either a white domed turban known as a *taqiyya* or a red bonnet with large tufts called a *zamt,*[5] and either the honorific *khil'a,* a sleeveless mantle draped over the shoulders that extends to the waist, or the more elaborate and prestigious *kamiliyya,* a robe with broad sleeves.[6] Most of them also have thin, long white scarves draped round their necks. The soldier standing directly behind Anianus is armed with a bow and arrow, placed inside an embroidered red quiver. Though most of the 29 figures in the painting are Mamluk, portraits of Venetian confraternity officers have been interspersed among them in the foreground.

Of all the Venetian painters who worked in the "Oriental mode" at the end of the 15th and the beginning of the 16th centuries, none was as fascinated with Mamluk costume as Mansueti, whose knowledge of contemporary Egypto-Syrian dress was remarkable (see also cats. 26–27, 51). In *St. Mark Baptizing Anianus,* he reveals his broader acquaintance with the Mamluks by including in the composition a minaret topped with a crescent; the blazon used by the last of the Mamluk sultans;[7] a metal mosque lamp; and a blue and white ceramic bowl of Near Eastern manufacture.

TK

1 The documents for the entire program are summarized in Fortini Brown 1988, pp. 92–94.
2 For the hypothesis that the *Storm at Sea* was initiated by Palma il Vecchio and finished by Paris Bordone, see Humfrey 1985, p. 232.
3 Lehmann 1977, pp. 1–9.
4 On Mansueti generally, see Miller 1978.
5 Raby 1982, pp. 40–41.
6 Petry 2001, p. 354.
7 For more on these blazons, see cat. 69.

29. Anonymous Venetian *The Reception of the Venetian Ambassadors in Damascus*

Venice, 1511
Oil on canvas
118 x 203 cm (46 1/2 x 80 in.)
Musée du Louvre, Paris
Inv. 100 (ill. p. 85)

During the past century, our knowledge about this Venetian painting has greatly increased due to the studies of scholars of the Islamic Near East, including most importantly L. A. Mayer, Jean Sauvaget, and Julian Raby.[1] Thanks to their insightful scholarship, the setting is now recognized as the Syrian city of Damascus in the final years of Mamluk rule, and the subject as the reception of a Venetian delegation by the powerful local governor, or *na'ib.* Questions of authorship and patronage remain, but the recent discovery of the date of 1511 on the painting sheds new light on its role in the development of Venetian Orientalist paintings in the late 15th and early 16th centuries. Rather than coming at the beginning of this trend, as has generally been assumed for the last 25 years, the painting appeared only towards its end. The work cannot be confidently attributed to any major Venetian Orientalist painters, including Gentile Bellini, Vittore Carpaccio, and Giovanni Mansueti, and, although dependent in part on their work, its topographical accuracy, airiness, and color palette mark a striking departure from most of its precedents.

Unlike every other large-scale Venetian narrative canvas from this period with a Near Eastern setting, the *Reception of the Venetian Ambassadors in Damascus* has a secular rather than religious subject. Without the obligation to unite East and West through architecture, as Gentile, Mansueti, and Cima da Conegliano had to do in their scenes from the life of St. Mark (see, for example, cats. 27–28), this painter had the freedom to create an "eyewitness" view of a contemporary Islamic city.[2] Whether he traveled to Damascus with the Venetian embassy or relied on secondhand information about the city from a Venetian diplomat or a print or drawing remains an open question.[3] Regardless of how he gained his knowledge, the artist created a well-informed view of Damascus as seen from the south side of the city's Great Umayyad Mosque. From this angle, one can see the mosque's original cupola (destroyed by fire in 1893 and later rebuilt), lead roof, three minarets, and façade; the public bath with two domes adjacent to the grain market; modest homes with wooden balconies with *mashrabiyya* openwork shutters, and rooftop terraces; a great palace complex with a ceremonial *iwan*; a garden enclosed by a crenellated wall; and another minaret. In the background are Mt. Qasiyun and the domed steam room of another public bathhouse.[4] Finely observed details include the blazon of Sultan Qa'itbey or one his successors (see cat. 69); the rug covered dias upon which the *na'ib* and his two attendants sit; the variety of turbans worn by the different classes of Mamluk society; the lush gardens for which Damascus has long been famous; and the circular metal finials atop the city's domes and minarets. The inscriptions above and beside the archway of the *iwan*, however, have not been accurately copied, and cannot be read, even in reverse, as has recently been claimed.[5]

Though it incorporates a large number of figures and animals, the scene is not nearly as crowded as the compositions of most other Venetian Orientalist paintings, particularly those of Gentile and Mansueti (see, for example, cats. 27–28). Moreover, unlike Carpaccio, who usually placed the protagonists of his stories in the immediate foreground (see, for example, cats. 30–31), here the most important figures are positioned in the middle ground. This invites the viewer to linger over the painting, admiring each vignette one by one. Despite his unique way of arranging the composition, the anonymous painter of the *Reception* appears to have shared pattern drawings, or *simili*, for the figures, architectural details, and exotic animals with the now better-known Venetian Orientalist painters (see, for example, cat. 51).[6]

The pale, luminous colors and clear tonality of the canvas also distinguish this painting from the other large-scale narrative paintings for Venetian devotional confraternities, which feature gold, ochre, and a far more extensive use of a deep, rich red. The light pink, blue, and green worn by the turbaned trio of men in the center foreground and used elsewhere in this composition are unusual for this genre, and reflect the more nuanced use of color by a new generation of Venetian painters led by Giovanni Bellini and Giorgione.[7]

Also unlike the canvases painted for the confraternities, or *scuole*, this painting is not known to have been part of a larger series. Most likely it originally hung in the palace of one of the Venetian diplomats in the black robes and hats, pictured before the *na'ib*, or else in the residence of the figure dressed in the red senatorial robe, who has been identified as Pietro Zen (1458–1539), a man deeply involved in the political machinations of the Near East between 1510 and 1512.[8] In theme, the painting appears to draw inspiration from the scenes involving ambassadors from Carpaccio's St. Ursula cycle of the 1490s.[9]

The Reception of the Venetian Ambassadors is significant above all for capturing a moment in time that represented the end of an era for Mamluk-Venetian trade. Just a few years after it was painted, Egypt and Syria fell to the Ottomans, and Venice began losing ground in the spice trade to the Portuguese. The economic partnership between the Mamluks and the Venetians, which had been so carefully nurtured through diplomacy, thus came to an abrupt finish, and a new dynamic in East-West trade emerged in the 16th century.[10]

SC / TK

1 Mayer 1933, 1952; Sauvaget 1945–46; Raby 1982, 1991.
2 See the essay by Schmidt-Arcangeli in this volume.
3 For more on this issue, see Campbell and Chong 2005, p. 22.
4 For the identification of the buildings, see Sauvaget 1945–46; Raby 1981; Cuneo 1991.
5 The assertion is made in Campbell and Chong 2005, p. 22.
6 On the use of *simili* drawings by Venetian Orientalist painters, see also cats. 52–53. The standard treatment of the subject remains Tietze and Tietze-Conrat 1944.
7 For the change of color preferences in Venetian painting in the early 16th century, see Hills 1999, especially pp. 133–53.
8 On Pietro Zen in these years, see Campbell and Chong 2005, pp. 22–23; Howard in this volume.
9 Especially *The Return of the Ambassadors* and *Reception of the Ambassadors* (Venice, Gallerie dell'Accademia).
10 On trade between Venice and the Mamluks and of the importance of Damascus as a commercial center, see Howard 2000, 2003, 2005 and her essay in this volume (all with earlier bibliography). See also the essay by Hocquet.

30. Vittore Carpaccio (1460–1525) and collaborators
The Sermon of Saint Stephen

Venice, ca. 1514
Oil on canvas
148 x 194 cm (58 1/4 x 76 3/8 in.)
Musée du Louvre, Paris
Inv. 181 (ill. p. 133)

Between 1511 and 1520, Carpaccio decorated the meeting hall of the Scuola di Santo Stefano, one of the oldest devotional confraternities in Venice, with scenes from the life of its patron saint, St. Stephen. Five canvases originally made up the cycle, although only four survived until the early 19th century, when the confraternity was suppressed and the paintings were dispersed to museums outside Venice.[1] This exhibition reunites two of the remaining canvases, *The Sermon of St. Stephen* and *The Stoning of St. Stephen* (cat. 31), both major examples of the "Oriental mode" in Venetian Renaissance painting.

By the time he began working for the Scuola di Santo Stefano, Carpaccio had inherited Gentile Bellini's status in Venice as the painter *par excellence* of large-scale narrative canvases. He had already completed cycles for the Scuola di Sant'Orsola, the Scuola di San Giorgio degli Schiavoni, and the Scuola degli Albanesi, as well as contributed to the decoration of the Scuola di San Giovanni Evangelista and the Great Council Hall in the Palazzo Ducale. From these previous commissions, Carpaccio had amassed a large stock of his own drawings and German prints, both of which he drew upon for figural, architectural, topographical, and costume details for the Santo Stefano cycle.[2] Numerous surviving drawings by Carpaccio and his followers, including two in this exhibition (cats. 52–53), can be associated with paintings in this series. In addition, Erhard Reuwich's woodcut illustrations in Bernard von Breydenbach's *Peregrinationes in Terram Sanctam* (Pilgrimages to the Holy Land), published in Mainz in 1486, served as one of Carpaccio's most important sources.[3] With its cityscape of Jerusalem, the place where St. Stephen lived and died in the 1st century AD, and representations of its inhabitants, the popular German illustrated book helped Carpaccio create the setting for his paintings. For the narrative itself, Carpaccio relied on both the biblical Acts of the Apostles and the more recent account of St. Stephen's life in Jacopo da Varagine's *Golden Legend*.

In the *Sermon of St. Stephen*, the second in the cycle's sequence of canvases, Carpaccio depicts the youthful protagonist of the story striking an orator's pose atop a crumbling ancient pedestal, where a Roman statue would have once stood. Clad in a richly ornamented deacon's dalmatic, St. Stephen addresses an attentive crowd of both men and women in a wide variety of costumes. Among them are Christian pilgrims from Western Europe, Byzantine Greeks—including two wearing headgear like that seen in Pisanello's 15th-century medals and drawings of Emperor John Palaeologus—and men capped with Ottoman and Mamluk turbans. The women, seated on the ground, are all Muslims. Four of the five females have pulled back their veils so that their *tarturs*, or tall brimless and ornamented hats, and faces are exposed, which typically they would not have done in public.[4] The background of the painting is populated with men, women, and children in Near Eastern dress.

The architectural backdrop of the scene features several buildings borrowed directly from Reuwich's view of Jerusalem, including the Holy Sepulcher, the Dome of the Rock, Mamluk minarets, and numerous edifices crowned with small hemispherical domes. In the center of it all, Carpaccio places a Roman triumphal arch and classical column.[5] Absent from Reuwich's woodcut, these latter details refer in a general way to the monuments and remnants of Antiquity visible in the Near East that so fascinated Northern Italian visitors to the Levant, such as the Venetian merchant-diplomat Giosafat Barbaro and the artist-antiquarian Cyriacus da Ancona.[6]

When each of its parts is analyzed individually, Carpaccio's *Sermon of St Stephen* emerges as a great amalgam of elements culled from a wide variety of sources. The result is a kaleidoscopic vision of the Holy City. As his mentors Gentile and Giovanni Bellini did a few years earlier in *St Mark Preaching in Alexandria* (fig. 7, p. 129), Carpaccio mixes antique, Christian, and Islamic architecture, people, and motifs in his depiction of an Eastern locale that he never visited. Never more than an armchair traveler, Carpaccio nonetheless was privy to a great deal of information about the Near East simply by virtue of being Venetian. Indeed, in 1511, the same year he started the Santo Stefano cycle, Carpaccio felt so well informed about Jerusalem that he offered to paint a view of the city for the palace of Francesco II Gonzaga in Mantua.[7]

TK

1 On the history of the cycle, see Fortini Brown 1988, pp. 296-98; Green 1995; Mason 2000, pp. 196–99.
2 Tietze and Tietze-Conrat 1944, pp. 138-57; Ames-Lewis 1990; Fletcher 1973.
3 First observed by Sidney Colvin, (1897). See more recently, Marshall 1984.
4 Mayer 1952, pp. 71, 73; Raby, 1982, pp. 41, 66.
5 As Zampetti first noted, the Roman gateway resembles the Arch of Trajan in Ancona south of Venice. Zampetti 1963 and 1997.
6 Fortini Brown 1996, pp. 81–91, 150–56; Lehmann 1977.
7 Bourne 1999.

31. Vittore Carpaccio (ca. 1465–1525) and collaborators
Stoning of St. Stephen

Venice, 1520
Oil on canvas
149 x 170 cm (58 5/8 x 66 7/8 in.)
Staatsgalerie, Stuttgart
Inv. 311 (ill. p. 27)

The Stoning of St. Stephen is the final painting in the narrative sequence of Carpaccio's Scuola di Santo Stefano cycle and is believed to have been the last of the five canvases in the series to be completed by the artist. In the late 18th century, the date 1520 was still visible on the cartouche depicted at the bottom of the painting.[1] As in the

Sermon of St. Stephen, the setting for the *Stoning* is Jerusalem.

In this scene of mob violence, St. Stephen, wrongly accused of blasphemy against God and Moses, has been driven outside the walls of the city, which appears in the distance in the upper left corner. Kneeling on the right, with his hands and head raised to heaven and asking God to have mercy on his executioners, St. Stephen is surrounded by men hurling stones at him with great force. Like a fulcrum, a faceless, turbaned figure dressed in red occupies the center of the composition. Closer to the viewer, on the opposite side of the canvas, priests and soldiers stand as witness to the martyrdom.

In earlier scenes in this cycle, St. Stephen is shown in the company of Christians, Jews, and Muslims. In Carpaccio's day, as today, the population of Jerusalem represented a mixture of these three different religious groups.[2] Though according to the bible, Jews stoned St. Stephen, Carpaccio instead represents the executioners as Ottomans, recognizable by their bulbous turbans, which are wrapped around a *taj,* or ribbed red cap.[3] Indeed, men in this distinctive style of Islamic dress dominate the composition. Recent interpretations of the painting have emphasized its anti-Semitic overtones;[4] yet, it may be more apt to view it as emblematic of Venetian concern about the increasing military strength of the Ottomans, who overtook Jerusalem and the rest of the Mamluk Empire in 1517, just three years before Carpaccio completed this canvas.

TK

1 Zanetti 1771.
2 Burgoyne 1987, p. 61.
3 Mamluk turbans lack the *taj.*
4 Gentili 1996, pp. 136–38.

32. Lorenzo Lotto (ca. 1480–1556) *Giovanni della Volta with his Wife and Children*

Venice, 1547
Oil on canvas
104.5 x 138.5 cm (41 1/8 x 54 1/2 in.)
Signed L. LOTTO
The National Gallery, London
Gift of Miss Sarah Solly, 1879
Inv. NG 1047 (ill. p. 126)

Lorenzo Lotto lived in Venice and neighboring Treviso during most of the 1540s, a decade difficult for him in terms of both health and career. In late 1545 he moved into a house near the Rialto Bridge owned by Giovanni della Volta, for whom he painted this unusual family portrait in late 1546 and into 1547, probably in lieu of rent. The work, along with its textile cover or *timpano,* is recorded in the artist's expense book in September 1547 as "a painting of [della Volta's] portrait from life and that of his wife with two children, altogether comprising four figures."[1] As Venetian family portraits are very rare at this date, it is likely that the commission arose because of a certain degree of intimacy between the artist and his landlord. Almost like bookends, the husband and wife tenderly bracket the figures of a young girl seated on a table reaching for a bowl of cherries, and a figure of a lively toddler whose pose seems inspired by a sculptural source. As with other late portraits by Lotto, the adults seem preoccupied and somber, despite their rich clothing and jewelry.

Draping the table is one of the six Oriental carpets that appear in Lotto's paintings, rugs that are so accurately depicted that they "can serve as documents for the history of carpet weaving," and of which one group became known as "Lotto" carpets.[2] "Lotto" carpets have distinctive Turkish designs, probably originally from the Ushak region of Anatolia, many of them made for export to Italy and elsewhere in Europe. The center fields of these carpets are elaborate, but without a fixed beginning or end, and, as here, often have pseudo-kufic borders; a comparable extant example dated to the 16th century shows a similar color scheme of reds and yellows (cat. 84).[3] In a study of these carpets, Charles Grant Ellis has described a *kilim* subtype of the "Lotto" characterized by serrated elements, here seen in bands at the edges of the principal field; these may have been made in Transylvania or another southeastern European region under Ottoman control.[4]

While the carpets in Lotto's portraits and devotional paintings may have belonged to the patrons who commissioned them, the artist was certainly sensitive to their beauty, as his depictions of them—such as that of the turned back edge of the re-entrant prayer rug in his *Mystic Marriage of St. Catherine, with the Donor Niccolò Bonghi* (Accademia Carrara, Bergamo)—makes clear. Lotto himself owned a large Turkish carpet that he pawned in the ghetto in Venice in 1548 to make cash loans to two friends but later recovered. The artist shared this admiration with other Venetians. "Mosque" and "Turkish" carpets (*tapedi a moschetti,* or *turchesco*), as well as others clearly of mid-Eastern origin, appear in various Venetian inventories, such as that of Francesco Badoer, who owned eight in 1521, and it appears that such carpets could even be rented. The carpets were often described according to their function or size, as suitable "for floor," "for table," "for armchair," or "for chest."[5] Thus Lotto's portrayal of one atop a table follows a known custom, one that is also seen ubiquitously in Dutch paintings of the following century.

AB

1 For an overview of the painting's history see the full account in Penny 2004, pp. 92–102.
2 Mack in Washington 1997–98, p. 59.
3 This carpet can also be compared to that portrayed in Lotto's *St. Antoninus* altarpiece of 1542 (Venice, Santi Giovanni e Paolo); see Mack 2002, p. 88.
4 Ellis 1975, pp. 20–22.
5 Penny 2004, p. 264.

°33. Cesare Vecellio (1521–1601) *Family Portrait*

Venice, ca. 1555–70
Oil on canvas
113 x 180 cm (44 1/2 x 70 7/8 in.)
Museo Civico Correr, Venice
Inv. 254 (ill. p. 63)

In the mid-16th century, Cesare Vecellio painted this family portrait which, like his famous costume book published several decades later (cat. 63), provides valuable insight into the material culture of Renaissance Venice.

Vecellio had strong professional and familial affiliations with Titian, but with this painting he reveals his admiration for other contemporary artists including, most importantly, Lorenzo Lotto and Paolo Veronese. Vecellio is one of many 16th-century painters in northeast Italy who borrowed Lotto's formula of depicting fashionably dressed families gathered around a table draped with a fine Oriental carpet (see cat. 32). The idealized figure types in this portrait, on the other hand, most closely resemble Veronese's, as seen, for example, in the *Portrait of the Bella Nani* of 1555 (Musée du Louvre, Paris,) and the *Cuccina Family presented to the Virgin and Child by Faith, Hope, and Charity* of 1570 (Staatliche Gemäldegalerie, Dresden).

Meant to hang in the most public part of the private palace, this type of group portrait commemorates the family portrayed while also celebrating its prosperity and fecundity.[1] Among Venetians, family portraits were most popular with the upper middle class, who had usually arrived at their elevated social position thanks to trade, often with the Islamic Near East.[2] The coat of arms in the background of this portrait has yet to be identified, and therefore the name and precise status of the family remains unknown.[3] Given Vecellio's lifelong connection to his hometown, however, it cannot be ruled out that this family is from Pieve di Cadore or its environs in the Veneto rather than from Venice itself.[4]

Three generations of a single family are represented here, including the elderly patriarch on the extreme left, his offspring, their spouses, and their young children. Prior to the mid-16th century, women rarely appear in Venetian portraiture of any kind,[5] but here they play a prominent role, even if it is primarily to demonstrate the affluence of their male relatives. In contrast to the somber black and gray costume of the men, the women wear conspicuous *scarlatto* dresses accented with lace and slit sleeves,[6] and their poses and gestures are calculated to call attention to their rings, broaches, and necklaces. Five of the six women wear pearl necklaces, most likely imported from the East and presented to them upon their nuptials.[7] The small children before the table show signs of tenderness and affection, while the young boy in the center gazing out towards the viewer holds a tray of sweets, perhaps marzipan.[8]

A major protagonist in this portrait is the *tappeto da tavola,* the imported carpet draped over the long table, a signifier of good taste and wealth.[9] Previously mistaken as an Ushak carpet from Anatolia,[10] it is instead a northwest Persian medallion carpet, a type more rare and highly valued in Renaissance Venice (and Europe in general).[11] Characterized by an elegant central medallion surrounded by a red field with floral or vegetal scrolls, an arabesque border, and inner and outer guard bands, Persian medallion carpets are finely ornamented, extraordinarily luxurious, and monumental in scale.[12] Venetian merchants and diplomats, including Marco Polo and Giosafat Barbaro, had high praise for the marketplace of Tabriz, where northwest Persian medallion carpets were probably made.[13] Members of the family depicted in this portrait may have frequented Tabriz's bazaars themselves and purchased this carpet there. Regardless of the manner in which they acquired it, however, its prominence in the painting leaves no doubt that the family considered their Persian carpet a prized possession.

TK

1 Hughes 1986; Rogers 1993; Fortini Brown 1997, p. 167; de Maria 2003, pp. 262–65.
2 De Maria, pp. 275–81; Fortini Brown 2004, pp. 16–19.
3 Conte 2001, p. 179.
4 As suggested in Mariacher 1957, pp. 225–26.
5 Fortini Brown 1997, pp. 162–64; Goffen 1999.
6 For more on the costumes, see Davanzo Poli 1980.
7 Fortini Brown 2004, p. 17.
8 This is a counterpart to the fruit bowl in Lotto's della Volta family portrait (cat. 32) and in Bernardino Licinio's family portrait in the Collection of Her Majesty the Queen. In Licinio's *Portrait of Arrigo Licinio* and his family, a boy presents flowers to his mother.
9 On the manner in which Oriental carpets were displayed in Renaissance Italy, see Mack 2002, pp. 73–93, who also explains how expensive these imported works of art were in comparison to other objects from the period.
10 Berlin 1989a, p. 621.
11 I owe the proper identification of this carpet to Daniel Walker. For the relative rarity of Persian carpets in Venice, see Curatola's essay in this volume.
12 King 1983, pp. 84–89. An extant carpet in The Metropolitan Museum of Art, for example, is more than 12 meters long (inv. 64.311).
13 Howard 2000, pp. 47–48, 60.

°34. Paolo Caliari, called the Veronese (1528–1588)
Allegory of the Battle of Lepanto

Venice, ca. 1571–72
Oil on canvas
169 x 137 cm (66 1/2 x 54 in.)
Gallerie dell'Accademia, Venice
Inv. 284 (ill. p. 93)

On May 25, 1571, a military alliance of Catholic maritime powers known as the Holy League formed with the goal of halting Ottoman expansion in the Mediterranean. Motivated by the loss of the strategic outpost of Cyprus to the Ottomans the previous winter, Venice contributed more money, ships, and soldiers to the effort than any other member state except the Hapsburg Empire.[1] The Papal States, led by the crusading Pope Pius IV, represented the third largest supporter. United, the Holy League accomplished what none of its members could have done singlehandedly, decisively defeating a larger Turkish fleet at the Battle of Lepanto in the Gulf of Corinth on October 7, 1571. Vivid descriptions of the event quickly reached Venice and inspired processions, epic poems, songs, commemorative medals, and paintings celebrating Christendom's victory over the Ottoman sultan.[2]

In subsequent years, Paolo Veronese represented the Battle of Lepanto on numerous occasions, including in drawings and large-scale paintings.[3] The present, relatively small painting appears to have been executed in the immediate, exhilarating wake of the triumph in 1571–72. In the lower half of the canvas, large galleys with tall masts evoke the magnitude of the event by filling the gulf as far as the eye can see. Amid the chaos of sinking ships and cannon fire, Ottoman golden crescents and red Venetian flags depicting St. Mark's lion can still be discerned. The clouds above serve as a stage for the Virgin Mary (whom the Holy League credited for its victory, along with Santa Giustina, on whose feast day the battle occurred); SS. Peter, James, and Mark—the patron saints of the Papal States, the Hapsburg Empire, and Venice, respectively; Faith (shrouded in white); and a chorus of music-making angels. To underscore the role of divine intervention in the battle, one of the angels launches fiery arrows at Ottoman ships below, while the clouds strategically shower them with rain. By contrast, in a signature example of Veronese's theatrical use of light, the ships of the Holy League are bathed in sunshine.

The original location of this painting remains unknown. Prior to entering the Gallerie dell'Accademia in the early 19th century, it stood above an altar in the Church of San Pietro Martire in Murano, which was closed in 1808–13 and its works of art dispersed. It was long believed to have been an ex-voto commissioned by a local man who had distinguished himself in the battle, but Mason rightlynoted that there is no donor figure in the composition.[4] The painting instead appears to celebrate the victory of the Holy League more generally, and therefore may have been painted for the Venetian State and only later deposited in the church.

Venice basked in the Ottoman defeat at home, but its foreign policy took a fascinating turn in the years after Lepanto. Proving that the city valued its role as the bazaar of Europe more than as militant defender of the Catholic faith, Venice withdrew from the Holy League in 1573 and signed a secret pact with the Ottomans, accepting the loss of Cyprus and paying Sultan Selim II a substantial tribute to protect Venetian commercial privileges in Turkish territories.[5]

TK

1 For an overview of Venice's role in the Holy League and its commercial relations with the Ottomans in this period, see Mantran 1986 and Knapton 1986, both with earlier bibliography. See also the essays in this volume by Raby and Hocquet.
2 Muir 1981, p. 15; Cecconi 1986; Cecconi 1986a.
3 On the development of the battle's iconography in these years, see Mason Rinaldi 1986; Keil 1986; Rearick 1988, pp. 102–11.
4 Mason Rinaldi 1986, pp. 29–30, with a review of earlier theories about the patronage and original location of the painting.
5 Hess 1972, pp. 54, 63.

35–38. Attributed to an Anonymous Painter from Verona or Follower
Four Portraits from a Series of Ottoman Rulers

Venice, 1578 or later
Each painting, oil on canvas
ca. 69 x 54 cm (27 1/4 x 21 1/4 in.)
Bayerische Staatsgemäldesammlungen, Staatsgalerie in der Residenz Würzburg, Munich
(ill. p. 110)

Orhan (r. 1324–60)
Inscribed ORCANE II
Inv. 2236

Mehmet I (r. 1403)
Inscribed MAVMETO PRI° VII
Inv. 2241

Bayezid II (r. 1481–1512)
Inscribed BAIAZETH SEC° X
Inv. 2246

Murad III (r. 1574–95)
Inscribed AMVRATH. SEC.VIII
Inv. 2239

These portraits belong to a larger Ottoman dynastic series preserved in its entirety in the Bayerische Staatsgemäldesammlungen. In addition to the selection of four sultans exhibited here, the set includes the entire house of the Ottomans down to the 1570s, that is, eight other sultans, Osman I, Murad I, Bayezid I, Murad II, Mehmet II, Selim I, Süleyman II, and Selim II, and two interregnum rulers, Musa Celebi VI and Isa Celebi V. Existing in multiple copies, versions of these portraits were well known during the late 16th century in Venice and Istanbul, and they exerted a lasting influence on the portrait traditions in both Italy<loyed in his household a "young Veronese painter" who is believed to be the author of the series. It is highly unlikely that this artist was the great Paolo Veronese himself (1528–1588), as is often claimed, who, incidentally, was not a young man in the late 1570s. Regardless of his identity, the painter clearly strove to produce lively, individualized portraits, creating a staccato rhythm by alternating three-quarter and profile views of the figures. The emphasis on the diagonal in several of the portraits, such as those of Orhan and Mehmet I, is unusual and striking, and the bulbous and bejeweled white turbans set against the dark background add drama as well. As is common in portraits of Ottoman rulers painted in both the East and the West, the facial expressions of the sitters are uniformly stern.

What is perhaps most striking is the similarity between the depiction of Murad III and contemporary Ottoman portraits of him, although it is unclear precisely how the Italian artist learned of the reigning sultan's arched brows, heavy eyelids, flat nose, and short beard. For many of the likenesses, including those of Orhan and Bayezid II, the artist depended on earlier European printed portrait series, evidently readily available on the lagoon or specifically procured for this commission.[2] Little could have been known about the appearance of the earliest Ottoman sultans anywhere in Europe in the late 16th century, and thus portraits of figures like Orhan and Mehmet I in this series are indubitably fanciful.

Present in Germany since at least 1636, the Munich portrait series is most likely a contemporaneous or a slightly later Venetian copy rather than the original set sent to Istanbul in 1579. The paintings that arrived at the Sublime Porte, which may be represented by works still in the Topkapı Sarayi Müzesi in Istanbul,[3] served immediately as the models for the sultan portraits in the deluxe illustrated history of the Ottoman Dynasty known as the *Şema'ilname* (cats. 8–10). In accordance with his native artistic tradition, Nakkaş Osman (active ca. 1560–81), the renowned court artist who illustrated the earliest versions of the manuscript, infused the likenesses with pure color and abandoned the European bust format in favor of poses and gestures that had become conventional in Ottoman royal portraiture in the period of Süleyman the Magnificent.[4]

TK

1 The documents, found in the Archivio di Stato di Venezia, Dispacci da Costantinopoli and the Senato Deliberazioni Costantinopoli (Secreta), are discussed in Raby 2000, pp. 150–52.
2 Istanbul 2000, pp. 253, 255; Raby 2000b.
3 There are 16th-century versions of these portraits from two different cycles now in the Topkapı Sarayi Müzesi, Istanbul.
4 Çağman 2000, pp. 164–87.

39. Giovanni Antonio Guardi (1699–1760) or Francesco Guardi (1712–1793)
Odalisques Playing a Mancala Game in the Harem

Venice, 1742–43
Oil on canvas
45.5 x 64 cm (18 x 25 1/4 in)
Gemäldegalerie, Stiftung Museum Kunst Palast, Düsseldorf
Inv. Nr. M 24 (ill. p. 138)

Between February 1, 1742, and December 15, 1743, Field Marshal Johann Matthias von der Schulemberg (1661–1747) paid Giovanni Antonio Guardi, then head of the Guardi family workshop, for 43 Turkish scenes of the same size and horizontal format.[1] During the past half-century, many of these paintings, known collectively as the *quadri turcheschi*, have appeared on the art market, capturing the attention of collectors and scholars alike.[2] Comparisons of the canvases reveal that Giovanni Antonio's younger brother Francesco and at least one anonymous painter helped complete the series, but there is as yet no agreement about how to divide up the hands. For many of the scenes, the Guardi and their assistant(s) relied on the engravings first published in 1714 in the *Recueil de cent Estampes représentant différentes Nations du Levant*, which themselves were based on paintings that the French ambassador to the Ottoman Empire, Charles de Ferriol, had commissioned from the Franco-Flemish artist Jean-Baptiste Van Mour (1671–1737) in 1707–8.[3] Thus, as they had been for Carpaccio in the late Quattrocento, prints proved to be a useful source for the costume and customs of the Islamic world for later Venetian artists who also had never traveled to the Near East.

With their signature loose brushwork and silvery palette, the Guardi *bottega* transformed the rather dry and sober French engravings into captivating vignettes. In this canvas, one of two paintings from the Schulenburg series now in the Kunstmuseum Düsseldorf,[4] the Guardi combined the figures and props from two prints, to which they added new elements and sumptuous color.[5] Especially in scenes like this one, in which odalisques are shown in a comfortable, well-appointed interior, the beautiful setting has the melancholic air of a gilded cage thanks to the bars on the windows. The focus of this composition is the two women in the center who pass the time playing a *mancala* game (from the Arabic *manqala*, lit. "a stopping place") on the divan. On the right, a woman stands by idly while another, seen from the rear, smokes a long pipe. In other harem scenes from this series, women play musical instruments, drink coffee or wine, entertain soldiers, and bathe. A wide variety of additional themes are treated in the cycle as well, including processions, the reception of ambassadors, and whirling dervishes.[6]

That Marshal Schulenburg wanted paintings such as these to decorate his Venetian residence, the Palazzo Loredan, is in itself fascinating. An Austrian aristocrat and professional soldier, he served the Saxon and Venetian armies in the early 18th century, and earned a prominent place in Venetian history thanks to his successful defense of Corfu, then under Venetian control, against the Ottoman siege of 1716. Thereafter he resided in Venice and became an important art collector, patronizing virtually every major artist in the city.[7] For 15 years, from 1730 to 1745, Schulenburg employed Giovanni Antonio Guardi to copy other artists' works. Though they too are not entirely original, the *quadri turcheschi* are among the most compelling paintings to emerge from this long-term relationship. Indeed, few other examples of Rococo exoticism from Italy are to be found, and the harem scenes in particular, such as the *Odalisques Playing Mancala,* offer insight into Western European perceptions of the seraglio prior to the new Orientalism of the 19th century.

TK

1 Binion 1990, p. 107.
2 Bettagno in Venice 1993a.
3 This relationship was first noted in Watson 1960; see now also Venice 1993a.
4 For both works, see Venedigs Ruhm 1991, pp. 140–43, cat. 26–27; Venice 1993a, pp. 44–47, cat. 8–9.
5 For the sources of this painting, see Venice 1993a, pp. 44–45, cat. 8; Fortini Brown 1993.
6 Venice 1993a; Chiappini di Sorio 2002.
7 On Schulenburg as a patron of art, see Binion 1970; Haskell 1980, pp. 310–15; Binion 1990.

40. Giambattista Tiepolo (1696–1770) *Two Orientals under a Tree*

Venice, ca. 1742–45
Oil on canvas
160 x 53 cm (63 x 21 in.)
The National Gallery, London
Purchased in 1960
Inv. NG6306 (ill. p. 137)

One of Giambattista Tiepolo's most captivating series of canvases represents scenes from Torquato Tasso's *Gerusalemme liberata* (published in 1581) painted for a Venetian palace in the 1740s. In his reconstruction of the cycle George Knox[1] united 12 paintings from various collections[2] that included four narrative scenes of the encounter of the Christian knight Rinaldo and the pagan enchantress Armida (Cantos 14–16), three overdoors of satyrs and putti, four vertical canvases that probably flanked the two smaller narrative scenes, and a splendid allegorical ceiling. Knox believed that the series was painted for the *salone,* or reception hall, of the Palazzo Dolfin Manin on the Grand Canal near the Rialto Bridge, but as Barcham has shown, an inventory of the palace in 1799 lists only the ceiling, calling into question—although not entirely ruling out—its identification as the original location.[3]

The number of works revolving around Rinaldo and Armida seems to hint that Tasso's Crusaders found their strongest opponents in enchantresses and magicians in their attempt to capture Jerusalem in 1099. Their primary enemies, however, were the Saracens (the term commonly used for the Muslims fighting with the Crusaders), who held the city under their leader Aladine and were supported by the Egyptians of Gaza whose warriors were ready to fight for the city. Two of the four upright canvases in London, one of which is *Two Orientals under a Tree,* are not part of the narrative of Rinaldo and Armida and are probably meant to evoke the Saracens. In each, two figures are shown in exotic dress and headgear, three of the four figures wearing turbans. In the *Two Orientals* the figures sit under a fir tree; the one facing the viewer has a large jar by his side. Comparable imagery is to be found in Tiepolo's prints and drawings, in particular the group of etchings known as *Scherzi di fantasia* (ca. 1743–57; DV 13–35), where various figures wear turbans, are associated with jars and urns, and are shown in sketchily described landscapes dominated by spindly pines (for the tree, see for example DV 22). Similar figures also appear in drawings, such as sheets from the volume *Vari studi e pensieri* in the Victoria and Albert Museum where exotically dressed, gesturing figures include some with turbans.[4] All of these are examples of *capricci,* or fantastical, enigmatic subjects; it may be that the *Scherzi* allude to themes of ancient Egyptian necromancy and magic.[5] It is interesting to note a similarly turbaned figure, seen from the rear, as the lancer in an important drawing by Giandomenico, Giambattista's son (see cat. 55), which documents a contemporary historical event in Malta, the *Consilium in arena.*[6] Again, in one of Giandomenico's drawings from the "Scenes of Contemporary Life," the *Concertino* in the Correr Museum in Venice, some members of the sparse audience listening to the singers and musicians are Eastern in appearance, two of them turbaned. These scenes suggest that the entire Tiepolo workshop could have been familiar with the representation of figures in Eastern garb.

Levey noted that the condition and quality of *Two Orientals Seated under a Tree* separates it somewhat from the other three, better-preserved, canvases of the commission currently in London.[7] He also pointed out that the other three are reproduced in etchings by Giandomenico and Lorenzo, Giambattista's other son. Levey argued that the four paintings should be dated around 1757, comparing the imagery with that of the brilliant frescoes of scenes from *Gerusalemme Liberata* at the Villa Valmarana of that date. Recently, however, the entire cycle has been more commonly dated ca. 1742–45, and Barcham has noted that the etchings made after the paintings in London were done before 1750.[8]

AB

1 Knox 1978.
2 The Art Institute of Chicago; Galleria d'Arte Nazionale, Rome; Norton Simon Art Foundation, Pasadena; National Gallery, London.
3 Barcham 1997.
4 See two examples in Knox 1960, figs. 273, 282.
5 Christiansen in New York 1997, cat. 60a–w, pp. 358–69.
6 Musei Civici, Udine. Pavanello in Venice 2004, cat. 102, pp. 160–61.
7 Levey 1971.
8 Barcham 1997, p. 134.

CARTOGRAPHY

41. Workshop of Pietro Vesconte *City views of Jerusalem and Acre*

Marin Sanudo Torsello (ca. 1270–1338)
Liber secretorum fidelium crucis
Venice, ca. 1330
Ink and colors on paper
35 x 25.5 cm (13 3/4 x 10 in.)
The British Library, Manuscript Collections, London
Inv. Add. MS 27376*, fol. 190 (ill. p. 62)

The scion of a noble Venetian family, Marin Sanudo Torsello (Marin Sanudo the Elder) came of age in a turbulent period in Mediterranean history. Around 1285, while still a teenager, he traveled to the Near East to learn the art of maritime trade,[1] spending long periods of time in Alexandria and Acre ('Akko in modern-day Israel). His family appears to have had business interests in Acre, a major port in the Crusader Kingdom, where Venetians paid low customs duties and tolls on goods coming from Damascus, Baghdad, and other points east. When Acre fell to the Mamluks in 1291, bringing with it an end to Frankish rule in the Holy Land, Sanudo felt the loss both economically and emotionally and he subsequently became one of the most significant Crusader propagandists of his day. In 1307, he submitted his first treatise, *Conditiones terrae sanctae* (Conditions of the Holy Land), to Pope Clement V, who welcomed Crusade proposals. Fifteen years later Sanudo presented a second, far more elaborate, treatise to Pope John XXII: the *Liber secretorum fidelium crucis* (Book of the Secrets of the Faithful of the Cross), which is notable for its extensive information about the history, trade routes, major port cities, and commodities of the Near East. In an effort to gain broad support for the Crusade, Sanudo also distributed his text to other European potentates, including this famous copy now in the British Museum.[2]

The *Liber secretorum* features an impressive series of portolans, *mappamundi,* and views of Near Eastern cities commissioned from the workshop of Pietro Vesconte, the celebrated Genoese cartographer who resided in Venice.[3] Exhibited here are the maps of Jerusalem and Acre, which likely reflect Sanudo's own recollections about the two former Crusader cities. Pilgrimage sites receive the greatest prominence in the view of Jerusalem,[4] while much more detailed information is given about the layout, shape, and size of Acre, a city with commercial rather than religious significance.[5] The various quarters within Acre's fortified walls are indicated, including the neighborhood of the Templars and Hospitalers as well as the new suburb of Montmusard. The communities of the major Italian maritime powers, Pisa, Genoa, and Venice, are also shown. Because they so frequently lent naval forces to the Crusader Kingdom, the Venetians enjoyed both a larger sector of the city than their rivals, and an enviable position on Acre's inner harbor. Each community had its own bakery, church, market, and lodging.[6] Throughout the Eastern Mediterranean, Venetians established this kind of merchant colony, which enabled them to achieve commercial supremacy in the region.

Keen to recapture Acre and the rest of the Holy Land, Sanudo called for a European-wide embargo of Egypt to weaken the Mamluk sultanate to the point that its entire territory could be conquered. Ironically, but indicative of a broader ambivalence about launching a holy war among Europeans, at the same time that Sanudo received encouragement to compose his treatises, his Venetian compatriots negotiated extensive trading privileges with Mamluk Egypt. The desire for immediate economic gain proved stronger than religious zeal. Despite his ambitious efforts, Sanudo died in 1338 without seeing his dream of a new Crusade fulfilled.

TK

1 On the education of Venetian merchants active in the Near East, see Howard 2000, pp. 19–22.
2 Tyerman 1982; pp. 65–68; Howard 2000, p. 175.
3 Harding and Micklewright 1997, pp. 51, 55.
4 Berlin 1989, pp. 687–88, cat. 7/10.
5 Folda 2005, p. 490.
6 Jacoby 1989, 1989a; Howard 2000, p. 30.

42. Francesco de Cesanis *Portolan*

Venice, 1421
Ink and colors on vellum
58 x 96.6 cm (22 7/8 x 38)
Venice, Museo Civico Correr
Inv. Portolano no. 13 (ill. p. 55)

Bustling maritime trade in the Mediterranean in the late medieval era gave rise to the development of a special kind of map known as the portolan. Sailors and merchants used these nautical charts to navigate the coastline of the sea and to find the best route between port cities. To increase legibility, principal trading centers are picked out with red lettering, written inland at a right angle to the shore, while smaller settlements appear in black. Islands are carefully noted in a variety of contrasting colors, and major and minor wind directions are indicated with red, green, and black or brown rhumb lines. These highly detailed maps were used in conjunction with compasses and texts, which provided more specific information about harbors, difficult passages, anchorage, and the political situation on land. Precocious in their precision, portolans were highly accurate at a time when *mappamundi* still were not, an indication of just how intimately known and extensively traveled the Mediterranean region was in comparison to the rest of the world before 1492.

Venice, along with Catalonia, emerged early on as one of the most prolific and important centers of portolan production, reflecting the great activity and interest which these cities had in long-distance commercial shipping in the Mediterranean. There are a few early Arab examples, all made in North Africa, but in general portolans do not appear to have been made in great numbers in the Islamic world until the early 16th century, when the Ottoman Turks, who were great seafarers, began producing comparable nautical charts and maps (cats. 46, 47).[1]

This early 15th-century Venetian portolan belongs to a type first made popular over a century earlier by the famous mapmaker Pietro Vesconte (active 1310–30).[2] An array of flags indicates the allegiance of the major ports. No flag is bigger or flies higher than the bright red one of Venice with the golden winged lion, the symbol of Mark the Evangelist, the city's patron saint. A similar but smaller flag appears next to the city of Zara, indicating Venetian rule over this part of the Dalmatian coast. Other prominent flags represented here include those of Trebizond in the nearby Black Sea (gold with a red eagle); Alexandria (white with red stripes) Tripoli de Barbaria in the south (white with a black lion); Malaga (gold with a black lion) in the west; and Genoa (white with a red cross) in the north.

Many portolans, including this example, were drawn in ink on vellum, and have one pointed end, or "neck." This map's tattered edges and numerous holes provide tangible evidence of the frequency with which it was once used shipboard.

TK

1 Soucek 1996, pp. 10–33.
2 Biadene 1990, pp. 46–47, no. 3.

43. *Atlante di tre carte nautiche (Atlas with Three Portolans)*

Venice, first half of the 15th century
Ink and colors on parchment; leather binding
31.4 x 20.5 cm (12 1/4 x 8 in.)
Biblioteca Nazionale Marciana, Venice
Inv. Cod. Marc It. IV, 9 (=5090) (ill. p. 63)

This early Quattrocento Venetian sea atlas consists of three portolans bound together in one volume. The first represents the British Isles, the west coast of mainland Europe, and Morocco; the second focuses on the Central Mediterranean; and the third shows the Eastern Mediterranean and the Black Sea.

Close in date to Francesco de Cesanis' portolan (cat. 42), this trio of nautical maps nonetheless displays many different features. Most noticeably, these portolans are more colorful and richly embellished, successfully combining the arts of mapmaking and manuscript illumination. This is especially true of the elaborate second map, which includes symbols of the four Evangelists in the corners as well as vignettes of two great Italian seaports, Venice and Genoa, and one inland center, probably Paris. Venice, surrounded by its lagoon, is the largest and most boldly delineated of these cities and thus also the most prominent and eye-catching.

Whereas Francesco de Cesanis' portolan is somewhat archaic, still deeply rooted in 14th-century tradition, the maps in this atlas reflect important new developments in the field of cartography. They employ, for example, the compass rose, a new Catalan invention, whose central star points north. Usefully, this atlas also indicates the location of shoals hazardous to large ships with dotted red lines.

The gathering of these three portolans in a book-like format has undoubtedly contributed to their survival to the present day and excellent state of preservation. Long after they were used on a ship, these maps found a place on dry land, upon the bookshelves of an early collector or bibliophile, and eventually entered the Biblioteca Marciana.

TK

°44. Matteo Pagano *La Vera Descritione de la Gran Cita del Caiero*

Venice, 1549 (?)
Woodcut
98.5 x 198 cm (38 3/4 x 78 in.) on 21 sheets
Staatliche Museen zu Berlin, Kupferstichkabinett, Berlin
Inv. 924-100 (ill. p. 74)

This vast bird's-eye view of Cairo presents the city from the west with the River Nile in the foreground and the Muqattam Hills in the background. The major urban centers of al-Qahira, Bulaq, and Babylon are clearly visible, together with smaller settlements such as Matariya, Rawda, Memphis, Imbaba, and Shubra. In addition to the Italian title, one of the dual names of the city (al-Qahira and Misr) is rendered at the top of the view in the Hebrew, Arabic, Greek, Ethiopic, Armenian, Syriac, Arabic, Glagolitic, and Cyrillic alphabets.

The dense matrix of buildings that make up the city is broken by a network of streets that is a remarkably accurate reflection of the topography of the medieval city. Clearly distinguishable are the Shari^c al-A^czam, the central north-south spine of the city with the Bayn al-Qasreyn at its center, the Darb al-Ahmar and the Shari^c Saliba, as well as numerous other smaller arteries. The eastern and southern cemetery areas are differentiated, as are a number of the urban lakes (such as al-Azbakiya and al-Ratli) and the two major canals running inland from the Nile (the Khalij al-Masri and the Khalij al-Nasiri). Certain major landmarks are also individually portrayed and labeled. These include the Citadel, the aqueduct, the *madrasa* of Sultan Hasan, the hospital of Sultan Qalawun, the Fatimid city gates, the northern and eastern city walls, and many bridges over the canals. Mosques are given the generic label *"gema"* (Arabic *jami^c*). Also shown are the signal monuments of Ancient Egypt: the obelisk at Heliopolis, the pyramids, and the Sphinx.

Thirty-four numbered captions, of varying length, and vignettes of an historical and ethnographic nature are also placed on the view. Of particular interest are vignettes showing the defeat of the Mamluks by the Ottomans in 1517, and scenes of horsemanship, date picking, water transport, and other daily-life activities, intended to imbue the view with a greater veracity. Also highlighted are exotic flora and fauna such as camels, crocodiles, and cassia trees. The captions relate to a descriptive Latin pamphlet, entitled *Descriptio Alcahir: Urbis qui Mizir, et Mazar, dicitur*, published separately by Matteo Pagano in 1549 and surviving in three copies. In the absence of any date on the view itself, the pamphlet provides the only dating criterion for the work. Although the author of the *Descriptio* is anonymous, the work has been repeatedly attributed to the French cosmographer and Orientalist Guillaume Postel.

While the view was printed in the mid-16th century, it is likely that the representation portrays Cairo at the end of the 15th century, probably during the reign of Sultan Qa'itbey, when Venetian relations with Egypt were particularly strong. Another, much smaller view of the city from an identical viewpoint is found in a Venetian pilgrimage manual printed by Niccolò Zoppino in 1519. Documentary evidence regarding the city-views painted for Gonzaga palaces in Mantua in the 1490s and 1500s suggests that a major printed city-view of Cairo, now lost, was then in circulation. This could have provided the inspiration for later views of Cairo, such as that of Pagano. The name of Giovanni Domenico Zorzi, an artist employed by the Council of Ten, also appears on Pagano's view, and he is probably the draftsman who transferred the view onto the printing blocks prior to their being cut.

Pagano (active 1538–62) is known for his production of large multi-part woodblock prints, such as a view of Venice after Jacopo de' Barbari and a four-meter-long print of a procession of the Doge. He also produced specialty prints, such as portraits of Süleyman the Magnificent and Roxelana, and pattern books. Both of his characteristic trademarks representing "Faith" (a female figure holding a chalice and a pair of clasped hands) appear on the view, as well as his trading address. It is not known how may impressions of the Cairo view were originally made; only one other example survives in the collection of the Arcadian Library in London.[1]

NW

1 The basic bibliography on the prints is: Warner 2006; Blanc et al. 1981; Codazzi 1952.

45. Hajji Ahmed (Nicolò Cambi, Michele Membré, Marc'Antonio Giustiniani) *Six woodblocks and print of the "Perfect and complete engraving and description of the entire world"*

Venice, printed in 1795 from wood blocks carved in Venice in 1559–60
Carved wood and ink on paper
110 x 106 cm (43 1/4 x 41 3/4 in.)
Biblioteca Nazionale Marciana, Venice
(Ill. p. 106)

The story of this renowned heart-shaped map of the world, known as the *mappamondo* of Hajji Ahmed, is complex and spans more than 200 years, from the mid-16th to the late 18th centuries. Carved in Venice in 1559–60, the six wood blocks from which the map was made were kept in the archives of the Council of Ten until 1795, when they were transferred to their present location in the Biblioteca Marciana. In addition to the cordiform projection, in the lower part of the map there are two celestial globes and a small armillary sphere.

All the geographical names are indicated in Arabic, while the continuous text around and inside the map is in

Ottoman Turkish. General notes about geography and the continents, a description of the 12 better-known countries in the 16th century, and the names of the seven greatest kings accompany the cartographical representation. Following ancient tradition, the 12 countries and the seven kings were linked with the 12 houses of the zodiac and the seven planets.[1] In the accompanying text, Hajji Ahmed also writes about his life, claiming to be a slave from Tunis educated in Fez. His owner, despite being a Frankish "infidel," is described as a cultured and good man who allowed Hajji Ahmed to continue practicing his religion.

Scholars now believe that Hajji Ahmed was simply the pen name of three enterprising Venetians: Nicolò Cambi, the senior dragoman of the Venetian Republic; Michele Membré, the Republic's official Persian translator; and Marc'Antonio Giustiniani, a local printmaker specializing in Hebrew books. Together they founded a society with the purpose of creating and printing this map for sale in the Muslim world, and in particular to Ottoman sultans and princes who had demonstrated a special interest in Venetian cartography in the mid-16th century.[2] The fact that heart-shaped maps were known and used only in Europe in this period supports the theory that this *mappamondo* was made in Venice. Other evidence includes the many grammatical mistakes in both Arabic and Turkish in the text, the Western terminology used for geographical names with the exception of Venice (called al-Bunduqiyya), and the blessing after the name of Christ but not after that of Muhammad. Most importantly, archival evidence related to the production of this map in Venice in the mid-16th century has been found.[3]

In 1568, the Venetian Senate granted Marc'Antonio Giustiniani a monopoly for printing this map, but shortly thereafter the Council of Ten confiscated the wood blocks for it from his house because he was suspected of practicing illegal activities. After an investigation, Giustiniani was once again authorized to print the map, although it is unclear if he ever did.[4] In 1795, when the original wood blocks were rediscovered in the Council of Ten archives, the Republic's official printmaker created 24 new impressions of the map, of which the present copy is one of 11 known surviving examples.[5]

RM

1 Bellingeri and Vercellin 1985, p.155.
2 Arbel 2002; see also Raby's essay in this volume.
3 Ménage 1958.
4 Fabris 1989, p. 3.
5 Gasparrini-Sitran 1988, p. 224; Arbel 2002, p. 26, note 1.

46a-b. *"View of Istanbul" and "View of Alexandria"*

Two folios from a copy of the *Kitab-i bahriye* ("The Book of the Sea") by Piri Re'is (ca. 1465–1554/55)
fols. 3v-4r and 45r
Turkey, ca. 1670
Ink, gouache, and watercolor on paper
Each folio: 34 x 24 cm (13 3/8 x 9 in.)
The Nasser D. Khalili Collection of Islamic Art, London
Inv. MSS 718 (46b, ill. p. 75)

Piri Re'is, the nephew of a well-known Turkish mariner, learned seafaring and navigation from his uncle while both were serving in the Ottoman navy. In 1511, Piri Re'is returned to his hometown of Gallipoli on the Dardanelles and began making the maps and charts that made him famous. In 1513, he created his first important work, a world map of which only one third has survived in the Topkapı Palace Library; however, Piri Re'is is better known for another work dedicated to the art of seafaring: the *Kitab-i bahriye*, or "The Book of the Sea." The text is divided into chapters with maps and commentary texts that, while clearly indebted to previous cartographic works, were innovative and fundamental for contemporary Islamic geographical literature.

At the time of Piri Re'is, marine cartography consisted mainly of portolans and portolan charts, which had been in use since the 13th century. Written almost exclusively by Europeans in Italian and Catalan, portolans focused on the Mediterranean, but also included the trade routes along the Black Sea and the Atlantic coasts of Europe and northwestern Africa (see cats. 42–43). Another less widespread genre of medieval cartography was *isolarii*, which, as their name indicates, concentrated on islands. Venice played a major role in maritime cartography between the 14th and the 16th centuries, producing world maps, portolans, and *isolarii* (see cat. 62). Venetians such as Pietro Vesconte (cat. 41), Battista Agnese (a Genoese active in Venice), Alvise Ca' da Mosto, Bartolommeo da li Sonnetti, and Benedetto Bordone produced excellent examples of the different cartographic genres.[1]

Piri Re'is collected earlier maps and took inspiration from them for his *Kitab-i bahriye,* which focuses on the Mediterranean like portolans and subdivides it into chapters with maps and commentary texts like *isolarii.* Yet the book of Piri Re'is is more literary, intimate, and historically significant than most portolans and *isolarii.* He wrote an entertaining cartographic work whose intended audience was the Ottoman court and high society rather than seamen.

Piri Re'is compiled two versions of the *Kitab-i bahriye* (in 1521 and in 1526) with some variations. In both cases, the book starts from the Dardanelles and proceeds counterclockwise describing the coasts of the Mediterranean. The most relevant variation in the second version is the addition of the topographical views of Venice and Cairo. The Khalili Collection manuscript is an unsigned and untitled version of the *Kitab-i bahriye.*[2] The topographic view of Istanbul, which includes the Yeni Cami mosque completed in 1665, and the addition of Candia, taken by the Ottoman army in 1667, to the chart supports a mid- to late 17th century date for this work.

Additional realistic and topographically accurate drawings are those depicting Istanbul (cat. 46a), Galata, Venice, Cairo, and Alexandria (cat. 46b). Istanbul is drawn from a bird's-eye perspective, possibly taken from the Tower of Galata in the city, which is represented in another folio. The city is surrounded by walls: the two walls encompassing the Topkapı Palace and the Yedikule fortress are the most visible features of the plan and occupy two corners of the triangular-shaped metropolis. Noteworthy are the representations of two Byzantine landmarks, now in ruin: the column of Arcadius, in the city center, and the Tekfur Sarayi (as the Turks called the Byzantine palace of the Blachernae) near the walls. On the left are the Anatolian shores of Üsküdar and the Princes' Islands with a group of galleys sailing west.

The important port of Alexandria is represented on a long span of coast characterized by the two main gulfs between which the city lies. A large beautiful galley, one of the ships most frequently represented in the book, is shown on the sea in front of the main port. The inclusion of a windrose on the right lower corner of the folio is reminiscent of earlier Catalan and Venetian portolans (see cat. 43).[3]

MAM

1 Venice 2001.
2 Rogers 1995, p. 121, fig. 75, folios 3b-4a.
3 Soucek 1996.

47. Seyyed Nuh *Kitab al-bahr al-aswad wa al-abyad (The Book of the Black and White Sea)*

Istanbul, Turkey, second half of 17th century
Ink and colors on paper
42 x 27.3 cm (16 1/2 x 10 3/4 in.)
Biblioteca Universitaria, Bologna
Inv. Ms 3609, fol. 55v-56r (ill. p. 13)

In the Islamic world, marine geography first flourished in the Ottoman Empire in the 16th century. Following earlier Italian, Spanish, and Portuguese portolans, Ottoman mapmakers produced accurately detailed topographic drawings, the most famous of all being the *Kitab-i bahriyye* by Piri Re'is (see cats. 46a, 46b). During the same period, Ibn Majid and his younger colleague Süleyman al-Mahri, widely renowned sea captains who traveled between the Red Sea and the Indian Ocean, wrote many of the best Islamic nautical geographical treatises, focusing on the Indian Ocean trade route.

The aforementioned works served as models for these 17th-century drawings by Seyyed Nuh in his "Book of the Black and White Sea."[1] Compiled early in the reign of Sultan Mehmet IV (1648–1687), this sailor's handbook follows the same counter-clockwise representation of the Mediterranean as Piri Re'is's *Kitab-i bahriyye.* Many noteworthy illustrations fill the treatise, including this colored view of Venice. Identified in the caption,[2] the city, made up of many different islands, is depicted at the center of the lagoon. Prominent details are the two columns of Piazza San Marco and an imaginary version of the Basilica of San Marco with a gabled roof in the city center. In addition to Venice's many fortified barrier islands, on the far left Chioggia appears, while on the far right Murano and the Cathedral of Torcello (labeled *munastir*) are represented.[3] According to the title page, written in Turkish, Seyyed Nuh himself had traveled to all the places he

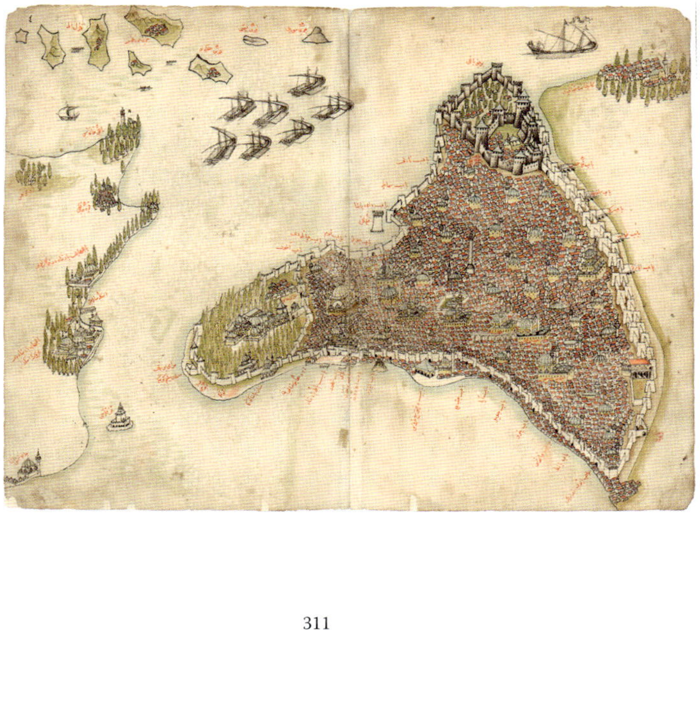

cat. 46a

represented in his sea atlas, and presumably this includes Venice itself.

MAM

1 Babinger 1955.
2 "*ishkal shahr venedik*" ("figure of the city of Venice"), with Venice taking its German name "Venedig."
3 Curatola 1993, pp. 409-10, cat. 262.

48. *Map with* qibla-*indicator*

Istanbul, Turkey, AH 1151 / AD 1738
Ink and colors on paper glued on a wooden support; housed in a painted wooden case
76.5 x 36 cm (30 x 14 1/4 in.)
Museo Civico Correr, Venice
Inv. Cl. XXIX 53 (ill. p. 108)

This intriguing work is a *qibla*-indicator, a tool used to locate Mecca from other places in the world.[1] Two medallions, both divided horizontally into hemispheres, are arranged one above the other in the main panel of a wooden framed triptych. Naturalistic flowers inspired by European designs fill the negative space around the medallions and decorate the frame.[2] The top half of the upper medallion shows an image of the sanctuary of the Ka'ba surrounded by other important places in Mecca, each identified by an inscription. The lengthy text in the lower half of this medallion, which describes the function of this object and how it works, includes the name of the designer and maker, a certain al-Barun al-Mukhtari; the place of production, Istanbul; and the year of manufacture, AH 1151 / 1738 AD.

The upper half of the lower medallion shows a European-style map of the lands north of the equator between West Africa and Japan,[3] with principal cities indicated with a numerical notation. A magnetic compass is inserted at its apex, and a pointer, its pivot fixed on Mecca, can be oscillated over the map. Below is a table with 20 columns containing the names of 392 cities and their corresponding numerical value on the map; for example, Istanbul = 1. To find the direction of Mecca from a given city, the pointer is oriented towards the location in question on the map (using the table for reference); then the map is moved around until the compass's needle is parallel to the pointer. The reading on the compass thus gives the angle of the direction of prayer.

Al-Barun al-Mukhtari made and signed a very similar but smaller handheld device now in the Chester Beatty Library (Dublin) with the map on the base of the object and the image of the Ka'ba on the inside of the once-hinged lid.[4] In the text he discusses his interest in geography and astronomy, as well as a commission to invent a *qibla*-indicator that would be useful in all lands. Completed in 1738, the Museo Correr's *qibla*-indicator map seems to be a variation of the Chester Beatty's portable instrument.

In its visual organization, this *qibla*-indicator recalls a *hilye*, or a verbal portrait of the Prophet Muhammad, a type of production distinctive to Ottoman Turkey from the last quarter of the 17th century.[5]

QA

1 Venice 1993, pp. 406–7, no. 260; Vienna 1983, p. 363, cat. 27/16, fig. p. 365.
2 Venice 1993, pp. 406–7.
3 King 1999, p. 97.
4 Minorsky 1958, pp. 78–80, no. 443, pl. 36; King 1999, fig. 2.8.10.
5 Derman 1998, pp. 35–36.

•49. *Firman including a treaty granted by Süleyman the Magnificent to the Republic of Venice*

Istanbul, October 2, 1540
Ink, gold, and blue, green, and red colors on paper lined with red silk
507 x 35.5 cm (199 1/2 x 14 in.)
Bibliothèque Nationale de France, département des Manuscrits orientaux, Paris
Inv. Suppl. turc 727 (ill. p. 45)

Ottoman imperial edicts, known in general as firmans,[1] encompassed nearly every aspect of public and private life, from politics to economics to religion.[2] The *tuğra*, the sultan's elaborate calligraphic signature, completes such documents and serves as the authoritative mark of the Ottoman Empire. The *tuğra* first began to be used by the Ottomans in the mid-14th century, was further developed in the time of Mehmet the Conqueror (r. 1451–81), and reached its most sumptuous form during the reign of Süleyman the Magnificent (r. 1520–66).[3]

Firmans were usually written in *divani*, or "chancery," script. The most elaborate and splendid ones, showing an artistically accomplished *tuğra* at the beginning of the long scroll as seen here, were often agreements between sovereigns. Among the Turkish documents of the Archivio di Stato in Venice is the original version of this firman in which Sultan Süleyman the Magnificent granted a peace treaty to Doge Pietro Lando, through the diplomatic work of *baili* Tomaso Contarini and Alvise Badoer, on October 2, 1540, following the Venetian-Ottoman war of 1537–40.[4] Technically, it is not a peace agreement co-signed by the sultan and the doge, but rather a commitment from Süleyman to honor a number of stipulations with the Venetians. The negotiations had started in April 1540, when Badoer reached Istanbul. On April 25, Süleyman received him and agreed to the doge's requests, at the same time requiring that the Venetians hand over Nauplia and Malvasia in the Peloponnesus to the Ottomans. The Venetian Senate consented to the transfer of ownership of the two areas and the negotiations proceeded without obstacles. This agreement led to the treaty, which guaranteed Venice a series of trade benefits. The dragoman Giannettino Salvago carried this important document to Venice.[5] The firman includes paragraphs on the consequences of the recent clashes between Venice and the Ottomans, regulations of the navigation in the Eastern Mediterranean, and rules for maritime cooperation and protection of trade in order to benefit both powers.

The present document, most likely one of the copies made immediately after the original to be distributed to Venetian diplomats in Turkey, found its way to Carpentras in southern France where it was acquired by the Bibliothèque Nationale at the end of the 19th century.[6] It features Süleyman the Magnificent's lavishly decorated *tuğra*, painted in blue and gold and set against a light blue and gold background. Tight spirals, sprouting small rosettes and leaves, fill the negative space around the calligraphic loop. This motif inspired ceramic decoration of the time, which took the name "*tugrakeş* spiral style" (see cat. 173). The three long vertical letters of the *tuğra* are capped with a curious lobed design, which presents the same red-and-gold color scheme of the two small six-pointed stars occupying the document's upper corners. The large vines of leaves and flowers, echoing the calligraphic decoration, framing the top of the document seem to be later additions.

RM / SC

1 In Turkish there are distinctions among different types of documents: a *ferman* is an imperial edict; a *berat* is a document granting an imperial title, privilege, or property; a *menşur* is an imperial appointment.
2 Rogers and Ward 1988, p 56.
3 Derman 1998, pp. 37–39.
4 Bombaci 1943.
5 Ibid., p. 379.
6 Paris 1990, p. 46, cat. 25. Two other copies, both acquired in Cairo, are listed by Bombaci 1943, p. 374.

DRAWINGS, ENGRAVINGS, AND PRINTS

•50. Giovanni Bellini (ca. 1431/36–1516) *Miracle of St. Mark: The Healing of the Cobbler Anianus* (recto)*; Fragmentary Design of Ornamental Spiral* (verso)

Venice, mid-1480s
Pen and brown ink (recto); black chalk (verso); fragment of partly illegible watermark of circle and mount
18.4 x 17.2 cm (7 1/4 x 63/4 in.), max. sheet
Staatliche Museen zu Berlin, Kupferstichkabinett, Berlin,
Inv. KdZ 1357r (ill. p. 131)

According to Jacopo da Varagine's life of St. Mark in the *Golden Legend*, while in Alexandria the evangelist Mark miraculously cured the cobbler Anianus, who had injured his hand with an awl as he repaired the saint's shoe. Following the miracle, Anianus converted to Christianity and later succeeded Mark as bishop of Alexandria.[2] With a profoundly moving expressive beauty, this exceedingly rare sketch of the Venetian Quattrocento tells the story of St Mark, dressed in a Roman toga, healing the hand of the recumbent Anianus, attended by at least two witnesses who wear distinctly Mamluk costume. Never disputed since its modern attribution to Giovanni Bellini by Detlev von Hadeln in 1925, this important work is among the fewer than 20 drawings convincingly attributed to the artist.[3]

The relief-like conception of form and space in Bellini's drawing has led art historians to connect it to the sculpted reliefs on the exterior of the Scuola Grande of San Marco in Venice (see fig. 1, p. 13), which was rebuilt beginning in 1489, first by Pietro Lombardo and his sons, and then, on their dismissal in 1490, by Mauro Coducci.[4] Tulio Lombardo's relief of 1488–90 of the same subject as Bellini's drawing, but with a composition in mirror design orientation, flanks the secondary entrance in the façade of the Scuola Grande of San Marco.[5] Hans and Erica Tietze thought Bellini's drawing was intended as the guiding design for one of the lost reliefs by Antonio Rizzo, thus they dated it to 1476; the only support for their argument, however, is the very general reference to Rizzo's commission of a spiral staircase and pulpit with ornamental reliefs for the Scuola Grande of San Marco in a document of July 1476, which notes that the sculptor was to follow a drawing provided by Giovanni's brother Gentile, who at the time was dean of the confraternity.[6] Yet the extant lunette relief by Rizzo of *St. Mark Healing Anianus* at the Scuola dei Calegheri (see fig. 6, p. 16), the confraternity of cobblers,[7] of about 1479, clearly demonstrates in its still Gothic-style figural proportions just how far Rizzo's sensibility seems to have been from Bellini's monumental classical vocabulary, which was in no small way indebted to Andrea Mantegna, his brother-in-law. As two recent scholars have rightly emphasized, the Berlin drawing accords better with the grandeur of expression of Giovanni's graphic style of the mid-1480s, and the formal similarities in the drawing are really with the façade relief that is still *in situ* today at the Scuola Grande of San Marco, attributed to Tullio Lombardo.[8] The Antique-style motif of ornament drawn on the verso of the Berlin sheet generally agrees with the refined classicism of Venetian architectural sculpture in the 1480s–90s.[9]

CB

1 Provenance: Samuel Woodburn, London (1780–1853; stamp Lugt 2584); Marquis Philippe de Chennevières, Paris (1820–99;

stamp Lugt 2072/2073); Alphonse Wyatt Thibaudeau, Paris and London (c. 1840-c. 1892; stamp Lugt 2473); by bequest 1880 Kupferstichkabinett Berlin. Selected Bibliography: Von Hadeln 1925, pp. 46–47, pl. 68; Schulze Altcappenberg 1995, no. 8, pp. 66–68, 189 (with much previous bibliography); W. R. Rearick in Paris 1993, p. 276, under no. 9; Goldner 2004, pp. 242–44, 318 (note 13), fig. 83.

2 Voragine 1969, pp. 239–40.

3 Schulze Altcappenberg 1995; Goldner 2004.

4 The documented chronology of the façade is discussed in Sohm 1982, pp. 110–62, 271 (document no. 57).

5 Cf. Wilk 1978, pp. 17–18; Luchs 1995, pp. 39–41.

6 Cf. Tietze and Tietze-Conrat 1944, p. 83. Document of July 1476 about Antonio Rizzo now published in detail in Schulz 1983, p. 125.

7 See Schulz pp. 66-69, pls. 123–24.

8 See W. R. Rearick in Paris 1993; Goldner 2004, p. 243.

9 Illustrated in Schulze Altcappenberg 1995.

•51. Attributed to Giovanni Mansueti (1485–1526) *Three Standing Mamluk Dignitaries*

Venice, early 16th century, before 1526
Brush and brown wash, black chalk, on buff paper.
30.7 x 17.9 cm. (12 1/16 x 7 1/16 inches), max. sheet.
The Royal Collection, Windsor Castle[1]
Inv. RL 062, P&W1 (ill. p. 87)

In his late 16th-century printed costume book (cat. 63), Cesare Vecellio identifies the costume worn by one of the figures in this drawing as that of "Admirals and Counselors" (*Armiragli, et Conseglieri*) to the great sultan of Cairo (fol. 479v). The precisely observed details of the Syro-Egyptian costumes in this drawing independently confirm that the three figures are Mamluk.[2] In contrast to the obvious variety of headdresses portrayed in Vecellio's woodcut and the robes of ornate silk patterns, all three figures in the Windsor sheet wear robes of plain cloth and subtly varied examples of the *taqiyya*, or tall domed hat—often stuffed with paper and trimmed with beaver—that was adopted by the military class under the Circassian Mamluk dynasty (1389–1517).[3]

Scholars have most often associated this drawing with the Mamluk onlookers at the extreme right of the *Reception of the Venetian Ambassadors in Damascus* of 1511 (cat. 29). Hovever, on close analysis—motif by motif—the figures in the painting are actually too different to regard the drawing as dependent on the Louvre picture. More recently, this drawing has also been considered a conflation of figures from Giovanni Mansueti's *Arrest and Trial of St. Mark* of 1499 (cat. 27) and the *Scenes from the Life of St. Mark,* canvases which teem with Mamluk motifs.[4] Yet the level of individualized detail and the tactile description of textures in this drawing seems to go beyond any of the painted adaptations of Mamluk costume in Mansueti's canvases, and that fact speaks strongly for this particular draftsman's quest of an authenticity of detail (regardless of the perceived graphic shortcomings noted by A. E. Popham and Johannes Wilde).[5]

Given the apparently authoritative observation of Mamluk costume, not to mention the refined execution, and the fact that no extant painting seems to reprise exactly the motifs in the Windsor sheet, one should reconsider the merits of attributing the drawing to Mansueti himself, as argued by Hans and Erica Tietze in 1944. Even if one may disagree with some particulars of their thesis, the Tietzes made an important contribution to the discussion by identifying the role of pattern drawings, or *simili,* in Venetian 15th-century artistic practice.[6] As a rule, Venetian artists of Mansueti's generation still regarded drawings as models or exemplars for reuse in paintings (none more valuable, one may argue, than a representation of Mamluk costumes), rather than as serving a purely exploratory, or creative, one-time purpose. The conception of the Windsor drawing as a *simile* would go a long way in explaining its copy-like accuracy. While it is true that securely attributed drawings by Mansueti are practically non-existent save for a sheet sometimes ascribed to him in Florence (Uffizi inv. 1293 E), and in sharp contrast, for example, to the exceptionally prolific draftsman Vittore Carpaccio, who was a significant utilizer of *simili* drawings (cats. 52–53), the Windsor sheet nevertheless manifests the shadow of Gentile Bellini's artistic vocabulary that generally characterizes Mansueti's work.[7] Indeed, Mansueti declared himself to be a pupil of Gentile Bellini in the signature on two of his paintings, the *Miracle of the True Cross at the Campo di San Lio* of 1494 (Gallerie dell'Accademia, Venice) from the Scuola Grande of San Giovanni Evangelista; and in a *St. Mathew Enthroned,* last recorded in a private collection in Venice.[8]

The question of dating the Windsor sheet must presently remain open, in view of Mansueti's long career (he died in 1526/27), because ongoing scientific investigation of Venetian pictures from the 1480s to 1520s continues to lead to major historical reassessments.

CB

1 Provenance: probably Royal Collection by ca. 1810. Selected Bibliography: Tietze and Tietze-Conrat 1944, pp. 189-90, no. 801, plate 154 (Mansueti); Popham and Wilde 1949, p. 171, no. 1 (after Gentile Bellini); Raby 1982, pp. 40, 60–61, fig. 43 (Mansueti); Meyer zur Capellen 1985, p. 174, no. F 10 (Mansueti); Campbell and Chong 2005, pp. 23–24, under no. 2 (as after Giovanni Mansueti).

2 Raby 1982, pp. 43, 48, and fig. 25.

3 Raby 1982, p. 40.

4 On Mansueti's use of the Mamluk mode, Raby 1982, pp. 35–49; Mack 2002, pp. 160–62. On the debate regarding the Windsor sheet, Campbell and Chong 2005, pp. 23–24, under no. 2.

5 Popham and Wilde 1949, p. 171, no. 1.

6 Tietze and Tietze-Conrat 1944, pp. 10–13, 189–90, no. 801.

7 The Uffizi sheet is illustrated and discussed in Petrioli Tofani 1987, pp. 538–39, no. 1293 E.

8 Miller 1978, p. 78.

52. Vittore Carpaccio (ca. 1465–1525) *Two Standing Women, One in Mamluk Dress* (recto); *Head of a Man, Head of a Lion* (verso)

Pen and dark brown ink, brush and pale gray-brown wash, highlighted with white gouache, over black chalk, on light brown paper (recto); black chalk, brush and pale gray-brown wash, highlighted with white gouache (verso)
22.9 x 12 cm (9 x 4 3/4 in.), max. sheet
Princeton University Art Museum, Princeton
Gift of Frank Jewett Mather, Jr.[1]
Inv. 1944-274 (ill. p. 130)

One of the finest drawings by Carpaccio in the United States,[2] this double-sided sheet of studies sheds significant light on the prolific Venetian artist's working practices. The motifs on the sheet were produced as *simili*, or pattern drawings,[3] and this explains why the two sides of the paper offer designs used at widely different points in Carpaccio's career.

Cesare Vecellio's *Degli habiti antichi et moderni* (cat. 63) clearly identifies the exotic attire of the woman seen at right on the recto of Carpaccio's drawing as Egyptian (*Donna del Cairo*), on folio 481 recto; thus she conforms to a Mamluk model, a fact that can be confirmed independently from descriptions by such early authors as Arnold von Harff and Leo Africanus.[4] The motif of the two Egyptian women also appears in the retinue at extreme left in Carpaccio's *Triumph of St. George*, in the Scuola of San Giorgio degli Schiavoni,[5] although their designs are somewhat overlapped and in reversed order and the painted figures exhibit small differences of detail in their costumes. The quick preliminary composition sketch for the scene of the *Triumph of St. George*, drawn in pen and ink on the recto of another double-sided sheet (Uffizi inv. 1287 E, Florence), depicts the figures at extreme left much as in the Princeton sheet,[6] but must have preceded it. Carpaccio derived the motif of the two Egyptian women from a woodcut by Erhard Reeuwich portraying the "*Sarraceni,*" or Saracen inhabitants of the Holy Land, published on folio 64r of Bernhard von Breydenbach's highly popular *Peregrinatio in terram sanctam* of 1486.[7] Carpaccio also relied on Reeuwich's woodcuts in portraying the buildings seen in the background of his *Triumph of St. George* Uffizi sketch and in the final canvas, but the artist was conflating Eastern Mediterranean and North African elements in his rendition of the legend of St. George.[8] Regarding the Mamluk female figures on the Princeton recto, however, only the black chalk underdrawing in the study—that which the artist drew first on the sheet—shows the haloed headdress of the woman at left and the squat proportions of the *tartur* (a fairly tall hat) of the woman at right as in Reeuwich's woodcut of 1486 (and as in Carpaccio's own Uffizi composition sketch, which makes it clearly preliminary to the Princeton sheet); thus, it is evident that the overall function of Carpaccio's Princeton drawing was to serve primarily in the process of adaptation, Reeuwich's print providing only a starting point, as a good part of it was actually modified by Carpaccio when he developed the Princeton drawing in the final ink with wash layers.[9] The Venetian artist was interested in a harmonic consistency of costume for the two women as he portrayed them in a large retinue. The preliminary layer of black chalk underdrawing in the Princeton sheet is rather abraded, and as a result the study may look somewhat crude and mechanical in photographs since most of what remains is the top layer of pen and ink. Also dressed exactly as the woman at right in Carpaccio's Princeton drawing are the Egyptian women gathered at center in Gentile and Giovanni Bellini's *St. Mark Preaching in Alexandria* of 1504–7 (fig. 7, p. 129). Rather perplexingly, as there is no more than an extremely generic similitude of pose (certainly, none of costume), the motif on the Princeton recto drawing has also been connected to the women attendants at center in Carpaccio's *St. George Baptizing the King and Princess,* another of the canvases of the Scuola of San Giorgio degli Schiavoni cycle, and to two conversing women in the background to the right of center in the *Visitation* painted for the Scuola degli Albanesi (Museo Correr, Venice).[10] The Mamluk styling of the women seen in the Princeton sheet would have had no iconographic application in the Scuola degli Albanesi cycle, which is dedicated to the Life of the Virgin Mary.[11]

The head of the man on the verso of Carpaccio's Princeton sheet has suffered slight abrasion of the drawing surface affecting the passages of intermediate shadows. Following Hans and Erica Tietze, this male head has usually been identified with the portrait of an onlooker at extreme left in Carpaccio's *Engaged Couple Saying Farewell* scene of the Scuola di Sant' Orsola cycle (Gallerie dell'Accademia, Venice), which is dated 1495.[12]

As the lion was the attribute of the evangelist St. Mark and the symbol of the Republic of Venice, any reasonably detailed drawing of such a feline made an intrinsically useful stock pattern, or *simile,* for a Venetian artist to keep in his studio, and it is probable, though not certain, that the study of the lion's head on the verso of the Princeton sheet relates to the designing of Carpaccio's heavily restored monumental canvas, the *Lion of St. Mark* of 1516 (Palazzo Ducale, Venice).[13] Like the Palazzo Ducale canvas, the Princeton verso is greatly more iconic in conception than that of Carpaccio's recently discovered study of a lion of ca. 1502, which may be based from life.[14]

CB

1 Provenance: based on letter of July 14, 1943, by Frank Jewett Mather, Jr., Princeton University Art Museum file, Alessandro Maggiori, Faenza and Rome (late 18th century–early 19th century); Guastalla; Arthur Frothingham; Frank Jewett Mather, Jr., Washington Crossing, Pennsylvania (stamp Lugt suppl. 1853a). Selected Bibliography: Tietze and Tietze-Conrat 1944, pp. 156–57, no. 640; Gibbons 1977, vol. 1, pp. 54–55, no. 148 recto and verso (with much of the earlier bibliography), illustrated vol. 2, pl. 148; Muraro 1977, pp. 73–74; Raby 1982, pp. 41–43, 66; Gealt 1983, pp. 22–23, no. 4; Ames-Lewis 1990, pp. 681, 685 (note 89); Blass-Simmen 1991, pp. 52–55; Nepi Scirè 2004, pp. 90, 110; Humfrey 2005, p. 99, no. 29.
2 Bean 1966.
3 As first defined in Tietze and Tietze-Conrat 1944, pp. 10–13. See Ames-Lewis 1990, pp. 657–58; Brooke 2004, pp. 304–6.
4 As rightly emphasized in Raby 1982, p. 41.
5 See documented chronology of this painted cycle in Fortini Brown 1988, pp. 287–90, no. XVII; and Mason 2004, pp. 73–77.
6 Lauts 1962, p. 268, no. 13, pls. 111 and 115; Petrioli Tofani 1987, p. 535, no. 1287 E.
7 See Arcangeli's essay in this volume. A copy of the *Peregrinatio* is in The Metropolitan Museum of Art (no. 19.49.3).
8 Cf. Raby 1982, pp. 66–67; Humfrey 2005, pp. 21–23; Lauts 1962, p. 268, pl. 115.
9 Microscopic analysis of the Princeton drawing facilitated by Laura Giles and Calvin Brown.
10 Cf. Humfrey 2005, pp. 98–99, 110, under no. 29.
11 Documented chronology in Fortini Brown 1988, pp. 290–91, no. XVIII; and Nepi Scirè 2004, pp. 99—101.
12 Illustrated as a detail in Gealt 1983, p. 22.
13 Lauts 1962, p. 249, no. 77, pl. 188.
14 Private Collection, Switzerland. Goldner 2005, p. 26, no. 3.

°53. Attributed to Vittore Carpaccio (Venice, ca. 1465–1525) *Six Turkish Figures, One on Horseback* (verso)*; Eight Sketches of Figures* (recto)

Venice, ca. 1500–10
Pen and brown ink, brush and gray-brown wash, over traces of black chalk (recto and verso)
11.3 x 28 cm. (4 7/16 x 11 inches), max. sheet
Musée du Louvre, Collection Edmond de Rothschild, Paris[1]
Inv. 765 D (ill. p. 134)

In his famous costume book (cat. 63), Cesare Vecellio declares that the sultan of Turkey invited a "certain Vittore Scarpe, who was an excellent painter in his time" (*un certo Vittore Scarpe, il quale era diligentissimo pittore dei tempi suoi*).[2] While all later editions of Vecellio's book in 1598 and 1604 omit this statement, and while modern art historians have dismissed the idea that the artist actually traveled to the Islamic world, it is undeniable that Carpaccio's drawings and paintings bear vivid testimony to his fascination with Near Eastern imagery, most often of the Mamluk mode that gained predominance in Venetian painting by the first years of the Cinquecento.[3] Although his imagery seems to have been primarily based on secondhand visual sources (see cats. 30 and 52), indiscriminately combining at times elements of costume of the Mamluk and Ottoman worlds, as is true of the present drawing, the artist must have also gained some direct knowledge of Eastern cultures from the Muslim presence in Venice at the time.[4] At least two, possibly three, standing figures in Carpaccio's drawing in the Edmond de Rothschild Collection wear headgear conforming to Ottoman fashion: a small turban wound around a cap with vertical ribbing (counting from the left border, the figures are second, fifth, and sixth). The old bearded man standing fourth from the left, in full frontal pose, at center, is patently derived from Erhard Reeuwich's woodcut of the *Sarraceni* (see cat. 52). However, the horseman at extreme left and another figure second to his right wear the *zamt* (bonnet), a typical headgear of the Mamluk military, which beyond Carpaccio's lifetime was also illustrated in Pierre Belon's *Observations* ("Portraict d'un Villageois Arabe"), a late 16th-century sourcebook.[5] Carpaccio's drawing therefore offers a composite of Ottoman and Mamluk motifs that is not rigorous if measured by the yardstick of the strictly consistent Mamluk setting seen in the Louvre *Reception of the Venetian Ambassadors in Damascus* (cat. 29) of 1511, which also portrays a horseman with onlookers.

Although rejected from the Carpaccio corpus by Michelangelo Muraro in 1977 on account of its "linearity and vacuity," the surprisingly little-studied, double-sided sheet of sketches displays the self-assured control of outline with a quick, summary openness of contour strokes and economic use of wash combined with parallel hatching typical of the artist's late period.[6] It is fully comparable in this to the elaborate composition sketches that are firmly datable: the *Funeral of St. Jerome* (University Library, Uppsala) and the *St. Augustine in his Study* (British Museum, London) of 1502–7, and *Pope Alexander III Presenting to the Doge Sebastiano Ziani with the Ceremonial Sunshade* (E. B. Crocker Art Gallery, Sacramento, California) of 1507.[7]

As is true of most of Carpaccio's drawings of figures, particularly of those in exotic Eastern dress, the function of the motifs on both sides of the Paris sheet falls somewhere between that of *simili* or pattern drawings and that of free exploratory sketches; they most often provide the design of "filler" motifs in the background of his paintings. Sketchily painted horsemen and spectators in similar dress to those in the Paris recto populate the distant landscapes in the canvases of the *Funeral of St. Jerome*, the *Triumph of St. George*, and *St. George Baptizing the Pagan King and Queen* of 1502–7 in the Scuola of San Giorgio degli Schiavoni.[8] The monastic figures on the Paris verso are quickly reprised in the background of *St. Jerome and the Lion,* another canvas from the same cycle.[9] Probably stimulating Carpaccio's pictorial cycle, the patrician Paolo Valaresso (commander of the Venetian fortresses in Modone and Corone when they fell to the Ottomans in 1499) presented to the Scuola of San Giorgio degli Schiavoni in 1502 a relic of St. George obtained from the Patriarch of Jerusalem.[10] Some of the exotic figures in the Paris recto were also reused in part, and in slightly different arrangements, much later in the background of two canvases of 1514 from the Scuola di Santo Stefano, the *Sermon of St. Stephen* (cat. 30) and the *Disputation of St. Stephen* (Pinacoteca di Brera, Milan).[11] The Ottoman costume of the standing man at extreme right in the Paris recto is identical to those worn by the Infidel aggressors in the *Stoning of St. Stephen* (cat. 31), probably of 1520, a canvas exhibiting Eastern riders in the distant left as well. One may broadly conclude therefore that Carpaccio's practice of using and reusing sheets with closely observed *simile* sketches and drawings of Oriental figures, over long periods of time, appears to speak of his and his patrons' ambitions in deliberately constructing a mood of authenticity in the narrative painting cycles that were being commissioned. While this drawing seems distinctly later (ca. 1500–1502), and more pictorially free, its iconography relates to a group of studies of Ottoman soldiers on horseback and on foot of 1500–1502 (Musée du Louvre inv. 3094, Paris), which was drawn by Carpaccio on a sheet of reused paper whose verso is inscribed with records of payments for the years 1469 and 1470.[12]

CB

1 Provenance: Jonathan Richardson, Sr., London (1665–1745; stamp Lugt 2183); Thomas Hudson, London (1701–79; stamp Lugt 2432); Sir Joshua Reynolds, London (1723–92; stamp Lugt 2364); William Esdaile, Clapham Common, London (1758-1837; stamp Lugt 2617); Sir Thomas Lawrence, London (1769-1830; stamp Lugt 2446); Charles Gasc, Paris (doc. ca. 1850; stamp Lugt 544); von Gottlob [according to Tietze and Tietze-Conrat 1944]; Emile Galichon, Paris (1829–75; version of stamp Lugt 1058); baron Edmond James de Rothschild, Boulogne-sur-Seine (1845–1934); by bequest to the Musée du Louvre, 1936. Selected Bibliography: Tietze and Tietze-Conrat 1944, p. 155, no. 634 (Carpaccio); Lauts 1962, p. 275, no. 44 (Carpaccio); Muraro 1977, pp. 71–72, figs. 65, 65 (as Benedetto Carpaccio ?); Brooke 2004, pp. 306, 313 (note 18), figs. 6–7 (Carpaccio).
2 Cf. Tietze and Tietze-Conrat 1944, pp. 141-42; Raby 1982, p. 66.
3 Discussed in Raby 1982, p. 66.
4 See Howard's essays in this volume.
5 Raby 1982, pp. 41, 51 (fig. 30).
6 Muraro 1977, p. 72: *"uno stile grafico tutto linearismi e vacuità."*
7 See Brooke 2004, 303–9; and Humfrey 2005, pp. 89, 90, 118, nos. 23, 24, 43.
8 See documented chronology of this narrative cycle in Fortini Brown 1988, pp. 287–90, no. XVII; Nepi Scirè 2004, pp. 73–77.
9 Brooke 2004, pp. 306–9.
10 Fortini Brown 1988, p. 288.
11 Cf. Lauts 1962, p. 236, nos. 26, 27, pls. 160, 169; and Fortini Brown 1988, pp. 296–98, no. XXII.
12 Lauts 1962, p. 275, no. 42, pl. 116.

°54. *"Interior of a house in Cairo"* Alessandro Magno, *Travel Diary*

Venice, Southeastern Mediterranean, Brescia, and London, ca. 1557–65
Ink on paper; parchment binding
20.5 x 15.5 cm (8 x 6 1/8 in.)
Folger Shakespeare Library, Washington, D.C.
Inv. Ms. V.a. 259, fol. 127r (ill. p. 62)

The young Venetian patrician Alessandro Magno (1538–1576) will not have a place in history as an accomplished draftsman but his lively accounts and ink sketches of his travels around the Mediterranean and Europe provide important insights into a traveling merchant's experience in the mid-16th century. His *Travel Diary,* annotated on the flyleaf by a later owner as an "Account of the journey to Cyprus and other journeys until the return to Venice of a patrician from the Veneto,"[1] was in a Venetian library until the late 18th century, when it was acquired by the book collector Matteo Luigi Canonici (d. 1805). It then found its way to England, where Henry Folger bought it in 1924 before taking it to the United States.

The diary is written in a neat and methodical script in Italian with recurrent use of Venetian dialectal terms. While still a young man, between 1557 and 1565, his far-flung travels ranged from the islands of Cyprus and Zante (Zakynthos) in the East to London in the North, and, closer to the home, to the Brescian territory after he gained the title of *camerlingo* (chancellor).[2] Of specific interest here is his journey to Alexandria and Cairo, or *"Viaggio di Alessandria"* (fols. 110–40), setting sail on the *Santa Maria* at two in the morning of Good Friday April 4, 1561, arriving at Alexandria on May 1 after a stopover on the island of Zante, and traveling to and from Cairo and Alexandria from June 29 to August 14. The purpose of the journey was to conduct business and trade goods he brought with him—among which were wool and silk fabrics, copper vessels, glass beads, paper, and coral (fol. 111)—in return for spices such as pepper, ginger, and cinnamon (fol. 137v–138r). The young Alessandro, however, was a curious traveler who wanted to make the most of his trip to Egypt and, in addition to visiting the Venetian *fondachi,* trading, and dealing with the local authorities, he was similar to a modern enterprising tourist. In Alexandria, he visited the sacred sites of St. Mark's preaching and martyrdom, including the Church of Saba and the Coptic catacombs; saw and sketched the obelisk and Pompeius's column (fols. 118–19); passed through Rosetta; and enjoyed sailing on the Nile. In Cairo, he visited affluent houses and described their interiors with colored *qamariyya* windows (fols. 126–27); went to the main market, the Khan al-Khalili (*"il Cancali"*; fol. 126v); was unable to enter the mosques ("Entering is dangerous; either one converts, or ends up dead");[3] and was beaten after returning late from Matariyya because of the curfew (fol. 128). Magno also went to see the stepped pyramid at Saqqara and was quite impressed at the sight of the Sphinx near the pyramids, which he entered, sketching all of the above (fols. 129–33). Finally, he saw a giraffe and an elephant, mummies, and the flooding of the Nile before returning to Alexandria (fols. 134–36).

The drawing on fol. 127r illustrates the *qa'a*, or reception room, of a wealthy house (*"sala delle case al Cairo"*).[4] Alessandro was impressed by the fountain's jets and the water systems, which he described and drew accurately. Particularly well observed are the beamed ceiling with corner pendentives[5] and polygonal opening in the center, the geometric patterns of the glass windows,[6] and the two divans. Only the stool and "Mamluk" medallion carpet (see cat. 81) draped over the table in the Venetian fashion (see cats. 32–33) look out of place in this context and may not stem from Magno's direct observations.

We can assume that Alessandro Magno expired of an illness when he was not yet 40 years old in 1576. Had he not died so young, he probably would have become an active member of the Venetian oligarchy and would have made a name for himself in the Senate. Fortunately, we are left with a spirited account of his early years as a well-trained, curious, and bright Venetian nobleman and merchant.

SC

1 *"Relazione del viaggio di Cipro, di quell'isola, e d'altri viaggi fino al ritorno in Ven.ª di un Patrizio Veneto."*

2 Barron, Coleman, and Cobbi 1983; Naar 2002.

3 *"Lo andarvi entro è pericoloso, o di farsi moro, o esser ucciso"* (fol. 127r).

4 Previously published in Howard 2000, p. 39, fig. 36.

5 *"La travamenta poi è tutta lavorata, e di colore azuro, e d'oro dipenta a pitture, e lavori moreschi."* (The beamed ceiling is ornamented and painted in blue and gold with Moorish decorations), fol. 126r.

6 *". . . percioche son fatti a modi diversi altri tondi, qual quadri, molti in stella, altri a similitudine di core, et altri a piu modi fatti con gelosie, co' fogliami, con groppi, e diversi altri lavori fatti di gesso, e li vedri in esso di piu colori."* (. . . some are circular, other square, many star-shaped, others cordiform, and others decorated with leaves and knots, and many other works made of plaster with multicolored glass in them.), fol. 126r.

55. Giandomenico Tiepolo (1727–1804) *Turkish Lancer and Onlookers Approaching a Town*

Venice, ca. 1760–70
Pen and brown ink, brush and pale brown wash, over traces of black chalk; framing outlines by the artist in pen and brown ink
Unknown watermark (not in Briquet)
28.6 x 41.1 cm (11 1/4 x 16 3/16 in.) max. sheet
Signed in pen and dark brown ink at lower left: "Dom.° Tiepolo f."
The Metropolitan Museum of Art, Rogers Fund, 1937, New York
Inv. 37.165.671 (ill. p. 137)

This sheet belongs to a group of drawings of Ottoman Turkish horsemen and chieftains riding or resting in idyllic landscapes, accompanied by exotically clad attendants, by Giandomenico Tiepolo, son of the famous Giambattista (1696–1770). His compositions generally reflect the contemporary artistic and literary taste in Venice for tales of exotic Eastern romance.[2] In 1741–43, for instance, the Venetian Antonio Guardi painted a series of 43 pictures, called in documents of the time the *quadri de costumi dei Turchi* (scenes on the habits of the Turks), for field marshal Johann Matthias von der Schulenburg (cat. 39).[3] Editions of *Gerusalemme Liberata*, Torquato Tasso's 16th-century epic poem recounting the delivery of the Holy Land from Muslim hands, were also being republished in Venice at this time (see cat. 40). Less serious than Tasso's poem, and not far from Giandomenico Tiepolo's own artistic temperament, Count Carlo Gozzi's *fiabe* (fables), dramatic pieces fusing the fantasy and the magic of Eastern fairy tales with contemporary themes and characters of the Venetian theater, were popular in the 1750s and 1760s, and Gozzi's *Memoirs* tell of his contact with the Ottoman Empire during his three-year military service in Dalmatia.[4]

Tiepolo's *Turkish Lancer and Onlookers Approaching a Town* offers a more ambitious elaboration of the motif of the mounted Turkish lancer also explored by the artist in a smaller, probably preliminary, sketch also in The Metropolitan Museum of Art (no. 35.42.2) drawn with darker brown washes on thin paper with a more simplified mountainous landscape. In the present sheet, the turbaned lancer on horseback is accompanied at right by two standing onlookers in Arabian dress (but not distinctively Ottoman Turkish) that conform to exotic figural types recurring in paintings by the artist's father, Giambattista, most prominently among the spectators in the allegorical portrayals of the continents Africa and Asia on the ceiling frescoes of the staircase of the Residenz in Würzburg, a documented project of 1752–53 in which Giandomenico also assisted. At left, in the middle ground of the drawn composition, a town emerges between softly curving mountains, most likely set in the Friuli region (northeast of Venice), judging from the style and detailing of the buildings (the short towers with hip-roofs stand on pilasters). But the scene, like its exotic characters, is a fanciful composite, a *capriccio* (or *fiaba*, to borrow Gozzi's literary term) based on carefully observed individual elements. The artist probably developed the design of the townscape separately from a preliminary on-site study; analogous views of towns and rural buildings from the Veneto and Friuli appear in sheets that probably once comprised a sketchbook, attributed to both Tiepolos, father and son, from 1757–59.[5]

On good-quality, thick paper and in a large size, this vigorous drawing was clearly intended to be a finished work itself; it is executed with a stunning verve of outline and virtuoso effects of flickering light. Like this sheet and its companion, the other variations on the theme of Turkish horseman in action or at rest are undated as well, and may not have all been produced during the same period of the artist's career.[6] Although the drawing has been reasonably dated to after 1770 by some scholars,[7] it is possible that *Turkish Lancer and Onlookers Approaching a Town* is instead from a decade earlier, from around the time of the Tiepolo family's departure for Spain in 1762, or from shortly before, due to the light wash technique; the stylistic links to some of Giandomenico's early religious drawings; the detailed, apparently site-specific portrayal of the town; and the airy conception of space and landscape.[8]

CB

1 The provenance is as follows: Baron Louis-Auguste de Schwiter, Nienburg and Paris (1805–1889; his stamp at lower right, Lugt 1768); his sale Hôtel Drouot, Paris, salle 3, 20–21 April, 1883, no. 149; Marquis de Biron, Paris and Geneva (ca. 1850s–late 1930s).

2 Bean with Griswold 1990, no. 261, pp. 262–63 (with previous bibliography); Wolk-Simon 1996, p. 53, fig. 80; Knox and Gealt 1996–97, p. 240, no. 20.

3 Pedrocco and Montecuccoli degli Erri 1992, pp. 39, 130–32, cats. 60–78.

4 Gozzi 1890, vol. 1, pp. 229–78.

5 For example, Knox 1975, cats. 54, 56, 57.

6 The Metropolitan Museum of Art no. 35.42.1; The Metropolitan Museum of Art, Robert Lehman Collection, 1975.1.515; Gabinetto Disegni e Stampe degli Uffizi, inv. 7805 S and 7810 S, Florence; Musée des Beaux-Arts D 3017, Besançon; and private collection. Christie's, New York, January 12, 1995, lot 56; Knox and Gealt 1996–97, no. 121.

7 Wolk-Simon 1996, p. 53, no. 80.

8 A tentative earlier dating, as suggested above, is also supported by Catherine Whistler and Bozena Anna Kowalczyk (written communications to the author, April 20 and May 3, 2006).

56. Anonymous Venetian *The Doge in the Bucintoro being Rowed to the Marriage of the Sea*

Venice, ca. 1501–21
Woodcut
49.3 x 112 cm (19 3/8 x 44 1/8 in.)
The British Museum, London
Inv. PD1866-07-14.48 (ill. p. 74)

Each spring, the merchant galleys of Venice departed for the markets of the Near East after the celebration of the Marriage of the Sea on the feast of the Ascension.[1] On this day, the doge made a ritual voyage to the Lido, where the lagoon opens to the Adriatic, and cast a golden ring into the water, thereby wedding the city and the sea. The ring also served as a conciliatory measure to insure the safety of Venetians about to sail across the Mediterranean. Before returning to the Palazzo Ducale, the doge celebrated at San Nicolò on the Lido. The origins of this ceremony, known as the *Sensa,* have been traced to the late 12th century, when Venice first asserted her supremacy over the northern Adriatic. Centuries later, even after Venice had ceased to be one of the world's great maritime powers, the ritual continued to be performed every year.

Long before the *Sensa* became a favorite subject of Canaletto and other Venetian *vedutisti*,[2] this woodcut commemorates the spirited festival in the early Cinquecento, probably during the dogate of Leonardo Loredan (r. 1501–21).[3] At the center of activity is the *Bucintoro*, the gilded ceremonial galley powered by 200 oarsmen that transported the doge and other noblemen to and from the Lido.[4] Private gondolas surround the *Bucintoro* in the water and spectators line the embankment. Among them are foreigners, including several turbaned men from the Near East. Peering out from windows draped with Oriental carpets, Venetian women both observe and become part of the spectacle. While it captures the frenzy and excitement of the *Sensa,* the scene is at least in part anachronistic. The route from the Palazzo Ducale to the Lido, for instance, did not require the *Bucintoro* to pass through a canal,[5] as it does here, and the buildings are a pastiche of structures from around the city rather than a representation of a specific quay.[6]

Combining religious and political ceremony with commerce as only Venice could, the Marriage of the Sea marked not only the beginning of the sailing season, but also the commencement of a 15-day market in Piazza San Marco, which drew thousands of foreign shoppers to buy the latest goods "the bazaar of Europe" had to offer.[7] The international fame of the piazza as a marketplace had been established earlier, as the frontispiece of the Bodleian manuscript of Marco Polo's *Il Milione* from ca. 1400 attests (cat. 15).

TK

1 On the Marriage of the Sea, see Mazzarotto 1961, pp. 180–205; Muir 1981, pp. 119–34.
2 See, for example, Canaletto's *The Bacino di San Marco on Ascension Day* from ca. 1733–34 (Royal Collection, England, C/L 335).
3 Huse and Wolters 1990, pp. 3–5.
4 On the ritual use of the *Bucintoro*, see Fortini Brown 1990.
5 For the precise route, see the map in Muir 1981, p. 9.
6 The traditional identification of the setting as the Riva degli Schiavoni thus appears to be incorrect.
7 On the *Sensa* fair, see most recently Welch 2005, pp. 177–84, 238. The appellation of Venice as the "bazaar of Europe" comes from Howard 2006.

57. Johannes de Ketham (Johannes von Kirckheim?) *"The Zodiac Man"*

fol. 8r from *Fascicolo di Medicina*
Venice, Johannes and Gregorius de Gregoriis, February 5, 1493
Printed book with woodcut illustrations
41.9 x 29.8 cm (16 1/2 x 11 3/4 in.)
The Metropolitan Museum of Art, New York
Harris Brisbane Dick Fund, 1938
Inv. no. 38.52 (ill. p. 69)

First published in Latin in 1491, the *Fascicolo di Medicina* is a compilation of medical texts on surgery, urology, herbal remedies, obstetrics, and gynecology. The first edition was associated with Johannes de Ketham, who has been tentatively identified with the 15th-century Viennese professor of medicine Johannes Kelner von Kirchheim (d. 1470), but his name was omitted from the Italian edition of 1493. This second enlarged edition, with additional texts and new woodcuts, is particularly renowned for the beauty of its illustrations, which have been called the finest examples of the so-called "classical" school of 15th-century Venetian woodcut illustration.[1]

Although in the latest Renaissance style, these illustrations may be heir to a tradition that dates back to Hellenic Alexandria, where in 300 BC anatomy was first taught from the cadaver, and two famous anatomists are reputed to have used illustrations in their lectures.[2] A standard set of "squatting" figures has been identified in medieval manuscripts that demonstrate the locations of the arteries, veins, bones, nerves, muscles, and viscera. These figures are found in Persian, Arabic, and Indian manuscripts as well as European, suggesting that they go back to a common Alexandrian or possibly Arabic source.[3] Although no longer "squatting" the series in Ketham relates to these medieval cycles, which often included a disease man, wound man, and zodiac man.

The *Zodiac Man*, in which each part of the body is associated with a specific zodiac sign, was used by doctors in conjunction with a calendar to determine the best time to operate on or let blood from certain organs—when the moon was in the sign of the organ, treatment was to be avoided. While there are literary sources testifying to the relationship between astrology and bloodletting as far back as Egyptian and Babylonian medicine, no representations of the zodiac man earlier than the 13th century have been found. However, the fact that some of the medieval zodiac men are shown in the squatting pose suggests the possibility of a Greek source.[4]

Even if the zodiac man were a medieval invention, it represents the coming together of two fields of knowledge, astrology and medicine, that had been lost to the West after the 5th century and was transmitted to Europe in the Middle Ages through Arabic and Persian manuscripts (see cat. 14). By the 11th century, some of the Arabic translations of lost Greek texts were translated into Latin and began to circulate in Europe under the Latinized names of Arabic authors such as Avicenna (Ibn Sina, 980–1037) and Ibn Zakariya, also known as Rhazes (ca. 854–925). Even the writings of the ancient Greek physician Galen (AD 129–200), which formed the framework of Western medical studies, came to Europe in the Middle Ages via Arabic texts (where he is called Jalinus) that had been edited and interpreted by Arabic medical writers, who supplemented them with their clinical experience and left out that which did not interest them.[5] The frontispiece to the *Fascicolo di Medicina* furnishes proof of the importance of the Arabic sources. Pietro da Montagnana, a Paduan grammarian renowned for his knowledge of Greek, Latin, and Hebrew, is illustrated in the act of transcribing or translating a text.[6] On the shelf above his head appears an ideal medical library, which not only includes Galen but also four Arabic authors, Avicenna, ʿAli ibn ʿAbbas (d. 994), Rhazes, and Averroës (Ibn Rushd, d. 1198).

WT

1 Hind 1935, II, p. 494; Essling 1908, II, pp. 54–57; Singer 1925, I, p. 9.
2 Herrlicher 1970, p. 9.
3 Roberts and Tomlinson 1992, p. 19.
4 Herrlicher 1970, pp. 26–28.
5 Jones 1984, pp. 22–27.
6 Pesenti 1985, pp. 15–25.

58. Giovanni Antonio Tagliente (ca. 1465–1527) *Arabesque Interlace in Circle, signature B7 and Arabesque and Classical Ornament, signature C6v and C7*

Opera nuova che insegna a le donne a cuscire . . . laqual e intitolata Esempio di raccammi *(A New Work that Teaches Women how to Sew . . . Entitled "Samples of Embroidery")*

Venice, Giovanantonio e i Fratelli da Sabbio, 1530
Text printed using Tagliente's italic font
Woodcuts engraved by Piron da Carpi
19.8 x 15.7 (7 13/16 x 6 3/16 in.)
The Metropolitan Museum of Art, New York
Harris Brisbane Dick Fund, 1935
Inv. no. 35.75.3 (ill. p. 29)

Giovanni Antonio Tagliente, who had experience as a writing instructor, seems to have had a genuine interest in pedagogy and in his later years became a pioneer in the production of instructional booklets. His publications of the 1520s include an accounting manual that was the first with both single- and double-entry bookkeeping, a calligraphy book that was a landmark in its field, a unique volume for teaching reading at home, a letter-writing manual, and a model-book for love letters that was perhaps the first of its kind.[1]

His book of designs for needlework, first published in 1527, was the earliest Italian example of what would become a very popular genre in Venice. Tagliente probably knew similar German books that had been published in Augsburg and Nuremberg as early as 1523. Setting the tone for future Venetian sewing books, Tagliente expresses his hope that his book will "render beautiful women most beautiful and charming ones most charming."[2] In Lodovico Dolce's 1547 treatise on women's education, the author has his female interlocutor claim that knowing how to sew is as important for women as knowing how to write is for men.[3] Of course, as Tagliente notes, these designs could be useful for craftsmen of all kinds, for the patterns could easily be applied to metalwork (see cats. 120–21), architectural ornament, ceramics, and even printed ornament in other books.

Among the models offered by Tagliente are many *groppi moreschi & arabeschi*—Moorish knots and arabesques. While arabesque ornament had been applied to Italian bindings as early as the 15th century (cats. 130–31) and the first printed Arabic ornament had appeared as decorative woodcut borders in an Arabic Book of Hours published in 1514 (and was likely known to Tagliente),[4] this publication was the first pattern book to supply such designs as models for use in other media. Some of Tagliente's patterns are faithful copies of Islamic designs, characterized by the strict geometry that controls the complex interlaced pattern of leaves, while others combine Islamic and classical decorative vocabularies.[5] The knot engravings of the Leonardo school could have been another source of inspiration and Tagliente's explanation of a technical shortcut for producing interlace patterns may owe something to a lost text by Leonardo himself.[6]

WT

1 Osley 1972, pp. 15–16; Schutte 1986.
2 "*le belle Donne renderle bellisime & leggiadre leggiadrissime*" (verso of title page).
3 Fortini Brown 2004, pp. 112–13.
4 Morison 1955, pp. 9–10.
5 Snodin and Howard 1996, pp. 195–97.
6 Bambach 1991.

59. Anonymous Venetian *Sultan Süleyman the Magnificent Wearing the Jewel-Studded Helmet*

Venice, ca. 1532
Woodcut
92 x 55.8 cm (36 1/4 x 21 15/16 in.) two sheets
The Metropolitan Museum of Art, New York
Harris Brisbane Dick Fund, 1942
Inv. 42.41.1 (ill. p. 112)

The magnificent head ornament depicted in this print, with its fine workmanship and extraordinary collection of diamonds, pearls, and other precious gems, was the work of Venetian goldsmiths, including Luigi Caorlini and Vincenzo Levriero, who, together with merchants active in Venice and Istanbul, planned to sell it to Sultan Süleyman the Magnificent for over 100,000 ducats. Marin Sanudo, the Venetian diarist who provides us with much of this information, reported that the object was brought to the Doge's Palace for public display on March 16, 1532.[1] It must have been on this occasion that the crown was carefully drawn in order to create this woodcut. Given its topical nature, the print was probably issued soon after the sale to the sultan (for 116,000 ducats) was confirmed.

Beneath the crown, Süleyman's profile, apart from the mustache, resembles a painted portrait in Vienna that derives from the one in Paolo Giovio's collection, recorded in a woodcut by Tobias Stimmer,[2] although it has also been identified as a product of Titian's studio.[3] By 1538 Titian had created a new image of the sultan that could be replicated on request and was said to be based on a medal (see cat. 119) and on another portrait,[4] quite possibly a copy of Giovio's.[5] If Titian's portrait was not yet in existence by 1532, the designer of this print may have relied on the same models; given Titian's involvement in the production of monumental woodcuts in this period, the design may well have originated in his circle. The cutting has been compared with works by Giovanni Britto,[6] but this German wood engraver's presence in Venice is not confirmed before 1536.

Otto Kurz, who first published the documents concerning the manufacture and sale of this splendid headgear, noted that crowns were not worn in the Islamic world and that the piece was used mainly for display—worn by a page in a ceremonial parade and exhibited in the sultan's tent to impress Austrian ambassadors.[7] More recently Gülru Necipoğlu has argued persuasively that the object, produced in collaboration with the sultan's Grand Vizier Ibrahim Pasha, was intended to send a clear message to Süleyman's European rivals. Süleyman's indignation that Charles V, crowned Holy Roman Emperor by Pope Clement VII in Bologna in 1530, should presume to the title of Caesar was part of the motivation for his planned attack on Austria and the papal territories. As Süleyman progressed towards Vienna, Ibrahim Pasha orchestrated triumphal entries and ambassadorial audiences that included a staggering display of wealth, among which the head ornament that fused the form of Charles V's imperial miter-crown with the tiara of his ally excited much comment. With its four crowns, the helmet offered a challenge to the three-tiered papal tiara and was understood by European observers—who assumed it was the Ottoman imperial crown—to symbolize Süleyman's claim to universal sovereignty. Even those aspects of the crown most in accordance with Ottoman tradition, the helmet base and the plume at top, can be seen as echoes of the pseudo-Roman helmet worn by Charles V at his coronation parade. No reports of the object have come down to us from Islamic observers, nor is the crown depicted in miniatures illustrating Süleyman's Viennese campaign.[8]

WT

1 Kurz 1969, p. 250.
2 Meyer and Bağci in Kangal 2000, cat. 17, p. 114.
3 Roxburgh 2005, cat. 284, pp. 448–49.
4 Cavalcaselle and Crowe 1974, p. 440, n. 1.
5 Meyer and Bağci in Kangal 2000, p. 100.
6 Rosand and Muraro 1976, pp. 208–9.
7 Kurz 1969, pp. 251–56.
8 Necipoğlu 1989, pp. 401–17.

60. Qur'an Printed in Arabic *Paganino and Alessandro Paganini*

Venice, 1537–38
Ink on paper; cardboard binding
27.6 x 19.4 cm (10 7/8 x 7 5/8 in.)
Provincia Veneta di S. Antonio dell'Ordine dei Frati Minori, Venice
Inv. coll. A.V. 22 (ill. p. 30)

This copy of the Qur'an, printed with mobile letters on expensive paper by the Venetian publisher Paganino Paganini and his son Alessandro Paganini in 1537–38, is of paramount importance in the history of the transmission of Islamic culture to Europe through Venice, because it represents the earliest printed Arabic edition ever produced. It is well known that printing did not become popular in the Islamic world until the 19th century, particularly because of the sacred nature of calligraphy and its relation to the copying of the Qur'an. Late 15th- and early 16th-century Venice was the right place for such an initiative because the city was at the avant-garde in printing techniques and polyglot enterprises.[1]

Before the Paganini Qur'an was printed, there had been previous successful attempts in Venice to incorporate Arabic words in Francesco Colonna's *Hypnerotomachia Poliphili* published by Aldo Manuzio in 1499; the first entire printed Arabic text is the *Kitab salat al-sawaʿi* (*Horologium*) of 1514.[2] The Republic had also been asked to grant the monopoly on prints in the "Arabic, Moorish, Syrian, Armenian, and Barbaric languages" (!) by a certain Democrito Terracina in 1498,[3] who apparently never produced such texts, given his basic ignorance of Near Eastern written idioms.

Printing a copy of the Qur'an, however, was a different matter. It was an endeavor that went beyond a simple commercial enterprise, assuming that the intended market was Ottoman Istanbul, similar to the heart-shaped map devised in Venice just two decades later (cat. 45). Angela Nuovo perceptively wrote that "the history of this Arabic Qur'an is the peculiar Venetian history of a profit-yielding sector, the typographic business, which was ingenious and strongly dynamic because it was driven by relentless competition."[4] On the other hand, the Paganinis may have underestimated the inevitable opposition to a printed Qur'an in the Muslim world, considering that practical typographic problems as well as the unavailability of a competent Arabic editor resulted in several errors and lacunae, which would have been unacceptable to any Muslim. In other words, if this Qur'an was expected to make the world best seller list because of its potential audience, it was inevitably destined to fail; this might be one reason why the present copy is the only one known to have survived.[5]

Paganino Paganini was a printer from Brescia who began conducting business in Venice in 1509. The family was involved in the export of good quality paper especially to the Near East (paper was also among the goods sold by the merchant Alessandro Magno in 1561; see cat. 54) and the father and son may have obtained through their business one or more Qur'an manuscripts that could have prompted the idea to print the text. It has been suggested that the Paganini Qur'an, like the original manuscripts, might have been intended for hand-illumination after printing, given its wide margins that traditionally would have included medallions marking verse separations and a richly decorated initial double page.[6]

Although likely unsuccessful, the Paganinis' effort probably inspired the first Italian translation of the Qur'an in 1547 as well as a later Arabic print in Rome in the late 16th century.[7] Its groundbreaking importance was recognized immediately by the Orientalist Teseo Ambrogio degli Albonesi (1469–1540), who acquired this very copy of the Paganini Qur'an shortly after its publication and cited it in one of his works printed in 1539 as an *"Alcorani typis impressis"* (a printed Qur'an).[8]

SC

1 From this period are also the earliest printed books in Cyrillic and Armenian characters, in addition, of course, to the earlier Greek and Hebrew texts. See Zorzi 2000.
2 It was published at Fano on the Adriatic coast in Central Italy by Gregorio de Gregori who was mostly active in Venice; see Galbiati 1946. Both books are in Venice 2000, pp. 164–65, cat. 104–5; Vercellin 2000, pp. 54–55.
3 *"in lingua Arabica, moresca, sorian, armenicha et barbaresca"*; Zorzi 2000, p. 26.
4 Nuovo 1990, p. 119.
5 Although its existence was known since 1539 from Teseo Ambrogio degli Albonesi (see below), it was Nuovo's fortunate discovery in the library of the small convent of San Michele on the homonymous island of Venice's famous cemetery that brought this copy to the attention of scholars.
6 Bobzin 1995, p. 197.
7 For the translation, see Venice 2000, p. 163, cat. 102. The later print was the work of Giovan Battista Raimondi for the Stamperia Orientale Medicea, starting in 1584; see Venice 1993, pp. 297–98, cat. 298.
8 This Qur'an includes Teseo's autograph note of ownership at fol. [aa]4v; see Venice 2000, pp. 167–68, cat. 110.

61. Anonymous *Il volo del turco*

Venice, 1816 (after original of ca. 1548)
Engraving on paper
3.85 x 5.9 cm (1.5 x 2 3/8 in.)
Museo Civico Correr, Venice
Inv. St. P.D. 8114

The annual pre-Lenten festival of Carnival began in Venice on December 26 and reached its dramatic climax during the week preceding Ash Wednesday, starting with *giovedì grasso*, or Shrove Thursday.[1] This engraving commemorates a lively *giovedì grasso* spectacle known as *il volo del turco*, or the flight of the Turk, introduced during the dogate of Francesco Donà (r. 1545–53). A Turkish tightrope walker originally performed this three-part feat in the theater-like Piazzetta.[2] From a floating dock offshore, the Turk ascended to the belfry of San Marco's bell tower on a rope; then he descended, turning somersaults, on a different rope into the second-floor gallery of the Palazzo Ducale, landing at the doge's feet. There the Turk presented the doge with sonnets and the dogaressa with a bouquet of flowers in exchange for money; finally he climbed back to the belfry before sliding down to where he began in the *bacino*. Although aided by pulleys and rings, the tightrope walker appeared miraculously to fly, and over time the stunts became ever more dangerous and thrilling.[3]

In this print, the tightrope walker, balancing himself with a pole, is making the perilous journey towards the campanile. Three turbaned men, presumably also Turkish, operate the pulleys from the floating dock offshore. Members of the populace watch from the Piazzetta below and in gondolas on the water, while government officials and the nobility observe from the privileged perspective of the Palazzo Ducale's *piano nobile*.

In mid 16th-century Italy, Turks appear to have been admired for their acrobatic skill and showmanship, and those who performed in Venice were handsomely paid.[4] In his famous portrait gallery in Como, Paolo Giovio had a portrait of "Ali Turco," a Turkish aerialist believed to have been painted from life in Rome in 1547.[5] The Ottoman court may well have fostered the development of tightrope acts for their own entertainment, and it is possible that Venetian merchants and diplomats first saw spectacles similar to *il volo del turco* performed in Istanbul.[6] On Venetian soil, however, the act became more than mere amusement; it had a political charge as well. Tightrope walkers and other street performers, such as jugglers, singers, musicians, and buffoons, were considered uncivil and full of vice.[7] By hiring a Turk to perform as an acrobat, Venetians appear to have been declaring their sense of moral superiority over the Ottomans as a people. Adding another layer of meaning, the author of this print depicts the Turkish tightrope walker as he reached the halfway point between the Piazzetta's Columns of Justice, the place were criminals were subjected to public ridicule and executed.[8] In the playful and uninhibited atmosphere of Carnival, Venetians expressed their ambivalence about their Muslim neighbors and trading partners through this spectacle.

Attesting to its enduring popularity, *il volo del turco* continued to be performed in Venice for centuries, although locals

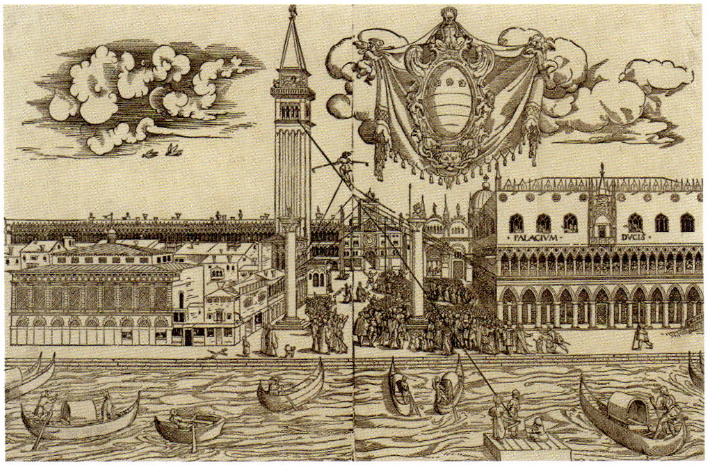

cat. 61

eventually took over the role and then, because of the inherent danger, a puppet was used instead.[9] *Il volo della colombina*, the flight of the dove, of today's Venetian Carnival represents a reinterpretation of the original spectacle.

Several later representations of *il volo del turco* are known,[10] but the first edition of this print may be among the very earliest. Doge Donà's coat of arms provide it with a *terminus ante quem* of 1553, and the fact that it records Sansovino's Marciana Library, begun in 1537, in its initial phase of construction, with only the first ten bays completed, suggests the print could have been made in the late 1540s.[11] In 1816, after Venice had lost its liberty and Carnival celebrations temporarily ceased, the print was reissued, either as a reminder of the city's glorious past or because of a renewed interest in Orientalist themes (or both). The Correr's print belongs to the early 19th-century edition.[12]

TK

1 Muir 1981, pp. 156–81.
2 Michiel 1829, pp. 57–59.
3 Mazzarotto 1961, pp. 34–35; Norris 1983, p. 38.
4 In 1564, for example, the tightrope walker who performed *il volo del turco* received 100 ducats (Muir 1981, p. 171, n. 100).
5 De Vecchi 1977; p. 95, cat. 59; Klinger 1991, p. 9.
6 A tightrope spectacle performed above water is illustrated, for example, in the *Surname* in Topkapı Sarayı Müzesi (A.3593, fols. 139v-40r). Though later than the advent of *il volo del turco*, the manuscript depicts traditional festivals organized by the Ottoman state. See Atıl 1993.
7 See generally, Kenaan-Kedar 1992.
8 On public performances of justice between the Piazzetta's columns, see Johnson 2000, pp. 444–46.
9 Pignatti 1975, p. 208.
10 Reproduced in Mazzarotto 1961, p. 34; Norris 1983, p. 39.
11 Howard 1974, fig. 10 identifies the coat of arms as Francesco Donà's.
12 Lorenzetti 1928–29, p. 85.

62. Giovanni Francesco Camocio (active 1552–75) *"Finial of Turkish Standard Given to the Venetian Senate after Victory at Lepanto, 1571,"* pl. 67

Isole famose, porti, fortezze, terre maritime della Repubblica di Venetia et altri principi Cristiani, et al Sig.or Turco novamente poste in luce (Famous Islands, Ports, Fortresses, Maritime Lands of the Republic of Venice, of Other Christian Princes, and of the Turkish Lord, Newly Described)
Publisher: Donato Bertelli (active 1558–1623), Venice, Alla libraria del segno di San Marco, after August 1574
Biblioteca Nazionale Marciana, Venice
Inv. Rari V. 244 (ill. p. 92)

Giovanni Francesco Camocio was a bookseller and publisher of prints, maps, and books. He published a wide variety of prints, from devotional images to reproductions of Titian paintings, yet he is most admired for his cartographic activities in a period when Venice was preeminent in the field. Although Camocio is usually identified as the author of this book, only 12 of the plates bear his name and the address on the title page is the bookshop of his competitor Donato Bertelli. It has been persuasively argued that after Camocio's death—which seems to have occurred in the great plague of 1575—Bertelli acquired Camocio's plates and published this compendium.[1] The earliest print dates to 1566 and the latest to 1574 but most of the prints are from 1571.

Although not accompanied by a separate text, the maps tell the story of the progressive conquest of Venetian lands by the Ottomans, with occasional Venetian successes. Many of the maps would have originally been issued like newspaper reports to document the ongoing power struggle.[2] The climax of the narrative comes with the Battle of Lepanto in 1571 (see cat. 34), a surprising reversal in which the Venetians took enormous pride. The victorious Venetian warriors had returned dressed in Ottoman garb, dragging the standards of their enemy behind them.[3]

Among the most curious and handsome images in the *Isolario* is the engraving of a gilded silver finial captured from the Ottomans in this battle. The inscription states that it comes from the standard of the commander of the Ottoman armada: it had been donated to the Venetian governing council by the goldsmiths Paolo and Bernardino Sancto, it was three times the size of the print, and it was entirely covered with Turkish writing. This writing has been accurately transcribed and translated, although the engraver, who took care to incise the Italian text in reverse so that it would read correctly, has not thought to reverse the Arabic calligraphy, which appears in mirror image. The profession of faith, "There is no god but Allah and Muhammad is the Prophet of Allah," is the phrase most frequently found on Ottoman flags and finials and the other devotional text is characteristic of the type of inscriptions used in this context: "A divine protection and ornament for the faithful; in the worthy enterprise, Allah favors Muhammad."[4] In a report sent to Vienna in 1571 by the Imperial ambassadors in Venice, mention is made of a gilded silver finial that bears exactly the same inscriptions. Donated to the Signoria by an unnamed goldsmith, who had purchased it from a soldier for 50 ducats, the standard was to have been installed in a public place, presumably the Sala d'Armi of the Doge's Palace, where many such trophies were displayed. The report does not mention that the finial had come from the commander's standard, but this may not have been immediately recognized. If this account, which describes the finial as circular, does not refer to the very same object illustrated here, it certainly gives a fuller picture of the circumstances of its donation.[5]

WT

1 Gallo 1950, pp. 96–100; Sman 2000, pp. 239, 242.
2 Woodward 1996, pp. 93–99; Witcombe 2004, p. 244.
3 Wilson 2005, p. 149.
4 Zygulski 1992, pp. 34–35.
5 De Lucia 1908, p. 147.

63. Cesare Vecellio (ca. 1521–1601) *"La Favorita del Turco" De gli habiti antichi et moderni di diverse parti del mondo libri due . . .* (Of Ancient and Modern Dress from Diverse Parts of the World in Two Books . . .)

Publisher: Damiano Zenaro, Venice, 1590
Printed book with woodcuts by Christoph Krieger [Cristoforo Guerra]
16.9 x 13 cm (6 3/4 x 5 1/8 in.)
The Metropolitan Museum of Art, New York
Museum accession, 1921
Inv. 21.36.146, fol. 391v (ill. p. 113)

Cesare Vecellio was a distant relative of Titian (Tiziano Vecellio, 1490–1576), who joined Titian's workshop in Venice and probably remained there until the master's death. As a painter, he carried out a number of significant commissions in both oil (cat. 33) and fresco, particularly in his native Cadore,[1] but he is best known as the author and illustrator of this important costume book.

Vecellio's book is, in many ways, the culmination of a trend that began in the mid-16th century with a series of engravings of European costumes attributed to Enea Vico. Although the set was never completed, the Vico prints were in wide circulation by 1558, providing models for costume books from the very first such book, published in Paris in 1562, right through to Vecellio. The source for most 16th-century representations of Turkish costumes was Nicolas de Nicolay's illustrated account of his travels in the Ottoman Empire as part of the retinue of Francis I. First published in Lyon in 1567, the book went through numerous editions, including a Venetian one of 1580. In the 1570s and '80s, new costume books appeared in Germany, Italy, and the Netherlands, among which the volumes of Boissard and De Bruyn stand out for their finely engraved illustrations.[2] While most of these costume books were essentially collections of plates, Vecellio's thick quarto volume is a true treatise on costume, which even attempts to address the historical evolution of national dress. For his plates, Vecellio drew from all the earlier costume books, but also added new material. Although he traveled little—he is known to have been to Augsburg with Titian in 1548—Vecellio had the opportunity to observe foreign visitors in Venice and could rely on a wide range of informants, many of them artists capable of providing him with sketches.[3] The first section of Vecellio's book covers the costumes of Europe, concluding with a section on Turkish costume. The short second section (or book) on Africa and Asia includes the dress of Persians, Armenians, Ethiopians, Moors, and Arabs.

Among the Turkish women Vecellio illustrates is one labeled "*Favorita del Turco.*" By calling her "the favorite" here and in his accompanying text, Vecellio calls to mind the woman known as Roxelane (which may mean Ruthenian maiden) and as Hurrem or "the Merry One," who rose from being a slave and concubine to become the wife and confidant of Süleyman the Magnificent. Hurrem created a stir in the Muslim world for breaking with numerous Ottoman traditions—bearing more than one son to the sultan, becoming a free woman and his legal wife, leaving the seraglio to live in the palace with the sultan, and not accompanying any of her sons when they were assigned provincial posts. Remaining in her husband's palace, she was the one who kept Süleyman informed about conditions in Istanbul when he was away.[4] This powerful unseen woman fascinated the Venetians, who needed to court her favor. Titian painted her portrait—probably largely from imagination—which survives in many copies. Vecellio, as a member of Titian's studio, would have known this work as well as the woodcut issued by Mattheo Pagani at mid-century and identified as *la più bella e più favorita donna del gran Turcho dita la Rossa* (The most beautiful and favorite woman of the Great Turk, nicknamed the Red-Haired).[5] While Vecellio's "favorite" is similarly labeled, in most details he follows an image in Boissard's costume book of 1581 that is identified as Süleyman's daughter Camilla.[6] Süleyman never had a child named Camilla, but his only daughter Mihrimah became his confidant after her mother's death in 1558.[7] A powerful princess and an important patron of architecture, she too was portrayed by Titian, as we know from Vasari and a number of surviving portrait replicas identified as Süleyman's daughter.[8] Vecellio probably did not intend to provide a portrait of either Roxelane or Mihrimah, but rather to represent the splendor of dress characteristic of the Ottoman woman closest to the sultan.

WT

1 Conte 2001.
2 Guérin-Dalle Mese 1998, pp. 12–17; Olian 1977; Gomez-Gérard and Yérasimos 1989.
3 Guérin-Dalle Mese 1998, pp. 48–50.
4 Pierce 1988, pp. 58–65; Pierce 1992.
5 Sman 2003, pp. 186–87.
6 Boissard 1581, n.p.
7 Pierce 1988, p. 65.
8 Sman 2003, p. 186.

64. Avicenna (Ibn Sina) (980–1037)

Canon (Avicennae Arabum medicorum principis Ex Gerardi Cremonensis versione et Andreae Alpagi Bellunensis castigatione)

Venice, 1595
Printed book
36 x 25 cm (14 1/4 x 9 7/8 in.)
Bibliothèque interuniversitaire de medicine, Paris
Inv. 99 (ill. p. 70)

Between 1487 and 1517, the Bellunese physician Andrea Alpago (d. 1522) served the Venetian merchant colony in Damascus, where he learned Arabic and the tenets of Islamic medicine well enough to complete an entirely new Latin translation of Avicenna's *Canon*, which superceded the previous one by Gerard da Cremona (d. 1187).[1] In medieval and Renaissance Italy, the *Canon*, an encyclopedia of Greco-Arabic medicine noted for its comprehensiveness and excellent organization, served as one of the principal textbooks for medical students, including those at the University of Padua.[2] In 1521, the Junta printing house in Venice first published Alpago's translation of the *Canon*, and that same year the College of Philosophers and Physicians in Padua both endorsed it and hired him as a professor.[3] After his death, Alpago's nephew Paolo continued issuing new annotated editions of his translation with the Junta press, one of the leading publishers of medical texts in the Veneto.[4] Their 1544 edition opens with six engraved images, stacked in vertical rows across two pages; these illustrations also appear in several successive editions, including the one of 1595, exhibited here.[5]

In European manuscripts and printed books of the *Canon*, author portraits of Avicenna are relatively common, as are representations of him presiding over a council of other famous physicians and philosophers.[6] In this instance, however, all six engravings show the implementation of medical procedures described in the *Canon*, emphasizing the practical application of Avicenna's text by the primary audience of this edition, University of Padua students. In each scene, a turbaned doctor attempts to realign his patient's spine using different contraptions as well as by simply walking barefoot upon his back. It is unclear whether the doctor-chiropractor is intended to be Avicenna himself. In any event, the presence of turbaned figures in the composition emphasizes the Islamic pedigree of the medical text that follows and hence its sophistication. The most prominent kind of turban illustrated in the engravings is voluminous and wrapped around a *taj* in the Ottoman fashion, the type of Muslim headgear with which Venetians were probably most familiar in the 16th century.

TK

1 Lucchetta 1964; Siraisi 1987, pp. 104, 145–46; Paris 1996.
2 Siraisi 1987.
3 Ibid., pp. 8, 94, 96
4 Ibid., pp. 133–134; Burnett 1999, pp. 190–91.
5 Siraisi 1987, p. 134; Paris 1996, p. 300, fig. 209.
6 Hasse 1997.

65. Giacomo Franco (1550–1620)

"Schiac Appas, Re di Persia" (Shah ᶜAbbas, King of Persia)

Effigie naturali dei maggior prencipi et più valorosi capitani di questa età con l'armi loro, raccolte et con dilegentia intagliate da Giacomo Franco (Natural Likenesses of the Major Princes and Most Valorous Captains of This Age, with Their Arms, Collected and Diligently Engraved by Giacomo Franco).
Published in Venice, 1596
Engraving
30.6 x 20.8 (12 x 8 1/4 in.)
The Metropolitan Museum of Art, New York
The Elisha Whittelsey Collection, The Elisha Whittelsey Fund, 1957
Inv. no. 57.506, fol. 32 (ill. p. 81)

Giacomo Franco was the natural son and sole heir of the painter and printmaker Battista Franco, known as "Il Semolei." Through the mid-1590s, Giacomo was active as an engraver of frontispieces, book illustrations, topical prints, and maps. Among his most impressive works are the full-page illustrations for Anguillara's translation of Ovid's *Metamorphoses* (Venice, 1584) and for Torquato Tasso's *La Gerusalemme Liberata* (Genoa, 1590; see cat. 40).[1] In the 1590s, Franco turned to publishing his own works. Although his 1591 request for a privilege to publish a book of women's costumes was denied, by the time he issued this collection of portraits in 1596, Franco had already published a two-volume writing book and a sewing book for women.[2]

Franco's decision to publish a series of portraits of individuals famous for their leadership or martial valor must be understood in the framework of an increasing interest in such effigies, stimulated especially by the well-known collection of portraits assembled by Paolo Giovio and exhibited in his private museum at Como. In 1575 a new edition of Giovio's *Elogia virorum bellica virtute illustrium* (Tribute to the Men of War Celebrated for their Virtues) was published in Basel, illustrated with woodcuts by Tobias Stimmer that reproduce Giovio's portraits of men distinguished for their skill at war. These cuts appeared again, without Giovio's text, in a work entitled *Musaei ioviani imagines* (Illustrations from Giovio's Museum; Basel, 1577).[3] Among its 133 images of powerful rulers and military men are represented seven "Turkish emperors," the most recent being Süleyman the Magnificent, and three "Persian kings," along with eight other powerful figures from the Muslim world.[4] Franco's book can be seen as a supplement to this volume, for whereas Giovio's collection was historical, providing images of rulers as far back as Romulus and Alexander the Great, Franco's smaller book is limited to contemporary rulers, most of whom had come to power since 1577. Assembled from diverse sources, all the rulers are represented in a dignified and imposing manner, many holding staffs and all accompanied by their coats of arms—those from Islamic countries are provided with imaginary ones. While the figures are engraved in a controlled style, the backgrounds are frequently enlivened with etched scenes of military exercises. Franco's collection includes an even higher proportion of Eastern rulers than Giovio's, eight of thirty-five, including the current Ottoman sultan Mehmet II, with three of his military leaders, and the current "King of Persia," Shah ᶜAbbas I (r. 1588–1629).

While the attitude of Venetians towards the Ottoman Empire was ambivalent—peaceful relations were necessary to assure trade yet the Turks threatened Venetian territory—the Venetian view of the Persians, who had never exercised aggression against Venice but had at times challenged the authority of the Ottomans, was much more positive. Shah ᶜAbbas I was a declared enemy of the Ottoman Empire. Although the Venetians would resist his attempts to enlist them in his battle strategy, they admired his valor and were grateful that he kept the Ottoman forces occupied in battling the Persian army. His ambassadors received a royal welcome in Venice (see cat. 83) and the assurances of ᶜAbbas I that Venetian merchants would always be welcome in Persia guaranteed a flourishing trade between the nations. Armenians from Persia had long had a presence in Venice. Many passed through as merchants and ambassadors and some settled there, such as a Cristoforo from Tabriz who in 1557 translated a Persian novel into Italian.[5]

WT

1 Pasero 1936.
2 Witcombe 2004, pp. 291–93.
3 Wilson 2005, p. 201.
4 Muller 1577. (The Metropolitan Museum's copy 21.36.34).
5 Benzoni 1985b, pp. 80–82.

66. Attributed to Francesco Basilicata (active in the first half of the 17th century)

Turk on a Horse

Venice, 1618
Print
37 x 49 cm (14 5/8 x 19 3/8 in.)
Museo Civico Correr, Venice
Inv. St. Correr 4731 (ill. p. 34)

As in many other Islamic cultures, Ottoman Turkey had a rich equestrian tradition, and Turkish cavalrymen enjoyed international renown for their prowess. In preparation for military battle, they often learned *cirit*, a dangerous equine game played with wooden spears and javelins that required a high degree of athleticism.[1] The sport was also popular at the Ottoman court, where it was performed after weddings and on holidays, especially from the 16th to the 18th century. Transformed into a proper spectacle, *cirit* demanded even greater virtuosity, with the riders taking extraordinary risks by riding backwards, vaulting, and somersaulting on horses galloping at full speed. Numerous European ambassadors to the court, including Venetians such as Pietro Zen,[2] witnessed such displays of horsemanship. Evidently awestruck, they meticulously recorded details about the riders' feats, costumes, weapons, and thoroughbred horses.[3]

This intriguing print of a Turkish rider mounted upon a horse has been attributed to Francesco Basilicata, a cartographer and military engineer to the Venetian Republic in the early 17th century. From ca. 1612 to 1638 he lived on the Venetian colony of Crete, where he supervised and improved the island's defense system. By this time, the Ottoman Empire dominated the Eastern Mediterranean and Crete remained Venice's only major possession in the region. Venetians considered a Turkish attack of Crete inevitable, and their worst fears were realized when the Ottomans invaded the island in 1645.[4]

Francesco Basilicata is best known for his interest in Crete's fortification prior to its fall to the Turks, yet he also concerned himself with its feudal cavalry.[5] Given his position, Basilicata would have been well aware of the formidability of the Ottoman Empire's own cavalry and its importance within the Ottoman military. Basilicata's representation of a Turkish rider in all his glory upon a quickly galloping horse, cape blowing in the wind, weapons in both hands, and standing erect on the animal's back serves as a visual complement to the written descriptions of Turkish riders recorded by European ambassadors. The print, however, takes on distinctly more ominous tones, given that it appears to have been made at a time when the Venetians had a heightened fear of Ottoman military might.

TK

1 Rogers 1996, p. 182.
2 Ibid., p. 183, n. 41.
3 Ibid., p. 176.
4 See Clutton 1978 for the broader historical context.
5 Ibid., pp. 278–80.

67. Vincenzo Maria Coronelli (1650–1718)

"Turkish banner"

Description géographique et historique de la Morée, reconquise par les Vénitiens... (Geographic and Historical Description of the Morea, Again Conquered by the Venetians..."), pl. 17
Nicolas Langlois publisher, Paris, 1687
38.5 x 25.5 cm (15 1/8 x 10 in.); fold-out

plate 38.5 x 54 cm (15 1/8 x 21 1/4 in.)
Biblioteca Nazionale Marciana, Venice
Inv. 203.D.23 (ill. p. 47)

This is one of 103 engravings in the *Description géographique et historique de la Morée, reconquise par les Vénitiens,* a volume published in Paris in 1687 by the Venetian geographer and cosmographer Vincenzo Coronelli.[1] The subject is the 1685 Venetian victory over the Ottoman Turks at Corone, a city in the Morea (the Greek peninsula also known as the Peloponnesus). The Captain-General of the Venetian forces, Francesco Morosini (1618–1694), who later became doge of Venice, led the military expedition to recapture the Morea, which had been under Turkish domination since 1485.[2] When he returned victoriously to Venice, Morosini's booty included a large group of Turkish banners. The Venetians celebrated the arrival of these banners with fireworks, processions, concerts, and a solemn mass in St. Mark's Basilica, and public alms were administered. One banner was exhibited on St. Mark's façade before being transferred to the altar of St. Gaetano in the Church of the Tolentini.

A large banner decorated with geometric and foliate patterns and an Arabic inscription with the profession of the Muslim faith ("There is no God but Allah and Muhammad is His Prophet") dominates the composition of this print. Beneath the banner, small putti, typical Baroque embellishments, hold two standards. The standard on the left bears the saying, "In the name of Allah, the most Gracious, the most Merciful. Help from Allah and a victory near at hand. And give good news to the Believers," followed by "Oh! Muhammad, Abu Bakr, ᶜUmar, ᶜUthman, ᶜAli." (Qur'an, Ch. 61, verse 13), while the one on the right is inscribed "There is no God but Allah and Muhammad is the messenger of Allah. Our Lord, decide between us and our people with truth, and You are the Best of Deciders" (Qur'an, 7:89). To the right of the large banner is a military scene showing Venetian soldiers actively defeating the Ottomans. A mustached Turk, who looks remarkably similar to the one represented on the figurehead of Francesco Morosini's *bastarda* ship (cat. 149), protects himself with a shield decorated with crescent moons, a Turkish symbol. While one Venetian attacks a turbaned Turk with a lance, others approach from behind, waving a banner with a winged lion, the symbol of Venice, and brandishing a large wooden cross, the emblem of Christianity. The battle takes place in front of a large Ottoman military tent with *tu* s (Turkish battle standards) marking its entrance.

The *Description . . . de la Morée* is based on Coronelli's earlier Italian publications, *Le Memorie istoriografiche del Regno di Morea e Negroponte* and *Le conquiste della Repubblica in Dalmazia, Epiro e Morea,* both of 1685.[3] These works enjoyed great success, as testified by their numerous editions and translations into German, English, and Flemish in addition to French.[4] Used repeatedly throughout Coronelli's work, the image of the captured Turkish banner became a powerful symbol of the Venetian Republic's military victories over the formidable Ottoman Empire in the late 17th century.

RM

1 Armao 1944.
2 Navari 1995, p. 505.
3 Stouraiti 2002, p. 143 ff.
4 Armao 1944. Among the 15 editions of *Le Memorie istoriografiche della Morea* three of them are *in folio* (one is in Venice, the other in Paris), ten are *in octavo* and two are *in sedicesimo.* Six of them are in Italian, six in French, and three respectively in English, German, and Flemish.

TEXTILES AND CARPETS

68. *Fragment of cloth from the tomb of Cangrande I della Scala* (d. 1329)

Possibly northwest Persia, early 14th century
Silk *lampas,* brocaded fabric with silver-gilt-wrapped silk thread
73 x 200 cm (28 3/4 x 78 3/4 in.)
Musei Civici, Museo di Castelvecchio, Verona
Inv. 36287 (ill. p. 64)

Can Francesco della Scala[1] (1291–1329), known as Cangrande, ruled Verona in the early 14th century and became an important patron of the poet Dante Alighieri when the latter sought refuge in Verona after being exiled from Florence. Cangrande stipulated a commercial treaty with Venice in 1323 and never set his eyes on the much more powerful Republic on the lagoon, but his short and tumultuous reign saw Verona in conflict with many of Venice's neighbors, especially Padua, Vicenza, Treviso, and Belluno. After his death in 1329, his body was eventually housed in a marble tomb over the entrance to the tomb of Santa Maria Antica in Verona.

Found in the bottom of the tomb in 1921, together with two smaller fragments from the same cloth, the present fabric was originally part of Cangrande's outer burial tunic while the two other pieces formed his hat.[2] Over time the metal hilt of the sword that was placed in the tomb made a circular hole near the left edge of the larger fabric. The design includes beautifully drawn four-lobed medallions with a central stylized flower, smaller circular medallions including a knotted pattern linking the larger motifs, and various paired animals (birds, fish, hares, and felines) in the voids left by the medallions. Clearly, the design is Islamic with Chinese inspiration, and the fabric is thought to have originated in Tabriz,[3] which in the early 14th century was under the rule of the Mongol Il-Khanid dynasty that had embraced Islam late in the previous century.[4] Paola Frattaroli made the colored reconstruction drawing for the catalogue of the recent exhibition dealing with Cangrande's life.[5]

Surviving Mongol brocaded silks in the *lampas* technique are relatively rare, but typically combine staggered rows of geometric decorative frames, such as small four-lobed medallions, with paired birds or animals, as seen here. Venetian commercial relations with Iran, while not of the same level as the Venetian Mediterranean maritime trade, did include Azerbaijan in northwestern Persia, where Khiyar and Tabriz were known for producing elegant textiles such as these. In the first half of the 14th century merchants selling linen or cotton cloth produced in Italy and in Champagne and exported through Constantinople reached markets as far away as Trebizond and Tabriz, and it is not at all surprising that on the return voyage luxury fabrics from the East made their way back to Venice and the *terraferma* in Verona. For Dante himself, the beneficiary of his fellow Ghibelline Cangrande's generosity, these Middle Eastern silks were a byword for color and luxury. In describing the pelt of the monster Gerione in the *Inferno* (XVII, lines 14–17), he says:

his back and chest as well as both his flanks
had been adorned with twining knots and circlets.
No Turks or Tartars ever fashioned fabrics more colorful in background and relief."[6]

WD / SC

1 See also the fragments of a beaker made in Venice with the coat of arms of the della Scala (cat. 159).
2 Sangiorgi 1921–22; see the reconstruction of the tunic and hat in a drawing in Magagnato 1983, p. 109.
3 Magagnato 1983, pp. 100–109; Verona 2004, pp. 287–88, cat. 27.
4 Komaroff and Carboni 2003, pp. 184, 260, cat. 70; see also Ashtor 1983, p. 394.
5 Verona 2004, fig. p. 90.
6 ". . . *lo dosso e 'l petto e ambedue le coste dipinti avea di nodi e di rotelle. Con più color, sommesse e sovraposte non fer mai drappi Tartari né Turchi,*" in Mandelbaum's translation.

69. *Textile fragment with Mamluk emblem*

Egypt, ca. 1468–96
Wool, plain weave and appliqué
22.9 x 30.5 cm (9 x 12 in.)
The Metropolitan Museum of Art, New York
Rogers Fund, 1972
Inv. 1972.120.3 (ill. p. 75)

The Mamluks (1250–1517) in Egypt and Syria developed a system of emblems or blazons that indicated the office of a particular emir at the court; for example, the diamond-shaped figure of a napkin (*buqja*) for the Master of the Robes (*jamdar*),[1] or a sword for the armor-bearer (*silahdar*). Since appointments at the court, including that of the sultan, were not hereditary, these symbols of office were not equivalent to the coats of arms of European families. In time, especially after the Circassian or Burji Mamluks came to power in 1391, these emblems grew in complexity and several symbols became incorporated in the same blazon, either because the emir had held different offices in the past or there existed a generic "logo"—irrespective of the office held—that linked a newly appointed emir to the sultan he served.[2]

This seems to be the case of the present textile fragment—either from a piece of clothing or furnishing—that is divided into three horizontal fields including a napkin on top, a cup with the symbol of the pen-box flanked by two horns or "Trousers of Nobility"[3] in the middle field, and a second cup at the bottom. The color combination of both the background and the single elements probably helped to identify this particular emir, who is unfortunately unknown to us. There is little doubt, however, that he was in the service of the sultan al-Ashraf Qa'itbey (r. 1468-96), since the few emirs who can be identified with this specific composite blazon were under his patronage.[4]

These late 15th-century emblems became familiar to the Venetian "Orientalist" painters, who probably interpreted them as coats of arms of the house of the Mamluks, through oral and written descriptions, colored sketches, objects, and textiles like the present one. The symbol of the cup flanked by two horns seems to have been particularly appealing to these painters. It became part of the architectural landscape in Giovanni Mansueti's anachronistic episodes from the life of St. Mark populated by a crowd in Mamluk costumes (see cats. 27–28). In the famous painting illustrating a contemporary scene, the anonymous *Reception of the Venetian Ambassadors in Damascus* (cat. 29)—dated 1511 toward the very end of the Mamluk Dynasty—the emblem depicted on the walls of the palace of the sultan's representative in Syria is the very same as the present textile, including the colors of the background of the three horizontal fields. Little is known about the emblems of the emirs under Sultan Qansuh al-Ghawri (r. 1501–16); they may have emulated those of earlier decades, but the close match with blazons related to Sultan Qa'itbey suggests that the Venetian painter—assuming he was indeed depicting an episode from the second decade of the 16th century— was relying on earlier visual documents in creating his Mamluk architecture.

SC

1 The *buqja* was a piece of cloth worn by the *jamdar* in which documents and other things were wrapped up, thus taking the stylized shape of a square or diamond.
2 The latter may have been individualized, making use of different colors.
3 Mayer 1933, pp. 19–22.
4 See, for example, Mayer 1933, pls. LXII:3 (Sibay ibn Bukht Jukha), LXIII (Qajmas al-Ishaqi), LXVI:3 (from the Khan al-Sabun in Aleppo).

70. *Ecclesiastical cope (piviale)*

Probably Bursa, Turkey, cut, assembled, and embroidered in Venice, mid-15th century
Silk velvet, cut, assembled, and embroidered with silk and silver-gilt-wrapped silk thread
H. ca. 140 cm (55 1/8 in.); W. ca. 297 cm (117 in.)
Basilica di Santa Maria Gloriosa dei Frari, Venice
(ill. p. 87)

Heavy silk velvet, a weaving technique practiced in Italy, Egypt, and the Ottoman realms in the 15th century, usually resulted in fabrics with large-scale designs and rich, if limited, coloration. They were especially suitable as furnishing fabrics and for showy outer garments with little tailoring used for ceremonies of all kinds in both East and West. Copes, dalmatics, and chasubles used in Roman Catholic ritual and made of Ottoman velvets woven in Bursa are today found in churches and museums in Sweden, Romania, Bosnia, Poland, Italy, and in museum collections as far afield as Cincinnati and Kansas City; Ottoman velvets were the primary fabric of choice for Russian Orthodox ceremonial vestments as well, and are preserved in significant numbers in various Russian collections.

The Frari *piviale* is of particular interest as the design suggests a mid-15th century origin for the fabric, using staggered rows of alternately red- and white-ground compartments set on a field of scrolling vines and flowers.[1] Venetian velvets in similar layout and style probably formed the inspiration for a group of central Anatolian carpets of the 17th and 18th centuries that took their designs from the more urban and opulent silk textiles.

Until recently, there was considerable confusion between Ottoman and Italian velvets, a problem exacerbated by the Italian practice of weaving velvets in Ottoman layouts and using what were even then recognized as emblematic Ottoman designs, and by the Ottoman adoption of Italian artistic motifs in the velvets of Bursa. In the present case, it seems that the silk velvet is probably from Bursa, less likely from Venice, but it was cut, assembled, and embroidered with silk and silver-gilt-wrapped silk thread in Venice.

WD

1 Venice 1993, p. 467, cat. 316; Melbourne 1997, p. 71, cat. 53 (where it is erroneously identified as Iranian).

°71. *Pieced panel of brocaded silk*

Turkey, Probably Bursa, second half of 16th century
Silk velvet pile and voided areas brocaded with silver-gilt-wrapped silk wefts
168 x 132 cm (66 1/8 x 52 in.)
The Metropolitan Museum of Art, New York
Rogers Fund; 1972
Inv. 17.29.10 (ill. p. 60)

Bursa, a mountainside city in northwest Anatolia about 60 kilometers away from Istanbul, was from the mid-15th to the 17th century the major source of Ottoman woven silk velvets. This splendid panel, composed of two loom-width pieces sewn together, typifies Bursa velvet weaving in the second half of the 16th century. In the large-scale and dramatic design, three pairs of leaves originally brocaded with brilliant shiny silver thread, now tarnished and corroded, were decorated with small crimson honeysuckles, rosebuds, and carnations. The leaves form embracing frames for small silver pinecone-like forms probably intended to represent artichokes, a favorite motif of 16th-century Ottoman weavers and ceramic artists.[1]

Fabrics such as this were primarily used in the Ottoman Empire for furnishings such as cushions, curtains, and wall hangings, in contrast to their use for ceremonial costume in European countries to which they were exported in large numbers. By the later 15th and throughout the 16th century, Ottoman velvets were in direct competition with their Italian counterparts. Probably as a consequence, relatively few examples of Ottoman silks have survived in Italy, most of them as decorative panels such as this example, or as untailored loom-width lengths of cloth, and we rarely if ever see depictions of recognizable Ottoman fabrics of the 16th century in Italian and Venetian paintings. By contrast, Italian velvets, some made in Ottoman designs specifically for the Ottoman market, were prized at the Ottoman court in the early to mid-16th century, and royal velvet kaftans made of Italian and French cloth greatly outnumber those made of Turkish velvet in the imperial collections surviving today in Istanbul's Topkapı Palace (cat. 80); in addition, Turkish weavers sometimes wove carpets inspired by Venetian velvets. By the later 16th century, the Ottomans has begun a self-conscious effort to promote their own styles and luxury products within their empire, a change doubtless prompted by bullionist economic policies.

WD

1 Atasoy et al. 2001, pp. 171–72, 182–90.

72. *Loom-width piece of brocaded silk fabric*

Probably Istanbul, mid-16th century
Silk *kemha* (lampas) fabric brocaded with silver-gilt-wrapped silk weft
141 x 66.2 cm (55 1/2 x 26 in.)
Topkapı Sarayı Müzesi, Istanbul
Inv. 13/1904 (ill. p. 184)

Ottoman multicolored *kemha* silks, in which contrasting figural designs including silver or gilt-silver-wrapped silk thread are brocaded against a shiny satin ground, were primarily produced in Istanbul, beginning in the second third of the 16th century, and usually reflect designs that originated in the *naqqashkhane,* or court design atelier, in Istanbul. The popular ogival layout was usually embellished with designs based either on the Chinese-inspired floral and leaf arabesques known as *saz,* which emerged in the second quarter of the 16th century, or on the popular and eventually almost emblematic Ottoman garden flowers, especially tulips, honeysuckles, hyacinths, roses and rosebuds, and carnations.

The design of the Topkapı example is a bridge between the two styles. The large central motif, a highly decorated tulip in form, actually recalls earlier Venetian velvet prototypes with large-calyx blossoms—the only easily identifiable Ottoman garden flower is the honeysuckle at the very top of each ogival medallion.[1] Several variants of this design are known in surviving Ottoman *kemha* examples, which use different colors but the same identical design within the ogival lattice frame, while often showing variations in the decoration of the bands of the lattice itself; this reuse of elements of a design in programming a velvet loom is typical of Bursa commercial practice. The secondary ornament of curved leaves and serrated palmettes is typical of the Ottoman court style of the second quarter of the 16th century.

WD

1 Atasoy et al. 2001, pp. 278–79, figs. 231–33.

73. *Loom-width piece of velvet fabric*

Turkey, probably Bursa, late 16th century
Silk velvet with voided areas brocaded with silver-gilt and silver-wrapped silk thread
162 x 65 cm (63 3/4 x 25 1/2 in.)
Museo Nazionale del Bargello, Florence
Inv. 2463 (ill. p. 189)

As Mackie has noted, what has been dubbed the "Italianate" style in Ottoman velvet weaving from Bursa persisted long after the emergence of a more typical Ottoman decorative vocabulary in the mid-16th century. Most of the examples of Bursa velvet presently in the Bargello are of the latter type—long pieces from bolts of velvet utilizing designs with rows of typical Ottoman carnations and other garden flowers. This piece, by contrast, shows the close design relationships between Italian, possibly Venetian, and Ottoman silks.[1] The small tulip in the very center of the ogival medallion is usually deemed to be typically Ottoman, although remarkable similar forms appear in Italian velvets long before the tulip became a stock item in the Ottoman decorative vocabulary in the mid-16th century; a mid-15th-century portrait of a young woman attributed to the Florentine Paolo Uccello (ca. 1397–1475) in the Gardner Museum, Boston, shows such a motif in a velvet garment.[2]

Other Italianate features of the Bargello velvet—whose attribution to Turkey is based on distinctive technical features in the way its brocaded wefts are bound or secured by warps—are the use of a motif to "bind" the scaled ogival bands together when they converge, and the large rosettes decorating those same bands midway between convergences.

WD

1 Suriano and Carboni 1999, p. 114, fig. 38; Atasoy et al. 2001, p. 303, fig. 306.
2 Hendy 1974, pp. 266–69, pl. 13.

74. *Chasuble embroidered with the arms of the Barbaro family*

Probably Istanbul, ca. 1570–80, embroidered in Venice, late 16th century
Kemha (lampas) brocaded silk with added appliqué satin border and silk embroidery
H. 102.5 cm (40 3/8 in.); W. 77 cm (30 1/4 in.)
Cividale del Friuli, Parrocchia Santa Maria Assunta
Arcidiocesi di Udine, Ufficio Arte Sacra e Beni Culturali
Inv. 23201 (ill. p. 185)

Donated together with a maniple and a *stola* to the Basilica of Santa Maria Assunta in Cividale by Francesco Barbaro during his tenure as Patriarch of Aquileia from 1592 to 1616, this sumptuous garment—made from an Ottoman silk fabric in a relatively rare variant of the *kemha* technique known as *serenk,* where golden yellow silk substitutes for metallic-enriched silk yarn—bears the embroidered coat of arms of the Barbaro family at the bottom, in the center.[1] Traditionally, this precious chasuble was worn only twice a year: during the festivities of San Donato (August 21) and Christmas.

Francesco Barbaro's father, Marcantonio, was the Venetian *bailo* in Istanbul from 1568 to 1574, during the reign of Sultan Selim II (r. 1566–74), and based on its style we may conjecture that the silk fabric from which this vestment was made was probably woven in Istanbul during the early 1570s and subsequently purchased there by the elder Barbaro. As such, it provides an interesting contrast to and balance with the sultan's kaftan (cat. 80), which is made of Italian, probably Venetian, velvet prized at the Ottoman court.

The familiar layout consists of ogival framing bands decorated with tiny prunus blossoms and carnations. Within each ogival compartment two huge leaves decorated with hyacinth sprays embrace a red-ground field decorated with cypress trees surrounded by sprays of six-petaled blossoms. The golden-yellow satin tape and the embroidered Barbaro coat of arms were added during the making of the chasuble, and represent Venetian work from the late 16th century.

WD

1 The emblem includes a cross, crosier, and sword. See A. Zorzi, handwritten catalogue cards, Archivio del Museo Nazionale di Cividale, 1899, card no. 18; Santangelo 1936, p. 34; Atasoy et al. 2001, p. 243, cat. 18.

75. *Loom-width piece of velvet fabric*

Bursa, Turkey, late 16th century
Silk velvet pile, voided ground with silver and gilt-silver-wrapped silk brocading
163 x 63 cm (64 1/8 x 24 3/4 in.)
Staatliche Museen zu Berlin
Kunstgewerbemuseum , Berlin
Inv. 1884.903 (ill. p. 186)

Closely related in design, conception, and scale to the contemporary velvet panel from The Metropolitan Museum (cat. 71), the Berlin velvet piece of a loom-width fabric is another splendid example of the large-scale designs so popular with Bursa velvet weavers in the later 16th century. Meant to be sewn into a wider panel, the design consists of a huge artichoke enclosed in two crescent-shaped *saz* leaves decorated with hyacinth sprays, with two small tulips ornamenting the stems at the base of the leaves, and a floral spray of two rosebuds and a carnation in the interstice directly above the top of the artichoke palmette.[1]

Although the details are in every respect typical of Ottoman design in the second half of the 16th century, the layout and the artichoke palmette itself are also strongly reminiscent of Venetian velvet design both in layout and in the use of the scaled palmette, here an artichoke but in Venetian textiles usually thought to represent a pomegranate.

WD

1 Atasoy et al. 2001, p. 128, pl. 78.

76. *Shield*

Turkey, mid-16th century
Wicker, wood, silk, steel, gold, rubies and turquoise
Diam. 58 cm (22 3/4 in.)
Topkapı Sarayi Müsezi, Istanbul
Inv. 1/2466 (ill. p. 238)

Widely used throughout Asia and the Middle East for centuries, the wicker shield, or *kalkan* in Turkish,[1] was specifically identified by Europeans with the Ottoman Turks, whose armies, deadly efficient and colorfully arrayed, were all too familiar to those defending the borders of Austria, Hungary, and the Balkans in the 16th and 17th centuries. Wicker shields were highly prized booty taken from the battlefields and are still found in large numbers in museums in Central and Eastern Europe. Italy, too, preserves significant examples, notably Francesco Morosini's collection in the Museo Civico Correr in Venice (see cat. 77) and the famous Bolognese collections formed by Marchese Ferdinando Cospi and Count Luigi Ferdinando Marsigli in the 17th century, and now preserved in the Museo Civico Medioevale, Bologna, among the oldest repertories of Ottoman trophies. The earliest, most splendid and best-preserved *kalkans*, however, are to be found, not surprisingly, in the Topkapı Palace Museum in Istanbul. Among them, the present shield stands out for its rich materials, refined design, and bold sense of color.

It is constructed in the usual manner of *kalkans*, composed of a thin coiled reed or cane, each ring stitched to the adjacent one and wound around a central wooden disk, covered on the outside with a metal plate or boss. This construction assured a sturdy but lightweight defense. Here, the cane is wrapped in yellow silk thread that serves as a background for the decorative motifs, also executed in silk and metallic thread, consisting of four Chinese-inspired red cloud bands that alternate with turquoise cartouches. The cloud bands are filled with blossoms, leaves, and triple balls (the *cintamani* motif) in white, yellow, and silver; the cartouches contain a Persian poem in elegant calligraphy, in silver thread with white foliate arabesques as a background. Narrow multicolored bands frame the outer edge and domed boss.

The bosses found on most *kalkans* are typically of plain polished iron or steel, though some examples are damascened in gold with delicate foliate or geometric designs. The boss on this shield is extraordinary in being covered with tooled gold sheet and set with red and blue precious and semiprecious stones, transforming it into a rich jewel. The boss echoes, both in color and geometry, the surrounding textile ornament, revealing the careful planning behind its design. Centered on a raised knob set with a ruby, the boss is decorated with an eight-point medallion issuing an oval lobed medallion from each of its points, the whole inscribed within a narrow jeweled border. The medallions and surfaces between them are covered with dense arabesques that include pairs of deer or fox and are set with rubies and turquoise. Atıl observed that the Persian verses and the introduction of animals into the foliate ornament are typical characteristics of Safavid design, thus suggesting that the shield may have been conceived by an Iranian artist in Istanbul or copied from a Safavid model.[2]

SP

1 For *kalkans* in general, see Atıl 1987, pp. 160–61 and Zygulski 1999.
2 Atıl 1987, p. 161. The shield was also recently published in Memphis 1992, p. 51.

77, 113, 134

77. *Shield*

Turkey, 17th century
Cane, wood, silk, steel, gold
Diam. 64 cm (25 1/4 in)
Museo Civico Correr, Venice
Inv. XVI n. 140 (ill. p. 65)

113. *Bow Case*

Ottoman Empire, possibly the Balkans, 17th century
Steel, leather, gold
L. 67 cm (26 3/8 in.); W. 28.5 cm (11 1/4 in.)
Museo Civico Correr, Venice
Inv. XIV. n. 1362 (ill. p. 238)

134. *Flask*

Turkey, 17th century
Leather, velvet, silver thread
H. 24 cm (9 1/2 in.); W. 18.3 cm (7 1/4 in.)
Museo Civico Correr, Venice
Inv. XVI n. 1431 (ill. p. 238)

These three objects belong to an important group of Ottoman military trophies that were captured by Francesco Morosini (1618–1694), admiral of the Venetian fleet, on campaigns in the Eastern Mediterranean during the second half of the 17th century. Popularly known as "the Peloponnesian" (*il Peloponnesiaco*), Morosini was the Serenissima's last great naval hero who succeeded in recapturing for Venice some of her overseas outposts, notably in the Morea (Peloponnesus), that had been lost to the Turks in the preceding centuries (see cat. 67). He was unanimously elected doge in 1688 while away at sea. The spoils of war he brought back to Venice remained in the Palazzo Morosini until the family became extinct in 1884; they were acquired by the Museo Civico Correr in 1895. Still awaiting proper study and publication, the Morosini trophies are the largest and most important holdings of Ottoman arms and military equipment in Italy. Indeed, they compare favorably with the great collections of Turkish booty taken during the relief of Vienna in 1683 and preserved principally in Karlsruhe, Vienna, Dresden, and Cracow.[1]

The circular shield is constructed in typical Ottoman fashion of a length of cane coiled around a wooden disk, the cane wrapped in colored thread and the center reinforced with a domed metal boss. The textile has an intricate radial pattern, consisting of six triangular areas filled with geometric designs alternating with stylized cypress-like trees with projecting branches. The designs are rendered in white, pale yellow, pale brown, blue, and silver (now tarnished black) against a deep red ground, producing a rich, carpet-like effect. The boss has a dark patinated surface damascened in gold with an Arabic inscription around the raised central knob ("Help from Allah and a victory near at hand. And give good news to the Believers"; Qur'an, 61:13, see also cat. 67), with another band of foliate ornament around the outer edge, and with four medallions set on the axes that connect the two concentric bands. The large rosette-shaped iron washers visible on the exterior served to attach the interior fittings, comprising a square arm pad, two cord loops for the arms, and a longer cord, or guige, that allowed the shield to be thrown over the shoulder. The dense patterning of the textile of this example and several others among the Morosini trophies[2] contrasts markedly with larger and more open patterns found on Ottoman shields of the previous century (cat. 76) and is typical of those captured at the siege of Vienna.[3] The gold-damascened boss complements the richness of the surrounding textile and reinforces the impression that this richly decorated example was originally carried by a Turkish soldier of high rank.

The flask is conical in shape and semicircular in section except at the back, which is flat.[4] It is constructed of two pieces of hard leather, one piece forming the front and sides, the other the back and bottom, their joins stitched and covered with polished leather piping. A hole for filling the flask is at the top (the stopper is missing), a short curved spout is inset in the front, and a thick handle of stitched red leather is attached at the back. The sides and bottom are covered with red silk velvet embroidered in silver-wrapped thread with a dense pattern of peonies, tulips, and carnations. The bottle is typical of much 17th-century Ottoman military equipment, especially bow cases and quivers, several examples of which are found among the Morosini spoils, that are essentially utilitarian objects transformed into luxury goods through the use of richly embroidered textiles.

The bow case is an unusual variant of a well-known type used throughout the Islamic world that was typically constructed of stitched leather panels whose outer side was variously tooled, fitted with decorative metal appliqués, stitched with openwork leather designs, or faced with velvet embroidered with metallic thread. This example, by contrast, is faced with thin steel sheet, formed of two vertically aligned plates, which have been incised and gilded. The decoration consists of a circular field inscribed within a wide border, the surfaces covered with foliate scrolls and palmettes, the motifs in dark metal against the contrasting gilt ground. Some of the ground is shaded by diagonal hatching, lending nuance and depth to the design. Narrow bands of dark metal incised with a guilloche design outline the border and medallion and give the impression that this is stitched and gilded leather rather than metal. The bow case's leather backing is stitched to the edges of the metal face, which is pierced with numerous holes for that purpose, and the join is covered with polished leather piping. The bow case was probably originally accompanied by a matching quiver, the two pieces forming a garniture that had been essential equipment for mounted archers in Asia and the Middle East for centuries.

Only two other examples of bow cases of similar construction and decoration are known, one in the Higgins Armory Museum, Worcester, Massachusetts (inv. 2394), the other in a private collection.[5] The example in Worcester is engraved with three lines of seemingly poetic verses in Persian or in Ottoman Turkish. The Morosini provenance of the example in Venice provides a probable date for the group to the late 17th century. Given the rarity of the type and the fact that Morosini was active in Greece and the Eastern Mediterranean, the bow case may be provincial Ottoman, possibly Balkan, in origin.

SP

1 A list of the contents of the Morosini collection is found in Correr 1899, pp. 79–95. Comparable collections of 17th-century Ottoman booty have been published in Petrasch, Sänger, and Zimmermann 1991; Hummelberger 1969; Vienna 1983; Schöbel 1974; and Dresden 1995.
2 For two similar shields from the Morosini group, see Venice 1993, pp. 405–6, no. 259. For cane shields in general, see Zygulski 1999.
3 For example, see Petrasch, Sänger, and Zimmermann 1991, pp. 172–78, nos. 118–25; Vienna 1983, pp. 196–97, nos. 16/83–84, 16/86–87. Schöbel 1974, pp. 40–41, nos. 3–4.
4 The Morosini flask was published in Venice 1993, pp. 404–5, no. 257, where similar flasks are cited.
5 Kindly pointed out by David Alexander.

78. *Fragment of velvet fabric*

Venice, 15th century
Silk velvet brocaded with gilt-silver-wrapped silk thread
82 x 55 cm (32 1/4 x 21 5/8 in.)
Museo di Palazzo Mocenigo, Venice
Inv. Cl. XXIII n.491/268 (ill. p. 53)

One of the striking aspects of 15th-century Venetian velvets, exemplified in this fragment, is an ambiguity between motif and background. The ogival layout created by the stem-like bands, with their rich crimson velvet pile and large composite blossoms, is by virtue of its color and luster the dominant aspect of the design at first glance. The ogival medallions created by the bands—voided and brocaded with gilt-silver-wrapped silk thread—contain a much larger design motif that is also iconographically more complex. A group of sinuous curved leaves, not unlike those of the later Ottoman *saz* style, forms the base of the composition in which a thick bifurcate stem rises through the middle of a crown, and at the apex of the design are three pomegranates.[1]

By contrast, the Ottoman velvet-weavers of Bursa never produced ogival velvet designs in which the framing so utterly dominated the ground visually, and they virtually never used ornaments of such size and prominence; moreover, Ottoman velvets of this type would have been designed so that loom widths could be sewn together side by side, and so would have repeated the ogival framing horizontally.

Nevertheless, early Venetian velvets like this seem to have had a profound impact on Ottoman velvet design, which apparently during the later 15th century moved from relatively small-scale repetitive designs, often employing the characteristic paired wavy bands and three balls known collectively as *cintamani*, to larger-scale ogival compositions such as this.

WD

1 Grube 1989, p. 208, fig. 1; Musei Civici 1988, p. 229, cat. 28.

79. *Loom-width piece of velvet*

Probably Bursa, Turkey, or possibly Venice, late 15th century
Silk velvet pile and voided areas brocaded with silver-gilt-wrapped silk wefts
109 x 65.5 cm (43 x 25 3/4 in.)
The Metropolitan Museum of Art, New York
Rogers Fund, 1953
Inv. 53.157 (ill. p. 80)

This splendid crimson velvet with pinkish voided areas and others brocaded with silver-wrapped yellow thread reflects the international style common in Ottoman Turkey, Timurid and Turkoman Iran, and Mamluk Syria and Egypt in the late 15th century. These velvets, with their many variants, may have been woven in Bursa and a few are found today in the Topkapı Sarayi Museum, but an Italian origin for some of them cannot be discounted.[1]

The technique, coloration, and tightly controlled design—in this case an overlapping double-ogival layout on a small scale—recall a number of other velvets in Turkish and European collections. The vocabulary of the design, including knotted motifs in both the primary and the secondary level of vine arabesques, the serrated palmettes at the junctures of the stems of the primary vine arabesques, and the long curled-edged leaves, is entirely Islamic, but the syntax and grammar—the mode of combining this vocabulary in an expressive whole—is common to the Eastern Mediterranean in the late 15th century.

WD

1 The present location of the textile in The Metropolitan Museum, for example, is in the Department of European Sculpture and Decorative Arts. See Atasoy et al. 2001, pp. 118-19, cats. 67–68 for an attribution of two similar examples to Bursa, ca. 1500.

80. *Silk velvet ceremonial robe (kaftan)*

Italian, lined in Istanbul, 16th century
Silk velvet with silver-gilt-wrapped brocaded wefts, tailored and lined with Ottoman *atlas* (satin)
L. 109 cm (43 in.)
Topkapı Sarayı Müzesi, Istanbul
Inv. 13/500 (ill. p. 188)

The popularity of Italian velvets at the Ottoman court is nowhere better attested than in this magnificent long-sleeved royal Ottoman kaftan made from a 15th-century Italian, probably Venetian, velvet fabric with a large-scale wavy-vine layout.[1] Most of the figured velvet kaftans now in the Topkapı Palace collections, including many with designs from the mainstream of Ottoman art, are made from Italian velvet instead of the less esteemed local production of Bursa. In the 15th-century, velvets such as these were recognized all over Europe as expensive Italian products, perhaps the first in a long historical line of luxury goods from Italy.

Similar Italian textiles, because of their association with wealth and luxury, were highly popular as furnishing and clothing fabrics in northern Europe, where they were commonly used in the later 15th and early 16th centuries as backdrops in paintings of the Madonna enthroned with the Christ Child, such as Hans Memling's famous St. John altarpiece in Bruges of 1479. A female donor in Petrus Christus's *A Goldsmith in his Shop* of 1445 in The Metropolitan Museum of Art wears a dress of Venetian velvet to proclaim her status, and Jean Fouquet's diptych of Etienne Chevalier and St. Stephen of ca. 1450 in the Gemäldegalerie in Berlin shows the martyr wearing a black robe trimmed with Venetian velvet. Many of the most famous paintings from the Northern Renaissance, from Hugo van der Goes's *Portinari Altarpiece* in the Uffizi to Rogier van der Weyden's *Deposition* in the Prado, show Italian velvets of the type found in the Topkapı kaftan. Thus what was valued in Bruges was also valued on the Bosphorus, and in the late 15th and early 16th centuries Italian, particularly Venetian, velvet was evidently not only highly prized at the Ottoman court, but was produced in Italy with Turkish designs specifically for the Turkish market.

WD

1 Atasoy et al. 2001, p. 182, fig. 36.

81. *"Mamluk" carpet*

Probably Cairo, Egypt, before 1541
Wool pile knotted on wool warp; wool weft
Ca. 970 x 375 cm (ca. 382 x 148 in.)
Scuola Grande di San Rocco, Venice
(ill. p. 178)

After the Ottoman conquest of Mamluk Egypt in the early 16th century, the weavers of Cairo continued to produce so-called Mamluk carpets such as this one in a variety of sizes and shapes, which were exported in significant numbers to Europe through Genoese and Venetian middlemen. Distinguished by their unusual palette of three colors—an insect-derived red, a blue, and a green, usually without white accents or any dark-brown outlining—and by their use of clockwise-spun ("S"-spun) wool yarns for pile, warp, and weft, the later tri-color Mamluk carpets represent a rarified taste at variance with the main carpet production of the time in Anatolia, Syria, and Iran.[1] The designs employ a highly characteristic border of elongated cartouches alternating with small eight-lobed medallions, central motifs usually octagonal in shape, and a decorative vocabulary of tiny fan-shaped motifs thought to represent Egyptian papyrus leaves.

According to Curatola, the Scuola di San Rocco probably purchased this carpet prior to 1541, using funds originally earmarked to buy two smaller carpets; the huge size of the carpet was evidently something of a major status symbol in Venice.[2] The carpet may have been displayed on the long and narrow table in the room where the Council used to meet (the Sala dell'Albergo, entirely painted by Tintoretto) on the upper floor of the Scuola. The dimensions of the table would allow the carpet to cover its surface as well as the side facing the entrance door, thus vertically displaying its magnificent decorative pattern to visitors entering the room. The table's size indicates it most likely was custom-made to accommodate the carpet.

By the end of the 16th century, many of the weavers of this kind of carpet in Cairo had switched to weaving designs provided by the Ottoman court in Istanbul, utilizing typical Ottoman court motifs such as the curved leaves and complex floral palmettes known as the *saz* style, or the stylized garden flowers that were to become emblematic of Ottoman culture in the later 16th century (see also cats. 174, 176–77). Some Mamluk weavers, along with a large quantity of their dyed wool, were summoned to the Ottoman court in Istanbul in the late 16th century, and there is a possibility that at least one Cairene weaver may have emigrated to Italy during the same general time (see cat. 82). Carpets with the subdued Cairene palette continued to be popular in Italy throughout the 16th century, and are documented in a small but significant number of Italian paintings.

WD

1 Pertegato 1998.
2 Curatola 1986.

82. *"Mamluk" synagogue carpet*

Probably Cairo, Egypt, mid-16th century
Wool pile knotted on wool warp; wool weft
138 x 109 cm (54 3/8 x 43 in.)
Comunità Ebraica di Padova, Padua
(ill. p. 182)

This small carpet from a synagogue in Padua has previously been identified as a *parokhet*, a curtain hung before the Holy Ark, the cabinet containing the Torah in the temple.[1] The textile's stiff structure, however, would make it difficult to draw it as a curtain. Thus it was more likely used as a decorative wall hanging instead.

Its rediscovery by Boralevi in 1982 constitutes one of the major events in carpet scholarship of the 20th century.[2] Boralevi attributes the carpet to Cairo and dates it to the second half of the 16th century on the basis of its technique; woven entirely in knotted pile of S-spun Egyptian wool in "three-color-Mamluk" coloration (see cat. 81), with typical 16th-century Mamluk borders, the Padua carpet underlines the role of the Oriental carpet as a bridge between cultures and civilizations, as well as religions, in the 16th-century Mediterranean.[3] The presence of some Ottoman decorative elements places it in the so-called transitional Mamluk group, which is characterized by a Mamluk structure and Ottoman ornament, having been manufactured in Cairo after the Ottoman conquest of Mamluk Syria and Egypt.[4]

This small carpet is woven in the size and arched layout of a *sajjada* or Islamic prayer rug, depicting a gateway to Paradise. Indeed, the inscription in Hebrew, from Psalm 118:20, translates "This is the gate of the Lord, through which the righteous shall enter." Set against a red background, a brazier, menorah, and crown (*keter torah*) appear in the center of the carpet. This kind of architectural frame is unique in the 16th-century Cairene carpet tradition. The iconography seems to derive from the frontispieces of Hebrew books printed in Venice in the 16th century, which depicted the "Gate of God" flanked by two spiral columns. They recall Jachin and Boaz, the two columns of the Temple of Solomon in Jerusalem. The spiral columns became very popular in Hebrew texts because European Jews compared the first page of a book to the entrance of a house. According to Boralevi, it is possible that a Venetian Jewish merchant brought a copy of the book, with the depiction of the Gate of God, to Egypt to be copied onto the textile.[5] The seven-branched *menorah* candlestick symbolizes Divine Light, as does the flaming brazier below, in the same way as the image of a lamp in a Muslim *sajjada* symbolizes God's presence. The flames in the brazier take their form from the twinned flame-bands of *çintamani*, a motif much used in Ottoman art of the time, originally derived from a Buddhist depiction of a flaming "auspicious jewel" that had been a good luck symbol in the Islamic world since the 9th century.

Some 16th-century Italian documents even state that a carpet weaver from Egypt, whose name suggests he was Jewish, was brought to Italy to weave carpets.[6] Other evidence points to the transmission of artistic ideas from Muslim Spain to Ottoman Turkey via the Spanish Jewish refugees expelled by Ferdinand and Isabella who were invited by the Ottoman sultan Bayezid II to settle in his realms. In sum, the Padua synagogue carpet, which almost certainly arrived in Europe via Venice, is a paradigm of the trans-cultural artistic richness of the early modern era, in which Venetian commerce and culture played such an important role.

WD / RM

1 Boralevi 1984, pp. 36, 40; Venice 1993, p. 328.
2 Boralevi 1984; Boralevi 1986.
3 Boralevi 1984, p. 38
4 Erdmann 1938, p.179.
5 Boralevi 1984, pp. 40–42. For more on the role of Jewish merchants in the Mediterranean carpet trade, see the essay by Giovanni Curatola in this volume.
6 See Denny's essay in this volume.

83. *"Presentation" carpet*

Iran, probably Kashan, later 16th century
Silk pile knotted on silk warp; silk weft; supplemental silver-wrapped silk brocading wefts
Ca. 258 x 181 cm (ca. 101 x 71 in.)
Procuratoria di San Marco, Venice
Inv. 26 (ill. p. 180)

Persian carpets woven with a silk pile from the 16th and 17th centuries are among the most rare and highly prized Islamic carpets in European collections. Dubbed "presentation carpets" by the German scholar Friedrich Spuhler, such items were probably woven in workshops under careful court control, and destined as presents, especially for foreign dignitaries. One later group, dubbed "Polonaise" or "Polish" carpets in the literature, was created primarily in the 17th century, and the presence of several important examples in Poland, some with Polish coats of arms incorporated in the design, lend them their name. Earlier examples such as this one in St. Mark's Basilica, probably woven in the north-central Persian city of Kashan, tend to be finer and incorporate large-scale floral and vegetal arabesques.

The large size and expensive materials of the San Marco carpet—one of five such items given to the doge through diplomatic gifts—whose design incorporates flat-woven areas brocaded with silk yarn wrapped with incredibly fine strips of silver foil that contrast with the areas of silk pile, together with its fragility, suggest that it may have been destined to be used only sporadically in front of the main altar of the church during special religious festivals, or as a floor covering to display objects from the Treasury, or was perhaps laid underneath a doge's bier on the occasion of a ducal funeral. Venice's well-known humidity undoubtedly contributed to the gradual tarnishing of the silver-wrapped thread, and exposure to light over the years has softened and muted the original colors, but the luxuriousness of this object fits perfectly with Venetian taste for opulent displays of artistic wealth in religious and civil ceremony.[1]

WD

1 Venice 1993, p. 431, cat. 277.

84. *Carpet with "Lotto" pattern or "Lotto carpet"*

Western Anatolia, early 16th century
Wool pile knotted on wool warp; wool weft
Ca. 170 x 109 cm (ca. 67 x 43 in.)
The Saint Louis Art Museum, St. Louis
Gift of James F. Ballard
Inv. 104-1929 (ill. p. 125)

Based on the evidence of numerous examples depicted in European, and especially Italian painting, the "Lotto" pattern in Turkish carpets seems to originate around 1500, and has a long history in Turkish weaving. Based on a curvilinear arabesque of split-leaf forms known in Turkish art as *rumi* and in Iranian art as *islimi*, the pattern derives its conventional name from the depiction of a carpet very similar to this example in a famous altarpiece painted in 1542 by Lorenzo Lotto, entitled *The Charity of St. Antoninus,* for the church of SS. Giovanni e Paolo in Venice; many other painters from Italy, the Low Countries, Germany, Hungary, Spain, and England have depicted carpets with this pattern, and unusually large numbers of small carpets with this motif have survived in Central European churches, to which they were evidently donated as votive gifts. Charles Grant Ellis classified Lotto carpets according to three subvariant design groups, of which that represented by the St. Louis carpet is the earliest.[1] Lotto's portrait of Giovanni della Volta with his family (The National Gallery, London) depicts a variant design with "thin" yellow arabesques on a red ground and a standard mid-16th century "plaited" border (cat. 32).

The earliest surviving Lotto carpets are distinguished by a border of white interlaced elements with decorated finials on a light-green ground, a decorative element derived from an elaborate monumental form of Kufic Arabic script, and sometimes termed "kufesque" in the literature. What might appear at first glance to be an inscription around the periphery of the carpet is therefore actually a decorative form that is meant to recall Arabic script, with all of its connotations of holiness, apotropaic protectiveness, and monumentality, without creating the problems that would arise from having potentially holy writing underfoot. The St. Louis carpet is unusual among early Lotto-pattern carpets in its small size; most surviving examples from this group are far larger.

WD

1 Dimand 1935, pl. 21; Mack 2002, p. 89, fig. 83.

85. *Prayer carpet* (sajjada)

Western Anatolia (probably Ushak district), ca. 1500–50
Wool pile knotted on wool warp; wool weft; loss of knotted pile on all four sides
Ca. 177 x 122 cm (ca. 70 x 48 in.)
Staatliche Museen zu Berlin,
Museum für Islamische Kunst, Berlin
Purchased by Wilhelm von Bode in Venice in 1888
Inv. I.24 (ill. p. 178)

The powerful design of this small carpet demonstrates the creativity of the commercial carpet weavers of Ushak in the 16th century.[1] Due to the niche-like layout, the design is easily recognizable as that of an individual prayer rug (*sajjada*), suitable for use by one person in performing the five daily Muslim prayers. As the carpet is missing edges on all four sides, it is not certain whether it was woven as an individual prayer rug, or represents one panel of a larger mosque rug incorporating multiple compartments in rows (*saff*).

All the elements of the design are taken from the early 16th-century Ottoman court design repertoire: stylized lotus palmette (on a red ground in the bottom), with smaller ones on light-blue stems in the dark-blue field, split-leaf arabesques known as *rumi* (in the red-ground spandrels of the arch at the top) and the light-blue convoluted cloud-band motif, ultimately derived from Chinese prototypes, which separates the bottom red-ground area from the dark blue area above it, and also occurs in the middle of the dark-blue field.

All of these elements have been shown in curvilinear form, but the coarseness of the weave, roughly 40 x 30 knots per square decimeter (120 knots per square inch) militates in the direction of geometric simplification. The layout and the form of the arch also recall Persian court prayer rugs from the 16th century, and the design of the Berlin rug may be regarded as a kind of bridge between Anatolian and Iranian traditions.

If the vocabulary of the design is typical of Ottoman court art from the first half of the 16th century, the syntax of the design by contrast shows a striking resemblance to the layout of the so-called Bellini carpets, which feature a protuberant element rising from the lower edge into the bottom third of the field. The original meaning of this form is still a subject of debate; it may derive from an East Asian depiction of a sacred mountain, or it may originally have been intended to represent an octagonal pool with a small canal emerging from it, thought to be an evocation of the fountain named Salsabil mentioned in the Qur'an as a feature of Paradise. The Islamic features of the carpet notwithstanding, it was in Venice that Wilhelm von Bode, scholar of Renaissance art, author of the first scholarly study of Islamic carpets, and founder of the Berlin museums, purchased the carpet in 1888.

WD

1 Enderlein 1955, no. 10.

86. *Dragon carpet with dragon design*

Eastern Transcaucasia, ca. 1700
Wool pile knotted on wool warp; wool wefts
Ca. 523 x 224 cm (ca. 206 x 88 in.)
Staatliche Museen zu Berlin,
Museum für Islamische Kunst, Berlin
Purchased by Wilhelm von Bode from a church in Burano; donated to the museum in 1905
Inv. I.2 (ill. p. 179)

The dragons and other animals, all ultimately of Chinese origin, that decorate the overall lattice layout of this large carpet, woven in Transcaucasia in the late 17th century, are highly stylized and reduced to simple geometric forms, and indeed might not evenbe recognized as animals by the casual viewer. The late American carpet scholar Charles Grant Ellis posited that the design and motifs of the Transcaucasian dragon carpets derived from central Persian prototypes woven in Kirman in the earlier 17th century. Weavers of the dragon carpets drastically altered the motifs, simplifying them and creating almost abstract geometric forms instead. The reasons for this transformation are not clear, but certainly the coarser weave of the dragon carpets and the subsequent discovery of many of them in Anatolian mosques (where easily recognizable animal images would have been forbidden) may be contributing factors.

There is a stylistic progression in the weaving of Transcaucasian dragon carpets spanning the period from the mid-17th to the late 19th centuries. This carpet, with its diamond-shaped lattice containing motifs of highly stylized dragons, antelopes, birds, and lions, dates to the end of the 17th century.

While Italian paintings depicting carpets document large numbers of Turkish carpets in Italy from the 15th century onwards, and smaller numbers of Persian carpets in Italy from the 16th century onwards, depictions of dragon carpets are conspicuously lacking. Nevertheless, carpets such as this one did make their way to Italy, probably through Venetian maritime commerce, and Bode discovered this example in a church on the Venetian island of Burano, most likely the Chiesa di San Martino, in the late 19th century.[1]

WD

1 Spuhler 1987, no. 103. The large 16th-century Church of San Martino seems to be the only building where von Bode might have acquired the carpet in Burano, the only other church on the island being the tiny 14th-century Church of St. Catherine. In San Martino's there were also paintings by Giovanni Mansueti, presently placed in the nearby Oratory of Santa Barbara.

STONE

87. *"Chair of St. Peter"*

Eastern Mediterranean, backrest ca. 11th-12th century assembled with earlier elements
Carved marble and sandstone
Ca. H. 140 cm (55 in.) max.; W. 74.5 cm (29 1/4 in.) max.; D. 52 cm (20 1/2 in.) max.
Basilica con Cattedrale di San Pietro di Castello, Venice
(ill. p. 14)

The most intriguing and mysterious object that incorporates elements of Islamic art today in Venice is the so-called Chair of St. Peter, a marble seat placed on the right wall near the entrance of San Pietro di Castello. The church, located behind the Arsenal in the Castello quarter of the city, is nowadays off the main tourist route and few people realize that it was the seat of the Patriarchate from 1451 to 1807.[1] For ships entering the lagoon on the side of San Nicolò at the Lido and the defensive Fort of Sant'Andrea, San Pietro was once the first important building to greet anyone's arrival.

The chair is composed of several parts in white marble that form its backrest, armrests, sides, and seat, and of a slab of pale pink sandstone that supports the front edge of the seat. The only decorated section is the backrest, the upper part of which is carved in relief on both sides with Arabic inscriptions within a complex geometric and pseudo-vegetal design, the most distinctive being large star patterns on the front side.[2] The text, which runs on both sides in a band along the curving shape of the backrest and inside the geometric figures, was copied in a nondescript style of Kufic script that can be attributed to the 11th or 12th century. The text is Qur'anic (sura 3, v. 192–94, sura 23, v. 118) and strongly suggests that the original function of this carved marble slab was that of a funerary stele planted in the ground, although it cannot be excluded—as was surmised in the past—that it formed the backrest of an Islamic throne or a *minbar* (pulpit). Strika has concluded that the backrest, originally a stele brought by the Venetians from the Eastern Mediterranean coasts at the time of the Crusades, can be attributed to the mid-11th century and belongs to the Seljuq period of rule of the greater Syrian area.[3] Since the Seljuq Syrian branch controlled the region roughly in the years 1076–1117, without challenging Strika's reasonable interpretation, its attribution can be extended to the late 11th as well as the early 12th century.

The mystery of the "Cattedra" lies in its traditional name, "St. Peter's Chair," which implies that it was the seat of the apostle and first patriarch; the Venetian legend tells us that this chair was his original seat in Antioch (Syria) and most sources agree that it was donated to a doge by a Byzantine emperor in the 9th century in appreciation of Venice's assistance in the effort to recapture Sicily from the Arabs. The earliest extant source for the presence of the chair in Venice seems to be Andrea Dandolo's (1307–1354; r. 1343–54) *Chronicle*, a compilation of earlier sources, mentioning the "marble chair in which Peter of Antioch used to sit, and which is presently placed behind the main altar of the Church of St. Peter."[4] Only in the 18th century was it finally noticed that Arabic could not have been used before the 7th century in Antioch and that there was something wrong with the traditional attribution of the seat.[5]

There might be a grain of truth in the various legends surrounding the chair; it is possible that the Kufic stele was a replacement for the backrest of an earlier marble seat that was originally in a church in Antioch (although an 11th-century source describes St. Peter's seat as made of palm wood covered with silver sheets)[6] and that was taken to Byzantium and subsequently given to Venice through diplomatic channels or taken from there during the Crusade of 1204 (see also cats. 88, 150). The truth may never be established, but just as the relics of the body of St. Mark were taken from Muslim-controlled Alexandria in 828, tradition holds that, at about the same time, St. Peter's Chair, decorated with a prominent Arabic inscription, also arrived in Venice. The doge's and the patriarch's effort to turn the city into the most important center of Christian pilgrimage and therefore of business and profit—even challenging papal Rome where, not surprisingly, another Chair of St. Peter was located—between the Orthodox denomination and Catholic Europe cannot be more manifest than in this case.[7]

SC

1 The Basilica of St. Mark was erected and functioned as the Doge's Chapel until it was chosen as the new seat of the patriarch. San Pietro di Castello Church had been for centuries the seat of the bishop, reporting to the patriarch in Grado, northeast of Venice, when Pope Nicholas V elevated the Venetian church to the patriarchate in 1451, choosing the future saint Lorenzo Giustiniani and current Venetian bishop, as the new patriarch.

2 Good drawings of the two sides are in Lanci 1846, pls. 17–18; a color illustration of the front side of the backrest is in Venice 1993, fig. p. 29. The star pattern and its astrological symbolism are thoroughly discussed in Strika 1978, pp. 32–78.

3 Strika 1978, p. 89.

4 *"Cathedram marmoream, in qua primum divus Petrus Antiochiae sedit, quae post altare majus in aede divi Petris nunc extat"*; Andrea Dandolo cited in *Rerum Italicarum Scriptores* (Milan), 1733, p. 172.

5 Corner 1758, pp. 25–26.

6 The source is Yahya ibn Saʿid al-Antaki; see Le Strange 1924.

7 Not to mention that the Treasury of St. Mark's also includes a carved marble "Chair of St. Mark"; see, for example, *Treasury* 1984, pp. 98–105, cat. 7.

88. *Rock crystal vase with mount*

Vase: Egypt, late 10th century; Mount: Venice, mid-13th century
Vase: carved rock crystal; Mount; silver-gilt with filigree work, pearl, and semi-precious stone insets
Vase: H. ca. 31 cm (12 in.), Diam. 17 cm max. (6 3/4 in.); with mount: H. 49 cm (19 1/4 in.)
Procuratoria di San Marco, Venice
Inv. 99 (ill. p. 19)

During the serious political and economic crisis that erupted in the Fatimid capital of Cairo in 1070–71 the dynasty's fabled treasury was looted, sold, and dispersed. The chronicles report that thousands of gold, silver, precious stone, and rock crystal objects either left Cairo or were melted down in those years.[1] The Fatimid Dynasty bounced back and ruled for another century, but the treasury was never recovered. The powerful Byzantine court was probably the first and foremost recipient of the precious goods dispersed from Cairo. A little over a century later, in 1204 during the Fourth Crusade, Venetian ships captured Constantinople and looted the city, bringing back what have since become emblems of Venice, such as the four bronze horses crowning St. Mark's façade. Many precious objects now in St. Mark's Treasury also undoubtedly came from this successful expedition and there is a distinct possibility that several Islamic rock crystal and cut glass objects (see cat. 150) may have originally come from late 11th-century Cairo.

Although the most celebrated Fatimid rock-crystal object in the Treasury is the splendid jug dedicated to the caliph al-ʿAziz billah (r. 975–96), one of only three extant such objects bearing a caliph's name, nine other important pieces can be found in St. Mark's.[2] The present cylindrical vase is outstanding not only because of its shape and decoration but also because it is the largest Islamic carved rock crystal known to have survived to the present day.[3] The decoration includes a crown of lanceolate leaves joined at the base creating three-quarter circular patterns, which derive directly from the artistic language created in 9th-century ʿAbbasid Iraq that was promptly adopted by the Tulunids in Egypt later in the century and by the early Fatimids in the 10th century. If the lanceolate leaf decoration suggests an early and possibly Iraqi origin for the vase, the Kufic inscription, verging on a floriated style, allows us to attribute it to the late 10th century and most likely to Fatimid Egypt.[4] Rather than diminishing the appeal of this large vase, the voided central band adds to the monumentality of the object, although it may have originally been filled with gold decoration. The present mid-13th-century silver-gilt mount set with filigree and precious stones, which hides the broken foot of the vase as well as the collar of the neck, has been defined by Hahnloser as one of the richest and more refined examples of *"opus venetum ad filum,"* or "Venetian work with filigree," emphasizing the preciousness of the rock crystal object.[5]

SC

1 Kahle 1935, citing in particular the chronicle by the 15th-century Egyptian historian al-Maqrizi; Shalem 1996, pp. 56-71.
2 Erdmann 1971, pp. 108-19, cat. 129, pls. 95–104.
3 Lamm 1929–30, pp. 202–3, pl. 68:17; Erdmann 1971, pp. 111–12, cat. 123, pls. 96–97; Venice 1993, pp. 145–46, cat. 55.
4 The inscription extols good wishes on the anonymous owner or patron: "Perpetual power and complete blessing and well-being to our lord."
5 Erdmann 1971, p. 112.

METALWORK

89. *Flask*

Khurasan or the Punjab, ca. 1200
Cast brass, inlaid with silver
H. 31.4 cm (12 3/8 in.)
The British Museum, London
Inv. OA 1883.10-19.7 (ill. p. 26)

By the 12th century the eastern provinces of the Islamic world had emerged as leading centers of metalwork inlaid with silver, copper, and gold.[1] The silver inlay of this cast brass flask highlights the inscription, simplified arabesques, and floral motifs distributed in bands around the body and rim and in cartouches along the sides.

Although this vessel has many unique features, such as the two goat-shaped loops and the square foot, its overall shape relates it to pilgrim flasks, bottles with two slightly convex sides, a short neck, low foot, and suspension loops used by travelers to carry drinking water.[2] Leather, ceramic, and metal pilgrim flasks had been made in the Mediterranean since Antiquity and later became relatively common in China and the Islamic world. Their interesting shape eventually spread to other media, including glassmaking, and later was adopted in Europe as well. An enameled and gilded glass flask produced in early 16th-century Venice (known locally as *inghistere fracade*) offers proof of the westward migration of this form (see cat. 167), as does a 17th-century Venetian maiolica pilgrim flask in the style of Ottoman Iznikware also included in this exhibition (cat. 192).

FL

1 Ward 1993, p. 72.
2 Carboni 2003.

• 90. *Astrolabe*

Face: Iraq, AH 706 / AD 1306–7; Tablets: Turkey, AH 1097 / AD 1685–86
Brass, hammered and engraved
Diam. 9.3 cm (3 5/8 in.)
Musée de l'Institut du Monde Arabe, Paris
Inv. AI 86-14 (ill. p. 70)

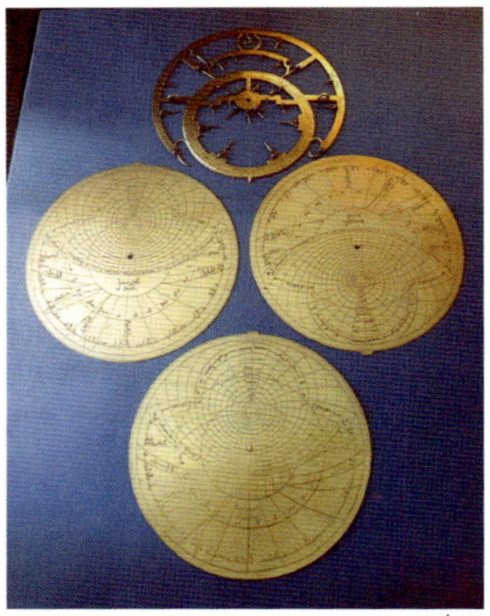

cat. 91

91. *Astrolabe*

Seville, Spain, probably 14th century
Brass, hammered and engraved
Diam. ca. 18 cm (7 1/8 in.)
Museo Storico Navale, Venice
Inv. 2094

The astrolabe—from the Arabic word *asturlab*—is one of the most sophisticated scientific tools of Antiquity. It was invented by the Greeks around 150 BC and was developed and modified in the early centuries of Islam as part of the great flowering of scientific studies that began with the ʿAbbasid caliphs in the late 8th century. Traditionally used to observe the positions of the stars and determine their altitude in relation to the horizon, its applications extended to terrestrial measurements, including the determination of the correct times for Muslim prayers. Spain served as the main gateway through which Islamic scientific contributions entered the West, including the astrolabe. These scientific instruments were accompanied by numerous treatises, composed from the 11th century on, which explained their use.

These two examples are different versions of the planispheric, or flat, astrolabe, the most common type used in the late Middle Ages in both Europe and the Near East, as proved by illustrations in Ptolemy's *Cosmographia* and the *Kitab al-bulhan* (see cats. 2, 16). The astrolabe in Paris bears the signatures of two different craftsmen; the so-called mother, the front side of the disk, is signed by Mahmud ibn Shawqa, whose family was from Baghdad, and dates to AH 706 (AD 1306–7), while the "spider"—the astrolabe's principal movable element—was made by Ahmad Ayyubi and it bears a much later date (AH 1097 / AD 1685–86) and a different place of production in Turkey.[1] Both the different geographical origins of the components and the chronological gap suggest a later replacement of a lost or damaged original spider. The second astrolabe, the only such example today in Venetian collections, is an unsigned and undated example of the rich and prolific Andalusian production during the Nasrid period and is datable to the 14th century.[2]

FL

1 Paris 1996, p. 222, cat. 177.
2 A comparative example in Genoa is in Venice 1993, pp. 345–46, cat. 206.

92. *Bowl*

Iran, probably Shiraz, mid-14th century
Cast brass inlaid with gold and silver
Diam. 24 cm (9 1/2 in.) max.; H. 10.5 cm (4 1/8 in.) max.
Staatliche Museen zu Berlin, Museum für Islamische Kunst, Berlin
Purchased by Friedrich Sarre in Venice in 1899
Inv. I.3580 (ill. p. 214)

Friedrich Paul Theodor Sarre (1865–1945) is one of the most familiar names to scholars and students of Islamic art and can rightly be regarded as a pioneer and founding father of this relatively new field of art history. His vast scholarship began with reports of his extensive archaeological and architectural travels in the Near and Middle East and continued until the end of his life. He dealt with all aspects of Islamic art, in particular carpets, metalwork, ceramics, and bookbindings. One of his frequent stops on his way to the Eastern Mediterranean was, of course, Venice, and it is in this city that he acquired the present inlaid metal bowl in 1899.[1] Venice must have been a treasure trove for those who developed a scholarly interest in Islamic art in the late 19th and early 20th centuries, which can be proved also by Wilhelm von Bode's acquisition of carpets from the city's churches (cats. 85–86).

Few works from Islamic Iran survive in Venetian collections today (see cats. 83, 114, 179, 180), a fact that does not accurately reflect their important place in trade and diplomatic exchanges throughout the centuries. This inlaid metal bowl, a good example of mid-14th century production in the southern province of Fars, a renowned Iranian metalworking center,[2] represents therefore a welcome addition to the small group of objects that we know passed through Venice at some point in history. The main decoration around the body of the bowl includes six circular medallions, each containing two figures conversing; between the roundels are polo players in full swing. The tapered shape of the walls, concave base, and straight lip at the mouth, combined with the dynamic figures around the body and a radiating geometric composition under the base, indicate a probable attribution to the second quarter of the 14th century or ca. 1350. Other details, such as the peonies under the base and the spiraling scrolls in the background of the main band help to confirm this dating.

SC

1 As reported in Sarre 1906, p. 22, cat. 44, pl. VII; the object is also published in *SPA*, vol. 6, pl. 1369.
2 See, for example, Melikian-Chirvani 1982, pp. 209–11, cats. 95–96; Allan 1999, pp. 106–09, cat. 24.

93. *Casket*

Southern Italy or Spain, probably late 13th or early 14th century
Silver with gilded and nielloed decoration
H. 8.2 cm; L. 14.2 cm; W. 9.5 cm (3 1/4 in. x 5 5/8 in. x 3 3/4 in.)
Procuratoria di San Marco, Venice
Inv. 132 (ill. p. 123)

This exquisitely decorated silver casket with a handle terminating in dragon-heads is related to the luxury boxes made of ivory and metal for courtly patrons in the medieval Islamic world, yet it appears to have been made by a Christian rather than Muslim artist.[1] Many different artistic traditions intermingle in the casket's imagery and motifs. This synthesis of cultures is typical of the art of medieval southern Italy (including Sicily), the most likely place of manufacture of the casket, although Spain, where a similar phenomenon occurred, cannot be ruled out. During the reign of Alfonso X (1221–84), King of Castile and León, there were especially strong contacts between Spain and southern Italy, making it difficult to attribute the casket with certainty.

The theme of paired musicians engraved on the lid is widely used in Islamic art, and can also be found in the Cappella Palatina in Palermo.[2] Islamic manuscripts, such as the 13th-century *Maqamat* by al-Hariri from Baghdad,[3] which was popular in Spain at the time of Alfonso X,[4] appear to have been important sources for the figures' poses and clothing with *tiraz* armbands and for the architectural frame that surrounds them. The accuracy of Islamic details—for example, the *cintamani* motif on the musicians' robes and their instruments (the harp known as *chang* or *jank* and a type of lute known as *rabab*)[5]—suggests that other Islamic manuscripts were also used as models for this casket.

Christian manuscripts, such as Alfonso X's *Cantigas de Santa Maria*, an illustrated collection of over 400 poems, also served as important references for the designer of this casket.[6] Mozarabic and Gothic manuscripts are the most likely source of the interlocking vegetal motifs and the harpies with human faces and reptilian tails on the casket's sides.[7]

The 1325 inventory of the Treasury of St. Mark's lists a *"capsicula argenti deaurata, cum literis de niello circundata, et cum figures in copertura"* (a gilded silver casket, surrounded by a nielloed inscription and figures on the lid), a reference that does not seem to have been taken into account in previous discussions of this work.[8] If indeed it refers to the casket, then it places the object in the treasury already by the first quarter of the 14th century and establishes a useful *terminus ante quem* for its execution.

FL

1 Beckwith 1960; Dodds 1992, pp. 41–47. The closest parallel is a brass casket with truncated pyramidal lid once in the Heeramaneck Galleries (Baer 1983, p. 4, fig. 54).
2 Baer 1983, p. 140, fig. 117; p. 226, fig. 187; Marshak 1986, figs. 158–60.
3 See in particular the 1334 copy in the Osterreichische Nationalbibliothek of Vienna, (Paris 1996, p. 171).
4 I would like to thank Dr. Francisco Prado-Vilar for this information, who first mentioned to me the connection between the *Maqamat* and the *Cantigas*.
5 They are also illustrated in a page from the *Mu'nis al-Ahrar* manuscript (Shiraz, 1341) today in the Cleveland Museum of Art (Carboni and Swietochowski 1994, pp. 30–31).
6 Fontana in Curatola 1993, pp. 477–80, cat. no. 297. See in particular *Cantigas* 1979, CVII, CXLXI, CLXIII and CLXXXIIII.
7 Mentré 1996, p. 85; pl. 49; see also the examples on late 10th-century Anglo-Saxon illumination (Pächt 1986, p. 182, fig. 188). For hybrids and harpies in 13th-and 14th-century Western manuscripts and architectural decoration see *Cantigas* 1979, LXX; Baltrušaitis 1981, pp. 13–18, 69, 103, 111; Camille 1992, pp. 11–55; von Folsach 2001, p. 158, no. 187; p. 159, no. 188; p. 305, no. 480.
8 Gallo 1967, p. 276, no. 6.

94. *Candlestick with the arms of a Venetian family*

Probably Damascus, Syria, ca. 1400
Brass incised and inlaid with silver and gold
H. 12.4 cm (4 7/8 in.) Max. diam. 8.3 cm (3 1/4 in.)
The British Museum, London
Inv. OA 1878.12-30.721 (ill. p. 217)

Like cats. 95 and 96, this small brass candlestick inlaid with silver and gold was made most likely in Damascus around 1400, and is one of the many Mamluk brass objects intended for the Italian market.[1] Already by the early 14th century, Islamic metalwork from Mamluk Egypt and Syria had found its way to Europe, where it was highly esteemed, and there can be no doubt that Mamluk artisans gradually started producing works specifically for European consumption. After the lifting of the papal embargo on trade with the Islamic world in the second half of the 14th century, Italian merchants began custom ordering Islamic metal objects.[2] The heraldic symbols they often bear may have been added after their arrival in Europe.

The coat of arms on this candlestick most likely belongs to the Venetian Boldù family. Precious metals were in short supply at this time, nonetheless, the object is lavishly inlaid in silver and gold. The tapering base and turned neck are characteristic Islamic candlestick features, already present in Ayyubid and Seljuk examples of the 12th and 13th centuries; however, in this case the neck is unusually tall in proportion to the rest of the elements. The base is decorated with scenes of animal battles, which, although widespread in earlier Islamic metalwork, had become somewhat antiquated by the 15th century.

A candlestick in the Victoria and Albert Museum shares many features with this one, including a similar profile, a Venetian coat of arms (in this case that of the Badoer family), and animal motifs.[3]

MAM

1 Ward 1993, p. 28, fig. 17.
2 Mack 2002, p. 141, fig. 149.
3 See Allan 1986, p. 53, figs. 39, 40 and 50.

95–96. *Two candlesticks with the arms of Venetian families*

Probably Damascus, Syria, early 15th century
Brass inlaid with gold and silver
Average heights 12.5 cm (5 in.), diams. 8.5 cm (3 3/8 in.)
Museo Civico Correr, Venice
Inv. Cl. XII, no. 22; Cl. XII, no. 23 (ill. p. 65)

Brass candlesticks were among the most common metal objects used in public as well as private, and secular as well as religious contexts, as much in the Middle East as in Europe in the medieval period. In the Mamluk territory, most likely in Syria, a specific type of candlestick with a truncated conical base, a large drip pan, and a tall neck was made in the first half of the 15th century. Every example is inlaid with silver, some are inlaid with gold, and many are decorated with Italian coats of arms, including those of Venetian families (see cat. 94). The Museo Correr owns four of these smallMamluk candlesticks,[1] two of which are presented here. The first (cat. 95) bears a circular medallion with diagonal stripes identified as the arms of the Malipiero or Contarini family, while the second (cat. 96) has a vortex star motif, the heraldic symbol of an unidentified Venetian family.

Until fairly recently it was believed that Muslim artisans working in Venice made these candlesticks and other brass objects, but this hypothesis is now obsolete since no written documents attest to the presence of craftsmen in the city. Had they established workshops in Venice and been accepted in the city's rigid guild system, they would have surely left traces in contemporary records.[2]

Imported Islamic candlesticks like those exhibited here no doubt influenced later, most likely Venetian examples that have a different, more elongated form but still imitate Islamic decoration (see cat. 121).

MAM

1 Venice 1993, pp. 488–89, cat. 306; Auld 2004, pp. 249–50, cat. 6.1, 6.3.
2 Huth 1970, pp. 58–68.

97. *Incense burner*

Probably Egypt, first half of the 14th century
Pierced brass, inlaid with gold and silver in two sections
Diam. 9 cm (3 1/2 in.)
Museo Correr, Venice
Inv. Cl.XII no. 9 (ill. p. 82)

This spherical incense burner conforms to Mamluk style in both its inscription and decorative details. Because it is more heavily pierced than most examples, it can emit greater amounts of fragrance.

A series of incomplete phrases, with no mention of the patron's name, comprise the inscription. The text can be translated as "the excellency, the sublime, the ruler, the learned, the just, the . . ." The script, with its repetitive upright *hastae* strokes, was either for decoration alone, or the anonymous craftsman ran out of space while copying the words and could not complete the inscription. Touches of gold in the whirling rosettes and in the center of the main roundels indicate the object's status as a luxury object. Large roundels with lotus blossoms, halved by the incense burner's midsection, were common circa 1320.

A basin made for Sultan Nasir al-Din Muhammad (r. 1293–1341), now in the British Museum (inv. no. 1851 1-4 1), is similarly engraved with small striations in the lotus' silver inlay, thus suggesting an attribution of the incense burner in the first half of the 14th century. Inlaid objects made for use in the Mamluk capital of Cairo originated in Egypt itself or in Syria, where there was a long tradition of high-quality metalwork.

SA

98. *Sprinkler* (qumqum)

Probably Egypt, 15th century
Brass inlaid with silver and a black compound
H. 23.7 cm (9 3/8 in.)
The British Museum, London
Inv. 1882 3-2 17.

This is one of a small group of inlaid brass bottles with a flattened ovoid body and a narrow tapered neck rising from a prominent knop.[1] Such metal flasks are similar in size, shape, and decoration to Mamluk glass perfume- or rosewater sprinklers known as *qumqum*. Distinguishing the metal examples from their glass counterparts is their lack of a spout, making their original function unclear. Metal *qumqums* could have been for ornament alone; two similar objects—one black, one red—are displayed upon a shelf in Carpaccio's *St. Augustine in His Study* of 1502 in the Scuola di San Giorgio degli Schiavoni in Venice.[2] The painting also provides valuable evidence that this kind of Mamluk metalwork was known in Renaissance Venice.

A decorative scheme similar to the one on this brass flask can be found on Mamluk round-bottomed boxes and lids. The motifs of guilloche knots and scrolling stems flanked by interlaced borders are almost universal in Mamluk metalwork.[3]

SA

1 Two examples are in Bologna, Museo Civico Medioevale, inv. nos. 2117 and 2118.
2 See also Schmidt Arcangeli's essay in this volume, esp. note 22.
3 Auld 2004, pp. 76 and 84, figs. 12 and 34; the present "sprinkler" is discussed on pp. 306–7, cat. 9.6.

99. *Box with lid*

Probably Egypt, 15th century
Brass engraved and inlaid with silver and a black compound
Diam. 11.4 cm (4 1/2 in.); H. 7.6 cm (3 in.)
The Metropolitan Museum of Art, New York
Rogers Fund, 1923
Inv. 23.67.5a (ill. p. 226)

The decoration of this lidded box is rooted in the same late Mamluk tradition as the *qumqum* in the British Museum (cat. 98). Here the main patterns consist of the dart-and-shield motif on the lid and the quatrefoil-shaped and elongated lobed cartouches around the box's walls. Scrolling stems, triangular knots, split-palmettes, guilloches, and rosettes ornament the exterior of both the lid and the box.[1] The decoration of the two parts is so similar and complementary that there can be no doubt that they belong together.

In the signed works of Mahmud al-Kurdi and Zain al-Din (cats. 103–5), two artists with a first hand-knowledge of the Mamluk metalworking tradition who likely worked elsewhere in the Near East, cartouches form a geometric mesh in silver inlay that stands out boldly against the extraordinarily subtle background decoration. In contrast, classic Mamluk objects like this box have a flatter background, which allows the viewer to get acquainted with the patterns and discover them little by little.

SC

1 Martin 1902, pl. 15, fig. 6; Auld 2004, pp. 166–67, cat. 2.35.

100. Mahmud al-Kurdi *Salver*

Possibly northwest Iran or southeast Anatolia, late 15th century
Brass engraved and inlaid with silver
Diam. 29 cm (11 3/8 in.)
Inscribed in Arabic across the centre *ʿamal al-muʿallim mahmud al-kurdi yarju al-maghfir* (the work of the master Mahmud the Kurd who hopes for forgiveness)
Musée du Louvre, Paris
Département des Arts de l'Islam
Inv. AO 7526 (ill. p. 219)

Flat, with a short vertical rim, this elaborately decorated tray was used to serve fine food in the Islamic world. An early 11th-century account refers to this kind of salver as a *sini*, defined as a "lunch" or "table-tray."[1] In late 15th-century Persian illustrated manuscripts, servants present similar trays laden with fruit or vessels to princes dining alfresco. During his sojourn in Tabriz, the Venetian Giosafat Barbaro experienced this luxurious style of picnicking firsthand at the court of Uzun Hasan, the Turkoman White Sheep leader.[2]

There are two other extant salvers signed by Mahmud al-Kurdi, one in the British Museum (cat. 101) and the other in the Hermitage Museum, St. Petersburg (inv. no. VC 235), which appear to belong to the same set. In both the Louvre and the Hermitage examples, the signature appears at the center of this object, an unusually prominent place for a craftsman's name. Lending credence to the idea that he worked in Northern Iran, Mahmud al-Kurdi always used a Persian signature.

All three trays in the set testify to Mahmud's love of different textures. Here the bold, silver-inlaid scrolling stems of the background are set against a central octagon and lime-shaped medallions. Important parallels for the equally bold inlaid border can be found in Qur'anic illumination, manuscript illustration, and the architectural decoration of 15th-century Tabriz and Herat.[3]

SA

1 Melikian-Chirvani 1982, pp. 399-400.
2 Barbaro and Contarini 1873, pp. 127-28.
3 Lentz and Lowry 1989; Auld 2004, pp. 11-28, 219-21, cat. 5.1-5.3.

101. Mahmud al-Kurdi
Salver

Possibly northwest Iran or southeast Anatolia, late 15th century
Brass engraved and inlaid with silver
H. 3 cm (1 1/8 in.); diam. 29.2 cm (11 1/2 in.)
Inscribed in Arabic across four roundels: "(1) *naqsh al-muʿallim* (2) *mahmud* (3) *al-kurdi yarju* (4) *al-maghfir* (?) *maulahi*" (the design of the master Mahmud the Kurd who hopes for forgiveness [from] his lord)
The British Museum, London
Inv. 1878 12-30 705 (ill. p. 220)

This salver is one of the finest examples of Mahmud al-Kurdi's work. Similarities between it and two other trays in Paris (cat. 100) and St. Petersburg (Hermitage Museum, inv. VC 235) suggest they once formed a set, perhaps with additional pieces. Carrying dishes presented successively to diners, the salvers would have been supported on a stand or laid on a carpet on the ground during the meal. The silver inlay would have protected the food from contamination, but these salvers were used to serve prepared food or to transport vessels with food inside and not for cooking.

Mahmud's design is in four parts and is centered on the same convex-sided octagon as cat. 100. His signature is divided between four separate roundels, each flanked by two crescents. The different sections are set between fillet borders in a way remarkably similar to the blazons of Mamluk rulers (see cat. 69). It is notable that the clearest script—because it is the least crowded—is used for Mahmud's own name. One of the reasons for a continuing discussion about the place of manufacture of this and related metal objects is their apparent reference to Mamluk protocol. There are also similarities between Mahmud al-Kurdi's border designs and those used in contemporary Qur'an illumination and on decorated stone domes in the Mamluk capital of Cairo, although it should be noted that these intertwined borders originated in Timurid and Turkoman Persia. On the outer rim of the salver is yet another reference to the style current in late 15th-century Cairo. Ten little lotus blossoms fill small roundels, a motif popular during Sultan Qa'itbey's reign (1468–96).

The use of inlay was relatively rare in the latter part of the 15th century. The salver, which does not bear the name or titles of a patron, could have been made for a court official, for its extensive silver inlay suggests it was still a luxury object.

SA

102. Mahmud al-Kurdi
Salver

Possibly northwest Iran or southeast Anatolia, late 15th century
Brass; engraved and inlaid with silver and a black compound
Inscribed in Arabic in cartouches: "1) *ʿamal al-muʿallim* 2) *mahmud al-kur* 3) *d* [*sic*] *yarju* 4) *al-maghfira* 5) *min maulahi* (the work of the master Mahmud the Kurd who hopes for forgiveness from his lord)
Diam. 53.5 cm (21 1/16 in.)
Parrocchia di Santa Maria Assunta, Arcidiocesi di Udine, Ufficio Arte Sacra e Beni Culturali, Cividale del Friuli
Inv. 23251 (ill. p. 229)

This salver has been present in the Church of Santa Maria Assunta in Cividale del Friuli since at least 1546, the year when it and a bucket (cat. 112) are referred to in an inventory as *"il bacil e calderol lavorati alla azimina son del q M. Daniel Gallicino"* (the inlaid salver and bucket belonging to Mr. Daniel Gallicino).[1] As a sign of his devotion, Gallicino might have given these luxurious metal objects to the church that year.

This salver consists of a repoussé central umbo (*omphalos*), low curving sides, and a broad, flat rim.[2] Silver inlay, organized into a radial pattern emanating from the center, decorates its face. Within each circular band are multi-lobed cartouches set against a ground of intricate arabesques. The inscription with Mahmud al-Kurdi's name appears discreetly along the side in five cartouches in the outermost register. This register bears a narrow band, defined by silver inlay and divided into sections by a sinuous knotted vine-form. These sections are alternately decorated with star-shaped patterns, split-palmettes, and inscriptions.

The underside of the salver is completely devoid of decoration, except for two single words inscribed on diametrically opposed sides along the rim. They are in bold Arabic cursive script and have been double-outlined, as if prepared for inlay. The words are difficult to decipher, and their endings in the letter *waw* ("o" or "oo") make it unlikely that they are native to the Arabic or Persian languages. They could, however, be read as transliterated Italian proper names, in which case one appears to be "Jacopo." If this interpretation is correct, then the presence of an Italian name written in Arabic would suggest that the salver was acquired in the Islamic world by a European traveler or merchant literate in Arabic. This richly decorated salver by a renowned craftsman would make a fine souvenir or a luxury gift, for display in a home or for use in a liturgical ceremony.

QA

1 Quoted in Santangelo 1936 from the *Inventario del 1546* in *Inventari raccolti da Giorgio Modana*, ms. copy in the Museo di Cividale. Strangely, the salver visible in Santangelo's photograph does not correspond to the object here under discussion although its dimensions are identical. The entry in Codroipo 1992 (p. 97) illustrates instead the correct salver.
2 Santangelo 1936, pp. 44–45; Codroipo 1992, p. 97, cat. II.39. The closest parallel is in the Isabella Stewart Gardner Museum, Boston; see Auld 2004, p. 224, no. 5.8 and Campbell and Chong 2005, pp. 33–35.

103. Mahmud al-Kurdi
Box with lid

Possibly northwest Iran or southeast Anatolia, late 15th century
Brass, engraved and inlaid with silver and a black compound.
H. 7.6cm (2 7/8 in.); diam. 15.8 cm (6 1/8 in.)
Inscribed in Arabic and in Latin on the upper rim of the box: "*ʿamal al-muʿallim mahmud yarju al-maghfira min maulahi* (the work of the master Mahmud who hopes for forgiveness from his lord); "*AMELEIMALENMAMUD*" (the work of the master Mahmud)
Courtauld Institute of Art Gallery, London
Inv. O.1966.GP.204 (ill. p. 221)

Purchased by the English collector Thomas Gambier-Parry in Zara (now Zadar) along the Dalmatian coast in 1858, this lidded box is now considered a key piece in the debate on where Mahmud al-Kurdi worked.[1] When the object was first published, its signature was thought to include the words "al-Kurdi."[2] In fact, only "Mahmud" appears, but the style and technique of the decoration link the work without question to the Kurdish master, who signed his full name on many other pieces (including cats. 101, 102, 104).[3] Here Mahmud is written in both Arabic and Latin, perhaps indicating that the box was intended for a European destination. The Roman characters spell out a transliterated Persian form of Mahmud's signature rather than a translation, which suggests that the recipient could speak but not read Persian or Arabic, or had a translator at hand.

The shape and size of this box conform to other examples in the British Museum analyzed by Ward and La Niece, who believed that they formed a distinct group made in Turkoman Iran.[4] Sweetmeats may have been served in these elegant little containers, but the similarity in their size and capacity lends support to the idea that they were used to transport prepacked *spezierie minute* or *sottili* (valuable spices exported in small quantities to Europe). The practice of producing containers of standard dimensions appears to have been widespread in the Mediterranean world. In Mamluk Egypt, for example, large bowls contained a specified weight of wheat for sale in the market and therefore were easy for inspectors to check. In Renaissance Italy, merchants learned from an early age how to gauge capacity by arithmetical means.

SA

1 Auld 1989, pp. 36–43; Auld 2004.
2 Robinson 1967, pp. 170–71.
3 Auld 2004, pp. 148–51, 219–21.
4 Ward and La Niece 1995.

104. Mahmud al-Kurdi
Box with lid

Possibly northwest Iran or southeast Anatolia, late 15th century
Brass; engraved and inlaid with silver and a black compound
H. 8.2 cm (3 1/4 in.); Diam. 13.7 cm (5 3/8 in.)
Inscribed in Arabic, on lid: "1) *ʿamal al-muʿallim mahmu* 2) *d al-kurdi yarju*" (the work of the master Mahmud al-Kurdi who hopes)
Inscribed in Arabic, on box: "1) *ʿamal al-muʿallim mahmud al-kurdi* 2) *yarju al-maghfira min maulahi*" (the work of the master Mahmud al-Kurdi who hopes for forgiveness from his lord)
Museo Archeologico Nazionale, Cividale del Friuli
Inv. 4441 (ill. p. 218)

This box with lid is signed in two places by the master Mahmud al-Kurdi, and is one of seven such boxes that bear his name (see cat. 103).[1] As is characteristic of Mahmud's work, the decoration of both the box and its lid is organized according to large geometric compositions outlined in silver, emanating from a central radial arabesque and terminating in shield-shaped sections. The inscriptions with the maker's name are placed between parallel lines within these shield-shaped medallions, their arrangement recalling the typical format of a Mamluk blazon.

Boxes with rounded bases and tight-fitting lids were a common type of al-Kurdi-related production in the 15th and 16th centuries but an unusual shape in contemporary Islamic metalwork. Owing to their rounded base, these boxes are inherently unstable and tend to tip sideways, and it is still unclear how they were used. One possibility is that they may have been supported on metal stands, but these boxes do not show any evidence of resulting abrasion and no stand for them is known to have survived.[2] They may have been used with a sectioned tray as coordinated sets. Although the term *tas* (cup) has been used to describe such boxes and a few paintings show rounded bowls as drinking vessels, the instability of these objects make them unsuitable for holding liquids. Their tightly fitted lids corroborate the suggestion that they contained goods, such as herbs, requiring assured freshness and safe transport.

QA

1 Auld 2004, p. 150, cat. 2.5; Scerrato 1966, pp. 140-41, fig. 61.
2 Auld 2004, p. 141.

105. Zain al-Din
Box with lid

Possibly northwest Iran or southeast Anatolia, late 15th - early 16th century
Brass, engraved and inlaid with silver
Inscribed in Arabic around the rim: *"naqsh al-ᶜabd al-faqir zain al-din yarju al-maghfira"* (the design of the poor slave Zain al-Din who hopes for forgiveness)
Diam. 15cm (6 3/4 in.)
Musée du Louvre, Paris
Inv. OA 6009 (ill. p. 224)

Unlike Mahmud al-Kurdi, whose signature on boxes was frequently hidden under the cover, Zain al-Din prominently placed his name in two sections on the bulging rim of this box. Muslim artists frequently referred to themselves as a "poor slave [of God]," as Zain al-Din does here, but the last part of his inscription, "who hopes for forgiveness," echoes Mahmud al-Kurdi (see cats. 100–104).

One of many boxes whose original function was to carry some precious substance, this elaborately decorated work is typical of Zain al-Din (see cat. 106), who seems to have taken inspiration from, and worked a little later, than Mahmud al-Kurdi.[1] The ornament consists of flowing interlaced wire and cusped figures set on a minutely engraved ground. Interestingly, Zain al-Din's example is the only box in this group to bear a European shield. The coat of arms on the lid in the form of a displayed heraldic bird, perhaps intended to be an eagle, has not yet been identified.

SA

1 Auld 2004, pp. 151–52, cat. 2.7.

106. Zain al-Din
Incense burner

Possibly northwest Iran or southeast Anatolia, late 15th - early 16th century
Pierced brass, engraved and inlaid with silver and a black compound
Inscribed in Arabic on both halves: *"naqsh zain al-din"* (the design of Zain al-Din)
H. 8.9 cm (3 1/2 in.); diam. 8.6 cm (3 3/8 in.)
The Walters Art Museum, Baltimore
Inv. 54.2236A and B (ill. p. 224)

This little brass ball is another example of a type known in the West under various names, including *scaldamano* (hand warmer), but intended originally to hold steady a burning, aromatic substance (see cat. 97).[1] The internal cardanic suspension system of rings with a central cup was attached to the rim by a single pin. The piercing occurs in the areas of the heavy inlaid arabesques, which are intertwined, crossing at the center to form a single knot.

Zain al-Din has signed the ball in two areas on both halves, in the narrow band surrounding the main roundel at the apex and base. He used the term *naqsh* to describe his work; this can mean either "design" or "decoration"; Mahmud al-Kurdi, on the other hand, commonly used the term *ᶜamal,* "work" (see cat,. 100, 102–104), although two salvers and a round-bottomed box in the Victoria and Albert Museum have *naqsh* instead (see cat. 101). The two terms therefore may have been interchangeable.

This example is inlaid with silver only, with elements of the design intersecting in two bands of decoration. The ornamentation is based on a circle but there is a fluidity of line that is different from the overtly geometric shapes of incense burners made by Mamluk craftsmen (compare cat. 97). Zain al-Din worked in the Turkoman-Iranian tradition of Mahmud al-Kurdi, but probably at a slightly later date.

SA

1 Auld 2004, pp. 116–17, cat. 1.2.

107. Zain al-Din cUmar
Box with lid

Possibly northwest Iran or southeast Anatolia, late 15th - early 16th century
Brass, engraved and inlaid with silver
Inscribed in Arabic under the lid: *"naqsh al-ᶜabd al-faqir al-muᶜallim zain al-din ᶜumar"* (the design of the poor slave, the master, Zain al-Din ᶜUmar)
H. 9.5 cm (3 3/4 in.); diam. 16.3 cm (6 3/8 in.)
Museo Nazionale del Bargello, Florence
Inv. B.317 (ill. p. 217)

This beautifully decorated box with a rounded base and tightly fitting flat lid was originally in the collection of Ferdinand I de' Medici (1549–1609), and from 1589 was kept in Florence in the Sala della Tribuna in the Uffizi, a place reserved for objects of special value.[1]

The artist's signature on the box is not immediately visible because it is hidden under the lid. Another round-bottomed box also signed by Zain al-Din ᶜUmar is in the Museo Civico Correr in Venice (inv. II 8), while another, signed by "Zain al-Din son of the master ᶜUmar the coppersmith" (*zain al-din ibn al-muᶜallim ᶜumar al-nahhas*), was sold at auction in London in 1986.[2] Working in a style close to master Zain al-Din (cats. 105–106), a relationship between the three artists—Zain al-Din, Zain al-Din ᶜUmar, and his son ibn ᶜUmar—seems probable. Family workshops were common when these lidded boxes were made in the second half of the 15th or early 16th century.

As in other examples of this type, the design of the lid is expanded to fill the base and walls of the box as well. In artistic terms, Zain al-Din ᶜUmar favors more flowing lines and better defined spaces within the four-part inlaid design as compared to the rather essential, more geometric, appearance of the works signed by Mahmud the Kurd.

SA

1 The original use of these lidded boxes is discussed in cat. 103.
2 Auld 2004, pp. 153–55, cat. 2.9 and 2.11.

108. Qasim
Ewer

Possibly northwest Iran or southeast Anatolia, late 15th - early 16th century
Brass, engraved and probably originally inlaid with silver; later gilding
H. 19.1 cm (7 1/2 in.)
Inscribed in Arabic inside the lip: *"naqsh al-muᶜallim qasim"* (the design of the master Qasim)
The Walters Art Museum, Baltimore
Inv. 54.2334 (ill. p. 26)

The original use of small ewers like this one is not clear. Several jugs in gold, hardstone, and zinc of similar size but with a straight neck over a bulging body and set with semi-precious stones are to be found in the Topkapı Museum in Istanbul.[1] These reflect a particular type of small jug from the Timurid period, of which many examples are known. This fluted ewer, however, is closer to Turkish ceramic objects, in particular a jug in the Victoria and Albert Museum, London, which however has no pouring spout.[2]

This is the only object known to bear Qasim's signature, which is expertly achieved inside the lip by means of parallel engraved lines; the script is clear, elegantly proportioned and with the points over individual letters carefully positioned, bearing some similarity with the supposed Italian owner's name on the underside of the salver in the Treasury of Cividale (cat. 102).[3] On a similarly shaped jug now in the Musée du Louvre, Paris (inv. R57) a transliterated "signature" has been added upside down, whereas Qasim's name may be read by anyone holding the object in his hand.[4]

SA

1 See, for example, *Palace of Gold and Light* 2000, p. 171, figs. E54, E55.
2 Petsopoulos 1982, p. 94, no. 95.
3 Auld 2004, p. 293, cat. 8.2.
4 Auld 2004, pp. 292–93, cat. 8.1.

109. *Salver*

Brass engraved and inlaid with silver
Possibly northwest Iran or southeast Anatolia, late 15th century
Diam. 41cm (16 1/8 in.)
Staatliche Museen zu Berlin, Museum für Islamische Kunst, Berlin
Inv. I.3615 (ill. p. 56)

Although the celebrated trays of Mahmud al-Kurdi have relatively small dimensions and short perpendicular walls (cats. 100–101), the most common shape for salvers that can be included in this group of possible northwestern Iranian or southwestern Anatolian origin is by far a large, flat plate with a shallow cavetto and a broad averted rim like this one in Berlin. Al-Kurdi himself was familiar with this kind of salver as is evident from the work in Cividale that bears his signature (cat. 102), which is even larger than the present example. Variation within this type is limited to the treatment of the central circle, which can be worked in repoussé (as in cat. 102) or inlaid with a coat of arms or a distinctive medallion.[1]

As for the decorative program, the majority of these salvers follow Islamic models in their arrangement in concentric circles, each containing mostly sequences of lobed cartouches boldly outlined in silver and filled within and without with fine vegetal patterns. Peculiar to this example is the large central medallion that departs from a 12-pointed star with guilloche knots radiating from its tips.[2] The variations of Islamic ornament are of course infinite and no plate is identical to another, but between the two other salvers of identical shape presented in this exhibition, the artistic intent of this object is much closer to the work of Mahmud al-Kurdi (cat. 102) than to the one with the Venetian coat of arms (cat. 120).

SC

1 An exhaustive survey is in Auld 2004, Ch. 5, pp. 219–45.
2 A detailed description of the pattern of this salver is in Auld 2004, p. 238, cat. 5.33.

110. Bucket

Probably Egypt or Syria, late 14th-early 15th century
Brass engraved and inlaid with silver
H. (without handle) 16 cm (6 1/4 in.); diam. 15cm (6 in.)
Staatliche Museen zu Berlin, Museum für Islamische Kunst, Berlin
Inv. B.72 (ill. p. 125)

With its bell-shaped angled walls, vertical neck, and bail handle (which may be a replacement) supported by brackets, this small bucket is close in shape to an example in the Victoria and Albert Museum, London.[1] In Persian, one type of bucket is referred to as *tas-i hammam* or "bath-house bucket," used to carry soap to the public baths; they appear in a late Timurid miniature painting, perhaps by Bihzad, dating to 1494;[2] however, the profile of the present bucket finds closer parallels in Egyptian or Syrian works and its original use is unclear. In Europe, where they were imported, these objects were used as holy-water receptacles,[3] and a similar one can be seen hanging beside the bed in Carpaccio's painting of *The*

Dream of St. Ursula of ca. 1495 in the Gallerie dell'Accademia, Venice.[4]

Once thought to be a European imitation of Islamic metalwork because the inscription around the base could not be deciphered,[5] Doris Behrens Abouseif has recently demonstrated that the script is indeed Arabic and includes several verses well known in Mamluk Egypt.[6]

The decoration of the bucket, however, is curiously different from the Mamluk metalwork design of this period, which is characterized by strict bands and interlacing knots, scrolls, and floral roundels. In this instance, the inlaid, loosely constructed lobed shapes and linked trefoils that cover the bucket's walls are closer to work signed by Mahmud al-Kurdi and Zain al-Din (see cats. 100–106). Another important parallel for the bucket's decoration can be found in the highly unusual manuscript illuminations of Ibrahim al-Amidi, or "from Amid," an area under the control of the Turkoman White Sheep, who worked in Cairo for a number of years before 1376. The bucket's decoration appears to reflect elements of the illuminator's designs, including the use of angular geometric shapes. Emblematic of Ibrahim al-Amidi's work is the frontispiece to a Qur'an now in the National Library, Cairo,[7] which was bequeathed by Sultan Shaban to his mother's religious school in 1369. Ibrahim al-Amidi's dotted white outlines set against a dark ground simulate the effect of silver inlay against an engraved metal ground, or one filled with a black compound.

SA

1 Inv. no. M.3-1946. See Auld 2004, p. 284, cat. 7.23.
2 The British Library, London, *Khamsa* of Nizami, Or.6810 f.27v; see Lentz and Lowry 1989, ill. p. 291.
3 For example, the bucket with aspergillum now in the Museo Diocesano in Treviso; see Venice 1993, pp. 313–15, cat. 180; Bertelli 2002, pp. 96–101, cat. 13.
4 See also Schmidt Arcangelis' essay in this volume, esp. note 21.
5 Auld 2004, pp. 283–84, cat. 7.22.
6 In an oral presentation during a symposium held at the Chester Beatty Library, Dublin, in September 2004.
7 Fols.1v-2r; see James 1988, cat. 31, fig. 142.

111. *Bucket*

Islamic Near East or possibly Venice, 16th century
Brass inlaid with silver
H. 13 cm (5 1/8 in.); diam. 22 cm (8 5/8 in.)
Inscribed in Latin on the upper section: "*MO DE RA TA*"; on the lower section: "*BEA TUS SOA VIR*"
Museo Nazionale del Bargello, Florence
Inv. 837 B (ill. p. 214)

Projecting ribs on the base and center as well as under the rim enliven the angled walls of this bucket.[1] Brackets soldered to the flaring lip show that the object once had a handle, now lost. In Persia, this type of bucket sometimes carries verses in praise of wine (see cat. 114); as a result it has been suggested they may have used as wine buckets (see cat. 112) but it is just as likely that their function was to collect water poured over the hands from a ewer, before and after eating. In Europe, priests used them for a similar purpose in preparation for the mass. In late medieval and Renaissance religious paintings, the buckets are symbols of purity and frequently used in association with the Virgin Mary and other female saints.[2]

At first glance the decoration of this bucket appears authentically Islamic, although its shape is unusual. A closer examination reveals Latin inscriptions set into small cartouches in the upper and lowest bands. There are four shield-shaped panels in the upper section, each carrying two letters: *"MO DE RA TA,"* thus apparently forming the feminine adjective *"moderata,"* meaning "temperate," or "restrained," or perhaps the proper name of a minor saint or of the original owner. On the curved section at the edge of the base there are four further panels; these have the letters: *"BEA TUS SOA VIR."* It is not clear what meaning can be taken from these letters. Presumably the first pairing produces *"beatus,"* "blessed." Perhaps *VIR* is a shortened form of *"virgo"* in which case *SOA* could be *"soave"* thus making it "sweet Virgin." But the adjective *beatus* is in the masculine form and cannot be associated with the feminine noun "virgin." The association of these objects with purity, however, seems underlined by the inclusion of these letters also because *"moderata"* can mean "sober."

The inclusion of Roman script may point to a Western place of manufacture, perhaps Venice. Another possibility is that the bucket was decorated in the East with implicit instructions to include Roman letters that had some specific meaning now unclear to us.

SA

1 Auld 2004, p. 279, cat. 7.15.
2 Auld 2004, p. 267, n. 267.

112. *Bucket*

Islamic Near East or possibly Venice, 16th century
Brass engraved and inlaid with silver and a black compound
H. (without handle) 11 cm (4 5/16 in.); diam. 25 cm (9 13/16 in.)
Parrocchia di Santa Maria Assunta, Arcidiocesi di Udine, Ufficio Arte Sacra e Beni Culturali, Cividale del Friuli
Inv. 23250 (ill. p. 56)

Like the salver in the same treasury (cat. 102), this bucket was listed in the 1546 inventory of Santa Maria Assunta as having been owned by Daniel Gallicino, who donated both objects to the church. The bucket has straight sides, a slightly rounded base, and a zoomorphic handle with two pairs of confronted serpents.[1] The exterior is decorated with a lavish ornamented pattern on its sides and base whereas the interior is unadorned. The walls bear alternating rectangular and octagonal lobed cartouches, defined in silver inlay, against a richly carved background of split-palmette scrolls. The cartouches are filled with knots, vegetal scrolls, and star-shaped motifs, demonstrating the range of the maker's skill. On the base, the ornament is organized in concentric bands surrounding a central radial design, each band further divided by lobed medallions with silver-inlaid outlines. The overall effect of this vessel is of luxury and sumptuousness, and of high-quality workmanship. Buckets such as this one may have been used for wine[2] or perhaps for collecting water poured over the hands from a ewer, before and after eating, or in bath-houses.

QA

1 Santangelo 1936, pp. 44–45; Codroipo 1992, p. 97, cat. II. 39.
2 Melikian-Chirvani 1982, p. 379.

113. See cat. 77

114. *Wine Cup*

Iran, late 16th - early 17th century
Metal alloy
H. 8.7 cm (3 3/8 in.); diam. 19.5 cm (7 5/8 in.)
Museo Civico Correr, Venice
Inv. Cl. XI, 778 (ill. p. 20)

Bowls and wide cups on a short foot (*badiye* and *jam* in Persian, respectively) enjoyed particular success in the Safavid period (1502–1722). Their decoration usually consists of an epigraphic band, vegetal scrolls, and geometric motifs, a combination that became standardized by the time of the long reign of Shah ʿAbbas I (r. 1588–1629).[1] This type of decoration originated in the Timurid period, which in its turn had drawn inspiration from Far-Eastern vegetal and floral motifs;[2] it also echoes the lobed scrolls that appear in Safavid manuscript illumination and architectural decoration, particularly from the period of Shah Tahmasp (r. 1524–76).[3]

In this cup, the decoration develops in a rhythmic succession of scrolls with bi-lobed and tri-lobed finials and palmettes that cover the entire surface; the foot-ring is engraved with a continuous pattern of Y-shaped motifs.[4] The verses of the celebrated 14th-century Persian poet Hafez, inscribed in elegant *nastaʿliq* inside 6 multi-lobed cartouches with intervening quatrefoils, run around the exterior rim and in the center medallion of the interior, openly referring to the cup's use:

"Oh cupbearer, enlighten my cup with the light of wine

And you, minstrel, proclaim a world fashioned in my way

In the cup I glanced the shadow of a friendly face

Oh thou, reluctant to the joy of my unexhausted drinking

Drunkenness is a pleasing thing for the beloved I love

Thus my reins are entrusted to drunkenness /

When my companion loses the cup, all the idols fall into pieces."[5]

This wine cup is one of the few works of Islamic art with a Safavid origin (see cat. 178) today in the Museo Correr—therefore presumably acquired by Teodoro Correr from a Venetian family—thus allowing a glimpse into the efforts of the Serenissima to seek alliance with the Iranian shah against the Ottomans.

FL

1 Melikian-Chirvani 1973, pp. 109; 120–21; Melikian Chirvani 1982, pp. 170, 266, 292–93, 301, 329–35, figs. 66, 69, cat. 126, 131, 149–54.
2 Melikian-Chirvani 1982, p. 256, 258, figs. 115A, 116; transitional examples between the Timurid and the Safavid decorative patterns can be found in Thompson and Canby 2003, pp. 2, 215, figs. 1.1, 8.10.
3 Thompson and Canby 2003, pp. 33, 85, 105, 151, figs. 2.9, 4.6, 4.20, 5.7.
4 See in particular Melikian-Chirvani 1973, pp. 120–21.
5 The inscription is transcribed in Persian and translated into Italian in Venice 1993, p. 432, cat. 279. The present English translation is mine.

°115. *Hanging Lamp*

Veneto region, mid- to late 15th century (excavated in Padua in 1908)
Cast and tooled bronze
H. 28 cm (11 1/16 in.); diam. of the mouth max. 26 cm (10 in.)
Inscription: AVE MARIA G[R]ACIA PLENA DOM/INVS TECUM BENEDI[C]TA T/V IN MULIERIBUS
Excavated in Padua in 1908
The Walters Art Museum, Baltimore
Inv. 54.259

The origins of vase-shaped lamps with a flaring neck, circular foot, globular body, and loops for suspension can be traced to early Islamic Iran, where they were made in both glass and metal.[1] This distinctive form of lighting device gradually spread to other regions of the Islamic world, and later appeared in ceramic as well.[2] Plainer specimens illuminated secular buildings, but those intended for mosques and other religious foundations often bore ornament and pious inscriptions.[3] The most elaborate examples are the famous enameled and gilded glass mosque lamps from Mamluk Egypt, which feature Qu'ranic verses in elegant calligraphy comparing God to the light of a glass lamp within a niche (see cats. 152–53).[4] Byzantine and medieval churches in the Latin West, such as Old St. Peter's in Rome, eventually adopted the form as well,[5] although it always remained more common in the Islamic world.

This little known vase-shaped bronze lantern inscribed in Latin represents an adaptation of the Islamic mosque lamp for a Christian religious setting in the Veneto. Excavated in Padua in 1908, packed in a box along with other liturgical treasures that were probably hidden

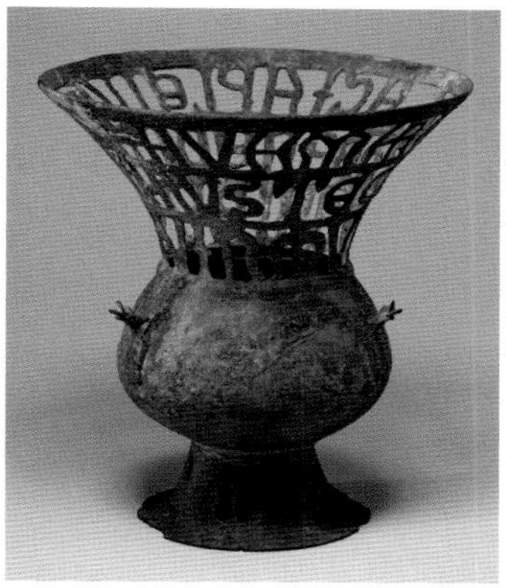

cat. 115

during the Napoleonic invasions, the lamp must have once illuminated an altar in the nearby church of San Felice.[6] An important indication of how it hung in its original setting is found in Giovanni Mansueti's early 16th-century altarpiece of *St. Mathew Enthroned with Five Saints and Music-Making Putti*.[7]

This lamp is difficult to date, but Padua became an important bronze-casting center only after Donatello's extended sojourn in the city between 1443 and 1453, which provides a possible *terminus ante quem*. It appears that an ambitious, anonymous local master working in the mid- to late Quattrocento modeled this work on an imported Islamic metal mosque lamp similar to examples now in the David Collection in Copenhagen, the Louvre in Paris, and the Gayer Anderson Museum in Cairo.[8] In addition to replicating the shape and function of his Near Eastern prototype, the Paduan bronze caster also pierced the thinly beaten metal to highlight the sacred text that runs around the neck in the same manner.[9] Some metal mosque lamps are more elaborate than this, including intricate geometric ornament as well as inscriptions, while others are much simpler, without any openwork. In his *St. Mark Baptizing Anianus* of ca. 1518 (cat. 28), Mansueti represents a solid, gilt metal mosque lamp suspended above the central scene, suggesting that a variety of these objects were known in the Veneto in this period.

The Latin inscription on this lamp is divided into three rows and consists of the Archangel Gabriel's greeting to the Virgin Mary at the Annunciation, an event theologically associated with Christ's Incarnation and therefore often recalled on or near Christian altars. An abbreviated version of the phrase also appears on a few late 13th- and early 14th-century Venetian enameled glass beakers (see, for example, cat. 157), which probably functioned as wine vessels during the celebration of the Mass. An even more direct parallel exists with a Venetian glass *cesendello* painted with the figures of both Gabriel and the Virgin (cat. 165), which also must have illuminated a church chapel.

TK

1 Behrens-Abouseif 1995, pp. 25–26; Carboni 2001, p. 165, cat. 38a.
2 Illustrated and discussed in Behrens-Abouseif 1995, pp. 26, 31, pl. 11.
3 Carboni and Whitehouse 2001, p. 227, cat. 113; Carboni 2003, p. 24. For ceramic examples, see Atasoy and Raby 1989, pp. 262–63.
4 Carboni 2003, pp. 24–26.
5 Rohauld de Fleury 1888, pls. CDXLI, CDXLV, and CDXLII.
6 Pellegrini 1911, pp. 308–10. Another, more elaborate vase-shaped lamp with a similar inscription was found in the same box in Padua and is also in the Walters Art Museum today (no. 54.258).
7 Illustrated in Berenson 1957, fig. 368.
8 Illustrated and discussed along with other comparable examples in Behrens-Abouseif 1995, pp. 25–41.
9 On this technique, see Behrens-Abouseif 1995, pp. 7–8,.

116–117. *Medals of Sultan Mehmet II*

Designed by Gentile Bellini (1429-1507)
Probably cast by Bartolomeo Bellano (ca. 1437/8–1496/7)
Istanbul, late 1479-early 1480
Bronze

116.

Diameter 9.5 cm (3 3/4 in.)
The British Museum, Department of Coins and Medals, London
Inv. 1883-3-1 (ill. p. 134)

117.

Diameter 9.3 cm (3 3/5 in.)
Galleria G. Franchetti alla Ca' d'Oro, Venice
Inv. ME 88[1] (ill. p. 134)

After peace was declared between Venice and the Ottoman Empire in 1479, ending 16 years of bitter conflict, Sultan Mehmet II sent a letter to the Venetian Senate requesting a painter, a sculptor, and a bronze founder. In response, the Senate sent to the sultan's court Gentile Bellini, the official painter to the Republic,[2] and Bartolomeo Bellano, Donatello's Paduan protégée, along with two assistants for each master.[3] By this date, Mehmet II had already developed a passionate interest in portrait medals and the skills he sought in these artists indicate that he specifically desired a new medallic portrait of himself.

Bellini, in the role of portraitist-designer, and Bellano, acting as the bronze caster, almost certainly collaborated on the medal, even if the painter's name alone appears on the final product and historically he has received sole credit for its production. The fact that Bellano remained in Istanbul for less than six months suggests that the first version of the medal was made no later than early in 1480. Additional examples may have been made thereafter, also after the return of the artists to Italy.

Two slightly different casts of the 15 known surviving examples of the Bellini-Bellano medal are shown here.[4] Among these two, the Ca' D'Oro medal (cat. 117) has a smaller diameter and the sultan's costume lacks embellishment. By contrast, the sultan wears a velvet costume with floral patterns in the larger medal in the British Museum (cat. 116). In both instances, the medal is pierced at top center, suggesting they were once hung.

Several artists from the Italian peninsula made medals depicting Mehmet II in the Quattrocento, but Gentile is one of the very few to have captured the sultan's likeness firsthand.[5] Interestingly, Costanzo da Ferrara (Costanzo di Moysis), who also stayed at Mehmet II's court and portrayed him from life, created a markedly different image than Bellini.[6] Sent to Istanbul by Ferdinand I of Naples sometime between 1464 and 1481, Costanzo depicted Mehmet II as a physically imposing man eminently worthy of the title "the Conqueror."[7] On the obverse of the medal, the sultan's prodigious turbaned head and broad shoulders dramatically bulge beyond the confines of the frame. Bellini's portrait lacks that monumentality: he depicted Mehmet II as a slighter man whose head and shoulders fit neatly within the medal's parameters. From this, Raby concluded that Costanzo captured the sultan's likeness before age and illness had diminished him in his final years.[8] While that may be true, it is also important to remember the different cultural backgrounds of the two artists. Costanzo worked primarily in Ferrara and Naples, where political power and ruler imagery were more readily associated with military prowess. In Venice, where a mature oligarchy prevailed, gently wizened features often figure prominently in dogal portraits (see cats. 21–22). Far more so than anywhere else in Italy, Venetians valued political leaders with the wisdom and experience that advanced age brings. Gentile therefore may have been flattering the sultan by depicting him in the same fashion as he represented revered Venetian doges.

The symbolism of the Bellini-Bellano medallic portrait relates it to Bellini's famous painted portrait of the sultan dated November 1480 (cat. 23). Like the painting, the medal features three crowns stacked one above the other on a blank field. The utter simplicity of the iconography—the three crowns refer to Greece, Asia, and Trebizond, the lands conquered by the sultan—renders these works immediately comprehensible and hence highly effective means of propaganda.[9]

Mehmet II, who seized the Byzantine capital of Constantinople in 1453 when he was just 21 years old, enjoyed international fame—or rather infamy—long before any Italian portrait of him was made, but his patronage of Costanzo da Ferrara and Gentile Bellini indicates the sultan's growing concern for controlling his image in Europe. Mehmet II could have been aware of such unflattering portrayals of him as the Florentine *Il Gran Turco* prints of ca. 1470;[10] if so, he would have wanted to counteract them with a more celebratory and dignified image of himself. Significantly, Florence became an important early destination for the Bellini-Bellano medal. Before his death in 1481, Mehmet II sent the medal through diplomatic channels to Lorenzo de' Medici, and eventually it served as the point of departure for Bertoldo di Giovanni's own medal of the sultan.[11] Not just Florentines, but many other powerful Europeans came to recognize Mehmet II's distinctive characteristics—his aquiline nose, overbite, bristled beard, pointed chin, and turban elegantly wrapped around a *taj*—thanks to the broad circulation of the Bellini-Bellano medallic portrait.

TK

1 Formerly in the Museo Archeologico, Venice.
2 For a discussion of the factors contributing to the Senate's selection of Gentile for the mission, see Chong 2005, p. 107.
3 The documents related to the artists' mission are published in Meyer zur Capellen 1985, pp. 109–111. For the broader context of Mehmet II's patronage of Italian artists, see Raby 1982a, Raby 1987, and Raby's essay in this volume.
4 The most recent survey of Gentile Bellini's medal is in Spinale 2003, who curiously omits the Ca' D'Oro example exhibited here. For that reason, see also Hill 1930, no. 432, which does include it.
5 For the other medals of Mehmet II, see especially Raby 1987a and Spinale 2003.
6 On Costanzo da Ferrara, see especially Andaloro 1980; Raby 1987, pp. 176–78; Washington 1991, pp. 211–12; Spinale 2003, pp. 112–53; Campbell and Chong 2005.
7 Underscoring this characterization, the inscription on the obverse of Costanzo's medal declares Mehmet II "the thunderbolt of war, [who] has laid low people and cities" (Washington 1991, p. 211).
8 Raby 1994, p. 89.
9 For an alternative interpretation of the significance of the crowns, see Pedani Fabris 1996–97 and Pedani Fabris 1999.
10 On these prints, one of which is in the Topkapı Palace Museum in Istanbul, see most recently Raby 2000a, pp. 64–65; Spinale 2003, pp. 99–110; Campbell and Chong 2005, pp. 66–69.
11 On Bertoldo's medal, see Draper 1992, pp. 95–101; Draper 1994, p. 127; Spinale 2003, pp. 177–88.

118. Ulocrino (active 1485–1530) *Aristotle and Alexander of Aphrodisias*

Padua, late 15th or early 16th century
Cast bronze
7cm x 5.5 cm (2 3/4 x 2 1/4 in.)
Museo Civico Correr, Venice,
Inv. Cl. XI n. 67

Between 1450 and 1575, Venetian and Paduan humanists published Greek editions and Latin translations of the writings of Aristotle and his 3rd-century commentator Alexander of Aphrodisias.[1] Renaissance humanist scholars also avidly collected bronze plaquettes, which could be held in the hand or hung on the walls of a *studiolo*.[2] Produced in multiple copies, many of which are

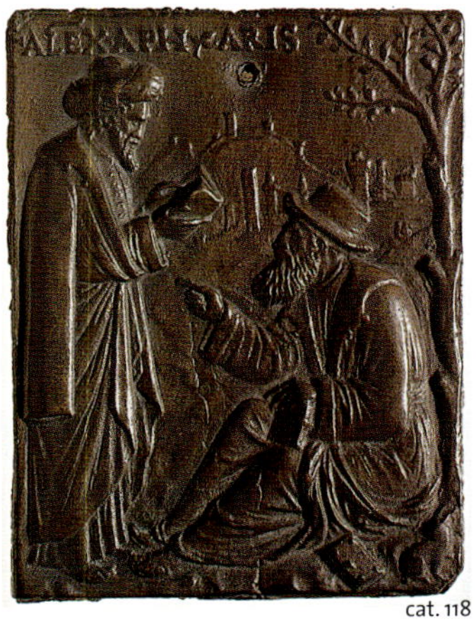

cat. 118

still extant, this magnificent little relief depicts Aristotle, seated on the right beneath a tree, directly addressing Alexander, standing on the left holding an open book.[3] The identification of Alexander of Aphrodisias is made certain by the Latin inscription in the upper left corner, *ALEX APH* (leaf) *ARIS*. The plaquette is emblematic of the sophisticated and learned milieu of Venetian Renaissance humanism.

Attributed to the Paduan sculptor known as Ulocrino,[4] the composition of the relief appears to depend upon the frontispiece of the first volume of the Morgan Aristotle (cat. 17), printed and probably illuminated in Venice in 1483, which depicts another one of Aristotle's respected commentators, Averroës, interacting with Aristotle.

The different headdresses of the two figures represented in Ulocrino's plaquette are of extraordinary interest. Aristotle wears a brimmed round hat like that often used in Venetian art to denote a figure's Greek origin, while Alexander, though he too was Greek, is crowned with a turban in the Ottoman style. In the art of Venetian humanist circles, the turban often evokes the wisdom and learning of the figure wearing it, labeling him as a veritable *hakim,* or sage. In illuminations from the same milieu, even Aristotle is sometimes depicted wearing a turban, and thus the head covering was universally appropriate for great thinkers and philosophers. For the Venetian humanists, who gained access to the writings of Aristotle and other classical authors in part through Arabic translations and commentaries, the ancient and Islamic intellectual traditions mingled fluidly with one another. Making sharp distinctions between the two cultures evidently was not yet always considered important or even necessary.

TK

1 Cranz 1958; Fortini Brown 1996, p. 272; Canova 2003.
2 Pope-Henessey 1964; Thornton 1997, pp. 85, 147–48.
3 Other examples are found in the National Gallery, Washington, D.C.; Victoria and Albert Museum, London; Museo Civico Correr, Venice; Ashmolean Museum, Oxford; and the Gilbert Collection, London. For a longer study of the plaquette, see Morison1990.
4 On Ulocrino, sometimes identified as Riccio's alter ego, see most recently Jesataz 1989, pp. 191–205 (with earlier bibliography).

119. *Portrait Medallion of Süleyman the Magnificent*

Probably Venice, after 1521
Bronze
Diam. 13 cm (5 1/8 inches)
The Metropolitan Museum of Art, New York
Rogers Fund, 1918
Inv. 18.70.8 (ill. p. 134)

With the exception of Mehmet II, Süleyman the Magnificent (r. 1520–66) is represented more frequently in Italian portrait medals than any other Ottoman sultan. Given their commemorative function, medals were eminently suited to portray these two great military conquerors who significantly expanded the extent of the Ottoman political realm. Whereas Mehmet II commissioned most of his own medals (see cats. 116–17), European patrons appear to have created the demand for those of Süleyman the Magnificent, who achieved international fame and notoriety early in his reign by capturing Belgrade in 1521 and the Kingdom of Hungary in 1526 and nearly taking Vienna in 1529. Rulers throughout Europe both admired and feared Süleyman, earning the Turkish sultan a place among the *viri illustri* of his time.

This unusually large uniface medal is known today in several different casts in European and American collections, among which the inscriptions and quality vary.[1] In this instance the sitter is identified simply as *SOLYMAN IMP TVR* ("Süleyman the Emperor") and presented in a stalwart fashion. Beyond the sultan's rotund, ribbed turban rendered in high relief, there is no further indication of costume, which is unusual in the realm of portraiture. Instead, the artist focused exclusively on the sultan's most prominent physical features: his long neck, aquiline nose, curled moustache, chiseled cheekbones, and crow's feet around the eyes. The representation does not glorify Süleyman the Magnificent, yet it does not outright satirize him either.

Earlier attributions of this medal to Leone Leoni (b. Arezzo 1509–d. Milan 1590) or Alfonso Lombardi (1487–1536) from the region of Emilia can be dismissed on the basis of both style and quality. Its affinities with contemporary Venetian painted and printed portraits of the sultan (see, for example, cat. 59) suggest the likely possibility that it was made by a now anonymous portrait medalist also working on the lagoon.

TK

1 For other versions and the different inscriptions, see Planiscig 1919, p. 185, no. 385; Hill 1926, p. 296; Middeldorf and Stiebral, no. LVIII; Pollard, 1984–85, p. 1482, cat. 873; Meyer zur Capellen in Istanbul 2000, p. 112, cat. 14 (with additional bibliography).

120. *Salver*

Venice, 16th century
Brass engraved and inlaid with silver
Diam. 45.7cm (18 in.)
Courtauld Institute of Art Gallery, London
Inv. O.1966.GP.202 (ill. 221)

The center of this salver has a European shield with the arms of the Giustiniani or Sagredo families of Venice. These appear to be original: hatching and cross-hatching on the arms give a three-dimensionality that is consistent with similar shading in other areas of the decoration. The function of the object is undoubtedly one of display; a platter like this would have been placed in a prominent position in the public rooms of a Venetian palace to underline the family's position and wealth. Contemporaneous paintings by Carpaccio represent similar display objects (see cats. 98, 110).

The inlaid silver decoration on the salver, though inspired by Islamic arabesques, is European. In view of the family crest, it is likely that the salver was made in Venice. Encircling the central area is a band that ultimately looks back to a classical Greek laurel wreath, bound with crossed ribbons. None of the individual elements of the ornamentation are based on a circle and there are tiny human masks, birds, and monstrous animals set among the scrolling stems. Similar heads and birds with entwined necks appear on a ceramic tile dated to 1509, also in the Courtauld Institute. These *grottesche* also have a classical origin, and were highly fashionable from the early years of the 16th century, when the subterranean rooms of the Domus Aurea ("Golden House" of Nero) were excavated in Rome. In his autobiography (written between 1558–62), Benvenuto Cellini described how in 1525 he came to own a number of small Turkish silver-inlaid daggers.[1] His own work in this style, he wrote, was not only more beautiful but also more durable because he undercut the ground metal more deeply to hold the precious metal. He listed a number of different leaf designs, used in varying areas—bryony, ivy, acanthus, arum, and sunflowers—advising that *"turchescha"* scrolling stems should be improved by the addition of "some little birds and different animals." He advocated a visual pun by including certain species: the common name for acanthus, then as now, was *brancaorsina* or bears' foot, and *salvatica* (snapdragon) was known as *bocche di lione* (lion's mouths), so the addition of bears or lions was appropriate. No inlaid objects by Cellini are known to have survived and there is no reason to suppose that this salver is his own work; nonetheless it demonstrates to perfection the style he was advocating.

SA

1 Auld 2004, pp. 229–30, cat. 5.18. See also Auld's essay in the present volume, esp. notes 15 and 23.

121. *Candlestick*

Europe, possibly Venice, 16th century
Brass engraved and inlaid with silver
H. 19.1 cm (7 1/2 in.); diam. 18 cm (7 in.)
The Metropolitan Museum of Art, New York,
Gift of J. Pierpont Morgan, 1917
Inv. 17.190.637 (ill. p. 28)

Unlike the majority of metalwork types under discussion here (cats. 94–112, 120–21), Islamic candlesticks can be distinguished from their European derivatives by their profile, rather than their surface decoration. Islamic candlesticks, in particular those made for foreign markets (cats. 94–96), all have a slightly splayed bell-shaped body, a flat drip-tray whose diameter approximately equals that of the base, and a vertical and narrow cylindrical shaft topped by a socket of larger diameter. European candlesticks, on the other hand, generally have a shorter, bulbous body; the drip-tray is sometimes convex with a smaller diameter than the base, while the shaft and socket are fused into a single section with a baluster- or vase-like profile.[1] In Western candlesticks, as seen here, the base, drip pan, and shaft are screwed together rather than soldered as they are in Mamluk examples. The shaft of the present candlestick, cast in one piece, is particularly elaborate; it has the profile of a vase surmounted by a three-lobed gadrooned socket of equal height.

Although the profile is European, the surface ornament of this and other related candlesticks recalls Islamic metalwork, especially the work by Mahmud al-Kurdi and his followers and forerunners (cats. 98–112). This candlestick's elaborate decoration,[2] which includes scrolling stems, rhomboid knots, quatrefoils, and strap-work panels, is closer to that found on the Islamic sprinkler in the British Museum (cat. 98) and the bucket in Cividale (cat. 112) than to the ornament of the Venetian salver in the Courtauld Insititute (cat. 120).

The Metropolitan's candlestick is without a doubt European and may be Venetian, an attribution supported not only by its shape but also by the coat of arms set within a "parchment" shield. It is particularly in Renaissance Venice that we would expect to find metalworkers using the candlesticks of the classic European shape ornamented with well-established Islamic decorative motifs.

SC

1 See in particular Mackay Thomas 1942; Auld 2004, pp. 260–64.
2 Described in Auld 2004, pp. 262–63, cat. 6.29.

122–123. *Morion and Shield*

Brescia, third quarter of the 16th century
Steel, gold, brass, leather
Shield: diam. 58.8 cm (23 1/3 in.)
Armeria di Palazzo Ducale, Venice
Inv. C27bis and J5 (ill. p. 28)

The decoration of the Italian armor of the 16th century, whether etched or embossed in relief, typically employed a limited vocabulary of Renaissance ornament. This included foliate scrollwork (*rinceaux*), candelabra designs, grotesques, trophies, and, on the more ambitious examples, figural ornament of classical or Biblical theme. Islamic ornament, on the other hand, and notably the arabesque (or moresque), is less frequently encountered despite its familiar presence in contemporary pattern books (see cat. 58). It appears most often on armor associated with soldiers in Venetian service, harnesses that were most likely made in the Venetian-governed city of Brescia, which (like its rival, Milan) was famed for the manufacture of armor. The helmet and shield are two such examples, both attributable to Brescia and distinctly Venetian in spirit and iconography.

The helmet is a morion, a form of head defense generally used for infantry service that is characterized by a semi-circular bowl or skull having a tall comb and a short brim with deeply concave profile that rises to an acute point at the front and back. The comb of this example is etched and gilt in the center with a medallion enclosing the winged lion of St. Mark, with trophies and shield-bearing putti holding palms of victory to either side. Similar trophies decorate the brim. The bowl is etched and gilt overall with meandering arabesques, distinctly Western in spirit but made up of tendrils and split leaves that ultimately derive from Ottoman design. Near the top on each side is etched a shield bearing the arms of the patrician da Mula family.[1] The round shield, or *brocchiere,* is of matching design, the border etched and gilt with trophies, the Lion of St. Mark, and the da Mula arms, with the center covered with gilt arabesques. The rise in the center was formerly fitted with a metal spike (*brocca*). Around the base of the helmet bowl and edge of the shield are lining rivets with decorative brass washers that formerly retained the padded linings, now lost.

These pieces belong to a series of three morions and two shields of identical design in the armory of the Palazzo Ducale.[2] A fourth morion is preserved in the Hofjajd- und Rüstkammer, Vienna.[3] Thus there must originally have been at least four sets, each composed of a morion and shield, which were presumably carried by a ceremonial guard that served one of the members of the da Mula family. The same family coat of arms appears on the gilt leather binding in Ottoman style that covered the official appointment of Antonio da Mula as procuratore of San Marco (fig. 1, p. 242). These sets appear to be unique, in so far as there are several known series of decorated helmets made as equipment for aristocratic bodyguards, but none paired with matching shields.[4] The prominent display of the Serenissima's emblem together with the da Mula arms suggests that this armor was intended for use in a public or official capacity and that the guard who wore it was of sufficient importance to warrant specially designed and finely made equipment. The prominence given the arabesque on armor of Brescian manufacture and its Venetian association demonstrates the everyday presence, acceptance, and assimilation of Islamic ornament in the area. A comparison between these etched arabesques and their more accurate rendering on the polychrome leather shields in the Palazzo Ducale (cats. 135–39) demonstrates the extremes of imitation and interpretation of this motif.

In addition to the da Mula morions and shields, only a handful of contemporary armors decorated with similar arabesque ornament are known. Among them is an armor made for a member of the noble Martinego family of Brescia,[5] a provenance that reinforces the Brescian attribution for this group. An armor for man and horse from the Farnese armory in the Museo Nazionale di Capodimonte, Naples, is not only etched overall with arabesques, but the bard is constructed of small rectangular plates connected by links of mail, in the manner of contemporary Ottoman armor. It is a rare example of an Italian armor that is both constructed and decorated in Islamic fashion.[6]

SP

1 Franzoi 1990, p. 81, cat. 100.
2 De Lucia 1908, p. 27, inv. nos. E 11–13 and p. 33, inv. nos. F 40–41; Franzoi 1990, pp. 80–81, cat. 97–99.
3 Gamber and Beaufort 1990, p. 118, inv. no. A 436.
4 Among these are the embossed burgonets worn by the guard of Pierluigi Farnese, Duke of Parma and Piacenza in 1545–47, and the series of etched burgonets made for the guard of Pope Julius III (1550–55), for which see Pyhrr 2000, pp. 23–24, cat. 32–33.
5 Mazzini et al. 1982, p. 330, cat. 25. Complete arm and leg defenses of matching design are in the Museo Poldi Pezzoli, Milan; see Boccia and Godoy, 1985, p. 120, cat. 300, figs. 324–26.
6 Naples 1996, pp. 311–12, cat. 9.7, color ill. p. 316.

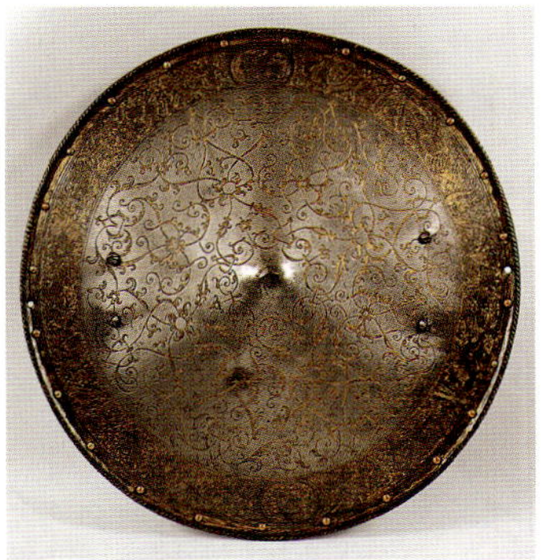
cat. 123

BOOKBINDINGS

124–125.

°124. *Second volume of a 30-volume Qur'an manuscript*

Egypt, late 14th century
Binding: Pasteboard lined with embossed, tooled, and gilded leather
36.9 x 26.3 cm (14 1/2 x 10 3/8 in.)
The Walters Art Museum, Baltimore
Inv. Ms. 561 (ill. p. 26)

• 125. *Twenty-first volume of a 30-volume Qur'an manuscript*

Egypt, ca. 1388–99
Binding: Pasteboard lined with tooled and gilded leather with sections cut out against green silk
37.3 x 26.4 cm (14 5/8 x 10 3/8 in.)
Manuscrits orientaux, Bibliothèque Nationale de France, Paris
MS. arabe 5845 (ill. p. 240)

Known for their religious zeal, the Mamluks founded an impressive number of mosques, *madrasas*, and other religious establishments, for which many Qur'ans were commissioned.[1] These two volumes from two different but roughly contemporaneous sets of 30-volume Qur'an manuscripts, which are among the best examples to survive from the 14th century, bear the name of the patron Amir Aytmish al-Bajasi (d. 1400; cat. 124) and the *waqf* (donation deed) of the Mamluk sultan Barquq (r. 1388–99; cat. 125), respectively.

Arabic bookbinding is generally austere and Mamluk manuscripts followed this trend. The Baltimore example (cat. 124), although keeping in line with a overall sobriety in the composition, is more elaborate than many others in the dense background filling of the flap, the borders, and the corners, and especially in the creation of a multi-lobed central medallion and quarter-medallions in the shape of flowers at the corners.[2]

The Paris binding (cat. 125) is instead exceptional for the richness of its ornament, the openwork pattern, and the elaborate techniques. Following established models, a central circular medallion and four corner-pieces constitute the main decoration, but the medallion, the quarter-medallions at each corner, and the flap contain cut-out floral designs set against a green silk background and the entire field and borders are tooled and stamped with additional geometric and floral motifs, thus emphasizing the complexity and elegance of the overall composition.[3]

Among the most portable examples of the arts of the Mamluk Sultanate, manuscripts with their binding reached Italy in large quantities via trade and as personal items, especially in the 15th century. Islamic binding techniques and decorations were particularly appealing to Italian craftsmen, especially in Florence, Padua, and Venice, and they promptly imitated them, thus providing some of the earliest examples of direct Islamic artistic influence on the lagoon (see cat. 130).[4]

MAM / SC

1 James 1992, p. 150.
2 Published in Baltimore 1957, pp. 28–29, no. 61, pl. XVII.
3 Paris 2001, pp. 144–45, fig. 105; Déroche 1985, n° 346.
4 Hobson 1989, pp. 111–17; Mack 2002, pp. 125–37.

126. Nizami' *Khamsa*

Iran, Shiraz, 1510
Binding, tooled and gilded leather; ink on paper
29.2 x 17.8 cm (11 1/2 x 7 in.)
The Metropolitan Museum of Art, New York
Gift of Alexander Smith Cochran, 1913
Inv. 13.228.6 (ill. p. 239)

This copy of Nizami's *Khamsa*, a famous collection of five epic tales, was produced in Shiraz in the early 16th century. Manuscripts from the Safavid capital, such as this one, are notable for their high quality illustrations and bindings.

The inner cover (or doublure) of this binding is elegantly decorated with a central almond-shaped medallion embellished with finials and corner pieces. A spare geometric design in gold is set against a blue background of intricate floral motifs and Chinese clouds. Characteristic of Persian doublures of this period is the contrasting colors: the burgundy of the leather, the blue of the center and corner-pieces, and the gilding. The linear gilding and discrete frames are standard features as well.[1]

Similar techniques of gilding leather bindings appeared in Europe in the 16th century in Cordoba, Spain and Venice, Italy. While the Cordovan school continued the Arabic bookbinding tradition developed in North Africa and Islamic Spain, the Venetian school was more influenced by the Islamic Middle East, and in particular by Ottoman and Safavid examples (see cats. 132, 133).[2]

MAM

1 Haldane 1983, pp. 67–136, ex. no. 79 for another example from Shiraz.
2 Hobson 1989, pp. 111–17.

127. Al-Bukhar *Sahīh*

Turkey, 1529
Binding: black morocco leather, stamped and gilt; doublures of reddish-brown morocco leather with filigree ornament
Boards: 29.2 x 18.5 cm (11 1/2 x 7 1/4 in.); flap: 29.2 x 8.5 cm (11 1/2x 3 3/8 in.)
The Nasser D. Khalili Collection of Islamic Art, London
Inv. MSS 203 (ill. p. 241)

Al-Bukhari (810–870) gained fame by compiling the *Sahīh*, a canonical collection of the Prophet Muhammad's sayings and deeds (known as *hadith*). Widely respected in the Muslim world, al-Bukhari's work was read in Ottoman imperial mosques on evenings in the months of Sahᶜban and Ramadan.

Carefully written in a cursive *nesih* (*naskh*) script, this manuscript copy of the *Sahīh* is dated Saturday, August 4, 1529 (AH 9 Zilhicce 935).[1] The stamped and gilded techniques used for its contemporaneous leather binding were common in the Middle East, especially in Safavid Iran (see cat. 126), where the art first developed, and Ottoman Turkey, where it was perfected. The central almond-shaped medallion (*şemse*) and the concave fillings in the four corners (*kösebent*) are common features of Islamic books, especially religious texts. The use of both pressure molding and gilding to create the center- and corner-pieces has its origins in Turkoman bindings of northwestern Iran, but was later adopted by Turkish artists during the reign of Sultan Bayezid II (r. 1481–1512) and became common in the Ottoman Empire in the following decades.[2] The curving scrolls with flowers and serrated leaves are also characteristic of Ottoman decorative arts of the 16th century, appearing in a wide variety of other media, including textiles, carpets, and ceramics.

Ottoman book covers with this kind of floral design and central pointed medallion with four corner-pieces inspired a great number of Italian bookbindings, especially in Renaissance Venice (see cat. 133).[3]

MAM

1 Rogers 1995, pp. 96–97, cat. 51, and p. 220, cat. 150.
2 Raby and Tanındı 1993, pp. 81–104.
3 Hobson 1989, pp. 111–17.

128. Sacdi *Bustan*

Istanbul, after 1530
Binding in pasteboard, the outer covers and flap painted with black lacquer decorated in contrasting tones of gold
Boards: 24.7 x 16.5 cm (9 3/4 x 6 1/2 in.); flap and fore-edge: 24.7 x 11 cm (9 3/4 x 4 3/8 in.)
The Nasser D. Khalili Collection of Islamic Art, London
Inv. MSS 712 (ill. p. 26)

Sa'di (d. Shiraz 1292) ranks as one of the most important Persian poets, and his *Bustan* (*Flower Garden*), a collection of stories and maxims, is among the most famous literary works ever produced in Iran. This copy of his text, dated 15 Sha'ban 936 (April 1, 1530), was written in Safavid Tabriz, although its illuminations and binding appear to have been added later in Istanbul at the Ottoman court.[1]

The manuscript's binding is painted with black lacquer and decorated with gold arabesques. Tabrizi craftsmen appear to have brought the technique to Istanbul, and this example of their work is impressive for its virtuosity. The overall pattern is rendered in the same detailed design of the manuscript's illuminations. Resembling 16th-century Ottoman *tuğras* (cat. 49) and the contemporary pottery (cat. 173) they inspired, the binding is densely decorated with spiraled stems studded with tiny flowers; Chinese-cloud motifs fill the corner-pieces and trefoil-shaped cartouches at the top and bottom of the almond-shaped central medallion.[2] The insertion of a flying goose in the very center of this medallion is significant; it is a chinoiserie motif that entered the Islamic artistic vocabulary and was commonly used in Persian and Ottoman bookbinding. Elegant arabesque motifs like those seen here traveled to the West, particularly influencing the production of arts and crafts in Italian cities such as Venice with strong commercial ties with the Middle East. An appreciation for arabesque designs is particularly evident in Venetian Renaissance bookbindings and furniture, which are lacquered with similar designs (cats. 144–48).[3] It is in the realm of the inlaid metalwork stemming from the workshop of Mahmud al-Kurdi, however, that the influence of the Islamic arabesque motif is most noticeable (cats. 100–112, 120–21).

MAM

1 Rogers 2000, pp. 222–23, fig. 152.
2 Petsopoulos 1982, p. 91.
3 See Grube 1989a; Allan 1989, Hobson 1989.

129. *Binding for a Qur'an*

Iran, late 16th century
Pasteboard lined with stamped, tooled, and gilded brown leather inset with turquoise
5.5 x 3.9 cm (14 x 10 in.)
The Metropolitan Museum of Art, New York
Rogers Fund, 1956
Inv. 56.222 (ill. p. 240)

The art of the book in Safavid times is usually associated with secular illustrated manuscripts, yet religious manuscripts were no less important and could be just as elaborately adorned and bound. This book cover was made for a Qur'an manuscript that has not survived: its border is decorated with elegant cursive Arabic inscriptions in broad cartouches including text from the sayings (*hadiths*) attributed to the Prophet Muhammad about the importance of reading the sacred book.

Virtually the entire surface is stamped and gilded. The two plates have a central almond-shaped medallion and corner-pieces of a peculiar type, the undulating lines in the corners creating an effect comparable to marbling. The stamped decoration in the central rectangular field features arabesques and cloud bands, a Chinese motif that passed to Safavid bookbinding through the Timurid and Turkoman traditions. In turn, Venetian artists working in various media copied the same arabesque and cloud-band motifs, particularly on shields produced in the Republic at the end of the 16th century (see cats. 135–40).[1]

The inlaid turquoise decoration that enriches the cover of this Qur'an may have been added in Ottoman Turkey. During the Ottoman-Persian wars, Persian manuscripts were brought to Turkey along with bookmakers—especially from the northwestern region of Tabriz—and further ornamented. The flap is also elaborately adorned, using the technique of gilt filigree over paper painted in various colors with an overall pattern of rhomboidal medallions. The use of the filigree technique on a polychrome painted ground was initiated in Shiraz bookbinding during the Timurid and Turkoman periods and became widespread in the second half of the 16th century.[2]

MAM

1 Grube 1989a, p. 217.
2 Tanındi 2003, pp. 155-83.

130. Virgil *Opera*

Binding: tooled and gilded leather
Venice, ca. 1460s
36.3 x 21.3 cm (14 3/8 x 8 3/8 in.)
The British Library, London
Inv. MS. Harley 3963 (ill. p. 240)

The popular phrase "never judge a book by its cover" is particularly apt for the present volume. Its blind-tooled and gilded leather exterior makes it appear to be a Mamluk Qu'ran (see cats. 124–25), so much so that a leading bookbinding expert asked whether it could have been made in Egypt or Syria.[1] Minor but telltale details in the execution, however, reveal that this binding is an early Venetian imitation of the Mamluk style.[2]

One of the most fascinating phenomena of the Venetian Renaissance is the adoption of Islamic-style bookbinding for classical and humanist texts. In the absence of ancient Roman and Greek models, Venetian and Paduan bibliophiles asked local craftsmen to mimic the most sophisticated examples available to them, the intricately worked leather bookbindings of the Islamic world, which arrived in the Veneto via trade with the Near East.[3] The text in this instance is Virgil's *Opera*, beautifully illuminated by the Venetian painter Cristoforo Cortese (ca. 1399–before 1445).

The Venetian binder of the British Library Virgil adopted numerous Mamluk patterns and techniques, including the circular centerpiece design with quarter-circle corner-pieces, rope and interlace boarders, and gold tooling. Nonetheless he employed dramatically different proportions for the ornament, revealing his own aesthetic sensibility. Instead of the delicate balance between pattern and void achieved in the Mamluk tradition, the oversized roundels dominate the composition, nearly filling it. Perhaps most importantly, the underlying geometry of Mamluk bindings, which typically begins with a pointed star in the center, is not evident here. A lotus flower, similar to those used as finials in cat. 125, is at the heart of this design. The calligraphy incorporated into the roundels is suitably elegant but illegible.[4] For all these reasons, it is clear that a Muslim master could not have made this work.

The survival of this binding to the present day is remarkable considering that it was once in the library of Lord Edward Harley (1689–1741), who rebound the majority of his manuscripts as a mark of his ownership.[5] Nonetheless, a 19th-century restorer did modify certain aspects of its structure. Most notably, the covers have been laid down over a modern binding and an outer gilt border added.[6]

TK

1 Hobson 1992, p. 32.
2 Hobson 1989, p. 114.
3 Hobson 1989, 1992; Mack 2002, pp. 125–34.
4 Ibid., p. 114.
5 Nuvolini 2000, p. 81.
6 Hobson 1992, p. 30.

• 131. Cicero *Epistolae ad familiares*

Venice or Padua, 1475
Tooled and gilded leather binding with the coat of arms of Peter Ugelheimer
29 x 15 cm (11 3/4 x 6 in.)
Bibliothéque Nationale de France, Paris
Livres rare
Inv. Vélins 1149 (ill. p. 240)

An astonishing number of the most sumptuous manuscripts and incunabula from late Quattrocento Venice and Padua bear the coat of arms of Peter Ugelheimer, a noble businessman from Frankfurt who resided in the Fondaco dei Tedeschi in Venice.[1] An entrepreneur, Ugelheimer invested in the Venetian publishing firm of Nicolaus Jensen, and in return received handsome and often extravagant editions for his own library.[2] In addition to the luxurious Aristotle illuminated for Ugelheimer (cat. 17), the present exhibition also includes this Cicero printed on parchment, one of many of his books bound in the Islamic style by local craftsmen. Thus, at the same time that he supported the burgeoning book-printing industry and humanism in Venice, the German merchant fostered the development of *alla damaschina* bookbinding there as well.[3]

The Cicero is magnificently bound in tooled and gilt brown leather. If it were not for the prominent placement of Ugelheimer's blazon in the very center of the composition, it would be easy to mistake the binding as Mamluk. Undeniably Islamic characteristics include the vesica-shaped centerpiece, the gilded ornament, fillet and lotus flower motifs, and the L-shaped segmented borders.

Thanks to the exquisite binding, which rivals imports from the Near East, this volume of Cicero's *Epistolae ad familiares* must have immediately made a profound impression when Jensen first presented it as a gift to Ugelheimer.

TK

1 An important group of Ugelheimer's books are published in Alexander 1994, pp. 190–205, cats. 96–101.
2 Alexander 1994, pp. 190–92, cat. 96.
3 Hobson 1989, pp. 112–13; Hobson 1992, pp. 38–41; Alexander 1994, pp. 190–98, cats. 96–98.

132. Fra Giovanni Giocondo da Verona *Syllogue*

Scribe: Bartolomeo Sanvito (ca. 1435–after Manuscript on vellum, 259 leaves
Bound in Venice ca. 1520–30, in red goatskin, tooled and painted
25.2 x 16.5 x 5.5 cm (9 7/8 x 6 1/2 x 2 1/8 in.)
Trustees of the Chatsworth Settlement, Chatsworth (ill. p. 239)

The architect and engineer Fra Giovanni Giocondo (ca. 1453–1515) and the calligrapher Bartolomeo Sanvito (ca. 1435–after 1518) belonged to the same formidable generation of Renaissance antiquarians and both moved in humanist circles in Padua, Venice, and Rome. The two shared a keen interest in classical epigraphy, and Sanvito scripted copies of all three recensions of Giocondo's *syllogue* of ancient inscriptions.[1] The first was dedicated to the illustrious Lorenzo de' Medici and the second, much larger one to Ludovico Agnelli, Archbishop of Cosenza and confidant of Francesco Gonzaga and Pope Sixtus IV, which demonstrates the elite audience for these manuscripts. Multiple surviving copies of the *syllogue* are beautifully bound, including the present example, which belongs to the third, incomplete recension.[2]

Only after the deaths of both Giocondo and Sanvito did this manuscript receive its extraordinary elegant leather binding.[3] In the early 16th century, Venetian merchants began having classical literature bound in Istanbul by Muslim craftsmen, which meant that examples of Ottoman bindings became more readily available on the lagoon for local craftsmen to copy in this period.[4] Bindings from elsewhere in the Islamic world, such as Persia and Egypt, were also arriving on Venetian shores through trade during this period. The binder of the Chatsworth manuscript clearly sought to emulate those sophisticated Islamic imports, and rose to the occasion, creating what is widely considered a masterpiece.[5] On the exterior, the composition closely resembles that of contemporary Turkish bindings, such as cat. 127, with a gilded, almond-shaped centerpiece decorated with scrolling flowers and framed by thin, dart-shaped fillets. Clearly borrowed from China by way of the Near East, the cloud-bands are an unusual feature in Venetian bindings.[6] The motif is common on Persian bindings (see, for example, cat. 129), which likely also served as the model in this instance.

The present binding is even more remarkable on its interior thanks to its ornamented doublure. A combination of gilt tooling and filigree has been used to create the center- and corner-pieces. The goatskin is cut away in an interlace pattern to reveal a deep blue and turquoise painted ground, creating a jewel-like effect. The technique derives from the Near Eastern bookbinding tradition,[7] and can be seen, for example, on the cover of an earlier Mamluk Qur'an in this catalogue (cat. 125). Known for their refined taste in all aspects of manuscript production, Paduan antiquarians were among the first Italians to appreciate filigree, and the Chatsworth *syllogue* is one of the earliest surviving Venetian bindings to incorporate it.[8]

TK

1 Hobson 1992, p. 7.
2 Ibid., pp. 79-82.
3 Ibid., pp. 82, 150.
4 Ibid., pp. 148, 150.
5 Ibid., pp. 150, 153; Mack 2002, pp. 132-33.
6 Hobson, p. 150.
7 Ibid., p. 42.
8 Ibid., p. 150.

133. Ludovico Dolce (1508–1568) *Le Trasformazioni*

Venice, 1553
Leather tooled and lacquered binding
25.8 x 18 cm (10 1/8 x 7 1/8 in.)
Fondazione Giorgio Cini, Venice
MS 216A/D47 (ill. p. 241)

One of the most important developments in leather bookbinding in Renaissance Venice occurred in the mid-16th century when local craftsmen mastered the lacquer technique. Ottoman and, to a lesser extent, Persian lacquerware served as the vehicle of transmission of this originally Far Eastern art form to Venice.[1] Most surviving Venetian lacquer bindings cover appointment documents (*commissioni*) of doges and other top officials like the procurators of Saint Mark's Basilica.[2] In this instance, however, the text inside is a mythological one from classical Antiquity, Ovid's *Metamorphoses*, which reminds us once again of the humanists' interest in Islamic-style bindings (see also cats. 130–32).[3] The translation of Ovid's poem, printed by the Venetian publisher Gioloto de Ferrari in 1553, is by the eminent humanist Lodovico Dolce, also of Venice.

The Cini Ovid is considered one of the finest surviving Venetian lacquered bindings, and was formerly owned by the distinguished connoisseur Tammaro De Marinis. Recently Susy Marcon has attributed it to the same workshop of another, slightly later masterpiece, the *Commissione* of Girolamo da Mula (fig. 1, p. 242).[4] As well as technique, the two share a similar layout and many motifs, including feathery *saz*-like leaves and flower blossoms on scrolling vines, derived from the Ottoman tradition. Furthermore, the center- and corner-pieces recall those on Ottoman bindings, for example, cat. 127. The design here is accented with red, green, and dark blue paint in addition to being enhanced by the golden varnish. Touches of color can also be found on Ottoman book covers from this period.

During the late 16th century, lacquerware with Islamizing motifs was in vogue in Venice. As numerous objects in the exhibition demonstrate, arms and armor, small furnishings, and musical instruments, as well as bookbindings, were similarly ornamented and varnished.

TK

1 See the essays by Grube and Rizzo in this volume; Mack 2002, pp. 133–34.
2 Hobson 1992, p. 153.
3 Hobson 1988, 1992.
4 Marcon 2003, p. 76.

134. See cat. 77

LEATHER-COVERED SHIELDS

135–139. *Five shields*

Venice, late 16th century

135.

Wood, leather, silver, polychromy
Diam. 53.2 cm (21 in.)
Armeria di Palazzo Ducale, Venice
Inv. J 16 (ill. p. 234)

136.

Wood, leather, silver, polychromy
Diam. 54.5 cm (21 1/2in.)
Armeria di Palazzo Ducale, Venice
Inv. J 17 (ill. p. 235)

137.

Papier maché, leather, gold, polychromy
Diam. 57.5 cm (22 5/8 in.)
Armeria di Palazzo Ducale, Venice
Inv. J 19 (ill. p. 236)

138.

Wood, leather, gold, polychromy
Diam. 54.5 cm (21 1/2 in.)
Armeria di Palazzo Ducale, Venice
Inv. J 21 (ill. p. 71)

139.

Papier maché, leather, iron, silver, polychromy
Diam. 62 cm (24 3/8 in.)
Armeria di Palazzo Ducale, Venice
Inv. J 26 (ill. p. 236)

Venice is not usually thought of as a center for manufacture of arms and armor. Instead, the city provisioned its naval and land forces with armaments made in Brescia, the famous arms-making city on the mainland that Venice had governed since 1516 (see cats. 122–23). Venice did, however, contribute to the history of arms and armor in the late 16th century by producing a distinctive series of round leather-covered shields decorated with gilded and polychrome ornament in the Ottoman style. Together with other Venetian leatherwork of the period, especially bookbinding (cats. 130–33)—but also quivers—these shields exemplify the art of *cuoridoro*, the gilded leather for which the city was famous. They demonstrate not only the strong influence of Islamic design, but also the sophisticated assimilation of the foreign style into works inherently Venetian in spirit. With their opulent use of precious metal and brilliant color, these shields were undoubtedly created for ceremonial use and belong more to the field of decorative art than defensive arms.

These five shields are representative of a group of 23 preserved in the Doge's Palace in Venice.[1] In material and construction they differ significantly from contemporary Turkish shields, which were typically made of coiled cane reinforced in the center with a metal boss (cats. 76, 77). The majority of the Venetian group, here represented by three examples (cats. 135–36, 138), were constructed with two overlapping layers of thin wood boards, glued together at right angles to one another and then shaped, presumably when humidified, into their distinctive convex form. The leather facings on the front and back were then glued over the wooden core. A second group, somewhat flatter than the first and here represented by two shields (cats. 137, 139), was constructed with a core of thick papier maché rather than of wood over which were glued two layers of leather, the lower one thicker and coarser, the upper one thinner and more finely finished. The second group is further distinguished by the presence of a domed metal boss nailed over the center on the front, undoubtedly in direct imitation of their Turkish counterparts. Curiously, all of the surviving Venetian examples have lost their bosses, suggesting that they had perhaps been made of precious metal, possibly gilt silver, which proved tempting to vandals.

The decoration of the leather surfaces is remarkably varied in color, design, and workmanship. On some of the shields the leather was covered with gold leaf as a ground color (cat. 139), whereas on others silver leaf was used and then covered with a translucent yellow varnish to give the appearance of gold (cat. 137). These metallic surfaces were typically covered with a further coat of translucent colored varnish, usually red, pink, or orange, as a ground for the ornament picked out in contrasting opaque colors. Other shields have grounds painted in dark, opaque colors as a foil for the gilt and varnished ornament (cat. 136). The designs, which are particularly faithful to Ottoman models, typically employ a 12-point-star foliate central medallion (replaced by the metal boss on the papier maché examples) with six smaller arabesque-filled medallions spaced equidistantly around it; the remaining surfaces are covered with various arrangements of rhythmically undulating and intersecting foliate tendrils, peonies, and Chinese-inspired cloud-bands. Most of the ornament is slightly raised in the tooled leather, although one example (cat. 137) has a completely flat surface. This polychrome decoration, and in particular the use of translucent varnishes on metallic ground, suggests intentional imitation of Ottoman lacquer. Apparently few Turkish arms with lacquer decoration survive, but a bow and matching bow case in the Hofjagd und Rüstkammer in Vienna, recorded in imperial Austrian collections since 1583, and lacquered in translucent and opaque colors, provide contemporary examples that may have served as inspiration to Venetian leather-workers.[2]

The backs of the shields are also covered with leather and have typical Italian-style leather-covered armpads nailed horizontally across the center, with remnants of the leather armstraps at either end. Many of the shield backs, including four of these five shields, have simple tooled and gilt borders filled with foliate ornament and a gilt lobed medallion filled with arabesques set above and below the armpad. This decoration is especially similar to that found on Ottoman bookbindings and their Venetian imitations. One of the shield backs (cat. 135) is painted instead with an overall "marbleized" design.

Despite the absence of contemporary documents referring to the manufacture and use of these shields in Venice,[3] there can be little doubt that they were made by specialized Venetian craftsman toward the end of the 16th century. One of the 23 shields in the Palazzo Ducale (inv. J 30) has its center medallion painted with the Lion of St. Mark, emblem of the city, and the initials *C.X.* referring to the Consiglio dei Dieci (Council of Ten), the ruling body of government, indicating that this unique shield, likely one of a series, was a state commission.[4] Another (inv. J 14) bears the same emblem and the initials *A.C.*, presumably a member of one of the local patrician families.[5] A further six shields, of which cat. 135 is one, are painted with the Foscarini arms and the initials *A.F.*, possibly referring to Antonio Foscarini (1570–1622).[6] The shields can also be compared in style and technique to the closely related group of painted quivers bearing the Lion of St. Mark (cats. 141–42), likewise in the Armory of the Palazzo Ducale, and to the series of shields thought to have been made for Wolf Dietrich von Raitenau, prince-archbishop of Salzburg, during his tenure from 1584 to 1611 (cat. 140).

SP

1 The first discussion of these shields in the context of Venetian "lacquer" is in Huth 1971, p. 4; Contadini 1989 includes the fundamental examination of their construction and decoration, mentioning 23 shields; De Lucia 1908, p. 32, nos. F 8–29 and Franzoi 1990, pp. 82–84, nos. 108–28 count only 21 examples.
2 Inv. nos. C 16 and C 93; see Huth, 1971, pl. 5; Gamber and Beaufort 1990, p. 225, pl. 131.
3 Franzoi 1990 (pp. 231–51) published transcriptions of the inventories of the Armory of the Palazzo Ducale for the years 1548, 1611, 1773, and 1799. The inventory of 1611, for example, contains references to many round shields (*rotelle*), but the descriptions are too brief to allow us to identify any of the Ottoman-inspired examples under discussion.
4 De Lucia 1908, p. 32, cat. no. F 30; Contadini 1989, p. 236; and Franzoi 1990, p. 83, cat. no. 123.
5 De Lucia 1908, p. 32, cat no. F 29; Huth 1971, color pl. II; Contadini 1989, p. 238, figs. 9, 10A, and 10B; and Franzoi 1990, p. 83, cat. no. 121, fig. 36.
6 De Lucia 1908, p. 32, cat. nos. F 21–25 and F 28; Contadini 1989, p. 238, figs. 4, 5A, and 5B; and Franzoi 1990, p. 82, cat. nos. 109 11, color pl. 25.

°140. *Parade Shield*

Venice, late 16th century
Wood, leather, iron, silver, varnish, and paint
59.8 x 56.8 cm (23 1/2 x 22 3/8 in.)
The Metropolitan Museum of Art, New York
Gift of Stephen Grincsay, 1942
Inv. 42.50.31 (ill. p. 233)

The Metropolitan's shield belongs to a large group of Ottoman-inspired shields that have long been thought to have served as equipment for the bodyguard of Wolf-Dietrich von Raitenau, prince-archbishop of Salzburg from 1587 to 1612.[1] Though now widely scattered in museums throughout Europe and North America, the majority of these shields, 94 in all, are preserved in the Museum Carolino Augusteum in Salzburg.[2] In construction and decoration these shields are very close to those in the Armory of the Palazzo Ducale in Venice discussed above (cats. 135–39) and have rightly been attributed to Venetian manufacture around 1600. The unprecedented size of this group—the largest known series of matching shields in Europe—attests to the prodigious scale of reproduction within the Venetian leatherworking industry, which is said to have numbered more than 70 shops in the 16th century.[3]

Like the shields in Venice this example is round and convex in section, its core formed of two layers of thin wood boards laid at right angles to one another that are reinforced around the rim with a narrow iron band. The exterior is overlaid with thin leather with tooled ornament in low relief, its surface covered with silver leaf that has been given a golden hue by means of translucent yellow varnish.[4] The designs are further highlighted with varnishes and opaque colors in imitation of lacquer. The interior is also covered with leather, which is gessoed and painted with an overall marbleized pattern in green, gray, and black. The leather-covered arm pad and two leather arm straps on the back are 19th-century restorations.

The design on the exterior is centered on a 12-point star medallion enclosing a raised European-style cartouche in which is a small applied iron boss with domed center, its surfaces etched with stylized foliage, which is held by a central rivet with a silvered head. Framed by raised cloud-bands, the medallion is filled with a foliate scroll formed of alternating lotuses and symmetrical flowers highlighted in opaque green and white. The main field consists of two concentric but offset rings each composed of six irregularly shaped medallions with raised cloud-band edges overlaid and interconnected by delicate foliate scrolls and peonies in opaque green, yellow, and white. The ground, now of a golden hue, was originally covered by a layer of translucent red glaze that has largely flaked off. The contrast between the ornament and the background would thus originally have been much more pronounced. Around the shield's edge are two concentric bands, the wider inner one painted with undulating foliate scrollwork like that of the central medallion, and the outer one painted with a continuous scroll in white against a black ground.

The design on the exterior is identical to two of the exhibited examples from the Palazzo Ducale (cats. 136, 139), whereas the original coloring of the ground, once ruby red, formerly resembled that of another (cat. 135). The border design of foliate scrolls also matches that of cat. 139, whereas the marbleized interior is found on cat. 135. There can be little doubt, therefore, that this shield and the nearly identical examples still in Salzburg were made in the same workshops as those in the Palazzo Ducale.

In the literature on European lacquer it has been asserted that the Salzburg shields were ordered in Venice for use by the archbishop's mounted bodyguard.[5] Unfortunately this statement is not supported by documentation. The only near-contemporary reference to these shields is found in an inventory of the Salzburg armory in 1664, which lists 398 "gilded and painted shields",[6] though it seems unlikely that so large a number could refer exclusively to these exquisitely made and undoubtedly expensive Venetian shields. Wolf Dietrich was a distinguished collector and patron of the arts and like other ruling princes of the era he maintained an expensively outfitted bodyguard, consisting of a traditional corps of halberdiers and another armed with carbines.[7] Shields were not typically carried by guards (and certainly not by those on horse) and, indeed, were not in general use in Europe by the late 16th century. Like those in Venice, the Salzburg shields were most likely used for ceremonial occasions, perhaps as accessories for pseudo-Turkish costume.[8]

SP

1 The shield was probably sold as a duplicate from the Salzburg museum in the 19th century like the two identical shields remaining in the Princely Collections of Liechtenstein (inv. 871, 881). Its previous owners are: the prince of Liechtenstein; in 1926, Bashford Dean, Curator of Arms and Armor at the Metropolitan Museum; on November 19–20, 1926, Clarence Mackay at auction at the American Art Association, New York (lot 138); in 1940, Stephen Grancsay, Dean's successor at the Metropolitan, who donated it in 1942.
2 For this series of shields, see Tietze 1919, p. 301, and especially von Gumppenberg 1987, p. 269.
3 Contadini 1989, p. 232.
4 The author is grateful to Richard Stone, Dept. of Objects Conservation, MMA, for having undertaken the x-ray and x-ray fluorescence examination of the shield.
5 Huth 1971, p. 4; Grube 1989, p. 217.
6 "*vergult und gemalte Schilt,*" cited in Tietze 1919, p. 301, n. 1.
7 Von Gumppenberg 1987, pp. 265–69, where the equipment of the archbishop's bodyguard is discussed.
8 See Grube's essay in this volume.

141–142. *Two Quivers*

Venice, second half of the 16th century
Wood, leather, gold, polychromy
H. 70 cm (27 1/2 in.)
Armeria di Palazzo Ducale, Venice
Inv. G 11, G 14 (ill. p. 99)

The Armory of the Doge's Palace preserves a unique group of 15 quivers that are very similar in material, technique, and style to the series of gilt leather shields of Ottoman inspiration discussed above (cats. 135–39).[1] Unmistakably Italian in form, the quivers are of cylindrical shape with flat backs and are constructed of wood covered with leather. Down the center of each is a design consisting of three lobed medallions framed and connected by interlacing bands. The larger center medallion encloses a Lion of St. Mark, symbol of Venice, and the medallions above and below are filled with peonies. Like the shields, the quivers are decorated with a narrow range of design that is nevertheless given variety by changing color combinations employing gold, translucent varnishes, and opaque paint. Cat. 141, for example, has a red-painted ground punctuated overall with gold dots, its medallions floating free in the center. Cat. 142, on the other hand, is painted green, its medallions with gold grounds outlined in red, the interlacing bands extending the full length of the face, with foliate tendrils emerging from the medallions and covering the sides.

The 1611 inventory of the Armory in the Doge's Palace records hundreds of quivers, all bristling with arrows, including "52 quivers, some of leather and others of gilt wood," but the descriptions are too brief to allow this distinctive group to be identified.[2] It seems likely, however, that they were originally accompanied by bows in the Turkish style decorated with matching arabesque ornament. Such elaborate and colorful archery equipment was probably used in Venice for sporting contests or on ceremonial occasions.

SP

1 For these quivers, see Huth 1971, p. 4, fig. 6; Contadini 1989, pp. 235, 238; Franzoi 1990, p. 121, cat. 381.
2 Franzoi 1990, p. 242 ("*Carcassi, alcuni de curame, et altri de legno indoradi n° cinquantadoi. . . .*").

PAINTED AND LACQUERED WOOD

143. Benedetto Floriani *Polygonal Virginal* (Spinetta)

Venice, 1572
Gilded and lacquered wood, ivory, ebony, and paint
H. 20 cm (7 7/8 in.); D. 53 cm (20 7/8 in.); L. 180.5 cm (71 1/16 in.)
On loan from the Musée des Arts decoratifs to the Musée de la Musique/ Cité de la Musique, Paris
Inv. D.AD.Pe.1803 (ill. p. 242)

Made in Venice in 1572, this handsome keyboard instrument is a polygonal virginal, or *spinetta*, a type of harpsicord. Numerous examples from the Renaissance survive, and in most instances they are rather simply finished. Only about 30 of the known examples are as elaborately decorated as this one.[1] The famous master instrument maker Benedetto Floriani constructed the instrument itself,[2] while an unknown but equally talented woodcarver built the case. Like the Metropolitan Museum's casket (cat. 147), this virginal has a lacquered exterior decorated with Islamic motifs borrowed from Ottoman and Venetian bookbindings from the same period (see cat. 133). Indeed, the panels across the front of the instrument inserted directly above the keys resemble the bookbinding format to the degree that each one has a central medallion and four corner medallions.

Beautifully crafted virginals like this one played a vital role in the public space of the Venetian *palazzo*, providing a source of entertainment while also enriching the interior. A painting by Ludovico Pozzoserrato of the late 1570s shows a festive gathering of a "merry company" around a virginal in a parlor, providing us with a glimpse of the social significance of this kind of musical instrument in its original setting. Among the ladies, who are all dressed in the latest Venetian fashion and richly adorned with lace and golden jewelry, one plays the virginal (not nearly as elaborately decorated as this one) while greeting new arrivals to the party.[3] Learning to play the *spinetta* appears to have been part of the education of many Venetian Renaissance women, and it allowed them to entertain both their families and their guests, either alone or with the accompaniment of singers.

According to Patricia Fortini Brown, "less than a third of the wealthy *cittadino* merchant families [in Venice] owned books, but all had at least two musical instruments."[4] Ironically, therefore, one could surmise that the designs on the bookbindings owned by the Venetian cultural elite were transferred to the musical instruments of the merchant classes. More to the point, these Islamic patterns had become so ubiquitous in Venice that they were employed on all types of decorated surfaces.

WK

1 www.denzilwraight.com/italpolyrectvirg.html.
2 Wraight 1992–1993.
3 Fortini Brown 2004, p. 174, fig. 197.
4 Fortini Brown 2004, p. 123.

144. *Pair of Doors*

Venice, ca. 1575–1600
Lacquered wood (perhaps poplar); ebony moldings and veneer, semi-precious stones, mother-of-pearl, partially gilded and painted; metal and iron
Each side: H.146.5 cm (57 5/8 in.); w. 52.5 cm (20 5/8 in.)
Rainer Zietz, Ltd., London (ill. p. 237)

Along with the St. Louis Casket (cat. 145) and the Collector's Cabinet from Berlin (cat. 146), these exceptionally well-preserved doors count among the most important works of art decorated with Venetian lacquer. The latter technique represents an early European attempt to imitate Oriental lacquerware through a distinctive decoration of leafy Islamic patterns painted in gold against a dark ground, which also recalls metalwork ornamented *"alla damaschina."*[1]

The original setting of these exceptional doors remains mysterious, however, their elaborate décor and high level of craftsmanship suggest they were intended for a palace, either of an affluent patron in Venice or as an extravagant diplomatic gift to the Ottoman Empire, as exemplified by similar doors in Levantine palaces such as the Topkapı Sarayi in Istanbul.[2] These doors could also have been commissioned by one of the hundreds of diplomats representing Western powers in Venice, who were able to sidestep strict local guild regulations and deal directly with merchants of luxury goods. Queen Elizabeth I of England, for example, regularly sent gifts of such magnitude to Muslim dignitaries and expressed her opinion in the turbulent climate of shifting alliances after the battle of Lepanto in 1571 through the statement "Better the turban than the tiara," the latter referring to the triple papal crown.[3] All sides of the doors, except the bottom, are decorated, making them suitable as independent works of art to be admired from every angle. Simultaneously, the lockable doors, which pivoted on now missing pegs, may have enshrined a built-in wall cabinet with shelves, thus securing the precious objects inside. By opening the doors, the objects could be displayed in this sumptuous environment. It is plausible that the doors concealed a curiosity cabinet holding exotic artifacts and *naturalia* from distant cultures, for which Venice (along with Portugal)[4] was one of the main ports of entry into Europe (see cat. 146).[5] Protecting a wide range of prized collector's items inside a space of great importance would underscore the search for humanist learning and ostentatious luxury display of the period. Holy relics and their valuable containers were stored in a comparable fashion in wall cupboards,[6] as were precious manuscripts and books, which then were considered "relics of knowledge."[7] A possible use as window shutters for these doors has also been suggested, however, the delicate golden paint and the other fragile materials make it unlikely.[8]

The foliate *a rabesco* embellishment of the geometric design of the moldings framing the semi-precious stones (mostly agate, jasper, and lapis lazuli), painted panels, or the areas ornamented with mother-of-pearl veneer between the oval and square tablets can be found on other objects with lacquered Islamicizing detailing, hence evoking their highly desired exotic appearance.[9] Not only this Oriental looking adornment but also the typical space allocation of geometric molding patterns can be observed in contemporary Venetian bookbinding (see cat. 133).[10] However, their distinguished Western layout reflects contemporary Venetian interior architectural elements, in particular the Renaissance coffered ceilings with inserted painting.[11] These doors were likely produced in a large *bottega* that employed specialist artisans for the decoration, the *pietre dure*, and the body construction as well as the mother-of-pearl cutting.

At a later time the reverse of the doors was cleaned in an effort to regain the daring juxtaposition of the iridescent sparkle of the exotic mother-of-pearl and the dark-ground wooden framework. Small areas were painted in and the large ovals in the center of each field were set with translucent agate tablets that were cut in a sophisticated manner called *"en papillion"* (like the "wings of a butterfly," or book-matched) resulting in a mirrored appearance of the stone's graining. These large ovals are surrounded in each section by four small raised agate applications with plain metal mounts in a way that can be seen on 18th-12 and 19th-century cabinets and caskets.[13] One of the rarest of all stones, lapis lazuli possesses, at least according to tradition, magical and medical powers including protection against melancholia and anxiety. Before large deposits were discovered in the Russian Ural Mountains in the 18th century, lapis lazuli—valued as much as gold—was imported to Europe through the Ottoman trade routes from Central Asia.[14]

WK

1 See the essays by Auld, Rizzo, and Grube in the present volume.
2 Sale catalogue, Christie's, New York, January 10, 1995, lot. 63; Auersperg-Trautson 1998, p. 14, figs. 9–11; for diplomatic gifts compare a "Renaissance Augsburg Elephant Automaton Clock" specifically made for Venice and to be presented to the Ottomans as indicated by a note in the *Codex Grevembroich*; see Koeppe 1992, no.U1, p. 269.
3 A papal tiara was last used during the coronation of John XXIII in 1958; Pope Paul VI banished this symbol of worldly power in 1963 and restricted its use to his coat of arms; Matar 1996, p. 42.
4 Vienna, 2000.
5 Koeppe 2004, pp. 80–89; with extensive literature.
6 Koeppe and Lupo 1991, pp. 35–56.
7 Fortini Brown 2004, fig. 243.
8 Auersperg-Trautson 1998, p. 11.
9 See Grube's essay in this volume; Fortini Brown 2004, pp. 108-12: Auersperg-Trautson 1998.
10 Fortini Brown 2004, p. 129, fig. 146.
11 Bassi 1987; see also the cofanetto, cat. 148.
12 Koeppe 1992, M141, p. 239.
13 Sale Catalogue, Christie's, London Dec. 26, 1997, lot. 756; Auersperg-Trautson 1998, p. 1.
14 Kappel 1998, p. 48. See also Berrie's essay in the present volume.

145. *Casket*

Venice, late 16th century
Lacquered wood, rock crystal; silver, partially gilded
47.6 x 73.3 x 47 cm (18 3/4 x 28 3/4 x 18 3/4 in.)
Saint Louis Art Museum, St. Louis
Inv. 346.1958 (ill. p. 105)

While preparing his *History of Venice* (published in 1581), Francesco Sansovino visited the shop of a jeweler of the Ruga dei Orefici in Venice, where he saw "a large casket of rock crystal made in such a manner that the contents could be seen through the crystal windows as if sculptured within."[1] Another contemporary document is a workshop version of Titian's portrait of his daughter Lavinia in which she holds up a similar casket with large rock crystal inserts.[2] The appearance and ostentatious positioning of such an object in written accounts and in a Venetian Renaissance painting point to the important role allocated to these caskets within the spectrum of luxury creations.

Hans Huth demonstrated that the St. Louis casket and others like it decorated with rock crystal (about half a dozen survive today)[3] relate to a tradition observed in high ecclesiastical circles from 1601 until 1880: "[The] popes followed the custom of presenting sets of baby linen which they had blessed (called *fascie benedette)* and other appropriate gifts to the male heirs of the great Catholic ruling houses of Europe. A set was even sent to Charles Edward, the Stuart Pretender. The custom of honoring distinguished persons by presenting them with [golden] roses blessed by the pope is well known [through surviving pieces in Royal treasuries. The first *fascie* are recorded in a protocol of 1601 in which] we are told that the papal nuncio extraordinary, Maffeo Barberini (later Pope Urban VIII), presented the gift of *fascie* to the [French] royal couple, Henry IV and Maria de' Medici, for their son, later Louis XIII [at the Louvre] on

December 16, 1606 . . . it was handed to them 'in a casket'."[4] Since Sansovino mentions a similar casket in 1581, they may have been around even earlier than the 17th century.

Using these lacquered and decorated caskets as reliquaries seems unlikely given the "pagan Turkish" embellishment that would have been inappropriate for such consecrated utensils in the decades after the Council of Trent. It may be surprising that the Holy See would order such sumptuous items in Venice instead of employing local Roman artisans, but a simple explanation may lay in the lagoon's long tradition of lapidary works and the monopoly-like ability of Venetian masters to imitate Near-Eastern lacquer.

Most of the nearly two hundred rock crystal pieces applied to this casket are facetted and almost flawless, their high quality suggesting they were probably mined in a quarry near the Saint Gotthard mountain in the Italian-Swiss Alps. The spiral columns (*colonna tortile* or *salomonica*)[5] and the golden décor paint are of greatest delicacy. The Islamic-inspired decoration is especially evident in the interior walls of the casket, which provide the framing for the large and small rock-crystal window panels. Intricate bands including scrolls with open flowers and leaves derived from the Ottoman *saz* pattern (see cat. 174) form the overall frame, while the larger panels between the windows present a dense symmetric motif of peonies and confronted birds against a scrolling background. When reflecting the sun rays by day or the flickering candlelight by night, the casket's overall appearance must have changed constantly, thus resulting in firework-like sparkles that would have entranced its admirers with its "exotic" fascination.

WK

1 "*. . . una cassa di cristallo molto grande fatta di modo che le cose si ripongono dentro appariscano tutti scolpiti di fuori,*" after Huth 1971, p. 8.
2 Huth 1968, p. 46, fig. 3; Grube 1989, p. 33, fig. 19.
3 Huth 1968, p. 43; Lorenzelli and Veca 1984, pp. 155–57; other examples include a silver mounted version with glass in the Metroplitan Museum (no. 1985.195.4) and two boxes that recently appeared on the Paris (Jacques Kugel) and London (Rainer Zietz) art market.
4 Huth 1968; Huth 1971, pp. 8–9.
5 A name adopted from the spiral columns that originally flanked the *memoria* in the old Church of St. Peter in Rome, which inspired Bernini to use this motive for the expressive torsion of the gigantic supports of his bronze *baldacchino* above the high altar of the new church.

146. *Collector's Cabinet*

Venice, 1565–1680
Secondary wood: coniferous wood (fir?), poplar and alder; veneer: fruitwood (possibly pear), painted and lacquered, semi-precious stones, mother-of-pearl, partially gilded and painted; yellow metal and iron
H. 81 cm (31 7/8 in.), H. 159 cm (62 5/8 in.) with front vertically opened; W.112.2 cm (44 1/8 in.; D. 48.8 cm (19 1/4 in.)
Staatliche Museen zu Berlin, Stiftung Preussischer Kulturbesitz, Kunstgewerbemuseum, Berlin Inv. no. 1933,26 (ill. p. 232)

Beginning in the mid-16th century, collecting the extraordinary, mysterious, and extravagant with an encyclopedic scope became a major goal of humanists.[1] The three elements of a collection consisted of *naturalia* (products of nature), *artificialia* (products of man), and *scientifica* (man's ability to measure and dominate nature with clocks, astrolabes, and other scientific instruments). Gathered into a room known as the *Kunst-und Wunderkammer*, these objects underlined their powerful owners' status and sophistication.

Didactic curiosity rooms, however, were only within the reach of princely and upper class patrons. Those with smaller purses, like the urban patricians of Venice, instead had elaborate cabinets furnished with many drawers and secret compartments filled with objects of a similar kind. These masterpieces of cabinetmaking represented in miniature format the diversity of items found in an entire *Kunstkammer*.

Venetian cabinetmakers frequently took inspiration from contemporary palaces, replicating their designs on a smaller scale. In this way, the latest architectural fashion entered the *piano nobile* of the patrician residence. Because of their reduced size, these cabinets could be decorated with even more expensive materials than those used on palace façades. The model for this exquisitely decorated cabinet appears to have been Jacopo Sansovino's Ca' Corner della Regina on Venice's Grand Canal, begun around 1545. The cabinet's arcade has column-flanked niches and balustrades like those of the upper two floors of the Corner palace.[2]

When the front panel of this cabinet is fully opened, the finely detailed decoration of its interior is revealed. The distinct pattern of geometric roundels and a rhombus invite the viewer to examine the surface close-up.[3] The main reference to Islamic patterns is evident in the dense background decoration of the interior surface of the drop-down front panel, an ornament that is very similar to that of the interior of the large casket in St. Louis (cat. 145). Here, the gold-and- red scrolling pattern is even more elaborate, showing an array of flowers, leaves, and cloud patterns that are also reminiscent of the decoration on some of the most accomplished leather parade shields produced by Venetian craftsmen in those very years (cats. 135–140).

This extraordinary piece stands out among a dozen similar, mostly smaller collector's cabinets, including a recently identified variation in the collection of Michael Hall in New York City.[4] Another piece of great importance for future scientific analyses of the various lacquer and woodworking techniques is the small toilet cabinet from the *Kunstkammer* of Duke Ferdinand II of Tirol at Ambras Castle near Innsbruck. Today preserved at the Kunsthistorisches Museum in Vienna, it is listed in an inventory of 1596 and probably never left the Imperial Habsburg collection.[5]

The combination of the superbly chosen semi-precious stones (*naturalia*) and the refined design of the man-made artistic structure (*arteficialia*) make the work in Berlin a curiosity cabinet *par excellence*.

WK

1 Wolfram Koeppe, "Collecting for the Kunstkammer," in *Timeline of Art History*, The Metropolitan Museum of Art's website (www.metmuseum.org).
2 Fortini Brown 2004, p. 39, fig. 44; later examples are Sansovino's Marciana Library and the Procuratorie Nuove in St. Mark's Square; Fortini Brown 2004, p. 198, fig. 219; Hellbing 2005, pp. 20–24.
3 A very similar pattern is seen inside the doors of a cabinet in Vienna; see Windisch-Graetz 1983, p. 244, pl. IV, fig. 95.
4 Windisch-Graetz 1983, pp. 242–44, pls. III–IV; Bert-Uwe Hellbing 2005 is the most detailed study of the Berlin Cabinet; Achim Stiegel of the Kunstgewerbemuseum in Berlin, is currently preparing a catalogue of the Berlin Renaissance furniture that includes the present object.
5 Windisch-Graetz 1983, p. 243, figs. 92–93.

147. Casket *(Cofanetto or Scrigno)*

Venice, ca. 1570–90
Beech wood, rosewood veneer, partially gilded painted, and lacquered, gold powder, gold leaf, silver flakes, silver-gilt, bronze, and yellow metal
H. 19.7 cm (7 3/4 in.); W. 41.8 cm (16 7/16 in.); D. 28.9 cm (11 3/8 in.)
The Metropolitan Museum of Art, New York
Rogers Fund, 1957
Inv. 57.25ab (ill. 246)

Like a *cassone* (a large receptacle for the bride's dowry) but much smaller,[1] the *cofanetto* (a luxury vanity case for toilet articles and personal items) and the *scrigno* (a strong box), are caskets locked with a key that were kept in a Renaissance woman's *camera* or bedroom.

A recent X-ray examination of this casket, which may be either a *cofanetto* or a *scrigno*, revealed grooves along its interior that represent fittings for combs like those of another *cofanetto* in The Metropolitan Museum (cat. 148).[2] In this instance, however, the grooves end at a considerable distance below the upper edges of all four sides, leaving enough space for a drop-in, removable tray to conceal the space. This now lost tray could have had a secondary function as well, perhaps serving as a small writing surface, to hide a game board, or possibly for the daily *coiffure* if covered with a resistant surface such as leather. The embroidered silk fabric that lines the area today was added later to obscure the original arrangement. In addition, an inset mirror in the lid can be detached to give access to a large hidden storage compartment in its attic space.

The density of the painted gold-leaf ornament that covers the surface bestows a rather distinctly Ottoman flavor on this elaborate object. Only the handle and escutcheon give away its European, distinctly Venetian, origin. The outstanding modeling of the silver-cast handle is a work of art in its own right, and attests to the inventiveness of contemporary Venetian sculptors and metal artisans while also adding to the sumptuousness of the casket.[3]

A surprising discovery emerging from the recent scientific examination was that the beech wood body is veneered on the outside with rosewood whose grain has a horizontal orientation.[4] Contrary to earlier assumptions, this veneer is not covered with a layer of dark lacquer to imitate exotic lacquer, but instead the cabinetmaker used the natural and rather eccentric looking grain of the rare wood that was merely covered by translucent lacquer and gold paint with Islamic-looking vegetal motifs. The latter are highlighted by areas of silver flakes (possibly imitating 16th-century Japanese examples containing gold dust), and relief accents of red and green glazes over the gilding as well as blue paint, thus creating a mesmerizing surface when closely examined.[5]

Related examples are in the Berlin Kunstgewerbemuseum[6] and the Museum für Angewandte Kunst in Vienna.[7] Nonetheless, the heavy silver-gilt mount and the attention to every detail set the Metropolitan Museum's casket apart. Moreover, thanks to the recent scientific analysis, this box can now be identified as a unique survival of the *petteniera turchesca* ("comb-casket in the Turkish manner"), one of the ultimate luxury arts produced in Renaissance Venice.

WK

1 Koeppe 1995; Fortini Brown 2004, pp. 102–107; Kisluk-Grosheide et al. 2006.
2 I am most grateful to Mechthild Baumeister, Conservator, Sherman Fairchild Center for Objects Conservation, who shared her research on the Berlin and Viennese pieces with me.
3 Mark T. Wypyski, Research Scientist, Department of Scientific Research, performed surface analysis using X-ray fluorescence spectrometry (XRF). Briefly, he found that the large escutcheon is composed of a brass alloy containing about 15% zinc and small amounts of iron, nickel, tin, antimony, and lead. The gilded front surface of the escutcheon was mercury- or fire-gilded. The handle on the cover appears to be silver-gilt with a small amount of copper in the alloy. The four small escutcheons on the corners of the interior mirror are also silver-gilt. The interior lock-plate is probably made of steel and inlaid with gold.
4 Marijn Manuels, Associate Conservator, and Dana Melchar, Conservation Intern, determined that the wood of the casket is Honduras rosewood (*Dalbergia stevensonii*) rather than the expected Indian rosewood (*Dalbergia latifolia*), although transverse and radial samples would need to be obtained for conclusive identification. The allocation of a South American species would imply an early trade connection with the Spanish Americas that seems to be hitherto unknown in the history of exotic wood trade. See also a comprehensive "Examination and Treatment Report" by Dana Melchar, April 25, 2006.

5 Windisch-Graetz 1983, p. 39; Mack 2002, p. 137, fig. 147; Fortini Brown 2004, p. 274, n. 61.
6 Huth 1971, p. 10; Berlin 1989, pp. 98–99, cat. 6.
7 Huth 1971, p. 6.

°148. *Casket (Cofanetto or Scrigno)*

Venice, ca. 1575–1600
Beech, ebony, painted and lacquered, decorated with incrustations of mother-of-pearl, ivory with gilding, and gouache miniatures on parchment under glass; later textile-lining
H. 7 3/4 in.; W. 15 1/2 in.; D. 11 in.
The Metropolitan Museum of Art, New York
Gift of J. Pierpont Morgan, 1917
Inv. no. 17.190.848 (ill. p. 247)

Mother-of-pearl, harvested mainly from the Red Sea, the Persian Gulf, and the Indian Ocean, was synonymous in the 16th and 17th centuries with rare and expensive materials; it alluded to the patron's wealth and interest in the exotic or even the bizarre. The ability to polish mother-of-pearl with abrasives, thus significantly enhancing its luster as well as the range of its iridescent color, added to the natural material's splendor.[1] This casket is adorned with mother-of-pearl tablets on both the outside and the inner surface of its lid. All the elements are connected by panels with Islamicizing, *"alla damaschina,"* decorative patterns like those on the pair of doors in this exhibition (cat. 144). A less elaborate and smaller box in the Metropolitan Museum (inv. 06.182) and a splendid virginal dated 1593 in the Royal College of Music, London have similar decorative layouts.[2] Here, the glistening framework enhances the look of the miniatures painted on parchment under glass with mythological themes, including the "love of the gods" and the celebration of female beauty. The inserts on the lid in ivory, a material that has also long been associated with the charismatic beauty of the female complexion, evokes similar ideas.[3]

The original inserted mirror (see cat. 147) was later substituted with colorful fabric to conceal the lid's "secret" compartment.[4] The interior would have held toilet articles and writing implements such as feather knives. Other compartments provided secure places for valuables within the lockable receptacle. Three narrow spaces probably protected ivory combs. A shallow drawer occupies the lower part of the base. A similar, though less elaborate box furnished with such items can be seen in an engraving published in Bartolomeo Scappi's *Opera* of 1570; there, a pair of scissors and a double-sided comb are also clearly visible within the casket.[5]

Beautiful nude allegorical figures surround the part of the lid where the mirror was once inserted. When the casket's female owner looked at her reflection, she would have been reminded to take care of her appearance, a sign of her family's high social status, but without succumbing to *vanitas.* Such a stylish casket was likely part of an aristocratic woman's trousseau or a wedding gift.

WK

1 Büttner 2000, pp. 7, 11.
2 Huth 1971, cat. 33; see also Lorenzelli and Veca 1984, p. 135, no. 178; Thornton 1984, p. 250, fig. 15.
3 Koeppe 2006.
4 The fitting style of the later embroidery of this casket is unusually close to that of the object cat. 147 and to an example in Vienna that has also lost its mirror; see Grube 1989, p. 224, fig. 10. I am grateful to Mechthild Baumeister for this observation. Future investigation may provide an answer to the question where and when such fabrics were produced and applied to refit these boxes, apparently in the same workshop.
5 Fortini Brown 2004, p. 82, fig. 88.

CARVED WOOD

149. *Stern decoration from the bastarda of Commander-in-Chief Francesco Morosini*

Venice, mid-17th century
Carved wood
L. ca. 310 cm (122 in.) max.; H. ca. 110 cm (43 1/4 in.)
Museo Storico Navale, Venice (inv. 1238)

Doge Francesco Morosini (1618-1694; r. 1688-94), known as the *Peloponnesiaco* and the Commander-in-Chief of the Venetian fleet on several occasions starting in 1657, was one of the greatest naval captains of the Serenissima. The majority of his spoils of war are presently in the Museo Correr (see cat. 77, 113, 134) but the Museo Storico Navale in Venice proudly owns the ship figureheads that decorated the two sides of the stern of his *bastarda*, the heavily armed war galley and admiral ship of the Venetian fleet. This roundship, together with the other heavy galleys (*galeazze*) in the fleet, had a similar function as World War I and II battleships, armed with exceptionally long-range, powerful, and precise artillery on board. Morosini's reputation after the victory in Morea (1687) was so great that his bronze bust was installed in the Ducal Palace even before he was elected doge, and the historian Andrea Da Mosto described him as "one of the greatest men of [the 17th] century".[1] After Morosini's election, which occurred while he was still fighting in the eastern Mediterranean in 1688, the symbols of Venetian rule—the dogal seal and the horned hat—were delivered to him at sea; and for the first time, in Venice the same person was appointed both Doge and Commander-in-Chief.[2]

Morosini was the hero of the Serenissima in the war against the Ottomans and it is not surprising to see a chained half-naked, bare-headed, slave-looking Turk as a symbolic and talismanic reminder of the expected victories of the Venetians in the islands of the Aegean and the Peloponnesus. Similar images are found as a symbol of his defeat over the Turks in the two lower corners of his medallion portrait published by Coronelli a few years after his death.[3] Embassies and diplomatic exchanges had become infrequent between the two powers in the 17th century, mostly because the Ottoman sultan regarded Venice as a secondary power on the European scene by that time, but the rhetoric of war was predominant on the lagoon where the loss of influence in the Mediterranean was painfully perceived.

One can imagine the building yards in the Arsenal busier than ever under Morosini's leadership, preparing both the heavy *galeazze* and the speedy galleys for setting sail. Among the hundreds of shipbuilders were also the woodcarvers working on the final touches of the ship figureheads and other decorations: these imposing sculptures (the present one is more than three meters long including the folded sail), the back of which had to be adapted to the shaped walls of the vessel, were no small feat for talented wood craftsmen who had to convey the puissance of the Venetian fleet.

SC

1 "*Si può dir uno tra primi huomini di questo secolo.*" Da Mosto 1983, p. 435.
2 A short account in English of Morosini's career as admiral of the fleet is in Topping 1976; see also Casini 2001 for an in-depth analysis of how his figure was perceived in Venice during his lifetime.
3 Vincenzo Coronelli, "Ritratto di Francesco Morosini", in *Ritratti de' celebri personaggi raccolti nell'accademia cosmografica degli Argonauti*, Venice, 1697, pl. 4.

GLASS

150. *Cup with mount*

Cup: Probably Iran, 9th-10th century or Egypt, 10th-11th century
Mount: Byzantine, 10th-11th century
Blown and tooled glass with incised decoration; mount in gilt silver with inlaid enamel, pearls, semiprecious stones, and glass
Cup: Diam. 13.1 cm (5 1/8 in.); H. 7 cm (2 3/4 in.)
With mount: Diam. 13.5 cm (5 3/8 in.); H. 18.5 cm (7 1/4 in.)
Procuratoria di San Marco, Venice
Inv. 76 (ill. p. 255)

In the Treasury of St. Mark's there are several works in glass, four of which are undisputably from the early Islamic period while the others are generally attributed to Byzantine factories.[1] The Islamic objects consist of two bowls, one cup, and the remaining half of a *navicella* (lit. "a small boat," a shallow elongated bowl), which imitate the color and texture of precious or semiprecious stones, respectively emerald, turquoise, rock crystal, and ruby.[2] They are all decorated in the lapidary technique—the glass was sculpted and cut at the wheel like a piece of stone—that represents one of the highest points of Islamic glassmaking during the 9th through the 11th centuries from Iran to Egypt.

The most celebrated and often reproduced work is the opaque pale blue, turquoise-like bowl with running hares in relief that is traditionally said to have been brought to Venice by the envoys of the Turkoman Aq-Qoyunlu sultan, Uzun Hasan in 1472. An inscription under its base reading "Khorasan," interpreted by some as a reference to the eastern region of Iran where turquoise was mined, deceivingly suggests that the bowl was made of the real semiprecious stone rather than being an imitation in glass.[3]

One wonders if this emerald-like glass cup—which may have originated in Fatimid Cairo like many other objects in the St. Mark's Treasury (see cat. 88)—was also perceived as the "real deal" in Venice. From a connoseuir's point of view, this dark and bright green bowl (the color, quite rare in the Islamic glass production, was obtained with a high percentage of lead oxide) is not as accomplished as the "turquoise" cup, mainly because its decoration of running hares is not carved in relief but simply incised on the surface of the glass, thus giving it a flatter and more stylized appearance.[4] Its hemispherical shape and the concentric circles carved at the base may suggest an Eastern Islamic origin following Sasanian prototypes; but it cannot be excluded that it could be the work of 10th-or 11th-century Cairene craftsmen under the Fatimids.

There is little doubt that the object was in Constantinople shortly after it was made and that it was used in an ecclesiastical context: its custom-made gilt-silver mount with pearls, stone, and glass insets has been attributed by André Grabar to the 10th or 11th centuries and includes enameled bands with a Greek inscription related to the consecration of the Eucharist.[5]

SC

1 The Treasury represents the largest repository of high quality Byzantine glass, a field of art history that is still far from being well understood. After closer examination, some of these "Byzantine" or "Sasanian" glass objects may be revealed as early Islamic.
2 Erdmann 1971, pp. 103–8, cat. 117–20, pls. 89–94; Carboni and Whitehouse 2001, pp. 176–79, 187–88, cats. 83–84, 92. The implications of their precious stone-like appearance are discussed in my paper entitled "Vetri preziosi: la circolazione del vetro di origine islamica in Italia" presented at the symposium "Dono, merce, bottino. Itinerari e fortuna di opere d'arte islamiche in Italia e nel Mediterraneo dal 1250 al 1500," Florence, March 2006.
3 Recently, see Shalem 1996, pp. 63–66; Carboni and Whitehouse 2001, pp. 176–78, cat. 83.
4 Pasini 1885–86, p. 57, pl. 45; Erdmann 1971, pp. 104–5, cat. 118, pls. 91–92; Gabrieli and Scerrato 1979, p. 477, fig. 485, fig. 586; Venice 1993, p. 100, cat. 27.
5 Erdmann 1971, p. 105.

151. *Two Beakers*[1]

Syria, ca. 1260
Yellowish colorless glass, green, yellow, blue, and white enamels and gold; free-blown, enameled and gilt; tooled on the pontil
The Walters Art Museum, Baltimore
Inv. 47.17, 47.18 (ill. p. 78)

151a.

H. 18.5 cm (7 5/16 in.); max. diam. 12.1 cm (4 3/4 in.)
Inscribed in Arabic, below rim: "Glory to our lord the sultan, the royal, the diligent, the wise, the defender, the protector of frontiers, the fortified by God, the triumphant."

151b.

H. 17 cm (6 5/8 in.); max. diam. 10.5 cm (4 1/8 in.)
Inscribed in Arabic, below rim, partially effaced: "Glory to our lord the sultan, the royal"

These identically shaped and similarly decorated beakers either form a pair or once belonged to a larger set of four.[2] Their enameled decoration is divided into three horizontal bands, with an architectural composition in the center and two bands of inscriptions above and below. Only parts of the inscriptions remain legible and are of a formulaic benedictory type commonly found on Ayyubid and Mamluk metal and glass. Each beaker features two domed buildings, prominent vegetation, and figures with small and large haloes. The scene on the smaller beaker (cat. 151b) has been identified as the Entry of Christ into Jerusalem; the buildings are perhaps the Tower of David and a minaret overshadowing the route down the Via Dolorosa. The slightly larger beaker (cat. 151a) bears images of the two most important monuments in the Holy Land—the central-plan building with three hanging lamps is the Anastasis rotunda of the Church of the Holy Sepulcher and the smaller octagonal building is the Templum Domini (the Dome of the Rock).[3] The subject matter recalls 13th-century Ayyubid inlaid metalwork, which was frequently decorated with Christian themes.[4] It is, however, relatively uncommon in enameled glass: only two other extant intact objects, a bottle in Liechtenstein and a drinking horn in the Hermitage Museum, are closely related to these beakers.[5]

There are still many questions surrounding the function, makers, and patrons of these objects. Beakers of this shape comprise one of the largest groups of enameled vessels and were widely produced from the late Ayyubid period (ca. 1225) to the middle of the Mamluk period (late 14th century).[6] The variation in their shapes and sizes suggests that they were used for ceremonial purposes and as gifts as well as for drinking. The beakers' decoration is the product of a visual culture remarkably unfettered by religious boundaries. Thus such objects may have been produced for local Christians,[7] for pilgrims returning from the Holy Land, for Crusaders settled in the Latin East who had developed a taste for local luxury goods,[8] and perhaps even for Muslims.[9] Their shape also became popular in Europe, especially in 13th-century Venice, as exemplified by the "Aldrevandin" group (cats. 156-159).

QA

1 They were sold as a pair in Baghdad in 1912 and entered the collection of G. Dattari in Cairo; Henry Walters acquired them in 1925.
2 Folda 2005, pp. 364–65, figs. 230–32; Carswell 1998, pp. 61-63, pl. L, figs. 15.1, 15.2; Atıl 1981, pp. 125–27 and 144, cat. nos. 44–45; Lamm 1929–30, pp. 330–31, nos. 8, 9, pl. 127: 8–9.
3 Carswell 1998; Georgopoulou 1999, pp. 303–15.
4 Hoffman 2004; Katzenstein and Lowry 1983; Baer 1989.
5 Carboni 2001, cat. no. 121 and fig. 102.
6 Kenesson 1998, p. 48.
7 Carboni 2001, p. 245.
8 Folda 2005, p. 363; Rogers 1998, p. 70.
9 Hoffman 2004, p. 132.

152-153. Two mosque lamps

152.

Cairo, Egypt, ca. 1329–35
Free-blown brownish colorless glass, tooled on the pontil; blue, grayish blue, red, white, yellow, and pink enamels, yellow and green stains and gold
H. 35.6 cm (14 in.); Diam. max. 23.9 cm (9 3/8 in.)
Inscriptions: In Arabic, around neck: "That which was made for his excellency, the exalted, the lord, the royal, the well-served Sayf al-Din Qawsun, the Cup-bearer of al-Malik al-Nasir";
Around the body: Qur'an, *sura* 24 (*Surat al-Nur*), beginning of verse 35: "God is the light of the heavens and the earth, the likeness of His light is as a wick-holder [wherein is a light (the light in a glass, the glass as it were a glittering star)]"; around foot: "The work of the poor slave [of God] ᶜAli ibn Muhammad al-Barmaki [?], may God safeguard him"
The Metropolitan Museum of Art, New York
Gift of J. Pierpont Morgan, 1917
Inv. 17.190.991 (ill. p. 254)

• 153.

Cairo, Egypt, ca. 1356–63
Free-blown brownish colorless glass, tooled on the pontil; blue and red enamels and gold
H. 40.7 cm (16 in.); Diam. max. 28.5 cm (11 1/4 in.)
Victoria and Albert Museum, London
Inv. 324-1900 (ill. p. 22)

Large and impressive glass lamps such as these in the shape of footed vases with enameled decoration and suspension rings attached around their body were commissioned by sultans and members of their court for mosques, *madrasas* (Qur'anic schools), tombs, hospices, and other public buildings in 14th-century Mamluk Cairo.

Dedicated to Qawsun (d. 1342), an emir of Sultan al-Nasir Muhammad ibn Qalaun (r. 1293–1341 with brief interruptions), the earlier lamp of these two lamps (cat. 152), was probably intended for one of his two architectural commissions in Cairo: the mosque (completed in 1329 and now mostly in ruins) or the tomb-hospice complex completed in 1335, of which only the minaret survives. The lamp's decoration is organized in registers. The neck bears part of the verses from the Qur'an's "Chapter of Light," which aptly uses the metaphor of a glass lamp to describe the divine light of God. The body features formulaic and benedictory inscriptions in bold cursive *thuluth* script, which recalls the inlaid metalwork with epigraphic decoration popular during the long reign of al-Nasir Muhammad.[1] This lamp bears the name of the patron, Amir Qawsun, states his office as "Cup-bearer" (*saqi*), and includes the name of the sultan he served. Heraldic symbols indicating rank in the Mamluk hierarchy also appear on objects and architecture from the period of al-Nasir Muhammad, and in this case a blazon with a cup, the symbol of Qawsun's highest office, is repeated six times on the neck and underside of the lamp. An unusual feature of this lamp is the artist's signature inscribed around the foot, which may belong to the glass-maker, the painter, or both. The *nisba* (patronymic or place of origin) of the craftsman, about whom little is known, is ambiguously written, and thus has given rise to varied interpretations.[2] A similar lamp in Cairo, which is contemporaneous with this one, bears the same signature.

The second, larger lamp (cat. 153) has no inscriptions and is entirely decorated, including its foot, with a dense background of leaves and vegetal patterns against which are dispersed large peonies seen in profile as well as opened six-petaled flowers. The lavish ornamentation is emphasized by the contrast of blue and gold. Lamps with the same decorative scheme are known to have hung from the ceilings of the madrasa of Sultan Malik Nasir Hasan (r. 1347–51 and 1354–61), the largest and most impressive building of Mamluk Cairo, which was begun in 1356 and finished in 1362–63 after his disappearance and presumed death. Two lamps with very similar decoration, which were taken directly from his madrasa, are today in the Museum of Islamic Art in Cairo, and several others are known in different collections.[3]

Glassmaking in Mamluk Cairo peaked in the 14th century and a decline in quantity and quality began already by the early 15th century. The main centers of enameled glass production shifted to Europe, especially Venice and Barcelona,[4] by the end of the century, and in the 16th century, "mosque" lamps became popular export items from Venice to the Near East (see cats. 162–63, 169–71).

QA / SC

1 Atıl 1981, nos. 25–32.
2 Carboni 2001, p. 234.
3 Wiet 1929, pp. 9–13, nos. 270 and 271, pls. XXII, XXIII; Lamm 1929–30, p. 454, nos. 109 and 110, pl. 193:3–4.
4 Carboni 2004, pp. 72–76.

154. *Ewer*

Syria or Egypt, ca. 1361–63
Blown glass with gilded decoration
H. 11.5 cm (4 1/2 in.); Diam. at rim 5.4 cm (2 1/8 in.)
The Ashmolean Museum of Art and Archaeology, Oxford
Inv. EA 1977.9 (ill. p. 122)

This small blue jug is a typical example of the dark-colored (blue or purple) glass vessels with gilded decoration created in the Syria and Egypti under the Ayyubids and the Mamluks (13th–15th centuries).[1] Even though most of it wore off, the gilded decoration is still legible becausethe gold was fired and therefore left a permanent impression on the surface. ment One can still see the the horizontal bands around the ewer's body and the lobed arches on its shoulder. In addition, there are inscriptions in cursive *naskh* around the neck and the lower part of the body, the latter including the name of the Mamluk sultan Salah al-Din Muhammad (r. 1361–63). This glass typology seems to be mostly Syrian, although fragments of blue or purple glass with gilding were also found at Fustat (Old Cairo), where the Cairene glass factories were located. According to the Ashmolean's records, the ewer was found in Iran, but there is no doubt that the vessel was made in the Mamluk sultanate.

In terms of shape, the ewer resembles the inlaid metal object signed by Qasim now in the Walters Art Museum in Baltimore (cat. 108). This form became popular not only in Egypt but also in Timurid and Turkoman Iran, which is strictly related to the production of the master Mahmud al-Kurdi and therefore also to Venetian works (cats. 100–112). A further connection to Venice is through the glass medium. A large number of enameled and gilded jugs of similar dimensions and profile (though mostly with a different foot and neck), including a few in dark blue glass, were made in Murano at the beginning of the 16th century and were often decorated a rabesche (see cat. 166).

RM / SC

1 Newby 1998, pp. 37–38, figs. 10.12–10.13; Newby 2000, pp. 42–43, cat. 32.

155. *Fragment from the pulpit of the Church of San Giovanni Fuorcivitas in Pistoia*

Pulpit by Guglielmo; glass decoration by Venetian craftsmen working in Pistoia, 1270
Carved marble with insets of glass tiles painted in gold on the reverse
H. 81 cm max. (31 7/8 in.); W. 101 cm max. (39 3/4 in.); Th. 6 cm (2 3/8 in.)
Museo Diocesano, Pistoia (ill. p. 256)

In an important article on 13th-century Italian glass decorated with incised gold-leaf designs on the reverse (a technique often called *verre eglomisé*) of 1970, Bertelli identified this fragment, originally part of the 1270 pulpit of the Church of San Giovanni Fuorcivitas in Pistoia, as one of the best examples of gilded glass from the 13th century. He also convincingly argued that Venetian craftsmen created its glass decoration, basing his statement on a comparison with illuminated borders of contemporaneous manuscripts and with details of local architectural decoration, but especially because of Venice's unique access to, and knowledge of, geometric patterns of Islamic origin.[1] The technique of *verre eglomisé* in late 13th-century Venice, a period when enameled and gilded glass based on Islamic models became popular in the city (see cats. 156–59), is also confirmed through archival documents.[2]

The overall geometric composition of the pulpit's glass decoration—a complex pattern that departs from six-pointed stars and intersects horizontally, vertically, and diagonally, creating small compartments of different shapes (rhomboids, diamonds, triangles, trapezoids, and elongated pentagons) filled with glass tiles—recalls some of the best achievements of Islamic designers in the creation of inlaid-wood *minbars* (pulpits) made for medieval Spanish, Moroccan, and Egyptian mosques.[3]

This large fragment (a rectangle with two missing corners and dimensions of 81 x 101 cm) was found together with two smaller triangular pieces, which had been buried in the floor of the pulpit when it was disassembled in order to prevent its destruction during World War II. Taken to the Opificio delle Pietre Dure in Florence for restoration, the three fragments were deposited in the Diocesan Museum in Pistoia in 1969.[4] Clearly, they belong to the original pulpit of 1270 designed by Guglielmo, a contemporary of the celebrated sculptors Nicola and Giovanni Pisano.

The stairway of the Pistoia pulpit, with its glass-inlaid marble parapet, appears to have been conceived much like a Muslim *minbar*, which gives it its distinctive appearance.

The glass tiles set into the grooved marble, the largest width of which is ca. 3.5 cm, are made of clear, rather bubbly glass whose surface is not perfectly flat. They were probably created with the "broad glass"[5] technique, which was also the leading one in the Islamic world.[6] The motifs, incised with a needle-like point in the graffito technique through the gold leaf applied on the reverse of each tile, include designs that are common to both Gothic and Islamic art, such as paired animals among leafage, palmettes, and geometric patterns. The Near Eastern connection is even more evident when one observes that the best comparison for the use of painted glass tiles set against a geometric background can be found in Mamluk Cairo only two decades later, in the decoration of the *qibla* wall of a small mausoleum dated to 1291.[7]

The pulpit of San Giovanni Fuorcivitas, therefore, epitomizes the influence of Islamic religious art among the leading sculptors in Tuscany in the second half of the 13th century and at the same time the role of Venetian glassmakers—the only ones who had the necessary skills and knowledge—in achieving the designer's artistic intent.

SC

1 Bertelli 1970, pp. 75-76.
2 In the inventory of Pope Bonifacius VIII of 1295 there is an "icon made in Venice with a central figure *in majestatis* surrounded by pearls and other [figures] in *verre eglomisé*" ("*unam iconam de opera veneticorum de una tabula in qua est figyura maiestatis in medio et plures perle, alie in vitro ad aurum*"); Pettenato 1973, p. 72.
3 See, in general, Bloom et al. 1998 with its bibliography.
4 Bertelli 1970, p. 71, n. 5. Given its "Islamic" appearance, it was exhibited in the museum with the label "Moorish art, 12th century".
5 In the broad glass technique the enflated glass bubble is elongated in order to form a cylinder that is cut lengthwise and then flattened.
6 Carboni 2003b, pp. 129-30.
7 Carboni 2003a, esp. pp. 78-79.

156–159. *Three beakers and a fragmentary beaker*

Venice, late 13th–early 14th century
Free-blown and enameled glass, tooled on the pontil

• 156.

H. 13 cm (5 1/8 in.); Diam. 10.9 cm max. (4 1/4 in.)
The British Museum, London
Inv. MME 1876.11–04.0003 (ill. p. 257)

157.

H. 11.3 cm (4 1/2 in.); Diam. 9.5 cm (3 3/4 in.)
Museum für Angewandte Kunst, Frankfurt a. M.
Inv. 6770 (ill. p. 258)

158.

H. 8 cm (3 1/8 in.); Diam. 7.7 cm max. (3 in.)
Karl Amendt Collection, Krefeld, on loan to the Museum Kunst Palast, Glasmuseum Hentrich, Düsseldorf
Inv. L 1989-1 (Sig. Amendt) (ill. p. 257)

159.

Largest fragment: H. 8.7 cm (3 1/2 in.); Diam. ca. 7.9 cm (reconstructed max.) (3 1/8 in.)
Soprintendenza per Beni Archeologici del Veneto, Verona
Inv. IG 156322 (ill. p. 257)

These four beakers belong to a distinctive group of enameled glass objects, the great majority of them drinking glasses, that has recently received scholarly attention and found its proper place in the history of Venetian glass production. A few of these objects have been known since the early 20th century and were classified as "Syro-Frankish" by Carl Johan Lamm, who believed they had been produced in Ayyubid or Mamluk Syria for a European clientele shortly before the last Crusaders abandoned the region in the early 1290s.[1] In the 1970s, Luigi Zecchin published both important archival notices for "painters of beakers" active on the lagoon between 1280 and 1351 and early descriptions of the vessels, which made the connection between Lamm's "Syro-Frankish" group and Venice evident.[2] Since then, the only serious challenge to a Venetian origin for these beakers has come from scholars who suggest that a share of the production, though inspired by the Venetian objects, may have been manufactured in Germanic Central Europe.[3]

The four beakers in the present exhibition represent the initial Islamic inspiration of their technology and iconography (cat. 158), the adaptation of motifs to a European taste (cat. 157), the full integration of Western themes (cat. 156), and the archaeological evidence that completes and corroborates Zecchin's archival discoveries (cat. 159). Their chronology, however, is not clearly understood and the sequence above is not an attempt to propose one on the basis of these beakers' decoration; as a matter of fact, the only chronological distinction suggested thus far by the present author, which partially contradicts the list above, relates to the possibility of an earlier elongated and splayed profile of some of them versus the later stockier, straight-walled appearance of others and to the presence of gold paint on the exterior of examples belonging to the supposed earlier group.[4]

There is no doubt, however, that the Venetian glassmakers and painters had direct knowledge of the famed enameled and gilded glass that was a specialty of Islamic craftsmen (see cats. 151–53). This is confirmed not only by the long history of importation of both cullet and raw materials from the Near East but also by scientific analyses of the composition of the glass and the enamels.[5] That one of the surviving beakers depicts a caravan-like sequence of three camels around its walls (cat. 158) is a wonderful reminder of the ancestral place of production of these objects, the mercantile nature of its transmission, and the way such an image echoed on the lagoon.[6]

A similar iconographic parallel can be postulated for one of the better preserved and most accomplished beakers of the group (cat. 157) representing an interpretation of the ancient classical image of the griffin that became popular in medieval Islamic art and was subsequently transmitted to Europe, where it turned into a powerful heraldic symbol. Here, the Venetian painter chose a profile view of the mythical half-lion/half-eagle beast, using a fanciful range of five colors (black, white, red, green, and yellow) to depict a lion's body with a long curling tail and a bird's forepart with spread wings. The Ancient Greek, Byzantine, Near Eastern, and later Islamic lion's forepaws of the griffin are here replaced with naively drawn eagle's claws, thus giving the impression that the beast is composed of two separate halves rather than being a truly hybrid animal.[7] This is the most common medieval European iconography of the griffin, a transformation that may have happened in Norman or Swabian Southern Italy in the 12th century, and this Venetian beaker represents an early example of such image.[8] An Islamic connection is stressed by the slender, elegant profile of the object, a typical Near Eastern shape that became popular in the late 12th and 13th centuries for drinking vessels that were often produced in sets of four or more glasses of different sizes nesting into one another (see cat. 151).[9] The nearly perfect state of preservation of the object in Frankfurt, which is shared with only two other known beakers (including cat. 156), points to the high esteem in which these objects were held over the centuries. This work used to be in the collection of the Hohenzollern princely family in Sigmaringen, Germany, and while its earlier history is unknown, one of these three well-preserved beakers, similar to an Islamic glass once treasured in a Central Italian church, was found behind the altar of St. Anthony in St. Thomas's Church in the Swiss town of Sevgein.[10] In ecclesiastical settings, these beakers may have assumed a role in the Mass. The Frankfurt beaker is one of several with the Latin inscription, *AVE MARIA GRATIA PLENA* (Hail Mary, full of grace), Archangel Gabriel's greeting to the Virgin during the Annunciation, here written in white letters below the rim.

Definitely more secular in tone is the most famous object of this group (cat. 156), the so-called Aldrevandin Beaker after its maker's or painter's signature copied in the same kind of band as Gabriel's salutation on the Frankfurt piece (*MAGISTER ALDREVANDIN ME FECI[T]* (Master Aldrevandin made me).[11] Paying homage to this object, acquired in Munich in 1876, these enameled works are often labeled today as "the Aldrevandin group" replacing Lamm's obsolete "Syro-Frankish" definition. Its artistic intent is rather removed from the Islamic models, both in its stockier profile and in the choice of European, although possibly meaningless,[12] coats of arms in the shape of pointed shields.

Unquestionably linked to a powerful Italian family is the fragmentary beaker that was excavated in the Cortile del Tribunale in Verona in 1982 (cat. 159), the object of this group that provides the most compelling archaeological evidence for a Venetian production, given Venice's geographical and political proximity to Verona and to the della Scala (or Scaligeri) family (see also cat. 68). The object can be reconstructed as originally including three pointed shields around its walls, which depict a gold ladder (*scala* in Italian) set vertically against a red field.[13] Its shape, slender with a splayed opening, together with the use of gilding, suggests a close connection with Islamic models. On the other hand, the use of less expensive yellow enamel in place of gold for most of its decoration and the indisputable political and diplomatic implication between Venice and Verona make this object entirely European, thus exemplifying the exchange and transition between the two great Eastern and Western glassmaking traditions.

1 Lamm 1929–30, pp. 278–79, pl. 99; Lamm 1941, pp. 77–99. For a general discussion of this group, see also Carboni and Barovier's essay in the present volume.
2 Zecchin 1969, 1970, 1973.
3 Baumgartner and Krueger 1988, pp. 126–60, nos. 72–119; Krueger 1998, p. 109.
4 Carboni 1998, esp. note 16.
5 See Verità's essay in the present volume.
6 A similar representation of a camel is carved in relief on a marble slab inserted on the façade of Palazzo Mastelli around the corner from Campo dei Mori ("of the Moors", traditionally identified as the three Mastelli brothers Rioba, Sandi, and Alfani, three merchants from Morea, Greece who arrived in Venice in the early 12th century). See also cat. 156, illustrated on p. 257.
7 According to the *Bestiario moralizzato*, a text compiled in the 13th or 14th century, the griffin is indeed described as having the rear of a lion and the fore of an eagle *(". . . l'arieri parte sì come leone, davante snbla l'aquilia volante")*; cited in Morini 1996, p. 509.
8 The relationship between the Islamic lion-legged griffin and the Medieval European equivalent with eagle's claws does not seem to have been properly studied. For a general background, see Nigg 1982 and Armour 1995.
9 Carboni 2001, pp. 334–35, cat. 87.
10 Baumgartner and Krueger 1988, p. 129, cat. 72. The beaker, now in the Treasury of the Cathedral of Chur, Switzerland, depicts three figures praying under arches. The Islamic beaker from a church in Orvieto is presently in the Louvre (inv. OA 6131); recently published in Paris 2001, p. 191, cat. 204.
11 See Carboni and Whitehouse 2001, pp. 302–3, cat. 151 (with bibliography).
12 The fact that there are three different shields, two of which seem to be related to Swabian families, makes it unlikely that it represents a specific commission; see Carboni and Whitehouse 2001, p. 303.
13 Most recently published in Baumgartner and Krueger 1988, p. 151, cat. 106; Carboni 1998, fig. 23.2.

160-161.

160. *Goblet*

Venice, late 15th century
Mold-blown colorless glass, tooled, enameled and gilded; applied foot
H. 16 cm (6 5/16 in.); Diam. 10 cm (4 in.)
Victoria and Albert Museum, London
Inv. 7536-1861 (ill. p. 260)

161. *Beaker*

Venice, late 15th century
Free-blown colorless glass, tooled, enameled and gilded; applied base
H. 10 cm (4 in.); Diam. 8 cm (3 3/16 in.)
Corning Museum of Glass, Corning, New York
Inv. 55.3.12 (ill. p. 264)

A distinctive type of drinking vessel produced in Venice in the wake of Angelo Barovier's "invention" of *cristallo* in the mid-15th century[1] is the clear-glass tumbler or goblet with a pinched "crown" at the base, a diamond or lattice pattern in relief (usually called *nipt-diamond-waies)* with enameled and gilded dots around the body filled,[2] and simple floral patterns on the rim.[3] Zecchin has convincingly argued that the creation of *cristallo* provided a new impetus in the last quarter of the 15th century for enameled glass,[4] a technique that Venetians had learned from Islamic craftsmen in the late 13th century, but which had largely fallen out of fashion in Venice by the late 14th century (see cats. 156–59).

Unquestionably Venetian in character, especially the tall bell-shaped foot in dark blue glass sprinkled with gold on the goblet in the Victoria and Albert Museum (cat. 160),[5] the group of drinking vessels also includes a handful of beakers, represented here by the one in the Corning Museum (cat. 161), with a reputed archaeological provenance from a Jewish cemetery in Damascus.[6] A specific link to the Jewish community in Damascus is only hearsay, although if true it would open a fascinating window on the ties between Venetian and Levantine Jews and their trading deals.[7] A Syrian provenance, however, seems more probable and can be supported with evidence from a few different sources. It has yet to be determined whether these vessels were diplomatic gifts, similar to a vase-shaped lamp sent to Damascus and mentioned in a document of 1480;[8] specific requests from the Mamluk elite in Damascus (like the mosque lamps and the *cesendelli* obtained in Ottoman Istanbul, see cats. 164–65, 169–71); or if they were simply luxury export objects. Whatever the answer, their significance lies mainly in the fact that they provide the earliest link in the chain of steady trade of Venetian glass in the Near East after Venice's glassmaking industry took an indisputable lead in the Mediterranean. The Ottomans were especially fond of Venetian glass, but these tumblers suggest that the late Mamluk elite enjoyed it as well. Especially in Syria, the Venetian vessels would have reminded consumers of their own great tradition of enameled and gilded glass, which was, in the 15th century, still a recent memory.

SC

1 *Cristallo* is a nearly colorless, bubble-free glass whose recipe was mastered by the famous Venetian glassmaker around 1450 and soon became a most prized export to Europe. See Zecchin 1967.
2 Or "nipped diamond-wise." The term was used for the first time by the glassmaker George Ravenscroft in London in his price list of 1677.
3 The floral motif is often the so-called lily-of-the-valley (see also cat. 163).
4 Zecchin 1968, p. 22.
5 Compare also the foot of the mosque lamp in Istanbul, cat. 171.
6 Charleston (1965, p. 161, pl. 49) mentions four of them and updates the number in Charleston 1974, pp. 245–48, also including a few fragments; see also Carboni 1989, p. 154. The airport road was paved over the Jewish cemetery in Damascus in the 1950s–60s and these glass beakers may have surfaced at that time.
7 See also Curatola's essay in the present volume.
8 Zecchin 1968a, p. 19; Carboni 1989, p. 150. The lamp was given by the traveler Santo Brasca (ca. 1444–1512) from Milan, to the Mamluk sultan Qa'itbey's representative in Damascus. His *Viaggio in Terrasanta* was published in 1481 and the most recent edition was edited by A. L. Momigliano Lepschy (Milan, 1966).

• 162. *Mosque lamp*

Probably Venice, late 15th–early 16th century
Free-blown glass tooled on the pontil; applied foot and suspension loops
H. 23.6 cm (9 1/4 in.); Diam. 17.7 cm max. (7 in.)
Victoria and Albert Museum, London
Inv. 332-1900 (ill. p. 260)

Mamluk mosque lamps made in the glass factories of Cairo are characterized by a large enameled and gilded vase with a splayed foot and suspension rings; they are also often inscribed with a sultan's or emir's name (cats. 152–53). While sharing the same distinctive shape, several mosque lamps in the Museum of Islamic Art in Cairo are by comparison rather plain. Faint traces of gilding exist on some examples, but otherwise they are either transparent with a slight yellow tinge or made of deep blue glass.[1] In the 19th century, these less ornate lamps were removed from several buildings in Egypt, namely, the mosque and *madrasa* of the sultan Qansuh al-Ghuri (the next to last Mamluk ruler before the advent of the Ottomans) built in 1503; the mausoleum of Imam Shafiʿi in Cairo; the mosque of Shaykh Ahmad Dar Tuqa in Rashid (Rosetta) on the Nile Delta; and the mosque of Sidi Sariya (also known as Süleyman Pasha al-Khadim) built in 1528 in the Cairo Citadel.[2]

Only a chemical analysis of the plain lamps in the Cairo museum could help us to determine whether they are of Mamluk or Venetian manufacture, yet, given the historical developments in the glassmaking industry in the late 15th and early 16th centuries, the latter now appears the most likely. The number of Venetian embassies to Cairo intensified in this period, almost as if merchants and diplomats felt the urgency of concluding deals and ratifying treaties before the inevitable Ottoman conquest of the Mamluk Empire occurred. At the same time, the Murano glass industry became the leader in the Mediterranean and its factories were exporting all kinds of luxury objects, including the enameled and gilded products that were once the pride of the Mamluk glassmakers (see cats. 160–61). There are no specific records indicating that Venetian glass lamps were ordered by Sultan Qansuh al-Ghuri's emissaries or that they were diplomatic gifts from the doge, but the late 15th and the early 16th centuries are most likely the period that Venice initiated its successful strategy for exporting lighting devices for religious and secular buildings to Islamic regions, including, at a slightly later date, Ottoman Istanbul (cats. 169–71).[3]

The mosque lamp in the Victoria and Albert Museum presented here, which is in many ways comparable to the transparent lamps in Cairo, as well as to one in the Museum of Turkish and Islamic Art in Istanbul,[4] seems to be of Venetian origin as well. The London lamp is colorless with a slight grayish tinge and has a conical "kick" (created by the pontil) at the base, a typical characteristic of European glass. Formerly in the Myers Collection, this lamp and one like it with a taller neck have been catalogued by the museum as "made for the Oriental market."[5]

SC

1 I had the opportunity to study four of these lamps (two are colorless, the other two are blue) plus two fragmentary blue ones in the storeroom of the museum (inv. nos. 1642, 3358, 2339, 2401, 2340, and 2341, respectively).
2 Wiet 1929 (pp. 116–17, 119–20, 127) where they are mentioned but not illustrated.
3 A document of 1466, for example, mentions that the Egyptian sultan asked for window glass from Venice in exchange of his gift of various valuable perfumes and spices. See Zecchin 1980, year 1466.
4 Inv. 1025; see also cats. 169–70.
5 The other lamp is inv. no. 331-1900.

163. *Mosque lamp*

Possibly Venice, ca. 1500
Free-blown and partly blown in a dip mold (*mezzaforma* technique); applied foot and suspension loops; enameled and gilded
H. 30.5 cm (12 in.), Diam. 18.4 cm (7 1/4 in.)
Museum Kunst Palast, Glasmuseum Hentrich, Düsseldorf
Inv. P1978-1 (Ill. p. 69)

This elaborately ornamented mosque lamp has been attributed either to Venice or to Barcelona, the two most important glass enameling centers of Renaissance Europe, with a general consensus that it can be dated to the very beginning of the 16th century. A few of the lamp's features are common to both glassmaking traditions, including the purple foot and the applied rings, the enameled "lily-of-the-valley" pattern set vertically along the ribs, and the band of tiny colored dots in the horizontal band at the base of the neck (see also cats. 160–61).[1] The ornamentation of the neck, especially the pseudo-inscriptional Arabic band near the opening, may fit better within the Islamicized environment of the Iberian peninsula. The complex manufacturing and decorative techniques, however, tip the balance in favor of a Venetian production, and specifically one made for export to the fading Mamluk dynasty. In this respect it is similar to the plain mosque lamp in this exhibition (cat. 162), but like the typical Islamic mosque lamp this example is enameled and gilded.[2] David Whitehouse has provided a detailed explanation of how the ribs of this lamp were created in a "half-mold" (*mezza forma* or *mezza stampaura,* a typical Venetian technique in use from the 15th century inherited from the Roman glass tradition), which allowed only the lower section of the body to be impressed with vertical ribs.[3]

This kind of decoration was carried out in three stages—first the gold foil, second the enamels, and third the liquid gold—all fired while the object was held at the end of the pontil and slowly rotated at the mouth of the kiln (the glory hole), a technique acquired from the Islamic glassmakers probably as early as the late 13th century (see cat. 156–59).

At some point in its history, this lamp was broken into many pieces, but has since been repaired. Most of the foot is a replacement, and much of the original gilding is now lost; its surface as well as the enamels, however, are still in good condition and allow a proper understanding of its original decorative program. The lamp survives as a very rare example of a European, most likely Venetian, glassmaker's effort to imitate the great Islamic tradition of enameled and gilded glass in the 16th century.

SC

1 For example, see Frothingham 1964, pls. 3–9; Tait 1991, figs. 199, 204.
2 Another, rather different, enameled lamp in the name of the sultan Qa'itbey (r. 1468–96) today in the Museum of Islamic Art in Cairo, represents another yet unresolved problem of attribution. It may well be that the Qa'itbey lamp is the last gasp of a dying Egyptian tradition whereas the object in Düsseldorf is the earliest known work of the rising European one. See Carboni 2004, pp. 73–75.
3 Carboni and Whitehouse 2001, pp. 304–5 cat. 152.

164–65. *Two hanging lamps (cesendelli)*

Venice, late 15th - early 16th century
Free-blown colorless glass, enameled and gilded; applied finial

°164.

H. 28.5 cm (11 1/4 in.); Diam. 7 cm (2 3/4 in.)
Museo Vetrario, Murano, Venice
Inv. Cl. VI, no. 2 (ill. p. 267)

165.

H. 36.2 cm (14 1/4 in.); Diam. 12.5 cm (5 in.)
The Metropolitan Museum of Art, New York
Rogers Fund, 1914
Inv. 14.83 (ill. p. 270)

The same document that includes a drawing of the mosque lamps requested by the Ottoman vizier Mehmet Sokollu Pasha in 1569 (see cats. 169–70) also contains a sketch of a long cylindrical hanging lamp with a decorative finial at the base and a splayed mouth that provides a protruding circle meant to accommodate a metal ring for suspension; this ring was then either attached to chains and hung from a ceiling or a niche, or soldered to a bracket and attached to a wall. This type of lamp was a common element in bronze chandeliers (in the shape of a large disk with a number of holes pierced in it, inside which were placed cylindrical glass lamps) in Roman and Byzantine times and also later in the Islamic world. In Renaissance Venice, this small lamp, called *cicindela* or "firefly" in Latin, developed into a fairly large object that constituted a lighting device on its own, still retaining the meaning of its original name as *zexendelo*[1] or *cesendello* (as it is now most commonly known). In the 1569 document in the Venetian State Archives mentioned above, the *bailo* Marcantonio Barbaro notes that the Ottoman vizier wanted to obtain from Murano "300 [lamps] of the elongated shape sketched below plus 300 more of the same type, only one-half bigger" (fig. 12, p. 270).[2]

In Venice, *cesendelli* were used both as votive lamps, as evident from many late 15th- and 16th-century paintings illustrating one above an altar and before the altarpiece,[3] and as private and public illumination. Even today, there is a *cesendello* hanging from every arch of the *Procuratorie,* the building that surrounds three sides of the city's Piazza San Marco.

Both the devotional and the secular uses of *cesendelli* are evident from these two objects, which represent the only two such works from the late 15th- or early 16th century to have survived until the present day. The *cesendello* today in the Metropolitan Museum of Art (cat. 165) depicts the Annunciation; the religious subject matter with Eucharistic connotations suggests that it was likely made for the private chapel of a Venetian family.[4] The lamp in the Museo Vetrario (cat. 164), instead, bears the arms of the powerful Tiepolo family set against a pattern of colored dots-and-scales typical of 15th- and 16th-century Muranese glass painters. Although it, too, could have been for an altar sponsored by the Tiepolo, it most likely was one of a pair, or one of a series, that illuminated and decorated the main entrance or the *piano nobile* of one of the family's palaces on the Grand Canal.

Definitely popular in Venice, these hanging lamps were without a doubt also fashionable in Istanbul, judging from Mehmet Sokollu Pasha's large order by of 1569 and from the specific mention of *cesendelli alla turchesca* in another document of the same year.[5] Providing further proof of their popularity among the Ottomans, a *cesendello* literally hangs from the sky in Bartolomeo Georgievitz's engraving *Libellus . . . de diversas res turcharum . . .* (The Booklet . . . of Various Turkish Matters . . .) published in Rome in 1552, which illustrates an open-air scene with Turks around a large fountain and a building in the foreground.[6] In the Topkapı Palace Museum, in addition to the Venetian mosque lamps with or without *redeselli* decoration (cats. 169–71), there are also two *cesendelli* with the same shape, including the bulbous finial, as the one sketched in 1569 and the two examples presented here. The decoration of these lamps consists of colorful vertical *redeselli* (white, red, and blue), and they are also rather tall (ca. 35 cm), neatly matching Barbaro's descriptions of objects ". . . of the same type, only one-half bigger" and "partly in plain glass and partly decorated *a redeselli.*"[7]

SC

1 Zecchin (1970, p. 26) quotes a document from 1469 mentioning *zexendeli da tre maneghi,* or "*cesendelli* with three handles," implying that they had suspension rings (similarly to the mosque lamps) rather than made to hang from a metal ring.
2 *". . . altri 300 della forma longa qui apresso disegnata, et altri 300 la mità piu grandi della sorte di questi longhi . . ."* ASV, *Deliberazioni del Senato – Secreta III – Costantinopoli,* filza 4ff, fol. 105v.
3 Just to mention two examples, Giovanni Bellini's *Madonna Enthroned with Saints* in the Church of San Zaccaria and Carpaccio's *Presentation in the Temple* now in the Gallerie dell'Accademia and originally in the Scuola degli Albanesi.
4 Some doubts have been raised suggesting that the enameled decoration may have been added at a later period, based on some iconographic details. A close inspection of the object by Lisa Pilosi, Conservator, revealed that the enamels seem to be consistent with a 16th-century attribution and there is no evidence of later firing of the object.
5 Zecchin 1970, p. 26.
6 Carboni 1989, p. 153, fig. 14.
7 Charleston 1966, p. 19; Carboni 1989, p. 152. A third similar *cesendello* was acquired by the Victoria and Albert Museum in 1964 (inv. 19-1965).

166. *Ewer*

Venice, early 16th century
Blown and tooled glass with enameled and gilded decoration; applied foot and handle
H. ca. 25 cm (10 in.)
Musée du Louvre, Département des Objets d'art, Paris
Inv. R104 (ill. p. 266)

Like the pilgrim flask (cat. 167), this enameled and gilded ewer exemplifies the exuberant creations of the glass painters of early 16th-century Venice.[1] The narrow and flared neck, the trailed double-rib collar below the rim, and the splayed foot distinguish its profile from the common Islamic shape, which has a low foot and a straight neck (see cats. 108, 154).[2] The lower end of the gilded handle, formed into a loop, was pulled out creating a grooved tail, a distinctive trait of these 16th-century ewers.[3]

The decoration is mainly floral and shares a few details with the "mosque" lamp in Düsseldorf, perhaps made in Venice for export to Mamluk Cairo (cat. 163), including the prominent lily-of-the-valley (*zigli* o *zii* in Venetian dialect)[4] motif that encircles the body at its widest point. The ornamentation around the neck is also comparable to the lamp in Germany with its bands of tiny colored dots on the top and bottom, the gilded patterns in the background, and the enameled circular medallions drawn at regular intervals within the main field. In general, the overall decoration is attuned to the geometric arrangement of the otherwise freely drawn vegetal patterns typical of Islamic art.

SC

1 Lanmon and Whitehouse 1993, fig. 3.5.
2 A few of these Venetian jugs are closer in profile to the Islamic models, such as one in the Museo della Certosa di San Martino in Naples; Carboni 1989, fig. 11. Another variation is that these jugs may have a trefoil-shaped mouth similar to the Greek *oinochoe,* which became fashionable also in maiolica examples in Italy; Lanmon and Whitehouse 1993, pp. 24–26, cat. 5 and figs. 5.1–5.2.
3 See two ewers in the Lehman Collection of The Metropolitan Museum (1975.1.1172 and 1975.1.1170); Lanmon and Whitehouse 1993, pp. 16–20, 24–26, cats. 3, 5, with additional examples.
4 See Barovier's and Carboni's essay in this volume.

167. *Pilgrim flask*

Venice, ca. 1500–25
Free-blown, tooled, enameled, and gilded colorless glass; applied foot and suspension loops
H. 31.4 cm (12 3/8 in.)
The Metropolitan Museum of Art, New York
Robert Lehman Collection, 1975
Inv. 1975.1.1167 (ill. p. 54)

The term "pilgrim flask" applies to bottles with compressed circular bodies that were originally inspired by similarly shaped leather or metal vessels, worn on the belt of ancient travelers to provide an emergency water supply. By adding a foot to help it stand upright, an elongated neck, and ornamentation, craftsmen transformed the flask into a purely decorative object, with the only allusions to the original function being the shape of the body and the small suspension loops. The pilgrim flask became so popular across different cultures and continents in the late medieval period that one can cite examples in pottery in Ilkhanid Iran (1256–1353),[1] in silver in 14th-century France,[2] and in enameled copper in Ming China.[3]

Even though the pilgrim flask had long been known in Europe, late 15th- and early 16th-century Venetian pilgrim flasks appear to have been influenced by Islamic examples not only in terms of shape but also as part of the general trend to incorporate foliate and floral patterns in the glassmakers' enameled and gilded works. Furthermore, in this period Venetian pilgrim flasks were made in pairs to celebrate marriages and specifically to wish fortune and prosperity on the newlyweds (especially when filled with good wine),[4] which recalls the astrological and therefore apotropaic and well-wishing significance of this kind of vessel in Islamic cultures.[5]

In Venice, the pilgrim flask was called *inghistera fracada* (*inghistera* being the general term for a bottle, *fracada* meaning "compressed"), as archival documents attest. All kinds of decorative types and techniques were used to ornament these vessels, including gilding alone, enameling on clear and *lattimo* glass,[6] *nipt-diamond-waies* patterns (see cats. 160–61), and *a redeselli* (see cats. 169–70). The *inghistera fracada* in the Lehman Collection provides an excellent example of the evolution of the decoration from medallion-like portraits of couples, to coats of arms of Venetian and German families, to exuberant vegetal patterns that make use of the designs available in the early 16th century, including Islamicizing *rabesche.*

SC

1 One example is in The Metropolitan Museum of Art, inv. 57.164; Carboni 1997, pp. 36–37, cat. 15.
2 Ottomeyer and Völker 2002, p. 189, cat. 88.
3 Giurescu Heller 2002, p. 88, cat. 28.
4 The most famous pair of Venetian pilgrim flasks are those still preserved in the Museo Civico di Arte Medievale in Bologna (inv. 1364, 1365), probably ordered to celebrate the marriage of Alessandro Bentivoglio and Ippolita Sforza in 1492. Recently, see Barovier Mentasti 1982, p. 62, fig. 43; Carboni 1989, pp. 154-55, fig. 16.
5 Carboni 2003, pp. 174–76.
6 On *lattimo,* see Barovier's and Carboni's essay in this volume.

168. *Ewer*

Venice, early 16th century
Free blown and tooled with applied foot, spout, and handle
H. 29.9 cm (11 3/4in.); Diam. 14.8 cm (5 3/4 in.)
The Corning Museum of Glass, Corning, New York
Inv. no. 2001.3.56 (ill. p. 261)

Because of their similarity to the translucent or milky grayish quartz found in the ancient city of Chalcedon in Asia Minor, marbleized colored glass objects such as this ewer are termed "calcedonio" or chalcedony. *Calcedonio* glass was reputedly invented around 1450–55 in Venice, the same period as the discovery of the formula for *cristallo* (see cats. 160–61), clearly a time of great creativity for the Murano glassmakers.

Together with enameled *cristallo* vessels, *calcedonio* was the most precious and expensive type of Venetian glass exported to Ottoman Istanbul as early as the second half of the 15th century. An interesting letter sent on April 28, 1473 from the Venetian merchant Antonio di Coradi, settled in Istanbul, to his brother-in-law and partner, at home in Venice, mentions that he wants to receive "large undecorated beakers with their lid, footed bowls, footless bowls, and jugs also in *cristallino* glass (of every type and color [white, green, red], and *calcedonio*)."[1] In Turkey, the merchant was hoping to sell these items *"il 300 per 100,"* or three times the original cost. Probably because of the difficult process involved, *calcedonio* glass generally commanded high prices even in Italy; two years later 11 vessels of this type produced in the furnace of Bartolomeo d'Angelo were sold and sent to Florence for 55 ducats.[2]

Although the present knowledge of glassmaking in Ottoman Turkey is very scant, the export of *calcedonio* and *lattimo* ("milky", or white opaque) glass from Venice may have stimulated the production of a number of flasks, with long necks, that seem to imitate the colors and textures of the Venetian examples and that have not yet found a precise attribution.[3]

The shape of this ewer, one of the most accomplished examples of early Venetian *calcedonio* glass, is Western and has perhaps little to do with Islamic models. It can be related, however, to a small group of vessels of similar shape in inlaid metal that combine the typical surface patterns of the so-called Mahmud al-Kurdi group and a Gothicizing handle and spout. One of these metal ewers bears the arms of the Molino family from Venice and it is assumed that they were created on the city on the lagoon for export to Northern Europe.[4]

SC

1 *"Goti grandi schieti, con el suo choverchio, taze, piadene sanze pie, ramini de vedro pur chrestalini schieti ... de chalzedonio."* Cited in Zecchin 1980, under year 1473. The term *ramini,* translated by Zecchin as "jugs," may also refer to the use of cuprous oxides (*ramina,* CuO and Cu_2O) that were used to obtain translucent red and aquamarine glass.
2 Zecchin 1980, under year 1473, citing Spallanzani 1978a, p. 165.
3 Few examples have been published, but they are found today in several collections around the world. See, for example, Rogers 1983, pl. 64, nos. 1–3; Jenkins 1986, p. 49, no. 55; Goldstein 2005, p. 298, no. 319.
4 See Liefkes (1997, pp. 50–51, figs. 54–55) who compares a *calcedonio* example that is very similar to the present object in the Corning Museum and the "Molino" ewer, both in the Victoria and Albert Museum, London.

169–70. *Two mosque lamps*

Venice, 16th century
Free-blown colorless glass decorated with twisted opaque white canes (*redeselli*) in the glass body; gilded on the surface; applied suspension rings
Dimensions: one is H. 28 cm (11 in.)
Topkapı Sarayi Müzesi, Istanbul
Inv. 34/468
(cat. 169, ill. p. 271; cat. 170, ill. p. 98)

Together the Topkapı Palace Museum and the Museum of Turkish and Islamic Art in Istanbul hold the largest collection of Venetian mosque lamps made for export to the Islamic world from the 16th century and later.[1] Numerous archival documents attest that the Ottoman court and their retinue were among the most avid consumers of the celebrated works created by the Murano factories and that there was a constant influx of glass objects from Venice, at least until the local Beykoz factories were established near Istanbul at the end of the 18th century.[2]

The most famous of these documents—because it includes actual drawings of the objects (fig. 11, p. 270)—is today in the Archivio di Stato of Venice. In the memorandum, the Venetian *bailo* Marcantonio Barbaro scribbled the request of 300 mosque lamps by the Ottoman vizier Mehmet Sokollu Pasha in 1569. Barbaro, or the vizier himself, drew the familiar shape of a lamp with a low tapered foot, a bulbous stocky vase, and a large splayed neck.[3]

In reference to the two lamps discussed here, the most interesting piece of information in Barbaro's note is that a total 900 lamps, including 600 *cesendelli* (see cats. 164–65), were meant to be "partly in plain glass and partly decorated *'a redeselli'* [lit. 'with fine nets']."[4] The term *redeselli* (or *filigrana*) refers to fine opaque glass canes that are manipulated and twisted in order to obtain a delicate pattern resembling a web or net, which are then worked into a glass object to create vertical or spiraling decorative designs. This is clearly the case for the two lamps in Istanbul with white *redeselli,* one of which includes a vertical pattern, whereas in the other the canes were twisted around the entire surface of the object. A Venetian origin is therefore certain, although it is not possible to establish whether the objects represent the sole survivors from the Barbaro-Sokollu Pasha transaction of 1569 or from another earlier or later shipment.

The Venice document succinctly describes the shape and type of glass requested but makes no mention that the surface of lamps were to be decorated with gilded patterns, as is the case with these two objects. It is possible that glass painters in Venice may have "improved" the aspect of the lamps made for export to the Ottomans by painting over in gold (and white enamel in the case of cat. 170) the typical floral and vegetal patterns they were familiar with from imported Iznik pottery (see cats. 174–75) as well as the many Venetian works inspired by such models. The combination of a bold, striking decoration such as that of the *redeselli* and a gilded, equally bold, pattern that provides a visual dissonance with the object itself, however, is not likely Venetian, therefore suggesting that the surface decoration was probably added in Istanbul at a later date. Two other lamps in Istanbul—one in the Topkapı Palace Museum, the other in the Turkish and Islamic Museum—show *redeselli* decoration but no gilding, further suggesting that the Ottomans received lamps, from Venice, whose surfaces were originally undecorated.[5]

SC

1 The only brief surveys of Venetian lamps in the Topkapı Sarayi are Rückert 1963, where five lamps are illustrated, including cat. 170 (fig. 7), and Charleston 1964, pp. 166–67, pl. 52a, b. Seven of them are usually on display in a case, including the present two as well as cat. 171. Five Venetian lamps are displayed in the Turkish and Islamic Art Museum nearby.
2 For archival documents, see Rogers 1983; see also the essay by Raby and the one by Barovier and Carboni in this volume. For Beykoz ware, see Bayramoğlu 1976; Carboni and Whitehouse 2001, pp. 280–81, 293–95, cat. 148–50.
3 Carboni 1989, fig. 7; see also Raby's essay in this volume.
4 *". . . si che in tutto siano 900 parte schietti et parte a redeselli."*
5 A stronger argument for a later addition could be made after a close inspection of the lamps in order to determine if the gilding was fixed without reheating the objects, as one would expect if they were decorated in Istanbul. Rückert (1963, p. 226) thought so, describing the technique as *"kalter Bemalung,"* or "cold enameling."

171. *Mosque lamp*

Venice, 16th century
Mold-blown colorless glass; applied foot in green glass with gold; applied suspension rings in blue glass; metal chains
H. 30 cm (11 3/4 in.)
Topkapı Sarayi Müsezi, Istanbul
(ill. p. 271)

Another type of mosque lamp that constituted a common Venetian export to Ottoman Istanbul during the 16th and 17th centuries was blown in a ribbed mold. Compared to the two lamps decorated *a redeselli* (cats. 169–70), this kind of lamp is unmistakably Renaissance European in character, with its tall bell-shaped foot, gracious profile, flaring neck, and wide open mouth, almost as if it were a flower vase rather than a lighting device. The chromatic contrast of the dark-colored foot decorated with gold leaf, dark suspension rings (in the present case, unusually of different colors, emerald green and dark blue), and a clear *cristallo* body are also typically Venetian and do not betray the fact that they were made for the Ottoman market or that they were meant to be hung in an Islamic religious setting.

Four lamps of this type are on display today in the museums of the Topkapı Palace and of Turkish and Islamic Art, including the present one,[1] and many more could probably be found in their storerooms. Except for the second one in the Topkapı, which presents a relief decoration of *"nipt-diamond-waie"* (see cats. 160–61), the other three show twisted ribs around their body and vertical ribs along the neck. Dark cobalt blue is clearly the predominant color for the foot and the suspension rings, the green foot of the present lamp providing the only exception. Two of these lamps also retain the original chains for suspension that may have been added when the objects reached their destination in the various mosques and other religious buildings for which the Ottoman elite had obtained them from Venice through a steady commercial supply.

SC

1 Published in Rückert 1963, pp. 223–26, fig. 4; see also Charleston 1965 and 1966.

CERAMICS

172. *Bowl*

Underglaze painted porcelain
China, late 15th century
Diameter: 35 cm (13 3/4 in.)
Topkapı Sarayi Müzesi, Istanbul
Inv. 15/1448 (ill. p. 88)

Chinese porcelain enjoyed extraordinary popularity in the Islamic Near East, and the large collection of it assembled by the Ottoman sultans in the Topkapı Sarayi Museum remains one of the richest in the world.[1] This Chinese porcelain bowl, with a lotus bouquet tied with a ribbon at the center and peonies around the rim, belongs to that collection, and provides important evidence of the relation between Chinese porcelain and Islamic and European, especially Venetian, pottery. The importation of Chinese blue-and-white porcelain to the Ottoman Empire reached its peak in the late 14th and 15th centuries, and at the same time Iznik potters adopted a similar style. Following the introduction of other Iznik designs in the 16th century, the blue-and-white style was largely eclipsed in Turkey, although it never disappeared entirely and copies of Chinese blue-and-white porcelain continued to be made there throughout the 16th century and after.[2]

The decoration of this plate is typical of late Ming blue-and-white porcelain produced between the end of the 15th and the beginning of the 16th centuries, much of which was intended for export to the Near East. The abstract decorative style of the wares appealed to Islamic taste.

The Ottoman Empire served as one of the principle channels through which Chinese pottery reached Europe. Italian ceramic production in turn imitated blue-and-white Ming porcelain with great freedom of interpretation. At the end of the 15th century, earthenware *alla porcellana* was made in Faenza, followed soon after by Tuscany and Venice. Blue-and-white predominated in Venice throughout the 16th century, revealing a discernable stylistic development: initially blue-and-white seemed more directly influenced by Chinese models (cats. 182–83), but from the 1540s the Ottoman manner, characterized by blue symmetrical arabesques on white (cats. 184–85), began to prevail.[3]

MAM

1 Krahl 1986.
2 Atasoy and Raby 1989, pp. 237–39.
3 Mack 2002, pp.105–7, fig. 107.

• 173. *Plate*

Iznik, Turkey, ca. 1535–45
Underglaze painted fritware
Diam. ca. 24.5 (9 3/4 in.)
The Ashmolean Museum of Art and Archaeology, Oxford
Inv. EAX.3724(ill. p. 122)

This plate belongs to a group of highly distinctive Ottoman ceramics decorated with cobalt blue stems in concentric rings against a white ground; tiny rosettes, small leaves, and semi-circular motifs sprout from the stems at regular intervals.[1] First appearing in the mid- to late 1520s, the style continued into the second half of the 16th century. The traditional appellation for these ceramics is "Golden Horn" ware although there is no evidence for their production in Istanbul. Because of the strong resemblance of its patterns to the illuminated background decoration of *tuğras*, the Ottoman imperial monograms used in official documents beginning with Sultan Süleyman the Magnificent (see cat. 49), the definition "*tuğrakeş* spiral style" is now considered more appropriate.[2]

The international Mediterranean ceramics trade resulted in a lively cross-cultural exchange of ideas, as exemplified by this Ottoman plate, which resembles an Italian *tondino* with its flat rim and semispherical cavetto (see cat. 184).[3] It is unclear whether Ottoman wares like this one were made specifically for the Italian market, as has often been suggested. What is certain, however, is that they reached Italy in significant numbers and were highly prized there. As early as the 1540s, Ottoman *tuğrakeş* spiral style ceramics were imitated in the Ligurian cities of Genoa and Savona on the northwestern coast of the Italian peninsula in addition to Venice.[4]

MAM

1 Allan 1991, pp. 68–66; Mack 2002, p. 108, fig. 111.
2 Atasoy and Raby 1989, pp. 110–13, 268; Venice 1993, p. 383.
3 For similar *tondini* with *tuğrakeş* style decoration, see Venice 1993, pp. 383–84, cat. 229.
4 Venice 1993, pp. 481–84.

174. *Fragment of a large plate*

Iznik, Turkey, ca. 1570
Underglaze painted fritware
Max. diam. ca. 10 cm (4 in.)
Museo Franchetti alla Ca'd'Oro, Venice
Collection Luigi Conton, excavated from an unknown location in the Venetian lagoon
Inv. C 3133 (ill. p. 63)

This fragment, made of an alkaline fritware, features decoration typical of late Iznik ceramics at the end of the 16th century, also known, misleadingly, as "Rhodian ware.[1]"The fragment was probably part of a large ceremonial platter set on a round foot with a polychrome decoration of vines curling around a serrated *saz* leaf. The pigments were cobalt blue, bluish green, and a red in slight relief (Armenian bole) with black outlining along the edges of the design.

Iznik (ancient Nicaea) was the most important center of ceramic production during the Ottoman period. Dishes were first painted in blue on a white ground (second half of the 15th century) then, from the mid-16th century onwards, were made in a great variety of forms (plates, bowls, flasks, bottles—sometimes large in size) characterized by an extraordinary profusion of decoration. Turkish workshops specialized in the production of tiles with floral motifs (tulips, carnations, small roses, hyacinths, peonies, and saz), designed to adorn walls, for which a characteristic red lacquer, or Armenian bole, was used.

A fairly large number of fragments of this type, now preserved in the Galleria G. Franchetti alla Ca' d'Oro, were found in the lagoon, testifying to the importance of Venetian importation of Anatolian ceramics in the late 16th and the 17th centuries.

FS

1 Atasoy and Raby 1989; Venice 1993, pp. 381–82 , cat. 230–234.

175. *Plate*

Iznik, Turkey, ca. 1575
Underglaze painted fritware
Diam. 36 cm (14 1/8 in.)
Scuola Grande di San Rocco, Venice
Inv. 96/c[1] (ill. p. 238)

Ottoman ceramic production is closely associated with its most important center, Iznik, whose brilliantly painted luxury wares appealed to both Ottoman and Western European tastes. This plate is indicative of the chromatic variety of Iznik ware in the second half of the 16th century, when thick red Armenian bole was added to the traditional palette of blues and greens. The decoration of the interior of this plate, a relatively recent but significant acquisition of the Scuola Grande di San Rocco (see also cat. 81), consists of a bouquet of carnations, tulips, and hyacinths springing from a tuft of leaves at the base and symmetrically arranged to fill the plate's inner surface. A stylized "wave-and-rock" border of Chinese inspiration decorates the narrow rim (see cats. 172, 176).

After the battle of Lepanto in 1571, European imports of Iznik ware increased and their popularity inspired interesting local imitations, including most importantly "Candiana" ware in the Veneto (cats. 188–92),[2] which closely copied Ottoman models but never successfully employed Armenian bole.

FL

1 Formerly in the Bisacco-Palazzi Collection, acquired in the early 20th century.
2 Fontana 1989; Mack 2002, pp. 107–11.

176. *Plate*

Iznik, Turkey, ca. 1580
Underglaze painted fritware
H. 5.2 (2 in.); Diam. 31 cm (12 1/4 in.)
Musée National de la Renaissance, Château d'Écouen
Inv. E.Cl8432 (Ill. p. 288)

Ottoman ceramic production reached its highest peak in the second half of the 16th century during Sultan Süleyman the Magnificent's reign. At this time Iznik potters developed a slip that did run around the glaze, which allowed them to use red pigment, a notoriously unstable color, successfully for the first time. The so-called Armenian bole red was obtained with high-ferrous clay that gave the color its intense coral hue and a density that results in relief decoration.[1] This red color characterized Iznik production for over a century. With its use came a new style called *quatre fleurs,* a combination of tulips, carnations, roses, and hyacinths, as can be seen in the present example. Compared to the *saz* style (see cat. 174), from which it originated, this new floral style was much more naturalistic. The "wave-and-rock" border, derived from Chinese porcelain decoration, also became common on plates from the third quarter of the 16th century (see cat. 175). This plate represents a classic example of the Iznik production during the reigns of the sultans Selim II (1566–74) and Murad III (1574–95).

MAM

1 The term *bolo armeno* was used by Cipriano Piccolpasso in his treatise *Li tre libri dell'arte del vasaio* ("The Three Books of the Art of the Potter"), written in Italy about 1550 (G. Conti [ed.], Florence, 1976).

177. *Bowl*

Iznik, Turkey, last quarter of the 16th century
Undeglaze painted fritware
H. 7cm (2 3/4 in.); Diam. 34 cm (13 3/8 in.)
Staatliche Museen zu Berlin, Kunstgewerbemuseum, Berlin
Inv. 1982.130 (ill. p. 289)

This Iznik bowl is roughly contemporaneous with the two previous examples (cats. 175–76) and very similar in design and composition, with its rock-and-wave border and the *saz* leaf that dominates the design like a feather floating in the foreground.[1] The sprigs that depart from the tuft of grass at the bottom include the familiar flora of carnations, tulips, and smaller flowers. Slightly different, however, is the use of color, here more contained and restricted to smaller areas and the effort to draw finer stems and leaves, which results in a less crowded design that grants greater prominence to the bright white background.

The potters from the Veneto who were responsible for the "Candiana" production (cats. 188–92) seem to have combined a taste for this type of finer stems and leaves with large flowers, which makes the design of many of the Italian wares seem oddly imbalanced in comparison to their Ottoman exemplars.

SC

1 Published in Mack 2002, p. 109, fig. 114.

178. *Bowl*

Iznik, Turkey, 17th century
Underglaze painted fritware
Diam. 43.5 cm (17 1/8 in.); H. 17.5 cm (6 7/8 in.)
Museo Civico Correr, Venice
Inv. CL. 1, V.70 (ill. p. 131)

In the 17th century the quality of the ceramic production in Iznik began to decline for several reasons. Initially, the Ottoman court, Iznik's great patron, complained that potters failed to fulfill orders; later, court patronage dwindled as fewer tiled royal buildings were commissioned. Reacting to imperial firmans issued from Istanbul that limited control over their products and fixed prices, the craftsmen of Iznik began to standardize designs and the quality of objects inevitably suffered.[1] The most visible sign of this change is the blurring of colors underneath the glaze, indicating a lack of control over the pigments. This technical flaw is evident in the decoration on the exterior of this early 17th-century bowl, although the quality is still high and the design is accurate.[2]

In addition to these developments, patronage patterns were also shifting from the Ottoman court to a broader foreign market, including Egypt, Crimea, the Balkans, and Europe.[3] Commercial contacts between Italy and the Ottoman Empire quickly resumed following the battle of Lepanto of 1571, and the import of Iznik ware to Venice increased thereafter. A shipment of ceramics from Iznik worth 100 ducats, for example, arrived in Venice in 1577. [4] It remains unclear when this particular bowl arrived on the lagoon, where Teodoro Correr (1750–1830), founder of the Correr Museum, presumably acquired it . Its very presence in Venice is indicative of a broader interest in Islamic ceramics in the city.

MAM

1 Atasoy and Raby 1989, pp. 273–78.
2 First published in Venice 1993, p. 386, cat. 234.
3 Atasoy and Raby 1989, pp. 273–80.
4 Sarre 1939, pp. 341–45.

179. *Bowl*

Iran, 17th century
Underglaze painted fritware
Diam. 42 cm (16 1/2 in.); H. 18 cm (7 1/4 in.)
Museo Civico Correr, Venice
Inv. CL. V n.136 (ill. p. 283)

For centuries Chinese porcelain, especially Ming blue-and-white, fascinated collectors and artists in the Middle East and Europe and often inspired imitations. In Safavid Iran (1501–1732), ceramicists copied Chinese techniques and styles so well that the Frenchman Jean Chardin (1643–1713) noted in his travel diary, ". . . we would not be able to distinguish [porcelain] coming from China from that of Persia."[1]

The composition and decoration of this large blue-and-white bowl demonstrate the high quality of Persian imitations already in the 17th century. The exterior is covered with repeating vegetal and floral motifs,[2] while on the interior a nine-pointed blue star is set against a white background and surrounded by six groups of flowers and leaves that extend up the sides. Stylized cloud motifs adorn both the inner and outer rims.

An increase in Persian ceramic production appears to have occurred during a period in which the Chinese industry declined (1652–83).[3] Exported to the Ottoman Empire and Western Europe, Persian blue-and-white quickly turned into a successful rival to Chinese wares.[4] It is unknown when this particular vessel arrived in Venice (see discussion under cat. 178), but blue-and-white ceramics from a wide range of Eastern sources, including China, Syria, and Persia certainly contributed to the development of the Italian city's own distinctive ceramic tradition.

FL

1 "*On est si fort trompé à cette porcelaine qu'on ne sauroit discerner celle de la Chine d'avec celle de Perse*" (Chardin 1711, II, p. 80). Venice 1993 p. 422; Mack 2002, pp. 109–11.
2 Similar decorative patterns recur on late 15th-century Ming vessels; see Krahl 1986, cats. 686, 729, 734–36.
3 Crowe 2002, pp. 9, 21.
4 Lane 1957, p. 75; Krahl 1986; Venice 1993, pp. 424–27.

180. *Bottle*

Iran, 17th century
Luster-painted over a blue glaze
H. 30 cm (11 7/8 in.); Diam. 21 cm max (8 1/4 in.)
Scuola Grande di San Rocco, Venice
Inv. 363/c

Attributed to 17th-century Safavid Iran, this small lusterware bottle with a globular body and high foot belongs to the small collection of late Islamic ceramics in the Scuola Grande di San Rocco and represents one of the few Persian objects from this period today in Venice.[1] This vessel is decorated with lustered flower bouquets and cypresses set against a shiny blue background. A brass neck engraved with scrolls ending in human figures and animals tops the bottle, but it was probably added during the Qajar dynasty (1775–1924) as a replacement for the original.[2]

FL

1 Vitali 1987, p. 40, cat. 8; Venice 1993, pp. 427–28, cat. 273b.
2 See Watson 1985, pl. P.

181a–d. *Four tiles from the floor of the Cappella Lando, Church of San Sebastiano, Venice*

Probably Venice, ca. 1510
Maiolica (underglaze painted tin-glazed earthenware)
Each tile: ca. 15.5 x 15.5 (6 1/8 x 6 1/8 in.); th. ca. 2.3 cm (1 in.)
Church of San Sebastiano, on loan to the Museo Franchetti alla Ca' d'Oro, Venice
Inv. 86 (d), 223 (c), 260 (a), 329 (b) (ill. p. 29)

Four of the 393 small maiolica tiles from the pavement of the Lando Chapel in the Venetian church of San Sebastiano are exhibited here.[1] Two others bear the date 1510, which make it possible to date the entire floor. A craftsmen probably trained in the Marches, perhaps in Pesaro or Fano, headed the Venetian workshop responsible for its manufacture.

The corners of the all the tiles are decorated with a quarter-flower motif: a central bud with trellised pattern and a projecting orange lozenge flanked by petals. A colorful range of pigments—yellow (antimony), green (copper), orange (antimony and iron), blue (cobalt), and purple (manganese)—has been used.

Tiles (a) and (b) are decorated *alla porcellana,* with blue vine shoots on a white ground, set in a polygonal frame. The foliage is arranged around a large central flower, respectively a blossom with four serrated petals (a) and a stylized peony (b). The open spaces are painted orange. The outer, circular frame is handled in a basketweave motif (a) and has blue leaves against white (b).

The ornament known generically as *alla porcellana* (or, in the term used in Picolpasso's 16th-century treatise, *alla porcellana tirata*)[2] had already been employed in the 15th century for Islamic-inspired

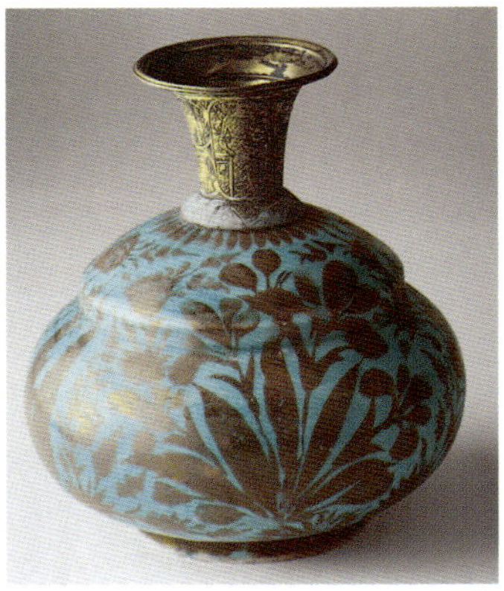

cat. 180

wares, called *alla damaschina* at the time, in various regions of Italy including Faenza, Montelupo, Siena, Casteldurante, Rome, Genoa, and Savona. This pattern was also widely used in Venice in the 16th century by its great maiolica masters. The motifs of foliage or clusters of leaves arranged around a large central flower were undoubtedly inspired by Ming porcelain and its Syrian and Anatolian imitators.[3] These three types have been documented, if in limited fashion, by archaeological finds in Venice,[4] testifying to the city's contacts with the Far East as well as the Near East.

Tile (c) bears the motif generally described by specialists as a classical leaf ornament; it is ringed by a polygonal pattern set inside a round *fiammanti* frame. Here again a decorative model of Islamic origin can be detected merely by recognizing its resemblance to certain half-palmette arabesques often found on Persian Il-khanid ceramics of the late 13th and 14th centuries,[5] as well as to the ornamentation later used in Mudejar Spain,[6] and finally to Turkish metalwork of the 16th century.[7] The intermediate areas are colored alternately in green and orange.

Tile (d), which depicts a hare looking over its shoulder, is ringed by a polygon pattern set inside a round overlapping-scale frame. The background shows a meadow with stylized bushes beneath a sky patterned with a three-dot motif. As in tile (c), the intermediate areas are colored alternately in green and orange. The hare, symbolizing fertility, was associated with femininity and, from an astrological standpoint, with the moon. It was widely employed in Eastern Islamic ceramics, from incised slipware and Aghkand-type sgraffito (12th–13th centuries) to the silhouetted hare under turquoise glaze on Seleucid ceramics and Il-khanid wares of the Sultanabad type from the first half of the 14th century,[8] and on, to later examples from the Safavid period in the 16th and 17th centuries.

FS

1 The recently restored paving was exhibited at the show organized by the Galleria G. Franchetti alla Ca d'Oro (Perissa and Saccardo, 2002). On the most recent theories of attribution, see Saccardo (forthcoming).
2 Piccolpasso 1976, p. 210.
3 Fehervari 1985, pp. 183–184; Faenza 1990, pp. 132–50; Venice 1993, p. 294, cat. 165.
4 On discoveries of porcelain in the lagoon, see Saccardo, Camuffo, and Gobbo 1992, fig. 2, no. 2.
5 Fehervari 1985, pp. 156–57.
6 Berlin 1986, fragment of stucco wall decoration, p. 112, cat. 190.
7 Ibid., p. 135, cat. 236.
8 Fehervari 1985, p. 173.

182. *Plate decorated* alla porcellana *with the arms of the Augsburg families Meuting and Hörwarth*

Maiolica (tin glazed earthenware)
Venice, ca. 1516
Diam. 21.7 cm (8 5/8 in.); H. 2.4 cm (1 in.)
The British Museum, London
Inv. MME 1878. 12-30, 435 (ill. p. 272)

As early as the 15th century Venice had established itself as the major European entrepôt of Chinese porcelain and Ottoman Iznik-ware, and wealthy connoisseurs, such as Filippo Strozzi of Florence, sent agents there to acquire new pieces for their collections.[1] The supply of these exotic wares in Venice never fully satisfied demand, however, and in the early 16th century industrious Venetian potters began producing comparable ceramics to fill the void. While still using the same tin-glazed earthenware techniques employed elsewhere on the Italian peninsula, the Venetian artisans adopted many of the color schemes and motifs of the porcelain and ceramics imported to their city from the Far and Middle East. The result was a distinctive kind of maiolica, known since the Renaissance as *alla porcellana.* It, too, became highly sought after, and was made for both home and export markets. Bavarian merchants active in Venice in particular appear to have purchased it in large quantities, especially pieces customized with their own coats of arms.

The wealthy Meuting family of Augsburg was likely among the very first of the German traders to acquire armorial sets of Venetian maiolica decorated *alla porcellana.*[2] This plate from the British Museum must have been part of a larger table service made to celebrate the 1516 marriage of Hans Meuting and Dorothea Hörwarth, also of Augsburg. The heraldic devices of their two families appear side by side in the plate's center; the pattern of its outer rim consists of scrolling vines and flowers. With its cobalt blue ornament set against an opaque white background, the plate's appearance is strikingly similar to that of 15th-century Ming blue-and-white porcelain and its Ottoman and Persian imitations (compare cats. 172–173). Though highly simplified, the floral and foliate pattern of the Venetian plate achieves a rhythm matching its Eastern prototypes.

TK

1 Carswell 1993, pp. 180–86; Spallanzani 1978, pp. 51–52, 55, 87, 165. See also Fontana's essay in this volume.

2 The earliest known Venetian plate decorated *"alla porcellana"* dates to 1515, and was also commissioned for a marriage, this time between a Meuting and a Lamparten von Greiffenstein of Augsburg (Frankfurt, Museum für Angewandtekunst), while another plate documents the 1540 marriage between Bernardo Meuting and Anna Maria Meuting (Berlin, Kunstgewerbemuseum); both are reproduced in Bortolotto 1981, plates XLVI and XLVIa.

183. *Plate decorated* alla porcellana *with arms of Andreas Imhoff and Ursula Schlaudersbach of Nuremburg*

Venice, ca. 1518–25
Maiolica (underglaze painted tin-glazed earthenware)
Diam. 42.8 cm (16 7/8 in); H. 6.4 cm (2 1/2 in.)
Fioritura Collection, Heinz and Jertha Kuckei Collection, Berlin (ill. p. 288)

This luminous plate with the arms of two wealthy Nuremburg families further attests to the popularity among German merchants of Venetian maiolica *alla porcellana* (see also cat. 182). In this instance, the heraldic plate celebrates the marriage of Andreas Imhoff (1491–1579) and Ursula Schlaudersbach (1501–1525). The object must date between 1518, the year the couple wed, and Ursula's untimely death in 1525. Several related, though not identical, Venetian plates with *alla porcellana* decoration and the same coats of arms survive in at least four other European collections.[1]

The inventory of Andreas Imhoff's possessions made after his death in 1579 reveals that during his lifetime he had collected a large quantity of Venetian maiolica, including examples explicitly described as *alla porcellana*.[2] As a young man, Andreas had represented his family's firm in Venice, where they traded a wide variety of goods at the Fondaco dei Tedeschi.[3] It is then and there that Andrea likely acquired his taste for Venetian ceramics. Other members of his family are known to have owned these wares as well.

This plate's exquisite design reflects Andreas Imhoff's sophisticated taste. On the flat rim is a lotus wreath with smaller buds and leaves set between a pair of double rings, obvious borrowings from Chinese porcelains brought to Venice via trade and diplomatic relations with the Islamic world. What is distinctly European about the plate is its use of heraldic devices as the centerpiece. By contrast, Ming porcelain often features a lotus pond, bouquet of flowers, or other naturalistic scene at its center (see cat. 172).

A classic example of Venetian maiolica *alla porcellana*, this plate is also decorated on its reverse with a garland of blue-and -white floral scrolls and sprays.

TK

1 The other objects are listed in Hausmann 2002, pp. 203–4, cat. no. 81.
2 The relevant excerpt from the document, dated October 24, 1579, is published in Alverà Bortolotto 1983, p. 310.
3 Ibid.

184. Attributed to Maestro Lodovico *Plate with tendrils* alla porcellana

Venice, ca. 1540–50
Maiolica (underglaze painted tin-glazed earthenware)
Diam. 24.5 cm
Fioritura Collection, Heinz and Jertha Kuckei Collection, Berlin (ill. p. 287)

Throughout the mid-16th century, Venetian ceramicists continued making traditional blue-and-white wares, but several virtuoso masters began adding small amounts of cobalt blue to their glazes, thereby giving their products a translucent light blue or lilac-gray tint. The distinctive type of maiolica that resulted, called *berettino*, appears to have first been made in Faenza, a major center of maiolica production in northern Italy, but soon spread to Venice, where it enjoyed equal if not greater popularity.[1] On the lagoon, potters must have must been particularly aware of the preciousness of cobalt, its Eastern source, and the value and beauty it added to their wares. In this period, most cobalt was mined in the mountains near Kashan in Central Iran and made its way to Venice via trade.

This elegant example of Venetian *berettino* not only incorporates a highly prized ore from the East, but also eastern motifs. The light, airy floral pattern with comma-shaped leaves betrays the potter's awareness of contemporary Ottoman "*tugrakeş* spiral style" wares (see cat. 173). The classic scroll and the shaded flowers set within double rings, however, recall Chinese Ming porcelain, as does the extraordinary thinness of the potting (see cat. 172).[2] Mixing and matching a wide variety of foreign elements and aspects with confidence and panache, the result is an object that is distinctly Venetian.

This kind of plate with a sunken well at its center is known as a *tondino*. At least two other similar Venetian plates—possibly part of the same service—were recorded in the early 20th century: one example had the exact same dimensions of the present plate (formerly Hermann Emden Collection), the second was slightly smaller (formerly Wilhelm von Bode Collection; see cats. 85–86 for two carpets from the same collection).[3]

Like cat. 185, this plate has been attributed to Maestro Lodovico, a master who signed and dated other *berettino* wares produced in Venice in the 1540s and 1550s. His workshop was located in the San Polo district of the city.

TK

1 Wilson 1987, p. 108.
2 Mallet and Dreyer 1998, p. 150.
3 Ibid.

185. Attributed to Maestro Lodovico *Plate*

Venice, ca. 1540–50
Maiolica (underglaze painted tin-glazed earthenware)
Diam. 50 cm (19 3/4 in.)
Musèe de la Renaissance, Écouen, Chateau d'Écouen
Inv. E.Cl 2415 (ill. p. 268)

This plate ascribed to Maestro Lodovico of Venice (see also cat. 184) attests that high quality Iznik-ware from its earliest phase—about 1470 until the late 1520s—had reached Venice through East-West trade no later than the mid-16th century. Inspired by Ming porcelain, Iznik potters of this period manufactured magnificent plates whose diameter often exceeds 45 cm.[1] They used a bright white slip, upon which they painted elaborate arabesques, floral scrolls, and lozenge panels in a deep cobalt blue, layering elements to give their designs a sense of depth and texture. With his own oversized plate, Maestro Lodovico imitated the distinctive effects of early Iznik pottery, by employing a blue-and-white palette and a dense but highly structured mixture of ornaments. The majority of motifs, such as the arabesques and the radial pattern, are Ottoman in inspiration as well, but the trophies, known as *trofei*, in the very center belong instead to the maiolica tradition of Cinquecento Italy. The plate thus represents a fascinating confluence of Islamic and Italian artistic styles.

TK

1 Raby and Atasoy 1989, p. 79.

186. *Fragment from a plate depicting a man with a turban*

Venice, second half of the 16th century
Underglaze painted fritware
21 x 22 cm (8 1/4 x 8 3/4 in.); diam. of foot 11.2 cm (4 3/8 in.)
Museo Franchetti alla Ca' d'Oro, Venice (C 2327)
Ex-Collection of Luigi Conton

This fragment comes from a plate with a slightly convex body, wide, flat rim, and annealed foot. It is decorated with both the fine-point *sgraffito* method and the *fonde ribassatto* technique (scraping away larger areas to produce a relief effect). The pinkish ochre ceramic is covered with a white slip and a shiny pale yellow glaze. Rust yellow, copper green, and cobalt blue were employed as colors. In the center of the fragment is the bust of a man wearing a turban, in profile facing right, placed in an architectural setting of Palladian inspiration.[1] This could be a portrait of Süleyman the Magnificent, (r. 1520–66), or his son and successor, Selim II (r. 1566–74). The first hypothesis seems the most plausible, judging from the similarity of pose and dress with a 1550 engraving of *"Sulimano Imperator dei Turchi . . . regnante nel 1519"* by the Venetian engraver Mathio Pagani (see cat. 63). It is true that Süleyman has a mustache and his hair is entirely covered by the turban in the engraving and not in the ceramic fragment; yet, when making this comparison, the Venetian manner of depicting Ottoman figures in the 16th and 17th centuries should be taken into account (see also cats. 116–17, 119, 187).[2]

FS

1 Conton 1982 p. 163, bottom; Saccardo 1998, n. 403. A "Turk" wearing a turban can be seen on another fragment held at the Ca' d'Oro (inv. C 2328), see Conton 1982, p. 89; see also the collective volume 1990, p. 102, top left (fragment of a Paduan sgraffito) and Alverá Bortolotto 1981 (maiolica albarello attributed to Maestro Domenico).
2 See also, for example, the paintings of Jacopo Ligozzi (1574–1625), originally from Verona.

187. Attributed to Domenico da Venezia (active 1540–68) *Albarello*

Venice, ca. 1560
Maiolica (underglaze painted tin-glazed earthenware)
H. 35 cm (13 3/4 in.); Diam. 27 cm (10 5/8 in.)
Inscribed: MOSTARDA F.
Musée National de Céramique, Sèvres
Inv. MNC 23119 (ill. p. 348)

This large Venetian albarello, or apothecary jar, has a tall, cylindrical body, concave walls, and a flanged top. It belongs to a distinctive type of glazed earthenware storage vessel likely invented by medieval Islamic potters. As early as the 9th century, albarelli were produced in central Asia and Iran and thereafter the form spread quickly to the rest of the Islamic world.[1] Medical advances, especially the development of new drugs, in this region created an ever-greater demand for the jars, which were made as beautiful as they were functional. By the 13th century, albarelli from Islamic Persia, Egypt, Syria, and Spain were regularly exported to Italy. After 1450, potters in the major ceramic centers of Renaissance Italy, including Venice, also began producing pharmaceutical jars in large numbers, using remarkably similar shapes, glazing and firing techniques, and colors.[2]

The Sèvres albarello is one of many splendid apothecary jars of various shapes and sizes now ascribed to Domenico da Venezia, whose prolific workshop was located in the San Polo district of Venice.[3] The potter employed a vivid palette of golden yellow, olive green, and cobalt blue as well as exuberant designs with daisies and bellflowers, curving scrolls, and large profile busts. The Sèvres albarello thus is highly typical of his oeuvre. In this instance, the portrait is of a man coiffed with a bulbous turban. Domenico da Venezia likely found inspiration for this image in depictions of the Ottoman sultan, Süleyman the Magnificent, who appeared in numerous Venetian paintings, prints, drawings, and medals of the 16th century (see cats. 59, 119, 186).[4]

The abbreviated inscription on the opposite side of this albarello indicates its original contents, *Mostarda fina*, or fine mustard, which was used to enliven the taste of fish and meats and to alleviate various human ailments. Although cultivated throughout Europe in this period, mustard seeds also arrived on the lagoon via Venice's vigorous spice trade with the Near East.

TK

1 For examples of early Islamic albarelli, see Paris 1996, pp. 147–56, cats. 68–86.
2 Drey 1978, pp. 21–65.
3 On Domenico da Venezia, see Pavone 1985, pp. 49–67.
4 For portraits of Süleyman the Magnificent, see Istanbul 2000, pp. 96–153.

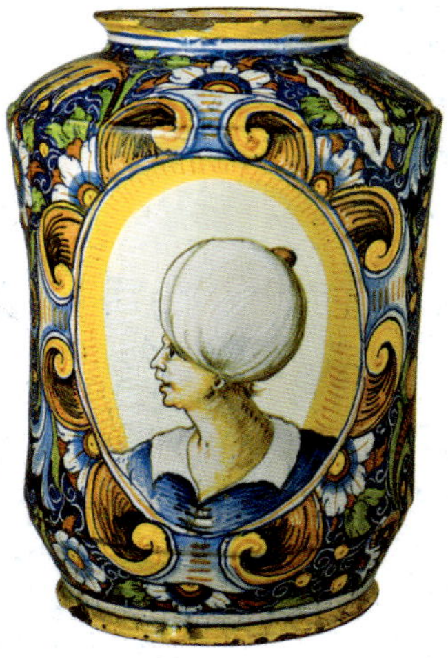
cat. 187

188. *Plate*

Veneto, 1633
Maiolica (underglaze painted tin-glazed earthenware)
Diam. 26 cm (10 1/4 in.)
Musée National de Céramique, Sèvres
Inv. 4617 (ill. p. 291)

Connoisseurs of Ottoman Iznik pottery identify the second half of the 16th century as the height of its production. Manufactured under the aegis of the sultans Selim II (r. 1566–74) and Murad III (r. 1574–95), Iznik-ware of this period features carnations, peonies, hyacinths, tulips, and serrated *saz* leaves, all painted in bold colors—primarily blue, green, and red—over a pristine white slip. Venetians were among the very first outside the Ottoman sphere to appreciate the extraordinary quality and beauty of this distinctive type of pottery, importing and collecting it from an early date. Indeed, Venetian demand for it was such that local potters began imitating its style in earnest at the beginning of the 17th century. For at least 100 years, these Venetian counterfeits enjoyed great popularity as well.

This particular plate represents one of the finest of the Venetian imitations of Iznik pottery ever produced. While it lacks the fluidity and delicate line of its Ottoman counterparts (exemplified by cats. 174–77), it nonetheless reproduces the floral design of late of late 16th-century Iznik with remarkable fidelity. Replicating Iznik's distinctive color palette, however, proved to be more challenging. Venetian potters never mastered the brilliant tomato red, made from Armenian bole, which played such a prominent role in the Iznik ceramic tradition. In its place, Venetians used a much less vibrant orange like that seen in this plate.

In the 16th and 17th centuries, Italian potters referred to their Iznik-style ceramics as maiolica *alla Turchesca*.[1] Late 19th-century connoisseurs called them instead Candiana ware, a term that remains in use today. The appellation is borrowed from the inscription on the reverse of this plate, which reads *"S. Chandiana 1633."* Long misinterpreted, the phrase is now recognized as a reference to Suor, or sister, Chandiana, a woman who evidently entered a convent in the Veneto, with this plate as part of her dowry, in 1633. Venetian maiolica dishes with the names of other nuns in this and other styles are known as well.[2] Evidently, this class of objects once had an important place on the refectory tables of the Veneto's best convents.[3]

TK

1 Poole 1997, p. 108.
2 See, for example, Banzato and Munarini 1995, pp. 161–62, and 176, cats. 232–33 and 263–64.
3 Soave and Siviero 1982.

189. *Two tiles*

Veneto, first half of the 17th century
Maiolica (underglaze painted tin-glazed earthenware)
Each tile: 17.7 x 17.7 (7 x 7 in.); th. 1.4 cm (1/2 in.)
Museo Franchetti alla Ca' d'Oro, Venice (inv. C2002)
Ex-Collection of Luigi Conton

These two square tiles come from a group of six previously in the Luigi Conton Collection.[1] Their earlier provenance is unknown, although they most likely came from the pavement of a Venetian palace. They represent important examples of Candiana ware (see cats. 188–92), a term applied Venetian ceramics inspired by the polychrome floral clusters of imported Ottoman Iznik "Rhodian ware." Candiana ware was produced in many cities in the Veneto, including Bassano,[2] Padua, and Venice itself. Dated examples, held in various European museums, range from 1603 to 1705.[3]

One tile is ornamented with hyacinths and peonies on long, slender stems that go back to a shared root, while the other is decorated with carnations and tulips around a central flower handled in a more elaborate way, with stem, serrated leaves, and buds. In both tiles, small flowers flanked by tiny leaves fill the corners. The colors used are brown, yellow, blue, and green.

FS

1 Conton 1982, p. 151.
2 Kiln-wasters were probably reused by the Manardi workshop; see Stringa 1987, pp. 63–70.
3 Moschetti 1933; Conton 1982, pp. 117–22; Fontana 1993, pp. 483–84; Padua 1995, cats. 263–65, 269–70, 272–76.

190. *Bowl*

Veneto, 17th century
Maiolica (underglaze painted tin-glazed earthenware)
Diam. 31.2 cm (12 1/4 in.); H. 9.8 cm (4 in.); Diam. foot 8.8 cm (3 1/2in.)
Museo d'Arte Medievale e Moderna, Padua
Inv. 843 (ill. p. 290)

In Italian, the word *crespa* means pleat or wrinkle, and bowls such as this one, with a series of convex lobes resembling deep pleats, are known as *crespine.* Employing molds, Italian potters appear to have invented this unique form, which first became popular in the 16th century. In many Renaissance paintings of banquets or informal meals, *crespine* can be seen set on tables with a bounty of fruit inside.[1]

This *crespina* represents another important example of Venetian Candiana ware. Together with the other objects in the same style in the exhibition (cats. 188–89, 191–92), this lobed bowl helps demonstrate just how varied the production of this distinctive class of Venetian maiolica was. Numerous other shapes, including ewers and vases, also survive. Candiana ceramics therefore could be found in a wide range of settings and serving many different purposes. The sheer number of extant examples in modern museums leaves no doubt that the pottery was produced in large quantities, and the range in quality—from exquisite to poor—suggests that a wide spectrum of the Venetian and Veneto populace could have owned it. Indeed, the formula of naturalistic floral motifs rendered in a brilliant array of colors first developed in the ceramic workshops of Iznik in the mid-16th century clearly had a broad appeal in the Veneto towards the end of the Renaissance.

TK

1 Hess 2004, p. 25

°191. *Barber's dish*

Veneto, 17th century
Maiolica (underglaze painted tin-glazed earthenware)
Diam. 37 cm (14 1/2 in.); H. 15 cm (5 7/8 in.)
Museo Civico Correr, Venice
Inv. Cl. IV n. 180 (ill. p. 61)

This distinctively shaped dish provides evidence that Candiana wares were not exclusively used in convents (see cat. 188). Its deep well and wide brim with a cavity designed to cradle a man's neck indicate that it was once used in a barber's shop.

The shape of this utilitarian Venetian object has no counterpart in Islamic pottery, but its decoration clearly depends heavily on Iznik-ware. The dish's interior is painted in the classic Iznik style, with a bold blue and green *saz* leaf in the center, surrounded by peonies, carnations, and tulips. The bleeding of the blue cobalt that occurred when the bowl was fired is the only detail marring its beauty. From extant evidence, it is clear that the potters of Iznik generally exercised greater control over their colors during production than their Venetian counterparts.

TK

192. *Pilgrim flask*

Veneto, 17th century
Maiolica (underglaze painted tin-glazed earthenware)
H. 25 cm (9 7/8 in.); Diam. of base 10.2 cm (4 in.)
Museo d'Arte Medievale e Moderna, Padua
Acquired by G. Sanario, 1929
Inv. 844 (Ill. p. 291)

Bulbous bottles of this form, with a long neck, a low oval foot, and four looped handles, are related to those called pilgrim flasks, *guastade*, or *inghistere fracade*[1] which have two flattened sides. The shape is of Islamic origin (see cat. 89), but by the late 15th century had spread to Venice and elsewhere in Europe. Italian enthusiasm for pilgrim flasks is evident in the great number of surviving examples in many different mediums, including inlaid metal, painted and enameled glass (see cat. 167), porcelain, and glazed pottery. Fragile examples, like this one made of maiolica, however, were intended instead to be part of an elegant table service. In such a setting, they most likely functioned as wine decanters.[2]

In both the Islamic world and Italy, these bottles could be simply or elaborately decorated. In this instance, the flask is richly ornamented in the Candiana style. Here, the typical Iznik saz leaf, carnations, and peonies are rendered in a particularly vivacious and lively manner.

TK

1 Carboni 2003.
2 Ibid., p. 172.

Appendices

Bibliography

Marin Sanudo, *Diarii*

Chronology

Bibliography

AB
Art Bulletin

Abulafia 1987
David Abulafia, "Asia, Africa and the trade of medieval Europe", in *Cambridge Economic History of Europe*, vol. 2, 1987, pp. 402-73

Abulafia 1994
David Abulafia, "The role of trade in Muslim-Christian contact during the Middle Ages", in D.A. Agius and R. Hitchcock (eds.), *The Arab Influence in Medieval Europe, Folia Scholastica Mediterranea*, Reading, 1994, pp. 1-24

Aikema and Martin 1999
Bernard Aikema and Andrew John Martin, "Crosscurrents with Germany: The spread of the Venetian Renaissance", in B. Aikema and B.L. Brown (eds.), *Renaissance Venice and the North, Crosscurrents in the Time of Dürer, Bellini and Titian*, exh. cat., Palazzo Grassi, Venice, 1999, pp. 332-39

Alexander 1996
David Alexander (ed.), *Furusiyya: The Horse in the Art of the Near East*, Riyadh, 1996

Alexander 2002
David Alexander, "Armi da cerimonia e armi da guerra", in Florence 2002, pp. 41-47

Alexander 1969
Jonathan J. G. Alexander, "Notes on some Veneto-Paduan illuminated books of the Renaissance", *Arte Veneta*, 23, 1969, pp. 9-20 (repr. in J.J.G. Alexander, *Studies in Italian Manuscript Illumination*, London, 2002)

Alexander 1994
Jonathan J. G. Alexander (ed.), *The Painted Page: Italian Renaissance Book Illumination, 1450-1550*, exh. cat., Royal Academy of Arts, London and The Pierpont Morgan Library, New York, 1994

Al-Jazari 1974
Ibn al-Razzaq al-Jazari, *The Book of Knowledge of Ingenious Mechanical Devices (Kitab fi Macrifat al Hiyal al-Handasiya) by Ibn al-Razzaq al-Jazari*, D. R. Hill (ed. and transl.), Boston, 1974

Allan 1984
James W. Allan, "Shaʿbān, Barqūq, and the decline of the Mamluk metalworking industry", *Muqarnas*, 2, 1984, pp. 85-93

Allan 1986
James W. Allan, *Metalwork of the Islamic World. The Aaron Collection*, London, 1986

Allan 1989
James W. Allan, "Veneto-Saracenic metalwork: The problems of provenance", in Grube 1989, pp. 167-84

Allan 1991
James W. Allan, *Islamic Ceramics*, Oxford, 1991

Allan 1999
James W. Allan, *Islamic Metalwork. The Nuhad es-Said Collection*, (1st ed. 1982), London, 1999

Almagià 1959-1960
Roberto Almagià, "A proposito del mappamondo in lingua turca della Biblioteca Marciana", *Atti dell'Istituto Veneto di Scienze, Lettere et Arti. Classe di scienze morali, lettere ed arti*, 118, 1959-60, pp. 53-59

Alpers and Baxandall 1994
Svetlana Alpers and Michael Baxandall, *Tiepolo and the Pictorial Intelligence*, New Haven and London, 1994

Alverà Bortolotto 1981
Angelica Alverà Bortolotto, *Storia della ceramica a Venezia dagli albori alla fine della Repubblica*, Florence, 1981

Alverà Bortolotto 1983
Angelica Alverà Bortolotto, "A proposito dei piatti veneziani con decoro 'alla porcellana'", *Faenza*, 49, 1983, pp. 310-12

Alverà Bortolotto 1988
Angelica Alverà Bortolotto, *Maiolica a Venezia nel Rinascimento*, Bergamo, 1988

Ambrosini 1981
Federica Ambrosini, "Descrizioni del mondo nelle case venete dei secoli XVI e XVII", *AV*, ser. 5, 117, 1981, pp. 67-79

Ames-Lewis 1990
Francis Ames-Lewis, "Il disegno nella pratica della bottega del Quattrocento", in M. Lucco (ed.), *La pittura nel Veneto, il Quattrocento*, vol. 2, Milan, 1990, pp. 657-85

Andaloro 1980
Maria Andaloro, "Costanzo da Ferrara. Gli anni a Costantinopoli alla corte di Maometto II", *Storia dell'Arte*, 38, 1980, pp. 185-212

And 1985
Metin And, "17.yüzyıl Türk Çarşı Ressamları", *Tarih ve Toplum*, 167, 1985, pp. 40-45

Anderson 1997
Jaynie Anderson, *Giorgione, the Painter of "Poetic Brevity": Including Catalogue Raisonné*, New York, 1997

Angiolello 1909
Giovanni Maria Angiolello, *Historia turchesca (1300-1514)*, I. Ursa (ed.), Bucharest, 1909

AO
Ars Orientalis

Arabesques 1995
Arabesques, Decorative Panels of the Renaissance, Paris, 1995

Arbel 1992
Benjamin Arbel, "Nur Banu (c. 1580-83): A Venetian sultana", *Turcica*, 24, 1992, pp. 241-59

Arbel 1995
Benjamin Arbel, *Jews and Venetians in the Early Modern Eastern Mediterranean. Jewish Studies*, 14, Leiden, New York and Köln, 1995

Arbel 2002
Benjamin Arbel, "Maps of the world for Ottoman princes? Further evidence and questions concerning 'The mappamondo of Hajji Ahmed'", *Imago Mundi*, 54, 2002, pp. 19-29

Arbel 2004
Benjamin Arbel, "The last decades of Venice's trade with the Mamluks: Importations into Egypt and Syria", *MSR*, 8, 2004, pp. 37-86

Aretino 1913
Pietro Aretino, *Il Primo Libro delle Lettere*, F. Nicolini (ed.), Bari, 1913

Aretino 1971
Pietro Aretino, *Teatro, tutte le opere di Pietro Aretino*, G. Petrocchi (ed.), Verona, 1971

Aretino 1997
Pietro Aretino, *Lettere, tomo I, libro I*, P. Procacciolo (ed.), Rome, 1997

Armao 1944
Ermanno Armao, *Vincenzo Coronelli*, Florence, 1944

Armour 1995
Peter Armour, "Griffins", in J. Cherry (ed.), *Mythical Beasts*, London, 1995, pp. 72-103

Armstrong 1994
Lillian Armstrong, "Aristotle, *Works*; Porphyrius, *Isagoge*", in Alexander 1994, pp. 204-05

Armstrong 1994a
Lillian Armstrong, "The hand-illumination of printed book in Italy, 1465-1515", in Alexander 1994, pp. 35-47

Ashtor 1976
Eliyahu Ashtor, *A Social and Economic History of the Near East in the Middle Ages*, London, 1976

Ashtor 1976a
Eliyahu Ashtor, "Observations on Venetian trade in the Levant in the XIVth century", *Journal of European Economic History*, 5, 1976, pp. 533-86

Ashtor 1977
Eliyahu Ashtor, "L'apogée du commerce vénitien au Levant. Un nouvel essai d'explication", in Beck, Manoussacas, and Pertusi 1977, vol. 1, pp. 307-26

Ashtor 1978
Eliyahu Ashtor, "L'exportation de textiles occidentaux dans le Proche-Orient musulman au bas Moyen Âge (1370-1517)", in L. de Rosa et al. (eds.), *Studi in memoria di Federigo Melis*, vol. 2, Naples, 1978, pp. 303-77 (Reprinted in Ashtor 1986)

Ashtor 1978a
Eliyahu Ashtor, *Studies on the Levantine Trade in the Middle Ages*, London, 1978

Ashtor 1983
Eliyahu Ashtor, *The Jews and the Mediterranean Economy (10th-15th centuries)*, London, 1983

Ashtor 1983a
Eliyahu Ashtor, *Levant Trade in the Later Middle Ages*, Princeton, 1983

Ashtor 1986
Eliyahu Ashtor, *East-West Trade in the Medieval Mediterranean*, B. Z. Kedar (ed.), London, 1986

ASV
Archivio di Stato di Venezia

Atasoy 1997
Nurhan Atasoy, *1582. Surname-i Humayun: An Imperial Celebration*, Istanbul, 1997

Atasoy 2002
Nurhan Atasoy, *A Garden for the Sultan, Gardens and Flowers in Ottoman Culture*, Istanbul, 2002

Atasoy et al. 2001
Nurhan Atasoy, Julian Raby, Louise Mackie et al., *IPEK. The Crescent and the Rose. Imperial Ottoman Silk and Velvets*, London, 2001

Atasoy and Raby 1989
Nurhan Atasoy and Julian Raby, *Iznik: The Pottery of Ottoman Turkey*, Y. Petsopoulos (ed.), London, 1989

Atıl 1973
Esin Atıl, "Ottoman miniature painting under Sultan Mehmed II", *AO*, 9, 1973, pp. 103-21

Atıl 1981
Esin Atıl, *Renaissance of Islam: Art of the Mamluks*, exh. cat., Smithsonian Institution, Washington, D.C, 1981

Atıl 1987
Esin Atıl (ed.), *The Age of Süleyman the Magnificent*, exh. cat., Washington, D.C., 1987

Atıl 1993
Esin Atıl "The story of an eighteenth-century Ottoman festival", *Muqarnas*, 10, 1993, pp. 181-200

Auersperg-Trautson 1998
Johannes Auersperg-Trautson, "A pair of Venetian lacquer-work doors", *Studiolo*, London, 1998, pp. 1-16

Auld 1986
Sylvia Auld, "Kuficising inscriptions in the work of Gentile da Fabriano", *Oriental Art* (n.s.), 32/3, 1986, pp. 246-65

Auld 1989
Sylvia Auld, "Master Mahmud: Objects fit for a prince", in Grube 1989, pp. 185-201

Auld 1990-1991
Sylvia Auld, "The Mamluks and Venetians: Commercial interchange: The visual evidence", in *Palestine Exploration Quarterly*, 1990-1991, pp. 84-102

Auld 2004
Sylvia Auld, *Renaissance Venice, Islam and Mahmud the Kurd. A Metalworking Enigma*, London, 2004

Auld (forthcoming)
Sylvia Auld, "From pattern to production: The cast of three unfinished trays", forthcoming in E. Wright (ed.), *Metals and Metalworking in Islamic Iran*, Dublin, forthcoming

Auriemma 1999
Rita Auriemma, *Il carico e la dotazione di bordo*, in *Operazione Iulia Felix dal mare al museo: lo scavo, il recupero e il progetto di musealizzazione della nave romana rinvenuta al largo di Grado*, Monfalcone, 1999, pp. 47-62

AV
Archivio Veneto

Ayalon 1979
David Ayalon, *The Mamluk Military Society*, London, 1979

Aymard 1966
Maurice Aymard, *Venise, Raguse et le commerce du blé pendant la seconde moitié du XVIe siècle*, Paris, 1966

Babinger 1931
Franz Babinger, *Zur Geschichte der Papier-*

zeungung im osmanischen Reiche, Berlin, 1931
Babinger 1952
Franz Babinger, "Vier Bauvorschläge Lionardo da Vinci's am Sultan Bajezid II. (1502/3)", *Nachrichten der Akademie der Wissenschaften in Göttingen I. phil-hist. Klasse,* 1952
Babinger 1955
Franz Babinger, "Seyyid Nuh and his Turkish sailing handbook", *Imago Mundi,* 12, 1955, pp. 180-82
Babinger 1956
Franz Babinger, *Mehmed der Eroberer und seine Zeit: Weltenstürmer einer Zeitenwende,* Munich, 1956
Babinger 1961
Franz Babinger, *Johannes Darius, 1414-1494: Sachwalter Venedigs im Morgenland, und sein griechischer Umkreis,* Munich, 1961
Babinger 1963
Franz Babinger, *Spätmittelalterliche fränkische Briefschaften aus dem grossherrlichen Seraj zu Stambul, Südosteuropäische Arbeiten,* 61, Munich, 1963
Babinger 1963a
Franz Babinger, "Lionardo da Vinci's Bauvorschläge an Sultan Bâjezid II. (1502/3)" (revised version of Babinger 1952), in Babinger 1963, pp. 120-35
Babinger 1978
Franz Babinger, *Mehmet the Conqueror and His Time,* transl. from Babinger 1956 by R. Manheim, W. Hickman (ed.), Princeton, 1978
Baer 1968
Eva Baer, "Fish-pond ornaments on Persian and Mamluk metal vessels", *BSOAS,* 31/1, 1968, pp. 14-28
Baer 1983
Eva Baer, *Metalwork in Medieval Islamic Art,* Albany, 1983
Baer 1989
Eva Baer, "Ayyubid metalwork with Christian images", *Studies in Islamic Art and Architecture,* supplement to *Muqarnas,* 4, Leiden and New York, 1989
Baker 1991
Patricia A. Baker, "Islamic honorific garments", *Costume,* 25, 1991, pp. 25-35
Baker and Henry 2001
Christopher Baker and Tom Henry (eds.), *The National Gallery Complete Illustrated Catalogue,* London, 2001
Balbi 1590
Gasparo Balbi, *Viaggio dell'Indie orientali,* Venice, 1590
Balducci Pegolotti 1936
Francesco Balducci Pegolotti, *La pratica della mercatura,* A. Evans (ed.), Cambridge, MA, 1936
Ballardini 1925
Gaetano Ballardini, "Ceramiche cosiddette 'di Rodi'", *Faenza,* 13, 1925, pp. 13-18
Ballardini 1938
Gaetano Ballardini, *La maiolica italiana dalle origini alla fine del Cinquecento,* Florence, 1938
Ballardini 1940
Gaetano Ballardini, "'Candiana', ma non tutto 'Candiana'", *Faenza,* 28, 1940, pp. 39-47
Baltimore 1957
The History of Bookbinding 525-1950 A.D., exh. cat., Baltimore Museum of Art, Baltimore, 1957
Baltrušaitis 1981
Jurgis Baltrušaitis, *Le Moyen Âge fantastique: Antiquites et exotisme dans l'art gothique,* Paris, 1981
Bambach 1991
Carmen Bambach, "Leonardo, Tagliente, and Dürer: 'La scienza del far di groppi'", *Achademia Leonardi Vinci,* 4, 1991, pp. 72-98
Bambach and Whitaker 1991
Carmen Bambach and Lucy Whitaker, "The lost knots", *Achademia Leonardi Vinci,* 4, 1991, pp. 107-10
Barbaro and Contarini 1873
Josafat Barbaro and Ambrogio Contarini, *Travels to Tana and Persia,* L. Stanley (ed.), W. Thomas and S.A. Roy (transl.), London, 1873
Barbieri 1991
Edoardo Barbieri, "La tipografia Araba a Venezia nel XVI secolo: Una testimonianza d'archivio dimenticata", *QSA,* 9, 1991, pp. 127-31
Barcelona 2004
David Abulafia et al., *Mediterraneum. El esplendor del Mediterráneo medieval, S. XIII-XV,* exh. cat., History Museum of Catalunya and Maritime Museum of Barcelona, Barcelona, 2004
Barcham 1997
William Barcham, "The Tasso Cycle", in New York 1997, pp. 134-47
Barkan 1979
Ömer Lutfi Barkan, "Istanbul Saraylarına ait Muhasebe Defterleri", *Belgeler,* 9/3, 1979, pp. 1-38
Barker 1990
Nicolas Barker, "Italian writing books 1522-39: An attempted chronology", in S. Morison (ed.), *Early Italian Writing-Books: Renaissance to Baroque,* London and Verona, 1990, pp. 151-204
Barkeshli, Zain and Zekrgoo 2000
Mandana Barkeshli, Dzul Haimi bin. Md. Zain and Amir Hossein Zekrgoo, "Materials used for decoration of Quran", in *Nur Al-Quran,* exh. cat., Islamic Arts Museum, Kuala Lumpur, 2000, pp. 15-26
Barovier Mentasti 1982
Rosa Barovier Mentasti, *Il vetro veneziano,* Milan, 1982
Barovier Mentasti 2001
Rosa Barovier Mentasti, "Dalla pittura al vetro", in *Per l'arte da Venezia all'Europa, Studi in onore di Giuseppe Maria Pilo,* Gorizia, 2001, vol. 1, pp. 187-90
Barral I Altet 1985
Xavier Barral I Altet, *Les mosaïques de pavement medievales de Venise, Murano, Torcello,* Paris, 1985
Barron, Coleman and Cobbi 1983
Caroline Barron, Christopher Coleman and Claire Cobbi (eds.), *The London Journal of Alessandro Magno, 1562,* London, 1983
Barry 2004
Michael Barry, *Figurative Art in Medieval Islam and the Riddle of Bihzâd of Herât (1465-1535),* Paris, 2004
Bartsch 1978
The Illustrated Bartsch, vol. 27, K. Oberhuber (ed.), New York, 1978
Bassi 1987
Elena Bassi, *Palazzi di Venezia: Admiranda urbis venetae,* Venice, 1987
Batari 1994
Ferenc Batari, *Ottoman Turkish Carpets,* Budapest, 1994
Bauer et al. 1987
Rotraud Bauer et al., *Weltliche und Geistliche Schatzkammer, Bildführer,* Vienna, 1987
Bauer-Eberhardt 1984
Ulrike Bauer-Eberhardt, "Die Rothschild-Miscellanea in Jerusalem Hauptwerk des Leonardo Bellini", *Pantheon,* 42, 1984, pp. 229-308
Baumgartner and Krueger 1988
Erwin Baumgartner and Ingeborg Krueger, *Phönix aus Sand und Ashe: Glas des Mittelalters,* exh. cat., Rheinisches Landesmuseum, Bonn and Historisches Museum, Basel, 1988
Bayramoğlu 1976
Fuat Bayramoğlu, *Turkish Glass Art and Beykoz-Ware,* Istanbul, 1976
Bean 1966
Jacob Bean, *Italian Drawings in the Art Museum, Princeton University; 106 Selected Examples,* New York, 1966
Bean 1990
Jacob Bean with William Griswold, *18th Century Italian Drawings in The Metropolitan Museum of Art,* New York, 1990
Beattie 1964
May Hamilton. Beattie, "Britain and the Oriental carpet", *Leeds Art Calendar,* 55, 1964, pp. 4-15
Beck, Manoussacas and Pertusi 1977
Hans-Georg Beck, Manoussos Manoussacas and Agostino Pertusi (eds.), *Venezia: Centro di mediazione tra oriente e occidente (secoli XV-XVI): Aspetti e problemi,* 2 vols., Florence, 1977
Beckwith 1960
John Beckwith, *Caskets from Cordoba,* London, 1960
Behrens-Abouseif 1995
Doris Behrens-Abouseif, *Mamluk and Post-Mamluk Metal Lamps,* Cairo, 1995
Behrens-Abouseif 2004
Doris Behrens-Abouseif, "European arts and crafts at the Mamluk court", *Muqarnas,* 21, 2004, pp. 45-54
Bellieni 1990
Andrea Bellieni, "1.5.5. Graffita rinascimentale a Treviso", in Ericani and Marini 1990, pp. 138-43
Bellingeri and Vercellin 1985
Giampiero Bellingeri and Giorgio Vercellin, "Note sul mappamondo turco a forma di cuore", in Tenenti 1985, pp. 154-59
Benvenuti and Romano 1998
Feliciano Benvenuti and Sergio Romano, *Per Vittorio Cini: nel ventesimo anniversario della morte,* Venice, 1998
Benzoni 1974
Gino Benzoni, *Il Mediterraneo nella seconda metà del '500 alla luce di Lepanto,* Florence, 1974
Benzoni 1985
Gino Benzoni, "Il 'farsi turco', ossia l'ombra del rinnegato", in Tenenti 1985, pp. 56-69
Benzoni 1985a
Gino Benzoni, "Venezia e la Persia", in *L'Oriente: Storie di viaggiatori italiani,* Milan, 1985, pp. 70-82
Berchet 1864
Guglielmo Berchet, *Del commercio dei Veneti nell'Asia,* Venice, 1864
Berchet 1865
Guglielmo Berchet, *La Repubblica di Venezia e la Persia,* Turin 1865
Berghe, Maquoi, and Wouters 2004
Ina Vanden Berghe, Marie-Christine Maquoi, and Jan Wouters, "Dye analysis of Ottoman silks", in De Jonghe et al. 2004, pp. 49-60
Berindei 1989
Mihnea Berindei, "Les Vénitiens en Mer Noire XVIe-XVIIe siècles", *Cahiers du Monde Russe et Soviétique. Hommage à Alexandre Benningsen,* 30, no. 3-4, 1989, pp. 207-23
Berlin 1986
Islamische Kunst Verborgene Schatze, exh. cat., Museum für Islamische Kunst, Berlin, 1986
Berlin 1989
Schatzkästchen und Kabinettschrank, exh. cat., Kunstgewerbemuseum, Berlin, 1989
Berlin 1989a
Hendrik Budde and Gereon Sievernich (eds.), *Europa und der Orient: 800-1900,* exh. cat., Martin-Gropius-Bau, Berlin, Gütersloh, 1989
Berlin 2002
Hans Ottomeyer and Michaela Völker, *Die öffentliche Tafel. Tafelzeremoniell in Europa 1300-1900,* exh. cat., Kronprinzenpalais, Berlin, 2002
Berliner 1926
Rudolf Berliner, *Ornamentale Vorlageblätter des 15. bis 18. Jahrhunderts,* 2 vols., Leipzig, 1926
Bernari and De Vecchi 1970
Carlo Bernari and Pierluigi De Vecchi, *L'opera completa del Tintoretto,* Milan, 1970
Bernini 1988
Dante Bernini (ed.), *Laboratorio di Restauro 2,* Rome, 1988
Bertelè 1932
Tommaso Bertelè, *Il Palazzo degli Ambasciatori di Venezia a Costantinopoli e sue antiche memorie,* Bologna, 1932
Bertelli 1970
Carlo Bertelli, "Vetri italiano a fondo d'oro del secolo XIII", *JGS,* 12, 1970, pp. 70-78
Bertelli 2002
Carlo Bertelli (ed.), *Restituzioni 2002: Capolavori restaurati,* Vicenza, 2002
Bertelli 2003
Carlo Bertelli, "Il Cairo di Gentile Bellini", in M. V. Fontana and B. Genito (eds.), *Studi in onore di Umberto Scerrato*

per il suo settantacinquesimo compleanno, Naples, 2003, pp. 105-20

Berti and Gelichi 1995
Graziella Berti and Sauro Gelichi, "Ceramiche, ceramisti e trasmissioni tecnologiche tra il XII e XIII secolo nell'Italia centro settentrionale", in *Miscellanea in memoria di Giuliano Cremonesi*, Pisa, 1995, pp. 409-45

Berti and Gelichi 1997
Graziella Berti and Sauro Gelichi, "'Zeuxippus Ware' in Italy", in H. Maguire (ed.), *Materials Analysis of Byzantine Pottery. Papers from a Colloquium held at Dumbarton Oaks, April 1-2, 1995*, Washington, D.C., 1997, pp. 85-104.

Berti and Gelichi 2000
Graziella Berti and Sauro Gelichi, "Considerazioni sulla cosiddetta 'ceramica crociata', in P. Peduto and F. Widemann (eds.), *L'ambiente culturale. Ravello nel medioevo. Il caso della famiglia Rufolo*, Bari, 2000, pp. 245-56

Berti and Gelichi 2001
Graziella Berti and Sauro Gelichi, "Trasmissioni di tecnologie nel Medioevo: Tendenze e linee di ricerca attuali", in *Atti del XXXII Convegno Internazionale della Ceramica Albisola 1999*, Albisola, 2001, pp. 23-41

Berti, Gelichi, and Mannoni 1997
Graziella Berti, Sauro Gelichi, and Tiziano Mannoni, "Trasformazioni tecnologiche nelle prime produzioni italiane con rivestimenti vetrificati (secc. XII-XIII)", in G. Démians d'Archimbaud (ed.), *La céramique médiévale en Méditerranée, Actes du VIe Congrès de l'AIECM2*, Aix-en-Provence, 1997, pp. 383-403

Bettagno 1993
Alessandro Bettagno, "Guardi: Quadri turcheschi", in Venice 1993a, pp. 17-28

Biadene 1990
Susanna Biadene, *Carte da navigar, portolani e carte nautiche del Museo Correr 1319-1732*, Venice, 1990

Bianchi and Howard 2003
Francesco Bianchi and Deborah Howard, "Life and death in Damascus: The material culture of Venetians in the Syrian capital in the mid-fifteenth century", *SV*, 46, 2003, pp. 233-300

Bini 1854
Telesforo Bini, *I Lucchesi a Venezia, Reale Accademia Lucchese*, 15, 1854

Binion 1970
Alice Binion, "From Schulenburg's gallery and records", *BM*, 112, no. 806, May 1970, pp. 297-303

Binion 1990
Alice Binion, *La galleria scomparsa del maresciallo von der Schulenburg: un mecenate nella Venezia del Settecento*, Milan, 1990

Binney 1979
Edwin Binney, *Turkish Treasures from the Collection of Edwin Binney, 3rd*, Portland, OR, 1979

Biringuccio 1540
Vannuccio Biringuccio, *De la Pirotechnia*, Venice, 1540 [A. Carugo (ed.), Milan, 1977]

Birley 1970
Robert Birley, *One Hundred Books in Eton College Library. Selected and Annotated by Robert Birley*, Eton, 1970

Bistort 1912
Giulio Bistort, *Il Magistrato alle Pompe nella Repubblica di Venezia: Studio storico*, Venice, 1912

Björkman 2000
Walther Björkman, "Tulband", in , *EI²* vol.10 , pp. 608-615

Blair and Bloom 1994
Sheila S. Blair and Jonathan M. Bloom, *The Art and Architecture of Islam 1250-1800*, New Haven and London, 1994

Blake 1971
Hugo Blake, "Descrizione provvisoria delle ceramiche assisiane e discussione sulla maiolica arcaica", in *Atti del IV Convegno Internazionale della Ceramica Albisola 1971*, Centro Ligure per la storia della ceramica, Albisola, 1971, pp. 363-92

Blake 1980
Hugo Blake, "The 'bacini' of North Italy", in *La céramique médiévale en Méditerranée occidentale Xᵉ-XVᵉ siècles. Actes du 1ᵉʳ colloque international*, Paris, 1980, pp. 93-111

Blake, Tonghini, and Vannini 1998
Hugo Blake, Cristina Tonghini, and Guido Vannini, "The impact of Islamic culture in Southern Europe: An archaeological view", in M. Pierce and M. Tosi (eds.), *Papers from the EEA Third Annual Meeting at Ravenna 1997*, 2, *Classical and Medieval*, Oxford, 1998, pp. 146-47

Blanc et al. 1981
B. Blanc, S. Denoix, J-C. Garcin and R. Gordiani, 'À propos de la carte du Caire de Matheo Pagano", *Annales Islamologiques*, 17, 1981 pp. 203-85

Blass-Simmen 1991
Brigit Blass-Simmen, *Sankt Georg: Drachenkampf in der Renaissance; Carpaccio, Raffael, Leonardo*, Berlin, 1991

Bloom 1999
Jonathan M. Bloom, "Mamluk art and architectural history: A review article", *MSR*, 3, 1999, pp. 31-58

Bloom et al. 1998
Jonathan M. Bloom et al., *The Minbar from the Kutubiyya Mosque*, New York, 1998

BM
The Burlington Magazine

Boalch 1995
Donald H. Boalch, *Makers of the Harpsichord and Clavicord 1440-1840*, (1st ed. 1956), Oxford, 1995

Boas 1994
Adrian J. Boas, "The import of Western ceramics to the Latin Kingdom of Jerusalem", *Israel Exploration Journal*, 44, 1994, pp. 102-22

Bobzin 1995
Hartmut Bobzin, *Der Koran im Zeitalter der Reformation: Studien zur Frühgeschichte der Arabistik und Islamkunde in Europa*, Beirut and Stuttgart, 1995

Boccia 1975
Lionello G. Boccia, *Il Museo Stibbert a Firenze: L'Armeria europea*, vol. 3, Florence, 1975

Boccia and Godoy 1985
Lionello G. Boccia and José A. Godoy, *Museo Poldi Pezzoli, Armeria*, vol. 1, Milan, 1985

Bode and Kühnel 1984
Wilhelm von Bode and Ernst Kühnel, *Antique Rugs from the Near East*, C. G. Ellis (ed. and transl.), London, 1984

Boesen 1960
Gudmund Boesen, *Venetianske Glas på Rosenborg*, Copenhagen, 1960

Böhmer and Karadağ 1993
Harald Böhmer and Recep Karadağ, "Dye-analyses of Ottoman brocades and velvets from the Topkapı Museum, Istanbul, and other silk textiles", in *7th International Conference on Oriental Carpets*, Hamburg and Berlin, 1993, pp. 69-78

Boissard 1581
Jean-Jacques Boissard, *Habitus Variarum Orbis Gentium*, Maline, 1581

Bollati 2004
Milvia Bollati (ed.), *Dizionario biografico dei miniatori italiani*, Milan, 2004

Bombaci 1943
Alessio Bombaci, "Ancora sul trattato turco-veneto del 2 ottobre 1540", *Rivista degli Studi Orientali*, 20, 1943, pp. 373-83

Bombaci 1949
Alessio Bombaci, "La collezione di documenti turchi dell'Archivio di Stato di Venezia", *Rivista degli Studi Orientali*, 24, 1949, pp. 95-107

Bombaci 1965
Alessio Bombaci, "Les thougres enluminés da la collection de documents turcs des Archives d'Etat de Venise", in *Atti del Secondo Congresso Internazionale d'Arte Turca*, Naples, 1965, pp. 41-55

Bonito Fanelli 1981
Rosalia Bonita Fanelli, *Five Centuries of Italian Textiles: 1300-1800*, Florence, 1981

Bonito Fanelli 1994
Rosalia Bonita Fanelli, "I 'doni dall'Oriente e da Champagne, Provins et Ultramonti': Commerci, chiesa e moda", in M. Ciatti (ed.), *"Drappi, velluti, taffetta et altre cose." Antichi tessuti a Siena e nel suo territorio*, Siena, 1994, pp. 50-59

Boralevi 1984
Alberto Boralevi, "Un tappeto ebraico italo-egiziano", *Critica d'Arte*, Jun-Sep 1984, pp. 34-47

Boralevi 1986
Alberto Boralevi, "Three Egyptian carpets in Italy", *OCTS*, 2, 1986, pp. 205-20

Borgherini Scarabellin 1925
Maria Borgherini Scarabellin, *Il magistrato dei cinque savi alla mercanzia*, Venice, 1925

Born 1937
Wolfgang Born, "Early European automatons", *Connoisseur*, 100, 1937, pp. 123-29, 246-52

Bosch, Carswell and Petherbridge 1981
Gulnar Bosch, John Carswell and Guy Petherbridge, *Islamic Bindings & Bookmaking, A Catalogue of an Exhibition*, exh. cat., The Oriental Institute, The University of Chicago, Chicago, 1981

Boschini 1966
Marco Boschini, *La carta del navegar pitoresco*, (1st ed. Venice, 1659), A. Pallucchini (ed.), Venice, 1966

Boskovits and Brown 2003
Miklâos Boskovits and David Alan Brown, *Italian Paintings of the Fifteenth Century*, Washington,
D. C. and New York, 2003

Botti 1992
Isabella Botti, "Tra Venezia e Alessandria: I teleri belliniani per la Scuola Grande di San Marco", *Venezia Cinquecento*, 3, 1992, pp. 333-73

Bourne 1999
Molly Bourne, "Francesco II Gonzaga and maps as palace decoration in Renaissance Mantua", *Imago Mundi*, 51, 1999, pp. 51-82

Branca 1963
Vittore Branca,: "Ermolao Barbaro e l'umanesimo veneziano", in V. Branca (ed.), *Umanesimo europeo e umanesimo veneziano*, Florence, 1963

Brandt 2003
Kathleen Weil-Garris Brandt, "Raphael's Portrait of Bindo Altoviti as a Young Man", in Chong, Pegazzano, and Zikos 2003, pp. 374-77

Braudel 1949
Fernand Braudel, *La méditerranée et le monde méditerranéen à l'époque de Philippe II*, Paris, 1949

Braudel 1966
Revised edition of Braudel 1949, 2 vols., Paris, 1966

Braudel 1972-73
Fernand Braudel, *The Mediterranean and the Mediterranean World in the Age of Philip II*, S. Reynolds (transl.), 2 vols., London, 1972-73

Brill 1967
Robert H. Brill, "A great slab from ancient Galilee", *Archaeology*, 20, 1967, pp. 88-95

Brill 1999
Robert H. Brill, *Chemical Analyses of Early Glasses*, 2 vols., Corning, 1999

Brooke 2004
Caroline Brooke, "Vittore Carpaccio's method of composition in his drawings for the Scuola di S. Giorgio 'Teleri'", *Master Drawings*, 42, no. 4, 2004, pp. 302-14

Brown 1993
Beverly Louise Brown, "Venice. Guardi exhibitions", *BM*, 135, no. 1089, Dec 1993, pp. 850-51

Brown 1920
Horatio Brown, "The Venetians and the Venetian quarter in Constantinople to the close of the twelfth century,' *JHS*, 40, 1920, pp. 68-88

Brunello 1986
Franco Brunello, *Marco Polo e le merci dell'Oriente*, Vicenza, 1986

BSOAS
Bulletin of the School of Oriental and African Studies

Burgoyne 1987
Michael Hamilton Burgoyne, *Mamluk Jerusalem, an Architectural Study*, London, 1987

Burnett 1999
Charles Burnett, "The second revelation of Arabic philosophy and science: 1492-1562", in Burnett and Contadini 1999, pp. 185-98

Burnett and Contadini 1999
Charles Burnett and Anna Contadini (eds.), *Islam and the Italian Renaissance. Warburg Institute Colloquia*, 5, London, 1999

Burnham 1980
Dorothy K. Burnham, *Warp and Weft. A Textile Terminology*, Toronto, 1980

Bury 2001
Michael Bury, *The Print in Italy, 1550-1620*, London, 2001

Buss, Butazzi and Pertegato 1983
Chiara Buss, Grazietta Butazzi and Francesco Pertegato, *Tessuti serici italiani,1450-1530*, Milan, 1983

Butler et al. 1983
Anthony R. Butler, Christopher Glidewell, Joseph Needham, and Sharee Pritchard, "Mosaic gold in Europe and China", *Chemistry in Britain*, 19/2, 1983, pp. 132-35

Büttner 2000
Andreas Büttner, *Perlmutt, von der Faszination eines göttlichen Materials*, Petersberg, 2000

Çağman 2000
Filiz Çağman, "Portrait series of Nakka Osman", in Istanbul 2000, pp. 164-87

Çağman and Tanındı 1979
Filiz Çağman and Zeren Tanındı, *Topkapı Saray Museum, Islamic Miniature Painting*, Istanbul, 1979

Cahen 1977
Claude Cahen, *Makhzumiyyat. Études sur l'histoire économique et financière de l'Égypte médiévale*, Leiden, 1977

Cacciavillani 1995
Ivone Cacciavillani, *Andrea Gritti nella vita di Nicolò Barbarigo*, Venice, 1995

Camille 1992
Michael Camille, *Image on the Edge: The Margins of Medieval Art*, London, 1992

Campbell and Chong 2005
Caroline Campbell and Alan Chong, *Bellini and the East*, exh. cat., Isabella Stewart Gardner Museum, Boston and National Gallery, London, 2005

Canby 1998
Sheila R. Canby, *Princes, Poets and Paladins: Islamic and Indian Paintings from the Collection of Prince and Princess Sadruddin Aga Khan*, exh. cat., London, 1998

Canova 1969
Giordana Mariani Canova, *La miniatura veneta del Rinascimento, 1450-1500*, Venice, 1969

Canova 2003
Giordana Mariani Canova, "Illuminated miniatures—vehicles for antiquity", in Mina Gregori (ed.), *In the Light of Apollo: Italian Renaissance and Greece*, exh. cat., National Gallery-Alexandros Soutzos Museum, Athens, Milan, 2003, pp. 258-60

Cantigas 1979
Alfonso X el Sabio, *Cantigas de Santa María: Edición facsímil del Códice T.I.1 de la Biblioteca de San Lorenzo el Real de El Escorial, siglo XIII*, Madrid, 1979

Capodimonte 1996
Museo Nazionale di Capodimonte. La Collezione Farnese. Le arti decorative, Naples, 1996

Carboni 1988
Il Kitab al-Bulhan di Oxford, Quaderni del Dipartimento di Studi Eurasiatici - Università degli Studi di Venezia, 6, Turin, 1988

Carboni 1989
Stefano Carboni, "Oggetti decorati a smalto di influsso islamico nella vetraria muranese: Tecnica e forma", in Grube 1989, pp. 147-66

Carboni 1989a
Stefano Carboni, "Le 'lampade egizie' della Murano ottocentesca", in *La conoscenza dell'Asia e dell'Africa in Italia nei secoli XVIII e XIX*, vol. 3, II, Naples, 1989, pp. 935-59

Carboni 1997
Stefano Carboni, *Following the Stars: Images of the Zodiac in Islamic Art*, exh. cat., The Metropolitan Museum of Art, New York, 1997

Carboni 1998
Stefano Carboni, "Gregorio's tale: Or, of enamelled glass production in Venice", in Ward 1998, pp. 101-06

Carboni 2001
Stefano Carboni, *Glass from Islamic Lands. The Al-Sabah Collection, Kuwait National Museum*, New York, 2001

Carboni 2003
Stefano Carboni, "A *guastada* with images of the zodiac", in M. V. Fontana and B. Genito (eds.), *Studi in onore di Umberto Scerrato per il suo settantacinquesimo compleanno*, vol. 1, Naples, 2003, pp. 167-80

Carboni 2003a
Stefano Carboni, *Mamluk Enamelled and Gilded Glass in the Museum of Islamic Art, Qatar*, London, 2003

Carboni 2003b
Stefano Carboni, "The painted-glass decoration of the mausoleum of Ahmad ibn Sulayman al-Rifaʿi in Cairo", *Muqarnas*, 20, 2003, pp. 61-84

Carboni 2003c
Stefano Carboni, "The use of glass as architectural decoration in the Islamic world", in *Annales du 15e Congrès de l'Association Internationale pour l'Histoire du Verre*, New York and Corning, 2001, Nottingham, 2003, pp. 127-32

Carboni 2004
Stefano Carboni, "Fifteenth-century enameled glass and gilded glass made for the Mamluks: The end of an era, the beginning of a new one," *Orient*, 39, 2004, pp. 69-78

Carboni and Swietochowski 1994
Stefano Carboni and Marie Lukens Swietochowski, *Illustrated Poety and Epic Images: Persian Painting of the 1330s and 1340s*, exh. cat., The Metropolitan Museum of Art, New York, 1994

Carboni and Whitehouse 2001
Stefano Carboni and David Whitehouse (eds.), *Glass of the Sultans*, exh. cat., The Corning Museum of Glass, Corning, NY, The Metropoltian Museum of Art, and Benaki Museum, Athens, New Haven, 2001

Carr 1997
Dawson W. Carr, *Andrea Mantegna: The Adoration of the Magi*, Los Angeles, 1997

Carswell 1993
John Carswell, "'The Feast of the Gods': The porcelain trade between China, Istanbul, and Venice", *Asian Affairs*, 1993, pp. 180-85

Carswell 1998
John Carswell, "The Baltimore beakers," in Ward 1998, pp. 61-63

Casini 2001
Matteo Casini, "Immagini dei capitani generali 'da Mar' a Venezia in età barocca", in M. Fantoni (ed.), *Il "Perfetto Capitano". Immagini e realtà (secoli XV-XVII)*, Rome, 2001, pp. 219-70

Cavalcaselle and Crowe 1974
Giovanni Battista Cavalcaselle and Joseph Archer Crowe, *Tiziano: La sua vita e i suoi tempi*, (1st ed. in English London, 1881), Florence, 1974

Cecchetti 1883
"C" (= Bartolomeo Cecchetti), "Testamento di Pietro Vioni veneziano fatto a Tauris (Persia) MMCCLXIV, X dicembre", *AV*, 26, 1883, pp. 161-65

Cecchetti 1886
Bartolomeo Cecchetti, *La vita dei veneziani nel 1300: Le vesti*, Venice, 1886

Cecconi 1986
Giovanna Cecconi, "Avvisi, lettere, ragguagli, canzoni: i 'successi' in Levante da Nicosia a Lepanto", in *Venezia e Levante* 1986, pp. 32-35

Cecconi 1986a
Giovanna Cecconi, "Le voci e gli echi: Antologia di testi per l'audio", in *Venezia e Levante* 1986, pp. 36-46

Cellini 1891
Benvenuto Cellini, *La Vita*, B. Bianchi (ed.), Florence, 1891

Cellini 1956
Benvenuto Cellini' Autobiography, G. Bull (transl.), Harmondsworth, 1956

Cessi 1985
Roberto Cessi, *Venezia nel Duecento: tra Oriente e Occidente*, Venice, 1985

Chardin 1711
John Chardin, *Voyages de Monsieur le Chevalier Chardin en Perse et autres lieux de l'Orient*, Amsterdam, 1711

Charleston 1959
Robert J. Charleston, "Souvenirs of the grand tour", *JGS*, 1, 1959, pp. 62-82

Charleston 1965
Robert J. Charleston, "The import of Venetian glass into the Near East, 15th-16th century", *Annales du 3e Congrès des Journées Internationales du Verre*, Liège, 1965, pp. 158-68

Charleston 1966
Robert J. Charleston, "The import of Western glass into Turkey: Sixteenth-eighteenth centuries", *Connoisseur*, 162, no. 651, May 1966, pp. 19-26

Charleston 1974
Robert J. Charleston, "Types of glass imported into the Near East, and some fresh examples; 15th - 16th century", in A. Ohm and H. R. Hamburg (eds.), *Festschrift für Peter Wilhelm Meister zum 65. Geburtstag am 16. Mai 1974*, Hamburg, 1974, pp. 245-51

Charleston, Archer and Marcheix 1977
Robert J. Charleston, Michael Archer and Madeleine Marcheix, *The James A. de Rothschild Collection at Waddesdon Manor, Glass and Stained Glass, Limoges and Other Painted Enamels*, London, 1977

Charrière 1848-1860
Ernest Charrière, *Négociations de la France dans le Levant*, Collection de documents inédits sur l'histoire de France, sér. I, 4 vols., Paris, 1848-1860

Chiappini di Sorio 2002
Ileana Chiappini di Sorio, "Alcune osservazioni sulle 'Turcherie'", in A. Bettagno (ed.), *I Guardi: Vedute, capricci, feste, disegni e 'quadri turcheschi'*, Venice, 2002, pp. 165-78

Chicago 1985
John Carswell, *Blue and White. Chinese Porcelain and Its Impact on the Western World at the David and Alfred Smart Gallery, The University of Chicago*, exh. cat., Chicago, 1985

Chong 2005
Alan Chong, "Gentile Bellini in Istanbul: Myths and misunderstandings", in Campbell and Chong 2005, pp. 106-29

Chong, Pegazzano, and Zikos 2003
Alan Chong, Donatella Pegazzano, and Dimitrios Zikos (eds.), *Raphael, Cellini, and a Renaissance Banker: The Patronage of Bindo Altoviti*, exh. cat., Isabella Stewart Gardner Museum, Boston and Museo Nazionale del Bargello, Florence, 2003

Cisotto Nalon and Barovier Mentasti 2002
Mirella Cisotto Nalon and Rosa Barovier Mentasti, *Suggestioni, colori e fantasie. I vetri dell'Ottocento muranese*, Milan, 2002

Clarke 1974
Timothy H. Clarke, "Lattimo. A group of Venetian glass enameled on an opaque-white ground", *JGS*, 16, 1974, pp. 22-56

Clayton and Wace 1938
Muriel Clayton andAlan John Bayard Wace , "A tapestry at Powis Castle", *BM*, 73, no. 425, 1938, pp. 64-66, 69

Clot 1992
André Clot, *Suleiman the Magnificent*, M. J. Reisz (transl.), New York, 1992

Clutton 1978
Elizabeth Clutton, "Political conflict and military strategy: The case of Crete as exemplified by Basilicata's *Relatione* of 1630", *Transactions of the Institute of British Geographers*, n.s. 3, no. 3, 1978, pp. 274-84

Clutton 1982
Elizabeth Clutton, "Some seventeenth-century images of Crete: A comparative analysis of the manuscript maps by Francesco Basilicata and the printed maps

by Marco Boschini", *Imago Mundi*, 34, 1982, pp. 48-65

Cocke 2001
Richard Cocke, *Paolo Veronese: Piety and Display in an Age of Religious Reform*, Aldershot, 2001

Coco and Manzonetto 1985
Carla Coco and Flora Manzonetto, *Baili veneziani alla Sublime Porta. Storia e caratteristiche dell'ambasciata veneta a Costantinopoli*, Venice, 1985

Codazzi 1952
Angela Codazzi, "Una 'descrizione' del Cairo di Guglielmo Postel" in *Studi in onore di Cesare Manaresi*, Milan, 1952, pp. 169-206

Cohen 1995
Simona Cohen, "A new perspective on Giorgione's *Three Philosophers*", *GBA*, ser. 6, 126, Sep 1995, pp. 53-64

Colle 1996
Enrico Colle, *Museo d'Arti Applicate: mobili e intagli lignei*, Milan, 1996

Colle 1998
Enrico Colle, *Scrigni e stipi, i tesori della collezione Mosca*, Pesaro, 1998

Colleoni and Errera 1868
Antonio Colleoni and Alberto Errera, *Sulla Seconda Esposizione Vetraria del 1869 in Murano. Discorsi, notizie e relazione, a cura del Municipio dell'Isola*, Venice, 1868

Collins 1970
Howard Collins, "Gentile Bellini: A monograph and catalogue of works", Ph.D. Dissertation, University of Pittsburgh, 1970

Colvin 1897
Sidney Colvin, "Uber einige Zeichnungen des Carpaccio in England", *Jahrbuch der Königlichen Preussischen Kunstsammlungen*, 18, 1897, pp. 193-204

Colonna 2004
Francesco Colonna, *Hypnerotomachia Poliphili*, (1st ed. Venice, 1499), M. Ariani and M. Gabriele (eds.), 2 vols., Milan, 2004

Concina 1984
Ennio Concina, "Fra Oriente e Occidente: Gli Zen, un palazzo e il mito di Trebisonda", in M. Tafuri (ed.), *"RENOVATIO URBIS". Venezia nell'età di Andrea Gritti (1523-1538)*, Rome, 1984, pp. 265-90

Concina 1994
Ennio Concina, *Il doge e il sultano: mercatura, arte e relazioni nel primo '500. Doç ve Sultan. 16 yuuzyıl başlarında ticaret, sanat ve ilişkiler*, S. Postacioğlu Banon (transl.), Rome, 1994

Concina 1997
Ennio Concina, *Fondaci: Architettura, arte e mercatura tra Levante, Venezia e Alemagna*, Venice, 1997

Concordia 1989
Pierangela Croce da Villa (ed.), *La città nella città. Un intervento di archeologia urbana in Concordia Sagittaria: materiali romani e rinascimentali dallo scavo di Piazza della Cattedrale*, exh. cat., Concordia Sagittaria, Basilica paleocristiana, s.l., 1989

Condivi 1746
Ascanio Condivi, *Vita di Michelagnolo Buonarroti, pittore, scultore, architetto e gentiluomo fiorentino*, Florence, 1746

Condivi 1999
Ascanio Condivi, *The Life of Michelangelo*, H. Wohl (ed.), A.S. Wohl (transl.), (1st ed. in Italian, Rome, 1553), University Park, PA, 1999

Constable 2001
Olivia Remie Constable, "*Funduq, fondaco* and *khān* in the wake of Christian commerce and Crusade", in A. E. Laiou and R. P. Mottahedeh (eds.), *The Crusades from the Perspective of Byzantium and the Muslim World*, Washington, D.C., 2001, pp. 145-56

Constable 2003
Olivia Remie Constable, *Housing the Stranger in the Mediterranean World: Lodging, Trade and Travel in Late Antiquity and the Middle Ages*, Cambridge, 2003

Contadini 1988
Anna Contadini, "Due pannelli di cuoio dorato nel Museo Civico Medievale di Bologna", *Annali di Ca' Foscari*, 27, no. 3, 1988, pp. 127-42

Contadini 1989
Anna Contadini, "Cuoridoro: tecnica e decorazione di cuoi dorati veneziani e italiani con influssi islamici", in Grube 1989, pp. 231-51

Contadini 1999
Anna Contadini, "Artistic contacts: Current scholarship and future tasks", in Burnett and Contadini 1999, pp. 1-60

Conte 2001
Tiziana Conte (ed.), *Cesare Vecellio, 1521c.-1601*, Belluno, 2001

Contò and Quaquarelli 1995
Agostino Contò and Leonardo Quaquarelli (eds.), *L'"Antiquario" Felice Feliciano Veronese, tra epigrafia antica, letteratura e arti del libro. Atti del Convegno di Studi*, Padua, 1995

Conton 1940
Luigi Conton, *Le antiche ceramiche veneziane scoperte nella Laguna*, Venice, 1940

Conton 1982
Reprint of Conton 1940

Corner 1758
Flaminio Corner, *Notizie storiche delle chiese e monasteri di Venezia e Torcello*, Padua, 1758

Corning 2004
Jutta-Annette Page, *Beyond Venice: Glass in Venetian Style, 1500-1750*, exh. cat., Corning Museum of Glass, Corning, NY, 2004

Correr 1899
Museo Civico e Raccolta Correr, Elenco degli oggetti esposti, Venice, 1899

Cozzi 1963-64
Gaetano Cozzi, "Cultura, politica e religione nella 'pubblica storiografia' veneziana del '500", *Bollettino dell'Istituto di Storia della Società e dello Stato Veneziano*, 5-6, 1963-64, pp. 243-55

Cozzi 1987
Gaetano Cozzi (ed.), *Gli Ebrei e Venezia. Secoli XIV-XVIII*, Milan, 1987

Cozzi 1997
Gaetano Cozzi, "Dalla riscoperta della pace all'inestinguibile sogno di dominio", *SVe*, 7, 1997, pp. 3-104

Cozzi and Knapton 1986
Gaetano Cozzi and Michael Knapton, *Storia della Repubblica di Venezia, dalla guerra di Chioggia alla riconquista della terraferma. Storia d'Italia*, vol. 12/1, Turin, 1986

Cozzi and Prodi 1994
Gaetano Cozzi and Paolo Prodi (eds.), *Storia di Venezia. Vol VI. Dal Rinascimento al barocco*, Rome, 1994

Cozzi, Knapton and Scarabello 1992
Gaetano Cozzi, Michael Knapton and Giovanni Scarabello, *La Repubblica di Venezia nell'età moderna, dal 1517 alla fine della Repubblica. Storia d'Italia*, vol. 12/2, Turin, 1992

Craddock, La Niece and Hook 1998
Paul T. Craddock, Susan La Niece and Duncan R. Hook, "Brass in the medieval Islamic world", in P. T. Craddock (ed.), *2000 Years of Zinc and Brass*, British Museum Occasional Paper, 50, 2nd ed., London, 1998, pp. 73-113

Cranston 2003
Jodi Cranston, "Desire and gravitas in Bindo's portraits", in Chong, Pegazzano, and Zikos 2003, pp. 115-32

Cranz 1958
Edward F. Cranz, "The prefaces to the Greek editions and Latin translations of Alexander of Aphrodisias, 1450-1575", *Proceedings of the American Philosophical Society*, 102/5, Oct 1958, pp. 510-46

Crouzet-Pavan 1992
Élisabeth Crouzet-Pavan, "*Sopra le acque salse*": *Espaces, pouvoir et société à Venise à la fin du moyen âge*, 2 vols., Rome, 1992

Crowe 1976
Yolande Crowe, "The Islamic potter and China", *Apollo*, 103, no. 170, 1976, pp. 296-301

Crowe 2002
Yolande Crowe, *Persia and China. Safavid Blue and White Ceramics in the Victoria and Albert Museum. 1501-1738*, Switzerland and London, 2002

Cuneo 1991
Paolo Cuneo, "Sulla raffigurazione della città di Damasco in una tela di scuola belliniana conservata al Louvre", in C. Muscarà (ed.), *Venezia e l'oriente vicino: Città e civiltà*, Venice, 1991, pp. 43-51

Curatola 1985
Giovanni Curatola, "Tessuti e artigianato turco nel mercato veneziano", in Tenenti 1985, pp. 185-92

Curatola 1986
Giovanni Curatola, "Four carpets in Venice", *OCTS*, 2, 1986, pp. 123-30

Curatola 1991
Giovanni Curatola, "I tappeti, Venezia e l'Oriente", in *Arabeschi. Tappeti classici d'Oriente dal XVI al XIX secolo*, Venice, 1991, pp. 15-27

Curatola 1999
Giovanni Curatola, "Ebrei, turchi e veneziani a Rialto. Qualche documento sui tessili", in Burnett and Contadini 1999, pp. 105-12

Curatola 2003
Giovanni Curatola, "Con più color, sommesse e sovrapposte / non fer mai drappi Tartari né Turchi", in E. Carbonell, R. Cassanelli and T. Velmans (eds.), *Il Rinascimento in Oriente e Occidente, 1250-1490*, Milan, 2003, pp. 168-79

Curatola 2004
Giovanni Curatola, "A sixteenth-century quarrel about carpets", *Muqarnas*, 21, 2004, pp. 129-37

Curatola 2004a
Giovanni Curatola, "Tappeti orientali a Venezia", in N.-E. Vanzan Marchini (ed.), *Rotte mediterranee e baluardi di sanità. Venezia e i lazzaretti mediterranei*, Geneva and Milan, 2004, pp. 130-37

Curatola and Spallanzani 1981
Giovanni Curatola and Marco Spallanzani, *Metalli islamici dalle collezioni granducali*, Museo Nazionale del Bargello, Florence, 1981

Curtin 1984
Philip D. Curtin, *Cross-cultural Trade in World History*, Cambridge, 1984

Dalla Santa 1916-17
G. Dalla Santa, "Commerci, vita privata e notizie politiche dei giorni della lega di Cambrai", *Atti del Reale Istituto Veneto di Scienze, Lettere ed Arti*, 76, 1916-1917, pp. 1547-1605

Damisch 1984
Hubert Damisch, "Le théâtre de peinture", in D. Rosand (ed.), *Interpretazioni veneziane, Studi di storia dell'arte in onore di Michelangelo Muraro*, Venice, 1984, pp. 137-43

Da Mosto 1983
Andrea Da Mosto, *I dogi di Venezia nella vita pubblica e privata*, (1st ed. Venice, 1939), Florence, 1983

Dandolo 1938-52
Andrea Dandolo (ca. 1350), *Chronica per extensum descripta*, E. Pastorello (ed.), in L.A. Muratori (ed.), *Rerum italicarum scriptores*, n.s. 13, 1, 1938-52

Daniele and Schmidt Arcangeli 1998
Umberto Daniele and Catarina Schmidt Arcangeli, *Tarsie lignee della Basilica di San Marco*, Milan, 1998

D'Arcais 1992
Francesca d'Arcais, "Venezia", in M. Lucco (ed.), *La pittura nel Veneto, il Trecento*, vol. 1, Milan, 1992, pp. 17-87

Darrag 1961
Ahmad Darrag, *L'Égypte sous le règne de Barsbay (825-841 / 1422-1438)*, Damascus, 1961

Davanzo Poli 1980
Doretta Davanzo Poli, "La moda nella Venezia del Palladio, 1550 - ca. 1580", in L. Puppi (ed.), *Architettura e utopia nella Venezia del Cinquecento*, exh. cat., Palazzo Ducale, Venice, Milan, 1980, pp. 219-34

Davanzo Poli 1997
Doretta Davanzo Poli (ed.), *Seta e oro: La collezione tessile di Mariano Fortuny*, Venice, 1997

Davanzo Poli 2001
Doretta Davanzo Poli, *Abiti antichi e moderni dei veneziani*, Vicenza, 2001

Davies 1961
Martin Davies, *The Earlier Italian Schools*, (1st ed. London, 1951), London, 1961

De Busbecq 1881
The Life and Letters of Ogier Ghiselin de Busbecq, by C. T. Forster and F. H. B. Daniell (eds. and transl.), 2 vols., London, 1881
De' Conti 1929
Nicolò de' Conti, *Viaggi in Persia, India e Giava*, M. Longhena (ed.), Milan, 1929
Degenhart and Schmitt 1980
Bernhard Degenhart and Annegrit Schmitt, *Corpus der italienischen Zeichnungen 1300-1450, Teil II. Venedig. Addenda zu Süd- und Mittelitalien, Venedig 1300-1400*, Berlin, 1980
Degenhart and Schmitt 1990
Bernhard Degenhart and Annegrit Schmitt, *Corpus der italienischen Zeichnungen 1300-1450, Teil II, Venedig, Jacopo Bellini*, Berlin, 1990
De Jonghe et al. 2004
Daniël De Jonghe et al., *The Ottoman Silk Textiles of the Royal Museums of Art and History in Brussels*, Brepols, 2004
De Liesville 1878
A. R. De Liesville, "Exposition universelle, la ceramique moderne, verrerie", *GBA*, Nov. 1878, pp. 695-701
De Lucia 1908
Giuseppe de Lucia, *La sala d'armi nel Museo dell'Arsenale di Venezia; Catalogo storico, descritto, documentato e con una appendice di Mario Nani Mocenigo*, Rome, 1908
De Maria 2003
Blake de Maria, "The Merchants of Venice: A Study in Sixteenth-Century Cittadino Patronage", Ph.D. Dissertation, Princeton University, 2003
De Marinis 1955
Tammaro De Marinis, *Rilegature veneziane del XV al XVI secolo*, Venice, 1955
De Marinis 1960
Tammaro de Marinis, *La legatura artistica in Italia nei secoli XV e XVI*, Florence, 1960
De Marinis 1966
Tammaro de Marinis, "L'influsso orientale sull'arte della legatura a Venezia", in Pertusi 1966, pp. 547-53
Demus 1960
Otto Demus, *The Church of San Marco in Venice: History, Architecture, Sculpture*, Washington, D.C., 1960
Denny 1983
Walter Denny, "Dating Ottoman Turkish works in the *Saz* style", *Muqarnas*, 1, 1983, pp. 103-21
Denny 1999
Walter B. Denny, "Anatolian rugs with textile patterns", in N. Ölçer and W.B. Denny, *Masterpieces of Anatolian Carpets from the Museum of Turkish and Islamic Art, Istanbul*, vol. 1, Bern, 1999, pp. 50-55
Denny 2002
Walter B. Denny, *The Classical Tradition in Anatolian Carpets*, Washington, D.C. and London, 2002
Derenzini 1996
Giovanna Derenzini, "Tolomeo tra antico e nuovo: Una miniatura del codice *Marc. gr. Z. 388*", in *Bisanzio e L'occidente: arte, archeologia, storia. Studi in onore di Fernanda de Maffei*, Rome, 1996, pp. 559-73
Derman 1998
M. Uğur Derman, *Letters in Gold: Ottoman Calligraphy from the Sakip Sabanci Collection, Istanbul*, exh. cat., The Metropolitan Museum of Art, New York, 1998
Déroche 1985
François Déroche, *Catalogue des manuscrits arabes, 2e partie. Les manuscrits du Coran. 2. Du Maghreb à l'Insulinde*, Bibliothèque Nationale de France, Paris, 1985
Deschodt and Davanzo Poli 2001
Anne-Marie Deschodt and Doretta Davanzo Poli, *Fortuny*, New York, 2001
De Vecchi 1977
Pier Luigi De Vecchi, "Il Museo Gioviano e le 'vere imagines' degli uomini illustrati", in *Omaggio a Tiziano. La cultura artistica milanese nell'età di Carlo V*, Milan, 1977, pp. 87-96
De Voragine 1969
Jacopus de Voragine, *The Golden Legend*, G. Ryan and H. Ripperger (eds.), New York, 1969
Diacono 1890
Giovanni Diacono, "*Cronaca Veneziana*", in *Cronache veneziane antichissime*, G. Monticolo (ed.), *Fonti per la storia d'Italia*, Rome, 1890, pp. 57-171
Di Crollalanza 1888
G. B. Di Crollalanza, *Dizionario storico-blasonico delle famiglie nobili e notabili italiane estinte e fiorenti*, Pisa, 1888
Dimand 1935
Maurice S. Dimand, *The Ballard Collection of Oriental Rugs in the City Art Museum of Saint Louis*, St. Louis, 1935
Dodds 1992
Jerrilyn Dodds (ed.), *Al-Andalus: The Art of Islamic Spain*, exh. cat., Alhambra, Granada and The Metropolitan Museum of Art, New York, 1992
Dorigo 2003
Wladimiro Dorigo, *Venezia romanica. La formazione della città medioevale fino all'età gotica*, 2 vols., Venice and Verona, 2003
Dorini and Bertelé 1956
Umberto Dorini and Tommaso Bertelé, *Il Libro dei conti di Giacomo Badoer (Costantinopoli 1436-1440), Il Nuovo Ramusio*, 3, Rome, 1956
Drake 1868
William Richard Drake, *Notes on Venetian Ceramics*, London, 1868
Draper 1992
James David Draper, *Bertoldo di Giovanni. Sculptor of the Medici Household*, Columbia, MO, 1992
Draper 1994
James David Draper, "Bertoldo di Giovanni", in Scher 1994, pp. 126-32
Drey 1978
Rudolph E. A. Drey, *Apothecary Jars: Pharmaceutical Pottery and Porcelain in Europe and the East, 1150-1850*, London and Boston, 1978
Dufournier, Flambard, and Noyé 1986
Daniel Dufurnier, Anne-Marie Flambard and Ghislaine Noyé, "A propos de céramique 'RMR': Problèmes de définition et de classement, problèmes de répartition", in *La ceramica medievale nel Mediterraneo occidentale. Atti del III Congresso Internazionale*, Florence, 1986, pp. 251-77
Dursteler 2001
E. R. Dursteler, "The bailo in Constantinople: Crisis and career in Venice's early modern diplomatic corps", *Mediterranean Historical Review*, 16, no. 2, 2001, pp. 1-30
Dutschke 1998
Consuelo E. Dutschke, "The truth in the book: The Marco Polo texts in Royal 19.D.I and Bodley 264", *Scriptorium*, 1998, 52, no. 2, pp. 278-300
Edhem and Stchoukine 1933
Fehmi Edhem and Ivan Stchoukine, *Les manuscripts orientaux illustrés de la Bibliothèque de l'Université de Stamboul*, Paris, 1933
EI2
Encyclopaedia of Islam, new edition, H.A.R. Gibb et al. (eds.), Leiden, 1960-2002
Eickhoff 1991
Ekkehard Eickoff, *Venezia, Vienna e i turchi. Bufera nel sud-est europeo (1645-1700)*, Milan, 1991
Eisler 1989
Colin T. Eisler, *The Genius of Jacopo Bellini: The Complete Paintings and Drawings*, New York, 1989
Eldem 1999
Edhem Eldem, *French Trade in Istanbul in the Eighteenth Century*, Leiden, 1999
Ellis 1975
Charles Grant Ellis, "The 'Lotto' pattern as a fashion in carpets", in A. Ohm and H. R. (eds.), *Festschrift für Peter Wilhelm Meister zum 65. Geburtstag am 16. Mai 1974*, Hamburg, 1975, pp. 19-31
Enderlein 1955
Volkmar Enderlein, *Wilhelm von Bode und die Berliner Teppichsammlung*, Museum für Islamische Kunst, Berlin, 1955
Erber 1993
Christian Erber (ed.), *A Wealth of Silk and Velvet, Ottoman Fabrics and Embroideries*, Bremen, 1993
Erdmann 1938
Kurt Erdmann, "Kairener Teppiche, Teil I: Europäische und islamische Quellen des 15.-18. Jahrhunderts", *Ars Islamica*, 5, 1938, pp. 179-206
Erdmann 1962
Kurt Erdmann, *Europa und der Orientteppich*, Berlin and Mainz, 1962
Erdmann 1966
Kurt Erdmann, "Venezia e il tappeto orientale", in Pertusi 1966, pp. 529-45
Erdmann 1970
Kurt Erdmann, *Seven Hundred Years of Oriental Carpets*, Berkeley and Los Angeles, 1970
Erdmann 1971
Kurt Erdmann with André Grabar and Hans R. Hahnloser, "Opere islamiche", in H. R. Hahnloser, *Il Tesoro e il Museo*, vol. 2 of *Il Tesoro di San Marco*, Florence, 1971, pp. 101-27
Ericani 1990
Giuliana Ericani, "1.6.4. Graffita Rinascimentale tarda e ceramica dipinta nel Veneto occidentale, nel Padovano, nel Bellunese e a Oderzo", in Ericani and Marini 1990, pp. 155-71
Ericani 1990a
Giuliana Ericani, "2.9. Maioliche 'alla turchesca'. La porcellana tenera", in Ericani and Marini 1990, pp. 233-43
Ericani and Marini 1990
Giuliana Ericani and Paola Marini (eds.), *La ceramica nel Veneto. La terraferma dal XIII al XVIII secolo*, Verona, 1990
Ettinghausen 1950
Richard Ettinghausen, *Studies in Muslim Iconography, I: The Unicorn*, Freer Gallery of Art Occasional Papers, vol. 1, no. 3, Washington, D.C., 1950
Ettinghausen 1959
Richard Ettinghausen, "Near Eastern bookcovers and their influence on European bindings", *AO*, 3, 1959, pp. 113-31
Evans 1975
Joan Evans, *Pattern: A Study of Ornament in Western Europe from 1180-1900*, New York, 1975
Eyice 1967
Semavi Eyice, "La verrerie en Turquie de l'époque byzantine à l'époque turque", in *Annales du 4e Congrès des Journées Internationales du verre, Ravenne-Venise 1967*, Liège, 1967, pp. 162-82
Fabris 1989
Antonio Fabris, "Note sul mappamondo cordiforme di Haci Ahmed di Tunisi", *QSA*, 7, 1989, pp. 3-17
Fabris 1990
Antonio Fabris, "Un caso di pirateria veneziana: La cattura della galea del bey di Gerba (21 ottobre 1584)", *QSA*, 8, 1990, pp. 91-112
Fabris 1991
Antonio Fabris, "Artisanat et Culture: Recherches sur la production Venitienne et le marché Ottoman au XVIe siècle", *Arab Historical Review for Ottoman Studies*, 3-4, Dec 1991, pp. 51-60
Faenza 1990
Paola Torre, *Le Mille e una Notte. Ceramiche persiane, turche e ispano-moresche*, exh. cat., Museo delle Ceramiche, Faenza, 1990
Fedalto 1977
Giorgio Fedalto, "Le minoranze straniere a Venezia tra politica e legislazione", in Beck, Manoussacas, and Pertusi 1977, vol. 1, pp. 143-62
Fedalto 1980
Giorgio Fedalto, "Stranieri a Venezia e a Padova", in G. Arnaldi and M. P. Stocchi (eds.), *Storia della Cultura Veneta*, vol. 3/1, Vicenza, 1980, pp. 499-535
Fehérvári 1985
Géza Fehérvári, *La ceramica islamica*, Milano, 1985
Felton 1997
Anton Felton, *Jewish Carpets*, London, 1997
Fenerci 1986
Mehmed Fenerci, *Osmanlı kıyafetleri: aslı Rahmi M. Koç özel kitaplığında bulunan, Fenerci Mehmed tarafından resimlendirilmiş Osmanlı kıyafetleri*

albümünün tıpkı basımıdır / Fenerci Mehmed albümü = Ottoman Costume Book: A Facsimile Edition of Osmanlı Kıyafetleri by Fenerci Mehmed, the Original of which is in the Private Collection of Rahmi M. Koç, Istanbul, 1986

Fenlon 1988
Iain Fenlon, "Lepanto: The arts of celebration in Renaissance Venice", *Proceedings of the British Academy*, 73, 1988, pp. 201-36

Ferino-Pagden and Nepi Sciré 2004
Sylvia Ferino-Pagden and Giovanna Nepi Sciré (eds.), *Giorgione, Myth and Enigma*, exh. cat., Kunsthistorisches Museum Vienna, Vienna, 2004

Ferriguto 1933
Arnaldo Ferriguto, *Attraverso i "misteri" di Giorgione*, Castelfranco Veneto, 1933

Finlay 1984
Robert Finlay, "Al servizio del sultano: Venezia, i turchi e il mondo cristiano, 1523-1538", in M. Tafuri (ed.), *"Renovatio urbis": Venezia nell'età di Andrea Gritti (1523-1538)*, Rome, 1984, pp. 78-117

Fioravanti 1562
Leonardo Fioravanti, *Compendio de' secreti rationali*, Venice, 1562

Fioravanti 1572
Leonardo Fioravanti, *Dello specchio di scientia universale, dell'eccell...M. Leonardo Fioravanti bolognese libri tre*, 3 vols., Venice, 1572

Fioravanti 1675
Reprint of Fioravanti 1562, , 5 vols.

Fiore 1999-2001
Giovanni Fiore da Cropani, *Della Calabria illustrata*, Ulderico Nisticò (ed.) 3 vols., Catanzaro, 1999-2001

FitzHugh 1988
Elisabeth West FitzHugh, "Study of pigments on selected paintingsfrom the Vever Collection (Appendix 9)", in G. Lowry and M. C. Beach (eds.), *An Annotated and Illustrated Checklist of the Vever Collection*, Seattle and London, 1988

Fleming and Honour 1989
John Fleming and Hugh Honour, *The Penguin Dictionary of Decorative Arts*, new edition, London, 1989

Fletcher 1973
Jennifer Fletcher, "Sources of Carpaccio in German woodcuts", *BM*, 115, no. 846, Sep 1973, pp. 599-601

Florence 2002
Islam specchio d'Oriente, rarità e preziosi nelle collezioni statali fiorentine, exh. cat., Palazzo Pitti, Florence, 2002

Folda 2005
Jaroslav Folda, *Crusader Art in the Holy Land, From the Third Crusade to the Fall of Acre, 1187-129*, Cambridge and New York, 2005

Fontana 1989
Maria Vittoria Fontana, "Rapporti artistici fra ceramica islamica e ceramica veneta fra il Quattrocento e il Seicento", in Grube 1989, pp. 125-46

Fontana 1993
Maria Vittoria Fontana, "L'influsso dell'arte islamica in Italia", in Venice 1993, pp. 455-98

Fontana and Heise 1998
Eszter Fontana and Birgit Heise, *Pleasure for Both Eye and Ear, Musical Instruments of Five Centuries*, Leipzig, 1998

Fortini Brown 1988
Patricia Fortini Brown, *Venetian Narrative Painting in the Age of Carpaccio*, New Haven and London, 1988

Fortini Brown 1990
Patricia Fortini Brown, "Measured friendship, calculated pomp: The ceremonial welcomes of the Venetian Republic", in B. Wisch and S. Scott Munshower (eds.), *"All the world's a stage..." Art and Pageantry in the Renaissance and Baroque, Part I: Triumphal Celebrations and the Rituals of Statecraft*, University Park, PA, 1990, pp. 136-86

Fortini Brown 1996
Patricia Fortini Brown, *Venice and Antiquity; The Venetian Sense of the Past*, New Haven and London, 1996

Fortini Brown 1997
Patricia Fortini Brown, *Art and Life in Renaissance Venice*, New York, 1997

Fortini Brown 2004
Patricia Fortini Brown, *Private Lives in Renaissance Venice: Art, Architecture, and the Family*, New Haven and London, 2004

Fortnum 1896
Charles Drury Edward Fortnum, *Majolica. A Historical Treatise on the Glazed and Enamelled Earthenwares of Italy, with Marks and Monograms. Also Some Notice of the Persian Damascus, Rodhian and Hispano-Moresque Wares*, Oxford, 1896

Franco 1998
Tiziana Franco, *Michele Giambono e il monumento a Cortesia da Serego in Santa Anastasia a Verona*, Padua, 1998

Franzoi 1990
Umberto Franzoi, *L'Armeria del Palazzo Ducale a Venezia*, Venice, 1990

Frescobaldi, Gucci and Sigoli 1948
Leonardo Frescobaldi, Giorgio Gucci and Simone Sigoli, *Visit to the Holy Places of Egypt, Sinai, Palestine and Syria in 1384*, T. Bellorini and E. Hoade (transl.), Jerusalem, 1948

Freestone 2001
Ian C. Freestone, "Primary glass sources in the mid first millennium AD", *Annales du 15ᵉ Congrès de l'Association Internationale pour l'Histoire du Verre*, New York and Corning, 2001, Nottingham, 2003, pp. 111-15

Freestone 2002
Ian C. Freestone, "Composition and affinities of glass from the furnaces on the island site, Tyre", *JGS*, 44, 2002, pp. 67-77

Freestone and Gorin-Rosen 1999
Ian C. Freestone and Yael Gorin-Rosen, "The great slab at Bet She'arim, Israel: An early Islamic glassmaking experiment?", *JGS*, 41, 1999, pp. 105-16

Freestone, Gorin-Rosen and Hughes 2000
Ian C. Freestone, Yael Gorin-Rosen and Michael J. Hughes, "Primary glass from Israel and the production of glass in late antiquity and the early Islamic period", *Travaux de la Maison de l'Orient Méditerranéen*, 33, 2000, pp. 66-83

Freestone, Greenwood and Gorin-Rosen 2002
Ian C. Freestone, R. Greenwood and Yael Gorin-Rosen, "Byzantine and early Islamic glassmaking in the Eastern Mediterranean: Production and distribution of primary glass", in G. Kordas (ed.), *Proceedings of the 1st International Conference Hyalos, Vitrum, Glass*, Athens, 2002, pp. 167-74

Freestone and Stapleton 1998
Ian C. Freestone and Colleen P. Stapleton, "Composition and technology of Islamic enamelled glass of the thirteenth and fourteenth centuries", in Ward 1998, pp. 122-28.

Frey 1899
Karl Frey, *Sammlung ausgewählter Briefe an Michelangelo Buonarroti*, Berlin, 1899

Frick 1968-2003
The Frick Collection: An Illustrated Catalogue, New York, 1968-2003

Frothingham 1951
Alice Wilson Frothingham, *Lustreware of Spain*, New York, 1951

Frothingham 1964
Alice Wilson Frothingham, *Spanish Glass*, London, 1964

Fuess 2001
Albrecht Fuess, "Rotting ships and razed harbors: The naval policy of the Mamluks", *MSR*, 5, 2001, pp. 45-71

Gabriele 2004
Mino Gabriele, "The 'Three Philosophers', the Magi and the nocturnal", in Ferino-Pagden and Nepi Sciré 2004, pp. 79-83

Gabrieli 1966:
Francesco Gabrieli, "Venezia e i mamelucchi", in Pertusi 1966, pp. 417-32

Gabrieli and Scerrato 1979
Francesco Gabrieli and Umberto Scerrato, *Gli Arabi in Italia: Cultura, contatti e tradizioni*, Milan, 1979

Galanté 1941-42
Abraham Galanté, *Histoire des Juifs d'Istanbul depuis la prise de cette ville, en 1453, par Fatih Mehmed II, jusqu'à nos jours*, Istanbul, 1941-42

Galbiati 1946
Giovanni Galbiati, *La prima stampa in arabo. Miscellanea Giovanni Mercati*, vol. 6, Vatican City, 1946

Gallo 1950
Rodolfo Gallo. "Gian Francesco Camocio and his large map of Europe", *Imago Mundi*, 7, 1950, pp. 96-100

Gallo 1967
Rodolfo Gallo, *Il tesoro di San Marco e la sua storia*, Venice and Rome, 1967

Gamber and Beaufort 1990
Ortwin Gamber and Christian Beaufort with Matthias Pfaffenbichler, *Kunsthistorisches Museum, Wien, Hofjagd und Rüsthammer: Katalog der Leibrüstkammer*, vol. 2, *Der Zietraum von 1530-1560*, Vienna and Busto Arsizio, 1990

Garcin 1995-2000
Jean-Claude Garcin (ed.), *États, sociétés et cultures du monde musulman médiéval (Xᵉ-XVᵉ siècles)*, 3 vols., Paris, 1995-2000

Garton 2003
John Garton, "Paolo Veronese's portraits: Their creation and context", Ph.D. Dissertation, New York University, Institute of Fine Arts, 2003

Garzoni 1587
Tommaso Garzoni, *La piazza universale di tutte le professioni del mondo*, Venice, 1587

Garzoni 1589
Tommaso Garzoni, *La piazza universale di tutte le professioni del mondo, Nuovamente ristampata, & posta in luce da Thomaso Garzoni da Bagnacauallo, con l'aggiunta d'alcune bellissime annotationi a discorso per discorso*, (1st ed. 1585), Venice, 1589

Gasparetto 1973
Astone Gasparetto, "The Gnalić wreck. Identification of the ship", *JGS*, 15, 1973, pp. 79-84

Gasparetto 1976
Astone Gasparetto, "Vetri veneziani da un naufragio in Dalmazia e da documenti dell'ultimo Cinquecento", *SV*, 17-18, 1976, pp. 411-66

Gaudefroy-Demombynes 1923
Maurice Gaudefroy-Demombynes, *La Syrie à l'époque des Mamelouks d'après les auteurs arabes*, Paris, 1923

Gayraud 1986
Roland Pierre Gayraud, "Importations de céramiques occidentales dans l'Empire des Mamelouks (résumé)", in *La ceramica medievale nel Mediterraneo occidentale. Atti del III Congresso Internazionale*, Florence, 1986, p. 611

GBA
Gazette des Beaux Arts

Gealt 1984
Adelheid M. Gealt, *Italian Portrait Drawings, 1400-1800, from North American Collections*, exh. cat., Indiana University Art Museum, Bloomington, 1984

Gealt and Knox 1996
Adelheid M. Gealt and George Knox, *Domenico Tiepolo: Master Draftsman*, exh. cat., Castello di Udine and Indiana University Art Museum, Bloomington, 1996

Gelichi 1983-84
Sauro Gelichi, "I bacini della chiesa di San Bartolo a Ferrara", *Bollettino Annuale dei Musei Ferraresi*, 13, 1983-84, pp. 71-92

Gelichi 1986
Sauro Gelichi, "La ceramica ingobbiata medievale nell'Italia nord-orientale", in *La ceramica medievale nel Mediterraneo occidentale. Atti del III Congresso Internazionale*, Florence, 1986, pp. 353-407

Gelichi 1991
Sauro Gelichi, "La ceramica nell'Italia centro-settentrionale nel tardo medioevo tra oriente e occidente", in *Actas do IV Congresso Internacional a cerâmica medieval no Mediterrâneo ocidental*, Mértola, 1991, pp. 339-48

Gelichi 1991a
Sauro Gelichi, "Ceramiche e commerci con il Mediterraneo orientale nel tardomedioevo (XII-XIII secolo)", in *XXXVIII Corso di cultura sull'arte ravennate e bizan-*

tina, Seminario internazionale di studi sul tema: "La Grecia insulare tra Tardoantico e Medioevo", Ravenna, 1991, pp. 197-208

Gelichi 1993
Sauro Gelichi, "La ceramica bizantina in Italia e la ceramica italiana nel Mediterraneo orientale tra XII e XIII secolo: Stato degli studi e proposte di ricerca, in S. Gelichi (ed.), *La ceramica nel mondo bizantino tra XI e XV secolo e i suoi rapporti con l'Italia, Atti del Seminario di Pontignano*, Florence, 1993, pp. 9-46

Gelichi 1993a
Sauro Gelichi, "Ceramiche 'tipo Santa Croce'. Un contributo alla conoscenza delle produzioni venete tardo-medievali", *Archeologia medievale*, 20, 1993, pp. 229-301

Geneva 1985
Toby Falk (ed.), *Treasures of Islam*, exh. cat., Musée Rath, Geneva, 1985

Gentili 1996
Augusto Gentili, *Le Storie di Carpaccio: Venezia, i Turchi, gli Ebrei*, Venice, 1996

Gentili 2004
Augusto Gentili, "Traces of Giorgione, Jewish culture and astrological science", in Ferino-Pagden and Nepi Scirè 2004, pp. 57-69

Georgopulou 1999
Maria Georgopulou, "Orientalism and Crusader art: Constructing a new canon", *Medieval Encounters*, 5, no. 3, 1999, pp. 289-321

Gerlach 1674
Stephan Gerlach, *Stephan Gerlachs dess Aelten Tage-Buch ...*, Frankfurt-am-Main, 1674

Gerspach 1885
Edouard Gerspach, *L'art de la verrerie*, Paris, 1885

Gibbons 1977
Felton Gibbons, *Catalogue of Italian Drawings in the Art Museum, Princeton University*, 2 vols., Princeton, 1977

Gibbs-Smith and Rees 1978
Charles Harvard Gibbs-Smith and Gareth Rees (eds.), *The Inventions of Leonardo da Vinci*, Oxford, 1978

Gobbo 1998
Vincenzo Gobbo, "Distribuzione areale della ceramica ispano-moresca nel Veneto orientale e nel Friuli", in *Atti XXXI Convegno Internazionale della Ceramica Albisola 1998*, Albisola, 1999, pp. 223-31

Goffen 1975
Rona Goffen, "Icon and vision: Giovanni Bellini's half-length Madonnas", *AB*, 57, Dec 1975, pp. 487-518

Goffen 1989
Rona Goffen, *Giovanni Bellini*, New Haven and London, 1989

Gökbilgin 1964
M. Tayyip Gökbilgin, "Venedik devlet aráivindeki vesikalar kulliyatında Kanuni Sultan Süleyman devri belgeler", *Belgeler*, 1/2, 1964, pp. 119-220

Gökbilgin 1979
M. Tayyip Gökbilgin, "Le relazioni veneto-turche nell'età di Solimano il Magnifico", *Il Veltro. Rivista della Civiltà Italiana*, 23, nos. 2-4, Mar-Aug 1979, pp. 277-91

Golden 2005
Peter B. Golden, "The Turks: A historical overview", in London 2005, pp. 18-31

Goldner 2004
George R. Goldner, "Bellini's Drawings", in P. Humfrey (ed.), *The Cambridge Companion to Giovanni Bellini*, Cambridge, 2004, pp. 226-55

Goldner 2005
George R. Goldner, "Vittore Carpaccio, study of a lion", in P. Costamagna, F. Härb and S. Prosperi Valenti Rodinò (eds.), *Disegno, giudizio e bella maniera: Studi sul disegno italiano in onore di Catherine Monbeig Goguel*, Milan, 2005, cat. 3, p. 26

Goldschmidt 1928
Ernst Philip Goldschmidt, *Gothic and Renaissance Bookbindings: Exemplified and Illustrated from the Author's Collection*, 2 vols., London, Boston and New York, 1928

Goldstein 2005
Sidney M. Goldstein, *Glass. From Sasanian Antecedents to European Imitations*, The Nasser D. Khalili Collection of Islamic Art, vol. 15, London, 2005

Golombek, Mason and Bailey 1996
Lisa Golombek, Robert B. Mason and Gauvin A. Bailey, *Tamerlane's Tableware: A New Approach to the Chinoiserie Ceramics of Fifteenth- and Sixteenth-Century Iran. Islamic Art and Architecture Series*, 6, Costa Mesa, 1996

Gombrich 1967
Ernst H. Gombrich, "Celebrations in Venice of the Holy League and of the victory of Lepanto", in M. Kitson and J. Shearman (eds.), *Studies in Renaissance & Baroque Art presented to Anthony Blunt on his 60th Birthday*, New York, 1967, pp. 62-68

Gombrich 1984
Ernst H. Gombrich, *The Sense of Order: A Study in the Psychology of Decorative Art*, (1st ed. Ithaca, NY, 1979), Oxford, 1984

Gombrich 1986
Ernst H. Gombrich, "A Note on Giorgione's 'Three Philosophers'", *BM*, 128, no. 1000, Jul 1986, p. 48

Gomez-Gérard and Yérasimos 1989
Marie-Christine Gomez-Gerard and Stéphane Yérasimos (eds.), *Nicolas de Nicolay: Dans l'Empire de Soliman le Magnifique*, Paris, 1989

Gonzales Clavijo 1990
Ruy de Gonzales Clavijo, *La route de Samarkand au temps de Tamerlan*, Lucien Kehren (trans.), Paris, 1990

González Martí 1944
Manuel González Martí, *Cerámica del Levante español. Siglos medievales. Loza*, Barcelona, 1944

González Martí 1948
Manuel González Martí, "Azulejos valencianos exportados a Italia", *Faenza*, 34, 1948, pp. 91-92

González-Palacios 1996
Alvar González-Palacios, *I mobili italiani*, Milan, 1996

Gottlieb 1913
Theodor Gottlieb, "Venezianische Einbände des XV. Jahrhunderts", *Kunst und Kunsthandwerk*, 16, 1913, pp. 153-76

Gould 1976
Cecil Gould, "The oriental element in Titian", in *Tiziano e Venezia. Convegno Internazionale di Studi, Venezia, 1976*, Vicenza, 1976, pp. 233-35

Gozzi 1890
Carlo Gozzi, *The Memoirs of Count Carlo Gozzi; Translated into English by John Addington Symmonds*, 2 vols., London, 1890

Grabar 1984
Oleg Grabar, "Reflections on Mamluk art", *Muqarnas*, 2, 1984, pp. 1-12

Grabar 1992
Oleg Grabar, *The Mediation of Ornament*, Princeton and Oxford, 1992

Grafton 1993
Anthony Grafton (ed.), *Rome Reborn: The Vatican Library and Renaissance Culture*, exh. cat., Library of Congress, Washington, D.C., 1993

Granzotto 1995
Orfea Granzotto, "Alcune note su Feliciano Legatore", *L'Antiquario*, 1995, pp. 221-29

Gratuze et al. 1996
Bernard Gratuze, Isabelle Soulier, Marise Blet, and Lucy Vallauri, "De l'origine du cobalt: du verre à la céramique", *Revue d'Archéométrie*, 20, 1996, pp. 77-94

Green 1995
Michael Green, "La scuola di Santo Stefano in Venezia: Sede delle ultime storie di Vittore Carpaccio", *SV*, 29, 1995, pp. 143-66

Grevembroch 1764
Giovanni Grevembroch, *Varie venete curiosità sacre e profane*, Biblioteca del Museo Correr, MS. Gr. Dolfin 65/III, Venice, 1764

Gronau 1903
Georg Gronau, "Tizians Bildnisse türkischer Sultaninnen", *Beiträge zur Kunstgeschichte*, 1903, pp. 131-37

Grube 1974
Ernst J. Grube, "A lacquered panel painting from the collection of Lester Wolfe in the Museum of the University of Notre-Dame", in J.M. Barral (ed.), *Orientalia Hispanica, sive studia M. F. Pareja octogenaro dicata*, vol. 1 (Arabica-Islamica), Leiden, 1974, pp. 376-97

Grube 1982
Ernst J. Grube, "Traditionalism or forgery: Lacquered painting in 19th-century Iran", in W. Watson (ed.), *Lacquerwork in Asia and Beyond. Colloquies on Art & Archaeology in Asia*, 11, Percival David Foundation of Chinese Art -School of Oriental and African Studies, London, 1982, pp. 277-300

Grube 1986
Ernst J. Grube, *Arte Veneziana*, Venice, 1986

Grube 1987
Ernst J. Grube, "The date of the Venice *Iskandar-nama*", *Islamic Art*, 2, 1987, pp. 187-202

Grube 1989
Ernst J. Grube (ed.) with Stefano Carboni and Giovanni Curatola, *Venezia e l'Oriente Vicino: Atti del primo simposio sull'arte veneziana e l'arte islamica, Venice, Ateneo Veneto, 1986*, Venice, 1989

Grube 1989a
Ernst J. Grube, "Lacche veneziane e i loro modelli islamici", in Grube 1989, pp. 217-29

Grube 1989b
Ernst J. Grube, "Apporti orientali nella decorazione della graffita veneta", in *Atti del convegno "La ceramica graffita medievale e rinascimentale nel Veneto"*, Padua, 1989, pp. 145-57

Grube and Sims (forthcoming)
Ernst J. Grube and Eleanor Sims, "From 'The Bloody and Cruell Turke' to Turquerie: Some thoughts on the perception of the Turk in European imagination, art, and history", in *Tulips, Carnations and Roses. Festschrift for Tadeusz Majda*, forthcoming

Guâerin-Dalle Mese 1998
Jeannine Guâerin-Dalle Mese, *L'occhio di Cesare Vecellio: abiti e costumi esotici nel '500*, Alessandria, 1998

Guidoni 1995-96
Enrico Guidoni, "I Tre Filosofi: Pitagora, Tolomeo, Copernico", in E. Guidoni (ed.), *Studi su Giorgione e sulla pittura del suo tempo: Conferenze 1995-96*, 5 vols., Rome, 1995-96, vol. 4, pp. 3-14

Gullino 1996
Giuseppe Gullino, "Le frontiere navali", in *SVe*, 4, 1996, pp. 12-111

Gullino 1997
Giuseppe Gullino, "Foscari, Francesco", in *Dizionario Biografico degli Italiani*, vol. 49, pp. 306-14

von Gumppenberg 1987
Georg Frerherr von Gumppenberg, "Wachen und Waffen um 1600", in Salzburg 1987, pp. 265-69

Gyselen 1999
Rika Gyselen (ed.), *La science[s] des cieux: sages, mages, astrologues*, Bures-sur-Yvette, 1999

Hasse 1997
Dag Nikolaus Hasse, "King Avicenna: The iconographic consequences of a mistranslation", *Journal of the Warburg and Courtald Institutes*, 60, 1997, pp. 230-43

Haldane 1983
Duncan Haldane, *Islamic Bookbindings in the Victoria and Albert Museum*, London, 1983

Hale 1994
John R. Hale, "La guerra e la pace", in Cozzi and Prodi 1994, pp. 239-52

Hamilton Beattie 1964
May Hamilton Beattie, "Britain and the Oriental Carpet", *Leeds Art Calendar*, 55, 1964, pp. 4-15

Han 1973
Verena Han, "Fifteen[th] and sixteen[th] century trade in glass between Dubrovnik and Turkey", *Balcanica*, 4, 1973, pp. 163-78

Harding and Micklewright 1997
Catherine Harding and Nancy Micklewright, "Mamluks and Venetians: An international perspective on fourteenth-century material culture in the

Mediterranean", *Revue d'art canadienne*, 24, no. 2, 1997, pp. 47-66

Hare 1935
W. Loftus Hare, "The Portrait of Muhammed II by Gentile Bellini", *Apollo*, 20, 1934, p. 249

Harthan 1961
John P. Harthan, *Bookbindings*, London, 1961

Haskell 1980
Francis Haskell, *Patrons and Painters, A Study in the Relations Between Art and Society in the Age of the Baroque*, (1st ed. London, 1963), New Haven and London, 1980

Hausmann 2002
Tjark Hausmann, *Fioritura: Blütezeiten der Majolika: eine Berliner Sammlung*, Berlin, 2002

Heck and Hoffmann 2000
M. Heck and P. Hoffmann, "Coloured opaque glass beads of the Merovingians", *Archaeometry*, 42, 2000, pp. 341-57

Hein 1984
Jørgen Hein, *Venetianske Glas Rosenborg*, Copenhagen, 1984

Hein 1992
Jørgen Hein, "Venetian or Saxon: Early Saxon glass in the glass room at Rosenborg Palace", *JGS*, 34, 1992, pp. 63-78

Heinemann 1962
Fritz Heinemann, *Giovanni Bellini e i belliniani*, Venice, 1962

Hellbing 2005
Bert-Uwe Hellbing, "Ein venezianischer Kabinettschrank mit Steineinlagen und Goldlackmalerei aus der zweiten Hälfte des 16. Jahrhunderts", Ph.D. Dissertation, Fachhochschule Potsdam, Berlin, 2005

Heller 1961
Erdmute Heller, *Venedische Quellen zur Lebensgeschichte des Ahmed Pasa Hersekoghlu*, Munich, 1961

Henderson, McLoughlin and McPhail 2004
Julian Henderson, Sean D. McLoughlin and David S. McPhail, "Radical changes in Islamic glass technology: Evidence for conservatism and experimentation with new glass recipes from early and middle Islamic Raqqa, Syria", *Archaeometry*, 46, 2004, pp. 439-68

Hendy 1974
Philip Hendy, *European and American Paintings in the Isabella Stewart Gardner Museum*, Boston, 1974

Herrlicher 1970
Robert Herrlicher, *History of Medical Illustration from Antiquity to 1600*, New York, 1970

Hess 1972
Andrew Hess, "The battle of Lepanto and its place in Mediterranean history", *Past and Present*, 57, Nov 1972, pp. 53-73

Hess 2004
Catherine Hess, "Brilliant achievements: The journey of Islamic glass and ceramics to Renaissance Italy", in C. Hess (ed.), *The Arts of Fire: Islamic Influences on Glass and Ceramics of the Italian Renaissance*, exh. cat., J. Paul Getty Museum, Los Angeles, 2004, pp. 1-33

Hetteš 1960
Karel Hetteš, *Benátské Sklo - Venetian Glass*, Prague, 1960

Heyd 1866-68
Wilhelm von Heyd, *Le colonie commerciali degli Italiani in Oriente nel Medio Evo*, 2 vols., Venice and Turin, 1866-68

Heyd 1885-86
Wilhelm Heyd, *Histoire du commerce du Levant au Moyen Age*, F. Raynaud (transl.), Leipzig, 1885-86

Heyd 1923
Reprint of Heyd 1885-86

Heyd 1936
Reprint of Heyd 1885-86

Hill 1926
George Francis Hill, "Medals of Turkish sultans", *Numismatic Chronicle*, ser. 5, 6, 1926, pp. 287-98

Hill 1930
George Francis Hill, *A Corpus of Italian Medals of the Renaissance before Cellini*, 2 vols., London, 1930

Hillenbrand 1999
Carole Hillenbrand, *The Crusades. Islamic Perspectives*, Edinburgh, 1999

Hillenbrand 1994
Robert Hillenbrand, *Islamic Architecture: Form, Function, Meaning*, Edinburgh, 1994

Hills 1999
Paul Hills, *Venetian Colour: Marble, Mosaic, Painting and Glass, 1250-1550*, New Haven, 1999

Hills 2002
Paul Hills, "Interpreting Renaissance colour", in A. J. Grieco, M. Rocke and F. Gioffredi Superbi (eds.), *The Italian Renaissance in the Twentieth Century: Acts of an International Conference, Florence, Villa I Tatti, June 9-11, 1999*, Florence, 2002

Hitzel 2001
Frédéric Hitzel, *L'Empire ottoman, XVe-XVIIIe siècles*, Paris, 2001

Hobson 1989
Anthony Hobson, "Islamic influence on Venetian Renaissance bookbinding", in Grube 1989, pp. 111-23

Hobson 1992
Anthony Hobson, *Humanists and Bookbinders. The Origin and Diffusion of the Humanistic Bookbinding, 1459-1559, with a Census of Historiated Plaquette and Medallion Bindings of the Renaissance*, (1st ed. 1989), Cambridge, 1992

Hocquet 1978-79
Jean Claude Hocquet, *Le sel et la fortune de Venise*, vol. 1; *Production et monopole*, vol. 2. *Voiliers et commerce en Méditerranée 1200-1650*, Lille, 1978-79

Hocquet 1999
Jean Claude Hocquet, *Denaro, navi e mercanti a Venezia*, Rome, 1999

Hocquet 2002
Jean Claude Hocquet, *Comercio marítimo en el Mediterráneo medieval y moderno*, Granada, 2002

Hocquet 2004
Jean-Claude Hocquet, *Venise au Moyen Age*, Paris, 2004

Hocquet (forthcoming)
Jean-Claude Hocquet, *Venise et la mer*, Paris, forthcoming

Hoeniger 1992
Cathleen Hoeniger, "Le stoffe nella pittura veneziana nel Trecento", in M. Lucco (ed.), *La pittura nel Veneto, Il Trecento*, vol. 2, Milan, 1992, pp. 442-62

Hofenk de Graaff 2004
Judith H. Hofenk de Graaff, *The Colourful Past. Origins, Chemistry and Identification of Natural Dyestuffs*, Riggisberg and London, 2004

Hoffman 2001
Eva R. Hoffman, "Pathways of portability: Islamic and Christian interchange from the tenth to the twelfth century", *Art History*, 24, 2001, pp. 17-50

Hoffman 2004
Eva R. Hoffman, "Christian-Islamic encounters on thirteenth-century Ayyubid metalwork: Local culture, authenticity, and memory", *Gesta*, 43, no. 2, 2004, pp. 129-42

Hope 1983
Charles Hope, *Benvenuto Cellini*, London, 1983

Howard 1974
Deborah Howard, "Two notes on Jacopo Sansovino", *Architectura*, 4, 1974, pp. 137-46

Howard 2000
Deborah Howard, *Venice & the East: The Impact of the Islamic World on Venetian Architecture 1100-1500*, New Haven and London, 2000

Howard 2003
Deborah Howard, "Death in Damascus: Venetians in Syria in the mid-fifteenth century", *Muqarnas*, 20, 2003, pp. 143-57

Howard 2003a
Deborah Howard, "Venice between East and West: Marc'Antonio Barbaro and Palladio's Church of the Redentore", *Journal of the Warburg and Courtauld Institutes*, 62, no. 3, 2003, pp. 306-25

Howard 2005
Deborah Howard, "Venice, the bazaar of Europe", in Campbell and Chong 2005, pp. 12-31

Humfrey 1983
Peter Humfrey, *Cima da Conegliano*, New York, 1983

Humfrey 1985
Peter Humfrey, "The Bellinesque life of St. Mark cycle for the Scuola Grande di San Marco in Venice in its original arrangement", *Zeitschrift für Kunstgeschichte*, 48, 1985, pp. 225-42

Humfrey 2005
Peter Humfrey, *Carpaccio*, London, 2005

Hummelberger 1969
Walter Hummelberger, "Die Türkenbeute im Historischen Museum der Stadt Wien, Das 17. Jahrhundert", *Vaabenhistoriske Aarboger*, 15, 1969, pp. 7-97

Huse and Wolters 1990
Norbert Huse and Wolfgang Wolters, *The Art of Renaissance Venice*, E. Jephcott (transl.), Chicago and London, 1990

Huth 1968
Hans Huth, "A Venetian Renaissance casket", *Museum Monographs*, 1, The City Art Museum of Saint Louis, St. Louis, 1968, pp. 41-50

Huth 1970
Hans Huth, "Sarazenen in Venedig?", in P. Bloch and G. Zick (eds.), *Festschrift für Hans Ladendorf*, Cologne and Vienna, 1970, pp. 58-68

Huth 1971
Hans Huth, *Lacquer of the West. The History of a Craft and an Industry, 1550-1950*, Chicago, 1971

Ibn Battuta 1958-94
Ibn Battuta, *The Travels of Ibn Battuta AD 1325-1354*, C. F. Beckingham (transl.), H.A.R. Gibb (ed.), 4 vols., *Haklyut Society*, ser. 2, nos. 110, 117, 141, and 178, 1958-94

Ibn Khaldun 1967
Ibn Khaldun, *The Muqaddimah: An Introduction to History*, F. Rosenthal (transl.), (1st ed. New York, 1958), 3 vols., Princeton, 1967

Ibrahim 1984
Leila 'Ali Ibrahim, "Residential architecture in Mamluk Cairo", *Muqarnas*, 2, 1984, pp. 47-59

Ilg 2004
Ulrike Ilg, "The cultural significance of costume books in sixteenth-century Europe", in C. Richardson (ed.), *Clothing culture, 1350-1650*, London, 2004, pp. 29-47

Imhaus 1997
Brunehilde Imhaus, *Le minoranze orientali a Venezia, 1300-1510*, Rome, 1997

Inalcik 1966
Halil Inalcik, "Harir", in *EI²*, vol. 3, pp. 209-18

Inalcik 1977
Halil Inalcik, "An outline of Ottoman-Venetian relations", in Beck, Manoussacas and Pertusi 1977, vol. 1, pp. 83-90

Inalcik 1978
Halil Inalcik, *The Ottoman Empire. Conquest, Organization and Economy*, London, 1978

Inalcik 1986
Halil Inalcik, "The Yürüks: Their origins, expansion and economic role", *OCTS*, 2, 1986, pp. 39-66

Inalcik 1994
Halil Inalcik, *An Economic and Social History of the Ottoman Empire, 1300-1600*, vol. 1, Cambridge, 1994

Ingolstadt 1979
Osmanisch-Türkisches Kunsthandwerk aus suddeutschen Sammlungen. Katalog zur Ausstellung im Bayerischen Armeemuseum Ingolstadt, Neues Schloss, exh. cat., Bayerischen Armeemuseum Ingolstadt, Neues Schloss, Munich, 1979

Irwin 1986
Robert Irwin, *The Middle East in the Middle Ages: The Early Mamluk Sultanate 1250-1382*, Carbondale and Edwardsville, 1986

Isphording and von Arnim 1987
Edouard Isphording and Manfred von Arnim, *Fünf Jahrhunderte Buchillustra-*

tion: Meisterwerke der Buchgraphik aus der Bibliothek Otto Schäfer, Nürnberg, 1987

Istanbul 1983
The Anatolian Civilisations, III: Seljuq/ Ottoman, exh. cat., Topkapı Palace Museum, Istanbul, 1983

Istanbul 1999
War and Peace, Ottoman-Polish Relations in the 15th-19th Centuries, exh. cat., Museum of Turkish and Islamic Art, Istanbul, 1999

Istanbul 2000
The Sultan's Portrait. Picturing the House of Osman, exh. cat., Topkapı Palace Museum, Istanbul, 2000

Istanbul 2003
From the Medicis to the Savoias: Ottoman Splendour in Florentine Collections, exh. cat., Sakip Sabancı Museum, Istanbul, 2003

Ivanoff 1976
Nicola Ivanoff, "The paintings in San Giorgio Maggiore", *Apollo*, 104, no. 173, Jul 1976, pp. 39-47

Jacoby 1979
David Jacoby, *Recherches sur la Méditerranée orientale du XIIe au XVe siècle. Peuples, sociétés, économies*, London, 1979

Jacoby 1989
David Jacoby, "Les Communes italiennes et les ordres militaires à Acre à l'époque des croisades", in M. Balard (ed.), *Etat et colonisation au Moyen Age*, Lyon, 1989, pp. 193-214 (Reprinted in D. Jacoby, *Trade, Commodities and Shipping in the Medieval Mediterranean*, Hampshire, 1997)

Jacoby 1989a
David Jacoby, "L'évolution urbaine et la fonction méditerranéenne d'Acre à l'époque des croisades", in E. Poleggi (ed.), *Città portuali del Mediterraneo, storia e archeologia. Atti del Convegno Internazionale di Genova 1985*, Genoa, 1989, pp. 95-109 (Reprinted in D. Jacoby, *Trade, Commodities and Shipping in the Medieval Mediterranean*, Hampshire, 1997)

Jacoby 1993
David Jacoby, "Raw materials for the glass industries of Venice and the Terraferma, about 1370-about 1460", *JGS*, 35, 1993, pp. 65-90

James 1988
David James, *Qur'ans of the Mamluks*, London, 1988

James 1992
David James, *The Master Scribe. Qur'ans of the 10th to 14th Centuries AD, Nasser D. Khalili Collection of Islamic Art*, vol. 2, London, 1992

JGS
Journal of Glass Studies

Jenkins 1984
Marilyn Jenkins [Madina], "Mamluk underglaze-painted pottery: Foundations for future study", *Muqarnas*, 2, 1984, pp. 95-114

Jenkins 1986
Marilyn Jenkins [Madina], *Islamic Glass. A Brief History*, The Metropolitan Museum of Art Bulletin, 44, no. 2, Fall 1986

Jestaz 1989
Bertrand Jestaz, "Riccio et Ulocrino", in A. Luchs (ed.), *Italian Plaquettes. Studies in the History of Art*, vol. 22, Washington, D.C., 1989, pp. 191-205

Jestaz 1990
Bertrand Jestaz, "Porcelaine de Chine et bronze islamique à Venise. La collection Redaldi (1527)", *Annali della Scuola Normale Superiore di Pisa*, ser. 3, 20, part 1, 1990, pp. 23-60

JHS
Journal of Hellenic Studies

Johnson 2000
Eugene J. Johnson, "Jacopo Sansovino, Giacomo Torelli, and the theatricality of the Piazzetta in Venice", *JSAH*, 59, no. 4, Dec 2000, pp. 436-53

Jones 1984
Peter Murray Jones, *Medieval Medical Miniatures*, London, 1984

JSAH
Journal of the Society of Architectural Historians

Kafadar 1986
Cemal Kafadar, "A death in Venice (1575). Anatolian Muslim merchants trading in the Serenissima", *Journal of Turkish Studies*, 10, 1986, pp. 191-218

Kaftal 1978
George Kaftal with Fabio Bisogni, *Iconography of the Saints in the Painting of North East Italy*, Florence, 1978

Kahle 1935
Paul Kahle, "Die Schatze der Fatimiden", *Zeitschrift der Deutschen Morgenländischen Gesellschaft*, 89, 1935, pp. 329-62

Kappel 1998
Jutta Kappel, *Deutsche Steinschnitte aus dem Grünen Gewölbe zu Dresden*, Idar-Oberstein and Dresden, 1998

Karpov 1986
Sergej P. Karpov, *L'Impero di Trebisonda, Venezia, Genova e Roma, 1204-1461. Rapporti politici, diplomatici e commerciali*, Rome, 1986

Katzenstein and Lowry 1983
Ranee A. Katzenstein and Glenn D. Lowry, "Christian themes in thirteenth century Islamic metalwork", *Muqarnas*, 1, 1983, pp. 53-68

Keil 1986
Robert Keil, "Einige Ikonographische Bemerkungen zur 'Schlacht von Lepanto' von Paolo Veronese in der Gallerie dell Accademia in Venedig", *Arte Veneta*, 40, 1986, pp. 85-94

Kenaan-Kedar 1992
Nurith Kenaan-Kedar, "The margins of society in marginal Romanesque sculpture", *Gesta*, 31, no. 1, 1992, pp. 15-24

Kenesson 1998
Summer S. Kenesson, "Islamic enamelled beakers: A new chronology", in Ward 1998, pp. 45-49

Kennedy 1981
Hugh Kennedy, *The Early ^cAbbasid Caliphate: A Political History*, London and Totowa, NJ, 1981

Ker 1977
Neil R. Ker, *Medieval Manuscripts in British Libraries*, Oxford, 1977

Kertesz 2005
Andrei Kertesz, "Transylvania and the Turkish rugs", in S. Ionesco (ed.), *Antique Ottoman Rugs in Transylvania*, Rome, 2005, pp. 19-40

Khalili 1997
Nasser D. Khalili, *Lacquer of the Islamic Lands. Nasser D. Khalili Collection of Islamic Art*, vol. 22, pt. 2, 2 vols., Oxford, 1997

Khalili, Robinson and Stanley 1996
Nasser D. Khalili, B.W. Robinson and Tim Stanley, *Lacquer of the Islamic Lands. Nasser D. Khalili Collection of Islamic Art*, vol. 22, London and New York, 1996

King 1999
David King, *World Maps for Finding the Direction and Distance to Mecca. Innovation and Tradition in Islamic Science*, Leiden, 1999

King 1982
Donald King, "The inventories of the carpets of King Henry VIII", *Hali*, 5, no. 3, 1983, pp. 293-302

King 1983
Donald King, "The carpets in the exhibition", in London 1983, pp. 24-105

Kisluk-Grosheide, Koeppe and Rieder 2006
Daniëlle Kisluk-Grosheide, Wolfram Koeppe and William Rieder, *European Furniture in The Metropolitan Museum of Art*, New Haven and London, 2006

Kissling 1961
Hans Joachim Kissling, "Das Renegantum in der Glanzeit des Osmanischen Reiches", *Scientia*, 1961, pp. 18-26

Klauner 1955
Friderike Klauner, "Zur Symbolik von Giorgiones 'Drei Philosophen', *Jahrbuch der Kunsthistorischen Sammlungen in Wien*, 51, 1955, pp. 145-68

Klesse 1967
Brigitte Klesse, *Seidenstoffe in der italienischen Malerei des vierzehnten Jahrhunderts*, Bern, 1967

Klesse and Mayr 1987
Brigitte Klesse and Hans Mayr, *European Glass from 1500-1800, The Ernesto Wolf Collection*, Vienna, 1987

Klinger 1991
Linda Susan Klinger, "The Portrait Collection of Paolo Giovio", Ph.D. Dissertation, Princeton University, Princeton, 1991

Knapton 1986
Michael Knapton, "Lo stato veneziano fra la battaglia di Lepanto e la guerra di Candia (1571-1644)", in *Venezia e Levante* 1986, pp. 233-41

Knox 1960
George Knox, *Catalogue of the Tiepolo Drawings in the Victoria and Albert Museum*, London, 1960

Knox 1975
George Knox, *Un Quaderno di vedute di Giambattista e Domenico Tiepolo*, Venice, 1975

Knox 1978
George Knox, "The Tasso Cycles of Giambattista Tiepolo and Giannantonio Guardi", *Museum Studies*, 9, 1978, pp. 49-95

Koeppe 1992
Wolfram Koeppe, "Die Lemmers-Danforth-Sammlung Wetzlar", *Heidelberg*, 1992, no. U1, p. 269

Koeppe 1995
Wolfram Koeppe, "The chest in the Italian and Central European bedchamber from the 15th to the 17th century", in M. Chilton (ed.), *The Bedroom from the Renaissance to Art Deco*, Toronto, 1995, pp. 13-24

Koeppe 2004
Wolfram Koeppe, "Exotica and the Kunstkammer: 'Snake stones, iridescent sea snails, and eggs of the giant iron-devouring bird'", in *Princely Splendor, The Dresden Court 1580-1620*, exh. cat., The Metropolitan Museum of Art, New York, 2004, pp. 80-89

Koeppe 2006
Wolfram Koeppe, "Collector's cabinet", in Kisluk-Grosheide, Koeppe and Rieder 2006, pp. 40-43

Koeppe and Lupo 1991
Wolfram Koeppe and Michelangelo Lupo, "Lo Heiltumsaltar nella sacrestia della cattedrale di Trento", in E. Castelnuovo (ed.), *Ori e Argenti dei Santi*, Trento, 1991, pp. 35-56

Komaroff and Carboni 2002
Linda Komaroff and Stefano Carboni, *The Legacy of Genghis Khan. Courtly Art and Culture in Western Asia, 1256-1353*, exh. cat., The Metropolitan Museum of Art, New York and Los Angeles County Museum of Art, Los Angeles, 2002

Kopplin 1998
Monika Kopplin, *Europäische Lackkunst*, Münster, 1998

Krahl 1986
Regina Krahl, *Chinese Ceramics in the Topkapı Saray Museum, Istanbul: A Complete Catalogue*, London and New York, 1986

Krahn 2001
Volker Krahn, "Bartolomeo Bellano", in *Donatello e il suo tempo, Il bronzetto a Padova nel Quattrocento e nel Cinquecento*, exh. cat., Musei Civici, Padua, 2001, pp. 63-91

Krek 1979
Miroslav Krek, "The enigma of the first Arabic book printed from movable type", *Journal of Near Eastern Studies*, 38, 1979, pp. 203-12

Krekić 1997
Bariša Krekić, *Dubrovnik: A Mediterranean Urban Society, 1300-1600*, London, 1997

Krueger 1998
Ingeborg Krueger, "An enamelled beaker from Stralsund: A spectacular new find", in Ward 1998, pp. 107-09

Kühnel 1949
Ernst Kühnel, *Die Arabeske: Sinn und Wandlung eines Ornaments*, Wiesbaden, 1949

Kupelwieser 1899
Luise Kupelwieser, *Die Kämpfe Österreichs mit den Osmanen vom Jahre 1526 bis 1537*, Vienna and Leipzig, 1899

Kurtzman and Koldau 2002
Jeffrey Kurtzman and Linda Maria

Koldau, "*Trombe, trombe d'argento, trombe squarciate, tromboni* and *pifferi* in Venetian processions and ceremonies of the 16th and 17th centuries", *Journal of Seventeenth-Century Music*, 8, no. 1, 2002, pp. 1-46

Kurz 1969
Otto Kurz, "A gold helmet made in Venice for Sultan Sulayman the Magnificent", *GBA*, ser. 6, 74, 1969, pp. 249-58 (Reprinted in Kurz 1977)

Kurz 1975
Otto Kurz, *European Clocks and Watches in the Near East*, London, 1975

Kurz 1977
Otto Kurz, *The Decorative Arts of Europe and the Islamic East. Selected Studies*, London, 1977

Kurz & Kurz 1972
Otto Kurz & Hilde Schueller Kurz, "The Turkish dresses in the costume book of Rubens", *Nederlands Kunsthistorisch Jaarboek*, 23, 1972, pp. 275-90

Labib 1965
Subhi Y. Labib, *Handelsgeschichte Ägyptens im Spätmittelalter (1171-1517)*, Wiesbaden, 1965

Lace 2006
William W. Lace, *The Unholy Crusade: The Ransacking of Medieval Constantinople*, San Diego, 2006

Lamm 1929-30
Carl J. Lamm, *Mittelalterliche Gläser und Steinschnittarbeiten aus dem Nahen Osten*, 2 vols., Berlin, 1929-30

Lamm 1941
Carl J. Lamm, *Oriental Glass of Medieval Date Found in Sweden and the Early History of Lustre-Painting*, Kungl. Vitterhets Historie och Antikvitets Akadamiens Handlingar, 50, no. 1, Stockholm, 1941

Lanci 1846
Michelangelo Lanci, *Trattato delle simboliche rappresentanze arabiche e della varia generazione de' musulmani caratteri sopra differenti materie operati*, 3 vols., Paris, 1846

Land 1974
Norman Land, "Michele Giambono: A Catalogue Raisonné", Ph.D. Dissertation, University of Virginia, 1974

Landau and Parshall 1994
David Landau and Peter Parshall, *The Renaissance Print, 1470-1550*, New Haven, 1994

Lane 1957
Arthur Lane, *Later Islamic Pottery*, London, 1957

Lane 1957a
Arthur Lane, "The Ottoman pottery of Isnik", *AO*, 2, 1957, pp. 247-81

Lane 1957b
Frederic C. Lane, "Fleets and fairs", in *Studi in onore di Armando Sapori*, vol. 1, Milan and Varese, 1957, pp. 651-63 (Reprinted in F.C. Lane, *Venice and History*, Baltimore, 1966)

Lane 1963
Arthur Lane, *La porcellana italiana*, (1st ed. London, 1954), Florence, 1963

Lane 1973
Frederic C. Lane, *Venice, a Maritime Republic*, Baltimore and London, 1973

Lane 1978
Frederic C. Lane, *Storia di Venezia*, Turin, 1978

Lane 1982
Frederic C. Lane, *I mercanti di Venezia*, Turin, 1982

Lanmon and Whitehouse 1993
Dwight P. Lanmon with David B. Whitehouse, *The Robert Lehman Collection*, vol. 11, *Glass*, New York, 1993

Larner 1999
John Larner, *Marco Polo and the Discovery of the World*, New Haven and London, 1999

Laurie 1935
Arthur Pillans Laurie, "Materials in Persian miniatures", *Technical Studies in the Field of the Fine Arts*, 3, no. 3, 1935, pp. 146-56

Lauts 1962
Jan Lauts, *Carpaccio, Paintings and Drawings*, London, 1962

Lavagna 1992
Rita Lavagna, "Tipologie della maiolica ligure del Cinquecento negli scavi del Priamàr a Savona", in *Atti XXV Convegno Internazionale della Ceramica Albisola 1992*, Albisola, 1995, pp. 135-47

Lavagna and Varaldo 1986
Rita Lavagna and Carlo Varaldo, "La graffita arcaica tirrenica di produzione savonese alla luce degli scarti di fornace dei secoli XII e XIII", in *Atti XIX Convegno Internazionale della Ceramica Albisola 1986*, Albisola, 1989, pp. 119-30

Lavoix 1862
Henri Lavoix, "Lez Azziminists", *GBA*, 3, 1862, pp. 64-74

Lazari 1859
Vincenzo Lazari, *Notizie delle opere d'arte e d'antichità della raccolta Correr*, Venice, 1859

Lazzarini 1989
Lorenzo Lazzarini, "Nuovi dati sulla nascita e sviluppo del graffito veneziano", in *Atti del convegno "La ceramica graffita medievale e rinascimentale nel Veneto"*, Padua, 1989, pp. 19-28

Lazzarini and Canal 1983
Lorenzo Lazzarini and Ernesto Canal, "Ritrovamenti di ceramica graffita bizantina in laguna e la nascita del graffito veneziano", *Faenza*, 49, 1983, pp. 19-59

Lebe 1981
Reinhard Lebe, *Quando San Marco approdò a Venezia. Il culto dell'Evangelista e il miracolo politico della Repubblica di Venezia*, Rome, 1981

Ledermuseum 1974
Deutsches Ledermuseum, Katalog Heft 1: Leder, Bucheinband, Lederschnitt, Handvergoldung, Lederwaren, Taschen, Offenbach, 1974

Le Goff 1957
Jacques Le Goff, *Les intellectuels au Moyen Age*, Paris, 1957

Lehmann 1977
Phyllis Williams Lehmann, *Cyriacus of Ancona's Egyptian Visit and Its Reflections in Gentile Bellini and Hieronymous Bosch*, Locust Valley, NY, 1977

Lemay 1962
Richard Lemay, *Abu Ma'shar and Latin Aristotelianism in the Twelfth Century, The Recovery of Aristotle's Natural Philosophy through Arabic Astrology*, Beirut, 1962

Lentz and Lowry 1989
Thomas W. Lentz and Glenn D. Lowry, *Timur and the Princely Vision. Persian Art and Culture in the Fifteenth Century*, exh. cat., Los Angeles County Museum of Art, Los Angeles and Arthur M. Sackler Gallery, Smithsonian Institution, Washington, D.C., 1989

Le Strange 1924
Guy Le Strange, "Histoire de Yahya ibn Sa'id d'Antioche, continuateur de Sa'id ibn Bitriq", in J. Kratchowski and A. Vasiliev (eds.), *Patrologia Orientalis*, 18, no. 5, 1924, pp. 699-833

Lesure 1972
Michel Lesure, "Notes et documents sur les relations vénéto-ottomanes 1570-1573 (I)", *Turcica*, 4, 1972, pp. 134-64

Lesure 1976
Michel Lesure, "Notes et documents sur les relations vénéto-ottomanes 1570-1573 (II)", *Turcica*, 8, no. 1, 1976, pp. 117-56

Letosnikova 1968
Ludise Letosnikova, *Restaurierung im Kunstgewerbe, Ausstellung veranstaltet vom Zentrum der Staatlichen Denkmalpflege des MittelböhmischenKreises*, Prague, 1968

Lewis 1978
Archibald Lewis, "Mediterranean maritime commerce: A.D. 300-1100: Shipping and trade", in *La navigazione mediterranea nell'alto medioevo. Settimane di studio del Centro italiano di studi sull'alto Medioevo*, 25, Spoleto, 1978, pp. 480-501

Levey 1971
Michael Levey, *National Gallery Catalogues. The Seventeenth and Eighteenth Century Italian Schools*, London, 1971

Levey 1996
Santina M. Levey, "Italy: Textiles", in Jane Turner (ed.), *The Dictionary of Art*, vol. 16, London, 1996, p. 753

Levi d'Ancona 1964
Mirella Levi d'Ancona, "Postille a Girolamo da Cremona", in *Studi di bibliografia e di storia in onore di Tommaso de Marinis*, vol. 3, Verona, 1964, pp. 45-104

Levy 1994
Avigdor Levy, *The Jews of the Ottoman Empire*, Princeton, 1994

Liefkes 1997
Reino Liefkes (ed.), *Glass*, Victoria and Albert Museum, London, 1997

Lightbrown 1986
Ronald W. Lightbrown, *Mantegna: With a Complete Catalogue of the Paintings, Drawings and Prints*, Berkeley, 1986

Little 1970
Donald Presgrave Little, *An Introduction to Mamluk Historiography: An Analysis of Arabic Annalistic and Biographical Sources for the Reign of al-Mamluk an-Nasir Muhammad ibn Qala'un*, Wiesbaden and Montreal, 1970

Liverani 1937
Giuseppe Liverani, "Sull'origine della maiolica italiana", *Faenza*, 25, 1937, pp. 3-17

Livingston 1912
Arthur Livingston, "Sebastiano Rossi imitatore e plagiario di Gian Francesco Busenello", *Nuovo Archivio Veneto*, 23, 1912, pp. 163-88

Lloyd 1993
Christopher Lloyd, *Italian Paintings before 1600 in the Art Institute of Chicago, A Catalogue of the Collection*, Princeton, 1993

Lockhart 1960
Laurence Lockhart, *Persian Cities*, London, 1960

Lockhart and Morozzo della Rocca 1973
Laurence Lockhart, Raimondo Morozzo della Rocca and Maria Francesca Tiepolo (eds.), *I viaggi in Persia degli ambasciatori veneti Barbaro e Contarini*, Rome, 1973

Lokman 1987
Seyyid Lokman, *Kıyâfetü'l-insâniyye fî şemâili'l-osmâniyye*, Istanbul, 1987

London 1981
David Chambers and Jane Martineau (eds.), *Splendours of the Gonzaga*, exh. cat., Victoria and Albert Museum, London, 1981

London 1983
Donald King and David Sylvester (eds.), *The Eastern Carpet in the Western World*, exh. cat., Hayward Gallery, London, 1983

London 1987
Timothy Wilson, *Ceramic Art of the Italian Renaissance*, exh. cat., British Museum, London, 1987

London 2005
David J. Roxburgh (ed.), *Turks. A Journey of a Thousand Years, 600-1600*, exh. cat., Royal Academy of Arts, London, 2005

Longo 1994-95
Oddone Longo, "Una 'soasa' per il Conquistatore: Gentile Bellini e Maometto II", *Atti dell'Istituto Veneto di scienze, lettere ed arti: Classe di scienze morali, lettere ed arti*, 153, 1994-95, pp. 509-30

Lopez 1988
Robert S. Lopez, "I successori di Marco Polo e la febbre della seta", in Zorzi 1988, pp. 289-90

Lopez and Raymond 1955
Robert S. Lopez and Irving W. Raymond, *Medieval Trade in the Mediterranean World*, New York and Oxford, 1955

Lorenzelli and Veca 1984
Pietro Lorenzelli and Alberto Veca (eds.), *Tra/E: Teche, pissidi, cofani e forzieri dall'Alto Medioevo al Barocco*, Bergamo and London, 1984

Lorenzetti 1928-29
Giulio Lorenzetti, "La libreria Sansoviniana di Venezia", *Accademie e biblioteche d'Italia*, 2, no. 6, 1928-29, pp. 73-98

Lozzi 1900
Carlo Lozzi, "Cesare Vecellio e i suoi disegni e intagli per libri di costumi e di merletti", *La Bibliofilia*, 1, 1900, pp. 3-11

Lucchetta 1964
Francesca Lucchetta, *Il medico e filosofo bellunese Andrea Alpago (†1522) traduttore di Avicenna. Profilo biografico*, Padua, 1964

Lucchetta 1969
Francesca Lucchetta, "'L'affare Zen' in

Levante nel primo Cinquecento", *SV*, 10, 1969, pp. 109-219
Lucchetta 1979
Francesca Lucchetta, "Recenti studi sull'averroismo padovano", in *L'Averroismo in Italia: Atti dei Convegni Lincei no. 40, 1977,* Rome, 1979, pp. 91-120
Luchs 1995
Alison Luchs, *Tullio Lombardo and Ideal Portrait Sculpture in Renaissance Venice, 1490-1530*, Cambridge and New York, 1995
Luzzatto 1995
Gino Luzzatto, *Storia economica di Venezia dall'XI al XVI secolo*, Venice, 1995
MacLennan and Kilpatrick 2001
Neil MacLennan and Ross. Kilpatrick, "King Solomon and the temple builders: A biblical reading of Giorgione's painting 'The Three Philosophers'", *Heredom*, 9, 2001, pp. 111-34
Mack 1997
Rosamond E. Mack, "Lotto: A carpet connoisseur", in Washington 1997, pp. 59-67
Mack 2002
Rosamond E. Mack, *Bazaar to Piazza: Islamic Trade and Italian Art, 1300-1600,* Berkeley, Los Angeles, and London, 2002
Mackay Thomas 1942
W. G. Mackay Thomas, "Old English candlesticks and their Venetian prototypes", *BM*, 80, no. 471, 1942, pp. 145-51
Mackie 1984
Louise W. Mackie, "Toward an understanding of Mamluk silks: National and international considerations", *Muqarnas*, 2, 1984, pp. 127-45
Mackie 2001
Louise W. Mackie, "Italian silks for the Ottoman market", in Atasoy et al. 2001, pp. 182-90
Mäesalu 1999
Ain Mäesalu, "Emailbemalte Glasbecher aus Tartu", in R. Vissak and A. Mäesalu (eds.), *The Medieval Town in the Baltic: Hanseatic History and Archaeology*, Tartu, 1999, pp. 75-84
Majer 2000
Hans Georg Majer, "Giovio, Veronese und die Osmanen. Zum Sultansbild der Renaissance", in B. Guthmüller and W. Kühlmann (eds.), *Europa und die Türken in der Renaissance*, Tübingen, 2000, pp. 345-71
Malipiero 1843-44
Domenico Malipiero, *Annali veneti dall'anno 1457 al 1500 del Senatore Domenico Malipiero ordinati e abbreviati dal Senatore Francesco Longo, Archivio Storico Italiano*, 7, 1843-44
Mallett and Dreyer 1998
J.V.G. Mallet and Franz Adrian Dreyer, *The Hockemeyer Collection, Maiolica and Glass*, Bremen, 1998
Mallett and Hale 1984
Michael Mallett and John R. Hale, *The Military Organization of a Renaissance State: Venice c. 1400 to 1617*, Cambridge, 1984
Mallory 1975
Michael Mallory, "Thoughts concerning the 'Master of the Glorification of St. Thomas'", *AB*, 57, no. 1, Mar 1975, pp. 9-20
Manno 1999
Antonio Manno with Giandomenico Romanelli and Guido Tigler, *Il poema del tempo, i capitelli del Palazzo Ducale di Venezia, storia e iconografia*, Venice, 1999
Mantran 1982
Robert Mantran, "Foreign merchants and the minorities in Istanbul during the sixteenth and seventeenth centuries", in B. Braude and B. Lewis (eds.), *Christians and Jews in the Ottoman Empire. The Functioning of a Plural Society*, vol. 1, New York, 1982, pp. 127-37
Mantran 1986
Robert Mantran, "L'impero ottomano, Venezia e la guerra (1570-1670)", in *Venezia e Levante* 1986, pp. 227-32
Mantran 1989
Robert Mantran, *Histoire de l'Empire ottoman*, Paris, 1989
Marcon 2003
Susy Marcon, "Figure, tra pennelli e legni", in M. Zorzi (ed.), *La Vita nei Libri: Edizioni illustrate a stampa del Quattro e Cinquecento dalla Fondazione Giorgio Cini*, exh. cat., Biblioteca Nazionale Marciana, Venice, 2003, pp. 54-79
Marcon 2004
Susy Marcon, "Leonardo Bellini", in M. Bollati (ed.), *Dizionario biografico dei miniatori italiani*, Milan, 2004, pp. 76-78
Mariacher 1957
Giovanni Mariacher, *l Il Museo Correr di Venezia, Dipinti dal XIV al XVI secolo*, Venice, 1957
Mariacher 1958
Giovanni Mariacher, "I lattimi di Miotti al Museo Vetrario di Murano", *Bollettino dei Musei Civici Veneziani*, 2, 1958, pp. 5-12
Marini 1990
Paola Marini, "2.10. La manifattura Manardi, i 'latesini' e il cosiddetto 'stile angarano'", in Ericani and Marini 1990, pp. 244-74
Marino 2005-06
Maria Antonietta Marino, "La ceramica mamelucca bianca e blu e suoi derivati", Ph.D. Dissertation, Università degli Studi di Napoli "L'Orientale", Naples, 2005-06
Marshak 1986
Boris I. Marshak, *Silberschätze des Orients: Metallkunst des 3.-13. Jahrhunderts und ihre Kontinuität*, Leipzig, 1986
Martin 1902
Fredrik Robert Martin, *Ältere Kupfer-Arbeiten aus dem Orient*, Stockholm, 1902
Marzinot 1979
Federico Marzinot, *Ceramica e ceramisti di Liguria*, Genoa, 1979
Marzinot 1982
Federico Marzinot, "L'influenza della ceramica veneta su quella ligure del XVI secolo. Bartolomeo Guidobono e il repertorio callottiano nel suo affresco della Cappella della Crocetta in Savona", in *Atti XI Convegno Internazionale della Ceramica Albisola 1978*, Albisola, 1982, pp. 133-40
Mason 2000
Stefania Mason [Rinaldi], *Carpaccio, The Major Pictorial Cycles*, Milan, 2000
Mason Rinaldi 1986
Stefania Mason Rinaldi, "Le virtù della Repubblica e le gesta dei capitani. Dipinti votivi, ritratti, pietà", in *Venezia e Levante* 1986, pp. 13-31
Matar 1996
Nabil I. Matar, "Renaissance England and the turban", in *Images of the Others, Cairo Papers in Social Science*, 19, 1996, p. 42
Matthew 1998
Louisa C. Matthew, "The painter's presence: Signatures in Venetian Renaissance pictures", *AB*, 80, 1998, pp. 616-48
Matthew 2002
Louisa C. Matthew "'Vendecolori a Venezia': Reconstruction of a profession", *BM*, 144, no. 1196, 2002, pp. 680-86
Matthew and Berrie 2005
Louisa C. Matthew and Barbara H. Berrie, "Memoria de colori che bisognino torre a Vinetia", unpublished paper read at the conference "Trade in Painters' Materials: Markets and Commerce in Europe to 1700", The National Gallery and The Courtauld Institute, London, 2005
Mayer 1933
Leo Ary Mayer, *Saracenic Heraldry: A Survey*, Oxford, 1933
Mayer 1952
Leo Ary Mayer, *Mamluk Costume: A Survey*, Geneva, 1952
Mayes 1956
Stanley Mayes, *An Organ for the Sultan*, London, 1956
Mazzarotto 1961
Bianca Tamassia Mazzarotto, *Le feste veneziane*, Florence, 1961
Mazzini et al. 1982
Franco Mazzini et al., *L'Armeria Reale di Torino*, Busto Arsizio, 1982
McAndrew 1980
John McAndrew, *Venetian Architecture of the Early Renaissance*, Cambridge, MA and London, 1980
McConnell 1976
James McConnell (ed.), *Treasures of Eton*, London, 1976
McCray, Osborne and Kingery 1995
W. Patrick McCray, Zoe Osborne and W. David Kingery, "The culture and technology of Renaissance Venetian chalcedony glass", *RSSV*, 5/6, 1995, pp. 25-78
McNeill 1974
William Hardy McNeill, *Venice: The Hinge of Europe, 1081-1797*, Chicago, 1974
Meilman 2000
Patricia Meilman, *Titian and the Altarpiece in Renaissance Venice*, Cambridge, 2000
Meiss 1933
Millard Meiss, "The problem of Francesco Traini", *AB*, 6, no. 2, Jun 1933, pp. 97-173
Melegati 1998
Luca Melegati, *Giovanni Vezzi e le sue porcellane*, Milan, 1998
Melikian-Chirvani 1973
Assadullah Souren Melikian-Chirvani, *Le bronze iranien*, Paris, 1973
Melikian-Chirvani 1974
Assadullah Souren Melikian-Chirvani, "Venise entre l'orient et l'occident", *Bulletin des Études Orientales*, 27, 1974, pp. 109-26
Melikian-Chirvani 1982
Assadullah Souren Melikian-Chirvani, *Islamic Metalwork from the Iranian World 8th-18th Centuries*, Victoria and Albert Museum, London, 1982
Meller 1981
Peter Meller, "I 'Tre filosofi'di Giorgione", in R. Pallucchini (ed.), *Giorgione e l'umanesimo veneziano*, Florence, 1981, pp. 227-47
Memphis 1992
Nurhan Atasoy, *Splendors of the Ottoman Sultans*, T. Artan (ed. and transl.), exh. cat., Memphis, 1992
Ménage 1958
Victor L. Ménage, "The map of Hajji Ahmed and its makers", *BSOAS*, 21, 1958, pp. 291-314
Merkel 2001
Ettore Merkel, "Le tre 'Storie di Maria e dell'infanzia di Cristo' di Giovanni Mansueti nella chiesa di San Martino in Burano", in M. Piantoni (ed.), *Per l'arte. Da Venezia all'Europa. Studi in onore di Giuseppe Maria Pilo /1. Dall'antichità al Caravaggio*, Venice, 2001, pp. 143-47
Merrifield 1849
Mary Philadelphia Merrifield, *Original Treatises Dating from the XII to the XVIII Centuries on the Art of Painting*, 2 vols., London, 1849
Mentré 1996
Mireille Mentré, *The Illuminated Manuscripts of Medieval Spain*, New York, 1996
Meyer zur Capellen 1981
Jürg Meyer zur Capellen, "Zum venezianischen Dogenbild des Quattrocento", *Konsthistorik Tidskrift*, 50, 1981, pp. 70-86
Meyer zur Capellen 1985
Jürg Meyer zur Capellen, *Gentile Bellini*, Stuttgart, 1985
Michelangelo 1967
Giovanni Poggi, Paola Barocchi and Renzo Ristori (eds.), *Il carteggio di Michelangelo*, Florence, 1967
Michiel 1829
Giustina (Renier) Michiel, *Origine delle feste veneziane*, 6 vols., Milan, 1829
Middeldorf and Stiebral 1983
Ulrich Middeldorf and Dagmar Stiebral, *Renaissance Medals and Plaquettes*, Florence, 1983
Mignucci 2002
Anna Mignucci, "The 13th-14th century Venetian ceramic production of 'graffita a spirale-cerchio', 'graffita S. Bartolo' and glazed ceramic: A new reference group and an attribution", in V. Kilikoglou, A. Hein, and Y. Maniatis (eds.), *Modern Trends in Scientific Studies on Ancient*

Ceramics, Papers presented at the 5th European Meeting on Ancient Ceramics, Athens 1999, Oxford, 2002, pp. 245-52

Miller 1978
Sandra Miller, "Giovanni Mansueti, a little master of the Venetian Quattrocento," *Revue Roumaine d'Histoire de lAart*, 15, 1978, pp. 77-115

Mills 1978
John Mills, "'Small pattern Holbein' carpets in Western paintings", *Hali*, 1, no. 4, 1978, pp. 326-34

Mills 1981
John Mills, "'Lotto' carpets in Western paintings", *Hali*, 3, no. 4, 1981, pp. 278-89

Mills 1983
John Mills, "The coming of the carpet to the West", in D. King and D. Sylvester (eds.), London 1983, pp. 11-23

Mills 1986
John Mills, "Near Eastern carpets in Italian paintings", *OCTS*, 2, 1986, pp. 109-23

Mills 1991
John Mills, "Carpets in paintings: the 'Bellini', 'keyhole', or 're-entrant' rugs", *Hali*, 58, 1991, pp. 86-103

Mills and White 1994
John S. Mills and Raymond White, *The Organic Chemistry of Museum Objects*, (1st ed. 1987), Oxford, 1994

Millwright 2001
Marcus Millwright, "Balsam in the mediaeval Mediterranean: A case study of information and commodity exchange", *Journal of Mediterranean Archeaology*, 14, 2001, pp. 3-23

Molà 2000
Luca Molà, *The Silk Industry in Renaissance Venice*, Baltimore and London, 2000

Molino et al. 1986
Antonio e Paolo Molino et al., "Il relitto del vetro. Relazione preliminare", *Archeologia Subacquea, 3*, (and *Bollettino d'Arte*, suppl. 37-38), 1986, pp. 179-94

Molmenti 1905-08
Pompeo Molmenti, *Venezia nella vita privata,*. 3 vols., Bergamo, 1905-08

Molmenti 1910-12
Pompeo Molmenti, *La storia di Venezia nella vita privata dalle origini alla caduta della Repubblica*, 3 vols., (1st ed. 1905), Bergamo, 1910-12

Monnas 1988
Lisa Monnas, "Loom widths and selvedges prescribed by Italian silk weaving statutes, 1265-1512. A preliminary investigation", *Bulletin du CIETA*, 66, 1988, pp. 35-44

Monneret de Villard 1950
Ugo Monneret de Villard, *Le pitture musulmane al soffitto della Cappella Palatina in Palermo*, Rome, 1950

Monticolo 1905
Giovanni Monticolo, *I capitolari delle Arti Veneziane sottoposti alla Giustizia Vecchia dalle origini al MCCCXXX* (*Capitolare Depentori, cap. XVI-XVIII-XX-XXII-LIII*), vol. 2, Rome, 1905

Moore 1999
John C. Moore (ed.), *Pope Innocent III and his World*, Brookfield, 1999

Moore 2003
John C. Moore, *Pope Innocent III (1160/61-1216): To Root up and to Plant*, Leiden, 2003

Moore Valeri 1997
Anna Moore Valeri, "Venetian beakers with enamel decoration and Tuscan mold-blown vessels in an early 16th-century wall painting in Florence", *JGS*, 39, 1997, pp. 200-06

Morazzoni 1955
Giuseppe Morazzoni, *La maiolica antica veneta*, vol. 1, Milan, 1955

Morgan 1994
Peter Morgan, "Sgraffiato: Types and distribution", in E. J. Grube, *Cobalt and Lustre. The First Centuries of Islamic Pottery, The Nasser D. Khalili Collection of Islamic Art*, vol. 9, London, 1994, pp. 119-23

Morin 1985
Marco Morin, "La battaglia di Lepanto", in Tenenti 1985, pp. 210-31

Morini 1996
Luigina Morini (ed.), *Bestiari medievali*, Turin, 1996

Morison 1929
Stanley Morison, *Eustachio Celebrino da Udene: Calligrapher, Engraver and Writer for the Venetian Printing Press*, Paris, 1929

Morison 1955
Stanley Morison, *Venice and the Arabesque*, London, 1955

Morison 1990
Stanley Morison, *Early Italian Writing-Books: Renaissance to Baroque*, London and Verona, 1990

Morrison 1990
Donald Morrison, "'Aristotle and Alexander of Aphrodisias' by Ulocrino", in R. Sorabji (ed.), *Aristotle Transformed, The Ancient Commentators and their Influence*, Ithaca, NY, 2000, pp. 481-84

Morozzo della Rocca 1957
Raimondo Morozzo della Rocca (ed.), *Lettere di mercanti a Pignol Zucchello (1336-1350)*, Venice, 1957

Morozzo della Rocca and Lombardo 1940
Raimondo Morozzo della Rocca and Antonino Lombardo, *Documenti del commercio veneto dei sec. XI-XIII*, 2 vols., Turin, 1940

Morozzo della Rocca and Lombardo 1953
Raimondo Morozzo della Rocca and Antonino Lombardo, *Nuovi documenti del commercio veneto dei sec. XI-XIII*, Venice, 1953

Moschetti 1931
Andrea Moschetti, "Delle maioliche dette 'Candiane'", in *Bollettino del Museo Civico di Padova*, n.s. 7, 1931, pp. 1-58

Moschetti 1932
Andrea Moschetti, "Le ceramiche di Candiana", *Faenza*, 20, 1932, pp. 137-44

Mottola Molfino 1976
Alessandra Mottola Molfino, *L'Arte della porcellana in Italia, il Veneto e la Toscana*, Milan, 1976

Mraz 1980
Gottfried Mraz, "Die Rolle der Uhrwerke in der kaiserlichen Türkenverehrung im 16.Jahrhundert", in K. Maurice and O. Mayr (eds.) *Die Welt als Uhr*, exh. cat., Bayerisches National Museum, Munich and National Museum of History and Technology, Smithsonian Institution, Washington, D.C., 1980, pp. 39-54

MSR
Mamluk Studies Review

Muir 1979
Edward Muir, "Images of power: Art and pageantry in Renaissance Venice", *American Historical Review*, 84, 1979, pp. 16-52

Muir 1981
Edward Muir, *Civic Ritual in Renaissance Venice*, Princeton, 1981

Muller 1577
Theobaldus Muller, *Musæ Ioviani Imagines: Artifice manu ad vivum expressæ*, Basel, 1577

Munarini 1983
Michelangelo Munarini, "Su alcune ceramiche anatoliche conservate in due musei del Padovano", *Bollettino del Museo Civico di Padova*, 72, 1983, pp. 155-73

Munarini 1990
Michelangelo Munarini, "1.5.2. Graffita rinascimentale canonica", in Ericani and Marini 1990, pp. 81-96

Munarini 1990a
Michelangelo Munarini, "2.3. Maiolica rinascimentale a Venezia e in terraferma", in Ericani and Marini 1990, pp. 190-95

Munarini 1990b
Michelangelo Munarini, "2.4. Maiolica istoriata in terraferma", in Ericani and Marini 1990, pp. 195-209

Munarini 1990c
Michelangelo Munarini, "2.5.1 Maiolica berettina a Padova", in Ericani and Marini 1990, pp. 213-17

Munarini 1998
Michelangelo Munarini, "Alcune riflessioni sulle importazioni di ceramiche spagnole in area veneta", in *Atti XXXI Convegno Internazionale della Ceramica Albisola 1998*, Albisola, 1999, pp. 233-40

Müller-Wiener 1992
Martina Müller-Wiener, *Eine Stadtgeschichte Alexandrias von 564/1169 bis in die Mitte des 9. /15. Jahrhunderts*, Berlin, 1992

Muraro 1977
Michelangelo Muraro, "Questioni 'islamiche' nell'arte Veneziana", in *Actas del XXIII Congresso Internacional de Historia del Arte - Granada, 1973*, Granada, 1977, pp. 156-67

Muraro 1977a
Michelangelo Muraro, *I disegni di Vittore Carpaccio*, Florence, 1977

Musei Civici 1988
Una città e il suo museo: un secolo e mezzo di collezioni civiche veneziane, Special issue, *Bollettino dei Civici Musei Veneziani d'arte e di storia*, n.s. 30, 1-4, 1986, Venice, 1988

Naar 2002
Wilfred Naar (ed. and transl.), *Alessandro Magno. Voyages 1557-1565*, Brindisi and Paris, 2002

Nani 1997
Giacomo Nani, *Della difesa di Venezia*, G. Filippi (ed.), Istituto Veneto di Scienze, Lettere ed Arti, Classe di scienze morali, lettere ed arti, Memorie, vol. 72, Venice, 1997

Nardi 1955
Bruno Nardi, "I 'Tre filosofi' di Giorgione", *Il Mondo*, Aug 23, 1955

Navari 1995
Leonora Navari, "Vincenzo Coronelli and the Iconography of the Venetian Conquest of the Morea: A Study in Illustrative Methods," *British School at Athens* 90,1995, pp. 505-519

Necipoğlu 1989
Gülru Necipoğlu, "Suleyman the Magnificent and the representation of power in the context of Ottoman-Hapsburg-Papal rivalry", *AB*, 71, no. 3, 1989, pp. 401-27

Necipoğlu 1995
Gülru Necipoğlu, *The Topkapı Scroll. Geometry and Ornament in Islamic Architecture*, Santa Monica, 1995

Necipoğlu 2000
Gülru Necipoğlu, "A period of transition: portraits of Selim II", in Istanbul 2000, pp. 202-07

Necipoğlu 2000a
Gülru Necipoğlu, "Word and image: The serial portraits of Ottoman sultans in comparative perspective", in Istanbul 2000, pp. 22-63

Necipoğlu 2005
Gülru Necipoğlu, *The Age of Sinan, Architectural Culture in the Ottoman Empire*, London, 2005

Nepoti 1986
Silvio Nepoti, "Ceramiche tardo medievali spagnole ed islamiche orientali nell'Italia centro-settentrionale adriatica", in *Segundo Coloquio Internacional de Cerámica Medieval en el Mediterráneo Occidental*, Madrid, 1986, pp. 353-63

Neri 1612
Antonio Neri, *L'arte vetraria*, Florence, 1612 (English version transl. and annotated by P. Engle, *L'Arte Vetraria - The Art of Glass by Antonio Neri*, vol. 1, Hubbardston, 2003)

Newby 1998
Martine Newby, "The Cavour Vase and gilt and enamelled Mamluk coloured glass", in Ward 1998, pp. 35-39

Newby 2000
Martine Newby, *Glass of Four Millennia*, Oxford, 2000

Newett 1907
M. Margaret Newett (ed.), *Canon Pietro Casola's Pilgrimage to Jerusalem*, Manchester, 1907

Newton 1988
Stella Mary Newton, *The Dress of the Venetians 1495-1525*, Aldershot and Brookfield, VT, 1988

New York 1973
Alexandrine N. St. Clair, *The Image of the*

Turk in Europe, exh. cat., The Metropolitan Museum of Art, New York, 1973

New York 1984
The Treasury of San Marco Venice, exh. cat., (English edition), The Metropolitan Museum of Art, New York, Milan, 1984

New York 1997
Keith Christiansen (ed.), *Giambattista Tiepolo*, exh. cat., The Metropolitan Museum of Art, New York, 1997

New York 2002
Ena Giurescu Heller, *Icons or Portraits? Images of Jesus and Mary from the collection of Michael Hall*, exh. cat., The Gallery of the American Bible Society, New York, 2002

New York 2004
Helen C. Evans (ed.), *Byzantium Faith and Power (1261-1557)*, exh. cat., The Metropolitan Museum of Art, New York, 2004

Nicol 1988
Donald M. Nicol, *Byzantium and Venice: A Study in Diplomatic and Cultural Relations*, Cambridge, 1988

Niero 1992
Antonio Niero, "Il culto di S. Marco (da Alessandria a Venezia)", in *Storia e arte del patriarcato di Aquileia*, Udine, 1992, pp. 15-40

Nigg 1982
Joe Nigg, *The Book of Gryphons*, Cambridge and Watertown, 1982

Norris 1983
D. Richard Norris, "Venice: Masked lion of the Adriatic", *Arts Quarterly of the New Orleans Museum of Art*, 5, no.1, 1983, pp. 30-41

Northedge 1996
Alastaire Northedge, "Friedrich Sarre's *Die Keramik von Samarra* in perspective", in K. Bartl and S. R. Hauser (eds.), *Continuity and Change in Northern Mesopotamia from the Hellenistic to the Early Islamic Period (Colloquium)*, Berlin, 1996, pp. 229-58

Nuovo 1990
Angela Nuovo, *Alessandro Paganino (1509-1538)*, Padua, 1990

Nuvolini 2000
Laura Nuvolini, "Commissioni Dogali: Venetian bookbinding in the British Library", in D. Pearson (ed.), *"For the Love of Binding". Studies in Bookbinding History Presented to Mirjam Foot*, London, 2000, pp. 81-109

Nystazopoulou Pélékidis 1973
Marie Nystazopoulou Pélékidis, "Venise et la Mer Noire du XIe au XVe siècle", in Pertusi 1973-74, vol. 1, part 2, pp. 541-82

OCTS
Oriental Carpet and Textile Studies

O'Kane 1996
Bernard O'Kane, "Monumentality in Mamluk and Mongol art and architecture", *Art History*, 19, 1996, pp. 499-522

Olian 1977
Jo Anne Olian, "Sixteenth-century costume books", *Dress*, 3, 1977, pp. 20-48

Olivieri 1979
Achille Olivieri, "Un 'modello' mediterraneo: la città 'nave' in Cristoforo da Canal", *Il Veltro. Rivista della Civiltà Italiana*, 23/2-4, Mar-Aug 1979, pp. 229-41

Olschki 1937
Leonardo Olschki, *Storia Letteraria delle scoperte geografiche: Studi e ricerche*, Florence, 1937

Olschki 1960
Leonardo Olschki, *Marco Polo's Asia: An Introduction to His "Description of the World" Called "Il Milione"*, Berkeley and Los Angeles, 1960

Orfali 2002
Moises Orfali, "Doña Gracia Mendes and the Ragusan Republic: The successful use of economic institutions in 16th-century commerce", in E. Horowitz and M. Orfali (eds.), *The Mediterranean and the Jews. Society, Culture and Economy in Early Modern Times*, vol. 2, Ramat Gan, 2002, pp. 175-201

Origo 1986
Iris Origo, *The Merchant of Prato*, (1st ed. 1957), Harmondsworth, 1986

Ortalli 1996
Gherardo Ortalli, "Venice and papal bans on trade with the Levant: The role of the jurist", in B. Arbel (ed.), *Intercultural Contacts in the Medieval Mediterranean*, London, 1996, pp. 242-58

Osley 1972
A.S. Osley, *Luminario*
An Introduction to the Italian Writing Books of the Sixteenth and Seventeenth Centuries, Nieuwkoop, 1972

Osma 1980
Guillermo de Osma, *Fortuny: Mariano Fortuny, His Life and Work*, New York, 1980

Öz 1950
Tahsin Öz, *Turkish Textiles and Velvets, XIV-XVI Centuries*, Ankara, 1950

Paci 1971
Renzo Paci, *La "scala" di Spalato e il commercio veneziano nei Balcani fra Cinque e Seicento*, Venice, 1971

Pächt 2003
Otto Pächt, *Venetian Painting in the 15th Century: Jacopo, Gentile, and Giovanni Bellini and Andrea Mantegna*, London, 2003

Padua 1991
Alessandro Ballarin and Davide Banzato (eds.), *Da Bellini a Tintoretto. Dipinti dei Musei Civici di Padova dalla metà del Quattrocento ai primi del Settecento*, exh. cat., Musei Civici, Padua, 1991

Padua 1992
Michelangelo Munarini (ed.), *Ceramiche medievali dei Musei Civici di Padova*, exh. cat., Oratorio di S. Rocco, Padua, 1992

Padua 1993
Michelangelo Munarini and Davide Banzato (eds.), *Ceramiche rinascimentali dei Musei Civici di Padova*, exh. cat., Musei Civici, Padua, 1993

Padua 1995
Davide Banzato and Michelangelo Munarini, *Ceramiche del '600 e '700 dei Musei Civici di Padova*, exh. cat., Palazzo della Ragione, Padua, 1995

Pagani 2001
Catherine Pagani, *Eastern Magnificence & European Ingenuity*, Ann Arbor, 2001

Palace 2000
Palace of Gold and Light. Treasures from the Topkapı, Istanbul, exh. cat., Washington, D.C., 2000

Pallucchini 1961
Rodolfo Pallucchini, *I Vivarini (Antonio, Bartolomeo, Alvise)*, Venice, 1961

Pallucchini and Perocco 1961
Rodolfo Pallucchini and Guido Perocco, *I teleri del Carpaccio in San Giorgio degli Schiavoni*, Milan, 1961

Panofsky 1971
Erwin Panofsky, *Early Netherlandish Painting. Its Origins and Character*, 2 vols., New York, Hagerstown, San Francisco and London, 1971

Paris 1878
L'Esposizione di Parigi del 1878 illustrata, Milan, 1878-79

Paris 1990
Soliman le Magnifique, exh. cat., Grand Palais, Paris, 1990

Paris 1993
Michel Laclotte and Giovanna Nepi Scirè (eds.), *Le Siècle de Titien: L'âge d'or de la peinture à Venise*, exh. cat., Grand Palais, Paris, 1993

Paris 1996
La Médecine au temps des califes: à l'ombre d'Avicenne, exh. cat., Institut du Monde Arabe, Paris, 1996

Paris 2001
L'Orient de Saladin. L'art des Ayyoubides, exh. cat., Institut du Monde Arabe, Paris, 2001

Paris 2001a
Marie-Geneviève Guesdon and Annie Vernay-Nouri (eds.), *L'Art du livre arabe: Du manuscrit au livre d'artiste*, Bibliothèque Nationale de France, Paris, 2001

Pasero 1936
Carlo Pasero, "Giacomo Franco, editore, incisore e calcografo nei secoli XVI e XVII", *La Bibliofilia*, 37, 1935, pp. 332-56

Passeri 1758
Giovan Battista Passeri, *Istoria delle Pitture in Majolica fatte in Pesaro, e ne' Luoghi circonvicini*, Venice, 1758

Patey 1978
Carol Patey, *Musical Instruments at the Victoria and Albert Museum. An Introduction*, London, 1978

Patitucci Uggeri 1997
Stella Patitucci Uggeri (ed.), *Protomaiolica. Bilancio e aggiornamenti. Quaderni di Archeologia Medievale*, 2, Florence, 1997

Pavone 1985
Maria Pia Pavone, "Maestro Domenico da Venezia e la spezieria del grande ospedale di Messina", *Faenza*, 71, 1985, pp. 49-67

Paynter et al. 2004
S. Paynter et al., "The production technology of Iznik pottery: A reassessment", *Archaeometry*, 46, 2004, pp. 421-37

Pedani 1994
Maria Pia Pedani [Fabris], *In nome del Gran Signore. Inviati ottomani a Venezia dalla caduta di Costantinopoli alla guerra di Candia*, Venice, 1994

Pedani Fabris 1994
Maria Pia Pedani Fabris, *I 'documenti turchi' dell'Archivio di Stato di Venezia*, Rome, 1994

Pedani Fabris 1996
Maria Pia Pedani Fabris, "Ottoman envoys to Venice (1384-1644)", *Arab Historical Review for Ottoman Studies*, 13-14, 1996, pp. 111-15

Pedani Fabris 1996-97
Maria Pia Pedani Fabris, "Simbologia ottomana nell'opera di Gentile Bellini", in *Atti Istituto Veneto di scienze lettere ed arti. Classe di scienze morali lettere ed arti*, 155, no. 1, 1996-97, pp. 2-29

Pedani Fabris 1999
Maria Pia Pedani Fabris, "The portrait of Mehmed II: Gentile Bellini. The making of an imperial image", in F. Déroche et al. (eds.), *Turkish Art. 10th International Congress of Turkish Art, Geneva, 17-23 September 1995*, Geneva, 1999, pp. 555-58

Pedani 2000
Maria Pia Pedani [Fabris], "Safiye's household and Venetian diplomacy", *Turcica*, 32, 2000, pp. 9-32

Pedrocco and Montecuccoli degli Erri 1992
Filippo Pedrocco and Federico Montecuccoli degli Erri, *Antonio Guardi*, Milan, 1992

Pellegrini 1911
G. Pellegrini, "Bronzi artistici medievali scoperti in Padova", *Bollettino d'Arte*, 5, 1911, pp. 308-10

Penny 2004
Nicholas Penny, *National Gallery Catalogues. The Sixteenth Century Italian Paintings, vol. I. Painting from Bergamo, Brescia and Cremona*, London, 2004

Perkins 1868
Charles Perkins, *Italian Sculptors*, London, 1868

Pertegato 1998
Francesco Pertegato, "Restauro di un tappeto mamelucco del XVI secolo", *Kermes: Arte, Conservazione, Restauro*, 11, no. 31, 1998, pp. 1-15

Pertusi 1966
Agostino Pertusi (ed.), *Venezia e l'Oriente fra tardo medioevo e rinascimento*, Florence, 1966

Pertusi 1973-74
Agostino Pertusi (ed.), *Venezia e il Levante fino al secolo XV. Atti del I Convegno internazionale di storia della civiltà veneziana promosso e organizzato dalla Fondazione Giorgio Cini, Venezia, 1-5 giugno 1968*, Civiltà veneziana. Studi 27, 2 vols., Florence, 1973-74

Pesaro 1992
Cristina Pesaro, "Michele Giambono", *Saggi e memorie di storia dell'arte*, 18, 1992, pp. 13-69

Petrarca 1906
Francesco Petrarca, *De sui ipsius et multorum aliorum ignorantia*, (1st ed. Venice, 1501), L.M. Capelli (ed.), Paris, 1906

Petrasch, Sanger and Zimmermann 1991
Ernst Petrasch, Reinhard Sanger, Eva Zimmermann, *Badisches Landesmuseum Karslruhe, Die Karlsruher Türkenbeute, Die "Türkische Kammer" des Markgrafen Ludwig Wilhelm von Baden-Baden, Die "Türkischen Curiositaeten" des Markgrafen von Baden-Durlach*, Munich, 1991

Petricioli 1973
Sofija Petricioli, "The Gnalić wreck: The glass", *JGS*, 15, 1973, pp. 85-92

Petrioli Tofani 1987
Annamaria Petrioli Tofani, *Gabinetto disegni e stampe degli Uffizi: Inventario 2: Disegni esposti*, Florence, 1987

Petry 1998
Carl F. Petry (ed.), *Islamic Egypt (640-1517). The Cambridge History of Egypt*, 1, Cambridge, 1998

Petry 2001
Carl F. Petry, "Robing ceremonials in late Mamluk Egypt: Hallowed traditions, shifting protocols", in S. Gorden (ed.), *Robes and Honor: The Medieval World of Investiture*, New York, 2001, pp. 353-77

Petsopoulos 1982
Yanni Petsopoulos (ed.), *Tulips, Arabesques & Turbans. Decorative Arts from the Ottoman Empire*, New York, 1982

Pettenato 1973
Silvana Pettenato, "Vetri a oro del Trecento padano", *Paragone*, 275, 1973, pp. 71-80

Phillips 2004
Jonathan Phillips, *The Fourth Crusade and the Sack of Constantinople*, New York, 2004

Piccolpasso 1976
Cipriano Piccolpasso, *Li tre libri dell'arte del vasaio* (printed edition of the ms. in the Victoria and Albert Museum, London), G. Conti (ed.), Florence, 1976

Piemontese 1557
Alessio Piemontese, *Secreti del reverendo donno Alessio Piemontese*, Pesaro, 1557

Pierce 1988
Leslie Pierce, "Shifting boundaries: Images of Ottoman royal women in the 16th and 17th Centuries", *Critical Matrix*, 4, Fall-Winter 1988, pp. 43-82

Pierce 1992
Leslie Pierce, *The Imperial Harem: Women and Sovereignty in the Ottoman Empire*, New York and Oxford, 1992

Pignatti 1953
Terisio Pignatti, "A rediscovered portrait by Gentile Bellini", *BM*, 95, no. 600, Mar 1953, pp. 93-95

Pignatti 1975
Terisio Pignatti, "Venetian festivals and amusements", *Apollo*, 102 1975, pp. 208-15

Pingree 1968
David Pingree, *The Thousands of Abu Ma'shar*, London, 1968

Pinner and Denny 1986
Robert Pinner and Walter B. Denny (eds.), *Oriental Carpet & Textile Studies, II, Carpets of the Mediterranean Countries 1400-1600*, London, 1986

Pinto 1966
Olga Pinto, "Viaggiatori veneti in Oriente dal secolo XIII al XVI", in Pertusi 1966, pp. 389-402

Pixley 2003
Mary L. Pixley, "Islamic artifacts and cultural currents in the art of Carpaccio", *Apollo*, 158, no. 501, Nov 2003, pp. 9-18

Planiscig 1919
Leo Planiscig, *Die Estensische Kunstsammlung*, vol. 1,Vienna, 1919

Poldi Pezzoli 1985
Musei e Gallerie d'Italia. Il Museo Poldi Pezzoli: Armeria, vol. 1, Milan, 1985

Pollard 1984-85
John Graham Pollard, *Medaglie italiane del rinascimento nel Museo Nazionale del Bargello*, Florence, 1984-85

Polzer 1995
Joseph Polzer, "Andrea di Bonaiuto's Via Veritatis and Dominican thought in late Medieval Italy", *AB*, 77, no. 2, Jun 1995, pp. 262-87

Poole 1997
Julia Poole, *Italian Maiolica*, New York, 1997

Pope 1956
John Alexander Pope, *Chinese Porcelains from the Ardabil Shrine*, Washington, D.C., 1956

Pope 1972
John Alexander Pope, "Chinese influences on Iznik pottery: A re-examination of an old problem", in R. Ettinghausen (ed.), *Islamic Art in the Metropolitan Museum of Art*, New York, 1972, pp. 125-39

Pope-Hennessey 1964
John Pope-Hennessey, "The Italian plaquette", *Proceedings of the British Academy*, 1, 1964, pp. 63-76 (Reprinted in J. Pope-Hennessey, *The Study and Criticism of Italian Sculpture*, Princeton, 1980)

Popham and Wilde 1949
Arthur Ewart Popham and Johannes Wilde, *The Italian Drawings of the XV and XVI Centuries in the Collection of His Majesty the King at Windsor Castle*, London, 1949

Prawer 1973
Joshua Prawer, "Veneziani e colonie veneziane nel Regno di Gerusalemme", in Pertusi 1973-74, vol. 1, pp. 625-56

Preto 1975
Paolo Preto, *Venezia e i Turchi*, Florence, 1975

Preto 1993
Paolo Preto, "Relations between the papacy, Venice, and the Ottoman empire in the age of Süleymân the Magnificent", in H. Inalcık and C. Kafadar (eds.), *Süleyman the Second and his Time*, Istanbul, 1993, pp. 195-202

Preto 1994
Paolo Preto, "Le paure della società veneziana, le calamità, le sconfitte, i nemici esterni ed interni", in Cozzi and Prodi 1994, pp. 3-125

Preto 1994
Paolo Preto, *I servizi segreti di Venezia*, Milan, 1994

Preyger 1973
Firuze Preyger, "Bayram Taht", *Türk Etnoğrafya Dergisi*, 13, 1973, pp. 71-77

Pringle 1986
Denys Pringle, "Pottery as evidence for trade in the Crusader states", in G. Airaldi and B.Z. Kedar (eds.), *I Comuni Italiani nel Regno Crociato di Gerusalemme. Atti del Colloquio "The Italian Communes in the Crusading Kingdom of Jerusalem"*, Genoa, 1986, pp. 449-75

Pryor 1988
John. H. Pryor, *Geography, Technology and War. Studies in the Maritime History of the Mediterranean, 649-1571*, Cambridge, 1988

Purinton and Watters 1991
Nancy Purinton and Mark Watters, "A study of the materials used by Persian painters", *Journal of the American Institute for Conservation*, 30, no. 2, 1991, pp. 125-44

Qadi Ahmad 1959
Qadi Ahmad, *Calligraphers and Painters. A Treatise by Qadi Ahmad, Son of Mir-Munshi (circa A.H. 1015 / A.D. 1606)*, V. Minorsky (transl.), Freer Gallery of Art Occasional Papers, vol. 3, no. 2, Washington, D.C., 1959

QSA
Quaderni di Studi Arabi

Rabbat 1995
Nasser Rabbat, *The Citadel of Cairo: A New Interpretation of Royal Mamluk Architecture*, Leiden, 1995

Raby 1980
Julian Raby, "El Gran Turco. Mehmed the Conqueror as a patron of the arts of Christendom", D.Phil. thesis, University of Oxford, 1980

Raby 1981
Julian Raby, "Fatih and the Fatih Album", *Islamic Art*, 1, 1981, pp. 42-49

Raby 1982
Julian Raby, *Venice, Dürer, and the Oriental Mode. The Hans Huth Memorial Studies*, 1, Totowa, NJ, 1982

Raby 1982a
Julian Raby, "A Sultan of paradox: Mehmed the conqueror as a patron of the arts", *Oxford Art Journal*, 5, no. 1, 1982, pp. 3-8

Raby 1985
Julian Raby, "Exotica from Islam", in O. Impey and A. MacGregor (eds.), *The Origins of Museums: The Cabinet of Curiosities in Sixteenth- and Seventeenth-Century Europe*, Oxford, 1985, pp. 251-58

Raby 1986
Julian Raby, "Court and export: Part I: Market demands in Ottoman carpets 1450-1550", *OCTS*, 2, 1986, pp. 29-38

Raby 1986a
Julian Raby, "Court and export: Part II: The Ushak Carpets", *OCTS*, 2, 1986, pp. 177-187

Raby 1987
Julian Raby, "Pride and prejudice. Mehmed the conqueror and the Italian portrait medal", in J. G. Pollard (ed.), *Italian Medals, Studies in the History of Art*, vol. 21, Washington, D.C., 1987, pp. 171-94

Raby 1991
Julian Raby, "Picturing the Levant", in *Circa 1492, Art in the Age of Exploration*, exh. cat., National Gallery of Art, Washington, D.C., 1991, pp. 77-81

Raby 1994
Julian Raby, "Costanzo da Ferrara", in Scher 1994, pp. 87-89

Raby 1995
Julian Raby, "Terra Lemnia & the potteries of the Golden Horn. An antique revival under Ottoman auspices", in S. Euthymiades, C. Rapp and D. Tsougarakis (eds.), *Bosphorus. Essays in Honour of Cyril Mango, Byzantinsiche Forschungen*, Amsterdam, 1995, pp. 305-42

Raby 2000
Julian Raby, "Opening gambits", in Istanbul 2000, pp. 64-91

Raby 2000a
Julian Raby, "From Europe to Istanbul", in Istanbul 2000, pp. 136-63

Raby and Tanındı 1993
Julian Raby and Zeren Tanındı, *Turkish Bookbinding in the Fifteenth Century. The Foundation of an Ottoman Court Style*, London, 1993

Raby and Yücel 1983
Julian Raby and Ünsal Yücel, "Blue-and-white, celadon and whitewares Iznik's debt to China", *Oriental Art*, 29, 1983, pp. 38-48

Rackham 1910
Bernard Rackham, "Two Seicento porcelain bowls", *BM*, 17, no. 87, 1910, pp. 163-65, 169

Rackham 1936
Bernard Rackham, "Paduan maiolica of the so-called 'Candiana' type", *BM*, 28, no. 396, Mar 1936, pp. 113-14

Rackham 1940
Bernard Rackham, *Victoria and Albert Museum. Catalogue of Italian Maiolica*, 2 vols., London, 1940

Rackham 1952
Bernard Rackham, *Italian Maiolica*, London, 1952

Raymond 1984
André Raymond, "Cairo's area and population in the early fifteenth century", *Muqarnas*, 2, 1984, pp. 21-31

Rava 1916
Beatrix Rava, *Venise dans la littérature francaise depuis les origines jusqu'à la mort de Henri IV, avec un recueil de textes dont plusieurs rares et inédits*, Paris, 1916

Ravanelli Guidotti 1992
Carmen Ravanelli Guidotti (ed.), *MediTERRAneum. Ceramica spagnola in Italia tra Medioevo e Rinascimento*, Viterbo, 1992

Ravanelli Guidotti 2000
Carmen Ravanelli Guidotti, "Maioliche faentine del Rinascimento 'famiglia gotico-floreale a tavolozza fredda: gruppo italo-moresco'", in *Atti XXXIII Convegno Internazionale della Ceramica Albisola 2000*, Albisola, 2001, pp. 369-82

Reath 1927
Nancy Reath, "Velvets of the Renaissance from Europe and Asia Minor", *BM*, 50, no. 291, Jun 1927, pp. 298-304

Renan 1852
Ernest Renan, *Averroès et l'Averroïsme*, Paris, 1852

Renouard 1955
Yves Renouard, "Mercati e mercanti veneziani alla fine del Duecento", in *La civiltà di Venezia del secolo di Marco Polo*, Venice, 1955, pp. 85-108. (Reprinted in V. Branca [ed.], *Storia della civiltà veneziana: Dalle origini al secolo di Marco Polo*, vol. 1, Florence, 1979)

Riavez 2001
Pietro Riavez, "'Atlit-Ceramica Port St Symeon, 1217-1291', graffite 'crociate' del Mediterraneo orientale", *Archeologia Medievale*, 28, 2001, pp. 500-32

Riccardi-Cubitt 1992
Monique Riccardi-Cubitt, *The Art of the Cabinet*, London, 1992

Rice 1955
David Storm Rice, "Studies in Islamic metalwork 5", *BSOAS*, 17, 1955, pp. 206-31

Ridolfi 1994
Carlo Ridolfi, *Vite dei Tintoretto da Le meraviglie dell'arte, ouero, Le vite de gl'illvstri pittori veneti, e dello stato*, (1st ed. Venice, 1648), Venice, 1994

Rolland 1903-26
Victor Rolland, *Armoiries des familles contenues dans l'Armorial général de J.B. Rieststap*, 6 vols., Paris, 1903-26

Rispoli Fabris 1974
Annamaria Rispoli Fabris, *L'arte della lacca*, Milan, 1974

Rizzi 1987
Alberto Rizzi, *Scultura esterna a Venezia, Corpus delle sculture erratiche all'aperto di Venezia e sulla laguna*, Venice, 1987

Roberts and Tomlinson 1992
K. B. Roberts and J. D. W. Tomlinson, *The Fabric of the Body: European Traditions of Anatomical Illustration*, Oxford, 1992

Robinson 1967
B.W. Robinson, "Oriental metalwork in the Gambier Parry Collection", *BM*, 109, no. 768, Mar 1967, pp. 169-73

Rogers 1993
Mary Rogers, "An ideal wife at the Villa Maser: Veronese, the Barbaros and Renaissance theorists of marriage", *Renaissance Studies*, 7, no. 4, 1993, pp. 379-97

Rogers 1982
J. Michael Rogers, "The state and the arts in Ottoman Turkey. Part 2. The furniture and decoration of Süleymaniye", *International Journal of Middle East Studies*, 14, no. 3, 1982, pp. 283-313

Rogers 1983
J. Michael Rogers, "Glass in Ottoman Turkey", *Istanbuler Mitteilungen*, 33, 1983, pp. 239-66

Rogers 1986
J. Michael Rogers, "Carpets in the Mediterranean countries 1450-1550. Some historical observations", *OCTS*, 2, 1986, pp. 13-28

Rogers 1990-92
J. Michael Rogers: "To and fro: Aspects of Mediterranean trade and consumption in the 15th and 16th centuries", in *Villes au Levant: Hommage à André Raymond*, special issue of *Revue du Monde Musulman et de la Méditerranée*, 55-56, 1990-92, pp. 57-74

Rogers 1995
J. Michael Rogers, *Empire of the Sultans: Ottoman art from the collection of Nasser D.Khalili*, exh. cat., London, 1995

Rogers 1998
J. Michael Rogers, "European inventories as a source for the distribution of Mamluk enamelled glass", in Ward 1998, pp. 69-73

Rogers 1999
J. Michael Rogers, "Ornament prints, patterns and designs East and West", in Burnett and Contadini 1999, pp. 133-65

Rogers 2005
J. Michael Rogers, "Mehmed the Conqueror: Between East and West", in Campbell and Chong 2005, pp. 80-97

Rogers and Köseoğlu 1987
J. Michael Rogers and Cengiz Köseoğlu, *Topkapı. The Treasury*, Istanbul and London, 1987

Rogers and Ward 1988
J. Michael Rogers and Rachel M. Ward, *Süleyman the Magnificent*, exh. cat., British Museum, London, 1988

Rohault de Fleury 1888
Charles Rohault de Fleury, *Le messe; études archéologiques sur ses monuments, par Ch. Rohault de Fleury... continuées par son fils*, vol. 6, Paris, 1888

Romanelli 1985
Giandomenico Romanelli, *Correr Museum*, Milan, 1985

Romanin 1973
Samuele Romanin, *Storia documentata di Venezia*, 10 vols., (1st ed. 1853-61), Venice, 1973

Rosand 1983
David Rosand, "The portrait, the courtier, and death", in R. Hanning and D. Rosand (eds.), *Castiglione, The Ideal and the Real in Renaissance Culture*, New Haven and London, 1983, pp. 91-130

Rosand 2001
David Rosand, *Myths of Venice: The Figuration of a State*, Chapel Hill and London, 2001

Rosand and Muraro 1976
David Rosand and Michelangelo Muraro, *Titian and the Venetian Woodcut*, exh. cat., Washington, D.C., 1976

Rossabi 2002
Morris Rossabi, "The Mongols and their legacy", in Komaroff and Carboni 2002, pp. 13-35

Rossi 1937
Ettore Rossi, "Parafrasi turca del 'De Senectute' presentata a Solimano il Magnifico dal Bailo Marino Cavalli (1559)", *Reale Accademia dei Lincei. Rendiconti della Classe di Scienze morali, storiche e filologiche*, ser.VI, 12, no. 7-10, 1937, pp. 1-77

Rossi 1938
Ettore Rossi, "Una parafrasi turca del 'De Senectute' datata 1559", in *Atti del IV Congresso Nazionale di Studi Romani*, Rome, 1938, pp. 1-77

Rossi 1953
Ettore Rossi, "La sultana Nūr Bānū (Cecilia Venier-Baffo) moglie di Selīm II (1566-1574) e madre di Murād III (1574-1595)", *Oriente Moderno*, 33, 1953, pp. 433-35

Rossi 1922-23
Filippo Rossi, "Le legature italiane del '500", *Dedalo*, 3, 1922-23, pp. 373-96

Rota 2002
Giorgio Rota, "Diplomatic relations between Safavid Persia and the Republic of Venice: An overview", in H. C. Güzel, C. C. Oguz and O. Karatay (eds.), *The Turks*, vol. 2, Ankara, 2002, pp. 580-87

Rouleau 1954
Francis A. S. J. Rouleau, "The Yangchow Latin tombstone as a landmark of medieval Christianity in China", *Harvard Journal of Asiatic Studies*, 17, 1954, pp. 346-65

Roxburgh 2005
David J. Roxburgh, *The Persian Album 1400-1600, from Dispersal to Collection*, New Haven and London, 2005

Rozen 1993
Minna Rozen, "La vie économique des Juifs du bassin méditerranéen, de l'expulsion d'Espagne (1492) à la fin du XVIIIe siècle", in S. Trigano (ed.), *La société juive à travers l'histoire*, Paris, 1993, pp. 296-570

RSSV
Rivista della Stazione Sperimentale del Vetro

Rückert 1963
Rainer Rückert, "Venezianische Moscheeampeln in Istanbul", in *Sonderdruck aus der Festschrift für Harald Keller*, Darmstadt, 1963, pp. 223-34

Rugiadi 2001-02
Martina Rugiadi, "Vasellame da tavola invetriato da Qal'at Homs (XI-XIV secolo)", M.A. Thesis, Università degli Studi di Napoli "L'Orientale", Naples, 2001-02

Rugiadi (forthcoming)
Martina Rugiadi, "The emergence of siliceous-body ceramics in Iran and contemporary glazed wares: First remarks on the excavated material from the *Masjed-e jom'e* of Esfahān", in B. Genito (ed.), Tehran, forthcoming

Saccardo 1993
Francesca Saccardo, "Contesti medievali nella laguna e prime produzioni graffite veneziane", in S. Gelichi (ed.), *La ceramica nel mondo bizantino tra XI e XV secolo e i suoi rapporti con l'Italia, Atti del Seminario di Pontignano*, Florence, 1993, pp. 201-39

Saccardo 1995
Francesca Saccardo, "Ceramiche tardomedievali veneziane e d'importazione dal ritrovamento di Malomocco-Forte, al Lido di Venezia", *Archeologia Uomo e Territorio*, 14, 1995, pp. 161-82

Saccardo 1996
Francesca Saccardo, "Nuovi dati sulla ceramica tardomedievale veneziana: il ritrovamento di Malamocco", in *Atti XXVI Convegno Internazionale della Ceramica "I bacini murati medievali. Problemi e stato della ricerca" Albisola 1993*, Albisola, 1996, pp. 353-72

Saccardo 1997
Francesca Saccardo, "Contributo alla conoscenza della ceramica invetriata veneziana 'tipo Santa Croce', XIII secolo", in S. Gelichi (ed.), *Atti del I Congresso nazionale di Archeologia Medievale, Pisa 1997*, Florence, 1997, pp. 409-15

Saccardo 1998
Francesca Saccardo, "Venezia. Le importazioni ceramiche tra XII e XIII secolo", in S. Gelichi (ed.), *Ceramiche, città e commerci nell'Italia tardo-medievale*, Mantua, 1998, pp. 49-73

Saccardo (forthcoming)
Francesca Saccardo, "Il pavimento della Cappella Lando a San Sebastiano", proceedings of the symposium *I Vasai del Leone*, Venice, 2004, forthcoming

Saccardo, Camuffo and Gobbo 1995
Francesca Saccardo, Sergio Camuffo and Vincenzo Gobbo, "La maiolica a smalto berettino di Venezia", *Atti del XXV Convegno Internazionale della Ceramica Albisola 1992*, Albisola, 1995, pp. 59-83

Saccardo, Lazzarini and Munarini 2003
Francesca Saccardo, Lorenzo Lazzarini and Michelangelo Munarini, "Ceramiche importate a Venezia e nel Veneto tra X e XIV secolo", in *VIIe Congrès International sur la Céramique Médiévale en Méditerranée*, Athens, 2003, pp. 395-420

Sagredo and Berchet 1860
Agostino Sagredo and Federico Berchet, *Il Fondaco dei Turchi in Venezia: studi storici e artistici con documenti inediti e tavole illustrative*, Milan, 1860

Saliba 1985
George Saliba (tr. and ed.), *The crisis of the 'Abbasid Caliphate*, Albany, 1985 (Al-Tabari, *Ta'rikh al-rusul wa al-muluk*, SUNY Series in Near Eastern Studies, Bibliotheca Persica, vol. 35)

Salinger 1938
Margaretta M. Salinger, "A gift of two Italian paintings", *Bulletin of the Metropolitan Museum of Art*, 23, . no. 3/1, 1938, pp. 6-10

Salzburg 1987
Fürsterzbischof Wolf Dietrich von Raitenau, Gründer des barocken Salzburg, exh. cat., Salzburger Landesausstellung, Residenz-Neugebau and Dommuseum, Salzburg, 1987

Sansovino 1581
Francesco Sansovino, *Venezia, città nobilissima*, Venice, 1581

Sansovino 1993
Francesco Sansovino, *Venezia città nobilissima et singolare*, G. Martinioni (ed.), 2 vols., Venice, 1993

Santini 2003
Clara Santini, *Le lacche dei veneziani: oggetti d'uso quotidiano nella Venezia del Settecento*, Modena, 2003

Sanudo 1879-1902
Marin Sanudo (Sanuto) il giovane, *I diarii di Marino Sanuto*, R. Fulin et al. (eds.), 58 vols., Venice, 1879-1902

Sanudo 1980
Marin Sanudo (Sanuto) il giovane, *De origine, situ et magistratibus urbis Venetae ovvero la città di Venezia (1493-1530)*, A. Carriciolo Aricò (ed.), Milan, 1980

Sarre 1906
Friedrich Sarre, *Erzeugnisse islamischer Kunst I. Metall*, Berlin, 1906
Sarre 1909
Friedrich Sarre, "Michelangelo und der türkische Hof", *Repertorium für Kunstwissenschaft*, 32, 1909, pp. 61-66
Sarre 1933
Friedrich Sarre, "Der Import orientalischer Keramik nach Italien im Mittelalter und in der Renaissance", *Forschungen und Fortschritte*, 9/29, 1933, pp. 423-24
Sarre 1939
Friedrich Sarre, "Die Fayencen von Nicaea und ihr Export nach dem Abendland", *Pantheon*, 24, 1939, pp. 341-45
Sauerlandt 1929
Max Sauerlandt, "Ceramiche italiane nei musei tedeschi", *Faenza*, 17, 1929, pp. 71-85
Saxl 1937
Fritz Saxl, "Costumes and festivals of Milanese society under Spanish rule", *Proceedings of the British Academy*, 23, 1937, pp. 401-56 (Also published separately as *The Annual Italian lecture*, 18 November 1936, Oxford, 1938)
Saxl et al. 1987
Fritz Saxl et al., *Il Libro del Sarto della Fondazione Querini Stampalia di Venezia*, Modena, 1987
Scarazzolo 2003
Michela Scarazzolo, "Suggestioni Islamiche nei dipinti delle Galleria dell'Accademia. Alcune proposte per un itinerario", *Dal Museo alla Città. Itinerari didattici*, 10, 2003, pp. 120-49
Scarpa 1994
Jacopo Scarpa, "Giorgione e Abelardo, *I tre filosofi* di Vienna", *Arte Documento*, 8, 1994, pp. 59-66
Scerrato 1966
Umberto Scerrato, *Metalli islamici*, Milan, 1966
Scher 1994
Stephen Scher (ed.), *The Currency of Fame, Portrait Medals of the Italian Renaissance*, exh. cat., National Gallery of Art, Washington D.C. and The Frick Collection, New York, London, 1994
Schmidt 1911
Robert Schmidt, "Die Venezianischen Emailgläserdes XV. und XVI Jahrhunderts", *Jahrbuch der Königlich Preussischen Kunstsammlungen*, 32, 1911, pp. 249-86
Schmidt Arcangeli 1998
Catarina Schmidt Arcangeli, "L'iconografia marciana nella sagrestia della Basilica di San Marco", in A. Niero (ed.), *San Marco: Aspetti storici e agiografici*, Milan, 1998, pp. 223-29
Schmidt Arcangeli 2005
Catarina Schmidt Arcangeli, "'Una sacra conversazione in famiglia', zum Bildnis des Dogen Leonardo Loredan in der Berliner Gemäldegalerie", in M. Gaier, B. Nicolai, and T. Weddigen (eds.), *Der unbestechliche Blick: Festschrift zu Ehren von Wolfgang Wolters zu seinem siebzigsten Geburtstag/ Lo sguardo incorruttibile, Studi di storia dell'arte in onore di Wolfgang Wolters in occasione del settantesimo compleanno*, Trier, 2005, pp. 283-91
Schmitt 1979
Charles B. Schmitt, "Renaissance Averroism studied through the Venetian editions of Aristotle-Averroes" in *L'Averroismo in Italia: Atti dei Convegni Lincei no. 40, 1977*, Rome, 1979, pp. 121-42
Schöbel 1974
Johannes Schöbel, *Türkenschatz aus dem Historischen Museum der Staatlichen Kunstsammlungen Dresden, Die Schatzkammer*, vol. 29, Leipzig, 1974
Schulz 1995
Juergen Schulz, "The restoration of the Fondaco dei Turchi", *Annali di Architettura*, 7, 1995, pp. 19-38
Schulze Altcappenberg 1995
Hein-Th. Schulze Altcappenberg, *Die italienischen Zeichnungen des 14. und 15. Jahrhunderts im Berliner Kupferstichkabinett: Kritischer Katalog*, Berlin, 1995
Schutte 1986
Anne Jacobson Schutte, "Teaching adults to read in sixteenth-century Venice: Giovanni Antonio's Libro Maistrevole", *Sixteenth Century Journal*, 17, 1986, pp. 3-16
Schweppe 1997
Helmut Schweppe, "Indigo and Woad", in E.W. FitzHugh (ed.), *Artists' Pigments: A Handbook of Their History and Characteristics*, Washington, 1997, pp. 81-108
Schwoebel 1967
Robert Schwoebel, *The Shadow of the Crescent: the Renaissance Image of the Turk (1453-1517)*, Nieuwhokop, 1967
Scott 1996
Kathleen L. Scott, *A Survey of Manuscripts Illuminated in the British Isles. Vol. VI: Later Gothic Manuscripts, 1390-1490*, vol. 2, London, 1996
Setton 1976-84
Kenneth M. Setton, *The Papacy and the Levant (1204-1571)*, 4 vols., Philadelphia, 1976-84
Setton 1991
Kenneth M. Setton, *Venice, Austria, and the Turks in the 17th Century*, Philadelphia, 1991
Sgarbi 1984
Vittorio Sgarbi, *Ca' Dario: Mito e storia di Giovanni Dario e del suo palazzo tra Oriente e Venezia*, Milan, 1984
Shalem 1998
Avinoam Shalem, *Islam Christianized: Islamic Portable Objects in the Medieval Church Treasuries of the Latin West*, (1st ed. 1996), Frankfurt am Main, 1998
Shalem 2002
Avinoam Shalem, "The portraiture of objects: A note on representations of Islamic objects in European painting of the 14th-16th centuries", in M. Bernardini et al (eds.), *Europa e l'Islam tra i secoli XIV e XVI / Europe and Islam between 14th and 16th centuries*, Naples, 2002, pp. 497-521
Siciliano 1978
Italo Siciliano, *Commemorazione di Vittorio Cini*, Venice, 1978
Sigoli 1944
Simone Sigoli, *Viaggi in Terrasanta*, C. Angelini (ed.), Florence, 1944
Simon 1984
Bruno Simon, "Contribution à l'étude du commerce vénitien dans l'Empire Ottoman au milieu du seizème siècle (1558-1560)", in *Mélanges de l'Ecole Française de Rome, Moyen Age - Temps Modernes*, 96/2, 1984, pp. 973-1020
Simon 1985
Bruno Simon, "I rappresentanti diplomatici veneziani a Costantinopoli", in Tenenti 1985, pp. 56-69
Simon 1997
Erika Simon, "Das 'Götterfest' des Giovanni Bellini und die osmanische Türkei", in G. Erath, M. Lehner and G. Schwarz (eds.), *KOSMOS, Festschrift für Thuri Lorenz zum 65. Geburtstag*, Vienna, 1997, pp. 305-12
Sims 1990
Eleanor Sims, "The 'Doria Velvet': An Ottoman velvet in the Detroit Institute of Arts", in T. Majda (ed.), *Seventh International Congress of Turkish Art*, Warsaw, 1990, pp. 215-20
Sinding-Larsen 1956
Staale Sinding-Larsen, "The changes in the iconography and composition of Veronese's allegory of the Battle of Lepanto in the Doge's Palace", *Journal of the Warburg & Courtauld Institutes*, 19, no. 3/4, 1956, pp. 298-302
Siraisi 1987
Nancy G. Siraisi, *Avicenna in Renaissance Italy, The Canon and Medical Teaching in Italian Universities after 1500*, Princeton, 1987
Skilliter 1976
Susan A. Skilliter, "The Sultan's messenger, Gabriel Defrens: an Ottoman master-spy of the sixteenth century", *Wiener Zeitschrift für die Kunde des Morgenlandes*, 68, 1976, pp. 47-59
Skilliter 1977
Susan A. Skilliter, *Life in Istanbul 1588. Scenes from a Traveller's Picture Book*, Oxford, 1977
Skilliter 1977a
Susan A. Skilliter, *William Harborne and the Trade with Turkey, 1578-1582. A Documentary Study of the First Anglo-Ottoman Relations*, Oxford, 1977
Skilliter 1982
Susan A. Skilliter, "The letters of the Venetian 'Sultana' Nūr Bānū and her Kira to Venice", in A. Gallotta and U. Marazzi (eds.), *Studia Turcologica Memoriae Alexii Bombaci dicata*, Naples, 1982, pp. 515-36
Skilliter 1982a
Susan A. Skilliter, "Three letters from the Ottoman 'Sultana' Safiye to Queen Elizabeth I", in S. M. Stern (ed.), *Documents from Islamic Chanceries*, Oxford, 1982, pp. 119-57
Sman 2000
Gert Jan van der Sman, "Print publishing in Venice in the second half of the sixteenth century", *Print Quarterly*, 17, 2000, pp. 235-47
Sman 2003
Gert Jan van der Sman, *Le Siècle de Titien: Gravures vénitiennes de la Renaissance*, Zwolle, 2003
Snodin and Howard 1996
Michael Snodin and Maurice Howard, *Ornament: A Social History Since 1450*, New Haven and London, 1996
Soave and Siviero 1985
Decio Soave and Giovanni Battista Siviero, "Il grande servizio conventuale del Museo Civico di Padova e considerazioni sulla ceramica conventuale veneta", *Atti XV Convegno Internazionale della Ceramica Albisola 1982*, 1985, pp. 113-66
Sohm 1982
Philip L. Sohm, *The Scuola Grande di San Marco 1437-1550. The Architecture of a Venetian Lay Confraternity*, New York, 1982
Soucek 1996
Svat Soucek, *Piri Reis and Turkish Mapmaking After Columbus, The Khalili Portolan Atlas*, London, 1996
Southern 1962
Richard William Southern, *Western Views of Islam in the Middle Ages*, Cambridge, MA and London, 1962
SPA
Arthur Upham Pope (ed.), *A Survey of Persian Art, from Prehistoric Times to the Present*, Tokyo, 1964
Spagni 1900
Emilio Spagni, "Una sultana veneziana", *Nuovo Archivio Veneto*, 19, 1900, pp. 341-48
Spallanzani 1978
Marco Spallanzani, *Ceramiche orientali a Firenze nel Rinascimento*, Florence, 1978
Spallanzani 1978a
Marco Spallanzani, "Un invio di maioliche ispano-moresche a Venezia negli anni 1401-1402", *Archeologia Medievale*, 5, 1978, pp. 529-41
Spallanzani 1985
Marco Spallanzani, "Il piatto islamico Venier-Molin del Bargello", in A. Morrogh et al. (eds.), *Renaissance Studies in Honour of Craig Hugh Smyth*, vol. 2, Florence, 1985, pp. 465-72
Spallanzani 1989
Marco Spallanzani, "Fonti archivistiche per lo studio dei rapporti fra l'Italia e l'Islam: le arti minori nei secoli XIV-XVI", in Grube 1989, pp. 83-100
Spallanzani 1994
Marco Spallanzani, *Ceramiche alla corte dei Medici nel Cinquecento*, Florence, 1994
Spallanzani 1997
Reprint of Spallanzani 1978
Speziale 2005
Fabrizio Speziale, "I codici persiani miniati della Fondazione", in *Lettera da San Giorgio*, Fondazione Giorgio Cini, 7, no. 12, Mar-Aug 2005, pp. 10-13
Spinale 2003
Susan Spinale, "The portrait medals of Ottoman sultan Mehmed II (r. 1451-81)", Ph.D. Dissertation, Harvard University, Cambridge, MA, 2003
Spremić 1971
Momcilo Spremić, "I tributi veneziani nel Levante nel XV secolo", *SV*, 13, 1971, pp. 221-52
Spriggs 1965
S. I. Spriggs, "Oriental porcelain in western paintings", *Transactions of the*

Oriental Ceramic Society, 36, 1965, pp. 73-84
Spuhler 1987
Friedrich Spuhler, *Oriental Carpets in the Museum of Islamic Art, Berlin,* Washington, D.C., 1987
Stazzi 1967
Francesco Stazzi, *Porcellane della casa eccellentissima Vezzi (1720 - 1727),* Milan, 1967
Stouraiti 2002
Anastasia Stouraiti, "Propaganda figurata: geometrie di dominio e ideologie veneziane nelle carte di Vincenzo Coronelli", *SV,* 44, 2002, pp. 129-55
Stowasser 1984
Karl Stowasser, "Manners and customs at the Mamluk court", *Muqarnas,* 2, 1984, pp. 13-20
Strika 1978
Vincenzo Strika, *La "Cattedra" di S. Pietro a Venezia. Note sulla simbologia astrale nell'arte islamica, Annali dell'Istituto Orientale di Napoli,* suppl. 15, vol. 38, fasc. 2, Naples, 1978
Stringa 1987
Nadir Stringa, *La famiglia Manardi e la ceramica a Bassano nel '600 e '700,* Bassano, 1987
Stussi 1965
Alfredo Stussi (ed.), *Testi veneziani del Duecento e dei primi del Trecento,* Pisa, 1965
Suriano 1949
Fra Francesco Suriano, *Treatise on the Holy Land,* T. Bellorini OFM and E. Hoade OFM (transl.), Jerusalem, 1949
Suriano and Carboni 1999
Carlo Maria Suriano and Stefano Carboni with Paolo Peri, *La seta islamica. Temi ed influenze culturali / Islamic Silk. Design and Context,* Florence, 1999
SV
Studi Veneziani
SVe
Storia di Venezia, Istituto della Enciclopedia Italiana
Swerdlow 1993
Noel M. Swerdlow, "The recovery of the exact sciences of antiquity: Mathematics, astronomy, geography", in Grafton 1993, pp. 157-68
Świechowski and Rizzi 1982
Zygmunt Świechowski and Alberto Rizzi, *Romanische Reliefs von venezianischen Fassaden. "Patere e Formelle",* Wisbaden, 1982
Taeschner 1925
Franz Taeschner, *Alt-Stambuler Hof-und Volksleben. Ein türkisches Miniaturen-Album aus dem 17.Jahrhundert,* Hanover, 1925
Tafuri 1985
Manfredo Tafuri, *Venezia e il Rinascimento,* Rome and Bari, 1985
Tait 1979
Hugh Tait, *The Golden Age of Venetian Glass,* London, 1979
Tait 1991
Hugh Tait (ed.), *Glass 5,000 Years,* New York, 1991
Tait 1999
Hugh Tait, "Venice: Heir to the glass-makers of Islam or of Byzantium", in Burnett and Contadini 1999, pp. 77-104
Tanındı 2003
Zeren Tanındı, "Safavid bookbinding", in Thompson and Canby 2003, pp. 155-83
Tenenti 1985
Alberto Tenenti (ed.), *Venezia e i Turchi: Scontri e confronti di due civiltà,* Milan, 1985
Tenenti 1999
Alberto Tenenti, *Venezia e il senso del mare. Storia di un prisma culturale dal XIII al XVIII secolo,* Naples, 1999
Tenenti and Tucci 1991
Alberto Tenenti and Ugo Tucci (eds.), *Il mare, storia di Venezia, temi,* Rome, 1991
Tezcan 1980
Hülye Tezcan and Selma Delibas, *The Topkapı Saray Museum. Costumes, Embroideries and other Textiles,* J. M. Rogers (transl.), Boston, 1980
Thénaud 1530
Jean Thénaud, *Le voyage et itinéraire de oustre mer,* Paris, ca.1530
Thénaud 1884
Jean Thénaud, *Le voyage d'outremer, suivi de la relation de l'Ambassade de Domenico Trevisan auprès du Soudan d'Egypte, 1512,* C. Schefer (ed.), Paris, 1884
Theuerkauf-Liederwald 1994
Anna-Elisabeth Theuerkauf-Liederwald, *Venezianisches Glas der Kunstsammlungen der Veste Coburg,* Lingen, 1994
Thomas 1880
Georg Martin Thomas, *Diplomatarium Veneto-Levantinum: Acta et Diplomata res Venetas Graecas atque Levantis illustrantia,* 2 vols., Venice, 1880
Thomas d'Aquin 1998
Saint Thomas d'Aquin, *De unitate intellectus contra Averroistas / Trattato sull'unità dell'intelletto contro gli averroisti,* B. Nardi (ed.) and P. Mazzantini (re-ed.), Spoleto, 1998
Thompson and Canby 2003
Jon Thompson and Sheila R. Canby (eds.), *Hunt for Paradise, Court Art of Safavid Iran 1501-1576,* exh. cat., Asia Society, New York and Museo Poldi Pezzoli and Palazzo Reale, Milan, 2003
Thornton 1990
Dora Frieda Thornton, "The study room in Renaissance Italy with particular reference to Venice circa 1560-1620", Ph.D. Dissertation, Warburg Institute, London, 1990
Thornton 1997
Dora Frieda Thornton, *The Scholar in His Study: Ownership and Experience in Renaissance Italy,* New Haven and London, 1997
Thornton 1984
Peter Thornton, "Cassoni, forzieri, goffani and cassette, terminology and its problems", *Apollo,* 120, Oct 1984, pp. 246-51
Thornton 1991
Peter Thornton, *The Italian Renaissance Interior, 1400-1600,* New York, 1991
Thuasne 1888
Louis Thuasne, *Gentile Bellini et Sultan Mohammed II. Notes sur le séjour du peintre venitien à Constantinople (1479-1480) d'après les documents originaux en partie inédits,* Paris, 1888
Tiepolo 2002
Maria Francesca Tiepolo, "Greci nella cancelleria veneziana: Giovanni Dario", in M. F. Tiepolo and E. Tonetti (eds.), *I Greci a Venezia,* Venice, 2002, pp. 257-314
Tietze 1919
Hans Tietze, *Die Kunstsammmlungen der Stadt Salzburg. Österreichische Kunsttopographie,* 16, Vienna, 1919
Tietze and Tietze-Conrat 1944
Hans Tietze and Erika Tietze-Conrat, *The Drawings of the Venetian Painters of the 15th and 16th Centuries,* New York, 1944
Tognetti 1985
Giampaolo Tognetti, "Venezia e le profezie sulla conversione dei turchi", in Tenenti 1985, pp. 86-90
Tonghini 1999
Cristina Tonghini, "Fatimid ceramics from Italy: The archaeological evidence", in M. Barrucand (ed.), *L'Égypte fatimide, son art et son histoire. Actes du colloque organisé à Paris les 28, 29 et 30 mai 1998,* Paris, 1999, pp. 285-97
Toniolo 2003
Federica Toniolo, "Petrus de Abano (Abano 1257-Padua c. 1315), *Expositio problematum Aristotelis cum textu*", in Athens 2003, pp. 263-64
Toniolo 2004
Federica Toniolo, "Girolamo da Cremona", in Bollati 2004, pp. 310-15
Torrini Perissa 2004
Annalisa Perissa Torrini, "Documents and sources", in Ferino-Pagden and Nepi Scirè 2004, pp. 21-30
Topping 1976
Peter Topping, "Venice's last imperial venture", *Proceedings of the American Philosophical Society,* 120, no. 3, Jun 1976, pp. 159-65
Trevor-Roper 1961
H. R. Trevor-Roper, "Doge Francesco Foscari", in R. M. Ketchum (ed.), *The Horizon Book of the Renaissance,* New York, 1961, pp. 272-80
Tucci 1957
Ugo Tucci (ed.), *Lettres d'un marchand vénitien Andrea Berengo (1553-56),* Paris, 1957
Tucci 1973
Ugo Tucci, "The psychology of the Venetian merchant in the sixteenth century", in J. R. Hale (ed.), *Renaissance Venice,* London, 1973, pp. 346-78
Tucci 1985
Ugo Tucci, "Tra Venezia e il mondo turco", in Tenenti 1985, pp. 38-55
Turan 1968
Şerafettin Turan, "Venedik'te Türk ticaret merkezi (Fondaco dei Turchi)", *Belleten,* 32, 1968, pp. 247-83
Turkische Kunst 1985
Turkische Kunst und Kultur aus osmanischer Zeit, exh. cat., Museum für Kunsthandwerk, Frankfurt am Main, and Villa Hügel e.V., Essen, Recklinghausen, 1985
Tyerman 1982
Christopher J. Tyerman, "Marino Sanudo Torsello and the lost Crusade: Lobbying in the fourteenth century", *Transactions of the Royal Historical Society,* 5th series, vol. 32, London, 1982, pp. 57-73
Ünver 1958
Süheyl Ünver, *Geçmiş yüzyıllarda kıyafet resimlerimiz,* Atatürk Kültür, Dil ve Tarih Yüksek Kurumu, Türk Tarih Kurumu Yayınları VII. dizi-Sa.36a, Ankara, 1958
Urbani de Ghelthof 1877
Giuseppe Marino Urbani de Ghelthof, "Una fabbrica di porcellana in Venezia nel 1740", *Bollettino di arti, industrie e curiosità veneziane,* 1, 1877, pp. 78-82
Uzunçarşılı 1960
Ismail Hakkı Uzunçarşılı, "Iran Şahına iltica etmiş olan Şehzade Beyazit'in teslimi için Sultan Süleyman ve oğlu Selim tarafından Şaha gönderilen altın ve kıymetli hediyeler", *Belleten,* 24, no. 93, 1960, pp. 103-10
Vaghi, Verità and Zecchin 2004
Francesca Vaghi, Marco Verità and Sandro Zecchin, "Silver stain on medieval window glass excavated in the Venetian lagoon", *JGS,* 46, 2004, pp. 105-08
Valensi 1987
Lucette Valensi, *Venise et la Sublime Porte. La naissance du despote,* Paris, 1987
Valensi 1989
Lucette Valensi, *Venezia e la Sublime Porta,* Bologna, 1989
Valier 1787
Agostino Valier, *Dell'utilità che si può trarre dalle cose operate dai veneziani,* Padua, 1787
Vallet 1999
Eric Vallet, *Marchands vénitiens en Syrie à la fin du XVe siècle,* Paris, 1999
Vanzan Marchini 2004
Nelli-Elena Vanzan Marchini (ed.), *Rotte mediterranee e baluardi di sanità. Venezia e i lazzaretti mediterranei,* Geneva and Milan, 2004
Vasari 1550
Giorgio Vasari, *Le vite de' piu eccellenti architetti, pittori, et scultori italiani,* Florence, 1550
Venedigs Ruhm 1991
Venedigs Ruhm im Norden, Die grossen venezianischen Maler der 18. Jahrhunderts ihre Auftraggeber und ihre Sammler, Forum des Landesmuseums Hannover and Kunstmuseum Düsseldorf im Ehrenhof, exh. cat., Landesmuseum, Hannover and Kunstmuseum, Düsseldorf, Hannover, 1991
Venezia e Levante1986
Venezia e la difesa del Levante, da Lepanto a Candia 1570-1670, Venice, 1986
Venice 1963
Pietro Zampetti (ed.), *Vittore Carpaccio, catalogo della mostra,* exh. cat., Palazzo Ducale, Venice, 1963
Venice 1982
Rosa Barovier Mentasti et al. (eds.), *Mille anni di arte del vetro a Venezia,* exh. cat., Palazzo Ducale, Venice, 1982
Venice 1993
Giovanni Curatola (ed.), *Eredità dell'Islam. Arte islamica in Italia,* exh. cat., Venice, Palazzo Ducale, 1993

Venice 1993a
Guardi: Quadri Turcheschi, exh. cat., Galleria di Palazzo Cini, Venice, 1993

Venice 1999
Maurizio Barberis et al. (eds.), *Mariano Fortuny*, exh. cat., Palazzo Fortuny, Venice, 1999

Venice 2000
Simonetta Pelusi (ed.), *La civiltà del libro e la stampa a Venezia. Testi sacri cristiani, ebraici, islamici dal Quattrocento al Settecento*, exh. cat., Biblioteca Nazionale Marciana, Venice, 2000

Venice 2001
Camillo Tonini and Pietro Lucchi (eds.), *Navigare e descrivere. Isolari e portolani del Museo Correr di Venezia XV-XVIII secolo*, exh. cat., Musei Civici Veneziani, Venice, 2001

Venice 2004
Adriano Mariuz and Giuseppe Pavanello (eds.), *Tiepolo. ironia e comico*, exh. cat., Fondazione Giorgio Cini, Venice, 2004

Venice 2004a
Giovanna Nepi Scirè, *Carpaccio: Pittore di storie*, exh. cat., Gallerie dell'Accademia, Venice, 2004

Vercellin 1979
Giorgio Vercellin, "Mercanti turchi a Venezia alla fine del Cinquecento", *Il Veltro*, 23, no. 2-4, 1979, pp. 243-75

Vercellin 1980
Giorgio Vercellin, "Mercanti turchi e sensali a Venezia", *SV*, 4, 1980, pp. 45-78

Vercellin 2000
Giorgio Vercellin, "Venezia e le origini della stampa in caratteri arabi", in Venice 2000, pp. 53-64

Verità 1985
Marco Verità, "L'invenzione del cristallo muranese: una verifica analitica delle fonti storiche", *RSSV*, 15, 1985, pp. 17-29

Verità 1995
Marco Verità, "Analytical investigation of European enameled beakers of the 13th and 14th centuries", *JGS*, 37, 1995, pp. 83-98

Verità 1998
Marco Verità, "Analyses of early enamelled Venetian glass: a comparison with Islamic glass", in Ward 1998, pp. 129-34, 212

Verità 1999
Marco Verità, "Analisi di tessere musive vitree del Battistero della Basilica di San Marco a Venezia", in E. Vio and A. Lepschy (eds.), *Scienza e tecnica del restauro della Basilica di San Marco*, Venice, 1999, pp. 567-85

Verità and Toninato 1990
Marco Verità and Tullio Toninato, "A comparative analytical investigation on the origins of Venetian glassmaking", *RSSV*, 20, 1990, pp. 169-76

Verità, Zecchin and Renier 2002
Marco Verità, Sandro Zecchin and Alessandro Renier, "Chemical analyses of ancient glass finds excavated in the Venetian lagoon", *Journal of Cultural Heritage*, 3, 2002, pp. 261-71

Verona 1983
Licisco Magagnato (ed.), *Le Stoffe di Cangrande*, exh. cat., Boggian di Castelvecchio, Verona, 1983

Verona 2004
Paola Marini, Ettore Napione and Gian Maria Varanini (eds.), *Cangrande della Scala: La morte e il corredo di un principe nel medioevo europeo*, exh. cat., Museo di Castelvecchio, Verona, 2004

Viallon 1995
Marie F. Viallon, *Venise et la Porte Ottomane (1453-1566): Un siècle de relations vénéto-ottomanes de la prise de Constantinople à la mort de Soliman*, Paris, 1995

Vienna 1983
Die Türken vor Wien, Europa und die Entscheidung an der Donau 1683, exh. cat., Sonderausstellung des Historischen Museums der Stadt Wien, Vienna, 1983

Vienna 2000
Wilfried Seipel (ed.), *Exotica. Portugals Entdeckungen im Spiegel fürstlicher Kunst- und Wunderkammern der Renaissance*, exh. cat., Kunsthistorisches Museum Vienna, Vienna, 2000

Viggiano 1996
Alfredo Viggiano, "Critica delle istituzioni e progetti politici, Giacomo Nani, le isole Ionie e la Morea nel Settecento", in M. Costantini and A. Nikiforou, *Levante veneziano: Aspetti di storia delle Isole Ionie al tempo delle Serenissima*, Rome, 1996, pp. 123-47

Villain-Gandossi 1969
Christiane Villain-Gandossi, "Contribution à l'étude des relations diplomatiques et commerciales entre Venise et la Porte ottomane au XVIe siècle: III. Firmans du Sultan Murad III", *Südost-Forschungen*, 28, 1969, pp. 13-47

von Folsach 2001
Kjeld von Folsach, *Art from the World of Islam in the David Collection*, Copenhagen, 2001

Von Hadeln 1925
Detlev Von Hadeln, *Venezianische Zeichnungen des Quattrocento*, Berlin, 1925

VS
Vetro e silicati

Waagé 1934
Frederick O. Waagé, "Preliminary report on the Medieval pottery from Corinth", *Hesperia*, 3, 1934, pp. 129-39

Walker 2000
Bethany J. Walker, "Rethinking Mamluk textiles", *MSR*, 4, 2000, pp. 167-95

Wansbrough 1961
John Wansbrough, "A Mamluk letter of 877/1473", *BSOAS*, 24, 1961, pp. 200-13

Wansbrough 1963
John Wansbrough, "A Mamluk ambassador to Venice in 913/1507", *BSOAS*, 26, 1963, pp. 503-30

Wansbrough 1965
John Wansbrough, "Venice and Florence in the Mamluk commercial privileges", *BSOAS*, 28, 1965, pp. 483-523

Wansbrough 1965a
John Wansbrough, "A Mamluk commercial treaty concluded with the Republic of Florence 894/1489", in S. M. Stern (ed.), *Documents from Islamic Chanceries, Oriental Studies*, 3, Oxford, 1965, pp. 39-80

Ward 1993
Rachel Ward, *Islamic Metalwork*, New York, 1993

Ward 1998
Rachel Ward (ed.), *Gilded and Enamelled Glass from Middle East*, London, 1998

Ward et al.. 1995
Rachel Ward et al., "Veneto-Saracenic metalwork: An analysis of the bowls and incense burners in the British Museum", in D. R. Hook and D. Gaimster (eds.), *Trade and Discovery: The Scientific Study of Artefacts from Post-Medieval Europe and Beyond*, British Museum Occasional Papers, 109, London, 1995, pp. 235-58

Wardwell 1989
Anne E. Wardwell, "*Panni tartarici*: Eastern Islamic silks woven with gold and silver (13th and 14th centuries)", *Islamic Art*, 3, 1989, pp. 95-173

Warner 2006
Nicholas Warner, *The True Description of Cairo: A Sixteenth-Century Venetian View*, Studies in the Arcadian Library, 2, Oxford, 2006

Washington 1966
Art Treasures of Turkey, exh. cat., Smithsonian Institution, Washington, D.C., 1966

Washington 1991
Circa 1492: Art in the Age of Exploration, exh. cat., National Gallery of Art, Washington, D.C., 1991

Washington 1997
David Alan Brown, Peter Humfrey and Mauro Lucco, *Lorenzo Lotto: Rediscovered Master of the Renaissance*, exh. cat., National Gallery of Art, Washington, D.C., New Haven, 1997

Watson 1960
F. Watson, "A series of 'turqueries' by Francesco Guardi", *The Baltimore Museum of Art News Quarterly*, 24, no. 1, 1960, pp. 3-13

Watson 1985
Oliver Watson, *Persian Lustre Ware*, London and Boston, 1985

Wearden 1985
Jennifer Wearden, "Siegmund von Herberstein: An Italian velvet in the Ottoman court", *Costume*, 19, 1985, pp. 22-29

Wedepohl 1997
Karl Hans Wedepohl, "Chemical composition of medieval glass from excavations in West Germany", *Glastechnische Berichte / Glass Science and Technology*, 70, 1997, pp. 246-55

Weigel 1997
Thomas Weigel, *Die Reliefsäulen des Hauptsaltarciborium von San Marco in Venedig*, Münster, 1997

Welch 1976
Anthony Welch, *Artists for the Shah. Late Sixteenth-Century Painting at the Imperial Court of Iran*, New Haven and London, 1976

Welch 2005
Evelyn Welch, *Shopping in the Renaissance: Consumer Cultures in Italy, 1400-1600*, New Haven and London, 2005

Wenzel 1988
Marian Wenzel, "Islamic gold sandwich glass: Some fragments in the David Collection, Copenhagen", *Journal of the Royal Asiatic Society*, 1, 1988, pp. 45-72

Wethey 1971
Harold E. Wethey, *The Paintings of Titian: Complete Edition*, London, 1971

Whitehouse 1967
David Whitehouse, "The medieval glazed pottery of Lazio", *Papers of the British School at Rome*, 35, 1967, pp. 40-86

Whitehouse 1972
David Whitehouse, "La Liguria e la ceramica medievale nel Mediterraneo", in *Atti IV Convegno Internazionale della Ceramica Albisola 1971*, Albisola, 1972, pp. 263-94

Whitehouse 1980
David Whitehouse, "Proto-maiolica", *Faenza*, 66, 1980, pp. 77-89

Whitehouse 2002
David Whitehouse, "The transition from natron to plant ash in the Levant", *JGS*, 44, 2002, pp. 193-96

Wiener Zeughaus 1977
Das Wiener Bürgerliche Zeughaus, Rüstungen und Waffen aus fünf Jahrhunderten, 49. Sonderausstellung des Historischen Museums der Stadt Wien in Schloss Schallaburg bei Melk, Vienna, 1977

Wiet 1929
Gaston Wiet, *Catalogue général du Musée arabe du Caire. Lampes et bouteilles en verre émaillé*, Cairo, 1929

Wilde 1932
Johannes Wilde, "Röntgenaufnahmen der 'Drei Philosophen' Giorgiones und der Zigeunermadonna Tizians", *Jahrbuch der Kunsthistorischen Sammlungen in Wien*, 6, 1932, pp. 141-54

Wilk 1978
Sarah Wilk, *The Sculpture of Tullio Lombardo: Studies in Sources and Meaning*, New York, 1978

Williams 1984
John Alden Williams, "Urbanization and monument construction in Mamluk Cairo", *Muqarnas*, 2, 1984, pp. 33-45

Wilson 2003
Bronwen Wilson, "Reflecting on the Turk in sixteenth-century Venetian portrait-books", *Word & Image*, 19, no. 1-2, 2003, pp. 38-58

Wilson 2004
Bronwen Wilson, "Reproducing the contours of Venetian identity in sixteenth-century costume books", *Studies in Iconography*, 25, 2004, pp. 221-74

Wilson 2005
Bronwen Wilson, *The World in Venice: Print, the City, and Early Modern Identity*, Toronto, 2005

Windisch-Graetz 1983
Franz Windisch-Graetz, *Möbel Europas, Renaissance und Manierismus: vom 15. Jahrhundert bis in die erste Hälfte des 17. Jahrhunderts*, Munich, 1983

Witcombe 2004
Christopher Witcombe, *Copyright in the Renaissance: Prints and the Privilegio in Sixteenth-Century Venice and Rome*, Leiden and Boston, 2004

Witschnitzer-Bernstein 1945
R. Witschnitzer-Bernstein, "The 'Three

Philosophers'", *GBA*, X, 6th ser., 27 , no. 87, 1945, pp. 193-212

Wittek 1952
Paul Wittek, "A letter of Murad III to the Doge of Venice, of 1580", *BSOAS*, 14, 1952, pp. 381-83

Woodward 1996
David Woodward, *Maps and Prints in the Italian Renaissance: Makers, Distributors, & Consumers*, London, 1996

Wolk-Simon 1996
Linda Wolk Simon, *Domenico Tiepolo: Drawings, Prints, and Paintings in The Metropolitan Museum of Art. The Metropolitan Museum of Art Bulletin*, 54, no. 3, Winter 1996-97, New York, 1996

Wolters 1976
Wolfgang Wolters, *La scultura veneziana gotica (1330-1460)*, Venice, 1976

Wraight 1992-93
Denzil Wraight, "Two harpsichords by Giovanni Celestini", *Galpin Society Journal*, 46, 1993, pp. 120-36

Yriarte 1885
Charles Yriarte, *Vie d'un patricien de Venise au XVIe siècle*, Paris, 1885

Yucel 1977
Unal Yucel, "Turkische Waffen vom 16. bis zum 18. Jahrhundert", in *Wiener Zeughaus* 1977, pp. 54-59

Zachariadou 1976
Elizabeth A. Zachariadou, "Sept traités inédits entre Venise et les émirats d'Aydin et de Menteşe (1331-1407)", in A. Gallotta (ed.), *Studi preottomani e ottomani. Atti del convegno di Napoli*, Istituto Universitario Orientale, Naples, 1976, pp. 229-40

Zachariadou 1983
Elizabeth A. Zachariadou, *Trade and Crusade. Venetian Crete and the Emirates of Menteshe and Aydin (1300-1415)*, Venice, 1983

Zampetti 1969
Pietro Zampetti (ed.), *Libro di spese diverse*, Venice, 1969

Zampetti 1977
Pietro Zampetti, "Carpaccio, Bellini e Ancona", *Arte Documento*, 2, 1977, pp. 77-85

Zanetti 1771
Antonio Maria Zanetti, *Della pittura veneziana e delle opere pubbliche dei veneziani maestri libri V*, Venice, 1771

Zanetti 1869
Vincenzo Zanetti, *Delle attuali condizioni dell'industria vetraria nelle venete lagune*, Venice, 1869

Zecchin 1967
Luigi Zecchin, "Nascita del cristallo veneziano", *VS*, 66, 1967, pp. 20-23 (Reprinted in Zecchin 1987-90, vol. 1, pp. 237-41)

Zecchin 1968
Luigi Zecchin, "Cristallini dorati e smaltati", *VS*, 68, 1968, pp. 22-25 (Reprinted in Zecchin 1987-90, vol. 3, pp. 109-13)

Zecchin 1968a
Luigi Zecchin, "I primi cristalli muranesi giunti in Oriente", *VS*, 71, 1968, pp. 17-20 (Reprinted in Zecchin 1987-90, vol. 1, pp. 242-45)

Zecchin 1969
Luigi Zecchin, "Un decoratore di vetri a Murano alla fine del Duecento", *JGS*, 11, 1969, pp. 39-42 (Reprinted in Zecchin 1987-90, vol. 3, pp. 114-16)

Zecchin 1970
Luigi Zecchin, "Cesendelli, inghistere, moioli", *VS*, 80, 1970, pp. 25-28 (Reprinted in Zecchin 1987-90, vol. 3, pp. 161-65)

Zecchin 1973
Luigi Zecchin, "Cronologia vetraria veneziana e muranese", *RSSV*, 1973, pp. 19-22, 63-66, 119-22, 165-68, 213-16, 257-60 (Reprinted in Zecchin 1987-90, vol. 1, nos. 144-49, p. xxiii)

Zecchin 1974
Luigi Zecchin, "Cronologia vetraria veneziana e muranese", *RSSV*, 1974, 4, nos. 2-3 and 5, pp. 63-66, 115-18, 217-20 (Reprinted in Zecchin 1987-90, vol. 1, nos. 150-53, p. xxiii)

Zecchin 1976
Luigi Zecchin, "L'arte vetraria muranese all'inizio del 1469", *RSSV*, 1976, 6, no. 5, pp. 253-56 (Reprinted in Zecchin 1987-90, vol. 3, pp. 374-78)

Zecchin 1979
Luigi Zecchin, "Decoratori di vetri a Murano fra il 1470 e il 1520", *RSSV*, 1979, 9, no. 2, pp. 63-68 (Reprinted in Zecchin 1987-90, vol. 3, pp. 125-30)

Zecchin 1980
Luigi Zecchin, "Prodotti vetrari nei documenti veneziani (1457-1468)", *RSSV*, 10, no. 1, 1980, pp. 17-22 (Reprinted in Zecchin 1987-90, vol. 3, pp. 145-48)

Zecchin 1986
Luigi Zecchin, *Il Ricettario Darduin, un codice vetrario del Seicento trascritto e commentato*, R. Barovier Mentasti, A. Tucci and M. Verità (eds.), Venice, 1986

Zecchin 1987-90
Luigi Zecchin, *Vetro e vetrai di Murano*, vols. 1-3, Venice, 1987, 1989, 1990

Zele 1989
Walter Zele, "Aspetti delle legazioni ottomane nei *Diarii* di Marin Sanudo", *SV*, 18, 1989, pp. 241-84

Zeri 1973
Federico Zeri, *Italian Paintings: A Catalogue of the Collection of The Metropolitan Museum of Art. Venetian School*, Vicenza, 1973

Zick-Nissen 1972
Johanna Zick-Nissen, catalogue entries in *Das Tier in der Kunst Irans.*, exh. cat., Linden-Museum, Stuttgart, 1972

Zorzi 1988
Alvise Zorzi (ed.), *Venezia e l'Oriente: Arte, commercio, civiltà al tempo di Marco Polo*, Milan, 1988

Zorzi 1988a
Alvise Zorzi, "Marco Polo e la Venezia del suo tempo", in Zorzi 1988, pp. 13-40

Zorzi 1987
Marino Zorzi, *La Libreria di San Marco. Libri, lettori, società nella Venezia dei Dogi*, Milan, 1987

Zorzi 2000
Marino Zorzi, "Il libro religioso nella storia della stampa veneziana", in Venice 2000, pp. 17-28

Zuliani 2000
Fulvio Zuliani, "Conservazione e innovazione nel lessico architettonico veneziano del XIII e XIV secolo", in F. Valcanover and W. Wolters (eds.), *L'architettura gotica a Venezia*, Venice, 2000, pp. 29-34

Zygulski 1992
Zdzislaw Zygulski, *Ottoman Art in the Service of the Empire*, New York, 1992

Zygulski 1999
Zdzislaw Zygulski, "The kalkan—the shield of the Orient", in Istanbul 1999, pp. 70-79

Marin Sanudo, *Diarii*[1]

Introduction to the Appendix

The presence of Marin Sanudo the Younger (1476–1533) permeates the pages of this book. Elected senator in 1498, he carefully recorded facts, as well as moods and gestures that occurred in front of his eyes, while noting stories and rumors that circulated in the Doge's Palace, until his death at the age of 67. This chronicle, often peppered with witty remarks, has come down to us in the form of his *Diarii,* which were eventually published between 1879 and 1902 in 58 volumes (Sanudo 1879–1902, edited among others by Rinaldo Fulin). Scholars have long recognized the importance of Sanudo's testimony, although its interpretation has been hindered by its extensiveness and by an objective complexity in translating—and sometimes even reading in the original language—his wonderful mixture of Renaissance Italian and Venetian dialect. In the present Appendix, edited by Giovanni Curatola, who has painstakingly extrapolated references to textiles in particular, but also to other works that reveal information about Venice's relationship with the Islamic Near East, the reader can have a glimpse of Sanudo's style as well as of the impracticality of a translation. Although they are in the original language, it is hoped that the following extracts will be of interest, amusement, and help to a wide range of readers.

SC

Vol. 2, col. 615-16

Dono del sultano mamelucco alla Signoria, aprile 1499: "*Una sella d'arzento dorado; uno pannello; una coverta de troncha fila, quatro peze de zambeloto, benzoloi rotoli 15 cajerini; legno aloe rotoli 10, camerini; zibelo, uno corno, quatro onchie; sesse*[1] *de 50 pichi, peze do; sesse de 40 pichi peze do; porzelane merzori otto; porzelane, piadane quattro; porzelane scude due*". *[...]* "*Una vesta de seda moresca de più colori, fodrada da armellini; una sella da cavallo coverta di veludi cremesin, lavorada larzon, davanti e da drio d'arzento dorato al consueto, con la sua coverta de cuoro, tamen senza pannicello sotto; una coverta di gropa de cavalo, lavorada ad ago, d'oro con suoi fiochi di seda; peze quatro de zambeloti bianchi de seda, voltadi in le sue carte; peze 4 de sessa; pezi 14 de porzelana e un corneto di zibetto sopra ligado, el qual fu posto in la busteta del benzoi e aloe; una busteta ne la qual è un pezo de benzoi pesato libre 15, e pezeti di legno aloe libre 9 onze 3, ne la qual busta è il dito corneto di zibetto; una scatoletta con bussoli 10 de thjriacha, et pirioli 4 de vero, dicono essere polvere da ochi, excepto una di 10 ne la qual sono pirioli 3 e li 2 bussoleti de thjriacha; et in cadauna de le dite 10 scatole, ne la parte sopra sono certi pezeti de legni et misture in pocha quantità. E questo è il presente de il signor soldam*".

Vol. 5, col. 50

Dono per il Sultano offerto dall'ambasciatore Beneto Sanudo, 1503: "*veste 6 tra panni d'oro richi e poveri e restagni*[2] *veste 10 di veludi de diversi colori, veste 30 tra scarlati e paonazzi, zebelinim 120, vari 300, formazi peze 40, che fu bellissimo presente era più di 110 homeni che lo portavano*".

Vol. 5, col. 116

Dono del sultano mamelucco a Soranzo, ambasciatore al Cairo, 1503: "*Una vesta d'oro fodrà meza de armellini; una coperta da cavalo, mezo d'oro et meza de veludo paonazzo; quattro peze de tabi;*[3] *quattro peze de sessa; una sela de cavalo, fornita d'arzento dorata; quatro pezi de legno aloe, pesa marchi 19 ½ ; tre pezi de belzuì, marchi 26; uno corneto de zibeleto scemo; 8 piaddene de porzelana grande; 2 scudeloti picoli; 10 scatole con busoli de turinga numero 38 et cum imponete 40. Tute le soprascrite robe sono stà consignate in man del patron de la nave Bernarda*"

Vol. 5, col. 993

Dono dell'ambasciatore ottomano a Venezia, marzo 1504: "*Cavezi* [scampoli] *5 de brochà d'oro de Bursa, dei quali uno è più richo degli altri, et uno altro e etiam brochà d'arzento; uno fazuol de seda da cenzer; cinque cavezi de damaschin de diversi colori fatti in Bursa, tra i quali n'è uno de broccatello d'oro et paonazzo, con forami turchini; quatro peze de zambeloto, do paonazze, una più scura di l'altra; et le altre do verde, una più scura di l'altra*".

Vol. 7, col. 636-37

Doni scambiati a Costantinopoli fra l'ambasciatore persiano e il sultano ottomano, settembre 1508: "*A dì XI lujo zonse in Costantinopoli l'orator dil signor Sophi, acceptato onorevolmente. A dì 16 bassò la mano al signor turco, et presentò le lettere del signor suo, insieme con molti presenti. Presenti fati per l'orator dil Sophi al signor turco: peze 40 damaschini a la persiana, con fiori d'oro; peze 30 rasi; peze 15 talassi fini; XII casachi, o ver fazuoli da zenzer, bellissimi de valuda de aspri 6 in 7 milia l'uno; alcune sexe da tulipani* [turbanti] *fine*".

"*Presenti fati per el signor turco al ditto orator: aspri XXV milia per sue spexe, oltra le spexe ordinarie; do veste de brocato d'oro a la turchescha; 4 mastrapani d'argento; 4 tapsi d'argento; 8 taze d'argento; aspri 30 milia in contadi; a la fameia soa, a chi 4, 5 et 6000 aspri per uno, secondo la conditione di le persone*"

Vol. 9, col. 546-47

Doni dell'ambasciatore mamelucco al sulltano ottomano a Edirne, febbraio 1510: "*Questi sono li presenti portati al Signor turco per l'orator dil signor soldan: uno pavion*[4] *con alcuni belli lavori; do schiaveti negri eunuchi; cavalli sie, uno con la sella et coperta d'oro, uno coperto de armadura de piastre, et altri quatro con le coperte di seda; gambelli tre coradori; tre simitare fornide d'oro; do bisachi; tre coraze de piastre dorade; quatro targe lavorade a la damaschina; uno ciminier azalin [acciaio] belissimo; alcuni ferri de lanze; alcune peze de ormesini,*[5] *et altri lavori de seda de molto valor; alcune casse con cose odorifere; alcune pignate de confetion; diexe tepsi grandi de porzelana*".

Vol. 14, col. 501

Osservazioni dell'ambasciatore veneziano Domenico Trevisan alloggiato nella dimora del sultano mamelucco ad Alessandria, 1511: "*andasemo ad alozar in una casa dil Soldan la più bella sia in Alessandria fata aparechiar per sua magnificentia, tuta quanta piena de porfidi, serpentini et tute le porte lavorade intarsià de ebano, avuolio et li salizi a foza doi quelli dela chiesia de San Marco*"

Vol. 14, col. 502

Doni offerti all'emir mamelucco da Domenico Trevisan nella stessa occasione, prima di partire per il Cairo: "*una vesta de restagno d'oro, una veste de pano d'oro sopra rizo*[6] *cremesi, 3 veste de seda, 3 de scarlatto, 3 de pano paonazo et 6 peze de formazo piasentin*"

Riceve in cambio: "*10castroni et 10 para de galine et un par de porchi, pan pure e grandissima quantità di erbazi*".

Vol. 15, col. 194-95

L'alloggio del Cairo nelle osservazioni di Domenico Trevisan nel corso della stessa visita, 1512: "*fu fata far per il Soldan vechio Chait bei, a istanzia di la soldonessa sua moier madre del soldaneto. La qual fabricha è da una spexa estrema, e tuta salizada in ogni canto di marmori, porfidi e serpentini, come la chiexia da San Marcho, e molto meglio lavorati che è nostri, soffittà tutta d'oro con lavori a la damaschina con intagli, né hanno sparagnato spexa alcuna, fino li lochi comuni* [toilette] *sono salizadi di porfidi e sofità d'oro... Fu adornata per l'orator con le sue tapezarie, che sono cose nuove in quelli paexi e molto apreciate da mori, e li piacevano assai, e li consoli e marchadanti hanno trovato tapedi da terra grandi che un triumpho a intrar in questa caxa*".

Vol. 15, col. 195

Doni del sultano mamelucco Qansuh al-Ghawri a Trevisan, 10 giugno 1512: "*il presente dil signor Soldan fu: 100 veste portate a questo modo, 8 d'oro, 14 di veludo de diversi colori, 28 de raxi e damaschini, 32 di scarlato, 18 di paonazzi, messi in sti soi schafazi di datoleri, e portati discoperti, che tutti vedeano. Oltre di questo, messeno le pelatarie, 120 pesi de zibellini, 400 pezi de armellini, 4500 vari e dossi*[7] *molto fini e belli, et 50 pezi de formazo piasentin, e tutto questo presente fo portà per mori su la testa che tutti el vedeva, e andavano avanti l'ambasador a do a do, che era un triumpho a veder*".

Vol. 17, col. 521

Doni dell'ambasciatore ottomano Alì Bey al doge, 1 febbraio 1514: "*10 pezze tra panno d'oro, cremesin, turchesco, paonazo, et altri colori di panni di seda, numero peze 10 che cadaun portava la sua; poi 3 quali portavano do peze di zambeloto fine per uno, paonazze e negre e uno portava uno fazuol rosso con oro turchesco, e uno altro uno tappedo piccolo*"

Vol. 17, col. 545-46

Doni del doge ad Ali Bey nella stessa occasione: "*cinque veste, zoè do di panno d'oro e una de veludo cremexin, a doi soi dil zarchular d'oro in testa una veste di damaschin per uno, al resto di la fameia una di scarlato per uno*".

Vol. 25, col. 131-33

Doni del rappresentante ottomano Selim al Cairo agli ambasciatori veneziani Bortolomeo Contarini e Alvise Mocenigo, 1517: "*14 veste, 4 di alto basso d'oro, 6 di alto basso appizolado di pocho pretio, et 4 di damaschino pocho miglio che carta. Deteno a li ambassadori ducati 120 per uno di questo paese, che sono 80 de li nostri; per li doi secretari notati 40 per uno, et al turciman* [interprete] *40*".

Vol. 28, col. 675-76).

Doni, per una spesa di 700 ducati, inviati dal Consiglio dei Dieci al sangiacco di Bosnia per mezzo del segretario Vincenzo Guidotto, 10 maggio 1520: "*Pani di seda compradi per mandar a donar (...): Damaschin alexandrin braza*[8] *28, ha pagato 27.2 a ducati 1 grossi 2... ducati 29.19 / damaschin limonzin braza 28, ha pagato 27.2 a ducati 1 g. 2....ducati 29.19 / Damaschin verde braza 14, ha pagato 27.2 a ducati 1 g. 2....ducati 14.21 / Raso paonazo braza 14, ha pagato 13.3 a ducati 1 g. 12.... ducati 20.15 / Tabì verde braza 20, ha pagato 19.3 a ducati ... g.15.....ducati 12.8 / Tabì rosso braza 20, ha pagato 19.3 a ducati ...g. 18....ducati 14.2 / da sier Jacomo di Pizoni da la Seda....../...../ ducati 12.26 / Veludo paonazzo braza 14, ha pagato 13.3, a ducati 3 grossi 4....ducati 43.13 / da sier Gabriel Moro et cavalier e fradelli. / Veludo pelo de Lion braza 14, ha pagato 19.3 a ducati 3 g. 2 .... ducati 30.8 / da sier Santo de Zuane da la Seda. / Veludo cremexin braza 14, ha pagato 13.3 a ducati 4....ducati 55.- / Alto e basso cremexin braza 13.2, ha pagato 13.3 ½ a ducati 5 g. 6....ducati 68.21 / Damaschin paonazo braza 14, ha pagato 13.3 a ducati 1 g. 17....ducati 23.12 / Raxo cremexin braza 14, ha pagato 13.3 a ducati 1. g. 17....ducati 23.12 / Damaschin cremexin braza 14, ha pagato 13.3 a ducati 2 g. 2..... ducati 28.15 / da sier Jacomo di Zuane e nevodi da la Seda. / Pano scarlatin peze 1 braza 37.2, ha pagato 36 a grossi 23.....ducati 24.15 / da sier Alvise da la Gata drapier. / Pano paonazo di 80 braza 15, ha pagato g. 14.2 a ducati 42.....ducati 25.9 / da sier Polo Valaresso qu. sier Ferigo. / pano scarlato di 100 braza 10, ha pagato g. 9.2 a ducati 4 monta.... ducati 38.- / da sier Bortolo Zane e fradelli. / Pano paonazzo di 100 braza 15, ha pagato 14.2 a ducati 2.6....ducati 32.15 / da sier Agustin di Franceschin drapier. / Carixee peza una scarlattina /....../ Carixee peza una biava.....per ducati 18 ½ / da sier Daniel de Bombergo / Item, da sier Gabriel Moro el cavalier e fratelli per conto de spiziarie. / Pani 200 di zucharo fin pexo neto, lire 237 a ducati 16 el 100....ducati 37.2 / Specie dolce e forte lire 34.4, a ducati 7 la lira ....ducati 10.- / Pevere intrigo lire 50, a ducati 8 la lira....ducati 16.16. / E per spexe.....ducati 2.21 / Summa summarum ducati 612, grossi 25 /*"

Vol. 39, col. 23-24; 37, 39, 42

Nel 1525 giunge un altro ambasciatore turco a Venezia e viene alloggiato alla Giudecca in Cà Dandolo.[9] Viene ricevuto ed è vestito con "*habito turchesco pizolato*" e quelli del seguito portano "*casache di velludo cremisino*". Al momento del congedo "*iusta il consueto*" gli verranno donate vesti di seta scarlatte e denaro per la somma di 500 ducati. Visita la Merceria[10] per l'occasione abbellita con tessuti di pregio e tappeti.

Vol. 43, col. 599

Gennaio 1527: "*Questa matina vidi in la sala di Pregadi una bella cossa; uno scachier grando bellissimo in tondo et alto lavorado d'arzento et d'oro con calzedonie, diaspri et altre zoie, et li scacchi di cristallo finissimo, fo di sier Jacopo Loredan. Fo portado perché sier Piero Lando lo volse monstrar al Serenissimo e al Collegio si volevano comprar per mandarlo a donar al Signor turco con sier Marco Minio va orator in Costantinopoli, qual fu fatto per mandarlo a vender al soldan Gauri. Et dimandano di questo ducati 5000*"

Vol. 43, col. 725

Il bailo Piero Zen a Costantinopoli, gennaio 1527: "*ha dato l'orologio a Mustafà bassà, qual ringrazia la Signoria*"

Vol. 43, col. 766

Alla partenza di Marco Minio, 1527: "*...oltra li presenti soliti, li fo dato di zoie...et uno bazil d'argento bellissimo, et uno spechio...et altre cose da donar a parte a Imbraim bassà per ducati 800*"

Vol. 45, col. 271

Da Costantinopoli, 27 aprile 1527 "*si conteniva che era zonto uno azamin con assà zoie, il qual avia donato al magnifico Imbraim bassà un pero* [forse un pendente] *di carati 40, una perla di carati 20, do balassi di carati 100 l'uno, diamanti etc. Et havia fatto un merchado con il Signor di zoie per ducati 130 milia, et assà altre ne haved*".

Vol. 46, col. 414

Doni dell'inviato del sangiaccato di Charzego a Venezia, 1527: "*et portò a presentar do astori, do archi, do mazi de freze, do peze di zambeloto, quatro tapedi novi turcheschi et uno grande assà. Tutte queste cose fo portà da li soi turchi in Collegio*"

Vol. 47, col.135

Il visir ottomano Ibrahim Pasha dona al figlio naturale del doge, Alvise Gritti, marzo 1528: "*peze 2000 di zambeloti*".

Vol. 53, col. 344

Ottobre 1528: "*In questa matina, avendo l'orator del bassà di Tossina mandato a donar al Serenissimo per nome de la Signoria una cassetta d'arzento benissimo lavorata con l'arma del Papa de Medici, in la qual è del legno di la Croxe un bon pezo, zoè...parse al Serenissimo con il Collegio mandar per il Patriarca, il qual vene, et in camera di Soa Serenità con li consieri fu fatto experientia; posto in fuoco et non si brusone, poi butano in uno bazil d'arzento, si smorzò il foco, et rimase intacto, facendo tremolii et gonfii ne l'acqua*".

Vol. 53, col. 536

La vicenda del "*liocorno*". Piero Zen e Tomà Mozenigo, in una lettera da Costantinopoli, 9 giugno 1530: "*... el magnifico Imbraim averli richiesti con grandissime persuasion parte del liocorno che nui havemo*".

Settembre 1530: "*Imbraim si ha dolesto, la Signoria non li ha mandà il liocorno richiesto ... et da mò sia preso che li sia mandato il liocorno bianco..., perochè in le zoie sono 3 alicorni: uno, il vecchio, che fo robado; l'altro, quel dete Domenego di Zorzi a la Signoria; il terzo, quel si have da Corfù mediante sier Bernardo Barbarico. Et questo terzo se li mandà*".

Vol. 54, col. 291

Febbraio 1531: "*portar a presentar al Signor turcho il liocorno, iusta la deliberation fatta per questo Conseio, et atenta la in stantia fece il magnifico Imbraim fosse mandato né vol acetar li presenti, sono de li mandati per la Signoria, fino non zonzi il ditto liocorno*"

Vol. 55, col. 178

Lettera da Costantinopoli di Piero Zen, oratore, e Francesco Bernardo, bailo, 7 ottobre 1531: " *Hor, posto ordine di essere insieme un altro zorno, andono da soa magnificentia, tolto fuora di la cassa lo alicorno; et ge lo mostrò, el qual lo tolse in man et disse: 'Questo è bello e di gran precio'. Et riguardandolo ben, disse: 'Questo è bello sì nel color come in venesee'. Dicendo: 'Il Gran Signor ne ha uno molto più grosso, come havea il brazo, et è in do pezi perché sultam Mameth lo taiò e fece manegi di pugnali, e questo Signor à fato far manegi forniti a centure et anelli d'archo di parte di quello'. Poi disse, non credesse l'havesse dito questo per sminuir la beleza di questo simel dono, ch'è grandissimo segno e demostration di una summa benevolentia di la Signoria che la portava a questo Gran Signor, hessendo stà esso alicorno grandissimo tempo ne le cose pompose et zoie di quel Stado, et privarse di questo e mandarlo a questo imperador: e tanto è più degno presente, quanto che mai se habbi udito dir né letto, che alcun principe, in alcun tempo, habbi mandato a uno altro simel presente rarissimo maxime di beleza come erra questo.*"

A selection by Giovanni Curatola

Notes

1. Sanudo 1879–1902.
2. What Dutch and English merchants called "chintz."
3. Fabric of silk and gold.
4. A kind of moiré taffeta.
5. Perhaps a banner, although in Silician dialect this term can also mean "flag."
6. A type of silk whose name comes from the port of Ormuz, in Persia. In the Cannaregio district of Venice, near the bridge leading to the Ghetto, is a Calle [street] degli Ormesini, a Fondamenta [quay] degli Ormesini, and a Rio [canal] degli Ormesini.
7. *Soprarizzo* is a kind of velvet (Davanzo and Poli, 2001, pp. 203–4).
8. Squirrel or rabbit fur.
9. The Venetian *braza* measured 63.8 cm for silk and 68.2 cm for wool.
10. Since Giudecca is an island, its residents could be monitored easily.
11. The Merceria is the main street linking the Rialto to St. Mark's Square.

Chronology

Venice

9th century

828
The relics of St. Mark are translated from Alexandria to Venice.

832
Construction of St. Mark's Basilica, which is enlarged in 976 and then rebuilt in the 11th century.

11th century

1082
The Byzantine emperor (*basileus*) grants a *chrysobull* (golden bull) to the doge, awarding Venice trading rights that open the gateway to the East.

1096–97
First Crusade—the Venetian fleet ferries Crusaders eastward.

12th century

1104
Venice's Arsenal is established, and is later enlarged in the 14th century.

First half of 12th century
Venetians are present in the main Levantine ports, Alexandria and Beirut. Like Pisa and Genoa, Venice obtains its own quarters in Acre and other main cities and ports in the Holy Land.

1123
During Doge Domenico Michiel's term of office, the Venetian fleet comes to the aid of Jaffa, which the Fatimid caliph of Cairo, al-Amir, attempts to recapture from the Crusaders.

1124
Tyre is besieged by the Crusaders with the help of the Venetian fleet.

12th century through first third of the 13th century
Venice establishes its presence in North Africa.
The Byzantine emperor challenges the privileges accorded to Venice.

13th century

1202–4
The Venetians build and equip a fleet for the Fourth Crusade. The sack of Constantinople strengthens the Venetian presence in the Mediterranean. Byzantine and Islamic works of art are brought back from Constantinople and deposited in the Treasury of St. Mark's Basilica. The four bronze horses, also removed from Constantinople, are installed on the façade of St. Mark's Basilica.

1207
First commercial treaty with the Ayyubid sultanate of Aleppo.

1215
A "colony" of Venetians, residing in a *fondaco*, is established in Alexandria.

1231
A trade treaty is signed between the Doge and Abu Zakariya Yahya I, the Hafsid monarch of Tunisia, Tripoli, and Kabylia.

1261
The emperor of Nicaea, Michael Paleologus, recaptures Constantinople and expels the Venetians.

1284
Venice strikes its first gold ducats.

1291
The Council of Venice orders the transfer of glasshouses from the area of Rialto to the island of Murano.

14th century

1347–48
Black Death and famine.

1378–1400
Reconstruction of the Palazzo Ducale in Venice.

1381
The Peace Treaty of Turin between Venice and Genoa is a setback for Venice and benefits Genoa.

1388
Commercial treaty with the Turks.

1396
Decline of Genoa as a Mediterranean power.

15th century

1404
The Most Serene Republic increases its *terra firma* (the Italian provinces in the Veneto).

1406
Election of Gregory XII, the first Venetian pope.

1415
Commercial treaty with the Mamluk sultan, al-Mu'ayyad. Second third of 15th century the Senate opens the Barbary and Trafego trade routes.

1468
The Marciana Library is founded.

16th century

1503
The Republic signs a peace treaty with the Ottoman Empire, losing some of its possessions in southern Greece (Modon and Coron).

1507
Trade treaty with the Mamluk sultan Qansuh al-Ghawri.

1514
The Rialto Bridge burns down.

1538
The Republic is defeated at Prevesa (Epirus) by the Turkish fleet of Admiral Haireddin Barbarossa.

1569
A fire badly damages the Arsenal.

1571
The Holy League, including Venice, inflicts a naval defeat on the Ottoman fleet at the battle of Lepanto.

1575–77
Outbreak of plague in Venice; construction of the church of the Redeemer (il Redentore) on the island of Giudecca.

Late 16th century
The Republic achieves domination over Cyprus, Crete, Corfu, and part of the Dalmatian coast.

17th and 18th centuries

1630
Major epidemic of plague. Construction of the church of Santa Maria della Salute.

1646–69
The Turks besiege Candia (Crete). The Venetians surrender.

1684–1716
War in the Peloponnesus (Morea) opposes Venetians and Ottomans.

ca. 1716
Shipbuilding activities cease in the Arsenal.

1784–92
War against Barbary pirates and the bey of Tunis. Venice negotiates a peace treaty that requires payment of heavy tributes.

1797
French troops under Napoleon Bonaparte occupy the Veneto and declare war on Venice. End of the Venetian Republic.

Islamic World

9th century

800–909
reign of the Aghlabid dynasty in Ifriqiya (now Tunisia), which conquers Sicily.

9th–10th century
Treaties are signed between the Republic of Venice and the Islamic sovereigns of North Africa, Syria, and Egypt.

827–29
Alexandria is placed under the authority of the ʿAbbasid governor of Cairo.

10th century

921
Al-Mahdiyah in North Africa becomes the first capital of the Fatimid dynasty.

969–1171
The Fatimids reign over Egypt and Syria.

969
Cairo is founded by Fatimid caliph al-Mu'izz.

970–72
Construction of the Al-Azhar Mosque in Cairo.

11th century

1034
The Oghuz Turks enter Iran.
Third quarter of 11th century
The Fatimid treasury in Cairo is dispersed after a period of civil unrest. Some works originally in the treasury will be later looted by the Venetians during the Fourth Crusade in 1204 and deposited in the Treasury of St. Mark's Basilica.

1055
Beginning of the Seljuq sultanate in Syria and Iraq. Toghril Beg captures Baghdad from the Buyids.

1099
The Crusaders take Jerusalem, creating trade opportunities for Venetian merchants, who obtain the right to establish a *fondaco* in the city as well as elsewhere in the Kingdom of Jerusalem.

12th century

1123
Al-Amir, the Fatimid caliph in Cairo, attempts to retake Jaffa from the Crusaders.

1124
Crusaders besige Tyre with Venetian backing.

1171–1260
Reign of the Ayyubid dynasty, which extends its control over Jerusalem.

1231
Beginning of rule of the Hafsid dynasty in Ifriqiya.

13h century

1250–1517
The Mamluks reign over Egypt and Syria, becoming the Venetians' main trading partners.

1258
The Il-Khanid ruler Hulegu (son of Genghis Khan) sacks Baghdad and puts an end to the ʿAbbasid dynasty.

1260
The Mamluks defeat the Mongols at ʿAyn Jalut.

1270
The Venetians establish a port of call at Ras al-Makhbaz (Tunisia), a terminus of African caravan routes.

1280
The caravan routes are extended to Bone (Annaba) and Bougie (Bejaia).

1281
The Ottoman Empire is founded, and will steadily extend its hegemony.

1284–85
Construction of the Mamluk sultan Qala'un's complex in Cairo, which includes a hospital, a *madrasa,* and a mausoleum.

1291
Acre brought under Mamluk control.

14th century

1326–44
Papal embargo on trade with Egypt.

1326–66
Bursa becomes the capital of the Ottoman Empire.

1366
The Ottoman capital is transferred to Edirne.

1375
Venetian consuls (*baili*) are present in Alexandria, Cairo, Damascus, and Beirut.

15th century

1426
The Mamluks conquer Cyprus.

1453
Mehmet II the Conqueror captures Constantinople, which becomes the new Ottoman capital. The sultan signs commercial treaties with Venice. Ottoman troops take Trebizond and Morea.

1479–81
Gentile Bellini stays at the court of Sultan Mehmet II in Istanbul. Venice enters into an alliance with Uzun Hasan, ruler of the "White Sheep" federation of Turkmen, in an effort to counter the Ottomans.

16th century

1512–20
Selim I extends Ottoman domination by seizing Syria, Egypt, central Anatolia, and Azerbaijan.

1514
The battle of Çaldiran (Iran) results in the victory of the Ottomans (Selim I) over the Safavids.

1516
The Ottomans defeat the Mamluks, and occupy Aleppo and Damascus.

1517
Ottoman conquest of Cairo.

1518
A new shipyard is built in Istanbul.

1520–66
Reign of Süleyman the Magnificent, who extended his domination to Iraq, Yemen, and North Africa (except Morocco).

1530s
Algiers is in the hands of the corsair Haireddin Barbarossa, Süleyman's lieutenant. Tunis is captured (but lost to the Crusaders in 1535).

1537
Süleyman the Magnificent besieges Corfu.

1550
The Süleyman Mosque is built in Istanbul by the architect Sinan.

1565– 79
Vizierate of Sokollu Mehmet Pasha.

1568
Sinan begins building the Selim II Mosque in Edirne.

1570
Süleyman orders the seizure of Venetian ships in the Bosphorus and the Dardanelles.

1571
The Ottomans are defeated at Lepanto. The Turks lay siege to Famagusta (Cyprus).

1574
The Ottomans under Uluj Ali capture Tunis and Goletta.
Late 16th century
the Ottoman Empire stretches from Budapest to Baghdad, from Damascus to Algiers, into the Balkans and the Danube plain, and over to Eastern Asia, the Near East, Egypt, and parts of North Africa.

17th century

1603
Ambassadors of the Iranian Shah ʿAbbas I arrive in Venice to negotiate an agreement to resist Ottoman hegemony.

1609
Beginning of the construction of Sultan Ahmed I's "Blue Mosque" in Istanbul.

1646
The Turks arrive in Crete, Venice's last Greek possession, and lay siege to Candia. The Ottoman Empire builds a major fleet.

18th century:

1714–16
The Turks besiege Morea and the most recent Venetian conquests in the Peloponnesus.

1717–29
First Turkish printing shop that uses the Arabic alphabet.

1784–92
Wars against the Barbary pirates and the bey of Tunis. Venice negotiates a peace treaty that requires payment of heavy tributes.

Photographic Credits

Baltimore
The Walters Art Museum: cat. 106, 108, 115, 124, 151 a-b, fig. 8, p. 224

Berlin
PBK / dist. RMN: fig. 4, p. 124; fig. 5, p. 126
PBK, Berlin, dist. RMN / Photo Jörg P. Anders: cat. 44, 50, 75, 110
PBK, Berlin, dist. RMN / Photo Ingrid Geske: cat. 86, 92, 109, 177
PBK, Berlin, dist. RMN / Photo Georg Niedermeiser: cat. 85
Staatliche Museen zu Berlin, Gemäldegalerie / Photo Jörg P. Anders, Berlin: cat. 20

Bologna
Biblioteca Universitaria: cat. 47
Museo Civico d'Arte Medievale: fig. 8, p. 263

Brussels
Musées Royaux d'Art et d'Histoire / Kmkg-mrah: fig. 8, p. 82

Cairo
Museum of Islamic Art: fig. 7, p. 260

Cambridge
Faculty of Architecture and History of Art, University of Cambridge: fig. 1, p. 60; fig. 2-3, p. 76

Chatsworth
The Devonshire Collection. Reproduced by permission of the Chatsworth Settlement Trustees: cat. 132

Chicago
The Newberry Library: fig. 1, p. 242

Cividale del Friuli
Cathedral: cat. 74
Cathedral Treasury: cat. 102, 112; fig. 1-2, p. 228
Museo Archeologico Nazionale: cat. 104

Corning
The Corning Museum of Glass: cat. 161, 168

Düsseldorf
Gemäldegalerie, Stiftung Museum Kunst Palast: cat. 39, 158, 163

Florence
Galleria degli Uffizi, Gabinetto disegni e stampe: fig. 11, p. 132
Scala: cat. 25
Scala 1990: cat. 155; fig. 7, p. 70
Scala / Venice, Gallerie dell'Accademia: fig. 3, p. 177; fig. 2, p. 216
Scala / Venice, Scuola di San Giorgio degli Schiavoni: fig. 9-10, p. 132
Scala / Verona, San Zeno: fig. 5, p. 181
Soprintendenza Speciale per il Polo Museale Fiorentino: cat. 107, 111

Frankfurt
Museum für Angewandte Kunst: cat. 157

Geneva
Aga Khan Trust for Culture, formerly in the collection of du Prince and Princess Sadruddin Aga Khan: cat. 7

Harvard
Journal of Asiatic Studies: fig. 2, p. 62

Istanbul
Topkapı Sarayı Müzesi: cat. 4-6, 8, 80

London
The Bridgeman Art Library / Venice, Cameraphoto Arte: fig. 6, p. 181
The Bridgeman Art Library / Christie's Images: fig. 3, p. 124
The Bridgeman Art Library / Milan, Pinacoteca di Brera: cat. 28; fig. 7, p. 129
The British Library: cat. 41, 130
The Trustees of The British Museum: cat. 56, 89, 94, 98, 101, 116, 156, 182; fig. 6, p. 223; fig. 3, p. 228
Courtauld Institute of Art Gallery: cat. 103, 120
The Nasser D. Khalili Collection of Islamic Art: cat. 10, 46a-b, 127-128
The National Gallery: cat. 23, 32, 40
Rainer Zietz Ltd.: Cat. 144
Victoria and Albert Museum: cat. 153, 160, 162
Wellcome Library: cat. 14

Munich
Bayerische Staatsgemäldesammlungen, Staatsgalerie Würzburg and Kunstdia-Archiv Artothek, D-Weilheim: cat. 35, 36, 37, 38

New York
Art Resource / Erich Lessing: fig. 2, p. 151
Art Resource / Florence, Scala: fig. 9, p. 83; fig. 6, p. 168
Art Resource / Venice, Cameraphoto Arte,: fig. 8, p. 129; fig. 1, p. 216
Cooper-Hewitt, National Design Museum, Smithsonian Institution: fig. 3, p. 192; fig. 5, p. 195
The Metropolitan Museum of Art: cat. 153; fig. 1, p. 176; fig. 2, p. 247; fig. 9, p. 264
Gift of Stephen V. Grancsay, 1942 / photo 2006, The Metropolitan Museum of Art: cat. 140
Gift of J. Pierpont Morgan, 1913 / photo 1991, The Metropolitan Museum of Art: cat. 126
Gift of J. Pierpont Morgan, 1917 / photo 1994, The Metropolitan Museum of Art: cat. 52
Gift of J. Pierpont Morgan, 1917 / photo 2006, The Metropolitan Museum of Art: cat. 121
Gift of J. Pierpont Morgan, 1937 / photo 1996, The Metropolitan Museum of Art: cat. 55
Gift of J. Pierpont Morgan, 1917 / photo 2003, The Metropolitan Museum of Art: cat. 148
Gift of J. Pierpont Morgan, 1957 / photo 1991, The Metropolitan Museum of Art: cat. 147
Gift of J. Pierpont Morgan, 1914 / photo 1982, The Metropolitan Museum of Art: cat. 165
Harris Brisbane Dick Fund, 1938 / photo 2006, The Metropolitan Museum of Art: cat. 57
Harris Brisbane Dick Fund, 1935 / photo 2006, The Metropolitan Museum of Art: cat. 58
Harris Brisbane Dick Fund, 1942 / photo 2006, The Metropolitan Museum of Art: cat. 59
Rogers Fund, 1906 / photo 2006, The Metropolitan Museum of Art: cat. 63
Rogers Fund, 1917 / photo 2006, The Metropolitan Museum of Art: cat. 71
Rogers Fund, 1918 / photo 2006, The Metropolitan Museum of Art: cat. 119
Rogers Fund, 1923 / photo 2006, The Metropolitan Museum of Art: cat. 99
Rogers Fund, 1953 / photo 2006, The Metropolitan Museum of Art: cat. 79
Rogers Fund, 1956 / photo 2006, The Metropolitan Museum of Art: cat. 129
Rogers Fund, 1972 / photo 2006, The Metropolitan Museum of Art: cat. 69
Robert Lehman Collection, 1975 / photo Sheldan Collins / 1993, The Metropolitan Museum of Art: cat. 167
The Elisha Whittelsey Collection, The Elisha Whittelsey Fund, 1957 / photo 2006, The Metropolitan Museum of Art: cat. 65
The Pierpont Morgan Library, 2006: cat. 17
The Pierpont Morgan Library, 2002: fig. 5, p. 168

Oxford
The Ashmolean Museum of Art and Archaeology, University of Oxford: cat. 154
The Ashmolean Museum of Art and Archaeology, University of Oxford / The Bridgeman Art Library: cat.. 154, 173
The Bodleian Library, University of Oxford: cat. 2, 15

Padua
Comunità Ebraica di Padova: cat. 82
Museo d'Arte Medievale e Moderna: cat. 190, 192

Paris
Akg-Images: cat. 9
Bibliothèque Interuniversitaire de Médecine: cat. 64
Bibliothèque Nationale de France: cat. 49, 125, 131, 194; fig. 3, p. 159
Collection Musée des Arts Décoratifs on loan to Musée de la Musique / photo J.-M. Anglès: cat. 143
Institut du Monde Arabe: cat. 91
Réunion des Musées Nationaux / M. Beck-Coppola: cat. 187, 188
Réunion des Musées Nationaux / J.-G. Berizzi: cat. 100, 105, 166; fig 4, p. 222
Réunion des Musées Nationaux / G. Blot: cat. 30, 185; fig. 2, p. 123; fig. 1, p. 147
Réunion des Musées Nationaux / G. Blot / J. Schormans: cat. 29
Réunion des Musées Nationaux / T. Le Mage: cat. 53
Réunion des Musées Nationaux / R.-G. Ojéda: cat. 176

Princeton
Princeton University Art Museum / photo Bruce M. White: cat. 52

Rome
Galleria Nazionale d'Arte Antica, Palazzo Barberini: cat. 19

St. Louis
Saint Louis Art Museum, Gift of James F. Ballard: cat. 84
Saint Louis Art Museum, Friends Fund: cat. 145

St. Petersburg
Hermitage Museum: fig. 5, p. 222; fig. 10, p. 267

Stuttgart
Staatgalerie: cat. 31

Venice
Archivio di Stato: fig. 11-12, p. 270
Armeria di Palazzo Ducale: cat. 122-123, 135-139, 141-142
Biblioteca dei frati minori di San Michele in Isola: cat. 60
Biblioteca Nazionale Marciana/ Soprintendenza Speciale per il Polo Museale Fiorentino: cat. 1, 3, 11, 13, 43, 45a, 45b, 62a, 62b, 67
Fondazione Giorgio Cini: cat. 12, 133
Galleria Franchetti alla Ca' d'Oro: 117, 174, 181a-d, 186, 189
Gallerie dell'Academia: cat. 34
Museo Civico Correr: cat. 18, 21-22, 33, 42, 48, 61, 66, 77-78, 95-97, 113-114, 118, 134, 178-179, 191
Museo Storico Navale: cat. 90, 149
Museo Vetrario: cat. 164
Procuratoria di San Marco: cat. 83, 88, 93, 150
Scuola Grande di San Rocco: cat. 81, 175, 180

Verona
Museo di Castelvecchio: cat. 26, 68a-b
Soprintendenza Archeologica per il Veneto: cat. 159

Vienna
Kunsthistorisches Museum mit MVK und ÖTM, 2006: cat. 193; fig. 4, p. 162
Sammlungen des Fürsten von und zu Liechtenstein: cat. 27

Washington, D.C.
The Folger Shakespeare Library: cat. 54

Windsor
Eton College Library: cat. 16
The Royal Collection, Windsor Castle, Her Most Gracious Majesty Queen Elizabeth the Second: cat. 51

S. Auld
Fig. 3, p. 219

Francesco Turio Bohm
Cat. 70, 87; fig. 1, p. 13; fig. 5, p. 12; fig. 2, p. 15; fig. 6, p. 16; fig. 4, p. 17; fig. 5, p. 17; fig. 7, p. 18; fig. 8, p. 23; fig. 10, p. 84; fig. 2, p. 94; fig. 1, p. 121; fig. 6, p. 128; fig. 1, p. 255; fig. 4-5, p. 259; fig. 6, p. 273

Osvaldo Bohm
Fig. 5, p. 66

Uwe Helbing
Cat. 146

J.-C. Hocquet
Fig. 1, p. 39; fig. 2, p. 40; fig. 3, p. 43; fig. 4, p. 44

D. Howard
Fig. 3-6, p. 66-67; 1, p. 76; fig. 5-6, p. 79

Sarah Quill
Fig. 4, p. 78

S. Sardjono
Fig. 1-5, p. 193-195

M. Verità
Fig. 1, p. 279

All Rights Reserved
Cat. 24, 183, 184; fig. 3, p. 15; fig. 9, p. 31; fig. 7, p. 81; fig. 1, p. 91; fig. 2, p. 177; fig. 4, p. 178; fig. 7, p. 186; fig. 8, p. 189; fig. 9, p. 190; fig. 7, p. 223; fig. 1, p. 247; fig. 2, p. 256; fig. 3, p. 257; fig. 13, p. 274; fig. 1-6, p. 283-291

Typesetting: Dominique Guillaumin
Photoengraving: Arciel Graphic, Verona
Printing of this work was completed in December 2006
On the presses of GECA, Milan
Printed and bound in Italy
French legal registration of copyright: October 2006
ISBN: 978-0-300-12430-9
Library of Congress Number: 2006938864